D1566693

Baseball Weekly 2000 Almanac

Everything the baseball fan needs — all in one book

Edited by
Paul White
Editor, *Baseball Weekly*

With contributions from
the staffs of *Baseball Weekly*
and USA TODAY Sports

Project Editor, Liz Barrett

Week-by-Week Notes Edited by
John Shostrom

A Balliett & Fitzgerald Book

Total Sports
New York

Published by
Total Sports, Inc.
100 Enterprise Dr.
Kingston, NY 12401

ISSN: 1091-7071
ISBN: 1-892129-16-7

First Edition—2000

Printed in the United States of America

10   9   8   7   6   5   4   3   2   1

Produced by Balliett & Fitzgerald, Inc.
Managing editor: Tom Dyja
Production editor: Michael Walters
Production staff: Erin Monty, Meghan Murphy
Copyeditor: Peter Pullman
Proofreader: Kevin Kerr
Editorial assistant: Ed H. Foley, Weston Minissali

Acknowledgments
We would like to thank Paul White and especially Keith Cutler for making this
    possible, as well as Barbara Jean Germano, Greg L'Heureux, and Susan Mayoralgo.

Major league statistics provided by Elias Sports Bureau.
Minor league statistics provided by Howe SportsData International.
Record book, historical statistics, and disabled list information provided by
    Pete Palmer and Garry Gillette of Total Sports.
Photographs of Major League Baseball are used with the permission of
    Major League Baseball.
Rotisserie values provided by John Hunt

Contents

2000 Baseball Weekly Almanac

Leading off

▶**Baseball Weekly
editor Paul White
on the heroes of
the game**

USA SNAPSHOTS®

A look at statistics that shape the sports world

Decade of dominance

The Atlanta Braves have made it to the postseason every year this decade except once (1990). Because of the strike, playoffs weren't held in 1994. Teams with the most postseason appearances in the 1990s:

Atlanta Braves — 8

Cleveland Indians — 5

N.Y. Yankees — 5

Boston Red Sox — 4

Source: Elias Sports Bureau   By Scott Boeck and Genevieve Lynn, USA TODAY

Heroes will continue to thrill, captivate us

Todd Pratt rounded first base and hesitated. No fan, whether rooting for the New York Mets or not, dared breathe. The anticipation—to see whether leaping Arizona center fielder Steve Finley would pull back the series-winning home run—was every bit as delicious as a belt-high fastball or hanging curve heading toward Mark McGwire or Sammy Sosa. Pratt got the home run, of course, the fourth he had hit all year. McGwire and Sosa combined for 128 homers in 1999 and now rank 3-4, behind themselves, in single-season, longball performances.

Heroes all, the backup catcher and two superstars who seem to have changed the game forever. But think again. McGwire and Sosa really haven't changed the game. In fact, they merely are an extension of what continues to draw fans to baseball, what has brought back those disenchanted by money, labor issues and corporate ownership.

Heroes. It can be Pedro Martinez mesmerizing fans as adeptly as he confuses hitters during a 23-4 season. Or 35-year-old Jim Morris pitching his way to the majors and validating the dream of even those who have been little boys—in baseball terms, at least—for several decades.

Excite us, surprise us, thrill us so much that we wonder if anyone understands the catch in the throat, the moisture at the corner of the eye. We want heroes, whether we see them as reflections of ourselves or as the bigger-than-life shadows they cast. That's why Cal Ripken is credited with pulling the game back from the edge of oblivion, and Mark and Sammy for leading the burst into the next century.

To be sure, the things fans despise—or at least hate to acknowledge—won't go away. More corporate owners will come along, although the Southern California experience proves that Angels aren't always heavenly and "Dodger blue" can be as much a feeling as a tradition. Except to the fans of those teams, their disappointing results probably are a good thing. Fans want to believe money can't buy everything. Small-revenue teams will continue to have difficulty competing, or even surviving, but the Cincinnati Reds and Oakland A's remind us that underdogs will always be able to get our attention and sometimes catch up with the big guys. But what 1999 has shown us is that the sport is healthy—because fans want it to be healthy. It's healthy because of people, the ones who play it and the ones who love it. And those aren't mutually exclusive groups. That's how it always has been.

Some of us saw Willie, Mickey and the Duke. Others learned the words to the song before understanding those heroes' deeds. Regardless, we embrace the idea of heroes. Mark and Sammy—doesn't that roll off the tongue now every bit as easily as Willie, Mickey and the Duke?—already are a part of the lore.

Where have you gone, Joe DiMaggio?

You're Cal Ripken now, and soon you'll probably be Jeter and A-Rod, Nomar and Pedro, Bernie and Chipper. Notice how they don't require full names.

Just as importantly, we continue to find a compelling story like Morris, a tale of perseverance like Jeff Zimmerman, the "Who-the-heck-is-this-guy?" emergence of Erubiel Durazo. And we marvel at Manny Ramirez driving in so many runs, Randy Johnson's dazzling strikeout totals, Rickey Henderson finding another gear beyond the age of 40.

All that and more is why there's plenty of hope in baseball—always has been, always will be. The game, the people, the performances are bigger than the money and the power. Fans will never let it be otherwise.

—by Paul White, editor

Inside pitch

2000 Baseball Weekly Almanac

- ▶The Mac & Sammy show—again
- ▶1999: Field notes from the regular season
- ▶All-century teams (a few)
- ▶Baseball's famous flakes

USA SNAPSHOTS®

A look at statistics that shape the sports world

Future inductees

Hall of Famers Hank Aaron, Willie Mays and Stan Musial are all tied for most All-Star Game appearances with 24. Most All-Star selections for players on this year's rosters:

Cal Ripken	17
Tony Gwynn	15
Mark McGwire	11
Roberto Alomar	10
Ken Griffey, Jr.	10
Barry Larkin	10

Photo reference: AP

Source: Major League Baseball

By Scott Boeck and Bob Laird, USA TODAY

1999 Homer race: Play it again, Sam & Mac

Sammy Sosa finished 1999 with 63 homers.

Mark McGwire won the race with 65.

The Great Home Run Race of 1999 came to an anticlimactic end amid rain, thunder and lightning at Busch Stadium. Mark McGwire hit his 65th home run in the first, and two innings later Sammy Sosa hit his 63rd. The Cardinals won the game 9-5 when it was called in the middle of the fifth inning after a rain delay of one hour, 24 minutes.

Perhaps it is just as well.

McGwire wanted to finish the game, but he also said 1999 was one of his longest and most difficult seasons.

He said 50 home runs was and will always be his goal. But to do that, he said, "the work ethic has to be dead-on every day. Only Sammy and I know what it feels like. It is hard to describe."

McGwire's final home run of 1999 came against the Cubs' Steve Trachsel, who gave up Big Mac's historic No. 62 on Sept. 8, 1998. McGwire took an easy cut on this last of 1999 and the ball took off on a line drive estimated at 461 feet to straightaway center. Fireworks exploded.

The home run was career No. 522 for McGwire, moving him past Ted Williams and Willie McCovey into 10th place by himself on the all-time list.

McGwire became the first National League player to win consecutive home run titles since Dale Murphy in 1984-85.

Sosa's home run in the third inning, against the Cardinals' Larry Luebbers, was a fly ball that towered above Busch Stadium before crashing into the lower deck in left field. It was only his second homer in his last 11 games. Nobody was happier to see Sosa's homer than Leonel Antonio Fernandez, president of the Dominican Republic, Sosa's home country. His face lit up when he talked about Sosa.

"Sammy is the symbol of the Dominican Republic, and he has the support of my country's people," said Fernandez, who grew up wearing No. 27 in honor of Juan Marichal.

"It doesn't matter who finishes first or second. McGwire and Sosa are remarkable."

Sosa was honored to have the president in town. President Clinton saw him hit a home run at Wrigley Field, "and now my president sees me hit a home run," Sosa said.

After the game McGwire answered reporters' questions. Then he took off. "I'm exhausted," he said. "I can't wait to get home." But he'll be back for Home Run Derby III, starting April 3, 2000, at Busch Stadium when the Cardinals open against the Cubs.

—by Mel Antonen, USA TODAY

1999: Field notes from the regular season

And you thought Yankee fans were wild?

Minnesota Twins rookie first baseman Doug Mientkiewicz said there was no pressure in his major league debut, compared with an international tournament in Nicaragua when he played for Team USA.

"We were in a room about as big as [the Twins'] clubhouse," Mientkiewicz said. "There were windows all around, and people were banging on them. There were bomb threats. They busted a guy with an assault rifle and twenty rounds of ammo on a catwalk over our dugout before the first game."

Curt Schilling read his 'Top 10' on the Letterman show.

Get to the Parque on time

White Sox pitcher Jim Parque was scheduled to start April 13 in Boston, but was stuck in traffic. When he finally arrived, the gate attendant refused to let him enter because his player's ID card had expired. After arguing for 15 minutes, the attendant went to call security and Parque "just charged right in," said the attendant. Parque went 6⅔ innings, giving up three runs on five hits.

Crime Dog has a record

Tampa Bay's Fred McGriff set a major league record May 7 with a two-run homer at Jacobs Field. It was the 34th ballpark in which he hit a regular season home run, snapping a tie with the Cubs' Gary Gaetti and the Giants' Ellis Burks. The opposing pitcher was Cleveland's Dwight Gooden, a childhood friend and foe from Tampa. McGriff was homerless against Gooden in 34 previous at-bats, but folks still talk about the mammoth dinger McGriff hit in 1981, when he was a senior at Jefferson High and Gooden was a junior at Hillsborough High.

Schilling's Top 10 list

Phillies pitcher Curt Schilling appeared on David Letterman and read his "Top 10" list of pregame rituals:

▶10. Sit naked for an hour in a giant tub of Philadelphia Cream Cheese.

▶9. Caress old Mike Schmidt mustache clippings.

▶8. Call Pete Rose to see what the line is on the game.

▶7. Kiss all 200 of my cuddly, adorable Beanie Babies.

▶6. Smoke one of those weird cigarettes Allen Iverson gave me.

▶5. Wolf down burritos I shoplifted from Wawa.

▶4. Sing Boyz II Men song, "I'll Make Love to You," over stadium P.A. system.

▶3. Run through stadium parking lot snapping off antennas.

▶2. Learn what not to do by watching a tape of a Mets game.

▶1. Go rough up some snot-nosed Swarthmore punks.

The nerve, wasting beer!

The Cubs implemented tighter security measures at Wrigley Field, including restricting beer sales and increasing the ranks of security personnel. The crackdown came May 15, ten days after a game against Colorado was delayed in the eighth inning when fans, upset over a call, pelted the field with balls, bottles, coins, and beer. Seventy-five people were ejected but there were no arrests.

The Cubs' vice president of business operations said the team would keep a closer eye on the notorious "Bleacher Bums." Fans seen throwing objects onto the field now face arrest. Unless, of course, that object is an opposing team's home run ball. Fans are still allowed to throw those back.

More bite than your average baseball fight

The fights on the *Jerry Springer Show* are real, at least judging by the teeth marks on Cleveland assistant Ray Negron's thumb. Several Indians' players and Negron went to a filming of the show last week while the team was in Chicago. The show, "Why People Cheat on Their Spouses," aired July 26. Springer wanted a Cleveland player to serve as a celebrity bouncer.

"None of the players would do it, but they volunteered me," said Negron, an assistant to the team psychologist. Negron found himself rolling around in front of a TV camera with his right thumb in a woman's mouth as he tried to break up a fight, while Dwight Gooden, David Justice, Kenny Lofton, Steve Karsay, and Richie Sexson cheered him on.

Minnesota blimp a hit with Mieske

Seattle outfielder Matt Mieske was stretching before a game against Minnesota when the Twins' remote-controlled blimp hit him. He never thought about getting out of the way.

"I looked up and it was coming right at

The Twins' blimp whacked Seattle's Matt Mieske.

By Tom DiPace

me and lowering and lowering and lowering," he said. "I knew the guy was in the upper deck with the controller. It crashed right into me. So I just pushed it up into the air, and then two guys came out and got it fixed. I thought they were just messing around. And the guy said they didn't do it on purpose; it broke. It's really light. It didn't hurt. It was funny more than anything."

It must not have done much damage. Mieske had three hits, three runs and four RBI.

It ain't the pits any more

Rookie groundskeeper Heather Nabozny got rave reviews for renovating the mound at Tiger Stadium.

"In the past, the mound was horrible here," Mariners pitcher Jamie Moyer said. "After three or four innings, there was a deep hole in front of the rubber, and the landing area was all dust."

Nabozny, 28, the first female groundskeeper in the major leagues, said it's all in the clay.

"We're mixing some of the old clays with some of the new clays I brought in," she said. "Plus, we put an old tarp over

[the mound] during batting practice. That keeps the moisture in."

Nabozny, who spent five years as head groundskeeper for the West Michigan Whitecaps, a Tigers minor league affiliate, said she started buying Canadian clay after a Michigan supplier ran out.

"Whatever she's doing, it's perfect," Detroit reliever Doug Brocail said. "Even the bullpen mounds are better."

"You have to give him credit. Most guys don't start cheating until later in their career."

—Cubs' Mark Grace, on Diamondbacks reliever Byung-Hyun Kim. In the sixth game of his big-league career, Kim was ejected when a bandage with a gooey substance flew out from his uniform. Kim said he forgot to take it off.

El Duque: Mi White House no es su White House

It has been quite a journey for Yankees ace Orlando "El Duque" Hernandez. Less than two years ago, he was exiled in Costa Rica, waiting for a chance to pitch in the majors. In June 1999, he was with his teammates in the Rose Garden of the White House, shaking hands with President Clinton.

It wasn't the first time Hernandez visited with a nation's chief executive. But Hernandez, known for his voracious appetite, found something missing in the ceremony, which didn't include lunch.

"Mrs. Clinton asked El Duque what was the difference from the American White House and the center of government in Cuba when he was there with the national team," Yankees first base coach Jose Cardenal told the *Hartford Courant*. "He told her, 'The difference is that, in Cuba, they gave us food.'"

Hindsight is 30-30-30

The Toronto Blue Jays had tried 12 different players at DH by July.

"We have used everyone, and no one has really stepped up and taken the job," Blue Jays manager Jim Fregosi said. Meanwhile, their former DH, Jose Canseco, hit his 30th home run with the Tampa Bay Devil Rays, becoming the first player in big-league history to reach the mark with four different teams. What did that prove?

"I've been traded a lot," Canseco said.

Big, bad and bald

Sandy Alomar was in Boston during the All-Star break for an event to raise money for charity—and raise hair on his head.

The Cleveland catcher was one of seven big-leaguers who agreed to take Propecia for a year. In exchange, Propecia donated $25,000 to each player's favorite charity.

At the 2000 All-Star Game, the seven players will be judged to see whose hair improved the most, and Propecia will donate another $200,000 to the winner's charity.

The other players: Anaheim's Todd Greene, Atlanta's John Smoltz and Walt Weiss, the Cubs' Gary Gaetti, Boston's Bret Saberhagen, and San Francisco's Stan Javier.

Mariners fans: Don't read this

Seattle's Ken Griffey Jr. was named baseball's most marketable player in a survey of 90 industry experts conducted by the *Sports Business Daily*.

Griffey, who also earned the distinction in 1997, placed ahead of, in order: Mark McGwire, Sammy Sosa, Derek Jeter, Cal Ripken, and Griffey teammate Alex Rodriguez. NBC Sports president Ken Schanzer called Griffey "the gold standard, the best player of this generation."

However, some panelists suggested that Griffey could increase his visibility by playing in a larger market. Said Sportscrop president Marc Ganis: Griffey "needs to

leave Seattle to maximize his marketability, both for himself and for baseball."

Yer outta here! (Not)

When Anaheim Angels leadoff hitter Orlando Palmeiro was called out on strikes Aug. 4 and dropped his bat at home plate, umpire Tim Tschida viewed it as an act of defiance and ejected him. But Palmeiro was simply leaving the bat there for No. 2 hitter, Gary DiSarcina, who left it for the next batter, who left it for the next.

Batting coach Rod Carew had come up with the idea of using a single bat through the starting lineup as a way to loosen up the team. After DiSarcina and manager Terry Collins convinced Tschida that Palmeiro wasn't trying to show him up, the umpire rescinded the ejection.

"Once they make the decision, they don't change it. I don't think that's ever happened," said Palmeiro. "It may be a first, but I don't want to be famous for that."

By Tom DiPace

Brian McRae played for three different teams in 10 days.

Home sweet home

Frequent business travelers know what it's like to wake up in a hotel room and momentarily forget what city they're in. But outfielder Brian McRae went through a 10-day period in which he almost forgot where home was.

McRae played for three teams between July 31 and Aug. 9, going from the Mets to the Rockies to the Blue Jays. He never got to play a home game for Colorado, which was on a long road trip when he arrived, and his first three games with Toronto also were on the road. Considering that the Mets were on the road when he was traded, McRae went 15 days without playing a home game.

"I might never get to wear a white jersey again," he said.

He finally wore some home whites Aug. 13 in his SkyDome debut.

Notching up zeroes

Seven career milestones were reached over a four-day span beginning Aug. 5,

when Mark McGwire hit his 500th career home run.

The Yankees' Tino Martinez quietly hit career homer No. 200 Aug. 5, and Tony Gwynn reached 3,000 hits the following day. The day after that, Wade Boggs hit his 118th career home run to join the 3,000-hit club, and the White Sox's Frank Thomas connected on career home run No. 300.

Two more marks were reached Aug. 8, when the Giants' Ellis Burks collected his 250th career home run and the Red Sox's Pedro Martinez notched his 100th career win.

What's that smell?

Players never forget their debuts, but Rangers pitcher Doug Davis would like to give it a try. Davis, 23, made his debut Aug. 9. Damage report: $2\frac{1}{3}$ innings, 11 hits, 10 runs (all earned) and three home runs. On the plus side, he struck out two batters and walked none, but it wasn't enough. He was optioned back to AAA Oklahoma the next day.

A little history lesson

The Mets' Shawon Dunston lost track, and Mark McGwire lost a piece of history.

When McGwire hit a pair of homers—Nos. 49 and 50—at Shea Stadium, he became the first player to hit 50 home runs in four consecutive seasons. The 50th landed in the center field bleachers, where a fan caught it momentarily and dropped it. Dunston picked up the ball and flipped it to a man holding a child.

"I thought it was 51," Dunston said."I didn't know. I felt so bad."

When Dunston reached base later in the game, he apologized to McGwire, who later said of home run No. 50: "If the father and the young kid have it, so be it. Let them cherish it."

No. 49 was already long gone—it flew at least 502 feet, breaking a lightbulb halfway up the scoreboard in right-center.

Awesome autographs

Rockies right fielder Larry Walker, who asks that $25 be donated to a children's charity when people request autographs through the mail, received a stern letter from Larry Sanders of Loveland, Colo. It turns out that Sanders donated $25, but still had not received the autograph.

Walker telephoned Sanders, apologized, and not only immediately sent him the autographed baseball card, but also an autographed bat.

Walker thought no more about it until Aug. 18, when he opened his mail and found an autographed picture of Babe Ruth with his wife and daughter. "It turns out he was a friend of Ruth's daughter," Walker said. "Unbelievable. I can't believe he did this. This is awesome."

Who knew?

"I'm not worried about [the Reds]," Houston's Jose Lima said in August. "If we play like we can play, it doesn't matter what the Reds do, because we're going to win the division.

"We're still the team to beat," he added. "The Reds have been playing good base-

By Michael Schwarz, USA TODAY

Jose Lima said the Reds were no threat to his Astros.

ball, but they aren't the best team in the division. The Astros are."

Lima's a pretty brash player. But he wasn't the only Astro who believed the Red menace would be thwarted.

"I still believe we have the best team in the Central Division and I still believe we're going to win the division," manager Larry Dierker said. At the time, Houston had a 19-29 mark against teams with a record over .500.

Sveum back in the swing

Dale Sveum just wanted to keep making a living in baseball. Now he's made history, although he's taken a roundabout route.

The Yankees released Sveum in 1998, but he stayed on as bullpen coach. He had accepted a scouting job with Milwaukee for 1999, but Arizona invited him to spring training. Sveum played in AAA for the Diamondbacks and was released after a month.

Pittsburgh signed him to a minor league contract and recalled him in July. In August, Sveum became the second Pittsburgh player this century to homer from both sides of the plate in the same game.

All he's cracked up to be

Arizona's Rob Ryan was smashing in his September big-league debut, if you ask Joe Oliver. Ryan swung at a pitch and connected with the Pittsburgh catcher's head. Oliver staggered off, dazed. He autographed his cracked catcher's helmet, "Rob Ryan, first major league hit" and sent it to Ryan. "I think he was looking to take my head off," Oliver told *The Beaver County Times*, "so he could put it on his mantel as a souvenir."

Greg Maddux (above) and Charles Nagy are the only pitchers with 15 wins in each of the past five seasons.

Maddux and that Nagy guy

Charles Nagy and Greg Maddux may not be best friends, but they do share something special: They're the only pitchers who have won at least 15 games every year for the past five seasons.

Nagy is used to not getting much respect. He was even able to joke about it when asked about the key to consistency.

"With other guys, it's the way they pitch," he told the (Akron) *Beacon Jour-nal*. "With me, it's the run support." Of course, Maddux's streak is just a little more special—he's won 15 games every year since 1988.

Jordan put the 'run' back in home run

Philadelphia infielder Kevin Jordan is doing his part to speed up the game. According to the Phillies' cable TV station, Jordan circled the bases in a tidy 17 seconds after homering in a game against San Francisco in September. Compare that to Barry Bonds, who homered four times in the first two games of the same series, and took nearly twice as long as Jordan to navigate the bases. Bonds averaged 31 seconds per home-run trot.

No cheers for the Bronx

Ken Griffey Jr. didn't say where he'll go when he leaves the Mariners but you can cross out the Bronx. He still holds a grudge against George Steinbrenner for ordering him off the field as a 12-year-old during batting practice when Ken Griffey Sr. played for the Yankees.

"Steinbrenner sent a security guard to tell my father that 'George didn't want him on the field,' meaning me," Griffey said. "Graig Nettles' kid was on the field and nothing was said to him. I never stepped on the field [again] in the Stadium until I was a Mariner."

All together now, 1-2-3

When you're out of contention in September, sometimes it's easier to count the number of days until vacation than the number of outs in an inning.

San Diego's Reggie Sanders began running for the outfield after being retired in a game against Montreal. Problem was, he was only the second out.

Later in that game, Sanders struck out to conclude the seventh inning. But play continued. Veteran plate umpire Jerry Layne's indicator read two outs, and none of the Expos headed for the dugout, either.

Here's a new one: Brick day

The verdict is in: The Brewers will play Opening Day in Miller Park—in 2001. The team will have to play the 2000 opener at County Stadium because the new ballpark won't be ready. Fans thought the Oct. 3 game against Cincinnati would be the last in County Stadium, so 53,000 bought tickets for the contest. The Brewers tried to make amends by offering $1 parking, $1 hot dogs and a County Stadium brick.

Mood music

Houston's Billy Wagner and the Yankees' Mariano Rivera had Metallica's "Enter Sandman" piped over the sound system as they warmed up for appearances in 1999. More closers' favorites:
▶John Franco, New York Mets, "Johnny B. Goode" by Chuck Berry
▶Trevor Hoffman, San Diego, "Hell's Bells" by AC/DC
▶Jose Mesa, Seattle, "Smoke on the Water" by Deep Purple
▶Robb Nen, San Francisco, "Enter Sandman" by Metallica
▶Troy Percival, Anaheim, "Smoke on the Water" by Deep Purple
▶John Rocker, Atlanta, "I Wanna Rock" by Twisted Sister
▶Scott Williamson, Cincinnati, "Hell's Bells" by AC/DC

Teaching by example

High school baseball coach Jim Morris never made it above Class A in the '80s, but he bet his Regan County High School baseball team in West Texas that if they made the state playoffs, he would go to an upcoming Tampa Bay Devil Rays tryout camp. They did, and he did.

The Devil Rays were impressed by his 98-mph fastballs and signed him, playing him first in AA Orlando, then AAA Durham. The 35-year-old left-hander became the oldest rookie in the majors in 29 years when he struck out Royce Clayton in a late-September game against Texas. He was the oldest rookie since 36-year-old Minnie Mendoza with Minnesota in 1970 and the oldest rookie pitcher since 41-year-old Diomedes Oliva with Pittsburgh in 1960. "I felt like my heart was going to jump out of my chest," Morris said.

> *"I've always prided myself on never striking out four times in a game. And I still haven't."*
>
> **—Philadelphia's Scott Rolen** after striking out five times in a game against the Padres.

In the (twilight) zone

Pirates reliever Brad Clontz took the mound Oct. 3 with the bases loaded against the Mets and the score tied. He bounced his first pitch to the backstop and the winning run scooted home—keeping the Mets' season alive for another day.

Watching behind home plate at Shea Stadium was former Brooklyn Dodger Ralph Branca, who exactly 48 years earlier had tossed a letter-high fastball that Bobby Thomson smashed to launch the famous cry, "The Giants win the pennant! The Giants win the pennant!"

Branca looked up when Clontz took the mound and saw that it was 4:46 p.m. Eastern Daylight Time. Branca's brush with infamy happened at 3:46 p.m., Eastern Standard Time, meaning Clontz was about to throw a baseball at precisely the same moment of the day that Bianca had thrown his.

"I was saying Oct. 3 owes this family one," said Branca, whose son-in-law is Mets manager Bobby Valentine. The Mets made the playoffs the next day by beating the Reds, 5-0.

Torre's iron man streak

Yankees manager Joe Torre gave almost all of his regulars a day off Oct. 3. Then he gave himself a break, too. With the Yankees already assured home-field advantage throughout the AL playoffs, Torre turned the helm over to outfielder Paul O'Neill.

O'Neill, who had bruised his right side and lower back when he crashed into a fence the night before, filled Torre's role as manager as the Yankees, using a lineup featuring just one regular—catcher Jorge Posada.

"We're looking forward to the playoffs, so you can have fun with this game," said O'Neill, who joked that his teammates wouldn't play for him. "I'm walking around before the game asking guys if they will do this for me; they'd say 'No.' It was quite a challenge and we didn't live up to it." The Yankees lost 6-2.

Camped out on the Corner

The Tigers couldn't quite say goodbye in their final game at Tiger Stadium, so the trio of closer Todd Jones, pitcher Brian Moehler, and pitching coach Dan Warthen spent the night at the stadium.

"We were going to get a tent and sleep on the field," Jones said, "but the stadium operations director caught wind of it and bagged that idea. So we came back about 1 a.m., walked around the stadium and then slept in the clubhouse. It was awesome, sleeping in her lap on the last night."

Hats off to Wells. (Gloves and jerseys, too)

David Wells has a thirst for baseball memorabilia.

Who can forget the day he wore one of Babe Ruth's caps on the mound while he was a Yankee?

On the last week of the 1999 season, Wells added a number of items to his collection, courtesy of an auction in New York. He is now the proud owner of a glove worn by Ruth; the jersey Rickey Henderson wore May 29, 1990, when he broke Ty Cobb's American League stolen-base record with Wells on the mound; and a Phil Rizzuto glove.

The items will be kept at Wells's Palm Harbor, Fla., home, where he has spent $70,000 on a room that will house his baseball treasures.

Straw's stirring blast

Darryl Strawberry's towering home run Oct. 1 at Tropicana Field brought back memories of past moonshots—like the one in 1988 that he nearly drove out of Montreal's Olympic Stadium and the one he smacked off the clock tower at Busch Stadium in St. Louis. But the Yankee also had a less pleasant reason for reflection, as Oct. 1 marked the one-year anniversary of his cancer diagnosis.

Strawberry said he is reminded of his bout with colon cancer every time he looks at the nasty scar that runs the length of his abdomen. "It was a real bad time. I was in a lot of pain—physically and mentally," said Strawberry.

For a night, at least, he could forget. Strawberry sent a fastball crashing off a pole that connects the roof of the dome to a catwalk 120 feet above right field.

"That's the best I've ever hit a ball," said Strawberry. "That's a once-in-a-lifetime thing."

While stadium officials estimated Strawberry's blast at 425 feet, few accepted that calculation.

"They were off by about 100 feet," Yankees pitcher David Cone said.

Kersee got Jordan back on track

Atlanta's Brian Jordan finally figured out how to play through the pain in his right hand with an assist from personal trainer and Olympic coach Bob Kersee. For 30 minutes every day, Kersee manipulated Jordan's hand and wrist, massaging the stiffness.

Jordan had hit .140 with five RBI in the first half of September. He went 8-for-24 with seven RBI and six runs scored after the treatment began. He homered Sept. 28 for the first time since Aug. 15.

No 'I' in team

Colorado's Larry Walker isn't a player wrapped up in his own stats, even though he hit .379 for the season and won his second consecutive NL batting title.

Couldn't he savor, if only for a moment, such a sweet year?

"No, no sweetness involved," Walker said. "When you're talking about all of us going home Oct. 3, what's the use of what you did individually?"

Bob Wickman set a save—and handshake—record.

A man of the people

Milwaukee closer and native Wisconsinite Bob Wickman is a fan favorite at County Stadium, and how he celebrated setting the Brewers' single-season save record shows why. Wickman shook hands with teammates on the field—and then shook hands with ushers, fans, and a groundskeeper on his way to the dugout.

Junior-ball

Meet manager Ken Griffey Jr.

Yes, Junior.

Seattle manager Lou Piniella let Griffey make out the Mariners' lineup card for the season finale against Oakland.

"I thought about pitching," Griffey said with a smile, "but then I decided [starter John] Halama had to hit, and he didn't want to do that."

Outfielder Jay Buhner coached at first base for one inning.

"It was Junior's lineup today, he made it up all himself," Piniella said. "Unfortunately, it counts on my record." Seattle lost 3-1.

Thanks for your patience

Only 23,892 fans attended the Phillies' Fan Appreciation Day, as the team wrapped up its 12th losing season in 13 years. Among the signs: "Wait Till Next Century."

Rankings rankle Schmidt

While fans ranked the top 100 players in baseball history for what would become Major League Baseball's official All-Century Team, Philadelphia Hall of Famer Mike Schmidt wondered how anyone could possibly measure players from different eras.

"How can I compare Sammy Sosa to Roberto Clemente?" Schmidt asked.

"I mean, you can, but realistically it's tough. Sosa plays when the ball goes 10 yards further and the fences are 10 feet shorter.

"And when I played we flew charters while Eddie Mathews rode a train.

"I'd hit 35 home runs and drive in 110 runs and I'd be an MVP candidate. With those numbers today, I'd be a No. 8-hole hitter."

Major League Baseball All-Century Team

Final selections for the All-Century Team:
▶**Pitcher:** Roger Clemens, Bob Gibson, Lefty Grove, Walter Johnson, Sandy Koufax, Christy Mathewson, Nolan Ryan, Warren Spahn, Cy Young.
▶**Catcher:** Johnny Bench, Yogi Berra.
▶**First Base:** Lou Gehrig, Mark McGwire.
▶**Second Base:** Rogers Hornsby, Jackie Robinson.
▶**Shortstop:** Ernie Banks, Cal Ripken Jr., Honus Wagner.
▶**Third Base:** Brooks Robinson, Mike Schmidt.
▶**Outfield:** Hank Aaron, Ty Cobb, Joe DiMaggio, Ken Griffey, Jr., Mickey Mantle, Willie Mays, Stan Musial, Pete Rose, Babe Ruth, Ted Williams.

Fans' voting results

Final results of fan balloting:
▶**Catcher:** 1. Johnny Bench, 1,010,403; 2. Yogi Berra, 704,208; 3. Carlton Fisk, 322,384; 4. Roy Campanella, 247,909; 5. Josh Gibson, 233,288; 6. Mickey Cochrane, 75,344; 7. Bill Dickey, 74,295; 8. Gabby Hartnett, 24,198.
▶**First Base:** 1. Lou Gehrig, 1,207,992; 2. Mark McGwire, 517,181; 3. Jimmie Foxx, 351,488; 4. Harmon Killebrew, 185,622; 5. Eddie Murray, 161,564; 6. Hank Greenberg, 114,317; 7. Willie McCovey, 106,717; 8. George Sisler, 28,378; 9. Buck Leonard, 20,091; 10. Bill Terry, 12,976.
▶**Second Base:** 1. Jackie Robinson, 788,116; 2. Rogers Hornsby, 630,761; 3. Joe Morgan, 608,660; 4. Rod Carew, 430,267; 5. Nap Lajoie, 90,402; 6. Eddie Collins, 58,836; 7. Charlie Gehringer, 45,663; 8. Frankie Frisch, 27,527.
▶**Shortstop:** 1. Cal Ripken Jr., 669,033; 2. Ernie Banks, 598,168; 3. Ozzie Smith, 589,025; 4. Honus Wagner, 526,740; 5. Robin Yount, 134,655; 6. Luis Aparicio, 129,328; 7. Luke Appling, 28,877; 8. Joe Cronin, 27,789.
▶**Third Base:** 1. Mike Schmidt, 855,654; 2. Brooks Robinson, 761,700; 3. George

Brett, 656,511; 4. Eddie Mathews, 174,529; 5. Paul Molitor, 160,271; 6. Pie Traynor, 96,699.
▶**Outfield:** 1. Babe Ruth, 1,158,044; 2. Hank Aaron, 1,156,782; 3. Ted Williams, 1,125,583; 4. Willie Mays, 1,115,896; 5. Joe DiMaggio, 1,054,423; 6. Mickey Mantle, 988,168; 7. Ty Cobb, 777,056; 8. Ken Griffey Jr., 645,389; 9. Pete Rose, 629,742; 10. Roberto Clemente, 582,937; 11. Stan Musial, 571,279; 12. Joe Jackson, 326,415; 13. Reggie Jackson, 296,039; 14. Tony Gwynn, 232,476; 15. Carl Yastrzemski, 222,082; 16. Frank Robinson, 220,226; 17. Rickey Henderson, 180,940; 18. Barry Bonds, 173,279; 19. Lou Brock, 131,361; 20. Billy Williams, 97,911; 21. Tris Speaker, 84,461; 22. Willie Stargell, 71,585; 23. Al Kaline, 67,719; 24. Duke Snider, 63,410; 25. Cool Papa Bell, 59,189; 26. Mel Ott, 51,748; 27. Ralph Kiner, 32,302; 28. Al Simmons, 15,930; 29. Paul Waner, 15,057; 30. Oscar Charleston, 13,893; 31. Joe Medwick, 11,238; 32. Wee Willie Keeler, 10,553; 33. Goose Goslin, 9,475; 34. Harry Heilmann, 9,415.
▶**Pitcher:** 1. Nolan Ryan, 992,040; 2. Sandy Koufax, 970,434; 3. Cy Young, 867,523; 4. Roger Clemens, 601,244; 5. Bob Gibson, 582,031; 6. Walter Johnson, 479,279; 7. Greg Maddux, 431,751; 8. Steve Carlton, 405,365; 9. Satchel Paige, 399,657; 10. Warren Spahn, 337,215; 11. Tom Seaver, 330,219; 12. Whitey Ford, 253,120; 13. Bob Feller, 252,115; 14. Christy Mathewson, 249,747; 15. Jim Palmer, 158,266; 16. Grover Cleveland Alexander, 151,255; 17. Dennis Eckersley, 143,710; 18. Lefty Grove, 142,169; 19. Dizzy Dean, 130,389; 20. Juan Marichal, 122,366; 21. Rollie Fingers, 106,416; 22. Carl Hubbell, 54,618; 23. Mordecai Brown, 31,432; 24. Robin Roberts, 23,366; 25. Eddie Plank, 13,195; 26. Ed Walsh, 12,687.

Reporters select Latin American all-century team

As a protest to the absence of Roberto Clemente on Major League Baseball's All-Century Team, a group of 21 Latin American sports reporters chose the "Latin American Ideal 20th Century Team." The reporters sent a letter to Commissioner Bud Selig expressing "the most fervent disappointment for the unjustifiable exclusion of Roberto Clemente."

Said Hall of Fame broadcaster Jaime Jarrin: "We still cannot believe the omission of such a great ballplayer, who among other things opened the doors for the major leagues to benefit from the incomparable contributions of the great Latin American players."

▶**Catcher:** Ivan Rodriguez, Manny Sanguillen
▶**First base:** Orlando Cepeda, Andres Galarraga
▶**Second base:** Rod Carew, Roberto Alomar
▶**Shortstop:** Luis Aparicio, David Concepcion, Alfonso Carrasquel
▶**Third base:** Tony Perez, Vinny Castilla
▶**Outfield:** Roberto Clemente, Sammy Sosa, Juan Gonzalez, Tony Oliva, Bernie Williams, Minnie Minoso
▶**Pitcher:** Juan Marichal, Luis Tiant, Fernando Valenzuela, Dennis Martinez, Martin DiHigo, Mike Cuellar, Mariano Rivera, Camilo Pascual, Roberto Hernandez
▶**Pinch-hitter:** Manny Mota
▶**Designated hitter:** Edgar Martinez, Jose Canseco
▶**Latin American player of the century:** Clemente

The Joe Black all-century team

Also selecting an All-Century Team was former major leaguer Joe Black, who was in the major leagues from 1952-57 after pitching in the Negro Leagues from 1943-1950.

Black, 75, was the first African-American pitcher to win a World Series game. His Brooklyn Dodgers lost to the New York Yankees in the 1952 World Series, in which Black, a reliever, was called on to start three games in seven days. Black won a 4-2 decision before losing 2-0 and 4-2.

Black was voted the 1952 National League Rookie of the Year after winning 15 games as a reliever. He also roomed that year with the legendary Jackie Robinson.

▶**Catcher:** Josh Gibson, Johnny Bench
▶**First base:** Lou Gehrig, Hank Greenberg
▶**Second base:** Jackie Robinson, Joe Morgan
▶**Shortstop:** Ozzie Smith, Honus Wagner
▶**Third base:** Mike Schmidt, Pie Traynor
▶**Outfield:** Willie Mays, Hank Aaron, Frank Robinson, Mickey Mantle, Joe DiMaggio, Ted Williams, Babe Ruth, Ty Cobb, Stan Musial, Roberto Clemente
▶**Pitcher:** Cy Young, Lefty Grove, Satchel Paige, Robin Roberts, Steve Carlton, Sandy Koufax, Juan Marichal, Warren Spahn, Bob Gibson, Christy Mathewson
—from staff and wire reports

The other all-century team: A tip of the propeller cap to baseball's famous flakes

Former Detroit Tiger ace Mark Fidrych's 45th birthday took place in 1999. And while there is no distinct definition of a flake, Fidrych surely qualified as one by talking to baseballs before he hurled them from the mound. His career was short-lived, but the memory of his antics lives on. In his honor, the following players are nominated to join him on the starting lineup of the All-Century All-Star All-Flake team.

▶**Danny Gardella:** Before a 1945 road game with the New York Giants in Cincinnati, he left a suicide note for teammate Nat Reyes. He also left the window of their hotel room open. When Reyes looked out that window, a grinning Gardella was hanging from the ledge.

▶**Jimmy Piersall:** Upon hitting his 100th career homer in 1963, Piersall ran the bases facing backward. He also once doused an umpire with a squirt gun, occasionally threw balls at the exploding Comiskey Park scoreboard (it irritated him) and, called upon to make the ceremonial first pitch at the 1974 Babe Ruth League World Series, chucked the ball into the parking lot.

▶**Norm Cash:** Realizing he had no chance to avoid being the final out of a Nolan Ryan no-hitter in 1973, Cash went to the plate with a table leg instead of a bat.

▶**Jerry Coleman:** Flakiness did not manifest itself in Coleman, a '50s infielder for the Yankees, until he became a broadcaster for the Padres in the '70s. Then, he started saying things like "Randy Jones, the left-hander with the Karl Marx hairdo"; "Grubb goes back. He's under the warning track"; "There's someone warming up in the bullpen, but he's obscured by his number"; and "He slides into second with a standup double."

▶**Dock Ellis:** In 1970, Ellis no-hit the Padres, then later admitted he took LSD before the game. Which perhaps explains his eight walks. In 1974, Ellis began a game by intentionally hitting three Reds. Tony Perez ducked Ellis's beanballs and walked, then Johnny Bench dodged two more head-hunting pitches before Ellis was removed.

▶**Tug McGraw:** This southpaw reliever once said he didn't need uppers because "just being left-handed is like taking a greenie a day." When asked whether he preferred artificial or natural turf, McGraw replied, "I don't know. I never smoked Astroturf." He called his fastball the "Lady Godiva" because there was nothing on it.

▶**Dizzy Dean:** The National League's last 30-game winner always was a proud advocate of the philosophy that too much thinking gets in the way of good pitching. He once proclaimed, "The doctors X-rayed my head and found nothing." As an announcer, he was known to talk about "testicle fortitude."

▶**Bill Lee:** The "Spaceman" was once the presidential candidate of the Rhinoceros Party, running on the platform of "No guns, no butter." When his Boston Red Sox switched to a two-tone cap, he protested by wearing a propeller atop his.

▶**Marv Throneberry:** "Marvelous Marv" epitomized the 1962 Mets by once failing to touch first and second base on the way to a would-be triple. The initials of Marvin Eugene Throneberry spell MET. His flakiness earned him appearances in 13 beer commercials. And George Brett swung a T-85 Throneberry-model bat when he hit his infamous pine-tar home run.

Sources: The Cultural Encyclopedia of Baseball; Pep Talk; Baseball's Greatest Quotations; The Baseball Timeline.
　　　　—by Tom Weir, USA TODAY

NL/AL beat

▶Features

▶1999 Hall of Fame
 inductees

▶All-Star Game

▶1999 award winners

▶Division wrap-ups

▶1999 league leaders

▶Obituaries

USA SNAPSHOTS®

A look at statistics that shape the sports world

Hits on deck

The late Joe DiMaggio has the famous record for consecutive games with a hit at 56. Who holds the record for consecutive at-bats with a hit?

Pinky Higgins, Red Sox (1938)	12
Walt Dropo, Tigers (1952)	12
Tris Speaker, Indians (1920)	11
Johnny Pesky, Red Sox (1946)	11

Source: *Total Baseball*   By Scott Boeck and Kevin Rechin, USA TODAY

Boggs retires after 18 years and 3,000 hits

Wade Boggs was one of the best hitters this century.

There were times Wade Boggs made hitting look so easy. Give Boggs a pitch he could handle and he'd line it off Fenway's Green Monster or drive it to the gap in right-center. Make a tough, two-strike pitch on him and he'd still flick it to the opposite field for a single.

Clearly, hitting a baseball came easily for Boggs. Stepping away from his playing career did not. But Boggs did just that on Nov. 11.

"It wasn't an easy decision," he said. "An athlete can always look in the mirror and say, 'OK, I can still play.' Deep down inside, probably I thought I still could. Even at 41, I still want to get to the ballpark early, put on the uniform, go out, take batting practice and ground balls. It's still fun."

Boggs, who batted .328 for his career, hoped to play one more season, but Tampa Bay suggested that to do so, he would have to do it elsewhere. So Boggs elected to remain in his hometown and become a special assistant to Devil Rays' GM Chuck LaMar. He'd like to become a broadcaster.

"I guess I could have turned this down and gone elsewhere and tried to play and not done well and struggled," Boggs said.

"Why not go out on top?"

Boggs freely admitted that he could have hit for more power during his career, but he made his living getting on base. Particularly at Fenway Park, he viewed his function at the top of the batting order to be a table-setter. Six times he led the American League in on-base percentage. Not only did he hit .361 or higher four times, he led the league in doubles and runs in 1988 and 1989.

For years, Boggs was renowned for his achievements with the bat. Blessed with extraordinary hand-eye coordination, he became the only player this century to collect 200 hits in seven consecutive seasons, and notched an astonishing 240 hits, batting .368, in 1985.

But he worked at all phases of his game, including his defense. Plagued by an erratic arm early in his career, Boggs steadily improved to the point where he won his first of two Gold Gloves with the Yankees in 1994. At age 36, on his way to playing 78 consecutive errorless games, Boggs became the oldest non-pitcher to win a Gold Glove.

Boggs came up through the Boston system, but after he hit just .259 in an injury-plagued 1992 season, the Red Sox figured he might be washed up and let him go to New York as a free agent.

He hit higher than .300 each of the next four years, including .342 in the strike-interrupted 1994 season, and was named to his 12th consecutive All-Star team in 1996.

He celebrated his first World Series championship by riding around Yankee Stadium on horseback in October 1996. He was a Devil Ray when he became the first major leaguer to make his 3,000th career hit a home run. But it was his accomplishments in that Red Sox uniform—five batting titles in six seasons—that likely will earn him a ticket to Cooperstown sooner rather than later.

—by Seth Livingstone

Terry Steinbach played in three World Series.

Steinbach, McGee declare retirement

Minnesota Twins catcher Terry Steinbach, 37, retired from baseball after 11 years with the Oakland A's organization and three with the Minnesota Twins. Steinbach made his major league debut with Oakland in 1986, hitting a home run in his first at-bat. He played in three World Series with the A's (1988, 1989, 1990), winning a title in 1989. He signed with the Twins as a free agent in 1996 and finished his career with a .271 batting average and 162 home runs, including eight grand slams. His best season was 1996, when he set an American League record for catchers with 34 home runs.

St. Louis Cardinals outfielder Willie McGee, 41, announced his retirement in a live television interview with KSDK-TV.

Willie McGee was MVP and won two batting titles.

"I knew a while ago that this was probably going to be it," McGee said. "The way my season went, it seems like it's just time. I tried to trick myself and find something inside to get me motivated, but it's just not there."

McGee was a World Series hero as a rookie for the 1982 title-winning Cardinals. He was the National League MVP in 1985, batting .353 with 216 hits, won two NL batting titles during his career, and finished 1999 with a career .295 batting average. His performance had slipped the past two years—he hit .251 in 1999—but Cardinals manager Tony La Russa had said McGee would have a job next season if he wanted one.

Players' Choice: Griffey best in '90s

Ken Griffey, Jr., the Seattle Mariners outfielder who asked his team to trade him, was voted player of the 1990s by fellow major leaguers in the Players' Choice Awards. Griffey beat out Atlanta Braves pitcher Greg Maddux and San Francisco Giants outfielder Barry Bonds. Boston Red Sox ace Pedro Martinez won player of the year, and Chicago Cubs outfielder Sammy Sosa won man of the year for performance on the field and contributions to the community.

Among 1999 American League awards, Cleveland Indians outfielder Manny Ramirez was named outstanding player, Martinez was outstanding pitcher, Kansas City Royals outfielder Carlos Beltran was outstanding rookie, and Oakland A's first baseman John Jaha was comeback player.

In the National League, Atlanta third baseman Chipper Jones was voted outstanding player, Houston Astros' Mike Hampton was outstanding pitcher, Florida Marlins outfielder Preston Wilson was outstanding rookie, and Florida pitcher Alex Fernandez was comeback player.

Balloting was conducted by the players' association in September, with players on all 30 teams eligible to vote.

By Barbara Jean Germano, *Baseball Weekly*

Mark Grace didn't get to the World Series, but he finished the 1990s with more hits than anybody.

Grace has most hits of the decade

Chicago Cubs first baseman Mark Grace finished the 1990s with more hits than any other major league ballplayer. His 1,754 hits were seven ahead of Texas Rangers' Rafael Palmeiro. Grace also led in doubles with 364, two more than Houston's Craig Biggio. Every player who has led a decade in hits, except career hits leader Pete Rose, is in the Hall of Fame. Grace, who has always played in the shadow of such Cubs greats as Andre Dawson, Ryne Sandberg and Sammy Sosa, was keenly aware of his new place in history. "I'm not a spectacular player," he said. "I'm not a flashy player. I don't do dances. I don't wear fancy sunglasses or fancy earrings. But one thing you can depend on is that I'll be out there playing first base and that I'll be getting a lot of hits." Grace has been with the Cubs since 1988 and he's only the second player in team history to be the opening-day starter at the same position for an entire decade. In addition to the decade hits and doubles mark, Grace got his 2,000th hit on Aug. 2. He batted .309 with 16 home runs and 91 RBI in 1999.

Y2K managers

Following are the major league baseball managers for the 2000 season.

American League
- Anaheim: Mike Scioscia
- Baltimore: Mike Hargrove
- Boston: Jimy Williams
- Chicago: Jerry Manuel
- Cleveland: Charlie Manuel
- Detroit: Phil Garner
- Kansas City: Tony Muser
- Minnesota: Tom Kelly
- New York: Joe Torre
- Oakland: Art Howe
- Seattle: Lou Piniella
- Tampa Bay: Larry Rothschild
- Texas: Johnny Oates
- Toronto: Jim Fregosi

National League
- Arizona: Buck Showalter
- Atlanta: Bobby Cox
- Chicago: Don Baylor
- Cincinnati: Jack McKeon
- Colorado: Buddy Bell
- Florida: John Boles
- Houston: Larry Dierker
- Los Angeles: Davey Johnson
- Milwaukee: Davey Lopes
- Montreal: Felipe Alou
- New York: Bobby Valentine
- Philadelphia: Terry Francona
- Pittsburgh: Gene Lamont
- St. Louis: Tony La Russa
- San Diego: Bruce Bochy
- San Francisco: Dusty Baker

Slam happy

Aug. 9 marked the first time five grand slams were hit on the same day.
- **Fernando Tatis**, St. Louis, vs. Billy Brewer, Philadelphia.
- **Jose Vidro**, Montreal, vs. Carlos Almanzar, San Diego.
- **Mike Lowell**, Florida, vs. John Johnstone, San Francisco.
- **Bernie Williams**, New York Yankees, vs. Mike Oquist, Oakland.
- **Jay Buhner**, Seattle, vs. John Snyder, Chicago White Sox.

Who wants to be a millionaire?

More than twice as many major league players earned $1 million or more in 1999 than earned the $200,000 minimum. According to USA TODAY's survey of all major league salaries, 342 players made at least $1 million, while only 145 got the minimum. The Boston Red Sox and New York Mets had the most millionaires with 20 each; the Florida Marlins had the fewest with just two. The average salary for the 920 major league players on Aug. 31 rosters and disabled lists was $1,571,107, based on an industry payroll of $1,445,418,343. The average salary increased 13.24 percent this year, the largest jump since 1997, when it went up 19.33 percent. Including $3,860,246 in termination pay, the World Series champion New York Yankees became the first team in history to pass the $90 million mark. Their payroll was $91,990,955, a disparity of $77,340,955 between them and the Florida Marlins, who had the lowest payroll of the 30 teams at $14,650,000.

—by Hal Bodley, USA TODAY

1999 team payrolls

Playoff teams in ALL CAPS

Team	Actual	Term.	Total
Ana	$49,868,166	$1,472,131	$51,340,297
ARI	69,945,999	100,819	70,046,818
ATL	74,965,000	4,291,599	79,256,599
Bal	70,593,363	4,850,000	75,443,363
BOS	71,470,000	860,656	72,330,656
ChiC	24,535,000	—	24,535,000
ChiWS	55,368,500	51,148	55,419,648
Cin	42,142,761	-4,111,476	38,031,285
Cle	73,417,962	113,730	73,531,692
Col	54,367,504	—	54,367,504
Det	34,934,666	2,020,000	36,954,666
Fla	15,150,000	-500,000	14,650,000
Hou	55,439,000	950,000	56,389,000
K.C.	16,557,000	—	16,557,000
L.A.	71,115,786	5,491,461	76,607,247
Mil	42,927,395	49,180	42,976,575
Min	16,345,000	-500,000	15,845,000
Mon	16,338,000	-1,322,750	15,015,250
NYM	71,281,425	229,098	71,510,523
NYY	88,130,709	3,860,246	91,990,955
Oak	24,150,333	1,058,525	25,208,858
Phil	30,441,500	—	30,441,500
Pit	24,167,666	-485,246	23,682,420
St. L	46,173,195	163,934	46,337,129
S.D.	45,832,179	675,000	46,507,179
S.F.	45,934,557	57,377	45,991,934
Sea	44,246,336	1,104,918	45,351,254
T.B.	37,737,500	121,951	37,860,451
Tex	80,801,598	—	80,801,598
Tor	48,065,333	781,967	48,847,300
Totals	$1,442,443,433	$21,385,268	$1,463,828,701

SOURCE: *Major League Baseball*

Average player salaries

Year	Average	Inc./dec.	Median
1976	$52,300	—	—
1977	74,000	41.49%	
1978	97,800	32.16%	
1979	121,900	24.64%	
1980	146,500	20.18%	
1981	196,500	34.13%	
1982	245,000	24.68%	
1983	289,000	17.96%	$207,500
1984	325,900	12.77%	229,750
1985	368,998	13.22%	265,833
1986	410,517	11.25%	275,000
1987	402,579	-1.93%	235,000
1988	430,688	6.98%	235,000
1989	489,539	13.66%	280,000
1990	589,483	20.42%	350,000
1991	845,383	43.41%	412,000
1992	1,012,424	19.76%	392,500
1993	1,062,780	4.97%	371,500
1994	1,154,486	8.63%	450,000
1995	1,094,440	-5.20%	275,000
1996	1,101,455	0.64%	300,000
1997	1,314,420	19.33%	400,000
1998	1,384,530	5.33%	427,500
1999	1,567,873*	13.24%	495,000

At season's end, including players added to rosters in September.

1999 Milestones: Pitching masterpieces...

David Cone breezed through New York's steamy mid-July heat to pitch a perfecto against the Expos.

Perfect game: David Cone

Former Yankee Don Larsen threw out the ceremonial first pitch to ex-battery mate Yogi Berra before the July 18 game at Yankee Stadium. Then, as Berra would say, it was deja vu all over again. On a 95-degree afternoon, Cone pitched the 14th perfect game of the century. He needed just 88 pitches—nine fewer than Larsen had thrown in his 1956 World Series—to beat the Montreal Expos 6–0 and complete the third perfect game in Yankee history.

"You probably have a better chance of winning the lottery than having this happen," Cone said. "It makes you stop and think about Yankee magic and the mystique of this ballpark. You can't help but get caught up in it now."

When former Yankee David Wells threw a perfect game against Minnesota in 1998, it was Cone who sat next to him in the dugout, calming him between innings. After Cone's perfecto, Wells called from Toronto to congratulate one of his best friends.

"I've got bigger goose bumps than you do," Wells bellowed into the phone. "I'm glad you did it. Welcome to the club."

Armed with his best slider, Cone confused the Expos with his wide array of arm angles and deliveries. He struck out 10 batters and never went to a three-ball count. Following a 33-minute rain delay

in the middle of the third inning, he needed just seven pitches to get through the fourth.

"He didn't get away with any bad pitches," Montreal catcher Chris Widger said. "He just didn't throw any bad pitches."

—by Bill Koenig, with wire reports and the Westchester Journal News

No-hitters: Jose Jimenez, Eric Milton

After struggling through much of his rookie season, St. Louis right-hander Jose Jimenez pitched a no-hitter on June 25 against Arizona ace Randy Johnson and the National League leaders in batting average, runs, hits and home runs.

Jimenez struck out eight, walked two and hit a batter in the first Cardinal no-hitter in 16 years. Only one runner got as far as second base.

Jimenez entered the game with an 8.04 ERA and an NL-high 60 runs allowed in his previous 11 starts. But manager Tony La Russa had faith in Jimenez, who was 1998 Texas League Pitcher of the Year.

The no-hitter was the first by a rookie since 1991 (White Sox lefty Wilson Alvarez) and the first by a St. Louis rookie since 1934 (Paul Dean).

Three months after Jimenez's feat, Minnesota's Eric Milton pitched the fifth no-hitter in Twins' history. Facing the Anaheim Angels on Sept. 11, Milton struck out a career-high 13 batters, walked only two, and faced only one more than the minimum 27.

Milton dominated the Angels with his fastball, change-up and curve, and got stronger as the game went on—his blazing fastball hit a game-high 94 mph in the ninth inning. He completed the game by striking out the final batter.

Milton was the prized prospect the Twins received in the Chuck Knoblauch trade in 1997. The no-hitter, first for the Twins since 1974, was Milton's second consecutive shutout of the Angels in 1999.

... and exceptional batting performances

Mark McGwire, the 16th major leaguer to hit 500 home runs, did it quicker than anyone in history.

Aug. 6, 7: Gwynn, Boggs join 3,000-hit club

After a disappointment in St. Louis the night before, Tony Gwynn singled to right-center off Montreal's Dan Smith on Aug. 6 and became the 22nd major leaguer to collect 3,000 career hits.

The next night, Tampa Bay third baseman Wade Boggs became the exclusive 3,000-hit club's 23rd member with a two-run homer off Cleveland's Chris Haney.

Gwynn finished the season in 18th place on the all-time hit list with 3,067, while Boggs, who retired after the season, finished in 21st place with 3,010.

Aug. 5: McGwire hits 500th career home run

Mark McGwire launched what would become a three-day run for the record book with his 500th career home run against the San Diego Padres on Aug. 5.

McGwire's third-inning blast set off three minutes of fireworks, streamers and a loud celebration among the sellout crowd (45,106) at Busch Stadium. When he gave the joyous crowd an encore— No. 50—in the eighth inning, the stadium went wild again.

The atmosphere was reminiscent of September 1998, when McGwire tied—and eventually obliterated—Roger Maris's single-season home run record.

McGwire, the 16th player to reach the 500-homer milestone, got there faster than any player in history. He needed just 5,487 at-bats, while Babe Ruth needed 5,801. The next closest was Jimmie Foxx, with 7,074.

Meanwhile, San Diego right fielder Tony Gwynn hoped to get his 3,000th career hit during the game, but he went 1-for-4 with a two-run double in the ninth inning and had to settle for 2,999. The crowd gave Gwynn a standing ovation anyway.

Tony Gwynn got his 3,000th career hit in August.

Tatis smashes two grand slams in one inning

On April 23, St. Louis Cardinal Fernando Tatis did what no major league ballplayer had ever done before: He hit two grand slams in one inning. Major leaguers had swatted 4,777 grand slams with no player ever accomplishing the feat. Tatis's eight RBI from the two homers—both off the Dodgers' Chan Ho Park in the third inning—topped the modern-day RBI mark for an inning by two.

By Charles Krupa, AP/Wide World Photos

Hall of Fame inductees: Orlando Cepeda (left), Robin Yount, Nolan Ryan and George Brett.

Clear-cut class voted into Hall

Nolan Ryan, Orlando Cepeda, George Brett, and Robin Yount led the Hall of Fame's seven-man Class of 1999. Cepeda was a premier National League slugger in the late 1950s and 1960s, Yount won MVP trophies at two positions, Ryan is baseball's undisputed strikeout king, and Brett owned a .337 career postseason batting average. Also enshrined were umpire Nestor Chylak, manager Frank Selee, and Negro Leagues pitcher Smokey Joe Williams. The ceremony set records for fans (50,000) and media (more than 900). There also were 34 Hall of Famers present.

Inductees talk about baseball, retirement, each other

▶"I'd go home and dream of playing in a major league game. I was lucky. That dream came true. I dreamed of hitting a home run in the World Series. I was lucky. That dream came true. I dreamed of catching the last ball (in the World Series) and being mobbed by my teammates. Well, I guess all my dreams didn't come true."
—*Robin Yount, whose Brewers lost the 1982 Series to St. Louis in seven games*
▶"The first time I saw George Brett in 1974, I said, 'This kid is never gonna make it.' Sometimes you make mistakes."
—*Orlando Cepeda*

"I'm glad you don't scout for the Royals, Orlando."
—*Brett's response*
▶"Hitting against Nolan Ryan was like eating soup with a fork."
—*Cepeda*
▶"When I retired...I can honestly say, it took two full years to get over the fact that I was no longer a baseball player."
—*Nolan Ryan*

Plaques cite achievements

Excerpts from Hall of Fame plaques:
▶**George Brett**
"Played each game with ceaseless intensity and unbridled passion. ...A 13-time All-Star and the first player to win batting titles in three decades (1976, '80, '90)."
▶**Orlando Cepeda**
"A powerful first baseman and consistent run producer for 17 major league seasons. ...Unanimous selection for both the 1958 N.L. Rookie of the Year award and 1967 MVP honors."
▶**Nolan Ryan**
"One of baseball's most intimidating figures on the pitching mound for four decades...benchmarks include 5,714 strikeouts, seven no-hitters and 12 one-hitters in 27 seasons pitched. Led league in strikeouts 11 times and fanned 300 batters in a season on six occasions. ...Strikeout victims totaled 1,176 different players."
▶**Robin Yount**
"A prolific hitter ... equally graceful at shortstop and in center field. One of three players to earn MVP honors at two positions. Produced 3,142 hits, seventh most in American League history. Hit .300 six times, 40 doubles four times, 20 HR four times and scored 100 runs five times."

1999 Hall of Famers' career statistics

George Brett

Year	Team	AB	R	H	HR	RBI	AVG
1973	KC	40	2	5	0	0	.125
1974	KC	457	49	129	2	47	.282
1975	KC	634	84	195	11	89	.308
1976	KC	645	94	215	7	67	.333
1977	KC	564	105	176	22	88	.312
1978	KC	510	79	150	9	62	.294
1979	KC	645	119	212	23	107	.329
1980	KC	449	87	175	24	118	.390
1981	KC	347	42	109	6	43	.314
1982	KC	552	101	166	21	82	.301
1983	KC	464	90	144	25	93	.310
1984	KC	377	42	107	13	69	.284
1985	KC	550	108	184	30	112	.335
1986	KC	441	70	128	16	73	.290
1987	KC	427	71	124	22	78	.290
1988	KC	589	90	180	24	103	.306
1989	KC	457	67	129	12	80	.282
1990	KC	544	82	179	14	87	.329
1991	KC	505	77	129	10	61	.255
1992	KC	592	55	169	7	61	.285
1993	KC	560	69	149	19	75	.266
Totals		**10,349**	**1,583**	**3,154**	**317**	**1,595**	**.305**

Robin Yount

Year	Team	AB	R	H	HR	RBI	AVG
1974	Mil	344	48	86	3	26	.250
1975	Mil	558	67	149	8	52	.267
1976	Mil	638	59	161	2	54	.252
1977	Mil	605	66	174	4	49	.288
1978	Mil	502	66	147	9	71	.293
1979	Mil	577	72	154	8	51	.267
1980	Mil	611	121	179	23	87	.293
1981	Mil	377	50	103	10	49	.273
1982	Mil	635	129	210	29	114	.331
1983	Mil	578	102	178	17	80	.308
1984	Mil	624	105	186	16	80	.298
1985	Mil	466	76	129	15	68	.277
1986	Mil	522	82	163	9	46	.312
1987	Mil	635	99	198	21	103	.312
1988	Mil	621	92	190	13	91	.306
1989	Mil	614	101	195	21	103	.318
1990	Mil	587	98	145	17	77	.247
1991	Mil	503	66	131	10	77	.260
1992	Mil	557	71	147	8	77	.264
1993	Mil	454	62	117	8	51	.258
Totals		**11,008**	**1,632**	**3,142**	**251**	**1,406**	**.285**

Orlando Cepeda

Year	Team	AB	R	H	HR	RBI	AVG
1958	SF	603	88	188	25	96	.312
1959	SF	605	92	192	27	105	.317
1960	SF	569	81	169	24	96	.297
1961	SF	585	105	182	46	142	.311
1962	SF	625	105	191	35	114	.306
1963	SF	579	100	183	34	97	.316
1964	SF	529	75	161	31	97	.304
1965	SF	34	1	6	1	5	.176
1966	SF	49	5	14	3	15	.286
1966	StL	452	65	137	17	58	.303
1967	StL	563	91	183	25	111	.325
1968	StL	600	71	149	16	73	.248
1969	Atl	573	74	147	22	88	.257
1970	Atl	567	87	173	34	111	.305
1971	Atl	250	31	69	14	44	.276
1972	Atl	84	6	25	4	9	.298
1972	Oak	3	0	0	0	0	.000
1973	Bos	550	51	159	20	86	.289
1974	KC	107	3	23	1	18	.215
Totals		**7,927**	**1,131**	**2,351**	**379**	**1,365**	**.297**

Nolan Ryan

Year,	Team	W-L	SO	ERA
1966	NYM	0-1	6	15.00
1968	NYM	6-9	133	3.09
1969	NYM	6-3	92	3.54
1970	NYM	7-11	125	3.41
1971	NYM	10-14	137	3.97
1972	Cal	19-16	329	2.28
1973	Cal	21-16	383	2.87
1974	Cal	22-16	367	2.89
1975	Cal	14-12	186	3.45
1976	Cal	17-18	327	3.36
1977	Cal	19-16	341	2.77
1978	Cal	10-13	260	3.71
1979	Cal	16-14	223	3.59
1980	Hou	11-10	200	3.35
1981	Hou	11-5	140	1.69
1982	Hou	16-12	245	3.16
1983	Hou	14-9	183	2.98
1984	Hou	12-11	197	3.05
1985	Hou	10-12	209	3.80
1986	Hou	12-8	194	3.34
1987	Hou	8-16	270	2.76
1988	Hou	12-11	228	3.52
1989	Tex	16-10	301	3.20
1990	Tex	13-9	232	3.44
1991	Tex	12-6	203	2.91
1992	Tex	5-9	157	3.83
1993	Tex	5-5	46	4.88
Totals		**324-292**	**5,714**	**3.19**

No-hitters:
American League
May 15, 1973, California, at Kansas City, 3-0; July 15, 1973, California, at Detroit, 6-0; Sept. 28, 1974, California, vs. Minnesota, 4-0; June 1, 1975, California, vs. Baltimore, 1-0; June 11, 1990, Texas, at Oakland, 5-0; May 1, 1991, Texas, vs. Toronto, 3-0
National League
Sept. 26, 1981, Houston, vs. Los Angeles, 5-0

Numbers represent only statistics compiled during the regular season.

All-Star Game

American 4, National 1

National	0	0	1	0	0	0	0	0	1	4
American	2	0	0	2	0	0	0	0	x	4

National	AB	R	H	RBI	BB	SO	LOB	AVG
Larkin ss	3	0	1	1	0	1	1	.333
a-A Gonzalez ph-ss	1	0	0	0	0	0	1	.000
Walker rf	2	0	0	0	0	1	1	.000
L Gonzalez lf	2	0	1	0	0	0	1	.500
Sosa cf	3	0	0	0	0	2	2	.000
Guerrero rf	1	0	0	0	0	0	2	.000
McGwire 1b	2	0	0	0	1	2	2	.000
Casey 1b	1	0	0	0	0	0	0	.000
Williams 3b	3	0	1	0	0	1	1	.333
Sprague 3b	1	0	0	0	0	0	0	.000
Bagwell dh	3	0	1	0	0	2	2	.333
b-Sheffield ph-dh	1	0	0	0	0	0	0	.000
Piazza c	2	0	1	0	0	1	0	.500
Lieberthal c	1	0	0	0	0	0	1	.000
Nilsson c	1	0	0	0	0	1	0	.000
Burnitz lf-rf	2	1	1	0	0	0	3	.500
Jordan cf	1	0	1	0	1	0	0	1.000
Bell 2b	1	0	0	0	1	1	1	.000
Kent 2b	1	0	0	0	1	0	1	.000
Totals	32	1	7	1	4	12	19	

a-popped to second for Larkin in the 7th; b-grounded to shortstop for Bagwell in the 8th.
BATTING—2B: Burnitz (1, Cone); L Gonzalez (1, Mussina). **RBI:** Larkin (1). **2-out RBI:** Larkin. Runners left in scoring position, 2 out: Burnitz 2, McGwire 2, Guerrero 1. **GIDP:** Lieberthal, Kent. Team LOB: 8. **BASERUNNING—CS:** Williams (1, 2nd base by Martinez/Rodriguez); Jordan (1, 2nd base by Zimmerman/Ausmus). **FIELDING—E:** Williams (1, ground ball).

National	IP	H	R	ER	BB	SO	HR	ERA
Schilling	2	3	2	2	1	3	0	9.00
Johnson	1	0	0	0	0	1	0	0.00
Bottenfield	1	1	2	2	1	2	0	18.00
Lima	1	1	0	0	0	0	0	0.00
Millwood	1	1	0	0	0	1	0	0.00
Ashby	.1	0	0	0	0	0	0	0.00
Hampton	.2	0	0	0	0	0	0	0.00
Hoffman	.1	0	0	0	0	1	0	0.00
Wagner	.2	0	0	0	0	2	0	0.00

By Robert Deutsch, USA TODAY

Pedro Martinez struck out the first four batters and was MVP.

Martinez sets blazing pace for 4-1 AL victory at Fenway

The 70th All-Star Game was a Boston Red Sox festival. A tribute to Fenway Park and Hall of Famer Ted Williams quickly became a coronation of Red Sox ace Pedro Martinez in a 4-1 American League victory.

Martinez gave Boston fans what they wanted from the majors' winningest (15) starter. He struck out the first four he faced—an All-Star Game record—and five of six he faced, tying an AL All-Star record.

"Right now he's the top pitcher in the game and will be for a long time," National League outfielder Larry Walker said. "He's dominating."

The AL's domination extended its All-Star winning streak to three games and nine wins in the last 12 games. It was an appropriate end to the last All-Star Game in Fenway Park, due to be replaced, and Red Sox legend Williams, who threw out the first pitch.

Martinez's victims included Sammy Sosa and Mark McGwire. Martinez had a chilling effect on the NL's power-packed lineup. NL hitters struck out 12 times in all.

"He has the best pitches in baseball," McGwire said. "Right now he's devastating."

No argument from the AL starting catcher. "He's the best pitcher in the game," Ivan Rodriguez said. "His first two pitches, I wasn't sure I could even see them."

A total of 22 batters struck out, an All-Star Game record. The AL scored twice in the first inning against

Curt Schilling and twice more in the fourth against Kent Bottenfield. The NL struck back for one run against David Cone in the third inning.

Randy Johnson, the NL's second pitcher, had to enjoy it. It was the first run scored for Johnson since the third inning in a start June 20, a run of 34 innings of nonsupport by his Arizona mates.

That was all as Baltimore's Mike Mussina, Kansas City's Jose Rosado, Texas' Jeff Zimmerman and Tampa Bay's Roberto Hernandez followed Cone effectively.

—by Rod Beaton, USA TODAY

1999 MVP Pedro Martinez

On a night when baseball honored a century of its greatest players, pitcher Pedro Martinez brought back memories of the 1934 All-Star Game. Martinez, from the hometown Boston Red Sox, earned the All-Star Most Valuable Player award by striking out five of the six NL batters he faced in two innings, including the game's first four batters—the first time that's been done.

"Pedro dominated and got everyone fired up," said American League first baseman Jim Thome of the Cleveland Indians.

—by Mel Antonen, USA TODAY

Latino ballplayers take charge

The All-Star Game was another step in the Latinization of baseball. Six starters were Latinos, most notably American League starting pitcher Pedro Martinez. The others: Cleveland right fielder Manny Ramirez, Cubs right fielder Sammy Sosa, Cleveland second baseman Roberto Alomar, Texas catcher Ivan "Pudge" Rodriguez and Texas first baseman Rafael Palmeiro. Martinez, Ramirez and Sosa are Dominican natives; Alomar and Rodriguez are natives of Puerto Rico; and Palmeiro was born in Cuba.

Fourteen All-Stars came from Latin American countries, 15 if you include sidelined Tampa Bay/AL DH Jose Canseco, born in Cuba.

"It's good to see that," said Toronto third baseman Tony Fernandez, the all-time Dominican hits leader. "I think sometimes as a minority you don't get second chances, the same opportunity as other players. I think we [Latinos] deserve a chance to succeed in this game, just like anybody else. It's nice to see we're getting a chance like anyone else." "We're taking over," Houston All-Star Jose Lima said. "We have to be proud of what is happening. There are many more coming."

—by Rod Beaton, USA TODAY

American	AB	R	H	RBI	BB	SO	LOB	AVG
Lofton lf-cf	3	1	1	0	0	1	2	.333
Williams cf	1	0	0	0	0	1	1	.000
Garciaparra ss	2	0	0	0	0	0	1	.000
Jeter ss	1	0	0	0	0	1	2	.000
Vizquel ss	1	0	0	0	0	0	0	.000
Griffey cf	2	0	0	0	0	1	1	.000
Surhoff lf	2	0	0	0	0	0	0	.000
Ramirez rf	1	1	0	0	1	1	0	.000
Green rf	1	0	1	0	0	0	1	1.000
Ordonez rf	1	0	0	0	0	0	0	.000
Thome 1b	2	1	1	1	1	0	1	.500
Coomer 1b	1	0	0	0	0	1	0	.000
Ripken 3b	1	1	1	1	0	0	0	1.000
Fernandez 3b	2	0	0	0	0	1	1	.000
Palmeiro dh	2	0	1	1	0	0	2	.500
a-Baines ph-dh	1	0	1	0	0	0	0	1.000
c-Jaha ph-dh	1	0	0	0	0	1	0	.000
Rodriguez c	2	0	0	0	0	1	2	.000
Ausmus c	1	0	0	0	0	0	1	.000
Alomar 2b	2	0	1	0	1	0	2	.000
b-Offerman ph-2b	1	0	0	0	0	0	0	.000
Totals	**31**	**4**	**6**	**4**	**2**	**10**	**16**	

a-singled for Palmeiro in the 6th; b-grounded to pitcher for Alomar in the 6th; c-struck out for Baines in the 8th. **BATTING—RBI:** Thome (1), Ripken (1), Palmeiro (1), Alomar (1). **2-out RBI:** Thome, Ripken. Runners left in scoring position, 2 out: Palmeiro 1, Jeter 1, Williams 1. **Team LOB:** 6. **BASERUNNING—SB:** Lofton (1, 2nd base off Schilling/Piazza). **FIELDING—E:** Alomar (1, bobble); Offerman (1, throw). **DP:** 3 (Rodriguez-Alomar, Fernandez-Alomar-Thome, Wetteland-Vizquel-Coomer).

American	IP	H	R	ER	BB	SO	HR	ERA
Martinez	2	0	0	0	0	5	0	0.00
Cone	2	4	1	1	0	3	0	4.50
Mussina	1	1	0	0	1	2	0	0.00
Rosado (H)	1	1	0	0	0	1	0	0.00
Zmmrmn (H)	1	0	0	0	2	0	0	0.00
Hrnndz (H)	1	0	0	0	0	0	0	0.00
Wetteland (S)	1	1	0	0	0	1	0	0.00

WP: Martinez. **HBP:** Ripken (by Bottenfield). **Pitches-strikes:** Martinez 28-19; Cone 39-26; Mussina 21-13; Rosado 15-10; Zimmerman 20-9; Hernandez 7-6; Wetteland 19-14; Schilling 37-25; Johnson 9-6; Bottenfield 30-20; Lima 12-9; Millwood 25-15; Ashby 5-4; Hampton 4-2; Hoffman 5-4; Wagner 10-7. **Ground balls-fly balls:** Martinez 0-0; Cone 2-1; Mussina 1-0; Rosado 2-0; Zimmerman 1-1; Hernandez 3-0; Wetteland 2-0; Schilling 2-1; Johnson 1-1; Bottenfield 0-1; Lima 2-1; Millwood 2-0; Ashby 1-0; Hampton 1-1; Hoffman 0-0; Wagner 0-0. **Batters faced:** Martinez 6; Cone 11; Mussina 5; Rosado 3; Zimmerman 5; Hernandez 3; Wetteland 3; Schilling 10; Johnson 3; Bottenfield 7; Lima 4; Millwood 4; Ashby 1; Hampton 2; Hoffman 1; Wagner 2.

UMPIRES—HP: Jim Evans. **1B:** Terry Tata. **2B:** Dale Ford. **3B:** Angel Hernandez. **LF:** Mark Johnson. **RF:** Larry Vanover. **GAME DATA—T:** 2:53. **Att:** 34,187.

Rodriguez, Jones win 1999 MVP awards

Catcher Ivan Rodriguez's hot bat and solid arm helped the Texas Rangers win the division title.

American League MVP: Ivan Rodriguez, Texas

Texas catcher Ivan Rodriguez won the 1999 American League MVP award, even though Boston pitcher Pedro Martinez had more first-place votes.

Rodriguez, who hit .332 with 35 homers and 113 RBI, finished with seven first-place votes and 252 points in balloting by the Baseball Writers' Association of America. Martinez, who won the AL Cy Young Award after going 23–4 with a 2.07 ERA and 313 strikeouts, had eight first-place votes and 239 points. Voters list their top 10, and Rodriguez won largely because he was listed on the ballots of all 28 voters while Martinez was not listed by two: George King of the *New York Post* and La Velle Neal of the *Minneapolis Star Tribune*.

"Everybody that was in the pile was good enough to be MVP so I don't hold anything against anybody," Martinez said.

Rodriguez's batting average was the highest by an AL catcher since the Yankees' Bill Dickey hit .362 in 1936. Rodriguez also became the first AL catcher to hit .300 and reach 100 in runs (116) and RBI. He threw out 39 of 72 (54 percent) runners trying to steal.

National League MVP: Chipper Jones, Atlanta

Chipper Jones—who hit 45 homers and carried Atlanta to an eighth straight division title—won the 1999 National League MVP award in a landslide. He got 29 of 32 first-place votes and finished with 432 points.

"It's awfully hard to believe," Jones said. "To have this in your corner, to always be able to say you won an MVP, is a tremendous honor."

Houston first baseman Jeff Bagwell was second with one first-place vote and 276 points, followed by Arizona third baseman Matt Williams, who had two firsts and 269 points.

"Matt Williams is one of the guys I try to be like. Just to be in the hunt with him is an honor in itself," Jones said. "I didn't have a real good first half. Baggy put together a full year."

The 27-year-old third baseman hit .319 with 110 RBI, 116 runs, 25 steals and 126 walks. He finished third in homers (behind Mark McGwire and Sammy Sosa) and walks; fourth in slugging percentage (.633), on-base average (.441) and total bases (359); seventh in runs; and 10th in batting.

After June 15, Jones hit 30 homers and drove in 79 runs.

Chipper Jones's second-half surge carried the Braves to their eighth consecutive division title.

AL Cy Young Award:
Pedro Martinez, Boston

There was no doubt about this one. Boston right-hander Pedro Martinez, who earned pitching's "Triple Crown" by leading the American League in victories (23), ERA (2.07) and strikeouts (313)—was the unanimous choice for the Cy Young Award.

Martinez's season was truly historic. Since Fenway's Green Monster was erected in 1934, the Red Sox have never led the league in ERA—until 1999, when Martinez's mark lowered the staff ERA by a full third of a run.

Randy Johnson's dominant first year in the National League led Arizona to a division title.

By Tom DiPace

NL Cy Young Award:
Randy Johnson, Arizona

This was the year of "double-winners." Randy Johnson and Pedro Martinez became the second and third pitchers ever to win the Cy Young Award in both leagues.

Johnson, who signed with Arizona as a free agent after spending his entire career with the Seattle Mariners in the American League, went 17-9 with a 2.48 ERA and 364 strikeouts in 271⅔ innings. Those numbers are striking, but his value to the Diamondbacks was even greater than his record shows.

"There's numbers you don't see," Johnson said during the season, "like a stretch where I had 14 consecutive starts where I gave up two or less runs."

Johnson also helped his team by saving the bullpen—he led the league in complete games with 12. And he kept batters off the bases. He finished 19 strikeouts short of the single-season record set by Nolan Ryan in 1973 and struck out 10 or more 23 times, matching Ryan's 1973 record.

Johnson became only the second pitcher since 1991 to break the hold on the award by Atlanta's pitchers. The only other non-Brave to win the NL award during that time was 1999 AL winner Pedro Martinez, who took the Cy Young with Montreal in 1997.

Pedro Martinez had one of the best seasons in history and led the Red Sox to a wild card.

By H. Darr Beiser, USA TODAY

Martinez's figure was 1.37 runs better than any other AL pitcher's, the greatest winning margin this century. His 2.07 ERA was compiled in a circuit where the league ERA approached 5.00. In a league in which the average hitter batted .274 and no regular hit below .232, he held batters to a .205 average, which dropped to .134 in the late innings of close games. In fact, Martinez's major league-best 23-4 record might have been even better with a little luck. In his four losses, he compiled a 3.86 ERA while walking four and striking out 45 in 28 innings. The only truly poor start he had all year was on July 18, one of only two starts all year in which he allowed more than three runs.

Future stars: 1999 Rookies of the Year

Switch-hitting Carlos Beltran had 108 RBI and scored 112 runs for the Kansas City Royals.

AL: Carlos Beltran

Carlos Beltran of the Kansas City Royals was a nearly unanimous choice for American League Rookie of the Year. He was the first rookie with 100 runs and 100 RBI since Boston's Fred Lynn in 1975 and only the eighth overall in a group that includes Ted Williams and Joe DiMaggio.

"He kind of came out of nowhere, but the players and pitchers who compete against him know who he is and where he is," Royals manager Tony Muser said.

Beltran hit .293 for Kansas City, with 22 homers, 108 RBI, 112 runs and 27 stolen bases in 35 attempts. Together with second baseman Carlos Febles, the strong-armed center fielder helped form what is arguably the most potent 1-2 rookie punch on one team since Boston's Lynn and Jim Rice.

"The scouts and the development people need to be given some credit," Muser said. "It was their tutoring and their teaching and disciplining that got them so far so fast." Beltran is the third Royals player to win the award, joining Lou Piniella in 1969 and Bob Hamelin in 1994.

—by Chuck Johnson, USA TODAY

NL: Scott Williamson

Cincinnati Reds reliever Scott Williamson, who went from unknown to All-Star, capped an outstanding season by winning the National League Rookie of the Year Award. Williamson, 23, wasn't even on the Reds' roster when the season began, but he finished 12-7 with a 2.41 ERA and 19 saves as a key reliever.

He pitched 23⅓ consecutive scoreless innings from April 30 to June 11—the NL's longest streak of the year.

A former starter, Williamson made the NL All-Star team after going 7-4 with a 1.66 ERA and 11 saves in the first half. He tied an NL record for relievers by striking out six consecutive batters May 27 against the Dodgers.

"I want to benefit the team the best I can," Williamson said. "If it's relieving, I want to relieve. If it's starting, I'll start."

Although a sore arm slowed him late in the season, Williamson ended up leading NL rookie pitchers in wins, saves and winning percentage and led all NL relievers in ERA and strikeouts with 107 in 93⅓ innings.

Williamson credited former teammate Stan Belinda with helping him succeed: "He taught me so much about baseball; I don't think I would be receiving this award if it weren't for him."

—by Chuck Johnson, USA TODAY

Scott Williamson was a key reliever for the Reds.

AL Manager of the Year: Jimy Williams, Boston

Jimy Williams was named the American League Manager of the Year after leading the Boston Red Sox into the playoffs despite the loss of slugging first baseman Mo Vaughn to free agency.

"Certainly Mo was an integral part of this ballclub in the past years, but wasn't with our team [in 1999]," Williams said. "He was with another team, and you have to move on."

After the Manager of the Year votes were cast, the Red Sox overcame a 2-0 deficit to beat the Indians in their best-of-5 first-round Division Series, then lost to the Yankees in the AL Championship Series.

"As far as I'm concerned, this is a team award," Williams said. "It's pretty special."

Williams received 20 first-place votes and five seconds for 115 points from the Baseball Writers' Association of America. Oakland's Art Howe finished second after keeping the Athletics in contention until September despite a $25.2 million payroll, 24th among the 30 major league teams; Joe Torre of the World Series champion New York Yankees, last year's winner, was third.

NL Manager of the Year: Jack McKeon, Cincinnati

Jack McKeon, whose low-budget Cincinnati Reds caught most opponents by surprise when they almost became a wild-card playoff team, said those tactics won't work next season.

"It's going to be a lot tougher trying to repeat what we did," McKeon said. "So many times in the past it's been difficult for teams to repeat. We have to improve, to seek to be better."

McKeon guided the Reds, who had one of baseball's lowest payrolls at $38 million, to 96 victories and into a one-game playoff with the New York Mets for the NL wild-card berth. They lost that game 5-0.

McKeon, 69, said his patience with young players was the key ingredient to the Reds' unexpected success.

"We let them be aggressive and be on their own," he said. "We let them build up confidence and didn't restrict them from doing things they're capable of doing. Allowing them to make a mistake here and there, not jumping all over them and showing faith in them was important." McKeon, 69, is the third-oldest manager in major league history behind Connie Mack, 88, and Casey Stengel, 75. McKeon received 17 first-place votes, nine seconds and three thirds for 115 points to beat Atlanta's Bobby Cox by 17 points.

1999 Gold Glove winners

AMERICAN LEAGUE

C	Ivan Rodriguez	Texas
1B	Rafael Palmeiro	Texas
2B	Roberto Alomar	Cleveland
SS	Omar Vizquel	Cleveland
3B	Scott Brosius	New York
OF	Ken Griffey, Jr.	Seattle
OF	Bernie Williams	New York
OF	Shawn Green	Toronto
P	Mike Mussina	Baltimore

NATIONAL LEAGUE

C	Mike Lieberthal	Philadelphia
1B	J.T. Snow	SF
2B	Pokey Reese	Cincinnati
SS	Rey Ordonez	New York
3B	Robin Ventura	New York
OF	Andruw Jones	Atlanta
OF	Larry Walker	Colorado
OF	Steve Finley	Arizona
P	Greg Maddux	Atlanta

1998 Silver Slugger winners

AMERICAN LEAGUE

1B	Carlos Delgado	Toronto
2B	Roberto Alomar	Cleveland
SS	Alex Rodriguez	Seattle
3B	Dean Palmer	Detroit
DH	Rafael Palmeiro	Texas
OF	Ken Griffey, Jr.	Seattle
OF	Manny Ramirez	Cleveland
OF	Shawn Green	Toronto
C	Ivan Rodriguez	Texas

NATIONAL LEAGUE

1B	Jeff Bagwell	Houston
2B	E. Alfonzo	New York
SS	Barry Larkin	Cincinnati
3B	Chipper Jones	Atlanta
OF	Sammy Sosa	Chicago
OF	Larry Walker	Colorado
OF	V. Guerrero	Montreal
C	Mike Piazza	New York
P	Mike Hampton	Houston

AL East: Boston was the big surprise

It couldn't be as easy. And it wasn't. But the New York Yankees won the American League East again, won the pennant again, and won the World Series again. No 125-victory juggernaut like the 1998 version, these Yankees still won a league-high 98 games. Yet, they didn't clinch the division until the final Thursday of the season. They spent most of the year trying to shake the Boston Red Sox, a team that was supposed to be worse than the previous year but rode the Cy Young Award dominance of Pedro Martinez to the wild card and a finish just four games behind the Yankees.

Despite adding Roger Clemens, the Yankees' pitching was far less consistent than it had been in 1998. But they generally remained in control of the division during the first half of the season as shortstop Derek Jeter led the offense. Jeter reached base in the first 53 games of the season, the longest streak in the major leagues in 1999. He finally was stopped June 6 in an interleague game against the Mets.

STANDINGS AT THE ALL-STAR BREAK

	W	L	Pct.	GB
New York	52	34	.605	—
Boston	49	39	.557	4
Toronto	47	43	.522	7
Tampa Bay	39	49	.443	14
Baltimore	36	51	.414	16.5

Still, at that point, the Yankees had been trailing Boston for nearly three weeks in the division race. They finally got back on top three days later when they won 11-5 at Philadelphia, and never again relinquished the lead.

It wasn't until mid-August that Boston took command of second place, and it took another few weeks for the Red Sox to solidify the wild-card spot.

The Red Sox were a surprise because they were supposed to falter after losing slugging first baseman Mo Vaughn to free agency. But Martinez and a patchwork staff kept Boston at or near the top of the league in pitching all season. The other surprise was the improving Toronto Blue Jays. Despite making a last-minute managerial change during spring training, replacing Tim Johnson with Jim Fregosi, the Blue Jays rode the hitting of Shawn Green and Carlos Delgado into wild-card contention for much of the season.

It was another year of expensive under-achieving for the Baltimore Orioles, who added Albert Belle as a free agent but lost Robbie Alomar and Rafael Palmeiro—both strong MVP candidates. The Orioles were themselves in last place at the beginning of September, and only a fast finish brought them to a semi-respectable 78-84. Still, that wasn't enough to save the jobs of manager Ray Miller and general manager Frank Wren at the end of the season.

Tampa Bay's dreams of escaping last place in just their second season faded quickly in September, though the highlight of the Devil Rays' year, other than Wade Boggs's 3,000th hit, was twice nearly sweeping the Yankees in the final two weeks. They first took three of four games in New York (losing the fourth in 11 innings after blowing a two-run lead in the ninth) then two of three in St. Petersburg.

In addition to their division race, the New York and Boston shortstops, Jeter and Nomar Garciaparra, staged a tight race for the batting title with Garciaparra winning .357-.349, and Bernie Williams of the Yankees finishing third.

FINAL STANDINGS

	W	L	Pct.	GB
New York	98	64	.605	—
Boston	94	68	.580	4
Toronto	84	78	.519	14
Baltimore	78	84	.481	20
Tampa Bay	69	93	.426	29

AL Central: All Cleveland, all the time

The American League Central Division remains baseball's foregone conclusion—but even with four consecutive division titles, the Indians had a nagging concern they had underachieved for the past couple of seasons. Lack of a World Series title was part of the frustration, but Cleveland players also thought their regular-season performances hadn't fully proven how much better they were than their division competition.

Mission accomplished.

The Indians moved into first place for good on April 8, spent all but two days on top of the division, got off to a franchise-best 26-9 start and romped home 21½ games ahead of the second-place Chicago White Sox.

That was nothing new. Since 1995, Cleveland has owned—or tied for—first place in the division 818 of the 881 days, 83 games better than the second-place White Sox. Their big blemish was a 10-22 record against the league's other playoff teams—the Yankees, Rangers and Red Sox. It was a warning worth heeding; The Indians were upset by wild-card Boston in the Division Series, a loss that cost manager Mike Hargrove his job.

STANDINGS AT THE ALL-STAR BREAK

	W	L	Pct.	GB
Cleveland	56	31	.644	—
Chicago	42	43	.494	13
Detroit	36	52	.409	20.5
Kansas City	35	52	.402	21
Minnesota	34	52	.395	21.5

The rest of the division jockeyed for position behind Cleveland—way behind Cleveland. None of the other teams could play .500 baseball, but the White Sox likely came away with the most, as a collection of talented young players contributed to their 75 victories.

Outfielder Magglio Ordonez blossomed into an All-Star for the White Sox, who also saw young Paul Konerko and Carlos Lee become major contributors. Chicago will need more improvement from their young pitchers to even think about slicing into Cleveland's advantage.

Kansas City and Minnesota both lost 97 times but were buoyed by their own developing players, led by center fielder Carlos Beltran in Kansas City and pitcher Eric Milton in Minnesota.

Detroit managed to finish third, a two-slot improvement over the previous season. But the year was considered a major disappointment because the Tigers entered the season as the team most likely to make significant gains on the Indians. About the only highlight was the fanfare marking the closing of Tiger Stadium, but the overall disappointment quickly was underscored by the October firing of manager Larry Parrish and the hiring of ex-Milwaukee skipper Phil Garner.

Still, the division remains all about Cleveland. The Indians were better than ever on offense with four players contributing 100 or more RBI on a team that scored 1,009 times. Right fielder Manny Ramirez drove in 165, the most in the AL since Jimmie Foxx in 1938.

But pitching was a concern all season. Bartolo Colon won 18 games but injuries and general ineffectiveness led Cleveland to use 25 pitchers during the season.

The Indians got away with some of their mound deficiencies through brute force. They became the first team in major league history to come back and win three games in one season in which they trailed by eight or more runs, including a game against Tampa Bay in which they became the first team to trail by eight and win by nine in the same game.

FINAL STANDINGS

	W	L	Pct.	GB
Cleveland	97	65	.599	—
Chicago	75	86	.466	21.5
Detroit	69	92	.429	27.5
Kansas City	64	97	.398	32.5
Minnesota	63	97	.394	33

AL West: Oakland hounded the Rangers

The Texas Rangers set an American League West record, clinching the division earlier than any team since the league went to the three-division format in 1994. They controlled the division, but it should also be noted that the clincher didn't come until the 155th game of the season.

The bigger surprise is that when the Rangers clinched in a head-to-head game with the second-place team, they were playing the Oakland Athletics.

Texas had first place since the eighth game of the season and never saw its lead shrink below 4½ games after the All-Star break. As the Rangers marched along to a franchise-record 95 victories, the teams expected to be their pursuers—Anaheim and Seattle—never seriously got into the race.

But Oakland did, chasing Boston deep into September in the wild-card race and never letting Texas get too comfortable—until the Rangers scored 32 runs to sweep a three-game series with the A's Sept. 24-26 and officially end the suspense. It was the first time in the past five seasons that Texas wrapped up with its own victory.

The heavy-hitting Rangers overcame pitching problems—their 5.07 earned run average was the second-worst ever for a playoff team behind Baltimore's 5.14 in 1996—to compile a 47-28 record after the All-Star break and go 27-18 after Aug. 15.

STANDINGS AT THE ALL-STAR BREAK

	W	L	Pct.	GB
Texas	48	39	.552	—
Oakland	43	44	.494	5
Seattle	42	45	.483	6
Anaheim	41	45	.477	6.5

The Rangers led the majors with a .293 batting average and became the seventh team in major league history to have six players with 20 or more home runs. Free-agent Rafael Palmeiro led the way with 47, followed by Juan Gonzalez (39), Ivan Rodriguez (35), Lee Stevens and Todd Zeile (24), and Rusty Greer (20).

That a serious division race never materialized was a testament to turmoil in Anaheim. The trouble began on Opening Day when off-season signing Mo Vaughn slipped into the dugout while catching a foul ball and injured his ankle. It took more than half of the season for him to approach his usual prolific production. But by then, the most prolific element of the Angels was infighting. In a clubhouse of volatile personalities led by high-strung manager Terry Collins, losing was cause for explosion. Collins quit before the season ended and general manger Bill Bavasi was gone soon after.

Oakland, meanwhile, struck a blow for small-market teams. The A's were supposed to be an up-and-coming franchise because of the young talent they were developing. But 1998 Rookie of the Year Ben Grieve had a horrendous first half and 1999 candidate Eric Chavez started slowly. Both began to produce later in the season, just in time to bolster a team hanging close thanks to huge seasons from reclamation project John Jaha, veteran Tony Phillips, and holdover sluggers Matt Stairs and Jason Giambi.

The Mariners never advanced beyond the fringes of the race. Early in the season shortstop Alex Rodriguez was injured and second baseman Carlos Guillen was lost for the season. The Mariners were six games back when they moved into Safeco Field at the All-Star break, but they quickly faded despite the development of rookie pitchers Freddy Garcia and John Halama.

FINAL STANDINGS

	W	L	Pct.	GB
Texas	95	67	.586	—
Oakland	87	75	.537	8
Seattle	79	83	.488	16
Anaheim	70	92	.432	25

NL East: Mets couldn't topple Atlanta

The Braves won their eighth consecutive division championship in 1999, but the late-September charge from the New York Mets may have been what pushed Atlanta into the World Series. For the second consecutive season, the Braves dominated the Mets down the stretch, but this time the division title was on the line, not just a New York bid for a wild card.

With 12 games remaining in the season, the Mets came to Atlanta trailing the first-place Braves by one game. That's when Chipper Jones took over.

Jones hit home runs in the first and eighth innings to give the Braves a 2-1 victory in the opening game of the series. He then hit home runs in each of the next two games as the Braves completed the sweep. By the time the Mets lost two of three to the Braves at Shea Stadium the following week, the division race was long over—the Braves were eight games ahead. They finished with a major league-high 103 victories.

STANDINGS AT THE ALL-STAR BREAK				
	W	L	Pct.	GB
Atlanta	55	34	.616	—
New York	50	39	.562	5
Philadelphia	46	40	.535	7.5
Montreal	33	51	.393	19.5
Florida	32	56	.364	22.5

The collapse nearly cost the Mets their playoff berth because they also lost three in a row at Philadelphia between the two Atlanta series. But New York regrouped and swept the final three games from Pittsburgh to tie Cincinnati for the wild-card spot. The Mets then won a one-game playoff at Cincinnati to reach the postseason.

Atlanta moved into first place on April 24 with an 8-7 victory at Florida and held the top spot until a July 30 loss at Philadelphia.

The Braves had been playing all season without first baseman Andres Galarraga, who learned in spring training he had cancer, and 1998 closer Kerry Ligtenberg, who suffered from elbow ligament damage. When they lost catcher Javy Lopez

for the season in late July with knee problems, some of the Braves players admitted they had reached a low point.

But as they found themselves in as tough a race as they've had in several years, the Braves responded. Trailing by a game on Aug. 19, Atlanta went on a 10-game winning streak and won 13 of 14 to grab the lead for good. The Mets got within one game four different times in September—the last occasion was the eve of their head-to-head meeting.

The only other NL East team to have a hand in the division race was Philadelphia. In fact, the Phillies were just five games behind Atlanta at the beginning of August. The Phillies were unsuccessful in convincing the Yankees to trade pitcher Andy Pettitte at the July 31 trading deadline and, after ace Curt Schilling went down with an injury, their hopes were slim.

The Phillies dropped out of the race with a 10-17 August, losing 10½ games in the standings as Atlanta went on a 21-7 run. It got worse in September, and Philadephia's final 77-85 record wasn't indicative of the improvements the team had made. Montreal and Florida never got into the race and, from the beginning, had their own private battle to avoid the basement. The Expos won that consolation prize, finishing four games ahead of last-place Florida. Both managed to avoid triple-digit losses, the Marlins by a mere two games.

FINAL STANDINGS				
	W	L	Pct.	GB
Atlanta	103	59	.636	—
New York	97	66	.595	7
Philadelphia	77	85	.475	26
Montreal	68	94	.420	35
Florida	64	98	.395	39

NL Central: Reds gave Houston a wild ride

This was supposed to be the Houston Astros' division and, in the end, it was. But not until an emotional ride finished with a down-to-the-wire race thanks to a spirited challenge from one of the last places they expected. Even after a 12-game winning streak between Sept. 3 and 14 opened a four-game lead, The Astros' unlikely rivals—the Cinderella Reds—wouldn't go away.

By the time Cincinnati came to the Astrodome—where they had swept four earlier games—there were just five days remaining in the season and the two teams were tied atop the division. The Reds took sole possession of first place after the first night, but the Astros won the next, to regain a tie.

STANDINGS AT THE ALL-STAR BREAK				
	W	L	Pct.	GB
Cincinnati	49	36	.576	—
Houston	50	37	.575	—
Pittsburgh	43	44	.494	7
St. Louis	43	45	.489	7.5
Milwaukee	42	44	.488	7.5
Chicago	41	44	.482	8

Both teams also were involved with the East Division's New York Mets in the battle for the wild-card berth. After Cincinnati left town, Houston lost the opener of the final regular-season series in the Astrodome to the Dodgers while the Reds fell at Milwaukee. Jose Lima shut out Los Angeles the next night while the Reds were losing again, putting Houston on top for good and the Reds into a tie with the Mets.

Houston clinched the division on Sunday afternoon with a 9-4 rout of the Dodgers while the Mets were winning at home against Pittsburgh. The Reds were scheduled for an afternoon game at Milwaukee but had to wait out a six-hour rain delay just for the opportunity to tie the Mets for the wild card. Cincinnati eventually won that game and returned home for a one-game playoff the next night, but lost to the Mets.

The Astros had a 6½-game lead on June 20, but it shrunk to a half-game within two weeks. Manager Larry Dierker had surgery following a seizure in the Astrodome dugout and missed 27 days, and shortstop Ricky Gutierrez was on the disabled list for the second time, joining third baseman Ken Caminiti. Outfielder Moises Alou and catcher Mitch Meluskey were out for the season. Outfielders Derek Bell and Carl Everett plus catcher Tony Eusebio also landed on the DL, and outfielder Richard Hidalgo was lost for the year in August.

Cincinnati also had it's share of injury problems, patching together a pitching rotation that was consistently bailed out by manager Jack McKeon's deep and effective bullpen. The Reds made their late push when Pete Harnisch got hot, Steve Parris returned from an injury, and Juan Guzman was acquired from Baltimore at the trading deadline.

No other team was a threat. Pittsburgh finished third despite a season-ending injury to catcher and team leader Jason Kendall on July 4; the Cardinals were immersed in the middle of the Mac and Sammy Show II, but injuries decimated their pitching staff; and the Brewers fired manager Phil Garner and GM Sal Bando before they even finished what was supposed to be their final season at County Stadium. (A construction accident pushed back the opening of Miller Field until Opening Day 2001.) The biggest fall hit the Chicago Cubs, who lost phenom Kerry Wood to spring surgery and, despite Sammy Sosa's homers, finished with the league's second-worst record.

FINAL STANDINGS				
	W	L	Pct.	GB
Houston	97	65	.599	—
Cincinnati	96	67	.589	1.5
Pittsburgh	78	83	.484	18.5
St. Louis	75	86	.466	21.5
Milwaukee	74	87	.460	22.5
Chicago	67	95	.414	30

NL West: Arizona won battle of big spenders

When Raul Mondesi stunned the Arizona Diamondbacks on Opening Day with a game-tying home run in the ninth inning and a game winner in extra innings, that was how the National League West was supposed to work. The Los Angeles Dodgers had won the inaugural battle of the big spenders in a marquee matchup of free-agent pitchers Kevin Brown and Randy Johnson.

What happened instead showed how baseball has changed. The second-year Diamondbacks staged the biggest one-year turnaround in major league history and the Dodgers were never a significant factor in the race. And Arizona got to the postseason faster than any expansion team in history.

But it wasn't until the second half of the season that the Diamondbacks looked like a championship team. They struggled through the first half as their bullpen blew late-inning leads and Johnson got no run support.

STANDINGS AT THE ALL-STAR BREAK				
	W	L	Pct.	GB
San Francisco	50	38	.568	—
Arizona	48	41	.539	2.5
San Diego	43	43	.500	6
Colorado	40	46	.465	9
Los Angeles	39	47	.453	10

After the All-Star break, though, the division belonged to the Diamondbacks. On July 9, they got closer Matt Mantei in a trade with the Florida Marlins. On July 20, Johnson pitched a shutout against his former team, Seattle. After that, the Diamondbacks went 51-17—a .750 winning percentage—and ended up cruising to a 14-game margin over the Giants. In fact, Arizona clinched the division with a Sept. 24 victory at San Francisco.

Arizona became the sixth team to go from worst to first, all of them coming in the 1990s. The last three have come in consecutive years in the NL West: first the Giants, then the San Diego Padres, and now the Diamondbacks.

San Francisco and its weak pitching staff, plus a lineup that missed slugger Barry Bonds for large chunks of the season, managed to hang close into August. The Giants entered the month playing at a .538 pace and matched that during August, but that was no match for Arizona's hot streak.

The rest of the division had long been out of the race, with the most surprising laggard being the Dodgers. Despite preseason predictions of a trip to the World Series—many from within the Dodgers camp itself—the team hit, pitched, and generally played at a mediocre level. The high-priced roster didn't turn into a troubled clubhouse, as some skeptics had warned it would, until deep into August, when a struggling Mondesi demanded to be traded. He was still there at season's end, as was the team's mediocre play.

San Diego, dismantled after its run to the 1998 World Series, actually made a stronger bid than the Dodgers with a hot streak in June. But most of the Padres' success came against weak teams and they faded quickly when they had to face other contenders.

If there could be a bigger disappointment than the Dodgers, it would have to be the Colorado Rockies. New manager Jim Leyland became so frustrated with the big-hitting, poor-pitching, seldom-winning Rockies that he announced near season's end that he didn't want to honor the rest of his contract.

Meanwhile, the Diamondbacks were proving that NL teams need a lot more than hitting. Arizona finished third in the league in batting, behind Colorado and the New York Mets, and second only to Atlanta in pitching.

FINAL STANDINGS				
	W	L	Pct.	GB
Arizona	100	62	.617	—
San Francisco	86	76	.531	14
Los Angeles	77	85	.475	23
San Diego	74	88	.457	26
Colorado	72	90	.444	28

AL batting leaders

BATTING AVERAGE

Garciaparra, Bos.	.357
Jeter, N.Y.	.349
Williams, N.Y.	.342
Martinez, Sea.	.337
M. Ramirez, Cle.	.333
Vizquel, Cle.	.333
Rodriguez, Tex.	.332
Fernandez, Tor.	.328
Gonzalez, Tex.	.326
Palmeiro, Tex.	.324

HOME RUNS

Griffey, Sea.	48
Palmeiro, Tex.	47
Delgado, Tor.	44
M. Ramirez, Cle.	44
Green, Tor.	42
A. Rodriguez, Sea.	42
Gonzalez, Tex.	39
Palmer, Det.	38
Stairs, Oak.	38
Belle, Bal.	37

TRIPLES

Offerman, Bos.	11
Damon, K.C.	9
Febles, K.C.	9
Jeter, N.Y.	9
Durham, Chi.	8
Dye, K.C.	8
Polonia, Det.	8
Randa, K.C.	8
5 tied	7

DOUBLES

Green, Tor.	45
Dye, K.C.	44
Sweeney, K.C.	44
Garciaparra, Bos.	42
Fernandez, Tor.	41
Greer, Tex.	41
Zeile, Tex.	41
R. Alomar, Cle.	40
4 tied	39

RUNS BATTED IN

M. Ramirez, Cle.	165
Palmeiro, Tex.	148
Delgado, Tor.	134
Griffey, Sea.	134
Gonzalez, Tex.	128
Giambi, Oak.	123
Green, Tor.	123
R. Alomar, Cle.	120
Dye, K.C.	119
Belle, Bal.	117

RUNS SCORED

R. Alomar, Cle.	138
Green, Tor.	134
Jeter, N.Y.	134
M. Ramirez, Cle.	131
Griffey, Sea.	123
Knoblauch, N.Y.	120
Rodriguez, Tex.	116
Williams, N.Y.	116
Giambi, Oak.	115
Gonzalez, Tex.	114

HITS

Jeter, N.Y.	219
Surhoff, Bal.	207
Williams, N.Y.	202
Velarde, Ana.-Oak.	200
Rodriguez, Tex.	199
Randa, K.C.	197
Beltran, K.C.	194
Vizquel, Cle.	191
Garciaparra, Bos.	190
Green, Tor.	190

BASES ON BALLS

Thome, Cle.	127
Giambi, Oak.	105
Belle, Bal.	101
Jaha, Oak.	101
Williams, N.Y.	100
R. Alomar, Cle.	99
Martinez, Sea.	97
Palmeiro, Tex.	97
4 tied	96

STOLEN BASES

Hunter, Det.-Sea.	44
Vizquel, Cle.	42
Goodwin, Tex.	39
R. Alomar, Cle.	37
Stewart, Tor.	37
Anderson, Bal.	36
Damon, K.C.	36
Durham, Chi.	34
Encarnacion, Det.	33
Bush, Tor.	32

SLUGGING PERCENTAGE

M. Ramirez, Cle.	.663
Palmeiro, Tex.	.630
Garciaparra, Bos.	.603
Gonzalez, Tex.	.601
Green, Tor.	.588
A. Rodriguez, Sea.	.586
Griffey, Sea.	.576
Delgado, Tor.	.571
Rodriguez, Tex.	.558
Jaha, Oak.	.556

ON-BASE AVERAGE

Martinez, Sea.	.447
M. Ramirez, Cle.	.442
Jeter, N.Y.	.438
Williams, N.Y.	.435
Fernandez, Tor.	.427
Thome, Cle.	.426
R. Alomar, Cle.	.422
Giambi, Oak.	.422
Palmeiro, Tex.	.420
Garciaparra, Bos.	.418

EXTRA-BASE HITS

Green, Tor.	87
Delgado, Tor.	83
M. Ramirez, Cle.	81
Dye, K.C.	79
Palmeiro, Tex.	78
Griffey, Sea.	77
Gonzalez, Tex.	76
Belle, Bal.	74
Garciaparra, Bos.	73
2 tied	70

SINGLES

Velarde, Ana.-Oak.	152
Jeter, N.Y.	149
Vizquel, Cle.	146
Stewart, Tor.	144
Williams, N.Y.	143
Surhoff, Bal.	140
Beltran, K.C.	138
Randa, K.C.	137
Rodriguez, Tex.	134
Durham, Chi.	130

LEAD-ASSUMING RBI

M. Ramirez, Cle.	41
Vaughn, Ana.	33
Green, Tor.	32
Griffey, Sea.	32
Palmeiro, Tex.	31
Delgado, Tor.	30
Belle, Bal.	29
Palmer, Det.	28
Gonzalez, Tex.	27
Ordonez, Chi.	27

GAME-WINNING RBI

M. Ramirez, Cle.	21
Palmeiro, Tex.	20
Stairs, Oak.	17
Vaughn, Ana.	16
R. Alomar, Cle.	15
Belle, Bal.	15
Delgado, Tor.	15
Griffey, Sea.	15
4 tied	14

SACRIFICE HITS

Vizquel, Cle.	17
D. Cruz, Det.	14
Lewis, Bos.	14
R. Alomar, Cle.	12
Febles, K.C.	12
Caruso, Chi.	11
Martinez, T.B.	10
Sanchez, K.C.	10
Wilson, Sea.	10
5 tied	9

SACRIFICE FLIES

R. Alomar, Cle.	13
Gonzalez, Tex.	12
Beltran, K.C.	10
Bordick, Bal.	10
Flaherty, T.B.	10
O'Neill, N.Y.	10
Brosius, N.Y.	9
Palmeiro, Tex.	9
M. Ramirez, Cle.	9
8 tied	8

INTENTIONAL WALKS

Griffey, Sea.	17
Williams, N.Y.	17
Belle, Bal.	15
Palmeiro, Tex.	14
Thomas, Chi.	13
Thome, Cle.	13
Fernandez, Tor.	11
Justice, Cle.	11
McGriff, T.B.	11
Stevens, Tex.	10

HIT-BY-PITCH

Anderson, Bal.	24
Knoblauch, N.Y.	21
Easley, Det.	19
Delgado, Tor.	15
Saenz, Oak.	15
Ausmus, Det.	14
M. Ramirez, Cle.	13
Jeter, N.Y.	12
3 tied	11

GROUND OUTS

Caruso, Chi.	230
Ordonez, Chi.	216
Tejada, Oak.	209
Rodriguez, Tex.	202
Anderson, Ana.	201
Hunter, Det.-Sea.	197
Durham, Chi.	193
Stewart, Tor.	192
O'Neill, N.Y.	191
D. Cruz, Det.	186

AIR OUTS

Knoblauch, N.Y.	230
Surhoff, Bal.	222
Palmeiro, Tex.	206
Bordick, Bal.	204
Randa, K.C.	204
Bell, Sea.	199
Griffey, Sea.	194
Vizquel, Cle.	194
Anderson, Bal.	188
Belle, Bal.	187

STRIKEOUTS

Thome, Cle.	171
Palmer, Det.	153
Glaus, Ana.	143
Delgado, Tor.	141
Canseco, T.B.	135
Clark, Det.	133
Stevens, Tex.	132
M. Ramirez, Cle.	131
Jaha, Oak.	129
Vaughn, Ana.	127

GROUNDED INTO DP

Rodriguez, Tex.	31
Bordick, Bal.	25
O'Neill, N.Y.	24
Ordonez, Chi.	24
Cordova, Min.	22
O'Leary, Bos.	21
Sweeney, K.C.	21
Zeile, Tex.	20
5 tied	19

CAUGHT STEALING

Caruso, Chi.	14
Stewart, Tor.	14
Encarnacion, Det.	12
Offerman, Bos.	12
Rodriguez, Tex.	12
Durham, Chi.	11
Goodwin, Tex.	11
Lewis, Bos.	10
Walker, Min.	10
Williams, N.Y.	10

AL pitching leaders

MOST WINS
P. Martinez, Bos.	23
Colon, Cle.	18
Mussina, Bal.	18
Sele, Tex.	18
Garcia, Sea.	17
Hernandez, N.Y.	17
Nagy, Cle.	17
Wells, Tor.	17
Appier, K.C.-Oak.	16
3 tied	15

MOST LOSSES
Moehler, Det.	16
Parque, Chi.	15
Witt, T.B.	15
Appier, K.C.-Oak.	14
Fassero, Sea.-Tex.	14
Hawkins, Min.	14
Radke, Min.	14
Rosado, K.C.	14
3 tied	13

MOST STRIKEOUTS
P. Martinez, Bos.	313
Finley, Ana.	200
Sele, Tex.	186
Cone, N.Y.	177
Burba, Cle.	174
Mussina, Bal.	172
Garcia, Sea.	170
Wells, Tor.	169
Clemens, N.Y.	163
Milton, Min.	163

MOST COMPLETE GAMES
Wells, Tor.	7
Erickson, Bal.	6
Ponson, Bal.	6
P. Martinez, Bos.	5
Milton, Min.	5
Rosado, K.C.	5
6 tied	4

MOST SAVES
Rivera, N.Y.	45
Hernandez, T.B.	43
Wetteland, Tex.	43
Jackson, Cle.	39
Mesa, Sea.	33
Koch, Tor.	31
Percival, Ana.	31
Jones, Det.	30
Howry, Chi.	28
Timlin, Bal.	27

MOST GAMES STARTED
Helling, Tex.	35
Appier, K.C.-Oak.	34
Burba, Cle.	34
Erickson, Bal.	34
Hentgen, Tor.	34
Milton, Min.	34
Wells, Tor.	34
9 tied	33

LOWEST ERA
P. Martinez, Bos.	2.07
Cone, N.Y.	3.44
Mussina, Bal.	3.50
Radke, Min.	3.75
Rosado, K.C.	3.85
Moyer, Sea.	3.87
Colon, Cle.	3.95
Sirotka, Chi.	4.00
Garcia, Sea.	4.07
Hernandez, N.Y.	4.12

BATTING AVERAGE AGAINST
P. Martinez, Bos.	.205
Cone, N.Y.	.229
Hernandez, N.Y.	.233
Colon, Cle.	.242
Milton, Min.	.243
Finley, Ana.	.246
Rosado, K.C.	.248
Burba, Cle.	.254
Clemens, N.Y.	.261
Garcia, Sea.	.263

FEWEST HITS PER 9 INNINGS
P. Martinez, Bos.	6.75
Cone, N.Y.	7.63
Hernandez, N.Y.	7.85
Colon, Cle.	8.12
Milton, Min.	8.29
Finley, Ana.	8.31
Rosado, K.C.	8.52
Burba, Cle.	8.63
Clemens, N.Y.	8.87
Mussina, Bal.	9.16

FEWEST HOME RUNS PER 9 INNINGS
P. Martinez, Bos.	0.38
Mussina, Bal.	0.71
Garcia, Sea.	0.80
Olivares, Ana.-Oak.	0.83
Moyer, Sea.	0.91
Sele, Tex.	0.92
Pettitte, N.Y.	0.94
Clemens, N.Y.	0.96
Finley, Ana.	0.97
Cone, N.Y.	0.98

FEWEST WALKS PER 9 INNINGS
Heredia, Oak.	1.53
P. Martinez, Bos.	1.56
Radke, Min.	1.81
Moyer, Sea.	1.89
Mussina, Bal.	2.30
Wells, Tor.	2.41
Irabu, N.Y.	2.44
Sirotka, Chi.	2.45
Nagy, Cle.	2.63
Suppan, K.C.	2.67

MOST STRIKEOUTS PER 9 INNINGS
P. Martinez, Bos.	3.20
Finley, Ana.	8.44
Cone, N.Y.	8.24
Sele, Tex.	8.17
Clemens, N.Y.	7.82
Mussina, Bal.	7.61
Garcia, Sea.	7.60
Burba, Cle.	7.12
Milton, Min.	7.11
Irabu, N.Y.	7.07

MOST EXTRA-BASE HITS
Helling, Tex.	98
Fassero, Sea.-Tex.	82
Sele, Tex.	82
D. Wells, Tor.	82
Appier, K.C.-Oak.	81
Radke, Min.	80
Baldwin, Chi.	79
Hentgen, Tor.	79
Heredia, Oak.	79
Nagy, Cle.	77

MOST HOME RUNS
Helling, Tex.	41
Fassero, Sea.-Tex.	35
Ponson, Bal.	35
Baldwin, Chi.	34
Hentgen, Tor.	32
Wells, Tor.	32
Burba, Cle.	30
Blair, Det.	29
Hawkins, Min.	29
Navarro, ChiA	29

MOST HIT-BY-PITCH
Weaver, Det.	17
Arrojo, T.B.	14
Milcki, Det.	12
Rupe, T.B.	12
Sele, Tex.	12
Cone, N.Y.	11
Erickson, Bal.	11
Navarro, Chi.	11
3 tied	10

MOST GROUNDED INTO DP
Erickson, Bal.	41
Olivares, Ana.-Oak.	31
Pettitte, N.Y.	28
Suppan, K.C.	27
Witt, T.B.	27
Alvarez, T.B.	25
Moyer, Sea.	25
Halama, Sea.	24
Morgan, Tex.	23
Mussina, Bal.	23

MOST STOLEN BASES
Wells, Tor.	37
Wakefield, Bos.	35
Gooden, Cle.	27
Rapp, Bos.	27
Garcia, Sea.	26
Appier, K.C.-Oak.	24
Fassero, Sea.-Tex.	23
Cone, N.Y.	22
Navarro, Chi.	22
4 tied	21

MOST CAUGHT STEALING
Helling, Tex.	14
Ponson, Bal.	14
Finley, Ana.	13
Burba, Cle.	12
Clemens, N.Y.	11
Escobar, Tor.	11
Witt, T.B.	11
5 tied	10

MOST PICKOFFS
Lowe, Chi.	6
Halama, Sea.	5
Hentgen, Tor.	5
Olivares, Ana.-Oak.	5
Pettitte, N.Y.	5
Rogers, Oak.	5
Helling, Tex.	4
Moyer, Sea.	4
Sparks, Ana.	4
15 tied	3

MOST BALKS
Garcia, Sea.	3
Nitkowski, Det.	3
10 tied	2

MOST WILD PITCHES
Finley, Ana.	15
Burba, Cle.	13
Candiotti, Oak.-Cle.	13
Garcia, Sea.	12
Baldwin, Chi.	11
Snyder, Chi.	11
Suzuki, Sea.-K.C.	11
Appier, K.C.-Oak.	10
Erickson, Bal.	10
6 tied	9

LOWEST BATTING AVERAGE VS. LEFT-HANDERS
P. Martinez, Bos.	.221
Burba, Cle.	.224
Hudson, Oak.	.234
Hill, Ana.	.240
Cone, N.Y.	.245
Mays, Min.	.255
Garcia, Sea.	.255
Colon, Cle.	.255
Suppan, K.C.	.259
Rapp, Bos.	.262

LOWEST BATTING AVERAGE VS. RIGHT-HANDERS
Hernandez, N.Y.	.187
Cone, N.Y.	.213
Colon, Cle.	.229
Milton, Min.	.240
Finley, Ana.	.249
Rosado, K.C.	.250
Alvarez, T.B.	.257
Appier, K.C.-Oak.	.262
Nagy, Cle.	.263
Hentgen, Tor.	.265

NL batting leaders

BATTING AVERAGE

Walker, Col.	.379
Gonzalez, Ari.	.336
Abreu, Phi.	.335
Casey, Cin.	.332
Cirillo, Mil.	.326
Grudzielanek, L.A.	.326
Everett, Hou.	.325
Glanville, Phi.	.325
Helton, Col.	.320
C. Jones, Atl.	.319

HOME RUNS

McGwire, St.L	65
Sosa, Chi.	63
C. Jones, Atl.	45
Vaughn, Cin.	45
Bagwell, Hou.	42
V. Guerrero, Mon.	42
Piazza, N.Y.	40
Giles, Pit.	39
Bell, Ari.	38
Walker, Col.	37

TRIPLES

Abreu, Phi.	11
Perez, Col.	11
Finley, Ari.	10
Womack, Ari.	10
Cameron, Cin.	9
Kotsay, Fla.	9
Gonzalez, Fla.	8
Martin, Pit.	8
4 tied	7

DOUBLES

Biggio, Hou.	56
Gonzalez, Ari.	45
Vidro, Mon.	45
Grace, Chi.	44
Jenkins, Mil.	43
Casey, Cin.	42
Alfonzo, N.Y.	41
C. Jones, Atl.	41
Young, Pit.	41
2 tied	40

RUNS BATTED IN

McGwire, St.L	147
Williams, Ari.	142
Sosa, Chi.	141
Bichette, Col.	133
V. Guerrero, Mon.	131
Bagwell, Hou.	126
Piazza, N.Y.	124
Ventura, N.Y.	120
Vaughn, Cin.	118
Giles, Pit.	115

RUNS SCORED

Bagwell, Hou.	143
Bell, Ari.	132
Alfonzo, N.Y.	123
Biggio, Hou.	123
Abreu, Phi.	118
McGwire, St.L	118
C. Jones, Atl.	116
Helton, Col.	114
Sosa, Chi.	114
Gonzalez, Ari.	112

HITS

Gonzalez, Ari.	206
Glanville, Phi.	204
Cirillo, Mil.	198
Casey, Cin.	197
V. Guerrero, Mon.	193
Perez, Col.	193
Alfonzo, N.Y.	191
Williams, Ari.	190
Biggio, Hou.	188
Helton, Col.	185

BASES ON BALLS

Bagwell, Hou.	149
McGwire, St.L	133
C. Jones, Atl.	126
Olerud, N.Y.	125
Abreu, Phi.	109
Sheffield, L.A.	101
Giles, Pit.	95
Larkin, Cin.	93
Burnitz, Mil.	91
Biggio, Hou.	88

STOLEN BASES

Womack, Ari.	72
Cedeno, N.Y.	66
Young, L.A.	51
Castillo, Fla.	50
Cameron, Cin.	38
Reese, Cin.	38
Henderson, N.Y.	37
Renteria, St.L	37
Mondesi, L.A.	36
Sanders, S.D.	36

SLUGGING PERCENTAGE

Walker, Col.	.710
McGwire, St.L	.697
Sosa, Chi.	.635
C. Jones, Atl.	.633
Giles, Pit.	.614
V. Guerrero, Mon.	.600
Bagwell, Hou.	.591
Helton, Col.	.587
Piazza, N.Y.	.575
Everett, Hou.	.571

ON-BASE AVERAGE

Walker, Col.	.458
Bagwell, Hou.	.454
Abreu, Phi.	.446
C. Jones, Atl.	.441
Olerud, N.Y.	.427
McGwire, St.L	.424
Henderson, N.Y.	.423
Giles, Pit.	.418
Sheffield, L.A.	.407
Tatis, St.L	.404

EXTRA-BASE HITS

Sosa, Chi.	89
C. Jones, Atl.	87
McGwire, St.L	87
V. Guerrero, Mon.	84
Helton, Col.	79
Bagwell, Hou.	77
Bell, Ari.	76
Finley, Ari.	76
Giles, Pit.	75
Gonzalez, Ari.	75

SINGLES

Glanville, Phi.	149
Cirillo, Mil.	147
Perez, Col.	143
Gonzalez, Ari.	131
Womack, Ari.	131
Casey, Cin.	127
Hamilton, Col.-N.Y.	127
Loretta, Mil.	126
Larkin, Cin.	125
Grudzielanek, L.A.	124

LEAD-ASSUMING RBI

Williams, Ari.	39
Bichette, Col.	37
V. Guerrero, Mon.	37
McGwire, St.L	35
Gonzalez, Ari.	31
Jordan, Atl.	31
Sosa, Chi.	31
C. Jones, Atl.	30
3 tied	28

GAME-WINNING RBI

Williams, Ari.	19
V. Guerrero, Mon.	17
Bagwell, Hou.	16
Bonds, S.F.	16
C. Jones, Atl.	16
Bell, Hou.	15
Jordan, Atl.	15
Piazza, N.Y.	15
Sheffield, L.A.	15
Ventura, N.Y.	15

SACRIFICE HITS

Reynolds, Hou.	17
Brown, L.A.	13
Lima, Hou.	13
Maddux, Atl.	13
Nunez, Pit.	13
Karl, Mil.	12
Schmidt, Pit.	12
4 tied	11

SACRIFICE FLIES

Bichette, Col.	10
Grace, Chi.	10
Alfonzo, N.Y.	9
Bell, Ari.	9
Jordan, Atl.	9
Kotsay, Fla.	9
Sheffield, L.A.	9
6 tied	8

INTENTIONAL WALKS

McGwire, St.L	21
C. Jones, Atl.	18
Bagwell, Hou.	16
V. Guerrero, Mon.	14
Casey, Cin.	13
Beltre, L.A.	12
Ordonez, N.Y.	12
A. Jones, Atl.	11
Piazza, N.Y.	11
2 tied	10

HIT-BY-PITCH

Sprague, Pit.	17
Burnitz, Mil.	16
Tatis, St.L	16
Gonzalez, Fla.	12
Kendall, Pit.	12
Walker, Col.	12
Young, Pit.	12
8 tied	11

GROUND OUTS

Perez, Col.	218
Castillo, Fla.	207
Castilla, Col.	202
Womack, Ari.	194
Olerud, N.Y.	193
Ordonez, N.Y.	191
Larkin, Cin.	188
Biggio, Hou.	186
Casey, Cin.	184
Glanville, Phi.	180

AIR OUTS

Perez, Col.	238
Alfonzo, N.Y.	231
Grace, Chi.	215
Loretta, Mil.	213
Sheffield, L.A.	206
Womack, Ari.	198
Williams, Ari.	197
Cirillo, Mil.	193
Aurilia, S.F.	188
Reese, Cin.	188

STRIKEOUTS

Sosa, Chi.	171
Wilson, Fla.	156
Cameron, Cin.	145
Hernandez, Chi.-Atl.	145
Rivera, S.D.	143
McGwire, St.L	141
Vaughn, Cin.	137
Mondesi, L.A.	134
Bell, Ari.	132
Brogna, Phi.	132

GROUNDED INTO DP

Piazza, N.Y.	27
Olerud, N.Y.	22
Bell, Hou.	20
C. Jones, Atl.	20
Brogna, Phi.	19
Bagwell, Hou.	18
Barrett, Mon.	18
V. Guerrero, Mon.	18
Karros, L.A.	18
3 tied	17

CAUGHT STEALING

Young, L.A.	22
Castillo, Fla.	17
Cedeno, N.Y.	17
Veras, S.D.	17
Benard, S.F.	14
Biggio, Hou.	14
Henderson, N.Y.	14
Sanders, S.D.	13
Womack, Ari.	13
2 tied	12

NL pitching leaders

MOST WINS

Hampton, Hou.	22
Lima, Hou.	21
Maddux, Atl.	19
Bottenfield, St.L	18
Brown, L.A.	18
Millwood, Atl.	18
Ortiz, S.F.	18
Astacio, Col.	17
Johnson, Ari.	17
Daal, Ari.	16

MOST LOSSES

Trachsel, Chi.	18
Springer, Fla.	16
Meadows, Fla.	15
Benson, Pit.	14
Hermanson, Mon.	14
Hitchcock, S.D.	14
Jimenez, St.L	14
Reynolds, Hou.	14
Valdes, L.A.	14
3 tied	13

MOST STRIKEOUTS

Johnson, Ari.	364
Brown, L.A.	221
Astacio, Col.	210
Millwood, Atl.	205
Reynolds, Hou.	197
Hitchcock, S.D.	194
Lima, Hou.	187
Lieber, Chi.	186
Hampton, Hou.	177
Park, L.A.	174

MOST COMPLETE GAMES

Johnson, Ari.	12
Schilling, Phi.	8
Astacio, Col.	7
Brown, L.A.	5
Ashby, S.D.	4
Maddux, Atl.	4
Reynolds, Hou.	4
Trachsel, Chi.	4
7 tied	3

MOST SAVES

Urbina, Mon.	41
Hoffman, S.D.	40
Wagner, Hou.	39
Rocker, Atl.	38
Nen, S.F.	37
Wickman, Mil.	37
Shaw, L.A.	34
Mantei, Fla.-Ari.	32
Veres, Col.	31
Graves, Cin.	27

MOST GAMES STARTED

Brown, L.A.	35
Glavine, Atl.	35
Johnson, Ari.	35
Lima, Hou.	35
Reynolds, Hou.	35
Astacio, Col.	34
Hampton, Hou.	34
Hermanson, Mon.	34
Trachsel, Chi.	34
11 tied	33

LOWEST ERA

Johnson, Ari.	2.48
Millwood, Atl.	2.68
Hampton, Hou.	2.90
Brown, L.A.	3.00
Smoltz, Atl.	3.19
Ritchie, Pit.	3.49
Schilling, Phi.	3.54
Maddux, Atl.	3.57
Lima, Hou.	3.58
Daal, Ari.	3.65

BATTING AVERAGE AGAINST

Millwood, Atl.	.202
Johnson, Ari.	.208
Brown, L.A.	.222
Daal, Ari.	.236
Schilling, Phi.	.237
Hampton, Hou.	.241
Ortiz, S.F.	.244
Smoltz, Atl.	.245
Benson, Pit.	.249
Harnisch, Cin.	.252

FEWEST HITS PER 9 INNINGS

Millwood, Atl.	6.63
Johnson, Ari.	6.86
Brown, L.A.	7.49
Hampton, Hou.	7.76
Daal, Ari.	7.88
Schilling, Phi.	7.94
Smoltz, Atl.	8.11
Ortiz, S.F.	8.19
Benson, Pit.	8.42
Harnisch, Cin.	8.62

FEWEST HOME RUNS PER 9 INNINGS

Hampton, Hou.	0.45
Maddux, Atl.	0.66
Holt, Hou.	0.66
Smoltz, Atl.	0.68
Brown, L.A.	0.68
Glavine, Atl.	0.69
Hershiser, N.Y.	0.70
Benson, Pit.	0.73
Oliver, St.L	0.73
Leiter, N.Y.	0.80

FEWEST WALKS PER 9 INNINGS

Reynolds, Hou.	1.44
Maddux, Atl.	1.52
Lima, Hou.	1.61
Woodard, Mil.	1.75
Smoltz, Atl.	1.93
Lieber, Chi.	2.04
Brown, L.A.	2.10
Schilling, Phi.	2.20
Johnson, Ari.	2.32
Millwood, Atl.	2.33

MOST STRIKEOUTS PER 9 INNINGS

Johnson, Ari.	12.06
Hitchcock, S.D.	8.49
Lieber, Chi.	8.23
Nomo, Mil.	8.22
Astacio, Col.	8.15
Millwood, Atl.	8.09
Park, L.A.	8.06
Brown, L.A.	7.88
Reynolds, Hou.	7.65
Schilling, Phi.	7.59

MOST EXTRA-BASE HITS

Astacio, Col.	94
Ogea, Phi.	89
Lima, Hou.	88
Bohanon, Col.	86
Schmidt, Pit.	86
Tomko, Cin.	86
Williams, S.D.	83
Park, L.A.	81
Byrd, Phi.	79
3 tied	78

MOST HOME RUNS

Astacio, Col.	38
Ogea, Phi.	36
Benes, Ari.	34
Byrd, Phi.	34
Kile, Col.	33
Williams, S.D.	33
Trachsel, Chi.	32
Valdes, L.A.	32
3 tied	31

MOST HIT-BY-PITCH

Byrd, Phi.	17
Bohanon, Col.	14
Park, L.A.	14
Astacio, Col.	11
Hershiser, N.Y.	11
Jimenez, St.L	11
Oliver, St.L	11
Spradlin, S.F.	10
3 tied	9

MOST GROUNDED INTO DP

Hampton, Hou.	38
Clement, S.D.	28
Kile, Col.	28
Karl, Mil.	26
Reynolds, Hou.	26
Ritchie, Pit.	25
Leiter, NY-N	24
Mulholland, Chi.-Atl.	24
Holt, Hou.	23
2 tied	22

MOST STOLEN BASES

Johnson, Ari.	42
Nomo, Mil.	41
Leiter, N.Y.	26
Valdes, L.A.	26
Bohanon, Col.	25
Ortiz, S.F.	25
Thurman, Mon.	25
Astacio, Col.	24
Ashby, S.D.	23
3 tied	21

MOST CAUGHT STEALING

Johnson, Ari.	17
Springer, Fla.	17
Astacio, Col.	14
Park, L.A.	14
Oliver, St.L	11
6 tied	10

MOST PICKOFFS

Park, L.A.	7
Ritchie, Pit.	7
Abbott, Mil.	6
Estes, S.F.	6
Oliver, St.L	6
Villone, Cin.	6
Johnson, Ari.	5
Sanchez, Fla.	5
15 tied	4

MOST BALKS

Dreifort, L.A.	4
Schmidt, Pit.	4
Byrd, Phi.	3
Darensbourg, Fla.	3
Pavano, Mon.	3
Perez, L.A.	3
Perez, Atl.	3
Silva, Pit.	3
Trachsel, Chi.	3
16 tied	2

MOST WILD PITCHES

Estes, S.F.	15
Hitchcock, S.D.	15
Kile, Col.	13
Ortiz, S.F.	13
Williamson, Cin.	13
Byrd, Phi.	11
Clement, S.D.	11
Park, L.A.	11
3 tied	10

LOWEST BATTING AVERAGE VS. LEFT-HANDERS

Millwood, Atl.	.230
Vazquez, Mon.	.234
Bottenfield, St.L	.245
Schilling, Phi.	.246
Tomko, Cin.	.250
Ortiz, S.F.	.251
Brown, L.A.	.255
Harnisch, Cin.	.256
Williams, S.D.	.260
Reynoso, Ari.	.263

LOWEST BATTING AVERAGE VS. RIGHT-HANDERS

Millwood, Atl.	.175
Brown, L.A.	.189
Park, L.A.	.207
Villone, Cin.	.212
Johnson, Ari.	.219
Benson, Pit.	.225
Smoltz, Atl.	.229
Byrd, Phi.	.230
Nomo, Mil.	.235
Clement, S.D.	.235

By Russell Becker, Baseball Weekly

Joe DiMaggio combined elegance and excellence as a ballplayer and as a cultural icon.

Baseball mourns Yankee great Joe DiMaggio

Joe DiMaggio was much more than a mere Hall of Fame ballplayer. He was an icon of an era when America's greatest heroes took on mythical status. And no one dwelled higher on sport's Olympus.

He came along in 1936 at a time when America desperately needed something or someone to take its mind off its troubles. He responded with valor on the field and virtue off it.

DiMaggio nursed baseball through the Great Depression, then helped it celebrate postwar prosperity. DiMaggio led his team to the World Series with uncommon regularity and his 1941 hitting streak left the number 56 engraved on our national conscience.

Despite missing three years during World War II, DiMaggio finished his 13-year career with a .325 batting average, 361 home runs and 1,537 RBI. He totaled 2,214 hits, and his .579 slugging percentage ranks sixth all-time. An 11-time All-Star, DiMaggio won American League Most Valuable Player awards in 1939, 1941 and 1947. He won two batting titles, hitting a career-high .381 in 1939 and .352

the following year. He led the league with 46 home runs in 1937 (still a Yankees' record for a right-handed hitter) and with 39 in 1948.

Author David Halberstam described how Nobel physics laureate Edward Mills Purcell ran all of baseball's great records through his computer. The computer responded that only one achievement—DiMaggio's 56-game hitting streak—defied mathematical probability. He hit .408 (91-for-223) during that streak, with 16 doubles, four triples, 15 home runs and 55 RBI. He walked 21 times and struck out just five. He hit .575 (23-for-40) the last 10 games of the streak. He was so unfazed when his streak ended, he began a 16-gamer the next day.

But it wasn't just about the playing field. DiMaggio was a cultural icon. He has been celebrated in literature, in song, and on the screen. His marriage to actress Marilyn Monroe was the ultimate union of sports god and screen goddess. It lasted less than a year, but when Monroe died in 1962, DiMaggio took care of her funeral arrangements, keeping it from becoming a media circus. Then for the next 20 years, he had a single rose placed on her grave twice a week. He never remarried.

When 84-year-old DiMaggio lost his battle with lung cancer on March 8, President Bill Clinton declared: "Today, America lost one of the century's most beloved heroes, Joe DiMaggio. This son of Italian immigrants gave every American something to believe in. He became the very symbol of American grace, power, and skill. I have no doubt that when future generations look back at the best of America in the 20th century, they will think of the Yankee Clipper and all that he achieved."

Hear, hear.

—by Bill Koenig

Here's to you, Catfish

Jim "Catfish" Hunter is famous for three things: He helped create a dynasty in Oakland, he helped resuscitate another one in the Bronx, and he changed players' salaries forever with baseball's first multi-million-dollar contract. But those are broad strokes, and Catfish Hunter made a career out of perfectly executed details.

Mixing speeds and location, the right-handed pitcher could paint the corners like Degas. Efficient rather than over-powering, he never walked more than 85 batters in a full season. He won five World Series rings, captured the 1974 American League Cy Young Award, made eight All-Star teams and pitched a perfect game against Minnesota in 1968.

Yet friends remember Hunter as a humble man, totally unaffected by celebrity. During spring training with the Yankees, he used to help clubhouse attendant Nick Priore with his chores.

Hunter was always a regular guy—and a great teammate. After he pitched his perfect game with Oakland, A's owner Charlie Finley wanted to give him a $5,000 bonus right on the field, in front of all the fans.

"What about my catcher Jim Pagliaroni?" Hunter asked.

"The catcher doesn't get anything," Finley snorted.

"Either my catcher does—or I don't," Hunter replied. Finley had no choice but to split the pot.

The Oakland years were something out of *The Wild Bunch*. The only thing the A's did better than win was party; Hunter usually was in the middle of it. But the party ended after the 1974 World Series, when arbitrator Peter Seitz ruled that Finley had breached Hunter's contract. Seitz declared him a free agent, allowing him to negotiate with any team he chose.

Every team in baseball entered the bidding war, and on New Year's Eve, 1974, a special bulletin preceded the national telecast of the Sugar Bowl: Catfish Hunter had signed an unprecedented five-year, $3.75 million contract with the New York Yankees. The deal was three times the amount of any previous contract, and cleared the way for full-blown free agency in 1976.

Hall of Famer Jim "Catfish" Hunter was one of the most dominant pitchers of the 1970s.

Hunter led the league with 23 victories in his first season with the Yankees, then helped the club into three consecutive World Series in 1976-77-78.

"Catfish Hunter was the cornerstone of the Yankees' success the last quarter century," Yankees' owner George Steinbrenner said. "We were not winning before Catfish arrived, and since he arrived the Yankees have the best record in baseball. He exemplified class and dignity, and taught us how to win."

Hunter was always in control. On the mound, in the clubhouse, in private. He didn't lose control until Lou Gehrig's disease attacked him in the fall of 1998. It began in the prized right arm that won 224 games, then spread to his left side. He slipped off his porch steps Aug. 8, struck his head and never really recovered. He died Sept. 9. He was 53.

"You only live one day at a time," he said the spring before he died. "Sometimes you want to cry and other times you look around and are thankful you're living."

Catfish, we're thankful we knew you.

—by Bill Koenig

'The Brat' Stanky dies of heart attack at age 83

Eddie Stanky, the feisty second baseman whose combative style earned him the nickname "The Brat," died of a heart attack June 6 in his hometown, Fairhope, Ala. He was 83.

Stanky's all-out style helped three of his teams—the Brooklyn Dodgers (1947), Boston Braves (1948), and New York

> *"What do I need Humphrey for? He can't hit."*
>
> **—Eddie Stanky,** refusing to allow Vice President Hubert Humphrey into the Cardinals' clubhouse during the 1967 pennant race.

Giants (1951)—win pennants during his 11-year playing career.

The 5-8, 160-pound Stanky had a career average of .268 and held the NL single-season record with 148 walks from 1945 until Barry Bonds passed him in 1996, followed by Mark McGwire in 1998.

Dodgers president Branch Rickey once said: "He can't hit, he can't throw and he can't outrun his grandmother. But if there's a way to beat the other team, he'll find it."

As an infielder, Stanky often stood directly up the middle, behind the pitcher and jumped up and down to distract the hitter. If a runner was leading off second, Stanky frequently called for a pickoff just so he had a chance to swipe his glove across the opponent's face and goad him into a fight. That way he could tag the runner when he wandered off the base. In the 1951 World Series, he kicked the ball out of Yankee shortstop Phil Rizzuto's glove.

Stanky kept his combative style as manager, first with the Cardinals from 1952 to 1955, then the White Sox from 1966 to July 1968. Neck and neck with Boston in the standings in 1967, he tried to disrupt

Red Sox star Carl Yastrzemski by calling him "an All-Star from the neck down."

In 1969, Stanky began a new career as the baseball coach at the University of South Alabama, but for one June day in 1977, he was drawn back into the major leagues as manager of the Texas Rangers. The Rangers hired him to replace Frank Lucchesi, but one game convinced Stanky that he couldn't relate to players of that era.

Throughout his career, Stanky had a singular philosophy: "Baseball is not a game to me," he said. "It's a business. And a bloodthirsty business, at that."

—from staff and wire reports

Early Wynn dead at age 79

Hall of Fame pitcher Early Wynn, a 300-game winner and one of the fiercest competitors of his time, died April 4 in Venice, Florida. He was 79.

Wynn pitched from 1939 to 1963, winning 20 or more games for the Cleveland Indians four times and for the Chicago White Sox once in the 1950s. He was 23-11 in 1954, when the Indians won the AL pennant with a league record 111 wins in a 154-game season. In 1959, he won the Cy Young Award for the pennant-winning White Sox, posting a 22-10 record.

Wynn was also a good hitter, with 17 career home runs and a batting average one season of .319. Managers would sometimes use him as a pinch-hitter.

In 1963, at age 43, Wynn he returned to the Indians, needing one more win to reach 300. He reached the milestone July 13, 1963, pitching the first five innings of a 5-4 Indians victory in Kansas City against the Athletics.

After he retired, Wynn was a pitching coach for the Indians and the Minnesota Twins. He was inducted into the Hall of Fame in 1972.

—from staff and wire reports

'Little Colonel'
Pee Wee Reese dies at 81

Pee Wee Reese's Hall of Fame plaque reads: "Harold Henry 'Pee Wee' Reese, Brooklyn, N.L., 1940-1957, Los Angeles, N.L., 1958. Shortstop and captain of great Dodger teams of 1940s and '50s. Intangible qualities of subtle leadership on and off the field, competitive fire and professional pride complemented dependable glove, reliable baserunning and clutch hitting as significant factors in seven Dodger pennants. Instrumental in easing acceptance of Jackie Robinson as baseball's first black performer."

In one of Reese's first steps toward supporting the bold move by Dodgers executive Branch Rickey to integrate the major leagues, he refused to sign a petition in which several teammates threatened a boycott if Robinson was called up from Brooklyn's Montreal farm club.

Roger Kahn, author of *The Boys of Summer*, a 1971 best-seller about the 1950s Dodgers, said, "The momentum of the petition stopped right there."

The most symbolic moment underscoring the relationship between Reese and Robinson occurred during the Dodgers' first trip to Cincinnati's Crosley Field in 1947. The racial taunting had gone on all day—the organist had played "Bye Bye Blackbird." Finally, in the sixth inning, Reese walked toward second base from his shortstop position, put his hand on Robinson's shoulder and spoke briefly — a heartfelt gesture that immediately unplugged the crowd.

In a 1961 interview with broadcaster Jack Buck, Robinson said of Reese: "He's a real man. He didn't even look into the dugout. He walked over to my position, put his hand on my shoulder, said something. ...His actions indicated that the only thing he was asking was that Jackie Robinson continue to play baseball in the best manner he could."

"Pee Wee didn't ask for credit," pitcher Carl Erskine, who played with Reese and Robinson for nine seasons, said in 1997, the 50th anniversary of Robinson's first major league season. "I never heard him say one word that he was able to help Jackie. He helped all of us, by his leadership, his consistent play and just by being a good human being."

On the field, the 5-10 shortstop known as "The Little Colonel" was considered the heart and soul of one of baseball's most beloved teams. He frequently batted leadoff in a lineup studded with such Hall of Famers as Duke Snider, Jackie Robinson and Roy Campanella; played one of the game's most important positions; and was an eight-time NL All-Star. He died Aug. 14 at his Louisville home. He was 81.

Selected major leaguers who died in 1999

Joe Adcock: May 3, Coushatta, La.; 1950-66, Reds, Braves, Indians, Angels
Dewey Adkins: Dec. 26, 1998, Santa Monica, Calif.; 1942-49, Senators, Cubs
Clay Bryant: April 9, Boca Raton, Fla.; 1935-40, Cubs
Paul Calvert: Feb. 1, Sherbrooke, Quebec; 1942-51, Indians, Senators, Tigers
Joe DiMaggio: March 8, Hollywood, Fla.; 1936-51, Yankees
Len Dondero: Jan. 1, Fremont, Calif.; 1929, Browns
Jim Dunn: Jan. 6, Gadsden, Ala.; 1952, Pirates
Jim Dyck: Jan. 11, Cheney, Wash.; 1951-56, Browns, Indians, Orioles, Reds
Arnold Earley: Sept. 29, Flint, Mich.; 1960-67, Red Sox, Cubs, Astros
Dee Fondy: Aug. 19, Redlands, Calif.; 1951-58, Cubs, Pirates, Reds
Denny Galehouse: Dec. 12, 1998, Doylestown, Ohio; 1934-49, Indians, Red Sox, Browns
Bob Garber: June 7, Redwood City, Calif.; 1956, Pirates
Greek George: Aug. 15, Metairie, La.; 1935-45, Indians, Dodgers, Cubs, Athletics
Oscar Georgy: Jan. 15, New Orleans, La.; 1938, Mets
George Gill: Feb. 21, Jackson, Miss.; 1937-39, Tigers, Browns
Johnny Gorsica: Dec. 16, 1998, Charlottesville, Va.; 1940-47, Tigers

Paul Gregory: Sept. 16, Southaven, Miss.; 1932-33, White Sox

Lee Grissom: Oct. 4, 1998, Corning, Calif.; 1934-41, Reds, Yankees, Dodgers, Phillies

Doug Hansen: Sept. 16, Orem, Utah; 1951, Indians

Phil Haugstad: Oct. 21, 1998, Black River Falls, Wis.; 1947-52, Dodgers, Reds

Randy Heflin: Aug. 17, Fredericksburg, Va.; 1945-46, Red Sox

Clarence Heise: May 30, Winter Park, Fla.; 1934, Cardinals

Earl Huckleberry: Feb. 25, Seminole, Okla.; 1935, Athletics

Catfish Hunter: Sept. 9, Hertford, N.C.; 1965-79, Athletics, Yankees

Warren Huston: Aug. 30, Wareham, Mass.; 1937-44, Athletics, Braves

Ike Kahdot: March 31, Oklahoma City, Okla.; 1922, Indians

Ray Katt: Oct. 19, New Braunfels, Texas; 1952-59, Giants, Cardinals

Tim Layana: June 26, Bakersfield, Calif.; 1990-93, Reds, Giants

Ad Liska: Nov. 30, 1998, Portland, Ore.; 1929-33, Senators, Phillies

Bill Lohrman: Sept. 13, Poughkeepsie, N.Y.; 1934-44, Phillies, Giants, Cardinals, Dodgers, Reds

Doc Marshall: Sept. 1, Lake San Marcos, Calif.; 1929-32, Giants

Vinegar Bend Mizell: Feb. 21, Kerrville, Texas; 1952-62, Cardinals, Pirates, Mets

Pat Mullin: Aug. 14, Brownsville, Pa.; 1940-53, Tigers

Hal Newhouser: Nov. 10, 1998, Detroit, Mich.; 1939-55, Tigers, Indians

Bill Peterman: March 13, Philadelphia, Pa.; 1942, Phillies

Elmo Plaskett: Nov. 2, 1998, Christiansted, U.S. Virgin Islands; 1962-63, Pirates

Boots Poffenberger: Sept. 1, Williamsport, Md.; 1937-39, Tigers, Dodgers

Dave Pope: Aug. 28, Cleveland, Ohio; 1952-56, Indians, Orioles

Carl Powis: May 10, Houston, Texas; 1957, Orioles

Pee Wee Reese: Aug. 14, Louisville, Ky.; 1940-58, Dodgers

Johnny Riddle: Dec. 15, 1998, Indianapolis, Ind.; 1930-48, White Sox, Senators, Braves, Reds, Pirates

Kenny Robinson: Feb. 28, Tucson, Ariz.; 1995-97, Blue Jays, Royals

Cliff Ross: April 13, Philadelphia, Pa.; 1954, Reds

Joe Rossi: Feb. 20, Oakland, Calif.; 1952, Reds

George Schmees: Oct. 30, 1998, Oakland, Calif.; 1952, Browns, Red Sox

Strick Shofner: Oct. 10, 1998, Crawford, Texas; 1947, Red Sox

Dick Sisler: Nov. 20, 1998, Nashville, Tenn.; 1946-53, Cardinals, Phillies, Reds

Bernie Snyder: April 15, Havertown, Pa.; 1935, Athletics

Eddie Stanky: June 6, Fairhope, Ala.; 1943-53, Cubs, Dodgers, Braves, Giants, Cardinals

Carl Sumner: Feb. 8, Chatham, Mass.; 1928, Red Sox

Ben Taylor: May 11, Alma, Okla.; 1951-55, Browns, Tigers, Braves

Birdie Tebbetts: March 24, Manatee, Fla.; 1936-52, Tigers, Red Sox, Indians

Bob Thurman: Oct. 31, 1998, Wichita, Kan.; 1955-59, Reds

Paul Toth: March 20, Anaheim, Calif.; 1962-64, Cardinals, Cubs

Earl Turner: Oct. 20, Lee, Mass.; 1948-50, Pirates

Jim Turner: Nov. 29, 1998, Nashville, Tenn.; 1937-45, Braves, Reds, Yankees

Harry Walker: Aug. 8, Birmingham, Ala.; 1940-55, Cardinals, Phillies, Cubs, Reds

Ace Williams: Sept. 16, Kalooza Harbor, Mass.; 1940-46, Braves

Johnnie Wittig: Feb. 24, Nassawadox, Va.; 1938-49, Giants, Red Sox

Al Wright: Nov. 13, 1998, Oakland, Calif.; 1933, Braves

Whit Wyatt: July 16, Carrollton, Ga.; 1929-45, Tigers, White Sox, Indians, Dodgers, Phillies

Early Wynn: April 4, Venice, Fla.; 1939-63, Senators, Indians, White Sox

Norm Zauchin: Jan. 31, Birmingham, Ala.; 1951-59, Red Sox, Senators

—compiled by Bill Carle

Postseason

▶ **AL and NL Division Series stories and stats**
▶ **ALCS and NLCS stories and stats**

▶ **World Series game-by-game wrap-ups, box scores, MVP and composite player statistics**

USA SNAPSHOTS®

A look at statistics that shape the sports world

Baseball ticket inflation

The average 1999 major league ticket is up 10% to $14.91. The price is up 72.6% since 1991 vs. an 18.7% rise in the Consumer Price Index. Most, least expensive teams:

COSTLIEST

Boston	N.Y. Yankees	Texas
(+16.6%)	(+13.8%)	(+20.9%)
$24.05	$23.33	$19.93

CHEAPEST

Minnesota	Montreal[1]	Cincinnati
(+2.9%)	(-6%)	(+16%)
$8.46	$9.38	$9.71

1 – Only Montreal, Oakland and Tampa Bay cut prices for 1999

Source: *Team Marketing Report*   By Scott Boeck and Gary Visgaitis, USA TODAY

Player statistics

BOSTON 3, CLEVELAND 2

SERIES BATTING / BOSTON

	G	AB	R	H	2B	3B	HR	RBI	BB	SO	AVG
Hatteberg	1	1	1	1	0	0	0	1	0	0	1.000
Sadler	2	2	1	1	0	0	0	0	0	1	.500
Stanley	5	20	4	10	2	1	0	2	2	3	.500
Garciaparra	4	12	6	5	2	0	2	4	3	3	.417
Offerman	5	18	4	7	1	0	1	6	7	0	.389
Lewis	4	16	5	6	1	0	0	2	0	2	.375
Merloni	3	6	1	2	0	0	0	1	1	1	.333
Valentin	5	22	6	7	2	0	3	12	0	4	.318
Daubach	4	16	3	4	2	0	1	3	0	7	.250
Varitek	5	21	7	5	3	0	1	3	0	4	.238
Nixon	5	14	5	3	3	0	0	6	4	5	.214
Huskey	2	5	0	1	0	0	0	0	0	1	.200
O'Leary	5	20	4	4	0	0	2	7	2	3	.200
Buford	1	3	0	0	0	0	0	0	0	1	.000
Totals	5	176	47	56	17	1	10	47	19	35	.318

SERIES PITCHING / BOSTON

	G	CG	IP	H	R	ER	BB	SO	W-L	SV	ERA
P. Martinez	2	0	10	3	0	0	4	11	1-0	0	0.00
Cormier	2	0	4	2	0	0	1	4	0-0	0	0.00
Beck	2	0	2	2	0	0	0	2	0-0	0	0.00
R. Martinez	1	0	5.2	5	2	2	3	6	0-0	0	3.18
Garces	2	0	2.1	2	1	1	3	2	1-0	0	3.86
Lowe	3	0	8.1	6	7	4	1	7	1-1	0	4.32
Gordon	2	0	2	1	1	1	1	3	0-0	0	4.50
Mercker	1	0	1.2	3	2	2	3	1	0-0	0	10.80
Wakefield	2	0	2	3	3	3	4	4	0-0	0	13.50
Sbrhqn	2	0	3.2	9	11	11	4	2	0-1	0	27.00
Wasdin	2	0	1.2	2	5	5	4	1	0-0	0	27.00
Totals	5	0	43.1	38	32	29	28	43	3-2	0	6.02

SERIES BATTING / CLEVELAND

	G	AB	R	H	2B	3B	HR	RBI	BB	SO	AVG
Cordero	3	9	3	5	0	0	1	2	1	2	.556
R. Alomar	5	19	4	7	4	0	0	3	2	3	.368
Baines	4	14	1	5	0	0	1	4	2	1	.357
Thome	5	17	7	6	0	0	4	10	4	5	.353
Fryman	5	15	2	4	0	0	1	4	3	2	.267
Vizquel	5	21	3	5	1	1	0	3	2	3	.238
Sexson	3	6	1	1	0	0	0	1	1	3	.167
S. Alomar	5	14	1	2	0	0	0	1	2	6	.143
Lofton	5	16	5	2	1	0	0	1	5	6	.125
M. Ramirez	5	18	5	1	1	0	0	1	4	8	.056
Diaz	2	1	0	0	0	0	0	0	0	0	.000
Justice	3	8	0	0	0	0	0	1	2	2	.000
Roberts	2	3	0	0	0	0	0	0	0	2	.000
Wilson	3	2	0	0	0	0	0	0	0	0	.000
Totals	5	163	32	38	7	1	7	31	28	43	.233

SERIES PITCHING / CLEVELAND

	G	CG	IP	H	R	ER	BB	SO	W-L	SV	ERA
Burba	1	0	4	1	0	0	1	0	0-0	0	0.00
DePaula	3	0	5	2	1	1	3	5	0-0	0	1.80
Jackson	2	0	2	2	1	1	1	1	0-0	0	4.50
Nagy	2	0	10	11	9	8	2	6	1-0	0	7.20
Colon	2	0	9	11	9	9	4	12	0-1	0	9.00
Karsay	2	0	3	5	3	3	1	3	0-0	0	9.00
Shuey	3	0	4	4	5	4	4	5	1-1	0	11.25
Wright	1	0	2	4	5	5	1	1	0-1	0	22.50
Assnmchr	1	0	1	5	3	3	0	0	0-0	0	27.00
Reed	2	0	2.1	9	8	8	1	1	1-0	0	30.86
Rincon	1	0	.2	2	3	3	1	1	0-0	0	40.50
Totals	5	0	43	56	47	46	19	35	2-3	0	9.63

Same old story for Cleveland, as Boston takes Division Series

The Cleveland Indians' impressive resume—five consecutive American League Central Division championships, two World Series appearances, and two trips to the AL Championship Series—made them heavy favorites to advance to the ALCS for the fourth time since 1995. But they blew a 2-0 lead against the Boston Red Sox in the best-of-five Division Series and finished this postseason like every other they've played in the past 48 years: as also-rans. The Indians were in a position to sweep, but when the score was tied 3-3 in the seventh inning of Game Three, manager Mike Hargrove decided to save his top relief pitchers and went with Jaret Wright and Ricardo Rincon instead. The results were disastrous: a six-run seventh inning gave the Red Sox the game and a ticket to Game Four. Hargrove played down the importance of his decision in Game Three and called Game Four—a 23-7 rout—"an aberration." That description might have been easier to swallow if the Red Sox hadn't gone on to pound the Indians' pitching staff for 12 runs in Game Five. "Nothing matters," shortstop Omar Vizquel said afterward. "You can win 125 games or be ahead by 21 games in your division. If you don't play well in the playoffs, so what?"

—by Deron Snyder

Red Sox/Indians notebook

▶**Martinez saves the season:** After their Game Five victory, the jubilant Red Sox encircled Pedro Martinez in their clubhouse, pouring champagne on their star pitcher. If Martinez didn't completely exorcise Boston's curse, he certainly found a temporary cure. Just three days after he and his team were both counted out, Martinez made a surprise relief appearance, pitching six hitless innings and striking out eight batters.

▶**Boston massacre:** The 23-7 Game Four rout was the most lopsided postseason victory ever. The Red Sox broke the record for postseason runs set by the 1936 New York Yankees. John Valentin had two homers, a double and seven RBI. Mike Stanley had five hits while Valentin and Jason Varitek each had four of Boston's 24 hits—another postseason record.

▶**O'Leary makes Indians pay:** Troy O'Leary supplied the offense for Boston in Game Four, twice thwarting the Indians' strategy of intentionally walking Nomar Garciaparra by driving in seven runs with a pair of homers—including the first postseason grand slam in Red Sox history.

Texas slump lets Yanks sweep again

In getting swept again by the New York Yankees, the Texas Rangers ran their postseason losing streak to nine games. They have scored just two runs in 60 innings of Division Series play. As stunned manager Johnny Oates said: "It's mind-boggling. Just through pure luck we should do more offensively." His players were just as shell-shocked.

"I cannot explain how we scored one run in three games," designated hitter Rafael Palmeiro said. "I'll think about it all winter." In 1998, the Rangers hit .141 (13-for-92) in their quiet exodus. In 1999, they were exactly one hit better (14-for-92), at .152. That postseason slump is inexplicable for a team that led the majors with a .293 team batting average and scored a club-record 945 runs.

Since winning Game One of the 1996 Division Series, the Rangers are 11-32 against New York (regular and postseason combined).

"We know in our hearts that we can play with these guys," Oates said, "but until we start doing it, there's always going to be some doubt." The Rangers came into the series with confidence, but they were stymied by the end of Game One. Oates said his players tried being patient at the plate—they got seven walks—but with just two hits, they were shut out 8-0. They reverted to free-swinging form in Game Two, but squandered their best chance—second and third, nobody out in the fifth inning—by chasing balls out of the strike zone and striking out. Oates was asked before Game Three if he had any tricks left in his back pocket. "No," he replied. "Everybody has seen all of my tricks. They're old and worn out. They're not even feeling well today."

—by Bill Koenig

Yankees/Rangers notebook

▶**The last Straw:** In 1998, Darryl Strawberry announced he had colon cancer the day before New York played Game Three in Texas. The Yankees finished a first-round sweep the next day and dedicated the victory to him. In 1999, his three-run homer in Game Three gave New York the win, the sweep, and the division title.

▶**Rocket launch:** Seven shutout innings in Game Three gave Roger Clemens his first postseason win since 1986, satisfying Yankee fans who had been waiting all year for him to show the form that won five Cy Youngs.

▶**As good as it gets:** With his 8-0 victory in Game One, Yankees ace Orlando "El Duque" Hernandez brought his perfect postseason record to 3-0 with a near-perfect 0.41 ERA (one run in 20 innings).

Player statistics

NEW YORK 3, TEXAS 0

SERIES BATTING / NEW YORK

	G	AB	R	H	2B	3B	HR	RBI	BB	SO	AVG
Jeter	3	11	3	5	1	1	0	0	2	3	.455
Williams	3	11	2	4	1	0	1	6	1	2	.364
Davis	1	3	0	1	0	0	0	0	0	2	.333
Strawberry	2	6	2	2	0	0	1	3	1	0	.333
Ledee	3	11	1	3	2	0	0	2	1	5	.273
O'Neill	2	8	2	2	0	0	0	0	1	1	.250
Posada	1	4	0	1	1	0	0	0	0	0	.250
Martinez	3	11	2	2	0	0	0	0	2	2	.182
Knoblauch	3	12	1	2	0	0	0	0	1	3	.167
Brosius	3	10	0	1	1	0	0	1	0	0	.100
Curtis	3	3	1	0	0	0	0	0	0	0	.000
Girardi	2	6	0	0	0	0	0	0	0	1	.000
Leyritz	2	2	0	0	0	0	0	0	1	1	.000
Bellinger	1	0	0	0	0	0	0	0	0	0	—
Totals	3	98	14	23	6	1	2	13	10	19	.235

SERIES PITCHING / NEW YORK

	G	CG	IP	H	R	ER	BB	SO	W-L	SV	ERA
Clemens	1	0	7	3	0	0	2	2	1-0	0	0.00
Hernandez	1	0	8	2	0	0	6	4	1-0	0	0.00
Nelson	3	0	1.2	1	0	0	1	3	0-0	0	0.00
Rivera	2	0	3	1	0	0	0	3	0-0	2	0.00
Pettitte	1	0	7.1	7	1	1	0	5	1-0	0	1.23
Totals	3	0	27	14	1	1	9	17	3-0	2	0.33

SERIES BATTING / TEXAS

	G	AB	R	H	2B	3B	HR	RBI	BB	SO	AVG
Kelly	1	3	0	1	0	0	0	0	0	2	.333
Palmeiro	3	11	0	3	0	0	0	0	1	1	.273
Rodriguez	3	12	0	3	1	0	0	0	0	2	.250
Gonzalez	3	11	1	2	0	0	1	1	1	3	.182
Goodwin	3	7	0	1	0	0	0	0	0	1	.143
Greer	3	9	0	1	0	0	0	0	3	1	.111
Stevens	3	9	0	1	1	0	0	0	1	2	.111
McLemore	3	10	0	1	0	0	0	0	1	3	.100
Zeile	3	10	0	1	0	0	0	0	2	1	.100
Clayton	3	10	0	0	0	0	0	0	0	1	.000
Totals	3	92	1	14	2	0	1	1	9	17	.152

SERIES PITCHING / TEXAS

	G	CG	IP	H	R	ER	BB	SO	W-L	SV	ERA
Patterson	1	0	1	1	0	0	0	0	0-0	0	0.00
Venafro	2	0	1	2	2	0	1	0	0-0	0	0.00
Wetteland	1	0	1	0	0	0	0	1	0-0	0	0.00
Zmmmrn	1	0	1	1	0	0	0	1	0-0	0	0.00
Helling	1	0	6.1	5	2	2	1	8	0-1	0	2.84
Loaiza	1	0	7.1	7	1	3	1	4	0-1	0	3.86
Crabtree	2	0	1.2	1	2	1	1	1	0-0	0	5.40
Sele	1	0	5	6	4	3	5	3	0-1	0	5.40
Fassero	1	0	1	2	1	1	1	1	0-0	0	9.00
Totals	3	0	25	23	14	10	10	19	0-3	0	3.60

Player statistics

NEW YORK 3, ARIZONA 1

SERIES BATTING / NEW YORK

	G	AB	R	H	2B	3B	HR	RBI	BB	SO	AVG
Olerud	4	16	3	7	0	0	1	6	3	2	.438
Henderson	4	15	5	6	0	0	0	1	3	1	.400
Agbayani	4	10	1	3	1	0	0	1	0	3	.300
Cedeno	4	7	1	2	0	0	0	2	1	1	.286
Ordonez	4	14	1	4	1	0	0	2	0	5	.286
Alfonzo	4	16	6	4	1	0	3	6	3	2	.250
Piazza	2	9	0	2	0	0	0	0	0	4	.222
Ventura	4	14	1	3	2	0	0	1	4	2	.214
Dunston	4	6	0	1	0	0	0	0	0	1	.167
Hamilton	4	8	0	1	0	0	0	2	2	0	.125
Pratt	3	8	2	1	0	0	1	1	2	1	.125
Bonilla	2	1	1	0	0	0	0	0	1	0	.000
Mora	3	1	1	0	0	0	0	0	1	0	.000
M. Franco	1	0	0	0	0	0	0	0	0	0	—
Totals	**4**	**134**	**22**	**34**	**5**	**0**	**5**	**22**	**21**	**28**	**.254**

SERIES PITCHING / NEW YORK

	G	CG	IP	H	R	ER	BB	SO	W-L	SV	ERA
Benitez	2	0	2.1	2	0	0	1	2	0-0	0	0.00
Cook	1	0	1.2	1	0	0	1	1	0-0	0	0.00
J. Franco	3	0	3.2	1	0	0	0	2	1-0	0	0.00
Hershiser	1	0	1	0	0	0	0	1	0-0	0	0.00
Wendell	2	0	2	0	0	0	2	0	1-0	0	0.00
Reed	1	0	6	4	2	2	3	2	1-0	0	3.00
Leiter	1	0	7.2	3	3	3	3	4	0-0	0	3.52
Mahomes	1	0	1.2	3	1	1	0	1	0-0	0	5.40
Yoshii	1	0	5.1	6	4	4	0	3	0-0	0	6.75
Rogers	1	0	4.1	5	4	4	2	6	0-1	0	8.31
Dotel	1	0	.1	2	2	2	0	0	0-0	0	54.00
Totals	**4**	**0**	**36**	**26**	**16**	**16**	**14**	**22**	**3-1**	**0**	**4.00**

50

SERIES BATTING / ARIZONA

	G	AB	R	H	2B	3B	HR	RBI	BB	SO	AVG
Ward	3	2	2	1	0	0	1	3	1	0	.500
Colbrunn	2	5	1	2	1	0	1	2	2	2	.400
Finley	4	13	0	5	1	0	0	5	3	1	.385
Williams	4	16	3	6	1	0	0	0	0	1	.375
Bell	4	14	3	4	1	0	0	3	1	0	.286
Gonzalez	4	10	3	2	1	0	1	2	5	1	.200
Durazo	2	7	1	1	0	0	1	1	1	0	.143
Stinnett	4	14	1	2	1	0	0	0	1	4	.143
Womack	4	18	2	2	0	1	0	0	0	6	.111
Fox	1	3	0	0	0	0	0	0	0	1	.000
Frias	4	7	0	0	0	0	0	0	0	3	.000
Gilkey	2	6	0	0	0	0	0	0	0	0	.000
Harris	2	2	0	0	0	0	0	0	0	0	.000
Totals	**4**	**126**	**16**	**26**	**7**	**1**	**4**	**16**	**17**	**33**	**.206**

SERIES PITCHING / ARIZONA

	G	CG	IP	H	R	ER	BB	SO	W-L	SV	ERA
Olson	2	0	.1	0	1	0	1	0	0-0	0	0.00
Swindell	3	0	3.1	1	0	0	3	1	0-0	0	0.00
Stottlemyre	1	0	6.2	4	1	1	5	6	1-0	0	1.35
Anderson	1	0	7	7	2	2	0	4	0-0	0	2.57
Chouinard	2	0	2	3	1	1	0	1	0-0	0	4.50
Mantei	1	0	2	1	1	1	3	1	0-1	0	4.50
Daal	1	0	4	6	3	3	3	4	0-1	0	6.75
Johnson	1	0	8.1	8	7	7	3	11	0-1	0	7.56
Holmes	1	0	1.1	1	4	4	3	0	0-0	0	27.00
Plesac	1	0	.1	3	2	2	0	0	0-0	0	54.00
Totals	**4**	**0**	**36.2**	**34**	**22**	**21**	**21**	**28**	**1-3**	**0**	**5.16**

Arizona's series just out of grasp

When the Diamondbacks won the National League West, they became the first team to reach the playoffs in just their second season. And they did it big: They won 100 games, marking the greatest turnaround in baseball history, after a 65-97 record in 1998. They had every reason to believe they were capable of winning the World Series, but they wilted in the Division Series, losing three games to one to the New York Mets. The Diamondbacks insist they had a better team than the Mets. Yet, in the Division Series they didn't play the way they had all season. They didn't hit (.206), they didn't pitch (5.16 ERA), and they didn't play their usual solid defense (four errors in four games). But Tony Womack, who ignited the Arizona offense during the regular season, will probably be the one who unfairly gets the blame. His dropped fly ball in the final game may become the next "Buckner ball." The Diamondbacks had a 3-2 lead, just six outs away from sending the series back to Arizona. But everything started to unravel when manager Buck Showalter summoned lefty Greg Swindell to face John Olerud, who hit a slicing drive to the right-center gap. Womack raced over to the warning track, put his glove up in the air at eye level, opened it, and started to let the ball nestle into the pocket. Just as the ball was falling into his glove, Womack shut it. The ball clanked to the ground. The crowd of 56,177 screamed. The Mets suddenly had runners at second and third with no outs, and once Roger Cedeno tied the game with a sacrifice fly to center, the Diamondbacks were finished. "I dropped it, I just dropped it," Womack said afterward, never lifting his head. Did the sun get in his eyes? "I just dropped it." Were there any shadows? "I just dropped it." Was he fooled at all? "Look, I just dropped it, that's it," Womack repeated. "I dropped it. I dropped it. I dropped it." And the Mets took off for Atlanta.

—by Bob Nightengale

Mets/Diamondbacks notebook

▶**More Mets miracles:** The improbable playoff team had an unlikely hero in Todd Pratt, who replaced injured Mike Piazza for the second straight day and smacked the 10th-inning homer that won the Division Series for the Mets. It was just the fourth homer in baseball history that ended a postseason series.

Postseason a different ball game for Astros

When Jeff Bagwell and Craig Biggio—the Houston Astros' Killer Bs—went 4-for-32 (.125) with no RBI in the Division Series against the Atlanta Braves, nobody in Houston was really shocked. In three consecutive postseason series, they have combined to hit .123 (10-for-81). "I'm not going to lie to you. I'm frustrated," Bagwell said after his team was eliminated in four games. "I didn't want to suck again." Said Biggio, "I guess we have to take the heat." But the two shouldn't beat themselves up too much over their postseason problems. Atlanta's Chipper Jones fell victim to the same strategy. He hit .231 in the series. "Don't give Chipper Jones anything to hit," said Astros right-hander Shane Reynolds. "That's been the game plan from the start." Atlanta made no secret of taking the same approach with Bagwell and Biggio. Braves catcher Eddie Perez was blunt: "We were not going to pitch to Bagwell," he said. "We wanted him to swing at some bad pitches. If he walked, we'd get the next guy." "Biggio and Bagwell have nothing to hang their heads about," said right-hander John Smoltz, who earned the win in the clinching Game Four. "Our whole plan was to get them out. We were determined not to let them beat us." And the Astros were facing the likes of Smoltz, Kevin Millwood, Tom Glavine and Greg Maddux. Poor Biggio faced Millwood, Maddux and Glavine in Game Three alone. As upset as Astros fans were following the series, nobody was clamoring to trade either player. As Bagwell says, "This isn't like basketball or hockey, where a lot of teams make the playoffs. . . . If you change personnel, you might not get back." You'd better believe manager Larry Dierker wants Bagwell and Biggio with him when the Astros move into their new downtown ballpark, Enron Field, in 2000. Maybe the new environment will bring a new mentality.

—by Chris Colston

Braves/Astros notebook

▶**Not with a bang, but a whimper:** A crowd of 48,553—about 6,000 short of capacity—headed quietly for the exits after the final game of the Division Series, the last ever to be played in the Astrodome. The world's first domed stadium was dubbed the Eighth Wonder of the World when it opened in 1965.
▶**No choke:** The Astros have been to the postseason six times without ever winning a series, but the Division Series has never been much of an obstacle for the Braves, who have an overall record of 15-2 since the expanded playoffs began in 1995.

Player statistics
ATLANTA 3, HOUSTON 1

SERIES BATTING / ATLANTA

	G	AB	R	H	2B	3B	HR	RBI	BB	SO	AVG
Nixon	1	1	1	1	0	0	0	0	0	0	1.000
Boone	4	19	3	9	1	0	0	1	0	4	.474
Jordan	4	17	2	8	1	0	1	7	1	2	.471
Williams	4	18	2	7	1	0	0	3	0	3	.389
Klesko	4	12	3	4	0	0	0	1	1	4	.333
Perez	4	16	1	4	0	0	0	3	0	3	.250
C. Jones	4	13	2	3	0	0	0	1	5	2	.231
A. Jones	4	18	1	4	1	0	0	2	1	3	.222
Weiss	3	6	1	1	0	0	0	0	0	2	.167
Hernandez	4	11	1	1	0	0	0	0	1	3	.091
Battle	1	1	0	0	0	0	0	0	0	0	.000
Guillen	1	1	0	0	0	0	0	0	0	0	.000
Hunter	3	4	0	0	0	0	0	0	1	3	.000
Lockhart	3	1	0	0	0	0	0	0	0	1	.000
Totals	4	148	18	45	5	0	1	18	11	35	.304

SERIES PITCHING / ATLANTA

	G	CG	IP	H	R	ER	BB	SO	W-L	SV	ERA
McGlinchy	1	0	.1	0	0	0	0	0	0-0	0	0.00
Rocker	2	0	3.1	0	0	0	2	5	1-0	1	0.00
Springer	1	0	1	2	0	0	1	1	0-0	0	0.00
Millwood	2	1	10	1	1	1	0	9	1-0	1	0.90
Maddux	2	0	7	10	2	2	5	5	0-1	0	2.57
Glavine	1	0	6	5	2	2	3	6	0-0	0	3.00
Smoltz	1	0	7	6	4	4	3	3	1-0	0	5.14
Remlinger	2	0	3.2	4	4	4	3	4	0-0	0	9.82
Mulholland	2	0	.2	3	2	2	0	0	0-0	0	27.00
Totals	4	1	37	31	15	15	17	33	3-1	2	3.62

SERIES BATTING / HOUSTON

	G	AB	R	H	2B	3B	HR	RBI	BB	SO	AVG
Johnson	2	1	0	1	0	0	0	1	0	0	1.000
Bogar	2	4	0	3	1	0	0	1	1	0	.750
Caminiti	4	17	3	8	0	0	3	8	2	1	.471
Bell	2	3	0	1	0	0	0	0	0	0	.333
Javier	4	11	1	3	0	0	0	0	1	1	.273
Spiers	4	11	0	3	0	0	0	1	0	1	.273
Eusebio	4	15	2	4	0	0	1	3	1	2	.267
Bagwell	4	13	3	2	0	0	0	0	5	4	.154
Ward	3	7	1	1	0	0	1	1	0	2	.143
Everett	4	15	2	2	0	0	0	1	2	8	.133
Biggio	4	19	1	2	0	0	0	0	1	5	.105
Barker	2	3	1	0	0	0	0	0	0	2	.000
Gutierrez	3	10	0	0	0	0	0	0	2	5	.000
Mieske	2	4	1	0	0	0	0	0	1	0	.000
Totals	4	141	15	31	2	0	5	15	17	33	.220

SEIRES PITCHING / HOUSTON

	G	CG	IP	H	R	ER	BB	SO	W-L	SV	ERA
Cabrera	1	0	2	2	0	0	6	0-0	0	0.00	
Henry	2	0	3.2	1	0	0	3	2	0-0	0	0.00
Miller	2	0	1.1	1	0	0	0	2	0-0	0	0.00
Wagner	1	0	1	0	0	0	0	1	0-0	0	0.00
Elarton	2	0	2.1	4	1	1	1	3	0-0	0	3.86
Hampton	1	0	7	6	3	3	1	9	0-0	0	3.86
Reynolds	2	0	11	16	5	5	3	5	1-1	0	4.09
Lima	1	0	6.2	9	4	4	2	4	0-1	0	5.40
Powell	3	0	3	3	2	2	1	3	0-1	0	6.00
Holt	1	0	0	3	3	3	0	0	0-0	0	—
Totals	4	0	37	45	18	18	11	35	1-3	0	3.60

Player statistics

NEW YORK 4, BOSTON 1

SERIES BATTING/NEW YORK

	G	AB	R	H	2B	3B	HR	RBI	BB	SO	AVG
Jeter	5	20	3	7	1	0	1	3	2	3	.350
Knoblauch	5	18	3	6	1	0	0	1	3	0	.333
Strawberry	3	6	1	2	0	0	1	1	1	2	.333
O'Neill	5	21	2	6	0	0	0	1	1	5	.286
Martinez	5	19	3	5	1	0	1	3	2	4	.263
Girardi	3	8	0	2	0	0	0	0	0	2	.250
Ledee	3	8	2	2	0	0	1	4	1	4	.250
Williams	5	20	3	5	1	0	1	2	2	5	.250
Brosius	5	18	3	4	0	1	2	3	1	4	.222
Spencer	3	9	1	1	0	0	0	0	1	6	.111
Posada	3	10	1	1	0	0	1	2	1	2	.100
Davis	5	11	0	1	0	0	0	1	3	4	.091
Bellinger	3	1	0	0	0	0	0	0	0	1	.000
Curtis	3	6	1	0	0	0	0	0	0	2	.000
Sojo	2	1	0	0	0	0	0	0	0	0	.000
Totals	5	176	23	42	4	1	8	21	18	44	.239

SERIES PITCHING/NEW YORK

	G	CG	IP	H	R	ER	BB	SO	W-L	SV	ERA
Rivera	3	0	4.2	5	0	0	0	3	1-0	2	0.00
Mendoza	2	0	2.1	0	0	0	0	2	0-0	1	0.00
Watson	3	0	1	2	0	0	2	1	0-0	0	0.00
Nelson	2	0	.2	0	0	0	0	0	0-0	0	0.00
Stanton	3	0	.1	1	0	0	1	0	0-0	0	0.00
Hernandez	2	0	15	12	4	3	6	13	1-0	0	1.80
Pettitte	1	0	7.1	8	2	2	1	5	1-0	0	2.45
Cone	1	0	7	7	2	2	3	9	1-0	0	2.57
Irabu	1	0	4.2	13	8	7	0	3	0-0	0	13.50
Clemens	1	0	2	6	5	5	2	2	0-1	0	22.50
Totals	5	0	45	54	21	19	15	38	4-1	3	3.80

SERIES BATTING/BOSTON

	G	AB	R	H	2B	3B	HR	RBI	BB	SO	AVG
Offerman	5	24	4	11	0	1	0	2	1	3	.458
Buford	4	5	1	2	0	0	0	0	0	2	.400
Garciaparra	5	20	2	8	2	0	2	5	2	2	.400
O'Leary	5	20	2	7	3	0	0	1	2	5	.350
Valentin	5	23	3	8	2	0	1	5	2	4	.348
Nixon	4	14	2	4	2	0	0	0	0	5	.286
Stanley	5	18	1	4	0	0	0	1	2	4	.222
Huskey	4	5	1	1	1	0	0	0	1	1	.200
Varitek	5	20	1	4	1	1	1	1	1	4	.200
Daubach	5	17	2	3	1	0	1	3	1	4	.176
Lewis	5	17	2	2	1	0	0	1	0	3	.118
Hatteberg	3	1	0	0	0	0	0	0	0	1	.000
Merloni	1	0	0	0	0	0	0	0	1	0	—
Sadler	2	0	0	0	0	0	0	0	0	0	—
Totals	5	184	21	54	13	2	5	19	15	38	.293

SERIES PITCHING/BOSTON

	G	CG	IP	H	R	ER	BB	SO	W-L	SV	ERA
P. Martinez	1	0	7	2	0	0	2	12	1-0	0	0.00
Cormier	4	0	3.2	3	0	0	3	4	0-0	0	0.00
Rapp	1	0	1	0	0	0	1	0	0-0	0	0.00
Lowe	3	0	6.1	6	3	1	2	7	0-0	0	1.42
Saberhagn	1	0	6	5	3	1	1	5	0-1	0	1.50
R. Martinez	1	0	6.2	6	3	3	3	5	0-1	0	4.05
Mercker	2	0	7.2	12	4	4	4	5	0-1	0	4.70
Garces	2	0	3	3	5	4	1	2	0-0	0	12.00
Gordon	3	0	2	3	3	3	1	3	0-0	0	13.50
Beck	2	0	.2	2	2	2	0	1	0-1	0	27.00
Totals	5	0	44	42	23	18	18	44	1-4	0	3.68

Yankee fans gloat over the "Curse of the Bambino."

By Eileen Blass, USA TODAY

Boston loses series on field of nightmares

The Boston Red Sox didn't need a long epitaph for the 1999 American League Championship Series. Just a capital E and a zero would do. E as in E-4, E-3. Zero as in 0-for-10 with men in scoring position.

The Red Sox committed an LCS-record 10 errors in their five-game defeat to the New York Yankees, including two miscues in Game Five that contributed to their 6-1 loss.

And as in Game Two in New York, the Red Sox couldn't produce a base hit with men in scoring position and were shut down with the bases loaded in the eighth inning by Yankees setup man Ramiro Mendoza.

Amid the season-ending hugs and handshakes in the quiet Boston clubhouse was a disappointment that the team didn't play its best when it mattered most.

"We didn't lose to a better team, we just didn't play well enough to win," said Boston shortstop Nomar Garciaparra.

As with their four errors in Game Four, the Red Sox bunched the miscues in pairs to create two unearned runs in Game Five.

In the seventh, first baseman Mike Stanley failed to catch Garciaparra's hard, high throw after Derek Jeter's grounder, and Jose Offerman booted a routine grounder, helping New York pad its lead to 4-0.

"Is that the biggest reason why we're going home now? I don't know," said Stanley. "We just didn't score any runs to give our pitchers some confidence out there."

—by Mike Dodd, USA TODAY

Opinion: Curse of the umpires

A lack of clutch hitting and crucial errors pushed Boston to the edge of elimination in the ALCS, but blown calls by the umpires pushed them over.

It happened twice in Game Four. The Red Sox were trailing 3-2 with Jose Offerman on first and one out in the eighth when John Valentin hit a grounder to second baseman Chuck Knoblauch, who swiped a tag at Offerman and threw to first to complete a double play. Second base ump Tim Tschida called Offerman out, but the TV replay showed a lot of daylight between Knoblauch's glove and Offerman. Later the ump said he blew the call.

In the ninth, with the Yankees up 9-2, first base umpire Dale Scott called leadoff batter Nomar Garciaparra out at first. Replays showed he was safe.

Bad calls also hurt the Sox in Game One. With the score tied 3-3 in the 10th inning, Boston got a leadoff single from Offerman, but umpire Rick Reed called him out at second on a force. Replays showed Knoblauch dropped the ball and didn't have possession. After the game, won by the Yankees on Bernie Williams's leadoff homer in the bottom of the 10th, Reed admitted he missed the call and said, "I feel terrible."

—by Hal Bodley, USA TODAY

Yankees/Red Sox notebook

▶**Curse or crock?** Former Red Sox catcher Carlton Fisk called the Curse of the Bambino "a crock." Then, to further annoy the baseball gods, Boston tried to reverse the curse by letting Babe Ruth's 82-year-old daughter, Julia Ruth Stevens, throw out the first pitch in Game Five—and we all know how that turned out. Crock? You make the call.

▶**Homer sweet homer:** Darryl Strawberry's seven LCS homers put him third on the career list, two behind George Brett and one behind Steve Garvey. New York's Ricky Ledee joined Baltimore's pitcher Mike Cuellar (1970), California's Don

Baylor (1982) and Cleveland's Jim Thome (1998) as the only players with ALCS grand slams. Boston's Rod Beck allowed two homers on his first three pitches of the series.

Orlando Hernandez stayed cool under pressure and pitched the Yankees to another AL title.

POSTSEASON

By Robert Deutsch, USA TODAY

53

'El Duque' named series MVP

Orlando Hernandez wrapped up the New York Yankees' record 36th American League pennant in typical fashion. He pitched them past the Red Sox 6-1 and earned the series Most Valuable Player award.

Less than a year and a half after his major league debut, Hernandez finished his second ALCS 4-0 in postseason play with a 0.97 ERA—nearly halfway to Whitey Ford's franchise record of 10 postseason wins. Toying with major league hitters he allowed just four earned runs in 37 innings.

Nothing seems to rattle "El Duque." On a staff that struggled for consistency at times, he became the anchor, never going more than three starts without a win after mid-May. In 1998, Hernandez was the savior, starting against Cleveland with the Yankees' season suddenly starting to slip away and beating the Indians to even the ALCS at 2-all.

Last year was guts, this was glory.

Player Statistics

Atlanta 4, New York 2

SERIES BATTING / ATLANTA

	G	AB	R	H	2B	3B	HR	RBI	BB	SO	AVG
E. Perez	6	20	2	10	2	0	2	5	1	3	.500
Hernandez	2	2	0	1	0	0	0	2	0	1	.500
Lockhart	3	5	0	2	0	1	0	1	0	2	.400
Guillen	3	3	0	1	0	0	0	1	0	0	.333
Weiss	6	21	2	6	2	0	0	1	2	4	.286
C. Jones	6	19	3	5	2	0	0	1	9	7	.263
A. Jones	6	23	5	5	0	0	0	1	4	3	.217
Jordan	6	25	3	5	0	0	2	5	3	5	.200
Boone	6	22	2	4	1	0	0	1	1	7	.182
Williams	6	28	4	5	2	0	0	1	2	2	.179
Klesko	4	8	1	1	0	0	1	1	2	1	.125
Hunter	6	10	1	1	0	0	0	2	5	2	.100
Maddux	2	5	0	0	0	0	0	0	0	4	.000
Millwood	2	4	0	0	0	0	0	0	1	0	.000
Battle	3	2	0	0	0	0	0	0	0	2	.000
Fabregas	2	2	0	0	0	0	0	0	0	1	.000
Myers	2	2	0	0	0	0	0	0	1	1	.000
Glavine	1	2	0	0	0	0	0	0	0	1	.000
Smoltz	3	2	0	0	0	0	0	0	0	0	.000
McGlinchy	1	1	0	0	0	0	0	0	0	1	.000
Nixon	2	0	1	0	0	0	0	0	0	0	—
Totals	6	206	24	46	9	1	5	22	31	47	.223

SERIES PITCHING / ATLANTA

	G	CG	IP	H	R	ER	BB	SO	W-L	SV	ERA
Springer	2	0	2	0	0		1	1	1-0	0	0.00
Mulholland	2	0	2.2	1	0	0	1	2	0-0	0	0.00
Rocker	6	0	6.2	3	2	0	2	9	0-0	2	0.00
Glavine	1	0	7	7	0	0	1	8	1-0	0	0.00
Maddux	2	0	14	12	3	3	1	7	1-0	0	1.93
Remlinger	5	0	5.2	3	2	2	3	4	0-1	0	3.18
Millwood	2	0	12.2	13	6	5	1	9	1-0	0	3.55
Smoltz	3	0	8.2	8	6	6	0	8	0-0	1	6.23
McGlinchy	1	0	1	2	2	2	4	1	0-1	0	18.00
Totals	6	0	60.1	49	21	18	14	49	4-2	3	2.69

By Michael Schwarz, USA TODAY

The National League's MVP, Jones did not carry the Braves.

Braves' unsung heroes lead NLCS

Chipper Jones swung the biggest bat for the Atlanta Braves all season, so few thought they would reach the World Series without a major contribution from their star switch-hitter.

"But that's why this team is as good as it is," Jones said in the jubilant aftermath of the Braves' 10-9 Game Six victory in 11 innings over the New York Mets, a thriller that clinched the National League Championship Series. "It's not always the so-called big bats that have carried us."

Players such as Gerald Williams, Jose Hernandez, Brian Hunter, and Ozzie Guillen played integral roles in Game Six.

Williams was in a 1-for-21 funk when he led off the 11th with a double off Mets left-hander Kenny Rogers. A sacrifice and two intentional walks later, he scored the winning run when Rogers walked Andruw Jones. Hernandez spent much of the NLCS on the bench as shortstop Walt Weiss' backup, but his two-out, two-run pinch-hit single in the sixth made the lead 7-3 after the Mets had cut a 5-0 deficit to 5-3. Hunter's first hit of the postseason was a one-out RBI single off John Franco in the eighth, tying the score 8-8 after the Mets had taken their first lead. The Braves trailed 9-8 when Guillen's pinch-hit single off reliever Armando Benitez tied it again in the 10th.

And don't forget Eddie Perez, the former backup catcher who hit .500 (10-for-20) with two homers and five RBI, reaching base safely in five of the six games. Quite a performance, considering Perez hit just .249 with seven homers and 30 RBI in the regular season while starting a career-high 86 games.

—by Chuck Johnson, USA TODAY

Amazing resolve kept Mets alive

After the final game of the NLCS, most of the Mets looked defeated, but within a half-hour or so, the last comeback of their remarkable 1999 season began.

A small group of pitchers encircled the locker of Rick Reed, who would have started Game Seven. The group grew to a dozen players, and the laughter got louder as they talked about the past month's wild ride from the driver's seat of a postseason limo to the back seat of an off-season hearse. The farther they got from the deflating final loss, the more they appreciated their accomplishment in simply reaching Game Six.

On Sept. 21 the Mets were just one game behind Atlanta in the NL East. They had a three-game lead for the wild card, but seven straight losses left them two games back with three left to play. Unable to afford one more loss, the Mets swept the Pirates at Shea to force a one-game playoff in Cincinnati, where they blew out the Reds. Then they flew to Arizona, where they beat the Diamondbacks to win the Division Series in four games—and face the Braves again.

Trailing 3-0 in the NLCS, the miracle Mets came from behind to win Games Four and Five and force Game Six in Atlanta.

"There have been a lot of times we could've crawled into a shell," Mets reliever John Franco said. "Everybody was counting us out, but we never counted ourselves out."

—by Deron Snyder

MVP Perez finally in spotlight

Mental and physical toughness, patience and the dutiful prayers of his beloved family carried Braves' backup catcher Eddie Perez to the top of the baseball world in 1999. Before the NLCS, the 31-year-old from Venezuela was a virtual unknown. Then he hit .500 against the Mets and was named the Most Valuable Player, a crowning achievement for a player whose primary job had been to back up starter Javy Lopez throughout his minor and major league career.

When Lopez suffered a season-ending knee injury July 24, Perez came to the rescue with solid defense and a masterful job handling the Braves' pitching staff.

Several weeks before the playoffs, Perez knew he needed knee surgery and extensive work on his painful left elbow. But he postponed that until the offseason.

"We're winning, and I've finally got a chance to play every day," said Perez. "Why would I throw in the towel now? If I can stand up, I'm going to play."

—by Jill Lieber, USA TODAY

Player Statistics

SERIES BATTING / NEW YORK

	G	AB	R	H	2B	3B	HR	RBI	BB	SO	AVG
Cedeno	5	12	2	6	1	0	0	1	0	1	.500
M. Franco	5	2	1	1	0	0	0	1	0		.500
Pratt	4	2	0	1	0	0	0	3	1	1	.500
Mora	6	14	3	6	0	0	1	2	2	2	.429
Hamilton	5	17	0	6	1	0	0	2	0	4	.353
Bonilla	3	3	0	1	0	0	0	0	0	2	.333
Olerud	6	27	4	8	0	0	2	6	2	3	.296
Alfonzo	6	27	2	6	4	0	0	1	1	9	.222
Henderson	6	23	2	4	1	0	0	1	0	5	.174
Piazza	6	24	1	4	0	0	1	4	1	6	.167
Dunston	5	7	2	1	0	0	0	0	0	2	.143
Agbayani	4	7	2	1	0	0	0	0	4	2	.143
Ventura	6	25	2	3	1	0	0	1	2	5	.120
Ordonez	6	24	0	1	0	0	0	0	0	2	.042
Mahomes	3	2	0	0	0	0	0	0	0	2	.000
Rogers	3	1	0	0	0	0	0	0	0	1	.000
Yoshii	2	3	0	0	0	0	0	0	0	1	.000
Leiter	2	2	0	0	0	0	0	0	0	1	.000
Hershiser	2	1	0	0	0	0	0	0	0	0	.000
Reed	1	2	0	0	0	0	0	0	0	0	.000
Totals	6	225	21	49	9	0	4	21	14	49	.218

SERIES PITCHING / NEW YORK

	G	CG	IP	H	R	ER	BB	SO	W-L	SV	ERA
Cook	3	0	1.1	1	0	0	2	1	0-0	0	0.00
Hershiser	2	0	4.1	1	0	0	3	5	0-0	0	0.00
Benitez	5	0	6.2	3	1	1	2	9	0-0	1	1.35
Mahomes	3	0	6.1	4	1	1	3	3	0-0	0	1.42
Reed	1	1	7	3	2	2	0	5	0-0	0	2.57
Dotel	1	0	3	4	1	1	2	5	1-0	0	3.00
J. Franco	3	0	2.2	3	1	1	1	3	0-0	0	3.38
Yoshii	2	2	7.2	9	4	4	3	4	0-1	0	4.70
Wendell	5	0	5.2	2	3	3	4	5	1-0	0	4.76
Rogers	3	1	7.2	11	5	5	7	2	0-2	0	5.87
Leiter	2	2	7	5	6	5	4	5	0-1	0	6.43
Totals	6	6	59.1	46	24	23	31	47	2-4	1	3.49

Game 1

New York 4, Atlanta 1

New York	000	000	040 – 4
Atlanta	000	100	000 – 1

BATTING

NEW YORK	AB	R	H	RBI	BB	SO	LOB	AVG
Knoblauch 2b	4	1	0	0	0	0	3	.000
Jeter ss	4	1	2	1	1	1	1	.500
O'Neill rf	4	0	1	2	0	1	1	.250
BWilliams cf	2	0	0	0	2	1	1	.000
Martinez 1b	3	0	0	0	1	2	4	.000
Posada c	4	0	0	0	0	1	5	.000
Ledee lf	3	0	0	0	0	1	1	.000
b-Leyritz ph	0	0	0	1	1	0	0	.000
Nelson p	0	0	0	0	0	0	0	.000
Stanton p	0	0	0	0	0	0	0	.000
Rivera p	0	0	0	0	0	0	0	.000
Brosius 3b	4	1	3	0	0	1	3	.750
OHernandez p	1	0	0	0	0	0	1	.000
a-Strawberry ph	0	0	0	0	1	0	0	.000
Curtis pr-lf	1	1	0	0	0	0	0	.000
Totals	30	4	6	4	6	8	20	

a-walked for OHernandez in the 8th; b-walked for Ledee in the 8th.
▶**BATTING: S** - OHernandez, Knoblauch. **RBI** - Jeter (1), O'Neill 2 (2), Leyritz (1). **2-out RBI** - Leyritz. **Runners left in scoring position, 2 out** - BWilliams 1, Jeter 1, Ledee 1, Brosius 2. **GIDP** - Posada. **Team LOB** - 7.
▶**BASERUNNING: SB** - Jeter (1, 2nd base off Maddux/Perez); BWilliams (1, 2nd base off Maddux/Perez). **CS** - Jeter (1, 2nd base by Remlinger).

ATLANTA	AB	R	H	RBI	BB	SO	LOB	AVG
GWilliams lf	4	0	0	0	0	2	0	.000
Boone 2b	4	0	1	0	0	2	0	.250
CJones 3b	2	1	1	1	2	1	0	.500
Jordan rf	4	0	0	0	0	1	3	.000
Klesko 1b	3	0	0	0	0	0	1	.000
Hunter 1b	0	0	0	0	0	0	0	.000
e-Myers ph	1	0	0	0	0	0	2	.000
AJones cf	2	0	0	0	1	1	0	.000
Perez c	2	0	0	0	1	2	1	.000
Weiss ss	2	0	0	0	0	1	0	.000
a-Guillen ph	0	0	0	0	0	0	0	.000
b-JHrndz ph-ss	1	0	0	0	0	1	1	.000
Maddux p	2	0	0	0	0	2	0	.000
Rocker p	0	0	0	0	0	0	0	.000
c-Battle ph	0	0	0	0	0	0	0	.000
d-Lockhart ph	1	0	0	0	0	0	1	.000
Remlinger p	0	0	0	0	0	0	0	.000
Totals	28	1	2	1	4	13	9	

a-pinch-hit for Weiss in the 8th; b-struck out for Guillen in the 8th; c-pinch-hit for Rocker in the 8th; d-grounded to first for Battle in the 8th; e-fouled to third for Hunter in the 9th.
▶**BATTING: HR** - CJones (1, 4th inning off OHernandez 0 on, 1 out). **RBI** - CJones (1). **Runners left in scoring position, 2 out** - Myers 1. **Team LOB** - 4.
▶**BASERUNNING: CS** - CJones (1, 2nd base by OHernandez/Posada).
▶**FIELDING: E** - Hunter 2 (2, ground ball, throw). **DP** - 1 (Boone-Weiss-Klesko).

PITCHING

NEW YORK	IP	H	R	ER	BB	SO	BF	ERA
OHrnndz (W, 1-0)	7	1	1	1	2	10	23	1.29
Nelson (H, 1)	.1	0	0	0	1	1	2	0.00
Stanton (H, 1)	.1	0	0	0	0	1	1	0.00
Rivera (S, 1)	1.1	1	0	0	1	1	6	0.00

ATLANTA	IP	H	R	ER	BB	SO	BF	ERA
Maddux (L, 0-1)	7	5	4	2	3	5	29	2.57
Rocker	1	1	0	0	2	3	6	0.00
Remlinger	1	0	0	0	1	0	3	0.00

Maddux pitched to 4 batters in the 8th.
▶**UMPIRES: HP:** Randy Marsh. **1B:** Rocky Roe. **2B:** Steve Rippley. **3B:** Derryl Cousins. **LF:** Gerry Davis. **RF:** Jim Joyce.
▶**GAME DATA: T:** 2:57. **Att:** 51,342. **Weather:** 49 degrees, clear. **Wind:** 15 mph, left to right.

Orlando Hernandez beat the Braves with masterful control.

By Robert Hanashiro, USA TODAY

Yanks sweep into history

The Yankees sweep of the Atlanta Braves marked their second consecutive year of undefeated play in the World Series. It was their third Series crown in four years and 25th in this century, more championships than any organization in professional sports.

Game One: Big win for 'El Duque'

Orlando Hernandez struck out eight of the first 11 Braves he faced before he gave up a solo homer to Chipper Jones— his only mistake in a 4-1 victory over the Braves and pitcher Greg Maddux. "El Duque" Hernandez felt all his pitches—a variety of curves, sliders, fastballs and changeups—were working for him, ". . .but what was really working was my control," he said. "I had good placement of my pitches." Did he ever. Hernandez struck out Gerald Williams, Bret Boone and Jones in the first inning. He struck out the side again in the third (Walt Weiss, Maddux and Williams). He got Boone on strikes to start the fourth before Jones launched a towering home run into the right-field seats. After that, Hernandez retired 10 of 11 Braves batters. It took a while for the Yankees to figure out Maddux. Finally, in the eighth inning, Scott Brosius singled, pinch-hitter Darryl Strawberry walked and Chuck Knoblauch reached on an error. Derek Jeter singled to tie the game and knock Maddux out of it. Then Paul O'Neill hit a two-run single against lefty relief ace John Rocker. O'Neill took second on a throwing error, Bernie Williams was intentionally walked, and Rocker retired Tino Martinez and Jorge Posada before walking pinch-hitter Jim Leyritz to force in the winning run.

—by Mel Antonen, USA TODAY

Tino Martinez helps the Yanks score early—and often.

Game Two: Cone's one-hit shutout

The Yankees were on the top step of their dugout as baseball's "All-Century Team" was introduced before Game Two. The Yankees applauded politely, even reverently, as Vin Scully introduced some of the game's greatest heroes. But once the pageantry was over and the field cleared, they made their own point about what it takes to be the team of the century. Another round of excellent starting pitching, combined with a big first inning, put the Yankees halfway to their 25th World Series title. Three batters, three hits. Three runs before the Atlanta Braves got to bat. A 7-2 victory, a 2-0 World Series lead, a 10-game winning streak in World Series play (including seven on the road). The Yanks greeted Braves starter Kevin Millwood rudely in the opening inning, batting around and scoring three times before Cone even took the mound. Tino Martinez and Scott Brosius delivered RBI singles with two outs in the first. Ricky Ledee's double chased Millwood in the third, and it was 7-0 by the fifth. It's a baseball axiom that good pitchers can neutralize, even dominate, good hitters. Both teams had great pitching, but the Yankees found ways around it. Their first 12 hits in the World Series were singles. By the time Ricky Ledee doubled, New York had one victory plus a 3-0 lead. They'll beat you any way you want to play—and probably would be even more successful in the National League than they are in the American League.

—from staff reports and Paul White

Game 2

New York 7, Atlanta 2

New York	3 0 2	1 1 0	0 0 0 — 7
Atlanta	0 0 0	0 0 0	0 0 2 — 2

BATTING

NEW YORK	AB	R	H	RBI	BB	SO	LOB	AVG
Knoblauch 2b	4	1	2	1	1	1	2	.250
Jeters s	5	2	2	0	0	1	2	.444
O'Neill rf	4	0	1	1	1	0	1	.250
BWilliams cf	4	1	3	0	1	0	1	.500
Martinez 1b	5	2	2	2	0	1	4	.250
Ledee lf	4	0	2	1	1	2	2	.286
Brosius 3b	5	1	2	1	0	2	3	.556
Girardi c	4	0	0	0	0	1	4	.000
Cone p	4	0	0	0	0	0	3	.000
Mendoza p	1	0	0	0	0	0	1	.000
Nelson p	0	0	0	0	0	0	0	.000
Totals	40	7	14	6	4	8	23	

▶**BATTING – 2B:** Ledee (1, Millwood); Jeter (1, Mulholland); Brosius (1, Mulholland). S-Girardi. **RBI:** O'Neill (1), Martinez 2 (2), Brosius (1), Ledee (1), Knoblauch (1). **2-out RBI:** Martinez, Brosius, Knoblauch. Runners left in scoring position, 2 out–Girardi 1, O'Neill 1, Knoblauch 1, Martinez 1, Mendoza 1. **GIDP:** BWilliams. **Team LOB:** 11.
▶**BASERUNNING – SB:** Knoblauch (1, 2nd base off Millwood/Myers).
▶**FIELDING – E:** Cone (1, throw). **DP:** 3 (Jeter-Martinez, Brosius-Knoblauch-Martinez, Knoblauch-Jeter-Martinez).

ATLANTA	AB	R	H	RBI	BB	SO	LOB	AVG
GWilliams lf	4	0	0	0	0	1	2	.000
Guillen ss	4	0	0	0	0	0	1	.000
CJones 3b	3	1	1	0	1	0	0	.400
Jordan rf	3	0	0	0	1	0	2	.000
Klesko 1b	4	0	0	0	0	1	3	.000
Lockhart 2b	2	1	0	0	2	0	1	.000
Myers c	3	0	2	1	1	0	1	.500
AJones cf	3	0	0	0	0	1	4	.000
McGlinchy p	0	0	0	0	0	0	0	.000
b-Boone ph	1	0	1	1	0	0	0	.400
Millwood p	0	0	0	0	0	0	0	.000
Mulholland p	0	0	0	0	1	0	0	.000
a-Fabregas ph	1	0	0	0	0	1	0	.000
Springer p	0	0	0	0	0	0	0	.000
Nixon cf	2	0	1	0	0	0	2	.500
Totals	30	2	5	2	6	4	16	

a-struck out for Mulholland in the 5th; b-doubled for McGlinchy in the 9th.
▶**BATTING – 2B:** Boone (1, Nelson). **RBI:** Myers (1), Boone (1). **2-out RBI:** Myers, Boone. **Runners left in scoring position, 2 out:** Jordan 1, AJones 1, Nixon 2. **GIDP:** Guillen, AJones, GWilliams. **Team LOB:** 7.
▶**FIELDING – E:** Guillen (1, line drive). **DP:** 1 (Guillen-Klesko).

PITCHING

NEW YORK	IP	H	R	ER	BB	SO	BF	ERA
Cone (W, 1-0)	7	1	0	0	5	4	26	0.00
Mendoza	1.2	3	2	2	1	0	8	10.80
Nelson	.1	1	0	0	0	0	2	0.00

ATLANTA	IP	H	R	ER	BB	SO	BF	ERA
Millwood (L, 0-1)	2	8	5	4	2	2	15	18.00
Mulholland	3	3	2	2	1	3	14	6.00
Springer	2	1	0	0	0	1	7	0.00
McGlinchy	2	2	0	0	1	2	9	0.00

Millwood pitched to 3 batters in the 3rd.

▶**UMPIRES – HP:** Rocky Roe. **1B:** Steve Rippley. **2B:** Derryl Cousins. **3B:** Gerry Davis. **LF:** Jim Joyce. **RF:** Randy Marsh.
▶**GAME DATA T:** 3:14. **Att:** 51,226. Weather: 54 degrees, partly cloudy. Wind: 4 mph, left to right.

Game 3

New York 6, Atlanta 5

```
Atlanta   1 0 3  1 0 0  0 0 0  0 - 5
New York  1 0 0  0 1 0  1 2 0  1 - 6
```

BATTING

ATLANTA	AB	R	H	RBI	BB	SO	LOB	AVG
GWilliams lf	5	2	2	0	0	0	3	.154
Boone 2b	5	1	4	1	0	0	0	.600
Nixon pr	0	0	0	0	0	0	0	.500
Lockhart 2b	0	0	0	0	0	0	0	.000
CJones 3b	4	0	1	1	1	1	1	.333
Jordan rf	3	1	1	1	2	0	1	.100
AJones cf	5	1	1	0	0	0	2	.100
JHernandez dh	4	0	1	2	0	1	2	.200
a-Guillen ph-dh	1	0	0	0	0	1	0	.000
Perez c	4	0	1	0	0	1	1	.167
b-Klesko ph-1b	1	0	1	0	0	0	0	.125
Hunter 1b	4	0	1	0	0	1	2	.250
c-Myers ph-c	1	0	0	0	0	0	1	.400
Weiss ss	4	0	1	0	0	0	0	.167
Totals	**41**	**5**	**14**	**5**	**3**	**5**	**13**	

a-struck out for JHernandez in the 10th; b-singled for Perez in the 10th; c-grounded to first for Hunter in the 10th.
▶**BATTING – 2B:** Boone 3 (4, Pettitte 3); JHernandez (1, Pettitte). **3B:** GWilliams (1, Pettitte). **RBI:** CJones (2), Jordan (1), JHernandez 2 (2), Boone (2). **Runners left in scoring position, 2 out:** JHernandez 2, GWilliams 2, Hunter 1, AJones 1. **GIDP:** Jordan. **Team LOB:** 9.
▶**BASERUNNING – SB:** JHernandez (1, 3rd base off Pettitte/Girardi). **CS:** Boone (1, 3rd base by Pettitte/Girardi); Nixon (1, 2nd base by Rivera/Girardi).
▶**FIELDING: E -** Jordan (1, line drive). **DP:** 2 (Hunter, Hunter-Weiss-Boone).

NEW YORK	AB	R	H	RBI	BB	SO	LOB	AVG
Knoblauch 2b	4	2	2	2	0	0	1	.333
Jeter ss	4	0	1	0	0	1	1	.385
O'Neill rf	4	0	1	1	0	0	1	.250
BWilliams cf	4	0	0	0	0	1	0	.300
Davis dh	4	0	0	0	0	2	0	.000
Martinez 1b	4	1	1	1	0	0	0	.250
Brosius 3b	4	0	0	0	0	1	0	.385
Curtis lf	4	2	2	2	0	0	0	.400
Girardi c	3	1	2	0	0	0	0	.286
Totals	**35**	**6**	**9**	**6**	**0**	**4**	**4**	

▶**BATTING – 2B:** Knoblauch (1, Glavine). **HR:** Curtis 2 (2, 5th inning off Glavine, 0 on, 2 out, 10th inning off Remlinger 0 on, 0 out); Martinez (1, 7th inning off Glavine 0 on, 1 out); Knoblauch (1, 8th inning off Glavine, 1 on, 0 out). **RBI:** O'Neill (4), Curtis 2 (2), Martinez (3), Knoblauch 2 (2). **2-out RBI:** Curtis. **Runners left in scoring position, 2 out:** Curtis. **Team LOB:** 2.
▶**FIELDING – DP:** 1 (Jeter-Martinez).

PITCHING

ATLANTA	IP	H	R	ER	BB	SO	BF	ERA
Glavine	7	7	5	4	0	3	28	5.14
Rocker	2	1	0	0	0	1	6	0.00
Remlinger (L, 0-1)	0	1	1	1	0	0	1	9.00

NEW YORK	IP	H	R	ER	BB	SO	BF	ERA
Pettitte	3.2	10	5	5	1	1	21	12.27
Grimsley	2.1	2	0	0	2	0	10	0.00
Nelson	2	0	0	0	0	2	6	0.00
Rivera (W, 1-0)	2	2	0	0	0	2	7	0.00

Glavine pitched to 2 batters in the 8th.
Remlinger pitched to 1 batter in the 10th.

UMPIRES: HP: Steve Rippley. **1B:** Derryl Cousins. **2B:** Gerry Davis. **3B:** Jim Joyce. **LF:** Randy Marsh. **RF:** Rocky Roe.
GAME DATA – T: 3:16. **Att:** 56,794. **Weather:** 62 degrees, clear. **Wind:** 10 mph, left to right.

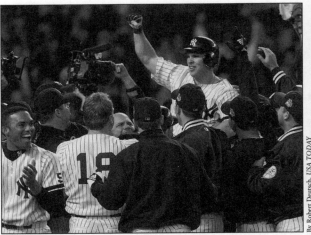

Chad Curtis (center) smashed two homers for the Yanks.

Game Three: Curtis blasts Braves

For most of the night, Game Three looked like a lock for the Atlanta Braves. They got hitting, they got pitching, they even got New York fans mad enough to boo their hometown heroes.

Braves starter Tom Glavine, scratched from Game One due to the flu, fortified himself with a plate of ravioli and helped Atlanta look every bit like the team that led the majors with 103 wins. Bret Boone hit three doubles in the first four innings against Andy Pettitte and finished with four hits.

Every Atlanta batter had a hit by the fifth, and by then it was 5-1 and the sellout crowd of 56,794 was booing.

Then the Yankees struck back. Chad Curtis homered in the fifth to begin New York's comeback, and homers from Tino Martinez and Chuck Knoblauch tied it. Knoblauch's two-run homer was a high drive to right field that bounced out of Brian Jordan's glove and into the stands.

Curtis led off the 10th inning with his second home run of the night and the Yankees beat the Braves 6-5 to move within one victory of a second straight World Series sweep.

"I have a tendency when I get up there in that situation, I try to hit a home run," Curtis said. "So I went up there and tried to hit it up the middle and I hit a home run."

Curtis's blast was the first game-ending homer in the Series since Joe Carter's Game Six shot won it all for Toronto in 1993. In his first-ever start in the World Series, Chad Curtis ended up as the hero.

—from staff reports

By H. Darr Beiser, USA TODAY

Roger Clemens' first World Series victory won the title for the Yanks.

Game Four: At last, Clemens wins

Roger Clemens had waited too long not to savor every moment of this glorious night. With the final out of the World Series, he bolted for the mound and, flanked by two of his sons, grabbed manager Joe Torre in a bear hug and found it hard to let go. Then, while his teammates were still dousing each other with champagne, Clemens sprinted back out to the field, climbed on the dugout roof and ran back and forth, slapping every outstretched hand in the front row. The Rocket had landed. The ring was his. Clemens pitched the Yankees to their second straight World Series sweep, shutting down the Atlanta Braves 4-1 and ending his quest for the one and only prize that had eluded him. "This must be what it's like to be a Yankee," Clemens said. "This is what everybody said it was all about." Clemens spent the game shouting to his fielders and offering congratulations. "I just wanted to fit in with these guys," Clemens said. All his life, Clemens had hoped for this chance and, at last, he commanded the October stage. Showing the form that earned him five Cy Young Awards and 247 wins in 16 seasons, he outdueled the Braves' formidable John Smoltz. "It seemed like a perfect setup," Torre said. "I couldn't see it not happening tonight, not with the way his career had gone." Clemens recalled seeing his teammates get their 1998 World Series rings in April, and being a bit envious. "I was sitting there watching them receive them. They said, 'We're going to get you one,'" he said. At age 37, in the last major league baseball game of the 20th century, Roger Clemens won his first world championship.
—from USA TODAY staff reports

Game 4

New York 4, Atlanta 1

Atlanta	000	000 010	– 1
New York	003	000 01x	– 4

BATTING

ATLANTA	AB	R	H	RBI	BB	SO	LOB	AVG
GWilliams lf	4	0	1	0	0	1	0	.176
Boone 2b	3	0	1	1	1	1	0	.538
CJones 3b	4	0	0	0	0	0	3	.231
Jordan rf	3	0	0	0	1	1	0	.077
Klesko 1b	4	0	1	0	0	0	1	.167
Lockhart dh	4	0	1	0	0	0	1	.143
Perez c	2	0	0	0	0	0	2	.125
a-Myers ph-c	1	0	0	0	0	0	0	.333
AJones cf	3	0	0	0	0	1	0	.077
Weiss ss	3	1	1	0	0	0	0	.222
Totals	31	1	5	1	2	4	7	

a-grounded to pitcher for Perez in the 8th.

▶BATTING: RBI – Boone (3). **2-out RBI:** Boone. **Runners left in scoring position, 2 out:** CJones 1. GIDP: Perez. **Team LOB:** 5.

NEW YORK	AB	R	H	RBI	BB	SO	LOB	AVG
Knoblauch 2b	4	1	1	0	0	2	1	.313
Sojo 2b	0	0	0	0	0	0	0	.000
Jeter ss	4	1	1	0	0	0	1	.353
O'Neill rf	3	0	0	0	1	1	3	.200
BWilliams cf	3	1	0	0	1	1	1	.231
Martinez 1b	3	0	1	2	1	1	0	.267
Strawberry dh	3	0	1	0	0	2	2	.333
a-Leyritz ph-dh	1	1	1	1	0	0	0	1.000
Posada c	4	0	2	1	0	2	2	.250
Ledee lf	3	0	0	0	0	1	4	.200
b-Curtis ph-lf	1	0	0	0	0	1	0	.333
Brosius 3b	3	0	1	0	0	1	2	.375
Totals	32	4	8	4	3	11	17	

a-homered for Strawberry in the 8th; b-fouled to first for Ledee in the 8th.

▶BATTING - **2B:** Posada (1, Mulholland). **HR:** Leyritz (1, 8th inning off Mulholland, 0 on, 2 out). **RBI:** Martinez 2 (5), Posada (1), Leyritz (2). **2-out RBI:** Posada, Leyritz. **Runners left in scoring position, 2 out:** Brosius 1, Ledee 1, O'Neill 1, Curtis 1. **Team LOB:** 7.
▶BASERUNNING - **SB:** Jeter 2 (3, 2nd base off Smoltz/Perez 2).
▶FIELDING - **DP:** 1 (Brosius-Knoblauch-Martinez).

PITCHING

ATLANTA	IP	H	R	ER	BB	SO	BF	ERA
Smoltz (L, 0-1)	7	6	3	3	3	11	30	3.86
Mulholland	.2	2	1	1	0	0	4	7.36
Springer	.1	0	0	0	0	0	1	0.00

NEW YORK	IP	H	R	ER	BB	SO	BF	ERA
Clemens (W, 1-0)	7.2	4	1	1	2	4	28	1.17
Nelson (H, 2)	0	1	0	0	0	0	1	0.00
Rivera (S, 2)	1.1	0	0	0	0	0	4	0.00

Nelson pitched to 1 batter in the 8th.

UMPIRES - HP: Derryl Cousins. **1B:** Gerry Davis. **2B:** Jim Joyce. **3B:** Randy Marsh. **LF:** Rocky Roe. **RF:** Steve Rippley.
GAME DATA – T: 2:58. **Att:** 56,752. **Weather:** 52 degrees, partly cloudy. Wind - 14 mph, left to right.

Rivera earns Series MVP with one win, two saves

Roger Clemens won the final game of the series for the Yankees, but it was closer Mariano Rivera who got the final out in the eighth inning and pitched a scoreless ninth to earn the save—and the MVP award. Rivera saved Game One, getting the last four outs. Then he pitched two scoreless innings and recorded the win in Game Three. In Game Four, he came on in the eighth inning with the tying runs on base and retired Chipper Jones on a grounder to end Atlanta's last threat. Then he breezed through the ninth and for the second straight year he was on the mound when the last out was recorded, securing the championship with a 4-1 victory.

Rivera was the obvious MVP choice, but he gave credit where he felt it was due.

"We all were MVP," he said. "The whole thing: manager, coaches, the 25 guys that were on the field."

World Series: Composite player statistics

NEW YORK 4, ATLANTA 0

NEW YORK YANKEES

Batting	G	AB	R	H	2B	3B	HR	RBI	BB	SO	AVG
Leyritz	2	1	1	1	0	0	1	2	1	0	1.000
Brosius	4	16	2	6	1	0	1	0	5	.375
Jeter	4	17	4	6	1	0	0	1	1	3	.353
Strawberry	2	3	0	1	0	0	0	0	1	2	.333
Curtis	3	6	3	2	0	0	2	2	0	0	.333
Knoblauch	4	16	5	5	1	0	1	3	1	3	.313
Girardi	2	7	1	2	0	0	0	0	0	1	.286
Martinez	4	15	3	4	0	0	1	5	2	4	.267
Posada	2	8	0	2	1	0	0	1	0	3	.250
B.Williams	4	13	2	3	0	0	0	4	2	.231
Ledee	3	10	0	2	1	0	0	1	1	4	.200
O'Neill	4	15	0	3	0	0	0	4	2	2	.200
O.Hernandez	1	1	0	0	0	0	0	0	0	0	.000
Mendoza	1	1	0	0	0	0	0	0	0	0	.000
Cone	1	4	0	0	0	0	0	0	0	1	.000
Davis	1	4	0	0	0	0	0	0	0	0	.000
Sojo	1	0	0	0	0	0	0	0	0	0	—
Totals	4	137	21	37	5	0	5	20	13	31	.270

Pitching	G	CG	IP	H	R	ER	BB	SO	W-L	SV	ERA
Cone	1	0	7	1	0	0	5	4	1-0	0	0.00
Rivera	3	0	4.2	3	0	0	1	3	1-0	2	0.00
Nelson	4	0	2.2	2	0	0	1	3	0-0	0	0.00
Grimsley	1	0	2.1	2	0	0	2	0	0-0	0	0.00
Stanton	1	0	.1	0	0	0	0	1	0-0	0	0.00
Clemens	1	0	7.2	4	1	1	2	4	1-0	0	1.17
O.Hernandez	1	0	7	1	1	1	2	10	1-0	0	1.29
Mendoza	1	0	1.2	3	2	2	1	0	0-0	0	10.80
Pettitte	1	0	3.2	10	5	5	1	1	0-0	0	12.27
Totals	4	0	37	26	9	9	15	26	4-0	2	2.19

ATLANTA BRAVES

Batting	G	AB	R	H	2B	3B	HR	RBI	BB	SO	AVG
Boone	4	13	1	7	4	0	0	3	1	3	.538
Nixon	2	2	0	1	0	0	0	0	0	0	.500
Myers	4	6	0	2	0	0	0	1	1	0	.333
Hunter	2	4	0	1	0	0	0	0	0	1	.250
C. Jones	4	13	2	3	0	0	1	2	4	2	.231
Weiss	3	9	1	2	0	0	0	0	0	1	.222
J.Hernandez	2	5	0	1	1	0	0	2	0	2	.200
GWilliams	4	17	2	3	0	1	0	0	0	4	.176
Klesko	4	12	0	2	0	0	0	0	0	1	.167
Lockhart	4	7	1	1	0	0	0	0	2	0	.143
Perez	3	8	0	1	0	0	0	0	1	3	.125
A. Jones	4	13	1	1	0	0	0	0	1	3	.077
Jordan	4	13	1	1	0	0	0	1	4	2	.077
Fabregas	1	1	0	0	0	0	0	0	0	1	.000
Maddux	1	2	0	0	0	0	0	0	0	2	.000
Guillen	3	5	0	0	0	0	0	0	0	1	.000
Battle	1	0	0	0	0	0	0	0	0	0	—
Mulholland	2	0	0	0	0	0	0	0	1	0	—
Totals	4	130	9	26	5	1	1	9	15	26	.200

Pitching	G	CG	IP	H	R	ER	BB	SO	W-L	SV	ERA
Rocker	2	0	3	2	0	0	2	4	0-0	0	0.00
Springer	2	0	2.1	1	0	0	1	0	0-0	0	0.00
McGlinchy	1	0	2	2	0	0	1	2	0-0	0	0.00
Maddux	1	0	7	5	4	2	3	5	0-1	0	2.57
Smoltz	1	0	7	6	3	3	11	0-1	0	3.86
Glavine	1	0	7	7	5	4	0	3	0-0	0	5.14
Mulholland	2	0	3.2	5	3	3	1	3	0-0	0	7.36
Remlinger	2	0	1	1	1	1	0	0	0-0	0	9.00
Millwood	1	0	2	8	5	4	2	2	0-1	0	18.00
Totals	4	0	35	37	21	17	13	31	0-4	0	4.37

SCORE BY INNINGS

New York	405	120	170	1 -	21
Atlanta	103	200	012	0 -	9

DP: New York 5, Atlanta 4. **CS:** Jeter, CJones, Boone, Nixon. **IBB:** off Rocker (BWilliams), off Mulholland (BWilliams), off Smoltz (BWilliams). **Umpires:** Randy Marsh (NL), Rocky Roe (AL), Steve Rippley (NL), Derryl Cousins (AL), Gerry Davis (NL), Jim Joyce (AL).

For the record

▶Active-player career records
▶All-time single-season and club records

▶Career records
▶Top fielding marks
▶All no-hitters
▶Award winners

Record qualifications

All-time records:
1,000 games played minimum for BA, OBA and SP.
1,500 innings pitched minimum for ERA.
100 wins minimum for winning percentage.

Active-player records:
One-half of above all-time minimum requirements.

Club records:
Same as active-player records, except pitchers winning percentage (40 wins minimum).

Season records:
3.1 plate appearances per game played by team for BA, OBA and SP.
1 inning pitched per game played by team for ERA.
15 victories for winning percentage.

Active-player records

Players listed through 1999 season.

Hitters

Games played: Most, career

2790	Cal Ripken, 1981-1999
2733	Rickey Henderson, 1979-1999
2702	Harold Baines, 1980-1999
2502	Gary Gaetti, 1981-1999
2440	Wade Boggs, 1982-1999
2436	Chili Davis, 1981-1999
2353	Tim Raines, 1979-1999
2333	Tony Gwynn, 1982-1999
2201	Willie McGee, 1982-1999
2161	Tony Phillips, 1982-1999
2082	Tony Fernandez, 1983-1999
2000	Barry Bonds, 1986-1999
1940	Rafael Palmeiro, 1986-1999
1930	Ozzie Guillen, 1985-1999
1906	Bobby Bonilla, 1986-1999

At-bats: Most, career

10765	Cal Ripken, 1981-1999
9911	Rickey Henderson, 1979-1999
9541	Harold Baines, 1980-1999
9180	Wade Boggs, 1982-1999
9059	Tony Gwynn, 1982-1999
8941	Gary Gaetti, 1981-1999
8694	Tim Raines, 1979-1999
8673	Chili Davis, 1981-1999
7788	Tony Fernandez, 1983-1999
7649	Willie McGee, 1982-1999
7617	Tony Phillips, 1982-1999
7281	Rafael Palmeiro, 1986-1999
7244	Julio Franco, 1982-1999
6976	Barry Bonds, 1986-1999
6800	Bobby Bonilla, 1986-1999

Runs: Most, career

2103	Rickey Henderson, 1979-1999
1561	Cal Ripken, 1981-1999
1548	Tim Raines, 1979-1999
1513	Wade Boggs, 1982-1999
1455	Barry Bonds, 1986-1999
1361	Tony Gwynn, 1982-1999
1300	Tony Phillips, 1982-1999
1270	Harold Baines, 1980-1999
1240	Chili Davis, 1981-1999
1157	Rafael Palmeiro, 1986-1999
1130	Gary Gaetti, 1981-1999
1120	Craig Biggio, 1988-1999
1117	Roberto Alomar, 1988-1999
1108	Will Clark, 1986-1999
1104	Julio Franco, 1982-1999

Hits: Most, career

3067	Tony Gwynn, 1982-1999
3010	Wade Boggs, 1982-1999
2991	Cal Ripken, 1981-1999
2816	Rickey Henderson, 1979-1999
2783	Harold Baines, 1980-1999
2561	Tim Raines, 1979-1999
2380	Chili Davis, 1981-1999
2280	Gary Gaetti, 1981-1999
2254	Willie McGee, 1982-1999
2240	Tony Fernandez, 1983-1999
2177	Julio Franco, 1982-1999
2158	Rafael Palmeiro, 1986-1999
2058	Mark Grace, 1988-1999
2040	Will Clark, 1986-1999
2023	Tony Phillips, 1982-1999

Total bases: Most, career

4856	Cal Ripken, 1981-1999
4474	Harold Baines, 1980-1999
4242	Rickey Henderson, 1979-1999
4156	Tony Gwynn, 1982-1999
4064	Wade Boggs, 1982-1999
3914	Chili Davis, 1981-1999
3898	Barry Bonds, 1986-1999
3881	Gary Gaetti, 1981-1999
3733	Rafael Palmeiro, 1986-1999
3708	Tim Raines, 1979-1999
3510	Fred McGriff, 1986-1999
3363	Jose Canseco, 1985-1999
3329	Will Clark, 1986-1999
3316	Ken Griffey, 1989-1999
3316	Mark McGwire, 1986-1999

2B: Most, career

578	Wade Boggs, 1982-1999
571	Cal Ripken, 1981-1999
522	Tony Gwynn, 1982-1999
474	Harold Baines, 1980-1999
472	Rickey Henderson, 1979-1999
443	Gary Gaetti, 1981-1999
426	Rafael Palmeiro, 1986-1999
424	Chili Davis, 1981-1999
423	Barry Bonds, 1986-1999
419	Tim Raines, 1979-1999
415	Mark Grace, 1988-1999
410	Will Clark, 1986-1999
410	Tony Fernandez, 1983-1999
392	Wally Joyner, 1986-1999
392	Paul O'Neill, 1985-1999

3B: Most, career

117	Lance Johnson, 1987-1999
112	Tim Raines, 1979-1999
94	Willie McGee, 1982-1999
92	Tony Fernandez, 1983-1999
85	Steve Finley, 1989-1999

84	Tony Gwynn, 1982-1999
69	Ozzie Guillen, 1985-1999
68	Devon White, 1985-1999
65	Barry Bonds, 1986-1999
65	Barry Larkin, 1986-1999
65	Luis Polonia, 1987-1999
64	Brady Anderson, 1988-1999
64	Dave Martinez, 1986-1999
63	Delino DeShields, 1990-1999
62	Jose Offerman, 1990-1999

HR: Most, career

522	Mark McGwire, 1986-1999
445	Barry Bonds, 1986-1999
431	Jose Canseco, 1985-1999
402	Cal Ripken, 1981-1999
398	Ken Griffey, 1989-1999
390	Fred McGriff, 1986-1999
373	Harold Baines, 1980-1999
361	Rafael Palmeiro, 1986-1999
360	Gary Gaetti, 1981-1999
358	Albert Belle, 1989-1999
350	Chili Davis, 1981-1999
340	Juan Gonzalez, 1989-1999
336	Sammy Sosa, 1989-1999
335	Darryl Strawberry, 1983-1999
334	Matt Williams, 1987-1999

RBI: Most, career

1583	Harold Baines, 1980-1999
1571	Cal Ripken, 1981-1999
1372	Chili Davis, 1981-1999
1340	Gary Gaetti, 1981-1999
1309	Jose Canseco, 1985-1999
1299	Barry Bonds, 1986-1999
1277	Mark McGwire, 1986-1999
1227	Rafael Palmeiro, 1986-1999
1192	Fred McGriff, 1986-1999
1152	Ken Griffey, 1989-1999
1136	Albert Belle, 1989-1999
1135	Will Clark, 1986-1999
1124	Bobby Bonilla, 1986-1999
1104	Tony Gwynn, 1982-1999
1099	Paul O'Neill, 1985-1999

SB: Most, career

1334	Rickey Henderson, 1979-1999
807	Tim Raines, 1979-1999
620	Otis Nixon, 1983-1999
460	Barry Bonds, 1986-1999
433	Kenny Lofton, 1991-1999
393	Delino DeShields, 1990-1999
382	Marquis Grissom, 1989-1999
377	Roberto Alomar, 1988-1999
352	Willie McGee, 1982-1999
347	Eric Davis, 1984-1999
346	Craig Biggio, 1988-1999
345	Barry Larkin, 1986-1999

62

2000 BASEBALL WEEKLY ALMANAC

335	Chuck Knoblauch, 1991-1999
325	Lance Johnson, 1987-1999
325	Devon White, 1985-1999

BB: Most, career

1972	Rickey Henderson, 1979-1999
1430	Barry Bonds, 1986-1999
1412	Wade Boggs, 1982-1999
1319	Tony Phillips, 1982-1999
1290	Tim Raines, 1979-1999
1194	Chili Davis, 1981-1999
1185	Mark McGwire, 1986-1999
1080	Cal Ripken, 1981-1999
1076	Frank Thomas, 1990-1999
1045	Fred McGriff, 1986-1999
1018	Harold Baines, 1980-1999
885	Jeff Bagwell, 1991-1999
877	Edgar Martinez, 1987-1999
868	Will Clark, 1986-1999
852	Bobby Bonilla, 1986-1999

HBP: Most, career

153	Craig Biggio, 1988-1999
136	Brady Anderson, 1988-1999
113	Chuck Knoblauch, 1991-1999
97	Mike Macfarlane, 1987-1999
96	Gary Gaetti, 1981-1999
91	Jeff Blauser, 1987-1999
89	Jason Kendall, 1996-1999
87	Ed Sprague, 1991-1999
86	Rickey Henderson, 1979-1999
82	Jeff Bagwell, 1991-1999
82	Mo Vaughn, 1991-1999
80	Larry Walker, 1989-1999
79	Jose Canseco, 1985-1999
74	Devon White, 1985-1999
73	Fernando Vina, 1993-1999

GIDP: Most, career

325	Cal Ripken, 1981-1999
290	Harold Baines, 1980-1999
255	Julio Franco, 1982-1999
254	Tony Gwynn, 1982-1999
236	Wade Boggs, 1982-1999
236	Gary Gaetti, 1981-1999
232	Chili Davis, 1981-1999
184	Paul O'Neill, 1985-1999
177	Terry Steinbach, 1986-1999
176	Albert Belle, 1989-1999
176	Fred McGriff, 1986-1999
169	Rafael Palmeiro, 1986-1999
167	Jose Canseco, 1985-1999
167	Mark Grace, 1988-1999
163	Wally Joyner, 1986-1999

BA: Highest, career

.339	Tony Gwynn, 1982-1999
.329	Mike Piazza, 1992-1999
.328	Wade Boggs, 1982-1999
.320	Frank Thomas, 1990-1999
.320	Edgar Martinez, 1987-1999
.318	Derek Jeter, 1995-1999
.312	Jason Kendall, 1996-1999
.312	Larry Walker, 1989-1999
.310	Mark Grace, 1988-1999
.310	Kenny Lofton, 1991-1999
.309	Rusty Greer, 1994-1999
.308	Alex Rodriguez, 1994-1999
.308	Manny Ramirez, 1993-1999
.307	Jeff Cirillo, 1994-1999
.305	Hal Morris, 1988-1999

On-base avg: Highest, career

.440	Frank Thomas, 1990-1999
.426	Edgar Martinez, 1987-1999
.416	Jeff Bagwell, 1991-1999
.415	Wade Boggs, 1982-1999
.412	Jim Thome, 1991-1999
.410	Barry Bonds, 1986-1999
.406	John Olerud, 1989-1999
.405	Rickey Henderson, 1979-1999
.399	Manny Ramirez, 1993-1999
.399	Jason Kendall, 1996-1999
.394	Mark McGwire, 1986-1999
.394	Chipper Jones, 1993-1999
.393	Rusty Greer, 1994-1999
.393	Tim Salmon, 1992-1999
.393	Gary Sheffield, 1988-1999

Slug pct: Highest, career

.587	Mark McGwire, 1986-1999
.576	Manny Ramirez, 1993-1999
.575	Mike Piazza, 1992-1999
.573	Albert Belle, 1989-1999
.573	Frank Thomas, 1990-1999
.572	Juan Gonzalez, 1989-1999
.569	Ken Griffey, 1989-1999
.567	Larry Walker, 1989-1999
.559	Barry Bonds, 1986-1999
.551	Alex Rodriguez, 1994-1999
.547	Jim Thome, 1991-1999
.545	Jeff Bagwell, 1991-1999
.538	Mo Vaughn, 1991-1999
.531	Carlos Delgado, 1993-1999
.529	Chipper Jones, 1993-1999

Extra-base hits: Most, career

1017	Cal Ripken, 1981-1999
933	Barry Bonds, 1986-1999
896	Harold Baines, 1980-1999
842	Gary Gaetti, 1981-1999
820	Rafael Palmeiro, 1986-1999
810	Rickey Henderson, 1979-1999
804	Chili Davis, 1981-1999
768	Mark McGwire, 1986-1999
764	Fred McGriff, 1986-1999
759	Jose Canseco, 1985-1999
757	Wade Boggs, 1982-1999
748	Ken Griffey, 1989-1999
739	Tony Gwynn, 1982-1999
730	Albert Belle, 1989-1999
723	Bobby Bonilla, 1986-1999

Pitchers

Games: Most, career

1090	Jesse Orosco, 1979-1999
884	Paul Assenmacher, 1986-1999
878	John Franco, 1984-1999
835	Mike Jackson, 1986-1999
822	Dan Plesac, 1986-1999
792	Doug Jones, 1982-1999
714	Eric Plunk, 1986-1999
700	Jeff Montgomery, 1987-1999
678	Rick Aguilera, 1985-1999
611	Mike Stanton, 1989-1999
581	Gregg Olson, 1988-1999
567	Tony Fossas, 1988-1999
562	Chuck McElroy, 1989-1999
559	Norm Charlton, 1988-1999
556	John Wetteland, 1989-1999

Complete games: Most, career

115	Roger Clemens, 1984-1999
93	Greg Maddux, 1986-1999
81	Mark Langston, 1984-1999
76	Bret Saberhagen, 1984-1999
68	Tom Candiotti, 1983-1999
68	Dwight Gooden, 1984-1999
68	Orel Hershiser, 1983-1999
68	Randy Johnson, 1988-1999
66	Kevin Brown, 1986-1999
62	Jack McDowell, 1987-1999
57	Chuck Finley, 1986-1999
57	Curt Schilling, 1988-1999
56	David Cone, 1986-1999
47	Scott Erickson, 1990-1999
47	John Smoltz, 1988-1999
47	Bobby Witt, 1986-1999

Saves: Most, career

416	John Franco, 1984-1999
304	Jeff Montgomery, 1987-1999
301	Doug Jones, 1982-1999
296	John Wetteland, 1989-1999
289	Rick Aguilera, 1985-1999
260	Rod Beck, 1991-1999
234	Roberto Hernandez, 1991-1999
228	Trevor Hoffman, 1993-1999
217	Gregg Olson, 1988-1999
185	Robb Nen, 1993-1999

154	Dan Plesac, 1986-1999
149	Jeff Brantley, 1988-1999
141	Jesse Orosco, 1979-1999
139	Troy Percival, 1995-1999
138	Mike Jackson, 1986-1999

Shutouts: Most, career

45	Roger Clemens, 1984-1999
28	Greg Maddux, 1986-1999
25	Orel Hershiser, 1983-1999
25	Randy Johnson, 1988-1999
24	Dwight Gooden, 1984-1999
22	David Cone, 1986-1999
20	Ramon Martinez, 1988-1999
18	Tim Belcher, 1987-1999
18	Tom Glavine, 1987-1999
18	Mark Langston, 1984-1999
16	Kevin Brown, 1986-1999
16	Scott Erickson, 1990-1999
16	Bret Saberhagen, 1984-1999
14	Chuck Finley, 1986-1999
14	Mike Mussina, 1991-1999
14	John Smoltz, 1988-1999

Wins: Most, career

247	Roger Clemens, 1984-1999
221	Greg Maddux, 1986-1999
203	Orel Hershiser, 1983-1999
188	Dwight Gooden, 1984-1999
187	Tom Glavine, 1987-1999
180	David Cone, 1986-1999
179	Mark Langston, 1984-1999
166	Bret Saberhagen, 1984-1999
165	Chuck Finley, 1986-1999
160	Randy Johnson, 1988-1999
157	Kevin Brown, 1986-1999
157	John Smoltz, 1988-1999
151	Tom Candiotti, 1983-1999
142	Tim Belcher, 1987-1999
141	David Wells, 1987-1999

Losses: Most, career

180	Mike Morgan, 1978-1999
164	Tom Candiotti, 1983-1999
158	Mark Langston, 1984-1999
155	Bobby Witt, 1986-1999
145	Orel Hershiser, 1983-1999
140	Chuck Finley, 1986-1999
135	Tim Belcher, 1987-1999
134	Roger Clemens, 1984-1999
126	Greg Maddux, 1986-1999
120	Jaime Navarro, 1989-1999
119	Andy Benes, 1989-1999
116	Tom Glavine, 1987-1999
115	Terry Mulholland, 1986-1999
115	Bret Saberhagen, 1984-1999
113	John Smoltz, 1988-1999
113	Todd Stottlemyre, 1988-1999

HR allowed: Most, career

311	Mark Langston, 1984-1999
256	Tim Belcher, 1987-1999
254	Chuck Finley, 1986-1999
251	Mike Morgan, 1978-1999
250	Tom Candiotti, 1983-1999
250	David Wells, 1987-1999
242	Bobby Witt, 1986-1999
234	Roger Clemens, 1984-1999
234	Greg Swindell, 1986-1999
230	Orel Hershiser, 1983-1999
224	Todd Stottlemyre, 1988-1999
221	Jamie Moyer, 1986-1999
219	Andy Benes, 1989-1999
215	Bret Saberhagen, 1984-1999
212	David Cone, 1986-1999

BB: Most career

1344	Bobby Witt, 1986-1999
1289	Mark Langston, 1984-1999
1118	Chuck Finley, 1986-1999
1102	Roger Clemens, 1984-1999
1013	Randy Johnson, 1988-1999
993	Orel Hershiser, 1983-1999
985	David Cone, 1986-1999
910	Dwight Gooden, 1984-1999
900	Tom Glavine, 1987-1999
883	Tom Candiotti, 1983-1999
872	Mike Morgan, 1978-1999
838	Tim Belcher, 1987-1999
807	Tom Gordon, 1988-1999
788	Ken Hill, 1988-1999
774	John Smoltz, 1988-1999

K: Most, career

3316	Roger Clemens, 1984-1999
2693	Randy Johnson, 1988-1999
2464	Mark Langston, 1984-1999
2420	David Cone, 1986-1999
2238	Dwight Gooden, 1984-1999
2160	Greg Maddux, 1986-1999
2151	Chuck Finley, 1986-1999
2098	John Smoltz, 1988-1999
2001	Orel Hershiser, 1983-1999
1918	Bobby Witt, 1986-1999
1735	Tom Candiotti, 1983-1999
1721	Andy Benes, 1989-1999
1705	Bret Saberhagen, 1984-1999
1701	Kevin Brown, 1986-1999
1659	Tom Glavine, 1987-1999

Wild pitches: Most, career

129	David Cone, 1986-1999
124	Bobby Witt, 1986-1999
120	Tom Candiotti, 1983-1999
119	Orel Hershiser, 1983-1999
119	John Smoltz, 1988-1999
117	Chuck Finley, 1986-1999
105	Juan Guzman, 1991-1999
100	Mike Morgan, 1978-1999

91	Tom Gordon, 1988-1999
91	Jaime Navarro, 1989-1999
90	Roger Clemens, 1984-1999
89	Mark Langston, 1984-1999
83	Darryl Kile, 1991-1999
82	Kevin Brown, 1986-1999
76	David Wells, 1987-1999

Win pct: Highest, career

.682	Pedro Martinez, 1992-1999
.673	Mike Mussina, 1991-1999
.648	Roger Clemens, 1984-1999
.645	Randy Johnson, 1988-1999
.642	Kirk Rueter, 1993-1999
.638	David Cone, 1986-1999
.638	Andy Pettitte, 1995-1999
.637	Dwight Gooden, 1984-1999
.637	Greg Maddux, 1986-1999
.619	Mike Hampton, 1993-1999
.617	Tom Glavine, 1987-1999
.616	Ramon Martinez, 1988-1999
.600	Denny Neagle, 1991-1999
.594	Kenny Rogers, 1989-1999
.593	Jack McDowell, 1987-1999

ERA: Lowest, career

2.64	John Franco, 1984-1999
2.81	Greg Maddux, 1986-1999
2.83	Pedro Martinez, 1992-1999
3.03	Jesse Orosco, 1979-1999
3.04	Roger Clemens, 1984-1999
3.17	Jeff Brantley, 1988-1999
3.19	David Cone, 1986-1999
3.26	Randy Johnson, 1988-1999
3.26	Doug Jones, 1982-1999
3.26	Mike Jackson, 1986-1999
3.27	Kevin Brown, 1986-1999
3.27	Jeff Montgomery, 1987-1999
3.33	Bret Saberhagen, 1984-1999
3.35	John Smoltz, 1988-1999
3.38	Curt Schilling, 1988-1999

Innings: Most, career

3462.1	Roger Clemens, 1984-1999
3105.2	Orel Hershiser, 1983-1999
3068.2	Greg Maddux, 1986-1999
2962.2	Mark Langston, 1984-1999
2725	Tom Candiotti, 1983-1999
2695.2	Dwight Gooden, 1984-1999
2675	Chuck Finley, 1986-1999
2659.2	Tom Glavine, 1987-1999
2598.2	Mike Morgan, 1978-1999
2590	David Cone, 1986-1999
2547.2	Bret Saberhagen, 1984-1999
2430.2	Kevin Brown, 1986-1999
2414.1	John Smoltz, 1988-1999
2406.1	Bobby Witt, 1986-1999
2402	Tim Belcher, 1987-1999

AL single-season records

ACTIVE PLAYERS in caps

Hitters

At-bats: Most

705	Willie Wilson, KC-1980
692	Bobby Richardson, NY-1962
691	Kirby Puckett, Min-1985
689	Sandy Alomar, Cal-1971
687	TONY FERNANDEZ, Tor-1986
686	Horace Clarke, NY-1970
686	ALEX RODRIGUEZ, Sea-1998
684	NOMAR GARCIAPARRA, Bos-1997
680	Kirby Puckett, Min-1986
679	Harvey Kuenn, Det-1953
679	Bobby Richardson, NY-1964
677	Don Mattingly, NY-1986
677	Jim Rice, Bos-1978
673	Bill Buckner, Bos-1985
673	B.J. SURHOFF, Bal-1999

Runs: Most

177	Babe Ruth, NY-1921
167	Lou Gehrig, NY-1936
163	Lou Gehrig, NY-1931
163	Babe Ruth, NY-1928
158	Babe Ruth, NY-1920
158	Babe Ruth, NY-1927
152	Al Simmons, Phi-1930
151	Joe DiMaggio, NY-1937
151	Jimmie Foxx, Phi-1932
151	Babe Ruth, NY-1923
150	Babe Ruth, NY-1930
150	Ted Williams, Bos-1949
149	Lou Gehrig, NY-1927
149	Babe Ruth, NY-1931
147	Ty Cobb, Det-1911

Hits: Most

257	George Sisler, StL-1920
253	Al Simmons, Phi-1925
248	Ty Cobb, Det-1911
246	George Sisler, StL-1922
241	Heinie Manush, StL-1928
240	WADE BOGGS, Bos-1985
239	Rod Carew, Min-1977
238	Don Mattingly, NY-1986
237	Harry Heilmann, Det-1921
236	Jack Tobin, StL-1921
234	Kirby Puckett, Min-1988
233	Joe Jackson, Cle-1911
232	Earl Averill, Cle-1936
232	Nap Lajoie, Phi-1901
231	Earle Combs, NY-1927

Total bases: Most

457	Babe Ruth, NY-1921
447	Lou Gehrig, NY-1927
438	Jimmie Foxx, Phi-1932
419	Lou Gehrig, NY-1930
418	Joe DiMaggio, NY-1937
417	Babe Ruth, NY-1927
410	Lou Gehrig, NY-1931
409	Lou Gehrig, NY-1934
406	Jim Rice, Bos-1978
405	Hal Trosky, Cle-1936
403	Jimmie Foxx, Phi-1933
403	Lou Gehrig, NY-1936
399	ALBERT BELLE, Chi-1998
399	Babe Ruth, NY-1923
399	George Sisler, StL-1920

2B: Most

67	Earl Webb, Bos-1931
64	George Burns, Cle-1926
63	Hank Greenberg, Det-1934
60	Charlie Gehringer, Det-1936
59	Tris Speaker, Cle-1923
56	George Kell, Det-1950
55	Gee Walker, Det-1936
54	Hal McRae, KC-1977
54	JOHN OLERUD, Tor-1993
54	ALEX RODRIGUEZ, Sea-1996
53	Don Mattingly, NY-1986
53	Al Simmons, Phi-1926
53	Tris Speaker, Bos-1912
52	ALBERT BELLE, Cle-1995
52	Lou Gehrig, NY-1927
52	EDGAR MARTINEZ, Sea-1995
52	EDGAR MARTINEZ, Sea-1996
52	Tris Speaker, Cle-1921
52	Tris Speaker, Cle-1926

3B: Most

26	Sam Crawford, Det-1914
26	Joe Jackson, Cle-1912
25	Sam Crawford, Det-1903
24	Ty Cobb, Det-1911
24	Ty Cobb, Det-1917
23	Ty Cobb, Det-1912
23	Earle Combs, NY-1927
23	Sam Crawford, Det-1913
23	Dale Mitchell, Cle-1949
22	Bill Bradley, Cle-1903
22	Earle Combs, NY-1930
22	Birdie Cree, NY-1911
22	Elmer Flick, Cle-1906
22	Tris Speaker, Bos-1913
22	Snuffy Stirnweiss, NY-1945

HR: Most

61	Roger Maris, NY-1961
60	Babe Ruth, NY-1927
59	Babe Ruth, NY-1921
58	Jimmie Foxx, Phi-1932
58	Hank Greenberg, Det-1938
56	KEN GRIFFEY, Sea-1997
56	KEN GRIFFEY, Sea-1998
54	Mickey Mantle, NY-1961
54	Babe Ruth, NY-1920
54	Babe Ruth, NY-1928
52	Mickey Mantle, NY-1956
52	MARK McGWIRE, Oak-1996
51	Cecil Fielder, Det-1990
50	BRADY ANDERSON, Bal-1996
50	ALBERT BELLE, Cle-1995
50	Jimmie Foxx, Bos-1938

RBI: Most

184	Lou Gehrig, NY-1931
183	Hank Greenberg, Det-1937
175	Jimmie Foxx, Bos-1938
175	Lou Gehrig, NY-1927
174	Lou Gehrig, NY-1930
171	Babe Ruth, NY-1921
170	Hank Greenberg, Det-1935
169	Jimmie Foxx, Phi-1932
167	Joe DiMaggio, NY-1937
165	Lou Gehrig, NY-1934
165	MANNY RAMIREZ, Cle-1999
165	Al Simmons, Phi-1930
164	Babe Ruth, NY-1927
163	Jimmie Foxx, Phi-1933
163	Babe Ruth, NY-1931

SB: Most

130	RICKEY HENDERSON, Oak-1982
108	RICKEY HENDERSON, Oak-1983
100	RICKEY HENDERSON, Oak-1980
96	Ty Cobb, Det-1915
93	RICKEY HENDERSON, NY-1988
88	Clyde Milan, Was-1912
87	RICKEY HENDERSON, NY-1986
83	Ty Cobb, Det-1911
83	Willie Wilson, KC-1979
81	Eddie Collins, Phi-1910
80	RICKEY HENDERSON, NY-1985
79	Willie Wilson, KC-1980
78	Ron LeFlore, Det-1979
77	RICKEY HENDERSON, NY-Oak-1989
77	Rudy Law, Chi-1983

BB: Most

170	Babe Ruth, NY-1923
162	Ted Williams, Bos-1947
162	Ted Williams, Bos-1949
156	Ted Williams, Bos-1946
151	Eddie Yost, Was-1956
149	Eddie Joost, Phi-1949
148	Babe Ruth, NY-1920
146	Mickey Mantle, NY-1957
145	Harmon Killebrew, Min-1969
145	Ted Williams, Bos-1941
145	Ted Williams, Bos-1942
144	Babe Ruth, NY-1921
144	Babe Ruth, NY-1926
144	Ted Williams, Bos-1951
142	Babe Ruth, NY-1924

K: Most

186	Rob Deer, Mil-1987
185	Pete Incaviglia, Tex-1986
182	Cecil Fielder, Det-1990
179	Rob Deer, Mil-1986
175	JAY BUHNER, Sea-1997
175	JOSE CANSECO, Oak-1986
175	Rob Deer, Det-1991
175	Dave Nicholson, Chi-1963
175	Gorman Thomas, Mil-1979
172	Bo Jackson, KC-1989
172	Jim Presley, Sea-1986
171	Reggie Jackson, Oak-1968
171	JIM THOME, Cle-1999
170	Gorman Thomas, Mil-1980
169	Rob Deer, Det-Bos-1993

GIDP: Most

36	Jim Rice, Bos-1984
35	Jim Rice, Bos-1985
32	Jackie Jensen, Bos-1954
32	CAL RIPKEN, Bal-1985
31	Tony Armas, Bos-1983
31	Bobby Doerr, Bos-1949
31	Jim Rice, Bos-1983
31	IVAN RODRIGUEZ, Tex-1999
30	Billy Hitchcock, Phi-1950
30	Dave Winfield, NY-1983
30	Carl Yastrzemski, Bos-1964
29	George Bell, Chi-1992
29	Jimmy Bloodworth, Det-1943
29	Frank Howard, Was-1969
29	Frank Howard, Was-1971
29	Dave Philley, Phi-1952
29	Jim Presley, Sea-1985
29	Jim Rice, Bos-1982
29	Brooks Robinson, Bal-1960

BA: Highest

.426	Nap Lajoie, Phi-1901
.420	George Sisler, StL-1922
.420	Ty Cobb, Det-1911
.409	Ty Cobb, Det-1912
.408	Joe Jackson, Cle-1911
.407	George Sisler, StL-1920
.406	Ted Williams, Bos-1941
.403	Harry Heilmann, Det-1923
.401	Ty Cobb, Det-1922
.398	Harry Heilmann, Det-1927
.395	Joe Jackson, Cle-1912
.394	Harry Heilmann, Det-1921
.393	Babe Ruth, NY-1923
.393	Harry Heilmann, Det-1925
.390	Ty Cobb, Det-1913

On-base avg: Highest

.551	Ted Williams, Bos-1941
.545	Babe Ruth, NY-1923
.530	Babe Ruth, NY-1920
.526	Ted Williams, Bos-1957
.516	Babe Ruth, NY-1926
.513	Ted Williams, Bos-1954
.513	Babe Ruth, NY-1924
.512	Mickey Mantle, NY-1957
.512	Babe Ruth, NY-1921
.499	Ted Williams, Bos-1942
.499	Ted Williams, Bos-1947
.497	Ted Williams, Bos-1946
.497	Ted Williams, Bos-1948
.495	Babe Ruth, NY-1931
.493	Babe Ruth, NY-1930

Slug pct: Highest

.847	Babe Ruth, NY-1920
.846	Babe Ruth, NY-1921
.772	Babe Ruth, NY-1927
.765	Lou Gehrig, NY-1927
.764	Babe Ruth, NY-1923
.749	Jimmie Foxx, Phi-1932
.739	Babe Ruth, NY-1924
.737	Babe Ruth, NY-1926
.735	Ted Williams, Bos-1941
.732	Babe Ruth, NY-1930
.731	Ted Williams, Bos-1957
.730	MARK McGWIRE, Oak-1996
.729	FRANK THOMAS, Chi-1994
.721	Lou Gehrig, NY-1930
.714	ALBERT BELLE, Cle-1994

Extra-base hits: Most

119	Babe Ruth, NY-1921
117	Lou Gehrig, NY-1927
103	ALBERT BELLE, Cle-1995
103	Hank Greenberg, Det-1937
100	Jimmie Foxx, Phi-1932
100	Lou Gehrig, NY-1930
99	ALBERT BELLE, Chi-1998
99	Hank Greenberg, Det-1940
99	Babe Ruth, NY-1920
99	Babe Ruth, NY-1923
98	Hank Greenberg, Det-1935
97	JUAN GONZALEZ, Tex-1998
97	Babe Ruth, NY-1927
96	Joe DiMaggio, NY-1937
96	Hank Greenberg, Det-1934
96	Hal Trosky, Cle-1936

Pitchers

Games: Most

90	Mike Marshall, Min-1979
89	Mark Eichhorn, Tor-1987
88	MIKE MYERS, Det-1997
88	SEAN RUNYAN, Det-1998
88	Wilbur Wood, Chi-1968
85	Mitch Williams, Tex-1987
84	Dan Quisenberry, KC-1985
83	EDDIE GUARDADO, Min-1996
83	MIKE MYERS, Det-1996
83	Ken Sanders, Mil-1971
82	Eddie Fisher, Chi-1965
82	PAUL QUANTRILL, Tor-1998
81	KENNY ROGERS, Tex-1992
81	MIKE STANTON, Bos-Tex-1996
81	GREG SWINDELL, Min-Bos-1998
81	Duane Ward, Tor-1991
81	John Wyatt, KC-1964

Complete games: Most

48	Jack Chesbro, NY-1904
42	George Mullin, Det-1904
42	Ed Walsh, Chi-1908
41	Cy Young, Bos-1902
40	Cy Young, Bos-1904
39	Bill Dinneen, Bos-1902
39	Joe McGinnity, Bal-1901
39	Rube Waddell, Phi-1904
38	Walter Johnson, Was-1910
38	Jack Powell, NY-1904
38	Cy Young, Bos-1901
37	Bill Dinneen, Bos-1904
37	Case Patten, Was-1904
37	Eddie Plank, Phi-1904
37	Frank Smith, Chi-1909
37	Ed Walsh, Chi-1907

Saves: Most

57	Bobby Thigpen, Chi-1990
51	Dennis Eckersley, Oak-1992
48	Dennis Eckersley, Oak-1990
46	TOM GORDON, Bos-1998
46	Bryan Harvey, Cal-1991
46	JOSE MESA, Cle-1995
46	Dave Righetti, NY-1986
45	Dennis Eckersley, Oak-1988
45	JEFF MONTGOMERY, KC-1993
45	Randy Myers, Bal-1997
45	Dan Quisenberry, KC-1983
45	MARIANO RIVERA, NY-1999

45	Duane Ward, Tor-1993	
44	Dan Quisenberry, KC-1984	
43	Dennis Eckersley, Oak-1991	
43	ROBERTO HERNANDEZ, TB-1999	
43	DOUG JONES, Cle-1990	
43	MARIANO RIVERA, NY-1997	
43	JOHN WETTELAND, NY-1996	
43	JOHN WETTELAND, Tex-1999	

Shutouts: Most

13	Jack Coombs, Phi-1910
11	Dean Chance, LA-1964
11	Walter Johnson, Was-1913
11	Ed Walsh, Chi-1908
10	Bob Feller, Cle-1946
10	Bob Lemon, Cle-1948
10	Jim Palmer, Bal-1975
10	Ed Walsh, Chi-1906
10	Joe Wood, Bos-1912
10	Cy Young, Bos-1904
9	Bert Blyleven, Min-1973
9	Stan Coveleski, Cle-1917
9	Ron Guidry, NY-1978
9	Walter Johnson, Was-1914
9	Addie Joss, Cle-1906
9	Addie Joss, Cle-1908
9	Denny McLain, Det-1969
9	Bob Porterfield, Was-1953
9	Babe Ruth, Bos-1916
9	Nolan Ryan, Cal-1972
9	Luis Tiant, Cle-1968

Wins: Most

41	Jack Chesbro, NY-1904
40	Ed Walsh, Chi-1908
36	Walter Johnson, Was-1913
34	Joe Wood, Bos-1912
33	Walter Johnson, Was-1912
33	Cy Young, Bos-1901
32	Cy Young, Bos-1902
31	Jim Bagby, Cle-1920
31	Jack Coombs, Phi-1910
31	Lefty Grove, Phi-1931
31	Denny McLain, Det-1968
29	Eddie Cicotte, Chi-1919
29	George Mullin, Det-1909
29	Hal Newhouser, Det-1944
28	Eddie Cicotte, Chi-1917
28	Jack Coombs, Phi-1911
28	Lefty Grove, Phi-1930
28	Walter Johnson, Was-1914
28	Cy Young, Bos-1903

Losses: Most

26	Bob Groom, Was-1909
26	Happy Townsend, Was-1904
25	Pete Dowling, Mil-Cle-1901

25	Patsy Flaherty, Chi-1903
25	Fred Glade, StL-1905
25	Walter Johnson, Was-1909
25	Scott Perry, Phi-1920
25	Red Ruffing, Bos-1928
24	Joe Bush, Phi-1916
24	Pat Caraway, Chi-1931
24	Dolly Gray, StL-1931
23	Tom Hughes, NY-Was-1904
23	Beany Jacobson, Was-1904
23	George Mullin, Det-1904
23	Elmer Myers, Phi-1916
23	Rollie Naylor, Phi-1920
23	Case Patten, Was-1904
23	Eddie Rommel, Phi-1921

HR allowed: Most

50	Bert Blyleven, Min-1986
46	Bert Blyleven, Min-1987
43	Pedro Ramos, Was-1957
42	Denny McLain, Det-1966
41	RICK HELLING, Tex-1999
40	Shawn Boskie, Cal-1996
40	Fergie Jenkins, Tex-1979
40	Jack Morris, Det-1986
40	Orlando Pena, KC-1964
40	BRAD RADKE, Min-1996
40	Ralph Terry, NY-1962
39	Catfish Hunter, Oak-1973
39	Jack Morris, Det-1987
39	Jim Perry, Min-1971
39	Pedro Ramos, Min-1961

BB: Most

208	Bob Feller, Cle-1938
204	Nolan Ryan, Cal-1977
202	Nolan Ryan, Cal-1974
194	Bob Feller, Cle-1941
192	Bobo Newsom, StL-1938
183	Nolan Ryan, Cal-1976
181	Bob Turley, Bal-1954
179	Tommy Byrne, NY-1949
177	Bob Turley, NY-1955
171	Bump Hadley, Chi-StL-1932
168	Elmer Myers, Phi-1916
167	Bobo Newsom, Was-Bos-1937
165	Weldon Wyckoff, Phi-1915
162	Nolan Ryan, Cal-1973
160	Tommy Byrne, NY-1950

K: Most

383	Nolan Ryan, Cal-1973
367	Nolan Ryan, Cal-1974
349	Rube Waddell, Phi-1904
348	Bob Feller, Cle-1946
341	Nolan Ryan, Cal-1977
329	Nolan Ryan, Cal-1972
327	Nolan Ryan, Cal-1976
325	Sam McDowell, Cle-1965

313	Walter Johnson, Was-1910
313	PEDRO MARTINEZ, Bos-1999
308	RANDY JOHNSON, Sea-1993
308	Mickey Lolich, Det-1971
304	Sam McDowell, Cle-1970
303	Walter Johnson, Was-1912
302	Rube Waddell, Phi-1903

Win pct: Highest

.938	Johnny Allen, Cle-1937
.900	RANDY JOHNSON, Sea-1995
.893	Ron Guidry, NY-1978
.886	Lefty Grove, Phi-1931
.882	Bob Stanley, Bos-1978
.872	Joe Wood, Bos-1912
.862	Whitey Ford, NY-1961
.862	Bill Donovan, Det-1907
.857	ROGER CLEMENS, Bos-1986
.852	PEDRO MARTINEZ, Bos-1999
.850	Chief Bender, Phi-1914
.849	Lefty Grove, Phi-1930
.842	Ralph Terry, NY-1961
.842	Schoolboy Rowe, Det-1940
.842	Sandy Consuegra, Chi-1954

ERA: Lowest,

0.96	Dutch Leonard, Bos-1914
1.14	Walter Johnson, Was-1913
1.16	Addie Joss, Cle-1908
1.26	Cy Young, Bos-1908
1.27	Ed Walsh, Chi-1910
1.27	Walter Johnson, Was-1918
1.30	Jack Coombs, Phi-1910
1.36	Walter Johnson, Was-1910
1.39	Walter Johnson, Was-1912
1.39	Harry Krause, Phi-1909
1.41	Ed Walsh, Chi-1909
1.42	Ed Walsh, Chi-1908
1.48	Rube Waddell, Phi-1905
1.49	Joe Wood, Bos-1915
1.49	Walter Johnson, Was-1919

Innings: Most

464.0	Ed Walsh, Chi-1908
454.2	Jack Chesbro, NY-1904
422.1	Ed Walsh, Chi-1907
393.0	Ed Walsh, Chi-1912
390.1	Jack Powell, NY-1904
384.2	Cy Young, Bos-1902
383.0	Rube Waddell, Phi-1904
382.1	George Mullin, Det-1904
382.0	Joe McGinnity, Bal-1901
380.0	Cy Young, Bos-1904
376.2	Wilbur Wood, Chi-1972
376.0	Mickey Lolich, Det-1971

371.2   Walter Johnson, Was-1914
371.1   Bill Dinneen, Bos-1902
371.1   Bob Feller, Cle-1946
371.1   Cy Young, Bos-1901

AL club records

BA: Highest, season
.316   Detroit, 1921
.313   St. Louis, 1922
.309   New York, 1930
.308   Cleveland, 1921
.308   St. Louis, 1920

BA: Lowest, season
.211   Chicago, 1910
.214   New York, 1968
.217   Texas, 1972
.218   St. Louis, 1910
.221   Chicago, 1909

Slug pct: Highest, season
.489   New York, 1927
.488   New York, 1930
.485   Seattle, 1997
.484   Cleveland, 1994
.484   Seattle, 1996

On-base avg: Highest, season
.385   Boston, 1950
.385   Detroit, 1921
.384   New York, 1930
.383   Cleveland, 1921
.383   New York, 1927

Runs: Most, season
1067   New York, 1931
1065   New York, 1936
1062   New York, 1930
1027   Boston, 1950
1009   Cleveland, 1999

HR: Most, season
264   Seattle, 1997
257   Baltimore, 1996
245   Seattle, 1996
244   Seattle, 1999
243   Oakland, 1996

SB: Most, season
341   Oakland, 1976
288   New York, 1910
287   Washington, 1913
280   Chicago, 1901
280   Detroit, 1909

GIDP: Most, season
174   Boston, 1990
172   Minnesota, 1996
171   Boston, 1982
171   Boston, 1983
170   Philadelphia, 1950

Fielding avg: Highest, season
.987   Baltimore, 1998
.986   Baltimore, 1995
.986   Baltimore, 1994
.986   New York, 1995
.986   Toronto, 1990

Errors: Most, season
410   Detroit, 1901
401   Baltimore, 1901
393   Milwaukee, 1901
385   St. Louis, 1910
382   New York, 1912

Errors: Fewest, season
81   Baltimore, 1998
84   Minnesota, 1988
86   Toronto, 1990
87   Texas, 1996
87   Oakland, 1990
87   Baltimore, 1989

Double plays: Most, season
217   Philadelphia, 1949
214   New York, 1956
208   Philadelphia, 1950
207   Boston, 1949
206   Boston, 1980
206   Toronto, 1980

ERA: Lowest, season
1.78   Philadelphia, 1910
1.93   Philadelphia, 1909
1.99   Chicago, 1905
2.02   Cleveland, 1908
2.03   Chicago, 1910

ERA: Highest, season
6.37   Detroit, 1996
6.24   St. Louis, 1936
6.08   Philadelphia, 1936
6.01   St. Louis, 1939
6.00   St. Louis, 1937

Shutouts: Most, season
32   Chicago, 1906
28   Los Angeles, 1964
27   Cleveland, 1906
27   Philadelphia, 1907
27   Philadelphia, 1909

HR allowed: Most, season
241   Detroit, 1996
233   Minnesota, 1996
226   Baltimore, 1987
220   Kansas City, 1964
219   Cleveland, 1987
219   California, 1996

HR allowed: Fewest, season
6   Boston, 1913
7   St. Louis, 1908
8   Philadelphia, 1910

8   Chicago, 1909
8   Detroit, 1907
8   Cleveland, 1907

Walks allowed: Most, season
827   Philadelphia, 1915
812   New York, 1949
801   St. Louis, 1951
784   Detroit, 1996
779   Washington, 1949

NL single-season records

ACTIVE PLAYERS in caps

Hitters

At-bats: Most
701   Juan Samuel, Phi-1984
699   Dave Cash, Phi-1975
698   Matty Alou, Pit-1969
696   Woody Jensen, Pit-1936
695   Omar Moreno, Pit-1979
695   Maury Wills, LA-1962
690   NEIFI PEREZ, Col-1999
689   Lou Brock, StL-1967
687   Dave Cash, Phi-1974
682   LANCE JOHNSON, NY-1996
681   Jo-Jo Moore, NY-1935
681   Lloyd Waner, Pit-1931
680   Pete Rose, Cin-1973
680   Frank Taveras, Pit-NY-1979
679   Curt Flood, StL-1964

Runs: Most
192   Billy Hamilton, Phi-1894
166   Billy Hamilton, Phi-1895
165   Willie Keeler, Bal-1894
165   Joe Kelley, Bal-1894
162   Willie Keeler, Bal-1895
160   Jesse Burkett, Cle-1896
160   Hugh Duffy, Bos-1894
159   Hughie Jennings, Bal-1895
158   Chuck Klein, Phi-1930
158   Bobby Lowe, Bos-1894
156   Rogers Hornsby, Chi-1929
156   John McGraw, Bal-1894
155   Kiki Cuyler, Chi-1930
155   King Kelly, Chi-1886
153   Dan Brouthers, Det-1887
153   Jesse Burkett, Cle-1895
153   Billy Hamilton, Bos-1896
153   Willie Keeler, Bal-1896

Hits: Most
254   Lefty O'Doul, Phi-1929
254   Bill Terry, NY-1930
250   Rogers Hornsby, StL-1922
250   Chuck Klein, Phi-1930
241   Babe Herman, Bro-1930

240	Jesse Burkett, Cle-1896	26	Kiki Cuyler, Pit-1925	96	Omar Moreno, Pit-1980
239	Willie Keeler, Bal-1897	26	John Reilly, Cin-1890	94	Maury Wills, LA-1965
238	Ed Delahanty, Phi-1899	26	George Treadway, Bro-1894		
237	Hugh Duffy, Bos-1894	25	Roger Connor, NY-StL-1894		

Total bases: Most

450	Rogers Hornsby, StL-1922
445	Chuck Klein, Phi-1930
429	Stan Musial, StL-1948
423	Hack Wilson, Chi-1930
420	Chuck Klein, Phi-1932
416	Babe Herman, Bro-1930
416	SAMMY SOSA, Chi-1998
409	Rogers Hornsby, Chi-1929
409	LARRY WALKER, Col-1997
406	Joe Medwick, StL-1937
405	Chuck Klein, Phi-1929
400	Hank Aaron, Mil-1959
397	Lefty O'Doul, Phi-1929
397	SAMMY SOSA, Chi-1999
392	ELLIS BURKS, Col-1996
392	Bill Terry, NY-1930

2B: Most

64	Joe Medwick, StL-1936
62	Paul Waner, Pit-1932
59	Chuck Klein, Phi-1930
57	Billy Herman, Chi-1935
57	Billy Herman, Chi-1936
56	CRAIG BIGGIO, Hou-1999
56	Joe Medwick, StL-1937
55	Ed Delahanty, Phi-1899
54	MARK GRUDZIELANEK, Mon-1997
53	Stan Musial, StL-1953
53	Paul Waner, Pit-1936
52	Johnny Frederick, Bro-1929
52	Enos Slaughter, StL-1939
51	CRAIG BIGGIO, Hou-1998
51	Hugh Duffy, Bos-1894
51	MARK GRACE, Chi-1995
51	Stan Musial, StL-1944
51	Frank Robinson, Cin-1962
51	Pete Rose, Cin-1978

3B: Most

36	Chief Wilson, Pit-1912
31	Heinie Reitz, Bal-1894
29	Perry Werden, StL-1893
28	Harry Davis, Pit-1897
27	George Davis, NY-1893
27	Sam Thompson, Phi-1894
27	Jimmy Williams, Pit-1899

237	Joe Medwick, StL-1937
237	Paul Waner, Pit-1927
235	Rogers Hornsby, StL-1921
234	Lloyd Waner, Pit-1929
231	Matty Alou, Pit-1969
231	Freddie Lindstrom, NY-1928
231	Freddie Lindstrom, NY-1930

25	Larry Doyle, NY-1911
25	Buck Freeman, Was-1899
25	Tom Long, StL-1915
24	Ed McKean, Cle-1893

HR: Most

70	MARK McGWIRE, StL-1998
66	SAMMY SOSA, Chi-1998
65	MARK McGWIRE, StL-1999
63	SAMMY SOSA, Chi-1999
56	Hack Wilson, Chi-1930
54	Ralph Kiner, Pit-1949
52	George Foster, Cin-1977
52	Willie Mays, SF-1965
51	Ralph Kiner, Pit-1947
51	Willie Mays, NY-1955
51	Johnny Mize, NY-1947
50	GREG VAUGHN, SD-1998
49	Andre Dawson, Chi-1987
49	Ted Kluszewski, Cin-1954
49	Willie Mays, SF-1962
49	LARRY WALKER, Col-1997

RBI: Most

191	Hack Wilson, Chi-1930
170	Chuck Klein, Phi-1930
166	Sam Thompson, Det-1887
165	Sam Thompson, Phi-1895
159	Hack Wilson, Chi-1929
158	SAMMY SOSA, Chi-1998
154	Joe Medwick, StL-1937
153	Tommy Davis, LA-1962
152	Rogers Hornsby, StL-1922
151	Mel Ott, NY-1929
150	Andres Galarraga, Col-1996
149	George Foster, Cin-1977
149	Rogers Hornsby, Chi-1929
148	Johnny Bench, Cin-1970
147	Cap Anson, Chi-1886
147	MARK McGWIRE, StL-1998
147	MARK McGWIRE, StL-1999

SB: Most

118	Lou Brock, StL-1974
111	Billy Hamilton, Phi-1891
111	John Ward, NY-1887
110	Vince Coleman, StL-1985
109	Vince Coleman, StL-1987
107	Vince Coleman, StL-1986
104	Maury Wills, LA-1962
102	Jim Fogarty, Phi-1887
102	Billy Hamilton, Phi-1890
99	Jim Fogarty, Phi-1889
98	Billy Hamilton, Phi-1894
97	Billy Hamilton, Phi-1895
97	Ron LeFlore, Mon-1980

BB: Most

162	MARK McGWIRE, StL-1998
151	BARRY BONDS, SF-1996
149	JEFF BAGWELL, Hou-1999
148	Eddie Stanky, Bro-1945
148	Jimmy Wynn, Hou-1969
147	Jimmy Sheckard, Chi-1911
145	BARRY BONDS, SF-1997
144	Eddie Stanky, NY-1950
142	GARY SHEFFIELD, Fla-1996
137	Ralph Kiner, Pit-1951
137	Willie McCovey, SF-1970
137	Eddie Stanky, Bro-1946
136	Jack Clark, StL-1987
136	Jack Crooks, StL-1892
135	JEFF BAGWELL, Hou-1996

K: Most

189	Bobby Bonds, SF-1970
187	Bobby Bonds, SF-1969
180	Mike Schmidt, Phi-1975
174	SAMMY SOSA, Chi-1997
171	SAMMY SOSA, Chi-1998
171	SAMMY SOSA, Chi-1999
169	Andres Galarraga, Mon-1990
168	Juan Samuel, Phi-1984
163	Donn Clendenon, Pit-1968
162	RON GANT, StL-1997
162	Juan Samuel, Phi-1987
161	Dick Allen, Phi-1968
160	HENRY RODRIGUEZ, Mon-1996
158	JEROMY BURNITZ, Mil-1998
158	Andres Galarraga, Mon-1989

GIDP: Most

30	Ernie Lombardi, Cin-1938
29	Ted Simmons, StL-1973
28	Sid Gordon, Bos-1951
27	John Bateman, Mon-1971
27	Carl Furillo, Bro-1956
27	ERIC KARROS, LA-1996
27	MIKE PIAZZA, NY-1999
27	Ron Santo, Chi-1973
27	Ken Singleton, Mon-1973
26	JEFF CIRILLO, Mil-1998
26	Sid Gordon, NY-1943
26	Cleon Jones, NY-1970
26	Billy Jurges, NY-1939
26	Ernie Lombardi, Cin-1933
26	Willie Montanez, Phi-SF-1975
26	Willie Montanez, SF-Atl-1976
26	Dave Parker, Cin-1985
26	Joe Torre, Mil-1964

BA: Highest

.440	Hugh Duffy, Bos-1894
.424	Willie Keeler, Bal-1897
.424	Rogers Hornsby, StL-1924
.410	Ed Delahanty, Phi-1899
.410	Jesse Burkett, Cle-1896
.409	Jesse Burkett, Cle-1895
.407	Ed Delahanty, Phi-1894
.404	Billy Hamilton, Phi-1894
.404	Ed Delahanty, Phi-1895
.403	Rogers Hornsby, StL-1925
.401	Rogers Hornsby, StL-1922
.401	Bill Terry, NY-1930
.401	Hughie Jennings, Bal-1896
.398	Lefty O'Doul, Phi-1929
.397	Rogers Hornsby, StL-1921

On-base avg: Highest

.548	John McGraw, Bal-1899
.523	Billy Hamilton, Phi-1894
.507	Rogers Hornsby, StL-1924
.502	Joe Kelley, Bal-1894
.502	Hugh Duffy, Bos-1894
.500	Ed Delahanty, Phi-1895
.498	Rogers Hornsby, Bos-1928
.491	Arky Vaughan, Pit-1935
.490	Billy Hamilton, Phi-1895
.489	Rogers Hornsby, StL-1925
.486	Jesse Burkett, Cle-1895
.483	King Kelly, Chi-1886
.480	Billy Hamilton, Bos-1898
.478	Ed Delahanty, Phi-1894
.478	Billy Hamilton, Bos-1896

Slug pct: Highest

.756	Rogers Hornsby, StL-1925
.752	MARK McGWIRE, StL-1998
.750	JEFF BAGWELL, Hou-1994
.723	Hack Wilson, Chi-1930
.722	Rogers Hornsby, StL-1922
.720	LARRY WALKER, Col-1997
.710	LARRY WALKER, Col-1999
.702	Stan Musial, StL-1948
.697	MARK McGWIRE, StL-1999
.696	Rogers Hornsby, StL-1924
.694	Hugh Duffy, Bos-1894
.687	Chuck Klein, Phi-1930
.679	Rogers Hornsby, Chi-1929
.678	Babe Herman, Bro-1930
.677	BARRY BONDS, SF-1993

Extra-base hits: Most

107	Chuck Klein, Phi-1930
103	Chuck Klein, Phi-1932
103	Stan Musial, StL-1948
102	Rogers Hornsby, StL-1922
99	LARRY WALKER, Col-1997
97	Joe Medwick, StL-1937
97	Hack Wilson, Chi-1930
95	Joe Medwick, StL-1936

94	Babe Herman, Bro-1930
94	Rogers Hornsby, Chi-1929
94	Chuck Klein, Phi-1929
93	Jim Bottomley, StL-1928
93	ELLIS BURKS, Col-1996
92	Hank Aaron, Mil-1959
92	Stan Musial, StL-1953
92	Frank Robinson, Cin-1962

Pitchers

Games: Most

106	Mike Marshall, LA-1974
94	Kent Tekulve, Pit-1979
92	Mike Marshall, Mon-1973
91	Kent Tekulve, Pit-1978
90	Wayne Granger, Cin-1969
90	Kent Tekulve, Phi-1987
89	JULIAN TAVAREZ, SF-1997
87	Rob Murphy, Cin-1987
85	Kent Tekulve, Pit-1982
85	Frank Williams, Cin-1987
84	Ted Abernathy, Chi-1965
84	STAN BELINDA, Cin-1997
84	Enrique Romo, Pit-1979
84	Dick Tidrow, Chi-1980
83	Craig Lefferts, SD-1986

Complete games: Most

75	Will White, Cin-1879
73	Charley Radbourn, Pro-1884
72	Jim Galvin, Buf-1883
72	Jim McCormick, Cle-1880
71	Jim Galvin, Buf-1884
68	John Clarkson, Chi-1885
68	John Clarkson, Bos-1889
67	Bill Hutchison, Chi-1892
66	Jim Devlin, Lou-1876
66	Charley Radbourn, Pro-1883
65	Jim Galvin, Buf-1879
65	Bill Hutchison, Chi-1890
65	Jim McCormick, Cle-1882
64	Mickey Welch, Tro-1880
63	George Bradley, StL-1876
63	Charlie Buffinton, Bos-1884

Saves: Most

53	TREVOR HOFFMAN, SD-1998
53	Randy Myers, Chi-1993
51	ROD BECK, Chi-1998
48	ROD BECK, SF-1993
48	JEFF SHAW, Cin-LA-1998
47	Lee Smith, StL-1991
45	Bryan Harvey, Fla-1993
45	Bruce Sutter, StL-1984
44	JEFF BRANTLEY, Cin-1996
44	Mark Davis, SD-1989
44	Todd Worrell, LA-1996
43	Lee Smith, StL-1992

43	Lee Smith, StL-1993
43	JOHN WETTELAND, Mon-1993
43	Mitch Williams, Phi-1993

Shutouts: Most

16	Pete Alexander, Phi-1916
16	George Bradley, StL-1876
13	Bob Gibson, StL-1968
12	Pete Alexander, Phi-1915
12	Jim Galvin, Buf-1884
11	Tommy Bond, Bos-1879
11	Sandy Koufax, LA-1963
11	Christy Mathewson, NY-1908
11	Charley Radbourn, Pro-1884
10	John Clarkson, Chi-1885
10	Mort Cooper, StL-1942
10	Carl Hubbell, NY-1933
10	Juan Marichal, SF-1965
10	John Tudor, StL-1985
9	Pete Alexander, Phi-1913
9	Pete Alexander, Chi-1919
9	Tommy Bond, Bos-1878
9	Mordecai Brown, Chi-1906
9	Mordecai Brown, Chi-1908
9	George Derby, Det-1881
9	Bill Lee, Chi-1938
9	Joe McGinnity, NY-1904
9	Orval Overall, Chi-1909
9	Don Sutton, LA-1972
9	Cy Young, Cle-1892

Wins: Most

59	Charley Radbourn, Pro-1884
53	John Clarkson, Chi-1885
49	John Clarkson, Bos-1889
48	Charlie Buffinton, Bos-1884
48	Charley Radbourn, Pro-1883
47	Al Spalding, Chi-1876
47	John Ward, Pro-1879
46	Jim Galvin, Buf-1883
46	Jim Galvin, Buf-1884
45	George Bradley, StL-1876
45	Jim McCormick, Cle-1880
44	Bill Hutchison, Chi-1891
44	Mickey Welch, NY-1885
43	Tommy Bond, Bos-1879
43	Larry Corcoran, Chi-1880
43	Will White, Cin-1879

Losses: Most

48	John Coleman, Phi-1883
42	Will White, Cin-1880
40	George Bradley, Tro-1879
40	Jim McCormick, Cle-1879
37	George Cobb, Bal-1892
36	Bill Hutchison, Chi-1892
36	Stump Wiedman, KC-1886
35	Jim Devlin, Lou-1876

35	Red Donahue, StL-1897
35	Jim Galvin, Buf-1880
34	Bobby Mathews, NY-1876
34	Amos Rusie, NY-1890
33	Harry McCormick, Syr-1879
33	Lee Richmond, Wor-1882
33	Jim Whitney, Bos-1881

HR allowed: Most

46	Robin Roberts, Phi-1956
41	Phil Niekro, Atl-1979
41	Robin Roberts, Phi-1955
40	Phil Niekro, Atl-1970
40	Robin Roberts, Phi-1957
39	BRIAN ANDERSON, Ari-1998
39	PEDRO ASTACIO, Col-1998
39	Murry Dickson, StL-1948
38	PEDRO ASTACIO, Col-1999
38	Lew Burdette, Mil-1959
38	Warren Hacker, Chi-1955
38	Don Sutton, LA-1970
37	LIVAN HERNANDEZ, Fla-1998
37	MARK LEITER, SF-Mon-1996
36	Tom Browning, Cin-1988
36	Larry Jansen, NY-1949
36	Art Mahaffey, Phi-1962
36	CHAD OGEA, Phi-1999
36	Ed Whitson, SD-1987

BB: Most

289	Amos Rusie, NY-1890
270	Amos Rusie, NY-1892
262	Amos Rusie, NY-1891
227	Mark Baldwin, Pit-1891
218	Amos Rusie, NY-1893
213	Cy Seymour, NY-1898
203	John Clarkson, Bos-1889
200	Amos Rusie, NY-1894
199	Bill Hutchison, Chi-1890
194	Mark Baldwin, Pit-1892
191	Ted Breitenstein, StL-1894
190	Bill Hutchison, Chi-1892
189	Ed Crane, NY-1892
189	Tony Mullane, Cin-Bal-1893
187	Kid Gleason, StL-1893
187	Tony Mullane, Cin-1891

K: Most

441	Charley Radbourn, Pro-1884
417	Charlie Buffinton, Bos-1884
382	Sandy Koufax, LA-1965
369	Jim Galvin, Buf-1884
364	RANDY JOHNSON, Ari-1999
345	Mickey Welch, NY-1884
345	Jim Whitney, Bos-1883
341	Amos Rusie, NY-1890
337	Amos Rusie, NY-1891

335	Tim Keefe, NY-1888
323	Lady Baldwin, Det-1886
319	CURT SCHILLING, Phi-1997
317	Sandy Koufax, LA-1966
315	Charley Radbourn, Pro-1883
314	Bill Hutchison, Chi-1892

Win pct: Highest

.947	Roy Face, Pit-1959
.941	Rick Sutcliffe, Chi-1984
.905	GREG MADDUX, Atl-1995
.889	Freddie Fitzsimmons, Bro-1940
.880	Preacher Roe, Bro-1951
.875	Fred Goldsmith, Chi-1880
.870	DAVID CONE, NY-1988
.864	OREL HERSHISER, LA-1985
.857	DWIGHT GOODEN, NY-1985
.850	JOHN SMOLTZ, Atl-1998
.846	MIKE HAMPTON, Hou-1999
.842	Emil Yde, Pit-1924
.842	Ron Perranoski, LA-1963
.842	Tom Hughes, Bos-1916
.838	Bill Hoffer, Bal-1895

ERA: Lowest

1.04	Mordecai Brown, Chi-1906
1.12	Bob Gibson, StL-1968
1.14	Christy Mathewson, NY-1909
1.15	Jack Pfiester, Chi-1907
1.17	Carl Lundgren, Chi-1907
1.22	Pete Alexander, Phi-1915
1.23	George Bradley, StL-1876
1.28	Christy Mathewson, NY-1905
1.31	Mordecai Brown, Chi-1909
1.33	Jack Taylor, Chi-1902
1.38	George Bradley, Pro-1880
1.38	Charley Radbourn, Pro-1884
1.39	Mordecai Brown, Chi-1907
1.42	Ed Reulbach, Chi-1905
1.42	Orval Overall, Chi-1909

Innings: Most

680.0	Will White, Cin-1879
678.2	Charley Radbourn, Pro-1884
657.2	Jim McCormick, Cle-1880
656.1	Jim Galvin, Buf-1883
636.1	Jim Galvin, Buf-1884
632.1	Charley Radbourn, Pro-1883
623.0	John Clarkson, Chi-1885
622.0	Jim Devlin, Lou-1876
622.0	Bill Hutchison, Chi-1892
620.0	John Clarkson, Bos-1889
603.0	Bill Hutchison, Chi-1890
595.2	Jim McCormick, Cle-1882
595.0	John Ward, Pro-1880
593.0	Jim Galvin, Buf-1879
590.2	Lee Richmond, Wor-1880

NL club records

BA: Highest, season

.349	Philadelphia, 1894
.343	Baltimore, 1894
.337	Chicago, 1876
.331	Boston, 1894
.330	Philadelphia, 1895

BA: Lowest, season

.208	Washington, 1888
.208	Detroit, 1884
.210	Washington, 1886
.213	Brooklyn, 1908
.219	New York, 1963

Slug pct: Highest, season

.484	Boston, 1894
.483	Baltimore, 1894
.481	Chicago, 1930
.478	Colorado, 1997
.476	Philadelphia, 1894

On-base avg: Highest, season

.418	Baltimore, 1894
.414	Philadelphia, 1894
.401	Boston, 1894
.394	Philadelphia, 1895
.394	Baltimore, 1897

Runs: Most, season

1220	Boston, 1894
1171	Baltimore, 1894
1143	Philadelphia, 1894
1068	Philadelphia, 1895
1041	Chicago, 1894

HR: Most, season

239	Colorado, 1997
223	St. Louis, 1998
223	Colorado, 1999
221	New York, 1947
221	Cincinnati, 1956
221	Colorado, 1996

SB: Most, season

441	Baltimore, 1896
415	New York, 1887
409	Brooklyn, 1892
401	Baltimore, 1897
382	Chicago, 1887

GIDP: Most, season

166	St. Louis, 1958
161	Chicago, 1933
161	Cincinnati, 1933
157	Chicago, 1938
154	Atlanta, 1985

Fielding avg: Highest, season

.989	New York, 1999
.986	Cincinnati, 1995

.985	St. Louis, 1992
.985	Atlanta, 1998
.985	San Francisco, 1994

Errors: Most, season

639	Philadelphia, 1883
607	Pittsburgh, 1890
595	Chicago, 1884
584	Baltimore, 1892
565	New York, 1892

Errors: Fewest, season

68	New York, 1999
91	Atlanta, 1998
94	St. Louis, 1992
95	Cincinnati, 1977
96	Cincinnati, 1992
100	Arizona, 1998
100	Cincinnati, 1958

Double plays: Most, season

215	Pittsburgh, 1966
202	Colorado, 1997
198	Los Angeles, 1958
197	Atlanta, 1985
195	Pittsburgh, 1963
195	Pittsburgh, 1970

ERA: Lowest, season

1.22	St. Louis, 1876
1.61	Providence, 1884
1.64	Providence, 1880
1.67	Hartford, 1876
1.69	Louisville, 1876

ERA: Highest, season

6.71	Philadelphia, 1930
6.37	Cleveland, 1899
6.21	St. Louis, 1897
6.13	Philadelphia, 1929
6.01	Colorado, 1999

Shutouts: Most, season

32	Chicago, 1907
32	Chicago, 1909
30	Chicago, 1906
30	St. Louis, 1968
29	Chicago, 1908

HR allowed: Most, season

237	Colorado, 1999
221	Chicago, 1999
213	Milwaukee, 1999
212	Philadelphia, 1999
198	Colorado, 1996

HR allowed: Fewest, season

5	Cincinnati, 1909
6	Chicago, 1909
8	Philadelphia, 1908
11	Chicago, 1907
12	Pittsburgh, 1909

12	Pittsburgh, 1907
12	Chicago, 1906
12	Pittsburgh, 1905

Walks allowed: Most, season

737	Colorado, 1999
716	Montreal, 1970
715	San Diego, 1974
715	Florida, 1998
702	Montreal, 1969

Career records
ACTIVE PLAYERS in caps

Hitters

Games played: Most

3562	Pete Rose, 1963-1986
3308	Carl Yastrzemski, 1961-1983
3298	Hank Aaron, 1954-1976
3035	Ty Cobb, 1905-1928
3026	Eddie Murray, 1977-1997
3026	Stan Musial, 1941-1963
2992	Willie Mays, 1951-1973
2973	Dave Winfield, 1973-1995
2951	Rusty Staub, 1963-1985
2896	Brooks Robinson, 1955-1977
2856	Robin Yount, 1974-1993
2834	Al Kaline, 1953-1974
2826	Eddie Collins, 1906-1930
2820	Reggie Jackson, 1967-1987
2808	Frank Robinson, 1956-1976
2792	Honus Wagner, 1897-1917
2790	CAL RIPKEN, 1981-1999
2789	Tris Speaker, 1907-1928
2777	Tony Perez, 1964-1986
2733	RICKEY HENDERSON, 1979-1999

At-bats: Most

14053	Pete Rose, 1963-1986
12364	Hank Aaron, 1954-1976
11988	Carl Yastrzemski, 1961-1983
11434	Ty Cobb, 1905-1928
11336	Eddie Murray, 1977-1997
11008	Robin Yount, 1974-1993
11003	Dave Winfield, 1973-1995
10972	Stan Musial, 1941-1963
10881	Willie Mays, 1951-1973
10835	Paul Molitor, 1978-1998
10765	CAL RIPKEN, 1981-1999
10654	Brooks Robinson, 1955-1977
10430	Honus Wagner, 1897-1917
10349	George Brett, 1973-1993
10332	Lou Brock, 1961-1979
10278	Cap Anson, 1871-1897
10230	Luis Aparicio, 1956-1973
10195	Tris Speaker, 1907-1928
10116	Al Kaline, 1953-1974
10078	Rabbit Maranville, 1912-1935

Runs: Most

2246	Ty Cobb, 1905-1928
2174	Hank Aaron, 1954-1976
2174	Babe Ruth, 1914-1935
2165	Pete Rose, 1963-1986
2103	RICKEY HENDERSON, 1979-1999
2062	Willie Mays, 1951-1973
1996	Cap Anson, 1871-1897
1949	Stan Musial, 1941-1963
1888	Lou Gehrig, 1923-1939
1882	Tris Speaker, 1907-1928
1859	Mel Ott, 1926-1947
1829	Frank Robinson, 1956-1976
1821	Eddie Collins, 1906-1930
1816	Carl Yastrzemski, 1961-1983
1798	Ted Williams, 1939-1960
1782	Paul Molitor, 1978-1998
1774	Charlie Gehringer, 1924-1942
1751	Jimmie Foxx, 1925-1945
1736	Honus Wagner, 1897-1917
1729	Jim O'Rourke, 1872-1904

Hits: Most

4256	Pete Rose, 1963-1986
4189	Ty Cobb, 1905-1928
3771	Hank Aaron, 1954-1976
3630	Stan Musial, 1941-1963
3514	Tris Speaker, 1907-1928
3419	Carl Yastrzemski, 1961-1983
3418	Cap Anson, 1871-1897
3415	Honus Wagner, 1897-1917
3319	Paul Molitor, 1978-1998
3315	Eddie Collins, 1906-1930
3283	Willie Mays, 1951-1973
3255	Eddie Murray, 1977-1997
3242	Nap Lajoie, 1896-1916
3154	George Brett, 1973-1993
3152	Paul Waner, 1926-1945
3142	Robin Yount, 1974-1993
3110	Dave Winfield, 1973-1995
3067	TONY GWYNN, 1982-1999
3053	Rod Carew, 1967-1985
3023	Lou Brock, 1961-1979

Total bases: Most

6856	Hank Aaron, 1954-1976
6134	Stan Musial, 1941-1963
6066	Willie Mays, 1951-1973
5854	Ty Cobb, 1905-1928
5793	Babe Ruth, 1914-1935
5752	Pete Rose, 1963-1986
5539	Carl Yastrzemski, 1961-1983
5397	Eddie Murray, 1977-1997
5373	Frank Robinson, 1956-1976
5221	Dave Winfield, 1973-1995
5101	Tris Speaker, 1907-1928
5060	Lou Gehrig, 1923-1939
5044	George Brett, 1973-1993

5041	Mel Ott, 1926-1947
4956	Jimmie Foxx, 1925-1945
4884	Ted Williams, 1939-1960
4862	Honus Wagner, 1897-1917
4856	CAL RIPKEN, 1981-1999
4854	Paul Molitor, 1978-1998
4852	Al Kaline, 1953-1974

2B: Most

792	Tris Speaker, 1907-1928
746	Pete Rose, 1963-1986
725	Stan Musial, 1941-1963
724	Ty Cobb, 1905-1928
665	George Brett, 1973-1993
657	Nap Lajoie, 1896-1916
646	Carl Yastrzemski, 1961-1983
640	Honus Wagner, 1897-1917
624	Hank Aaron, 1954-1976
605	Paul Molitor, 1978-1998
605	Paul Waner, 1926-1945
583	Robin Yount, 1974-1993
581	Cap Anson, 1871-1897
578	WADE BOGGS, 1982-1999
574	Charlie Gehringer, 1924-1942
571	CAL RIPKEN, 1981-1999
560	Eddie Murray, 1977-1997
542	Harry Heilmann, 1914-1932
541	Rogers Hornsby, 1915-1937
540	Joe Medwick, 1932-1948
540	Dave Winfield, 1973-1995

3B: Most

309	Sam Crawford, 1899-1917
295	Ty Cobb, 1905-1928
252	Honus Wagner, 1897-1917
243	Jake Beckley, 1888-1907
233	Roger Connor, 1880-1897
222	Tris Speaker, 1907-1928
220	Fred Clarke, 1894-1915
205	Dan Brouthers, 1879-1904
194	Joe Kelley, 1891-1908
191	Paul Waner, 1926-1945
188	Bid McPhee, 1882-1899
187	Eddie Collins, 1906-1930
185	Ed Delahanty, 1888-1903
184	Sam Rice, 1915-1934
182	Jesse Burkett, 1890-1905
182	Ed Konetchy, 1907-1921
182	Edd Roush, 1913-1931
178	Buck Ewing, 1880-1897
177	Rabbit Maranville, 1912-1935
177	Stan Musial, 1941-1963

HR: Most

755	Hank Aaron, 1954-1976
714	Babe Ruth, 1914-1935
660	Willie Mays, 1951-1973
586	Frank Robinson, 1956-1976
573	Harmon Killebrew, 1954-1975
563	Reggie Jackson, 1967-1987
548	Mike Schmidt, 1972-1989

536	Mickey Mantle, 1951-1968
534	Jimmie Foxx, 1925-1945
522	MARK McGWIRE, 1986-1999
521	Willie McCovey, 1959-1980
521	Ted Williams, 1939-1960
512	Ernie Banks, 1953-1971
512	Eddie Mathews, 1952-1968
511	Mel Ott, 1926-1947
504	Eddie Murray, 1977-1997
493	Lou Gehrig, 1923-1939
475	Stan Musial, 1941-1963
475	Willie Stargell, 1962-1982
465	Dave Winfield, 1973-1995

RBI: Most

2297	Hank Aaron, 1954-1976
2213	Babe Ruth, 1914-1935
2076	Cap Anson, 1871-1897
1995	Lou Gehrig, 1923-1939
1951	Stan Musial, 1941-1963
1938	Ty Cobb, 1905-1928
1922	Jimmie Foxx, 1925-1945
1917	Eddie Murray, 1977-1997
1903	Willie Mays, 1951-1973
1860	Mel Ott, 1926-1947
1844	Carl Yastrzemski, 1961-1983
1839	Ted Williams, 1939-1960
1833	Dave Winfield, 1973-1995
1827	Al Simmons, 1924-1944
1812	Frank Robinson, 1956-1976
1732	Honus Wagner, 1897-1917
1702	Reggie Jackson, 1967-1987
1652	Tony Perez, 1964-1986
1636	Ernie Banks, 1953-1971
1609	Goose Goslin, 1921-1938

SB: Most

1334	RICKEY HENDERSON, 1979-1999
938	Lou Brock, 1961-1979
912	Billy Hamilton, 1888-1901
892	Ty Cobb, 1905-1928
807	TIM RAINES, 1979-1999
752	Vince Coleman, 1985-1997
745	Eddie Collins, 1906-1930
739	Arlie Latham, 1880-1909
738	Max Carey, 1910-1929
722	Honus Wagner, 1897-1917
689	Joe Morgan, 1963-1984
668	Willie Wilson, 1976-1994
657	Tom Brown, 1882-1898
649	Bert Campaneris, 1964-1983
620	OTIS NIXON, 1983-1999
616	George Davis, 1890-1909
594	Dummy Hoy, 1888-1902
586	Maury Wills, 1959-1972
583	George Vanhaltren, 1887-1903
580	Ozzie Smith, 1978-1996

BB: Most

2056	Babe Ruth, 1914-1935
2019	Ted Williams, 1939-1960
1972	RICKEY HENDERSON, 1979-1999
1865	Joe Morgan, 1963-1984
1845	Carl Yastrzemski, 1961-1983
1733	Mickey Mantle, 1951-1968
1708	Mel Ott, 1926-1947
1614	Eddie Yost, 1944-1962
1605	Darrell Evans, 1969-1989
1599	Stan Musial, 1941-1963
1566	Pete Rose, 1963-1986
1559	Harmon Killebrew, 1954-1975
1508	Lou Gehrig, 1923-1939
1507	Mike Schmidt, 1972-1989
1499	Eddie Collins, 1906-1930
1464	Willie Mays, 1951-1973
1452	Jimmie Foxx, 1925-1945
1444	Eddie Mathews, 1952-1968
1430	BARRY BONDS, 1986-1999
1420	Frank Robinson, 1956-1976

HBP: Most

287	Hughie Jennings, 1891-1918
272	Tommy Tucker, 1887-1899
267	Don Baylor, 1970-1988
243	Ron Hunt, 1963-1974
230	Dan McGann, 1896-1908
198	Frank Robinson, 1956-1976
192	Minnie Minoso, 1949-1980
183	Jake Beckley, 1888-1907
173	Curt Welch, 1884-1893
165	Kid Elberfeld, 1898-1914
153	CRAIG BIGGIO, 1988-1999
153	Fred Clarke, 1894-1915
151	Chet Lemon, 1975-1990
143	Carlton Fisk, 1969-1993
142	Nellie Fox, 1947-1965
141	Art Fletcher, 1909-1922
140	Bill Dahlen, 1891-1911
137	Frank Chance, 1898-1914
137	Andres Galarraga, 1985-1998
136	BRADY ANDERSON, 1988-1999

K: Most

2597	Reggie Jackson, 1967-1987
1936	Willie Stargell, 1962-1982
1883	Mike Schmidt, 1972-1989
1867	Tony Perez, 1964-1986
1816	Dave Kingman, 1971-1986
1765	JOSE CANSECO, 1985-1999
1757	Bobby Bonds, 1968-1981
1748	Dale Murphy, 1976-1993
1730	Lou Brock, 1961-1979
1710	Mickey Mantle, 1951-1968
1699	Harmon Killebrew, 1954-1975

1698	CHILI DAVIS, 1981-1999
1697	Dwight Evans, 1972-1991
1686	Dave Winfield, 1973-1995
1615	Andres Galarraga, 1985-1998
1599	GARY GAETTI, 1981-1999
1570	Lee May, 1965-1982
1556	Dick Allen, 1963-1977
1550	Willie McCovey, 1959-1980
1537	Dave Parker, 1973-1991

GIDP: Most

328	Hank Aaron, 1954-1976
325	CAL RIPKEN, 1981-1999
323	Carl Yastrzemski, 1961-1983
319	Dave Winfield, 1973-1995
315	Eddie Murray, 1977-1997
315	Jim Rice, 1974-1989
297	Brooks Robinson, 1955-1977
297	Rusty Staub, 1963-1985
290	HAROLD BAINES, 1980-1999
287	Ted Simmons, 1968-1988
284	Joe Torre, 1960-1977
277	George Scott, 1966-1979
275	Roberto Clemente, 1955-1972
271	Al Kaline, 1953-1974
270	Frank Robinson, 1956-1976
268	Tony Perez, 1964-1986
266	Dave Concepcion, 1970-1988
261	Ernie Lombardi, 1931-1947
256	Ron Santo, 1960-1974
255	Buddy Bell, 1972-1989
255	JULIO FRANCO, 1982-1999

BA: Highest

.366	Ty Cobb, 1905-1928
.359	Rogers Hornsby, 1915-1937
.356	Joe Jackson, 1908-1920
.346	Ed Delahanty, 1888-1903
.345	Tris Speaker, 1907-1928
.344	Ted Williams, 1939-1960
.344	Billy Hamilton, 1888-1901
.342	Dan Brouthers, 1879-1904
.342	Babe Ruth, 1914-1935
.342	Harry Heilmann, 1914-1932
.342	Pete Browning, 1882-1894
.341	Willie Keeler, 1892-1910
.341	Bill Terry, 1923-1936
.340	George Sisler, 1915-1930
.340	Lou Gehrig, 1923-1939
.339	TONY GWYNN, 1982-1999
.338	Jesse Burkett, 1890-1905
.338	Nap Lajoie, 1896-1916
.336	Riggs Stephenson, 1921-1934
.334	Al Simmons, 1924-1944

On-base avg: Highest

.482	Ted Williams, 1939-1960
.474	Babe Ruth, 1914-1935
.466	John McGraw, 1891-1906
.455	Billy Hamilton, 1888-1901
.447	Lou Gehrig, 1923-1939
.440	FRANK THOMAS, 1990-1999
.434	Rogers Hornsby, 1915-1937
.433	Ty Cobb, 1905-1928
.428	Jimmie Foxx, 1925-1945
.428	Tris Speaker, 1907-1928
.426	EDGAR MARTINEZ, 1987-1999
.424	Eddie Collins, 1906-1930
.424	Ferris Fain, 1947-1955
.423	Dan Brouthers, 1879-1904
.423	Joe Jackson, 1908-1920
.423	Max Bishop, 1924-1935
.421	Mickey Mantle, 1951-1968
.419	Mickey Cochrane, 1925-1937
.417	Stan Musial, 1941-1963
.416	JEFF BAGWELL, 1991-1999

Slug pct: Highest

.690	Babe Ruth, 1914-1935
.634	Ted Williams, 1939-1960
.632	Lou Gehrig, 1923-1939
.609	Jimmie Foxx, 1925-1945
.605	Hank Greenberg, 1930-1947
.587	MARK McGWIRE, 1986-1999
.579	Joe DiMaggio, 1936-1951
.577	Rogers Hornsby, 1915-1937
.573	ALBERT BELLE, 1989-1999
.573	FRANK THOMAS, 1990-1999
.572	JUAN GONZALEZ, 1989-1999
.569	KEN GRIFFEY, 1989-1999
.567	LARRY WALKER, 1989-1999
.562	Johnny Mize, 1936-1953
.559	Stan Musial, 1941-1963
.559	BARRY BONDS, 1986-1999
.558	Willie Mays, 1951-1973
.557	Mickey Mantle, 1951-1968
.554	Hank Aaron, 1954-1976
.548	Ralph Kiner, 1946-1955

Extra-base hits: Most

1477	Hank Aaron, 1954-1976
1377	Stan Musial, 1941-1963
1356	Babe Ruth, 1914-1935
1323	Willie Mays, 1951-1973
1190	Lou Gehrig, 1923-1939
1186	Frank Robinson, 1956-1976
1157	Carl Yastrzemski, 1961-1983
1136	Ty Cobb, 1905-1928
1131	Tris Speaker, 1907-1928
1119	George Brett, 1973-1993

1117	Jimmie Foxx, 1925-1945
1117	Ted Williams, 1939-1960
1099	Eddie Murray, 1977-1997
1093	Dave Winfield, 1973-1995
1075	Reggie Jackson, 1967-1987
1071	Mel Ott, 1926-1947
1041	Pete Rose, 1963-1986
1039	Andre Dawson, 1976-1996
1017	CAL RIPKEN, 1981-1999
1015	Mike Schmidt, 1972-1989

Pitchers

Games: Most

1090	JESSE OROSCO, 1979-1999
1071	Dennis Eckersley, 1975-1998
1070	Hoyt Wilhelm, 1952-1972
1050	Kent Tekulve, 1974-1989
1022	Lee Smith, 1980-1997
1002	Rich Gossage, 1972-1994
987	Lindy McDaniel, 1955-1975
944	Rollie Fingers, 1968-1985
931	Gene Garber, 1969-1988
906	Cy Young, 1890-1911
899	Sparky Lyle, 1967-1982
898	Jim Kaat, 1959-1983
884	PAUL ASSENMACHER, 1986-1999
880	Jeff Reardon, 1979-1994
878	JOHN FRANCO, 1984-1999
874	Don McMahon, 1957-1974
864	Phil Niekro, 1964-1987
858	Charlie Hough, 1970-1994
848	Roy Face, 1953-1969
835	MIKE JACKSON, 1986-1999

Complete games: Most

749	Cy Young, 1890-1911
646	Jim Galvin, 1875-1892
554	Tim Keefe, 1880-1893
531	Walter Johnson, 1907-1927
531	Kid Nichols, 1890-1906
525	Bobby Mathews, 1871-1887
525	Mickey Welch, 1880-1892
489	Charley Radbourn, 1880-1891
485	John Clarkson, 1882-1894
468	Tony Mullane, 1881-1894
466	Jim McCormick, 1878-1887
448	Gus Weyhing, 1887-1901
437	Pete Alexander, 1911-1930
434	Christy Mathewson, 1900-1916
422	Jack Powell, 1897-1912
410	Eddie Plank, 1901-1917
394	Will White, 1877-1886
393	Amos Rusie, 1889-1901
388	Vic Willis, 1898-1910
386	Tommy Bond, 1874-1884

Saves: Most

478	Lee Smith, 1980-1997
416	JOHN FRANCO, 1984-1999
390	Dennis Eckersley, 1975-1998
367	Jeff Reardon, 1979-1994
347	Randy Myers, 1985-1998
341	Rollie Fingers, 1968-1985
311	Tom Henke, 1982-1995
310	Rich Gossage, 1972-1994
304	JEFF MONTGOMERY, 1987-1999
301	DOUG JONES, 1982-1999
300	Bruce Sutter, 1976-1988
296	JOHN WETTELAND, 1989-1999
289	RICK AGUILERA, 1985-1999
260	ROD BECK, 1991-1999
256	Todd Worrell, 1985-1997
252	Dave Righetti, 1979-1995
244	Dan Quisenberry, 1979-1990
238	Sparky Lyle, 1967-1982
234	ROBERTO HERNANDEZ, 1991-1999
228	TREVOR HOFFMAN, 1993-1999
227	Hoyt Wilhelm, 1952-1972
218	Gene Garber, 1969-1988
217	GREGG OLSON, 1988-1999
216	Dave Smith, 1980-1992
201	Bobby Thigpen, 1986-1994
193	Roy Face, 1953-1969
193	Mike Henneman, 1987-1996
192	Mitch Williams, 1986-1997
188	Mike Marshall, 1967-1981
186	Jeff Russell, 1983-1996

Shutouts: Most

110	Walter Johnson, 1907-1927
90	Pete Alexander, 1911-1930
79	Christy Mathewson, 1900-1916
76	Cy Young, 1890-1911
69	Eddie Plank, 1901-1917
63	Warren Spahn, 1942-1965
61	Nolan Ryan, 1966-1993
61	Tom Seaver, 1967-1986
60	Bert Blyleven, 1970-1992
58	Don Sutton, 1966-1988
57	Jim Galvin, 1875-1892
57	Ed Walsh, 1904-1917
56	Bob Gibson, 1959-1975
55	Mordecai Brown, 1903-1916
55	Steve Carlton, 1965-1988
53	Jim Palmer, 1965-1984
53	Gaylord Perry, 1962-1983
52	Juan Marichal, 1960-1975
50	Rube Waddell, 1897-1910
50	Vic Willis, 1898-1910

Wins: Most

511	Cy Young, 1890-1911
417	Walter Johnson, 1907-1927
373	Pete Alexander, 1911-1930
373	Christy Mathewson, 1900-1916
365	Jim Galvin, 1875-1892
363	Warren Spahn, 1942-1965
361	Kid Nichols, 1890-1906
342	Tim Keefe, 1880-1893
329	Steve Carlton, 1965-1988
328	John Clarkson, 1882-1894
326	Eddie Plank, 1901-1917
324	Nolan Ryan, 1966-1993
324	Don Sutton, 1966-1988
318	Phil Niekro, 1964-1987
314	Gaylord Perry, 1962-1983
311	Tom Seaver, 1967-1986
309	Charley Radbourn, 1880-1891
307	Mickey Welch, 1880-1892
300	Lefty Grove, 1925-1941
300	Early Wynn, 1939-1963

Losses: Most

316	Cy Young, 1890-1911
310	Jim Galvin, 1875-1892
292	Nolan Ryan, 1966-1993
279	Walter Johnson, 1907-1927
274	Phil Niekro, 1964-1987
265	Gaylord Perry, 1962-1983
256	Don Sutton, 1966-1988
254	Jack Powell, 1897-1912
251	Eppa Rixey, 1912-1933
250	Bert Blyleven, 1970-1992
248	Bobby Mathews, 1871-1887
245	Robin Roberts, 1948-1966
245	Warren Spahn, 1942-1965
244	Steve Carlton, 1965-1988
244	Early Wynn, 1939-1963
237	Jim Kaat, 1959-1983
236	Frank Tanana, 1973-1993
232	Gus Weyhing, 1887-1901
231	Tommy John, 1963-1989
230	Bob Friend, 1951-1966
230	Ted Lyons, 1923-1946

HR allowed: Most

505	Robin Roberts, 1948-1966
484	Fergie Jenkins, 1965-1983
482	Phil Niekro, 1964-1987
472	Don Sutton, 1966-1988
448	Frank Tanana, 1973-1993
434	Warren Spahn, 1942-1965
430	Bert Blyleven, 1970-1992
414	Steve Carlton, 1965-1988
399	Gaylord Perry, 1962-1983
395	Jim Kaat, 1959-1983
389	Jack Morris, 1977-1994

383	Charlie Hough, 1970-1994
380	Tom Seaver, 1967-1986
374	Catfish Hunter, 1965-1979
372	Jim Bunning, 1955-1971
372	Dennis Martinez, 1976-1998
347	Dennis Eckersley, 1975-1998
347	Mickey Lolich, 1963-1979
346	Luis Tiant, 1964-1982
338	Early Wynn, 1939-1963

BB: Most

2795	Nolan Ryan, 1966-1993
1833	Steve Carlton, 1965-1988
1809	Phil Niekro, 1964-1987
1775	Early Wynn, 1939-1963
1764	Bob Feller, 1936-1956
1732	Bobo Newsom, 1929-1953
1707	Amos Rusie, 1889-1901
1665	Charlie Hough, 1970-1994
1566	Gus Weyhing, 1887-1901
1541	Red Ruffing, 1924-1947
1442	Bump Hadley, 1926-1941
1434	Warren Spahn, 1942-1965
1431	Earl Whitehill, 1923-1939
1408	Tony Mullane, 1881-1894
1396	Sam Jones, 1914-1935
1390	Jack Morris, 1977-1994
1390	Tom Seaver, 1967-1986
1379	Gaylord Perry, 1962-1983
1371	Mike Torrez, 1967-1984
1363	Walter Johnson, 1907-1927

Hit batsmen: Most

277	Gus Weyhing, 1887-1901
219	Chick Fraser, 1896-1909
210	Pink Hawley, 1892-1901
205	Walter Johnson, 1907-1927
190	Eddie Plank, 1901-1917
185	Tony Mullane, 1881-1894
179	Joe McGinnity, 1899-1908
174	Charlie Hough, 1970-1994
171	Clark Griffith, 1891-1914
163	Cy Young, 1890-1911
160	Jim Bunning, 1955-1971
158	Nolan Ryan, 1966-1993
156	Vic Willis, 1898-1910
155	Bert Blyleven, 1970-1992
154	Don Drysdale, 1956-1969
148	Adonis Terry, 1884-1897
147	Bert Cunningham, 1887-1901
146	Silver King, 1886-1897
144	Win Mercer, 1894-1902
142	Frank Foreman, 1884-1902

K: Most

5714	Nolan Ryan, 1966-1993
4136	Steve Carlton, 1965-1988
3701	Bert Blyleven, 1970-1992
3640	Tom Seaver, 1967-1986
3574	Don Sutton, 1966-1988

3534	Gaylord Perry, 1962-1983
3509	Walter Johnson, 1907-1927
3342	Phil Niekro, 1964-1987
3316	ROGER CLEMENS, 1984-1999
3192	Fergie Jenkins, 1965-1983
3117	Bob Gibson, 1959-1975
2855	Jim Bunning, 1955-1971
2832	Mickey Lolich, 1963-1979
2803	Cy Young, 1890-1911
2773	Frank Tanana, 1973-1993
2693	RANDY JOHNSON, 1988-1999
2583	Warren Spahn, 1942-1965
2581	Bob Feller, 1936-1956
2564	Tim Keefe, 1880-1893
2556	Jerry Koosman, 1967-1985

Wild pitches: Most

343	Tony Mullane, 1881-1894
277	Nolan Ryan, 1966-1993
274	Mickey Welch, 1880-1892
252	Bobby Mathews, 1871-1887
240	Tim Keefe, 1880-1893
240	Gus Weyhing, 1887-1901
226	Phil Niekro, 1964-1987
221	Mark Baldwin, 1887-1893
221	Jim Galvin, 1875-1892
221	Will White, 1877-1886
214	Charley Radbourn, 1880-1891
214	Jim Whitney, 1881-1890
206	Jack Morris, 1977-1994
206	Adonis Terry, 1884-1897
203	Matt Kilroy, 1886-1898
189	George Bradley, 1875-1888
187	Tommy John, 1963-1989
183	Steve Carlton, 1965-1988
182	John Clarkson, 1882-1894
179	Charlie Hough, 1970-1994
179	Toad Ramsey, 1885-1890

Win pct: Highest

.795	Al Spalding, 1871-1878
.717	Spud Chandler, 1937-1947
.690	Dave Foutz, 1884-1896
.690	Whitey Ford, 1950-1967
.688	Bob Caruthers, 1884-1893
.686	Don Gullett, 1970-1978
.682	PEDRO MARTINEZ, 1992-1999
.680	Lefty Grove, 1925-1941
.673	MIKE MUSSINA, 1991-1999
.672	Joe Wood, 1908-1922
.667	Vic Raschi, 1946-1955
.665	Larry Corcoran, 1880-1887
.665	Christy Mathewson, 1900-1916
.660	Sam Leever, 1898-1910
.657	Sal Maglie, 1945-1958
.656	Dick McBride, 1871-1876
.655	Sandy Koufax, 1955-1966
.654	Johnny Allen, 1932-1944
.651	Ron Guidry, 1975-1988
.650	Lefty Gomez, 1930-1943

ERA: Lowest

1.82	Ed Walsh, 1904-1917
1.89	Addie Joss, 1902-1910
2.04	Al Spalding, 1871-1878
2.06	Mordecai Brown, 1903-1916
2.10	John Ward, 1878-1884
2.13	Christy Mathewson, 1900-1916
2.14	Tommy Bond, 1874-1884
2.16	Rube Waddell, 1897-1910
2.17	Walter Johnson, 1907-1927
2.23	Orval Overall, 1905-1913
2.28	Will White, 1877-1886
2.28	Ed Reulbach, 1905-1917
2.30	Jim Scott, 1909-1917
2.35	Eddie Plank, 1901-1917
2.35	Larry Corcoran, 1880-1887
2.38	Eddie Cicotte, 1905-1920
2.38	George McQuillan, 1907-1918
2.38	Ed Killian, 1903-1910
2.39	Candy Cummings, 1872-1877
2.39	Doc White, 1901-1913

Innings: Most

7356.0	Cy Young, 1890-1911
6003.1	Jim Galvin, 1875-1892
5914.2	Walter Johnson, 1907-1927
5404.1	Phil Niekro, 1964-1987
5386	Nolan Ryan, 1966-1993
5350.1	Gaylord Perry, 1962-1983
5282.1	Don Sutton, 1966-1988
5243.2	Warren Spahn, 1942-1965
5217.1	Steve Carlton, 1965-1988
5190	Pete Alexander, 1911-1930
5056.1	Kid Nichols, 1890-1906
5049.2	Tim Keefe, 1880-1893
4970	Bert Blyleven, 1970-1992
4956	Bobby Mathews, 1871-1887
4802	Mickey Welch, 1880-1892
4782.2	Tom Seaver, 1967-1986
4780.2	Christy Mathewson, 1900-1916
4710.1	Tommy John, 1963-1989
4688.2	Robin Roberts, 1948-1966
4564	Early Wynn, 1939-1963

General club records

Highest winning percentage for league champion

.832	St. Louis, UA-1884
.798	Chicago, NL-1880
.788	Chicago, NL-1876
.777	Chicago, NL-1885
.763	Chicago, NL-1906

Lowest winning percentage for league champion

.509	New York, NL-1973
.525	Minnesota, AL-1987
.534	Cleveland, AL-1997
.551	New York, AL-1981
.556	Philadelphia, NL-1983
.556	Oakland, AL-1974

Most wins

116	Chicago, NL-1906
114	New York, AL-1998
111	Cleveland, AL-1954
110	Pittsburgh, NL-1909
110	New York, NL-1927

Fewest wins

36	Philadelphia, AL-1916
38	Washington, AL-1904
38	Boston, NL-1935
40	New York, NL-1962
42	Washington, AL-1909
42	Philadelphia, NL-1942
42	Pittsburgh, NL-1952

Most league championships

35	New York, AL
21	Brooklyn-Los Angeles, NL
19	New York-San Francisco, NL
16	Boston-Milwaukee-Atlanta, NL
16	Chicago, NL
15	St. Louis, NL
15	Philadelphia-Oakland, AL

Individual fielding records

Gold Gloves: Most, pitcher

16	Jim Kaat
9	Bob Gibson
9	GREG MADDUX
8	Bobby Shantz
7	MARK LANGSTON
5	Ron Guidry
5	Phil Niekro
4	Jim Palmer
3	Harvey Haddix
3	MIKE MUSSINA

Gold Gloves: Most, catcher

10	Johnny Bench
7	Bob Boone
7	IVAN RODRIGUEZ
6	Jim Sundberg

5	Bill Freehan
4	Del Crandall
4	CHARLES JOHNSON
4	Tony Pena
3	Earl Battey
3	Gary Carter
3	Sherm Lollar
3	Thurman Munson
3	TOM PAGNOZZI
3	Lance Parrish
3	BENITO SANTIAGO

Gold Gloves: Most, first base

11	Keith Hernandez
9	Don Mattingly
8	George Scott
7	Vic Power
7	Bill White
6	Wes Parker
4	Steve Garvey
4	MARK GRACE
4	J. T. SNOW
3	Gil Hodges
3	Eddie Murray
3	Joe Pepitone

Gold Gloves: Most, second base

9	Ryne Sandberg
8	Bill Mazeroski
8	Frank White
7	ROBERTO ALOMAR
5	Joe Morgan
5	Bobby Richardson
4	CRAIG BIGGIO
4	Bobby Grich
3	Nellie Fox
3	Davey Johnson
3	Bobby Knoop
3	Harold Reynolds
3	Manny Trillo
3	Lou Whitaker

Gold Gloves: Most, third base

16	Brooks Robinson
10	Mike Schmidt
6	Buddy Bell
5	Ken Boyer
5	Doug Rader
5	Ron Santo
5	ROBIN VENTURA
4	GARY GAETTI
4	MATT WILLIAMS
3	Frank Malzone
3	Terry Pendleton
3	Tim Wallach
3	KEN CAMINITI

Gold Gloves: Most, shortstop

13	Ozzie Smith
9	Luis Aparicio
8	Mark Belanger
6	OMAR VIZQUEL
5	Dave Concepcion
4	Tony Fernandez
4	Alan Trammell
3	BARRY LARKIN

3	Roy McMillan
2	Gene Alley
2	Larry Bowa
2	Don Kessinger
2	REY ORDONEZ
2	CAL RIPKEN
2	Maury Wills
2	Zoilo Versalles

Gold Gloves: Most, outfield

12	Roberto Clemente
12	Willie Mays
10	Al Kaline
9	KEN GRIFFEY, JR.
8	Paul Blair
8	BARRY BONDS
8	Andre Dawson
8	Dwight Evans
8	Garry Maddox
7	Curt Flood
7	Dave Winfield
7	DEVON WHITE
7	Carl Yastrzemski

Assists: Most, pitcher

227	Ed Walsh, Chi/A-1907
223	Will White, Cin/A-1882
190	Ed Walsh, Chi/A-1908
178	Harry Howell, StL/A-1905
177	Tony Mullane, Lou/A-1882
174	John Clarkson, Chi/N-1885
172	John Clarkson, Bos/N-1889
166	Jack Chesbro, NY/A-1904
163	George Mullin, Det/A-1904
160	Ed Walsh, Chi/A-1911

Assists: Most, catcher

238	Bill Rariden, New/F-1915
215	Bill Rariden, Ind/F-1914
214	Pat Moran, Bos/N-1903
212	Oscar Stanage, Det/A-1911
212	Art Wilson, Chi/F-1914
210	Gabby Street, Was/A-1909
204	Frank Snyder, StL/N-1915
203	George Gibson, Pit/N-1910
202	Bill Bergen, Bro/N-1909
202	Claude Berry, Pit/F-1914

Assists: Most, first base

184	Bill Buckner, Bos/N-1985
180	MARK GRACE, Chi/N-1990
167	MARK GRACE, Chi/N-1991
166	Sid Bream, Pit/N-1986
161	Bill Buckner, Chi/N-1983
159	Bill Buckner, Chi/N-1982
157	Bill Buckner, Bos/A-1986
155	Mickey Vernon, Cle/A-1949
152	Fred Tenney, Bos/N-1905
152	Eddie Murray, Bal/A-1985

Assists: Most, second base

641	Frankie Frisch, StL/N-1927
588	Hughie Critz, Cin/N-1926
582	Rogers Hornsby, NY/N-1927
572	Ski Melillo, StL/N-1930
571	Ryne Sandberg, Chi/N-1983

568	Rabbit Maranville, Pit/N-1924
562	Frank Parkinson, Phi/N-1922
559	Tony Cuccinello, Bos/N-1936
557	Johnny Hodapp, Cle/A-1930
555	Lou Bierbauer, Pit/N-1892

Assists: Most, shortstop

621	Ozzie Smith, SD/N-1980
601	Glenn Wright, Pit/N-1924
598	Dave Bancroft, Phi-NY/N-1920
597	Tommy Thevenow, StL/N-1926
595	Ivan DeJesus, Chi/N-1977
583	CAL RIPKEN, Bal/A-1984
581	Whitey Wietelmann, Bos/N-1943
579	Dave Bancroft, NY/N-1922
574	Rabbit Maranville, Bos/N-1914
573	Don Kessinger, Chi/N-1968

Assists: Most, third base

412	Graig Nettles, Cle/A-1971
410	Graig Nettles, NY/A-1973
410	Brooks Robinson, Bal/A-1974
405	Harlond Clift, StL/A-1937
405	Brooks Robinson, Bal/A-1967
404	Mike Schmidt, Phi/N-1974
399	Doug DeCinces, Cal/A-1982
396	Clete Boyer, NY/A-1962
396	Mike Schmidt, Phi/N-1977
396	Buddy Bell, Tex/A-1982

Assists: Most, outfield

50	Orator Shaffer, Chi/N-1879
48	Hugh Nicol, StL/A-1884
45	Hardy Richardson, Buf/N-1881
44	Tommy McCarthy, StL/A-1888
44	Chuck Klein, Phi/N-1930
43	Charlie Duffee, StL/A-1889
43	Jimmy Bannon, Bos/N-1894
42	Jim Fogarty, Phi/N-1889
41	Orator Shaffer, Buf/N-1883
41	Jim Lillie, Buf/N-1884

Assists: Most, pitcher, active players

71	Greg Maddux, Atl/N-1996
66	Kenny Rogers, Oak/A-1998
64	Greg Maddux, Chi/N-1992
63	Greg Maddux, Atl/N-1998
60	Orel Hershiser, LA/N-1988

Assists: Most, catcher, active players

103	Jason Kendall, Pit/N-1997
100	Benito Santiago, SD/N-1991
99	Mike Piazza, LA/N-1993
89	Rick Wilkins, Chi/N-1993
88	Pat Borders, Tor/A-1992

Assists: Most, first base, active players

180	Mark Grace, Chi/N-1990
167	Mark Grace, Chi/N-1991
147	Eric Karros, LA/N-1993
147	Rafael Palmeiro, Tex/A-1993
146	Todd Helton, Col/N-1998

Assists: Most, second base, active players

504	Craig Biggio, Hou/N-1997
494	Eric Young, Col-LA/N-1997
493	Randy Velarde, Ana-Oak/A-1999
475	Carlos Baerga, Cle/A-1992
473	Mark McLemore, Tex/A-1996

Assists: Most, shortstop, active players

583	Cal Ripken, Bal/A-1984
570	Ozzie Guillen, Chi/A-1988
534	Cal Ripken, Bal/A-1983
531	Cal Ripken, Bal/A-1989
528	Cal Ripken, Bal/A-1991

Assists: Most, third base, active players

389	Vinny Castilla, Col/N-1996
372	Robin Ventura, Chi/A-1992
368	Wade Boggs, Bos/A-1983
360	Gary Gaetti, Min/A-1983
353	Gary Gaetti, Cal/A-1991

Assists: Most, outfield, active players

21	Tim Raines, Mon/N-1983
20	Bobby Higginson, Det/A-1997
20	Andruw Jones, Atl/N-1998
20	Mark Kotsay, Fla/N-1998
19	Tony Gwynn, SD/N-1986
19	Bernard Gilkey, StL/N-1993
19	Manny Ramirez, Cle/A-1996
19	Kenny Lofton, Cle/A-1998
19	Mark Kotsay, Fla/N-1999

Putouts: Most, pitcher

57	Dave Foutz, StL/A-1886
54	Tony Mullane, Lou/A-1882
50	George Bradley, StL/N-1876
50	Guy Hecker, Lou/A-1884
49	Mike Boddicker, Bal/A-1984
47	Larry Corcoran, Chi/N-1884
45	Al Spalding, Chi/N-1876
45	Ted Breitenstein, StL/N-1895
44	Jim Devlin, Lou/N-1876
44	Dave Foutz, StL/A-1887
44	Bill Hutchison, Chi/N-1890

Putouts: Most, catcher

1135	Johnny Edwards, Hou/N-1969
1055	Mike Piazza, LA/N-1996
1051	Dan Wilson, Sea/A-1997
1045	Mike Piazza, LA/N-1997
1015	Jason Kendall, Pit/N-1998
1008	Johnny Edwards, Cin/N-1963

993	Javy Lopez, Atl/N-1996
984	Mike Piazza, LA-Fla-NY/N-1998
981	Darren Daulton, Phi/N-1993
978	Randy Hundley, Chi/N-1969
978	Javy Lopez, Atl/N-1998

Putouts: Most, first base

1846	Jiggs Donahue, Chi/A-1907
1759	George Kelly, NY/N-1920
1755	Phil Todt, Bos/A-1926
1710	Wally Pipp, Cin/N-1926
1697	Jiggs Donahue, Chi/A-1906
1691	Candy LaChance, Bos/A-1904
1687	Tom Jones, StL/A-1907
1682	Ernie Banks, Chi/N-1965
1667	Wally Pipp, NY/A-1922
1662	Lou Gehrig, NY/A-1927

Putouts: Most, second base

529	Bid McPhee, Cin/A-1886
484	Bobby Grich, Bal/A-1974
483	Bucky Harris, Was/A-1922
478	Nellie Fox, Chi/A-1956
472	Lou Bierbauer, Phi/A-1889
466	Billy Herman, Chi/N-1933
463	Bill Wambsganss, Bos/A-1924
461	Cub Stricker, Cle/A-1887
460	Buddy Myer, Was/A-1935
459	Bill Sweeney, Bos/N-1912

Putouts: Most, shortstop

425	Hughie Jennings, Bal/N-1895
425	Donie Bush, Det/A-1914
408	Joe Cassidy, Was/A-1905
407	Rabbit Maranville, Bos/N-1914
405	Dave Bancroft, NY/N-1922
405	Eddie Miller, Bos/N-1940
404	Monte Cross, Phi/N-1898
396	Dave Bancroft, NY/N-1921
395	Mickey Doolan, Phi/N-1906
392	Buck Weaver, Chi/A-1913

Putouts: Most, third Base

255	Denny Lyons, Phi/N-1887
251	Jimmy Williams, Pit/N-1899
251	Jimmy Collins, Bos/N-1900
243	Jimmy Collins, Bos/N-1898
243	Willie Kamm, Chi/A-1928
236	Willie Kamm, Chi/A-1927
233	Frank Baker, Phi/A-1913
232	Bill Coughlin, Was/A-1901
229	Ernie Courtney, Phi/N-1905
228	Jimmy Austin, StL/A-1911

Putouts: Most, outfield

547	Taylor Douthit, StL/N-1928
538	Richie Ashburn, Phi/N-1951
514	Richie Ashburn, Phi/N-1949
512	Chet Lemon, Chi/A-1977
507	Dwayne Murphy, Oak/A-1980
503	Dom DiMaggio, Bos/A-1948

503	Richie Ashburn, Phi/N-1956
502	Richie Ashburn, Phi/N-1957
496	Richie Ashburn, Phi/N-1953
495	Richie Ashburn, Phi/N-1958

Putouts: Most, pitcher, active players

41	Kevin Brown, LA/N-1999
40	Kevin Brown, Bal/A-1995
39	Greg Maddux, Chi/N-1990
39	Greg Maddux, Chi/N-1991
39	Greg Maddux, Atl/N-1993

Putouts: Most, catcher, active players

1055	Mike Piazza, LA/N-1996
1051	Dan Wilson, Sea/A-1997
1045	Mike Piazza, LA/N-1997
1015	Jason Kendall, Pit/N-1998
993	Javy Lopez, Atl/N-1996

Putouts: Most, first base, active players

1580	Mark Grace, Chi/N-1992
1528	Andres Galarraga, Col/N-1996
1520	Mark Grace, Chi/N-1991
1492	Will Clark, SF/N-1988
1487	Wally Joyner, Cal/A-1989

Putouts: Most, second base, active players

404	Fernando Vina, Mil/N-1998
400	Carlos Baerga, Cle/A-1992
361	Craig Biggio, Hou/N-1996
359	Craig Biggio, Hou/N-1999
347	Carlos Baerga, Cle/A-1993
347	Mike Lansing, Mon/N-1996

Putouts: Most, shortstop, active players

320	Shawon Dunston, Chi/N-1986
297	Cal Ripken, Bal/A-1984
297	Tony Fernandez, Tor/A-1990
294	Tony Fernandez, Tor/A-1986
291	Miguel Tejada, Oak/A-1999

Putouts: Most, third base, active players

146	Gary Gaetti, Min/A-1985
144	Scott Rolen, Phi/N-1997
142	Gary Gaetti, Min/A-1984
141	Wade Boggs, Bos/A-1984
141	Robin Ventura, Chi/A-1992

Putouts: Most, outfield, active players

492	Andruw Jones, Atl/N-1999
443	Devon White, Tor/A-1992
439	Rickey Henderson, NY/A-1985
439	Devon White, Tor/A-1991
438	Ray Lankford, StL/N-1992

Individual records

Hitters

Most consecutive games played, career

2632	CAL RIPKEN, 1982-1998
2130	Lou Gehrig, 1925-1939
1307	Everett Scott, 1916-1925
1207	Steve Garvey, 1975-1983
1117	Billy Williams, 1963-1970
1103	Joe Sewell, 1922-1930
895	Stan Musial, 1951-1957
829	Eddie Yost, 1949-1955
822	Gus Suhr, 1931-1937
798	Nellie Fox, 1955-1960

Longest hitting streak, season

56	Joe DiMaggio, NY/AL-1941
44	Willie Keeler, Bal/NL-1897
44	Pete Rose, Cin/NL-1978
42	Bill Dahlen, Chi/NL-1894
41	George Sisler, StL/AL-1922
40	Ty Cobb, Det/AL-1911
39	Paul Molitor, Mil/AL-1987
37	Tommy Holmes, Bos/NL-1945
36	Billy Hamilton, Phi/NL-1894
35	Fred Clarke, Lou/NL-1895
35	Ty Cobb, Det/AL-1917
34	George Sisler, StL/AL-1925
34	George McQuinn, StL/AL-1938
34	Dom DiMaggio, Bos/AL-1949
34	BENITO SANTIAGO, SD/NL-1987
33	Hal Chase, NY/AL-1907
33	George Davis, NY/NL-1893
33	Rogers Hornsby, StL/NL-1922
33	Heinie Manush, Was/AL-1933
31	Ed Delahanty, Phi/NL-1899
31	Nap Lajoie, Cle/AL-1906
31	Sam Rice, Was/AL-1924
31	Willie Davis, LA/NL-1969
31	Rico Carty, Atl/NL-1970
31	Ken Landreaux, Min/AL-1980
31	VLADIMIR GUERRERO, Mon/NL-1999
30	Cal McVey, Chi/NL-1876
30	Elmer Smith, Cin/NL-1898
30	Tris Speaker, Bos/AL-1912
30	Goose Goslin, Det/AL-1934
30	Stan Musial, StL/NL-1950
30	Ron LeFlore, Det/AL-1976
30	George Brett, KC/AL-1980
30	Jerome Walton, Chi/NL-1989
30	SANDY ALOMAR, JR., Cle/AL-1997
30	NOMAR GARCIAPARRA, Bos/AL-1997
30	ERIC DAVIS, Bal/AL-1998
30	LUIS GONZALEZ, Ari/NL-1999

Longest hitting streak, season, active players

34	Benito Santiago, SD/NL-1987
31	Vladimir Guerrero, Mon/NL-1999
30	Sandy Alomar, Jr., Cle/AL-1997
30	Nomar Garciaparra, Bos/AL-1997
30	Eric Davis, Bal/AL-1998
30	Luis Gonzalez, Ari/NL-1999
29	Hal Morris, Cin/NL-1996
28	Wade Boggs, Bos/AL-1985
28	Marquis Grissom, Atl/NL-1996
28	Garret Anderson, Ana/AL-1998
28	Shawn Green, Tor/AL-1999
27	John Flaherty, SD/NL-1996
27	Albert Belle, Chi/AL-1997
27	Jose Offerman, KC/AL-1998
26	John Olerud, Tor/AL-1993
26	Shannon Stewart, Tor/AL-1999
25	Tony Gwynn, SD/NL-1983
25	Wade Boggs, Bos/AL-1987
25	Lance Johnson, Chi/AL-1992

Most pinch hits, career

150	Manny Mota, 1962-1982
145	Smoky Burgess, 1949-1967
143	Greg Gross, 1973-1989
123	Jose Morales, 1973-1984
116	Jerry Lynch, 1954-1966
115	LENNY HARRIS, 1988-1999
114	Red Lucas, 1923-1938
113	Steve Braun, 1971-1985
108	Terry Crowley, 1969-1983
108	Denny Walling, 1975-1992
108	JOHN VANDER WAL, 1991-1999
107	Gates Brown, 1963-1975
103	Mike Lum, 1967-1981
102	Jim Dwyer, 1973-1990
100	Rusty Staub, 1963-1985
96	Dave Clark, 1986-1998
95	Larry Biittner, 1970-1983
95	Vic Davalillo, 1963-1980
95	Gerald Perry, 1983-1995
94	Jerry Hairston, 1973-1989

Most pinch hits, career active players

115	Lenny Harris, 1988-1999
108	John Vander Wal, 1991-1999
86	Dave Hansen, 1990-1999
81	John Cangelosi, 1985-1999
78	Thomas Howard, 1990-1999
77	Willie McGee, 1982-1999
69	Dave Magadan, 1986-1999

Most pinch hit home runs, career

20	Cliff Johnson, 1972-1986
18	Jerry Lynch, 1954-1966
16	Gates Brown, 1963-1975
16	Smoky Burgess, 1949-1967
16	Willie McCovey, 1959-1980
14	George Crowe, 1952-1961
13	JOHN VANDER WAL, 1991-1999
12	Joe Adcock, 1950-1966
12	Bob Cerv, 1951-1962
12	Jose Morales, 1973-1984
12	Graig Nettles, 1967-1988
11	Jeff Burroughs, 1970-1985
11	Jay Johnstone, 1966-1985
11	Candy Maldonado, 1981-1995
11	Fred Whitfield, 1962-1970
11	Cy Williams, 1912-1930
10	Mark Carreon, 1987-1996
10	Dave Clark, 1986-1997
10	Jim Dwyer, 1973-1990
10	Mike Lum, 1967-1981
10	Ken McMullen, 1962-1977
10	Don Mincher, 1960-1972
10	Wally Post, 1949-1964
10	Champ Summers, 1974-1984
10	Jerry Turner, 1974-1983
10	Gus Zernial, 1949-1959
10	GLENALLEN HILL, 1989-1999

Most pinch-hit home runs, career active players

13	John Vander Wal, 1991-1999
10	Glenallen Hill, 1989-1999
9	Paul Sorrento, 1989-1999
7	Jack Howell, 1985-1999
6	Kurt Abbott, 1993-1999
6	Thomas Howard, 1990-1999
6	Orlando Merced, 1990-1999
5	Chili Davis, 1981-1999
5	Matt Franco, 1995-1999
5	Kevin Jordan, 1995-1999
5	Terry Steinbach, 1986-1999
5	Mark Sweeney, 1995-1999
5	Rick Wilkins, 1991-1999
62	Mark Sweeney, 1995-1999
55	Harold Baines, 1980-1999
53	Keith Lockhart, 1994-1999

Pitchers

Most consecutive scoreless innings, season

59	OREL HERSHISER, LA/NL - Aug. 30 to Sept. 28, 1988 (end of season) (allowed a run in first inning of next start, April 5, 1989)
58	Don Drysdale, LA/NL - May 14 to June 8, 1968
55.2	Walter Johnson, Was/AL - April 10 to May 14, 1913

53 Jack Coombs, Phi/AL - Sept. 5 to 25, 1910

47 Bob Gibson, StL/NL - June 2 to 26, 1968

45.1 Carl Hubbell, NY/NL - July 13 to Aug. 1, 1933 (allowed a run charged to starter in a relief appearance on July 19, after 12 scoreless innings; had a 33-inning string afterward)

45 Cy Young, Bos/AL - April 25 to May 17, 1904

45 Doc White, Chi/AL - Sept. 12 to 30, 1904

45 Sal Maglie, NY/NL - Aug. 16 to Sept. 13, 1950

44 Ed Reulbach, Chi/NL - Sept. 17 to Oct. 3, 1908 (end of season) (added six more innings on April 17, 1909 for a total of 50 over two years)

43.2 Rube Waddell, Phi/AL - Aug. 22 to Sept. 5, 1905

42 Rube Foster, Bos/AL - May 1 to 26, 1914

41 Jack Chesbro, Pit/NL - June 26 to July 16, 1902

41 Grover Cleveland Alexander, Phi/NL - Sept. 7 to 24, 1911

41 Art Nehf, Bos/NL - Sept. 13 to Oct. 4, 1917

41 Luis Tiant, Cle/AL - April 28 to May 17, 1968

40 Walter Johnson, Was/AL - May 7 to 26, 1918

40 Gaylord Perry, SF/NL - Aug. 28 to Sept. 10, 1967

40 Luis Tiant, Bos/AL - Aug. 19 to Sept. 8, 1972

39.2 Mordecai Brown, Chi/NL - June 8 to July 8, 1908

39.2 Billy Pierce, Chi/AL - Aug. 3 to 19, 1953

39 Ed Walsh, Chi/AL - Aug. 10 to 22, 1906

39 Christy Mathewson, NY/NL - May 3 to 21, 1901

39 Don Newcombe, Bro/NL - July 25 to Aug. 11, 1956

39 Ray Culp, Bos/AL - Sept. 7 to 25, 1968

39 Gaylord Perry, SF/NL - Sept. 1 to 23, 1970

38.1 Bill Lee, Chi/NL - Sept. 5 to 26, 1938

38 Jim Galvin, Buf/NL - Aug. 2 to 8, 1884

38 John Clarkson, Chi/NL - May 18 to 27, 1885

38 Jim Bagby, Cle/AL - June 30 to July 16, 1917

38 Ray Herbert, Chi/AL - May 1 to 14, 1963

37 George Bradley, StL/NL - July 8 to 18, 1876

37 Cy Young, Bos/AL - June 13 to July 1, 1903

37 Walter Johnson, Was/AL - June 27 to July 13, 1913

37 Ed Walsh, Chi/AL - July 31 to Aug. 14, 1910

37 Joel Horlen, Chi/AL - May 11 to 29, 1968

37 Mike Torrez, Oak/AL - Aug. 29 to Sept. 15, 1976

36 Ed Morris, Pit/NL - Sept. 5 to 17, 1888

36 Hal Brown, Bal/AL - July 7 to Aug. 8, 1961 (allowed four runs on July 17 in a rained out game)

36 Jim McGlothlin, Cal/AL - May 22 to June 11, 1967

36 Charlie Hough, Tex/AL - Aug. 23 to Sept. 14, 1983 (GREGG OLSON, Bal/AL had a streak of 41 scoreless innings over two seasons from Aug. 4, 1989 to May 4, 1990, 26 in 1989 and 15 in 1990)

Most strikeouts, game

21 Tom Cheney, Was/AL - Sept. 12, 1962 (16 innings)

20 ROGER CLEMENS, Bos/AL - April 29, 1986

20 ROGER CLEMENS, Bos/AL - Sept. 18, 1996

20 KERRY WOOD, Chi/AL - May 6, 1998

19 Charlie Sweeney, Pro/NL - June 7, 1884

19 Hugh "One Arm" Daily, Chi/UA - July 7, 1884

19 Luis Tiant, Cle/AL - July 3, 1968 (10 innings)

19 Steve Carlton, StL/NL - Sept. 15, 1969

19 Tom Seaver, NY/NL - April 22, 1970

19 Nolan Ryan, Cal/AL - June 14, 1974 (12 innings)

19 Nolan Ryan, Cal/AL - Aug. 12, 1974

19 Nolan Ryan, Cal/AL - Aug. 20, 1974 (11 innings)

19 Nolan Ryan, Cal/AL - June 8, 1977 (10 innings)

19 DAVID CONE, NY/NL - Oct. 6, 1991

19 RANDY JOHNSON, Sea/AL - June 24, 1997

19 RANDY JOHNSON, Sea/AL - Aug. 8, 1997

18 Jim Whitney, Bos/NL - June 14, 1884 (15 innings)

18 Dupee Shaw, Bos/UA - July 19, 1884

18 Henry Porter, Mil/UA - Oct. 3, 1884

18 Jack Coombs, Phi/AL - Sept. 1, 1906 (24 innings)

18 Bob Feller, Cle/AL - Oct. 2, 1938 (1st game)

18 Warren Spahn, Bos/NL - June 14, 1952 (15 innings)

18 Sandy Koufax, LA/NL - Aug. 31, 1959

18 Sandy Koufax, LA/NL - April 24, 1962

18 Jim Maloney, Cin/NL - June 14, 1965 (11 innings)

18 Chris Short, Phi/NL - Oct. 2, 1965 (15 innings in an 18-inning game)

18 Don Wilson, Hou/NL - July 14, 1968

18 Nolan Ryan, Cal/AL - Sept. 10, 1976

18 Ron Guidry, NY/AL - June 17, 1978

18 Bill Gullickson, Mon/NL - Sept. 10, 1980

18 RAMON MARTINEZ, LA/NL - June 4, 1990

18 RANDY JOHNSON, Sea/AL - Sept. 27, 1992

18 ROGER CLEMENS, Tor/AL - Aug. 25, 1998

Most bases on balls, game

16 Bill George, NY/NL - May 30, 1887 (1st game)

16 George Van Haltren, Chi/NL - June 27, 1887

16 Henry Gruber, Cle/PL - April 19, 1890

16 Bruno Haas, Phi/AL - June 23, 1915

16 Tommy Byrne, NY/AL - Aug., 1951 (13 innings)

15 Carroll Brown, Phi/AL - July 12, 1913

14 Ed Crane, Was/NL - Sept. 1, 1886

14 Charlie Hickman, Bos/NL - Aug. 16, 1899 (2nd game)

14 Henry Mathewson, NY/NL - Oct. 5, 1906

14 Skipper Friday, Was/AL - June 17, 1923

13 Bill George, NY/NL - May 17, 1887

13 John Kirby, Ind/NL - June 9, 1887

13 Cy Seymour, NY/NL - May 24, 1899 (10 innings)

13 Mal Eason, Bos/NL - Sept. 3, 1902

13 Pete Schneider, Cin/NL - July 6, 1918

13 George Turbeville, Phi/AL - Aug. 24, 1935 (15 innings)

13   Tommy Byrne, NY/AL -
       June 8, 1949
13   Dick Weik, Was/AL -
       Sept. 1, 1949
13   Bud Podbielan, Cin/NL -
       May 18, 1953 (11 innings)

No-hit games, nine or more innings (number to left is career total if greater than 1)

Joe Borden, Phi vs Chi NA, 4-0;
   July 28, 1875.
George Bradley, StL vs Har NL, 2-0;
   July 15, 1876.
Lee Richmond, Wor vs Cle NL, 1-0;
   June 12, 1880 (perfect game).
Monte Ward, Pro vs Buf NL, 5-0;
   June 17, 1880 (perfect game).
Larry Corcoran, Chi vs Bos NL, 6-0;
   Aug. 19, 1880.
Jim Galvin, Buf at Wor NL, 1-0; Aug.
   20, 1880.
Tony Mullane, Lou at Cin AA, 2-0;
   Sept. 11, 1882.
Guy Hecker, Lou at Pit AA, 3-1;
   Sept. 19, 1882.
2 Larry Corcoran, Chi vs Wor NL, 5-
   0; Sept. 20, 1882.
Charley Radbourn, Pro at Cle NL, 8-
   0; July 25, 1883.
Hugh "One Arm" Daily, Cle at Phi NL;
   1-0; Sept. 13, 1883.
Al Atkisson, Phi vs Pit AA, 10-1;
   May 24, 1884.
Ed Morris, Col at Pit AA, 5-0;
   May 29, 1884.
Frank Mountain, Col at Was AA, 12-0;
   June 5, 1884.
3 Larry Corcoran, Chi vs Pro NL, 6-0;
   June 27, 1884.
2 Jim Galvin, Buf at Det NL, 18-0;
   Aug. 4, 1884.
Dick Burns, Cin at KC UA, 3-1;
   Aug. 26, 1884.
Ed Cushman, Mil vs Was UA, 5-0;
   Sept. 28, 1884.
Sam Kimber, Bro vs Tol AA, 0-0; Oct.
   4, 1884 (10 innings, darkness).
John Clarkson, Chi at Pro NL, 4-0;
   July 27, 1885.
Charlie Ferguson, Phi vs Pro NL, 1-0;
   Aug. 29, 1885.
2 Al Atkisson, Phi vs NY AA, 3-2;
   May 1, 1886.
Adonis Terry, Bro vs StL AA, 1-0;
   July 24, 1886.
Matt Kilroy, Bal at Pit AA, 6-0;
   Oct. 6, 1886.
2 Adonis Terry, Bro vs Lou AA, 4-0;
   May 27, 1888.
Henry Porter, KC at Bal AA, 4-0;
   June 6, 1888.
Ed Seward, Phi vs Cin AA, 12-2;
   July 26, 1888.
Gus Weyhing, Phi vs KC AA, 4-0;
   July 31, 1888.

Silver King, Chi vs Bro PL, 0-1;
   June 21, 1890, (8 innings, lost;
   bottom of 9th not played).
Cannonball Titcomb, Roch vs Syr
   AA, 7-0; Sept. 15, 1890.
Tom Lovett, Bro vs NY NL, 4-0; June
   22, 1891.
Amos Rusie, NY vs Bro NL, 6-0; July
   31, 1891.
Ted Breitenstein, StL vs Lou AA, 8-0;
   Oct. 4, 1891 (1st game, first start
   in major leagues).
Jack Stivetts, Bos vs Bro NL, 11-0;
   Aug. 6, 1892.
Ben Sanders, Lou vs Bal NL, 6-2;
   Aug. 22, 1892.
Bumpus Jones, Cin vs Pit NL, 7-1;
   Oct. 15, 1892 (first start in major
   leagues).
Bill Hawke, Bal vs Was NL, 5-0;
   Aug. 16, 1893.
Cy Young, Cle vs Cin NL, 6-0;
   Sept. 18, 1897 (1st game).
2 Ted Breitenstein, Cin vs Pit NL, 11-
   0; April 22, 1898.
Jim Hughes, Bal vs Bos NL, 8-0;
   April 22, 1898.
Red Donahue, Phi vs Bos NL, 5-0;
   July 8, 1898.
Walter Thornton, Chi vs Bro NL, 2-0;
   Aug. 21, 1898 (2nd game).
Deacon Phillippe, Lou vs NY NL, 7-0;
   May 25, 1899.
Noodles Hahn, Cin vs Phi NL, 4-0;
   July 12, 1900.
Earl Moore, Cle vs Chi AL, 2-4;
   May 9, 1901 (lost on two hits in
   the 10th).
Christy Mathewson, NY at StL NL, 5-
   0; July 15, 1901.
Nixey Callahan, Chi vs Det AL, 3-0;
   Sept. 20, 1902 (1st game).
Chick Fraser, Phi at Chi NL; 10-0;
   Sept. 18, 1903 (2nd game).
2 Cy Young, Bos vs Phi AL, 3-0;
   May 5, 1904 (perfect game).
Bob Wicker, Chi at NY NL, 1-0;
   June 11, 1904 (won in 12 innings
   after allowing one hit in the 10th).
Jesse Tannehill, Bos at Chi AL, 6-0;
   Aug. 17, 1904.
2 Christy Mathewson, NY at Chi NL,
   1-0; June 13, 1905.
Weldon Henley, Phi at StL AL, 6-0;
   July 22, 1905 (1st game).
Frank Smith, Chi at Det AL, 15-0;
   Sept. 6, 1905 (2nd game).
Bill Dinneen, Bos vs Chi AL, 2-0;
   Sept. 27, 1905 (1st game).
Johnny Lush, Phi at Bro NL, 6-0;
   May 1, 1906.
Mal Eason, Bro at StL NL, 2-0;
   July 20, 1906.
Harry McIntyre, Bro vs Pit NL, 0-1;
   Aug. 1, 1906 (lost on four hits in

13 innings after allowing the first
   hit in the 11th).
Frank (Jeff) Pfeffer, Bos vs Cin NL, 6-
   0; May 8, 1907.
Nick Maddox, Pit vs Bro NL, 2-1;
   Sept. 20, 1907.
3 Cy Young, Bos at NY AL, 8-0;
   June 30, 1908.
Hooks Wiltse, NY vs Phi NL, 1-0; July
   4, 1908 (1st game, 10 innings).
Nap Rucker, Bro vs Bos NL, 6-0;
   Sept. 5, 1908 (2nd game).
Dusty Rhoades, Cle vs Bos AL, 2-1;
   Sept. 18, 1908.
2 Frank Smith, Chi vs Phi AL, 1-0;
   Sept. 20, 1908.
Addie Joss, Cle vs Chi AL, 1-0; Oct.
   2, 1908 (perfect game).
Red Ames, NY vs Bro NL. 0-3; April
   15, 1909 (lost on seven hits in 13
   innings after allowing the first hit
   in the 10th).
2 Addie Joss, Cle at Chi AL, 1-0;
   April 20, 1910.
Chief Bender, Phi vs Cle AL, 4-0;
   May 12, 1910.
Tom L. Hughes, NY vs Cle AL, 0-5;
   Aug. 30, 1910 (2nd game) (lost
   on seven hits in 11 innings after
   allowing the first hit in the 10th)
Joe Wood, Bos vs StL AL, 5-0;
   July 29, 1911 (1st game).
Ed Walsh, Chi vs Bos AL, 5-0; Aug.
   27, 1911.
George Mullin, Det vs StL AL, 7-0;
   July 4, 1912 (2nd game).
Earl Hamilton, StL at Det AL, 5-1;
   Aug. 30, 1912.
Jeff Tesreau, NY at Phi NL, 3-0; Sept.
   6, 1912 (1st game).
Jim Scott, Chi at Was AL, 0-1;
   May 14, 1914 (lost on two hits in
   the 10th).
Joe Benz, Chi vs Cle AL, 6-1;
   May 31, 1914.
George Davis, Bos vs Phi NL, 7-0;
   Sept. 9, 1914 (2nd game).
Ed Lafitte, Bro vs KC FL, 6-2; Sept.
   19, 1914.
Rube Marquard, NY vs Bro NL, 2-0;
   April 15, 1915.
Frank Allen, Pit at StL FL, 2-0;
   April 24, 1915.
Claude Hendrix, Chi at Pit FL, 10-0;
   May 15, 1915.
Alex Main, KC at Buf FL, 5-0;
   Aug. 16, 1915.
Jimmy Lavender, Chi at NY NL, 2-0;
   Aug. 31, 1915 (1st game).
Dave Davenport, StL vs Chi FL, 3-0;
   Sept. 7, 1915.
2 Tom L. Hughes, Bos vs Pit NL, 2-0;
   June 16, 1916.
Rube Foster, Bos vs NY AL, 2-0;
   June 21, 1916.

Joe Bush, Phi vs Cle AL, 5-0;
Aug. 26, 1916.

Dutch Leonard, Bos vs StL AL, 4-0;
Aug. 30, 1916.

Eddie Cicotte, Chi at StL AL, 11-0;
April 14, 1917.

George Mogridge, NY at Bos AL, 2-1; April 24, 1917.

Fred Toney, Cin at Chi NL, 1-0;
May 2, 1917 (10 innings).

Hippo Vaughn, Chi vs Cin NL, 0-1;
May 2, 1917. (lost on two hits in the 10th, Toney pitched a no-hitter in this game).

Ernie Koob, StL vs Chi AL, 1-0;
May 5, 1917.

Bob Groom, StL vs Chi AL, 3-0;
May 6, 1917 (2nd game).

Ernie Shore, Bos vs Was AL, 4-0;
June 23, 1917 (1st game, perfect game). (Shore relieved Babe Ruth in the first inning after Ruth had been thrown out of the game for protesting a walk to the first batter. The runner was caught stealing, and Shore retired the remaining 26 batters in order.)

2 Dutch Leonard, Bos at Det AL, 5-0;
June 3, 1918.

Hod Eller, Cin vs StL NL, 6-0;
May 11, 1919.

Ray Caldwell, Cle at NY AL, 3-0;
Sept. 10, 1919 (1st game).

Walter Johnson, Was at Bos AL, 1-0;
July 1, 1920.

Charlie Robertson, Chi at Det AL, 2-0; April 30, 1922 (perfect game).

Jesse Barnes, NY vs Phi NL, 6-0;
May 7, 1922.

Sam Jones, NY at Phi AL, 2-0;
Sept. 4, 1923.

Howard Ehmke, Bos at Phi AL, 4-0;
Sept. 7, 1923.

Jesse Haines, StL vs Bos NL, 5-0;
July 17, 1924.

Dazzy Vance, Bro vs Phi NL, 10-1;
Sept. 13, 1925 (1st game).

Ted Lyons, Chi at Bos AL, 6-0;
Aug. 21, 1926.

Carl Hubbell, NY vs Pit NL, 11-0;
May 8, 1929.

Wes Ferrell, Cle vs StL AL, 9-0;
April 29, 1931.

Bobby Burke, Was vs Bos AL, 5-0;
Aug. 8, 1931.

Bobo Newsom, StL vs Bos AL, 1-2;
Sept. 18, 1934 (lost on one hit in the 10th).

Paul Dean, StL at Bro NL, 3-0;
Sept. 21, 1934 (2nd game).

Vern Kennedy, Chi vs Cle AL, 5-0;
Aug. 31, 1935.

Bill Dietrich, Chi vs StL AL, 8-0;
June 1, 1937.

Johnny Vander Meer, Cin vs Bos NL, 3-0; June 11, 1938

2 Johnny Vander Meer, Cin at Bro NL, 6-0; June 15, 1938 (next start after June 11)

Monte Pearson, NY vs Cle AL, 13-0;
Aug. 27, 1938 (2nd game).

Bob Feller, Cle at Chi AL, 1-0;
April 16, 1940 (opening day).

Tex Carleton, Bro at Cin NL, 3-0;
April 30, 1940.

Lon Warneke, StL at Cin NL, 2-0;
Aug. 30, 1941.

Jim Tobin, Bos vs Bro NL, 2-0;
April 27, 1944.

Clyde Shoun, Cin vs Bos NL, 1-0;
May 15, 1944.

Dick Fowler, Phi vs StL AL, 1-0;
Sept. 9, 1945 (2nd game).

Ed Head, Bro vs Bos NL, 5-0;
April 23, 1946.

2 Bob Feller, Cle at NY AL, 1-0;
April 30, 1946.

Ewell Blackwell, Cin vs Bos NL, 6-0;
June 18, 1947.

Don Black, Cle vs Phi AL, 3-0;
July 10, 1947 (1st game).

Bill McCahan, Phi vs Was AL, 3-0;
Sept. 3, 1947.

Bob Lemon, Cle at Det AL, 2-0;
June 30, 1948.

Rex Barney, Bro at NY NL, 2-0;
Sept. 9, 1948.

Vern Bickford, Bos vs Bro NL, 7-0;
Aug. 11, 1950.

Cliff Chambers, Pit at Bos NL, 3-0;
May 6, 1951 (2nd game).

3 Bob Feller, Cle vs Det NL, 2-1;
July 1, 1951 (1st game).

Allie Reynolds, NY at Cle AL, 1-0;
July 12, 1951.

2 Allie Reynolds, NY vs Bos AL, 8-0;
Sept. 28, 1951 (1st game).

Virgil Trucks, Det vs Was AL, 1-0;
May 15, 1952.

Carl Erskine, Bro vs Chi NL, 5-0;
June 19, 1952.

2 Virgil Trucks, Det at NY AL, 1-0;
Aug. 25, 1952.

Bobo Holloman, StL vs Phi AL, 6-0;
May 6, 1953 (first start in the major leagues).

Jim Wilson, Mil vs Phi NL, 2-0;
June 12, 1954.

Sam Jones, Chi vs Pit NL, 4-0;
May 12, 1955.

2 Carl Erskine, Bro vs NY NL, 3-0;
May 12, 1956.

Johnny Klippstein (seven innings), Hershell Freeman (one inning) and Joe Black (three innings), Cin at Mil NL, 1-2; May 26, 1956 (lost on three hits in 11 innings after allowing the first hit in the 10th)

Mel Parnell, Bos vs Chi AL, 4-0;
July 14, 1956.

Sal Maglie, Bro vs Phi NL, 5-0;
Sept. 25, 1956.

Don Larsen, NY AL vs Bro NL, 2-0;
Oct. 8, 1956 (World Series, perfect game).

Bob Keegan, Chi vs Was AL, 6-0;
Aug. 20, 1957 (2nd game).

Jim Bunning, Det at Bos AL, 3-0;
July 20, 1958 (1st game).

Hoyt Wilhelm, Bal vs NY AL, 1-0;
Sept. 20, 1958

Harvey Haddix, Pit at Mil NL, 0-1;
May 26, 1959 (lost on one hit in 13 innings after pitching 12 perfect innings).

Don Cardwell, Chi vs StL NL, 4-0;
May 15, 1960 (2nd game).

Lew Burdette, Mil vs Phi NL, 1-0;
Aug. 18, 1960.

Warren Spahn, Mil vs Phi NL, 4-0;
Sept. 16, 1960.

2 Warren Spahn, Mil vs SF NL, 1-0;
April 28, 1961.

Bo Belinsky, LA vs Bal AL, 2-0;
May 5, 1962.

Earl Wilson, Bos vs LA AL, 2-0;
June 26, 1962.

Sandy Koufax, LA vs NY NL, 5-0;
June 30, 1962.

Bill Monbouquette, Bos at Chi AL, 1-0; Aug. 1, 1962.

Jack Kralick, Min vs KC AL, 1-0;
Aug. 26, 1962.

2 Sandy Koufax, LA vs SF NL, 8-0;
May 11, 1963.

Don Nottebart, Hou vs Phi NL, 4-1;
May 17, 1963.

Juan Marichal, SF vs Hou NL, 1-0;
June 15, 1963.

Ken T. Johnson, Hou vs Cin NL, 0-1;
April 23, 1964 (lost the game).

3 Sandy Koufax, LA at Phi NL, 3-0;
June 4, 1964.

2 Jim Bunning, Phi at NY NL, 6-0;
June 21, 1964 (1st game, perfect game).

Jim Maloney, Cin vs NY NL, 0-1;
June 14, 1965 (lost on two hits in 11 innings after pitching 10 hitless innings).

2 Jim Maloney, Cin at Chi NL, 1-0;
Aug. 19, 1965 (1st game, 10 innings).

4 Sandy Koufax, LA vs Chi NL, 1-0;
Sept. 9, 1965 (perfect game).

Dave Morehead, Bos vs Cle AL, 2-0;
Sept. 16, 1965.

Sonny Siebert, Cle vs Was AL, 2-0;
June 10, 1966.

Steve D. Barber (8.2 innings) and Stu Miller (.1 inning) Bal vs Det AL, 1-2; April 30, 1967 (1st game, lost the game)

Don Wilson, Hou vs Atl NL, 2-0; June 18, 1967.

Dean Chance, Min at Cle AL, 2-1; Aug. 25, 1967 (2nd game).

Joe Horlen, Chi vs Det AL, 6-0; Sept. 10, 1967 (1st game).

Tom Phoebus, Bal vs Bos AL, 6-0; April 27, 1968.

Catfish Hunter, Oak vs Min AL, 4-0; May 8, 1968 (perfect game).

George Culver, Cin at Phi NL, 6-1; July 29, 1968 (2nd game).

Gaylord Perry, SF vs StL NL, 1-0; Sept. 17, 1968.

Ray Washburn, StL at SF NL, 2-0; Sept. 18, 1968.

Bill Stoneman, Mon at Phi NL, 7-0; April 17, 1969.

3 Jim Maloney, Cin vs Hou NL, 10-0; April 30, 1969.

2 Don Wilson, Hou at Cin NL, 4-0; May 1, 1969.

Jim Palmer, Bal vs Oak AL, 8-0; Aug. 13, 1969.

Ken Holtzman, Chi vs Atl NL, 3-0; Aug. 19, 1969.

Bob Moose, Pit at NY NL, 4-0; Sept. 20, 1969.

Dock Ellis, Pit at SD NL, 2-0; June 12, 1970 (1st game).

Clyde Wright, Cal vs Oak AL, 4-0; July 3, 1970.

Bill Singer, LA vs Phi NL, 5-0; July 20, 1970.

Vida Blue, Oak vs Min AL, 6-0; Sept. 21, 1970.

2 Ken Holtzman, Chi at Cin NL, 1-0; June 3, 1971.

Rick Wise, Phi at Cin NL, 4-0; June 23, 1971.

Bob Gibson, StL at Pit NL, 11-0; Aug. 14, 1971.

Burt Hooton, Chi vs Phi NL, 4-0; April 16, 1972.

Milt Pappas, Chi vs SD NL, 8-0; Sept. 2, 1972.

2 Bill Stoneman, Mon vs NY NL, 7-0; Oct. 2, 1972 (1st game).

Steve Busby, KC at Det AL, 3-0; April 16, 1973.

Nolan Ryan, Cal at KC AL, 3-0; May 15, 1973.

2 Nolan Ryan, Cal at Det AL, 6-0; July 15, 1973.

Jim Bibby, Tex at Oak AL, 6-0; July 30, 1973.

Phil Niekro, Atl vs SD NL, 9-0; Aug. 5, 1973.

2 Steve Busby, KC at Mil AL, 2-0; June 19, 1974.

Dick Bosman, Cle vs Oak AL, 4-0; July 19, 1974.

3 Nolan Ryan, Cal vs Min AL, 4-0; Sept. 28, 1974.

4 Nolan Ryan, Cal vs Bal AL, 1-0; June 1, 1975.

Ed Halicki, SF vs NY NL, 6-0; Aug. 24, 1975 (2nd game).

Vida Blue (five innings), Glenn Abbott (one inning), Paul Lindblad (one inning) and Rollie Fingers (two innings), Oak vs Cal AL, 5-0; Sept. 28, 1975.

Larry Dierker, Hou vs Mon NL, 6-0; July 9, 1976.

Blue Moon Odom (five innings) and Francisco Barrios (four innings), Chi at Oak AL, 2-1; July 28, 1976.

John Candelaria, Pit vs LA NL, 2-0; Aug. 9, 1976.

John Montefusco, SF at Atl NL, 9-0; Sept. 29, 1976.

Jim Colborn, KC vs Tex AL, 6-0; May 14, 1977.

Dennis Eckersley, Cle vs Cal AL, 1-0; May 30, 1977.

Bert Blyleven, Tex at Cal AL, 6-0; Sept. 22, 1977.

Bob Forsch, StL vs Phi NL, 5-0; April 16, 1978.

Tom Seaver, Cin vs StL NL, 4-0; June 16, 1978.

Ken Forsch, Hou vs Atl NL, 6-0; April 7, 1979.

Jerry Reuss, LA at SF NL, 8-0; June 27, 1980.

Charlie Lea, Mon vs SF NL, 4-0; May 10, 1981 (2nd game).

Len Barker, Cle vs Tor AL, 3-0; May 15, 1981 (perfect game).

5 Nolan Ryan, Hou vs LA NL, 5-0; Sept. 26, 1981.

Dave Righetti, NY vs Bos AL, 4-0; July 4, 1983.

2 Bob Forsch, StL vs Mon NL, 3-0; Sept. 26, 1983.

Mike Warren, Oak vs Chi AL, 3-0; Sept. 29, 1983.

Jack Morris, Det at Chi AL, 4-0; April 7, 1984.

Mike Witt, Cal at Tex AL, 1-0; Sept. 30, 1984 (perfect game).

Joe Cowley, Chi at Cal AL, 7-1; Sept. 19, 1986.

Mike Scott, Hou vs SF NL, 2-0; Sept. 25, 1986.

Juan Nieves, Mil at Bal AL, 7-0; April 15, 1987.

Tom Browning, Cin vs LA NL, 1-0; Sept. 16, 1988 (perfect game).

MARK LANGSTON (seven innings) and Mike Witt (two innings), Cal vs Sea AL, 1-0; April 11, 1990.

RANDY JOHNSON, Sea vs Det AL, 2-0; June 2, 1990.

6 Nolan Ryan, Tex at Oak AL, 5-0; June 11, 1990.

Dave Stewart, Oak at Tor AL, 5-0; June 29, 1990.

Fernando Valenzuela, LA vs StL NL, 6-0; June 29, 1990.

Andy Hawkins, NY at Chi AL, 0-4; July 1, 1990 (eight innings, lost the game; bottom of 9th not played).

TERRY MULHOLLAND, Phi vs SF NL, 6-0; Aug. 15, 1990.

Dave Stieb, Tor at Cle AL, 3-0; Sept. 2, 1990.

7 Nolan Ryan, Tex vs Tor AL, 3-0; May 1, 1991.

Tommy Greene, Phi at Mon NL, 2-0; May 23, 1991.

Bob Milacki (six innings), Mike Flanagan (one inning), Mark Williamson, (one inning) and GREGG OLSON (one inning), Bal at Oak AL, 2-0; July 13, 1991.

MARK GARDNER, Mon at LA NL, 0-1; July 26, 1991 (nine innings, lost on two hits in 10th, relieved by JEFF FASSERO, who allowed one more hit).

Dennis Martinez, Mon at LA NL, 2-0; July 28, 1991 (perfect game).

WILSON ALVAREZ, Chi at Bal AL, 7-0; Aug. 11, 1991.

BRET SABERHAGEN, KC vs Chi AL, 7-0; Aug. 26, 1991.

KENT MERCKER (six innings), MARK WOHLERS (two innings) and Alejandro Pena (one inning), Atl at SD NL, 1-0; Sept. 11, 1991.

Matt Young, Bos at Cle AL, 1-2; April 12, 1992 (1st game) (eight innings, lost the game, bottom of 9th not played).

Kevin Gross, LA vs SF NL, 2-0; Aug. 17, 1992.

Chris Bosio, Sea vs Bos AL, 7-0; April 22, 1993.

JIM ABBOTT, NY vs Cle AL, 4-0; Sept. 4, 1993.

DARRYL KILE, Hou vs NY NL, 7-1; Sept. 8, 1993.

KENT MERCKER, Atl at LA NL, 6-0; April 8, 1994.

SCOTT ERICKSON, Min vs Mil AL, 6-0; April 27, 1994.

KENNY ROGERS, Tex vs Cal AL, 4-0; July 28, 1994 (perfect game).

PEDRO MARTINEZ (nine innings) and MEL ROJAS (one inning), Mon at SD NL, 1-0; June 3,1995 (Martinez pitched nine perfect innings, but allowed a hit in the 10th, Rojas relieved and finished the game)

RAMON MARTINEZ, LA vs Fla NL, 7-0; July 14, 1995.

AL LEITER, Fla vs Col NL, 11-0; May 11, 1996.

DWIGHT GOODEN, NY vs Sea AL, 2-0; May 14, 1996.

HIDEO NOMO, LA at Col NL, 9-0; Sept. 17, 1996.

KEVIN BROWN, Fla at SF NL, 9-0; June 10, 1997.

FRANCISCO CORDOVA (nine innings) and RICARDO RINCON (one inning), Pit vs Hou NL, 3-0; July 12, 1997.

DAVID WELLS, NY vs Min AL, 4-0; May 17, 1998 (perfect game)

DAVID CONE, NY AL vs Mon NL, 6-0; July 18, 1999 (perfect game)

JOSE JIMENEZ, StL at Ari NL, 1-0; June 25, 1999

ERIC MILTON, Min vs Ana AL, 7-0; Sept. 11, 1999

No-hit games, less than nine innings

Larry McKeon, six innings, rain, Ind at Cin AA, 0-0; May 6, 1884.

Charlie Gagus, eight innings, darkness, Was vs Wil UA, 12-1; Aug. 21, 1884.

Charlie Getzien, six innings, rain, Det vs Phi NL, 1-0; Oct. 1, 1884.

Charlie Sweeney (two innings) and Henry Boyle (three innings), five innings, rain, StL vs StP UA, 0-1; Oct. 5,1884.

Dupee Shaw, five innings, agreement, Pro at Buf NL, 4-0; Oct. 7, 1885 (1st game).

George Van Haltren, six innings, rain, Chi vs Pit NL, 1-0, June 21,1888.

Ed Crane, seven innings, darkness, NY vs Was NL, 3-0; Sept. 27, 1888.

Matt Kilroy, seven innings, darkness, Bal vs StL AA, 0-0; July 29, 1889 (2nd game).

George Nicol, seven innings, darkness, StL vs Phi AA, 21-2; Sept. 23, 1890.

Hank Gastright, eight innings, darkness, Col vs Tol AA, 6-0; Oct. 12, 1890.

Jack Stivetts, five innings, called so Boston could catch train to Cleveland for Temple Cub playoffs, Bos at Was NL, 6-0; Oct. 15, 1892 (2nd game).

Elton Chamberlain, seven innings, darkness, Cin vs Bos NL, 6-0; Sept. 23, 1893 (2nd game).

Ed Stein, six innings, rain, Bro vs Chi NL, 6-0; June 2, 1894.

Red Ames, five innings, darkness, NY at StL NL, 5-0; Sept. 14, 1903 (2nd game, first game in the major leagues).

Rube Waddell, five innings, rain, Phi vs StL AL, 2-0; Aug. 15, 1905.

Jake Weimer, seven innings, agreement, Cin vs Bro NL, 1-0; Aug. 24, 1906 (2nd game).

Jimmy Dygert (three innings) and Rube Waddell (two innings), five innings, rain, Phi vs Chi AL, 4-3; Aug. 29,

1906. (Waddell allowed hit and two runs in sixth, but rain caused game to revert to five innings).

Stoney McGlynn, seven innings, agreement, StL at Bro NL, 1-1; Sept. 24, 1906 (2nd game).

Lefty Leifield, six innings, darkness, Pit at Phi NL, 8-0; Sept. 26, 1906 (2nd game).

Ed Walsh, five innings, rain, Chi vs NY AL, 8-1; May 26, 1907.

Ed Karger, seven perfect innings, agreement, StL vs Bos NL, 4-0; Aug. 11, 1907 (2nd game).

Howie Camnitz, five innings, agreement, Pit at NY NL, 1-0; Aug. 23, 1907 (2nd game).

Rube Vickers, five perfect innings, darkness, Phi at Was AL, 4-0; Oct. 5, 1907 (2nd game).

Johnny Lush, six innings, rain, StL at Bro NL, 2-0; Aug. 6, 1908.

King Cole, seven innings, called so Chicago could catch train, Chi at StL NL, 4-0; July 31, 1910 (2nd game).

Jay Cashion, six innings, called so Cleveland could catch train, Was vs Cle AL, 2-0; Aug. 20, 1912 (2nd game).

Walter Johnson, seven innings, rain, Was vs StL AL, 2-0; Aug. 25, 1924.

Fred Frankhouse, 7.2 innings, rain, Bro vs Cin NL, 5-0; Aug. 27, 1937.

John Whitehead, six innings, rain, StL vs Det AL, 4-0; Aug. 5, 1940 (2nd game).

Jim Tobin, five innings, darkness, Bos vs Phi NL, 7-0; June 22, 1944 (2nd game).

Mike McCormick, five innings, rain, SF at Phi NL, 3-0; June 12, 1959 (allowed a hit in sixth, but rain caused game to revert to five innings)

Sam Jones, seven innings, rain, SF at StL NL, 4-0; Sept. 26, 1959.

Dean Chance, five perfect innings, rain, Min vs Bos AL, 2-0; Aug. 6, 1967.

David Palmer, five perfect innings, rain, Mon at StL NL, 4-0; April 21, 1984 (2nd game).

Pascual Perez, five innings, rain, Mon at Phi NL, 1-0; Sept. 24, 1988.

Melido Perez, six innings, rain, Chi at NY AL, 8-0; July 12, 1990.

Most Valuable Player

Batting Stats: Average, HR, RBI
Pitching Stats: Wins, Losses, ERA

American League

1911	Ty Cobb	of	Det
	.420	8	127
1912	Tris Speaker	of	Bos
	.383	10	90
1913	W. Johnson	P	Was
	36-7	1.14	
1914	Eddie Collins	2b	Phi
	.344	2	85
1922	George Sisler	1b	StL
	.420	8	105
1923	Babe Ruth	of	NY
	.393	41	131
1924	Walter Johnson		Was
	23-7	2.72	
1925	R. Peckinpaugh	ss	Was
	.294	4	64
1926	G. Burns	1b	Cle
	.358	4	114
1927	Lou Gehrig	1b	NY
	.373	47	175
1928	M. Cochrane	c	Phi
	.293	10	57
1931	Lefty Grove	P	Phi
	31-4	2.06	
1932	Jimmie Foxx	1b	Phi
	.364	58	169
1933	Jimmie Foxx	1b	Phi
	.356	48	163
1934	M. Cochrane	c	Det
	.320	2	76
1935	H. Greenberg	1b	Det
	.328	36	170
1936	Lou Gehrig	1b	NY
	.354	49	152
1937	C. Gehringer	2b	Det
	.371	14	96
1938	Jimmie Foxx	1b	Bos
	.349	50	175
1939	J. DiMaggio	of	NY
	.381	30	126
1940	H. Greenberg	of	Det
	.340	41	150
1941	J. DiMaggio	of	NY
	.357	30	125
1942	Joe Gordon	2b	NY
	.322	18	103
1943	S. Chandler	P	NY
	20-4	1.64	
1944	H. Newhouser	P	Det
	29-9	2.22	
1945	H. Newhouser	P	Det
	25-9	1.81	
1946	Ted Williams	of	Bos
	.342	38	123
1947	J. DiMaggio	of	NY
	.315	20	97
1948	L. Boudreau	ss	Cle
	.355	18	106

Year	Player	Pos	Team	Stats
1949	Ted Williams	of	Bos	.343 43 159
1950	Phil Rizzuto	ss	NY	.324 7 66
1951	Yogi Berra	c	NY	.294 27 88
1952	B. Shantz	P	Phi	24-7 2.48
1953	Al Rosen	3b	Cle	.336 43 145
1954	Yogi Berra	c	NY	.307 22 125
1955	Yogi Berra	c	NY	.272 27 108
1956	M. Mantle	of	NY	.353 52 130
1957	M. Mantle	of	NY	.365 34 94
1958	J. Jensen	of	Bos	.286 35 122
1959	Nellie Fox	2b	Chi	.306 2 70
1960	Roger Maris	of	NY	.283 39 112
1961	Roger Maris	of	NY	.269 61 142
1962	M. Mantle	of	NY	.321 30 89
1963	E. Howard	c	NY	.287 28 85
1964	B. Robinson	3b	Bal	.317 28 118
1965	Z. Versalles	ss	Min	.273 19 77
1966	F. Robinson	of	Bal	.316 49 122
1967	C. Yastrzemski	of	Bos	.326 44 121
1968	D. McLain	P	Det	31-6 1.96
1969	H. Killebrew	3b	Min	.276 49 140
1970	Boog Powell	1b	Bal	.297 35 114
1971	Vida Blue	P	Oak	24-8 1.82
1972	Dick Allen	1b	Chi	.308 37 113
1973	R. Jackson	of	Oak	.293 32 117
1974	J. Burroughs	of	Tex	.301 25 118
1975	Fred Lynn	of	Bos	.331 21 105
1976	T. Munson	c	NY	.302 17 105
1977	Rod Carew	1b	Min	.388 14 100
1978	Jim Rice	of	Bos	.315 46 139
1979	Don Baylor	of	Cal	.296 36 139
1980	George Brett	3b	KC	.390 24 118
1981	Rollie Fingers	P	Mil	6-3 1.04
1982	Robin Yount	ss	Mil	.331 29 114
1983	Cal Ripken	ss	Bal	.318 27 102
1984	W. Hernandez	P	Det	9-3 1.92
1985	Don Mattingly	1b	NY	.324 35 145
1986	R. Clemens	P	Bos	24-4 2.48
1987	George Bell	of	Tor	.308 47 134
1988	J. Canseco	of	Oak	.307 42 124
1989	Robin Yount	of	Mil	.318 21 103
1990	R. Henderson	of	Oak	.325 28 61
1991	Cal Ripken	ss	Bal	.323 34 114
1992	D. Eckersley	P	Oak	7-1 1.91
1993	F. Thomas	1b	Chi	.317 41 128
1994	F. Thomas	1b	Chi	.353 38 101
1995	Mo Vaughn	1b	Bos	.300 39 126
1996	J. Gonzalez	of	Tex	.314 47 144
1997	Ken Griffey	of	Sea	.304 56 147
1998	J. Gonzalez	of	Tex	.318 45 157
1999	I. Rodriquez	c	Tex	.332 35 113

National League

Year	Player	Pos	Team	Stats
1911	F. Schulte	of	Chi	.300 21 107
1912	Larry Doyle	2b	NY	.330 10 90
1913	Jake Daubert	1b	Bro	.350 2 52
1914	Johnny Evers	2b	Bos	.279 1 40
1924	Dazzy Vance	P	Bro	28-6 2.16
1925	R. Hornsby	2b	StL	.403 39 143
1926	Bob O'Farrell	c	StL	.293 7 68
1927	Paul Waner	of	Pit	.380 9 131
1928	J. Bottomley	1b	StL	.325 31 136
1929	R. Hornsby	2b	Chi	.380 39 149
1931	F. Frisch	2b	StL	.311 4 82
1932	Chuck Klein	of	Phi	.348 38 137
1933	Carl Hubbell	P	NY	23-12 1.66
1934	Dizzy Dean	P	StL	30-7 2.66
1935	G. Hartnett	c	Chi	.344 13 91
1936	Carl Hubbell	P	NY	26-6 2.31
1937	Joe Medwick	of	StL	.374 31 154
1938	E. Lombardi	c	Cin	.342 19 95
1939	B. Walters	P	Cin	27-11 2.29
1940	F. McCormick	1b	Cin	.309 19 127
1941	Dolph Camilli	1b	Bro	.285 34 120
1942	Mort Cooper	P	StL	22-7 1.78
1943	Stan Musial	of	StL	.357 13 81
1944	Marty Marion	ss	StL	.267 6 63
1945	P. Cavarretta	1b	Chi	.355 6 97
1946	Stan Musial	1b	StL	.365 16 103
1947	Bob Elliott	3b	Bos	.317 22 113
1948	Stan Musial	of	StL	.376 39 131
1949	J. Robinson	2b	Bro	.342 16 124
1950	J. Konstanty	P	Phi	16-7 2.66
1951	R. Campanella	c	Bro	.325 33 108
1952	Hank Sauer	of	Chi	.270 37 121
1953	R. Campanella	c	Bro	.312 41 142
1954	Willie Mays	of	NY	.345 41 110
1955	R. Cmpanella	c	Bro	.318 32 107
1956	D. Newcombe	P	Bro	27-7 3.06
1957	Hank Aaron	of	Mil	.322 44 132
1958	Ernie Banks	ss	Chi	.313 47 129
1959	Ernie Banks	ss	Chi	.304 45 143
1960	Dick Groat	ss	Pit	.325 2 50
1961	F. Robinson	of	Cin	.323 37 124
1962	Maury Wills	ss	LA	.299 6 48
1963	S. Koufax	P	LA	25-5 1.88
1964	Ken Boyer	3b	StL	.295 24 119
1965	Willie Mays	of	SF	.317 52 112
1966	R. Clemente	of	Pit	.317 29 119
1967	O. Cepeda	1b	StL	.325 25 111

Year	Player	Pos	Team	AVG	HR	RBI
1968	Bob Gibson	P	StL	22-9	1.12	
1969	W. McCovey	1b	SF	.320	45	126
1970	J. Bench	c	Cin	.293	45	148
1971	Joe Torre	3b	StL	.363	24	137
1972	J. Bench	c	Cin	.270	40	125
1973	Pete Rose	of	Cin	.338	5	64
1974	Steve Garvey	1b	LA	.312	21	111
1975	Joe Morgan	2b	Cin	.327	17	94
1976	Joe Morgan	2b	Cin	.320	27	111
1977	G. Foster	of	Cin	.320	52	149
1978	Dave Parker	of	Pit	.334	30	117
1979	K. Hernandez	1b	St.L	.344	11	105
1979	Willie Stargell	1b	Pit	.281	32	82
1980	Mike Schmidt	3b	Phi	.286	48	121
1981	Mike Schmidt	3b	Phi	.316	31	91
1982	Dale Murphy	of	Atl	.281	36	109
1983	Dale Murphy	of	Atl	.302	36	121
1984	R. Sandberg	2b	Chi	.314	19	84
1985	Willie McGee	of	StL	.353	10	82
1986	Mike Schmidt	3b	Phi	.290	37	119
1987	A. Dawson	of	Chi	.287	49	137
1988	Kirk Gibson	of	LA	.290	25	76
1989	K. Mitchell	of	SF	.291	47	125
1990	Barry Bonds	of	Pit	.301	33	114
1991	T. Pendleton	3b	Atl	.319	22	86
1992	Barry Bonds	of	Pit	.311	34	103
1993	Barry Bonds	of	SF	.336	46	123
1994	Jeff Bagwell	1b	Hou	.368	39	116
1995	Barry Larkin	ss	Cin	.319	15	66
1996	Ken Caminiti	3b	SD	.326	40	130
1997	Larry Walker	of	Col	.366	49	130
1998	Sammy Sosa	of	Chi	.308	66	158
1999	C. Jones	3B	Atl	.319	45	110

Cy Young Award Winner

American League

Year	Player	Team	W-L	ERA
1958	Bob Turley	NY	21-7	2.97
1959	Early Wynn	Chi	22-10	3.17
1961	Whitey Ford	NY	25-4	3.21
1964	Dean Chance	LA	20-9	1.65
1967	Jim Lonborg	Bos	22-9	3.16
1968	Denny McLain	Det	31-6	1.96
1969	Mike Cuellar	Bal	23-11	2.38
1969	Denny McLain	Det	24-9	2.80
1970	Jim Perry	Min	24-12	3.04
1971	Vida Blue	Oak	24-8	1.82
1972	Gaylord Perry	Cle	24-16	1.92
1973	Jim Palmer	Bal	22-9	2.40
1974	Catfish Hunter	Oak	25-12	2.49
1975	Jim Palmer	Bal	23-11	2.09
1976	Jim Palmer	Bal	22-13	2.51
1977	Sparky Lyle	NY	13-5	2.17
1978	Ron Guidry	NY	25-3	1.74
1979	Mike Flanagan	Bal	23-9	3.08
1980	Steve Stone	Bal	25-7	3.23
1981	Rollie Fingers	Mil	6-3	1.04
1982	Pete Vuckovich	Mil	18-6	3.34
1983	LaMarr Hoyt	Chi	24-10	3.66
1984	W. Hernandez	Det	9-3	1.92
1985	B. Saberhagen	KC	20-6	2.87
1986	Roger Clemens	Bos	24-4	2.48
1987	Roger Clemens	Bos	20-9	2.97
1988	Frank Viola	Min	24-7	2.64
1989	B. Saberhagen	KC	23-6	2.16
1990	Bob Welch	Oak	27-6	2.95
1991	Roger Clemens	Bos	18-10	2.62
1992	D. Eckersley	Oak	7-1	1.91
1993	Jack McDowell	Chi	22-10	3.37
1994	David Cone	KC	16-5	2.94
1995	Randy Johnson	Sea	18-2	2.48
1996	Pat Hentgen	Tor	20-10	3.22
1997	Roger Clemens	Tor	21-7	2.05
1998	Roger Clemens	Tor	20-6	2.65
1999	Pedro Martinez	Bos	23-4	2.07

National League

Year	Player	Team	W-L	ERA
1956	D. Newcombe	Bro	27-7	3.06
1957	Warren Spahn	Mil	21-11	2.69
1960	Vern Law	Pit	20-9	3.08
1962	Don Drysdale	LA	25-9	2.83
1963	Sandy Koufax	LA	25-5	1.88
1965	Sandy Koufax	LA	26-8	2.04
1966	Sandy Koufax	LA	27-9	1.73
1967	M. McCormick	SF	22-10	2.85
1968	Bob Gibson	StL	22-9	1.12
1969	Tom Seaver	NY	25-7	2.21
1970	Bob Gibson	StL	23-7	3.12
1971	Fergie Jenkins	Chi	24-13	2.77
1972	Steve Carlton	Phi	27-10	1.97
1973	Tom Seaver	NY	19-10	2.08
1974	Mike Marshall	LA	15-12	2.42
1975	Tom Seaver	NY	22-9	2.38
1976	Randy Jones	SD	22-14	2.74
1977	Steve Carlton	Phi	23-10	2.64
1978	Gaylord Perry	SD	21-6	2.73
1979	Bruce Sutter	Chi	6-6	2.22
1980	Steve Carlton	Phi	24-9	2.34
1981	F. Valenzuela	LA	13-7	2.48
1982	Steve Carlton	Phi	23-11	3.10
1983	John Denny	Phi	19-6	2.37
1984	Rick Sutcliffe	Chi	16-1	2.69

1985	D. Gooden	NY
	24-4	1.53
1986	Mike Scott	Hou
	18-10	2.22
1987	S. Bedrosian	Phi
	5-3	2.83
1988	Orel Hershiser	LA
	23-8	2.26
1989	Mark Davis	SD
	4-3	1.85
1990	Doug Drabek	Pit
	22-6	2.76
1991	Tom Glavine	Atl
	20-11	2.55
1992	Greg Maddux	Chi
	20-11	2.18
1993	Greg Maddux	Atl
	20-10	2.36
1994	Greg Maddux	Atl
	16-6	1.56
1995	Greg Maddux	Atl
	19-2	1.63
1996	John Smoltz	Atl
	24-8	2.94
1997	Pedro Martinez	Mon
	17-8	1.90
1998	Tom Glavine	Atl
	20-6	2.47
1999	Randy Johnson	Ari
	17-9	2.48

Rookie of the Year

American League

1949	Roy Sievers	of	StL
	.306	16	91
1950	Walt Dropo	1b	Bos
	.322	34	144
1951	G. McDougald	3b	NY
	.306	14	63
1952	Harry Byrd	P	Phi
	15-15	3.31	
1953	H. Kuenn	ss	Det
	.308	2	48
1954	Bob Grim	P	NY
	20-6	3.26	
1955	Herb Score	P	Cle
	16-10	2.85	
1956	Luis Aparicio	ss	Chi
	.266	3	56
1957	Tony Kubek	of	NY
	.297	3	39
1958	A. Pearson	of	Was
	.275	3	33
1959	Bob Allison	of	Was
	.261	30	85
1960	Ron Hansen	ss	Bal
	.255	22	86
1961	Don Schwall	P	Bos
	15-7	3.22	
1962	Tom Tresh	ss	NY
	.286	20	93
1963	Gary Peters	P	Chi
	19-8	2.33	

1964	Tony Oliva	of	Min
	.323	32	94
1965	Curt Blefary	of	Bal
	.260	22	70
1966	Tommie Agee	of	Chi
	.273	22	86
1967	Rod Carew	2b	Min
	.292	8	51
1968	Stan Bahnsen	P	NY
	17-12	2.05	
1969	Lou Piniella	of	KC
	.282	11	68
1970	T. Munson	c	NY
	.302	6	53
1971	C. Chambliss	1b	Cle
	.275	9	48
1972	Carlton Fisk	c	Bos
	.293	22	61
1973	Al Bumbry	of	Bal
	.337	7	34
1974	Mike Hargrove	1b	Tex
	.323	4	66
1975	Fred Lynn	of	Bos
	.331	21	105
1976	Mark Fidrych	P	Det
	19-9	2.34	
1977	Eddie Murray	dh	Bal
	.283	27	88
1978	Lou Whitaker	2b	Det
	.285	3	58
1979	John Castino	3b	Min
	.285	5	52
1979	A. Griffin	3b	Tor
	.287	2	31
1980	J.Chrboneau	of	Cle
	.289	23	87
1981	Dave Righetti	P	NY
	8-4	2.05	
1982	Cal Ripken	ss	Bal
	.264	28	93
1983	Ron Kittle	of	Chi
	.254	35	100
1984	Alvin Davis	1b	Sea
	.284	27	116
1985	Ozzie Guillen	ss	Chi
	.273	1	33
1986	J. Canseco	of	Oak
	.240	33	117
1987	M. McGwire	1b	Oak
	.289	49	118
1988	Walt Weiss	ss	Oak
	.250	3	39
1989	Gregg Olson	P	Bal
	5-2	1.69	
1990	S. Alomar	c	Cle
	.290	9	66
1991	C. Knoblauch	2b	Min
	.281	1	50
1992	Pat Listach	ss	Mil
	.290	1	47
1993	Tim Salmon	of	Cal
	.283	31	95
1994	Bob Hamelin	dh	KC
	.282	24	65
1995	M. Cordova	of	Min
	.277	24	84

1996	Derek Jeter	ss	NY
	.314	10	78
1997	N.Garciaparra	ss	Bos
	.306	30	98
1998	Ben Grieve	of	Oak
	.288	18	89
1999	C. Beltran	of	KC
	.293	22	108

National League

1947	J.Robinson	1b	Bro
	.297	12	48
1948	Alvin Dark	ss	Bos
	.322	3	48
1949	D.Newcombe	P	Bro
	17-8	3.17	
1950	Sam Jethroe	of	Bos
	.273	18	58
1951	Willie Mays	of	NY
	.274	20	68
1952	Joe Black	P	Bro
	15-4	2.15	
1953	Jim Gilliam	2b	Bro
	.278	6	63
1954	Wally Moon	of	StL
	.304	12	76
1955	Bill Virdon	of	StL
	.281	17	68
1956	F. Robinson	of	Cin
	.290	38	83
1957	Jack Sanford	P	Phi
	19-8	3.08	
1958	O. Cepeda	1b	SF
	.312	25	96
1959	W. McCovey	1b	SF
	.354	13	38
1960	F. Howard	of	LA
	.268	23	77
1961	Billy Williams	of	Chi
	.278	25	86
1962	Ken Hubbs	2b	Chi
	.260	5	49
1963	Pete Rose	2b	Cin
	.273	6	41
1964	Dick Allen	3b	Phi
	.318	29	91
1965	Jim Lefebvre	2b	LA
	.250	12	69
1966	T. Helms	3b	Cin
	.284	9	49
1967	Tom Seaver	P	NY
	16-13	2.76	
1968	J. Bench	c	Cin
	.275	15	82
1969	Ted Sizemore	2b	LA
	.271	4	46
1970	Carl Morton	P	Mon
	18-11	3.60	
1971	Earl Williams	c	Atl
	.260	33	87
1972	Jon Matlack	P	NY
	15-10	2.32	
1973	G. Matthews	of	SF
	.300	12	58
1974	B. McBride	of	StL
	.309	6	56

1975	J.Montefusco P	SF
	15-9 2.88	
1976	B. Metzger P	SD
	11-4 2.92	
1977	A Dawson of	Mon
	.282 19 65	
1978	Bob Horner 3b	Atl
	.266 23 63	
1979	Rick Sutcliffe P	LA
	17-10 3.46	
1980	Steve Howe P	LA
	7-9 2.66	
1981	F. Valenzuela P	LA
	13-7 2.48	
1982	Steve Sax 2b	LA
	.282 4 47	
1983	D. Strawberry of	NY
	.257 26 74	
1984	D. Gooden P	NY
	17-9 2.60	
1985	V. Coleman of	StL
	.267 1 40	
1986	Todd Worrell P	StL
	9-10 2.08	
1987	B. Santiago c	SD
	.300 18 79	
1988	Chris Sabo 3b	Cin
	.271 11 44	
1989	J. Walton of	Chi
	.293 5 46	
1990	David Justice of	Atl
	.282 28 78	
1991	Jeff Bagwell 1b	Hou
	.294 15 82	
1992	Eric Karros 1b	LA
	.257 20 88	
1993	Mike Piazza c	LA
	.318 35 112	
1994	Raul Mondesi of	LA
	.306 16 56	
1995	Hideo Nomo P	LA
	13-6 2.54	
1996	T.Hllndswrth of	LA
	.291 12 59	
1997	Scott Rolen 3b	Phi
	.283 21 92	
1998	Kerry Wood P	Chi
	13-6 3.40	
1999	S. Williamson of	Cin
	12-7 2.41	

Manager of the Year

American League

1983	Tony La Russa	Chi
	99-63 1st W	
1984	S. Anderson	Det
	104-58 1st E	
1985	Bobby Cox	Tor
	99-62 1st E	
1986	J. McNamara	Bos
	95-66 1st E	
1987	S. Anderson	Det
	98-64 1st E	
1988	Tony La Russa	Oak
	104-58 1st W	
1989	Frank Robinson	Bal
	87-75 2nd E	
1990	Jeff Torborg	Chi
	94-68 2nd W	
1991	Tom Kelly	Min
	95-67 1st W	
1992	Tony La Russa	Oak
	96-66 1st W	
1993	Gene Lamont	Chi
	94-68 1st W	
1994	Buck Showalter	NY
	70-43 1st E	
1995	Lou Piniella	Sea
	79-66 1st W	
1996	Johnny Oates	Tex
	90-72 1st W	
1997	Davey Johnson	Bal
	98-64 1st E	
1998	Joe Torre	NY
	114-48 1st E	
1999	Jimy Williams	Bos
	91-67 2nd E	

National League

1983	Tom Lasorda	LA
	91-71 1st W	
1984	Jim Frey	Chi
	96-65 1st E	
1985	Whitey Herzog	StL
	101-61 1st E	
1986	Hal Lanier	Hou
	96-66 1st W	
1987	Buck Rodgers	Mon
	91-71 3rd E	
1988	Tom Lasorda	LA
	94-67 1st W	
1989	Don Zimmer	Chi
	93-69 1st E	
1990	Jim Leyland	Pit
	95-67 1st E	
1991	Bobby Cox	Atl
	94-68 1st W	
1992	Jim Leyland	Pit
	96-66 1st E	
1993	Dusty Baker	SF
	103-59 2nd W	
1994	Felipe Alou	Mon
	74-40 1st E	
1995	Don Baylor	Col
	77-67 2nd W	
1996	Bruce Bochy	SD
	91-71 1st W	
1997	Dusty Baker	SF
	90-72 1st W	
1998	Larry Dierker	Hou
	102-60 1st C	
1999	Jack McKeon	Cin
	96-66 2nd C	

Hall of Fame

The following abbreviations in parentheses designate the special committee that elected the inductee:
O-Old Timers
C-Centennial Commission
V-Veterans
N-Negro Leagues
S-Special election

1936

Ty Cobb	1905-1928
Outfield	
Walter Johnson	1907-1927
Pitcher	
Christy Mathewson	1900-1916
Pitcher	
Babe Ruth	1914-1935
Outfield	
Honus Wagner	1897-1917
Shortstop	

1937

Morgan Bulkeley (C)	1876-1876
Executive Ban Johnson (C)	
	1901-1927
Executive	
Nap Lajoie	1896-1916
Second base	
Connie Mack (C)	1894-1950
Manager	
John McGraw (C)	1891-1906
Manager	
Tris Speaker	1907-1928
Outfield	
George Wright (C)	1871-1882
Manager	
Cy Young	1890-1911
Pitcher	

1938

Grover C. Alexander	1911-1930
Pitcher	
Alexander Cartwright (C)	1845-1848
Executive	
Henry Chadwick (C)	1858-1908
Writer-statistician	

1939

Cap Anson (O)	1871-1897
First base	
Eddie Collins	1906-1930
Second base	
Charlie Comiskey (O)	1882-1894
Manager	
Candy Cummings (O)	1872-1877
Pitcher	
Buck Ewing (O)	1880-1897
Catcher	
Lou Gehrig (S)	1923-1939
First base	
Willie Keeler	1892-1910
Outfield	
Charley Radbourn (O)	1880-1891
Pitcher	

George Sisler 1915-1930
First base
Al Spalding (O) 1871-1878
Pitcher

1942
Rogers Hornsby 1915-1937
Second base

1944
Kenesaw M. Landis (O) 1920-1944
Commissioner

1945
Roger Bresnahan (O) 1897-1915
Catcher
Dan Brouthers (O) 1879-1904
First base
Fred Clarke (O) 1894-1915
Outfield
Jimmy Collins (O) 1895-1908
Third base
Ed Delahanty (O) 1888-1903
Outfield
Hugh Duffy (O) 1888-1906
Outfield
Hughie Jennings (O) 1891-1918
Shortstop
King Kelly (O) 1878-1893
Catcher
Jim O'Rourke (O) 1872-1904
Outfield
Wilbert Robinson (O) 1886-1902
Manager

1946
Jesse Burkett (O) 1890-1905
Outfield
Frank Chance (O) 1898-1914
First base
Jack Chesbro (O) 1899-1909
Pitcher
Johnny Evers (O) 1902-1929
Second base
Clark Griffith (O) 1891-1907
Manager
Tommy McCarthy (O) 1884-1896
Outfield
Joe McGinnity (O) 1899-1908
Pitcher
Eddie Plank (O) 1901-1917
Pitcher
Joe Tinker (O) 1902-1916
Shortstop
Rube Waddell (O) 1897-1910
Pitcher
Ed Walsh (O) 1904-1917
Pitcher

1947
Mickey Cochrane 1925-1937
Catcher
Frankie Frisch 1919-1937
Second base
Lefty Grove 1925-1941
Pitcher
Carl Hubbell 1928-1943
Pitcher

1948
Herb Pennock 1912-1934
Pitcher
Pie Traynor 1920-1937
Third base

1949
Mordecai Brown (O) 1903-1916
Pitcher
Charlie Gehringer 1924-1942
Second base
Kid Nichols (O) 1890-1906
Pitcher

1951
Jimmie Foxx 1925-1945
First base
Mel Ott 1926-1947
Outfield

1952
Harry Heilmann 1914-1932
Outfield
Paul Waner 1926-1945
Outfield

1953
Ed Barrow (V) 1903-1947
Manager
Chief Bender (V) 1903-1925
Pitcher
Tommy Connolly (V) 1898-1931
Umpire
Dizzy Dean 1930-1947
Pitcher
Bill Klem (V) 1905-1941
Umpire
Al Simmons 1924-1944
Outfield
Bobby Wallace (V) 1894-1918
Shortstop
Harry Wright (V) 1871-1893
Manager

1954
Bill Dickey 1928-1946
Catcher
Rabbit Maranville 1912-1935
Shortstop-Second base
Bill Terry 1923-1936
First base

1955
Frank Baker (V) 1908-1922
Third base
Joe DiMaggio 1936-1951
Outfield
Gabby Hartnett 1922-1941
Catcher
Ted Lyons 1923-1946
Pitcher
Ray Schalk (V) 1912-1929
Catcher
Dazzy Vance 1915-1935
Pitcher

1956
Joe Cronin 1926-1945
Shortstop
Hank Greenberg 1930-1947
First base

1957
Sam Crawford (V) 1899-1917
Outfield
Joe McCarthy (V) 1926-1950
Manager

1959
Zack Wheat (V) 1909-1927
Outfield

1961
Max Carey (V) 1910-1929
Outfield
Billy Hamilton (V) 1888-1901
Outfield

1962
Bob Feller 1936-1956
Pitcher
Bill McKechnie (V) 1922-1946
Manager
Jackie Robinson 1947-1956
Second base
Edd Roush (V) 1913-1931
Outfield

1963
John Clarkson (V) 1882-1894
Pitcher
Elmer Flick (V) 1898-1910
Outfield
Sam Rice (V) 1915-1934
Outfield
Eppa Rixey (V) 1912-1933
Pitcher

1964
Luke Appling 1930-1950
Shortstop
Red Faber (V) 1914-1933
Pitcher
Burleigh Grimes (V) 1916-1934
Pitcher
Miller Huggins (V) 1913-1929
Manager
Tim Keefe (V) 1880-1893
Pitcher
Heinie Manush (V) 1923-1939
Outfield
John Ward (V) 1878-1894
Pitcher

1965
Jim Galvin (V) 1875-1892
Pitcher

1966
Casey Stengel (V) 1934-1965
Manager
Ted Williams 1939-1960
Outfield

1967

Branch Rickey (V) 1913-1965
Manager
Red Ruffing 1924-1947
Pitcher
Lloyd Waner (V) 1927-1945
Outfield

1968

Kiki Cuyler (V) 1921-1938
Outfield
Goose Goslin (V) 1921-1938
Outfield
Joe Medwick 1932-1948
Outfield

1969

Roy Campanella 1948-1957
Catcher
Stan Coveleski (V) 1912-1928
Pitcher
Waite Hoyt (V) 1918-1938
Pitcher
Stan Musial 1941-1963
Outfield-First base

1970

Lou Boudreau 1938-1952
Shortstop
Earle Combs (V) 1924-1935
Outfield
Ford Frick (V) 1934-1965
Commissioner
Jesse Haines (V) 1918-1937
Pitcher

1971

Dave Bancroft (V) 1915-1930
Shortstop
Jake Beckley (V) 1888-1907
First base
Chick Hafey (V) 1924-1937
Outfield
Harry Hooper (V) 1909-1925
Outfield
Joe Kelley (V) 1891-1908
Outfield
Rube Marquard (V) 1908-1925
Pitcher
Satchel Paige (N) 1926-1953
Pitcher
George Weiss (V) 1932-1971
Executive

1972

Yogi Berra 1946-1965
Catcher
Josh Gibson (N) 1930-1946
Catcher
Lefty Gomez (V) 1930-1943
Pitcher
Will Harridge (V) 1931-1959
Executive
Sandy Koufax 1955-1966
Pitcher
Buck Leonard (N) 1933-1950
First base

Early Wynn 1939-1963
Pitcher
Ross Youngs (V) 1917-1926
Outfield

1973

Roberto Clemente (S) 1955-1972
Outfield
Billy Evans (V) 1906-1927
Umpire
Monte Irvin (N) 1938-1956
Outfield
George Kelly (V) 1915-1932
First base
Warren Spahn 1942-1965
Pitcher
Mickey Welch (V) 1880-1892
Pitcher

1974

Cool Papa Bell (N) 1922-1946
Outfield
Jim Bottomley (V) 1922-1937
First base
Jocko Conlan (V) 1941-1964
Umpire
Whitey Ford 1950-1967
Pitcher
Mickey Mantle 1951-1968
Outfield
Sam Thompson (V) 1885-1906
Outfield

1975

Earl Averill (V) 1929-1941
Outfield
Bucky Harris (V) 1924-1956
Manager
Billy Herman (V) 1931-1947
Second base
Judy Johnson (N) 1921-1938
Third base
Ralph Kiner 1946-1955
Outfield

1976

Oscar Charleston (N) 1915-1940
Outfield
Roger Connor (V) 1880-1897
First base
Cal Hubbard (V) 1936-1951
Umpire
Bob Lemon 1941-1958
Pitcher
Freddie Lindstrom (V) 1924-1936
Third base
Robin Roberts 1948-1966
Pitcher

1977

Ernie Banks 1953-1971
Shortstop-First base
Martin Dihigo (N) 1923-1945
Pitcher
John Henry Lloyd (N) 1905-1931
Shortstop-First base
Al Lopez (V) 1928-1947
Manager

Amos Rusie (V) 1889-1901
Pitcher
Joe Sewell (V) 1920-1933
Shortstop

1978

Addie Joss (V) 1902-1910
Pitcher
Larry MacPhail (V) 1934-1947
Executive
Eddie Mathews 1952-1968
Third base

1979

Warren Giles (V) 1946-1969
Executive
Willie Mays 1951-1973
Outfield
Hack Wilson (V) 1923-1934
Outfield

1980

Al Kaline 1953-1974
Outfield
Chuck Klein (V) 1928-1944
Outfield
Duke Snider 1947-1964
Outfield
Tom Yawkey (V) 1933-1976
Executive

1981

Rube Foster (V) 1902-1926
Manager
Bob Gibson 1959-1975
Pitcher
Johnny Mize (V) 1936-1953
First base

1982

Hank Aaron 1954-1976
Outfield
Happy Chandler (V) 1945-1951
Commissioner
Travis Jackson (V) 1922-1936
Shortstop
Frank Robinson 1956-1976
Outfield

1983

Walter Alston (V) 1954-1976
Manager
George Kell (V) 1943-1957
Third base
Juan Marichal 1960-1975
Pitcher
Brooks Robinson 1955-1977
Third base

1984

Luis Aparicio 1956-1973
Shortstop
Don Drysdale 1956-1969
Pitcher
Rick Ferrell (V) 1929-1947
Catcher
Harmon Killebrew 1954-1975
First base-Third base

Pee Wee Reese (V) 1940-1958
Shortstop

1985
Lou Brock 1961-1979
Outfield
Enos Slaughter (V) 1938-1959
Outfield
Arky Vaughan (V) 1932-1948
Shortstop
Hoyt Wilhelm 1952-1972
Pitcher

1986
Bobby Doerr (V) 1937-1951
Second base
Ernie Lombardi (V) 1931-1947
Catcher
Willie McCovey 1959-1980
First base

1987
Ray Dandridge (V) 1933-1949
Third base
Catfish Hunter 1965-1979
Pitcher
Billy Williams 1959-1976
Outfield

1988
Willie Stargell 1962-1982
Outfield-First base
1989
Al Barlick (V) 1940-1971
Umpire
Johnny Bench 1967-1983
Catcher
Red Schoendienst (V) 1945-1963
Second base
Carl Yastrzemski 1961-1983
Outfield

1990
Joe Morgan 1963-1984
Second base
Jim Palmer 1965-1984
Pitcher

1991
Rod Carew 1967-1985
First base-Second base
Fergie Jenkins 1965-1983
Pitcher
Tony Lazzeri (V) 1926-1939
Second base
Gaylord Perry 1962-1983
Pitcher
Bill Veeck (V) 1933-1980
Executive

1992
Rollie Fingers 1968-1985
Pitcher
Bill McGowan (V) 1925-1954
Umpire
Hal Newhouser (V) 1939-1955
Pitcher
Tom Seaver 1967-1986
Pitcher

1993
Reggie Jackson 1967-1987
Outfield

1994
Steve Carlton 1965-1988
Pitcher
Leo Durocher (V) 1939-1973
Manager
Phil Rizzuto (V) 1941-1956
Shortstop

1995
Richie Ashburn (V) 1948-1962
Outfield
Leon Day (V) 1934-1950
Pitcher
William Hulbert (V) 1877-1882
Executive
Mike Schmidt 1972-1989
Third base
Vic Willis (V) 1898-1910
Pitcher

1996
Jim Bunning (V) 1955-1971
Pitcher
Bill Foster (V) 1923-1937
Pitcher
Ned Hanlon (V) 1889-1907
Manager
Earl Weaver (V) 1968-1986
Manager

1997
Nellie Fox (V) 1947-1965
Second base
Tom Lasorda (V) 1976-1996
Manager
Phil Niekro 1964-1987
Pitcher
Willie Wells (V) 1924-1948
Shortstop

1998
George Davis (V) 1890-1909
Shortstop
Larry Doby (V) 1947-1959
Outfield
Lee MacPhail (V) 1941-1985
Executive
Bullet Joe Rogan (V) 1920-1938
Outfield-Pitcher
Don Sutton 1966-1988
Pitcher

1999
George Brett 1973-1993
Third base

Orlando Cepeda (V) 1958-1974
First base

Nestor Chylak (V) 1954-1978
Umpire

Nolan Ryan 1966-1993
Pitcher

Frank Selee (V) 1890-1905
Manager

Joe Williams (N, V) 1910-1932
Pitcher

Robin Yount 1974-1993
Shortstop-Outfield

World Series

1903	BOS (AL) over PIT (NL)	5-3
1905	NY (NL) over PHI (AL)	4-1
1906	CHI (AL) over CHI (NL)	4-2
1907	CHI (NL) over DET (AL) (one tie game)	4-0
1908	CHI (NL) over DET (AL)	4-1
1909	PIT (NL) over DET (AL)	4-3
1910	PHI (AL) over CHI (NL)	4-1
1911	PHI (AL) over NY (NL)	4-2
1912	BOS (AL) over NY (NL) (one tie game)	4-3
1913	PHI (AL) over NY (NL)	4-1
1914	BOS (NL) over PHI (AL)	4-0
1915	BOS (AL) over PHI (NL)	4-1
1916	BOS (AL) over BRO (NL)	4-1
1917	CHI (AL) over NY (NL)	4-2
1918	BOS (AL) over CHI (NL)	4-2
1919	CIN (NL) over CHI (AL)	5-3
1920	CLE (AL) over BRO (NL)	5-2
1921	NY (NL) over NY (AL)	5-3
1922	NY (NL) over NY (AL) (one tie game)	4-0
1923	NY (AL) over NY (NL)	4-2
1924	WAS (AL) over NY (NL)	4-3
1925	PIT (NL) over WAS (AL)	4-3
1926	STL (NL) over NY (AL)	4-3
1927	NY (AL) over PIT (NL)	4-0
1928	NY (AL) over STL (NL)	4-0
1929	PHI (AL) over CHI (NL)	4-1
1930	PHI (AL) over STL (NL)	4-2
1931	STL (NL) over PHI (AL)	4-3
1932	NY (AL) over CHI (NL)	4-0
1933	NY (NL) over WAS (AL)	4-1
1934	STL (NL) over DET (AL)	4-3
1935	DET (AL) over CHI (NL)	4-2

1936	NY (AL) over NY (NL)	4-2	1975	CIN (NL) over BOS (AL)	4-3
1937	NY (AL) over NY (NL)	4-1	1976	CIN (NL) over NY (AL)	4-0
1938	NY (AL) over CHI (NL)	4-0	1977	NY (AL) over LA (NL)	4-2
1939	NY (AL) over CIN (NL)	4-0	1978	NY (AL) over LA (NL)	4-2
1940	CIN (NL) over DET (AL)	4-3	1979	PIT (NL) over BAL (AL)	4-3
1941	NY (AL) over BRO (NL)	4-1	1980	PHI (NL) over KC (AL)	4-2
1942	STL (NL) over NY (AL)	4-1	1981	LA (NL) over NY (AL)	4-2
1943	NY (AL) over STL (NL)	4-1	1982	STL (NL) over MIL (AL)	4-3
1944	STL (NL) over STL (AL)	4-2	1983	BAL (AL) over PHI (NL)	4-1
1945	DET (AL) over CHI (NL)	4-3	1984	DET (AL) over SD (NL)	4-1
1946	STL (NL) over BOS (AL)	4-3	1985	KC (AL) over STL (NL)	4-3
1947	NY (AL) over BRO (NL)	4-3	1986	NY (NL) over BOS (AL)	4-3
1948	CLE (AL) over BOS (NL)	4-2	1987	MIN (AL) over STL (NL)	4-3
1949	NY (AL) over BRO (NL)	4-1	1988	LA (NL) over OAK (AL)	4-1
1950	NY (AL) over PHI (NL)	4-0	1989	OAK (AL) over SF (NL)	4-0
1951	NY (AL) over NY (NL)	4-2	1990	CIN (NL) over OAK (AL)	4-0
1952	NY (AL) over BRO (NL)	4-3	1991	MIN (AL) over ATL (NL)	4-3
1953	NY (AL) over BRO (NL)	4-2	1992	TOR (AL) over ATL (NL)	4-2
1954	NY (NL) over CLE (AL)	4-0	1993	TOR (AL) over PHI (NL)	4-2
1955	BRO (NL) over NY (AL)	4-3	1995	ATL (NL) over CLE (AL)	4-2
1956	NY (AL) over BRO (NL)	4-3	1996	NY (AL) over ATL (NL)	4-2
1957	MIL (NL) over NY (AL)	4-3	1997	FLA (NL) over CLE (AL)	4-3
1958	NY (AL) over MIL (NL)	4-3	1998	NY (AL) over SD (NL)	4-0
1959	LA (NL) over CHI (AL)	4-2	1999	NY (AL) over ATL (NL)	4-0
1960	PIT (NL) over NY (AL)	4-3			
1961	NY (AL) over CIN (NL)	4-1			
1962	NY (AL) over SF (NL)	4-3			
1963	LA (NL) over NY (AL)	4-0			
1964	STL (NL) over NY (AL)	4-3			
1965	LA (NL) over MIN (AL)	4-3			
1966	BAL (AL) over LA (NL)	4-0			
1967	STL (NL) over BOS (AL)	4-3			
1968	DET (AL) over STL (NL)	4-3			
1969	NY (NL) over BAL (AL)	4-1			
1970	BAL (AL) over CIN (NL)	4-1			
1971	PIT (NL) over BAL (AL)	4-3			
1972	OAK (AL) over CIN (NL)	4-3			
1973	OAK (AL) over NY (NL)	4-3			
1974	OAK (AL) over LA (NL)	4-1			

Major league report

2000 Baseball Weekly Almanac

▶1999 season
 wrap-ups
▶1999 team MVPs
▶Week-by-week
 season notes

▶Quotes of the year
▶Team rosters and
 statistics
▶Franchise records

New York Yankees

Derek Jeter's .349 batting average was the highest ever for a Yankees shortstop.

1999 Yankees: One more amazing season

From the moment they arrived in Florida, everything the New York Yankees did was geared toward champagne in October. It has been that way for much of the 20th century.

With their dismantling of the Atlanta Braves in the 95th World Series, the Yankees won a record 25th championship, the third in four years under manager Joe Torre.

"I'm still amazed, and yet, I'm not amazed because we grind," Torre said, defining the essence of his team. "I think the highest compliment I can pay our club is we go out there and play nine innings. And good things happen."

The Yankees pointed to that singleness of purpose as the foundation of their historic 1998 season, and said it was their compass in this tumultuous year. On the first day of spring training they traded 1998 ace David Wells to Toronto in a deal for five-time Cy Young Award winner Roger Clemens. It was the first of many thunderbolts, which included Torre's diagnosis of prostate cancer, the death of legend Joe DiMaggio, stretches on the disabled list for Clemens and Andy Pettitte (and trade rumors on the latter), the arrest of Darryl Strawberry, and endless comparisons to 1998.

After all that, the 1999 Yankees lost only one game in the playoffs and finished the year with a run of 18 victories in their last 19 postseason games. During the regular season, they won the AL East, their 37th first-place finish in franchise history, though Boston remained on their heels far longer than anyone expected.

No other team has more than 25 firsts. The Yankees' 98 wins give them 400 wins over the last four seasons, and they appeared in the postseason for the fifth consecutive year, something they haven't done since 1960-64.

The offense didn't quite compare to the wrecking crews that teams such as Cleveland and Texas put on the field. But it was formidable enough. Outfielders Bernie Williams (115) and Paul O'Neill

(110), first baseman Tino Martinez (105) and shortstop Derek Jeter (102) each recorded at least 100 RBI, the first time the Yankees have had such a quartet since 1939 (Joe DiMaggio, 126; Joe Gordon, 111; Bill Dickey, 105; and George Selkirk, 101).

It was Martinez's fifth consecutive 100-RBI season. Jeter's .349 average was the highest ever for a Yankees shortstop and was second only to Boston's Nomar Garciaparra in the batting race.

And the pitching certainly did its part. Closer Mariano Rivera became the first Yankee with consecutive 40-plus save seasons (45 and 45); and he didn't allow a run in his last 30⅔ innings, beginning July 21. He also was unscored-on in the postseason. David Cone, who became the second Yankee in as many seasons to throw a perfect game, had a 3.44 ERA, second best in the AL. And the depth of the rotation was an advantage over most other clubs, though Clemens had a sub-par season at 14-10 with a 4.60 ERA.

But the success still seems to revolve around Torre. It likely will remain so because owner George Steinbrenner appreciates Torre.

"The manager has a touch of genius to him," Steinbrenner says. "He just knows what to do. You can't say enough good about him."

1999 Yankees: Week-by-week notes

These notes were excerpted from the following issues of Baseball Weekly.

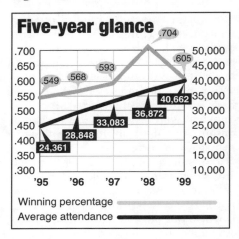

Five-year glance

Winning percentage
Average attendance

▶**April 7:** Owner George Steinbrenner ignited another firestorm on April 1 when he called right-hander Hideki Irabu a "fat, pussy toad" for not covering first base in an exhibition game. Irabu, his confidence crushed, stayed in Tampa when the Yankees left for Los Angeles.

▶**April 14:** The Yankees decided to stick with right-hander Ramiro Mendoza for his April 13 start against the Orioles, leaving Hideki Irabu to languish in the bullpen for at least another week. Mendoza, who was rushed into the rotation when Irabu was left in Tampa, pitched eight scoreless innings in a 4-0 victory over Oakland on April 7.

▶**April 21:** The Yanks lost 3-1 to Detroit on April 17 in a game twice interrupted by rain delays. But the nasty afternoon clouds had a silver lining—left-hander Andy Pettitte pitched six scoreless innings in his first start this season.

▶**April 28:** Chili Davis said he plans to retire after the season, and the DH was making memories with almost every swing of his bat. Davis was a scorching 7-for-16 during last week's homestand, with two home runs and seven RBI. In 16 games Davis, 39, was batting .389 with five home runs and a team-high 17 RBI.

▶**May 5:** The Yankees placed right-hander Roger Clemens on the 15-day DL and welcomed Hideki Irabu back to the rotation. Irabu had pitched well in his previous two relief outings, allowing only one run in eight innings.

▶**May 26:** There was never a question that Joe Torre would return to the Yankees, but he surprised his team on May 18 when he resumed his post as manager for the opener of a three-game series in Boston. Only two months after leaving the Yankees for prostate-cancer surgery, Torre was back in uniform and back in the dugout.

▶**June 2:** Roger Clemens still seemed to have a fire burning for his former team,

the Red Sox. He held Boston to two hits and one run for a 4-1 victory on May 26. In five starts against the Sox, Clemens was 3-0 with a 1.64 ERA and 52 strikeouts in 38 innings.

▶**June 9:** Shortstop Derek Jeter had a .374 batting average as of June 6 and had reached base safely in all 53 games, the longest streak on the Yankees since 1961.

▶**June 16:** Second baseman Chuck Knoblauch had dropped from leadoff hitter to the Yankees' nowhere man. Joe Torre bounced the slumping Knoblauch from the top spot to seventh during last week's interleague play, the first time he had been moved in his 200 games with the team. He was batting .259, far too low for a Yankee's leadoff hitter.

▶**June 30:** Right-hander Orlando Hernandez shut out the Devil Rays 7-0 on June 22 for the Yankees' first complete game in 67 starts—the club record for the longest stretch without one to open the season.

▶**July 15:** One published report last week had left-hander Andy Pettitte on the trading block, but the Yankees weren't ready to move him yet. Pettitte had struggled, losing five of his last seven decisions, so the top left-hander in the farm system, Ed Yarnall, was called up on July 11.

▶**July 21:** Closer Mariano Rivera suddenly went from automatic to erratic—a troubling development for the Yankees. Right-hander Rivera had converted 100 saves in

115 chances before his blown save on July 16 against the Braves. Rivera allowed a career-high four runs that day, then suffered consecutive losses for the first time in his career.

▶**July 28:** The Yankees romped to a 21-1 victory on July 24 against Cleveland, the most runs they had scored in the Bronx since 1931.

▶**Aug. 4:** Hideki Irabu won his seventh consecutive decision on July 30 against Boston. He had not lost in two months. In his last 11 starts Irabu was 7-0 with a 3.05 ERA, and was becoming entrenched as the club's No. 4 starter.

▶**Aug. 11:** One day after commissioner Bud Selig cleared DH Darryl Strawberry to play again following a suspension involving drug use, George Steinbrenner gave his approval for the outfielder to join AAA Columbus the following night (Aug. 4).

▶**Aug. 18:** Center fielder Bernie Williams finally seemed to be living up to the expectations of his $88 million contract. Before an 0-for-4 on Aug. 14, he was in a 20-for-35 groove with 22 RBI in 11 games. Williams also was third in the AL with a .352 average, behind teammate Derek Jeter and Boston's shortstop Nomar Garciaparra.

▶**Sept. 1:** Jeter scored his 100th run on Aug. 23, becoming the first Yankee to score 100 in four consecutive seasons since center fielder Mickey Mantle did it in nine consecutive seasons (1953-61).

▶**Sept. 8:** Roger Clemens was supposed to guarantee another title for New York, but his erratic performance had the Yankees are worried about him for the postseason. He failed to provide a strong showing for more than three innings on Sept. 1 as the Athletics stomped the Yankees 7-1. He was 12-7 with a 4.54 ERA.

▶**Sept. 15:** Strawberry had been almost unstoppable since he was called up on Sept. 1 from Columbus, and even a defensive shift employed by the Red Sox failed to slow him down. He scored twice on Sept. 11 and had now reached base safely 19 times in 27 plate appearances.

▶**Sept. 22:** Chuck Knoblauch committed his league-leading 26th error on Sept. 18, the most by a Yankee since third baseman Graig Nettles had 26 in 1973.

▶**Sept. 29:** Mariano Rivera had not allowed a run in his last 23 appearances, a span of 24⅔ innings. Left-handers were hitting .138 against him.

▶**Oct. 6:** Roger Clemens wound up 14-10 with a 4.60 ERA, the worst season of his 16-year career. Though Clemens has five Cy Young Awards to his credit, the Yankees decided to start ace Orlando Hernandez in Game One of the Division Series against Texas.

QUOTE OF THE YEAR

"I've had plenty of triples in my time."
—DH Chili Davis, saying he wanted to keep his 2,186-at-bat triple-less streak intact

Team Leaders

Batting avg.	Hits	Wins	Strikeouts
.349 Derek Jeter	219 Derek Jeter	17 Orlando Hernandez	177 David Cone
.342 Bernie Williams	202 Bernie Williams	14 Roger Clemens	163 Roger Clemens
		14 Andy Pettitte	

HR	Runs	Losses	Innings
28 Tino Martinez	134 Derek Jeter	11 Andy Pettitte	214.1 Orlando Hernandez
25 Bernie Williams	120 Chuck Knoblauch	10 Roger Clemens	193.1 David Cone

RBI	Stolen bases	ERA	Saves
115 Bernie Williams	28 Chuck Knoblauch	3.44 David Cone	45 Mariano Rivera
110 Paul O'Neill	19 Derek Jeter	4.12 Orlando Hernandez	3 Ramiro Mendoza

NEW YORK YANKEES 1999 final stats

BATTERS	BA	SLG	OBA	G	AB	R	H	TB	2B	3B	HR	RBI	BB	SO	SB	CS	E
Jimenez	.400	.500	.478	7	20	3	8	10	2	0	0	4	3	4	0	0	0
Jeter	.349	.552	.438	158	627	134	219	346	37	9	24	102	91	116	19	8	14
Williams	.342	.536	.435	158	591	116	202	317	28	6	25	115	100	95	9	10	5
Strawberry	.327	.612	.500	24	49	10	16	30	5	0	3	6	17	16	2	0	0
Knoblauch	.292	.454	.393	150	603	120	176	274	36	4	18	68	83	57	28	9	26
O'Neill	.285	.459	.353	153	597	70	170	274	39	4	19	110	66	89	11	9	8
Ledee	.276	.476	.346	88	250	45	69	119	13	5	9	40	28	73	4	3	9
Davis	.269	.445	.366	146	476	59	128	212	25	1	19	78	73	100	4	1	0
Martinez	.263	.458	.341	159	589	95	155	270	27	2	28	105	69	86	3	4	7
Curtis	.262	.369	.398	96	195	37	51	72	6	0	5	24	43	35	8	4	1
Sojo	.252	.346	.275	49	127	20	32	44	6	0	2	16	4	17	1	0	2
Brosius	.247	.414	.307	133	473	64	117	196	26	1	17	71	39	74	9	3	13
Posada	.245	.401	.341	112	379	50	93	152	19	2	12	57	53	91	1	0	5
Girardi	.239	.354	.271	65	209	23	50	74	16	1	2	27	10	26	3	1	8
Spencer	.234	.390	.301	71	205	25	48	80	8	0	8	20	18	51	0	4	0
Leyritz	.227	.318	.354	31	66	8	15	21	4	1	0	5	13	17	0	0	2
Bellinger	.200	.311	.217	32	45	12	9	14	2	0	1	2	1	10	1	0	0
Manto	.182	.273	.413	18	33	5	6	9	0	0	1	2	13	15	0	0	0
Tarasco	.161	.226	.229	14	31	5	5	7	2	0	0	3	3	5	1	0	0
Soriano	.125	.500	.125	9	8	2	1	4	0	0	1	1	0	3	0	1	1

PITCHERS	W-L	ERA	BA	G	GS	CG	GF	SH	SV	IP	H	R	ER	HR	BB	SO
Juden	0-1	1.59	.200	2	1	0	0	0	0	5.2	5	9	1	1	3	9
Rivera	4-3	1.83	.176	66	0	0	63	0	45	69.0	43	15	14	2	18	52
Watson	4-1	2.89	.254	24	0	0	8	0	0	37.1	36	17	12	8	13	32
Cone	12-9	3.44	.229	31	31	1	0	1	0	193.1	164	84	74	21	90	177
Grimsley	7-2	3.60	.231	55	0	0	25	0	1	75.0	66	39	30	7	40	49
Yarnall	1-0	3.71	.254	5	2	0	2	0	0	17.0	17	8	7	1	10	13
Erdos	0-0	3.86	.192	4	0	0	1	0	0	7.0	5	4	3	2	4	4
Hernandez	17-9	4.12	.233	33	33	2	0	1	0	214.1	187	108	98	24	87	157
Nelson	2-1	4.15	.245	39	0	0	8	0	1	30.1	27	14	14	2	22	35
Mendoza	9-9	4.29	.284	53	6	0	15	0	3	123.2	141	68	59	13	27	80
Stanton	2-2	4.33	.289	73	1	0	10	0	0	62.1	71	30	30	5	18	59
Naulty	1-0	4.38	.225	33	0	0	20	0	0	49.1	40	24	24	8	22	25
Buddie	0-0	4.50	.333	2	0	0	0	0	0	2.0	3	1	1	1	0	1
Clemens	14-10	4.60	.261	30	30	1	0	1	0	187.2	185	101	96	20	90	163
Pettitte	14-11	4.70	.289	31	31	0	0	0	0	191.2	216	105	100	20	89	121
Irabu	11-7	4.84	.267	32	27	2	2	1	0	169.1	180	98	91	26	46	133
Tessmer	0-0	14.85	.444	6	0	0	4	0	0	6.2	16	11	11	1	4	3
Fossas	0-0	36.00	.667	5	0	0	0	0	0	1.0	6	4	4	1	1	0

2000 preliminary roster

PITCHERS (22)
Ryan Bradley
Mike Buddie
Roger Clemens
David Cone
Luis De Los Santos
Craig Dingman
Darrell Einertson
Todd Erdos
Ben Ford
Jason Grimsley
Orlando Hernandez

Hideki Irabu
Jeff Juden
Ramiro Mendoza
Jeff Nelson
Todd Noel
Andy Pettitte
Mariano Rivera
Mike Stanton
Jay Tessmer
Allen Watson
Ed Yarnall

CATCHERS (1)
Jorge Posada

INFIELDERS (10)
Clay Bellinger
Scott Brosius
Derek Jeter
D'Angelo Jimenez
Nick Johnson
Chuck Knoblauch
Jim Leyritz
Tino Martinez

Wily Pena
Alfonso Soriano

OUTFIELDERS (6)
Ricky Ledee
Donzell McDonald
Paul O'Neill
Shane Spencer
Darrell Strawberry
Bernie Williams

Games played by position

PLAYER	G	C	1B	2B	3B	SS	OF	DH
Bellinger	32	0	8	1	16	1	2	0
Brosius	133	0	0	0	132	0	0	1
Curtis	96	0	0	0	0	0	81	14
Davis	146	0	0	0	0	0	0	141
Figga	2	2	0	0	0	0	0	0
Girardi	65	65	0	0	0	0	0	0
Jeter	158	0	0	0	0	158	0	0
Jimenez	7	0	0	1	6	0	0	0
Knoblauch	150	0	0	150	0	0	0	0
Ledee	88	0	0	0	0	0	77	5
Leyritz	31	1	9	0	1	0	0	14
Manto	6	0	3	0	1	0	0	0
Martinez	159	0	158	0	0	0	0	0
O'Neill	153	0	0	0	0	0	151	0
Posada	112	109	1	0	0	0	0	1
Sojo	49	0	4	16	20	6	0	0
Soriano	9	0	0	0	0	1	0	6
Spencer	71	0	0	0	0	0	64	3
Strawberry	24	0	0	0	0	0	0	17
Tarasco	14	0	0	0	0	0	12	0
Williams	158	0	0	0	0	0	155	2

Sick call: 1999 DL report

PLAYER	Days on the DL
Scott Brosius	15
Vidal Candelaria	64
Roger Clemens	23
Luis De Los Santos	18
Casey DeGroote	64
Darrell Einertson	104
Mike Jerzembeck	182
Jeff Nelson	86*
Andy Pettitte	12
Shane Spencer	24

Minor Leagues

Tops in the organization

BATTER	CLUB	AVG.	G	AB	R	H	HR	RBI
Johnson, Nick	Nrw	.345	132	420	114	145	14	87
Jimenez, D.	Col	.327	126	526	97	172	15	88
Raabe, Brian	Col	.327	130	493	93	161	11	77
Seabol, Scott	Grn	.315	138	543	86	171	15	89
Powell, Alonzo	Col	.315	130	470	97	148	24	90

HOME RUNS
Powell, Alonzo	Col	24
Bierek, Kurt	Col	23
Valencia, Victor	Nrw	22
Carpenter, B.	Col	22
Leon, Donny	Nrw	21

WINS
Beverlin, Jason	Nrw	15
Keisler, Randy	Nrw	14
Yarnall, Ed	Col	13
Zancanaro, Dave	Col	13
Several Players Tied at		11

RBI
Leon, Donny	Nrw	100
Bierek, Kurt	Col	95
Powell, Alonzo	Col	90
Seabol, Scott	Grn	89
Jimenez, D.	Col	88

SAVES
Ellison, Jason	Tam	35
Lisio, Joe	Nrw	33
Tessmer, Jay	Col	28
Weber, Brett	Grn	23
Several Players Tied at		9

STOLEN BASES
McDonald, D.	Nrw	54
Brown, Vick	Nrw	50
Smith, Rod	Nrw	40
Jimenez, D.	Col	26
Soriano, Alfonso	Col	25

STRIKEOUTS
Padua, Geraldo	Grn	155
Keisler, Randy	Nrw	152
Juden, Jeff	Col	151
Beverlin, Jason	Nrw	147
Yarnall, Ed	Col	146

PITCHER	CLUB	W-L	ERA	IP	H	BB	SO
Lail, Denny	Nrw	6-3	1.94	102	69	27	82
Padua, Geraldo	Grn	9-4	2.84	140	120	35	155
Dunn, Keith	Grn	9-9	3.13	135	134	16	109
Zancanaro, Dave	Col	13-3	3.22	157	149	60	106
Flores, Randy	Tam	11-5	3.43	160	150	49	118

1999 salaries

	Bonuses	Total earned salary
Bernie Williams, of		9,857,143
David Cone, p	1,500,000	9,500,000
Roger Clemens, p		8,250,000
Paul O'Neill, of		6,250,000
Chuck Knoblauch, 2b		6,000,000
Andy Pettitte, p		5,950,000
Scott Brosius, 3b		5,250,000
Derek Jeter, ss		5,000,000
Chili Davis, dh		4,333,333
Tino Martinez, 1b		4,300,000
Mariano Rivera, p		4,250,000
Joe Girardi, c		3,400,000
Hideki Irabu, p		3,125,000
Mike Stanton, p		2,016,667
Chad Curtis, of		2,000,000
Jim Leyritz, 1b		1,900,000
Orlando Hernandez, p		1,850,000
Jeff Nelson, p		1,816,666
Luis Sojo, 3b		800,000
Ramiro Mendoza, p		375,000
Jorge Posada, c		350,000
Jason Grimsley, p		350,000
Shane Spencer, of		204,050
Ricky Ledee, of		202,850
Allen Watson, p		200,000
Mike Jerzembeck, p		200,000
Vidal Candelaria, c		200,000
Casey DeGroote, ss		200,000

Average 1999 salary: $3,147,525
Total 1999 team payroll: $88,130,709
Termination pay: $3,860,246

New York (1903-1999)

100

Runs: Most, career

1959	Babe Ruth,	1920-1934
1888	Lou Gehrig,	1923-1939
1677	Mickey Mantle,	1951-1968
1390	Joe DiMaggio,	1936-1951
1186	Earle Combs,	1924-1935

Hits: Most, career

2721	Lou Gehrig,	1923-1939
2518	Babe Ruth,	1920-1934
2415	Mickey Mantle,	1951-1968
2214	Joe DiMaggio,	1936-1951
2153	Don Mattingly,	1982-1995

2B: Most, career

534	Lou Gehrig,	1923-1939
442	Don Mattingly,	1982-1995
424	Babe Ruth,	1920-1934
389	Joe DiMaggio,	1936-1951
344	Mickey Mantle,	1951-1968

3B: Most, career

163	Lou Gehrig,	1923-1939
154	Earle Combs,	1924-1935
131	Joe DiMaggio,	1936-1951
121	Wally Pipp,	1915-1925
115	Tony Lazzeri,	1926-1937

HR: Most, career

659	Babe Ruth,	1920-1934
536	Mickey Mantle,	1951-1968
493	Lou Gehrig,	1923-1939
361	Joe DiMaggio,	1936-1951
358	Yogi Berra,	1946-1963

RBI: Most, career

1995	Lou Gehrig,	1923-1939
1971	Babe Ruth,	1920-1934
1537	Joe DiMaggio,	1936-1951
1509	Mickey Mantle,	1951-1968
1430	Yogi Berra,	1946-1963

SB: Most, career

326	RICKEY HENDERSON,	1985-1989
251	Willie Randolph,	1976-1988
248	Hal Chase,	1905-1913
233	Roy White,	1965-1979
184	Ben Chapman,	1930-1936
184	Wid Conroy,	1903-1908

BB: Most, career

1847	Babe Ruth,	1920-1934
1733	Mickey Mantle,	1951-1968
1508	Lou Gehrig,	1923-1939
1005	Willie Randolph,	1976-1988
934	Roy White,	1965-1979

BA: Highest, career

.349	Babe Ruth,	1920-1934
.340	Lou Gehrig,	1923-1939
.325	Earle Combs,	1924-1935
.325	Joe DiMaggio,	1936-1951
.318	DEREK JETER,	1995-1999

On-base avg: Highest, career

.484	Babe Ruth,	1920-1934
.447	Lou Gehrig,	1923-1939
.421	Mickey Mantle,	1951-1968
.410	Charlie Keller,	1939-1952
.400	George Selkirk,	1934-1942

Slug pct: Highest, career

.711	Babe Ruth,	1920-1934
.632	Lou Gehrig,	1923-1939
.579	Joe DiMaggio,	1936-1951
.557	Mickey Mantle,	1951-1968
.526	Reggie Jackson,	1977-1981

Games started: Most, career

438	Whitey Ford,	1950-1967
391	Red Ruffing,	1930-1946
356	Mel Stottlemyre,	1964-1974
323	Ron Guidry,	1975-1988
319	Lefty Gomez,	1930-1942

Complete games: Most, career

261	Red Ruffing,	1930-1946
173	Lefty Gomez,	1930-1942
168	Jack Chesbro,	1903-1909
164	Herb Pennock,	1923-1933
164	Bob Shawkey,	1915-1927

Saves: Most, career

224	Dave Righetti,	1979-1990
151	Rich Gossage,	1978-1989
141	Sparky Lyle,	1972-1978
129	MARIANO RIVERA,	1995-1999
104	Johnny Murphy,	1932-1946

Shutouts: Most, career

45	Whitey Ford,	1950-1967
40	Red Ruffing,	1930-1946
40	Mel Stottlemyre,	1964-1974
28	Lefty Gomez,	1930-1942
27	Allie Reynolds,	1947-1954

Wins: Most, career

236	Whitey Ford,	1950-1967
231	Red Ruffing,	1930-1946
189	Lefty Gomez,	1930-1942
170	Ron Guidry,	1975-1988
168	Bob Shawkey,	1915-1927

K: Most, career

1956	Whitey Ford,	1950-1967
1778	Ron Guidry,	1975-1988
1526	Red Ruffing,	1930-1946
1468	Lefty Gomez,	1930-1942
1257	Mel Stottlemyre,	1964-1974

Win pct: Highest, career

.725	Johnny Allen,	1932-1935
.717	Spud Chandler,	1937-1947
.706	Vic Raschi,	1946-1953
.700	Monte Pearson,	1936-1940
.698	DAVID CONE,	1995-1999

ERA: Lowest, career

2.54	Russ Ford,	1909-1913
2.58	Jack Chesbro,	1903-1909
2.72	Al Orth,	1904-1909
2.73	Tiny Bonham,	1940-1946
2.73	George Mogridge,	1915-1920

Runs: Most, season

177	Babe Ruth,	1921
167	Lou Gehrig,	1936
163	Lou Gehrig,	1931
163	Babe Ruth,	1928
158	Babe Ruth,	1920
158	Babe Ruth,	1927

Hits: Most, season

238	Don Mattingly,	1986
231	Earle Combs,	1927
220	Lou Gehrig,	1930
219	DEREK JETER,	1999
218	Lou Gehrig,	1927

2B: Most, season

53	Don Mattingly,	1986
52	Lou Gehrig,	1927
48	Don Mattingly,	1985
47	Lou Gehrig,	1926
47	Lou Gehrig,	1928
47	Bob Meusel,	1927

3B: Most, season

23	Earle Combs,	1927
22	Earle Combs,	1930
22	Birdie Cree,	1911
22	Snuffy Stirnweiss,	1945
21	Earle Combs,	1928

HR: Most, season

61	Roger Maris,	1961
60	Babe Ruth,	1927
59	Babe Ruth,	1921
54	Mickey Mantle,	1961
54	Babe Ruth,	1920
54	Babe Ruth,	1928

RBI: Most, season

184	Lou Gehrig, 1931
175	Lou Gehrig, 1927
174	Lou Gehrig, 1930
171	Babe Ruth, 1921
167	Joe DiMaggio, 1937

SB: Most, season

93	RICKEY HENDERSON, 1988
87	RICKEY HENDERSON, 1986
80	RICKEY HENDERSON, 1985
74	Fritz Maisel, 1914
61	Ben Chapman, 1931

BB: Most, season

170	Babe Ruth, 1923
148	Babe Ruth, 1920
146	Mickey Mantle, 1957
144	Babe Ruth, 1921
144	Babe Ruth, 1926

BA: Highest, season

.393	Babe Ruth, 1923
.381	Joe DiMaggio, 1939
.379	Lou Gehrig, 1930
.378	Babe Ruth, 1924
.378	Babe Ruth, 1921

On-base avg: Highest, season

.545	Babe Ruth, 1923
.530	Babe Ruth, 1920
.516	Babe Ruth, 1926
.513	Babe Ruth, 1924
.512	Mickey Mantle, 1957

Slug pct: Highest, season

.847	Babe Ruth, 1920
.846	Babe Ruth, 1921
.772	Babe Ruth, 1927
.765	Lou Gehrig, 1927
.764	Babe Ruth, 1923

Games started: Most, season

51	Jack Chesbro, 1904
45	Jack Powell, 1904
42	Jack Chesbro, 1906
39	Pat Dobson, 1974
39	Whitey Ford, 1961
39	Catfish Hunter, 1975
39	Al Orth, 1906
39	Mel Stottlemyre, 1969
39	Ralph Terry, 1962

Complete games: Most, season

48	Jack Chesbro, 1904
38	Jack Powell, 1904
36	Al Orth, 1906
33	Jack Chesbro, 1903
31	Ray Caldwell, 1915

Saves: Most, season

46	Dave Righetti, 1986
45	MARIANO RIVERA, 1999
43	MARIANO RIVERA, 1997
43	JOHN WETTELAND, 1996
36	Dave Righetti, 1990
36	MARIANO RIVERA, 1998

Shutouts: Most, season

9	Ron Guidry, 1978
8	Whitey Ford, 1964
8	Russ Ford, 1910
7	Whitey Ford, 1958
7	Catfish Hunter, 1975
7	Allie Reynolds, 1951
7	Mel Stottlemyre, 1971
7	Mel Stottlemyre, 1972

Wins: Most, season

41	Jack Chesbro, 1904
27	Carl Mays, 1921
27	Al Orth, 1906
26	Joe Bush, 1922
26	Russ Ford, 1910
26	Lefty Gomez, 1934
26	Carl Mays, 1920

K: Most, season

248	Ron Guidry, 1978
239	Jack Chesbro, 1904
222	DAVID CONE, 1997
218	Melido Perez, 1992
217	Al Downing, 1964

Win pct: Highest, season

.893	Ron Guidry, 1978
.862	Whitey Ford, 1961
.842	Ralph Terry, 1961
.839	Lefty Gomez, 1934
.833	Spud Chandler, 1943

ERA: Lowest, season

1.64	Spud Chandler, 1943
1.65	Russ Ford, 1910
1.74	Ron Guidry, 1978
1.82	Jack Chesbro, 1904
1.83	Hippo Vaughn, 1910

Most pinch-hit homers, season

4	Johnny Blanchard, 1961

Most pinch-hit homers, career

9	Yogi Berra, 1946-1963
8	Bob Cerv, 1951-1962

Longest hitting streak

56	Joe DiMaggio, 1941
33	Hal Chase, 1907
29	Roger Peckinpaugh, 1919
29	Earle Combs, 1931
29	Joe Gordon, 1942

Most consecutive scoreless innings

33	Jack Aker, 1969
30.2	MARIANO RIVERA, 1999

No-hit games

Tom L. Hughes, NY vs Cle AL, 0-5; August 30, 1910 (2nd game) (lost on seven hits in 11 innings after allowing first hit in the 10th)

George Mogridge, NY at Bos AL, 2-1; April 24, 1917.

Sam Jones, NY at Phi AL, 2-0; September 4, 1923.

Monte Pearson, NY vs Cle AL, 13-0; August 27, 1938 (2nd game).

Allie Reynolds, NY at Cle AL, 1-0; July 12, 1951.

Allie Reynolds, NY vs Bos AL, 8-0; September 28, 1951 (1st game).

Don Larsen, NY AL vs Bro NL, 2-0; October 8, 1956 (World Series, perfect game).

Dave Righetti, NY vs Bos AL, 4-0; July 4, 1983.

Andy Hawkins, NY at Chi AL, 0-4; July 1, 1990 (8 innings, lost the game; bottom of 9th not played).

JIM ABBOTT, NY vs Cle AL, 4-0; September 4, 1993.

DWIGHT GOODEN, NY vs Sea AL, 2-0; May 14, 1996.

DAVID WELLS, NY vs Min AL, 4-0; May 17, 1998 (perfect game).

DAVID CONE, NY AL vs Mon NL, 6-0; July 18, 1999 (perfect game).

ACTIVE PLAYERS in caps.

Players' years of service are listed by the first and last years with this team and are not necessarily consecutive; all statistics record performances for this team only.

Boston Red Sox

By Barbara Jean Germano, Baseball Weekly

Pedro Martinez's Cy Young award-winning season was arguably the best in baseball, at any position.

1999 Red Sox: Teamwork was the key

Few forecasters picked Boston to finish higher than fourth in the AL East. The last time the Red Sox played when the autumn leaves were so close to peak color was in their World Series year of 1986. But when the 1999 American League Championship Series opened, it was the Sox and the New York Yankees.

Boston fell in five games, but the small consolation was they were the only club to defeat the Yankees in the postseason, in what turned out to be a mismatch between the reigning best pitcher in baseball, Pedro Martinez, and a man who once held the same title in the same uniform, Roger Clemens.

"We have to be proud of our season," said second baseman Jose Offerman, who was the unwitting victim of much preseason criticism after Boston signed him but lost Mo Vaughn to free agency. "Not too many people expected us to go this far."

The Red Sox probably won't be overlooked this spring. Not after going 94-68. Not with Martinez, plus the recovery of his brother, Ramon, from shoulder surgery, plus batting champion Nomar Garciaparra, plus a manager who seemed the perfect fit for his players in an "us against the world" season.

"I don't know what I do but watch them play," said AL Manager of the Year Jimy Williams. "It's a special group of guys that really became a unit to perform together daily."

It was a team of just two stars—Pedro Martinez and Garciaparra—and plenty of workmanlike teammates. That's how they held off wild-card challengers, Oakland and Toronto, and never let the Yankees pull away in the division race. Then the Red Sox eliminated Cleveland with three straight wins after losing the first two games of the Division Series.

How did the the Red Sox do it without Vaughn, their best home run hitter? Garciaparra won the batting title. His .357 average beat runner-up Yankee Derek Jeter's .349. And Pedro Martinez went 23-4, topping the AL in wins and

Team MVP

Pedro Martinez: No player at any position on any team was more dominant than Boston's pitching ace. He was the obvious Cy Young Award winner after an incredible 23-4 season with a 2.07 ERA, 313 strikeouts and just 37 walks in 213⅓ innings. The embodiment of a team that wouldn't quit, he pitched through a back injury to rally his team from a 2-0 deficit to a Division Series triumph.

strikeouts (313) and the majors with a 2.07 ERA.

The Red Sox led the AL East from May 18 through June 8, were in first or second from May 15 through July 24, and in second from Aug. 13 through the end of the season. They proved they could win big games by going 9-3 on a tough September road trip to Seattle, Oakland, New York and Cleveland.

The Red Sox also showed they could win without key players. Closer Tom Gordon missed more than half of the season with a strained elbow (Tim Wakefield, Derek Lowe and Rod Beck took turns filling his role). Bret Saberhagen had three stints on the disabled list. Ramon Martinez had surgery in June 1998 and didn't pitch until Sept. 2, 1999. Third baseman John Valentin was on the disabled list from Aug. 29 to Sept. 23 but was a playoff standout.

Boston led the AL with a 4.00 ERA, but the team still needs more hitting. Rookie Brian Daubach hit well but tailed off sharply the last month, and starting outfielders Darren Lewis and rookie Trot Nixon combined for just 17 homers. The good news was that Nixon established himself as the every-day right fielder and that Jason Varitek emerged as one of the AL's top catchers.

"I believe that our team is set up that we should be in the hunt every year," general manager Dan Duquette said.

1999 Red Sox: Week-by-week notes

These notes were excerpted from the following issues of Baseball Weekly.

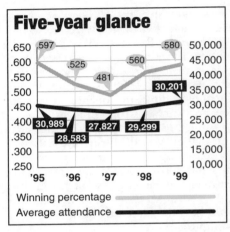

Five-year glance

Winning percentage ——————
Average attendance ——————

▶**April 14:** The Red Sox got off to a 5-0 start against the Royals and Devil Rays. With every starter working at least six innings, Sox pitchers gave up just 25 hits and had a 1.40 ERA in the five games.

▶**April 21:** The Red Sox got shortstop Nomar Garciaparra back from his hamstring strain on April 17, but they lost closer Tom Gordon later that afternoon. Right-hander Gordon was placed on the 15-day DL and underwent tests on his right elbow, which began acting up in spring training. It was expected that right-handers Derek Lowe and Jim Corsi would be among those used in ninth-inning situations.

▶**April 28:** Left fielder Troy O'Leary, who hit a career-high 23 home runs in 1998, belted his sixth homer of the season on April 24. The rest of the team had combined for five.

▶**May 5:** During April, Nomar Garciaparra did not homer and had only eight RBI, and third baseman John Valentin batted .195. A notoriously slow starter, Valentin's career average in April is .229.

▶**May 12:** Right-hander Pedro Martinez struck out a career-high 15 batters to overshadow first baseman Mo Vaughn's return to Fenway on May 7. Martinez, the AL Pitcher of the Month for April, tossed eight shutout innings to improve his record to 6-1.

▶**May 19:** On May 15 the Red Sox announced plans for a 44,000-seat stadium to be built on a parcel of land adjacent to Fenway Park. The $550 million plan, including $350 million for stadium construction alone, attempts to appease preservationists. It would retain much of the famed Green Monster in a park area. On the field, Pedro Martinez set a team record for strikeouts in consecutive games, with 30, by fanning 15 Mariners on May 12, and two days before, Nomar Garciaparra tied the team record for RBI in a game by driving in 10. He became the 18th player to hit two grand slams in

the same game, and he also hit a third home run that day.

▶**May 26:** The Red Sox bolstered their pitching by promoting from within. Right-handers John Wasdin (3-0), Juan Pena (2-0) and Brian Rose (1-0) made significant contributions since being called up from AAA Pawtucket. The Sox won 13 of 16 through May 22.

▶**June 2:** The Red Sox completed their stretch of 13 consecutive games against AL East rivals, going 6-1 against Toronto and 3-3 versus the New York. They followed that by winning the first two games of a three-game set in Cleveland, pulling out the May 29 game 4-2 behind the pitching of Pedro Martinez and a three-run eighth-inning homer by Nomar Garciaparra.

▶**June 9:** Tom Gordon's streak of 54 consecutive regular-season saves came to a halt on June 5 when the Braves strung together three two-out hits to beat him 6-5. The blown save was Gordon's first since April 14, 1998, his first full season as a closer.

▶**June 16:** Pedro Martinez's 10-game winning streak ended when he lost in his homecoming at Montreal. Martinez gave up four runs before the bullpen imploded in a 13-1 defeat. It capped the Expos' three-game sweep and extended the Boston's losing streak to five games.

▶**June 30:** Right-hander Bret Saberhagen's return from the DL helped the pitching

staff get its seventh shutout, on June 23 in Baltimore. Saberhagen, who missed two starts with a five-stitch cut on the bottom of his left foot, pitched 5⅓ innings in winning for the first time since April.

▶**July 7:** Pedro Martinez, named AL Pitcher of the Month for an unprecedented third consecutive time in June, began July by pitching eight innings of a 6-1 victory over the White Sox (July 2). Boston was struggling, though, falling four games behind the Yankees after losing four of six to Chicago and Tampa Bay.

▶**July 28:** After dropping 11 of 15 games to slip behind Toronto in the wild-card race, Boston broke out offensively in an 11-4 victory at Detroit on July 24. Boston hit seven homers, one shy of the team record. Rookie right fielder Trot Nixon hit three, as many as he'd hit in his previous 215 at-bats this season.

▶**Aug. 4:** After being benched for three games in favor of Donnie Sadler, second baseman Jose Offerman returned to the lineup on July 31 and reached base five times in a 6-5 come-from-behind victory against the Yankees.

▶**Aug. 18:** First baseman-DH Brian Daubach jumped into the AL Rookie of the Year race. He produced 11 RBI in two games in less than 24 hours, giving him 20 in a nine-game stretch.

▶**Aug. 25:** Right-hander Tim Wakefield made a start on Aug. 22 in Texas—his first since taking over the closer's role in May from the injured Tom Gordon—but he was ineffective in a 6-0 loss.

▶**Sept. 1:** New acquisition Kent Mercker, a left-hander, buoyed the rotation by providing six solid innings against Anaheim on Aug. 27. Boston rallied from a 3-0 deficit, winning 4-3 on Troy O'Leary's two-run double.

▶**Sept. 15:** The Red Sox retained control of the AL wild card and closed to within three games of the Yankees in the AL East with a three-game sweep at Yankee Stadium. Pedro Martinez pitched a one-hit masterpiece on Sept. 10, striking out a career-high 17 batters and retiring the last 22 Yankees.

▶**Sept. 29:** Pedro Martinez struck out 12 Blue Jays on Sept. 21 to reach the 300 mark, breaking Boston's single-season record of 291, held by right-hander Roger Clemens.

▶**Oct. 6:** On Sept. 29, the Red Sox qualified for postseason play for the second consecutive season, clinching the wild card. Nomar Garciaparra sat out the last five games of the season with a sore left wrist. He won the AL batting title, hitting .357 in 135 games.

Team Leaders

Batting avg.	Hits	Wins	Strikeouts
.357 Nomar Garciaparra	190 Nomar Garciaparra	23 Pedro Martinez	313 Pedro Martinez
.294 Jose Offerman	172 Jose Offerman	10 Bret Saberhagen	104 Tim Wakefield

HR	Runs	Losses	Innings
28 Troy O'Leary	107 Jose Offerman	12 Mark Portugal	213.1 Pedro Martinez
27 Nomar Garciaparra	103 Nomar Garciaparra	11 Tim Wakefield	150.1 Mark Portugal

RBI	Stolen bases	ERA	Saves
104 Nomar Garciaparra	18 Jose Offerman	2.07 Pedro Martinez	15 Derek Lowe
103 Troy O'Leary	16 Darren Lewis	2.63 Derek Lowe	15 Tim Wakefield

BOSTON RED SOX 1999 final stats

BATTERS	BA	SLG	OBA	G	AB	R	H	TB	2B	3B	HR	RBI	BB	SO	SB	CS	E
Garciaparra	.357	.603	.418	135	532	103	190	321	42	4	27	104	51	39	14	3	17
Daubach	.294	.562	.360	110	381	61	112	214	33	3	21	73	36	92	0	1	8
Offerman	.294	.435	.391	149	586	107	172	255	37	11	8	69	96	79	18	12	14
Veras	.288	.398	.323	36	118	14	34	47	5	1	2	13	5	14	0	2	6
Nunnally	.286	.357	.286	10	14	4	4	5	1	0	0	1	0	6	0	0	0
Huskey	.282	.492	.338	119	386	62	109	190	15	0	22	77	34	65	3	1	1
Stanley	.281	.466	.393	136	427	59	120	199	22	0	19	72	70	94	0	0	11
Frye	.281	.333	.362	41	114	14	32	38	3	0	1	12	14	11	2	2	4
Sadler	.280	.346	.313	49	107	18	30	37	5	1	0	4	5	20	2	1	9
O'Leary	.280	.495	.343	157	596	84	167	295	36	4	28	103	56	91	1	2	2
Jefferson	.277	.422	.338	83	206	21	57	87	13	1	5	17	17	55	0	0	0
Gubanich	.277	.426	.346	18	47	4	13	20	2	1	1	11	3	13	0	0	1
Hatteberg	.275	.375	.410	30	80	12	22	30	5	0	1	11	18	14	0	0	1
Nixon	.270	.472	.357	124	381	67	103	180	22	5	15	52	53	75	3	1	7
Varitek	.269	.482	.330	144	483	70	130	233	39	2	20	76	46	85	1	2	11
Merloni	.254	.333	.307	43	126	18	32	42	7	0	1	13	8	16	0	0	10
Valentin	.253	.398	.315	113	450	58	114	179	27	1	12	70	40	68	0	1	14
Buford	.242	.367	.294	91	297	39	72	109	15	2	6	38	21	74	9	2	3
Lewis	.240	.309	.311	135	470	63	113	145	14	6	2	40	45	52	16	10	2
Coleman	.200	.200	.333	2	5	1	1	1	0	0	0	0	1	0	0	0	0
Webster	.120	.140	.290	22	50	1	6	7	1	0	0	4	10	7	0	0	1
Fonville	.000	.000	.500	3	2	1	0	0	0	0	0	0	2	0	1	0	1
Lomasney	.000	.000	.000	1	2	0	0	0	0	0	0	0	0	2	0	0	0

PITCHERS	W-L	ERA	BA	G	GS	CG	GF	SH	SV	IP	H	R	ER	HR	BB	SO
Pena	2-0	0.69	.196	2	2	0	0	0	0	13.0	9	1	1	0	3	15
Garces	5-1	1.55	.171	30	0	0	4	0	2	40.2	25	9	7	1	18	33
Beck	0-1	1.93	.184	12	0	0	8	0	3	14.0	9	3	3	0	5	12
P. Martinez	23-4	2.07	.205	31	29	5	1	1	0	213.1	160	56	49	9	37	313
Lowe	6-3	2.63	.208	74	0	0	32	0	15	109.1	84	35	32	7	25	80
Saberhagen	10-6	2.95	.265	22	22	0	0	0	0	119.0	122	43	39	11	11	81
R. Martinez	2-1	3.05	.192	4	4	0	0	0	0	20.2	14	8	7	2	8	15
Mercker	2-0	3.51	.235	5	5	0	0	0	0	25.2	23	12	10	0	13	17
Cormier	2-0	3.69	.246	60	0	0	7	0	0	63.1	61	34	26	4	18	39
Wasdin	8-3	4.12	.236	45	0	0	17	0	2	74.1	66	38	34	14	18	57
Rapp	6-7	4.12	.263	37	26	0	3	0	0	146.1	147	78	67	13	69	90
Bullinger	0-0	4.50	.286	4	0	0	0	0	0	2.0	2	1	1	0	2	0
Florie	4-1	4.65	.288	41	5	0	10	0	0	81.1	94	50	42	8	35	65
Rose	7-6	4.87	.280	22	18	0	1	0	0	98.0	112	59	53	19	29	51
Wakefield	6-11	5.08	.266	49	17	0	28	0	15	140.0	146	93	79	19	72	104
Portugal	7-12	5.51	.292	31	27	1	1	0	0	150.1	179	100	92	28	41	79
Gordon	0-2	5.60	.246	21	0	0	15	0	11	17.2	17	11	11	2	12	24
Cho	2-3	5.72	.287	9	7	0	1	0	0	39.1	45	26	25	7	8	16
Guthrie	1-1	5.83	.275	46	0	0	15	0	2	46.1	50	32	30	9	20	36
Harikkala	1-1	6.23	.306	7	0	0	2	0	0	13.0	15	9	9	0	6	7
Ohka	1-2	6.23	.362	8	2	0	3	0	0	13.0	21	12	9	2	6	8
J. Santana	1-4	7.32	.300	22	5	0	7	0	0	55.1	66	49	45	10	32	34
Gross	0-2	7.82	.300	11	1	0	7	0	0	12.2	15	11	11	3	8	9
Wolcott	0-0	8.10	.333	4	0	0	1	0	0	6.2	8	6	6	1	3	2
M. Santana	0-0	15.75	.444	3	0	0	1	0	0	4.0	8	7	7	3	3	4

2000 preliminary roster

PITCHERS (19)
Rod Beck
Jin Ho Cho
Rheal Cormier
Paxton Crawford
Bryce Florie
Rich Garces
Tom Gordon
Derek Lowe
Pedro Martinez
Ramon Martinez
Tomokazu Ohka
Juan Pena
Brian Rose
Bret Saberhagen
Julio Santana
Jason Sekany
Tim Wakefield
John Wasdin
Tim Young

CATCHERS (4)
Scott Hatteberg
Shea Hillenbrand
Steve Lomasney
Jason Varitek

INFIELDERS (11)
Manny Alexander
Brian Daubach
David Eckstein
Jeff Frye
Nomar Garciaparra
Jose Offerman
Donnie Sadler
Mike Stanley
Dernell Stenson
John Valentin
Wilton Veras

OUTFIELDERS (7)
Jermaine Allensworth
Michael Coleman
Carl Everett
Butch Huskey
Darren Lewis
Trot Nixon
Troy O'Leary

Games played by position

PLAYER	G	C	1B	2B	3B	SS	OF	DH
Buford	91	0	0	0	0	0	84	5
Coleman	2	0	0	0	0	0	2	0
Daubach	110	0	61	0	1	0	2	48
Fonville	3	0	0	2	0	0	0	0
Frye	41	0	0	26	7	2	0	0
Garciaparra	135	0	0	0	0	134	0	0
Gubanich	18	14	0	0	1	0	0	2
Hatteberg	30	23	0	0	0	0	0	6
Huskey	45	0	0	0	2	0	4	37
Jefferson	83	0	2	0	0	0	0	58
Lewis	135	0	0	0	0	0	130	2
Lomasney	1	1	0	0	0	0	0	0
Merloni	43	0	1	8	9	24	1	0
Nixon	124	0	0	0	0	0	121	0
Nunnally	10	0	0	0	0	0	2	3
O'Leary	157	0	0	0	0	0	157	0
Offerman	149	0	8	128	0	0	0	18
Sadler	49	0	0	10	9	14	8	0
Stanley	136	0	111	0	0	0	0	22
Valentin	113	0	0	0	111	0	0	2
Varitek	144	140	0	0	0	0	0	2
Veras	36	0	0	0	35	0	0	0
Webster	6	6	0	0	0	0	0	0

Sick call: 1999 DL report

PLAYER	Days on the DL
Brian Barkley	73
Damon Buford	17
Jeff Frye	77
Tom Gordon	129*
Kip Gross	18
Mark Guthrie	20
Scott Hatteberg	112*
Shea Hillenbrand	34
Reggie Jefferson	11
Pedro Martinez	15
Ramon Martinez	150
Kent Mercker	16
Juan Pena	63*
Bret Saberhagen	63**
Julio Santana	74
Marino Santana	69
John Valentin	38*
John Wasdin	19

* Indicates two separate terms on Disabled List.
* * Indicates three separate terms on Disabled List.

1999 salaries

	Bonuses	Total earned salary
Pedro Martinez, p	100,000	11,100,000
John Valentin, 3b		6,350,000
Rod Beck, p		5,500,000
Jose Offerman, 2b	100,000	4,950,000
Tim Wakefield, p		4,000,000
Tom Gordon, p		3,750,000
Troy O'Leary, of		3,500,000
Bret Saberhagen, p		3,500,000
Mike Stanley, 1b		3,500,000
Reggie Jefferson, dh		3,400,000
Mark Portugal, p		2,700,000
Kent Mercker, p		2,500,000
Jeff Frye, 2b		2,400,000
Darren Lewis, of		2,100,000
Pat Rapp, p	400,000	1,650,000
Butch Huskey, of		1,500,000
Ramon Martinez, p		1,500,000
Nomar Garciaparra, ss	50,000	1,400,000
Bryce Florie, p		1,300,000
Damon Buford, of		1,100,000
Rheal Cormier, p	400,000	900,000
John Wasdin, p		500,000
Scott Hatteberg, c		350,000
Rich Garces, p		300,000
Julio Santana, p		272,500
Derek Lowe, p		245,000
Jason Varitek, c		237,500
Brian Daubach, 1b		215,000
Marino Santana, p		200,000
Trot Nixon, of		200,000
Donnie Sadler, ss		200,000
Wilton Veras, 3b		200,000
Shea Hillenbrand, c		200,000

Average 1999 salary: $2,173,333
Total 1999 team payroll:$71,720,000
Termination pay: $860,656

Minor Leagues

Tops in the organization

BATTER	CLUB	AVG.	G	AB	R	H	HR	RBI
Gonzalez, Raul	Tre	.335	127	505	80	169	18	103
Eckstein, David	Tre	.313	131	483	109	151	6	52
Kerrigan, Joseph	Aug	.300	72	277	45	83	0	20
Johnson, Rontrez	Sar	.300	132	494	97	148	8	59
Gibralter, David	Tre	.299	124	448	76	134	24	97

HOME RUNS

Burkhart, Morgan	Tre	35
Coleman, Michael	Paw	30
Alcantara, Israel	Paw	29
Chamblee, James	Paw	24
Gibralter, David	Tre	24

WINS

Ohka, Tomokazu	Paw	15
Fernandez, Jared	Paw	15
Sekany, Jason	Tre	14
Duchscherer, J.	Sar	11
Several Players Tied at		10

RBI

Burkhart, Morgan	Tre	108
Gonzalez, Raul	Tre	103
Gibralter, David	Tre	97
Stenson, Dernell	Paw	89
Chamblee, James	Paw	88

SAVES

Cisar, Mark	Aug	27
Bullinger, Kirk	Paw	25
Belovsky, Josh	Sar	20
Betancourt, Rafael	Tre	17
Several Players Tied at		7

STOLEN BASES

Eckstein, David	Tre	32
Soriano, Jose	Tre	27
Nunnally, Jon	Paw	26
Several Players Tied at		25

STRIKEOUTS

Norton, Jason	Aug	150
Miller, Greg	Aug	146
Duchscherer, J.	Sar	144
Kim, Sun	Tre	130
Lampley, Daniel	Sar	126

PITCHER	CLUB	W-L	ERA	IP	H	BB	SO
Ohka, Tomokazu	Paw	15-0	2.31	140	123	36	116
Norton, Jason	Aug	9-6	2.32	136	106	28	150
Surridge, Lance	Aug	9-5	3.05	106	102	38	88
Miller, Greg	Aug	10-6	3.10	137	109	56	146
Duchscherer, J.	Sar	11-7	3.35	153	122	38	144

Boston (1901-1999)

Runs: Most, career

1816	Carl Yastrzemski, 1961-1983
1798	Ted Williams, 1939-1960
1435	Dwight Evans, 1972-1990
1249	Jim Rice, 1974-1989
1094	Bobby Doerr, 1937-1951

Hits: Most, career

3419	Carl Yastrzemski, 1961-1983
2654	Ted Williams, 1939-1960
2452	Jim Rice, 1974-1989
2373	Dwight Evans, 1972-1990
2098	WADE BOGGS, 1982-1992

2B: Most, career

646	Carl Yastrzemski, 1961-1983
525	Ted Williams, 1939-1960
474	Dwight Evans, 1972-1990
422	WADE BOGGS, 1982-1992
381	Bobby Doerr, 1937-1951

3B: Most, career

130	Harry Hooper, 1909-1920
106	Tris Speaker, 1907-1915
90	Buck Freeman, 1901-1907
89	Bobby Doerr, 1937-1951
87	Larry Gardner, 1908-1917

HR: Most, career

521	Ted Williams, 1939-1960
452	Carl Yastrzemski, 1961-1983
382	Jim Rice, 1974-1989
379	Dwight Evans, 1972-1990
230	MO VAUGHN, 1991-1998

RBI: Most, career

1844	Carl Yastrzemski, 1961-1983
1839	Ted Williams, 1939-1960
1451	Jim Rice, 1974-1989
1346	Dwight Evans, 1972-1990
1247	Bobby Doerr, 1937-1951

SB: Most, career

300	Harry Hooper, 1909-1920
267	Tris Speaker, 1907-1915
168	Carl Yastrzemski, 1961-1983
141	Heinie Wagner, 1906-1918
134	Larry Gardner, 1908-1917

BB: Most, career

2019	Ted Williams, 1939-1960
1845	Carl Yastrzemski, 1961-1983
1337	Dwight Evans, 1972-1990
1004	WADE BOGGS, 1982-1992
826	Harry Hooper, 1909-1920

BA: Highest, career

.344	Ted Williams, 1939-1960
.338	WADE BOGGS, 1982-1992
.337	Tris Speaker, 1907-1915
.320	Pete Runnels, 1958-1962
.320	Jimmie Foxx, 1936-1942

On-base avg: Highest, career

.482	Ted Williams, 1939-1960
.429	Jimmie Foxx, 1936-1942
.428	WADE BOGGS, 1982-1992
.414	Tris Speaker, 1907-1915
.408	Pete Runnels, 1958-1962

Slug pct: Highest, career

.634	Ted Williams, 1939-1960
.605	Jimmie Foxx, 1936-1942
.542	MO VAUGHN, 1991-1998
.520	Fred Lynn, 1974-1980
.502	Jim Rice, 1974-1989

Games started: Most, career

382	ROGER CLEMENS, 1984-1996
297	Cy Young, 1901-1908
238	Luis Tiant, 1971-1978
232	Mel Parnell, 1947-1956
228	Bill Monbouquette, 1958-1965

Complete games: Most, career

275	Cy Young, 1901-1908
156	Bill Dinneen, 1902-1907
141	George Winter, 1901-1908
121	Joe Wood, 1908-1915
119	Lefty Grove, 1934-1941

Saves: Most, career

132	Bob Stanley, 1977-1989
104	Dick Radatz, 1962-1966
91	Ellis Kinder, 1948-1955
88	Jeff Reardon, 1990-1992
69	Sparky Lyle, 1967-1971

Shutouts: Most, career

38	ROGER CLEMENS, 1984-1996
38	Cy Young, 1901-1908
28	Joe Wood, 1908-1915
26	Luis Tiant, 1971-1978
25	Dutch Leonard, 1913-1918

Wins: Most, career

192	ROGER CLEMENS, 1984-1996
192	Cy Young, 1901-1908
123	Mel Parnell, 1947-1956
122	Luis Tiant, 1971-1978
117	Joe Wood, 1908-1915

K: Most, career

2590	ROGER CLEMENS, 1984-1996
1341	Cy Young, 1901-1908
1075	Luis Tiant, 1971-1978
1043	Bruce Hurst, 1980-1988
986	Joe Wood, 1908-1915

Win pct: Highest, career

.695	Roger Moret, 1970-1975
.684	Dave Ferriss, 1945-1950
.676	Joe Wood, 1908-1915
.659	Babe Ruth, 1914-1919
.640	Tex Hughson, 1941-1949

ERA: Lowest, career

1.99	Joe Wood, 1908-1915
2.00	Cy Young, 1901-1908
2.12	Ernie Shore, 1914-1917
2.13	Dutch Leonard, 1913-1918
2.19	Babe Ruth, 1914-1919

Runs: Most, season

150	Ted Williams, 1949
142	Ted Williams, 1946
141	Ted Williams, 1942
139	Jimmie Foxx, 1938
136	Tris Speaker, 1912

Hits: Most, season

240	WADE BOGGS, 1985
222	Tris Speaker, 1912
214	WADE BOGGS, 1988
213	Jim Rice, 1978
210	WADE BOGGS, 1983

2B: Most, season

67	Earl Webb, 1931
53	Tris Speaker, 1912
51	WADE BOGGS, 1989
51	Joe Cronin, 1938
47	WADE BOGGS, 1986
47	George Burns, 1923
47	Fred Lynn, 1975
47	JOHN VALENTIN, 1997

3B: Most, season

22	Tris Speaker, 1913
20	Buck Freeman, 1903
19	Buck Freeman, 1902
19	Buck Freeman, 1904
19	Larry Gardner, 1914
19	Chick Stahl, 1904

HR: Most, season

50	Jimmie Foxx, 1938
46	Jim Rice, 1978
44	MO VAUGHN, 1996
44	Carl Yastrzemski, 1967
43	Tony Armas, 1984
43	Ted Williams, 1949

RBI: Most, season

175	Jimmie Foxx, 1938
159	Vern Stephens, 1949
159	Ted Williams, 1949
145	Ted Williams, 1939
144	Walt Dropo, 1950
144	Vern Stephens, 1950

SB: Most, season

54	Tommy Harper, 1973
52	Tris Speaker, 1912
46	Tris Speaker, 1913
42	OTIS NIXON, 1994
42	Tris Speaker, 1914

BB: Most, season

162	Ted Williams, 1947
162	Ted Williams, 1949
156	Ted Williams, 1946
145	Ted Williams, 1941
145	Ted Williams, 1942

BA: Highest, season

.406	Ted Williams, 1941
.388	Ted Williams, 1957
.383	Tris Speaker, 1912
.369	Ted Williams, 1948
.368	WADE BOGGS, 1985

On-base avg: Highest, season

.551	Ted Williams, 1941
.526	Ted Williams, 1957
.513	Ted Williams, 1954
.499	Ted Williams, 1942
.499	Ted Williams, 1947

Slug pct: Highest, season

.735	Ted Williams, 1941
.731	Ted Williams, 1957
.704	Jimmie Foxx, 1938
.694	Jimmie Foxx, 1939
.667	Ted Williams, 1946

Games started: Most, season

43	Cy Young, 1902
42	Bill Dinneen, 1902
41	Babe Ruth, 1916
41	Cy Young, 1901
41	Cy Young, 1904

Complete games: Most, season

41	Cy Young, 1902
40	Cy Young, 1904
39	Bill Dinneen, 1902
38	Cy Young, 1901
37	Bill Dinneen, 1904

Saves: Most, season

46	TOM GORDON, 1998
40	Jeff Reardon, 1991
33	Jeff Russell, 1993
33	Bob Stanley, 1983
31	Bill Campbell, 1977
31	HEATHCLIFF SLOCUMB, 1996

Shutouts: Most, season

10	Joe Wood, 1912
10	Cy Young, 1904
9	Babe Ruth, 1916
8	ROGER CLEMENS, 1988
8	Carl Mays, 1918

Wins: Most, season

34	Joe Wood, 1912
33	Cy Young, 1901
32	Cy Young, 1902
28	Cy Young, 1903
26	Cy Young, 1904

K: Most, season

313	PEDRO MARTINEZ, 1999
291	ROGER CLEMENS, 1988
258	Joe Wood, 1912
257	ROGER CLEMENS, 1996
256	ROGER CLEMENS, 1987

Win pct: Highest, season

.882	Bob Stanley, 1978
.872	Joe Wood, 1912
.857	ROGER CLEMENS, 1986
.852	PEDRO MARTINEZ, 1999
.806	Dave Ferriss, 1946

ERA: Lowest, season

0.96	Dutch Leonard, 1914
1.26	Cy Young, 1908
1.49	Joe Wood, 1915
1.62	Ray Collins, 1910
1.62	Cy Young, 1901

Most pinch-hit homers, season

5	Joe Cronin, 1943
4	Del Wilber, 1953

Most pinch-hit homers, career

7	Ted Williams, 1939-1960
5	Joe Cronin, 1935-1945

Longest hitting streak

34	Dom DiMaggio, 1949
30	Tris Speaker, 1912
30	NOMAR GARCIAPARRA, 1997
28	WADE BOGGS, 1985
27	Dom DiMaggio, 1951

Most consecutive scoreless innings

45	Cy Young, 1904
42	Rube Foster, 1914
40	Luis Tiant, 1972
39	Ray Culp, 1968
37	Cy Young, 1903

No-hit games

Cy Young, Bos vs Phi AL, 3-0; May 5, 1904 (perfect game).

Jesse Tannehill, Bos at Chi AL, 6-0; August 17, 1904.

Bill Dinneen, Bos vs Chi AL, 2-0; September 27, 1905 (1st game).

Cy Young, Bos at NY AL, 8-0; June 30, 1908.

Joe Wood, Bos vs StL AL, 5-0; July 29, 1911 (1st game).

Rube Foster, Bos vs NY AL, 2-0; June 21, 1916.

Hubert (Dutch) Leonard, Bos vs StL AL, 4-0; August 30, 1916.

Ernie Shore, Bos vs Was AL, 4-0; June 23, 1917 (1st game, perfect game). (Shore relieved Babe Ruth in the first inning after Ruth had been thrown out of the game for protesting a walk to the first batter. The runner was caught stealing, and Shore retired the remaining 26 batters in order.)

Hubert (Dutch) Leonard, Bos at Det AL, 5-0; June 3, 1918.

Howard Ehmke, Bos at Phi AL, 4-0; September 7, 1923.

Mel Parnell, Bos vs Chi AL, 4-0; July 14, 1956.

Earl Wilson, Bos vs LA AL, 2-0; June 26, 1962.

Bill Monbouquette, Bos at Chi AL, 1-0; August 1, 1962.

Dave Morehead, Bos vs Cle AL, 2-0; September 16, 1965.

Matt Young, Bos at Cle AL, 1-2; April 12, 1992 (1st game) (eight innings, lost; bottom of ninth not played).

ACTIVE PLAYERS in caps.

Players' years of service are listed by the first and last years with this team and are not necessarily consecutive; all statistics record performances for this team only.

Toronto Blue Jays

Shawn Green had career highs in batting (.309), home runs (42) and RBI (123) for the Blue Jays.

By H. Darr Beiser, USA TODAY

1999 Blue Jays: Starting pitching a bust

The Toronto Blue Jays expected their starting pitching to lead them to the play-offs. But starting pitching ended up being the main reason they finished a disappointing 84-78, four wins fewer than last season.

"We had injuries, but we didn't get the type of consistent performances that we were hoping to get," Toronto general manager Gord Ash said.

Joey Hamilton, given a $17 million, three-year contract, pitched with shoulder pain throughout the season. Chris Carpenter had elbow pain in the second half. Both had season-ending operations in September. Kelvim Escobar (5.69 ERA) might have had the best stuff on the staff, but Ash said he lacked concentration and struggled with his mechanics. Former Cy Young Award winner Pat Hentgen (11-12 4.79 ERA) seems to be on the downside of his career.

David Wells (17-10 4.82 ERA), acquired from New York in the Roger Clemens deal, was every bit as effective as Clemens for much of the year, but that was only because neither came close to 1998 numbers. Wells had most of his best games mostly after the Blue Jays fell out of contention. That occurred in late August and early September, when the Blue Jays went only 11-24 anyhow.

"We had our opportunity and we choked," Wells said. "It's a shame but it's a learning experience for some of the younger guys. It's something to build on for next season. Once you get to July, there's not a lot of room for mistakes."

There were positives, though. The Blue Jays' offense scored the most runs in club history (883). Tony Fernandez flirted with .400 before tailing off in the second half. Second baseman Homer Bush, who turned out to be the most significant member of the Wells-Clemens deal, hit .320 in his first full season in the majors. Tony Batista, acquired from Arizona on June 12, finished with a combined 31 homers and 100 RBIs.

Best of all, Shawn Green became an All-Star. Green (.309, 42 homers, 123 RBI)

showed surprising power numbers and improved his outfield defense dramatically. Carlos Delgado regressed defensively at first base, but showed tremendous offense (.272, 44 HR, 134 RBI). The excitement over Green and Delgado was tempered, however, by persistent rumors that one or both would be traded. The pair was eligible for free agency after the 2000 season, and Green wanted to leave, so he was traded to Los Angeles while Delgado was re-signed.

Ash was clear that he would prefer to trade—sooner rather than later—any significant player he can't get under contract. The general manager said he would prefer not to let any distractions about free agency or trades carry into the season.

Manager Jim Fregosi called on Ash to resolve the two players' status. But Fregosi, who took over when Tim Johnson was fired during spring training, may have alienated Delgado and Green with his abrasive style.

Delgado was upset early in 1999 when Fregosi questioned his leadership, and Green was angry at the end of the season after Fregosi fired five of the coaches he inherited.

"I can't speak for others and I don't want to be controversial," Green said. "But I'm pretty upset by it. I know a lot of [other] guys are, too."

1999 Blue Jays: Week-by-week notes

These notes were excerpted from the following issues of Baseball Weekly.

▶**April 14:** With relievers Paul Quantrill, Bill Risley and Robert Person opening the season on the DL, the Jays' injury woes worsened last week. Second baseman Homer Bush injured the ligaments on his right index finger while sliding headfirst into second base on April 10 and would be lost for up to four weeks. Bush didn't even start that game. He entered to take over for Craig Grebeck, who left the game in the fourth inning with a bruised foot. Grebeck was listed as day-to-day.

▶**April 21:** Left-hander David Wells helped the Jays to get their fourth consecutive victory on April 17 with 6⅔ solid innings. He gave up two runs on six hits and three walks to Baltimore, leaving with a 3-2 lead. When Orioles' right-hander Doug Linton threw behind first baseman Carlos Delgado in the third inning after a homer by right fielder Shawn Green, Wells sent a message back, hitting right fielder Albert Belle to start the fourth.

▶**April 28:** The Blue Jays are not for sale "under any circumstances," Labatt boss Hugo Powell told Jays officials. Then came word that Labatt has a handshake agreement to sell half of its interest in the club to Howard Milstein, a part-owner of the NHL's New York Islanders.

▶**May 5:** In April the Blue Jays reeled off an eight-game winning streak. But then they dropped seven of the final eight games in the month, damaging illusions of competing with the first-place Yankees. Toronto's heralded starters had been far from outstanding. The Jays entered May ranked 10th in the AL, with a team ERA of 5.09.

▶**May 26:** The Jays had planned to have Tony Fernandez play a little third base, DH sometimes and have a bunch of days off to rest his 36-year-old body. But he has hit so well it has become difficult for manager Jim Fregosi to give him time off. Fernandez's .389 average led the AL as of May 23.

▶**June 2:** Shawn Green, the Jays' leader in

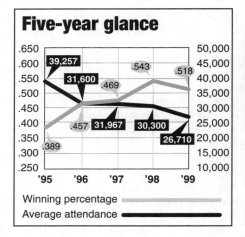

Five-year glance

Winning percentage
Average attendance

hits, home runs, doubles and almost every other offensive category, broke a small bone in his left wrist when he was hit by an Andy Pettitte pitch in the fourth inning of a May 28 Yankees game.

▶**June 16:** With shortstop Alex Gonzalez out for a month or longer with a shoulder injury, the Blue Jays dealt from strength to shore up two weak areas. They traded Dan Plesac, one of three lefties in the bullpen, to Arizona for shortstop Tony Batista and right-handed reliever John Frascatore. Batista hit 18 homers with 41 RBI while batting .273 with Arizona last year.

▶**June 30:** With their spring training site in Dunedin, Fla., the Blue Jays should know their way around the Tampa Bay area, but after an 8-0 loss on June 27, they are 1-8 at Tropicana Field against their division rivals. The Devil Rays hammered David Wells on June 24 and right-hander Kelvim Escobar the next day, and Tampa Bay's Fred McGriff homered to spark a 5-2 win on June 26.

▶**July 7:** Craig Grebeck contributed a 4-for-4 day as the DH on July 3 against Tampa Bay and drove in a run, but he admitted he's not DH material. Grebeck, 12-for-23 in six starts at DH, was hitting .398 (37-for-93) as a utility infielder through July 4. At 5-7 and 150 pounds, Grebeck is no long-ball threat—he hadn't homered even once in 1999.

▶**July 15:** General manager Gord Ash

improved his image immensely as his trades continued to help the Blue Jays. Recent acquisition Tony Batista provided steady defense and surprising offense (10 homers), while reliever John Frascatore, acquired in the same deal with Arizona, was 3-0 with a 3.60 ERA in 11 appearances.

▶**July 21:** The Marlins pounded rookie, righty closer Billy Koch for four runs in the ninth inning and won 8-6. For Koch it was his first major league loss, his third blown save in 17 opportunities and his worst outing since joining the Jays more than two months ago.

▶**July 28:** The Blue Jay's didn't appear to be lacking for confidence. They put together a three-game sweep against Atlanta, a two-game sweep versus Cleveland and two of three with a game still to go against the White Sox. Toronto had won 28 of 38 to move into wild-card contention.

▶**Sept. 1:** After winning four of six on the road, the Jays dropped three in a row after returning home against the Rangers over the weekend. With a 4-2 loss on Aug. 29, the Jays had dropped nine straight at SkyDome.

▶**Sept. 8:** The Jays got off to a rough start gearing up for a September run at the wild-card berth as right-handers Chris Carpenter and Joey Hamilton went down with injuries. Kelvim Escobar, banished to the bullpen two weeks earlier, pitched in place of Carpenter on Sept. 1 and threw seven shutout innings, limiting the Twins to four hits. Manager Jim Fregosi then brought Escobar back on three days' rest to pitch on Sept. 5 in Kansas City in what would have been Hamilton's spot. Escobar gave up four runs in four innings and took the loss.

▶**Sept. 22:** Chris Carpenter's season was over. Carpenter (9-8, 4.38 ERA) had an MRI that revealed bone spurs and chips in his right shoulder, and he subsequently underwent surgery.

▶**Sept. 29:** Carlos Delgado's outstanding season ended with a bad break. He suffered a fractured tibia when he fouled a ball off his right leg just above the ankle during a 14-9 Toronto win over Boston on Sept. 22. The injury left him tied with George Bell's single-season team RBI record of 134, set in 1987.

▶**Oct. 6:** Disappointed with the club's third-place finish in the AL East, the Jays' brass decided to gut the coaching staff. Jim Fregosi, hired during spring training with an intact staff, wanted to bring in people he knew better, so coaches Jim Lett, Gary Matthews, Lloyd Moseby, Marty Pevey and Mel Queen were to be offered other positions in the organization.

QUOTE OF THE YEAR

"They can't bring their clubs, but they can go to the pro shop and rent them."
—Manager Jim Fregosi, announcing his ban on golf clubs during road trips

---

Team Leaders

Batting avg.	Hits	Wins	Strikeouts
.328 Tony Fernandez	190 Shawn Green	17 David Wells	169 David Wells
.320 Homer Bush	185 Shannon Stewart	14 Kelvim Escobar	129 Kelvim Escobar

HR	Runs	Losses	Innings
44 Carlos Delgado	134 Shawn Green	12 Pat Hentgen	231.2 David Wells
42 Shawn Green	113 Carlos Delgado	11 Kelvim Escobar	199 Pat Hentgen

RBI	Stolen bases	ERA	Saves
134 Carlos Delgado	37 Shannon Stewart	4.79 Pat Hentgen	31 Billy Koch
123 Shawn Green	32 Homer Bush	4.82 David Wells	3 Graeme Lloyd

TORONTO BLUE JAYS 1999 final stats

BATTERS	BA	SLG	OBA	G	AB	R	H	TB	2B	3B	HR	RBI	BB	SO	SB	CS	E
Brown	.444	.667	.444	2	9	1	4	6	2	0	0	1	0	3	0	0	0
Grebeck	.363	.425	.443	34	113	18	41	48	7	0	0	10	15	13	0	0	5
Fernandez	.328	.449	.427	142	485	73	159	218	41	0	6	75	77	62	6	7	18
Bush	.320	.421	.353	128	485	69	155	204	26	4	5	55	21	82	32	8	16
Green	.309	.588	.384	153	614	134	190	361	45	0	42	123	66	117	20	7	1
Stewart	.304	.411	.371	145	608	102	185	250	28	2	11	67	59	83	37	14	5
Segui	.298	.468	.355	121	440	57	131	206	27	3	14	52	40	60	1	2	4
Gonzalez	.292	.416	.370	38	154	22	45	64	13	0	2	12	16	23	4	2	4
Fletcher	.291	.485	.339	115	412	48	120	200	26	0	18	80	26	47	0	0	2
Sanders	.286	.429	.286	3	7	1	2	3	1	0	0	2	0	2	0	0	0
Batista	.285	.565	.328	98	375	61	107	212	25	1	26	79	22	79	2	0	12
Delgado	.272	.571	.377	152	573	113	156	327	39	0	44	134	86	141	1	1	14
Kelly	.267	.483	.318	37	116	17	31	56	7	0	6	20	10	23	0	1	6
Borders	.265	.412	.286	12	34	3	9	14	0	1	1	6	1	5	0	1	2
V. Wells	.261	.352	.293	24	88	8	23	31	5	0	1	8	4	18	1	1	0
Blake	.256	.385	.293	14	39	6	10	15	2	0	1	1	2	7	0	0	0
Cruz	.241	.433	.358	106	349	63	84	151	19	3	14	45	64	91	14	4	3
Otanez	.237	.391	.293	71	207	28	49	81	11	0	7	24	15	46	0	0	6
Brumfield	.235	.353	.307	62	170	25	40	60	8	3	2	19	19	39	1	2	3
Woodward	.231	.269	.276	14	26	1	6	7	1	0	0	2	2	6	0	0	2
Hollins	.222	.333	.260	27	99	12	22	33	5	0	2	6	5	22	0	0	0
Martin	.222	.296	.364	9	27	3	6	8	2	0	0	4	4	4	0	0	1
Matheny	.215	.307	.271	57	163	16	35	50	6	0	3	17	12	37	0	0	2
Lennon	.207	.379	.281	9	29	3	6	11	2	0	1	6	2	12	0	0	0
Witt	.206	.324	.250	15	34	3	7	11	1	0	1	5	2	9	0	0	0
Greene	.204	.394	.266	81	226	22	46	89	7	0	12	41	20	56	0	0	1
McRae	.195	.366	.340	31	82	11	16	30	3	1	3	11	16	22	0	1	0
Berroa	.194	.290	.315	22	62	11	12	18	3	0	1	6	9	15	0	0	0
Dalesandro	.185	.185	.207	16	27	3	5	5	0	0	0	1	0	2	1	0	0
Butler	.143	.143	.250	8	7	1	1	1	0	0	0	1	0	0	0	0	0
Goodwin	.000	.000	.000	2	8	0	0	0	0	0	0	0	0	3	0	0	0

PITCHERS	W-L	ERA	BA	G	GS	CG	GF	SH	SV	IP	H	R	ER	HR	BB	SO
Glover	0-0	0.00	.000	1	0	0	1	0	0	1.0	0	0	0	0	1	0
Quantrill	3-2	3.33	.282	41	0	0	13	0	0	48.2	53	19	18	5	17	28
Koch	0-5	3.39	.235	56	0	0	48	0	31	63.2	55	26	24	5	30	57
Frascatore	7-1	3.41	.292	33	0	0	14	0	1	37.0	42	16	14	5	9	22
Lloyd	5-3	3.63	.250	74	0	0	25	0	3	72.0	68	36	29	11	23	47
Halladay	8-7	3.92	.270	36	18	1	2	1	1	149.1	156	76	65	19	79	82
Carpenter	9-8	4.38	.294	24	24	4	0	1	0	150.0	177	81	73	16	48	106
Spoljaric	2-2	4.65	.258	37	2	0	7	0	0	62.0	62	41	32	9	32	63
Hentgen	11-12	4.79	.286	34	34	1	0	0	0	199.0	225	115	106	32	65	118
D. Wells	17-10	4.82	.271	34	34	7	0	1	0	231.2	246	132	124	32	62	169
Escobar	14-11	5.69	.293	33	30	1	2	0	0	174.0	203	118	110	19	81	129
Munro	0-2	6.02	.318	31	2	0	9	0	0	55.1	70	38	37	6	23	38
Hamilton	7-8	6.52	.298	22	18	0	1	0	0	98.0	118	73	71	13	39	56
Plesac	0-3	8.34	.308	30	0	0	5	0	0	22.2	28	21	21	4	9	26
Person	0-2	9.82	.231	11	0	0	7	0	2	11.0	9	12	12	1	15	12
Romano	0-0	11.81	.364	3	0	0	1	0	0	5.1	8	8	7	1	5	3
Hudek	0-0	12.27	.471	3	0	0	1	0	0	3.2	8	5	5	1	1	2
Bale	0-0	13.50	.250	1	0	0	0	0	0	2.0	2	3	3	1	2	4
Rodriguez	0-1	13.50	.250	2	0	0	1	0	0	2.0	2	3	3	2	2	2
Ludwick	0-0	27.00	.500	1	0	0	0	0	0	1.0	3	3	3	0	2	0

2000 preliminary roster

PITCHERS (19)
Clayton Andrews
John Bale
Pedro Borbon
Chris Carpenter
Pasqual Coco
Matt DeWitt
Kelvim Escobar
Leoncio Estrella
John Frascatore
Gary Glover
Roy Halladay
Joey Hamilton

Billy Koch
Peter Munro
Lance Painter
Paul Quantrill
Nerio Rodriguez
John Sneed
David Wells

CATCHERS (3)
Alberto Castillo
Darrin Fletcher
Josh Phelps

INFIELDERS (11)
Tony Batista
Casey Blake
Homer Bush
Carlos Delgado
Alex Gonzalez
Craig Grebeck
Joe Lawrence
Willis Otanez
Kevin Witt
Chris Woodward
Mike Young

OUTFIELDERS (7)
Jose Cruz
Raul Mondesi
Anthony Sanders
Shannon Stewart
Andy Thompson
Vernon Wells
DeWayne Wise

Games played by position

PLAYER	G	C	1B	2B	3B	SS	OF	DH
Batista	98	0	0	0	0	98	0	0
Berroa	22	0	0	0	0	0	2	17
Blake	14	0	0	0	14	0	0	0
Borders	6	3	0	0	1	0	0	3
Brown	2	2	0	0	0	0	0	0
Brumfield	62	0	0	0	0	0	53	6
Bush	128	0	0	109	0	18	0	0
Butler	8	0	0	0	0	0	2	3
Cruz	106	0	0	0	0	0	106	0
Dalesandro	16	8	0	0	2	0	0	5
Delgado	152	0	147	0	0	0	0	5
Fernandez	142	0	0	1	132	0	0	11
Fletcher	115	113	0	0	0	0	0	0
Gonzalez	38	0	0	0	0	37	0	1
Goodwin	2	0	0	0	0	0	2	0
Grebeck	34	0	0	17	2	4	0	12
Green	153	0	0	0	0	0	152	0
Greene	81	0	0	0	7	0	3	52
Hollins	27	0	0	0	0	0	0	25
Kelly	37	0	0	35	0	0	0	2
Lennon	9	0	0	0	0	0	8	0
Martin	9	0	0	8	0	1	0	0
Matheny	57	57	0	0	0	0	0	0
McRae	31	0	0	0	0	0	13	15
Otanez	42	0	13	0	24	0	0	4
Sanders	3	0	0	0	0	0	1	2
Segui	31	0	4	0	0	0	0	25
Stewart	145	0	0	0	0	0	142	2
Wells	25	0	0	0	0	0	24	0
Witt	15	0	0	0	0	0	0	10
Woodward	14	0	0	0	2	10	0	0

Minor Leagues
Tops in the organization

BATTER	CLUB	AVG.	G	AB	R	H	HR	RBI
Wells, Vernon	Syr	.334	129	500	81	167	18	81
Phelps, Josh	Dun	.328	110	406	72	133	20	88
Lopez, Luis	Syr	.322	136	531	76	171	4	69
Young, Mike	Dun	.313	129	495	86	155	5	83
Giles, Tim	Knx	.311	133	505	76	157	18	114

HOME RUNS
Thompson, Andy	Syr	31	
Gibbons, Jay	Dun	25	
Witt, Kevin	Syr	24	
Blake, Casey	Stc	22	
Melhuse, Adam	Knx	21	

WINS
Coco, Pasqual	Dun	15
Estrella, Leo	Dun	14
Sneed, John	Knx	14
Cassidy, Scott	Hag	13
McClellan, Matt	Dun	13

RBI
Giles, Tim	Knx	114
Gibbons, Jay	Dun	108
Thompson, Andy	Syr	95
Gomez, Rudy	Knx	92
Phelps, Josh	Dun	88

SAVES
Kingrey, Jarrod	Hag	27
File, Bob	Dun	26
Smith, Brian	Syr	20
Sinclair, Steve	Syr	18
Bluma, Marc	Stc	13

STOLEN BASES
Nunez, Jorge	Hag	51
Davies, Justin	Hag	36
Abernathy, Brent	Knx	34
Izturis, Cesar	Dun	32
Young, Mike	Dun	30

STRIKEOUTS
Cassidy, Scott	Hag	178
Sneed, John	Knx	171
McClellan, Matt	Dun	146
Coco, Pasqual	Dun	142
Rodriguez, Nerio	Syr	137

PITCHER	CLUB	W-L	ERA	IP	H	BB	SO
Bleazard, David	Knx	11-9	2.75	177	154	64	107
Estrella, Leo	Dun	14-7	3.21	168	166	47	116
Cassidy, Scott	Hag	13-7	3.27	171	151	30	178
Coco, Pasqual	Dun	15-7	3.70	173	148	61	142
Sneed, John	Knx	14-3	3.75	154	140	57	171

Sick call: 1999 DL report

PLAYER	Days on the DL
Geronimo Berroa	106*
Homer Bush	33
Rob Butler	76
Chris Carpenter	25
Jose Cruz	15
Darrin Fletcher	31
Alex Gonzalez	140
Craig Grebeck	93*
Joey Hamilton	40
Dave Hollins	33
Willis Otanez	21
Robert Person	7
Paul Quantrill	71
Bill Risley	182
David Segui	25

Indicates two separate terms on Disabled List.

1999 salaries

	Bonuses	Total earned salary
Pat Hentgen, p		8,600,000
Carlos Delgado, 1b	50,000	5,075,000
David Wells, p	150,000	4,816,667
Joey Hamilton, p		4,250,000
Brian McRae, of		3,750,000
Shawn Green, of	75,000	3,125,000
Darrin Fletcher, c		2,625,000
David Segui, dh		2,500,000
Alex Gonzalez, ss		2,275,000
Tony Fernandez, 3b	25,000	2,250,000
Graeme Lloyd, p	50,000	1,025,000
Willie Greene, dh		1,000,000
Mike Matheny, c		600,000
Bill Risley, p		575,000
Craig Grebeck, 2b		550,000
Paul Quantrill, p		500,000
Chris Carpenter, p		483,333
Paul Spoljaric, p		450,000
Shannon Stewart, of		433,333
Tony Batista, ss		375,000
Kelvim Escobar, p		350,000
John Frascatore, p		345,000
Rob Butler, of		275,000
Pat Borders, c		270,000
Jacob Brumfield, of		240,000
Homer Bush, 2b		227,000
Willis Otanez, 3b		200,000
Pete Munro, p		200,000
Chris Woodward, ss		200,000
Roy Halladay, p		200,000
Billy Koch, p		200,000
Vernon Wells, of		200,000

Average 1999 salary: $1,505,167
Total 1999 team payroll: $48,165,333
Termination pay: $781,967

Toronto (1977-1999)

Runs: Most, career
- 768 Lloyd Moseby, 1980-1989
- 699 TONY FERNANDEZ, 1983-1999
- 641 George Bell, 1981-1990
- 578 Joe Carter, 1991-1997
- 538 Willie Upshaw, 1978-1987

Hits: Most, career
- 1565 TONY FERNANDEZ, 1983-1999
- 1319 Lloyd Moseby, 1980-1989
- 1294 George Bell, 1981-1990
- 1051 Joe Carter, 1991-1997
- 1028 Damaso Garcia, 1980-1986

2B: Most, career
- 287 TONY FERNANDEZ, 1983-1999
- 242 Lloyd Moseby, 1980-1989
- 237 George Bell, 1981-1990
- 218 Joe Carter, 1991-1997
- 213 JOHN OLERUD, 1989-1996

3B: Most, career
- 72 TONY FERNANDEZ, 1983-1999
- 60 Lloyd Moseby, 1980-1989
- 50 Alfredo Griffin, 1979-1993
- 42 Willie Upshaw, 1978-1987
- 36 ROBERTO ALOMAR, 1991-1995

HR: Most, career
- 203 Joe Carter, 1991-1997
- 202 George Bell, 1981-1990
- 179 Jesse Barfield, 1981-1989
- 149 CARLOS DELGADO, 1993-1999
- 149 Lloyd Moseby, 1980-1989

RBI: Most, career
- 740 George Bell, 1981-1990
- 736 Joe Carter, 1991-1997
- 651 Lloyd Moseby, 1980-1989
- 601 TONY FERNANDEZ, 1983-1999
- 527 Jesse Barfield, 1981-1989

SB: Most, career
- 255 Lloyd Moseby, 1980-1989
- 206 ROBERTO ALOMAR, 1991-1995
- 194 Damaso Garcia, 1980-1986
- 172 TONY FERNANDEZ, 1983-1999
- 126 DEVON WHITE, 1991-1995

BB: Most, career
- 547 Lloyd Moseby, 1980-1989
- 514 JOHN OLERUD, 1989-1996
- 438 TONY FERNANDEZ, 1983-1999
- 416 Rance Mulliniks, 1982-1992
- 403 Ernie Whitt, 1977-1989

BA: Highest, career
- .307 ROBERTO ALOMAR, 1991-1995
- .297 TONY FERNANDEZ, 1983-1999
- .293 JOHN OLERUD, 1989-1996
- .288 Damaso Garcia, 1980-1986
- .286 George Bell, 1981-1990

On-base avg: Highest, career
- .395 JOHN OLERUD, 1989-1996
- .389 FRED McGRIFF, 1986-1990
- .382 ROBERTO ALOMAR, 1991-1995
- .372 Otto Velez, 1977-1982
- .365 Rance Mulliniks, 1982-1992

Slug pct: Highest, career
- .531 CARLOS DELGADO, 1993-1999
- .530 FRED McGRIFF, 1986-1990
- .505 SHAWN GREEN, 1993-1999
- .486 George Bell, 1981-1990
- .483 Jesse Barfield, 1981-1989

Games started: Most, career
- 408 Dave Stieb, 1979-1998
- 345 Jim Clancy, 1977-1988
- 250 Jimmy Key, 1984-1992
- 222 PAT HENTGEN, 1991-1999
- 195 JUAN GUZMAN, 1991-1998

Complete games: Most, career
- 103 Dave Stieb, 1979-1998
- 73 Jim Clancy, 1977-1988
- 31 PAT HENTGEN, 1991-1999
- 28 Jimmy Key, 1984-1992
- 27 Luis Leal, 1980-1985

Saves: Most, career
- 217 Tom Henke, 1985-1992
- 121 Duane Ward, 1986-1995
- 52 MIKE TIMLIN, 1991-1997
- 31 BILLY KOCH, 1999
- 31 Joey McLaughlin, 1980-1984

Shutouts: Most, career
- 30 Dave Stieb, 1979-1998
- 11 Jim Clancy, 1977-1988
- 10 Jimmy Key, 1984-1992
- 9 PAT HENTGEN, 1991-1999
- 4 Jesse Jefferson, 1977-1980
- 4 TODD STOTTLEMYRE, 1988-1994

Wins: Most, career
- 175 Dave Stieb, 1979-1998
- 128 Jim Clancy, 1977-1988
- 116 Jimmy Key, 1984-1992
- 105 PAT HENTGEN, 1991-1999
- 76 JUAN GUZMAN, 1991-1998

K: Most, career
- 1658 Dave Stieb, 1979-1998
- 1237 Jim Clancy, 1977-1988
- 1030 JUAN GUZMAN, 1991-1998
- 995 PAT HENTGEN, 1991-1999
- 944 Jimmy Key, 1984-1992

Win pct: Highest, career
- .639 Doyle Alexander, 1983-1986
- .589 Jimmy Key, 1984-1992
- .580 PAT HENTGEN, 1991-1999
- .577 DAVID WELLS, 1987-1999
- .566 Dave Stieb, 1979-1998

ERA: Lowest, career
- 3.42 Dave Stieb, 1979-1998
- 3.42 Jimmy Key, 1984-1992
- 3.56 Doyle Alexander, 1983-1986
- 3.87 John Cerutti, 1985-1990
- 4.04 DAVID WELLS, 1987-1999

Runs: Most, season
- 134 SHAWN GREEN, 1999
- 121 Paul Molitor, 1993
- 116 DEVON WHITE, 1993
- 113 CARLOS DELGADO, 1999
- 111 George Bell, 1987

Hits: Most, season
- 213 TONY FERNANDEZ, 1986
- 211 Paul Molitor, 1993
- 200 JOHN OLERUD, 1993
- 198 George Bell, 1986
- 192 ROBERTO ALOMAR, 1993

2B: Most, season

54	JOHN OLERUD, 1993
45	SHAWN GREEN, 1999
43	CARLOS DELGADO, 1998
42	Joe Carter, 1991
42	CARLOS DELGADO, 1997
42	DEVON WHITE, 1993

3B: Most, season

17	TONY FERNANDEZ, 1990
15	Dave Collins, 1984
15	Alfredo Griffin, 1980
15	Lloyd Moseby, 1984
11	ROBERTO ALOMAR, 1991

HR: Most, season

47	George Bell, 1987
46	JOSE CANSECO, 1998
44	CARLOS DELGADO, 1999
42	SHAWN GREEN, 1999
40	Jesse Barfield, 1986

RBI: Most, season

134	George Bell, 1987
134	CARLOS DELGADO, 1999
123	SHAWN GREEN, 1999
121	Joe Carter, 1993
119	Joe Carter, 1992

SB: Most, season

60	Dave Collins, 1984
55	ROBERTO ALOMAR, 1993
54	Damaso Garcia, 1982
54	OTIS NIXON, 1996
53	ROBERTO ALOMAR, 1991

BB: Most, season

119	FRED McGRIFF, 1989
114	JOHN OLERUD, 1993
94	FRED McGRIFF, 1990
87	ROBERTO ALOMAR, 1992
86	CARLOS DELGADO, 1999

BA: Highest, season

.363	JOHN OLERUD, 1993
.341	Paul Molitor, 1994
.332	Paul Molitor, 1993
.328	TONY FERNANDEZ, 1999
.326	ROBERTO ALOMAR, 1993

On-base avg: Highest, season

.473	JOHN OLERUD, 1993
.427	TONY FERNANDEZ, 1999
.410	Paul Molitor, 1994
.408	ROBERTO ALOMAR, 1993
.405	ROBERTO ALOMAR, 1992

Slug pct: Highest, season

.605	George Bell, 1987
.599	JOHN OLERUD, 1993
.592	CARLOS DELGADO, 1998
.588	SHAWN GREEN, 1999
.571	CARLOS DELGADO, 1999

Games started: Most, season

40	Jim Clancy, 1982
38	Luis Leal, 1982
38	Dave Stieb, 1982
37	Jim Clancy, 1987
36	Doyle Alexander, 1985
36	Jim Clancy, 1984
36	Jimmy Key, 1987
36	Dave Stieb, 1983
36	Dave Stieb, 1985

Complete games: Most, season

19	Dave Stieb, 1982
15	Jim Clancy, 1980
14	Dave Stieb, 1980
14	Dave Stieb, 1983
12	Jerry Garvin, 1977
12	Tom Underwood, 1979

Saves: Most, season

45	Duane Ward, 1993
34	Tom Henke, 1987
34	Tom Henke, 1992
32	Tom Henke, 1990
32	Tom Henke, 1991

Shutouts: Most, season

5	Dave Stieb, 1982
4	Dave Stieb, 1980
4	Dave Stieb, 1983
4	Dave Stieb, 1988
3	Jim Clancy, 1982
3	Jim Clancy, 1986
3	ROGER CLEMENS, 1997
3	ROGER CLEMENS, 1998
3	PAT HENTGEN, 1994
3	PAT HENTGEN, 1996
3	PAT HENTGEN, 1997
3	Dave Lemanczyk, 1979

Wins: Most, season

21	ROGER CLEMENS, 1997
21	Jack Morris, 1992
20	ROGER CLEMENS, 1998
20	PAT HENTGEN, 1996
19	PAT HENTGEN, 1993

K: Most, season

292	ROGER CLEMENS, 1997
271	ROGER CLEMENS, 1998
198	Dave Stieb, 1984
194	JUAN GUZMAN, 1993
187	Dave Stieb, 1983

Win pct: Highest, season

.778	Jack Morris, 1992
.769	ROGER CLEMENS, 1998
.762	JUAN GUZMAN, 1992
.750	ROGER CLEMENS, 1997
.750	Dave Stieb, 1990

ERA: Lowest, season

2.05	ROGER CLEMENS, 1997
2.48	Dave Stieb, 1985
2.64	JUAN GUZMAN, 1992
2.65	ROGER CLEMENS, 1998
2.76	Jimmy Key, 1987

Most pinch-hit homers, season

3	WILLIE GREENE, 1999
2	Al Woods, 1977
2	Otto Velez, 1979
2	Rico Carty, 1979
2	Ernie Whitt, 1982
2	Jeff Burroughs, 1985

Most pinch-hit homers, career

4	Ernie Whitt, 1977-1989
4	Jesse Barfield, 1981-1989

Longest hitting streak

28	SHAWN GREENE, 1999
26	JOHN OLERUD, 1993
26	SHANNON STEWART, 1999
22	George Bell, 1989
21	Damaso Garcia, 1983
21	Lloyd Moseby, 1983
20	Damaso Garcia, 1980

Most consecutive scoreless innings

33	ROGER CLEMENS, 1998

No-hit game

Dave Stieb, Tor at Cle AL, 3-0;
September 2, 1990.

ACTIVE PLAYERS in caps.

Players' years of service are listed by the first and last years with this team and are not necessarily consecutive; all statistics record performances for this team only.

Baltimore Orioles

by H. Darr Beiser, USA TODAY

B.J. Surhoff played all 162 games, inheriting Cal Ripken's role as the Orioles' leader.

1999 Orioles: Bad timing was everything

The scenario is becoming familiar to the Baltimore Orioles. Salaries are high, along with ages and expectations. But after two disappointing seasons, it became apparent that the formula for success is much more complex than merely having owner Peter Angelos sign lots of big checks.

"It's happened two years in a row now. It's hard to pinpoint something," said pitcher Scott Erickson of a year that began 4-14 and didn't become respectable until a strong September. "Obviously, things just didn't go very well. We had a couple of good years, then somehow or another we switched things up and it went down the drain."

Manager Ray Miller was one casualty after the two sub-.500 seasons that followed Davey Johnson getting the Orioles to the AL Championship Series the previous two years. General Manager Frank Wren also got the boot.

While Wren's team slogged through the season, he made several moves to inject the Orioles with much-needed youth by trading starting pitcher Juan Guzman and 40-year-old designated hitter Harold Baines for prospects. The Orioles also took serious looks at several rookies, including second baseman Jerry Hairston, Jr., third baseman Ryan Minor, and center fielder Eugene Kingsale. But the team was locked into long-term commitments with several over-30 players: second baseman Delino DeShields, third baseman Cal Ripken, center fielder Brady Anderson, and first baseman Will Clark.

They did learn that B.J. Ryan, obtained in the Guzman trade, has the potential to be a solid closer. But Mike Timlin, who blew eight saves before the All-Star break and finished with a 3-9 record, signed a four-year deal last winter and was more consistent in the second half.

Albert Belle—who used a late surge to finish with 37 homers and 117 RBI—and B.J. Surhoff were the core of the offense, and Ripken hit well when his cranky back would allow him to be in the lineup. He reached the 400-homer plateau, but his march to 3,000 hits was put on hold when his back acted up again in September.

Team MVP

B.J. Surhoff: In 1999, B.J. Surhoff succeeded Cal Ripken as Baltimore's top offensive player and clubhouse leader. As a left fielder—unlike his earlier roles at catcher and third base—Surhoff was well over .300 all season, finishing at .308. Ironically, the only Oriole with a higher average was Ripken in his 86-game season. Surhoff played a Ripken-like 162 games with 207 hits, 28 homers and 107 RBI.

Sidney Ponson, who went 12-12 with six complete games, has one of the finest young arms in the American League. But Miller, a former pitching coach, couldn't get enough out of his staff in 1999. The Orioles had a club-record .279 batting average and set a franchise record with 1,572 hits. Baltimore had at least 10 hits in nearly half its games, but lost 24 games when it scored at least six runs.

"Everybody looks at how many runs we scored. A lot of runs doesn't win anything, as this year proves," ace Mike Mussina said. "You've got to pitch. It's as simple as that. The teams that pitch the best win the World Series every year."

Mussina went 18-7, so he gets no blame. But Erickson started 1-8 and Guzman didn't get his third win until June 12, which served to put a whole lot of early pressure on a bullpen that was suspect out of spring training.

"Our starting pitching didn't do too well early in the season, and the bullpen didn't pick up the pieces when it should have," Timlin said. "When the bullpen started doing well, it seemed like the starting pitching fell in line and then the hitting seemed to falter a little bit. We just didn't coordinate things at the same time."

For 2000, the Orioles hired a manager who has been able to put it all together: Mike Hargrove. They hired him just weeks after the Cleveland Indians let him go.

1999 Orioles: Week-by-week notes

These notes were excerpted from the following issues of Baseball Weekly.

▶**April 7:** Speaking publicly for the first time since the death of his father, Cal Ripken Sr., on March 25, third baseman Cal Ripken Jr. said that he feels "a little lost," but hopes baseball will help him deal with the loss. Ripken credited his father, above all others, for instilling the discipline and toughness to play 2,632 consecutive games.

▶**April 14:** Orioles ace Mike Mussina ended the pitching staff's ugly three-game slide with seven shutout innings against the Blue Jays on April 10. Before that game, Orioles starters had a 10.00 ERA and had pitched only 18 of a possible 36 innings. The Orioles played another sloppy game on the day after Mussina's win, leaving them 2-4 after the first week. Mussina had both of the team's victories.

▶**April 21:** Baltimore, off to its worst start since going 0-21 to begin the 1988 season, lost Cal Ripken and first baseman Will Clark for an undetermined time. Ripken missed his fourth game of the season on April 18 and was heading to Cleveland to have his back examined by a specialist. On the same day Clark fractured his left thumb on a grounder.

▶**May 5:** With losses piling up, manager Ray Miller finally snapped at his $84 million collection of ballplayers. After pitchers matched a club record by walking 14 in an 11-10 loss to the A's on April 25, Miller called them "unprofessional." The Orioles released reliever Heathcliff Slocumb on April 30, a day after he allowed seven runs in the ninth inning of a 15-5 loss to the Royals. Slocumb had allowed 26 baserunners in 8⅔ innings, and the Orioles had no choice but to eat his $1.1 million salary.

▶**May 12:** The Orioles won five in a row and six of seven the past week. They averaged 6.2 runs per game over their last nine, and the starting pitchers had a 2.72 ERA after having a 7.60 over their first 21 games.

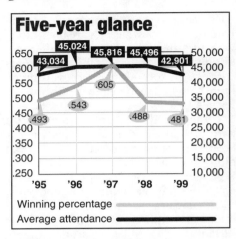

Five-year glance

	'95	'96	'97	'98	'99
Attendance	45,024	43,034	45,816	45,496	42,901
Winning pct.	.493	.543	.605	.488	.481

Winning percentage
Average attendance

▶**May 26:** To the surprise of some, Ray Miller retained his job after a 3-7 road trip left him admittedly running low on ideas to improve his club. Owner Peter Angelos refused to can Miller, instead focusing his scrutiny on general manager Frank Wren.

▶**June 9:** Ray Miller was tired of watching his veteran team make fundamental mistakes and said he would levy "blatant" fines for future blunders. The announcement came after the Orioles held on for a wild 14-11 victory over the Mariners, a game in which right-hander Juan Guzman failed to cover first on one play and lost track of outs on another. In his previous start, against the Angels, Guzman had been late in backing up the plate.

▶**June 23:** Left fielder B.J. Surhoff extended his career-high hitting streak to 21 games on June 20 and was making a strong bid for his first spot on the All-Star team. Hitting third regularly for the first time, he's batting .339 with 16 home runs and 50 RBI.

▶**June 30:** Three Orioles reached milestones during the past week. Left-hander Jesse Orosco made his 1,051th relief appearance, breaking Kent Tekulve's major league record. Center fielder Brady Anderson stole the 255th base of his Orioles career, breaking center fielder Al Bumbry's club record. Shortstop Mike Bordick got the 1,000th hit of his career.

▶**July 7:** The bullpen had fallen into com-

plete chaos by the end of the previous week, when it blew its 19th save in a 6-5 loss on July 3 to the Yankees, the Orioles' 10th straight defeat. The loss was the Orioles' 17th by one run this season.

▶**July 15:** The Orioles exercised their option on Cal Ripken's contract last week. Having resurrected his career with a blistering two-month run at the plate, Ripken will make $6.3 million to play his 19th season in 2000. After hitting .179 with two RBI before going on the DL in April, Ripken was at .310 with 12 homers and 38 RBI at the All-Star break.

▶**July 28:** In the wake of a June 4 incident in which right fielder Albert Belle made lewd gestures toward the Camden Yards crowd, the team began to explore the possibility of trading him despite the presence of a no-trade clause in his contract. Meanwhile, Belle was hot at the plate, going 13-for-33 with five home runs and 12 RBI over eight games.

▶**Aug. 11:** Bench coach Eddie Murray was named manager of the Arizona Fall League's Scottsdale Scorpions. Murray was considered a front-runner for the Orioles' job if Ray Miller was not to return next year.

▶**Aug. 25:** Will Clark was expected to miss the remainder of the season with bone chips in his elbow. Having battled a broken thumb, a swollen knee and an ailing elbow, Clark finished the season hitting .303 with 10 home runs and 29 RBI in 77 games. He was replaced by Jeff Conine, who outproduced him (.317, 12 homers, 55 RBI) in just a little more playing time.

▶**Sept. 8:** Cal Ripken became the 29th player in history to hit 400 home runs when he slammed a three-run blast on Sept. 2. Ripken, 39, was having one of his best years ever at the plate and his worst ever physically. He had missed 63 of 136 games through Sept. 5.

▶**Sept. 22:** By the first week of June, right-hander Scott Erickson was 1-8 with a 7.11 ERA and had allowed 89 hits in 69⅔ innings. He went 13-3 with a 3.65 ERA. He was leading the league in innings pitched and shutouts and was tied for the lead (with a teammate, right-hander Sidney Ponson) in complete games.

▶**Sept. 29:** The Orioles' 13-game winning streak, which ended on Sept. 23 when they dropped the first game of a doubleheader to the A's, matched the second longest in team history, behind only a 14-gamer in 1973. B.J. Surhoff reached 200 hits on Sept. 24, becoming just the third Oriole to reach that mark, after Cal Ripken (twice) and Al Bumbry.

▶**Oct. 6:** The Orioles set a club record for most hits in a season (1,572) and had their highest batting average ever (.279). They also led the league in fielding percentage (.986) and ranked fourth in the AL in team ERA (4.77). Yet they finished at 78-84 and came in a disappointing fourth.

Team Leaders

Batting avg.	Hits	Wins	Strikeouts
.308 B.J. Surhoff	207 B.J. Surhoff	18 Mike Mussina	172 Mike Mussina
.297 Albert Belle	181 Albert Belle	15 Scott Erickson	112 Sidney Ponson

HR	Runs	Losses	Innings
37 Albert Belle	109 Brady Anderson	12 Sidney Ponson	230.1 Scott Erickson
28 B.J. Surhoff	108 Albert Belle	12 Scott Erickson	210 Sidney Ponson

RBI	Stolen bases	ERA	Saves
117 Albert Belle	36 Brady Anderson	3.50 Mike Mussina	27 Mike Timlin
107 B.J.Surhoff	17 Albert Belle	4.71 Sidney Ponson	3 Arthur Rhodes

BALTIMORE ORIOLES 1999 final stats

BATTERS	BA	SLG	OBA	G	AB	R	H	TB	2B	3B	HR	RBI	BB	SO	SB	CS	E
Ripken	.340	.584	.368	86	332	51	113	194	27	0	18	57	13	31	0	1	13
Surhoff	.308	.492	.347	162	673	104	207	331	38	1	28	107	43	78	5	1	0
Clark	.303	.482	.395	77	251	40	76	121	15	0	10	29	38	42	2	2	3
Belle	.297	.541	.400	161	610	108	181	330	36	1	37	117	101	82	17	3	4
Conine	.291	.453	.335	139	444	54	129	201	31	1	13	75	30	40	0	3	7
Anderson	.282	.477	.404	150	564	109	159	269	28	5	24	81	96	105	36	7	1
Amaral	.277	.350	.348	91	137	21	38	48	8	1	0	11	15	20	9	6	0
Bordick	.277	.403	.334	160	631	93	175	254	35	7	10	77	54	102	14	4	9
Hairston	.269	.417	.323	50	175	26	47	73	12	1	4	17	11	24	9	4	0
May	.265	.510	.315	26	49	5	13	25	0	0	4	12	4	6	0	0	0
DeShields	.264	.364	.339	96	330	46	87	120	11	2	6	34	37	52	11	8	10
C. Johnson	.251	.413	.340	135	426	58	107	176	19	1	16	54	55	107	0	0	5
Kingsale	.247	.271	.301	28	85	9	21	23	2	0	0	7	5	13	1	3	1
Figga	.221	.302	.236	43	86	12	19	26	4	0	1	5	2	27	0	2	5
Garcia	.207	.414	.258	17	29	6	6	12	0	0	2	2	2	3	0	0	0
Minor	.194	.323	.241	46	124	13	24	40	7	0	3	10	8	43	1	0	5
Davis	.167	.167	.167	5	6	0	1	1	0	0	0	0	0	2	0	0	1
Reboulet	.162	.188	.317	99	154	25	25	29	4	0	0	4	33	29	1	0	2
Pickering	.125	.225	.314	23	40	4	5	9	1	0	1	5	11	16	0	0	2

PITCHERS	W-L	ERA	BA	G	GS	CG	GF	SH	SV	IP	H	R	ER	HR	BB	SO
Falkenborg	0-0	0.00	.200	2	0	0	0	0	0	3.0	2	0	0	0	2	1
Ryan	1-0	2.95	.150	13	0	0	3	0	0	18.1	9	6	6	0	12	28
Mussina	18-7	3.50	.268	31	31	4	0	0	0	203.1	207	88	79	16	52	172
Timlin	3-9	3.57	.221	62	0	0	52	0	27	63.0	51	30	25	9	23	50
Guzman	5-9	4.18	.265	21	21	1	0	1	0	122.2	124	63	57	18	65	95
Corsi	1-3	4.34	.288	36	0	0	8	0	0	37.1	40	19	18	6	20	22
Johns	6-4	4.47	.248	32	5	0	2	0	0	86.2	81	45	43	9	25	50
Ponson	12-12	4.71	.282	32	32	6	0	0	0	210.0	227	118	110	35	80	112
Erickson	15-12	4.81	.280	34	34	6	0	3	0	230.1	244	127	123	27	99	106
Reyes	2-3	4.85	.225	27	0	0	6	0	0	29.2	23	16	16	4	16	28
Kamieniecki	2-4	4.95	.250	43	3	0	18	0	2	56.1	52	32	31	4	29	39
Orosco	0-2	5.34	.239	65	0	0	12	0	1	32.0	28	21	19	5	20	35
Rhodes	3-4	5.43	.221	43	0	0	11	0	3	53.0	43	37	32	9	45	59
J. Johnson	8-7	5.46	.267	22	21	0	0	0	0	115.1	120	74	70	16	55	71
Fetters	1-0	5.81	.278	27	0	0	10	0	0	31.0	35	23	20	5	22	22
Linton	1-4	5.95	.296	14	8	0	0	0	0	59.0	69	41	39	14	25	32
Bones	0-3	5.98	.322	30	2	0	7	0	0	43.2	59	29	29	7	19	26
Molina	1-2	6.65	.256	20	0	0	7	0	0	23.0	22	19	17	4	16	14
Riley	0-0	7.36	.378	3	3	0	0	0	0	11.0	17	9	9	4	13	6
Coppinger	0-1	8.31	.294	11	2	0	7	0	0	21.2	25	21	20	8	19	17
Slocumb	0-0	12.46	.395	10	0	0	7	0	0	8.2	15	12	12	2	9	12

2000 preliminary roster

PITCHERS (19)
Juan Aracena
Radhames Dykhoff
Scott Erickson
Brian Falkenborg
Juan Guzman
Jimmy Hamilton
Doug Johns
Jason Johnson
Calvin Maduro
Chuck McElroy
Gabe Molina
Mike Mussina

Richard Negrette
Sidney Ponson
Al Reyes
Matt Riley
BJ Ryan
Mike Timlin
Mike Trombley

CATCHERS (1)
Charles Johnson

INFIELDERS (12)
Mike Bordick
Carlos Casimiro
Will Clark
Ivanon Coffie
Jeff Conine
Delino Deshields
Jesse Garcia
Jerry Hairston
Eddy Martinez
Ryan Minor
Calvin Pickering
Cal Ripken

OUTFIELDERS (8)
Wady Almonte
Rich Amaral
Brady Anderson
Harold Baines
Albert Belle
Eugene Kingsale
Luis Matos
B.J. Surhoff

Games played by position

PLAYER	G	C	1B	2B	3B	SS	OF	DH
Amaral	91	0	2	2	1	0	50	18
Anderson	150	0	0	0	0	0	136	10
Baines	107	0	0	0	0	0	0	96
Belle	161	0	0	0	0	0	154	7
Bordick	160	0	0	0	0	159	0	0
Clark	77	0	63	0	0	0	0	4
Conine	139	0	99	0	4	0	13	22
Davis	5	4	1	0	0	0	0	0
DeShields	96	0	0	93	0	0	0	0
Figga	41	41	0	0	0	0	0	0
Garcia	17	0	0	6	2	7	0	0
Hairston	50	0	0	50	0	0	0	0
Johnson	135	135	0	0	0	0	0	0
Kingsale	28	0	0	0	0	0	24	2
May	26	0	0	0	0	0	5	9
Minor	46	0	1	0	45	0	0	0
Otanez	29	0	5	0	22	0	0	3
Pickering	23	0	8	0	0	0	0	7
Reboulet	99	0	0	36	56	10	0	0
Ripken Jr	86	0	0	0	85	0	0	0
Surhoff	162	0	0	0	2	0	148	13
Webster	16	12	0	0	0	0	0	2

Sick call: 1999 DL report

PLAYER	Days on the DL
Ricky Bones	15
Will Clark	87*
Jim Corsi	15
Delino DeShields	62**
Mike Fetters	86
Scott Kamieniecki	33
Cal Ripken	56*
Lenny Webster	64

Indicates two separate terms on Disabled List.
**Indicates three separate terms on Disabled List.*

Minor Leagues
Tops in the organization

BATTER	CLUB	AVG.	G	AB	R	H	HR	RBI
Short, Rick	Bow	.314	112	392	60	123	16	62
Vinas, Julio	Roc	.312	126	484	67	151	20	83
Werth, Jayson	Bow	.294	101	357	59	105	4	41
Clark, Howie	Roc	.294	118	405	50	119	8	40
Almonte, Wady	Bow	.293	124	482	68	141	17	83

HOME RUNS

			WINS		
Minor, Ryan	Roc	21	Delahoya, Javier	Roc	13
Vinas, Julio	Roc	20	Riley, Matt	Bow	13
Casimiro, Carlos	Bow	18	Towers, Josh	Bow	12
Figueroa, Franky	Fre	17	Maduro, Calvin	Roc	11
Almonte, Wady	Bow	17			

RBI

			SAVES		
			Kohlmeier, Ryan	Bow	23
Almonte, Wady	Bow	83	Molina, Gabe	Roc	18
Vinas, Julio	Roc	83	Brown, Derek	Fre	14
Figueroa, Franky	Fre	78	McDougal, Mike	Bow	8
Matos, Luis	Bow	77	Rakers, Aaron	Del	8
Garabito, Eddy	Fre	77			

STOLEN BASES

			STRIKEOUTS		
Raines, Tim	Del	49	Stephens, John	Del	217
Matos, Luis	Bow	41	Riley, Matt	Bow	189
Garabito, Eddy	Fre	38	Maduro, Calvin	Roc	149
Diaz, Maikell	Del	31	Bechler, Steven	Del	139
Dent, Darrell	Roc	28	Guzman, Juan	Del	134

PITCHER	CLUB	W-L	ERA	IP	H	BB	SO
Riley, Matt	Bow	13-8	3.05	177	147	56	189
Stephens, John	Del	10-8	3.22	170	148	36	217
Douglass, Sean	Fre	5-6	3.32	98	101	35	89
Bechler, Steven	Del	8-12	3.54	152	137	58	139
Guzman, Juan	Del	9-5	3.55	124	124	44	134

1999 salaries

	Bonuses	Total earned salary
Albert Belle, of		11,949,794
Mike Mussina, p	75,000	6,623,143
Cal Ripken, 3b	100,000	6,500,000
Scott Erickson, p		6,079,931
Brady Anderson, of		5,674,897
Will Clark, 1b		4,920,840
Delino DeShields, 2b		3,719,758
B.J. Surhoff, of	50,000	3,705,516
Charles Johnson, c		3,600,000
Scott Kamieniecki, p		3,350,000
Mike Bordick, ss		3,083,334
Mike Timlin, p		2,250,000
Arthur Rhodes, p		2,200,000
Jeff Conine, 1b		1,960,000
Jesse Orosco, p		800,000
Mike Fetters, p		750,000
Jeff Reboulet, 3b		525,000
Rich Amaral, of		500,000
Doug Linton, p		400,000
Doug Johns, p		300,000
Al Reyes, p		252,500
Sidney Ponson, p		250,000
Jason Johnson, p	10,000	220,000
Mike Figga, c		203,650
Jim Corsi, p		200,000
Derrick May, dh		200,000
Eugene Kingsale, of		200,000
Ryan Minor, 3b		200,000
B.J. Ryan, p		200,000

Average 1999 salary: $2,442,013
Total 1999 team payroll: $70,818,363
Termination pay: $4,850,000

123

Baltimore (1954-1999), includes St. Louis Browns (1902-1953)

Runs: Most, career

1561	CAL RIPKEN, 1981-1999	
1232	Brooks Robinson, 1955-1977	
1091	George Sisler, 1915-1927	
1084	Eddie Murray, 1977-1996	
1013	Harlond Clift, 1934-1943	

Hits: Most, career

2991	CAL RIPKEN, 1981-1999
2848	Brooks Robinson, 1955-1977
2295	George Sisler, 1915-1927
2080	Eddie Murray, 1977-1996
1574	Boog Powell, 1961-1974

2B: Most, career

571	CAL RIPKEN, 1981-1999
482	Brooks Robinson, 1955-1977
363	Eddie Murray, 1977-1996
343	George Sisler, 1915-1927
294	Harlond Clift, 1934-1943

3B: Most, career

145	George Sisler, 1915-1927
88	Baby Doll Jacobson, 1915-1926
72	Del Pratt, 1912-1917
72	Jack Tobin, 1916-1925
70	Ken Williams, 1918-1927
68	Brooks Robinson, 1955-1977 (6)

HR: Most, career

402	CAL RIPKEN, 1981-1999
343	Eddie Murray, 1977-1996
303	Boog Powell, 1961-1974
268	Brooks Robinson, 1955-1977
185	Ken Williams, 1918-1927

RBI: Most, career

1571	CAL RIPKEN, 1981-1999
1357	Brooks Robinson, 1955-1977
1224	Eddie Murray, 1977-1996
1063	Boog Powell, 1961-1974
959	George Sisler, 1915-1927

SB: Most, career

351	George Sisler, 1915-1927
279	BRADY ANDERSON, 1988-1999
252	Al Bumbry, 1972-1984
247	Burt Shotton, 1909-1917
192	Jimmy Austin, 1911-1929

BB: Most, career

1080	CAL RIPKEN, 1981-1999
986	Harlond Clift, 1934-1943

889	Boog Powell, 1961-1974
886	Ken Singleton, 1975-1984
884	Eddie Murray, 1977-1996

BA: Highest, career

.344	George Sisler, 1915-1927
.326	Ken Williams, 1918-1927
.318	Jack Tobin, 1916-1925
.317	Baby Doll Jacobson, 1915-1926
.309	Bob Dillinger, 1946-1949
.305	HAROLD BAINES, 1993-1999 (8)

On-base avg: Highest, career

.403	Ken Williams, 1918-1927
.401	Frank Robinson, 1966-1971
.394	Harlond Clift, 1934-1943
.388	Ken Singleton, 1975-1984
.388	Randy Milligan, 1989-1992

Slug pct: Highest, career

.558	Ken Williams, 1918-1927
.545	RAFAEL PALMEIRO, 1994-1998
.543	Frank Robinson, 1966-1971
.512	Jim Gentile, 1960-1963
.509	HAROLD BAINES, 1993-1999

Games started: Most, career

521	Jim Palmer, 1965-1984
384	Dave McNally, 1962-1974
328	Mike Flanagan, 1975-1992
309	Scott McGregor, 1976-1988
283	Mike Cuellar, 1969-1976

Complete games: Most, career

211	Jim Palmer, 1965-1984
210	Jack Powell, 1902-1912
174	Barney Pelty, 1903-1912
150	Harry Howell, 1904-1910
143	Urban Shocker, 1918-1924

Saves: Most, career

160	GREGG OLSON, 1988-1993
105	Tippy Martinez, 1976-1986
100	Stu Miller, 1963-1967
76	Randy Myers, 1996-1997
74	Eddie Watt, 1966-1973

Shutouts: Most, career

53	Jim Palmer, 1965-1984
33	Dave McNally, 1962-1974
30	Mike Cuellar, 1969-1976
27	Jack Powell, 1902-1912
26	Milt Pappas, 1957-1965

Wins: Most, career

268	Jim Palmer, 1965-1984
181	Dave McNally, 1962-1974
143	Mike Cuellar, 1969-1976
141	Mike Flanagan, 1975-1992
138	Scott McGregor, 1976-1988

K: Most, career

2212	Jim Palmer, 1965-1984
1476	Dave McNally, 1962-1974
1325	MIKE MUSSINA, 1991-1999
1297	Mike Flanagan, 1975-1992
1011	Mike Cuellar, 1969-1976

Win pct: Highest, career

.673	MIKE MUSSINA, 1991-1999
.638	Jim Palmer, 1965-1984
.620	Wally Bunker, 1963-1968
.619	Dick Hall, 1961-1971
.619	Mike Cuellar, 1969-1976

ERA: Lowest, career

2.06	Harry Howell, 1904-1910
2.52	Fred Glade, 1904-1907
2.62	Barney Pelty, 1903-1912
2.63	Jack Powell, 1902-1912
2.67	Carl Weilman, 1912-1920
2.86	Jim Palmer, 1965-1984 (6)

Runs: Most, season

145	Harlond Clift, 1936
137	George Sisler, 1920
134	George Sisler, 1922
132	ROBERTO ALOMAR, 1996
132	Jack Tobin, 1921

Hits: Most, season

257	George Sisler, 1920
246	George Sisler, 1922
241	Heinie Manush, 1928
236	Jack Tobin, 1921
224	George Sisler, 1925
211	CAL RIPKEN, 1983 (10)

2B: Most, season

51	Beau Bell, 1937
49	George Sisler, 1920
47	Heinie Manush, 1928
47	CAL RIPKEN, 1983
47	Joe Vosmik, 1937

3B: Most, season

20	Heinie Manush, 1928
20	George Stone, 1906
18	George Sisler, 1920
18	George Sisler, 1921

18	George Sisler, 1922
18	Jack Tobin, 1921
12	Paul Blair, 1967 (24)

HR: Most, season

50	BRADY ANDERSON, 1996
49	Frank Robinson, 1966
46	Jim Gentile, 1961
43	RAFAEL PALMEIRO, 1998
39	RAFAEL PALMEIRO, 1995
39	RAFAEL PALMEIRO, 1996
39	Boog Powell, 1964
39	Ken Williams, 1922

RBI: Most, season

155	Ken Williams, 1922
142	RAFAEL PALMEIRO, 1996
141	Jim Gentile, 1961
134	Moose Solters, 1936
124	Eddie Murray, 1985

SB: Most, season

57	Luis Aparicio, 1964
53	BRADY ANDERSON, 1992
51	George Sisler, 1922
46	Armando Marsans, 1916
45	George Sisler, 1918

BB: Most, season

126	Lu Blue, 1929
121	Roy Cullenbine, 1941
118	Harlond Clift, 1938
118	Burt Shotton, 1915
118	Ken Singleton, 1975

BA: Highest, season

.420	George Sisler, 1922
.407	George Sisler, 1920
.378	Heinie Manush, 1928
.371	George Sisler, 1921
.358	George Stone, 1906
.328	Ken Singleton, 1977 (*)
.328	ROBERTO ALOMAR, 1996 (*)

On-base avg: Highest, season

.467	George Sisler, 1922
.452	Roy Cullenbine, 1941
.449	George Sisler, 1920
.442	Bob Nieman, 1956
.439	Ken Williams, 1923

Slug pct: Highest, season

.646	Jim Gentile, 1961
.637	BRADY ANDERSON, 1996
.637	Frank Robinson, 1966
.632	George Sisler, 1920
.627	Ken Williams, 1922

Games started: Most, season

40	Mike Cuellar, 1970
40	Mike Flanagan, 1978
40	Dave McNally, 1969
40	Dave McNally, 1970

40	Bobo Newsom, 1938
40	Jim Palmer, 1976

Complete games: Most, season

36	Jack Powell, 1902
35	Harry Howell, 1905
33	Red Donahue, 1902
33	Jack Powell, 1903
32	Harry Howell, 1904
25	Jim Palmer, 1975 (20)

Saves: Most, season

45	Randy Myers, 1997
37	GREGG OLSON, 1990
36	GREGG OLSON, 1992
34	Don Aase, 1986
33	Lee Smith, 1994

Shutouts: Most, season

10	Jim Palmer, 1975
8	Steve Barber, 1961
7	Milt Pappas, 1964
6	Fred Glade, 1904
6	Harry Howell, 1906
6	Dave McNally, 1972
6	Jim Palmer, 1969
6	Jim Palmer, 1973
6	Jim Palmer, 1976
6	Jim Palmer, 1978

Wins: Most, season

27	Urban Shocker, 1921
25	Steve Stone, 1980
24	Mike Cuellar, 1970
24	Dave McNally, 1970
24	Urban Shocker, 1922

K: Most, season

232	Rube Waddell, 1908
226	Bobo Newsom, 1938
218	MIKE MUSSINA, 1997
204	MIKE MUSSINA, 1996
202	Dave McNally, 1968

Win pct: Highest, season

.808	Alvin Crowder, 1928
.808	Dave McNally, 1971
.800	Jim Palmer, 1969
.792	Wally Bunker, 1964
.783	MIKE MUSSINA, 1992

ERA: Lowest, season

1.59	Barney Pelty, 1906
1.77	Jack Powell, 1906
1.89	Harry Howell, 1908
1.89	Rube Waddell, 1908
1.93	Harry Howell, 1907
1.95	Dave McNally, 1968 (7)

Most pinch-hit homers, season

3	Whitey Herzog, 1962
3	Sam Bowens, 1967
3	Pat Kelly, 1979

3	Jim Dwyer, 1986
3	Sam Horn, 1991

Most pinch-hit homers, career

9	Jim Dwyer, 1980-1988
7	Benny Ayala, 1979-1984

Longest hitting streak

41	George Sisler, 1922
34	George Sisler, 1925
34	George McQuinn, 1938
30	ERIC DAVIS, 1998
29	Mel Almada, 1938
28	Ken Williams, 1922

Most consecutive scoreless innings

41	GREGG OLSON, 1989-1990
36	Hal Brown, 1961

No-hit games

Earl Hamilton, StL at Det AL, 5-1; August 30, 1912.

Ernie Koob, StL vs Chi AL, 1-0; May 5, 1917.

Bob Groom, StL vs Chi AL, 3-0; May 6, 1917 (2nd game).

Bobo Newsom, StL vs Bos AL, 1-2; September 18, 1934 (lost on one hit in the 10th).

John Whitehead, six innings, rain, StL vs Det AL, 4-0; August 5, 1940 (2nd game).

Bobo Holloman, StL vs Phi AL, 6-0; May 6, 1953 (first start in the major leagues).

Hoyt Wilhelm, Bal vs NY AL, 1-0; September 20, 1958

Steve D. Barber (8⅔ innings) and Stu Miller (⅓ inning), Bal vs Det AL, 1-2; April 30, 1967 (1st game; lost the game)

Tom Phoebus, Bal vs Bos AL, 6-0; April 27, 1968.

Jim Palmer, Bal vs Oak AL, 8-0; August 13, 1969.

Bob Milacki (six innings), Mike Flanagan (one inning), Mark Williamson (one inning) and GREGG OLSON (one inning), Bal at Oak AL, 2-0; July 13, 1991.

ACTIVE PLAYERS in caps.

Players' years of service are listed by the first and last years with this team and are not necessarily consecutive; all statistics record performances for this team only.

Leader from the franchise's current location is included. If not in the top five, leader's rank is listed in parenthesis; asterisk (*) indicates player is not in top 25.

By Barbara Jean Germano, *Baseball Weekly*

After Jose Canseco was injured, Fred McGriff carried the full weight of the Devil Rays offense.

1999 Devil Rays: Still steadily improving

The Tampa Bay Devil Rays didn't promise a team that would win big right away, just one that would show steady improvement on the way to becoming a championship contender. From that standpoint 1999 was a success, despite another last-place finish in the AL East.

General manager Chuck LaMar said the team is building for long-term success and won't give in to the temptation to veer from its plan of getting better through a strong farm system.

"If I had to sum up a major accomplishment this year," LaMar said, "it's that we stayed with our philosophy, even though it's tempting sometimes to get away from it. In the long run, that's what's going to make this a championship organization."

Fred McGriff, who rebounded from a disappointing year to hit .310 with 32 homers and 104 RBI, signed a contract extension. The club also exercised its 2000 option on Jose Canseco, who led the AL in homers before back surgery sidelined him for six weeks. By season's end the Devil Rays had committed more than $33 million for next season to eight veterans who form their nucleus.

"I'm not satisfied with what we've done this year, but I'm satisfied knowing what we have to do to get to the level we need to play at," said manager Larry Rothschild. "Some of it will come from within, maybe with the ways that guys have coached things here, and some of it will come from outside."

The Devil Rays put a major-league-high 19 players on the disabled list and lost 16 of 19 games after a 22-20 start.

Highlights included Wade Boggs getting his 3,000th hit in his final season and taking three straight games from the playoff-bound Yankees in New York, where Tampa Bay had never won.

Closer Roberto Hernandez bounced back from a shaky 1998 to convert a career-high 43 of 47 save chances, the best percentage (91.5) in the AL. Catcher John Flaherty was another veteran who came

Team MVP

Fred McGriff: The perception that he was going home to play out his career went unrefuted in his first year with the Devil Rays (1998), but the veteran first baseman smashed the theory in 1999. He was the Tampa Bay offense—especially when injuries limited Jose Canseco's playing time—belting 32 homers with 104 RBI and a team-high .310 average. Plus, his 144 games played were tops on the club.

back to have a solid year. Right-hander Ryan Rupe (8-9, 4.55 ERA) became the first product of the farm system to make it to the majors.

But those highs were offset by the injuries that forced Rothschild to juggle the lineup and pitching plans much of the year. Left-hander Tony Saunders broke his pitching arm, top starter Wilson Alvarez served two stints on the DL, right-hander Rolando Arrojo missed part of the season with a sore shoulder and reliever Jim Mecir fractured his pitching elbow.

"I think we're a better team than the record shows," said Rothschild, "but I still think we have a long way to go. Whether injuries come into play or not, at some point you have to play .500 ball for a longer time against good competition."

Boggs, who had season-ending knee surgery a month after becoming the newest member of the 3,000-hit club, hit .301 in 90 games but retired after the season ended. The Devil Rays now will find out if youngster Bobby Smith can handle the job as a regular.

More than anything, though, Rothschild said the team needs to develop more toughness: "We've played good for stretches of 10 to 15 games at times, and then it's almost that we don't show up at times. . . . I want guys who will look you in the face and know that they will be there."

1999 Devil Rays: Week-by-week notes

These notes were excerpted from the following issues of Baseball Weekly.

▶**April 14:** Outfielder-DH Paul Sorrento figured nothing could be worse than the slump he suffered through in 1998. He was wrong. He pulled a hamstring while running the bases in the second game of the season and went on the 15-day DL. It was the first time in Sorrento's 11-year career that he had to go on the DL.

▶**April 21:** Saying they wanted to be cautious with their $35 million investment, the Rays put left-hander Wilson Alvarez on the DL after he felt pain in his shoulder following a workout. He missed two months last season with shoulder problems, but the Rays say that the two are unrelated.

▶**April 28:** DH Jose Canseco had the best start of his career with 10 home runs through the first 20 games. Canseco hit two completely out of Fenway Park, he hit the upper deck at SkyDome, and his three homers at Tropicana Field have each been more than 400 feet.

▶**May 5:** Right-hander Roberto Hernandez became the first Latin American pitcher to reach the 200-save mark when he closed a 4-3 victory against the Tigers on May 1. Hernandez had converted his first 10 save chances, a far cry from last season's 26 of 35.

▶**May 12:** Wade Boggs was still marching toward 3,000 hits, but not as quickly as before. The third baseman was on the DL with 2,943 hits after pulling a muscle in his left leg while running to first base. Another veteran, first baseman Fred McGriff, had 11 home runs through 32 games and was already halfway past his 1998 total of 19.

▶**June 2:** Quinton McCracken was most likely lost for the season after tearing the anterior cruciate ligament in his right knee while trying to make a leaping catch of a Juan Gonzalez home run. Next, right-hander Rolando Arrojo went on the DL with inflammation in his shoulder after starting the year 2-5 with a 7.31 ERA. Then, left-hander Tony Saunders went

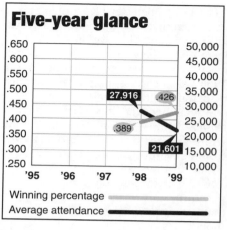

Five-year glance

27,916　　426

.389

21,601

'95　'96　'97　'98　'99

Winning percentage

Average attendance

down on May 26 with a broken arm, which made him the fourth member of the rotation to land on the DL.

▶**June 23:** The injury situation had reached absurd proportions. The Rays had put 18 players on the DL, including 14 since the start of the season. Both figures led the majors.

▶**June 30:** Rookie right-hander Ryan Rupe (4-3, 4.04 ERA) was emerging as the ace of the staff. Rupe, 24, had quality starts in his first 10 outings and had held opponents to a .232 average. Rupe was the first player produced by the farm system to reach the majors. A sixth-round pick, he was the third player from the 1998 draft to reach the majors, following J.D. Drew of St. Louis and Detroit's Jeff Weaver.

▶**July 7:** Second baseman Miguel Cairo seemed to have found a new home in the leadoff spot. The Rays had moved him to leadoff and Randy Winn to No. 9 against left-handers, but the lineup had worked so well—the Rays scored 30 runs in their first three games with it—that Cairo hit at the top for the rest of the week. Through July 4 he was hitting a team-high .324 and had nine steals.

▶**July 15:** It might have been the single greatest upset of the first half. Red Sox right-hander Pedro Martinez was attempting to win his 16th game before the All-Star break. Right-hander Dave Eiland was attempting to win a game for the first time

in four years, and he threw six innings of two-run ball as the Rays beat the Red Sox 3-2 on July 7.

▶**July 21:** The optimistic view was that Jose Canseco would be able to rejoin the Rays in early September, but he is finding it difficult to be optimistic these days. He had surgery on July 11 to repair a herniated disk in his lower back. At the time, he was leading the AL with 31 home runs and was two days away from making his first All-Star appearance in seven years.

▶**Aug. 4:** As he closed in on 3,000 hits, Wade Boggs knew that his next career milestone would be retirement, but he is not about to predict when that will occur. The Rays had an option on Boggs, 41, for next season, but they probably would not exercise it.

▶**Aug. 18:** A few days after reaching 3,000 hits, Wade Boggs took the mound in a 17-1 loss to Baltimore. It was his second pitching appearance. He threw a scoreless inning for New York a few years ago. Boggs came in with two outs and the bases loaded in the eighth and got catcher Charles Johnson to fly out, but he yielded a run on three hits in the ninth.

▶**Sept. 1:** Third baseman Bobby Smith had one month left to salvage what had been a disastrous season. One of the top rookies in the AL in 1998 with a .276 average and 11 homers, Smith had been expected to platoon again this year with Wade Boggs at third base. Instead, he was hitting .161 with two home runs and 50 strikeouts in 161 at-bats.

▶**Sept. 8:** Less than a month after making history, Wade Boggs found out that his season was history. Whether his career is also over remained to be seen. The third baseman had arthroscopic surgery on his right knee, ending his season soon after he reached the 3,000-hit milestone. He finished the year with 3,010 career hits and a .301 season average, the 15th time he has hit over .300.

▶**Sept. 22:** The Rays had two of the most prolific and well-traveled home run hitters ever. Fred McGriff hit his 30th home run on Sept. 19, becoming just the second player in history to have a 30-homer season for four different teams. The only other player to perform the feat? Jose Canseco.

▶**Sept. 29:** Roberto Hernandez was on target to set an AL record for percentage of team wins saved. He had 42 saves among Tampa Bay's 67 victories, for 62.7 percent. The league high was 60.6 percent, by Chicago's Bobby Thigpen, who had 57 saves among the team's 94 wins in 1990.

QUOTE OF THE YEAR

"He's busted his ass, but he's not an outfielder."
—Manager Larry Rothschild, on career first baseman Paul Sorrento's struggles in the field

Team Leaders

Batting avg.	Hits	Wins	Strikeouts
.310 Fred McGriff	164 Fred McGriff	9 Wilson Alvarez	128 Wilson Alvarez
.295 Miguel Cairo	146 Dave Martinez	8 Ryan Rupe	123 Bobby Witt

HR	Runs	Losses	Innings
34 Jose Canseco	79 Dave Martinez	15 Bobby Witt	180.1 Bobby Witt
32 Fred McGriff	75 Fred McGriff	12 Rolando Arrojo	160 Wilson Alvarez
	75 Jose Canseco		

RBI		ERA	Saves
104 Fred McGriff	Stolen bases	4.22 Wilson Alvarez	43 Roberto Hernandez
95 Jose Canseco	22 Miguel Cairo	5.84 Bobby Witt	1 Albie Lopez
	13 Dave Martinez		1 Jeff Sparks

TAMPA BAY DEVIL RAYS 1999 final stats

BATTERS	BA	SLG	OBA	G	AB	R	H	TB	2B	3B	HR	RBI	BB	SO	SB	CS	E
Graffanino	.315	.492	.364	39	130	20	41	64	9	4	2	19	9	22	3	2	5
McGriff	.310	.552	.405	144	529	75	164	292	30	1	32	104	86	107	1	0	13
DiFelice	.307	.469	.346	51	179	21	55	84	11	0	6	27	8	23	0	0	5
Boggs	.301	.377	.377	90	292	40	88	110	14	1	2	29	38	23	1	0	9
Stocker	.299	.370	.369	79	254	39	76	94	11	2	1	27	24	41	9	7	16
Cairo	.295	.368	.335	120	465	61	137	171	15	5	3	36	24	46	22	7	9
Trammell	.290	.505	.384	82	283	49	82	143	19	0	14	39	43	37	0	2	1
Martinez	.284	.387	.361	143	514	79	146	199	25	5	6	66	60	76	13	6	4
Canseco	.279	.563	.369	113	430	75	120	242	18	1	34	95	58	135	3	0	0
Flaherty	.278	.415	.310	117	446	53	124	185	19	0	14	71	19	64	0	2	6
Winn	.267	.366	.307	79	303	44	81	111	16	4	2	24	17	63	9	9	1
Ledesma	.265	.316	.305	93	294	32	78	93	15	0	0	30	14	35	1	1	10
Lowery	.259	.384	.330	66	185	25	48	71	15	1	2	17	19	53	0	2	3
Perry	.254	.397	.331	66	209	29	53	83	10	1	6	32	16	42	0	0	5
McCracken	.250	.324	.317	40	148	20	37	48	6	1	1	18	14	23	6	5	1
Guillen	.244	.339	.312	47	168	24	41	57	10	0	2	13	10	36	0	0	3
Sorrento	.235	.401	.351	99	294	40	69	118	14	1	11	42	49	101	1	1	5
Lamb	.226	.306	.284	55	124	18	28	38	5	1	1	13	10	18	0	1	9
Cox	.211	.263	.211	6	19	0	4	5	1	0	0	0	0	2	0	0	0
Clyburn	.198	.358	.270	28	81	8	16	29	4	0	3	5	7	21	0	0	0
Smith	.181	.256	.244	68	199	18	36	51	4	1	3	19	16	64	4	4	11
Butler	.150	.200	.227	7	20	2	3	4	1	0	0	0	2	4	0	0	0
Franco	.000	.000	.000	1	1	0	0	0	0	0	0	0	1	0	0	0	0

PITCHERS	W-L	ERA	BA	G	GS	CG	GF	SH	SV	IP	H	R	ER	HR	BB	SO
Gaillard	1-0	2.08	.324	8	0	0	1	0	0	8.2	12	9	2	1	4	7
Mecir	0-1	2.61	.205	17	0	0	3	0	0	20.2	15	7	6	0	14	15
Hernandez	2-3	3.07	.245	72	0	0	66	0	43	73.1	68	27	25	1	33	69
Duvall	1-1	4.05	.293	40	0	0	7	0	0	40.0	46	21	18	5	27	18
White	5-3	4.08	.304	63	1	0	11	0	0	108.0	132	56	49	8	38	81
Alvarez	9-9	4.22	.260	28	28	1	0	0	0	160.0	159	92	75	22	79	128
Charlton	2-3	4.44	.257	42	0	0	9	0	0	50.2	49	29	25	4	36	45
Rupe	8-9	4.55	.253	24	24	0	0	0	0	142.1	136	81	72	17	57	97
Lopez	3-2	4.64	.263	51	0	0	14	0	1	64.0	66	40	33	8	24	37
Aldred	3-2	5.18	.274	37	0	0	9	0	0	24.1	26	15	14	1	14	22
Arrojo	7-12	5.18	.296	24	24	2	0	0	0	140.2	162	84	81	23	60	107
Sparks	0-0	5.40	.171	8	0	0	2	0	1	10.0	6	6	6	1	12	17
Eiland	4-8	5.60	.294	21	15	0	0	0	0	80.1	98	59	50	8	27	53
Morris	0-0	5.79	.167	5	0	0	3	0	0	4.2	3	3	3	1	2	3
Rekar	6-6	5.80	.313	27	12	0	2	0	0	94.2	121	68	61	14	41	55
Witt	7-15	5.84	.304	32	32	3	0	2	0	180.1	213	130	117	23	96	123
Wheeler	0-4	5.87	.287	6	6	0	0	0	0	30.2	35	20	20	7	13	32
Yan	3-4	5.90	.326	50	1	0	15	0	0	61.0	77	41	40	8	32	46
Saunders	3-3	6.43	.315	9	9	0	0	0	0	42.0	53	39	30	6	29	30
Boggs	0-0	6.75	.429	1	0	0	1	0	0	1.1	3	1	1	0	0	1
Newman	2-2	6.89	.333	18	0	0	5	0	0	15.2	22	12	12	2	9	20
Lidle	1-0	7.20	.364	5	1	0	1	0	0	5.0	8	4	4	0	2	4
Callaway	1-2	7.45	.357	5	4	0	0	0	0	19.1	30	20	16	2	14	11

2000 preliminary roster

PITCHERS (18)
Wilson Alvarez
Todd Belitz
Cedrick Bowers
Mike Duvall
Roberto Hernandez
Cory Lidle
Albie Lopez
Jim Mecir
Jim Morris
Chad Ogea
Chris Reitsma
Bryan Rekar

Ryan Rupe
Tony Saunders
Jeff Sparks
Dan Wheeler
Rick White
Esteban Yan

CATCHERS (3)
Mike DiFelice
Mike Figga
John Flaherty

INFIELDERS (10)
Miguel Cairo
Vinny Castilla
Steve Cox
Tony Graffanino
David Lamb
Fred McGriff
Herbert Perry
Jared Sandberg
Robert Smith
Kevin Stocker

OUTFIELDERS (9)
Jose Canseco
Jose Guillen
Dave Martinez
Quinton McCracken
Alex Sanchez
Bubba Trammell
Greg Vaughn
Luke Wilcox
Randy Winn

Games played by position

PLAYER	G	C	1B	2B	3B	SS	OF	DH
Boggs	90	0	4	0	74	0	0	0
Butler	7	0	0	0	0	0	6	0
Cairo	120	0	0	117	0	0	0	2
Canseco	113	0	0	0	0	0	6	109
Clyburn	28	0	0	0	0	0	24	4
Cox	6	0	4	0	0	0	2	0
DiFelice	51	51	0	0	0	0	0	0
Flaherty	117	115	0	0	0	0	0	1
Franco	1	0	1	0	0	0	0	0
Graffanino	39	0	0	17	1	17	0	0
Guillen	47	0	0	0	0	0	47	0
Lamb	55	0	0	15	0	35	0	3
Ledesma	93	0	4	17	26	50	0	0
Lowery	66	0	0	0	0	0	60	0
Martinez	143	0	0	0	0	0	140	0
McCracken	40	0	0	0	0	0	40	0
McGriff	144	0	125	0	0	0	0	18
Perry	66	0	14	0	42	0	6	10
Smith	68	0	0	13	59	0	0	0
Sorrento	99	0	27	0	0	0	57	9
Stocker	79	0	0	0	0	76	0	0
Trammell	82	0	0	0	0	0	74	7
Winn	79	0	0	0	0	0	77	0

Sick call: 1999 DL report

PLAYER	Days on the DL
Wilson Alvarez	38*
Rolando Arrojo	51
Wade Boggs	46*
Rich Butler	11
Miguel Cairo	39*
Mickey Callaway	17
Jose Canseco	41
Mike Duvall	27
Dave Eiland	30*
Rick Gorecki	182
David Lamb	18
Aaron Ledesma	37
Cory Lidle	166
Albie Lopez	39
Quinton McCracken	132
Jim Mecir	145
Herb Perry	41
Julio Santana	21
Tony Saunders	130
Paul Sorrento	15
Kevin Stocker	74
Esteban Yan	28

* Indicates two separate terms on Disabled List.

Minor Leagues
Tops in the organization

Batter	Club	Avg.	G	AB	R	H	HR	RBI
Cox, Steve	Dur	.341	134	534	107	182	25	127
Beinbrink, Andrew	HdV	.339	76	292	46	99	11	51
Lowery, Terrell	Dur	.335	71	275	69	92	15	57
Graffanino, Tony	Dur	.313	87	345	66	108	9	58
Hamilton, Josh	HdV	.312	72	308	56	96	10	55

HOME RUNS

Wilcox, Luke	Dur	29
McClain, Scott	Dur	28
Cox, Steve	Dur	25
Wilson, Tom	Dur	23
Grummitt, Dan	HdV	23

WINS

Standridge, J.	StP		13
Tatis, Ramon	Dur		12
James, Delvin	StP		11
Harper, Travis	Orl		11
Several Players Tied at			10

RBI

Cox, Steve	Dur	127
McClain, Scott	Dur	104
Wilcox, Luke	Dur	96
Sandberg, Jared	StP	96
Huff, Aubrey	Orl	78

SAVES

Reyes, Eddy	Orl	27
Gaillard, Eddie	Dur	26
Haines, Talley	CSC	18
Daniels, John	Orl	14
Nunez, Maximo	Orl	118

STOLEN BASES

Sanchez, Alex	Dur	48
Soler, Ramon	CSC	46
Moore, Frank	HdV	24
Hoover, Paul	StP	23
Mann, Derek	CSC	22

STRIKEOUTS

Harper, Travis	Orl	147
Bowers, Cedrick	Orl	138
Kofler, Ed	CSC	136
Belitz, Todd	Orl	11
James, Delvin	StP	112

Pitcher	Club	W-L	ERA	IP	H	BB	SO
Standridge, J.	StP	13-5	2.57	164	129	51	110
Kennedy, Joe	HdV	6-5	2.65	95	78	26	101
Rosario, Juan	StP	5-3	2.67	94	80	25	37
Enders, Trevor	Orl	8-2	3.30	95	86	33	63
James, Delvin	StP	11-8	3.59	175	160	37	112

1999 salaries

	Bonuses	Total earned salary
Roberto Hernandez, p	130,000	6,180,000
Fred McGriff, 1b		5,250,000
Wilson Alvarez, p		4,500,000
Jose Canseco, dh	1,300,000	3,325,000
Paul Sorrento, of		3,000,000
Kevin Stocker, ss		2,400,000
Dave Martinez, of		2,000,000
Quinton McCracken, of		1,850,000
John Flaherty, c		1,280,000
Bobby Witt, p	750,000	1,100,000
Wade Boggs, 3b		750,000
Albie Lopez, p	80,000	630,000
Norm Charlton, p	200,000	500,000
Jose Guillen, of		375,000
Dave Eiland, p		280,000
Tony Saunders, p		277,500
Mike DiFelice, c		267,500
Jim Mecir, p		267,500
Tony Graffanino, 2b		262,500
Rick White, p		255,000
Rolando Arrojo, p	10,000	250,000
Aaron Ledesma, ss	10,000	237,500
Miguel Cairo, 2b		235,000
Bobby Smith, 3b		235,000
Bubba Trammell, of	10,000	230,000
Esteban Yan, p		225,000
Mike Duvall, p	15,000	215,000
Cory Lidle, p		210,000
Rick Gorecki, p		210,000
Herbert Perry, 3b	10,000	210,000
Terrell Lowery, of		205,000
Alan Newman, p		200,000
David Lamb, ss		200,000
Ryan Rupe, p		200,000

Average 1999 salary: $1,112,133
Total 1999 team payroll: $37,812,500
Termination pay: $122,951

Tampa Bay (1998-1999)

Runs: Most, career

148	FRED McGRIFF, 1998-1999	
110	MIGUEL CAIRO, 1998-1999	
110	DAVE MARTINEZ, 1998-1999	
97	QUINTON McCRACKEN, 1998-1999	
95	RANDY WINN, 1998-1999	

Hits: Most, career

324	FRED McGRIFF, 1998-1999
275	MIGUEL CAIRO, 1998-1999
225	DAVE MARTINEZ, 1998-1999
216	QUINTON McCRACKEN, 1998-1999
210	WADE BOGGS, 1998-1999

2B: Most, career

63	FRED McGRIFF, 1998-1999
44	QUINTON McCRACKEN, 1998-1999
41	MIGUEL CAIRO, 1998-1999
41	PAUL SORRENTO, 1998-1999
37	WADE BOGGS, 1998-1999
37	BUBBA TRAMMELL, 1998-1999

3B: Most, career

13	RANDY WINN, 1998-1999
10	MIGUEL CAIRO, 1998-1999
8	QUINTON McCRACKEN, 1998-1999
5	WADE BOGGS, 1998-1999
5	DAVE MARTINEZ, 1998-1999
5	KEVIN STOCKER, 1998-1999

HR: Most, career

51	FRED McGRIFF, 1998-1999
34	JOSE CANSECO, 1999
28	PAUL SORRENTO, 1998-1999
26	BUBBA TRAMMELL, 1998-1999
17	JOHN FLAHERTY, 1998-1999

RBI: Most, career

185	FRED McGRIFF, 1998-1999
99	PAUL SORRENTO, 1998-1999
95	JOSE CANSECO, 1999
95	JOHN FLAHERTY, 1998-1999
86	DAVE MARTINEZ, 1998-1999

SB: Most, career

41	MIGUEL CAIRO, 1998-1999
35	RANDY WINN, 1998-1999
25	QUINTON McCRACKEN, 1998-1999
21	DAVE MARTINEZ, 1998-1999
14	KEVIN STOCKER, 1998-1999

BB: Most, career

165	FRED McGRIFF, 1998-1999
103	PAUL SORRENTO, 1998-1999
95	DAVE MARTINEZ, 1998-1999
84	WADE BOGGS, 1998-1999
59	BUBBA TRAMMELL, 1998-1999

BA: Highest, career

.296	FRED McGRIFF, 1998-1999
.295	AARON LEDESMA, 1998-1999
.289	WADE BOGGS, 1998-1999
.288	BUBBA TRAMMELL, 1998-1999
.283	QUINTON McCRACKEN, 1998-1999

On-base avg: Highest, career

.388	FRED McGRIFF, 1998-1999
.366	BUBBA TRAMMELL, 1998-1999
.360	WADE BOGGS, 1998-1999
.351	DAVE MARTINEZ, 1998-1999
.331	QUINTON McCRACKEN, 1998-1999

Slug pct: Highest, career

.531	BUBBA TRAMMELL, 1998-1999
.496	FRED McGRIFF, 1998-1999
.403	PAUL SORRENTO, 1998-1999
.394	QUINTON McCRACKEN, 1998-1999
.393	MIKE DIFELICE, 1998-1999

Games started: Most, career

56	ROLANDO ARROJO, 1998-1999
53	WILSON ALVAREZ, 1998-1999
40	TONY SAUNDERS, 1998-1999
32	BOBBY WITT, 1999
27	BRYAN REKAR, 1998-1999

Complete games: Most, career

4	ROLANDO ARROJO, 1998-1999
3	BOBBY WITT, 1999
2	TONY SAUNDERS, 1998-1999
1	WILSON ALVAREZ, 1998-1999
1	BRYAN REKAR, 1998-1999
1	JULIO SANTANA, 1998-1999
1	DENNIS SPRINGER, 1998

Saves: Most, career

69	ROBERTO HERNANDEZ, 1998-1999
2	ALBIE LOPEZ, 1998-1999
1	JEFF SPARKS, 1999
1	ESTEBAN YAN, 1998-1999

Shutouts: Most, career

2	ROLANDO ARROJO, 1998-1999
2	BOBBY WITT, 1999

Wins: Most, career

21	ROLANDO ARROJO, 1998-1999
15	WILSON ALVAREZ, 1998-1999
10	ALBIE LOPEZ, 1998-1999
9	TONY SAUNDERS,
8	BRYAN REKAR, 1998-1999
8	RYAN RUPE, 1999
8	ESTEBAN YAN, 1998-1999

K: Most, career

259	ROLANDO ARROJO, 1998-1999
235	WILSON ALVAREZ, 1998-1999
202	TONY SAUNDERS, 1998-1999
124	ROBERTO HERNANDEZ, 1998-1999
123	BOBBY WITT, 1999
123	ESTEBAN YAN, 1998-1999

Win pct: Highest, career

.700	JIM MECIR, 1998-1999
.625	ALBIE LOPEZ, 1998-1999
.500	ESTEBAN YAN, 1998-1999
.471	RYAN RUPE, 1999
.467	ROLANDO ARROJO, 1998-1999

ERA: Lowest, career

3.51	ALBIE LOPEZ, 1998-1999
3.55	ROBERTO HERNANDEZ, 1998-1999
3.97	RICK WHITE, 1998-1999
4.23	ROLANDO ARROJO, 1998-1999
4.46	WILSON ALVAREZ, 1998-1999

Runs: Most, season

79	DAVE MARTINEZ, 1999
77	QUINTON McCRACKEN, 1998
75	JOSE CANSECO, 1999
75	FRED McGRIFF, 1999
73	FRED McGRIFF, 1998

Hits: Most, season

179	QUINTON McCRACKEN, 1998
164	FRED McGRIFF, 1999
160	FRED McGRIFF, 1998
146	DAVE MARTINEZ, 1999
138	MIGUEL CAIRO, 1998

2B: Most, season

38	QUINTON McCRACKEN, 1998	
33	FRED McGRIFF, 1998	
30	FRED McGRIFF, 1999	
27	PAUL SORRENTO, 1998	
26	MIGUEL CAIRO, 1998	

3B: Most, season

9	RANDY WINN, 1998
7	QUINTON McCRACKEN, 1998
5	MIGUEL CAIRO, 1998
5	MIGUEL CAIRO, 1999
5	DAVE MARTINEZ, 1999

HR: Most, season

34	JOSE CANSECO, 1999
32	FRED McGRIFF, 1999
19	FRED McGRIFF, 1998
17	PAUL SORRENTO, 1998
14	JOHN FLAHERTY, 1999
14	BUBBA TRAMMELL, 1999

RBI: Most, season

104	FRED McGRIFF, 1999
95	JOSE CANSECO, 1999
81	FRED McGRIFF, 1998
71	JOHN FLAHERTY, 1999
66	DAVE MARTINEZ, 1999

SB: Most, season

26	RANDY WINN, 1998
22	MIGUEL CAIRO, 1999
19	MIGUEL CAIRO, 1998
19	QUINTON McCRACKEN, 1998
13	MIKE KELLY, 1998
13	DAVE MARTINEZ, 1999

BB: Most, season

86	FRED McGRIFF, 1999
79	FRED McGRIFF, 1998
60	DAVE MARTINEZ, 1999
58	JOSE CANSECO, 1999
54	PAUL SORRENTO, 1998

BA: Highest, season

.310	FRED McGRIFF, 1999
.295	MIGUEL CAIRO, 1999
.292	QUINTON McCRACKEN, 1998
.284	DAVE MARTINEZ, 1999
.284	FRED McGRIFF, 1998

On-base avg: Highest, season

.405	FRED McGRIFF, 1999
.371	FRED McGRIFF, 1998
.369	JOSE CANSECO, 1999
.361	DAVE MARTINEZ, 1999
.335	MIGUEL CAIRO, 1999

Slug pct: Highest, season

.563	JOSE CANSECO, 1999
.552	FRED McGRIFF, 1999
.443	FRED McGRIFF, 1998
.410	QUINTON McCRACKEN, 1998
.387	DAVE MARTINEZ, 1999

Games started: Most, season

32	ROLANDO ARROJO, 1998
32	BOBBY WITT, 1999
31	TONY SAUNDERS, 1998
28	WILSON ALVAREZ, 1999
25	WILSON ALVAREZ, 1998

Complete games: Most, season

3	BOBBY WITT, 1999
2	ROLANDO ARROJO, 1998
2	ROLANDO ARROJO, 1999
2	TONY SAUNDERS, 1998
1	WILSON ALVAREZ, 1999
1	JULIO SANTANA, 1998
1	DENNIS SPRINGER, 1998

Saves: Most, season

43	ROBERTO HERNANDEZ, 1999
26	ROBERTO HERNANDEZ, 1998
1	ALBIE LOPEZ, 1998
1	ALBIE LOPEZ, 1999
1	ESTEBAN YAN, 1998

Shutouts: Most, season

2	ROLANDO ARROJO, 1998
2	BOBBY WITT, 1999

Wins: Most, season

14	ROLANDO ARROJO, 1998
9	WILSON ALVAREZ, 1999
8	RYAN RUPE, 1999
7	ROLANDO ARROJO, 1999
7	ALBIE LOPEZ, 1998
7	JIM MECIR, 1998
7	BOBBY WITT, 1999

K: Most, season

172	TONY SAUNDERS, 1998
152	ROLANDO ARROJO, 1998
128	WILSON ALVAREZ, 1999
123	BOBBY WITT, 1999
107	WILSON ALVAREZ, 1998
107	ROLANDO ARROJO, 1999

Win pct: Highest, season

.538	ROLANDO ARROJO, 1998

ERA: Lowest, season

3.56	ROLANDO ARROJO, 1998
4.12	TONY SAUNDERS, 1998
5.84	BOBBY WITT, 1999

Most pinch-hit homers, season

2	PAUL SORRENTO, 1998
1	BUBBA TRAMMELL, 1998

Most pinch-hit homers, career

2	PAUL SORRENTO, 1998
1	BUBBA TRAMMELL, 1998

Longest hitting streak

18	QUINTON McCRACKEN, 1998
14	AARON LEDESMA, 1998

Most consecutive scoreless innings

18	ROLANDO ARROJO, 1998
14.1	ESTBAN YAN, 1998

No-hit games

By Barbara Jean Germano, Baseball Weekly

Manny Ramirez drove in 165 runs for the Indians—more than any AL player in over a half-century.

1999 Indians: Nowhere near the champagne

General manager John Hart and his Cleveland Indians once again left the postseason party with no rings on their fingers—and this time they blew it before they even got to the League Championship Series. That irked Hart so badly he fired manager Mike Hargrove before the fizz went out of Boston's Division Series champagne.

The Indians were heavy favorites to advance to the ALCS for the fourth time since 1995, especially after they piled up wins all year on their puny division rivals. They won the American League Central by 21½ games and spent all but two days in first place.

The Indians were the first club since the 1950 Red Sox to score more than 1,000 runs (1,009) and just the seventh overall to accomplish the feat. They set club records for most players with more than 100 RBI and most players with more than 100 runs scored (five).

But there were indicators that the Indians' shiny exterior might be covering some rust spots. They showed up most in the bullpen, which injuries and poor performances had turned into a patchwork group over the season.

The pitching staff was tired—and the club is getting tired, too, of these same old endings. Gaudy stats and records and win totals. But the numbers are hollow with nothing but another champagneless clubhouse in the end.

"Even though you put up great numbers, records mean nothing if you don't do it in the playoffs," shortstop Omar Vizquel said. "Nothing matters. You can win 125 games or be ahead by 21 games in your division. If you don't play well in the playoffs, so what?"

This is the Indians second first-round knockout in the postseason, after the Orioles bounced them from the Division Series in 1996. First baseman Jim Thome, who has been a part of each postseason team since 1995, says all the aborted endings are frustrating. He's well aware, as are all his teammates, that there were high expectations for the Indians. But he emphasized that no matter how teams

---

Team MVP

Manny Ramirez: The way the Indians produce runs, it's often difficult to separate one of their bashers from the rest of the pack. Manny Ramirez made it easy. His 165 RBI were the most in the American League in more than 50 years. Plus, he led the team in batting average at .333, in home runs with 44 and in total bases with 346. He also was named the AL's top player at the annual Players' Choice Awards.

---

seem to match up in the playoffs, there are no guarantees.

"Once you get to the postseason anything can happen," Thome said. "Everyone in the playoffs has a good team or they wouldn't be there. It takes breaks, little breaks here and there."

Still, Thome says this isn't the most exasperating outcome, despite the 2-0 advantage.

"The toughest part was in the '97 Series, when we were one out away from winning it. That was worse than this. But we've had some great teams here, and I believe our time will come."

There will be some debate on whether the Indians are considered a great team. Even the Braves have had to hear it, but at least Atlanta has one World Series title to go with its eight consecutive postseason visits.

In Travis Fryman's mind, no team can be considered great—and that includes the Indians—until they've won it all. "I reserve the term greatness for teams that win the World Series," he said.

"We were expected to go to the World Series," catcher Sandy Alomar said. "It's tough. We were up two games to none, but believe me we didn't take anything for granted. They just took it to us."

Hart's parting words as he left the clubhouse following the final game: "We'll be back."

1999 Indians: Week-by-week notes

These notes were excerpted from the following issues of Baseball Weekly.

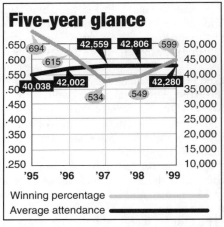

Five-year glance

Winning percentage
Average attendance

▶**April 14:** The Tribe offense hadn't missed injured left fielder David Justice. In their first six games the Indians scored 58 runs. Shortstop Omar Vizquel had seven RBI in the first two games, and right fielder Manny Ramirez had 11 in six games.

▶**April 21:** Last year first baseman Jim Thome won the home opener with a three-run homer in the 10th inning against Anaheim. This year third baseman Travis Fryman won the home opener with a three-run homer in the 10th against Kansas City.

▶**April 28:** The injuries were mounting. Catcher Sandy Alomar (back spasms) missed the Boston series, while Omar Vizquel (right quadriceps) sat out two games. Alomar was set to rejoin the lineup but reinjured his back during a fight at Fenway Park. Vizquel had been trying to play with his injury, but manager Mike Hargrove finally benched him.

▶**May 5:** When the Indians completed a four-game sweep of the Oakland on April 29, it gave them a 16-5, to match their best start in franchise history after 21 games. "It's a lot better than being 5-16," said Mike Hargrove.

▶**May 12:** The Indians had their biggest comeback in Jacobs Field history on May 7, overcoming a 10-2 deficit to beat Tampa Bay, 20-11. They won it by scoring 18 runs on 16 hits in the final three innings. In those three frames they sent 33 men to the plate.

▶**May 19:** Owner Dick Jacobs, who in 12 years had guided the Indians from the bottom to the top of the baseball world, announced on May 13 that he was selling the team. Jacobs, 73, and his late brother, David, purchased the Indians in December 1986 for an estimated $40 million. Some experts say he could get as much as $300 million for the club today.

▶**May 26:** Sandy Alomar had knee surgery for the seventh time and would be out for

four to six weeks. Rookie Einar Diaz and career backup Chris Turner took over for Alomar behind the plate.

▶**June 2:** Right-hander Jaret Wright was scheduled to meet AL president Gene Budig on June 1 in New York. Budig wanted to know why Wright had been in the middle of two bench-clearing beanball fights since April 23. Mike Hargrove was set to accompany Wright.

▶**June 9:** Jaret Wright was still in the rotation despite four poor starts, claims of head-hunting and his visit with Gene Budig. Wright blew a 4-0 first-inning lead in his last start, allowing seven runs on six hits in 3⅓ innings on June 2 in Yankee Stadium.

▶**June 23:** Right-hander Charles Nagy's five-game winning streak ended on June 18 against Seattle. Nagy, who led the club with eight wins, had been bothered by bursitis in his right shoulder since beating the Yankees on May 31.

▶**July 7:** The Indians were on pace for 106 victories, but they continued losing key players to injuries. They placed right-hander Steve Karsay on the DL on July 3 with a strained left oblique muscle. Karsay was 7-1 with a 2.63 ERA and led the bullpen with 54 innings. Travis Fryman sprained his right knee in a collision that day with Royals first baseman Jeremy Giambi and was also put on the DL.

▶**July 15:** Rookie Enrique Wilson, a short-

stop disguised as a utility infielder, was making a strong case for Mike Hargrove to keep him at third. He entered the All-Star break hitting .309 (51-for-165).

▶**July 28:** The Indians, in their worst stretch this season, lost nine of their first 11 games following the All-Star break—and the players weren't the only ones responsible. Against the Toronto on July 22 in Jacobs Field, an incorrect lineup card filled out by Mike Hargrove forced the Indians to play without the DH and bat Charles Nagy in the seventh spot in the lineup in a 4-3 loss.

▶**Aug. 4:** The July 31 deadline for making nonwaiver trades passed without the Indians' participation. They had talked seriously to the Angels about left-hander Chuck Finley but never made a deal.

▶**Aug. 11:** Outfielder-first baseman Richie Sexson, who started the season with 93 days' service in the majors, was on pace to hit 30 homers and drive in 100.

▶**Aug. 18:** Steve Karsay won his first start in more than a year on Aug. 14. Karsay, 8-1 with a 2.66 ERA, has been one of the best long relievers in baseball. He pitched five innings in a 7-1 victory over Baltimore.

▶**Sept. 1:** DH Harold Baines knows how to make an entrance. Several hours after being told he'd been traded from Baltimore to Cleveland, Baines walked onto Jacobs Field on Aug. 27 and hit a two-run first-inning single to lead Cleveland to a 2-1 victory against Tampa Bay. The next day he singled home another run in his new team's 3-0 win.

▶**Sept. 8:** The rotation was limping. Right-hander Dwight Gooden came off the DL last week, but Jaret Wright (right shoulder) and left-hander Mark Langston (left quadriceps) were still out. The new starting rotation was right-hander Bartolo Colon, Charles Nagy, righty Dave Burba, Gooden and lefty Chris Haney. The Indians were counting on Wright to fill the fourth spot in the postseason.

▶**Sept. 22:** When Jim Thome doubled home a run in the first inning on Sept. 18, it gave the Indians four players with 100 or more RBI for the first time in club history. Manny Ramirez had 146; Richie Sexson, 110; second baseman Roberto Alomar, 109; and Thome, 103.

▶**Sept. 29:** Benched for lack of hustle on Sept. 23 when he jogged after a foul ball in right field, Manny Ramirez responded by driving in 10 runs during his next five at-bats in two games against Toronto. He had 160 RBI through Sept. 26, two shy of the club record set by first-baseman Hal Trosky in 1936.

▶**Oct. 6:** The Indians picked up a cool grand on Oct. 1 against the Blue Jays: They became the seventh team in this century to score 1,000 runs and just the first since the Red Sox in 1950. The Indians ended the season with 1,009 runs.

QUOTE OF THE YEAR

"Every time I swing the bat, I'm trying to hit a home run."

—Right-hander Dwight Gooden, after hitting the eighth homer of his career

Team Leaders

Batting avg.	Hits	Wins	Strikeouts
.333 Manny Ramirez	191 Omar Vizquel	18 Bartolo Colon	174 Dave Burba
.333 Omar Vizquel	182 Roberto Alomar	17 Charles Nagy	161 Bartolo Colon

HR	Runs	Losses	Innings
44 Manny Ramirez	138 Roberto Alomar	11 Charles Nagy	220 Dave Burba
33 Jim Thome	131 Manny Ramirez	10 Jaret Wright	205 Bartolo Colon

RBI	Stolen bases	ERA	Saves
165 Manny Ramirez	42 Omar Vizquel	3.95 Bartolo Colon	39 Mike Jackson
120 Roberto Alomar	37 Roberto Alomar	4.25 Dave Burba	6 Paul Shuey

CLEVELAND INDIANS 1999 final stats

BATTERS	BA	SLG	OBA	G	AB	R	H	TB	2B	3B	HR	RBI	BB	SO	SB	CS	E
McDonald	.333	.333	.333	18	21	2	7	7	0	0	0	0	0	3	0	1	1
M. Ramirez	.333	.663	.442	147	522	131	174	346	34	3	44	165	96	131	2	4	7
Vizquel	.333	.436	.397	144	574	112	191	250	36	4	5	66	65	50	42	9	15
Cruz	.330	.511	.368	32	88	14	29	45	5	1	3	17	5	13	0	2	0
R. Alomar	.323	.533	.422	159	563	138	182	300	40	3	24	120	99	96	37	6	6
Baines	.312	.533	.387	135	430	62	134	229	18	1	25	103	54	48	1	2	0
S. Alomar	.307	.533	.322	37	137	19	42	73	13	0	6	25	4	23	0	1	7
Lofton	.301	.432	.405	120	465	110	140	201	28	6	7	39	79	84	25	6	3
Cordero	.299	.500	.364	54	194	35	58	97	15	0	8	32	15	37	2	0	1
A. Ramirez	.299	.474	.327	48	97	11	29	46	6	1	3	18	3	26	1	1	2
Justice	.287	.476	.413	133	429	75	123	204	18	0	21	88	94	90	1	3	4
Diaz	.281	.362	.328	119	392	43	110	142	21	1	3	32	23	41	11	4	10
Thome	.277	.540	.426	146	494	101	137	267	27	2	33	108	127	171	0	6	6
Wilson	.262	.352	.310	113	332	41	87	117	22	1	2	24	25	41	5	4	8
Sexson	.255	.514	.305	134	479	72	122	246	17	7	31	116	34	117	3	3	7
Fryman	.255	.410	.309	85	322	45	82	132	16	2	10	48	25	57	2	1	6
Roberts	.238	.308	.281	41	143	26	34	44	4	0	2	12	9	16	11	3	0
Baerga	.228	.281	.274	22	57	4	13	16	0	0	1	5	4	10	1	1	1
Branyan	.211	.342	.286	11	38	4	8	13	2	0	1	6	3	19	0	0	1
Turner	.190	.190	.227	12	21	3	4	4	0	0	0	0	1	8	1	0	2
Cabrera	.189	.216	.231	30	37	6	7	8	1	0	0	0	1	8	3	0	1
Whiten	.160	.320	.250	8	25	2	4	8	1	0	1	4	3	4	0	0	0
Levis	.154	.154	.214	10	26	0	4	4	0	0	0	3	1	6	0	0	0
Houston	.148	.296	.233	13	27	2	4	8	1	0	1	3	3	11	0	0	0

PITCHERS	W-L	ERA	BA	G	GS	CG	GF	SH	SV	IP	H	R	ER	HR	BB	SO
Karsay	10-2	2.97	.247	50	3	0	13	0	1	78.2	71	29	26	6	30	68
Shuey	8-5	3.53	.223	72	0	0	28	0	6	81.2	68	37	32	8	40	103
Colon	18-5	3.95	.242	32	32	1	0	1	0	205.0	185	97	90	24	76	161
Jackson	3-4	4.06	.232	72	0	0	65	0	39	68.2	60	32	31	11	26	55
Wagner	1-0	4.15	.263	3	0	0	1	0	0	4.1	5	4	2	0	3	0
Reed	3-2	4.23	.285	63	0	0	15	0	0	61.2	69	33	29	10	20	44
Burba	15-9	4.25	.254	34	34	1	0	0	0	220.0	211	113	104	30	96	174
Rincon	2-3	4.43	.248	59	0	0	14	0	0	44.2	41	22	22	6	24	30
Rakers	0-0	4.50	.250	1	0	0	0	0	0	2.0	2	1	1	1	1	0
Brower	3-1	4.56	.270	9	2	0	1	0	0	25.2	27	13	13	8	10	18
DePaula	0-0	4.63	.200	11	0	0	4	0	0	11.2	8	6	6	0	3	18
Haney	0-2	4.69	.270	13	4	0	1	0	0	40.1	43	22	21	3	16	22
Nagy	17-11	4.95	.293	33	32	1	0	0	0	202.0	238	120	111	26	59	126
Langston	1-2	5.25	.288	25	5	0	2	0	0	61.2	69	40	36	9	29	43
Wright	8-10	6.06	.277	26	26	0	0	0	0	133.2	144	99	90	18	77	91
Gooden	3-4	6.26	.282	26	22	0	0	0	0	115.0	127	90	80	18	67	88
DeLucia	0-1	6.75	.317	6	0	0	2	0	0	9.1	13	7	7	4	9	7
Candiotti	4-6	7.32	.300	18	13	0	1	0	0	71.1	86	64	58	14	30	41
Assenmacher	2-1	8.18	.347	55	0	0	8	0	0	33.0	50	32	30	6	17	29
Riske	1-1	8.36	.333	12	0	0	3	0	0	14.0	20	15	13	2	6	16
Martin	0-1	8.68	.325	6	0	0	0	0	0	9.1	13	9	9	2	3	8
Stevens	0-0	10.00	.286	5	0	0	0	0	0	9.0	10	10	10	1	8	6
Poole	1-0	18.00	.667	3	0	0	0	0	0	1.0	2	2	2	0	3	0
Spradlin	0-0	18.00	.400	4	0	0	1	0	0	3.0	6	6	6	1	3	2
Tam	0-0	81.00	1.000	1	0	0	0	0	0	0.1	2	3	3	0	1	0

2000 preliminary roster

PITCHERS (20)
Danny Baez
J.D. Brammer
Jim Brower
Jamie Brown
Dave Burba
Bartolo Colon
Sean DePaula
Chuck Finley
Scott Kamieniecki
Steve Karsay
Tom Martin
Willie Martinez

Charles Nagy
Steve Reed
Ricky Rincon
David Riske
Paul Shuey
Justin Speier
Martin Vargas
Jaret Wright

CATCHERS (2)
Sandy Alomar
Einar Diaz

INFIELDERS (10)
Roberto Alomar
Russell Branyan
Jolbert Cabrera
Travis Fryman
Tyler Houston
John McDonald
Richie Sexson
Jim Thome
Omar Vizquel
Enrique Wilson

OUTFIELDERS (8)
Jacob Cruz
David Justice
Kenny Lofton
Scott Morgan
Danny Peoples
Alex Ramirez
Manny Ramirez
David Roberts

Games played by position

PLAYER	G	C	1B	2B	3B	SS	OF	DH
R. Alomar	159	0	0	156	0	0	0	3
S. Alomar	37	35	0	0	0	0	0	1
Baerga	22	0	0	6	15	0	0	1
Baines	28	0	0	0	0	0	0	33
Borders	6	5	0	0	0	0	0	0
Branyan	11	0	0	0	8	0	0	3
Cabrera	30	0	0	6	0	0	16	0
Cordero	54	0	0	0	0	0	29	26
Cruz	32	0	0	0	0	0	24	3
Diaz	119	119	0	0	0	0	0	0
Fryman	85	0	0	0	85	0	0	0
Houston	13	1	0	0	10	0	0	0
Justice	133	0	0	0	0	0	93	36
Levis	10	9	0	0	0	0	0	0
Lofton	120	0	0	0	0	0	119	1
Manto	12	0	1	0	10	0	0	0
McDonald	18	0	0	7	0	6	0	0
M. Ramirez	147	0	0	0	0	0	146	2
A. Ramirez	48	0	0	0	0	0	29	14
Roberts	41	0	0	0	0	0	39	0
Sexson	134	0	61	0	0	0	49	25
Thome	146	0	111	0	0	0	0	36
Turner	12	12	0	0	0	0	0	0
Vizquel	144	0	0	0	0	143	1	0
Whiten	8	0	0	0	0	0	7	0
Wilson	113	0	0	21	61	35	0	0

Minor Leagues

Tops in the organization

BATTER	CLUB	AVG.	G	AB	R	H	HR	RBI
McDonald, John	Buf	.307	121	463	61	142	1	51
Ramirez, Alex	Buf	.305	75	305	50	93	12	50
Selby, Bill	Buf	.295	122	447	75	132	20	85
Betances, Junior	Akr	.294	89	306	41	90	2	28
Gonzalez, Luis	Clm	.293	84	300	41	88	7	50

HOME RUNS

Morgan, Scott	Buf	34
Branyan, Russell	Buf	30
Manto, Jeff	Buf	23
Peoples, Danny	Akr	21
Selby, Bill	Buf	20

WINS

Watson, Mark	Akr	15
Rigdon, Paul	Buf	14
Drew, Tim	Kin	13
Pugmire, Robert	Kin	13
Bautista, Martin	Kin	12

RBI

Morgan, Scott	Buf	101
Perry, Chan	Buf	89
Edwards, Mike	Kin	89
Selby, Bill	Buf	85
Peoples, Danny	Akr	78

SAVES

DeLucia, Rich	Buf	19
Mays, Jarrod	Kin	19
Riske, David	Buf	18
Aracena, Juan	Clm	18
Several Players Tied at		12

STOLEN BASES

Pratt, Scott	Kin	47
Requena, A.	MhV	44
Roberts, David	Buf	39
Sherrill, J.J.	MhV	28
Huelsmann, Mike	Akr	26

STRIKEOUTS

Pugmire, Robert	Kin	160
Spiegel, Mike	Kin	141
Drew, Tim	Kin	125
Drese, Ryan	Kin	122
Turnbow, Mark	Akr	121

PITCHER	CLUB	W-L	ERA	IP	H	BB	SO
Spiegel, Mike	Kin	7-3	3.02	131	96	65	141
Pugmire, Robert	Kin	13-2	3.28	154	128	39	160
Rigdon, Paul	Buf	14-4	3.35	153	134	38	85
Watson, Mark	Akr	15-8	3.40	153	171	48	97
Drew, Tim	Kin	13-5	3.73	169	154	60	125

Sick call: 1999 DL report

PLAYER	Days on the DL
Sandy Alomar	118
Wil Cordero	91
Jacob Cruz	82*
Travis Fryman	79*
Dwight Gooden	28
Steve Karsay	52*
Mark Langston	46*
Kenny Lofton	32*
Tom Martin	126
Willie Martinez	64
Jason Rakers	34
Ricardo Rincon	33
David Riske	16
Paul Shuey	15
Mark Whiten	79
Jaret Wright	47*

Indicates two separate terms on Disabled List.

1999 salaries

	Bonuses	Total earned salary
Jim Thome, 1b		8,225,000
Kenny Lofton, of	50,000	7,550,000
David Justice, of		7,000,000
Roberto Alomar, 2b	425,000	7,049,966
Charles Nagy, p		6,000,000
Travis Fryman, 3b		5,250,000
Dave Burba, p	166,664	4,666,664
Manny Ramirez, of	200,000	4,350,000
Omar Vizquel, ss		3,050,000
Sandy Alomar, c	100,000	2,800,000
Dwight Gooden, p		2,637,500
Mike Jackson, p	100,000	2,100,000
Harold Baines, dh	215,000	1,730,000
Paul Assenmacher, p	32,000	1,507,000
Steve Reed, p	66,666	1,366,666
Paul Shuey, p	50,000	1,117,666
Jaret Wright, p		812,500
Tyler Houston, 3b		715,000
Bartolo Colon, p		625,000
Chris Haney, p	50,000	550,000
Carlos Baerga, 3b		500,000
Wil Cordero		500,000
Steve Karsay, p	100,000	500,000
Ricardo Rincon, p		450,000
Jesse Levis, c		400,000
Mark Langston, p	50,000	350,000
Richie Sexson, 1b		219,000
Enrique Wilson, 3b		214,000
Einar Diaz, c		209,000
Alex Ramirez, of		205,000
Jacob Cruz, of		205,000
Jason Rakers, p		203,000
Jim Poole, p		200,000
David Roberts, of		200,000
Sean DePaula, p		200,000
David Riske, p		200,000

Average 1999 salary: $2,052,999
Total 1999 team payroll: $73,907,962
Termination pay: $113,730

Cleveland (1901-1999)

Runs: Most, career

1154	Earl Averill, 1929-1939
1079	Tris Speaker, 1916-1926
942	Charlie Jamieson, 1919-1932
865	Nap Lajoie, 1902-1914
857	Joe Sewell, 1920-1930

Hits: Most, career

2046	Nap Lajoie, 1902-1914
1965	Tris Speaker, 1916-1926
1903	Earl Averill, 1929-1939
1800	Joe Sewell, 1920-1930
1753	Charlie Jamieson, 1919-1932

2B: Most, career

486	Tris Speaker, 1916-1926
424	Nap Lajoie, 1902-1914
377	Earl Averill, 1929-1939
375	Joe Sewell, 1920-1930
367	Lou Boudreau, 1938-1950

3B: Most, career

121	Earl Averill, 1929-1939
108	Tris Speaker, 1916-1926
106	Elmer Flick, 1902-1910
89	Joe Jackson, 1910-1915
83	Jeff Heath, 1936-1945

HR: Most, career

242	ALBERT BELLE, 1989-1996
226	Earl Averill, 1929-1939
216	Hal Trosky, 1933-1941
215	Larry Doby, 1947-1958
214	Andy Thornton, 1977-1987

RBI: Most, career

1084	Earl Averill, 1929-1939
919	Nap Lajoie, 1902-1914
911	Hal Trosky, 1933-1941
884	Tris Speaker, 1916-1926
869	Joe Sewell, 1920-1930

SB: Most, career

404	KENNY LOFTON, 1992-1999
254	Terry Turner, 1904-1918
240	Nap Lajoie, 1902-1914
233	Ray Chapman, 1912-1920
207	Elmer Flick, 1902-1910

BB: Most, career

857	Tris Speaker, 1916-1926
766	Lou Boudreau, 1938-1950
725	Earl Averill, 1929-1939
712	Jack Graney, 1908-1922
703	Larry Doby, 1947-1958

BA: Highest, career

.375	Joe Jackson, 1910-1915
.354	Tris Speaker, 1916-1926
.339	Nap Lajoie, 1902-1914
.327	George Burns, 1920-1928
.323	Ed Morgan, 1928-1933

On-base avg: Highest, career

.444	Tris Speaker, 1916-1926
.441	Joe Jackson, 1910-1915
.412	JIM THOME, 1991-1999
.405	Ed Morgan, 1928-1933
.399	MANNY RAMIREZ, 1993-1999

Slug pct: Highest, career

.580	ALBERT BELLE, 1989-1996
.576	MANNY RAMIREZ, 1993-1999
.551	Hal Trosky, 1933-1941
.547	JIM THOME, 1991-1999
.542	Joe Jackson, 1910-1915

Games started: Most, career

484	Bob Feller, 1936-1956
433	Mel Harder, 1928-1947
350	Bob Lemon, 1941-1958
320	Willis Hudlin, 1926-1940
305	Stan Coveleski, 1916-1924

Complete games: Most, career

279	Bob Feller, 1936-1956
234	Addie Joss, 1902-1910
194	Stan Coveleski, 1916-1924
188	Bob Lemon, 1941-1958
181	Mel Harder, 1928-1947

Saves: Most, career

129	DOUG JONES, 1986-1998
104	JOSE MESA, 1992-1998
94	MIKE JACKSON, 1997-1999
53	Ray Narleski, 1954-1958
48	Steve Olin, 1989-1992

Shutouts: Most, career

45	Addie Joss, 1902-1910
44	Bob Feller, 1936-1956
31	Stan Coveleski, 1916-1924
31	Bob Lemon, 1941-1958
27	Mike Garcia, 1948-1959

Wins: Most, career

266	Bob Feller, 1936-1956
223	Mel Harder, 1928-1947
207	Bob Lemon, 1941-1958
172	Stan Coveleski, 1916-1924
164	Early Wynn, 1949-1963

K: Most, career

2581	Bob Feller, 1936-1956
2159	Sam McDowell, 1961-1971
1277	Bob Lemon, 1941-1958
1277	Early Wynn, 1949-1963
1161	Mel Harder, 1928-1947

Win pct: Highest, career

.682	OREL HERSHISER, 1995-1997
.667	Vean Gregg, 1911-1914
.663	Johnny Allen, 1936-1940
.630	Cal McLish, 1956-1959
.623	Addie Joss, 1902-1910

ERA: Lowest, career

1.89	Addie Joss, 1902-1910
2.31	Vean Gregg, 1911-1914
2.39	Bob Rhoads, 1903-1909
2.45	Bill Bernhard, 1902-1907
2.50	Otto Hess, 1902-1908

Runs: Most, season

140	Earl Averill, 1931
138	ROBERTO ALOMAR, 1999
137	Tris Speaker, 1920
136	Earl Averill, 1936
133	Tris Speaker, 1923

Hits: Most, season

233	Joe Jackson, 1911
232	Earl Averill, 1936
227	Nap Lajoie, 1910
226	Joe Jackson, 1912
225	Johnny Hodapp, 1930

2B: Most, season

64	George Burns, 1926
59	Tris Speaker, 1923
52	ALBERT BELLE, 1995
52	Tris Speaker, 1921
52	Tris Speaker, 1926

3B: Most, season

26	Joe Jackson, 1912
23	Dale Mitchell, 1949
22	Bill Bradley, 1903
22	Elmer Flick, 1906
20	Jeff Heath, 1941
20	Joe Vosmik, 1935

HR: Most, season

50	ALBERT BELLE, 1995
48	ALBERT BELLE, 1996
45	MANNY RAMIREZ, 1998
44	MANNY RAMIREZ, 1999
43	Al Rosen, 1953

RBI: Most, season

165	MANNY RAMIREZ, 1999
162	Hal Trosky, 1936
148	ALBERT BELLE, 1996
145	MANNY RAMIREZ, 1998
145	Al Rosen, 1953

SB: Most, season

75	KENNY LOFTON, 1996
70	KENNY LOFTON, 1993
66	KENNY LOFTON, 1992
61	Miguel Dilone, 1980
60	KENNY LOFTON, 1994

BB: Most, season

127	JIM THOME, 1999
123	JIM THOME, 1996
120	JIM THOME, 1997
111	Mike Hargrove, 1980
109	Andy Thornton, 1982

BA: Highest, season

.408	Joe Jackson, 1911
.395	Joe Jackson, 1912
.389	Tris Speaker, 1925
.388	Tris Speaker, 1920
.386	Tris Speaker, 1916

On-base avg: Highest, season

.483	Tris Speaker, 1920
.479	Tris Speaker, 1925
.474	Tris Speaker, 1922
.470	Tris Speaker, 1916
.469	Tris Speaker, 1923

Slug pct: Highest, season

.714	ALBERT BELLE, 1994
.690	ALBERT BELLE, 1995
.663	MANNY RAMIREZ, 1999
.644	Hal Trosky, 1936
.627	Earl Averill, 1936

Games started: Most, season

44	George Uhle, 1923
42	Bob Feller, 1946
41	Gaylord Perry, 1973
40	Stan Coveleski, 1921
40	Bob Feller, 1941
40	Gaylord Perry, 1972
40	Dick Tidrow, 1973
40	George Uhle, 1922

Complete games: Most, season

36	Bob Feller, 1946
35	Bill Bernhard, 1904
34	Addie Joss, 1907
33	Otto Hess, 1906
32	George Uhle, 1926

Saves: Most, season

46	JOSE MESA, 1995
43	DOUG JONES, 1990
40	MIKE JACKSON, 1998
39	MIKE JACKSON, 1999
39	JOSE MESA, 1996

Shutouts: Most, season

10	Bob Feller, 1946
10	Bob Lemon, 1948
9	Stan Coveleski, 1917
9	Addie Joss, 1906
9	Addie Joss, 1908
9	Luis Tiant, 1968

Wins: Most, season

31	Jim Bagby, 1920
27	Bob Feller, 1940
27	Addie Joss, 1907
27	George Uhle, 1926
26	Bob Feller, 1946
26	George Uhle, 1923

K: Most, season

348	Bob Feller, 1946
325	Sam McDowell, 1965
304	Sam McDowell, 1970
283	Sam McDowell, 1968
279	Sam McDowell, 1969

Win pct: Highest, season

.938	Johnny Allen, 1937
.783	BARTOLO COLON, 1999
.773	Bill Bernhard, 1902
.773	CHARLES NAGY, 1996
.767	Vean Gregg, 1911
.767	Bob Lemon, 1954

ERA: Lowest, season

1.16	Addie Joss, 1908
1.59	Addie Joss, 1904
1.60	Luis Tiant, 1968
1.71	Addie Joss, 1909
1.72	Addie Joss, 1906

Most pinch-hit homers, season

3	Gene Green, 1962
3	Fred Whitfield, 1965
3	Ted Uhlaender, 1970
3	Ron Kittle, 1988

Most pinch-hit homers, career

8	Fred Whitfield, 1963-1967
5	Chuck Hinton, 1965-1971

Longest hitting streak

31	Nap Lajoie, 1906
30	SANDY ALOMAR JR., 1997
29	Bill Bradley, 1902
28	Joe Jackson, 1911
28	Hal Trosky, 1936

Most consecutive scoreless innings

41	Luis Tiant, 1968
38	Jim Bagby, 1917

No-hit games

Earl Moore, Cle vs Chi AL, 2-4; May 9, 1901 (lost on two hits in the 10th).

Dusty Rhoades, Cle vs Bos AL, 2-1; September 18, 1908.

Addie Joss, Cle vs Chi AL, 1-0; October 2, 1908 (perfect game).

Addie Joss, Cle at Chi AL, 1-0; April 20, 1910.

Ray Caldwell, Cle at NY AL, 3-0; September 10, 1919 (1st game).

Wes Ferrell, Cle vs StL AL, 9-0; April 29, 1931.

Bob Feller, Cle at Chi AL, 1-0; April 16, 1940 (opening day).

Bob Feller, Cle at NY AL, 1-0; April 30, 1946.

Don Black, Cle vs Phi AL, 3-0; July 10, 1947 (1st game).

Bob Lemon, Cle at Det AL, 2-0; June 30, 1948.

Bob Feller, Cle vs Det AL, 2-1; July 1, 1951 (1st game).

Sonny Siebert, Cle vs Was AL, 2-0; June 10, 1966.

Dick Bosman, Cle vs Oak AL, 4-0; July 19, 1974.

Dennis Eckersley, Cle vs Cal AL, 1-0; May 30, 1977.

Len Barker, Cle vs Tor AL, 3-0; May 15, 1981 (perfect game).

ACTIVE PLAYERS in caps.

Players' years of service are listed by the first and last years with this team and are not necessarily consecutive; all statistics record performances for this team only.

By Barbara Jean Germano, *Baseball Weekly*

All-Star right fielder Magglio Ordonez emerged as the best of the White Sox's up-and-coming young players.

1999 White Sox: Experienced help wanted

The Chicago White Sox developed players. They sorted. They mixed. They matched. And they learned who can do what—and who can't—during manager Jerry Manuel's second season of rebuilding. The next step, Manuel says, is a step toward contention.

"I feel somewhat satisfied to have players evolve and develop into major league personnel. We feel we did that with our offense and pitching," Manuel said after a 75-86 season. "I'd like to win every game, but things don't work that way. I think we did a good job of developing the talent we had."

Since losing Albert Belle and Robin Ventura after the 1998 season, Manuel has been searching for more punch in the lineup, saying it's a must if the White Sox are to compete in the American League Central.

"Basically the big thing is the experience," Manuel said. "That experience factor has really weighed on us a lot. You have to have some experience at some positions in order to survive."

But Manuel's big-name veteran didn't produce in 1999. Frank Thomas hit only 15 homers. After making an error in Oakland, Thomas said he should be a DH instead of a first baseman, even though he was a much better hitter when he played in the field. Thomas and Manuel debated all season. After the manager sent the two-time MVP home for refusing to pinch-hit in the second game of a September doubleheader—saying his ankle was hurt—Thomas returned to Chicago and underwent ankle surgery that caused him to miss the final three weeks of the season.

The White Sox found some good young hitters for their future. All-Star right fielder Magglio Ordonez hit 30 homers and drove in 117 runs while batting .301. Carlos Lee, who played left and then ended up at first, hit 16 homers and drove in 84 runs after being called up in May. Center fielder Chris Singleton, the biggest surprise of all, batted .301 with 17 homers. Paul Konerko,

Team MVP

Magglio Ordonez: The White Sox's best 1999 player is part of the team's next wave of bright, young talent. Ordonez became the every-day right fielder in 1998 and advanced to become an All-Star in '99. Only veteran Frank Thomas had a higher batting average on the team, .305 to .301. But Ordonez had twice as many homers (30) and easily out-distanced Thomas in RBI, 117-77.

obtained in a trade for Mike Cameron, hit 24 homers and batted .294

A glaring problem spot was the left side of the infield—third baseman Greg Norton made a league-leading 27 errors and shortstop Mike Caruso had 24. The White Sox will try Konerko at third.

Starting pitching is a problem, too. Jaime Navarro—who has one year left on a $20 million, four-year contract—pitched so poorly (8-13, 6.09 ERA) that for the second straight season he ended up in the bullpen. James Baldwin had another miserable first half but won eight of his final 10 decisions to finish 12-13; lefty Jim Parque didn't win a game after July 7. On the plus side, lefty Mike Sirotka won 11 games, and Kip Wells and Aaron Myette look promising.

The bullpen was the strength of the team, with Keith Foulke, Sean Lowe, Bill Simas and Bobby Howry (28 saves) forming the nucleus.

Catcher Brook Fordyce, splitting time with Mark Johnson, hit .297 but threw out only 22 percent of runners. Second baseman Ray Durham, an All-Star in 1998, batted .296.

After his 80-82 rookie season, Manuel said he wouldn't "be satisfied if we're not [in a position to win a championship] in two years." If the White Sox are going to satisfy Manuel's timetable in 2000, he's got a big job ahead of him.

1999 White Sox: Week-by-week notes

These notes were excerpted from the following issues of Baseball Weekly.

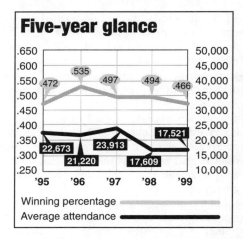

Five-year glance

Winning percentage

Average attendance

▶**April 14:** First baseman-DH Frank Thomas got off to a strong start, hitting .563 with six RBI in the first five games. Thomas hit .265 last season, an 82-point drop from his 1997 AL-batting-title figure.

▶**April 28:** White Sox pitchers were 10th in the AL in team ERA a year ago (4.73). Now, thanks to the relievers, under 3.00 collectively, and to strong efforts last week from the rotation—right-handers James Baldwin, Jaime Navarro and John Snyder, and lefties Jim Parque and Mike Sirotka—they're third at 3.96.

▶**May 5:** First baseman-DH Paul Konerko, third baseman Greg Norton and outfielder Jeff Abbott hit a combined .367 in spring training with seven home runs and 36 RBI, but they were at .207 with two homers and 13 RBI during April in the 5-6-7 lineup spots. No one had struggled more than Abbott, a career .340 minor league hitter who hit .143 in April.

▶**May 12:** Manager Jerry Manuel didn't think he had an ace when he started the season. That's history. John Snyder was 5-1 with a 1.81 ERA, and he's only 24. Meanwhile, Frank Thomas broke shortstop Luke Appling's club record for extra-base hits with No. 588, doing it in 1,259 games to Appling's 2,422.

▶**June 2:** Just when the White Sox were beginning to think they should have kept Robin Ventura, Greg Norton responded with five home runs in three games while playing flawless third base. Norton's eight homers in 148 at-bats were one shy of his total last season.

▶**June 9:** After settling down from a wild streak, Bobby Howry was ready to regain his job as closer. He allowed one run in 6⅓ innings after surrendering nine runs and 10 walks in his previous seven appearances.

▶**June 16:** Right fielder Magglio Ordonez was far exceeding expectations in his second full season. Moved to cleanup when Paul Konerko failed there, Ordonez was

on pace for 30 home runs and 110 RBI. Mike Sirotka was challenging Red Sox right-hander Pedro Martinez for the league ERA title. Sirotka's mark dropped to 2.41 on June 12 despite his having a 5-6 record because of lack of run support. He not only shut the Cubs out for 7⅔ innings in an 8-2 romp, but he also hit two singles.

▶**June 23:** Jerry Manuel was concerned with the .295 on-base percentage of his No. 2 hitter, shortstop Mike Caruso, who went 0-for-17 after hitting a game-winning two-run homer against the Cubs. Frank Thomas had a 21-game hitting streak, longest in the league this season. He batted .402 during the tear.

▶**June 30:** Center fielder Chris Singleton proved to be another reason the youth movement is blossoming. An acquisition from the Yankees for a minor league pitcher, he was expected to push fellow prospects Brian Simmons and McKay Christensen in spring training. Instead, he kept them in the minors with his .302 average and fine defensive play.

▶**July 7:** The Sox demoted John Snyder to AAA Charlotte when his record fell to 7-6 and his ERA rose to 5.81, after he had started 6-1 and 2.00. The team also threatened slumping James Baldwin with a trip to the bullpen.

▶**July 21:** Greg Norton and Mike Caruso lost their spots in the lineup because of a combined .247 batting average and 36

errors. Jerry Manuel went with Craig Wilson and Liu Rodriguez. Caruso was the toughest in the league to strike out, with just one every 21.9 at-bats, but he had drawn only seven walks in 304 at-bats for a .281 on-base percentage.

▶**July 28:** The club needed more production from left fielder Carlos Lee, who was a high-average, RBI hitter in the minor leagues but had only five homers and 38 RBI in 256 at-bats with the Sox.

▶**Aug. 4:** Paul Konerko batted .420 in July to lift his average to .305 from .256. The White Sox considered leaving Konerko at first base and keeping Frank Thomas at DH, which was fine with Thomas, who hadn't played first since July 18, when he hit a foul off his already sore right foot.

▶**Aug. 11:** The club wants Jaime Navarro to succeed because he has another year on his four-year, $20 million contract, but his ERA of 5.71 through 22 starts wasn't much different from the 6.36 and 5.79 marks he had posted the past two years.

▶**Aug. 18:** Frank Thomas's reluctance to return to first base after committing a crucial error at Oakland during a seven-game losing stretch became a club distraction. He wanted to remain a DH. But manager Jerry Manuel pointed to Thomas's .346 average when he played first base (in 1999) compared with his .299 as the DH; his slugging percentage is almost 100 points higher when he's in the field.

▶**Sept. 1:** The club was watching to see if Magglio Ordonez could turn around his second-half tumble once he has topped 100 RBI. Ordonez had been hitting just .229 in the second half after batting .332 in the first and being named an All-Star.

▶**Sept. 15:** Frank Thomas's season-ending foot surgery and the removal of a "significant" bone spur (and a little-toe corn) had Jerry Manuel wondering where the team's power will come from next season. Late-season slumps from Magglio Ordonez and Paul Konerko didn't help. Thomas finished with the second-lowest batting average (.305) of his 10-year career and his lowest full-season totals in home runs (15) and RBI (77).

▶**Sept. 22:** The White Sox planned to increase their payroll by at least $10 million next season—to about $36 million.

▶**Oct. 6:** Chicago was second in the AL Central for the fourth consecutive year but finished at 75-86. James Baldwin and Jim Parque went in opposite directions during the second half. Baldwin was 8-4 with a 3.56 ERA after going 4-9 and 6.62 in the first half. Parque lost his last nine decisions after going 8-5 with a 3.81 ERA in his first 15 starts.

QUOTE OF THE YEAR

"John has catapulted himself into the elite ranks of today's pitchers."

—Manager Jerry Manuel, early in the season on right-hander John Snyder, who finished 9-12 with a 6.68 ERA

145

Team Leaders

Batting avg.	Hits	Wins	Strikeouts
.305 Frank Thomas	188 Magglio Ordonez	12 James Baldwin	125 Mike Sirotka
.301 Magglio Ordonez	181 Ray Durham	11 Mike Sirotka	123 Keith Foulke
			123 James Baldwin

HR	Runs	Losses	Innings
30 Magglio Ordonez	109 Ray Durham	15 Jim Parque	209 Mike Sirotka
24 Paul Konerko	100 Magglio Ordonez	13 Mike Sirotka	199.1 James Baldwin
		13 James Baldwin	

RBI	Stolen bases	ERA	Saves
117 Magglio Ordonez	34 Ray Durham	4.00 Mike Sirotka	28 Bobby Howry
84 Carlos Lee	20 Chris Singleton	5.10 James Baldwin	9 Keith Foulke

CHICAGO WHITE SOX 1999 final stats

BATTERS	BA	SLG	OBA	G	AB	R	H	TB	2B	3B	HR	RBI	BB	SO	SB	CS	E
Thomas	.305	.471	.414	135	486	74	148	229	36	0	15	77	87	66	3	3	4
Ordonez	.301	.510	.349	157	624	100	188	318	34	3	30	117	47	64	13	6	3
Singleton	.300	.490	.328	133	496	72	149	243	31	6	17	72	22	45	20	5	4
Fordyce	.297	.459	.343	105	333	36	99	153	25	1	9	49	21	48	2	0	8
Durham	.296	.435	.373	153	612	109	181	266	30	8	13	60	73	105	34	11	19
Konerko	.294	.511	.352	142	513	71	151	262	31	4	24	81	45	68	1	0	4
Lee	.293	.463	.312	127	492	66	144	228	32	2	16	84	13	72	4	2	5
Jackson	.275	.430	.288	73	149	22	41	64	9	1	4	16	3	20	4	1	3
Norton	.255	.424	.358	132	436	62	111	185	26	0	16	50	69	93	4	4	27
Caruso	.250	.297	.280	136	529	60	132	157	11	4	2	35	20	36	12	14	24
Liefer	.248	.327	.295	45	113	8	28	37	7	1	0	14	8	28	2	0	0
Wilson	.238	.325	.301	98	252	28	60	82	8	1	4	26	23	22	1	1	7
Rodriguez	.237	.333	.343	39	93	8	22	31	2	2	1	12	12	11	0	0	3
Simmons	.230	.397	.281	54	126	14	29	50	3	3	4	17	9	30	4	0	2
Johnson	.227	.338	.344	73	207	27	47	70	11	0	4	16	36	58	3	1	3
Christensen	.226	.302	.271	28	53	10	12	16	1	0	1	6	4	7	2	1	3
Paul	.222	.278	.222	6	18	2	4	5	1	0	0	1	0	4	0	0	0
Abbott	.158	.263	.222	17	57	5	9	15	0	0	2	6	5	12	1	1	1
Dellaero	.091	.091	.114	11	33	1	3	3	0	0	0	2	1	13	0	0	4

PITCHERS	W-L	ERA	BA	G	GS	CG	GF	SH	SV	IP	H	R	ER	HR	BB	SO
Davenport	0-0	0.00	.200	3	0	0	2	0	0	1.2	1	0	0	0	2	0
Sturtze	0-0	0.00	.200	1	1	0	0	0	0	6.0	4	0	0	0	2	2
Foulke	3-3	2.22	.188	67	0	0	31	0	9	105.1	72	28	26	11	21	123
Howry	5-3	3.59	.229	69	0	0	54	0	28	67.2	58	34	27	8	38	80
Lowe	4-1	3.67	.262	64	0	0	13	0	0	95.2	90	39	39	10	46	62
Simas	6-3	3.75	.263	70	0	0	21	0	2	72.0	73	36	30	6	32	41
Sirotka	11-13	4.00	.283	32	32	3	0	1	0	209.0	236	108	93	24	57	125
Wells	4-1	4.04	.248	7	7	0	0	0	0	35.2	33	17	16	2	15	29
Daneker	0-0	4.20	.255	3	2	0	1	0	0	15.0	14	8	7	1	6	5
Baldwin	12-13	5.10	.278	35	33	1	1	0	0	199.1	219	119	113	34	81	123
Parque	9-15	5.13	.299	31	30	1	0	0	0	173.2	210	111	99	23	79	111
Pena	0-0	5.31	.259	26	0	0	1	0	0	20.1	21	15	12	3	23	20
Castillo	2-2	5.71	.274	18	2	0	6	0	0	41.0	45	26	26	10	14	23
Navarro	8-13	6.09	.313	32	27	0	1	0	0	159.2	206	126	108	29	71	74
Myette	0-2	6.32	.266	4	3	0	0	0	0	15.2	17	11	11	2	14	11
Snyder	9-12	6.68	.311	25	25	1	0	0	0	129.1	167	103	96	27	49	67
Rizzo	0-2	6.75	.500	3	0	0	2	0	0	1.1	4	2	1	0	3	2
Ward	0-1	7.55	.368	40	0	0	8	0	0	39.1	63	36	33	10	11	35
Eyre	1-1	7.56	.339	21	0	0	8	0	0	25.0	38	22	21	6	15	17
Lundquist	1-1	8.59	.315	17	0	0	7	0	0	22.0	28	21	21	3	12	18
Bradford	0-0	19.64	.474	3	0	0	0	0	0	3.2	9	8	8	1	5	0

2000 preliminary roster

PITCHERS (21)
James Baldwin
Lorenzo Barcelo
Kevin Beirne
Chad Bradford
Carlos Castillo
Pat Daneker
Joe Davenport
Scott Eyre
Keith Foulke
Bobby Howry
Sean Lowe
Aaron Myette
Jaime Navarro
Jim Parque
Jesus Pena
Jason Secoda
Bill Simas
Mike Sirotka
John Snyder
Tanyon Sturtze
Kip Wells

CATCHERS (3)
Brook Fordyce
Mark Johnson
Josh Paul

INFIELDERS (9)
Mike Caruso
Joe Crede
Jason Dellaero
Ray Durham
Paul Konerko
Jeff Liefer
Greg Norton
Frank Thomas
Craig Wilson

OUTFIELDERS (6)
Jeff Abbott
McKay Christensen
Carlos Lee
Magglio Ordonez
Brian Simmons
Chris Singleton

Games played by position

PLAYER	G	C	1B	2B	3B	SS	OF	DH
Abbott	17	0	0	0	0	0	17	0
Caruso	136	0	0	0	0	132	0	2
Christensen	28	0	0	0	0	0	27	0
Dellaero	11	0	0	0	0	11	0	0
Durham	153	0	0	148	0	0	0	4
Fordyce	105	103	0	0	0	0	0	0
Jackson	73	0	0	0	0	0	64	3
Johnson	73	72	0	0	0	0	0	2
Konerko	142	0	92	0	1	0	0	54
Lee	127	0	5	0	0	0	105	16
Liefer	45	0	15	0	0	0	17	9
Norton	132	0	26	0	120	0	0	1
Ordonez	157	0	0	0	0	0	153	2
Paul	6	6	0	0	0	0	0	0
Rodriguez	39	0	0	22	1	14	0	0
Simmons	54	1	0	0	0	0	46	3
Singleton	133	0	0	0	0	0	127	2
Thomas	135	0	49	0	0	0	0	83
Wilson	98	0	1	7	72	22	0	0

Sick call: 1999 DL report

PLAYER	Days on the DL
Scott Eyre	26
Darren Hall	182
Darrin Jackson	17
Brian Simmons	23

Minor Leagues
Tops in the organization

BATTER	CLUB	AVG.	G	AB	R	H	HR	RBI
Valenzuela, Mario	Bur	.323	122	477	89	154	10	70
Mottola, Chad	Cha	.321	140	511	95	164	20	94
Brito, Tilson	Cha	.318	111	406	60	129	11	58
Durham, Chad	Bur	.314	75	303	69	95	0	36
Merriman, Terrell	Bur	.306	109	382	77	117	15	85

HOME RUNS
Raven, Luis	Cha	33
Valdez, Mario	Cha	26
Rowand, Aaron	WS	24
Lydy, Scott	Brm	22
Mottola, Chad	Cha	20

WINS
Wells, Kip	Brm	13
Fogg, Josh	Brm	13
Myette, Aaron	Brm	12
Several Players Tied at		10

RBI
Raven, Luis	Cha	125
Mottola, Chad	Cha	94
Battersby, Eric	Bur	93
Rowand, Aaron	WS	88
Several Players Tied at		85

SAVES
Whatley, Brannon	Bur	20
Andujar, Luis	Cha	16
Tokarse, Brian	Brm	14
Guerrier, Matt	WS	12
Davenport, Joe	Brm	10

STOLEN BASES
Durham, Chad	Bur	59
Ramirez, Dan	Cha	51
Connacher, Kevin	Brm	28
Merriman, Terrell	Bur	27
Gomez, Ramon	Brm	26

STRIKEOUTS
Figueroa, Juan	WS	189
Fogg, Josh	Brm	149
Wells, Kip	Brm	139
Myette, Aaron	Brm	135
Scott, Brian	WS	132

PITCHER	CLUB	W-L	ERA	IP	H	BB	SO
Almonte, Edwin	Bur	9-12	3.03	116	107	28	85
Wells, Kip	Brm	13-8	3.29	156	127	65	139
Roberts, Mark	Brm	5-8	3.40	124	108	41	84
Scott, Brian	WS	8-8	3.41	148	135	60	132
Chantres, Carlos	Brm	6-8	3.50	141	122	61	105

1999 salaries

	Bonuses	Total earned salary
Frank Thomas, dh		7,000,000
Jaime Navarro, p		5,000,000
Ray Durham, 2b		3,400,000
James Baldwin, p		1,900,000
Bill Simas, p	50,000	1,150,000
Darren Hall, p		850,000
Mike Sirotka, p		500,000
Darrin Jackson, of	25,000	425,000
Magglio Ordonez, of	15,000	305,000
Mike Caruso, ss		275,000
Greg Norton, 3b		255,000
Keith Foulke, p		255,000
Carlos Castillo, p		250,000
Scott Eyre, p		240,000
Bobby Howry, p		235,000
Brook Fordyce, c		230,000
John Snyder, p		230,000
Jim Parque, p		230,000
Paul Konerko, 1b		215,000
Craig Wilson, 3b		205,000
Sean Lowe, p		200,000
Jesus Pena, p		200,000
Chris Singleton, of		200,000
Carlos Lee, of		200,000
Mark Johnson, c		200,000
Liu Rodriguez, 2b		200,000
Brian Simmons, of		200,000

Average 1999 salary: $909,259
Total 1999 team payroll: $24,550,000

Chicago (1901-1999)

Runs: Most, career

1319	Luke Appling, 1930-1950
1187	Nellie Fox, 1950-1963
1065	Eddie Collins, 1915-1926
968	FRANK THOMAS, 1990-1999
893	Minnie Minoso, 1951-1980

Hits: Most, career

2749	Luke Appling, 1930-1950
2470	Nellie Fox, 1950-1963
2007	Eddie Collins, 1915-1926
1749	HAROLD BAINES, 1980-1997
1608	OZZIE GUILLEN, 1985-1997

2B: Most, career

440	Luke Appling, 1930-1950
335	Nellie Fox, 1950-1963
317	FRANK THOMAS, 1990-1999
314	HAROLD BAINES, 1980-1997
266	Eddie Collins, 1915-1926

3B: Most, career

104	Shano Collins, 1910-1920
104	Nellie Fox, 1950-1963
102	Luke Appling, 1930-1950
102	Eddie Collins, 1915-1926
82	Johnny Mostil, 1918-1929

HR: Most, career

301	FRANK THOMAS, 1990-1999
220	HAROLD BAINES, 1980-1997
214	Carlton Fisk, 1981-1993
171	ROBIN VENTURA, 1989-1998
154	Bill Melton, 1968-1975

RBI: Most, career

1116	Luke Appling, 1930-1950
1040	FRANK THOMAS, 1990-1999
966	HAROLD BAINES, 1980-1997
808	Minnie Minoso, 1951-1980
804	Eddie Collins, 1915-1926

SB: Most, career

368	Eddie Collins, 1915-1926
318	Luis Aparicio, 1956-1970
250	Frank Isbell, 1901-1909
226	LANCE JOHNSON, 1988-1995
206	Fielder Jones, 1901-1908

BB: Most, career

1302	Luke Appling, 1930-1950

1076	FRANK THOMAS, 1990-1999
965	Eddie Collins, 1915-1926
668	ROBIN VENTURA, 1989-1998
658	Nellie Fox, 1950-1963
658	Minnie Minoso, 1951-1980

BA: Highest, career

.340	Joe Jackson, 1915-1920
.331	Eddie Collins, 1915-1926
.320	FRANK THOMAS, 1990-1999
.317	Zeke Bonura, 1934-1937
.315	Bibb Falk, 1920-1928

On-base avg: Highest, career

.440	FRANK THOMAS, 1990-1999
.426	Eddie Collins, 1915-1926
.407	Joe Jackson, 1915-1920
.399	Luke Appling, 1930-1950
.397	Minnie Minoso, 1951-1980

Slug pct: Highest, career

.573	FRANK THOMAS, 1990-1999
.518	Zeke Bonura, 1934-1937
.499	Joe Jackson, 1915-1920
.470	Ron Kittle, 1982-1991
.468	HAROLD BAINES, 1980-1997

Games started: Most, career

484	Ted Lyons, 1923-1946
483	Red Faber, 1914-1933
390	Billy Pierce, 1949-1961
312	Ed Walsh, 1904-1916
301	Doc White, 1903-1913

Complete games: Most, career

356	Ted Lyons, 1923-1946
273	Red Faber, 1914-1933
249	Ed Walsh, 1904-1916
206	Doc White, 1903-1913
183	Eddie Cicotte, 1912-1920
183	Billy Pierce, 1949-1961

Saves: Most, career

201	Bobby Thigpen, 1986-1993
161	ROBERTO HERNANDEZ, 1991-1997
98	Hoyt Wilhelm, 1963-1968
75	Terry Forster, 1971-1976
57	Wilbur Wood, 1967-1978

Shutouts: Most, career

57	Ed Walsh, 1904-1916
42	Doc White, 1903-1913
35	Billy Pierce, 1949-1961
29	Red Faber, 1914-1933
28	Eddie Cicotte, 1912-1920

Wins: Most, career

260	Ted Lyons, 1923-1946
254	Red Faber, 1914-1933
195	Ed Walsh, 1904-1916
186	Billy Pierce, 1949-1961
163	Wilbur Wood, 1967-1978

K: Most, career

1796	Billy Pierce, 1949-1961
1732	Ed Walsh, 1904-1916
1471	Red Faber, 1914-1933
1332	Wilbur Wood, 1967-1978
1098	Gary Peters, 1959-1969

Win pct: Highest, career

.648	Lefty Williams, 1916-1920
.644	Virgil Trucks, 1953-1955
.616	Jim Kaat, 1973-1975
.615	Juan Pizarro, 1961-1966
.611	JACK McDOWELL, 1987-1994

ERA: Lowest, career

1.81	Ed Walsh, 1904-1916
2.18	Frank Smith, 1904-1910
2.25	Eddie Cicotte, 1912-1920
2.30	Jim Scott, 1909-1917
2.30	Doc White, 1903-1913

Runs: Most, season

135	Johnny Mostil, 1925
126	RAY DURHAM, 1998
120	Zeke Bonura, 1936
120	Fielder Jones, 1901
120	Johnny Mostil, 1926
120	Rip Radcliff, 1936

Hits: Most, season

224	Eddie Collins, 1920
218	Joe Jackson, 1920
208	Buck Weaver, 1920
207	Rip Radcliff, 1936
204	Luke Appling, 1936

2B: Most, season

48	ALBERT BELLE, 1998
46	FRANK THOMAS, 1992
45	ALBERT BELLE, 1997
45	Floyd Robinson, 1962
44	Ivan Calderon, 1990
44	Chet Lemon, 1979

3B: Most, season

21	Joe Jackson, 1916
20	Joe Jackson, 1920
18	Jack Fournier, 1915
18	Harry Lord, 1911

| 18 | Minnie Minoso, 1954 |
| 18 | Carl Reynolds, 1930 |

HR: Most, season

49	ALBERT BELLE, 1998
41	FRANK THOMAS, 1993
40	FRANK THOMAS, 1995
40	FRANK THOMAS, 1996
38	FRANK THOMAS, 1994

RBI: Most, season

152	ALBERT BELLE, 1998
138	Zeke Bonura, 1936
134	FRANK THOMAS, 1996
128	Luke Appling, 1936
128	FRANK THOMAS, 1993

SB: Most, season

77	Rudy Law, 1983
56	Luis Aparicio, 1959
56	Wally Moses, 1943
53	Luis Aparicio, 1961
53	Eddie Collins, 1917

BB: Most, season

138	FRANK THOMAS, 1991
136	FRANK THOMAS, 1995
127	Lu Blue, 1931
125	TONY PHILLIPS, 1996
122	Luke Appling, 1935
122	FRANK THOMAS, 1992

BA: Highest, season

.388	Luke Appling, 1936
.382	Joe Jackson, 1920
.372	Eddie Collins, 1920
.360	Eddie Collins, 1923
.359	Carl Reynolds, 1930

On-base avg: Highest, season

.487	FRANK THOMAS, 1994
.474	Luke Appling, 1936
.461	Eddie Collins, 1925
.460	Eddie Collins, 1915
.459	FRANK THOMAS, 1996

Slug pct: Highest, season

.729	FRANK THOMAS, 1994
.655	ALBERT BELLE, 1998
.626	FRANK THOMAS, 1996
.611	FRANK THOMAS, 1997
.607	FRANK THOMAS, 1993

Games started: Most, season

49	Ed Walsh, 1908
49	Wilbur Wood, 1972
48	Wilbur Wood, 1973
46	Ed Walsh, 1907
43	Wilbur Wood, 1975

Complete games: Most, season

42	Ed Walsh, 1908
37	Frank Smith, 1909
37	Ed Walsh, 1907
34	Frank Owen, 1904
33	Ed Walsh, 1910
33	Ed Walsh, 1911

Saves: Most, season

57	Bobby Thigpen, 1990
38	ROBERTO HERNANDEZ, 1993
38	ROBERTO HERNANDEZ, 1996
34	Bobby Thigpen, 1988
34	Bobby Thigpen, 1989

Shutouts: Most, season

11	Ed Walsh, 1908
10	Ed Walsh, 1906
8	Reb Russell, 1913
8	Ed Walsh, 1909
8	Wilbur Wood, 1972

Wins: Most, season

40	Ed Walsh, 1908
29	Eddie Cicotte, 1919
28	Eddie Cicotte, 1917
27	Ed Walsh, 1911
27	Ed Walsh, 1912
27	Doc White, 1907

K: Most, season

269	Ed Walsh, 1908
258	Ed Walsh, 1910
255	Ed Walsh, 1911
254	Ed Walsh, 1912
215	Gary Peters, 1967

Win pct: Highest, season

.842	Sandy Consuegra, 1954
.806	Eddie Cicotte, 1919
.774	Clark Griffith, 1901
.759	Richard Dotson, 1983
.750	Reb Russell, 1917
.750	Bob Shaw, 1959
.750	Monty Stratton, 1937
.750	Doc White, 1906

ERA: Lowest, season

1.27	Ed Walsh, 1910
1.41	Ed Walsh, 1909
1.42	Ed Walsh, 1908
1.52	Doc White, 1906
1.53	Eddie Cicotte, 1917

Most pinch-hit homers, season

3	Ron Northey, 1956
3	John Romano, 1959
3	Oscar Gamble, 1977

Most pinch-hit homers, career

| 7 | Jerry Hairston, 1973-1989 |
| 5 | Smoky Burgess, 1964-1967 |

Longest hitting streak

27	Luke Appling, 1936
27	ALBERT BELLE, 1997
26	Guy Curtright, 1943
25	LANCE JOHNSON, 1992
23	Minnie Minoso, 1955

Most consecutive scoreless innings

45	Doc White, 1904
39	Billy Pierce, 1953
39	Ed Walsh, 1906
38	Ray Herbert, 1963
37	Ed Walsh, 1910
37	Joe Horlen, 1968

No-hit games

Nixey Callahan, Chi vs Det AL, 3-0; September 20, 1902 (1st game).

Frank Smith, Chi at Det AL, 15-0; September 6, 1905 (2nd game).

Ed Walsh, five innings, rain, Chi vs NY AL, 8-1; May 26, 1907.

Frank Smith, Chi vs Phi AL, 1-0; September 20, 1908.

Ed Walsh, Chi vs Bos AL, 5-0; August 27, 1911.

Jim Scott, Chi at Was AL, 0-1; May 14, 1914 (lost on 2 hits in the tenth).

Joe Benz, Chi vs Cle AL, 6-1; May 31, 1914.

Eddie Cicotte, Chi at StL AL, 11-0; April 14, 1917.

Charlie Robertson, Chi at Det AL, 2-0; April 30, 1922 (perfect game).

Ted Lyons, Chi at Bos AL, 6-0; August 21, 1926.

Vern Kennedy, Chi vs Cle AL, 5-0; August 31, 1935.

Bill Dietrich, Chi vs StL AL, 8-0; June 1, 1937.

Bob Keegan, Chi vs Was AL, 6-0; August 20, 1957 (2nd game).

Joe Horlen, Chi vs Det AL, 6-0; September 10, 1967 (1st game).

Blue Moon Odom (5 innings) and Francisco Barrios (4 innings), Chi at Oak AL, 2-1; July 28, 1976.

Joe Cowley, Chi at Cal AL, 7-1; September 19, 1986.

Melido Perez, six innings, rain, Chi at NY AL, 8-0; July 12, 1990.

WILSON ALVAREZ, Chi at Bal AL, 7-0; August 11, 1991.

ACTIVE PLAYERS in caps.

Detroit Tigers

Tony Clark was the Tigers hit leader and No.2 in average, homers and RBI.

1999 Tigers: Minor leaguers took over

After the Detroit Tigers finished 65-97 in 1998, team owner Mike Ilitch decided to open his wallet and put his team on the rise when it moved into its new stadium in 2000. He let general manager Randy Smith add $12 million, bringing the Tigers' payroll to $35 million.

The Tigers didn't get much in return—a 69-92 record—but they did move up in the standings from fifth to third in the American League Central Division.

"Not what we expected, that's for sure," Smith said.

And not nearly good enough for 2000, when the Tigers move into Comerica Park. Ilitch has at least $145 million of his own money invested in the new stadium, and it's a given that without a vastly improved team on the field, he could face financial problems.

"We're a club that has to get better, period," Smith said. "We'll look at any possibility to make us better."

The first move was hiring Phil Garner to replace Larry Parrish as manager, a move that rankled Commissioner Bud Selig because he felt the Tigers failed to consider minority candidates.

Pitching is the Tigers' greatest need. Their rotation is thin and their bullpen is weak. There was no left-handed reliever on the team over the final month.

When they broke spring camp, hopes were high. There were some promising young arms on the pitching staff, the club was solid in the infield and at catcher, and the outfield—anchored by Bobby Higginson—looked at least promising.

The hopes were dashed in a heartbeat. Right-hander Seth Greisinger, the Tigers' first-round draft pick in 1996 and the projected No. 3 starter, missed the entire season with a sore elbow. Lefty Justin Thompson, who has a history of arm and shoulder trouble, missed the final two months with a sore neck. Willie Blair, acquired in the off-season to bolster the rotation, went 3-11 with a 6.85 ERA. As a result, the Tigers were forced to call up minor leaguers who really weren't ready for the big leagues

A prime example was right-hander Jeff

Weaver, the club's top draft pick in 1998. Less than a year out of college, he had pitched just six minor league games when he was catapulted from Class AA into the Tigers' rotation. He got off to a 6-3 start before he suffered a five-game losing streak and was benched. He finished 9-12.

The Tigers' most effective starter turned out to be Dave Mlicki (14-12), acquired from the Los Angeles Dodgers in April.

The outfield also was sprinkled with players who probably should have stayed in the minors, especially Karim Garcia and Gabe Kapler—who also had to make the jump from AA to the majors. But when Higginson missed almost the entire second half with a toe injury, the Tigers had no choice. Youngsters were forced to learn the basics in the majors.

To make matters worse, some veteran players, like Tony Clark were slow getting on track. By the time they did, the season was beyond hope. Though Clark finished with 31 homers, 99 RBI and a .280 average, he was hitting just .240 with only eight homers and 38 RBI at the All-Star break. By then, the Tigers were already 16 games under .500 and 20½ games out of first place.

The Tigers did find a DH in veteran Luis Polonia, who was in their farm system after two years in the Mexican League, and free agents third baseman Dean Palmer and catcher Brad Ausmus also performed well.

1999 Tigers : Week-by-week notes

These notes were excerpted from the following issues of Baseball Weekly.

▶**April 14:** After winning on opening day in Texas, the club went into a tailspin, losing its next four games to Texas and New York. It brought back ugly memories of 1998, when the club got off to a 4-17 start and never recovered. Starting pitching was the team's major concern. With right-handers Seth Greisinger and Bryce Florie on the DL, the Rangers called up righty Beiker Graterol from Toledo for his first major league start on April 9. Graterol allowed seven earned runs in four innings, surrendering three homers in a 12-3 loss to the Yankees.

▶**April 21:** Not long ago it was unthinkable that Detroit would trade three minor league prospects for two veteran pitchers coming off sub-par seasons. But with the rotation depleted by injuries and the club off to a slow start, general manager Randy Smith traded minor leaguers Robinson Checo, Apostol Garcia, and Rick Roberts to Los Angeles for right-hander Dave Mlicki and righty reliever Mel Rojas.

▶**April 28:** Detroit won five of six games, with the staff allowing just six runs. The pitching was great; the batting was awful. Right fielder Bobby Higginson and backup infielder Frank Catalanotto were the only batters above .250 as the club was shut out five times in its first 17 games.

▶**May 5:** After allowing just 19 runs in its previous 11 games, the pitching staff yielded 30 runs in back-to-back losses at Seattle. In a 22-6 loss on April 29, Mel Rojas allowed 11 earned runs, becoming the 11th pitcher to allow 10 or more earned runs in an appearance since the start of the 1997 season.

▶**May 12:** Right-handed closer Todd Jones was pitching the best baseball of his career. He had converted 15 consecutive save opportunities, and his ERA was 2.08, compared with 4.97 last season.

▶**May 19:** First baseman Tony Clark and Bobby Higginson, expected to be the team's top run producers, were struggling.

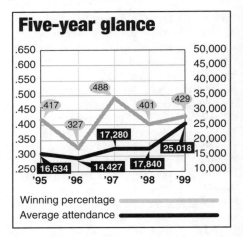

Five-year glance

Winning percentage
Average attendance

At one point, the Tigers went 117 at-bats without a home run until rookie outfielder Gabe Kapler broke through with a two-run shot off the Indians' right-hander Charles Nagy on May 14.

▶**May 26:** To inject more life into a sluggish offense, manager Larry Parrish moved All-Star second baseman Damion Easley to short and inserted Frank Catalanotto at second. The odd man out was Deivi Cruz, the starting shortstop since 1997. The move proved beneficial when Catalanotto went 4-for-4 and hit two home runs in his first start, on May 21, in a 9-6 victory at Cleveland.

▶**June 2:** Catcher Brad Ausmus observed that rookie right-hander Jeff Weaver—6-3 with a 2.89 ERA—had incredible confidence. "He is absolutely not intimidated by anybody or anything when he is out there on the mound," Ausmus said.

▶**June 9:** After right-handed reliever Matt Anderson had several rough outings, the club considered sending him to the minors. He went through a five-game stretch in which he allowed 11 earned runs on 10 hits (including three home runs) and five walks in three innings.

▶**June 16:** Randy Smith conceded that he might shake up the team if the Tigers continued to labor far below .500 after increasing their payroll from $23 million in 1998 to $35 million this year.

▶**June 23:** Larry Parrish benched slumping

Bobby Higginson indefinitely, hoping that a few days off would help him regain his form. Higginson was hitting .249 with eight home runs and 30 RBI. Since the 1998 All-Star break, he had hit .243 with 17 home runs and 69 RBI in 523 at-bats.

▶July 7: Team president John McHale Jr. was frustrated with the club's performance but said Larry Parrish's and Randy Smith's jobs were secure. The Tigers had been shut out 10 times in their first 82 games.

▶July 21: The return from the All-Star break couldn't have gone worse. Three consecutive losses at Houston on July 15-17 left the players, management, and coaching staff shaking their heads.

▶July 28: Tony Clark had gotten on track. In a seven-game stretch beginning on July 18 at Cincinnati, the switch-hitter went 10-for-29 (.345) with five home runs and 13 RBI. Clark had entered the All-Star break on pace for only 15 home runs and 68 RBI after averaging 33 home runs and 110 RBI in his first two full seasons.

▶Aug. 11: Parrish decided to skip Jeff Weaver's start on Aug. 11, hoping it would help him rebound from a seven-game skid in which his ERA was 10.69. During one stretch Weaver allowed 10 home runs in a span of 57 hitters.

▶Aug. 25: Justin Thompson's season was over. The left-hander (9-11, 5.11 ERA) had a tear in the labrum of his shoulder that would require surgery.

▶Sept. 8: Dave Mlicki had become the Tigers' ace, as he won six starts in a row through Sept. 5 and was working on a stretch of 25 innings in which he hadn't issued a walk. Mlicki was 11-10 with a 4.89 ERA with Detroit.

▶Sept. 15: Deivi Cruz was the team's most improved player. He was hitting .286 and had already surpassed his career highs in home runs with 12.

▶Sept. 22: Bobby Higginson's season ended with toe surgery on Sept. 15. Outfielder Karim Garcia, making a bid to stick around next season, had essentially taken Higginson's at-bats. Inserted regularly in the lineup on Aug. 30, Garcia hit .310 with four home runs and eight RBI in the next 17 games, raising his totals to .241 with 12 homers and 27 RBI.

▶Sept. 29: Jeff Weaver would most likely get one more start in 1999, after relieving on Sept. 26. He was 2-9 with an 8.92 ERA over his last 14 starts.

▶Oct. 6: Tiger Stadium's finale was an emotional one. The club beat Kansas City on a dramatic late-inning grand slam by rookie DH Robert Fick and went on to win the season's last four games at Minnesota and Kansas City.

153

QUOTE OF THE YEAR

"This was a great experience for us this year."
—President John McHale Jr., summing up the team's 69-92 last season at Tiger Stadium

Team Leaders

Batting avg.
.284 Deivi Cruz
.280 Tony Clark

HR
38 Dean Palmer
31 Tony Clark

RBI
100 Dean Palmer
99 Tony Clark

Hits
150 Tony Clark
147 Deivi Cruz
147 Dean Palmer

Runs
92 Dean Palmer
83 Damian Easley

Stolen bases
33 Juan Encarnacion
17 Luis Polonia

Wins
14 Dave Mlicki
10 Brian Moehler

Losses
16 Brian Moehler
12 Dave Mlicki
12 Jeff Weaver

ERA
4.60 Dave Mlicki
5.04 Brian Moehler

Strikeouts
119 Dave Mlicki
114 Jeff Weaver

Innings
196.1 Brian Moehler
191.2 Dave Mlicki

Saves
30 Todd Jones
2 Doug Brocail

DETROIT TIGERS 1999 final stats

BATTERS	BA	SLG	OBA	G	AB	R	H	TB	2B	3B	HR	RBI	BB	SO	SB	CS	E
Polonia	.324	.526	.357	87	333	46	108	175	21	8	10	32	16	32	17	9	1
D. Cruz	.284	.427	.302	155	518	64	147	221	35	0	13	58	12	57	1	4	12
Clark	.280	.507	.361	143	536	74	150	272	29	0	31	99	64	133	2	1	10
Catalanotto	.276	.458	.327	100	286	41	79	131	19	0	11	35	15	49	3	4	5
Ausmus	.275	.415	.365	127	458	62	126	190	25	6	9	54	51	71	12	9	2
Haselman	.273	.413	.320	48	143	13	39	59	8	0	4	14	10	26	2	0	1
Easley	.266	.434	.346	151	549	83	146	238	30	1	20	65	51	124	11	3	8
Palmer	.263	.518	.339	150	560	92	147	290	25	2	38	100	57	153	3	3	19
Encarnacion	.255	.450	.287	132	509	62	130	229	30	6	19	74	14	113	33	12	9
Macias	.250	1.000	.250	5	4	2	1	4	0	0	1	2	0	1	0	0	0
Kapler	.245	.447	.315	130	416	60	102	186	22	4	18	49	42	74	11	5	6
K. Garcia	.240	.441	.288	96	288	38	69	127	10	3	14	32	20	67	2	4	7
Higginson	.239	.382	.351	107	377	51	90	144	18	0	12	46	64	66	4	6	3
Fick	.220	.439	.327	15	41	6	9	18	0	0	3	10	7	6	1	0	0
Alvarez	.208	.377	.250	22	53	5	11	20	3	0	2	4	3	9	0	0	0
Jefferies	.200	.327	.258	70	205	22	41	67	8	0	6	18	13	11	3	4	0
Bartee	.195	.286	.279	41	77	11	15	22	1	3	0	3	9	20	3	3	1
Wood	.159	.250	.196	27	44	5	7	11	1	0	1	8	2	13	0	0	4
L. Garcia	.111	.222	.111	8	9	0	1	2	1	0	0	0	0	2	0	0	0

PITCHERS	W-L	ERA	BA	G	GS	CG	GF	SH	SV	IP	H	R	ER	HR	BB	SO
Brocail	4-4	2.52	.206	70	0	0	22	0	2	82.0	60	23	23	7	25	78
Cordero	2-2	3.32	.284	20	0	0	4	0	0	19.0	19	7	7	2	18	19
Runyan	0-1	3.38	.237	12	0	0	2	0	0	10.2	9	4	4	2	3	6
Jones	4-4	3.80	.259	65	0	0	62	0	30	66.1	64	30	28	7	35	64
Nitkowski	4-5	4.30	.213	68	7	0	7	0	0	81.2	63	44	39	11	45	66
Mlicki	14-12	4.60	.276	31	31	2	0	0	0	191.2	209	108	98	24	70	119
Moehler	10-16	5.04	.294	32	32	2	0	2	0	196.1	229	116	110	22	59	106
Thompson	9-11	5.11	.274	24	24	0	0	0	0	142.2	152	85	81	24	59	83
Hiljus	0-0	5.19	.241	6	0	0	0	0	0	8.2	7	5	5	2	5	1
Weaver	9-12	5.55	.278	30	29	0	1	0	0	163.2	176	104	101	27	56	114
N. Cruz	2-5	5.67	.281	29	6	0	10	0	0	66.2	74	44	42	11	23	46
Anderson	2-1	5.68	.232	37	0	0	9	0	0	38.0	33	27	24	8	35	32
Brunson	1-0	6.00	.367	17	0	0	1	0	0	12.0	18	9	8	3	6	9
Borkowski	2-6	6.10	.283	17	12	0	2	0	0	76.2	86	58	52	10	40	50
Kida	1-0	6.26	.289	49	0	0	21	0	1	64.2	73	48	45	6	30	50
Blair	3-11	6.85	.308	39	16	0	8	0	0	134.0	169	107	102	29	44	82
Lira	0-0	10.80	.389	2	0	0	0	0	0	3.1	7	5	4	2	2	3
Roberts	0-0	13.50	.500	1	0	0	0	0	0	1.1	3	4	2	0	0	0
Graterol	0-1	15.75	.250	1	1	0	0	0	0	4.0	4	7	7	3	4	2
Rojas	0-0	22.74	.387	5	0	0	2	0	0	6.1	12	16	16	3	4	6

2000 preliminary roster

PITCHERS (19)
Matt Anderson
Willie Blair
David Borkowski
Doug Brocail
Seth Greisinger
Shane Heams
Erik Hiljus
Mark Johnson
Todd Jones
Kris Keller
Masao Kida
Dave Mlicki
Brian Moehler
C.J. Nitkowski

Danny Patterson
Willis Roberts
Sean Runyan
Victor Santos
Ramon Tatis
Brandon Villafuerte
Jeff Weaver

CATCHERS (5)
Brad Ausmus
Javier Cardona
Robert Fick
Eric Munson
Gregg Zaun

INFIELDERS (7)
Gabe Alvarez
Tony Clark
Deivi Cruz
Damion Easley
Dean Palmer
Pedro Santana
Rob Sasser

OUTFIELDERS (7)
Juan Encarnacion
Karim Garcia
Juan Gonzalez
Bobby Higginson
Gregg Jefferies
Luis Polonia
Chris Wakeland

Games played by position

PLAYER	G	C	1B	2B	3B	SS	OF	DH
Alvarez	22	0	0	0	2	0	5	12
Ausmus	127	127	0	0	0	0	0	0
Bartee	41	0	0	0	0	0	38	1
Catalanotto	100	0	32	32	21	0	0	0
Clark	143	0	132	0	0	0	0	12
Cruz	155	0	0	0	0	155	0	0
Easley	151	0	0	147	0	19	0	0
Encarnacion	132	0	0	0	0	0	131	0
Fick	15	4	0	0	0	0	0	8
L. Garcia	8	0	0	1	0	7	0	0
K. Garcia	96	0	0	0	0	0	81	6
Haselman	48	39	0	0	0	0	0	11
Higginson	107	0	0	0	0	0	88	17
Hunter	18	0	0	0	0	0	18	0
Jefferies	70	0	3	2	0	0	2	45
Kapler	130	0	0	0	0	0	128	2
Macias	5	0	0	1	0	0	0	0
Palmer	150	0	0	0	141	0	0	9
Polonia	87	0	0	0	0	0	40	51
Wood	27	0	5	1	9	9	0	0

Sick call: 1999 DL report

PLAYER	Days on the DL
Raul Casanova	98
Tony Clark	15
Robert Fick	155
Bryce Florie	31
Seth Greisinger	182
Bob Higginson	31
Gregg Jefferies	47**
Masao Kida	28
Sean Runyan	150
Justin Thompson	49
Jason Wood	36

* Indicates three separate terms on Disabled List.

Minor Leagues

Tops in the organization

BATTER	CLUB	AVG.	G	AB	R	H	HR	RBI
Cardona, Javier	Jax	.309	108	418	84	129	26	92
Gillespie, Eric	Jax	.306	118	474	80	145	19	88
Gomez, Richard	WM	.303	130	479	89	145	8	81
Lennon, Pat	Tol	.287	111	414	75	119	30	83
Besco, Derek	Lkl	.287	122	456	70	131	9	66

HOME RUNS
			WINS			
McCarty, Dave	Tol	31	Darwin, David	Jax	14	
Lennon, Pat	Tol	30	Maroth, Mike	Jax	14	
Cardona, Javier	Jax	26	Pettyjohn, Adam	Jax	12	
Alvarez, Gabe	Tol	21	Santos, Victor	Jax	12	
Several Players Tied at		19	Johnson, Craig	Lkl	11	

RBI
			SAVES			
Cardona, Javier	Jax	92	Cordero, F.	Jax	27	
Gillespie, Eric	Jax	88	Watson, Gregory	One	19	
Lennon, Pat	Tol	83	Snyder, Bill	Jax	18	
Gomez, Richard	WM	81	Rodney, F.	Lkl	11	
Rivera, Mike	Lkl	78	Hearns, Shane	WM	10	

STOLEN BASES
			STRIKEOUTS			
Gomez, Richard	WM	66	Santos, Victor	Jax	146	
Lindsey, Rodney	Lkl	61	Pettyjohn, Adam	Jax	143	
Torres, Andres	WM	39	Sismondo, Bobby	WM	135	
Freeman, Terrance	Lkl	37	Cornejo, Nate	WM	125	
Santana, Pedro	Jax	34	Hiljus, Erik	Tol	110	

PITCHER	CLUB	W-L	ERA	IP	H	BB	SO
Bernero, Adam	WM	8-4	2.54	96	75	23	80
Santos, Victor	Jax	12-6	3.49	173	150	58	146
Borkowski, David	Tol	6-8	3.50	126	119	43	94
Darwin, David	Jax	14-12	3.56	187	194	58	100
Sismondo, Bobby	WM	9-12	3.67	169	153	62	135

1999 salaries

	Bonuses	Total earned salary
Dean Palmer, 3b		5,000,000
Bobby Higginson, of		3,825,000
Willie Blair, p		3,750,000
Damion Easley, 2b	100,000	3,350,000
Todd Jones, p		2,500,000
Tony Clark, 1b	100,000	2,362,500
Dave Mlicki, p		2,250,000
Brad Ausmus, c	175,000	2,200,000
Masao Kida, p	100,000	1,600,000
Gregg Jefferies, dh		1,375,000
Doug Brocail, p	100,000	1,000,000
Justin Thompson, p		650,000
Bill Haselman, c		650,000
Brian Moehler, p		466,666
Deivi Cruz, ss		430,000
Luis Polonia, dh		300,000
C.J. Nitkowski, p		300,000
Sean Runyan, p		280,000
Karim Garcia, of		270,000
Kimera Bartee, of		240,000
Seth Greisinger, p		240,000
Matt Anderson, p		240,000
Frank Catalanotto, 2b		237,500
Juan Encarnacion, of		233,000
Nelson Cruz, p		210,000
Francisco Cordero, p		200,000
Gabe Kapler, of		200,000
Dave Borkowski, p		200,000
Robert Fick, dh		200,000
Jeff Weaver, p		200,000

Average 1999 salary: $1,165,322
Total 1999 team payroll: $34,959,666
Termination pay: $2,020,000

Detroit (1901-1999)

Runs: Most, career

2088	Ty Cobb, 1905-1926	
1774	Charlie Gehringer, 1924-1942	
1622	Al Kaline, 1953-1974	
1386	Lou Whitaker, 1977-1995	
1242	Donie Bush, 1908-1921	

Hits: Most, career

3900	Ty Cobb, 1905-1926
3007	Al Kaline, 1953-1974
2839	Charlie Gehringer, 1924-1942
2499	Harry Heilmann, 1914-1929
2466	Sam Crawford, 1903-1917

2B: Most, career

665	Ty Cobb, 1905-1926
574	Charlie Gehringer, 1924-1942
498	Al Kaline, 1953-1974
497	Harry Heilmann, 1914-1929
420	Lou Whitaker, 1977-1995

3B: Most, career

284	Ty Cobb, 1905-1926
249	Sam Crawford, 1903-1917
146	Charlie Gehringer, 1924-1942
145	Harry Heilmann, 1914-1929
136	Bobby Veach, 1912-1923

HR: Most, career

399	Al Kaline, 1953-1974
373	Norm Cash, 1960-1974
306	Hank Greenberg, 1930-1946
262	Willie Horton, 1963-1977
245	Cecil Fielder, 1990-1996

RBI: Most, career

1805	Ty Cobb, 1905-1926
1583	Al Kaline, 1953-1974
1442	Harry Heilmann, 1914-1929
1427	Charlie Gehringer, 1924-1942
1264	Sam Crawford, 1903-1917

SB: Most, career

865	Ty Cobb, 1905-1926
400	Donie Bush, 1908-1921
317	Sam Crawford, 1903-1917
294	Ron LeFlore, 1974-1979
236	Alan Trammell, 1977-1996

BB: Most, career

1277	Al Kaline, 1953-1974
1197	Lou Whitaker, 1977-1995
1186	Charlie Gehringer, 1924-1942
1148	Ty Cobb, 1905-1926
1125	Donie Bush, 1908-1921

BA: Highest, career

.368	Ty Cobb, 1905-1926
.342	Harry Heilmann, 1914-1929
.337	Bob Fothergill, 1922-1930
.325	George Kell, 1946-1952
.321	Heinie Manush, 1923-1927

On-base avg: Highest, career

.434	Ty Cobb, 1905-1926
.420	Johnny Bassler, 1921-1927
.412	Hank Greenberg, 1930-1946
.412	Roy Cullenbine, 1938-1947
.410	Harry Heilmann, 1914-1929

Slug pct: Highest, career

.616	Hank Greenberg, 1930-1946
.518	Harry Heilmann, 1914-1929
.516	Ty Cobb, 1905-1926
.503	TONY CLARK, 1995-1999
.503	Rudy York, 1934-1945

Games started: Most, career

459	Mickey Lolich, 1963-1975
408	Jack Morris, 1977-1990
395	George Mullin, 1902-1913
388	Hooks Dauss, 1912-1926
373	Hal Newhouser, 1939-1953

Complete games: Most, career

336	George Mullin, 1902-1913
245	Hooks Dauss, 1912-1926
213	Bill Donovan, 1903-1918
212	Hal Newhouser, 1939-1953
200	Tommy Bridges, 1930-1946

Saves: Most, career

154	Mike Henneman, 1987-1995
125	John Hiller, 1965-1980
120	Willie Hernandez, 1984-1989
89	TODD JONES, 1997-1999
85	Aurelio Lopez, 1979-1985

Shutouts: Most, career

39	Mickey Lolich, 1963-1975
34	George Mullin, 1902-1913
33	Tommy Bridges, 1930-1946
33	Hal Newhouser, 1939-1953
29	Bill Donovan, 1903-1918

Wins: Most, career

223	Hooks Dauss, 1912-1926
209	George Mullin, 1902-1913
207	Mickey Lolich, 1963-1975
200	Hal Newhouser, 1939-1953
198	Jack Morris, 1977-1990

K: Most, career

2679	Mickey Lolich, 1963-1975
1980	Jack Morris, 1977-1990
1770	Hal Newhouser, 1939-1953
1674	Tommy Bridges, 1930-1946
1406	Jim Bunning, 1955-1963

Win pct: Highest, career

.654	Denny McLain, 1963-1970
.639	Aurelio Lopez, 1979-1985
.629	Schoolboy Rowe, 1933-1942
.626	Mike Henneman, 1987-1995
.616	Harry Coveleski, 1914-1918

ERA: Lowest, career

2.34	Harry Coveleski, 1914-1918
2.38	Ed Killian, 1904-1910
2.42	Ed Summers, 1908-1912
2.49	Bill Donovan, 1903-1918
2.61	Ed Siever, 1901-1908

Runs: Most, season

147	Ty Cobb, 1911
144	Ty Cobb, 1915
144	Charlie Gehringer, 1930
144	Charlie Gehringer, 1936
144	Hank Greenberg, 1938

Hits: Most, season

248	Ty Cobb, 1911
237	Harry Heilmann, 1921
227	Charlie Gehringer, 1936
226	Ty Cobb, 1912
225	Ty Cobb, 1917
225	Harry Heilmann, 1925

2B: Most, season

63	Hank Greenberg, 1934
60	Charlie Gehringer, 1936
56	George Kell, 1950
55	Gee Walker, 1936
50	Charlie Gehringer, 1934
50	Hank Greenberg, 1940
50	Harry Heilmann, 1927

3B: Most, season

26	Sam Crawford, 1914
25	Sam Crawford, 1903
24	Ty Cobb, 1911
24	Ty Cobb, 1917
23	Ty Cobb, 1912
23	Sam Crawford, 1913

HR: Most, season

58	Hank Greenberg, 1938
51	Cecil Fielder, 1990
45	Rocky Colavito, 1961
44	Cecil Fielder, 1991
44	Hank Greenberg, 1946

RBI: Most, season

183	Hank Greenberg, 1937
170	Hank Greenberg, 1935
150	Hank Greenberg, 1940
146	Hank Greenberg, 1938
140	Rocky Colavito, 1961

SB: Most, season

96	Ty Cobb, 1915
83	Ty Cobb, 1911
78	Ron LeFlore, 1979
76	Ty Cobb, 1909
74	BRIAN HUNTER, 1997

BB: Most, season

137	Roy Cullenbine, 1947
135	Eddie Yost, 1959
132	TONY PHILLIPS, 1993
125	Eddie Yost, 1960
124	Norm Cash, 1961

BA: Highest, season

.420	Ty Cobb, 1911
.409	Ty Cobb, 1912
.403	Harry Heilmann, 1923
.401	Ty Cobb, 1922
.398	Harry Heilmann, 1927

On-base avg: Highest, season

.487	Norm Cash, 1961
.486	Ty Cobb, 1915
.481	Harry Heilmann, 1923
.475	Harry Heilmann, 1927
.468	Ty Cobb, 1925

Slug pct: Highest, season

.683	Hank Greenberg, 1938
.670	Hank Greenberg, 1940
.668	Hank Greenberg, 1937
.662	Norm Cash, 1961
.632	Harry Heilmann, 1923

Games started: Most, season

45	Mickey Lolich, 1971
44	George Mullin, 1904
42	Mickey Lolich, 1973
42	George Mullin, 1907
41	Joe Coleman, 1974
41	Mickey Lolich, 1972
41	Mickey Lolich, 1974
41	Denny McLain, 1968
41	Denny McLain, 1969
41	George Mullin, 1905

Complete games: Most, season

42	George Mullin, 1904
35	Roscoe Miller, 1901
35	George Mullin, 1905
35	George Mullin, 1906
35	George Mullin, 1907

Saves: Most, season

38	John Hiller, 1973
32	Willie Hernandez, 1984
31	Willie Hernandez, 1985
31	TODD JONES, 1997
30	TODD JONES, 1999

Shutouts: Most, season

9	Denny McLain, 1969
8	Ed Killian, 1905
8	Hal Newhouser, 1945
7	Billy Hoeft, 1955
7	George Mullin, 1904
7	Dizzy Trout, 1944

Wins: Most, season

31	Denny McLain, 1968
29	George Mullin, 1909
29	Hal Newhouser, 1944
27	Dizzy Trout, 1944
26	Hal Newhouser, 1946

K: Most, season

308	Mickey Lolich, 1971
280	Denny McLain, 1968
275	Hal Newhouser, 1946
271	Mickey Lolich, 1969
250	Mickey Lolich, 1972

Win pct: Highest, season

.862	Bill Donovan, 1907
.842	Schoolboy Rowe, 1940
.838	Denny McLain, 1968
.808	Bobo Newsom, 1940
.784	George Mullin, 1909

ERA: Lowest, season

1.64	Ed Summers, 1908
1.71	Ed Killian, 1909
1.78	Ed Killian, 1907
1.81	Hal Newhouser, 1945
1.91	Ed Siever, 1902

Most pinch-hit homers, season

3	Dick Wakefield, 1948
3	Gus Zernial, 1958
3	Norm Cash, 1960
3	Charlie Maxwell, 1961
3	Vic Wertz, 1962
3	Gates Brown, 1968
3	Frank Howard, 1963
3	Ben Oglivie, 1976
3	John Grubb, 1984
3	Larry Herndon, 1986

Most pinch-hit homers, career

16	Gates Brown, 1963-1975
8	Norm Cash, 1960-1974

Longest hitting streak

40	Ty Cobb, 1911
35	Ty Cobb, 1917
30	Goose Goslin, 1934
30	Ron LeFlore, 1976
29	Dale Alexander, 1930
29	Pete Fox, 1935

Most consecutive scoreless innings

33	Harry Coveleski, 1914

No-hit games

George Mullin, Det vs StL AL, 7-0; July 4, 1912 (2nd game).

Virgil Trucks, Det vs Was AL, 1-0; May 15, 1952.

Virgil Trucks, Det at NY AL, 1-0; August 25, 1952.

Jim Bunning, Det at Bos AL, 3-0; July 20, 1958 (1st game).

Jack Morris, Det at Chi AL, 4-0; April 7, 1984.

ACTIVE PLAYERS in caps.

Players' years of service are listed by the first and last years with this team and are not necessarily consecutive; all statistics record performances for this team only.

Kansas City Royals

By Tom DiPace

Jermaine Dye topped his superb defense for the Royals with a breakthrough year at the plate.

1999 Royals: The bullpen from hell

The Kansas City Royals started 1999 with the best record in spring training, 22-9. In late May, they were two games over .500 and in second place in the American League Central.

By the end of the year, for the first time in team history, the Royals had three players with more than 100 RBI and had scored a team-record 856 runs. And with all that—thanks in part to a horrifying bullpen—they had a 64-97 record, tying the team mark for defeats in a single season.

"If somebody had told me we would have three players drive in 100 runs," said general manager Herk Robinson, "the favorite for Rookie of the Year (Carlos Beltran), that Joe Randa would have such a fine year, that Rey Sanchez and Carlos Febles would establish themselves the way they did, and that we would have four fairly good starters . . . but still lose almost a hundred games, I'd have told them they were nuts."

The bullpen blowing 30 save chances helped the Royals give up a team-record 921 runs. The bullpen ERA was 5.77. Jeff Montgomery, the team's career saves leader, was as ineffective as everyone else. He blew seven of his 19 save opportunities and retired from the game with 304 saves.

"It's almost like there was a curse over the entire [bullpen]," Robinson said. "You could almost count the number of good outings on one hand. It was just a big, deep, dark hole. The confidence level fell so badly, they hated to hear the phone ring."

On the bright side, Jermaine Dye, Mike Sweeney and Beltran all drove in more than 100 runs. Randa and Sanchez also had their finest seasons. Sweeney, Dye and Beltran all topped the 20-homer and 100-RBI marks. Sweeney, serving as DH most of the season, led the club with a .322 average, while third baseman Randa was close behind at .314.

Dye had the breakthrough season the Royals had been looking for since they sent Michael Tucker to Atlanta in a trade that no longer looks bad for Kansas City.

Beltran fell just six hits short of being the first rookie since Joe DiMaggio in

1936 to drive in 100 runs, score 100 runs and compile 200 hits. He also played a fine center field and proved himself a top base runner. He was the almost unanimous choice for Rookie of the Year.

In addition to Beltran's big year, fellow rookie Febles became the regular second baseman. The two youngsters had a lot to do with Kansas City complementing the team's solid hitting with an improved running game. Johnny Damon was tops on the team with 36 stolen bases, though Beltran had 27 and Febles added 20 while playing sparkling defense at second base.

The Royals expect future lineups for a lot of seasons to feature Febles as the leadoff hitter and Beltran in the crucial No. 3 slot. The Royals will go into spring training next year with a more settled rotation than they had last March despite sending veteran Kevin Appier to Oakland in July. Jay Witasick, acquired in April from Oakland, was spotty early but was 4-1 in September to join Jose Rosado and Jeff Suppan as the rotation's top three.

Rosado's record was a misleading 10-14, though his ERA was 3.85 and he allowed opposing batters just a .248 average. Suppan was the only other 10-game winner for the Royals, who went through 27 pitchers during the season, more than half of whom had ERAs over 6.00.

1999 Royals: Week-by-week notes

These notes were excerpted from the following issues of Baseball Weekly.

▶**April 14:** The Royals began the season by getting swept at home by the Red Sox. In the three-game series the Royals scored just four runs, with only one earned run in the final 26 innings, and the pitchers allowed 15 runs on 36 hits and nine walks.
▶**April 28:** Left fielder Johnny Damon, who hit .277 with 18 home runs and 104 runs last year, was off to a slow start this year. In the first 16 games he was hitting .169 with no home runs and three RBI.
▶**May 5:** General manager Herk Robinson was criticized after trading right fielder Michael Tucker to Atlanta for right fielder Jermaine Dye in spring training 1997. The critics were wrong: Dye blasted six homers and drove in 20 runs in April.
▶**May 12:** Rookie center fielder Carlos Beltran had quite a week. He was down 0-2 with two out in the ninth on May 4 before stroking a game-winning three-run triple off Tampa Bay closer Roberto Hernandez. He then extended his hitting streak to a career-high 12 games with a three-run homer and a double on May 7.
▶**May 19:** Johnny Damon went 0-for-5 on May 13, snapping his 16-game hitting streak, his career high and the longest in the AL this season. Damon went 27-for-67 (.403) with five home runs, 17 runs and 19 RBI during the streak.
▶**May 26:** First baseman Jeff King, plagued by chronic back problems, retired unexpectedly after the Royals' 5-4 win against Seattle on May 23. King, 34, had just 72 at-bats in 1999, batting .236 with three home runs and 11 RBI.
▶**June 2:** Right-hander Kevin Appier was 4-0 with a 2.36 ERA in his past five starts and continued to be trade bait for teams willing to give up two blue-chip prospects.
▶**June 9:** The Royals was powerless on a West Division trip, going 1-8 at Texas, Anaheim and Oakland. The Royals hit .212 in the nine games and scored just 19 runs in the eight losses.
▶**June 16:** Third baseman Joe Randa set a

Five-year glance

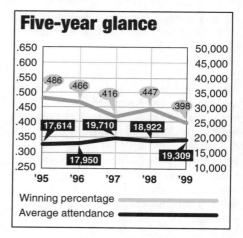

Winning percentage
Average attendance

Royals record with 10 consecutive hits over four games, June 8-12. Randa had been dropped from second to seventh and eighth in the order after a 9-for-44 slide. The previous record of eight consecutive hits was shared by center fielder Amos Otis (1970) and third baseman George Brett (1980).
▶**June 30:** For seven innings on June 26, In-dians right-handed starter Bartolo Colon had the Royals under control. He was working on a two-hitter in the eighth when the Royals exploded for 10 runs for an 11-7 victory.
▶**July 7:** DH Mike Sweeney set a club record by driving in at least one run in 13 consecutive games through July 4, with 17 RBI during the streak. Sweeney hit in a career-high 14 straight games, going 24-for-56 (.429).
▶**July 28:** A 3-5 trip to Milwaukee, Chicago and Detroit after the All-Star break was not what Kansas City had in mind to start the second half. They hit .296 and scored 50 runs in the eight games, but pitching did the club in. The staff had a 6.58 ERA, allowing 49 earned runs in 67 innings.
▶**Aug. 4:** The Kevin Appier era was over. Appier, scheduled to start on Aug. 1, was preparing to chart pitches for Kansas City on July 31 in Texas. In the first inning manager Tony Muser informed Appier that he had been traded to Oakland.

Kansas City received three right-handed pitchers—Blake Stein, Brad Rigby and Jeff D'Amico—for Appier, the Royals' all-time strikeout leader who had a 114-89 record with them in 10 seasons.

▶**Aug. 11:** Royals relievers had a 5.76 ERA, second worst in the AL, with 24 blown saves and 23 defeats. On Aug. 6 the Royals blew a 7-1 lead in a 9-8 home loss to the Twins. The next day the Royals had a three-run advantage in the eighth, but bullpen newcomer Brad Rigby failed to hold it, giving up a three-run homer to left fielder Marty Cordova.

▶**Aug. 18:** Mike Sweeney had his 25-game hitting streak snapped on Aug. 14 when he went 0-for-4 against the Devil Rays. His streak matched the third longest in Royals history. During the stretch Sweeney hit .412 with 10 doubles, one triple, six home runs, 23 runs and 25 RBI.

▶**Aug. 25:** In Blake Stein's past three starts—against Minnesota, Tampa Bay and New York—he allowed three runs on nine hits in 21 innings for a 1.29 ERA. His only problem was an occasional wild streak. He walked 12 and hit three batters in the three outings.

▶**Sept. 8:** Catcher Chad Kreuter was hitless in 38 consecutive at-bats through Sept. 5 since getting an Aug. 10 single against Boston. It was the longest hitless streak in the majors since Dan Howitt went 0-for-43 with Oakland and Seattle in 1992.

▶**Sept. 15:** It was a long time coming, but Blake Stein nailed down a major league victory for the first time in 13 months. In seven starts since being traded from the A's, he had a 2.31 earned run average. In only one of those starts, an Aug. 29 loss at Minnesota, had he allowed more than two runs.

▶**Sept. 22:** Left fielder Mark Quinn did not get a hit in his first big league at-bat. But before his first game as a Royal was over on Sept. 14, he had doubled in his second at-bat and finished the night with a pair of two-run homers against the Angels, becoming the third player in modern history to homer twice in his first major league game.

▶**Sept. 29:** Closer Jeff Montgomery decided to retire. He had 304 saves, ninth on the all-time list, but this season he was only 12-for-19 in save situations and had a 6.34 ERA. The league hit .342 against him, and he has missed a month with a hip injury.

▶**Oct. 6:** The Royals finished with their worst record in franchise history, 64-97, a .398 winning percentage. They can trace their poor record to inadequate pitching. The team set a club record by scoring 856 runs, but their staff ERA was 5.35, the worst in club history.

161

QUOTE OF THE YEAR

"Tony has done a great job molding the 1999 Royals."
—General manager Herk Robinson, on manager Tony Muser, midway through the team's 64-97 season

Team Leaders

Batting avg.	Hits	Wins	Strikeouts
.322 Mike Sweeney	197 Joe Randa	10 Jeff Suppan	141 Jose Rosado
.314 Joe Randa	194 Carlos Beltran	10 Jose Rosado	103 Jeff Suppan

HR	Runs	Losses	Innings
27 Jermaine Dye	112 Carlos Beltran	14 Jose Rosado	208.2 Jeff Suppan
22 Mike Sweeney	101 Mike Sweeney	12 Jeff Suppan	208 Jose Rosado
22 Carlos Beltran	101 Johnny Damon	12 Jay Witasick	

RBI	Stolen bases	ERA	Saves
			12 Jeff Montgomery
119 Jermaine Dye	36 Johnny Damon	3.85 Jose Rosado	8 Scott Service
108 Carlos Beltran	27 Carlos Beltran	4.53 Jeff Suppan	

KANSAS CITY ROYALS 1999 final stats

BATTERS	BA	SLG	OBA	G	AB	R	H	TB	2B	3B	HR	RBI	BB	SO	SB	CS	E
Lopez	.400	.500	.429	7	20	2	8	10	0	1	0	3	0	5	0	0	0
Quinn	.333	.733	.385	17	60	11	20	44	4	1	6	18	4	11	1	0	1
Sweeney	.322	.520	.387	150	575	101	185	299	44	2	22	102	54	48	6	1	12
Randa	.314	.473	.363	156	628	92	197	297	36	8	16	84	50	80	5	4	22
Damon	.307	.477	.379	145	583	101	179	278	39	9	14	77	67	50	36	6	4
Dye	.294	.526	.354	158	608	96	179	320	44	8	27	119	58	119	2	3	6
Sanchez	.294	.370	.329	134	479	66	141	177	18	6	2	56	22	48	11	5	13
Beltran	.293	.454	.337	156	663	112	194	301	27	7	22	108	46	123	27	8	12
Giambi	.285	.368	.373	90	288	34	82	106	13	1	3	34	40	67	0	0	2
Pose	.285	.307	.377	86	137	27	39	42	3	0	0	12	21	22	6	2	1
Holbert	.280	.310	.330	34	100	14	28	31	3	0	0	5	8	20	7	4	2
Febles	.256	.411	.336	123	453	71	116	186	22	9	10	53	47	91	20	4	14
King	.236	.389	.385	21	72	14	17	28	2	0	3	11	15	10	2	0	2
Fasano	.233	.517	.373	23	60	11	14	31	2	0	5	16	7	17	0	1	0
Sutton	.225	.343	.308	43	102	14	23	35	6	0	2	15	13	17	1	0	3
Kreuter	.225	.318	.309	107	324	31	73	103	15	0	5	35	34	65	0	0	3
Spehr	.206	.426	.324	60	155	26	32	66	7	0	9	26	22	47	1	0	3
Scarsone	.206	.279	.295	46	68	2	14	19	5	0	0	6	9	24	1	0	3
Leius	.203	.257	.244	37	74	8	15	19	1	0	1	10	4	8	1	0	2
Hansen	.203	.329	.289	49	79	16	16	26	1	0	3	5	10	32	0	1	1
Vitiello	.146	.244	.222	13	41	4	6	10	1	0	1	4	2	9	0	0	0
Martinez	.143	.143	.143	6	7	1	1	1	0	0	0	0	0	0	0	0	0
Brown	.080	.080	.148	12	25	1	2	2	0	0	0	0	2	7	0	0	1

PITCHERS	W-L	ERA	BA	G	GS	CG	GF	SH	SV	IP	H	R	ER	HR	BB	SO
Durbin	0-0	0.00	.125	1	0	0	0	0	0	2.1	1	0	0	0	1	3
Wallace	0-1	3.24	.259	8	0	0	4	0	0	8.1	7	4	3	2	5	5
Santiago	3-4	3.42	.251	34	0	0	15	0	0	47.1	46	23	18	7	14	15
Rosado	10-14	3.85	.248	33	33	5	0	0	0	208.0	197	103	89	24	72	141
Morman	2-4	4.05	.307	49	0	0	2	0	1	53.1	66	27	24	6	23	31
Mathews	2-1	4.38	.289	24	1	0	7	0	1	39.0	44	21	19	4	17	19
Suppan	10-12	4.53	.274	32	32	4	0	1	0	208.2	222	113	105	28	62	103
Stein	1-2	4.56	.241	13	12	0	0	0	0	73.0	65	38	37	11	47	47
Rigby	4-6	5.06	.303	49	0	0	11	0	0	83.2	102	51	47	11	31	36
Carter	0-1	5.06	.167	6	0	0	3	0	0	5.1	3	3	3	2	3	3
Witasick	9-12	5.57	.304	32	28	1	2	1	0	158.1	191	108	98	23	83	102
Moreno	0-0	5.63	.143	7	0	0	3	0	0	8.0	4	5	5	1	6	7
Service	5-5	6.09	.294	68	0	0	29	0	8	75.1	87	51	51	13	42	68
Whisenant	4-4	6.35	.267	48	0	0	21	0	1	39.2	40	28	28	4	26	27
Murray	0-0	6.48	.265	4	0	0	0	0	0	8.1	9	8	6	4	4	8
Suzuki	2-5	6.79	.286	38	13	0	6	0	0	110.0	124	92	83	16	64	68
Montgomery	1-4	6.84	.343	49	0	0	36	0	12	51.1	72	40	39	7	21	27
Pittsley	1-2	6.94	.337	5	5	0	0	0	0	23.1	33	22	18	2	15	7
Fussell	0-5	7.39	.329	17	8	0	3	0	2	56.0	72	51	46	9	36	37
Byrdak	0-3	7.66	.308	33	0	0	5	0	1	24.2	32	24	21	5	20	17
Pisciotta	0-2	8.64	.281	8	0	0	3	0	0	8.1	9	8	8	1	10	3
Ray	1-0	8.74	.460	13	0	0	4	0	0	11.1	23	12	11	2	6	0
Reichert	2-2	9.08	.327	8	8	0	0	0	0	36.2	48	38	37	2	32	20
Wengert	0-1	9.25	.376	11	1	0	2	0	0	24.1	41	26	25	6	5	10
Barber	1-3	9.64	.383	8	3	0	1	0	1	18.2	31	20	20	6	10	7
Rusch	0-1	15.75	.368	3	0	0	1	0	0	4.0	7	7	7	1	3	4

2000 preliminary roster

PITCHERS (24)
Tim Byrdak
Lance Carter
Jeff D'Amico
Chad Durbin
Chris Fussell
Tyler Green
Justin Lamber
David Lundquist
Orber Moreno
Scott Mullen
Dan Murray
Jason Rakers

Ken Ray
Dan Reichert
Brad Rigby
Jose Rosado
Jose Santiago
Jerry Spradlin
Blake Stein
Jeff Suppan
Mac Suzuki
Jamie Walker
Derek Wallace
Jay Witasick

CATCHERS (2)
Sal Fasano
Brian Johnson

INFIELDERS (6)
Carlos Febles
Ray Holbert
Joe Randa
Jeff Reboulet
Rey Sanchez
Mike Sweeney

OUTFIELDERS (9)
Carlos Beltran
Dee Brown
Johnny Damon
Todd Dunwoody
Jermaine Dye
Jeremy Giambi
Scott Pose
Mark Quinn
Goefrey Tomlinson

Games played by position

PLAYER	G	C	1B	2B	3B	SS	OF	DH
Beltran	156	0	0	0	0	0	154	2
Brown	12	0	0	0	0	0	3	2
Damon	145	0	0	0	0	0	140	4
Dye	158	0	0	0	0	0	157	1
Fasano	23	23	0	0	0	0	0	0
Febles	123	0	0	122	0	0	0	0
Giambi	90	0	26	0	0	0	5	52
Hansen	49	1	0	21	4	10	2	3
Holbert	34	0	0	11	1	22	0	0
King	21	0	20	0	0	0	0	1
Kreuter	107	101	0	0	0	0	0	1
Leius	37	0	13	1	10	2	0	0
Lopez	7	0	0	6	0	1	0	0
Martinez	6	0	0	1	0	2	0	0
Pose	86	0	0	0	0	0	25	20
Quinn	17	0	0	0	0	0	15	1
Randa	156	0	0	0	156	0	0	0
Sanchez	134	0	0	0	0	134	0	0
Scarsone	46	0	12	9	3	16	0	0
Spehr	60	59	0	0	0	0	0	0
Sutton	43	0	30	0	0	0	1	5
Sweeney	150	4	74	0	0	0	0	75
Vitiello	13	0	10	0	0	0	0	2

Sick call: 1999 DL report

PLAYER	Days on the DL
Carlos Febles	27
Jeremy Giambi	40
Jeff King	20
Scott Leius	92
Terry Mathews	40
Jeff Montgomery	31
Orber Moreno	116
Hipolito Pichardo	182
Dan Reichert	41
Jose Santiago	85
Larry Sutton	51

Minor Leagues

Tops in the organization

BATTER	CLUB	AVG.	G	AB	R	H	HR	RBI
Quinn, Mark	Oma	.360	107	428	67	154	25	84
Brown, Dee	Wch	.331	126	456	107	151	25	102
Medrano, Tony	Oma	.331	106	369	59	122	7	55
Ellis, Mark	SPO	.327	71	281	67	92	7	47
Vitiello, Joe	Oma	.318	122	447	70	142	28	98

HOME RUNS

McNally, Sean	Wch	36
Pellow, Kit	Oma	35
Gibralter, Steve	Oma	28
Vitiello, Joe	Oma	28
Several Players Tied at		25

WINS

Wilson, Kris	Wch	13
Gooding, Jason	Wch	13
Saier, Matt	Oma	13
Lineweaver, Aaron	Wch	12
Guerrero, Junior	Wil	11

RBI

McNally, Sean	Wch	109
Brown, Dee	Wch	102
Pellow, Kit	Oma	99
Vitiello, Joe	Oma	98
Amado, Jose	Wch	93

SAVES

Ray, Ken	Oma	15
Gehrke, Jay	SPO	13
Sonnier, Shawn	Wil	13
Carter, Lance	Wch	13
Morrison, Robbie	Wch	11

STOLEN BASES

Curry, Mike	Wil	85
Taveras, Jose	CWV	38
Calderon, Henry	CWV	33
Brown, Dee	Wch	30
Several Players Tied at		29

STRIKEOUTS

Guerrero, Junior	Wil	181
Gonzalez, Edwin	CWV	144
George, Chris	Wil	142
Thurman, Corey	Wil	131
Reichert, Dan	Oma	123

PITCHER	CLUB	W-L	ERA	IP	H	BB	SO
Guerrero, Junior	Wil	11-5	2.31	156	120	71	181
Gonzalez, Edwin	CWV	8-7	2.60	131	115	32	144
George, Chris	Wil	9-7	3.60	145	142	53	142
Reichert, Dan	Oma	9-2	3.71	112	92	50	123
Affeldt, Jeremy	CWV	7-7	3.83	143	140	80	111

1999 salaries

	Bonuses	Total earned salary
Hipolito Pichardo, p		2,625,000
Jeff Montgomery, p		2,500,000
Johnny Damon, of		2,100,000
Rey Sanchez, ss	100,000	1,200,000
Joe Randa, 3b	150,000	910,000
Chad Kreuter, c	150,000	875,000
Scott Service, p	25,000	745,000
Alvin Morman, p	100,000	365,000
Tim Spehr, c		330,000
Jose Rosado, p	30,000	300,000
Steve Scarsone, ss		275,000
Mike Sweeney, dh		265,000
Jermaine Dye, of		260,000
Scott Leius, 1b		250,000
Jeff Suppan, p		235,000
Scott Pose, of	10,000	225,000
Derek Wallace, p		216,000
Ray Holbert, ss		215,000
Mac Suzuki, p	10,000	212,000
Jay Witasick, p		210,000
Blake Stein, p		207,500
Jed Hansen, 2b		204,000
Brad Rigby, p		201,500
Jose Santiago, p		201,000
Carlos Febles, 2b		200,000
Orber Moreno, p		200,000
Tim Byrdak, p		200,000
Chris Fussell, p		200,000
Carlos Beltran, of		200,000
Jeremy Giambi, dh		200,000
Dan Reichert, p		200,000

Average 1999 salary: $534,097
Total 1999 team payroll: $16,557,000

Kansas City (1969-1999)

164

Runs: Most, career

1583	George Brett, 1973-1993
1074	Amos Otis, 1970-1983
1060	Willie Wilson, 1976-1990
912	Frank White, 1973-1990
873	Hal McRae, 1973-1987

Hits: Most, career

3154	George Brett, 1973-1993
2006	Frank White, 1973-1990
1977	Amos Otis, 1970-1983
1968	Willie Wilson, 1976-1990
1924	Hal McRae, 1973-1987

2B: Most, career

665	George Brett, 1973-1993
449	Hal McRae, 1973-1987
407	Frank White, 1973-1990
365	Amos Otis, 1970-1983
241	Willie Wilson, 1976-1990

3B: Most, career

137	George Brett, 1973-1993
133	Willie Wilson, 1976-1990
65	Amos Otis, 1970-1983
63	Hal McRae, 1973-1987
58	Frank White, 1973-1990

HR: Most, career

317	George Brett, 1973-1993
193	Amos Otis, 1970-1983
169	Hal McRae, 1973-1987
160	Frank White, 1973-1990
143	John Mayberry, 1972-1977

RBI: Most, career

1595	George Brett, 1973-1993
1012	Hal McRae, 1973-1987
992	Amos Otis, 1970-1983
886	Frank White, 1973-1990
552	John Mayberry, 1972-1977

SB: Most, career

612	Willie Wilson, 1976-1990
340	Amos Otis, 1970-1983
336	Freddie Patek, 1971-1979
201	George Brett, 1973-1993
178	Frank White, 1973-1990

BB: Most, career

1096	George Brett, 1973-1993
739	Amos Otis, 1970-1983
616	Hal McRae, 1973-1987
561	John Mayberry, 1972-1977
413	Freddie Patek, 1971-1979

BA: Highest, career

.305	George Brett, 1973-1993
.294	Kevin Seitzer, 1986-1991
.293	WALLY JOYNER, 1992-1995
.293	Hal McRae, 1973-1987
.290	Danny Tartabull, 1987-1991

On-base avg: Highest, career

.380	Kevin Seitzer, 1986-1991
.376	Danny Tartabull, 1987-1991
.375	Darrell Porter, 1977-1980
.374	John Mayberry, 1972-1977
.371	WALLY JOYNER, 1992-1995

Slug pct: Highest, career

.518	Danny Tartabull, 1987-1991
.487	George Brett, 1973-1993
.480	Bo Jackson, 1986-1990
.469	Willie Aikens, 1980-1983
.459	Steve Balboni, 1984-1988

Games started: Most, career

392	Paul Splittorff, 1970-1984
327	Mark Gubicza, 1984-1996
302	Dennis Leonard, 1974-1986
269	KEVIN APPIER, 1989-1999
226	BRET SABERHAGEN, 1984-1991

Complete games: Most, career

103	Dennis Leonard, 1974-1986
88	Paul Splittorff, 1970-1984
64	BRET SABERHAGEN, 1984-1991
61	Larry Gura, 1976-1985
53	Steve Busby, 1972-1980
53	Dick Drago, 1969-1973

Saves: Most, career

304	JEFF MONTGOMERY, 1988-1999
238	Dan Quisenberry, 1979-1988
58	Doug Bird, 1973-1978
49	Steve Farr, 1985-1990
40	Ted Abernathy, 1970-1972

Shutouts: Most, career

23	Dennis Leonard, 1974-1986
17	Paul Splittorff, 1970-1984
16	Mark Gubicza, 1984-1996
14	Larry Gura, 1976-1985
14	BRET SABERHAGEN, 1984-1991

Wins: Most, career

166	Paul Splittorff, 1970-1984
144	Dennis Leonard, 1974-1986
132	Mark Gubicza, 1984-1996
114	KEVIN APPIER, 1989-1999
111	Larry Gura, 1976-1985

K: Most, career

1451	KEVIN APPIER, 1989-1999
1366	Mark Gubicza, 1984-1996
1323	Dennis Leonard, 1974-1986
1093	BRET SABERHAGEN, 1984-1991
1057	Paul Splittorff, 1970-1984

Win pct: Highest, career

.593	Al Fitzmorris, 1969-1976
.587	Larry Gura, 1976-1985
.585	BRET SABERHAGEN, 1984-1991
.576	Doug Bird, 1973-1978
.576	Dennis Leonard, 1974-1986

ERA: Lowest, career

2.55	Dan Quisenberry, 1979-1988
3.20	JEFF MONTGOMERY, 1988-1999
3.21	BRET SABERHAGEN, 1984-1991
3.46	KEVIN APPIER, 1989-1999
3.46	Al Fitzmorris, 1969-1976

Runs: Most, season

133	Willie Wilson, 1980
119	George Brett, 1979
113	Willie Wilson, 1979
112	CARLOS BELTRAN, 1999
108	George Brett, 1985

Hits: Most, season

230	Willie Wilson, 1980
215	George Brett, 1976
212	George Brett, 1979
207	Kevin Seitzer, 1987
197	JOE RANDA, 1999

2B: Most, season

54	Hal McRae, 1977
46	Hal McRae, 1982
45	George Brett, 1978
45	George Brett, 1990
45	Frank White, 1982

3B: Most, season

21	Willie Wilson, 1985
20	George Brett, 1979
15	Willie Wilson, 1980
15	Willie Wilson, 1982
15	Willie Wilson, 1987

HR: Most, season

36	Steve Balboni, 1985
35	GARY GAETTI, 1995
34	John Mayberry, 1975
34	DEAN PALMER, 1998
34	Danny Tartabull, 1987

RBI: Most, season

133	Hal McRae, 1982
119	JERMAINE DYE, 1999
119	DEAN PALMER, 1998
118	George Brett, 1980
112	George Brett, 1985
112	Al Cowens, 1977
112	JEFF KING, 1997
112	Darrell Porter, 1979

SB: Most, season

83	Willie Wilson, 1979
79	Willie Wilson, 1980
66	TOM GOODWIN, 1996
59	Willie Wilson, 1983
59	Willie Wilson, 1987

BB: Most, season

122	John Mayberry, 1973
121	Darrell Porter, 1979
119	John Mayberry, 1975
103	George Brett, 1985
103	Paul Schaal, 1971

BA: Highest, season

.390	George Brett, 1980
.335	George Brett, 1985
.333	George Brett, 1976
.332	Hal McRae, 1976
.332	Willie Wilson, 1982

On-base avg: Highest, season

.454	George Brett, 1980
.436	George Brett, 1985
.421	Darrell Porter, 1979
.417	John Mayberry, 1973
.416	John Mayberry, 1975

Slug pct: Highest, season

.664	George Brett, 1980
.599	Bob Hamelin, 1994
.593	Danny Tartabull, 1991
.585	George Brett, 1985
.563	George Brett, 1979

Games started: Most, season

40	Dennis Leonard, 1978
38	Steve Busby, 1974
38	Dennis Leonard, 1980
38	Paul Splittorff, 1973
38	Paul Splittorff, 1978

Complete games: Most, season

21	Dennis Leonard, 1977
20	Steve Busby, 1974
20	Dennis Leonard, 1978
18	Steve Busby, 1975
16	Larry Gura, 1980
16	Dennis Leonard, 1976

Saves: Most, season

45	JEFF MONTGOMERY, 1993
45	Dan Quisenberry, 1983
44	Dan Quisenberry, 1984
39	JEFF MONTGOMERY, 1992
37	Dan Quisenberry, 1985

Shutouts: Most, season

6	Roger Nelson, 1972
5	Dennis Leonard, 1977
5	Dennis Leonard, 1979
4	Bill Butler, 1969
4	Dick Drago, 1971
4	Al Fitzmorris, 1974
4	Mark Gubicza, 1988
4	Larry Gura, 1980
4	Dennis Leonard, 1978
4	BRET SABERHAGEN, 1987
4	BRET SABERHAGEN, 1989

Wins: Most, season

23	BRET SABERHAGEN, 1989
22	Steve Busby, 1974
21	Dennis Leonard, 1978
20	Mark Gubicza, 1988
20	Dennis Leonard, 1977
20	Dennis Leonard, 1980
20	BRET SABERHAGEN, 1985
20	Paul Splittorff, 1973

K: Most, season

244	Dennis Leonard, 1977
207	KEVIN APPIER, 1996
206	Bob Johnson, 1970
198	Steve Busby, 1974
196	KEVIN APPIER, 1997

Win pct: Highest, season

.800	Larry Gura, 1978
.793	BRET SABERHAGEN, 1989
.769	BRET SABERHAGEN, 1985
.762	DAVID CONE, 1994
.727	Paul Splittorff, 1977

ERA: Lowest, season

2.08	Roger Nelson, 1972
2.16	BRET SABERHAGEN, 1989
2.46	KEVIN APPIER, 1992
2.56	KEVIN APPIER, 1993
2.69	Charlie Leibrandt, 1985

Most pinch-hit homers, season

2	Hal McRae, 1986
2	Carmelo Martinez, 1991

Most pinch-hit homers, career

2	Chuck Harrison, 1969-1971
2	Bob Oliver, 1969-1972
2	Amos Otis, 1970-1983
2	Hal McRae, 1973-1987
2	Steve Balboni, 1984-1988
2	Jim Eisenreich, 1987-1991
2	Carmelo Martinez, 1991
2	Bob Hamelin, 1993-1996

Longest hitting streak

30	George Brett, 1980
27	JOSE OFFERMAN, 1998
25	MIKE SWEENEY, 1999
22	BRIAN McRAE, 1991
19	Amos Otis, 1974

Most consecutive scoreless innings

31	BRET SABERHAGEN, 1989

No-hit games

Steve Busby, KC at Det AL, 3-0; April 16, 1973.

Steve Busby, KC at Mil AL, 2-0; June 19, 1974.

Jim Colborn, KC vs Tex AL, 6-0; May 14, 1977.

BRET SABERHAGEN, KC vs Chi AL, 7-0; August 26, 1991.

ACTIVE PLAYERS in caps.

Players' years of service are listed by the first and last years with this team and are not necessarily consecutive; all statistics record performances for this team only.

Minnesota Twins

Marty Cordova put up the best numbers during the Twins' dismal season, but became a free agent afterward.

1999 Twins: Nowhere to go but up

The Minnesota Twins had their worst season since 1982 and remained in many ways a team with an uncertain future.

Last in the American League Central, the Twins played 18 rookies in 1999, not because they were loaded with hot prospects but because owner Carl Pohlad ordered the payroll slashed. It was down to $19.1 million, third-lowest in the majors, on opening day.

"All those guys could have benefited by spending a little more time—maybe a lot more time—in the minor leagues," general manager Terry Ryan said. "But we don't have that luxury."

A sixth straight losing season was a foregone conclusion from the very start.

"These players got forced into this situation. They probably all should have been at Triple-A," said manager Tom Kelly. "On the one hand, they were maybe a little lucky to be in a situation where they got put into the big leagues. On the other hand, they were chosen to play at the big-league level. So, if that's earning it, I don't know."

Pohlad was trying to sell the team, but his best prospect was a deal contingent on St. Paul voters approving a half-percent sales tax increase on Nov. 2 to build a stadium along the banks of the Mississippi River. That failed.

The team's cloudy future made for muddied fortunes on the field in 1999. The only bright spots were Eric Milton's no-hitter against Anaheim on Sept. 11 and the emergence of a decent pitching staff. Milton (163), Brad Radke (121), Joe Mays (115), and LaTroy Hawkins (103) gave the Twins their first quartet of 100-strikeout pitchers since 1971 (Bert Blyleven, Jim Kaat, Jim Perry, and Tom Hall).

"When we left spring training, I think all of us involved in this organization felt that Radke and Milton were two guys that we could rely on and build around for the future," Ryan said. "Really out of nowhere Joe Mays ended up in this rotation. And he's had some really impressive games and also some not so impressive."

The Twins' outfield of Chad Allen,

Jacque Jones and Torii Hunter got invaluable experience, even though in most other organizations they wouldn't have been major league regulars.

"They all in essence skipped over the Triple-A level and that's a difficult thing to do," Ryan said. "If you're talking about New York, Cleveland and Baltimore, and many clubs with established veterans, 90 percent of these guys would have started at the minor league level, there's no doubt . . . but there were days they looked like they belonged."

Kelly, who will return for the final year of his contract, said: "There's a very long list of holes to fill. Leadoff hitter, a third hitter, a fourth hitter—I'd like to have some more power." In a season marked by an unprecedented number of major league home runs, Ron Coomer led the Twins with a meager 16.

Some good news: Among rookies, 21-year-old shortstop Cristian Guzman appears headed for stardom.

"As he gets a little older, a little stronger, a little more mature, a little smarter, a little more experience, he could turn into a pretty good player," Kelly said.

The Twins began to play decent ball over the summer, but a September swoon left them with their worst record since the '82 club, also loaded with youngsters, lost 102 games.

"We're so young, we'll do nothing but get better," Jones said.

167

MAJOR LEAGUE REPORT

MINNESOTA TWINS / AL CENTRAL

1999 Twins: Week-by-week notes

These notes were excerpted from the following issues of Baseball Weekly.

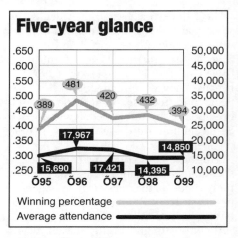

Five-year glance

Winning percentage
Average attendance

▶**April 7:** The Twins opened the season with a franchise-record 10 rookies on the roster.

▶**April 14:** The Twins had an $18 million payroll to start the season and wanted to slash it to $11 million as soon as possible, according to Jim Pohlad, the son of owner Carl Pohlad. The average age of the Twins was 26.6, while the pitching rotation averaged 24 years.

▶**April 21:** Don't blame right-hander Brad Radke for not wanting to see Cleveland again. He was shelled for 10 runs and 16 hits in 5⅔ innings in his two starts against the Indians this season. He was 5-10 for his career against them, 2-6 at Jacobs Field.

▶**April 28:** The Twins have a valuable commodity in right-hander Mike Trombley, who had been their best reliever and would inherit the closer's role if right-hander Rick Aguilera were traded. But the team had been unable to trade him and his $3.25 million salary. If they were unable to move Aguilera, they would possibly have no choice but to trade Trombley in order to trim the payroll. Trombley will earn $1.475 million this year.

▶**May 12:** The Twins, who rewarded right-hander LaTroy Hawkins with a two-year, $1.4 million contract last winter, had been befuddled by his continuing woes. Hawkins entered the week with a 1-5 record and a 9.49 ERA. He had just one victory in his past 17 starts, dating back to July 26, 1998.

▶**May 19:** Tom Kelly became the second manager in history to lose 1,000 games for the same team, have a losing record and not be fired. The other was Connie Mack, who managed the Philadelphia Athletics to a record of 3,582-3,814 (.474). He also owned the team. Kelly ended last week with a career 936-1,000 record (.483) but two World Series championships in 13 years with the Twins.

▶**May 26:** The Twins, were finally able to trade Rick Aguilera, slashing their payroll

to $16 million. They sent Aguilera and Class A right-hander Scott Downs to the Cubs for two fringe prospects: AA right-hander Jason Ryan and Class A righty Kyle Loshe. Aguilera, 37, was the Twins' final link to their 1991 championship team. He is the club's all-time leader in saves (254) and games pitched (490).

▶**June 2:** The Twins are becoming increasingly concerned with left-hander Ryan Mills, their $2 million bonus baby from the 1996 draft. Mills was 2-5 with an 8.17 ERA for Class A Fort Myers. He had walked or hit 44 batters while striking out 22 in 39 innings.

▶**June 9:** Mike Trombley, whose specialty is his split-finger pitch, apparently inherited closer duties. Left-hander Eddie Guardado, who was originally named the closer after the Aguilera trade, was on the DL.

▶**June 30:** Rookie right-hander Joe Mays, making just his second start for the Twins, won his first major league game at Tiger Stadium, a short trip from his hometown of Flint, Mich. Mays, who pitched six shutout innings for the victory in front of 30 friends and family, allowed just one run in 11 innings in his two starts.

▶**July 7:** The Twins reached an agreement to work exclusively with the city of St. Paul, and agreed to sell at least 49 percent of the club to another owner or group of owners by July 1, 2000. St. Paul Mayor Norm Coleman agreed to put an initia-

tive on the November ballot for city voters to decide whether to increase the sales tax by one-half cent for a new ballpark. The plan calls for the Twins to pay one-third of the cost, St. Paul to pay one-third and the state to pay one third.

▶July 21: The Twins were particularly impressed in the first half with shortstop Cristian Guzman, 21, who is becoming one of the league's finest defensive shortstops. All they needed was for him to start hitting. He entered July 19 with a .236 batting average and just one homer and 16 RBI.

▶July 28: Joe Mays, 3-1 with a 1.71 ERA since being promoted to the rotation, pitched 17⅓ scoreless innings in his past two starts, against the White Sox and the Cubs.

▶Aug. 4: LaTroy Hawkins suddenly started to turn around his season. He was 4-0 with a 4.18 ERA in his past six starts after going 3-8 with a 9.95 ERA in his first 15 starts. The Twins won 11 of his past 13 starts. The Twins went 15-11 in July—their first winning month since August 1996. They entered the week with a 26-22 record since June 5.

▶Aug. 11: The Twins' payroll of $16.8 million was the lowest in the AL, and Carl Pohlad has refused to grant Terry Ryan permission to offer Mike Trombley a multiyear contract. The Twins wanted to keep Trombley, but the delay left him just three months away from free agency. Trombley was seeking a three-year deal for about $6 million.

▶Sept. 1: Left-hander Eric Milton was pitching his best baseball of the season, yielding just two earned runs in his past 23⅓ innings for an 0.77 ERA. He has pitched seven or more innings in four consecutive starts.

▶Sept. 8: Terry Ryan, who impressed the front office and ownership with the progress of his rebuilding effort on a meager budget, was invited back for 2000, president Jerry Bell said. Ryan has held the position since September 1994.

▶Sept. 15: Eric Milton, in what he called the most wonderful day of his life, pitched the seventh no-hitter in Twins history on Sept. 12, a 7-0 gem against the Angels. Milton, the centerpiece of the Chuck Knoblauch trade with the Yankees, struck out a career-high 13 and yielded just two walks.

▶Oct. 6: NBA Minnesota Timberwolves owner Glen Taylor and Jac Sperling of the NHL's Minnesota Wild joined forces on a $120 million offer for the Twins that would have been finalized if a new stadium was approved in St. Paul. (The stadium was not approved.) Terry Ryan ended rumors that he might leave the Twins and rejoin former boss Andy MacPhail in the Cubs' front office.

QUOTE OF THE YEAR

"I would rather stay with the Twins and lose than go somewhere else and win."
—Closer Mike Trombley, on his desire to sign a contract extension

Team Leaders

Batting avg.	Hits	Wins	Strikeouts
.279 Todd Walker	148 Todd Walker	12 Brad Radke	163 Eric Milton
.277 Chad Allen	133 Chad Allen	10 LaTroy Hawkins	121 Brad Radke

HR	Runs	Losses	Innings
16 Ron Coomer	69 Chad Allen	14 Brad Radke	218.2 Brad Radke
14 Marty Cordova	62 Marty Cordova	14 LaTroy Hawkins	206.1 Eric Milton
	62 Todd Walker		

RBI	Stolen bases	ERA	Saves
70 Marty Cordova	26 Matt Lawton	3.75 Brad Radke	24 Mike Trombley
65 Ron Coomer	18 Todd Walker	4.37 Joe Mays	6 Rick Aguilera

MINNESOTA TWINS 1999 final stats

BATTERS	BA	SLG	OBA	G	AB	R	H	TB	2B	3B	HR	RBI	BB	SO	SB	CS	E
Koskie	.310	.468	.387	117	342	42	106	160	21	0	11	58	40	72	4	4	8
Jones	.289	.460	.329	95	322	54	93	148	24	2	9	44	17	63	3	4	5
Cordova	.285	.464	.365	124	425	62	121	197	28	3	14	70	48	96	13	4	3
Steinbach	.284	.391	.358	101	338	35	96	132	16	4	4	42	38	54	2	2	5
Walker	.279	.397	.343	143	531	62	148	211	37	4	6	46	52	83	18	10	7
Allen	.277	.395	.330	137	481	69	133	190	21	3	10	46	37	89	14	7	7
Pierzynski	.273	.364	.333	9	22	3	6	8	2	0	0	3	1	4	0	0	0
Hocking	.267	.378	.307	136	386	47	103	146	18	2	7	41	22	54	11	7	3
Coomer	.263	.424	.307	127	467	53	123	198	25	1	16	65	30	69	2	1	6
Cummings	.263	.342	.310	16	38	1	10	13	0	0	1	9	3	7	2	0	0
Lawton	.259	.355	.353	118	406	58	105	144	18	0	7	54	57	42	26	4	4
Hunter	.255	.380	.309	135	384	52	98	146	17	2	9	35	26	72	10	6	1
Gates	.255	.340	.328	110	306	40	78	104	13	2	3	38	34	56	1	3	3
Valentin	.248	.381	.313	78	218	22	54	83	12	1	5	28	22	39	0	0	1
Mientkiewicz	.229	.330	.324	118	327	34	75	108	21	3	2	32	43	51	1	1	3
Guzman	.226	.276	.267	131	420	47	95	116	12	3	1	26	22	90	9	7	24
Davidson	.136	.136	.136	12	22	3	3	3	0	0	0	3	0	4	2	0	1
Latham	.091	.091	.083	14	22	1	2	2	0	0	0	3	0	13	0	0	0
Ortiz	.000	.000	.200	10	20	1	0	0	0	0	0	0	5	12	0	0	0

PITCHERS	W-L	ERA	BA	G	GS	CG	GF	SH	SV	IP	H	R	ER	HR	BB	SO
Aguilera	3-1	1.27	.135	17	0	0	16	0	6	21.1	10	3	3	2	2	13
Miller	2-2	2.72	.284	52	0	0	12	0	0	49.2	55	19	15	3	16	40
Romero	0-0	3.72	.333	5	0	0	3	0	0	9.2	13	4	4	0	0	4
Radke	12-14	3.75	.280	33	33	4	0	0	0	218.2	239	97	91	28	44	121
Wells	8-3	3.81	.245	76	0	0	18	0	1	87.1	79	41	37	8	28	44
Trombley	2-8	4.33	.272	75	0	0	56	0	24	87.1	93	42	42	15	28	82
Mays	6-11	4.37	.270	49	20	2	8	1	0	171.0	179	92	83	24	67	115
Milton	7-11	4.49	.243	34	34	5	0	2	0	206.1	190	111	103	28	63	163
Guardado	2-5	4.50	.222	63	0	0	13	0	2	48.0	37	24	24	6	25	50
Ryan	1-4	4.87	.286	8	8	1	0	0	0	40.2	46	23	22	9	17	15
Carrasco	2-3	4.96	.261	39	0	0	10	0	1	49.0	48	29	27	3	18	35
Perkins	1-7	6.54	.326	29	12	0	7	0	0	86.2	117	69	63	14	43	44
Hawkins	10-14	6.66	.323	33	33	1	0	0	0	174.1	238	136	129	29	60	103
Lincoln	3-10	6.84	.321	18	15	0	0	0	0	76.1	102	59	58	11	26	27
Sampson	3-2	8.11	.351	30	4	0	2	0	0	71.0	107	65	64	17	34	56
Redman	1-0	8.53	.298	5	1	0	0	0	0	12.2	17	13	12	3	7	11
Rath	0-1	11.57	.300	5	1	0	1	0	0	4.2	6	6	6	1	5	1
Radlosky	0-1	12.46	.375	7	0	0	2	0	0	8.2	15	12	12	7	4	3

2000 preliminary roster

PITCHERS (21)
Sean Bergman
Hector Carrasco
Jack Cressend
Eddie Guardado
Latroy Hawkins
Matt Kinney
Mike Kusiewicz
Mike Lincoln
Joe Mays
Travis Miller
Eric Milton
Dan Perkins
Brad Radke

Scott Randall
Mark Redman
J.C. Romero
Jason Ryan
Benj Sampson
Johan Santana
Brent Stentz
Bob Wells

CATCHERS (3)
Chad Moeller
A.J. Pierzynski
Javier Valentin

INFIELDERS (10)
Ron Coomer
Cleatus Davidson
Cristian Guzman
Denny Hocking
Corey Koskie
Doug Mientkiewicz
David Ortiz
Luis Rivas
Mario Valdez
Todd Walker

OUTFIELDERS (6)
Chad Allen
Brian Buchanan
Midre Cummings
Torii Hunter
Jacque Jones
Matt Lawton

Games played by position

PLAYER	G	C	1B	2B	3B	SS	OF	DH
Allen	137	0	0	0	0	0	133	2
Coomer	127	0	71	0	57	0	1	0
Cordova	124	0	0	0	0	0	29	88
Cummings	16	0	0	0	0	0	6	5
Davidson	12	0	0	6	0	4	0	0
Gates	110	0	5	47	61	1	0	0
Guzman	131	0	0	0	0	131	0	0
Hocking	136	0	2	56	6	61	38	0
Hunter	135	0	0	0	0	0	130	0
Jones	95	0	0	0	0	0	93	0
Koskie	117	0	0	0	79	0	25	12
Latham	14	0	0	0	0	0	14	0
Lawton	118	0	0	0	0	0	109	6
Mientkiewicz	118	0	110	0	0	0	0	0
Ortiz	10	0	1	0	0	0	1	5
Pierzynski	9	9	0	0	0	0	0	0
Steinbach	101	96	0	0	0	0	0	1
Valentin	78	76	0	0	0	0	0	0
Walker	143	0	0	103	0	0	0	40

Sick call: 1999 DL report

PLAYER	Days on the DL
Hector Carrasco	81
Cleatus Davidson	5
Eddie Guardado	38
Cristian Guzman	15
Matt Lawton	39
Mark Redman	16
Terry Steinbach	34*

Indicates two separate terms on Disabled List.

Minor Leagues

Tops in the organization

BATTER	CLUB	AVG.	G	AB	R	H	HR	RBI
Salazar, Ruben	ELZ	.401	64	262	66	105	14	65
Cummings, Midre	SLk	.336	93	354	78	119	15	83
Scanlon, Matt	QC	.324	73	293	62	95	7	53
Latham, Chris	SLk	.322	94	382	93	123	15	51
Williams, Eddie	SLk	.316	97	345	56	109	17	57

HOME RUNS

Lecroy, Matthew	SLk	30
Ortiz, David	SLk	30
Hacker, Steve	SLk	29
Peterman, Tommy	NB	20
Several Players Tied at		19

WINS

Rincon, Juan	QC	14
Hoard, Brent	QC	12
Lohse, Kyle	NB	10
Davies, Bob	FtM	10
Several Players Tied at		9

RBI

Ortiz, David	SLk	110
Restovich, M.	QC	107
Hacker, Steve	SLk	100
Lecroy, Matthew	SLk	99
Peterman, Tommy	NB	84

SAVES

Rivera, Saul	QC	23
Fiore, Tony	SLk	19
Stentz, Brent	NB	12
Niedermaier, B.	NB	9
Romero, J.C.	SLk	8

STOLEN BASES

Davidson, C.	NB	40
Felston, Anthony	FtM	33
Rivas, Luis	NB	31
McMillin, Brian	QC	19
Latham, Chris	SLk	18

STRIKEOUTS

Rincon, Juan	QC	153
Hoard, Brent	QC	139
Cressend, Jack	NB	136
Lohse, Kyle	NB	115
Redman, Mark	SLk	114

PITCHER	CLUB	W-L	ERA	IP	H	BB	SO
Rincon, Juan	QC	14-8	2.92	163	146	66	153
Hoard, Brent	QC	12-7	3.43	150	143	64	139
Hooten, David	NB	6-6	3.56	104	94	49	89
Fisher, Peter	FtM	5-10	3.74	147	171	38	91
Radlosky, Rob	SLk	8-4	3.91	101	98	38	68

1999 salaries

	Bonuses	Total earned salary
Marty Cordova, dh		3,000,000
Brad Radke, p		2,225,000
Matt Lawton, of		1,700,000
Mike Trombley, p	25,000	1,500,000
Ron Coomer, 1b	50,000	1,150,000
Terry Steinbach, c	200,000	1,000,000
Eddie Guardado, p		850,000
Hector Carrasco, p		800,000
Brent Gates, 3b	100,000	425,000
Bob Wells, p		350,000
Dennis Hocking, ss		325,000
LaTroy Hawkins, p		300,000
Todd Walker, 2b		277,500
Eric Milton, p		240,000
Javier Valentin, c		207,500
Travis Miller, p		205,000
Dan Perkins, p		200,000
Torii Hunter, of		200,000
Jason Ryan, p		200,000
Corey Koskie, 3b		200,000
Cristian Guzman, ss		200,000
Joe Mays, p		200,000
Doug Mientkiewicz, 1b		200,000
Chad Allen, of		200,000
Jacque Jones, of		200,000

Average 1999 salary: $653,800
Total 1999 team payroll: $16,345,000
Termination pay: $500,000

171

Minnesota (1961-1999), includes Washington Senators (1901-1960)

Runs: Most, career

1466	Sam Rice, 1915-1933	
1258	Harmon Killebrew, 1954-1974	
1154	Joe Judge, 1915-1932	
1071	Kirby Puckett, 1984-1995	
1037	Buddy Myer, 1925-1941	

Hits: Most, career

2889	Sam Rice, 1915-1933
2304	Kirby Puckett, 1984-1995
2291	Joe Judge, 1915-1932
2100	Clyde Milan, 1907-1922
2085	Rod Carew, 1967-1978

2B: Most, career

479	Sam Rice, 1915-1933
421	Joe Judge, 1915-1932
414	Kirby Puckett, 1984-1995
391	Mickey Vernon, 1939-1955
329	Tony Oliva, 1962-1976

3B: Most, career

183	Sam Rice, 1915-1933
157	Joe Judge, 1915-1932
125	Goose Goslin, 1921-1938
113	Buddy Myer, 1925-1941
108	Mickey Vernon, 1939-1955
90	Rod Carew, 1967-1978 (8)

HR: Most, career

559	Harmon Killebrew, 1954-1974
293	Kent Hrbek, 1981-1994
256	Bob Allison, 1958-1970
220	Tony Oliva, 1962-1976
207	Kirby Puckett, 1984-1995

RBI: Most, career

1540	Harmon Killebrew, 1954-1974
1086	Kent Hrbek, 1981-1994
1085	Kirby Puckett, 1984-1995
1045	Sam Rice, 1915-1933
1026	Mickey Vernon, 1939-1955

SB: Most, career

495	Clyde Milan, 1907-1922
346	Sam Rice, 1915-1933
321	George Case, 1937-1947
276	CHUCK KNOBLAUCH, 1991-1997
271	Rod Carew, 1967-1978

BB: Most, career

1505	Harmon Killebrew, 1954-1974
1274	Eddie Yost, 1944-1958
943	Joe Judge, 1915-1932
864	Buddy Myer, 1925-1941
838	Kent Hrbek, 1981-1994

BA: Highest, career

.334	Rod Carew, 1967-1978
.328	Heinie Manush, 1930-1935
.323	Sam Rice, 1915-1933
.323	Goose Goslin, 1921-1938
.318	Kirby Puckett, 1984-1995

On-base avg: Highest, career

.393	Rod Carew, 1967-1978
.393	Buddy Myer, 1925-1941
.392	John Stone, 1934-1938
.391	CHUCK KNOBLAUCH, 1991-1997
.389	Eddie Yost, 1944-1958

Slug pct: Highest, career

.514	Harmon Killebrew, 1954-1974
.502	Goose Goslin, 1921-1938
.500	Roy Sievers, 1954-1959
.481	Jimmie Hall, 1963-1966
.481	Kent Hrbek, 1981-1994

Games started: Most, career

666	Walter Johnson, 1907-1927
433	Jim Kaat, 1959-1973
345	Bert Blyleven, 1970-1988
331	Camilo Pascual, 1954-1966
259	Frank Viola, 1982-1989

Complete games: Most, career

531	Walter Johnson, 1907-1927
206	Case Patten, 1901-1908
141	Bert Blyleven, 1970-1988
139	Tom Hughes, 1904-1913
133	Jim Kaat, 1959-1973

Saves: Most, career

254	RICK AGUILERA, 1989-1999
108	Ron Davis, 1982-1986
104	Jeff Reardon, 1987-1989
96	Firpo Marberry, 1923-1936
88	Al Worthington, 1964-1969

Shutouts: Most, career

110	Walter Johnson, 1907-1927
31	Camilo Pascual, 1954-1966
29	Bert Blyleven, 1970-1988
23	Jim Kaat, 1959-1973
23	Dutch Leonard, 1938-1946

Wins: Most, career

417	Walter Johnson, 1907-1927
190	Jim Kaat, 1959-1973
149	Bert Blyleven, 1970-1988
145	Camilo Pascual, 1954-1966
128	Jim Perry, 1963-1972

K: Most, career

3509	Walter Johnson, 1907-1927
2035	Bert Blyleven, 1970-1988
1885	Camilo Pascual, 1954-1966
1851	Jim Kaat, 1959-1973
1214	Frank Viola, 1982-1989

Win pct: Highest, career

.622	Firpo Marberry, 1923-1936
.602	Sam Jones, 1928-1931
.599	Walter Johnson, 1907-1927
.598	Earl Whitehill, 1933-1936
.588	Mudcat Grant, 1964-1967

ERA: Lowest, career

2.17	Walter Johnson, 1907-1927
2.64	Doc Ayers, 1913-1919
2.75	Harry Harper, 1913-1919
2.77	Charlie Smith, 1906-1909
2.83	Bert Gallia, 1912-1917
3.15	Jim Perry, 1963-1972 (10)

Runs: Most, season

140	CHUCK KNOBLAUCH, 1996
128	Rod Carew, 1977
127	Joe Cronin, 1930
126	Zoilo Versalles, 1965
122	Buddy Lewis, 1938

Hits: Most, season

239	Rod Carew, 1977
234	Kirby Puckett, 1988
227	Sam Rice, 1925
225	Paul Molitor, 1996
223	Kirby Puckett, 1986

2B: Most, season

51	Mickey Vernon, 1946
50	Stan Spence, 1946
46	MARTY CORDOVA, 1996
45	Joe Cronin, 1933
45	CHUCK KNOBLAUCH, 1994
45	Kirby Puckett, 1989
45	Zoilo Versalles, 1965

3B: Most, season

20	Goose Goslin, 1925	
19	Joe Cassidy, 1904	
19	Cecil Travis, 1941	
18	Joe Cronin, 1932	
18	Goose Goslin, 1923	
18	Sam Rice, 1923	
18	Howie Shanks, 1921	
18	John Stone, 1935	
16	Rod Carew, 1977 (11)	

HR: Most, season

49	Harmon Killebrew, 1964
49	Harmon Killebrew, 1969
48	Harmon Killebrew, 1962
46	Harmon Killebrew, 1961
45	Harmon Killebrew, 1963

RBI: Most, season

140	Harmon Killebrew, 1969
129	Goose Goslin, 1924
126	Joe Cronin, 1930
126	Joe Cronin, 1931
126	Harmon Killebrew, 1962

SB: Most, season

88	Clyde Milan, 1912
75	Clyde Milan, 1913
63	Sam Rice, 1920
62	CHUCK KNOBLAUCH, 1997
62	Danny Moeller, 1913

BB: Most, season

151	Eddie Yost, 1956
145	Harmon Killebrew, 1969
141	Eddie Yost, 1950
131	Harmon Killebrew, 1967
131	Eddie Yost, 1954

BA: Highest, season

.388	Rod Carew, 1977
.379	Goose Goslin, 1928
.376	Ed Delahanty, 1902
.364	Rod Carew, 1974
.359	Rod Carew, 1975

On-base avg: Highest, season

.454	Buddy Myer, 1938
.453	Ed Delahanty, 1902
.449	Rod Carew, 1977
.448	CHUCK KNOBLAUCH, 1996
.442	Goose Goslin, 1928

Slug pct: Highest, season

.614	Goose Goslin, 1928
.606	Harmon Killebrew, 1961
.590	Ed Delahanty, 1902
.584	Harmon Killebrew, 1969
.579	Roy Sievers, 1957

Games started: Most, season

42	Walter Johnson, 1910
42	Jim Kaat, 1965
41	Jim Kaat, 1966
40	Bert Blyleven, 1973
40	Bob Groom, 1912
40	Walter Johnson, 1914
40	Jim Perry, 1970

Complete games: Most, season

38	Walter Johnson, 1910
37	Case Patten, 1904
36	Walter Johnson, 1911
36	Walter Johnson, 1916
36	Al Orth, 1902
25	Bert Blyleven, 1973 (*)

Saves: Most, season

42	RICK AGUILERA, 1991
42	Jeff Reardon, 1988
41	RICK AGUILERA, 1992
38	RICK AGUILERA, 1998
34	RICK AGUILERA, 1993
34	Ron Perranoski, 1970

Shutouts: Most, season

11	Walter Johnson, 1913
9	Bert Blyleven, 1973
9	Walter Johnson, 1914
9	Bob Porterfield, 1953
8	Walter Johnson, 1910
8	Walter Johnson, 1917
8	Walter Johnson, 1918
8	Camilo Pascual, 1961

Wins: Most, season

36	Walter Johnson, 1913
33	Walter Johnson, 1912
28	Walter Johnson, 1914
27	Walter Johnson, 1915
26	Alvin Crowder, 1932
25	Jim Kaat, 1966 (6)

K: Most, season

313	Walter Johnson, 1910
303	Walter Johnson, 1912
258	Bert Blyleven, 1973
249	Bert Blyleven, 1974
243	Walter Johnson, 1913

Win pct: Highest, season

.837	Walter Johnson, 1913
.800	Stan Coveleski, 1925
.800	Firpo Marberry, 1931
.774	Frank Viola, 1988
.773	Bill Campbell, 1976

ERA: Lowest, season

1.14	Walter Johnson, 1913
1.27	Walter Johnson, 1918
1.36	Walter Johnson, 1910
1.39	Walter Johnson, 1912
1.49	Walter Johnson, 1919
2.49	Dave Goltz, 1978 (*)

Most pinch-hit homers, season

4	Don Mincher, 1964

Most pinch-hit homers, career

8	Bob Allison, 1961-1970
7	Don Mincher, 1961-1966

Longest hitting streak

33	Heine Manush, 1933
31	Sam Rice, 1924
31	Ken Landreaux, 1980
29	Sam Rice, 1920
28	Sam Rice, 1930

Most consecutive scoreless innings

55	Walter Johnson, 1913
40	Walter Johnson, 1918
37	Walter Johnson, 1913

No-hit games

Jay Cashion, six innings, called so Cleveland could catch train, Was vs Cle AL, 2-0; August 20, 1912 (2nd game).

Walter Johnson, Was at Bos AL, 1-0; July 1, 1920.

Walter Johnson, seven innings, rain, Was vs StL AL, 2-0; August 25, 1924.

Bobby Burke, Was vs Bos AL, 5-0; August 8, 1931.

Jack Kralick, Min vs KC AL, 1-0; August 26, 1962.

Dean Chance, five perfect innings, rain, Min vs Bos AL, 2-0; August 6, 1967.

Dean Chance, Min at Cle AL, 2-1; August 25, 1967 (2nd game).

SCOTT ERICKSON, Min vs Mil AL, 6-0; April 27, 1994.

ERIC MILTON, Min vs Ana AL, 7-0; September 11, 1999.

ACTIVE PLAYERS in caps.

Players' years of service are listed by the first and last years with this team and are not necessarily consecutive; all statistics record performances for this team only.

Leader from the franchise's current location is included. If not in the top five, leader's rank is listed in parenthesis; asterisk (*) indicates player is not in top 25.

Texas Rangers

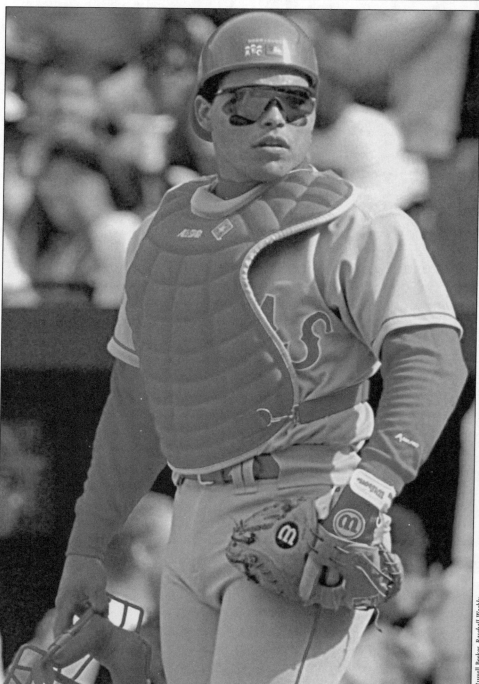

By Russell Becker, Baseball Weekly

American League MVP Ivan Rodriguez is as good as it gets—at the plate and behind it as well.

1999 Rangers: Pitching beats hitting

The Texas Rangers found themselves in a rut as their 1999 season ended—but not for long. Yes, the season ended with another American League West championship and a second consecutive three-game elimination in a Division Series at the hands of the New York Yankees.

But what was different was the reaction. New owner Tom Hicks made it clear: Enough is enough. General manager Doug Melvin got the message.

As the calendar was turned from the disappointment of October, the Rangers began November by sending slugging star Juan Gonzalez to the Detroit Tigers in a stunning nine-player trade.

Gonzalez was a key part of the powerful offense that carried the Rangers to the postseason and fell asleep in the playoffs. Texas scored just one run—on a homer by Gonzalez—in a three-game sweep by New York that was a replay of the previous October.

"I cannot explain what happened," said Rafael Palmeiro, who challenged for the team Triple Crown all season then had just three singles in the playoffs.

The Rangers won 95 games—the most in franchise history—behind an offense that averaged 5.83 runs per game and hit a major-league-best .293. Pitching and defense, the usual cornerstones for success in baseball, have never been Texas traditions. Bashing baseballs has always been the Rangers' style, for better or worse—mostly worse. But this year the Rangers bullpen was one of the success stories.

Well-traveled rookie Jeff Zimmerman was the best success story, winning nine games, saving three more, and allowing opposing batters just .166 as the primary set-up man for John Wetteland's 43 saves. Zimmerman, Wetteland, Mike Venafro, Tim Crabtree and Mike Munoz all had ERA under 4.00 and combined for a 23-12 record.

But as usual, the Rangers lived on their offense. Palmeiro and catcher Ivan Rodriguez were in the midst of the league MVP race all season (Rodriguez won). Despite being slowed by preseason knee

Team MVP

Ivan Rodriguez: There aren't any more ways Ivan Rodriguez can find to beat you—unless he takes up pitching. And he's actually a factor in that, because his defensive ability and throwing prowess almost completely eliminate opponents' running game. Now, he's become as complete an offensive player as exists in baseball. In 1999, he led Texas with a .332 batting average and hit 35 home runs with 113 RBI and 25 stolen bases.

surgery and limited to DH duty most of the season, Palmeiro returned as a free agent from Baltimore and hit .324 with 47 home runs and 148 RBI. Even with those numbers, he couldn't win the club triple crown—Rodriguez led in average at .332 and Gonzalez was second at .326. Palmeiro did lead in homers and RBI but not by much. In fact, Gonzalez added 128 RBI, Rodriguez 113 and Rusty Greer 101. Gonzalez added 39 home runs and Rodriguez 35.

All of that might be old hat to Texas fans. Attendance was down, with fewer than 40,000 fans attending crucial games in late September. Although the playoff game sold out, ticket sales went very slowly. And television ratings for the two road playoff games were down 19 percent from 1998.

Hicks isn't the kind of guy to let things stay in a rut for long. He's merging the Rangers' front office with the business side of his championship hockey team, the Dallas Stars. Hicks had said in the spring that Manager Johnny Oates and Melvin would be held accountable if Texas flopped again in the first round, though both got contract extensions late in the season.

Two fresh faces in 2000 will be in the outfield. Powerful Gabe Kapler was acquired in the Gonzalez deal and Ruben Mateo, who got a taste of the majors last season, has been the toast of the Texas farm system for several years.

1999 Rangers: Week-by-week notes

These notes were excerpted from the following issues of Baseball Weekly.

▶**April 14:** The Rangers allowed 36 runs in their first five games. Throw out one shutout—a combination seven-hitter by right-handers Aaron Sele, Tim Crabtree and Danny Patterson—and the staff gave up an average of nine runs per game.

▶**April 21:** Catcher Ivan Rodriguez needed just three innings of a 15-6 rout of the Mariners to collect a club-record nine RBI. He had a three-run homer in the first, a two-run single in the second and a grand slam in the third. Rodriguez had a chance to tie the major league record of 12 in his next at-bat when he came up with two men on, but he flied out.

▶**May 5:** In spring training, manager Johnny Oates had said that first baseman Lee Stevens could be a .300 hitter with power. Forced into full-time duty because of an Achilles tendon injury suffered by erstwhile platoon partner Mike Simms, Stevens spent April proving Oates right. He hit .354 with a team-leading eight homers and 17 RBI for the month.

▶**May 19:** Rookie reliever Jeff Zimmerman was 2-0 with a 0.69 ERA through May 16 and had held opponents to an .094 batting average. Right-handed closer John Wetteland had 11 saves, and the team was 8-1 in games in which they both pitched. But right-hander Rick Helling, a 20-game winner a year ago, had been 3-4 with a 6.34 ERA until he beat the Orioles 8-1 on May 15, typifying the problems of the rotation as a whole. Starters had an ERA over 6.00 and were averaging less than six innings per outing.

▶**May 26:** Right-hander John Burkett lost his spot in the rotation after yet another disastrous start and was replaced by rookie righty Ryan Glynn. Burkett was sent to the bullpen after giving up 12 runs in four innings of a 13-3 loss to Tampa Bay, setting a club record for most runs allowed in a game and lifting his ERA to 13.24.

▶**June 9:** The Rangers ran off a nine-game winning streak, the longest in the majors

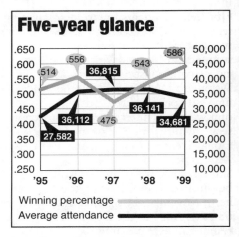

Five-year glance

	'95	'96	'97	'98	'99
Winning percentage	.514	.556	.475	.543	.586
Average attendance	27,582	36,112	36,815	36,141	34,681

Winning percentage
Average attendance

this year. The streak was built on the strength of the much-maligned rotation. The starters had a 4.07 ERA in 55 innings and pitched into the seventh inning seven times.

▶**June 16:** Jeff Zimmerman was 7-0 with an ERA of 1.13, the best among AL relievers. In all, the relievers were a big reason why the Rangers were leading the West. The bullpen was 16-1 with a 3.62 ERA through June 13, helping the club to go 20-8 in two-run games, 12-4 in one-run games and 5-0 in extra innings.

▶**June 23:** After his team lost for the 17th time in 21 games against the Yankees, including a sweep in the first round of the playoffs last year, Johnny Oates lost his cool. A postgame tirade after a 6-2 defeat included a couple of profanities and a baseball that he fired into a locker.

▶**June 30:** John Burkett rejoined the rotation when right-hander Mark Clark went on the DL. He responded with his best start of the season on June 24, holding the A's to two runs on six hits and no walks in six innings of a 5-2 victory. It was his first win of the year. He had managed a 3.00 ERA in five relief appearances covering 18 innings.

▶**July 7:** The Rangers went 15-13 in June and increased their lead in the West from three to five games despite playing 20 of 28 games on the road. The staff had a 4.13 ERA for the month, third in the AL.

Starting pitchers, the weak link for most of the season, were 9-4 with a 3.33 ERA in the last 15 games of June.

▶**July 28:** The Rangers were the hottest team in baseball after the All-Star break, winning 10 of their first 11 games to go a season-high 18 games over .500—and eight games up in the West. John Wetteland wasn't a big part of the winning streak. He failed in his first save opportunity after the break, his third consecutive blown save.

▶**Aug. 4:** Third baseman Todd Zeile hit .422 in the first 17 games after the All-Star break as the Rangers went 14-3 to build their big lead in the West. Overall, he was hitting .308 with 15 homers and 68 RBI through Aug. 1.

▶**Aug. 11:** Right fielder Juan Gonzalez continued to make news for the wrong reasons. He refused to dress for the Hall of Fame exhibition because his pants were too baggy, which caused an outcry even though he wasn't going to play because of a wrist injury.

▶**Aug. 18:** Ivan Rodriguez was hitting .326 with 26 homers and 82 RBI through Aug. 15. He was on pace to become the first catcher to both score and drive in 100 runs since the Royals' Darrell Porter in 1979. His real value comes on defense, though. He had thrown out 31 of 53 runners, a 58.5 percent success rate. The best percentage for a season since the statistic was first kept, in 1989, is 52.5 percent, by Rodriguez last year. He also hadn't allowed a passed ball.

▶**Aug. 25:** DH Rafael Palmeiro was batting .340 with 37 homers and 117 RBI. When Palmeiro hit two homers against the Red Sox on Aug. 21, he had six in his last six games and 11 in August. He hit another the next day, matching Juan Gonzalez's club record for a month.

▶**Sept. 1:** The Rangers claimed Jeff Fassero, a former ace left-hander struggling through a wretched season, on waivers from the Mariners and worked out a deal for a minor leaguer to be named. Fassero joined a rotation featuring Rick Helling, Aaron Sele and right-hander Esteban Loaiza, who were a combined 19-1 since the All-Star break after Sele defeated the Blue Jays on Aug. 28.

▶**Sept. 15:** Jeff Fassero earned a victory in his first start for the Rangers, limiting the White Sox to two runs in five innings to win for the first time since July 5, when he was with the Mariners.

▶**Sept. 29:** Aaron Sele was making a bid to be the team's No. 1 starter in the playoffs, with 11 wins in 13 decisions since July 3. Overall he was 18-8 with a 4.64 ERA.

▶**Oct. 6:** Rick Helling pitched horribly down the stretch, not a good sign for the No. 2 starter. Helling was 2-4 with a 7.68 ERA in his final six outings, giving up 15 home runs in those six starts and a club-record 41 for the year.

QUOTE OF THE YEAR

"You don't see real justice in the All-Star voting."

—Right fielder Juan Gonzalez, on trailing three Indians outfielders, including David Justice, in the balloting

Team Leaders

Batting avg.

.332 Ivan Rodriguez
.326 Juan Gonzalez

HR

47 Rafael Palmeiro
39 Juan Gonzalez

RBI

148 Rafael Palmeiro
128 Juan Gonzalez

Hits

199 Ivan Rodriguez
183 Juan Gonzalez
183 Rafael Palmeiro

Runs

116 Ivan Rodriguez
114 Juan Gonzalez

Stolen bases

39 Tom Goodwin
25 Ivan Rodriguez

Wins

18 Aaron Sele
13 Mike Morgan
13 Rick Helling

Losses

14 Jeff Fassero
11 Rick Helling

ERA

4.79 Aaron Sele
4.84 Rick Helling

Strikeouts

186 Aaron Sele
131 Rick Helling

Innings

219.1 Rick Helling
205 Aaron Sele

Saves

43 John Wetteland
3 Jeff Zimmerman

TEXAS RANGERS 1999 final stats

BATTERS	BA	SLG	OBA	G	AB	R	H	TB	2B	3B	HR	RBI	BB	SO	SB	CS	E
Simms	.500	.500	.500	4	2	0	1	1	0	0	0	0	0	1	0	0	0
Rodriguez	.332	.558	.356	144	600	116	199	335	29	1	35	113	24	64	25	12	7
Gonzalez	.326	.601	.378	144	562	114	183	338	36	1	39	128	51	105	3	3	4
Palmeiro	.324	.630	.420	158	565	96	183	356	30	1	47	148	97	69	2	4	1
Green	.308	.308	.357	18	13	4	4	4	0	0	0	0	1	2	0	1	0
Greer	.300	.493	.405	147	556	107	167	274	41	3	20	101	96	67	2	2	5
Kelly	.300	.448	.355	87	290	41	87	130	17	1	8	37	21	57	6	1	3
Zeile	.293	.488	.354	156	588	80	172	287	41	1	24	98	56	94	1	2	25
Clayton	.288	.445	.346	133	465	69	134	207	21	5	14	52	39	100	8	6	25
Shave	.288	.342	.350	43	73	10	21	25	4	0	0	9	5	17	1	0	5
Stevens	.282	.485	.344	146	517	76	146	251	31	1	24	81	52	132	2	3	8
McLemore	.274	.366	.363	144	566	105	155	207	20	7	6	45	83	79	16	8	12
Goodwin	.259	.341	.324	109	405	63	105	138	12	6	3	33	40	61	39	11	3
Zaun	.247	.323	.314	43	93	12	23	30	2	1	1	12	10	7	1	0	3
Mateo	.238	.451	.268	32	122	16	29	55	9	1	5	18	4	28	3	0	0
Alicea	.201	.317	.316	68	164	33	33	52	10	0	3	17	28	32	2	1	5
Dransfeldt	.189	.264	.232	16	53	3	10	14	1	0	1	5	3	12	0	0	3
Sheldon	.000	.000	.000	2	1	0	0	0	0	0	0	0	0	0	0	0	0

PITCHERS	W-L	ERA	BA	G	GS	CG	GF	SH	SV	IP	H	R	ER	HR	BB	SO
Zimmerman	9-3	2.36	.166	65	0	0	14	0	3	87.2	50	24	23	9	23	67
Perisho	0-0	2.61	.211	4	1	0	3	0	0	10.1	8	3	3	0	2	17
Venafro	3-2	3.29	.251	65	0	0	11	0	0	68.1	63	29	25	4	22	37
Crabtree	5-1	3.46	.280	68	0	0	21	0	0	65.0	71	26	25	4	18	54
Wetteland	4-4	3.68	.262	62	0	0	59	0	43	66.0	67	30	27	9	19	60
Munoz	2-1	3.93	.263	56	0	0	11	0	1	52.2	52	24	23	5	18	27
Loaiza	9-5	4.56	.275	30	15	0	4	0	0	120.1	128	65	61	10	40	77
Kolb	2-1	4.65	.268	16	0	0	6	0	0	31.0	33	18	16	2	15	15
Sele	18-9	4.79	.293	33	33	2	0	2	0	205.0	244	115	109	21	70	186
Helling	13-11	4.84	.272	35	35	3	0	0	0	219.1	228	127	118	41	85	131
Burkett	9-8	5.62	.307	30	25	0	1	0	0	147.1	184	95	92	18	46	96
Patterson	2-0	5.67	.304	53	0	0	18	0	0	60.1	77	38	38	5	19	43
Morgan	13-10	6.24	.323	34	25	1	1	0	0	140.0	184	108	97	25	48	61
Fassero	5-14	7.20	.318	37	27	0	2	0	0	156.1	208	135	125	35	83	114
Gunderson	0-0	7.20	.417	11	0	0	3	0	0	10.0	20	8	8	1	2	6
Glynn	2-4	7.24	.316	13	10	0	2	0	0	54.2	71	46	44	10	35	39
Clark	3-7	8.60	.329	15	15	0	0	0	0	74.1	103	73	71	17	34	44
Johnson	0-0	15.00	.529	1	0	0	0	0	0	3.0	9	5	5	0	2	3
Lee	0-1	27.00	.400	1	0	0	1	0	0	1.0	2	3	3	1	1	0
Davis	0-0	33.75	.600	2	0	0	0	0	0	2.2	12	10	10	3	0	3

2000 preliminary roster

PITCHERS (22)
Joaquin Benoit
Mark Clark
Francisco Cordero
Tim Crabtree
Doug Davis
David Elder
Ryan Glynn
Rick Helling
Jonathan Johnson
Danny Kolb
Corey Lee
Esteban Loaiza
Juan Moreno
Mike Munoz
Matt Perisho
Kenny Rogers
Brian Sikorski
Chuck Smith
Justin Thompson
Mike Venafro
John Wetteland
Jeff Zimmerman

CATCHERS (3)
Bill Haselman
Cesar King
Ivan Rodriguez

INFIELDERS (9)
Luis Alicea
Frank Catalanotto
Royce Clayton
Kelly Dransfeldt
Jason Grabowski
Mike Lamb
Rafael Palmeiro
Scott Sheldon
Lee Stevens

OUTFIELDERS (6)
Chad Curtis
Scarborough Green
Rusty Greer
Gabe Kapler
Ruben Mateo
Mike Simms

Games played by position

PLAYER	G	C	1B	2B	3B	SS	OF	DH
Alicea	68	0	0	37	10	0	1	0
Clayton	133	0	0	0	0	133	0	0
Dransfeldt	16	0	0	0	0	16	0	0
Gonzalez	144	0	0	0	0	0	131	16
Goodwin	109	0	0	0	0	0	107	0
Green	18	0	0	0	0	0	9	4
Greer	147	0	0	0	0	0	145	1
Kelly	87	0	0	0	0	0	85	0
Mateo	32	0	0	0	0	0	31	0
McLemore	144	0	0	135	0	0	11	0
Palmeiro	158	0	28	0	0	0	0	135
Rodriguez	144	141	0	0	0	0	0	1
Shave	43	0	9	1	6	24	0	0
Sheldon	2	0	0	0	2	0	0	0
Simms	4	0	1	0	0	0	1	2
Stevens	146	0	133	0	0	0	0	8
Zaun	43	37	0	0	0	0	0	2
Zeile	156	0	1	0	155	0	0	1

Sick call: 1999 DL report

PLAYER	Days on the DL
John Burkett	18
Mark Clark	106
Royce Clayton	20
Tom Goodwin	54*
Eric Gunderson	149
Danny Kolb	15
Esteban Loaiza	54
Ruben Mateo	76*
Mike Morgan	15
Mike Simms	155

* Indicates two separate terms on Disabled List.

Minor Leagues
Tops in the organization

BATTER	CLUB	AVG.	G	AB	R	H	HR	RBI
Mench, Kevin	Sav	.357	71	283	67	101	18	68
Cadiente, Brett	PUL	.354	68	274	69	97	7	48
Valdes, Pedro	Ok	.329	121	428	75	141	22	76
Lamb, Mike	Ok	.324	139	546	98	177	21	100
Romano, Jason	Chr	.312	120	459	84	143	13	71

HOME RUNS
Hafner, Travis	Sav	28
Sheldon, Scott	Ok	28
Brumbaugh, Cliff	Ok	25
Valdes, Pedro	Ok	22
Lamb, Mike	Ok	21

WINS
Perisho, Matt	Ok		15
Lundberg, Dave	Chr		14
Kosderka, Matt	Sav		12
Several Players Tied at			11

RBI
Hafner, Travis	Sav	111
Pena, Carlos	Chr	103
Lamb, Mike	Ok	100
Sheldon, Scott	Ok	97
Brumbaugh, Cliff	Ok	90

SAVES
McDill, Allen	Ok		18
Miller, Matt	Tul		15
Sollecito, Gabe	Tul		11
Dickey, R.a.	Ok		10
Frey, Steve	Ok		9

STOLEN BASES
Monroe, Craig	Ok	40
Romano, Jason	Chr	34
Myers, Adrian	Tul	33
Guerrero, Pedro	PUL	30
Green, S.	Ok	26

STRIKEOUTS
Davis, Doug	Ok		153
Hughes, Travis	Sav		150
Perisho, Matt	Ok		150
Lee, Corey	Ok		146
McGill, Frankie	Sav		128

PITCHER	CLUB	W-L	ERA	IP	H	BB	SO
Sollecito, Gabe	Tul	5-4	2.43	96	85	29	80
Davis, Doug	Ok	11-4	2.72	152	142	56	153
Hughes, Travis	Sav	11-7	2.81	157	127	54	150
Lundberg, Dave	Chr	14-7	2.83	156	162	44	81
Silva, Doug	Chr	4-5	3.62	112	118	28	73

1999 salaries

	Bonuses	Total earned salary
Rafael Palmeiro, dh	150,000	8,849,931
Ivan Rodriguez, c	300,000	8,950,000
Juan Gonzalez, of		8,500,000
John Wetteland, p	50,000	6,350,000
Aaron Sele, p		5,525,000
Jeff Fassero, p		5,016,667
Royce Clayton, ss		4,500,000
John Burkett, p		4,000,000
Mark Clark, p		4,000,000
Rusty Greer, of		3,300,000
Tom Goodwin, of		3,225,000
Todd Zeile, 3b		3,200,000
Mark McLemore, 2b		2,400,000
Rick Helling, p		2,250,000
Roberto Kelly, of		2,225,000
Lee Stevens, 1b	100,000	2,100,000
Esteban Loaiza, p		1,475,000
Mike Morgan, p	300,000	900,000
Luis Alicea, 2b		825,000
Tim Crabtree, p		670,000
Mike Simms, of		625,000
Mike Munoz, p	65,000	515,000
Eric Gunderson, p		450,000
Gregg Zaun, c	25,000	450,000
Jon Shave, ss		200,000
Ruben Mateo, of		200,000
Danny Kolb, p		200,000
Mike Venafro, p		200,000
Jeff Zimmerman, p		200,000

Average 1999 salary: $2,803,503
Total 1999 team payroll: $81,301,598

Texas (1972-1999), includes Washington (1961-1971)

Runs: Most, career

791	JUAN GONZALEZ, 1989-1999
649	IVAN RODRIGUEZ, 1991-1999
631	Toby Harrah, 1969-1986
571	Ruben Sierra, 1986-1992
567	RAFAEL PALMEIRO, 1989-1999

Hits: Most, career

1421	JUAN GONZALEZ, 1989-1999
1333	IVAN RODRIGUEZ, 1991-1999
1180	Jim Sundberg, 1974-1989
1174	Toby Harrah, 1969-1986
1141	Frank Howard, 1965-1972

2B: Most, career

282	JUAN GONZALEZ, 1989-1999
261	IVAN RODRIGUEZ, 1991-1999
226	Ruben Sierra, 1986-1992
204	RAFAEL PALMEIRO, 1989-1999
200	Jim Sundberg, 1974-1989

3B: Most, career

43	Ruben Sierra, 1986-1992
30	Chuck Hinton, 1961-1964
27	Ed Brinkman, 1961-1975
27	Jim Sundberg, 1974-1989
24	Ed Stroud, 1967-1970

HR: Most, career

340	JUAN GONZALEZ, 1989-1999
246	Frank Howard, 1965-1972
154	RAFAEL PALMEIRO, 1989-1999
154	DEAN PALMER, 1989-1997
153	Ruben Sierra, 1986-1992

RBI: Most, career

1075	JUAN GONZALEZ, 1989-1999
701	Frank Howard, 1965-1972
656	Ruben Sierra, 1986-1992
621	IVAN RODRIGUEZ, 1991-1999
579	RAFAEL PALMEIRO, 1989-1999

SB: Most, career

161	Bump Wills, 1977-1981
153	Toby Harrah, 1969-1986
144	Dave Nelson, 1970-1975
129	Oddibe McDowell, 1985-1994
98	JULIO FRANCO, 1989-1993

BB: Most, career

708	Toby Harrah, 1969-1986
575	Frank Howard, 1965-1972
544	Jim Sundberg, 1974-1989
435	Mike Hargrove, 1974-1978
422	RUSTY GREER, 1994-1999

BA: Highest, career

.319	Al Oliver, 1978-1981
.309	RUSTY GREER, 1994-1999
.308	WILL CLARK, 1994-1998
.307	JULIO FRANCO, 1989-1993
.303	Mickey Rivers, 1979-1984

On-base avg: Highest, career

.399	Mike Hargrove, 1974-1978
.395	WILL CLARK, 1994-1998
.393	RUSTY GREER, 1994-1999
.382	JULIO FRANCO, 1989-1993
.375	RAFAEL PALMEIRO, 1989-1999

Slug pct: Highest, career

.572	JUAN GONZALEZ, 1989-1999
.503	Frank Howard, 1965-1972
.499	RAFAEL PALMEIRO, 1989-1999
.489	RUSTY GREER, 1994-1999
.485	WILL CLARK, 1994-1998

Games started: Most, career

313	Charlie Hough, 1980-1990
269	BOBBY WITT, 1986-1998
190	Fergie Jenkins, 1974-1981
186	KEVIN BROWN, 1986-1994
155	Dick Bosman, 1966-1973

Complete games: Most, career

98	Charlie Hough, 1980-1990
90	Fergie Jenkins, 1974-1981
55	Gaylord Perry, 1975-1980
40	KEVIN BROWN, 1986-1994
36	Joe Coleman, 1965-1970

Saves: Most, career

134	Jeff Russell, 1985-1996
116	JOHN WETTELAND, 1997-1999
83	Ron Kline, 1963-1966
64	Darold Knowles, 1967-1977
58	Tom Henke, 1982-1994

Shutouts: Most, career

17	Fergie Jenkins, 1974-1981
12	Gaylord Perry, 1975-1980
11	Charlie Hough, 1980-1990
9	Dick Bosman, 1966-1973
8	Jim Bibby, 1973-1984

Wins: Most, career

139	Charlie Hough, 1980-1990
104	BOBBY WITT, 1986-1998
93	Fergie Jenkins, 1974-1981
78	KEVIN BROWN, 1986-1994
70	KENNY ROGERS, 1989-1995

K: Most, career

1452	Charlie Hough, 1980-1990
1405	BOBBY WITT, 1986-1998
939	Nolan Ryan, 1989-1993
895	Fergie Jenkins, 1974-1981
742	KEVIN BROWN, 1986-1994

Win pct: Highest, career

.603	DARREN OLIVER, 1993-1998
.597	RICK HELLING, 1994-1999
.578	KENNY ROGERS, 1989-1995
.567	Nolan Ryan, 1989-1993
.564	Fergie Jenkins, 1974-1981

ERA: Lowest, career

3.26	Gaylord Perry, 1975-1980
3.35	Dick Bosman, 1966-1973
3.41	Jon Matlack, 1978-1983
3.43	Nolan Ryan, 1989-1993
3.51	Joe Coleman, 1965-1970

Runs: Most, season

124	RAFAEL PALMEIRO, 1993
116	IVAN RODRIGUEZ, 1996
116	IVAN RODRIGUEZ, 1999
115	RAFAEL PALMEIRO, 1991
114	JUAN GONZALEZ, 1999

Hits: Most, season

210	Mickey Rivers, 1980
209	Al Oliver, 1980
203	RAFAEL PALMEIRO, 1991
203	Ruben Sierra, 1991
201	JULIO FRANCO, 1991

2B: Most, season

50	JUAN GONZALEZ, 1998
49	RAFAEL PALMEIRO, 1991
47	IVAN RODRIGUEZ, 1996
44	Ruben Sierra, 1991
43	Al Oliver, 1980

3B: Most, season

14	Ruben Sierra, 1989
12	Chuck Hinton, 1963
10	David Hulse, 1993
10	Ruben Sierra, 1986
10	Ed Stroud, 1968

HR: Most, season

48	Frank Howard, 1969
47	JUAN GONZALEZ, 1996
47	RAFAEL PALMEIRO, 1999
46	JUAN GONZALEZ, 1993
45	JUAN GONZALEZ, 1998

RBI: Most, season

157	JUAN GONZALEZ, 1998
148	RAFAEL PALMEIRO, 1999
144	JUAN GONZALEZ, 1996
131	JUAN GONZALEZ, 1997
128	JUAN GONZALEZ, 1999

SB: Most, season

52	Bump Wills, 1978
51	Dave Nelson, 1972
50	OTIS NIXON, 1995
45	Cecil Espy, 1989
44	Bill Sample, 1983

BB: Most, season

132	Frank Howard, 1970
113	Toby Harrah, 1985
109	Toby Harrah, 1977
107	Mike Hargrove, 1978
107	Mickey Tettleton, 1995

BA: Highest, season

.341	JULIO FRANCO, 1991
.333	Mickey Rivers, 1980
.332	RUSTY GREER, 1996
.332	IVAN RODRIGUEZ, 1999
.329	WILL CLARK, 1994

On-base avg: Highest, season

.432	Toby Harrah, 1985
.431	WILL CLARK, 1994
.420	Mike Hargrove, 1977
.420	RAFAEL PALMEIRO, 1999
.416	Frank Howard, 1970

Slug pct: Highest, season

.643	JUAN GONZALEZ, 1996
.632	JUAN GONZALEZ, 1993
.630	JUAN GONZALEZ, 1998
.630	RAFAEL PALMEIRO, 1999
.601	JUAN GONZALEZ, 1999

Games started: Most, season

41	Jim Bibby, 1974
41	Fergie Jenkins, 1974
40	Charlie Hough, 1987
37	Fergie Jenkins, 1975
37	Fergie Jenkins, 1979

Complete games: Most, season

29	Fergie Jenkins, 1974
22	Fergie Jenkins, 1975
21	Gaylord Perry, 1976
18	Jon Matlack, 1978
17	Charlie Hough, 1984

Saves: Most, season

43	JOHN WETTELAND, 1999
42	JOHN WETTELAND, 1998
40	Tom Henke, 1993
38	Jeff Russell, 1989
31	Mike Henneman, 1996
31	JOHN WETTELAND, 1997

Shutouts: Most, season

6	Bert Blyleven, 1976
6	Fergie Jenkins, 1974
5	Jim Bibby, 1974
5	Bert Blyleven, 1977
4	Tom Cheney, 1963
4	Joe Coleman, 1969
4	Fergie Jenkins, 1975
4	Fergie Jenkins, 1978
4	Doc Medich, 1981
4	Camilo Pascual, 1968
4	Gaylord Perry, 1975
4	Gaylord Perry, 1977

Wins: Most, season

25	Fergie Jenkins, 1974
21	KEVIN BROWN, 1992
20	RICK HELLING, 1998
19	Jim Bibby, 1974
19	AARON SELE, 1998

K: Most, season

301	Nolan Ryan, 1989
232	Nolan Ryan, 1990
225	Fergie Jenkins, 1974
223	Charlie Hough, 1987
221	BOBBY WITT, 1990

Win pct: Highest, season

.741	RICK HELLING, 1998
.708	KENNY ROGERS, 1995
.692	Fergie Jenkins, 1978
.676	Fergie Jenkins, 1974
.667	AARON SELE, 1999

ERA: Lowest, season

2.19	Dick Bosman, 1969
2.27	Jon Matlack, 1978
2.40	Dick Donovan, 1961
2.42	Rick Honeycutt, 1983
2.60	Pete Richert, 1965

Most pinch-hit homers, season

3	Don Lock, 1966
3	Brant Alyea, 1969
3	Rick Reichardt, 1970
3	Tom McCraw, 1971
3	Rusty Staub, 1980
3	Darrell Porter, 1987

Most pinch-hit homers, career

6	Brant Alyea, 1965-1969
6	Geno Petralli, 1985-1993

Longest hitting streak

24	Mickey Rivers, 1980
22	Jim Sundberg, 1978
21	Johnny Grubb, 1979
21	Buddy Bell, 1980
21	Al Oliver, 1980
21	JUAN GONZALEZ, 1996

Most consecutive scoreless innings

36	Charlie Hough, 1983

No-hit games

Jim Bibby, Tex at Oak AL, 6-0; July 30, 1973.

Bert Blyleven, Tex at Cal AL, 6-0; September 22, 1977.

Nolan Ryan, Tex at Oak AL, 5-0; June 11, 1990.

Nolan Ryan, Tex vs Tor AL, 3-0; May 1, 1991.

KENNY ROGERS, Tex vs Cal AL, 4-0; July 28, 1994 (perfect game).

ACTIVE PLAYERS in caps.

Players' years of service are listed by the first and last years with this team and are not necessarily consecutive; all statistics record performances for this team only.

Oakland Athletics

By Barbara Jean Germano, Baseball Weekly

Heir to Mark McGwire's first-base throne, Jason Giambi is key to the A's offense and a team. leader.

1999 Athletics: Best home record

It lasted for one day in August. Yet it provided what the Oakland Athletics hope was a glimpse into their future. The A's flirted with the playoffs and put together their first winning season since 1992 while improving by 13 games over 1998. It was the biggest improvement in the American League. And on Aug. 22 the A's defeated the Toronto Blue Jays 4-3, while Boston lost, to move Oakland into sole possession of the AL wild-card playoff spot.

Within a week, the A's were trailing the Red Sox for good, but the A's showed that a young, low-budget team can compete for a postseason spot. With a $22.8 million opening-day payroll that ranked among the five lowest in the majors—and with a team sprinkled with rookies and second-year players—Oakland had the best home record in the AL (52-29) and posted the league's third-best ERA (4.69).

Because of the success, the A's gave general manager Billy Beane a three-year contract extension through the 2005 season.

"It was a successful season, a big step in the right direction," manager Art Howe said. "I think these guys have had about as much enjoyment in this season as they've had in any season."

One of those enjoying it the most was Randy Velarde, traded from the Angels to the A's along with pitcher Omar Olivares on July 29. Instead of selling off players before the trade deadline, as they had in recent seasons, the A's obtained several players as part of their playoff push. In addition to Velarde and Olivares, the A's got Kevin Appier from the Royals and Jason Isringhausen from the Mets. Isringhausen, who was part of the trade that sent Kenny Rogers and Billy Taylor to the New York Mets, converted all eight of his save chances for Oakland.

"Coming over here rekindled my spirit and made me excited to play every day," Velarde said.

Velarde was one of several A's to put together a stellar season. He hit .317 and became the sixth major league player with 200 hits in a season in which he played for two clubs.

Jason Giambi hit .315, had 33 homers and drove in 123 runs, one short of the Oakland record set by Jose Canseco in 1988. John Jaha, signed as a free agent last winter when other teams rejected him because of foot problems, made the All-Star team, had 35 homers and 111 RBI, and was named Comeback Player of the Year at the Players Choice Awards.

Matt Stairs led the team with 38 homers and had 102 RBI. Ben Grieve overcame a deep slump in the first half of the season to hit 28 homers and drive in 86 runs.

On the mound, Gil Heredia went 13-8 and was the only pitcher to throw 200 innings for the A's. Tim Hudson, who started the season in Double-A, went 11-2 with a 3.23 ERA. Isringhausen had a 2.13 ERA in 20 appearances and made himself a top candidate to become the closer the A's have been searching for since the departure of Dennis Eckersley.

While the A's improved significantly on the field, the situation deteriorated off the field. A deal was finally worked out to sell the team to local buyers who promised to keep the club in Oakland, but major league owners tabled that deal and left the franchise's future in limbo. And while attendance improved to 1.4 million from 1.2 million the previous season, it was still one of the worst home attendance marks in the majors.

1999 Athletics: Week-by-week notes

These notes were excerpted from the following issues of Baseball Weekly.

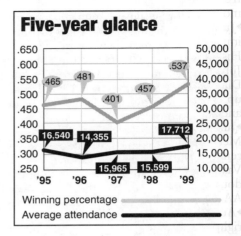

Five-year glance

Winning percentage
Average attendance

.465 .481 .401 .457 .537
16,540 14,355 15,965 15,599 17,712

'95 '96 '97 '98 '99

▶**April 7:** It appeared that left-hander Kenny Rogers would stay put for the time being. With Rogers eligible to be a free agent at the end of the year, however a trade at some point appeared likely.

▶**April 21:** In going 6-6, the A's relievers had been handed the lead six times and had allowed just one run in 14 innings. Overall, the bullpen ERA hadn't been that impressive—4.04—but 11 of the 17 runs given up by the pen have come in two blowout losses.

▶**April 28:** Manager Art Howe said he's thinking of "changing my middle name to Job" because of the patience required to manage the slumping young A's. Left fielder Ben Grieve and catcher A.J. Hinch were hitting well under .200 almost three weeks into the season.

▶**May 5:** Oakland's hitters floundered in the season's first month, standing as the major reason the A's were 11-15 through May 2. Oakland was hitting .246, dead last in the AL, with a .222 average with runners in scoring position.

▶**May 12:** Minor league journeyman Olmedo Saenz temporarily replaced Eric Chavez at third base. Saenz came into May 9 hitting .320 with two homers and 14 RBI. Chavez, the A's No. 1 draft pick in 1996, was hitting .253 with only four RBI.

▶**May 19:** City of Oakland and Alameda County politicians voted on May 10 to recommend a group headed by former A's executive Andy Dolich as its choice to buy the team. On the field the A's shook off slow starts by right-hander Tom Candiotti (2-4, 6.02) and Jimmy Haynes (1-5, 6.81) to post a 4.47 ERA, the third-best in the AL. Chiefly responsible were right-handers Gil Heredia and Mike Oquist, plus a bullpen that is the deepest in the AL West. Right-handed reliever T.J. Mathews had a great first six weeks. He's 5-0 with a 1.13 ERA, and hitters were averaging just .115 (6-for-52) against him.

▶**May 26:** Five days after moving into first place and six days after moving four games over .500, the A's were back under .500 and in third place in the West. After winning six straight games, the A's lost five in a row, including two extra-inning affairs in Minnesota.

▶**June 2:** The A's entered play on May 30 with the worst batting average in baseball and the worst defense in the AL. Yet the pitching had been exemplary, putting Oakland over .500 even after a season-worst six-game losing streak. Kenny Rogers ran off a streak of 20 scoreless innings and had a 1.04 May ERA after only a 5.59 mark in April.

▶**June 16:** Right-hander Tim Hudson, called up to replace Tom Candiotti (designated for assignment) in the rotation last week, made a powerful impression in his debut. He struck out 11 Padres, an A's record for a first game and only one strikeout shy of the AL debut record.

▶**June 30:** In the first 12 games of a season-longest 13-game road trip, the bullpen disintegrated in almost every way imaginable. They racked up five blown saves, four losses and a 5.40 ERA. They had 30 inherited baserunners, and the first hitters they faced went 13-for-23 with five walks, two sacrifice flies and 13 RBI. Offensively, DH John Jaha hit seven homers, Ben Grieve had six, and first baseman Jason Giambi hit five over the same stretch.

▶**July 7:** After getting off to a 5-0 start with a 1.08 ERA, T.J. Mathews was 1-3 with a 6.50 ERA in his last 18 games before going

on the DL on July 2 with right shoulder inflammation. Mathews had suffered from shoulder soreness for almost a month.

▶**July 15:** Tim Hudson had a stunning impact during his first month with the A's. His latest effort was 8⅔ shutout innings on July 10, beating Randy Johnson and the Diamondbacks in Phoenix. Hudson gave up just three hits and owns a 2.09 ERA and a 5-1 record in seven starts.

▶**July 28:** Kenny Rogers was traded to the Mets for minor league center fielder Terrence Long and lefty pitcher Leoner Vasquez. Long was hitting .326 with 20 doubles, four triples and seven homers for AAA Norfolk.

▶**Aug. 4:** On July 29 Oakland acquired right-hander Omar Olivares and second baseman Randy Velarde from Anaheim for three minor leaguers. Two days later, just two hours before the trading deadline, the A's picked up righty Kevin Appier from the Royals and right-handed relievers Jason Isringhausen and Greg McMichael from the Mets.

▶**Aug. 11:** After six years of finishing under .500, Oakland had its sights on the playoffs. Through Aug. 7, they had won eight of nine games. That sprint left Oakland seven games behind first-place Texas in the West, but only one game behind co-leaders Toronto and Boston in the AL wild-card race.

▶**Aug. 25:** Oakland was starting to push Tim Hudson for Rookie of the Year. At all levels—AA, AAA and the majors—his

record for the season was 15-1, with an 8-1 major league mark.

▶**Sept. 1:** Gil Heredia (11-5) had an eight-game winning streak and has not lost since dropping a 2-1 decision at San Diego on June 10. He had six no-decisions in that stretch, but he left most of those with leads.

▶**Sept. 15:** When Jason Giambi went deep in the first inning on Sept. 12, he gave Oakland three 30-homer players for just the second time. Right fielder Matt Stairs led the team with 34, and John Jaha had 32. For Stairs and Giambi the homer totals were career bests.

▶**Sept. 22:** The A's won their 82nd game on Sept. 19, guaranteeing the team its first winning season since 1992. One game under .500 at the All-Star break, the A's won 39 of 61 since then. Off the field, Major League Baseball scuttled the Dolich-Piccinini bid to buy the A's for $122.4 million. Owners voted 28-2 to table any vote on the proposed sale.

▶**Sept. 29:** Oakland was eliminated from the AL West race on Sept. 26 after losing to division-leading Texas, 10-3.

▶**Oct. 6:** The A's signed general manager Billy Beane to a three-year contract extension.

185

QUOTE OF THE YEAR

"My demotion really came out of left field."
—Center fielder Ryan Christenson, after going from A's starter to AAA Vancouver

Team Leaders

Batting avg.	Hits	Wins	Strikeouts
.317 Randy Velarde	200 Randy Velarde	16 Kevin Appier	132 Tim Hudson
.315 Jason Giambi	181 Jason Giambi	15 Omar Olivares	131 Kevin Appier

HR	Runs	Losses	Innings
38 Matt Stairs	115 Jason Giambi	14 Kevin Appier	209 Kevin Appier
35 John Jaha	105 Randy Velarde	12 Jimmy Haynes	205.2 Omar Olivares

RBI	Stolen bases	ERA	Saves
123 Jason Giambi	24 Randy Velarde	4.16 Omar Olivares	26 Billy Taylor
111 John Jaha	11 Tony Phillips	4.81 Gil Heredia	10 Doug Jones

OAKLAND ATHLETICS 1999 final stats

BATTERS	BA	SLG	OBA	G	AB	R	H	TB	2B	3B	HR	RBI	BB	SO	SB	CS	E
Velarde	.317	.455	.390	156	631	105	200	287	25	7	16	76	70	98	24	8	14
Giambi	.315	.553	.422	158	575	115	181	318	36	1	33	123	105	106	1	1	7
Hernandez	.279	.397	.363	40	136	13	38	54	7	0	3	21	18	11	1	0	6
Jaha	.276	.556	.414	142	457	93	126	254	23	0	35	111	101	129	2	0	0
Saenz	.275	.475	.363	97	255	41	70	121	18	0	11	41	22	47	1	1	8
Grieve	.265	.481	.358	148	486	80	129	234	21	0	28	86	63	108	4	0	3
Becker	.264	.312	.395	40	125	21	33	39	3	0	1	10	25	43	3	2	1
Stairs	.258	.533	.366	146	531	94	137	283	26	3	38	102	89	124	2	7	5
Tejada	.251	.427	.325	159	593	93	149	253	33	4	21	84	57	94	8	7	21
Chavez	.247	.427	.333	115	356	47	88	152	21	2	13	50	46	56	1	1	9
Phillips	.244	.433	.362	106	406	76	99	176	24	4	15	49	71	94	11	3	13
Macfarlane	.243	.372	.282	81	226	24	55	84	17	0	4	31	13	52	0	0	1
Spiezio	.243	.437	.324	89	247	31	60	108	24	0	8	33	29	36	0	0	7
Menechino	.222	.222	.222	9	9	0	2	2	0	0	0	0	0	4	0	0	0
Raines	.215	.341	.337	58	135	20	29	46	5	0	4	17	26	17	4	1	0
Hinch	.215	.346	.260	76	205	26	44	71	4	1	7	24	11	41	6	2	5
Christenson	.209	.306	.305	106	268	41	56	82	12	1	4	24	38	58	7	5	7
McDonald	.209	.278	.310	100	187	26	39	52	2	1	3	8	25	48	6	3	1
Velandia	.188	.208	.235	63	48	4	9	10	1	0	0	2	2	13	2	0	3

PITCHERS	W-L	ERA	BA	G	GS	CG	GF	SH	SV	IP	H	R	ER	HR	BB	SO
Mahay	2-0	1.86	.123	6	1	0	2	0	1	19.1	8	4	4	2	3	15
Isringhausen	0-1	2.13	.223	20	0	0	18	0	8	25.1	21	6	6	2	12	20
Hudson	11-2	3.23	.237	21	21	1	0	0	0	136.1	121	56	49	8	62	132
Jones	5-5	3.55	.267	70	0	0	35	0	10	104.0	106	43	41	10	24	63
Mathews	9-5	3.81	.215	50	0	0	15	0	3	59.0	46	28	25	9	20	42
Taylor	1-5	3.98	.287	43	0	0	38	0	26	43.0	48	23	19	3	14	38
Worrell	2-2	4.15	.256	53	0	0	17	0	0	69.1	69	38	32	6	34	62
Olivares	15-11	4.16	.276	32	32	4	0	0	0	205.2	217	105	95	19	81	85
Rogers	5-3	4.30	.288	19	19	3	0	0	0	119.1	135	66	57	8	41	68
Heredia	13-8	4.81	.283	33	33	1	0	0	0	200.1	228	119	107	22	34	117
Groom	3-2	5.09	.274	76	0	0	6	0	0	46.0	48	29	26	1	18	32
Appier	16-14	5.17	.279	34	34	1	0	0	0	209.0	230	131	120	27	84	131
Oquist	9-10	5.37	.283	28	24	0	1	0	0	140.2	158	86	84	18	64	89
McMichael	0-0	5.40	.283	17	0	0	4	0	0	15.0	15	9	9	3	12	3
Vizcaino	0-0	5.40	.231	1	0	0	1	0	0	3.1	3	2	2	1	3	2
Kubinski	0-0	5.84	.280	14	0	0	4	0	0	12.1	14	8	8	3	5	7
Haynes	7-12	6.34	.282	30	25	0	2	0	0	142.0	158	112	100	21	80	93
Harville	0-2	6.91	.310	15	0	0	8	0	0	14.1	18	11	11	2	10	15
Laxton	0-1	7.45	.316	3	2	0	0	0	0	9.2	12	12	8	1	7	9
Jarvis	0-1	11.57	.418	4	1	0	0	0	0	14.0	28	19	18	6	6	11

2000 preliminary roster

PITCHERS (18)
Kevin Appier
Eric DuBose
Chris Enochs
Kevin Gregg
Chad Harville
Gil Heredia
Tim Hudson
Jason Isringhausen
Doug Jones
Tim Kubinski
Brett Laxton
Mike Magnante

Ron Mahay
T.J. Mathews
Justin Miller
Ariel Prieto
Leoner Vasquez
Luis Vizcaino

CATCHERS (3)
Danny Ardoin
Ramon Hernandez
A.J. Hinch

INFIELDERS (12)
Eric Chavez
Josue Espada
Jason Giambi
John Jaha
Frank Menechino
Jose Ortiz
Adam Piatt
Olmedo Saenz
Scott Spiezio
Miguel Tejada
Jorge Velandia
Randy Velarde

OUTFIELDERS (7)
Rich Becker
Ryan Christenson
Mario Encarnacion
Ben Grieve
Terrence Long
Bo Porter
Matt Stairs

Games played by position

PLAYER	G	C	1B	2B	3B	SS	OF	DH
Becker	40	0	0	0	0	0	39	0
Chavez	115	0	0	0	105	2	0	3
Christenson	106	0	0	0	0	0	104	1
Giambi	158	0	142	0	1	0	0	15
Grieve	148	0	0	0	0	0	137	4
Hernandez	40	40	0	0	0	0	0	0
Hinch	76	73	0	0	0	0	0	0
Jaha	142	0	8	0	0	0	0	130
Macfarlane	81	79	0	0	0	0	0	1
McDonald	100	0	0	1	0	0	89	5
Menechino	9	0	0	0	1	5	0	0
Phillips	106	0	0	66	2	1	62	0
Raines	58	0	0	0	0	0	38	3
Saenz	97	0	28	0	56	0	0	8
Spiezio	89	0	10	42	31	0	0	0
Stairs	146	0	1	0	0	0	139	5
Tejada	159	0	0	0	0	159	0	1
Velandia	63	0	0	52	2	8	0	0
Velarde	61	0	0	61	0	0	0	0

Sick call: 1999 DL report

PLAYER	Days on the DL
Eric Chavez	29
Ramon Hernandez	32
Kevin Jarvis	46
Mike Macfarlane	15
T.J. Mathews	23
Tony Phillips	49
Ariel Prieto	182
Tim Raines	77
Olmedo Saenz	21
Eric Stuckenschneider	79
Jorge Velandia	58
Tim Worrell	19

Minor Leagues

Tops in the organization

BATTER	CLUB	AVG.	G	AB	R	H	HR	RBI
DaVanon, Jeff	Mid	.342	100	374	87	128	11	60
Piatt, Adam	Van	.340	135	494	129	168	39	138
Espada, Josue	Van	.336	119	461	87	155	6	51
Thomas, Gary	Mod	.323	99	344	69	111	7	38
Keith, Rusty	Vis	.313	124	448	87	140	10	62

HOME RUNS

Piatt, Adam	Van	39
Mensik, Todd	Vis	29
Landry, Jacques	Mod	27
Marcinczyk, T.R.	Mid	23
Several Players Tied at		21

WINS

Laxton, Brett	Van	13
Seaver, Mark	Mod	12
Several Players Tied at		10

RBI

Piatt, Adam	Van	138
Mensik, Todd	Vis	123
Hart, Jason	Mod	123
Marcinczyk, T.R.	Mid	111
Landry, Jacques	Mod	111

SAVES

Brink, Jim	Mod	29
Snow, Bert	Van	18
Harville, Chad	Van	18
Chavez, Anthony	Van	14
Several Players Tied at		11

STOLEN BASES

Rosario, Carlos	SOr	42
German, Esteban	Mod	40
Wenner, Michael	Ath	36
Byrnes, Eric	Mod	34
Garland, Tim	Mid	28

STRIKEOUTS

Colome, Jesus	Mod	127
Snow, Bert	Van	125
Jones, Marcus	Van	123
Gregg, Kevin	Van	118
Several Players Tied at		112

PITCHER	CLUB	W-L	ERA	IP	H	BB	SO
Nina, Elvin	Mid	8-4	2.87	103	95	59	92
Jarvis, Kevin	Van	10-2	3.27	110	114	27	74
Colome, Jesus	Mod	8-4	3.36	129	125	60	127
Laxton, Brett	Van	13-8	3.46	161	158	49	112
King, Bill	Van	9-6	3.49	98	105	22	60

1999 salaries

	Bonuses	Total earned salary
Kevin Appier, p		4,800,000
Jason Giambi, 1b		2,103,333
Greg McMichael, p		1,950,000
Matt Stairs, of		1,950,000
Omar Olivares, p	225,000	1,825,000
Randy Velarde, 2b	800,000	1,600,000
Tim Worrell, p	100,000	900,000
Buddy Groom, p		850,000
T.J. Mathews, p		750,000
Tony Phillips, 2b		700,000
Tim Raines, of		600,000
Mike Macfarlane, c		600,000
John Jaha, dh	125,000	525,000
Rich Becker, of		475,000
Jason Isringhausen, p	125,000	475,000
Mike Oquist, p		450,000
Gil Heredia, p	75,000	450,000
Doug Jones, p		400,000
Ben Grieve, of		300,000
Jimmy Haynes, p		280,000
Scott Spiezio, 2b		260,000
Olmedo Saenz, 3b	20,000	240,000
Miguel Tejada, ss		230,000
Jason McDonald, of		222,500
Ariel Prieto, p		210,000
Ryan Christenson, of		202,500
Jorge Velandia, 2b		201,000
Eric Chavez, 3b		201,000
Ramon Hernandez, c		200,000
Tim Hudson, p		200,000

Average 1999 salary: $805,011
Total 1999 team payroll: $24,150,333
Termination pay: $1,058,525

Oakland (1968-1999), includes Philadelphia (1901-1954) and Kansas City (1955-1967)

Runs: Most, career

1270	RICKEY HENDERSON, 1979-1998	
997	Bob Johnson, 1933-1942	
983	Bert Campaneris, 1964-1976	
975	Jimmie Foxx, 1925-1935	
969	Al Simmons, 1924-1944	

Hits: Most, career

1882 Bert Campaneris, 1964-1976
1827 Al Simmons, 1924-1944
1768 RICKEY HENDERSON, 1979-1998
1705 Jimmy Dykes, 1918-1932
1617 Bob Johnson, 1933-1942

2B: Most, career

365 Jimmy Dykes, 1918-1932
348 Al Simmons, 1924-1944
319 Harry Davis, 1901-1917
307 Bob Johnson, 1933-1942
292 Bing Miller, 1922-1934
289 RICKEY HENDERSON, 1979-1998 (6)

3B: Most, career

102 Danny Murphy, 1902-1913
98 Al Simmons, 1924-1944
88 Frank Baker, 1908-1914
85 Eddie Collins, 1906-1930
82 Harry Davis, 1901-1917
70 Bert Campaneris, 1964-1976 (12)

HR: Most, career

363 MARK McGWIRE, 1986-1997
302 Jimmie Foxx, 1925-1935
269 Reggie Jackson, 1967-1987
254 JOSE CANSECO, 1985-1997
252 Bob Johnson, 1933-1942

RBI: Most, career

1178 Al Simmons, 1924-1944
1075 Jimmie Foxx, 1925-1935
1040 Bob Johnson, 1933-1942
941 MARK McGWIRE, 1986-1997
796 Sal Bando, 1966-1976

SB: Most, career

867 RICKEY HENDERSON, 1979-1998
566 Bert Campaneris, 1964-1976
377 Eddie Collins, 1906-1930
232 Billy North, 1973-1978
223 Harry Davis, 1901-1917

BB: Most, career

1227 RICKEY HENDERSON, 1979-1998

1043 Max Bishop, 1924-1933
853 Bob Johnson, 1933-1942
847 MARK McGWIRE, 1986-1997
820 Elmer Valo, 1940-1956

BA: Highest, career

.356 Al Simmons, 1924-1944
.339 Jimmie Foxx, 1925-1935
.337 Eddie Collins, 1906-1930
.321 Mickey Cochrane, 1925-1933
.296 JASON GIAMBI, 1995-1999 (17)

On-base avg: Highest, career

.440 Jimmie Foxx, 1925-1935
.426 Ferris Fain, 1947-1952
.423 Eddie Collins, 1906-1930
.423 Max Bishop, 1924-1933
.409 RICKEY HENDERSON, 1979-1998 (6)

Slug pct: Highest, career

.640 Jimmie Foxx, 1925-1935
.584 Al Simmons, 1924-1944
.551 MARK McGWIRE, 1986-1997
.520 Bob Johnson, 1933-1942
.507 JOSE CANSECO, 1985-1997

Games started: Most, career

458 Eddie Plank, 1901-1914
340 Catfish Hunter, 1965-1974
288 Chief Bender, 1903-1914
267 Lefty Grove, 1925-1933
266 Rube Walberg, 1923-1933

Complete games: Most, career

362 Eddie Plank, 1901-1914
228 Chief Bender, 1903-1914
179 Lefty Grove, 1925-1933
168 Rube Waddell, 1902-1907
147 Eddie Rommel, 1920-1932
116 Catfish Hunter, 1965-1974 (8)

Saves: Most, career

320 Dennis Eckersley, 1987-1995
136 Rollie Fingers, 1968-1976
100 BILLY TAYLOR, 1994-1999
73 John Wyatt, 1961-1969
61 Jay Howell, 1985-1987

Shutouts: Most, career

59 Eddie Plank, 1901-1914
37 Rube Waddell, 1902-1907
36 Chief Bender, 1903-1914
31 Catfish Hunter, 1965-1974
28 Vida Blue, 1969-1977
28 Jack Coombs, 1906-1914

Wins: Most, career

284 Eddie Plank, 1901-1914
195 Lefty Grove, 1925-1933
193 Chief Bender, 1903-1914
171 Eddie Rommel, 1920-1932
161 Catfish Hunter, 1965-1974

K: Most, career

1985 Eddie Plank, 1901-1914
1576 Rube Waddell, 1902-1907
1536 Chief Bender, 1903-1914
1523 Lefty Grove, 1925-1933
1520 Catfish Hunter, 1965-1974

Win pct: Highest, career

.712 Lefty Grove, 1925-1933
.654 Chief Bender, 1903-1914
.637 Eddie Plank, 1901-1914
.632 Jack Coombs, 1906-1914
.628 George Earnshaw, 1928-1933
.615 Bob Welch, 1988-1994 (6)

ERA: Lowest, career

1.97 Rube Waddell, 1902-1907
2.15 Cy Morgan, 1909-1912
2.32 Chief Bender, 1903-1914
2.39 Eddie Plank, 1901-1914
2.60 Jack Coombs, 1906-1914
2.91 Rollie Fingers, 1968-1976 (8)

Runs: Most, season

152 Al Simmons, 1930
151 Jimmie Foxx, 1932
145 Nap Lajoie, 1901
144 Al Simmons, 1932
137 Eddie Collins, 1912
123 Reggie Jackson, 1969 (10)

Hits: Most, season

253 Al Simmons, 1925
232 Nap Lajoie, 1901
216 Al Simmons, 1932
214 Doc Cramer, 1935
213 Jimmie Foxx, 1932
187 JOSE CANSECO, 1988 (*)

2B: Most, season

53 Al Simmons, 1926
48 Nap Lajoie, 1901
48 Wally Moses, 1937
47 Harry Davis, 1905
47 Eric McNair, 1932
41 JASON GIAMBI, 1997 (15)

3B: Most, season

21 Frank Baker, 1912
19 Frank Baker, 1909
18 Danny Murphy, 1910

17	Danny Murphy, 1904
16	Bing Miller, 1929
16	Al Simmons, 1930
16	Amos Strunk, 1915

HR: Most, season

58	Jimmie Foxx, 1932
52	MARK McGWIRE, 1996
49	MARK McGWIRE, 1987
48	Jimmie Foxx, 1933
47	Reggie Jackson, 1969

RBI: Most, season

169	Jimmie Foxx, 1932
165	Al Simmons, 1930
163	Jimmie Foxx, 1933
157	Al Simmons, 1929
156	Jimmie Foxx, 1930
124	JOSE CANSECO, 1988 (13)

SB: Most, season

130	RICKEY HENDERSON, 1982
108	RICKEY HENDERSON, 1983
100	RICKEY HENDERSON, 1980
81	Eddie Collins, 1910
75	Billy North, 1976

BB: Most, season

149	Eddie Joost, 1949
136	Ferris Fain, 1949
133	Ferris Fain, 1950
128	Max Bishop, 1929
128	Max Bishop, 1930
118	Sal Bando, 1970 (10)

BA: Highest, season

.426	Nap Lajoie, 1901
.390	Al Simmons, 1931
.387	Al Simmons, 1925
.381	Al Simmons, 1930
.365	Eddie Collins, 1911
.325	RICKEY HENDERSON, 1990 (*)

On-base avg: Highest, season

.469	Jimmie Foxx, 1932
.467	MARK McGWIRE, 1996
.463	Jimmie Foxx, 1929
.463	Nap Lajoie, 1901
.461	Jimmie Foxx, 1935

Slug pct: Highest, season

.749	Jimmie Foxx, 1932
.730	MARK McGWIRE, 1996
.708	Al Simmons, 1930
.703	Jimmie Foxx, 1933
.653	Jimmie Foxx, 1934

Games started: Most, season

46	Rube Waddell, 1904
43	Eddie Plank, 1904
41	Catfish Hunter, 1974
41	Eddie Plank, 1905

Complete games: Most, season

39	Rube Waddell, 1904
37	Eddie Plank, 1904
35	Jack Coombs, 1910
35	Chick Fraser, 1901
35	Eddie Plank, 1905

Saves: Most, season

51	Dennis Eckersley, 1992
48	Dennis Eckersley, 1990
45	Dennis Eckersley, 1988
43	Dennis Eckersley, 1991
36	Bill Caudill, 1984
36	Dennis Eckersley, 1993

Shutouts: Most, season

13	Jack Coombs, 1910
8	Vida Blue, 1971
8	Joe Bush, 1916
8	Eddie Plank, 1907
8	Rube Waddell, 1904
8	Rube Waddell, 1906

Wins: Most, season

31	Jack Coombs, 1910
31	Lefty Grove, 1931
28	Jack Coombs, 1911
28	Lefty Grove, 1930
27	Eddie Rommel, 1922
27	Rube Waddell, 1905
27	Bob Welch, 1990

K: Most, season

349	Rube Waddell, 1904
302	Rube Waddell, 1903
301	Vida Blue, 1971
287	Rube Waddell, 1905
232	Rube Waddell, 1907

Win pct: Highest, season

.886	Lefty Grove, 1931
.850	Chief Bender, 1914
.849	Lefty Grove, 1930
.821	Chief Bender, 1910
.818	Bob Welch, 1990

ERA: Lowest, season

1.30	Jack Coombs, 1910
1.39	Harry Krause, 1909
1.48	Rube Waddell, 1905
1.55	Cy Morgan, 1910
1.58	Chief Bender, 1910

Most pinch-hit homers, season

4	Jeff Burroughs, 1982
3	Allie Clark, 1952
3	Kite Thomas, 1952
3	Bob Cerv, 1957
3	Frank Fernandez, 1970
3	Rich McKinney, 1977

Most pinch-hit homers, career

5	Mike Aldrete, 1993-1995

5	Jeff Burroughs, 1982-1984
5	Gus Zernial, Phi-KC-1951-1957

Longest hitting streak

29	Billy Lamar, 1925
28	Bing Miller, 1929
27	Socks Seybold,1901
27	Al Simmons, 1931
26	Bob Johnson, 1938

Most consecutive scoreless innings

53	Jack Coombs, 1910
43	Rube Waddell, 1905
37	Mike Torrez, 1976

No-hit games

Weldon Henley, Phi at StL AL, 6-0; July 22, 1905 (1st game).

Rube Waddell, five innings, rain, Phi vs StL AL, 2-0; August 15, 1905.

Jimmy Dygert (three innings) and Rube Waddell (two innings), five innings, rain, Phi vs Chi AL, 4-3; August 29, 1906. (Waddell allowed hit and two runs in sixth, but rain caused game to revert to five innings).

Rube Vickers, five perfect innings, darkness, Phi at Was AL, 4-0; October 5, 1907 (2nd game).

Chief Bender, Phi vs Cle AL, 4-0; May 12, 1910.

Joe Bush, Phi vs Cle AL, 5-0; August 26, 1916.

Dick Fowler, Phi vs StL AL, 1-0; September 9, 1945 (2nd game).

Bill McCahan, Phi vs Was AL, 3-0; September 3, 1947.

Catfish Hunter, Oak vs Min AL, 4-0; May 8, 1968 (perfect game).

Vida Blue, Oak vs Min AL, 6-0; September 21, 1970.

Vida Blue (five innings), Glenn Abbott (one inning), Paul Lindblad (one inning) and Rollie Fingers (two innings), Oak vs Cal AL, 5-0; September 28, 1975.

Mike Warren, Oak vs Chi AL, 3-0; September 29, 1983.

Dave Stewart, Oak at Tor AL, 5-0; June 29, 1990.

ACTIVE PLAYERS in caps.
Players' years of service are listed by the first and last years with this team and are not necessarily consecutive; all statistics record performances for this team only.

Leader from the franchise's current location is included. If not in the top five, leader's rank is listed in parentheses; asterisk (*) indicates player is not in top 25.

Seattle Mariners

By Neil Seiler, USA TODAY

Designated hitter Edgar Martinez was the most productive hitter for the Mariners in 1999.

1999 Mariners: New scenery didn't help

After their second straight disappointing season, the Mariners have decided that they're going to try to contend again. But the decision wasn't going to include Ken Griffey Jr. and Alex Rodriguez in Seattle.

Shortly after Pat Gillick became the general manager in October, he said he would honor Griffey's wish to be traded somewhere closer to his family's Florida home. Rodriguez and his agent, Scott Boras, said A-Rod would opt for free agency after 2000 whether or not he was traded.

"It's a sad day for me personally," the 24-year-old Rodriguez said on the final day of the season. "I came here as a young man and left as a grown man."

"You can't allow talent like that to walk away," manager Lou Piniella said. "It would set this organization back many, many years."

For the second year in a row, the Mariners failed on the field, finishing third in the AL West and under .500 at 79-83. A year after they traded Randy Johnson rather than risk losing him on the open market, the Mariners never even threatened Texas in the AL West, finishing 16 games back.

Facing cost overruns of $100 million at $517.6 million Safeco Field, the Mariners signed just one player, left-hander Jamie Moyer, during the season. Moyer won 14 games, but is 37 years old.

The new ballpark gave the Mariners other reasons to make changes as well. Players feel it is more of a pitcher's park than the Kingdome. The Mariners hit 75 home runs and .297 in 39 games at the Kingdome, but they had just 47 homers and hit .249 in 42 games after they moved to Safeco during the All-Star break. The team ERA was 6.67 in the Kingdome and 4.03 at Safeco.

But the move didn't hurt Griffey or Rodriguez in the power department. At the Kingdome, Griffey had 13 homers and Rodriguez seven. After the move to Safeco, Griffey had 14 homers at home and Rodriguez 13. Griffey won his third

Team MVP

Edgar Martinez: Who's better, the question in Seattle usually goes, Ken Griffey Jr. or Alex Rodriguez? Tote up their slugging percentages and on-base averages, a way to measure all-around achievement, and you'll likely be surprised—the answer is designated hitter Edgar Martinez. The former batting champ hit .337 and topped 1.000 in on-base plus slugging.

straight AL home-run title with 48, fourth in the majors, giving him 398 during 11 seasons in Seattle. Rodriguez matched his own career high with 42 homers even though he missed five weeks early in the season because of knee surgery.

Winners of their division in 1995 and 1997, the Mariners started out with a $53 million payroll. By season's end, they had traded away David Segui and Butch Huskey and had trimmed their active-player payroll to $40 million.

In September, Woody Woodward decided to retire after 11 seasons as general manager. The Mariners made a change at the top, as well, with Howard Lincoln replacing John Ellis as the chairman and chief executive officer. Lincoln announced that the Mariners had made offers to Griffey and Rodriguez that would make them the highest-paid players in baseball, but he didn't detail the offers. He also said he would boost the payroll to between $65 million and $75 million.

The Mariners did develop some outstanding young pitching during the season. Rookies Freddy Garcia and John Halama, who came over in the Johnson trade, won 17 and 11 games, respectively. Another rookie, Gil Meche, started the season in the minors and was 8-4 after being called up by the Mariners. Meche, 21, was 4-0 with a 3.19 ERA in September.

1999 Mariners: Week-by-week notes

These notes were excerpted from the following issues of Baseball Weekly.

►**April 7:** Two days before their first game, the Mariners finally unloaded reliever Bobby Ayala, shipping the right-hander to Montreal for 6-10 Class A right-hander Jimmy Turman. His departure left the Mariners with no relievers who pitched 25 innings in the bullpen last year, when Seattle had the worst relief corps in the AL.

►**April 14:** After undergoing surgery last week to repair torn cartilage in his left knee, Alex Rodriguez was uncertain how close he would be to the player who hit 42 homers and stole 46 bases last year. The Mariners expected their shortstop to miss at least a month. In his absence, rookie Carlos Guillen was to shift from second to shortstop and David Bell was to start at second. But Guillen was knocked out for the year on April 10 during a rundown play involving Oakland's Tony Phillips, injuring Guillen's anterior cruciate ligament.

►**April 28:** Seattle was getting minimal production from the top of its order in the absence of Carlos Guillen and Alex Rodriguez, so manager Lou Piniella penciled in shortstop Domingo Cedeno, outfielder Matt Mieske (whose leadoff chance was rained out in Chicago) and first baseman David Segui at the top of the lineup last week. Segui's leadoff appearance was the first of his 10-year career, and he marked the occasion with a three-run homer and two singles against Tampa Bay.

►**May 12:** Closer Jose Mesa got a measure of satisfaction by recording a save in his first outing against Cleveland, his old team. Jacobs Field fans booed him fiercely as he warmed up in the ninth inning on May 5, but Mesa delivered on his seventh save in as many opportunities.

►**May 19:** Alex Rodriguez returned to the lineup on May 14 and homered in his first at-bat. Rodriguez, who missed five weeks after surgery to repair torn cartilage in his left knee, figured he'd need about two weeks to regain confidence in his knee and be back to full strength.

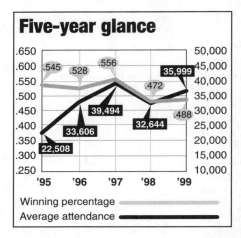

Five-year glance

.650 / .600 / .550 / .500 / .450 / .400 / .350 / .300 / .250

.545 / .528 / .556 / .472

35,999 / 39,494 / 33,606 / 32,644 / 22,508 / 488

50,000 / 45,000 / 40,000 / 35,000 / 30,000 / 25,000 / 20,000 / 15,000 / 10,000

'95 '96 '97 '98 '99

Winning percentage
Average attendance

►**June 2:** All Ken Griffey Jr. needed was a visit with dad. Since stopping by Cincinnati to see Ken Griffey Sr. on an off-day, May 4, the center fielder was virtually unstoppable, with a career-best 16-game hitting streak in which he batted .429 (27-for-63) with eight home runs and 21 RBI.

►**June 9:** When right fielder Jay Buhner went down with a hamstring injury in mid-May, Butch Huskey became a regular. He became a big contributor, batting .393 over 15 games with 20 RBI. Huskey has nine homers this year. The Mariners tied the major league record for homers in a month when they bashed 58 in May, the same as the Orioles hit in May 1987.

►**June 16:** Ken Griffey Jr. homered three times in Colorado, including a 478-foot blast off the facing of the third deck. The homers were his first in Colorado, giving him homers in every current park in which he had played.

►**June 23:** Left-hander Jeff Fassero, who had struggled since spring training, was shifted to the bullpen after a rough outing on June 14 in Detroit. In 15 starts Fassero was 3-7 with a 7.23 ERA and had allowed a major-league-high 25 home runs.

►**June 30:** The Mariners' struggling bullpen had an ERA about three runs higher than that of the division-leading Rangers. In back-to-back games last week, the Angels and the Rangers scored

20 runs off Seattle relievers in seven innings, earning come-from-behind victories in both.

▶**July 21:** Early returns confirmed suspicions that Safeco Field would be a pitchers' park. Only eight runs were scored in the first two games, and players were convinced several flyouts would have been home runs at the Kingdome.

▶**Aug. 4:** The Mariners dealt veteran talent at the deadline for the second year in a row. The club sent Butch Huskey to Boston for AAA left-hander Robert Ramsay, then shipped David Segui to Toronto for AAA right-hander Tom Davey and left-hander Steve Sinclair.

▶**Aug. 11:** Before struggling against the Yankees, the Mariners won their first five games of a 13-game homestand at Safeco. In those five games Seattle starters had a 1.60 ERA.

▶**Aug. 18:** Right-hander Todd Williams became the Mariners' 26th pitcher of the season when he made his debut, establishing a club record for pitchers used in one season. That record threatened the major league mark of 29 set by the 1996 Angels.

▶**Aug. 25:** Lefty Jamie Moyer had been solid in the rotation's No. 1 spot, and right-hander Freddy Garcia, 22, had held up well as a rookie. Rookie southpaw John Halama and right-hander Gil Meche had also been effective. On the other hand, Jeff Fassero almost certainly was history. The opening day starter, Fassero was shifted to the bullpen in early August but struggled there. He allowed nine earned runs in his first six relief innings, and his record was 4-14.

▶**Sept. 8:** Jamie Moyer had been one of the most dependable starters in baseball in the second half. After beating the Red Sox with a complete-game 2-1 victory on Sept. 3, Moyer was 5-1 with a 2.28 ERA since the All-Star break.

▶**Sept. 22:** Woody Woodward announced his retirement on Sept. 17 after more than a decade on the job. Woodward had the longest tenure of any active general manager, and he said he was worn out. The next Mariners GM would face the dual free agency of Ken Griffey Jr. and Alex Rodriguez after next season, plus this winter's free agency of DH Edgar Martinez.

▶**Oct. 6:** Insiders expected the Mariners' new chairman and CEO, Howard Lincoln, to be more hands-on than his predecessor, John Ellis. Lincoln announced that the Mariners will raise their payroll by 30 percent next season, to between $65 million and $70 million.

QUOTE OF THE YEAR

"We've had trouble finding ten good ones, so I don't know where we'll find an eleventh."
—Manager Lou Piniella, on the Mariners' search for pitchers

Team Leaders

Batting avg.	Hits	Wins	Strikeouts
.337 Edgar Martinez	173 Ken Griffey	17 Freddy Garcia	170 Freddy Garcia
.285 Ken Griffey	169 Edgar Martinez	14 Jamie Moyer	137 Jamie Moyer

HR	Runs	Losses	Innings
48 Ken Griffey	123 Ken Griffey	11 Jose Paniagua	228 Jamie Moyer
42 Alex Rodriguez	110 Alex Rodriguez	10 John Halama	201.1 Freddy Garcia

RBI	Stolen bases	ERA	Saves
134 Ken Griffey	44 Brian Hunter	3.87 Jamie Moyer	33 Jose Mesa
111 Alex Rodriguez	24 Ken Griffey	4.07 Freddy Garcia	3 Jose Paniagua
			3 Frankie Rodriguez

SEATTLE MARINERS 1999 final stats

BATTERS	BA	SLG	OBA	G	AB	R	H	TB	2B	3B	HR	RBI	BB	SO	SB	CS	E
Mieske	.366	.659	.395	24	41	11	15	27	0	0	4	7	2	9	0	0	0
Martinez	.337	.554	.447	142	502	86	169	278	35	1	24	86	97	99	7	2	0
Lampkin	.291	.495	.345	76	206	29	60	102	11	2	9	34	13	32	1	3	5
Griffey	.285	.576	.384	160	606	123	173	349	26	3	48	134	91	108	24	7	9
A. Rodriguez	.285	.586	.357	129	502	110	143	294	25	0	42	111	56	109	21	7	14
Bournigal	.274	.389	.317	55	95	16	26	37	5	0	2	14	7	6	0	0	3
Bell	.268	.432	.331	157	597	92	160	258	31	2	21	78	58	90	7	4	17
Wilson	.266	.382	.315	123	414	46	110	158	23	2	7	38	29	83	5	0	4
Ibanez	.258	.421	.313	87	209	23	54	88	7	0	9	27	17	32	5	1	3
Guevara	.250	.417	.250	10	12	2	3	5	2	0	0	2	0	2	0	0	3
Davis	.245	.435	.304	124	432	55	106	188	17	1	21	59	32	111	3	3	12
Mabry	.244	.401	.297	87	262	34	64	105	14	0	9	33	20	60	2	1	10
Blowers	.239	.391	.300	19	46	2	11	18	1	0	2	7	4	12	0	0	1
Jackson	.235	.279	.299	32	68	4	16	19	3	0	0	10	6	19	3	3	2
Hunter	.232	.301	.280	139	539	79	125	162	13	6	4	34	37	91	44	8	4
Gipson	.225	.338	.287	55	80	16	18	27	5	2	0	9	6	13	3	4	3
Buhner	.222	.421	.388	87	266	37	59	112	11	0	14	38	69	100	0	0	1
Cedeno	.214	.405	.313	21	42	4	9	17	2	0	2	8	5	9	1	1	4
Guillen	.158	.316	.200	5	19	2	3	6	0	0	1	3	1	6	0	0	1
Monahan	.133	.133	.133	16	15	3	2	2	0	0	0	0	0	6	0	0	0
Timmons	.114	.227	.188	26	44	4	5	10	2	0	1	3	4	12	0	1	0

PITCHERS	W-L	ERA	BA	G	GS	CG	GF	SH	SV	IP	H	R	ER	HR	BB	SO
Scheffer	0-0	1.93	.353	4	0	0	3	0	0	4.2	6	5	1	0	3	4
Abbott	6-2	3.10	.193	25	7	0	8	0	0	72.2	50	31	25	9	32	68
Moyer	14-8	3.87	.267	32	32	4	0	0	0	228.0	235	108	98	23	48	137
Paniagua	6-11	4.06	.264	59	0	0	16	0	3	77.2	75	37	35	5	52	74
Garcia	17-8	4.07	.263	33	33	2	0	1	0	201.1	205	96	91	18	90	170
Halama	11-10	4.22	.282	38	24	1	7	1	0	179.0	193	88	84	20	56	105
Williams	0-0	4.66	.289	13	0	0	7	0	0	9.2	11	5	5	1	7	7
Davey	2-1	4.71	.250	45	0	0	15	0	1	65.0	62	41	34	5	40	59
Meche	8-4	4.73	.237	16	15	0	0	0	0	85.2	73	48	45	9	57	47
Franklin	0-0	4.76	.238	6	0	0	2	0	0	11.1	10	6	6	2	8	6
Mesa	3-6	4.98	.305	68	0	0	60	0	33	68.2	84	42	38	11	40	42
Henry	2-0	5.04	.303	7	4	0	0	0	0	25.0	30	15	14	1	10	15
F. Rodriguez	2-4	5.65	.314	28	5	0	10	0	0	73.1	94	47	46	11	30	47
Ramsay	0-2	6.38	.324	6	3	0	1	0	0	18.1	23	13	13	3	9	11
Sinclair	0-1	6.52	.278	21	0	0	6	0	0	19.1	22	16	14	5	14	18
Leiter	0-0	6.75	.333	2	0	0	0	0	0	1.1	2	1	1	0	0	1
Zimmerman	0-0	7.88	.389	12	0	0	2	0	0	8.0	14	8	7	0	4	3
Carmona	1-0	7.94	.409	9	0	0	3	0	0	11.1	18	11	10	3	9	0
Cloude	4-4	7.96	.346	31	6	0	8	0	1	72.1	106	67	64	10	46	35
Hinchliffe	0-4	8.80	.323	11	4	0	2	0	0	30.2	41	31	30	10	21	14
Marte	0-1	9.35	.390	5	0	0	2	0	0	8.2	16	9	9	3	6	3
Stark	0-0	9.95	.370	8	0	0	2	0	0	6.1	10	8	7	0	4	4
Weaver	0-1	10.61	.318	8	0	0	2	0	0	9.1	14	12	11	2	8	14
Bunch	0-0	11.70	.426	5	1	0	4	0	0	10.0	20	13	13	3	7	4
Spencer	0-0	21.60	.556	2	0	0	0	0	0	1.2	5	4	4	0	3	2

2000 preliminary roster

PITCHERS (24)
Paul Abbott
Rafael Carmona
Ken Cloude
Tom Davey
Ryan Franklin
Brian Fuentes
Freddy Garcia
John Halama
Brett Hinchliffe
Kevin Hodges
Chris Mears
Gil Meche

Jose Mesa
Ivan Montane
Jamie Moyer
Jose Paniagua
Robert Ramsay
Frankie Rodriguez
Aaron Scheffer
Steve Sinclair
Sean Spencer
Dennis Stark
Todd Williams
Jordan Zimmerman

CATCHERS (2)
Tom Lampkin
Dan Wilson

INFIELDERS (7)
David Bell
Rafael Bournigal
Russ Davis
Carlos Guillen
Edgar Martinez
John Olerud
Alex Rodriguez

OUTFIELDERS (8)
Chad Alexander
Jay Buhner
Charles Gipson
Ken Griffey
Brian Hunter
Raul Ibanez
John Mabry
Shane Monahan

194

Games played by position

PLAYER	G	C	1B	2B	3B	SS	OF	DH
Bell	157	0	4	154	0	1	0	0
Blowers	19	0	14	0	4	0	0	1
Bournigal	55	0	0	17	8	28	1	0
Buhner	87	0	1	0	0	0	85	0
Cedeno	21	0	0	1	1	20	0	0
Davis	124	0	0	0	124	2	0	0
Gipson	55	0	0	3	17	3	28	0
Griffey	160	0	0	0	0	0	158	6
Guevara	10	0	0	0	0	9	0	0
Guillen	5	0	0	2	0	3	0	0
Hunter	121	0	0	0	0	0	121	0
Huskey	74	0	10	0	1	0	53	0
Ibanez	87	1	21	0	0	0	57	0
Jackson	32	0	29	0	0	0	1	0
Lampkin	76	56	0	0	0	0	2	2
Mabry	87	0	20	0	24	0	43	0
Martinez	142	0	5	0	0	0	0	143
Mieske	24	0	0	0	0	0	20	1
Monahan	16	0	0	0	0	0	9	3
Rodriguez	129	0	0	0	0	129	0	0
Segui	90	0	90	0	0	0	0	0
Timmons	26	0	1	0	0	0	17	5
Wilson	123	121	5	0	0	0	0	0

Sick call: 1999 DL report

PLAYER	Days on the DL
Jay Buhner	57
Rafael Carmona	59
Charles Gipson	52
Carlos Guillen	176
Butch Henry	126
Brian Lee Hunter	15
Raul Ibanez	16
Mark Leiter	178*
John Mabry	51
Alex Rodriguez	37
Eric Weaver	141
Jordan Zimmerman	33

Indicates two separate terms on Disabled List.

Minor Leagues
Tops in the organization

BATTER	CLUB	AVG.	G	AB	R	H	HR	RBI
Robinson, Bo	Wis	.329	138	499	101	164	13	102
Robinson, Kerry	Tac	.322	79	335	53	108	0	34
Williams, Peanut	Lnc	.316	77	304	66	96	28	66
Clark, Jermaine	Lnc	.315	126	502	112	158	6	61
Matos, Francisco	Tac	.310	100	393	43	122	3	33

HOME RUNS

Williams, Peanut	Lnc	28
Timmons, Ozzie	Tac	21
Bass, Jayson	NHv	21
Silvestre, Juan	Wis	21
Regan, Jason	Lnc	18

WINS

Torres, Melqui	Wis	13
Mears, Chris	Lnc	13
Several Players Tied at		10

RBI

Silvestre, Juan	Wis	107
Robinson, Bo	Wis	102
Connors, Greg	Lnc	84
Radmanovich, R.	Tac	80
Hargrove, Harvey	Lnc	80

SAVES

Kaye, Justin	Lnc	14
Montane, Ivan	NHv	13
Gryboski, Kevin	NHv	10
Holdridge, David	Tac	10
Scheffer, Aaron	Tac	9

STOLEN BASES

Valera, Ramon	Wis	46
Bass, Jayson	NHv	34
Clark, Jermaine	Lnc	33
Robinson, Kerry	Tac	30
Several Players Tied at		22

STRIKEOUTS

Anderson, Ryan	NHv	162
Parker, Brandon	Lnc	147
Matos, Josue	Wis	136
Torres, Melqui	Wis	129
Mears, Chris	Lnc	123

PITCHER	CLUB	W-L	ERA	IP	H	BB	SO
Ahearne, Pat	NHv	8-3	2.61	124	114	27	80
Bunch, Mel	Tac	10-2	3.10	125	112	40	117
Mears, Chris	Lnc	13-7	4.20	144	147	34	123
Hodges, Kevin	Tac	4-6	4.24	110	122	38	58
Wooten, Greg	Lnc	10-4	4.33	114	123	30	72

1999 salaries

	Bonuses	Total earned salary
Ken Griffey, of	125,000	8,760,532
Jay Buhner, of		4,816,804
Dan Wilson, c		3,625,000
Edgar Martinez, dh		3,500,000
Alex Rodriguez, ss		3,112,500
Mark Leiter, p		3,000,000
Jose Mesa, p	400,000	2,850,000
Russ Davis, 3b	150,000	2,350,000
Jamie Moyer, p		2,300,000
Brian Hunter, of		1,750,000
Butch Henry, p		1,500,000
John Mabry, of		1,400,000
David Bell, 2b		700,000
Tom Lampkin, c	25,000	625,000
Frankie Rodriguez, p		455,000
Rafael Bournigal, ss	50,000	400,000
Ken Cloude, p		275,000
Paul Abbott, p	15,000	235,000
Ryan Jackson, 1b		230,000
Jose Paniagua, p	15,000	230,000
Raul Ibanez, of	10,000	220,000
John Halama, p	15,000	215,000
Ozzie Timmons, of		210,000
Charles Gipson, of	5,000	210,000
Todd Williams, p		201,500
Eric Weaver, p		200,000
Carlos Guillen, ss		200,000
Freddy Garcia, p		200,000
Tom Davey, p		200,000
Gil Meche, p		200,000
Robert Ramsay, p		200,000

Average 1999 salary $1,431,333
Total 1999 team payroll: $44,371,336
Termination pay: $1,004,918

195

Seattle (1977-1999)

Runs: Most, career

1063	KEN GRIFFEY, 1989-1999
880	EDGAR MARTINEZ, 1987-1999
736	JAY BUHNER, 1988-1999
563	Alvin Davis, 1984-1991
543	Harold Reynolds, 1983-1992

Hits: Most, career

1742	KEN GRIFFEY, 1989-1999
1558	EDGAR MARTINEZ, 1987-1999
1163	Alvin Davis, 1984-1991
1153	JAY BUHNER, 1988-1999
1063	Harold Reynolds, 1983-1992

2B: Most, career

372	EDGAR MARTINEZ, 1987-1999
320	KEN GRIFFEY, 1989-1999
212	Alvin Davis, 1984-1991
209	JAY BUHNER, 1988-1999
200	Harold Reynolds, 1983-1992

3B: Most, career

48	Harold Reynolds, 1983-1992
30	KEN GRIFFEY, 1989-1999
26	Phil Bradley, 1983-1987
23	Spike Owen, 1983-1986
20	Ruppert Jones, 1977-1979

HR: Most, career

398	KEN GRIFFEY, 1989-1999
279	JAY BUHNER, 1988-1999
198	EDGAR MARTINEZ, 1987-1999
160	Alvin Davis, 1984-1991
148	ALEX RODRIGUEZ, 1994-1999

RBI: Most, career

1152	KEN GRIFFEY, 1989-1999
864	JAY BUHNER, 1988-1999
780	EDGAR MARTINEZ, 1987-1999
667	Alvin Davis, 1984-1991
463	ALEX RODRIGUEZ, 1994-1999

SB: Most, career

290	Julio Cruz, 1977-1983
228	Harold Reynolds, 1983-1992
167	KEN GRIFFEY, 1989-1999
118	ALEX RODRIGUEZ, 1994-1999
107	Phil Bradley, 1983-1987

BB: Most, career

877	EDGAR MARTINEZ, 1987-1999
747	KEN GRIFFEY, 1989-1999
721	JAY BUHNER, 1988-1999
672	Alvin Davis, 1984-1991
391	Harold Reynolds, 1983-1992

BA: Highest, career

.320	EDGAR MARTINEZ, 1987-1999
.308	ALEX RODRIGUEZ, 1994-1999
.301	Phil Bradley, 1983-1987
.299	KEN GRIFFEY, 1989-1999
.293	Joey Cora, 1995-1998

On-base avg: Highest, career

.426	EDGAR MARTINEZ, 1987-1999
.392	Ken Phelps, 1983-1988
.382	Phil Bradley, 1983-1987
.381	Alvin Davis, 1984-1991
.380	KEN GRIFFEY, 1989-1999

Slug pct: Highest, career

.569	KEN GRIFFEY, 1989-1999
.551	ALEX RODRIGUEZ, 1994-1999
.523	EDGAR MARTINEZ, 1987-1999
.521	Ken Phelps, 1983-1988
.496	JAY BUHNER, 1988-1999

Games started: Most, career

266	RANDY JOHNSON, 1989-1998
217	Mike Moore, 1982-1988
173	MARK LANGSTON, 1984-1989
147	Jim Beattie, 1980-1986
146	Glenn Abbott, 1977-1983

Complete games: Most, career

56	Mike Moore, 1982-1988
51	RANDY JOHNSON, 1989-1998
41	MARK LANGSTON, 1984-1989
30	Jim Beattie, 1980-1986
28	Glenn Abbott, 1977-1983

Saves: Most, career

98	Mike Schooler, 1988-1992
66	NORM CHARLTON, 1993-1997
56	BOBBY AYALA, 1994-1998
52	Bill Caudill, 1982-1983
36	Shane Rawley, 1978-1981

Shutouts: Most, career

19	RANDY JOHNSON, 1989-1998
9	MARK LANGSTON, 1984-1989
9	Mike Moore, 1982-1988
7	Floyd Bannister, 1979-1982
6	Jim Beattie, 1980-1986

Wins: Most, career

130	RANDY JOHNSON, 1989-1998
74	MARK LANGSTON, 1984-1989
66	Mike Moore, 1982-1988
56	Erik Hanson, 1988-1993
52	JAMIE MOYER, 1996-1999

K: Most, career

2162	RANDY JOHNSON, 1989-1998
1078	MARK LANGSTON, 1984-1989
937	Mike Moore, 1982-1988
740	Erik Hanson, 1988-1993
597	Matt Young, 1983-1990

Win pct: Highest, career

.684	JAMIE MOYER, 1996-1999
.637	RANDY JOHNSON, 1989-1998
.525	MARK LANGSTON, 1984-1989
.509	Erik Hanson, 1988-1993
.456	Bill Swift, 1985-1998

ERA: Lowest, career

3.42	RANDY JOHNSON, 1989-1998
3.69	Erik Hanson, 1988-1993
3.75	Floyd Bannister, 1979-1982
4.01	MARK LANGSTON, 1984-1989
4.13	Matt Young, 1983-1990

Runs: Most, season

141	ALEX RODRIGUEZ, 1996
125	KEN GRIFFEY, 1996
125	KEN GRIFFEY, 1997
123	KEN GRIFFEY, 1999
123	ALEX RODRIGUEZ, 1998

Hits: Most, season

215	ALEX RODRIGUEZ, 1996
213	ALEX RODRIGUEZ, 1998
192	Phil Bradley, 1985
185	KEN GRIFFEY, 1997
184	Harold Reynolds, 1989

2B: Most, season

54	ALEX RODRIGUEZ,	1996
52	EDGAR MARTINEZ,	1995
52	EDGAR MARTINEZ,	1996
46	EDGAR MARTINEZ,	1992
46	EDGAR MARTINEZ,	1998

3B: Most, season

11	Harold Reynolds,	1988
10	Phil Bradley,	1987
9	Ruppert Jones,	1979
9	Harold Reynolds,	1989
8	Phil Bradley,	1985
8	Al Cowens,	1982
8	Ruppert Jones,	1977
8	Spike Owen,	1984
8	Harold Reynolds,	1987

HR: Most, season

56	KEN GRIFFEY,	1997
56	KEN GRIFFEY,	1998
49	KEN GRIFFEY,	1996
48	KEN GRIFFEY,	1999
45	KEN GRIFFEY,	1993

RBI: Most, season

147	KEN GRIFFEY,	1997
146	KEN GRIFFEY,	1998
140	KEN GRIFFEY,	1996
138	JAY BUHNER,	1996
134	KEN GRIFFEY,	1999

SB: Most, season

60	Harold Reynolds,	1987
59	Julio Cruz,	1978
49	Julio Cruz,	1979
46	Julio Cruz,	1982
46	ALEX RODRIGUEZ,	1998

BB: Most, season

123	EDGAR MARTINEZ,	1996
119	JAY BUHNER,	1997
119	EDGAR MARTINEZ,	1997
116	EDGAR MARTINEZ,	1995
106	EDGAR MARTINEZ,	1998

BA: Highest, season

.358	ALEX RODRIGUEZ,	1996
.356	EDGAR MARTINEZ,	1995
.343	EDGAR MARTINEZ,	1992
.337	EDGAR MARTINEZ,	1999
.330	EDGAR MARTINEZ,	1997

On-base avg; Highest, season

.479	EDGAR MARTINEZ,	1995
.464	EDGAR MARTINEZ,	1996
.456	EDGAR MARTINEZ,	1997
.447	EDGAR MARTINEZ,	1999
.429	EDGAR MARTINEZ,	1998

Slug pct: Highest, season

.674	KEN GRIFFEY,	1994
.646	KEN GRIFFEY,	1997
.631	ALEX RODRIGUEZ,	1996
.628	EDGAR MARTINEZ,	1995
.628	KEN GRIFFEY,	1996

Games started: Most, season

37	Mike Moore,	1986
36	MARK LANGSTON,	1986
35	Floyd Bannister,	1982
35	JEFF FASSERO,	1997
35	STERLING HITCHCOCK, 1996
35	MARK LANGSTON,	1987
35	MARK LANGSTON,	1988
35	Matt Young,	1985

Complete games: Most, season

14	MARK LANGSTON,	1987
14	Mike Moore,	1985
13	Mike Parrott,	1979
12	Jim Beattie,	1984
12	Mike Moore,	1987

Saves: Most, season

33	JOSE MESA,	1999
33	Mike Schooler,	1989
30	Mike Schooler,	1990
26	Bill Caudill,	1982
26	Bill Caudill,	1983

Shutouts: Most, season

4	Dave Fleming,	1992
4	RANDY JOHNSON,	1994
3	Floyd Bannister,	1982
3	Brian Holman,	1991
3	RANDY JOHNSON,	1993
3	RANDY JOHNSON,	1995
3	MARK LANGSTON,	1987
3	MARK LANGSTON,	1988
3	Mike Moore,	1988
3	JAMIE MOYER,	1998

Wins: Most, season

20	RANDY JOHNSON,	1997
19	RANDY JOHNSON,	1993
19	MARK LANGSTON,	1987
18	Erik Hanson,	1990
18	RANDY JOHNSON,	1995

K: Most, season

308	RANDY JOHNSON,	1993
294	RANDY JOHNSON,	1995
291	RANDY JOHNSON,	1997
262	MARK LANGSTON,	1987
245	MARK LANGSTON,	1986

Win pct: Highest, season

.900	RANDY JOHNSON,	1995
.833	RANDY JOHNSON,	1997
.773	JAMIE MOYER,	1997
.704	RANDY JOHNSON,	1993
.680	FREDDY GARCIA,	1999

ERA: Lowest, season

2.28	RANDY JOHNSON,	1997
2.48	RANDY JOHNSON,	1995
3.19	RANDY JOHNSON,	1994
3.24	Erik Hanson,	1990
3.24	RANDY JOHNSON,	1993

Most pinch-hit homers, season

2	Leon Roberts,	1978
2	Gary Gray,	1981
2	Ken Phelps,	1986
2	Greg Briley,	1992
2	PAUL SORRENTO,	1997

Most pinch-hit homers, career

4	Ken Phelps, 1983-1988

Longest hitting streak

24	Joey Cora,	1997
21	Dan Meyer,	1979
21	Richie Zisk,	1982
20	ALEX RODRIGUEZ,	1996
19	Phil Bradley,	1986

Most consecutive scoreless innings

34	MARK LANGSTON, 1988

No-hit games

RANDY JOHNSON, Sea vs Det AL, 2-0; June 2, 1990.
Chris Bosio, Sea vs Bos AL, 7-0; April 22, 1993.

ACTIVE PLAYERS in caps.

Players' years of service are listed by the first and last years with this team and are not necessarily consecutive; all statistics record performances for this team only.

197

Anaheim Angels

In a miserable year for the Angels, Garret Anderson was the only batter to hit above .300.

1999 Angels: In a word, terrible

It wasn't exactly the Magic Kingdom. In fact the Anaheim Angels' anything-but-G-rated 1999 season didn't seem anything like the fare you'd expect from Disney, their owners.

The Angels, who have never made it to the World Series and haven't been to the postseason since 1986, had one of their worst seasons ever in 1999.

Early in spring training, shortstop and team leader Gary DiSarcina accidentally got whacked on the arm with a bat by coach George Hendrick. DiSarcina's broken arm sidelined him until June.

Newcomer Mo Vaughn didn't take long to discover the dark cloud hanging over the team. The $80 million free agent went tumbling into the visitors' dugout in his first inning as the Angels' first baseman and wound up with an ankle injury that sidelined him for two weeks. It bothered him most of the season.

Those and an assortment of other injuries played a role as the Angels, who were considered one of the favorites in the AL West, played well below expectations. That, in turn, led to dissension in the clubhouse. Frustrated by some players' attitudes, manager Terry Collins resigned Sept. 3. General manager Bill Bavasi followed at season's end.

A strong finish under interim manger Joe Maddon—who then watched a parade of outsiders interview for the permanent job—kept the Angels from having their worst season ever. But 70-92, 25 games behind AL West winner Texas, was plenty bad enough.

The Walt Disney Co., which bought control of the team in 1996, said it was willing to take the same route as Collins and Bavasi should a viable buyer be found.

Meanwhile, team president Tony Tavares said there need not be any delay in changing the roster.

"We need to look deeper than the talent issue," said Tavares, who at one point during the season called the often-volatile Angels' clubhouse a day-care center. "We have to address what's missing: discipline,

Team MVP

Garret Anderson: For several years, he has been a productive outfielder, but the one most often mentioned in trade rumors. In 1999, Anderson became the most consistent producer in the Anaheim offense. He was the only regular to bat better than .300, finishing at .303. His 21 homers were second on the club, and he topped the team with 36 doubles, 291 total bases, 188 hits, and 88 runs.

fundamentals, doing the right thing. The organization will go through introspection like never before. There's no kidding ourselves."

He called the season, in a word, "Terrible."

"I've had to go through a manager and general manager I believed in," he said. "With all the talent here, we ended up with one of the worst records in baseball."

Tavares admitted that Bavasi resigned on account of "philosophical differences" with him, and that left the pressure on Tavares.

"But I'm not going to be making the baseball decisions," Tavares said. "My only philosophy is, go get good people."

The Angels fell below .500 for good on April 18 and lost 11 straight games beginning July 16, putting them 16 games out of first place. They were 51-82 when Collins resigned.

Maddon, promoted from bench coach, put forth an upbeat demeanor and had a 19-10 record.

Asked if the Angels were relieved when the season was over, Maddon said, "Not necessarily. We'd like to play another month now. Some of the players are at the top of their game."

Outfielder Tim Salmon, who missed two months after spraining his left wrist on May 3, said, "A lot of guys are going to beat themselves up over the winter over what happened this season."

199

1999 Angels: Week-by-week notes

These notes were excerpted from the following issues of Baseball Weekly.

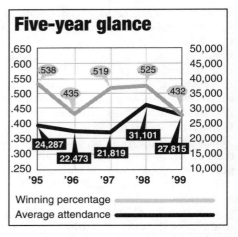

Five-year glance

Winning percentage
Average attendance

▶**April 14:** Days after first baseman Mo Vaughn hit the dirt, the Angels were struggling to get back up without their $80 million first baseman. Vaughn became the ninth Angel on the DL after he suffered a sprained left ankle when he fell into the Indians' dugout chasing a foul popup in the season opener.

▶**April 21:** Center fielder Jim Edmonds, still struggling to swing a bat without pain, said he feared his right shoulder might require season-ending surgery. Because of a recent gag order regarding injuries imposed by the front office, manager Terry Collins wouldn't comment on Edmonds's status. On the field, the bullpen (2.45 ERA in 36 innings through April 16) didn't allow a run in 20 innings during the team's 4-3 road trip through Texas and Oakland.

▶**April 28:** Third baseman Troy Glaus had been on a torrid hitting pace. Through April 20 he was fifth in the AL in batting (.400), first in doubles (10), first in extra-base hits (13), second in total bases (39) and second in slugging (.780).

▶**May 5:** Right fielder Tim Salmon finished April with a .349 average, seven home runs and 23 RBI—all career highs for the month. He had been a career .259 hitter in April.

▶**May 12:** When cleanup hitter Tim Salmon and No. 2 hitter Randy Velarde, the second baseman, were sidelined last week, the lineup went from hobbled to helpless. The Angels lost five of six, scoring only nine runs. They batted .183 (35-for-191) over those games as six opposing starters went 4-1 with a 1.29 ERA.

▶**May 19:** The Angels' sweep of the Yankees in New York—which finished with 19 shutout innings—was their first there since 1984. Left-hander Chuck Finley and right-hander Omar Olivares got back-to-back shutout victories in the series.

▶**June 2:** Closer Troy Percival put together

a hot streak in May. Since his lone blown save on May 1, he pitched 10 consecutive hitless appearances that included eight saves, 12 strikeouts and no walks in nine innings. Percival had 13 saves through May 29.

▶**June 23:** The fast-sinking Angels lost for the sixth consecutive time on June 19, their longest losing streak of the year. Until a 4-2 win against the Yankees the next day, the Angels had lost nine of 11 games, scoring just 20 runs in that span and batting .204.

▶**June 30:** The Angels surprised much of baseball by giving Terry Collins a contract extension believed to span two years with a club option for 2002. The deal ended three weeks of front-office silence following a meeting with general manager Bill Bavasi in which many veteran players aired concerns over Collins's managerial style.

▶**July 15:** The Angels surprised power-hitting DH Todd Greene when they optioned him to AAA Edmonton last week. He had been the cleanup hitter in 15 games, including as recently as four days before he was sent down. Greene was hitting .240 with 12 homers and 31 RBI, but he had just one hit in his last 19 at-bats and only two homers since May 31.

▶**July 28:** Barely a week after climbing out of last place for the first time in two months and taking aim at first-place

Texas, the Angels lost power and nose-dived to 10 consecutive losses. They dropped nine games further behind the Rangers to fall a season-high 15-games back and started to snap at each other in the clubhouse.

▶**Aug. 4:** The Angels sent a wrecking ball through their condemned season by trading their most productive pitcher and most productive position player. Omar Olivares (8-9, 4.05 ERA), who led the rotation in wins, and Randy Velarde, who led regulars in hitting (.306) and runs (57), went to Oakland for minor league outfielders Jeff DaVanon and Nathan Haynes and right-hander Elvin Nina.

▶**Aug. 11:** After an Angels stretch of 19 losses in 23 games, Angels' president Tony Tavares ended his yearlong silence and suggested that jobs were on the line, from the front office to the field, over the final two months. "There isn't anything sacred," he said.

▶**Aug. 25:** The Angels succeeded in winning back-to-back games for only the third time since the All-Star break when they beat Detroit on Aug. 20. But they followed that with another loss, falling to 9-28 in the second half through Aug. 22.

▶**Sept. 1:** Mo Vaughn's visit to Boston last weekend was only slightly more triumphant than the first one in May, when he was weakened with an ankle injury. Vaughn went 2-for-8 to finish 3-for-20 on the season as a visitor at Fenway Park.

▶**Sept. 8:** Terry Collins announced his sudden resignation/firing at a news conference on Sept. 3. Citing continued clubhouse infighting, Collins "agreed by mutual consent to resign," according to the club's press release, the day after the team lost its ninth consecutive game to drop its record to 51-82, worst in the majors.

▶**Sept. 22:** They might have played their last manager out of a job, but the Angels seemed to be supporting the long-term employment of interim manager Joe Maddon. They recently won nine of 10 games and closed out their best road trip in more than a year, at 6-2.

▶**Sept. 29:** Troy Percival finished his season with an inflamed shoulder and seven blown saves in his last 15 chances. He had a 6.23 ERA over that span, inflating his season's mark to 3.79.

▶**Oct. 6:** The resignation of Bill Bavasi may have been a sign of sweeping changes to come. Bavasi resigned with three games left in his sixth season as GM. The split apparently was a result of differences with Tony Tavares involving Bavasi's loyalty to the core of players he helped nurture during his tenure—outfielder Garret Anderson, shortstop Gary DiSarcina, Jim Edmonds, Chuck Finley, Troy Percival and Tim Salmon.

QUOTE OF THE YEAR

"As long as we win, I'll take the records"
—Knuckleballer Steve Sparks, after setting many hit-batsman records in an 8-6 victory

Team Leaders

Batting avg.	Hits	Wins	Strikeouts
.303 Garret Anderson	188 Garret Anderson	12 Chuck Finley	200 Chuck Finley
.281 Mo Vaughn	148 Darin Erstad	10 Mark Petkovsek	76 Ken Hill

HR	Runs	Losses	Innings
33 Mo Vaughn	88 Garret Anderson	11 Ken Hill	213.1 Chuck Finley
29 Troy Glaus	85 Troy Glaus	11 Steve Sparks	147.2 Steve Sparks
		11 Chuck Finley	

RBI	Stolen bases	ERA	Saves
108 Mo Vaughn	13 Darin Erstad	4.43 Chuck Finley	31 Troy Percival
80 Garret Anderson	10 Jeff Huson	4.77 Ken Hill	3 Lou Pote

ANAHEIM ANGELS 1999 final stats

BATTERS	BA	SLG	OBA	G	AB	R	H	TB	2B	3B	HR	RBI	BB	SO	SB	CS	E
Colangelo	.500	.500	.667	1	2	0	1	1	0	0	0	0	1	0	0	0	0
Anderson	.303	.469	.336	157	620	88	188	291	36	2	21	80	34	81	3	4	3
Luke	.300	.600	.344	18	30	4	9	18	0	0	3	6	2	10	0	0	0
Vaughn	.281	.508	.358	139	524	63	147	266	20	0	33	108	54	127	0	0	3
Palmeiro	.278	.331	.364	109	317	46	88	105	12	1	1	23	39	30	5	5	1
Salmon	.266	.490	.372	98	353	60	94	173	24	2	17	69	63	82	4	1	4
Huson	.262	.302	.307	97	225	21	59	68	7	1	0	18	16	27	10	1	5
Molina	.257	.337	.312	31	101	8	26	34	5	0	1	10	6	6	0	1	2
Erstad	.253	.374	.308	142	585	84	148	219	22	5	13	53	47	101	13	7	1
Edmonds	.250	.426	.339	55	204	34	51	87	17	2	5	23	28	45	5	4	1
Greene	.243	.436	.275	97	321	36	78	140	20	0	14	42	12	63	1	4	2
Unroe	.241	.333	.305	27	54	5	13	18	2	0	1	6	4	16	0	0	0
Walbeck	.240	.306	.308	107	288	26	69	88	8	1	3	22	26	46	2	3	5
Glaus	.240	.450	.331	154	551	85	132	248	29	0	29	79	71	143	5	1	19
Decker	.238	.333	.372	28	63	5	15	21	6	0	0	5	13	9	0	0	1
DiSarcina	.229	.273	.273	81	271	32	62	74	7	1	1	29	15	32	2	2	15
Williams	.222	.349	.286	30	63	8	14	22	1	2	1	6	5	21	2	1	1
DaVanon	.200	.450	.273	7	20	4	4	9	0	1	1	4	2	7	0	1	0
Sheets	.197	.275	.236	87	244	22	48	67	10	0	3	29	14	59	1	2	12
Durrington	.180	.197	.237	43	122	14	22	24	2	0	0	2	9	28	4	3	6
Pritchett	.156	.244	.188	20	45	3	7	11	1	0	1	2	2	9	1	1	1
Hemphill	.143	.143	.269	12	21	3	3	3	0	0	0	2	4	4	0	0	2
O'Brien	.097	.145	.136	27	62	3	6	9	0	0	1	4	1	12	0	0	1
Silvestri	.091	.182	.091	3	11	0	1	2	1	0	0	1	0	1	0	0	1

PITCHERS	W-L	ERA	BA	G	GS	CG	GF	SH	SV	IP	H	R	ER	HR	BB	SO
Pote	1-1	2.15	.219	20	0	0	10	0	3	29.1	23	9	7	1	12	20
Alvarez	0-1	3.00	.111	8	0	0	1	0	0	3.0	1	1	1	0	4	4
Magnante	5-2	3.38	.262	53	0	0	13	0	0	69.1	68	30	26	2	29	44
Levine	1-1	3.39	.247	50	1	0	12	0	0	85.0	76	40	32	13	29	37
Petkovsek	10-4	3.47	.269	64	0	0	18	0	1	83.0	85	37	32	6	21	43
Mintz	0-0	3.60	.381	3	0	0	2	0	0	5.0	8	2	2	1	2	2
Percival	4-6	3.79	.186	60	0	0	50	0	31	57.0	38	24	24	9	22	58
Finley	12-11	4.43	.246	33	33	1	0	0	0	213.1	197	117	105	23	94	200
Hill	4-11	4.77	.270	26	22	0	2	0	0	128.1	129	72	68	14	76	76
Cooper	1-1	4.88	.228	5	5	0	0	0	0	27.2	23	15	15	3	18	15
Hasegawa	4-6	4.91	.276	64	1	0	26	0	2	77.0	80	45	42	14	34	44
Fyhrie	0-4	5.05	.286	16	7	0	5	0	0	51.2	61	32	29	8	21	26
Washburn	4-5	5.25	.261	16	10	0	3	0	0	61.2	61	36	36	6	26	39
Sparks	5-11	5.42	.281	28	26	0	1	0	0	147.2	165	101	89	21	82	73
Schoeneweis	1-1	5.49	.294	31	0	0	6	0	0	39.1	47	27	24	4	14	22
Ortiz	2-3	6.52	.265	9	9	0	0	0	0	48.1	50	35	35	7	25	44
Belcher	6-8	6.73	.315	24	24	0	0	0	0	132.1	168	104	99	27	46	52
McDowell	0-4	8.05	.369	4	4	0	0	0	0	19.0	31	17	17	4	5	12
Holtz	2-3	8.06	.295	28	0	0	9	0	0	22.1	26	20	20	3	15	17

2000 preliminary roster

PITCHERS (19)
Juan Alvarez
Tim Belcher
Brian Cooper
Jason Dickson
Mike Fyhrie
Shigetoshi Hasegawa
Ken Hill
Mike Holtz
Al Levine
Elvin Nina
Ramon Ortiz
Troy Percival

Mark Petkovsek
Lou Pote
Scott Schoeneweis
Scot Shields
Derrick Turnbow
Jarrod Washburn
Matt Wise

CATCHERS (4)
Jason Dewey
Bret Hemphill
Ben Molina
Matt Walbeck

INFIELDERS (6)
Larry Barnes
Gary DiSarcina
Trent Durrington
Troy Glaus
Andy Sheets
Mo Vaughn

OUTFIELDERS (10)
Garret Anderson
Mike Colangelo
Jeff DaVanon
Jim Edmonds

Darin Erstad
Todd Greene
Elpidio Guzman
Norm Hutchins
Orlando Palmeiro
Tim Salmon

Games played by position

PLAYER	G	C	1B	2B	3B	SS	OF	DH
Anderson	157	0	0	0	0	0	153	4
Colangelo	1	0	0	0	0	0	1	0
DaVanon	7	0	0	0	0	0	5	2
Decker	28	17	6	0	0	0	0	3
DiSarcina	81	0	0	0	0	81	0	0
Durrington	43	0	0	41	0	0	0	0
Edmonds	55	0	2	0	0	0	42	9
Erstad	142	0	78	0	0	0	69	2
Glaus	154	0	0	0	153	0	0	1
Greene	97	12	0	0	0	0	30	44
Hemphill	12	12	0	0	0	0	0	0
Huson	97	0	8	41	9	22	2	10
Luke	18	0	4	0	0	0	6	0
Molina	31	30	0	0	0	0	0	0
O'Brien	27	27	0	0	0	0	0	0
Palmeiro	109	0	0	0	0	0	92	12
Pritchett	20	0	15	0	0	0	0	5
Salmon	98	0	0	0	0	0	89	9
Sheets	87	0	0	7	1	76	0	0
Silvestri	3	0	0	1	0	1	1	0
Unroe	27	0	0	1	3	0	12	0
Vaughn	139	0	72	0	0	0	0	70
Velarde	95	0	0	95	0	0	0	0
Walbeck	107	97	0	0	0	0	0	1
Williams	30	0	0	0	0	0	24	4

Sick call: 1999 DL report

PLAYER	Days on the DL
Justin Baughman	182
Tim Belcher	41
Mike Colangelo	112
Jason Dickson	182
Gary DiSarcina	78
Jim Edmonds	119
Darin Erstad	15
Pep Harris	182
Ken Hill	35*
Mike Holtz	16
Mike James	155
Matt Luke	69
Jack McDowell	109
Charlie O'Brien	50
Tim Salmon	74
Mo Vaughn	15
Reggie Williams	17

Indicates two separate terms on Disabled List.

Minor Leagues

Tops in the organization

BATTER	CLUB	AVG.	G	AB	R	H	HR	RBI
O'Keefe, Michael	Boi	.326	72	264	52	86	9	70
Quinlan, Robb	Boi	.322	73	295	51	95	9	77
Silvestri, Dave	Edm	.318	79	318	55	101	6	42
Simonton, Benji	LkE	.306	111	366	52	112	9	67
Rodriguez, Juan	LkE	.302	86	315	54	95	6	50

HOME RUNS

Kieschnick, B.	Edm	23
Barnes, Larry	Eri	20
Murphy, Nate	Eri	19
Wooten, Shawn	Eri	19
Christensen, Mike	CR	18

WINS

Bridges, Douglas	LkE	18	
Shields, Scot	Eri	14	
Ortiz, Ramon	Edm	14	
Cooper, Brian	Edm	12	
Fish, Steve	LkE	11	

RBI

Barnes, Larry	Eri	100
Wooten, Shawn	Eri	88
Quinlan, Robb	Boi	77
Murphy, Nate	Eri	76
Curtis, Matt	LkE	76

SAVES

Mintz, Steve	Edm	18
Demouy, Chris	CR	16
Brow, Scott	Edm	15
Jones, Greg	CR	13
Bovee, Mike	Eri	12

STOLEN BASES

Durrington, Trent	Eri	59
Castro, Nelson	LkE	53
Guzman, Elpidio	CR	52
Tolentino, Juan	Eri	47
Dougherty, Jeb	LkE	35

STRIKEOUTS

Shields, Scot	Eri	194
Fish, Steve	LkE	180
Cooper, Brian	Edm	175
Etherton, Seth	Edm	172
Bridges, Douglas	LkE	162

PITCHER	CLUB	W-L	ERA	IP	H	BB	SO
Shields, Scot	Eri	14-7	2.67	182	148	65	194
Ortiz, Ramon	Edm	14-7	3.24	155	134	59	150
Cooper, Brian	Edm	12-6	3.38	189	176	39	175
Fyhrie, Mike	Edm	9-5	3.47	114	90	40	113
Etherton, Seth	Edm	10-12	3.52	189	178	49	172

1999 salaries

	Bonuses	Total earned salary
Mo Vaughn, 1b		7,166,666
Chuck Finley, p		5,800,000
Tim Salmon, of		5,500,000
Ken Hill, p	50,000	5,500,000
Tim Belcher, p	50,000	4,650,000
Jim Edmonds, of		3,550,000
Gary DiSarcina, ss		3,125,000
Garret Anderson, of	100,000	2,200,000
Troy Percival, p	375,000	1,975,000
Steve Sparks, p	37,500	1,387,500
S. Hasegawa, p	150,000	900,000
Mark Petkovsek, p	50,000	850,000
Matt Walbeck, c		825,000
Mike James, p		805,000
Darin Erstad, 1b		800,000
Mike Magnante, p	175,000	775,000
Jason Dickson, p		375,000
Pep Harris, p		305,000
Mike Holtz, p		290,000
Jeff Huson, 2b		280,000
Orlando Palmeiro, of		276,000
Matt Luke, of		250,000
Andy Sheets, ss		230,000
Todd Greene, of		225,000
Jarrod Washburn, p		217,500
Justin Baughman, ss		215,000
Troy Glaus, 3b		212,500
Alan Levine, p		208,000
Lou Pote, p		200,000
Trent Durrington, 2b		200,000
Benjamin Molina, c		200,000
Ramon Ortiz, p		200,000
Michael Colangelo, of		200,000

Average 1999 salary: $1,511,914
Total 1999 team payroll: $49,893,166
Termination pay: $172,131

Anaheim (1997-1999), includes California (1965-1996) and Los Angeles (1961-1964)

Runs: Most, career

889	Brian Downing, 1978-1990	
691	Jim Fregosi, 1961-1971	
608	TIM SALMON, 1992-1999	
601	Bobby Grich, 1977-1986	
520	CHILI DAVIS, 1988-1996	

Hits: Most, career

1588	Brian Downing, 1978-1990
1408	Jim Fregosi, 1961-1971
1103	Bobby Grich, 1977-1986
1015	TIM SALMON, 1992-1999
973	CHILI DAVIS, 1988-1996

2B: Most, career

282	Brian Downing, 1978-1990
219	Jim Fregosi, 1961-1971
195	TIM SALMON, 1992-1999
184	GARY DiSARCINA, 1989-1999
183	Bobby Grich, 1977-1986

3B: Most, career

70	Jim Fregosi, 1961-1971
32	Mickey Rivers, 1970-1975
27	LUIS POLONIA, 1990-1993
27	Dick Schofield, 1983-1996
25	Bobby Knoop, 1964-1969

HR: Most, career

222	Brian Downing, 1978-1990
196	TIM SALMON, 1992-1999
156	CHILI DAVIS, 1988-1996
154	Bobby Grich, 1977-1986
141	Don Baylor, 1977-1982

RBI: Most, career

846	Brian Downing, 1978-1990
660	TIM SALMON, 1992-1999
618	CHILI DAVIS, 1988-1996
557	Bobby Grich, 1977-1986
546	Jim Fregosi, 1961-1971

SB: Most, career

186	Gary Pettis, 1982-1987
174	LUIS POLONIA, 1990-1993
139	Sandy Alomar, 1969-1974
126	Mickey Rivers, 1970-1975
123	DEVON WHITE, 1985-1990

BB: Most, career

866	Brian Downing, 1978-1990
630	Bobby Grich, 1977-1986
579	TIM SALMON, 1992-1999
558	Jim Fregosi, 1961-1971
493	CHILI DAVIS, 1988-1996

BA: Highest, career

.314	Rod Carew, 1979-1985
.300	GARRET ANDERSON, 1994-1999
.294	LUIS POLONIA, 1990-1993
.293	Juan Beniquez, 1981-1985
.291	TIM SALMON, 1992-1999

On-base avg: Highest, career

.393	TIM SALMON, 1992-1999
.393	Rod Carew, 1979-1985
.379	Albie Pearson, 1961-1966
.372	Brian Downing, 1978-1990
.370	Bobby Grich, 1977-1986

Slug pct: Highest, career

.524	TIM SALMON, 1992-1999
.498	JIM EDMONDS, 1993-1999
.464	CHILI DAVIS, 1988-1996
.463	Doug DeCinces, 1982-1987
.455	WALLY JOYNER, 1986-1991

Games started: Most, career

379	CHUCK FINLEY, 1986-1999
288	Nolan Ryan, 1972-1979
272	Mike Witt, 1981-1990
218	Frank Tanana, 1973-1980
210	MARK LANGSTON, 1990-1997

Complete games: Most, career

156	Nolan Ryan, 1972-1979
92	Frank Tanana, 1973-1980
70	Mike Witt, 1981-1990
57	CHUCK FINLEY, 1986-1999
51	Clyde Wright, 1966-1973

Saves: Most, career

139	TROY PERCIVAL, 1995-1999
126	Bryan Harvey, 1987-1992
65	Dave LaRoche, 1970-1980
61	Donnie Moore, 1985-1988
58	Bob Lee, 1964-1966

Shutouts: Most, career

40	Nolan Ryan, 1972-1979
24	Frank Tanana, 1973-1980
21	Dean Chance, 1961-1966
14	George Brunet, 1964-1969
14	CHUCK FINLEY, 1986-1999

Wins: Most, career

165	CHUCK FINLEY, 1986-1999
138	Nolan Ryan, 1972-1979
109	Mike Witt, 1981-1990
102	Frank Tanana, 1973-1980
88	MARK LANGSTON, 1990-1997

K: Most, career

2416	Nolan Ryan, 1972-1979
2151	CHUCK FINLEY, 1986-1999
1283	Mike Witt, 1981-1990
1233	Frank Tanana, 1973-1980
1112	MARK LANGSTON, 1990-1997

Win pct: Highest, career

.567	Frank Tanana, 1973-1980
.557	Andy Messersmith, 1968-1972
.553	Geoff Zahn, 1981-1985
.543	MARK LANGSTON, 1990-1997
.541	CHUCK FINLEY, 1986-1999

ERA: Lowest, career

2.78	Andy Messersmith, 1968-1972
2.83	Dean Chance, 1961-1966
3.07	Nolan Ryan, 1972-1979
3.08	Frank Tanana, 1973-1980
3.13	George Brunet, 1964-1969

Runs: Most, season

120	Don Baylor, 1979
120	JIM EDMONDS, 1995
119	TONY PHILLIPS, 1995
115	JIM EDMONDS, 1998
115	Albie Pearson, 1962

Hits: Most, season

202	Alex Johnson, 1970
189	GARRET ANDERSON, 1997
188	GARRET ANDERSON, 1999
188	Carney Lansford, 1979
186	Don Baylor, 1979
186	Billy Moran, 1962

2B: Most, season

42	Doug DeCinces, 1982
42	JIM EDMONDS, 1998
42	Johnny Ray, 1988
41	GARRET ANDERSON, 1998
39	GARY DiSARCINA, 1998
39	DARIN ERSTAD, 1998

3B: Most, season

13	Jim Fregosi, 1968	
13	Mickey Rivers, 1975	
13	DEVON WHITE, 1989	
12	Jim Fregosi, 1963	
11	Bobby Knoop, 1966	
11	Mickey Rivers, 1974	

HR: Most, season

39	Reggie Jackson, 1982
37	Bobby Bonds, 1977
37	Leon Wagner, 1962
36	Don Baylor, 1979
34	Don Baylor, 1978
34	WALLY JOYNER, 1987
34	TIM SALMON, 1995

RBI: Most, season

139	Don Baylor, 1979
129	TIM SALMON, 1997
117	WALLY JOYNER, 1987
115	Bobby Bonds, 1977
112	CHILI DAVIS, 1993

SB: Most, season

70	Mickey Rivers, 1975
56	Gary Pettis, 1985
55	LUIS POLONIA, 1993
51	LUIS POLONIA, 1992
50	Gary Pettis, 1986

BB: Most, season

113	TONY PHILLIPS, 1995
106	Brian Downing, 1987
96	Albie Pearson, 1961
95	Albie Pearson, 1962
95	TIM SALMON, 1997

BA: Highest, season

.339	Rod Carew, 1983
.331	Rod Carew, 1980
.330	TIM SALMON, 1995
.329	Alex Johnson, 1970
.326	Brian Downing, 1979

On-base avg; Highest, season

.429	TIM SALMON, 1995
.429	CHILI DAVIS, 1995
.420	Albie Pearson, 1961
.418	Brian Downing, 1979
.410	CHILI DAVIS, 1994

Slug pct: Highest, season

.594	TIM SALMON, 1995
.561	CHILI DAVIS, 1994
.548	Doug DeCinces, 1982
.543	Bobby Grich, 1981
.537	Bobby Grich, 1979

Games started: Most, season

41	Nolan Ryan, 1974
40	Bill Singer, 1973
39	Nolan Ryan, 1972
39	Nolan Ryan, 1973
39	Nolan Ryan, 1976
39	Clyde Wright, 1970

Complete games: Most, season

26	Nolan Ryan, 1973
26	Nolan Ryan, 1974
23	Frank Tanana, 1976
22	Nolan Ryan, 1977
21	Nolan Ryan, 1976

Saves: Most, season

46	Bryan Harvey, 1991
42	TROY PERCIVAL, 1998
37	Lee Smith, 1995
36	TROY PERCIVAL, 1996
31	Donnie Moore, 1985
31	TROY PERCIVAL, 1999

Shutouts: Most, season

11	Dean Chance, 1964
9	Nolan Ryan, 1972
7	Nolan Ryan, 1976
7	Frank Tanana, 1977
6	Jim McGlothlin, 1967

Wins: Most, season

22	Nolan Ryan, 1974
22	Clyde Wright, 1970
21	Nolan Ryan, 1973
20	Dean Chance, 1964
20	Andy Messersmith, 1971
20	Bill Singer, 1973

K: Most, season

383	Nolan Ryan, 1973
367	Nolan Ryan, 1974
341	Nolan Ryan, 1977
329	Nolan Ryan, 1972
327	Nolan Ryan, 1976

Win pct: Highest, season

.773	Bert Blyleven, 1989
.704	MARK LANGSTON, 1991
.692	Geoff Zahn, 1982
.690	Dean Chance, 1964
.682	MARK LANGSTON, 1995

ERA: Lowest, season

1.65	Dean Chance, 1964
2.28	Nolan Ryan, 1972
2.40	CHUCK FINLEY, 1990
2.43	Frank Tanana, 1976
2.52	Andy Messersmith, 1969

Most pinch-hit homers, season

4	JACK HOWELL, 1996
3	Joe Adcock, 1966
3	George Hendrick, 1987

Most pinch-hit homers, career

7	JACK HOWELL, 1985-1997
4	Ruppert Jones, 1985-1987
4	George Hendrick, 1985-1988

Longest hitting streak

28	GARRET ANDERSON, 1998
25	Rod Carew, 1982
23	JIM EDMONDS, 1995
22	Sandy Alomar, 1970
21	Bobby Grich, 1981
20	Bobby Grich, 1979

Most consecutive scoreless innings

36	Jim McGlothlin, 1967

No-hit games

Bo Belinsky, LA vs Bal AL, 2-0; May 5, 1962.

Clyde Wright, Cal vs Oak AL, 4-0; July 3, 1970.

Nolan Ryan, Cal at KC AL, 3-0; May 15, 1973.

Nolan Ryan, Cal at Det AL, 6-0; July 15, 1973.

Nolan Ryan, Cal vs Min AL, 4-0; September 28, 1974.

Nolan Ryan, Cal vs Bal AL, 1-0; June 1, 1975.

Mike Witt, Cal at Tex AL, 1-0; September 30, 1984 (perfect game).

MARK LANGSTON (seven innings) and Mike Witt (two innings), Cal vs Sea AL, 1-0; April 11, 1990

ACTIVE PLAYERS in caps.

Players' years of service are listed by the first and last years with this team and are not necessarily consecutive; all statistics record performances for this team only.

Atlanta Braves

Chipper Jones's masterful batting, speed, and defense for the Braves made him the National League MVP.

By Robert Deutsch, USA TODAY

1999 Braves: Another Series lost

With the Atlanta Braves three games down in the World Series, someone asked John Schuerholz about impending free agents.

"We're still trying to win a World Cham—" the Braves general manager said, stopping himself in mid-word. ". . .trying to win a World Series *game.*"

Schuerholz and his team never found that one victory—after 103 in the regular season and seven more in the National League playoffs—and never got close to that second World Championship in their eight-year playoff run. And never, it seems, will they be able to avoid questions about the failures made possible only by their successes.

The general manager had to poke around the inside pockets of his sports coat to find his roster, to count how many current Braves could be free agents. Six was the answer, with left fielder Gerald Williams the only every-day player among them. The others are shortstop Jose Hernandez, first baseman Brian Hunter, catcher Greg Myers, outfielder Otis Nixon, and pitcher Russ Springer.

Schuerholz's point in his remark was that he'd find time to be concerned about what changes could or should be made to his team once this World Series was over.

It would be over, of course, a few more agonizing hours later. A sweep.

Sweep: So ignominious, so ominous, so dominant in memory.

Yet, with three of the games decided in the late innings, wasn't the gulf between the Yankees and the Braves much narrower than it seemed?

"You mean the difference an Andres Galarraga and a Javy Lopez could make?" Schuerholz asked. He later added the name of 1998 closer Kerry Ligtenberg to the list, not claiming that the presence of the trio, missing because of illness and injury, necessarily would have changed the outcome against the Yankees.

The point was more applicable to the looming concern about where the Braves

Team MVP

Chipper Jones: The third baseman Chipper Jones led Atlanta to the NL East title with several key home runs in September showdown games with the New York Mets. But that was merely the icing on a sweet season. Despite being walked 126 times, Jones led the Braves with 45 home runs, 181 hits, 116 runs, 41 doubles, 359 total bases and a .319 batting average. He also had 110 RBI and 25 stolen bases.

go from here, whether they're running out of chances, whether eight opportunities is more than any franchise's fair share.

"It will be like signing three free agents for us," Schuerholz said of the expected return of catcher Lopez from knee surgery, first baseman Galarraga from cancer treatment and Ligtenberg from elbow surgery.

"We expect to be better," said club president Stan Kasten.

And the consensus in the Atlanta clubhouse was that they don't have to be a whole lot better after winning 103 games during the regular season.

"This was not our best team," said pitcher Greg Maddux. "But we played better as a team this year."

"This was a championship season," said third baseman Chipper Jones, who carried the injury-riddled Braves on his back and bat through a September division race with the New York Mets—and was rewarded with the league MVP trophy.

That also was the time of year when Kevin Millwood stepped up and became the team's best pitcher, no mean feat on a staff that includes Maddux, Tom Glavine and John Smoltz.

"At the risk of sounding arrogant," Schuerholz said, "We're very proud. But it's disappointing that we haven't won more than one world championship."

1999 Braves: Week-by-week notes

These notes were excerpted from the following issues of Baseball Weekly.

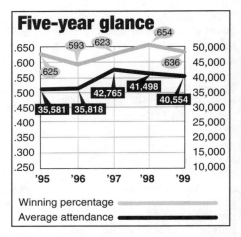

Five-year glance

Winning percentage ——————
Average attendance ——————

▶**April 14:** Closer Kerry Ligtenberg underwent successful "Tommy John" surgery on his elbow, but in the process he learned that he had a nearly complete tear of another elbow ligament and would need a full year to recover.

▶**April 21:** The Mark Wohlers experiment ended with the Braves trading away their former closer to Cincinnati for reliever John Hudek, after Wohlers refused his minor league assignment.

▶**April 28:** Left-hander Tom Glavine was frustrated about his 0-3 start—his worst since his rookie year, 1988— but he was trying not to let it get him down. "I can't get pulled into it because I'm not far off," said Glavine, whose ERA was 6.51. Glavine had not been getting the outside strike call that he was used to.

▶**May 12:** Without first baseman Andres Galarraga, out for the season with lymphoma, the Braves have sought more power from Ryan Klesko but hadn't been getting it until last week. Against the Padres on May 8, Klesko had a double, a triple and a home run—only one fewer extra-base hit than he'd had all year.

▶**May 19:** Eddie Perez believed one reason hitters had been getting to right-hander Greg Maddux this year was that umpires were calling automatic balls whenever a catcher went outside the lined catcher's box to get a pitch. Maddux, who gave up a career-high 14 hits to Chicago on May 15, was being hit for a .356 average, and his ERA was 4.83.

▶**May 26:** Manager Bobby Cox has replaced slumping Otis Nixon (.181 average) with Gerald Williams in left field.

▶**June 2:** Right-hander John Smoltz had thrown twice on the side and was prepared to return to the rotation on June 2 against the Rockies. Smoltz was 5-1 with a 2.59 ERA when he had to shut down with an inflamed elbow.

▶**June 9:** The Braves played some uncharacteristically flawed defense, as a pair of errors led to two losses to the Dodgers. Through 50 games last year, they had only 21 errors. This season through 50 games, they had committed 41.

▶**June 16:** Right fielder Brian Jordan was second to third baseman Chipper Jones on the Braves in home runs with 13 and was leading the team with 53 RBI. Jordan's 25 home runs last season with the Cardinals were a career high.

▶**June 23:** Lefty reliever Mike Remlinger had thrived since arriving in Atlanta from Cincinnati as part of the Bret Boone–Denny Neagle deal. Through June 19 his 1.38 ERA was the best on the staff, and his .202 opponents' average was second only to that of left-handed closer John Rocker (.157).

▶**June 30:** Chipper Jones might have found what he had been looking for most of this season: some rhythm from the left side. In three games against Montreal, the switch-hitter was 5-for-10, all against right-handed pitchers.

▶**July 15:** John Smoltz planned to pitch an inning on July 15 for AA Greenville to gauge how his elbow responds in a game situation and decide where to go next. Smoltz was on the DL for the second time this season with an inflamed elbow.

▶**July 21:** Ryan Klesko had three two-homer games, the latest on July 16, to bring his season total to 15 home runs. That was three fewer than he had all of

1998. He hit four homers in a span of three games.

▶**July 28:** The Braves got John Smoltz back on July 24 (in Philadelphia) but could have lost catcher Javy Lopez for the season. Lopez, who had been playing for a week on a sprained right knee, reinjured it landing on first base after beating out an infield hit.

▶**Aug. 11:** With the top of the lineup in a state of flux, Gerald Williams was the likely leadoff solution for Bobby Cox. Through Aug. 8 Williams was hitting .351 (33-for-94) over his past 40 games and was working on a career-high 11-game hitting streak.

▶**Aug. 18:** The roller-coaster ride continued for second baseman Bret Boone, who hit .270 in April and .302 in May, then .178 in June and .217 in July. He had hit .311 (14-for-45) with two home runs and 11 RBI this month through Aug. 15.

▶**Aug. 25:** In three outings at Coors Field this season, John Rocker was 0-2 with two blown saves. He had allowed seven runs in two-thirds of an inning for a 94.50 ERA.

▶**Sept. 1:** Setup man Rudy Seanez was on the DL with a stress fracture of his right elbow. In his absence the Braves used Russ Springer and Mike Remlinger to set up games for John Rocker.

▶**Sept. 8:** On Sept. 5 the ninth inning went from a breeze to a disaster in one pitch. With two out and nobody on and the Braves leading 5-4, Kelly Stinnett struck out on a pitch in the dirt against John Rocker. Eddie Perez retrieved the ball in front of the plate and threw the ball over first baseman Randall Simon's head into right field, allowing Stinnett to reach second. That led to a three-run Diamondbacks rally and a 7-5 loss for the Braves.

▶**Sept. 15:** Chipper Jones had already stolen a career-high 23 bases this season. Jones had been caught only three times, none in his last 16 attempts. Jones had also walked a career-high 110 times through Sept. 12 and had drawn walks in 16 consecutive games, tying the NL record set by Jack Clark of the Cardinals.

▶**Sept. 22:** Right-hander Kevin Millwood exceeded even his own expectations. He made his first National League All-Star team. Three times he flirted with no-hitters. Then he won six games in a row, including his 18th on Sept. 19 to top last year's total.

▶**Sept. 29:** After Chipper Jones hit four home runs and had seven RBI in a three-game sweep over the Mets, he was accused by the Mets of having been tipped off about the location of pitches. Jones pointed out that two of his homers came with the bases empty.

QUOTE OF THE YEAR

"I shouldn't dignify it with an answer because it's bush."

—Third baseman Chipper Jones, on the Mets' accusation that Jones was tipped off on pitch location

Team Leaders

Batting avg.	Hits	Wins	Strikeouts
.319 Chipper Jones	181 Chipper Jones	19 Greg Maddux	205 Kevin Millwood
.283 Brian Jordan	163 Brian Jordan	18 Kevin Millwood	156 John Smoltz
	163 Andruw Jonew		
HR		**Losses**	**Innings**
45 Chipper Jones	**Runs**	11 Tom Glavine	234 Tom Glavine
26 Andruw Jones	116 Chipper Jones	9 Greg Maddux	228 Kevin Millwood
	102 Bret Boone		
RBI		**ERA**	**Saves**
115 Brian Jordan	**Stolen bases**	2.68 Kevin Millwood	38 John Rocker
110 Chipper Jones	26 Otis Nixon	3.19 John Smoltz	3 Rudy Seanez
	25 Chipper Jones		

ATLANTA BRAVES 1999 final stats

BATTERS	BA	SLG	OBA	G	AB	R	H	TB	2B	3B	HR	RBI	BB	SO	SB	CS	E
Battle	.353	.529	.421	15	17	2	6	9	0	0	1	5	2	3	0	0	0
Lombard	.333	.333	.429	6	6	1	2	2	0	0	0	0	1	2	2	0	0
C. Jones	.319	.633	.441	157	567	116	181	359	41	1	45	110	126	94	25	3	17
Lopez	.317	.533	.375	65	246	34	78	131	18	1	11	45	20	41	0	3	4
Simon	.317	.459	.367	90	218	26	69	100	16	0	5	25	17	25	2	2	3
Klesko	.297	.532	.376	133	404	55	120	215	28	2	21	80	53	69	5	2	6
Jordan	.283	.465	.346	153	576	100	163	268	28	4	23	115	51	81	13	8	3
A. Jones	.275	.483	.365	162	592	97	163	286	35	5	26	84	76	103	24	12	10
Williams	.275	.457	.335	143	422	76	116	193	24	1	17	68	33	67	19	11	3
Hernandez	.266	.425	.339	147	508	79	135	216	20	2	19	62	52	145	11	3	17
Myers	.265	.370	.348	84	200	19	53	74	6	0	5	24	26	30	0	0	4
Lockhart	.261	.311	.337	108	161	20	42	50	3	1	1	21	19	21	3	1	1
Boone	.252	.416	.310	152	608	102	153	253	38	1	20	63	47	112	14	9	13
E. Perez	.249	.372	.299	104	309	30	77	115	17	0	7	30	17	40	0	1	5
Hunter	.249	.425	.367	114	181	28	45	77	12	1	6	30	31	40	0	1	4
Guillen	.241	.323	.284	92	232	21	56	75	16	0	1	20	15	17	4	2	7
Garcia	.235	.432	.261	57	132	17	31	57	5	0	7	24	5	42	0	0	2
Weiss	.226	.323	.315	110	279	38	63	90	13	4	2	29	35	48	7	3	12
Nixon	.205	.232	.309	84	151	31	31	35	2	1	0	8	23	15	26	7	1
Fabregas	.199	.299	.280	88	231	20	46	69	10	2	3	21	26	27	0	0	5
Matos	.125	.125	.125	6	8	0	1	1	0	0	0	2	0	1	0	0	0
DeRosa	.000	.000	.000	7	8	0	0	0	0	0	0	0	0	2	0	0	0

PITCHERS	W-L	ERA	BA	G	GS	CG	GF	SH	SV	IP	H	R	ER	HR	BB	SO
Remlinger	10-1	2.37	.215	73	0	0	14	0	1	83.2	66	24	22	9	35	81
Rocker	4-5	2.49	.180	74	0	0	61	0	38	72.1	47	24	20	5	37	104
Millwood	18-7	2.68	.202	33	33	2	0	0	0	228.0	168	80	68	24	59	205
McGlinchy	7-3	2.82	.255	64	0	0	21	0	0	70.1	66	25	22	6	30	67
Smoltz	11-8	3.19	.245	29	29	1	0	1	0	186.1	168	70	66	14	40	156
Seanez	6-1	3.35	.234	56	0	0	13	0	3	53.2	47	21	20	3	21	41
Springer	2-1	3.42	.185	49	0	0	8	0	1	47.1	31	20	18	5	22	49
Maddux	19-9	3.57	.294	33	33	4	0	0	0	219.1	258	103	87	16	37	136
Glavine	14-11	4.12	.287	35	35	2	0	0	0	234.0	259	115	107	18	83	138
Mulholland	10-8	4.39	.297	42	24	0	7	0	1	170.1	201	95	83	21	45	83
Cortes	0-0	4.91	.214	4	0	0	4	0	0	3.2	3	3	2	0	4	2
Bergman	5-6	5.21	.325	25	16	2	2	1	0	105.1	135	62	61	9	29	44
Chen	2-2	5.47	.208	16	7	0	3	0	0	51.0	38	32	31	11	27	45
Ebert	0-1	5.63	.300	5	0	0	3	0	1	8.0	9	5	5	2	5	4
Speier	0-0	5.65	.248	19	0	0	8	0	0	28.2	28	18	18	8	13	22
O. Perez	4-6	6.00	.275	18	17	0	0	0	0	93.0	100	65	62	12	53	82
Hudek	0-2	7.64	.325	17	0	0	12	0	0	17.2	25	17	15	2	14	18
Cather	1-0	10.13	.417	4	0	0	0	0	0	2.2	5	3	3	2	1	0
Stull	0-0	13.50	.500	1	0	0	0	0	0	0.2	2	3	1	0	2	0
Winkelsas	0-0	54.00	1.000	1	0	0	0	0	0	0.1	4	2	2	0	1	0

2000 preliminary roster

PITCHERS (23)
Winston Abreu
Bruce Chen
David Cortes
Richard Dishman
Derrin Ebert
Tom Glavine
Derrick Lewis
Kerry Ligtenberg
Greg Maddux
Jason Marquis
Kevin McGlinchy
Rafael Medina

Kevin Millwood
Damian Moss
Terry Mulholland
Jimmy Osting
Odalis Perez
Mike Remlinger
Luis Rivera
John Rocker
John Smoltz
Everett Stull
Ismael Villegas

CATCHERS (3)
Javier Lopez
Pascual Matos
Eddie Perez

INFIELDERS (10)
Bret Boone
Junior Brignac
Andres Galarraga
Freddy Garcia
Ozzie Guillen
Wes Helms
Chipper Jones

Keith Lockhart
Randall Simon
Walt Weiss

OUTFIELDERS (4)
Andruw Jones
Brian Jordan
Ryan Klesko
George Lombard

Games played by position

PLAYER	G	C	1B	2B	3B	SS	OF
Battle	15	0	0	0	6	0	0
Boone	152	0	0	151	0	0	0
DeRosa	7	0	0	0	0	2	0
Fabregas	6	4	1	0	0	0	0
Garcia	2	0	1	0	0	0	1
Guillen	92	0	0	1	6	53	0
Hernandez	48	0	1	0	0	45	1
Hunter	114	0	101	0	0	0	8
C. Jones	157	0	0	0	156	1	0
A. Jones	162	0	0	0	0	0	162
Jordan	153	0	0	0	0	0	150
Klesko	133	0	75	0	0	0	53
Lockhart	108	0	0	25	10	0	0
Lombard	6	0	0	0	0	0	4
Lopez	65	60	0	0	0	0	0
Matos	6	5	0	0	0	0	0
Myers	34	31	0	0	0	0	0
Nixon	84	0	0	1	0	0	52
Perez	104	98	2	0	0	0	0
Simon	90	0	70	0	0	0	0
Weiss	110	0	0	0	0	102	0
Williams	143	0	0	0	0	0	139

Sick call: 1999 DL report

PLAYER	Days on the DL
Andres Galarraga	182
Wes Helms	131*
John Hudek	44
Kerry Ligtenberg	182
Javier Lopez	95*
Damian Moss	57
Otis Nixon	34
Odalis Perez	73
Mike Remlinger	13
Rudy Seanez	44
John Smoltz	34*
Russ Springer	42
Walt Weiss	24

Indicates two separate terms on Disabled List.

Minor Leagues

Tops in the organization

BATTER	CLUB	AVG.	G	AB	R	H	HR	RBI
Giles, Marcus	MYR	.326	126	497	80	162	13	73
Furcal, Rafael	MYR	.322	126	519	105	167	1	41
Manning, Patrick	Mac	.313	67	259	46	81	8	38
Sisco, Steve	Rch	.311	128	495	80	154	18	76
Wilson, Travis	Mac	.309	90	363	65	112	11	63

HOME RUNS			WINS		
Battle, Howard	Rch	24	Osting, Jimmy	Mac	14
Hessman, Mike	MYR	23	Fleck, Will	MYR	10
Zapp, A.J.	Mac	22	Flach, Jason	Gvl	10
Cameron, Troy	Mac	22	Abreu, Winston	MYR	10
Tyler, Brad	Rch	21	Several Players Tied at		9

RBI			SAVES		
Tyler, Brad	Rch	79	Cortes, David	Rch	22
Johnson, Adam	Gvl	78	Greene, Ryan	MYR	16
Cameron, Troy	Mac	77	Milburn, Adam	Gvl	15
Sisco, Steve	Rch	76	Voyles, Brad	MYR	14
Battle, Howard	Rch	74	Corey, Michael	MYR	13

STOLEN BASES			STRIKEOUTS		
Furcal, Rafael	MYR	96	Abreu, Winston	MYR	171
Smith, Demond	Gvl	31	Sobkowiak, Scott	MYR	161
Ross, Jason	MYR	31	Osting, Jimmy	Mac	131
Brignac, Junior	MYR	28	Dishman, Richard	Gvl	131
Several Players Tied at		27	Ratliff, Jon	Rch	129

PITCHER	CLUB	W-L	ERA	IP	H	BB	SO
Lewis, Derrick	MYR	8-4	2.40	131	100	81	102
Abreu, Winston	MYR	10-4	2.48	138	94	67	171
Sobkowiak, Scott	MYR	9-4	2.84	139	100	63	161
Osting, Jimmy	Mac	14-4	2.88	147	130	30	131
Frachiseur, Zach	MYR	7-4	2.91	102	80	33	99

1999 salaries

	Bonuses	Total earned salary
Greg Maddux, p		10,600,000
Andres Galarraga, 1b		8,250,000
John Smoltz, p		7,750,000
Tom Glavine, p		7,000,000
Javy Lopez, c		5,250,000
Ryan Klesko, 1b		4,750,000
Brian Jordan, of		4,600,000
Chipper Jones, 3b	175,000	4,175,000
Walt Weiss, ss		3,000,000
Terry Mulholland, p		2,925,000
Bret Boone, 2b		2,900,000
Jose Hernandez, ss		2,400,000
Otis Nixon, of		1,500,000
Gerald Williams, of	75,000	1,475,000
Mike Remlinger, p		1,100,000
Keith Lockhart, 2b		1,000,000
Russ Springer, p		950,000
Greg Myers, c		850,000
Rudy Seanez, p	150,000	775,000
Eddie Perez, c	80,000	630,000
Ozzie Guillen, ss	50,000	550,000
Brian Hunter, 1b	75,000	375,000
Andruw Jones, of		330,000
Kerry Ligtenberg, p		255,000
Kevin Millwood, p		230,000
Mike Cather, p		225,000
John Rocker, p		217,500
Randall Simon, 1b		202,500
Jorge Fabregas, c		200,000
Bruce Chen, p		200,000
Odalis Perez, p		200,000
Kevin McGlinchy, p		200,000

Average 1999 salary: $2,345,781
Total 1999 team payroll: $75,065,000
Termination pay: $4,291,599

Atlanta (1966-1999), includes Boston (1876-1952) and Milwaukee (1953-1965)

Runs: Most, career

2107	Hank Aaron, 1954-1974
1452	Eddie Mathews, 1952-1966
1292	Herman Long, 1890-1902
1134	Fred Tenney, 1894-1911
1103	Dale Murphy, 1976-1990

Hits: Most, career

3600	Hank Aaron, 1954-1974
2201	Eddie Mathews, 1952-1966
1994	Fred Tenney, 1894-1911
1901	Herman Long, 1890-1902
1901	Dale Murphy, 1976-1990

2B: Most, career

600	Hank Aaron, 1954-1974
338	Eddie Mathews, 1952-1966
306	Dale Murphy, 1976-1990
295	Herman Long, 1890-1902
291	Tommy Holmes, 1942-1951

3B: Most, career

103	Rabbit Maranville, 1912-1935
96	Hank Aaron, 1954-1974
91	Herman Long, 1890-1902
80	John Morrill, 1876-1888
79	Bill Bruton, 1953-1960

HR: Most, career

733	Hank Aaron, 1954-1974
493	Eddie Mathews, 1952-1966
371	Dale Murphy, 1976-1990
239	Joe Adcock, 1953-1962
215	Bob Horner, 1978-1986

RBI: Most, career

2202	Hank Aaron, 1954-1974
1388	Eddie Mathews, 1952-1966
1143	Dale Murphy, 1976-1990
964	Herman Long, 1890-1902
927	Hugh Duffy, 1892-1900

SB: Most, career

433	Herman Long, 1890-1902
331	Hugh Duffy, 1892-1900
274	Billy Hamilton, 1896-1901
260	Bobby Lowe, 1890-1901
260	Fred Tenney, 1894-1911
240	Hank Aaron, 1954-1974 (6)

BB: Most, career

1376	Eddie Mathews, 1952-1966
1297	Hank Aaron, 1954-1974
912	Dale Murphy, 1976-1990
750	Fred Tenney, 1894-1911
598	Billy Nash, 1885-1895

BA: Highest, career

.339	Billy Hamilton, 1896-1901
.332	Hugh Duffy, 1892-1900
.327	Chick Stahl, 1897-1900
.317	Rico Carty, 1963-1972
.317	Ralph Garr, 1968-1975

On-base avg: Highest, career

.456	Billy Hamilton, 1896-1901
.398	Bob Elliott, 1947-1951
.394	CHIPPER JONES, 1993-1999
.394	Hugh Duffy, 1892-1900
.388	Rico Carty, 1963-1972

Slug pct: Highest, career

.567	Hank Aaron, 1954-1974
.533	Wally Berger, 1930-1937
.529	CHIPPER JONES, 1993-1999
.525	RYAN KLESKO, 1992-1999
.517	Eddie Mathews, 1952-1966

Games started: Most, career

635	Warren Spahn, 1942-1964
595	Phil Niekro, 1964-1987
501	Kid Nichols, 1890-1901
399	TOM GLAVINE, 1987-1999
356	JOHN SMOLTZ, 1988-1999

Complete games: Most, career

475	Kid Nichols, 1890-1901
374	Warren Spahn, 1942-1964
268	Vic Willis, 1898-1905
242	Jim Whitney, 1881-1885
226	John Clarkson, 1888-1892
226	Phil Niekro, 1964-1987

Saves: Most, career

141	Gene Garber, 1978-1987
112	MARK WOHLERS, 1991-1999
78	Cecil Upshaw, 1966-1973
62	BOB WICKMAN, 1998-1999
57	Rick Camp, 1976-1985

Shutouts: Most, career

63	Warren Spahn, 1942-1964
44	Kid Nichols, 1890-1901
43	Phil Niekro, 1964-1987
30	Lew Burdette, 1951-1963
29	Tommy Bond, 1877-1881

Wins: Most, career

356	Warren Spahn, 1942-1964
329	Kid Nichols, 1890-1901
268	Phil Niekro, 1964-1987
187	TOM GLAVINE, 1987-1999
179	Lew Burdette, 1951-1963

K: Most, career

2912	Phil Niekro, 1964-1987
2493	Warren Spahn, 1942-1964
2098	JOHN SMOLTZ, 1988-1999
1672	Kid Nichols, 1890-1901
1659	TOM GLAVINE, 1987-1999

Win pct: Highest, career

.712	GREG MADDUX, 1993-1999
.679	Fred Klobedanz, 1896-1902
.655	Harry Staley, 1891-1894
.645	John Clarkson, 1888-1892
.643	Kid Nichols, 1890-1901

ERA: Lowest, career

2.21	Tommy Bond, 1877-1881
2.34	GREG MADDUX, 1993-1999
2.49	Jim Whitney, 1881-1885
2.52	Art Nehf, 1915-1919
2.62	Dick Rudolph, 1913-1927

Runs: Most, season

160	Hugh Duffy, 1894
158	Bobby Lowe, 1894
153	Billy Hamilton, 1896
152	Billy Hamilton, 1897
149	Herman Long, 1893
131	Dale Murphy, 1983 (9)

Hits: Most, season

237	Hugh Duffy, 1894
224	Tommy Holmes, 1945
223	Hank Aaron, 1959
219	Ralph Garr, 1971
218	Felipe Alou, 1966

2B: Most, season

51	Hugh Duffy, 1894
47	Tommy Holmes, 1945
46	Hank Aaron, 1959
44	Wally Berger, 1931
44	Lee Maye, 1964
43	GEOFF JENKINS, 1999 (6)

3B: Most, season

20	Dick Johnston, 1887
20	Harry Stovey, 1891
19	Chick Stahl, 1899
18	Dick Johnston, 1888
18	Ray Powell, 1921
17	Ralph Garr, 1974 (6)

HR: Most, season

47	Hank Aaron, 1971
47	Eddie Mathews, 1953
46	Eddie Mathews, 1959

| 45 | Hank Aaron, 1962 |
| 45 | CHIPPER JONES, 1999 |

RBI: Most, season

145	Hugh Duffy, 1894
135	Eddie Mathews, 1953
132	Hank Aaron, 1957
132	Jimmy Collins, 1897
130	Hank Aaron, 1963
130	Wally Berger, 1935
127	Hank Aaron, 1966 (9)

SB: Most, season

84	King Kelly, 1887
83	Billy Hamilton, 1896
72	OTIS NIXON, 1991
68	King Kelly, 1889
66	Billy Hamilton, 1897

BB: Most, season

131	Bob Elliott, 1948
127	Jimmy Wynn, 1976
126	Darrell Evans, 1974
126	CHIPPER JONES, 1999
124	Darrell Evans, 1973
124	Eddie Mathews, 1963

BA: Highest, season

.440	Hugh Duffy, 1894
.387	Rogers Hornsby, 1928
.373	Dan Brouthers, 1889
.369	Billy Hamilton, 1898
.366	Billy Hamilton, 1896
.366	Rico Carty, 1970 (6)

On-base avg; Highest, season

.502	Hugh Duffy, 1894
.498	Rogers Hornsby, 1928
.480	Billy Hamilton, 1898
.478	Billy Hamilton, 1896
.462	Dan Brouthers, 1889
.454	Rico Carty, 1970 (7)

Slug pct: Highest, season

.694	Hugh Duffy, 1894
.669	Hank Aaron, 1971
.636	Hank Aaron, 1959
.633	CHIPPER JONES, 1999
.632	Rogers Hornsby, 1928

Games started: Most, season

72	John Clarkson, 1889
67	Charlie Buffinton, 1884
64	Tommy Bond, 1879
63	Jim Whitney, 1881
59	Tommy Bond, 1878
44	Phil Niekro, 1979 (22)

Complete games: Most, season

68	John Clarkson, 1889
63	Charlie Buffinton, 1884
59	Tommy Bond, 1879
58	Tommy Bond, 1877

57	Tommy Bond, 1878
57	Charley Radbourn, 1886
57	Jim Whitney, 1881
23	Phil Niekro, 1979 (*)

Saves: Most, season

39	MARK WOHLERS, 1996
38	JOHN ROCKER, 1999
37	BOB WICKMAN, 1999
33	MARK WOHLERS, 1997
30	Gene Garber, 1982
30	Kerry Ligtenberg, 1998

Shutouts: Most, season

11	Tommy Bond, 1879
9	Tommy Bond, 1878
8	Charlie Buffinton, 1884
8	John Clarkson, 1889
7	Kid Nichols, 1890
7	Togie Pittinger, 1902
7	Warren Spahn, 1947
7	Warren Spahn, 1951
7	Warren Spahn, 1963
7	Irv Young, 1905
6	Phil Niekro, 1974 (11)

Wins: Most, season

49	John Clarkson, 1889
48	Charlie Buffinton, 1884
43	Tommy Bond, 1879
40	Tommy Bond, 1877
40	Tommy Bond, 1878
24	JOHN SMOLTZ, 1996 (*)

K: Most, season

417	Charlie Buffinton, 1884
345	Jim Whitney, 1883
284	John Clarkson, 1889
276	JOHN SMOLTZ, 1996
270	Jim Whitney, 1884

Win pct: Highest, season

.905	GREG MADDUX, 1995
.850	JOHN SMOLTZ, 1998
.842	Tom Hughes, 1916
.826	GREG MADDUX, 1997
.810	Phil Niekro, 1982

ERA: Lowest, season

1.56	GREG MADDUX, 1994
1.63	GREG MADDUX, 1995
1.87	Phil Niekro, 1967
1.90	Bill James, 1914
1.96	Tommy Bond, 1879

Most pinch-hit homers, season

| 5 | Butch Nieman, Bos-1945 |
| 4 | Tommy Gregg, 1990 |

Most pinch-hit homers, career

7	Joe Adcock, Mil-1953-1962
6	Tommy Gregg, 1988-1997
6	Mike Lum, 1967-1981

Longest hitting streak

37	Tommy Holmes, Bos-1945
31	Rico Carty, 1970
29	Rowland Office, 1976
28	MARQUIS GRISSOM, 1996
27	Hugh Duffy, Bos-1893

Most consecutive scoreless innings

| 41 | Art Nehf, Bos-1917 |
| 29 | Phil Niekro, 1974 |

No-hit games

Jack Stivetts, Bos vs Bro NL, 11-0; August 6, 1892.

Frank (Jeff) Pfeffer, Bos vs Cin NL, 6-0; May 8, 1907.

George Davis, Bos vs Phi NL, 7-0; September 9, 1914 (2nd game).

Tom L. Hughes, Bos vs Pit NL, 2-0; June 16, 1916.

Jim Tobin, Bos vs Bro NL, 2-0; April 27, 1944.

Vern Bickford, Bos vs Bro NL, 7-0; August 11, 1950.

Jim Wilson, Mil vs Phi NL, 2-0; June 12, 1954.

Lew Burdette, Mil vs Phi NL, 1-0; August 18, 1960.

Warren Spahn, Mil vs Phi NL, 4-0; September 16, 1960.

Warren Spahn, Mil vs SF NL, 1-0; April 28, 1961.

Phil Niekro, Atl vs SD NL, 9-0; August 5, 1973.

KENT MERCKER (6 innings), MARK WOHLERS (2 innings) and Alejandro Pena (1 inning), Atl at SD NL, 1-0; September 11, 1991.

KENT MERCKER, Atl at LA NL, 6-0; April 8, 1994.

Jack Stivetts, five innings, called so Boston could catch train to Cleveland for Temple Cup play-offs, Bos at Was NL, 6-0; October 15, 1892 (2nd game).

Jim Tobin, five innings, darkness, Bos vs Phi NL, 7-0; June 22, 1944 (2nd game).

ACTIVE PLAYERS in caps.

Players' years of service are listed by the first and last years with this team and are not necessarily consecutive; all statistics record performances for this team only.

Leader from the franchise's current location is included. If not in the top five, leader's rank is listed in parenthesis; asterisk (*) indicates player is not in top 25.

New York Mets

Mike Piazza thrilled the Big Apple with big numbers, including 40 homers, 124 RBI, and a .305 average.

1999 Mets: The team that never gave up

The New York Mets had been rising from dead so often and for so long that people had come to expect it, especially the players themselves. It was almost surprising to finally end their season at Atlanta in extra innings of Game Six of the National League Championship Series, a game they had trailed 5-0 in a series they had once trailed 3-0.

But that was just how life went for the 1999 Mets.

They contended for most of the season, then had two head-to-head series with the Braves in the season's final two weeks—and the wild ride really began. A seven-game losing streak put them on the verge of wasting a wild-card lead for the second consecutive season, but a three-game sweep of Pittsburgh on the final weekend forced a playoff game at Cincinnati. The Mets won. Then they upset Arizona in a Division Series that began with Edgardo Alfonzo's ninth-inning grand slam and ended with Todd Pratt's 10th-inning homer.

"We've gone a lot of miles," said catcher Mike Piazza. "There's a lot of guys that matured in here. There's a lot of guys that have learned so much, not only about themselves, but what it takes to get to a World Series—not only the tangibles on the field, but the things that you don't see in a box score."

The Mets who began the season were a different team. They added Shawon Dunston, Darryl Hamilton, Orel Hershiser and Kenny Rogers. Benny Agbayani emerged during the season, and Melvin Mora and Pratt took star turns in the playoffs. Hamilton, acquired just before the July 31 trade deadline, talked about how many players "ran out of gas," that they were too banged up to perform up to their abilities. Piazza and many other Mets repeatedly said they "left it all on the field."

"It's a damn good stepping stone to get to the next level," pitcher Al Leiter said. "It's a great group of guys. With a tweak here and there, there's no question we can get to the next level."

The Mets knew their weak spots were outfield defense and starting pitching.

But the infield defense was among the best in baseball in decades. The signing of free agent third baseman Robin Ventura allowed the Mets to move Alfonzo from third to second. With fielding whiz Rey Ordonez already at shortstop and John Olerud at first base, the Mets led the league with only 68 errors.

Meanwhile relief pitching became a strength for much of the season, even with long-time closer John Franco losing time to injury and eventually losing his job to Armando Benitez.

Piazza remained the focal point of the offense, hitting .305 with 40 home runs and 124 RBI. But the Mets added a formidable dimension at the top of the order: Rickey Henderson. He signed on as a free agent and had his best season at the plate in several years, batting .314 to lead the regulars who were with the club all season. Henderson also did his thing on the bases, swiping 37. But he had to play second fiddle to Roger Cedeno, who came over in a trade from the Los Angeles Dodgers and excited the city by matching Henderson's .314 but topping him with 66 steals.

"I think every guy in this room should be proud of the way we handled ourselves," Franco said. "We're champions in our own hearts."

1999 Mets: Week-by-week notes

These notes were excerpted from the following issues of Baseball Weekly.

▶**April 7:** A terrible spring got left-hander Al Leiter's attention. The Mets' ace finished the exhibition season 0-4 with a 5.84 ERA. Leiter said he would take a step back from off-the-field obligations and the distractions that arose after he signed a four-year, $32 million contract in the off-season.

▶**April 14:** Catcher Mike Piazza was set to be sidelined two to three weeks after spraining ligaments in his right knee. The injury did not require surgery. The best news for the Mets last week was the play of Rickey Henderson. The ageless left fielder batted .471 (8-for-17) in his first six games, with four doubles, two homers and four RBI. He also walked eight times and had a .640 on-base percentage.

▶**April 21:** In six games, a span of 6⅔ innings, setup man Armando Benitez did not allow a run. He gave up just one hit and struck out 11 while walking only one. Meanwhile, closer John Franco recorded his 400th career save.

▶**May 12:** Mike Piazza was struggling after his return from the DL—aside from his clutch grand slam in the ninth inning that beat the Padres on April 28. The All-Star was just 8-for-44 in his first 11 games back.

▶**May 19:** Outfielder Roger Cedeno continued to shine playing in place of the injured Rickey Henderson. He tied a club record with four stolen bases on May 14. He had 15 for the year and was batting .337. Second baseman Edgardo Alfonzo had 10 RBI in a four-game stretch and was batting .339.

▶**May 26:** Third baseman Robin Ventura hit grand slams in both games of a doubleheader against the Brewers on May 20, becoming the first major leaguer to accomplish the feat. It gave Ventura 12 career grand slams, one behind active leader Harold Baines.

▶**June 2:** The real roadblock for Bobby Bonilla to get back in the lineup was Roger Cedeno, who stole two more bases

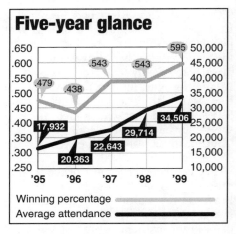

Five-year glance

Winning percentage
Average attendance

against Arizona, giving him a league-leading 28. Bonilla had struggled with injuries and was hitting .157.

▶**June 9:** General manager Steve Phillips fired three coaches on June 5, including pitching coach Bob Apodaca, who a few weeks earlier had been regarded as a guru by the organization. Also gone were hitting coach Tom Robson and assistant pitching coach Randy Niemann. Manager Bobby Valentine opposed the moves.

▶**June 16:** Piazza continued to sizzle. He hit safely in 17 consecutive games through June 13, highlighted by a game-tying homer off Boston's Tom Gordon in the ninth on June 11. Just as hot was outfielder Benny Agbayani. He homered on June 13 against the Red Sox—his 10th in 75 at-bats.

▶**June 23:** The maligned rotation suddenly hit its stride. After Orel Hershiser held the Cardinals to one hit in five shutout innings before leaving with back spasms on June 17 in St. Louis, the staff improved to 9-0 with a 2.82 ERA in 12 games.

▶**June 30:** The Mets entered a big showdown with the first-place Braves having won 14 of 17 games. After a 10-2 win in the opener, the Mets lost the second and third games of the series, spoiling the big-league debut of phenom Octavio Dotel on June 26. The right-hander lasted only 4⅓ innings and allowed six runs.

▶**July 7:** New York can't beat the Braves. Kevin Millwood and John Rocker combined on a three-hitter on July 3 to extend Atlanta's shutout streak against the Mets to 28 innings. The night before, the Braves beat the Mets 16-0, New York's worst shutout beating ever.

▶**July 15:** Mike Piazza was the hero of the first two games against the Yankees. He hit a three-run bomb off Roger Clemens that broke a 2-2 tie in the series opener, then a 482-foot, three-run homer the next day.

▶**July 28:** The Mets sought to bolster their rotation on July 23 when they brought Oakland's Kenny Rogers back to New York in return for AAA outfielder Terrence Long and AA pitcher Leoner Vasquez.

Aug. 4: The Mets addressed their bullpen needs by acquiring relief veterans Billy Taylor from the A's and Chuck McElroy from the Rockies. They also got Darryl Hamilton from Colorado and utility man Shawon Dunston from the Cardinals.

▶**Aug. 11:** At the end of a news conference on June 6, Bobby Valentine proclaimed, "If in the next 55 games we're not better, I shouldn't be the manager." The Mets became the best team in the majors after that. A 2-1 victory over the Dodgers left the Mets 40-15 during that span. They began the season 27-28.

▶**Aug. 18:** The offense was on fire. Through Aug. 15 Piazza was 12-for-18 (.667) with three homers and nine RBI in his last four games. Darryl Hamilton made his presence felt with 15 hits in 38 at-bats.

▶**Sept. 1:** Masato Yoshii was reinserted as a fill-in for right-hander Rick Reed, but he might have won a permanent job by allowing four earned runs in 22⅓ innings in his last three starts.

▶**Sept. 8:** Shortstop Rey Ordonez and understudy Luis Lopez got into a fistfight on the team bus last week. Ordonez suffered a cut above his left eye that required six stitches, but he was in the lineup on Sept. 3.

Sept. 22: Al Leiter allowed nine runs, eight earned, in the first inning of his last four starts. Leiter said he would start working on the problem in the wake of the three runs he allowed in the first inning against the Phillies on Sept. 17. Octavio Dotel, with a 7-2 record but a 5.35 ERA, was dropped from the rotation—possibly for the season.

▶**Oct. 6:** The Mets won the NL wild card on Oct. 4 by beating the Reds 5-0 in a one-game playoff. Even before the turn in fortunes, which started when the Mets snapped their seven-game losing streak with a win over the Braves on Sept. 29, co-owner Fred Wilpon made it clear that Bobby Valentine would return next season.

217

QUOTE OF THE YEAR

"The postseason is not an inevitable situation on this team."

—Manager Bobby Valentine, shortly before the Mets lost seven in a row down the stretch

Team Leaders

Batting avg.	Hits	Wins	Strikeouts
.315 Rickey Henderson	191 Edgardo Alfonzo	13 Al Leiter	162 Al Leiter
.315 Darryl Hamilton	177 Robin Ventura	13 Orel Hershiser	128 Armando Benitez

HR	Runs	Losses	Innings
40 Mike Piazza	123 Edgardo Alfonzo	12 Al Leiter	213 Al Leiter
32 Robin Ventura	107 John Olerud	12 Orel Hershiser	179 Orel Hershiser

RBI	Stolen bases	ERA	Saves
124 Mike Piazza	66 Roger Cedeno	4.23 Al Leiter	22 Armando Benitez
120 Robin Ventura	37 Rickey Henderson	4.40 Masato Yoshii	19 John Franco

NEW YORK METS 1999 final stats

BATTERS	BA	SLG	OBA	G	AB	R	H	TB	2B	3B	HR	RBI	BB	SO	SB	CS	E
Toca	.333	.333	.333	4	3	0	1	1	0	0	0	0	0	2	0	0	0
Dunston	.321	.453	.337	104	243	35	78	110	11	3	5	41	2	39	10	4	3
Henderson	.315	.466	.423	121	438	89	138	204	30	0	12	42	82	82	37	14	2
Hamilton	.315	.422	.386	146	505	82	159	213	19	4	9	45	57	39	6	8	0
Cedeno	.313	.408	.396	155	453	90	142	185	23	4	4	36	60	100	66	17	3
Alfonzo	.304	.502	.385	158	628	123	191	315	41	1	27	108	85	85	9	2	5
Piazza	.303	.575	.361	141	534	100	162	307	25	0	40	124	51	70	2	2	11
Ventura	.301	.529	.379	161	588	88	177	311	38	0	32	120	74	109	1	1	9
Olerud	.298	.463	.427	162	581	107	173	269	39	0	19	96	125	66	3	0	9
Pratt	.293	.386	.369	71	140	18	41	54	4	0	3	21	15	32	2	0	1
Agbayani	.286	.525	.363	101	276	42	79	145	18	3	14	42	32	60	6	4	2
Ordonez	.258	.317	.319	154	520	49	134	165	24	2	1	60	49	59	8	4	4
Payton	.250	.375	.333	13	8	1	2	3	1	0	0	1	0	2	1	2	0
M. Franco	.235	.364	.366	122	132	18	31	48	5	0	4	21	28	21	0	0	1
Allensworth	.219	.370	.310	40	73	14	16	27	2	0	3	9	9	23	2	1	0
Lopez	.212	.308	.308	68	104	11	22	32	4	0	2	13	12	33	1	1	4
Kinkade	.196	.413	.275	28	46	3	9	19	2	1	2	6	3	9	1	0	0
Mora	.161	.161	.278	66	31	6	5	5	0	0	0	1	4	7	2	1	0
Bonilla	.160	.303	.277	60	119	12	19	36	5	0	4	18	19	16	0	1	2
Long	.000	.000	.000	3	3	0	0	0	0	0	0	0	0	2	0	0	0
Halter	—	—	—	7	0	0	0	0	0	0	0	0	0	0	0	0	0
Wilson	—	—	—	1	0	0	0	0	0	0	0	0	0	0	0	0	0

PITCHERS	W-L	ERA	BA	G	GS	CG	GF	SH	SV	IP	H	R	ER	HR	BB	SO
Rusch	0-0	0.00	.333	1	0	0	1	0	0	1.0	1	0	0	0	0	0
Benitez	4-3	1.85	.148	77	0	0	42	0	22	78.0	40	17	16	4	41	128
J. Franco	0-2	2.88	.255	46	0	0	34	0	19	40.2	40	14	13	1	19	41
Wendell	5-4	3.05	.245	80	0	0	14	0	3	85.2	80	31	29	9	37	77
Tam	0-0	3.18	.150	9	0	0	3	0	0	11.1	6	4	4	3	3	8
Mahomes	8-0	3.68	.198	39	0	0	12	0	0	63.2	44	26	26	7	37	51
Cook	10-5	3.86	.216	71	0	0	12	0	3	63.0	50	27	27	11	27	68
Rogers	5-1	4.03	.253	12	12	2	0	1	0	76.0	71	35	34	8	28	58
Watson	2-2	4.08	.252	14	4	0	6	0	1	39.2	36	18	18	5	22	32
Leiter	13-12	4.23	.262	32	32	1	0	1	0	213.0	209	107	100	19	93	162
Yoshii	12-8	4.40	.260	31	29	1	1	0	0	174.0	168	86	85	25	58	105
Hershiser	13-12	4.58	.260	32	32	0	0	0	0	179.0	175	92	91	14	77	89
Reed	11-5	4.58	.281	26	26	1	0	1	0	149.1	163	77	76	23	47	104
McMichael	1-1	4.82	.270	19	0	0	4	0	0	18.2	20	10	10	3	8	18
Dotel	8-3	5.38	.226	19	14	0	1	0	0	85.1	69	52	51	12	49	85
McElroy	3-1	5.50	.286	56	0	0	19	0	0	54.0	60	34	33	9	36	44
Jones	3-3	5.61	.295	12	9	0	0	0	0	59.1	69	37	37	3	11	31
Manzanillo	0-0	5.79	.264	12	0	0	1	0	0	18.2	19	12	12	5	4	25
Isringhausen	1-3	6.41	.279	13	5	0	2	0	1	39.1	43	29	28	7	22	31
Taylor	0-1	8.10	.345	18	0	0	5	0	0	13.1	20	12	12	2	9	14
M. Franco	0-0	13.50	.429	2	0	0	2	0	0	1.1	3	2	2	1	3	2
Murray	0-0	13.50	.444	1	0	0	1	0	0	2.0	4	3	3	0	2	1

2000 preliminary roster

PITCHERS (19)
Armando Benitez
Leslie Brea
Eric Cammack
Dennis Cook
John Franco
Dicky Gonzalez
Mike Hampton
Bobby Jones
Al Leiter
Pat Mahomes
Jim Mann
Jesse Orosco

Rick Reed
Grant Roberts
Glendon Rusch
Bill Taylor
Turk Wendell
Paul Wilson
Masato Yoshii

CATCHERS (3)
Mike Piazza
Todd Pratt
Vance Wilson

INFIELDERS (10)
Edgardo Alfonzo
Matt Franco
Shane Halter
Mike Kinkade
Luis Lopez
Melvin Mora
Rey Ordonez
Jorge Toca
Robin Ventura
Todd Zeile

OUTFIELDERS (9)
Benny Agbayani
Derek Bell
Bobby Bonilla
Alex Escobar
Darryl Hamilton
Rickey Henderson
Juan LeBron
Jon Nunnally
Jay Payton

Games played by position

PLAYER	G	C	1B	2B	3B	SS	OF
Agbayani	101	0	0	0	0	0	80
Alfonzo	158	0	0	158	0	0	0
Allensworth	40	0	0	0	0	0	33
Bonilla	60	0	4	0	0	0	25
Cedeno	155	0	0	1	0	0	149
Dunston	42	0	0	0	1	0	27
Franco	122	0	19	0	12	0	19
Halter	7	0	0	0	0	1	2
Hamilton	55	0	0	0	0	0	52
Henderson	121	0	0	0	0	0	116
Kinkade	28	1	1	0	3	0	17
Long	3	0	0	0	0	0	0
Lopez	68	0	0	16	9	33	0
McRae	96	0	0	0	0	0	87
Mora	66	0	0	4	3	1	45
Olerud	162	0	160	0	0	0	0
Ordonez	154	0	0	0	0	154	0
Payton	13	0	0	0	0	0	6
Piazza	141	137	0	0	0	0	0
Pratt	71	52	1	0	0	0	1
Toca	4	0	1	0	0	0	0
Ventura	161	0	1	0	160	0	0
Wilson	1	1	0	0	0	0	0

Sick call: 1999 DL report

PLAYER	Days on the DL
Bobby Bonilla	80*
John Franco	63
Rickey Henderson	19
Brent Huff	37
Bobby Jones	109
Billy Martin	63
Scott McCrary	35
Greg McMichael	67
Jay Payton	64
Mike Piazza	15
Rick Reed	47*
Jeff Tam	41
Vance Wilson	38

Indicates two separate terms on Disabled List.

1999 salaries

	Bonuses	Total earned salary
Mike Piazza, c	50,000	7,171,428
Robin Ventura, 3b		7,000,000
Bobby Bonilla, of		5,900,000
Al Leiter, p		5,250,000
Kenny Rogers, p		5,000,000
Bobby Jones, p		4,866,666
John Olerud, 1b		4,250,000
Darryl Hamilton, of	80,000	3,613,333
John Franco, p	150,000	2,950,000
Edgardo Alfonzo, 2b		2,800,000
Billy Taylor, p		2,500,000
Orel Hershiser, p	500,000	2,500,000
Dennis Cook, p		2,000,000
Masato Yoshii, p		2,000,000
Armando Benitez, p	50,000	2,037,500
Rickey Henderson, of	100,000	1,900,000
Rick Reed, p		1,687,500
Rey Ordonez, ss		1,650,000
Turk Wendell, p	14,997	1,214,998
Chuck McElroy, p	50,000	1,050,000
Shawon Dunston, of	110,000	610,000
Luis Lopez, ss		575,000
Roger Cedeno, of		487,500
Todd Pratt, c		350,000
Pat Mahomes, p		310,000
Matt Franco, of		250,000
Jeff Tam, p		207,500
Octavio Dotel, p		200,000
Benny Agbayani, of		200,000
Vance Wilson, c		200,000
B.J. Huff, of		200,000
Scott McCrary, p		200,000
Billy Martin, 3b		200,000

Average 1999 salary: $2,161,558
Total 1999 team payroll: $71,331,425
Termination pay: $229,098

Minor Leagues
Tops in the organization

BATTER	CLUB	AVG.	G	AB	R	H	HR	RBI
Deschenes, Pat	PTF	.374	69	246	53	92	5	45
Long, Terrence	Nor	.326	78	304	41	99	7	47
Toca, Jorge	Nor	.319	124	455	85	145	25	96
Tomberlin, Andy	Nor	.316	106	332	64	105	17	65
Cole, Brian	CLB	.316	125	500	97	158	18	71

HOME RUNS

Snyder, Earl	CLB	28
Toca, Jorge	Nor	25
Gainey, Bryon	Bng	25
Erickson, Corey	CLB	23
Several Players Tied at		21

WINS

Gonzalez, Dicky	SLu	14
Strange, Patrick	CLB	12
Cook, Andy	CLB	12
Walker, Tyler	Bng	12
Murray, Dan	Nor	12

RBI

Snyder, Earl	CLB	97
Toca, Jorge	Nor	96
Jenkins, Brian	CLB	79
Gainey, Bryon	Bng	78
Bruce, Mo	Bng	76

SAVES

Bell, Heath	CLB	25
Henriquez, Oscar	Nor	23
Cammack, Eric	Nor	19
Riggan, Jerrod	SLu	12
Viole, Paul	CLB	11

STOLEN BASES

Cole, Brian	CLB	50
Tyner, Jason	Nor	49
Dina, Allen	Bng	43
Bruce, Mo	Bng	33
Several Players Tied at		29

STRIKEOUTS

Vega, Rene	CLB	148
Gonzalez, Dicky	SLu	146
Brea, Leslie	SLu	136
Saenz, Jason	CLB	125
Several players Tied at		124

PITCHER	CLUB	W-L	ERA	IP	H	BB	SO
Strange, Patrick	CLB	12-5	2.63	154	138	29	113
Brittan, Corey	Bng	2-4	2.78	91	84	23	60
Cook, Andy	CLB	12-7	2.83	150	150	42	124
Gonzalez, Dicky	SLu	14-10	2.83	175	161	31	146
Guerra, Mark	Nor	8-3	2.93	89	90	39	70

New York (1962-1999)

Runs: Most, career

662	DARRYL STRAWBERRY, 1983-1990
627	Howard Johnson, 1985-1993
592	Mookie Wilson, 1980-1989
563	Cleon Jones, 1963-1975
536	Ed Kranepool, 1962-1979

Hits: Most, career

1418	Ed Kranepool, 1962-1979
1188	Cleon Jones, 1963-1975
1112	Mookie Wilson, 1980-1989
1029	Bud Harrelson, 1965-1977
1025	DARRYL STRAWBERRY, 1983-1990

2B: Most, career

225	Ed Kranepool, 1962-1979
214	Howard Johnson, 1985-1993
187	DARRYL STRAWBERRY, 1983-1990
182	Cleon Jones, 1963-1975
170	Mookie Wilson, 1980-1989

3B: Most, career

62	Mookie Wilson, 1980-1989
45	Bud Harrelson, 1965-1977
33	Cleon Jones, 1963-1975
31	Steve Henderson, 1977-1980
30	DARRYL STRAWBERRY, 1983-1990

HR: Most, career

252	DARRYL STRAWBERRY, 1983-1990
192	Howard Johnson, 1985-1993
154	Dave Kingman, 1975-1983
124	TODD HUNDLEY, 1990-1998
122	Kevin McReynolds, 1987-1994

RBI: Most, career

733	DARRYL STRAWBERRY, 1983-1990
629	Howard Johnson, 1985-1993
614	Ed Kranepool, 1962-1979
521	Cleon Jones, 1963-1975
468	Keith Hernandez, 1983-1989

SB: Most, career

281	Mookie Wilson, 1980-1989
202	Howard Johnson, 1985-1993
191	DARRYL STRAWBERRY, 1983-1990
152	Lee Mazzilli, 1976-1989
116	Lenny Dykstra, 1985-1989

BB: Most, career

580	DARRYL STRAWBERRY, 1983-1990
573	Bud Harrelson, 1965-1977
556	Howard Johnson, 1985-1993
482	Wayne Garrett, 1969-1976
471	Keith Hernandez, 1983-1989

BA: Highest, career

.297	Keith Hernandez, 1983-1989
.292	DAVE MAGADAN, 1986-1992
.290	EDGARDO ALFONZO, 1995-1999
.283	Wally Backman, 1980-1988
.281	Cleon Jones, 1963-1975

On-base avg: Highest, career

.391	DAVE MAGADAN, 1986-1992
.387	Keith Hernandez, 1983-1989
.359	DARRYL STRAWBERRY, 1983-1990
.358	Rusty Staub, 1972-1985
.357	Lee Mazzilli, 1976-1989

Slug pct: Highest, career

.520	DARRYL STRAWBERRY, 1983-1990
.495	BOBBY BONILLA, 1992-1999
.460	Kevin McReynolds, 1987-1994
.459	Howard Johnson, 1985-1993
.453	Dave Kingman, 1975-1983

Games started: Most, career

395	Tom Seaver, 1967-1983
346	Jerry Koosman, 1967-1978
303	DWIGHT GOODEN, 1984-1994
250	Sid Fernandez, 1984-1993
241	Ron Darling, 1983-1991

Complete games: Most, career

171	Tom Seaver, 1967-1983
108	Jerry Koosman, 1967-1978
67	DWIGHT GOODEN, 1984-1994
65	Jon Matlack, 1971-1977
41	Al Jackson, 1962-1969

Saves: Most, career

268	JOHN FRANCO, 1990-1999
107	JESSE OROSCO, 1979-1987
86	Tug McGraw, 1965-1974
84	Roger McDowell, 1985-1989
69	Neil Allen, 1979-1983

Shutouts: Most, career

44	Tom Seaver, 1967-1983
26	Jerry Koosman, 1967-1978
26	Jon Matlack, 1971-1977
23	DWIGHT GOODEN, 1984-1994
15	DAVID CONE, 1987-1992

Wins: Most, career

198	Tom Seaver, 1967-1983
157	DWIGHT GOODEN, 1984-1994
140	Jerry Koosman, 1967-1978
99	Ron Darling, 1983-1991
98	Sid Fernandez, 1984-1993

K: Most, career

2541	Tom Seaver, 1967-1983
1875	DWIGHT GOODEN, 1984-1994
1799	Jerry Koosman, 1967-1978
1449	Sid Fernandez, 1984-1993
1159	DAVID CONE, 1987-1992

Win pct: Highest, career

.649	DWIGHT GOODEN, 1984-1994
.625	DAVID CONE, 1987-1992
.615	RICK REED, 1997-1999
.615	Tom Seaver, 1967-1983
.586	Ron Darling, 1983-1991

ERA: Lowest, career

2.57	Tom Seaver, 1967-1983
3.03	Jon Matlack, 1971-1977
3.08	DAVID CONE, 1987-1992
3.09	Jerry Koosman, 1967-1978
3.10	DWIGHT GOODEN, 1984-1994

Runs: Most, season

123	EDGARDO ALFONZO, 1999
117	LANCE JOHNSON, 1996
108	BERNARD GILKEY, 1996
108	Howard Johnson, 1991
108	DARRYL STRAWBERRY, 1987

Hits: Most, season

227	LANCE JOHNSON, 1996
197	JOHN OLERUD, 1998
191	EDGARDO ALFONZO, 1999
191	Felix Millan, 1975
185	Felix Millan, 1973

2B: Most, season

44	BERNARD GILKEY, 1996
41	EDGARDO ALFONZO, 1999
41	Howard Johnson, 1989
40	GREGG JEFFERIES, 1990
39	JOHN OLERUD, 1999

3B: Most, season

21	LANCE JOHNSON, 1996
10	Mookie Wilson, 1984
9	Steve Henderson, 1978
9	Charlie Neal, 1962
9	Frank Taveras, 1979
9	Mookie Wilson, 1982

HR: Most, season

41	TODD HUNDLEY, 1996
40	MIKE PIAZZA, 1999
39	DARRYL STRAWBERRY, 1987
39	DARRYL STRAWBERRY, 1988
38	Howard Johnson, 1991

RBI: Most, season

124	MIKE PIAZZA, 1999
120	ROBIN VENTURA, 1999
117	BERNARD GILKEY, 1996
117	Howard Johnson, 1991
112	TODD HUNDLEY, 1996

SB: Most, season

66	ROGER CEDENO, 1999
58	Mookie Wilson, 1982
54	Mookie Wilson, 1983
50	LANCE JOHNSON, 1996
46	Mookie Wilson, 1984

BB: Most, season

125	JOHN OLERUD, 1999
97	Keith Hernandez, 1984
97	DARRYL STRAWBERRY, 1987
96	JOHN OLERUD, 1998
95	Bud Harrelson, 1970

BA: Highest, season

.354	JOHN OLERUD, 1998
.340	Cleon Jones, 1969
.333	LANCE JOHNSON, 1996
.328	DAVE MAGADAN, 1990
.319	Cleon Jones, 1971

On-base avg; Highest, season

.447	JOHN OLERUD, 1998
.427	JOHN OLERUD, 1999
.423	RICKEY HENDERSON, 1999
.422	Cleon Jones, 1969
.417	DAVE MAGADAN, 1990

Slug pct: Highest, season

.583	DARRYL STRAWBERRY, 1987
.575	MIKE PIAZZA, 1999
.562	BERNARD GILKEY, 1996
.559	Howard Johnson, 1989
.551	JOHN OLERUD, 1998

Games started: Most, season

36	Jack Fisher, 1965
36	Tom Seaver, 1970
36	Tom Seaver, 1973
36	Tom Seaver, 1975
35	Ron Darling, 1985
35	Gary Gentry, 1969
35	DWIGHT GOODEN, 1985
35	Jerry Koosman, 1973
35	Jerry Koosman, 1974
35	Jon Matlack, 1976
35	Tom Seaver, 1968
35	Tom Seaver, 1969
35	Tom Seaver, 1971
35	Tom Seaver, 1972
35	Craig Swan, 1979
35	Frank Viola, 1990
35	Frank Viola, 1991

Complete games: Most, season

21	Tom Seaver, 1971
19	Tom Seaver, 1970
18	Tom Seaver, 1967
18	Tom Seaver, 1969
18	Tom Seaver, 1973

Saves: Most, season

38	JOHN FRANCO, 1998
36	JOHN FRANCO, 1997
33	JOHN FRANCO, 1990
31	JESSE OROSCO, 1984
30	JOHN FRANCO, 1991
30	JOHN FRANCO, 1994

Shutouts: Most, season

8	DWIGHT GOODEN, 1985
7	Jerry Koosman, 1968
7	Jon Matlack, 1974
6	Jerry Koosman, 1969
6	Jon Matlack, 1976

Wins: Most, season

25	Tom Seaver, 1969
24	DWIGHT GOODEN, 1985
22	Tom Seaver, 1975
21	Jerry Koosman, 1976
21	Tom Seaver, 1972

K: Most, season

289	Tom Seaver, 1971
283	Tom Seaver, 1970
276	DWIGHT GOODEN, 1984
268	DWIGHT GOODEN, 1985
251	Tom Seaver, 1973

Win pct: Highest, season

.870	DAVID CONE, 1988
.857	DWIGHT GOODEN, 1985
.783	Bob Ojeda, 1986
.781	Tom Seaver, 1969
.739	DWIGHT GOODEN, 1986
.739	AL LEITER, 1998

ERA: Lowest, season

1.53	DWIGHT GOODEN, 1985
1.76	Tom Seaver, 1971
2.08	Tom Seaver, 1973
2.08	Jerry Koosman, 1968
2.20	Tom Seaver, 1968

Most pinch-hit homers, season

4	Danny Heep, 1983
4	Mark Carreon, 1989

Most pinch-hit homers, career

8	Mark Carreon, 1987-1991
6	Ed Kranepool, 1962-1979
6	Rusty Staub, 1972-1985

Longest hitting streak

24	Hubie Brooks, 1984
24	MIKE PIAZZA, 1999
23	Cleon Jones, 1970
23	Mike Vail, 1975
23	JOHN OLERUD, 1998

Most consecutive scoreless innings

31	Jerry Koosman, 1973

No-hit games

ACTIVE PLAYERS in caps.

Players' years of service are listed by the first and last years with this team and are not necessarily consecutive; all statistics record performances for this team only.

Philadelphia Phillies

By Tom DiPace

The Phillies' Bobby Abreu finished among the top five batters in the National League.

1999 Phillies: Big bats and poor pitching

No matter what they do, the Philadelphia Phillies know they'll hear from their demanding fans. But the most demanding onlooker at the end of last season will be in uniform when the 2000 schedule opens.

"Offensively, we're one of the top clubs in the game," said Curt Schilling, the star pitcher who missed the last two months of the Phillies' 12th losing season in 13 years. "It's just going to come down to what the pitching staff looks like next season."

Depth is the key, says Schilling. He has been pressuring management to get him some help in the rotation and bullpen with varying degrees of urgency for several years.

"If we get it, we should be contenders for the title," Schilling said. "The division and the league title. . . . Starting next year, we need to win. I'd be very surprised if we're not contenders. A lot would have to go wrong for that not to happen."

With a potent lineup but little pitching to back up Schilling, the Phillies plummeted from 61-48 on Aug. 6 to 77-85 and 26 games behind the NL East champion Braves. Schilling made his last start of the season on Aug. 7, missing the final two months with a sore shoulder that is cause for concern about the enormous workload he has undertaken in recent years.

Of equal concern will be the result of General Manager Ed Wade's being given more latitude in pursuing trades and free agents.

"This is my first offseason to have this opportunity," said Wade, who aptly summarized his needs with five words: "Starting pitching and relief pitching."

The Phillies' ownership decided to grant Wade what he termed "financial flexibility" to improve the team. Wade quickly pointed out that the Phillies' payroll will not soar to the $70 million range from its last season's $26 million, one of the lowest in baseball.

The challenge for Wade is to find one, and possibly two starting pitchers to add to the top of the rotation and to find depth for a ragged bullpen. Chad Ogea, acquired from Cleveland to be the No. 2

starter behind Schilling, stumbled. He was second in the National League with 36 homers allowed despite being removed from the rotation in September.

The Phillies allowed a club record 212 homers, third in the league, and had a 4.92 ERA. Paul Byrd had a breakthrough year, going 15-11 and making the All-Star team, but he won only four games in the second half.

"I think we're close," outfielder Doug Glanville said. "We just need to add a couple of pieces. I don't think it has to be drastic."

Glanville was one of the many offensive bright spots for a team that suffered from mediocre attendance despite a wealth of young talent in the everyday lineup. He batted .325 with 11 homers and 73 RBI in the leadoff spot, stealing 34 bases in 36 attempts. With 204 hits, Glanville became the Phillies' first player with 200 hits since Pete Rose in 1979.

Catcher Mike Lieberthal was the sixth catcher in history to hit .300 with 30 homers. Bobby Abreu thrived in the No. 3 spot in the order at age 25.

But without pitching, all of it will add up to another lost season in 2000. Even manager Terry Francona, whose job is safe despite three straight losing seasons, knows that.

1999 Phillies: Week-by-week notes

These notes were excerpted from the following issues of Baseball Weekly.

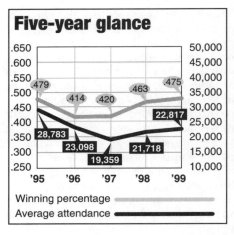

Five-year glance

Winning percentage
Average attendance

▶**April 7:** Aside from ace right-hander Curt Schilling, the rotation consisted of four largely unproven starters: righties Chad Ogea, Carlton Loewer and Paul Byrd, and lefty Paul Spoljaric.

▶**April 14:** The victory in the series finale against the Braves on April 8 was particularly emotional for Paul Byrd, who allowed three runs (two earned) on two hits through 7⅓ innings. The Phillies claimed Byrd last August after Atlanta placed him on waivers.

▶**April 28:** The Phillies had planned to give Paul Spoljaric an extended chance to prove whether he could switch from reliever to starter. But he was in limbo because in two starts, he was 0-2 with a 17.05 ERA and had allowed 17 hits in 6⅓ innings.

▶**May 5:** The Phillies knew they really couldn't afford significant injuries this season—like the torn labrum that sidelined closer Jeff Brantley for the season. Brantley missed most of 1997 following major shoulder surgery and wasn't fully recovered last season.

▶**May 19:** With at least 300 strikeouts in each of the last two seasons, Curt Schilling has been one of baseball's most dominant pitchers. Through his first eight starts in 1999, Schilling was averaging only 6.4 strikeouts per outing. But he also was 6-1 with a 2.80 ERA and had three complete games in his last four turns.

▶**May 26:** When April ended, left fielder Ron Gant was batting .132 with two homers and four RBI and was booed heartily by Veterans Stadium fans. In his first 16 games in May, Gant went 23-for-64 (.359) with five homers and 13 RBI.

▶**June 9:** For the second time in three starts, Curt Schilling was unable to hold a big lead late in the game. On June 3 against the Giants, he gave up four runs in the seventh inning after leading 4-1. Two starts earlier, he surrendered a 4-0 lead in the bottom of the ninth to the Mets.

▶**June 16:** To replace the injured Carlton Loewer in the rotation, the contract of left-hander Randy Wolf, 22, was purchased from AAA Scranton/Wilkes-Barre. Wolf won his debut against the Blue Jays on June 11. He pitched 5⅔ innings, allowing one run on six hits.

▶**June 30:** Manager Terry Francona didn't want to designate Wayne Gomes, 26, as his closer even though Gomes was 6-for-6 in converting saves in an eight-game stretch through June 25.

▶**July 7:** Third baseman Scott Rolen had a disappointing first half of the season, at least by his standards. Through June he batted .251, and he hadn't hit a home run in two weeks. So he came out for early batting practice on June 30 at Pittsburgh. Beginning the following night, he went 9-for-17 with four homers and 12 RBI in four games.

▶**July 15:** The Phillies had three players selected to the All-Star team: Curt Schilling, Mike Lieberthal, and Paul Byrd. It was the first time since 1995 that they had more than one player on the squad.

▶**July 28:** The Phillies managed to survive the first half of the season without many serious injuries to their key players. But then Curt Schilling turned up with tendinitis in his shoulder, Scott Rolen wrenched his back sliding into third base, and Mike Lieberthal woke up one morning with sharp pain in his elbow.

▶**Aug. 4:** Right fielder Bobby Abreu (.339)

and center fielder Doug Glanville (.325) had a chance to become the first pair of Phillies outfielders to bat at least .320 in the same season since Ethan Allen (.330) and Johnny Moore (.343) did it in 1934. In eight games filling in for Scott Rolen, Kevin Jordan went 13-for-33 (.394).

▶**Aug. 25:** Mike Lieberthal, part of the group that general manager Ed Wade hoped to keep intact, agreed on Aug. 20 to a three-year contract extension plus an option that could pay him $25.75 million through 2003. He is guaranteed at least $19 million over the next three years. Two days earlier Rico Brogna agreed to a one-year, $4.2 million extension.

▶**Sept. 1:** In his first eight games after signing a new contract, Rico Brogna went 21-for-39 (.538) with three homers and 15 RBI.

▶**Sept. 8:** The Phillies celebrated Curt Schilling's return from four weeks on the DL by breaking a seven-game losing streak on Sept. 3. Schilling pitched five dominant innings against the Reds before leaving as a precautionary measure after 75 pitches.

▶**Sept. 15:** The Phillies demonstrated how little they blame Terry Francona for the team's unexpected slump by extending his contract for two more years on Sept. 12.

He is now signed through 2002. The Phillies were 13 games over .500 on Aug. 6, then they lost 25 of 32.

▶**Sept. 22:** As if having lost 11 consecutive games and 18 of their last 19 wasn't enough, the Phillies decided on Sept. 15 to sit down their best pitcher and top position player for the rest of the year. Curt Schilling continued to have pain in his biceps after spending four weeks on the disabled list with an inflamed shoulder. Scott Rolen had been bothered by a strained lower back since July 21, and he hadn't played in three weeks.

▶**Sept. 29:** The Phillies lost 34 of 44 games between Aug. 6 and Sept. 23, assuring that the team would finish with a losing record for the 12th time in 13 years.

▶**Oct. 6:** The Phillies' limited partnership approved a significant payroll increase for the 2000 season, believed to be a 50 percent boost to about $45 million. It would be the highest payroll in club history.

QUOTE OF THE YEAR

"I just don't think we have the team to play .500 baseball."
—Catcher Mike Lieberthal, on the day the Phillies lost their 82nd game

Team Leaders

Batting avg.	Hits	Wins	Strikeouts
.335 Bobby Abreu	204 Doug Glanville	15 Curt Schilling	152 Curt Schilling
.325 Doug Glanville	183 Bobby Abreu	15 Paul Byrd	127 Robert Person

HR	Runs	Losses	Innings
31 Mike Lieberthal	118 Bobby Abreu	12 Chad Ogea	199.2 Paul Byrd
24 Rico Brogna	107 Ron Gant	11 Paul Byrd	180.1 Curt Schilling

RBI	Stolen bases	ERA	Saves
102 Rico Brogna	34 Doug Glanville	3.54 Curt Schilling	19 Wayne Gomes
96 Mike Lieberthal	27 Bobby Abreu	4.60 Paul Byrd	5 Jeff Brantley

PHILADELPHIA PHILLIES 1999 final stats

BATTERS	BA	SLG	OBA	G	AB	R	H	TB	2B	3B	HR	RBI	BB	SO	SB	CS	E
Magee	.357	.857	.400	12	14	4	5	12	1	0	2	5	1	4	0	0	0
Abreu	.335	.549	.446	152	546	118	183	300	35	11	20	93	109	113	27	9	3
Glanville	.325	.457	.376	150	628	101	204	287	38	6	11	73	48	82	34	2	8
Arias	.303	.401	.373	118	347	43	105	139	20	1	4	48	36	31	2	2	4
Lieberthal	.300	.551	.363	145	510	84	153	281	33	1	31	96	44	86	0	0	3
Jordan	.285	.386	.339	120	347	36	99	134	17	3	4	51	24	34	0	0	10
Brogna	.278	.454	.336	157	619	90	172	281	29	4	24	102	54	132	8	5	7
Sefcik	.278	.392	.368	111	209	28	58	82	15	3	1	11	29	24	9	4	2
G. Bennett	.273	.352	.298	36	88	7	24	31	4	0	1	21	4	11	0	0	4
Rolen	.268	.525	.368	112	421	74	113	221	28	1	26	77	67	114	12	2	14
Ducey	.261	.463	.383	104	188	29	49	87	10	2	8	33	38	57	2	1	0
Gant	.260	.430	.364	138	516	107	134	222	27	5	17	77	85	112	13	3	2
Anderson	.252	.361	.292	129	452	48	114	163	26	4	5	54	24	61	13	2	11
Relaford	.242	.327	.322	65	211	31	51	69	11	2	1	26	19	34	4	3	14
Lovullo	.211	.368	.268	17	38	3	8	14	0	0	2	5	3	11	0	0	0
Doster	.196	.309	.282	99	97	9	19	30	2	0	3	10	12	23	1	0	1
Estalella	.167	.167	.318	9	18	2	3	3	0	0	0	1	4	7	0	1	1
Prince	.167	.167	.286	4	6	1	1	1	0	0	0	0	1	1	0	0	0
Cedeno	.152	.258	.211	32	66	5	10	17	4	0	1	5	5	22	0	1	1

PITCHERS	W-L	ERA	BA	G	GS	CG	GF	SH	SV	IP	H	R	ER	HR	BB	SO
Montgomery	1-5	3.34	.229	53	0	0	21	0	3	64.2	54	25	24	10	31	55
Schilling	15-6	3.54	.237	24	24	8	0	1	0	180.1	159	74	71	25	44	152
Grahe	1-4	3.86	.308	13	5	0	4	0	0	32.2	40	16	14	1	17	16
Aldred	1-1	3.90	.277	29	0	0	5	0	1	32.1	33	15	14	1	15	19
Perez	3-1	3.94	.244	35	0	0	4	0	0	32.0	29	15	14	4	15	26
Gomes	5-5	4.26	.255	73	0	0	58	0	19	74.0	70	38	35	5	56	58
Person	10-5	4.27	.252	31	22	0	1	0	0	137.0	130	72	65	23	70	127
Schrenk	1-3	4.29	.223	32	2	0	8	0	1	50.1	41	24	24	6	14	36
Poole	1-1	4.33	.327	51	0	0	12	0	1	35.1	48	20	17	3	15	22
Byrd	15-11	4.60	.265	32	32	1	0	0	0	199.2	205	119	102	34	70	106
Loewer	2-6	5.12	.287	20	13	2	2	1	0	89.2	100	54	51	9	26	48
Brantley	1-2	5.19	.161	10	0	0	9	0	5	8.2	5	6	5	0	8	11
Wolf	6-9	5.55	.266	22	21	0	0	0	0	121.2	126	78	75	20	67	116
Ogea	6-12	5.63	.288	36	28	0	3	0	0	168.0	192	110	105	36	61	77
Telemaco	4-0	5.77	.259	49	0	0	10	0	0	53.0	52	34	34	10	26	43
Shumaker	0-3	5.96	.261	8	4	0	2	0	0	22.2	23	17	15	3	14	17
Ryan	1-2	6.32	.267	15	0	0	5	0	0	15.2	16	11	11	2	11	9
Brewer	1-1	7.01	.294	25	0	0	8	0	2	25.2	30	20	20	4	14	28
Politte	1-0	7.13	.275	13	0	0	0	0	0	17.2	19	14	14	2	15	15
Grace	1-4	7.69	.346	27	5	0	1	0	0	55.0	80	48	47	5	30	28
J. Bennett	2-1	9.00	.351	5	3	0	0	0	0	17.0	26	17	17	10	7	13
Spoljaric	0-3	15.09	.426	5	3	0	1	0	0	11.1	23	24	19	1	7	10

2000 preliminary roster

PITCHERS (20)
Scott Aldred
Andy Ashby
Manuel Barrios
Jeff Brantley
Jason Brester
Chris Brock
Mark Brownson
Paul Byrd
David Coggin
Wayne Gomes
Mike Jackson
Douglas Nickle
Robert Person
Cliff Politte
Carlos Reyes
Curt Schilling
Steve Schrenk
Anthony Shumaker
Amaury Telemaco
Randy Wolf

CATCHERS (3)
Gary Bennett
Mike Lieberthal
Tom Prince

INFIELDERS (11)
Marlon Anderson
Alex Arias
Rico Brogna
Pat Burrell
Carlos Duncan
Kevin Jordan
Felix Martinez
Desi Relaford
Scott Rolen
Jimmy Rollins
Kevin Sefcik

OUTFIELDERS (6)
Bob Abreu
Rob Ducey
Ron Gant
Doug Glanville
Wendell Magee
Reggie Taylor

Games played by position

PLAYER	G	C	1B	2B	3B	SS	OF
Abreu	152	0	0	0	0	0	146
Anderson	129	0	0	121	0	0	0
Arias	118	0	0	1	2	95	0
Bennett	36	32	0	0	0	0	0
Brogna	157	0	157	0	0	0	0
Cedeno	32	0	0	1	0	19	0
Doster	99	0	0	77	6	5	0
Ducey	104	0	0	0	0	0	58
Estalella	9	7	0	0	0	0	0
Gant	138	0	0	0	0	0	133
Glanville	150	0	0	0	0	0	148
Jordan	120	0	13	33	62	0	0
Lieberthal	145	143	0	0	0	0	0
Lovullo	17	0	6	6	0	0	0
Magee	12	0	0	0	0	0	4
Prince	4	4	0	0	0	0	0
Relaford	65	0	0	0	0	63	0
Rolen	112	0	0	0	112	0	0
Sefcik	111	0	0	15	0	0	64

Sick call: 1999 DL report

PLAYER	Days on the DL
Matt Beech	176
Jeff Brantley	150*
Bobby Estalella	24
Tyler Green	80
Carlton Loewer	92
Steve Montgomery	16
Yorkis Perez	94
Tom Prince	151
Desi Relaford	88
Curt Schilling	26

* Indicates two separate terms on Disabled List.

Minor Leagues
Tops in the organization

BATTER	CLUB	AVG.	G	AB	R	H	HR	RBI
Burrell, Pat	SWB	.320	127	450	88	144	29	94
Michaels, Jason	Clr	.306	122	451	91	138	14	65
Punto, Nick	Clr	.305	106	400	65	122	1	48
McMillon, Billy	SWB	.304	132	464	97	141	16	85
Kiil, Skip	Clr	.298	86	305	74	91	14	55

HOME RUNS

Burrell, Pat	SWB	29
Lovullo, Torey	SWB	21
Magee, Wendell	SWB	20
Valent, Eric	Clr	20
Several Players Tied at		16

WINS

Dodd, Robert	SWB	14
Turnbow, Derrick	Pie	12
Several Players Tied at		11

RBI

Lovullo, Torey	SWB	106
Valent, Eric	Clr	106
Burrell, Pat	SWB	94
Dominique, Andy	Clr	92
McMillon, Billy	SWB	85

SAVES

Nickle, Douglas	Clr	28
Hiles, Cary	Pie	26
Grahe, Joe	SWB	14
Scott, Darryl	SWB	10
Several Players Tied at		8

STOLEN BASES

Fajardo, Alejandro	Pie	44
Rojas, Alex	BAT	39
Taylor, Reggie	Rea	38
Huff, Larry	SWB	28
Several Players Tied at		27

STRIKEOUTS

Turnbow, Derrick	Pie	149
Kubes, Greg	Pie	147
Eaton, Adam	SWB	127
Thomas, Evan	Rea	127
Bennett, Joel	SWB	125

PITCHER	CLUB	W-L	ERA	IP	H	BB	SO
Baisley, Brad	Pie	10-7	2.26	148	116	55	110
Kubes, Greg	Pie	11-12	2.62	165	162	47	147
Dodd, Robert	SWB	14-2	3.04	110	97	29	102
Silva, Carlos	Pie	11-8	3.12	164	176	41	99
Thomas, Evan	Rea	9-5	3.25	127	123	50	127

1999 salaries

	Bonuses	Total earned salary
Ron Gant, of		6,000,000
Curt Schilling, p	50,000	5,250,000
Rico Brogna, 1b		3,200,000
Jeff Brantley, p		2,800,000
Mike Lieberthal, c	25,000	2,250,000
Chad Ogea, p		1,783,334
Scott Rolen, 3b		1,000,000
Alex Arias, ss	75,000	625,000
Kevin Jordan, 3b	50,000	550,000
Scott Aldred, p	120,000	545,000
Doug Glanville, of		541,666
Yorkis Perez, p		475,000
Kevin Sefcik, of		425,000
Bobby Abreu, of		400,000
Rob Ducey, of		400,000
Robert Person, p		379,000
Amaury Telemaco, p		325,000
Billy Brewer, p	20,000	320,000
Domingo Cedeno, ss		300,000
Tom Prince, c		300,000
Paul Byrd, p		297,500
Desi Relaford, ss		260,000
Wayne Gomes, p		260,000
Matt Beech, p		215,000
Carlton Loewer, p		215,000
Gary Bennett, c		200,000
Steve Schrenk, p		200,000
Joe Grahe, p		200,000
Steve Montgomery, p		200,000
Dave Doster, 2b		200,000
Marlon Anderson, 2b		200,000
Randy Wolf, p		200,000

Average 1999 salary: $953,641
Total 1999 team payroll: $30,516,500

Philadelphia (1883-1999)

228

Runs: Most, career

1506	Mike Schmidt, 1972-1989	
1367	Ed Delahanty, 1888-1901	
1114	Richie Ashburn, 1948-1959	
963	Chuck Klein, 1928-1944	
924	Sam Thompson, 1889-1898	

Hits: Most, career

2234	Mike Schmidt, 1972-1989
2217	Richie Ashburn, 1948-1959
2213	Ed Delahanty, 1888-1901
1812	Del Ennis, 1946-1956
1798	Larry Bowa, 1970-1981

2B: Most, career

442	Ed Delahanty, 1888-1901
408	Mike Schmidt, 1972-1989
337	Sherry Magee, 1904-1914
336	Chuck Klein, 1928-1944
310	Del Ennis, 1946-1956

3B: Most, career

157	Ed Delahanty, 1888-1901
127	Sherry Magee, 1904-1914
106	Sam Thompson, 1889-1898
97	Richie Ashburn, 1948-1959
84	Johnny Callison, 1960-1969

HR: Most, career

548	Mike Schmidt, 1972-1989
259	Del Ennis, 1946-1956
243	Chuck Klein, 1928-1944
223	Greg Luzinski, 1970-1980
217	Cy Williams, 1918-1930

RBI: Most, career

1595	Mike Schmidt, 1972-1989
1286	Ed Delahanty, 1888-1901
1124	Del Ennis, 1946-1956
983	Chuck Klein, 1928-1944
957	Sam Thompson, 1889-1898

SB: Most, career

508	Billy Hamilton, 1890-1895
411	Ed Delahanty, 1888-1901
387	Sherry Magee, 1904-1914
289	Jim Fogarty, 1884-1889
288	Larry Bowa, 1970-1981

BB: Most, career

1507	Mike Schmidt, 1972-1989
946	Richie Ashburn, 1948-1959
946	Roy Thomas, 1899-1911
693	Willie Jones, 1947-1959
643	Ed Delahanty, 1888-1901

BA: Highest, career

.361	Billy Hamilton, 1890-1895
.348	Ed Delahanty, 1888-1901
.338	Elmer Flick, 1898-1901
.333	Sam Thompson, 1889-1898
.326	Chuck Klein, 1928-1944

On-base avg: Highest, career

.468	Billy Hamilton, 1890-1895
.421	Roy Thomas, 1899-1911
.419	Elmer Flick, 1898-1901
.415	Ed Delahanty, 1888-1901
.400	John Kruk, 1989-1994

Slug pct: Highest, career

.553	Chuck Klein, 1928-1944
.530	Dick Allen, 1963-1976
.527	Mike Schmidt, 1972-1989
.510	Dolph Camilli, 1934-1937
.508	Ed Delahanty, 1888-1901

Games started: Most, career

499	Steve Carlton, 1972-1986
472	Robin Roberts, 1948-1961
301	Chris Short, 1959-1972
280	Pete Alexander, 1911-1930
262	Curt Simmons, 1947-1960

Complete games: Most, career

272	Robin Roberts, 1948-1961
219	Pete Alexander, 1911-1930
185	Steve Carlton, 1972-1986
165	Charlie Ferguson, 1884-1887
156	Bill Duggleby, 1898-1907

Saves: Most, career

103	Steve Bedrosian, 1986-1989
102	Mitch Williams, 1991-1993
94	Tug McGraw, 1975-1984
90	Ron Reed, 1976-1983
75	RICKY BOTTALICO, 1994-1998

Shutouts: Most, career

61	Pete Alexander, 1911-1930
39	Steve Carlton, 1972-1986
35	Robin Roberts, 1948-1961
24	Chris Short, 1959-1972
23	Jim Bunning, 1964-1971

Wins: Most, career

241	Steve Carlton, 1972-1986
234	Robin Roberts, 1948-1961
190	Pete Alexander, 1911-1930
132	Chris Short, 1959-1972
115	Curt Simmons, 1947-1960

K: Most, career

3031	Steve Carlton, 1972-1986
1871	Robin Roberts, 1948-1961
1585	Chris Short, 1959-1972
1458	CURT SCHILLING, 1992-1999
1409	Pete Alexander, 1911-1930

Win pct: Highest, career

.676	Pete Alexander, 1911-1930
.642	Tom Seaton, 1912-1913
.607	Charlie Ferguson, 1884-1887
.606	Charlie Buffinton, 1887-1889
.600	Red Donahue, 1898-1901
.600	Ron Reed, 1976-1983

ERA: Lowest, career

1.79	George McQuillan, 1907-1916
2.18	Pete Alexander, 1911-1930
2.48	Tully Sparks, 1897-1910
2.61	Frank Corridon, 1904-1909
2.63	Earl Moore, 1908-1913

Runs: Most, season

192	Billy Hamilton, 1894
166	Billy Hamilton, 1895
158	Chuck Klein, 1930
152	Chuck Klein, 1932
152	Lefty O'Doul, 1929

Hits: Most, season

254	Lefty O'Doul, 1929
250	Chuck Klein, 1930
238	Ed Delahanty, 1899
226	Chuck Klein, 1932
223	Chuck Klein, 1933

2B: Most, season

59	Chuck Klein, 1930
55	Ed Delahanty, 1899
50	Chuck Klein, 1932
49	Ed Delahanty, 1895
48	Dick Bartell, 1932

3B: Most, season

27	Sam Thompson, 1894
23	Nap Lajoie, 1897
21	Ed Delahanty, 1892
21	Sam Thompson, 1895
19	Juan Samuel, 1984
19	George Wood, 1887

HR: Most, season

48	Mike Schmidt, 1980
45	Mike Schmidt, 1979
43	Chuck Klein, 1929
41	Cy Williams, 1923
40	Dick Allen, 1966
40	Chuck Klein, 1930
40	Mike Schmidt, 1983

RBI: Most, season

170	Chuck Klein, 1930
165	Sam Thompson, 1895
146	Ed Delahanty, 1893
145	Chuck Klein, 1929
143	Don Hurst, 1932

SB: Most, season

111	Billy Hamilton, 1891
102	Jim Fogarty, 1887
102	Billy Hamilton, 1890
99	Jim Fogarty, 1889
98	Billy Hamilton, 1894
72	Juan Samuel, 1984 (7)

BB: Most, season

129	Lenny Dykstra, 1993
128	Mike Schmidt, 1983
126	Billy Hamilton, 1894
125	Richie Ashburn, 1954
121	Von Hayes, 1987

BA: Highest, season

.410	Ed Delahanty, 1899
.407	Ed Delahanty, 1894
.404	Billy Hamilton, 1894
.404	Ed Delahanty, 1895
.398	Lefty O'Doul, 1929

On-base avg; Highest, season

.523	Billy Hamilton, 1894
.500	Ed Delahanty, 1895
.490	Billy Hamilton, 1895
.478	Ed Delahanty, 1894
.472	Ed Delahanty, 1896
.465	Lefty O'Doul, 1929 (6)

Slug pct: Highest, season

.687	Chuck Klein, 1930
.657	Chuck Klein, 1929
.654	Sam Thompson, 1895
.646	Chuck Klein, 1932
.644	Mike Schmidt, 1981

Games started: Most, season

61	John Coleman, 1883
55	Kid Gleason, 1890
50	Ed Daily, 1885
49	Gus Weyhing, 1892
47	Charlie Ferguson, 1884
45	Pete Alexander, 1916 (8)

Complete games: Most, season

59	John Coleman, 1883
54	Kid Gleason, 1890
49	Ed Daily, 1885
46	Charlie Ferguson, 1884
46	Gus Weyhing, 1892
38	Pete Alexander, 1916 (13)

Saves: Most, season

43	Mitch Williams, 1993
40	Steve Bedrosian, 1987
34	RICKY BOTTALICO, 1996
34	RICKY BOTTALICO, 1997
32	HEATHCLIFF SLOCUMB, 1995

Shutouts: Most, season

16	Pete Alexander, 1916
12	Pete Alexander, 1915
9	Pete Alexander, 1913
8	Pete Alexander, 1917
8	Steve Carlton, 1972
8	Ben Sanders, 1888

Wins: Most, season

38	Kid Gleason, 1890
33	Pete Alexander, 1916
32	Gus Weyhing, 1892
31	Pete Alexander, 1915
30	Pete Alexander, 1917
30	Charlie Ferguson, 1886

K: Most, season

319	CURT SCHILLING, 1997
310	Steve Carlton, 1972
300	CURT SCHILLING, 1998
286	Steve Carlton, 1980
286	Steve Carlton, 1982

Win pct: Highest, season

.800	Tommy Greene, 1993
.800	Robin Roberts, 1952
.769	Charlie Ferguson, 1886
.760	Larry Christenson, 1977
.760	John Denny, 1983

ERA: Lowest, season

1.22	Pete Alexander, 1915
1.53	George McQuillan, 1908
1.55	Pete Alexander, 1916
1.83	Lew Richie, 1908
1.83	Pete Alexander, 1917

Most pinch-hit homers, season

5	Gene Freese, 1959
4	Rip Repulski, 1958
4	Del Unser, 1979

Most pinch-hit homers, career

9	Cy Williams, 1918-1930
6	Gavvy Cravath, 1912-1920
6	Rick Joseph, 1967-1970
6	Del Unser, 1973-1982

Longest hitting streak

36	Billy Hamilton, 1894
31	Ed Delahanty, 1899
26	Chuck Klein, 1930
26	Chuck Klein, 1930 (2nd streak)
24	Willie Montanez, 1974

Most consecutive scoreless innings

41	Grover Cleveland Alexander, 1911

No-hit games

Joe Borden, Phi vs Chi NA, 4-0; July 28, 1875.

Charlie Ferguson, Phi vs Pro NL, 1-0; August 29, 1885.

Red Donahue, Phi vs Bos NL, 5-0; July 8, 1898.

Chick Fraser, Phi at Chi NL; 10-0; September 18, 1903 (2nd game).

Johnny Lush, Phi at Bro NL, 6-0; May 1, 1906.

Jim Bunning, Phi at NY NL, 6-0; June 21, 1964 (1st game, perfect game).

Rick Wise, Phi at Cin NL, 4-0; June 23, 1971.

TERRY MULHOLLAND, Phi vs SF NL, 6-0; August 15, 1990.

Tommy Greene, Phi at Mon NL, 2-0; May 23, 1991.

ACTIVE PLAYERS in caps.

Players' years of service are listed by the first and last years with this team and are not necessarily consecutive; all statistics record performances for this team only.

Montreal Expos

By Tom DiPace

Vladimir Guerrero's 31-game hitting streak for the Expos was just part of a huge season at the plate.

1999 Expos: Short on wins, defense, fans

Bargain shoppers around the major leagues will be disappointed to learn that the days of fire sales in Montreal appear to be over. After years of threadbare management that led to the purging of such stars as Pedro Martinez, Larry Walker, Moises Alou and John Wetteland, the Expos could be on their way to a new ballpark and a new future. And contrary to the beliefs of the prevailing wisdom over the past couple of years, the ballpark and future are in Montreal.

A year ago, manager Felipe Alou appeared destined to leave the team and take over the Los Angeles Dodgers. Now, he is heading into the second year of a three-year deal with a young team that managed to improve a bit on 65 wins in 1998 with a 68-94 record in '99.

The combination of the uncertain status of the franchise's viability in Montreal and a young, inexperienced team on a shoestring budget led to the Expos' second straight season with less a million fans in attendance.

"I don't believe anybody wants to repeat the 1999 season . . ." Alou said. "We feel like it is time to win. We have been in a losing situation and a situation of uncertainty for a number of years. We know the reasons but the time is now."

Only 773,277 fans, the second-lowest attendance in the team's 31-year history, came out to see the Expos in 1999, despite the presence of 23-year-old superstar Vladimir Guerrero. Those on hand got to see Guerrero put together the best offensive season in team history. Guerrero batted .316 and set team records with 42 homers and 131 RBI.

Closer Ugueth Urbina had an inconsistent year, but still made the most of his limited opportunities and tied San Diego's Trevor Hoffman for the NL save lead with 41. That also matched Jeff Reardon for the second-most in Expos history behind Wetteland's 43 in 1993.

"I don't believe that there has ever been a team or a group of players that had to go through the kind of summer that our guys went through," Alou said, "and I

Team MVP

Vladimir Guerrero: He's the "Yeah, but . . ." leader of the National League. Talk to a manager or GM about one of the league's stars and he'll eventually say, "Yeah, but don't forget Guerrero." He hit .316 with 42 home runs, 131 RBI and 14 stolen bases. He was second in the NL with 366 total bases and had a season-high 31-game hitting streak.

have to congratulate them on the way they presented themselves and went about their business. Some of them got to be really good baseball players."

Second baseman Jose Vidro batted .304 with 45 doubles, and rookie Michael Barrett managed to hit .293 while bouncing back and forth between catching and playing third base. Look for Barrett to play at third base permanently next season with Chris Widger established as the number one catcher.

While staff ace Dustin Hermanson was a disappointing 9-14 with a 4.20 ERA, the Expos' young starting staff showed promise for the future. Javier Vazquez went 9-8 with a 5.00 ERA and pitched three complete games, including a one-hitter at Los Angeles.

The team's most glaring weakness was its inability to play consistent defense. The Expos led the majors with 160 errors, which included Guerrero's coming within one of becoming the first outfielder to reach 20 since Bob Johnson in 1935. With nine errors in April alone, Guerrero matched the post-World War II high of 19 (Lou Brock in 1966 and Chili Davis in 1988).

"That's something we have to be aware of," Alou said. "We're going to have to work hard and try to be better, starting next spring." If things turn out the way Alou hopes, he'll finally have the means to bring in the kind of experienced help that will make that happen.

1999 Expos: Week-by-week notes

These notes were excerpted from the following issues of Baseball Weekly.

▶**April 14:** Third baseman Shane Andrews requested a trade after manager Felipe Alou announced that Michael Barrett would be the opening-day third baseman. Barrett was also slated to see duty behind the plate.

▶**April 21:** Call Miguel Batista, 28, Mr. Better Late Than Never. Written off as a one-pitch journeyman reliever, the right-hander won a spot in the Expos' rotation in spring training and was dominant in his first two 1999 starts (2-0, 1.10 ERA).

▶**April 28:** Through 14 games the Expos had a major-league-leading 20 errors, six by second baseman Wilton Guerrero. Felipe Alou had said he wasn't going to use defensive replacements for first baseman Brad Fullmer or Guerrero late in the game, that it would be up to them to take his vote of confidence and run with it.

▶**May 5:** Right fielder Vladimir Guerrero's reputation as a five-tool player preceded him to the big leagues, but while his hitting had been brilliant, he had made nine errors through 21 games. Last season he led NL outfielders in errors, with 17.

▶**May 12:** The Expos concluded their longest homestand of the season with an embarrassing 2-10 record, and overall they had lost 15 of 19 at home. Olympic Stadium was turning into an ever-emptier tomb as the Expos' ownership stalemate drags on. A three-game series against Mark McGwire and the Cardinals drew just 37,291.

▶**May 26:** The woes of closer Ugueth Urbina continued. The 25-year-old fireballer, who had 34 saves in 38 opportunities last season, already had blown four of 11 save chances this season. He had allowed 13 earned runs this season, compared with just 10 in all of 1998.

▶**June 2:** Vladimir Guerrero and infielder Mike Mordecai hit two-run homers as the Expos swept their first series of the season on May 30 against San Francisco. Montreal had won eight of 11 since its record

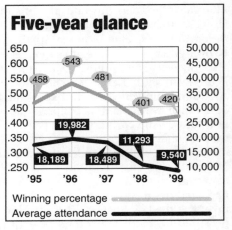

Five-year glance

Winning percentage
Average attendance

fell to 10-26 after its second seven-game losing streak.

▶**June 9:** Left fielder Orlando Merced's homer off Toronto's Joey Hamilton extended Montreal's team-record home run streak to 16 consecutive games. Outfielder Rondell White belted five of the 28 homers launched by 12 Expos, including the two-run shot off Philadelphia's Joel Bennett that started the streak on May 18.

▶**June 16:** The Expos' ace, right-hander Dustin Hermanson (2-6, 5.70 ERA), allowed six runs in two innings on June 6 in a 9-2 loss in Toronto and then allowed five runs—four earned—in 6⅓ innings in a 5-3 loss to Tampa Bay. He had an 8.77 ERA in his last five starts, allowing 25 runs in 25⅓ innings.

▶**June 23:** Right-hander Carl Pavano's career-high winning streak ended at three in a 5-2 loss in Houston on June 19. Pavano pitched a three-hitter for his first career complete game to beat Tampa Bay 4-0 in his previous start, on June 13.

▶**June 30:** Rondell White was placed on the 15-day DL on June 20 after missing the first six games of the road trip with a strained right hamstring. He suffered the injury while running in to make a sliding catch in a 4-0 win over Tampa Bay on June 13.

▶**July 7:** Vladimir Guerrero hit a game-winning three-run homer on June 29 as Montreal scored five runs in the ninth on

four hits off Braves closer John Rocker for a 6-5 victory. Guerrero homered again the next night as his 16th of the season cut Atlanta's lead to 5-2 in the fourth. The Expos moved their rally up an inning, scoring five against Kevin McGlinchy and Rudy Seanez in the eighth for a 7-5 win.

▶July 21: Vladimir Guerrero's NL-leading consecutive-game streak reached 234 on July 18 in New York. Guerrero was closing in on Rusty Staub's team-record 259-gamer of 1970-71.

▶July 28: Right-hander Javier Vazquez pitched a four-hitter for his first-ever complete game on July 23, beating Pittsburgh 5-1 to become the first Expos starter to win a complete game since Carl Pavano beat Florida 4-3 on June 25.

▶Aug. 11: Dustin Hermanson won for the first time in nearly three months on Aug. 2, coming within one out of pitching his first complete game of the season in beating the Cubs 5-1. He had gone 0-7 in his 14 previous starts.

▶Aug. 18: Felipe Alou was batting Rondell White leadoff for the first time in nearly three years. The move paid off in the first game as White went 3-for-4 and walked twice. White was 13-for-29 (.448) with a double, a triple, three homers and seven RBI in seven games out of the leadoff spot through Aug. 15.

▶Aug. 25: Reliever Steve Kline added his name to the record book on Aug. 17 as he struck out four Giants in one inning, the 36th time the feat has been accomplished and the first time for an Expo. The left-hander struck out six of the seven batters he faced in 1⅔ innings.

▶Sept. 1: Vladimir Guerrero, whose hitting streak ended at 31 games on Aug. 27, received curtain calls in three games last week. The Dominican superstar hit .386 during the streak with 49 hits in 127 at-bats, including 12 doubles, a triple, 11 homers and 27 RBI. A day after the streak ended, Guerrero hit a two-run homer with two outs in the ninth to give Montreal an 8-6 win over the Reds.

▶Sept. 8: Through Sept. 5 the Expos led the NL in doubles and triples with 275 and 42, respectively. Second baseman Jose Vidro led the way in doubles with 42, second in the league, while Wilton Guerrero's seven triples led the team.

▶Sept. 22: Javier Vazquez posted his first career shutout in style, one-hitting the Dodgers and outdueling Kevin Brown in a 3-0 win at Los Angeles on Sept. 14. Vazquez had a career-high 10 strikeouts.

▶Oct. 6: The best news for Expos fans last week was that prospective owner Jeffrey Loria met with the team's players on Sept. 30 in Philadelphia. Loria's meeting and optimistic statements by team chairman Jacques Menard and outgoing president Claude Brochu were clear indications that the much-anticipated change of ownership had never been closer to coming about.

233

QUOTE OF THE YEAR

"He's unaware of the world."
—Manager Felipe Alou, on first baseman Brad Fullmer's struggles before being demoted to the minors

Team Leaders

Batting avg.	Hits	Wins	Strikeouts
.316 Vladimir Guerrero	193 Vladimir Guerrero	9 Javier Vazquez	145 Dustin Hermanson
.312 Rondell White	168 Rondell White	9 Dustin Hermanson	113 Javier Vazquez

HR	Runs	Losses	Innings
42 Vladimir Guerrero	102 Vladimir Guerrero	14 Dustin Hermanson	216.1 Dustin Hermanson
22 Rondell White	83 Rondell White	11 Mike Thurman	154.2 Javier Vazquez

RBI	Stolen bases	ERA	Saves
131 Vladimir Guerrero	19 Manny Martinez	4.20 Dustin Hermanson	41 Ugueth Urbina
64 Rondell White	14 Vladimir Guerrero	5.00 Javier Vazquez	2 Anthony Telford

MONTREAL EXPOS 1999 final stats

BATTERS	BA	SLG	OBA	G	AB	R	H	TB	2B	3B	HR	RBI	BB	SO	SB	CS	E
V. Guerrero	.316	.600	.378	160	610	102	193	366	37	5	42	131	55	62	14	7	19
White	.312	.505	.359	138	539	83	168	272	26	6	22	64	32	85	10	6	11
Vidro	.304	.476	.346	140	494	67	150	235	45	2	12	59	29	51	0	4	11
Barrett	.293	.436	.345	126	433	53	127	189	32	3	8	52	32	39	0	2	14
W. Guerrero	.292	.403	.324	132	315	42	92	127	15	7	2	31	13	38	7	6	12
Fullmer	.277	.464	.321	100	347	38	96	161	34	2	9	47	22	35	2	3	7
Jones	.270	.317	.303	17	63	4	17	20	1	1	0	3	3	14	1	2	0
Merced	.268	.464	.353	93	194	25	52	90	12	1	8	26	26	27	2	1	5
Coquillette	.265	.327	.333	17	49	2	13	16	3	0	0	4	4	7	1	0	1
Widger	.264	.441	.325	124	383	42	101	169	24	1	14	56	28	86	1	4	6
Mouton	.262	.369	.364	95	122	18	32	45	5	1	2	13	18	31	6	2	1
Seguignol	.257	.486	.328	35	105	14	27	51	9	0	5	10	5	33	0	0	2
Cabrera	.254	.403	.293	104	382	48	97	154	23	5	8	39	18	38	2	2	10
Martinez	.245	.341	.279	137	331	48	81	113	12	7	2	26	17	51	19	6	8
Bergeron	.244	.289	.370	16	45	12	11	13	2	0	0	1	9	5	0	0	1
Blum	.241	.504	.327	45	133	21	32	67	7	2	8	18	17	25	1	0	10
Cox	.240	.400	.296	15	25	2	6	10	1	0	1	2	0	5	0	0	2
Mordecai	.235	.363	.297	109	226	29	53	82	10	2	5	25	20	31	2	5	7
McGuire	.221	.343	.347	88	140	17	31	48	7	2	2	18	27	33	1	1	2
Fernandez	.208	.292	.240	8	24	0	5	7	2	0	0	1	1	7	0	0	2
Machado	.182	.227	.250	17	22	3	4	5	1	0	0	0	2	6	0	0	0
Stowers	.000	.000	.000	4	2	0	0	0	0	0	0	0	0	0	0	0	0

PITCHERS	W-L	ERA	BA	G	GS	CG	GF	SH	SV	IP	H	R	ER	HR	BB	SO
Armas	0-1	1.50	.320	1	1	0	0	0	0	6.0	8	4	1	0	2	2
Mota	2-4	2.93	.257	51	0	0	18	0	0	55.1	54	24	18	5	25	27
Urbina	6-6	3.69	.208	71	0	0	62	0	41	75.2	59	35	31	6	36	100
Kline	7-4	3.75	.218	82	0	0	18	0	0	69.2	56	32	29	8	33	69
Telford	5-4	3.94	.295	79	0	0	21	0	2	96.0	112	52	42	3	38	69
Thurman	7-11	4.05	.251	29	27	0	1	0	0	146.2	140	84	66	17	52	85
Hermanson	9-14	4.20	.271	34	34	0	0	0	0	216.1	225	110	101	20	69	145
Strickland	0-1	4.50	.231	17	0	0	5	0	0	18.0	15	10	9	3	11	23
Powell	4-8	4.73	.302	17	17	0	0	0	0	97.0	113	60	51	14	44	44
Batista	8-7	4.88	.280	39	17	2	3	1	1	134.2	146	88	73	10	58	95
Vazquez	9-8	5.00	.255	26	26	3	0	1	0	154.2	154	98	86	20	52	113
Smart	0-1	5.02	.276	29	0	0	6	0	0	52.0	56	30	29	4	17	21
Pavano	6-8	5.63	.285	19	18	1	0	1	0	104.0	117	66	65	8	35	70
Smith	4-9	6.02	.293	20	17	0	0	0	0	89.2	104	64	60	12	39	72
Lilly	0-1	7.61	.309	9	3	0	1	0	0	23.2	30	20	20	7	9	28
Johnson	0-0	8.64	.324	3	1	0	0	0	0	8.1	12	8	8	2	7	6
Rojas	0-0	14.09	.313	8	0	0	3	0	0	7.2	10	12	12	3	5	4
Bennett	0-1	14.29	.444	5	1	0	1	0	0	11.1	24	18	18	4	3	4
DeHart	0-0	21.60	.545	3	0	0	0	0	0	1.2	6	4	4	2	3	1

2000 preliminary roster

PITCHERS (21)
Antonio Armas
Miguel Batista
Brent Billingsley
Matt Blank
Dustin Hermanson
Mike Johnson
Steve Kline
Ted Lilly
Maryt McLeary
Trey Moore
Guillermo Mota
Carl Pavano
Jeremy Powell

J.D. Smart
Dan Smith
Scott Strickland
Anthony Telford
Mike Thurman
Ugueth Urbina
Javier Vazquez
Jake Westbrook

CATCHERS (4)
Michael Barrett
Bob Henley
Brian Schneider
Chris Widger

INFIELDERS (10)
Jeff Blum
Orlando Cabrera
Trace Coquillette
Tomas De La Rosa
Brad Fullmer
Wilton Guerrero
Mike Mordecai
Talmadge Nunnari
Fernando Seguignol
Jose Vidro

OUTFIELDERS (5)
Peter Bergeron
Milton Bradley
Vladimir Guerrero
Manny Martinez
Rondell White

Games played by position

PLAYER	G	C	1B	2B	3B	SS	OF
Andrews	98	0	18	0	82	0	0
Barrett	126	59	0	0	66	2	0
Bergeron	16	0	0	0	0	0	13
Blum	45	0	0	2	0	42	0
Cabrera	104	0	0	0	0	102	0
Coquillette	17	0	0	6	11	0	0
Cox	15	14	0	0	0	0	0
Fernandez	8	0	0	0	6	0	0
Fullmer	100	0	94	0	0	0	0
W. Guerrero	132	0	0	54	0	0	22
V. Guerrero	160	0	0	0	0	0	160
Jones	17	0	0	0	0	0	17
Machado	17	17	0	0	0	0	0
Martinez	137	0	0	0	0	0	126
McGuire	88	0	58	0	0	0	23
Merced	93	0	7	0	0	0	44
Mordecai	109	0	1	38	32	38	0
Mouton	95	0	0	0	0	0	56
Seguignol	35	0	23	0	0	0	8
Stowers	4	0	0	0	0	0	2
Vidro	140	0	14	121	2	0	4
White	138	0	0	0	0	0	135
Widger	124	118	0	0	0	0	0

Sick call: 1999 DL report

PLAYER	Days on the DL
Shane Andrews	21
Michael Barrett	18
Miguel Batista	25
Orlando Cabrera	56
Darron Cox	99
Bob Henley	182
Steve Kline	16
Manny Martinez	15
Orlando Merced	27
Trey Moore	182
Carl Pavano	61
Fernando Seguignol	58
Rondell White	30*

Indicates two separate terms on Disabled List.

Minor Leagues
Tops in the organization

BATTER	CLUB	AVG.	G	AB	R	H	HR	RBI
Watson, M.	VMT	.380	70	284	55	108	7	47
Pascucci, V.	VMT	.351	72	259	62	91	7	48
Nunnari, T.	Har	.344	134	500	86	172	11	73
Bradley, Milton	Har	.329	87	346	62	114	12	50
Coquillette, Trace	Ott	.326	98	334	56	109	14	55

HOME RUNS
Tracy, Andy	Har	37	Blank, Matt	Har	15
Seguignol, F.	Ott	23	Tucker, T.J.	Har	13
Pittman, Thomas	CF	22	Westbrook, Jake	Har	11
Schneider, Brian	Har	17	Several Players Tied at		10
Hunter, Scott	Ott	16			

WINS
(see above)

RBI
Tracy, Andy	Har	128	Saylor, Ryan	Har	17
Pittman, Thomas	CF	97	Crumpton, Chuck	CF	12
Pond, Simon	Jup	77	Sheldon, Kyle	Jup	10
Benjamin, Al	CF	77	Strickland, Scott	Ott	10
Seguignol, F.	Ott	74	Several Players Tied at		8

SAVES
(see above)

STOLEN BASES
James, Kenny	Jup	44	Rodriguez, C.	CF	128
Hall, Noah	Jup	32	Tucker, T.J.	Har	120
Mateo, Henry	Jup	32	Johnson, Mike	Ott	120
Several Players Tied at		30	Serrano, Jim	Jup	118
			Hebson, Bryan	Jup	113

STRIKEOUTS
(see above)

PITCHER	CLUB	W-L	ERA	IP	H	BB	SO
Hebson, Bryan	Jup	7-7	2.17	137	107	43	113
Salyers, Jeremy	Har	3-3	2.38	95	88	31	48
Wamback, Trevor	CF	7-3	2.85	117	110	15	89
Armas, Tony	Har	9-7	2.89	150	123	55	106
Chiavacci, Ron	Jup	9-7	3.00	111	96	51	99

1999 salaries

	Bonuses	Total earned salary
Rondell White, of		3,000,000
Ugueth Urbina, p		2,200,000
Dustin Hermanson, p	25,000	2,075,000
Shane Andrews, 3b		1,250,000
Vladimir Guerrero, of	25,000	1,050,000
Chris Widger, c		900,000
Wilton Guerrero, 2b		340,000
Mike Mordecai, ss		325,000
Anthony Telford, p		320,000
Orlando Merced, of		300,000
Brad Fullmer, 1b		270,000
Steve Kline, p		260,000
Miguel Batista, p		250,000
James Mouton, of	25,000	250,000
Manny Martinez, of		225,000
Jose Vidro, 2b		225,000
Orlando Cabrera, ss		225,000
Ryan McGuire, 1b		225,000
Carl Pavano, p		225,000
Bob Henley, c		215,000
Mike Thurman, p		212,500
Darron Cox, c		210,000
Trey Moore, p		207,500
Fernando Seguignol, 1b		201,500
Jeremy Powell, p		201,000
Michael Barrett, 3b		200,500
Robert Machado, c		200,000
Dan Smith, p		200,000
Geoff Blum, ss		200,000
Scott Strickland, p		200,000

Average 1999 salary: $527,839
Total 1999 team payroll: $16,363,000
Termination pay: $1,322,750

Montreal (1969-1999)

Runs: Most, career

934	TIM RAINES, 1979-1990
828	Andre Dawson, 1976-1986
737	Tim Wallach, 1980-1992
707	Gary Carter, 1974-1992
446	Warren Cromartie, 1974-1983

Hits: Most, career

1694	Tim Wallach, 1980-1992
1598	TIM RAINES, 1979-1990
1575	Andre Dawson, 1976-1986
1427	Gary Carter, 1974-1992
1063	Warren Cromartie, 1974-1983

2B: Most, career

360	Tim Wallach, 1980-1992
295	Andre Dawson, 1976-1986
274	Gary Carter, 1974-1992
273	TIM RAINES, 1979-1990
222	Warren Cromartie, 1974-1983

3B: Most, career

81	TIM RAINES, 1979-1990
67	Andre Dawson, 1976-1986
31	Tim Wallach, 1980-1992
30	Warren Cromartie, 1974-1983
25	DELINO DeSHIELDS, 1990-1993
25	Mitch Webster, 1985-1988

HR: Most, career

225	Andre Dawson, 1976-1986
220	Gary Carter, 1974-1992
204	Tim Wallach, 1980-1992
118	Bob Bailey, 1969-1975
106	Andres Galarraga, 1985-1991

RBI: Most, career

905	Tim Wallach, 1980-1992
838	Andre Dawson, 1976-1986
823	Gary Carter, 1974-1992
552	TIM RAINES, 1979-1990
466	Bob Bailey, 1969-1975

SB: Most, career

634	TIM RAINES, 1979-1990
266	MARQUIS GRISSOM, 1989-1994
253	Andre Dawson, 1976-1986
187	DELINO DeSHIELDS, 1990-1993
139	Rodney Scott, 1976-1982

BB: Most, career

775	TIM RAINES, 1979-1990
582	Gary Carter, 1974-1992
514	Tim Wallach, 1980-1992
502	Bob Bailey, 1969-1975
370	Ron Fairly, 1969-1974

BA: Highest, career

.301	TIM RAINES, 1979-1990
.294	Rusty Staub, 1969-1979
.292	Moises Alou, 1990-1996
.292	RONDELL WHITE, 1993-1999
.288	Ellis Valentine, 1975-1981

On-base avg: Highest, career

.402	Rusty Staub, 1969-1979
.390	TIM RAINES, 1979-1990
.390	Ron Hunt, 1971-1974
.381	Ron Fairly, 1969-1974
.368	Bob Bailey, 1969-1975

Slug pct: Highest, career

.497	Rusty Staub, 1969-1979
.489	Moises Alou, 1990-1996
.483	LARRY WALKER, 1989-1994
.477	RONDELL WHITE, 1993-1999
.476	Andre Dawson, 1976-1986

Games started: Most, career

393	Steve Rogers, 1973-1985
233	Dennis Martinez, 1986-1993
193	Bryn Smith, 1981-1989
192	Steve Renko, 1969-1976
170	Bill Gullickson, 1979-1985

Complete games: Most, career

129	Steve Rogers, 1973-1985
46	Bill Stoneman, 1969-1973
41	Dennis Martinez, 1986-1993
40	Steve Renko, 1969-1976
31	Bill Gullickson, 1979-1985

Saves: Most, career

152	Jeff Reardon, 1981-1986
109	MEL ROJAS, 1990-1999
105	JOHN WETTELAND, 1992-1994
102	UGUETH URBINA, 1995-1999
101	Tim Burke, 1985-1991

Shutouts: Most, career

37	Steve Rogers, 1973-1985
15	Bill Stoneman, 1969-1973
13	Dennis Martinez, 1986-1993
8	Woodie Fryman, 1975-1983
8	Charlie Lea, 1980-1987
8	PEDRO MARTINEZ, 1994-1997
8	Scott Sanderson, 1978-1983
8	Bryn Smith, 1981-1989

Wins: Most, career

158	Steve Rogers, 1973-1985
100	Dennis Martinez, 1986-1993
81	Bryn Smith, 1981-1989
72	Bill Gullickson, 1979-1985
68	Steve Renko, 1969-1976

K: Most, career

1621	Steve Rogers, 1973-1985
973	Dennis Martinez, 1986-1993
843	PEDRO MARTINEZ, 1994-1997
838	Bryn Smith, 1981-1989
831	Bill Stoneman, 1969-1973

Win pct: Highest, career

.661	KEN HILL, 1992-1994
.625	PEDRO MARTINEZ, 1994-1997
.623	Tim Burke, 1985-1991
.581	Dennis Martinez, 1986-1993
.573	Charlie Lea, 1980-1987

ERA: Lowest, career

3.06	PEDRO MARTINEZ, 1994-1997
3.06	Dennis Martinez, 1986-1993
3.17	Steve Rogers, 1973-1985
3.20	JEFF FASSERO, 1991-1996
3.28	Bryn Smith, 1981-1989

Runs: Most, season

133	TIM RAINES, 1983
123	TIM RAINES, 1987
115	TIM RAINES, 1985
108	VLADIMIR GUERRERO, 1998
107	Andre Dawson, 1982

Hits: Most, season

204	Al Oliver, 1982
202	VLADIMIR GUERRERO, 1998
201	MARK GRUDZIELANEK, 1996
194	TIM RAINES, 1986
193	VLADIMIR GUERRERO, 1999

2B: Most, season

54	MARK GRUDZIELANEK, 1997
46	Warren Cromartie, 1979
45	MIKE LANSING, 1997
45	JOSE VIDRO, 1999
44	BRAD FULLMER, 1998
44	LARRY WALKER, 1994

3B: Most, season

13	TIM RAINES, 1985	
13	Rodney Scott, 1980	
13	Mitch Webster, 1986	
12	Andre Dawson, 1979	
11	Ron LeFlore, 1980	

HR: Most, season

42	VLADIMIR GUERRERO, 1999
38	VLADIMIR GUERRERO, 1998
36	HENRY RODRIGUEZ, 1996
32	Andre Dawson, 1983
31	Gary Carter, 1977

RBI: Most, season

131	VLADIMIR GUERRERO, 1999
123	Tim Wallach, 1987
113	Andre Dawson, 1983
109	VLADIMIR GUERRERO, 1998
109	Al Oliver, 1982

SB: Most, season

97	Ron LeFlore, 1980
90	TIM RAINES, 1983
78	MARQUIS GRISSOM, 1992
78	TIM RAINES, 1982
76	MARQUIS GRISSOM, 1991

BB: Most, season

123	Ken Singleton, 1973
112	Rusty Staub, 1970
110	Rusty Staub, 1969
100	Bob Bailey, 1974
97	Bob Bailey, 1971
97	TIM RAINES, 1983

BA: Highest, season

.339	Moises Alou, 1994
.334	TIM RAINES, 1986
.331	Al Oliver, 1982
.330	TIM RAINES, 1987
.324	VLADIMIR GUERRERO, 1998

On-base avg; Highest, season

.429	TIM RAINES, 1987
.426	Rusty Staub, 1969
.425	Ken Singleton, 1973
.422	Ron Fairly, 1973
.413	TIM RAINES, 1986

Slug pct: Highest, season

.600	VLADIMIR GUERRERO, 1999
.592	Moises Alou, 1994
.589	VLADIMIR GUERRERO, 1998
.587	LARRY WALKER, 1994
.562	HENRY RODRIGUEZ, 1996

Games started: Most, season

40	Steve Rogers, 1977
39	Bill Stoneman, 1971
38	Steve Rogers, 1974
37	Carl Morton, 1970
37	Steve Renko, 1971
37	Steve Rogers, 1979
37	Steve Rogers, 1980

Complete games: Most, season

20	Bill Stoneman, 1971
19	Ross Grimsley, 1978
17	Steve Rogers, 1977
14	Steve Rogers, 1980
14	Steve Rogers, 1982

Saves: Most, season

43	JOHN WETTELAND, 1993
41	Jeff Reardon, 1985
41	UGUETH URBINA, 1999
37	JOHN WETTELAND, 1992
36	MEL ROJAS, 1996

Shutouts: Most, season

5	Dennis Martinez, 1991
5	CARLOS PEREZ, 1997
5	Steve Rogers, 1979
5	Steve Rogers, 1983
5	Bill Stoneman, 1969

Wins: Most, season

20	Ross Grimsley, 1978
19	Steve Rogers, 1982
18	Carl Morton, 1970
18	Bryn Smith, 1985
17	Bill Gullickson, 1983
17	PEDRO MARTINEZ, 1997
17	Steve Rogers, 1977
17	Steve Rogers, 1983
17	Bill Stoneman, 1971

K: Most, season

305	PEDRO MARTINEZ, 1997
251	Bill Stoneman, 1971
222	JEFF FASSERO, 1996
222	PEDRO MARTINEZ, 1996
206	Steve Rogers, 1977

Win pct: Highest, season

.783	Bryn Smith, 1985
.762	KEN HILL, 1994
.704	Steve Rogers, 1982
.696	Dennis Martinez, 1989
.680	PEDRO MARTINEZ, 1997

ERA: Lowest, season

1.90	PEDRO MARTINEZ, 1997
2.39	Dennis Martinez, 1991
2.39	MARK LANGSTON, 1989
2.40	Steve Rogers, 1982
2.44	Pascual Perez, 1988

Most pinch-hit homers, season

4	Hal Breeden, 1973
3	CLIFF FLOYD, 1996

Most pinch-hit homers, career

5	Jose Morales, 1973-1977
4	Hal Breeden, 1972-1975
4	Jerry White, 1974-1983

Longest hitting streak

31	VLADIMIR GUERRERO, 1999
21	DELINO DeSHIELDS, 1993
19	Warren Cromartie, 1979
19	Andre Dawson, 1980
18	Pepe Mangual, 1975
18	Warren Cromartie, 1980
18	DAVID SEGUI, 1995
18	F. P. SANTANGELO, 1997

Most consecutive scoreless innings

32	Woodie Fryman, 1975

No-hit games

Bill Stoneman, Mon at Phi NL, 7-0; April 17, 1969.

Bill Stoneman, Mon vs NY NL, 7-0; October 2, 1972 (1st game).

Charlie Lea, Mon vs SF NL, 4-0; May 10, 1981 (2nd game).

MARK GARDNER, Mon at LA NL, 0-1; July 26, 1991 (9 innings, lost on 2 hits in 10th, relieved by JEFF FASSERO, who allowed 1 more hit).

Dennis Martinez, Mon at LA NL, 2-0; July 28, 1991 (perfect game).

PEDRO J. MARTINEZ (9 innings) and MEL ROJAS (1 inning), Mon at SD NL, 1-0; June 3,1995 (Martinez pitched 9 perfect innings, but allowed a hit in the tenth, Rojas relieved and finished the game)

David Palmer, five perfect innings, rain, Mon at StL NL, 4-0; April 21, 1984 (2nd game).

Pascual Perez, five innings, rain, Mon at Phi NL, 1-0; September 24, 1988.

ACTIVE PLAYERS in caps.

Players' years of service are listed by the first and last years with this team and are not necessarily consecutive; all statistics record performances for this team only.

Florida Marlins

Rookie Preston Wilson hit nearly twice as many home runs as anyone else on the Marlins.

By Steve Moore

1999 Marlins: Life after the fire sale

Florida Marlins fans were prepared for what happened in 1999. They knew up front that the team was deep into its rebuilding mode, which of course meant deep in the standings as well.

A full year removed from the World Series championship and former owner Wayne Huizenga's dismantling of the roster, new owner John Henry was sticking to his slow but sure approach of returning the Marlins at least to contention.

The missing part of that equation still is a new stadium, which was at the root of Huizenga's fire sale. While Henry made overtures to the community and local government in an attempt to get a facility built—and repair the franchise's seriously damaged image—general manager Dave Dombrowski quietly did what he does best: amass young talent.

The makings of a solid rotation began to take shape, led by the one significant holdover from the championship team, right-hander Alex Fernandez. He still wasn't fully returned to health from the arm injury he suffered during the 1997 playoff run, but he did get in 141 innings, and his 3.38 earned run average was heartening.

With the club going nowhere and some significant options on the roster, Dombrowski sent popular and coveted closer Matt Mantei to Arizona in the most crucial move of the Diamondbacks' drive to a division title. That July deal brought pitcher Vladimir Nunez to the Marlins. Nunez moved into the rotation and, belying his 7-10 record and 4.06 ERA, became more and more impressive as the season went on. The other key player in that deal was pitcher Brad Penny, who didn't get to the majors in 1999 but appeared for the Marlins in the Futures Game (top prospects) during the All-Star Game festivities.

Add young Ryan Dempster and A.J. Burnett and the Marlins' pitching future looks bright. And when Antonio Alfonseca took over as closer after Mantei's departure, he responded with 21 saves and a 3.24 ERA. Another closer candidate is Braden

Looper, acquired before the season in the deal that sent shortstop Edgar Renteria to St. Louis to make room for Alex Gonzalez. Gonzalez might have been a Rookie of the Year candidate, hitting .277 and playing nearly every day, had it not been for teammate Preston Wilson.

With Cliff Floyd injured for much of the season, Wilson became the top power threat in the lineup. He produced team highs in home runs (26) and RBI (71), edging an even bigger surprise, outfielder Bruce Aven, by one RBI for the lead in that category.

Aven collected his 70 RBI in just 381 at-bats and hit .289. That was second among regulars only to second baseman Luis Castillo, who finally began fulfilling the promise he has shown for several years by playing much more consistently and batting .302 with 50 stolen bases.

The best power prospect on the club could be third baseman Mike Lowell. He missed the first half of the season due to illness, but the rookie acquired from the Yankees hit 12 home runs in 97 games and was taking control of the starting job as the season wound down.

The season eventually did wind down to a last-place finish, though the Marlins battled the Montreal Expos to avoid that fate until the final two weeks of the season.

1999 Marlins: Week-by-week notes

These notes were excerpted from the following issues of Baseball Weekly.

▶**April 7:** Left fielder Cliff Floyd (sprained knee) was on the DL until at least April 14. Preston Wilson was playing left until Floyd returned. Second baseman Luis Castillo beat out incumbent Craig Counsell for the starting job by batting .345 with nine walks in 55 spring at-bats.

▶**April 14:** Right-hander Alex Fernandez pitched five strong innings (one run, five hits) on opening day against the Mets in his first start in 18 months since tearing his right rotator cuff. He topped out at 90 mph, just off his preinjury velocity.

▶**April 28:** Right-hander Brian Meadows (3-0, 2.53 ERA) has been sensational, but Florida's other starters were 2-9 with a 6.20 ERA.

▶**May 5:** The Marlins were hoping he can jump-start their moribund offense. Cliff Floyd returned from the DL on April 27 and went 4-for-16 with one RBI in his first five games. The problem was that Floyd's return sent Preston Wilson to the bench, taking five of the Marlins' 11 home runs with him.

▶**May 19:** Right-hander Matt Mantei had been one of the league's most overpowering closers, but not many knew that until recently. With the Marlins struggling, Mantei didn't get his first save opportunity until May 7 at Los Angeles. That started a mini-surge of five wins on a nine-game road trip, and Mantei got saves in all five.

▶**May 26:** Rookie shortstop Alex Gonzalez emerged as one of the game's top young players, batting .285 with five home runs and a team-best 19 RBI in 42 games. He reduced his strikeout ratio (26 in 172 at-bats) and learned to use the entire field.

▶**June 2:** Preston Wilson was finally emerging as the power-hitting force that the Mets hoped he would become when they drafted him in the first round in 1993. He was 17-for-35 (.486) with four home runs and nine RBI during a career-best nine-game hitting streak since replacing Todd Dunwoody in center field.

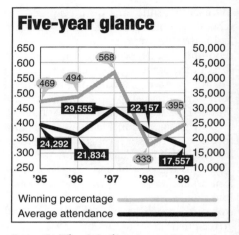

Five-year glance

.469 .494 .568 .395 .333

29,555 22,157 24,292 21,834 17,557

| | '95 | '96 | '97 | '98 | '99 |

Winning percentage
Average attendance

▶**June 9:** The Marlins were 14-14 since May 7. Since then, Matt Mantei has converted seven of eight saves, and the Marlins totaled 148 runs and 36 homers. In their first 28 games Florida was 6-22 with 92 runs and 11 homers.

▶**June 16:** Alex Fernandez's frustrations with restrictive pitch limits were apparent last week when he destroyed a television set in the clubhouse after being taken out of a game against Baltimore. He had pitched well, posting a 2.44 ERA. But he had only a 2-3 record, and he had been limited to 80-90 pitches per game by his surgeon.

▶**June 23:** Right-hander Livan Hernandez was on the trading block, according to an NL scouting official who was at Coors Field. Hernandez is in the final year of a four-year contract that will end up paying him more than $5 million when incentives are added.

▶**June 30:** The Marlins lost seven games with injured Cliff Floyd out of the lineup. Surprising rookie Bruce Aven will handle most of the left field duties until Floyd returns. Aven, 27, had a team-leading .345 average with seven home runs and 37 RBI in just 142 at-bats.

▶**July 7:** While the on-field losses mounted, the Marlins notched a big victory by signing Venezuelan shortstop phenom Miguel Cabrera, 16. The 6-2, 190-pound Cabrera drew comparisons to Alex Gonzalez

and Cal Ripken, and he received a $1.8 million bonus from the Marlins.

▶July 15: Matt Mantei became the latest name player traded by general manager Dave Dombrowski, who had both eyes on the future. He traded Mantei to the Diamondbacks for top right-handed prospect Brad Penny, right-handed reliever Vladimir Nunez and a player to be named.

▶July 28: The deconstruction of the 1997 World Series championship team continued when Livan Hernandez was traded to San Francisco for pitching prospects Jason Grilli and Nate Bump. The deal left the Marlins with only two members of their World Series roster: Cliff Floyd and reliever Antonio Alfonseca.

▶Aug. 4: Alfonseca was perfect in eight save opportunities since taking over as closer. After a poor first month, the 6-4 Alfonseca shed about 30 pounds, to get down to 248, and had a 1.60 ERA in his last 32 appearances.

▶Aug. 11: Alex Fernandez threw a 97-pitch three-hitter with no walks against Colorado on Aug. 6, his first complete game since his surgery in October 1997.

▶Aug. 25: Colorful and confident right-hander A.J. Burnett, 22, made a strong impression in his big league debut, shutting out the Dodgers for five innings before giving up a solo home run to Todd Hollandsworth. Tattooed, sporting pierced nipples and a mid-90s fastball, Burnett was charged with one run and five hits in 5⅔ innings at Dodger Stadium on Aug. 21.

▶Sept. 1: Pitching phenom Josh Beckett signed a four-year, $7 million major league contract with the Marlins on Aug. 28, two days before he was to start classes at junior college. Beckett, the No. 2 overall selection in the June draft, reaped a $3.625 million signing bonus.

▶Sept. 8: Right fielder Mark Kotsay figured to be one of Florida's cornerstones, but his weak bat has given Marlins officials reason to consider a trade. Kotsay was batting .263 with just seven home runs and 39 RBI in 426 at-bats through Sept. 5.

▶Sept. 15: Cliff Floyd returned after 11 weeks on the disabled list, only to be benched by manager John Boles in his first game back when he showed up late for pregame stretching.

▶Sept. 22: Alex Gonzalez was pulled from a game and benched by John Boles for an entire series in San Francisco after jogging to first base on an inning-ending ground-out in Cincinnati last week. It was the second time this season that the All-Star rookie was benched for loafing.

▶Oct. 6: Luis Castillo, who batted .302 with a .384 on-base percentage and 50 stolen bases, was scheduled for three to four months of rehab after Sept. 27 surgery on his dislocated left shoulder. The Marlins had their worst home attendance ever, 1.37 million, in the most rain-plagued of the team's seven seasons.

241

QUOTE OF THE YEAR

"We're challenging the Marlins to a seven-game series. And the winner stays [in the majors]. We'd beat them in six games."
—AAA Calgary first baseman Kevin Millar, before his call-up

Team Leaders

Batting avg.
.302 Luis Castillo
.280 Preston Wilson

HR
26 Preston Wilson
14 Alex Gonzalez

RBI
71 Preston Wilson
70 Bruce Aven

Hits
155 Alex Gonzalez
147 Luis Castillo

Runs
81 Alex Gonzalez
76 Luis Castillo

Stolen bases
50 Luis Castillo
11 Preston Wilson

Wins
11 Brian Meadows
7 Ryan Dempster
7 Alex Fernandez
7 Vladimir Nunez

Losses
16 Dennis Springer
15 Brian Meadows

ERA
4.86 Dennis Springer
5.60 Brian Meadows

Strikeouts
126 Ryan Dempster
86 Vladimir Nunez

Innings
196.1 Dennis Springer
178.1 Brian Meadows

Saves
21 Antonio Alfonseca
1 Brian Edmondson
1 Vladimir Nunez
1 Dennis Springer

FLORIDA MARLINS 1999 final stats

BATTERS	BA	SLG	OBA	G	AB	R	H	TB	2B	3B	HR	RBI	BB	SO	SB	CS	E
Floyd	.303	.518	.379	69	251	37	76	130	19	1	11	49	30	47	5	6	6
Castillo	.302	.366	.384	128	487	76	147	178	23	4	0	28	67	85	50	17	15
Redmond	.302	.351	.381	84	242	22	73	85	9	0	1	27	26	34	0	0	4
Aven	.289	.444	.370	137	381	57	110	169	19	2	12	70	44	82	3	0	3
Bautista	.288	.420	.303	70	205	32	59	86	10	1	5	24	4	30	3	0	3
Berg	.286	.382	.348	109	304	42	87	116	18	1	3	25	27	59	2	2	8
Millar	.285	.433	.362	105	351	48	100	152	17	4	9	67	40	64	1	0	4
Wilson	.280	.502	.350	149	482	67	135	242	21	4	26	71	46	156	11	4	9
Gonzalez	.277	.430	.308	136	560	81	155	241	28	8	14	59	15	113	3	5	27
Kotsay	.271	.402	.306	148	495	57	134	199	23	9	8	50	29	50	7	6	5
Orie	.254	.396	.322	77	240	26	61	95	16	0	6	29	22	43	1	0	7
Lowell	.253	.419	.317	97	308	32	78	129	15	0	12	47	26	69	0	0	4
A. Garcia	.250	.583	.333	10	24	6	6	14	0	1	2	2	3	11	0	0	3
G. Garcia	.250	.250	.250	4	4	0	1	1	0	0	0	0	0	2	0	0	0
Clapinski	.232	.321	.348	36	56	6	13	18	1	2	0	2	9	12	1	0	3
Hyers	.222	.370	.333	58	81	8	18	30	4	1	2	12	14	11	0	0	0
Dunwoody	.220	.317	.270	64	186	20	41	59	6	3	2	20	12	41	3	4	2
Lee	.206	.326	.263	70	218	21	45	71	9	1	5	20	17	70	2	1	3
Castro	.179	.328	.282	24	67	4	12	22	4	0	2	4	10	14	0	0	1
Roskos	.167	.333	.231	13	12	0	2	4	2	0	0	1	1	7	0	0	0
Ramirez	.143	.190	.182	15	21	3	3	4	1	0	0	2	1	6	0	1	1

PITCHERS	W-L	ERA	BA	G	GS	CG	GF	SH	SV	IP	H	R	ER	HR	BB	SO
Almanza	0-1	1.72	.154	14	0	0	2	0	0	15.2	8	4	3	1	9	20
Alfonseca	4-5	3.24	.274	73	0	0	49	0	21	77.2	79	28	28	4	29	46
Cornelius	1-0	3.26	.229	5	2	0	0	0	0	19.1	16	7	7	0	5	12
Fernandez	7-8	3.38	.252	24	24	1	0	0	0	141.0	135	60	53	10	41	91
Burnett	4-2	3.48	.242	7	7	0	0	0	0	41.1	37	23	16	3	25	33
Looper	3-3	3.80	.293	72	0	0	22	0	0	83.0	96	43	35	7	31	50
Nunez	7-10	4.06	.242	44	12	0	12	0	1	108.2	95	63	49	11	54	86
Almonte	0-2	4.20	.339	15	0	0	6	0	0	15.0	20	7	7	1	6	8
Dempster	7-8	4.71	.262	25	25	0	0	0	0	147.0	146	77	77	21	93	126
Springer	6-16	4.86	.303	38	29	3	3	2	1	196.1	231	121	106	23	64	83
Meadows	11-15	5.60	.302	31	31	0	0	0	0	178.1	214	117	111	31	57	72
Medina	1-1	5.79	.227	20	0	0	4	0	0	23.1	20	15	15	3	20	16
Edmondson	5-8	5.84	.290	68	0	0	14	0	1	94.0	106	65	61	11	44	58
Sanchez	5-7	6.01	.291	59	10	0	8	0	0	76.1	84	53	51	16	60	62
Corbin	0-1	7.29	.291	17	0	0	4	0	0	21.0	25	20	17	2	15	30
Darensbourg	0-1	8.83	.340	56	0	0	5	0	0	34.2	50	36	34	3	21	16
Tejera	0-0	11.37	.385	3	1	0	1	0	0	6.1	10	8	8	1	5	7
Ojala	0-1	14.34	.438	8	1	0	2	0	0	10.2	21	17	17	1	6	5
Billingsley	0-0	16.43	.379	8	0	0	3	0	0	7.2	11	14	14	3	10	3

2000 preliminary roster

PITCHERS (22)
Antonio Alfonseca
Armando Almanza
Hector Almonte
Josh Beckett
A.J. Burnett
Jared Camp
Scott Comer
Reid Cornelius
Vic Darensbourg
Ryan Dempster
Brian Edmondson
Alex Fernandez
Joe Fontenot

Gary Knotts
Nelson Lara
Braden Looper
Dan Miceli
Vladimir Nunez
Brad Penny
Jesus Sanchez
Michael Tejera
Claudio Vargas

CATCHERS (2)
Ramon Castro
Mike Redmond

INFIELDERS (9)
Dave Berg
Luis Castillo
Amaury Garcia
Alex Gonzalez
Derrek Lee
Mike Lowell
Kevin Millar
Pablo Ozuna
Nate Rolison

OUTFIELDERS (6)
Danny Bautista
Brant Brown
Cliff Floyd
Mark Kotsay
Julio Ramirez
Preston Wilson

Games played by position

PLAYER	G	C	1B	2B	3B	SS	OF
Aven	137	0	0	0	0	0	102
Bautista	70	0	0	0	0	0	60
Berg	109	0	0	29	19	37	3
Castillo	128	0	0	126	0	0	0
Castro	24	24	0	0	0	0	0
Clapinski	36	0	0	2	9	6	3
Counsell	37	0	0	12	0	0	0
Dunwoody	64	0	0	0	0	0	55
Fabregas	82	78	0	0	0	0	0
Floyd	69	0	0	0	0	0	62
A. Garcia	10	0	0	8	0	0	0
G. Garcia	4	3	0	0	0	0	0
Gonzalez	136	0	0	0	0	135	0
Hyers	58	0	14	0	0	0	15
Kotsay	148	0	19	0	0	0	129
Lee	70	0	66	0	0	0	0
Lowell	97	0	0	0	83	0	0
Millar	105	0	94	0	1	0	1
Orie	77	0	1	0	64	0	0
Ramirez	15	0	0	0	0	0	1
Redmond	84	82	0	0	0	0	0
Roskos	13	1	0	0	0	0	0
Wilson	149	0	0	0	0	0	136

Minor Leagues

Tops in the organization

BATTER	CLUB	AVG.	G	AB	R	H	HR	RBI
Roskos, John	Cal	.320	134	506	85	162	24	90
Garcia, Amaury	Cal	.317	119	479	94	152	17	53
Hill, Willy	KnC	.303	127	535	85	162	2	57
Rolison, Nate	Por	.299	124	438	71	131	17	69
Gload, Ross	BC	.298	133	490	80	146	10	74

HOME RUNS			WINS		
Norton, Chris	Por	38	Knotts, Gary	Por	15
Roskos, John	Cal	24	Tejera, Michael	Por	13
Lee, Derrek	Cal	19	Ludwick, Eric	Cal	11
Santos, Jose	KnC	19	Cornelius, Reid	Cal	10
Several Players Tied at		17	Several Players Tied at		9

RBI			SAVES		
Santos, Jose	KnC	105	Almonte, Hector	Por	23
Norton, Chris	Por	97	Ludwick, Eric	Cal	14
Roskos, John	Cal	90	McCurtain, Paul	BC	12
Aguila, Chris	KnC	78	Clackum, Scott	KnC	10
Gload, Ross	BC	74	Lara, Nelson	KnC	10

STOLEN BASES			STRIKEOUTS		
Ramirez, Julio	Por	64	Tejera, Michael	Por	157
Foster, Quincy	BC	56	Cornelius, Reid	Cal	135
Medrano, Jesus	KnC	42	Anderson, Wes	KnC	134
Hill, Willy	KnC	38	Knotts, Gary	Por	128
Several Players Tied at		33	Burnett, A.J.	Por	121

PITCHER	CLUB	W-L	ERA	IP	H	BB	SO
Comer, Scott	BC	9-4	2.35	130	120	5	85
Tejera, Michael	Por	13-6	3.13	164	156	49	157
Anderson, Wes	KnC	9-5	3.21	137	111	51	134
Noyce, David	KnC	7-3	3.30	101	82	29	86
Villafuerte, B.	Por	6-8	3.50	100	97	40	85

Sick call: 1999 DL report

PLAYER	Days on the DL
Archie Corbin	36*
Alex Fernandez	57**
Cliff Floyd	101*
Joe Fontenot	27
Mike Lowell	54
Kevin Orie	83*

Indicates two separate terms on Disabled List.
**Indicates three separate terms on Disabled List.*

1999 salaries

	Bonuses	Total earned salary
Alex Fernandez, p		7,000,000
Cliff Floyd, of		2,500,000
Danny Bautista, of		325,000
Mark Kotsay, of		280,000
Dennis Springer, p		275,000
Vic Darensbourg, p		265,000
Brian Meadows, p		265,000
Antonio Alfonseca, p		250,000
Brian Edmondson, p		240,000
Kevin Orie, 3b		240,000
Dave Berg, ss		235,000
Luis Castillo, 2b		225,000
Todd Dunwoody, of		222,000
Mike Redmond, c		220,000
Ryan Dempster, p		202,000
Vladimir Nunez, p		202,000
Preston Wilson, of		201,000
Alex Gonzalez, ss		201,000
Mike Lowell, 3b		201,000
Braden Looper, p		201,000
Chris Clapinski, 3b		200,000
Rafael Medina, p		200,000
Armando Almanza, p		200,000
Kevin Millar, 1b		200,000
Ramon Castro, c		200,000
Bruce Aven, of		200,000
A.J. Burnett, p		200,000

Average 1999 salary: $561,111
Total 1999 team payroll: $15,150,000
Termination pay: $500,000

MAJOR LEAGUE REPORT

243

FLORIDA MARLINS / NL EAST

Florida (1993-1999)

Runs: Most, career

365	GARY SHEFFIELD, 1993-1998	
337	JEFF CONINE, 1993-1997	
237	EDGAR RENTERIA, 1996-1998	
190	Chuck Carr, 1993-1995	
173	KURT ABBOTT, 1994-1997	

Hits: Most, career

737	JEFF CONINE, 1993-1997
538	GARY SHEFFIELD, 1 993-1998
450	EDGAR RENTERIA, 1996-1998
343	KURT ABBOTT, 1994-1997
339	GREG COLBRUNN, 1994-1996

2B: Most, career

122	JEFF CONINE, 1993-1997
98	GARY SHEFFIELD, 1993-1998
73	CLIFF FLOYD, 1997-1999
71	KURT ABBOTT, 1994-1997
60	CHARLES JOHNSON, 1994-1998

3B: Most, career

19	KURT ABBOTT, 1994-1997
17	MARK KOTSAY, 1997-1999
14	JEFF CONINE, 1993-1997
12	TODD DUNWOODY, 1997-1999
8	BENITO SANTIAGO, 1993-1994
8	EDGAR RENTERIA, 1996-1998
8	QUILVIO VERAS, 1995-1996
8	ALEX GONZALEZ, 1998-1999

HR: Most, career

122	GARY SHEFFIELD, 1993-1998
98	JEFF CONINE, 1993-1997
51	CHARLES JOHNSON, 1994-1998
45	GREG COLBRUNN, 1994-1996
40	KURT ABBOTT, 1994-1997

RBI: Most, career

422	JEFF CONINE, 1993-1997
380	GARY SHEFFIELD, 1993-1998
189	GREG COLBRUNN, 1994-1996
166	CHARLES JOHNSON, 1994-1998
158	CLIFF FLOYD, 1997-1999

SB: Most, career

115	Chuck Carr, 1993-1995
89	EDGAR RENTERIA, 1996-1998
86	LUIS CASTILLO, 1996-1999
74	GARY SHEFFIELD, 1993-1998
64	QUILVIO VERAS, 1995-1996

BB: Most, career

424	GARY SHEFFIELD, 1993-1998
277	JEFF CONINE, 1993-1997
163	CHARLES JOHNSON, 1994-1998
131	QUILVIO VERAS, 1995-1996
130	LUIS CASTILLO, 1996-1999

BA: Highest, career

.291	JEFF CONINE, 1993-1997
.288	GARY SHEFFIELD, 1993-1998
.288	EDGAR RENTERIA, 1996-1998
.284	GREG COLBRUNN, 1994-1996
.271	MARK KOTSAY, 1997-1999

On-base avg: Highest, career

.426	GARY SHEFFIELD, 1993-1998
.360	JEFF CONINE, 1993-1997
.342	EDGAR RENTERIA, 1996-1998
.335	ALEX ARIAS, 1993-1997
.330	CHARLES JOHNSON, 1994-1998

Slug pct: Highest, career

.543	GARY SHEFFIELD, 1993-1998
.467	JEFF CONINE, 1993-1997
.451	GREG COLBRUNN, 1994-1996
.428	KURT ABBOTT, 1994-1997
.416	CHARLES JOHNSON, 1994-1998

Games started: Most, career

115	PAT RAPP, 1993-1997
81	Chris Hammond, 1993-1998
70	LIVAN HERNANDEZ, 1996-1999
65	KEVIN BROWN, 1996-1997
62	BRIAN MEADOWS, 1998-1999

Complete games: Most, career

11	KEVIN BROWN, 1996-1997
11	LIVAN HERNANDEZ, 1996-1999
7	PAT RAPP, 1993-1997
6	ALEX FERNANDEZ, 1997-1999
5	Chris Hammond, 1993-1998
5	JOHN BURKETT, 1995-1996

Saves: Most, career

108	ROBB NEN, 1993-1997
51	Bryan Harvey, 1993-1995
29	ANTONIO ALFONSECA, 1997-1999
19	MATT MANTEI, 1995-1999
9	Jeremy Hernandez, 1994-1995

Shutouts: Most, career

5	KEVIN BROWN, 1996-1997
4	PAT RAPP, 1993-1997
3	Chris Hammond, 1993-1998
2	DENNIS SPRINGER, 1999-1999
1	Ryan Bowen, 1993-1995
1	Charlie Hough, 1993-1994
1	MARK GARDNER, 1994-1995
1	AL LEITER, 1996-1997
1	ALEX FERNANDEZ, 1997-1999

Wins: Most, career

37	PAT RAPP, 1993-1997
33	KEVIN BROWN, 1996-1997
29	Chris Hammond, 1993-1998
27	AL LEITER, 1996-1997
24	LIVAN HERNANDEZ, 1996-1999
24	ALEX FERNANDEZ, 1997-1999

K: Most, career

384	PAT RAPP, 1993-1997
364	KEVIN BROWN, 1996-1997
333	LIVAN HERNANDEZ, 1996-1999
332	Chris Hammond, 1993-1998
332	AL LEITER, 1996-1997

Win pct: Highest, career

.635	KEVIN BROWN, 1996-1997
.563	AL LEITER, 1996-1997
.475	Chris Hammond, 1993-1998
.463	PAT RAPP, 1993-1997

ERA: Lowest, career

2.30	KEVIN BROWN, 1996-1997
3.41	ROBB NEN, 1993-1997
3.51	ALEX FERNANDEZ, 1997-1999
3.51	AL LEITER, 1996-1997
4.18	PAT RAPP, 1993-1997

Runs: Most, season

118	GARY SHEFFIELD, 1996
90	EDGAR RENTERIA, 1997
88	Moises Alou, 1997
86	QUILVIO VERAS, 1995
86	GARY SHEFFIELD, 1997

Hits: Most, season

175	JEFF CONINE, 1996
174	JEFF CONINE, 1993
171	EDGAR RENTERIA, 1997
167	BOBBY BONILLA, 1997
166	CLIFF FLOYD, 1998

2B: Most, season

45	CLIFF FLOYD, 1998
39	BOBBY BONILLA, 1997
37	DEVON WHITE, 1996
33	GARY SHEFFIELD, 1996
32	Terry Pendleton, 1995
32	JEFF CONINE, 1996

3B: Most, season

9	MARK KOTSAY, 1999
8	ALEX GONZALEZ, 1999
7	KURT ABBOTT, 1995
7	QUILVIO VERAS, 1995
7	KURT ABBOTT, 1996
7	TODD DUNWOODY, 1998
7	MARK KOTSAY, 1998

HR: Most, season

42	GARY SHEFFIELD, 1996
27	GARY SHEFFIELD, 1994
26	JEFF CONINE, 1996
26	PRESTON WILSON, 1999
25	JEFF CONINE, 1995

RBI: Most, season

120	GARY SHEFFIELD, 1996
115	Moises Alou, 1997
105	JEFF CONINE, 1995
96	BOBBY BONILLA, 1997
95	JEFF CONINE, 1996

SB: Most, season

58	Chuck Carr, 1993
56	QUILVIO VERAS, 1995
50	LUIS CASTILLO, 1999
41	EDGAR RENTERIA, 1998
32	Chuck Carr, 1994
32	EDGAR RENTERIA, 1997

BB: Most, season

142	GARY SHEFFIELD, 1996
121	GARY SHEFFIELD, 1997
80	QUILVIO VERAS, 1995
79	WALT WEISS, 1993
73	BOBBY BONILLA, 1997

BA: Highest, season

.319	JEFF CONINE, 1994
.314	GARY SHEFFIELD, 1996
.302	JEFF CONINE, 1995
.302	LUIS CASTILLO, 1999
.301	Bret Barberie, 1994

On-base avg; Highest, season

.465	GARY SHEFFIELD, 1996
.424	GARY SHEFFIELD, 1997
.392	Jerry Browne, 1994
.384	LUIS CASTILLO, 1999
.384	QUILVIO VERAS, 1995

Slug pct: Highest, season

.624	GARY SHEFFIELD, 1996
.526	JEFF CONINE, 1994
.520	JEFF CONINE, 1995
.502	PRESTON WILSON, 1999
.493	Moises Alou, 1997

Games started: Most, season

34	Charlie Hough, 1993
33	Jack Armstrong, 1993
33	AL LEITER, 1996
33	KEVIN BROWN, 1997
33	LIVAN HERNANDEZ, 1998

Complete games: Most, season

9	LIVAN HERNANDEZ, 1998
6	KEVIN BROWN, 1997
5	KEVIN BROWN, 1996
5	ALEX FERNANDEZ, 1997
4	JOHN BURKETT, 1995

Saves: Most, season

45	Bryan Harvey, 1993
35	ROBB NEN, 1996
35	ROBB NEN, 1997
23	ROBB NEN, 1995
21	ANTONIO ALFONSECA, 1999

Shutouts: Most, season

3	KEVIN BROWN, 1996
2	Chris Hammond, 1995
2	PAT RAPP, 1995
2	KEVIN BROWN, 1997
2	DENNIS SPRINGER, 1999

Wins: Most, season

17	KEVIN BROWN, 1996
17	ALEX FERNANDEZ, 1997
16	AL LEITER, 1996
16	KEVIN BROWN, 1997
14	JOHN BURKETT, 1995
14	PAT RAPP, 1995

K: Most, season

205	KEVIN BROWN, 1997
200	AL LEITER, 1996
183	ALEX FERNANDEZ, 1997
162	LIVAN HERNANDEZ, 1998
159	KEVIN BROWN, 1996

Win pct: Highest, season

.667	KEVIN BROWN, 1997
.667	PAT RAPP, 1995
.607	KEVIN BROWN, 1996
.586	ALEX FERNANDEZ, 1997
.571	AL LEITER, 1996

ERA: Lowest, season

1.89	KEVIN BROWN, 1996
2.69	KEVIN BROWN, 1997
2.93	AL LEITER, 1996
3.44	PAT RAPP, 1995
3.59	ALEX FERNANDEZ, 1997

Most pinch-hit homers, season

3	PRESTON WILSON, 1999
2	KURT ABBOTT, 1996
2	Andre Dawson, 1996
2	BRUCE AVEN, 1999

Most pinch-hit homers, career

3	PRESTON WILSON, 1998-1999
2	KURT ABBOTT, 1994-1997
2	Andre Dawson, 1995-1996
2	JOHN CANGELOSI, 1997-1998
2	BRUCE AVEN, 1999

Longest hitting streak

22	EDGAR RENTERIA, 1996
22	LUIS CASTILLO, 1999
21	GREG COLBRUNN, 1996
17	GREG COLBRUNN, 1995
15	Bret Barberie, 1993
15	Chuck Carr, 1993

Most consecutive scoreless innings

26	Luis Aquino, 1994
24	PAT RAPP, 1995
24	CHRIS HAMMOND, 1994

No-hit games

ACTIVE PLAYERS in caps.

Players' years of service are listed by the first and last years with this team and are not necessarily consecutive; all statistics record performances for this team only.

Houston Astros

Jeff Bagwell led the Astros to a division title, playing every game and scoring the most runs in the league.

By Barbara Jean Germano, *Baseball Weekly*

1999 Astros: Last gasp in the Astrodome

"I'll be glad to leave the Astrodome," Houston Astros pitcher Jose Lima said. "I don't know if it's a curse or not. It's nothing against the Astrodome, but we don't want to come back."

Yet the Astros won another National League Central Division title, their third in succession, playing their final season in the Astrodome.

"We don't win here in the playoffs," Lima said.

After an emotional season, full of injuries and illnesses, Houston clinched the division on the final day of the season before losing a four-game Division Series to the Atlanta Braves. For a team becoming the regular participant in the postseason, division titles no longer provide much solace.

"I refuse to say it's choking," first baseman Jeff Bagwell said. "All I can tell you is I did the best I could. I just didn't get the hits when I needed to. But one thing you've got to understand is it's not that easy to get here. We're a winning team. We've won three division titles and we'll come through sooner or later."

Manager Larry Dierker said: "I'm sure if we get in next year, the stigma we came in with this year will come in even greater."

Bagwell, a contender for MVP in the regular season, is a career .304 hitter but he's only hitting .128 in the playoffs. Bagwell hit 42 homers and stole 30 bases in the regular season, joining Barry Bonds as the only 40-30 players to accomplish the feat twice in major league history.

Second baseman Craig Biggio led the majors with 56 doubles and became the first NL player since the Cardinals' Joe Medwick (in 1937) to hit that many doubles.

The Astros had 14 players spend time on the disabled list including two—Ricky Gutierrez and Jack Howell—who were there twice. Biggio and Bagwell were the only opening day starters who didn't go on the DL.

Houston played the entire season without All-Star left fielder Moises Alou, who hurt a knee before spring training. His

replacement, Richard Hidalgo, missed the final two months with an inflamed left knee. And third baseman Ken Caminiti hobbled through much of the season with a strained right calf muscle and didn't start producing until the playoffs.

Even the coaching staff got hurt. Dierker collapsed in the dugout from a seizure on June 13 and had to undergo brain surgery. Hitting coach Tom McCraw took a three-month leave for cancer treatment, and first-base coach Jose Cruz missed 34 games while receiving treatment for heart problems.

The Astros survived on a strong 1-2-3 pitching rotation of Mike Hampton (22-4), Lima (21-10) and Shane Reynolds (16-14) and closer Billy Wagner (39 saves). Promising Scott Elarton began the season as Wagner's setup man, then was promoted to the rotation.

Hampton's 22 victories broke by one the franchise record set by Joe Niekro in 1979. The Astros hit 168 homers, a club record, and they drew a franchise record 2,706,017 fans in their final year at the Astrodome before moving to their new downtown stadium.

"We came up a little short, but I think we're getting more out of our players' abilities," general manager Gerry Hunsicker said. But he added, "As long as the other teams are spending $10 million and $20 million more than we are, it's hard to think we won't continue to be the underdogs."

1999 Astros: Week-by-week notes

These notes were excerpted from the following issues of Baseball Weekly.

▶**April 14:** Three of the first four hitters in the lineup—second baseman Craig Biggio, first baseman Jeff Bagwell and third baseman Ken Caminiti—were a combined 10-for-58 (.172) with one homer and two RBI through April 10.

▶**April 21:** Jeff Bagwell was on a tear. After a mediocre first week he had an eight-game hitting streak through April 19 in which he was 12-for-25. During one stretch Bagwell reached base 10 consecutive times (five hits, five walks).

▶**April 28:** Jeff Bagwell became the Astros' all-time home run leader on April 21 with 225. He passed Jimmy Wynn, whose record of 224 stood for 25 years.

▶**May 5:** The Astros, already missing outfielder Moises Alou for up to four months with a knee injury, lost shortstop Ricky Gutierrez when he fractured his left hand on April 27 after being hit by a pitch from Arizona's Armando Reynoso. Gutierrez was hitting .357.

▶**May 12:** The Astros led the majors with a .352 (94-for-267) average against left-handers. Four starters—right fielder Derek Bell (.419), Craig Biggio (.414), Jeff Bagwell (.429) and center fielder Carl Everett (.407)—were over .400 against lefties through May 9.

▶**May 26:** The Astros put Ken Caminiti on the 15-day disabled list on May 22 because a strained right calf. After a slow start Caminiti had been playing well recently. Over his last 12 games Caminiti hit .375 (18-for-48) with nine RBI.

▶**June 16:** Right-hander Jose Lima tied Pedro Martinez for most wins in the majors when he got his 11th on June 12 against San Diego. Jeff Bagwell continued to stay ahead of his 1994 power pace, the year he won the MVP award after hitting .368 with 39 homers and a league-leading 116 RBI. He had 22 home runs and 61 RBI through June 13.

▶**June 23:** Manager Larry Dierker underwent surgery to have a lemon-sized lump of blood vessels removed from the front of his

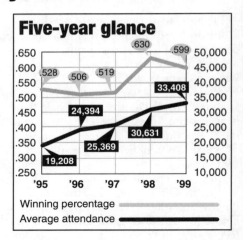

Five-year glance

Winning percentage ▬▬▬
Average attendance ▬▬▬

brain on June 15. The mass caused Dierker to have a seizure during the June 13 game against San Diego. Dierker was expected to be released from Methodist Hospital in Houston early this week, but he would not return to the field for at least another few weeks. Bench coach Matt Galante, a member of the Houston organization since 1980, was serving as interim manager.

▶**July 7:** Scott Elarton started on July 3 at Cincinnati in place of right-hander Sean Bergman, who was placed on the 15-day DL with a strained right forearm. Elarton, 5-3 with a 2.91 ERA as a reliever, is a former No. 1 draft pick.

▶**July 15:** The Astros lost two more players to injury. Ricky Gutierrez fractured the hamate bone in his left hand and would be out at least six weeks, and catcher Tony Eusebio returned to Houston to be examined by an ophthalmologist for swelling around his right eye. Eusebio wasn't placed on the DL but wouldn't return until after the All-Star break.

▶**July 21:** Derek Bell was dropped from second to sixth in the batting order, and he wasn't happy about it. Bell was hitting .245 through July 18 and led the league with 95 strikeouts.

▶**July 28:** The Astros had 10 players on the DL. To help plug the gaps, the Astros called up first baseman–outfielder Daryle Ward from AAA New Orleans. Ward was hitting .353 with 28 homers and 65 RBI.

▶**Aug. 4:** Mike Hampton has the league's

best record (16-3) and was third in ERA (2.97) through Aug. 1. The left-hander was 5-0 with a 2.77 ERA in 39 innings since the All-Star break. In 164⅓ innings he had allowed only seven homers and 62 walks, while striking out 111.

▶**Aug. 18:** Carl Everett had been the hottest hitter on the team since coming off the DL last week. Everett was out with a calf injury from July 16 to Aug. 5. In the eight games after he returned, Everett was 18-for-37 with three doubles, six homers and 19 RBI.

▶**Aug. 25:** The Astros received good and bad news on the injury front. Ken Caminiti returned after missing 79 games with a calf strain, but left fielder Richard Hidalgo could miss the remainder of the season and Moises Alou wouldn't be ready by Sept. 1, as previously hoped. Caminiti had only four hits in his first 20 at-bats, but counted a pair of game-winning hits among them, including a 16th-inning upper-deck home run on Aug. 20 at Florida.

▶**Sept. 1:** Through Aug. 29 Astros players had spent a club-record 698 games on the DL.

▶**Sept. 8:** The search for outfield help led to the acquisition of Stan Javier from the Giants for reliever Joe Messman (15 saves at Class A Kissimmee). Moises Alou's hopes of returning this season ended when he bruised his knee by falling off a bike while playing with his children.

▶**Sept. 15:** Jose Lima made good on his preseason prediction of winning 20 games. Lima and Mike Hampton had been getting notice as Cy Young candidates, but Larry Dierker believed that closer Billy Wagner (4-1, 1.72 ERA, 36 saves) also deserves a look.

▶**Sept. 22:** Mike Hampton became the first left-hander in franchise history to win 20 games, when he beat Philadelphia on Sept. 13. Hampton and teammate Jose Lima (20-8) each were looking to tie or break the club record for victories of 21, set by Joe Niekro in 1979.

▶**Sept. 29:** Right fielder Bill Spiers was attacked by a fan during the sixth inning of the Sept. 24 game in Milwaukee. Spiers lost a contact lens and had a sore neck from the attack, and the unidentified man was charged with assault.

▶**Oct. 6:** On Oct. 3 the Astros played their final regular-season game in the Astrodome, their home since 1965. Next year they'll move to a new downtown stadium. The day before, Billy Wagner extended his scoreless string to 23⅓ consecutive innings. Wagner didn't allow a run after Aug. 11.

QUOTE OF THE YEAR

*"It's not a he said–she said.
It's a he said–they said."*
—KTMD-TV general manager Marco Camacho,
about the evidence regarding remarks allegedly
made by Astros owner Drayton McLane Jr.
explaining why the team doesn't market to
Hispanic Americans

Team Leaders

Batting avg.	Hits	Wins	Strikeouts
.325 Carl Everett	188 Craig Biggio	22 Mike Hampton	197 Shane Reynolds
.304 Jeff Bagwell	171 Jeff Bagwell	21 Jose Lima	187 Jose Lima

HR	Runs	Losses	Innings
42 Jeff Bagwell	143 Jeff Bagwell	14 Shane Reynolds	246.1 Jose Lima
25 Carl Everett	123 Craig Biggio	13 Chris Holt	239 Mike Hampton

RBI	Stolen bases	ERA	Saves
126 Jeff Bagwell	30 Jeff Bagwell	2.90 Mike Hampton	39 Billy Wagner
108 Carl Everett	28 Craig Biggio	3.58 Jose Lima	4 Jay Powell

HOUSTON ASTROS 1999 final stats

BATTERS	BA	SLG	OBA	G	AB	R	H	TB	2B	3B	HR	RBI	BB	SO	SB	CS	E
Everett	.325	.571	.398	123	464	86	151	265	33	3	25	108	50	94	27	7	6
Bagwell	.304	.591	.454	162	562	143	171	332	35	0	42	126	149	127	30	11	8
Biggio	.294	.457	.386	160	639	123	188	292	56	0	16	73	88	107	28	14	12
Barker	.288	.356	.384	81	73	23	21	26	2	0	1	11	11	19	17	6	1
Spiers	.288	.389	.363	127	393	56	113	153	18	5	4	39	47	45	10	5	9
Caminiti	.286	.476	.386	78	273	45	78	130	11	1	13	56	46	58	6	2	14
Javier	.285	.365	.347	132	397	61	113	145	19	2	3	34	38	63	16	7	4
Mieske	.284	.468	.316	54	109	13	31	51	5	0	5	22	6	22	0	0	0
Johnson	.282	.442	.358	83	156	24	44	69	10	0	5	23	20	31	2	3	7
Ward	.273	.473	.311	64	150	11	41	71	6	0	8	30	9	31	0	0	2
Eusebio	.272	.356	.353	103	323	31	88	115	15	0	4	33	40	67	0	0	4
Gutierrez	.261	.336	.354	85	268	33	70	90	7	5	1	25	37	45	2	5	9
Bako	.256	.358	.332	73	215	16	55	77	14	1	2	17	26	57	1	1	6
Bogar	.239	.343	.328	106	309	44	74	106	16	2	4	31	38	52	3	5	9
Berkman	.237	.387	.321	34	93	10	22	36	2	0	4	15	12	21	5	1	2
Bell	.236	.350	.306	128	509	61	120	178	22	0	12	66	50	129	18	6	3
Hidalgo	.227	.420	.328	108	383	49	87	161	25	2	15	56	56	73	8	5	2
Diaz	.220	.320	.264	30	50	3	11	16	2	0	1	7	3	13	2	2	1
Howell	.212	.364	.366	37	33	2	7	12	2	0	1	1	8	9	0	0	0
Meluskey	.212	.333	.316	10	33	4	7	11	1	0	1	3	5	6	1	0	0
Thompson	.200	.400	.273	12	20	2	4	8	1	0	1	5	2	7	0	0	1
Knorr	.167	.200	.194	13	30	2	5	6	1	0	0	0	1	8	0	0	0
Hernandez	.143	.143	.143	16	14	4	2	2	0	0	0	1	0	0	3	1	1

PITCHERS	W-L	ERA	BA	G	GS	CG	GF	SH	SV	IP	H	R	ER	HR	BB	SO
Slusarski	0-0	0.00	.083	3	0	0	1	0	0	3.2	1	0	0	0	3	3
Wagner	4-1	1.57	.135	66	0	0	55	0	39	74.2	35	14	13	5	23	124
Cabrera	4-0	2.15	.196	26	0	0	11	0	0	29.1	21	7	7	3	9	28
Hampton	22-4	2.90	.241	34	34	3	0	2	0	239.0	206	86	77	12	101	177
Elarton	9-5	3.48	.238	42	15	0	8	0	1	124.0	111	55	48	8	43	121
Lima	21-10	3.58	.265	35	35	3	0	0	0	246.1	256	108	98	30	44	187
Reynolds	16-14	3.85	.275	35	35	4	0	2	0	231.2	250	108	99	23	37	197
Powell	5-4	4.32	.282	67	0	0	26	0	4	75.0	82	38	36	3	40	77
Williams	2-1	4.41	.272	50	0	0	15	0	0	67.1	69	35	33	4	35	53
Henry	2-3	4.65	.281	35	0	0	17	0	2	40.2	45	24	21	8	24	36
Holt	5-13	4.66	.303	32	26	0	2	0	1	164.0	193	92	85	12	57	115
T. Miller	3-2	5.07	.299	47	0	0	11	0	1	49.2	58	29	28	6	29	37
W. Miller	0-1	9.58	.362	5	1	0	2	0	0	10.1	17	11	11	4	5	8
McCurry	0-1	15.75	.478	5	0	0	1	0	0	4.0	11	8	7	1	2	3

2000 preliminary roster

PITCHERS (18)
Jose Cabrera
Octavio Dotel
Scott Elarton
Wayne Franklin
Jason Green
Doug Henry
Chris Holt
Eric Ireland
Jose Lima
Tony McKnight
Trever Miller
Wade Miller

Brian Powell
Jay Powell
Shane Reynolds
Jeriome Robertson
Wilfredo Rodriguez
Billy Wagner

CATCHERS (3)
Paul Bako
Tony Eusebio
Mitch Meluskey

INFIELDERS (10)
Jeff Bagwell
Craig Biggio
Tim Bogar
Ken Caminiti
Carlos Hernandez
Russ Johnson
Julio Lugo
Aaron McNeal
Bill Spiers
Chris Truby

OUTFIELDERS (7)
Moises Alou
Glen Barker
Lance Berkman
Roger Cedeno
Richard Hidalgo
Matt Mieske
Daryle Ward

Games played by position

PLAYER	G	C	1B	2B	3B	SS	OF
Bagwell	162	0	161	0	0	0	0
Bako	73	71	0	0	0	0	0
Barker	81	0	0	0	0	0	57
Bell	128	0	0	0	0	0	126
Berkman	34	0	1	0	0	0	27
Biggio	160	0	0	155	0	0	6
Bogar	107	0	0	1	12	90	0
Caminiti	78	0	0	0	75	0	0
Diaz	30	0	0	0	0	0	8
Eusebio	103	98	0	0	0	0	0
Everett	123	0	0	0	0	0	121
Gutierrez	85	0	0	0	1	80	0
Hernandez	16	0	0	7	0	2	0
Hidalgo	108	0	0	0	0	0	108
Howell	37	0	5	0	3	0	0
Javier	20	0	0	0	0	0	18
Johnson	83	0	0	15	36	2	0
Knorr	13	11	0	0	0	0	0
Meluskey	10	10	0	0	0	0	C
Mieske	54	0	0	0	0	0	37
Spiers	127	0	1	4	71	13	31
Thompson	12	0	0	0	0	0	10
Ward	64	0	10	0	0	0	31

Sick call: 1999 DL report

PLAYER	Days on the DL
Moises Alou	182
Glen Barker	15
Derek Bell	15
Sean Bergman	40
Ken Caminiti	86
Alex Diaz	71
Tony Eusebio	16
Carl Everett	21
Ricky Gutierrez	70*
Doug Henry	66
Richard Hidalgo	56
Jack Howell	107*
Mitch Meluskey	161
Joe Slusarski	15

Indicates two separate terms on Disabled List.

Minor Leagues

Tops in the organization

BATTER	CLUB	AVG.	G	AB	R	H	HR	RBI
Lugo, Julio	Jac	.319	116	445	77	142	10	42
Miles, Aaron	Mch	.317	112	470	72	149	10	71
McNeal, Aaron	Mch	.310	133	536	95	166	38	131
Thompson, Ryan	NO	.309	112	404	60	125	16	58
Turnquist, Tyler	Mch	.309	118	456	89	141	11	67

HOME RUNS

McNeal, Aaron	Mch	38
Ward, Daryle	NO	28
Truby, Chris	Jac	28
Johnson, J.J.	Jac	18
Porter, Colin	Mch	18

WINS

Rodriguez, W.	Kis	15
Robertson, J.	Jac	15
Oswalt, Roy	Mch	13
Miller, Wade	NO	11
Several Players Tied at		10

RBI

McNeal, Aaron	Mch	131
Truby, Chris	Jac	87
Cole, Eric	Jac	75
Miles, Aaron	Mch	71
Several Players Tied at		69

SAVES

Franklin, Wayne	Jac	21
Sessions, Doug	Kis	18
Ramirez, S.	MAR	17
Messman, Joe	Kis	15
Several Players Tied at		14

STOLEN BASES

De Aza, Modesto	AUB	34
Wright, Gavin	MAR	31
Topolski, Jon	AUB	27
Lugo, Julio	Jac	25
Rincon, Carlos	MAR	24

STRIKEOUTS

Nannini, Mike	Mch	154
Santana, Johan	Mch	150
Rodriguez, W.	Kis	148
Ireland, Eric	Kis	148
Oswalt, Roy	Mch	143

PITCHER	CLUB	W-L	ERA	IP	H	BB	SO
Ireland, Eric	Kis	10-8	2.24	185	164	32	148
McKnight, Tony	Jac	9-9	2.75	160	134	44	118
Navarro, Scott	Kis	8-3	2.88	113	108	17	86
Rodriguez, W.	Kis	15-7	2.88	153	108	62	148
Robertson, J.	Jac	15-7	3.06	191	184	45	133

1999 salaries

	Bonuses	Total earned salary
Jeff Bagwell, 1b		6,500,000
Craig Biggio, 2b		6,060,000
Moises Alou, of		5,000,000
Ken Caminiti, 3b		4,500,000
Derek Bell, of		4,500,000
Shane Reynolds, p	400,000	4,475,000
Mike Hampton, p	75,000	4,125,000
Carl Everett, of	100,000	2,500,000
Billy Wagner, p	125,000	2,250,000
Jose Lima, p	275,000	2,250,000
Ricky Gutierrez, ss		2,212,500
Stan Javier, of		1,750,000
Bill Spiers, 3b	100,000	1,600,000
Tony Eusebio, c	100,000	900,000
Jay Powell, p		800,000
Doug Henry, p		725,000
Tim Bogar, ss	150,000	700,000
Jack Howell, 1b		550,000
Matt Mieske, of		500,000
Brian Williams, p	100,000	375,000
Chris Holt, p	20,000	279,000
Ryan Thompson, of		275,000
Alex Diaz, of		275,000
Richard Hidalgo, of		260,000
Trever Miller, p		247,500
Paul Bako, c		230,000
Scott Elarton, p		230,000
Jose Cabrera, p		215,000
Russ Johnson, 3b		205,000
Mitch Meluskey, c		200,000
Glen Barker, of		200,000
Daryle Ward, of		200,000
Lance Berkman, of		200,000

Average 1999 salary: $1,683,758
Total 1999 team payroll: $55,564,000
Termination pay: $950,000

251

Houston (1962-1999)

Runs: Most, career

1120	CRAIG BIGGIO	1988-1999
921	JEFF BAGWELL	1991-1999
890	Cesar Cedeno	1970-1981
871	Jose Cruz	1975-1987
829	Jimmy Wynn	1963-1973

Hits: Most, career

1937	Jose Cruz	1975-1987
1868	CRAIG BIGGIO	1988-1999
1659	Cesar Cedeno	1970-1981
1448	Bob Watson	1966-1979
1447	JEFF BAGWELL	1991-1999

2B: Most, career

389	CRAIG BIGGIO	1988-1999
343	Cesar Cedeno	1970-1981
335	Jose Cruz	1975-1987
314	JEFF BAGWELL	1991-1999
241	Bob Watson	1966-1979

3B: Most, career

80	Jose Cruz	1975-1987
63	Joe Morgan	1963-1980
62	Roger Metzger	1971-1978
56	Terry Puhl	1977-1990
55	Cesar Cedeno	1970-1981
55	Craig Reynolds	1979-1989

HR: Most, career

263	JEFF BAGWELL	1991-1999
223	Jimmy Wynn	1963-1973
166	Glenn Davis	1984-1990
163	Cesar Cedeno	1970-1981
152	CRAIG BIGGIO	1988-1999

RBI: Most, career

961	JEFF BAGWELL	1991-1999
942	Jose Cruz	1975-1987
782	Bob Watson	1966-1979
778	Cesar Cedeno	1970-1981
719	Jimmy Wynn	1963-1973

SB: Most, career

487	Cesar Cedeno	1970-1981
346	CRAIG BIGGIO	1988-1999
288	Jose Cruz	1975-1987
219	Joe Morgan	1963-1980
217	Terry Puhl	1977-1990

BB: Most, career

885	JEFF BAGWELL	1991-1999
847	Jimmy Wynn	1963-1973
786	CRAIG BIGGIO	1988-1999
730	Jose Cruz	1975-1987
678	Joe Morgan	1963-1980

BA: Highest, career

.304	JEFF BAGWELL	1991-1999
.297	Bob Watson	1966-1979
.292	CRAIG BIGGIO	1988-1999
.292	Jose Cruz	1975-1987
.289	Cesar Cedeno	1970-1981

On-base avg: Highest, career

.416	JEFF BAGWELL	1991-1999
.380	CRAIG BIGGIO	1988-1999
.374	Joe Morgan	1963-1980
.372	BILL SPIERS	1996-1999
.364	Bob Watson	1966-1979

Slug pct: Highest, career

.545	JEFF BAGWELL	1991-1999
.483	Glenn Davis	1984-1990
.454	Cesar Cedeno	1970-1981
.445	Jimmy Wynn	1963-1973
.444	Bob Watson	1966-1979

Games started: Most, career

320	Larry Dierker	1964-1976
301	Joe Niekro	1975-1985
282	Nolan Ryan	1980-1988
267	Bob Knepper	1981-1989
259	Mike Scott	1983-1991

Complete games: Most, career

106	Larry Dierker	1964-1976
82	Joe Niekro	1975-1985
78	Don Wilson	1966-1974
76	J.R. Richard	1971-1980
42	Mike Scott	1983-1991

Saves: Most, career

199	Dave Smith	1980-1990
101	BILLY WAGNER	1995-1999
76	Fred Gladding	1968-1973
72	Joe Sambito	1976-1984
62	DOUG JONES	1992-1993

Shutouts: Most, career

25	Larry Dierker	1964-1976
21	Joe Niekro	1975-1985
21	Mike Scott	1983-1991
20	Don Wilson	1966-1974
19	J.R. Richard	1971-1980

Wins: Most, career

144	Joe Niekro	1975-1985
137	Larry Dierker	1964-1976
110	Mike Scott	1983-1991
107	J.R. Richard	1971-1980
106	Nolan Ryan	1980-1988

K: Most, career

1866	Nolan Ryan	1980-1988
1493	J.R. Richard	1971-1980
1487	Larry Dierker	1964-1976
1318	Mike Scott	1983-1991
1283	Don Wilson	1966-1974

Win pct: Highest, career

.634	MARK PORTUGAL, 1989-1993	
.633	MIKE HAMPTON	1994-1999
.609	Jim Ray	1965-1973
.601	J.R. Richard	1971-1980
.577	PETE HARNISCH	1991-1994

ERA: Lowest, career

2.53	Dave Smith	1980-1990
3.13	Nolan Ryan	1980-1988
3.15	Don Wilson	1966-1974
3.15	J.R. Richard	1971-1980
3.18	Ken Forsch	1970-1980

Runs: Most, season

146	CRAIG BIGGIO	1997
143	JEFF BAGWELL	1999
124	JEFF BAGWELL	1998
123	CRAIG BIGGIO	1995
123	CRAIG BIGGIO	1998
123	CRAIG BIGGIO	1999

Hits: Most, season

210	CRAIG BIGGIO	1998
198	DEREK BELL	1998
195	Enos Cabell	1978
191	CRAIG BIGGIO	1997
189	Jose Cruz	1983

2B: Most, season

56	CRAIG BIGGIO	1999
51	CRAIG BIGGIO	1998
48	JEFF BAGWELL	1996
44	Rusty Staub	1967
44	CRAIG BIGGIO	1994

3B: Most, season

14	Roger Metzger	1973
13	Jose Cruz	1984
13	STEVE FINLEY	1992
13	STEVE FINLEY	1993
12	Joe Morgan	1965
12	Craig Reynolds	1981

HR: Most, season

43	JEFF BAGWELL	1997
42	JEFF BAGWELL	1999
39	JEFF BAGWELL	1994
38	Moises Alou	1998
37	Jimmy Wynn	1967

RBI: Most, season

135	JEFF BAGWELL, 1997
126	JEFF BAGWELL, 1999
124	Moises Alou, 1998
120	JEFF BAGWELL, 1996
116	JEFF BAGWELL, 1994

SB: Most, season

65	Gerald Young, 1988
64	Eric Yelding, 1990
61	Cesar Cedeno, 1977
58	Cesar Cedeno, 1976
57	Cesar Cedeno, 1974

BB: Most, season

149	JEFF BAGWELL, 1999
148	Jimmy Wynn, 1969
135	JEFF BAGWELL, 1996
127	JEFF BAGWELL, 1997
110	Joe Morgan, 1969

BA: Highest, season

.368	JEFF BAGWELL, 1994
.334	DEREK BELL, 1995
.333	Rusty Staub, 1967
.325	CARL EVERETT, 1999
.325	CRAIG BIGGIO, 1998

On-base avg; Highest, season

.454	JEFF BAGWELL, 1999
.451	JEFF BAGWELL, 1994
.451	JEFF BAGWELL, 1996
.436	Jimmy Wynn, 1969
.425	JEFF BAGWELL, 1997

Slug pct: Highest, season

.750	JEFF BAGWELL, 1994
.592	JEFF BAGWELL, 1997
.591	JEFF BAGWELL, 1999
.582	Moises Alou, 1998
.571	CARL EVERETT, 1999

Games started: Most, season

40	Jerry Reuss, 1973
39	J.R. Richard, 1976
38	Joe Niekro, 1979
38	J.R. Richard, 1979
38	Joe Niekro, 1983
38	Joe Niekro, 1984
38	Bob Knepper, 1986

Complete games: Most, season

20	Larry Dierker, 1969
19	J.R. Richard, 1979
18	Don Wilson, 1971
17	Larry Dierker, 1970
16	Mike Cuellar, 1967
16	J.R. Richard, 1978
16	Joe Niekro, 1982

Saves: Most, season

39	BILLY WAGNER, 1999
36	DOUG JONES, 1992
33	Dave Smith, 1986
30	BILLY WAGNER, 1998
29	Fred Gladding, 1969

Shutouts: Most, season

6	Dave Roberts, 1973
5	Larry Dierker, 1972
5	Joe Niekro, 1979
5	Bob Knepper, 1981
5	Joe Niekro, 1982
5	Bob Knepper, 1986
5	Mike Scott, 1986
5	Mike Scott, 1988

Wins: Most, season

22	MIKE HAMPTON, 1999
21	JOSE LIMA, 1999
21	Joe Niekro, 1979
20	Larry Dierker, 1969
20	J.R. Richard, 1976
20	Joe Niekro, 1980
20	Mike Scott, 1989

K: Most, season

313	J.R. Richard, 1979
306	Mike Scott, 1986
303	J.R. Richard, 1978
270	Nolan Ryan, 1987
245	Nolan Ryan, 1982

Win pct: Highest, season

.846	MIKE HAMPTON, 1999
.818	MARK PORTUGAL, 1993
.731	DARRYL KILE, 1997
.704	SHANE REYNOLDS, 1998
.692	Mike Scott, 1985

ERA: Lowest, season

2.18	Bob Knepper, 1981
2.21	Danny Darwin, 1990
2.22	Mike Cuellar, 1966
2.22	Mike Scott, 1986
2.33	Larry Dierker, 1969

Most pinch-hit homers, season

5	Cliff Johnson, 1974
3	Joe Gaines, 1965

Most pinch-hit homers, career

8	Cliff Johnson, 1972-1977
6	Denny Walling, 1977-1992

Longest hitting streak

23	Art Howe, 1981
23	LUIS GONZALEZ, 1997
22	Cesar Cedeno, 1977
21	Lee May, 1973
21	Dickie Thon, 1982

Most consecutive scoreless innings

31	J. R. Richard, 1980

No-hit games

Don Nottebart, Hou vs Phi NL, 4-1; May 17, 1963.

Ken T. Johnson, Hou vs Cin NL, 0-1; April 23, 1964 (lost the game).

Don Wilson, Hou vs Atl NL, 2-0; June 18, 1967.

Don Wilson, Hou at Cin NL, 4-0; May 1, 1969.

Larry Dierker, Hou vs Mon NL, 6-0; July 9, 1976.

Ken Forsch, Hou vs Atl NL, 6-0; April 7, 1979.

Nolan Ryan, Hou vs LA NL, 5-0; September 26, 1981.

Mike Scott, Hou vs SF NL, 2-0; September 25, 1986.

DARRYL KILE, Hou vs NY NL, 7-1; September 8, 1993.

ACTIVE PLAYERS in caps.

Players' years of service are listed by the first and last years with this team and are not necessarily consecutive; all statistics record performances for this team only.

253

Cincinnati Reds

By Craig Ruttle, Cincinnati Enquirer

Sean Casey went from being a hot prospect in 1998 to driving the Reds' chase for a wild-card in 1999.

1999 Reds: Hot prospects helped the run

The Cincinnati Reds' wild ride was over. A crowd of 54,621 applauded them one last time following a loss to the New York Mets in a playoff to decide the National League wild-card berth.

"It wasn't so much losing as it was the season's over," first baseman Sean Casey said, his eyes brimming with tears. "It's tough when you realize that such a special season has come to an end."

But it may have been the year that turned Cincinnati back into a baseball town.

"This is certainly a springboard to leap off of," managing executive John Allen said. "Everybody I've talked to feels that crowd sent a message: Baseball is certainly not dead in Cincinnati."

There's new ownership, a new ballpark in the works and a sense that the franchise is headed in the right direction after years of lurching from crisis to crisis under former owner Marge Schott. New owner Carl Lindner plans to remain behind the scenes, allowing Allen and general manager Jim Bowden to continue rebuilding.

The Reds began slashing payroll and dove into a rebuilding program on July 31, 1997, when they traded pitcher John Smiley to Cleveland for prospects. They were aiming to be competitive by 2003, when the new ballpark is supposed to open and more money is available.

Despite a $35 million payroll, they figured out a way to contend while the ballpark was still on the drawing board. The offseason additions of Denny Neagle and Greg Vaughn, plus the unexpectedly rapid development of a young lineup—Casey, Aaron Boone, Pokey Reese, Dmitri Young, Scott Williamson—landed the Reds in a playoff race.

"They just developed earlier than we thought they would," Bowden said. "We thought some would develop this year, some next. What happened was that they all developed at one time, so we were very fortunate. We have a lot of good young players to build around now. Obviously it took our timetable of 2003 and pushed it up about four years."

Team MVP

Sean Casey: When the Reds got hot prospect Sean Casey from Cleveland in 1998, they couldn't have foreseen the impact he would have in 1999. But the big first baseman was the team's top offensive weapon the first half of the season and a major cog in their drive for a playoff berth. Casey hit .332 with 25 homers and 99 RBI. He also led the Reds with 197 hits, 103 runs and 42 doubles.

It was a bonus that they got to develop in the middle of a playoff race.

"This is an invaluable experience," said shortstop Barry Larkin, a member of the Reds' 1990 World Series title team. "To win early in your career is an experience you can bank on for years and years."

Manager Jack McKeon thinks the excitement of '99 will make his young players crave more: "It's a tremendous advantage as they try to get going along with their careers," McKeon said. "The pressure situations in close ball games and the way they've succeeded have got to be a plus for them."

In the short-term, it will be difficult for the Reds to repeat '99. Vaughn and starter Juan Guzman, obtained in a July 31 trade with Baltimore, were free agents. Keeping the young core intact will become expensive because of salary arbitration. The payroll may increase a little, but the Reds will remain a small-market club competing on a limited budget while they rebuild the farm system and prepare for a new ballpark.

"I'm not sure there can be any solid rationale for deviating from that plan after this season, based on what people saw," Allen said.

What they saw was a preview of the future.

"We weren't expected to do a lot, and it went down to the final game," Casey said. "Hopefully, this was such a special season that we'll be able to do it again next year."

1999 Reds: Week-by-week notes

These notes were excerpted from the following issues of Baseball Weekly.

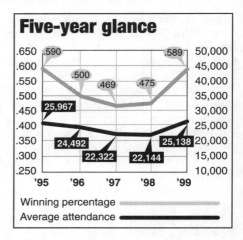

Five-year glance

Winning percentage
Average attendance

.590   .500   .469   .475   .589
25,967   24,492   22,322   22,144   25,138

'95   '96   '97   '98   '99

▶**April 7:** Left-hander Denny Neagle came to camp with a weak left shoulder, never pitched in an "A" exhibition game and was placed on the DL to start the season. Right-hander Pete Harnisch, scheduled to pitch opening day, was hit with back spasms and was shut down for 10 days.

▶**April 14:** If the Reds could have skipped the eighth inning, they might have started the season 5-0 instead of 1-4. In all four defeats they entered the eighth inning either tied or ahead, only to watch the bullpen blow up. In the four losses pitchers walked 28 batters and hit one, with 11 of those scoring. The bullpen pitched only 11⅔ innings, but walked 12.

▶**April 28:** Owner Marge Schott, facing another suspension from Major League Baseball if she didn't sell, agreed to sell five of her six shares (of 15 total shares) to three limited partners, Cincinnati billionaire Carl H. Lindner, George Strike and William Reik Jr., for $67 million.

▶**May 5:** His record was 1-2, but left-hander Steve Avery's ERA was 2.02. He was succeeding with a fastball that barely cracked 83 mph. In most starts he has used his changeup 40 percent of the time.

▶**May 12:** Sean Casey, among the top five NL hitters for the first five weeks of the season, is a man of little experience but lots of talent. The first baseman went on a two-day binge against the Cubs with five consecutive hits, including two home runs.

▶**May 19:** Right-hander Brett Tomko, exiled to AAA Indianapolis, was recalled on May 16 to pitch against San Diego, and he responded with 8⅔ innings of shutout ball. In seven starts earlier this season, Tomko was 0-1 with a 7.76 ERA.

▶**May 26:** With third-string right fielder Jeffrey Hammonds hitting a career-best three home runs and driving in five runs and Sean Casey hitting two homers and knocking in six, the Reds buried Colorado 24-12 in Coors Field on May 19. The lead-off hitter, center fielder Mike Cameron,

tied a major league record for a nine-inning game with eight plate appearances.

▶**June 2:** Through 46 games the team's bullpen led the league with a 2.97 ERA and was tied for the NL lead with 11 victories. Right-hander Danny Graves had four wins and rookie righty Scott Williamson had three, while Graves had six saves and Williamson five—as manager Jack McKeon mixed and matched the pair at the back end of games.

▶**June 16:** Catcher Eddie Taubensee was batting .253 when he began a career-best 15-game hitting streak that lifted his average to .324. And after hitting .182 through May 3, shortstop Barry Larkin went on a 33-game binge (45-123, .366) that pushed his average to .285.

▶**June 30:** Right-hander Steve Parris pushed his record to 5-1 by holding the Astros to one hit over seven innings. The Reds were 10 games over .500 (41-31) after beating Houston on June 27, their best margin since the end of their division-winning 1995 season, when they finished at 85-59.

▶**July 7:** On May 14 the Reds were 14-18 and in last place in the NL Central, seven games behind Houston. But an amazing turnaround, capped by a 10-game winning streak, pushed the Reds to first place on July 4.

▶**July 15:** Aaron Boone, in his first full season with the Reds, won the third base job

this spring, but he got off to a slow start (.218) and was demoted to Indianapolis on May 12. After returning later that month, Boone reached base safely in 34 of 35 games, hitting .364 to raise his average from .181 to .291.

▶July 21: After a sensational start that earned him a spot on the All-Star team, Scott Williamson blew four of five save opportunities through July 18. All four losses came on home runs.

▶July 28: There was no in-between for lefties Ron Villone and Steve Avery. In nine starts Villone held the opposition to one hit twice, two hits once and three hits once. In those four victories his ERA was 0.60; in his other five starts his ERA was 10.60. With Avery it was the first-inning blues. In 19 starts his ERA in the first inning was 11.81. In all other innings it was 3.46. In his 92 innings he gave up only 75 hits but walked 77.

▶Aug. 11: Eddie Taubensee rebounded from a wrist injury by driving in 33 runs in 33 games. Taubensee put together an eight-game hitting streak and hit safely in 25 of 28 starts (37-for-108, .343).

▶Aug. 18: With the addition of Juan Guzman and the return from the DL of Denny Neagle, the rotation solidified. Since the All-Star break starters went 12-4 with a 3.90 ERA, and this month they were 7-1 with a 2.30 ERA through Aug. 14.

▶Aug. 25: Pete Harnisch held Pittsburgh to one hit over eight innings Aug. 19 and got an eighth-inning home run from Sean Casey for a 1-0 victory. It was Harnisch's eighth consecutive victory, and the team is 11-1 in his last 12 starts.

▶Sept. 8: The Reds had a blast on Sept. 4 by hitting an NL-record nine home runs. Eight different players homered, setting a major league record in the 22-3 defeat of Philadelphia.

▶Sept. 22: After failing to hit a home run in 72 games, a career-worst stretch, Barry Larkin hit three in eight games and put together a nine-game hitting streak during which he hit .419 and scored 11 runs.

▶Oct. 6: The Reds lost 5-0 in a wild-card one-game playoff to the Mets on Oct. 4, after dropping two of three in the season-ending series against the Brewers to fall into a tie. It wasn't much consolation that Denny Neagle and left fielder Greg Vaughn won September honors as NL pitcher and player of the month, respectively. Vaughn led the majors with 14 homers, tying Frank Robinson's club record for most in a month, and drove in 33 runs. Neagle was 5-0 with a 2.00 ERA in five starts.

QUOTE OF THE YEAR

"I don't remember a thing that happened once I left the game and came up to the clubhouse."
—Right-hander Brett Tomko, on pitching eight innings in 100 degree-plus temperatures in Cincinnati

Team Leaders

Batting avg.	Runs	Losses	Strikeouts
.332 Sean Casey	108 Barry Larkin	10 Pete Harnisch	132 Brett Tomko
.293 Barry Larkin	104 Greg Vaughn	7 Steve Avery	120 Pete Harnisch
		7 Danny Graves	
HR	**Stolen bases**	7 Brett Tomko	**Innings**
45 Greg Vaughn	38 Mike Cameron	7 Ron Villone	198.1 Pete Harnisch
25 Sean Casey	38 Pokey Reese	7 Scott Williamson	172 Brett Tomko
RBI	**Wins**	**ERA**	**Saves**
118 Greg Vaughn	16 Pete Harnisch	3.68 Pete Harnisch	27 Danny Graves
99 Sean Casey	12 Scott Williamson	4.92 Brett Tomko	19 Scott Williamson
Hits			
197 Sean Casey			
171 Barry Larkin			

CINCINNATI REDS 1999 final stats

BATTERS	BA	SLG	OBA	G	AB	R	H	TB	2B	3B	HR	RBI	BB	SO	SB	CS	E
Sweeney	.355	.645	.429	37	31	6	11	20	3	0	2	7	4	9	0	0	0
Casey	.332	.539	.399	151	594	103	197	320	42	3	25	99	61	88	0	2	6
Taubensee	.311	.521	.354	126	424	58	132	221	22	2	21	87	30	67	0	2	9
Young	.300	.504	.352	127	373	63	112	188	30	2	14	56	30	71	3	1	4
Larkin	.293	.420	.390	161	583	108	171	245	30	4	12	75	93	57	30	8	14
Reese	.285	.417	.330	149	585	85	167	244	37	5	10	52	35	81	38	7	7
Morris	.284	.373	.348	80	102	10	29	38	9	0	0	16	10	21	0	0	1
Boone	.280	.445	.330	139	472	56	132	210	26	5	14	72	30	79	17	6	15
Hammonds	.279	.523	.347	123	262	43	73	137	13	0	17	41	27	64	3	6	0
Cameron	.256	.469	.357	146	542	93	139	254	34	9	21	66	80	145	38	12	8
Lewis	.254	.451	.280	88	173	18	44	78	16	0	6	28	7	24	0	0	6
Tucker	.253	.426	.338	133	296	55	75	126	8	5	11	44	37	81	11	4	2
Vaughn	.245	.535	.347	153	550	104	135	294	20	2	45	118	85	137	15	2	4
Stynes	.239	.301	.310	73	113	18	27	34	1	0	2	14	12	13	5	2	6
Johnson	.231	.419	.286	45	117	12	27	49	7	0	5	18	9	31	0	0	1
LaRue	.211	.389	.311	36	90	12	19	35	7	0	3	10	11	32	4	1	2
Dawkins	.143	.143	.250	7	7	1	1	1	0	0	0	0	0	4	0	0	0
Robinson	.000	.000	.000	9	1	4	0	0	0	0	0	0	0	1	0	1	0

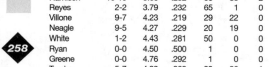

PITCHERS	W-L	ERA	BA	G	GS	CG	GF	SH	SV	IP	H	R	ER	HR	BB	SO
Williamson	12-7	2.41	.171	62	0	0	40	0	19	93.1	54	29	25	8	43	107
Sullivan	5-4	3.01	.217	79	0	0	16	0	3	113.2	88	41	38	10	47	78
Guzman	6-3	3.03	.238	12	12	1	0	0	0	77.1	70	33	26	10	21	60
Graves	8-7	3.08	.227	75	0	0	56	0	27	111.0	90	42	38	10	49	69
Parris	11-4	3.50	.260	22	21	2	0	1	0	128.2	124	59	50	16	52	86
Harnisch	16-10	3.68	.252	33	33	2	0	2	0	198.1	190	86	81	25	57	120
Reyes	2-2	3.79	.232	65	1	0	12	0	2	61.2	53	30	26	5	39	72
Villone	9-7	4.23	.219	29	22	0	2	0	2	142.2	114	70	67	8	73	97
Neagle	9-5	4.27	.229	20	19	0	0	0	0	111.2	95	54	53	23	40	76
White	1-2	4.43	.281	50	0	0	18	0	0	61.0	68	31	30	13	14	61
Ryan	0-0	4.50	.500	1	0	0	0	0	0	2.0	4	1	1	0	1	1
Greene	0-0	4.76	.292	1	0	0	0	0	0	5.2	7	4	3	2	1	3
Tomko	5-7	4.92	.263	33	26	1	1	0	0	172.0	175	103	94	31	60	132
Avery	6-7	5.16	.222	19	19	0	0	0	0	96.0	75	62	55	11	78	51
Belinda	3-1	5.27	.258	29	0	0	12	0	2	42.2	42	26	25	11	18	40
Wohlers	0-0	27.00	.333	2	0	0	0	0	0	0.2	1	2	2	0	6	0

2000 preliminary roster

PITCHERS (18)
Robbie Bell
Adrian Burnside
Elmer Dessens
Pat Flury
Eddie Gaillard
Danny Graves
Pete Harnisch
Heath Murray
Denny Neagle
Steve Parris
Dennys Reyes
John Riedling
Scott Sullivan
Brett Tomko
Ron Villone
Gabe White
Scott Williamson
Scott Winchester

CATCHERS (2)
Jason LaRue
Eddie Taubensee

INFIELDERS (10)
Aaron Boone
Sean Casey
Travis Dawkins
Adam Dunn
Barry Larkin
Brandon Larson
Mark Lewis
Hal Morris
Pokey Reese
Ron Wright

OUTFIELDERS (10)
Kimera Bartee
Dante Bichette
Mike Cameron
Brady Clark
D.T. Cromer
Mike Frank
Chris Stynes
Mark Sweeney
Michael Tucker
Dmitri Young

Games played by position

PLAYER	G	C	1B	2B	3B	SS	OF
Boone	139	0	0	0	136	6	0
Cameron	146	0	0	0	0	0	146
Casey	151	0	148	0	0	0	0
Dawkins	7	0	0	0	0	7	0
Hammonds	123	0	0	0	0	0	106
Johnson	45	39	0	0	0	0	0
Larkin	161	0	0	0	0	161	0
LaRue	36	35	0	0	0	0	0
Lewis	88	0	0	2	52	0	0
Morris	80	0	25	0	0	0	4
Reese	149	0	0	146	0	16	0
Robinson	9	0	0	0	0	0	2
Stynes	73	0	0	43	8	0	4
Sweeney	37	0	1	0	0	0	1
Taubensee	126	124	0	0	0	0	0
Tucker	133	0	0	0	0	0	114
Vaughn	153	0	0	0	0	0	144
Young	127	0	9	0	0	0	91

Sick call: 1999 DL report

PLAYER	Days on the DL
Steve Avery	71
Stan Belinda	81
Jason Bere	48
Brian Johnson	48
Ralph Milliard	42
Hal Morris	28
Denny Neagle	87*
Steve Parris	37
Scott Winchester	183
Mark Wohlers	171

Indicates two separate terms on Disabled List.

Minor Leagues
Tops in the organization

BATTER	CLUB	AVG.	G	AB	R	H	HR	RBI
Williams, Jason	Ind	.339	127	492	95	167	9	64
Broussard, Ben	Cht	.332	78	292	73	97	24	75
Hardtke, Jason	Ind	.329	101	416	74	137	12	61
Clark, Brady	Cht	.326	138	506	103	165	17	75
Goudie, Jaime	Cln	.322	85	342	56	110	3	51

HOME RUNS
Cromer, D.T.	Ind	30
Larson, Brandon	Cht	25
Peters, Samone	BIL	24
Broussard, Ben	Cht	24
Hiatt, Phil	Ind	18

WINS
Therneau, Dave	Ind	14
Harriger, Denny	Ind	14
Haring, Brett	Cht	12
Carrara, Giovanni	Ind	12
Several Players Tied at		11

RBI
Cromer, D.T.	Ind	107
Larson, Brandon	Cht	94
Wise, Dewayne	Rfd	81
Diaz, Alejandro	Cht	76
Several Players Tied at		75

SAVES
Puffer, Brandon	Cln	34
Williams, Todd	Ind	24
Flury, Pat	Ind	21
Meyer, Jake	Cht	16
Pike, Thomas	BIL	12

STOLEN BASES
Dawkins, Travis	Cht	53
Caceres, Wilmy	Cln	52
Perez, Antonio	Rfd	35
Wise, Dewayne	Rfd	35
Diaz, Alejandro	Cht	34

STRIKEOUTS
Therneau, Dave	Ind	139
Acevedo, Jose	Cln	136
Donaldson, Bo	Cht	117
Carrara, Giovanni	Ind	114
Averette, Robert	Cht	113

PITCHER	CLUB	W-L	ERA	IP	H	BB	SO
Hayden, Terry	Rfd	8-6	2.70	117	108	42	79
Averette, Robert	Cht	11-6	3.17	162	159	59	113
Haring, Brett	Cht	12-4	3.42	160	159	54	109
Carrara, Giovanni	Ind	12-7	3.47	158	144	58	114
Acevedo, Jose	Cln	8-6	3.77	134	119	43	136

1999 salaries

	Bonuses	Total earned salary
Greg Vaughn, of		5,615,428
Barry Larkin, ss		5,300,000
Juan Guzman, p		5,250,000
Mark Wohlers, p		5,200,000
Denny Neagle, p		4,750,000
Pete Harnisch, p		3,000,000
Jeffrey Hammonds, of		2,483,333
Michael Tucker, of		1,600,000
Eddie Taubensee, c		1,200,000
Stan Belinda, p		835,000
Brian Johnson, c	25,000	775,000
Steve Avery, p	250,000	750,000
Mark Lewis, 3b		500,000
Ron Villone, p		455,000
Hal Morris, 1b	50,000	450,000
Brett Tomko, p		400,000
Dmitri Young, of		375,000
Gabe White, p		300,000
Scott Sullivan, p		300,000
Mike Cameron, of		295,000
Steve Parris, p		275,000
Pokey Reese, 2b		270,000
Chris Stynes, 2b		270,000
Danny Graves, p		260,000
Sean Casey, 1b		220,000
Aaron Boone, 3b		210,000
Dennis Reyes, p		202,000
Scott Winchester, p		202,000
Jason LaRue, c		200,000
Scott Williamson, p		200,000

Average 1999 salary: $1,404,759
Total 1999 team payroll: $42,142,761
Termination pay: $4,111,476

Cincinnati (1890-1999)

Runs: Most, career

1741	Pete Rose, 1963-1986
1091	Johnny Bench, 1967-1983
1063	BARRY LARKIN, 1986-1999
1043	Frank Robinson, 1956-1965
993	Dave Concepcion, 1970-1988

Hits: Most, career

3358	Pete Rose, 1963-1986
2326	Dave Concepcion, 1970-1988
2048	Johnny Bench, 1967-1983
1934	Tony Perez, 1964-1986
1884	BARRY LARKIN, 1986-1999

2B: Most, career

601	Pete Rose, 1963-1986
389	Dave Concepcion, 1970-1988
381	Johnny Bench, 1967-1983
342	Vada Pinson, 1958-1968
339	Tony Perez, 1964-1986

3B: Most, career

152	Edd Roush, 1916-1931
115	Pete Rose, 1963-1986
112	Bid McPhee, 1890-1899
96	Vada Pinson, 1958-1968
94	Curt Walker, 1924-1930

HR: Most, career

389	Johnny Bench, 1967-1983
324	Frank Robinson, 1956-1965
287	Tony Perez, 1964-1986
251	Ted Kluszewski, 1947-1957
244	George Foster, 1971-1981

RBI: Most, career

1376	Johnny Bench, 1967-1983
1192	Tony Perez, 1964-1986
1036	Pete Rose, 1963-1986
1009	Frank Robinson, 1956-1965
950	Dave Concepcion, 1970-1988

SB: Most, career

406	Joe Morgan, 1972-1979
345	BARRY LARKIN, 1986-1999
337	Arlie Latham, 1890-1895
321	Dave Concepcion, 1970-1988
320	Bob Bescher, 1908-1913

BB: Most, career

1210	Pete Rose, 1963-1986
891	Johnny Bench, 1967-1983
881	Joe Morgan, 1972-1979
764	BARRY LARKIN, 1986-1999
736	Dave Concepcion, 1970-1988

BA: Highest, career

.332	Cy Seymour, 1902-1906
.331	Edd Roush, 1916-1931
.325	Jake Beckley, 1897-1903
.314	Bubbles Hargrave, 1921-1928
.311	Rube Bressler, 1917-1927

On-base avg: Highest, career

.415	Joe Morgan, 1972-1979
.390	Dummy Hoy, 1894-1902
.389	Frank Robinson, 1956-1965
.379	Pete Rose, 1963-1986
.379	Rube Bressler, 1917-1927

Slug pct: Highest, career

.554	Frank Robinson, 1956-1965
.514	George Foster, 1971-1981
.512	Ted Kluszewski, 1947-1957
.510	ERIC DAVIS, 1984-1996
.498	Wally Post, 1949-1963

Games started: Most, career

357	Eppa Rixey, 1921-1933
322	Paul Derringer, 1933-1942
321	Dolf Luque, 1918-1929
298	Tom Browning, 1984-1994
296	Bucky Walters, 1938-1948

Complete games: Most, career

209	Noodles Hahn, 1899-1905
195	Bucky Walters, 1938-1948
189	Paul Derringer, 1933-1942
188	Frank Dwyer, 1892-1899
184	Bob Ewing, 1902-1909

Saves: Most, career

148	JOHN FRANCO, 1984-1989
119	Clay Carroll, 1968-1975
88	JEFF BRANTLEY, 1994-1997
88	Rob Dibble, 1988-1993
88	Tom Hume, 1977-1987

Shutouts: Most, career

32	Bucky Walters, 1938-1948
30	Jim Maloney, 1960-1970
29	Johnny Vander Meer, 1937-1949
25	Ken Raffensberger, 1947-1954
24	Paul Derringer, 1933-1942
24	Dolf Luque, 1918-1929
24	Noodles Hahn, 1899-1905

Wins: Most, career

179	Eppa Rixey, 1921-1933
161	Paul Derringer, 1933-1942
160	Bucky Walters, 1938-1948
154	Dolf Luque, 1918-1929
134	Jim Maloney, 1960-1970

K: Most, career

1592	Jim Maloney, 1960-1970
1449	Mario Soto, 1977-1988
1289	Joe Nuxhall, 1944-1966
1251	Johnny Vander Meer, 1937-1949
1201	Jose Rijo, 1988-1995

Win pct: Highest, career

.674	Don Gullett, 1970-1976
.653	Pedro Borbon, 1970-1979
.623	Jim Maloney, 1960-1970
.623	Clay Carroll, 1968-1975
.621	Gary Nolan, 1967-1977

ERA: Lowest, career

2.18	Fred Toney, 1915-1918
2.37	Bob Ewing, 1902-1909
2.52	Noodles Hahn, 1899-1905
2.62	Hod Eller, 1917-1921
2.65	Pete Schneider, 1914-1918

Runs: Most, season

134	Frank Robinson, 1962
131	Vada Pinson, 1959
130	Pete Rose, 1976
129	Arlie Latham, 1894
126	Tommy Harper, 1965

Hits: Most, season

230	Pete Rose, 1973
219	Cy Seymour, 1905
218	Pete Rose, 1969
215	Pete Rose, 1976
210	Pete Rose, 1968
210	Pete Rose, 1975

2B: Most, season

51	Frank Robinson, 1962
51	Pete Rose, 1978
48	DMITRI YOUNG, 1998
47	Vada Pinson, 1959
47	Pete Rose, 1975

3B: Most, season

26	John Reilly, 1890
22	Bid McPhee, 1890
22	Sam Crawford, 1902
22	Mike Mitchell, 1911
22	Jake Daubert, 1922

HR: Most, season

52	George Foster, 1977
49	Ted Kluszewski, 1954
47	Ted Kluszewski, 1955
45	Johnny Bench, 1970
45	GREG VAUGHN, 1999

RBI: Most, season

149	George Foster, 1977
148	Johnny Bench, 1970
141	Ted Kluszewski, 1954
136	Frank Robinson, 1962
130	Deron Johnson, 1965

SB: Most, season

87	Arlie Latham, 1891
81	Bob Bescher, 1911
80	ERIC DAVIS, 1986
79	Dave Collins, 1980
76	Dusty Miller, 1896

BB: Most, season

132	Joe Morgan, 1975
120	Joe Morgan, 1974
117	Joe Morgan, 1977
115	Joe Morgan, 1972
114	Joe Morgan, 1976

BA: Highest, season

.377	Cy Seymour, 1905
.372	Bug Holliday, 1894
.351	Edd Roush, 1923
.351	Mike Donlin, 1903
.348	Edd Roush, 1924

On-base avg; Highest, season

.466	Joe Morgan, 1975
.449	Augie Galan, 1947
.444	Joe Morgan, 1976
.429	Cy Seymour, 1905
.428	Pete Rose, 1969

Slug pct: Highest, season

.642	Ted Kluszewski, 1954
.631	George Foster, 1977
.624	Frank Robinson, 1962
.611	Frank Robinson, 1961
.595	Frank Robinson, 1960

Games started: Most, season

49	Elton Chamberlain, 1892
47	Tony Mullane, 1891
45	Billy Rhines, 1890
43	Billy Rhines, 1891
42	Noodles Hahn, 1901
42	Pete Schneider, 1917
42	Fred Toney, 1917

Complete games: Most, season

45	Billy Rhines, 1890
43	Elton Chamberlain, 1892
42	Tony Mullane, 1891
41	Noodles Hahn, 1901
40	Billy Rhines, 1891

Saves: Most, season

44	JEFF BRANTLEY, 1996
42	JEFF SHAW, 1997
39	JOHN FRANCO, 1988

37	Clay Carroll, 1972
35	Wayne Granger, 1970

Shutouts: Most, season

7	Fred Toney, 1917
7	Hod Eller, 1919
7	Jack Billingham, 1973
6	Billy Rhines, 1890
6	Noodles Hahn, 1902
6	Jack Harper, 1904
6	Jake Weimer, 1906
6	Fred Toney, 1915
6	Dolf Luque, 1923
6	Johnny Vander Meer, 1941
6	Bucky Walters, 1944
6	Ewell Blackwell, 1947
6	Ken Raffensberger, 1952
6	Jim Maloney, 1963
6	Danny Jackson, 1988

Wins: Most, season

28	Billy Rhines, 1890
27	Pink Hawley, 1898
27	Dolf Luque, 1923
27	Bucky Walters, 1939
25	Eppa Rixey, 1922
25	Paul Derringer, 1939

K: Most, season

274	Mario Soto, 1982
265	Jim Maloney, 1963
244	Jim Maloney, 1965
242	Mario Soto, 1983
239	Noodles Hahn, 1901

Win pct: Highest, season

.826	Elmer Riddle, 1941
.821	Bob Purkey, 1962
.789	Don Gullett, 1975
.783	Tom Browning, 1988
.781	Paul Derringer, 1939

ERA: Lowest, season

1.58	Fred Toney, 1915
1.73	Bob Ewing, 1907
1.77	Noodles Hahn, 1902
1.82	Dutch Ruether, 1919
1.86	Andy Coakley, 1908

Most pinch-hit homers, season

5	Jerry Lynch, 1961
4	Bob Thurman, 1957

Most pinch-hit homers, career

13	Jerry Lynch, 1957-1963
7	Tony Perez, 1964-1986

Longest hitting streak

44	Pete Rose, 1978
30	Elmer Smith, 1898
29	HAL MORRIS, 1996
27	Edd Roush, 1920

27	Edd Roush, 1924
27	Vada Pinson, 1965

Most consecutive scoreless innings

32	Jim Maloney, 1968-69
27	Tom Seaver, 1977

No-hit games

Bumpus Jones, Cin vs Pit NL, 7-1; October 15, 1892 (first game in the major leagues).

Ted Breitenstein, Cin vs Pit NL, 11-0; April 22, 1898.

Noodles Hahn, Cin vs Phi NL, 4-0; July 12, 1900.

Fred Toney, Cin at Chi NL, 1-0; May 2, 1917 (ten innings).

Hod Eller, Cin vs StL NL, 6-0; May 11, 1919.

Johnny Vander Meer, Cin vs Bos NL, 3-0; June 11, 1938

Johnny Vander Meer, Cin at Bro NL, 6-0; June 15, 1938 (next start after June 11)

Clyde Shoun, Cin vs Bos NL, 1-0; May 15, 1944.

Ewell Blackwell, Cin vs Bos NL, 6-0; June 18, 1947.

Johnny Klippstein (7 innings), Hershell Freeman (1 inning) and Joe Black (3 innings), Cin at Mil NL, 1-2; May 26, 1956 (lost on 3 hits in 11 innings after allowing the first hit in the tenth)

Jim Maloney, Cin vs NY NL, 0-1; June 14, 1965 (lost on 2 hits in 11 innings after pitching 10 hit-less innings).

Jim Maloney, Cin at Chi NL, 1-0; August 19, 1965 (1st game, 10 innings).

George Culver, Cin at Phi NL, 6-1; July 29, 1968 (2nd game).

Jim Maloney, Cin vs Hou NL, 10-0; April 30, 1969.

Tom Seaver, Cin vs StL NL, 4-0; June 16, 1978.

Tom Browning, Cin vs LA NL, 1-0; September 16, 1988 (perfect game).

Elton Chamberlain, seven innings, darkness, Cin vs Bos NL, 6-0; September 23, 1893 (2nd game).

Jake Weimer, seven innings, agree-ment, Cin vs Bro NL, 1-0; August 24, 1906 (2nd game).

ACTIVE PLAYERS in caps.

Players' years of service are listed by the first and last years with this team and are not necessarily consecutive; all statistics record performances for this team only.

Pittsburgh Pirates

The move from Cleveland obviously was good for Brian Giles—he became the Pirates' top hitter.

By Tom DiPace

1999 Pirates: Improved but injured

If there is one image Pittsburgh Pirates fans will retain from 1999, it is that of Jason Kendall. Not Kendall lining a double or throwing out a base runner, but Kendall clutching a badly dislocated right ankle in agony behind first base on the Fourth of July. His season-ending injury cast a second half pall on a year filled with surprises and surgeries.

The Pirates jumped three places in the standings, from last to third in the NL Central, and bypassed two teams with much larger payrolls, the Cubs and the Cardinals. But the season ended poorly as the Pirates lost seven of their last 10 to finish below .500 for the seventh consecutive season. Their 78-83 record was 18½ games behind Houston.

"We're not Houston and we're not Cincinnati, but we're not far away," manager Gene Lamont said. "We're getting better, and I like to think that next year we'll have a contending team."

First, they might want to consider what went wrong and what went right in 1999.

What went wrong: The disabled list. The starting pitching. The defense.

What went right: Todd Ritchie's right-handed arm. Brian Giles's left-handed bat. The rookies.

"You could watch 'ER' every week and not see as many injuries as we had," said left fielder Al Martin, pointing to a disabled list that had as many as 13 players. Shortstop Pat Meares had hand surgery and played in only 17 games until making several late-season starts. Kendall (.332) was headed to the All-Star game until tearing up his ankle, an injury so severe it might have been career-threatening to an older player. Reliever Rich Loiselle had elbow surgery. Virtually all of the bullpen spent time on the disabled list: Jason Christiansen, Jeff Wallace, Mike Williams, Jose Silva, Chris Peters, Loiselle.

The injuries wrecked a pitching staff that was supposed to be the Pirates' strength, but wasn't. Jason Schmidt (13-11, 4.19) showed virtually no improvement and Francisco Cordova (8-10, 4.43) regressed

Team MVP

Brian Giles: He just needed to play every day. That was the familiar refrain when he platooned with the Indians, but what he did with that opportunity was more than even the Pirates could have hoped for. Brian Giles became Pittsburgh's No. 1 offensive threat, leading the team with a .315 average, 39 home runs, 115 RBI, 109 runs and 95 walks. His .614 slugging percentage ranked fifth in the league.

after once being expected to be the No. 1 starter.

But Ritchie, formerly a Twins reliever who had never started before in the majors, came out of nowhere to go 15-9, the most victories by a Pirates starter since Doug Drabek won 15 in 1992.

By season's end, Ritchie and rookie Kris Benson (11-14, 4.07) were the Pirates' best starters. Benson, the No. 1 pick in the 1996 draft, had to pitch his way onto the staff in spring training, but by September he was challenging top hitters. The big bullpen surprise was Rule 5 rookie Scott Sauerbeck (4-1, 2.00 ERA).

Giles, formerly a part-time outfielder with Cleveland, played every day, hitting .315 with 39 homers and 115 RBI. He was about to become the third Pirate in history to hit 40 homers, when a broken finger wiped out his final 11 games.

Rookie second baseman Warren Morris hit .300 most of the season until a September slump dropped him to .288. He has the power and the poise—if not the glove—of a Bill Mazeroski. First baseman Kevin Young hit .298 with 26 homers and 106 RBI, but his 23 errors were double those of any other NL first baseman. Ed Sprague, who missed most of September with a broken hand, had 22 homers and 81 RBI, but 29 errors at third.

263

1999 Pirates: Week-by-week notes

These notes were excerpted from the following issues of Baseball Weekly.

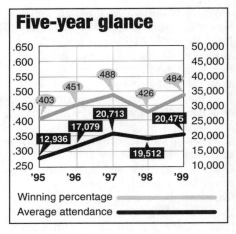

Five-year glance

Winning percentage

Average attendance

▶**April 14:** Right-hander Kris Benson made a successful debut on April 9, getting his first major league win in a 2-1 victory against the Chicago Cubs. Benson, the top overall pick in the 1996 draft, allowed two hits and a run in six innings. In the win, rookie second baseman Warren Morris, a teammate of Benson's on the 1996 Olympic team, hit his first major league home run.

▶**April 21:** The Pirates, who put right-hander Jose Silva on the DL late in spring training, added righty Francisco Cordova to the list on April 15. Cordova had inflammation in his right shoulder. Left-hander Pete Schourek struggled in his first two starts, allowing 14 hits and seven runs in eight innings.

▶**April 28:** The Pirates went 4-2 on their first road trip, placing a four-game winning streak between losses in Cincinnati and San Diego. That meant they'd already done something this season that they never did last year—win back-to-back series on the road. Over the last 39 innings the staff allowed only seven runs.

▶**May 5:** The Pirates, who'd gone 43 consecutive innings without having a multiple-run rally, scored three runs in the eighth inning on April 27 and beat Atlanta 5-3. It ended the team's four-game losing streak.

▶**May 12:** Left fielder Freddy Garcia had three run-scoring singles in a 13-3 victory on May 6 in St. Louis. Garcia came into the game hitting .100 (3-for-30) with 14 strikeouts.

▶**May 19:** Shortstop Pat Meares went down with a damaged tendon in his left hand that required surgery on May 14. He was set to be sidelined until mid-August. Abraham Nunez returned from AAA Nashville to replace Meares. Left-hander Jason Christiansen went on the DL with a neck strain. Right fielder Jose Guillen, sent down a month ago, returned from Nashville to take Christiansen's roster spot.

▶**May 26:** When Francisco Cordova returned to the rotation on May 19, right-hander Todd Ritchie stayed on as a starter and Jose Silva went to the bullpen. In his four starts Silva yielded 32 hits and 22 runs in 24 innings.

▶**June 2:** Pete Schourek was sent to the bullpen for the foreseeable future, and Jose Silva rejoined the rotation. Schourek was 2-5 with a 5.05 ERA in 10 starts. The Pirates signed closer Mike Williams to a two-year contract extension through 2001. That made him the 12th Pirate signed through at least 2000.

▶**June 9:** Manager Gene Lamont called his return last weekend to Comiskey Park "old news"—although it was his first trip there since June 2, 1995, when he was fired after three winning seasons and a division title as White Sox manager. Chicago won two out of three in the series.

▶**June 16:** Outfielder Brant Brown was on a mission to show the Pirates that they didn't err when they got him from the Cubs for Jon Lieber last winter. On June 18 Brown hit two homers and drove in three runs to help the Pirates beat Los Angeles 8-3. That put him at seven home runs and 25 RBI for the year.

▶**June 30:** The Pirates sent Jose Guillen to Nashville on June 24 for the second time this season, and there were indications that this exile would last longer than the first. Guillen batted .263 with one home run and 13 RBI in 95 Pirates at-bats.

►**July 7:** The Pirates suffered a major blow on July 4 when catcher Jason Kendall suffered a fractured and dislocated right ankle after stumbling over first base trying to beat out a bunt. Kendall has been the club's most productive hitter. He was batting .332 with eight homers and 41 RBI at the time of the injury.

►**July 28:** Catcher Keith Osik's injury on July 21 spurred the Pirates to acquire backstop Joe Oliver from Tampa Bay two days later in a four-player deal that sent Jose Guillen and minor league right-hander Jeff Sparks to the Devil Rays.

►**Aug. 11:** The Pirates hit five home runs in a game three times over an 82-game span between May 3 and Aug. 3. Before May 3 they also hit five home runs in a game three times—but it took them 2,702 games to do it, dating from June 3, 1979.

►**Aug. 25:** The Pirates placed Pete Schourek and Todd Ritchie on the DL on Aug. 21. Schourek had an inflammatory condition in his left shoulder, and Ritchie had a sore right shoulder.

►**Sept. 1:** Kris Benson turned in another strong start against Colorado on Aug. 24, allowing one run in eight innings, before losing to San Francisco on Aug. 29. Over a six-start span before that game, the rookie right-hander yielded only seven earned runs in 45 innings.

►**Sept. 8:** Center fielder Chad Hermansen, the Pirates' No. 1 pick in 1995, was expected to make his major league debut this week. At Nashville the center fielder

was hitting .274 with 31 home runs and 90 RBI. Incumbent center fielder Brian Giles reached the 100-RBI mark for the first time with his 34th home run on Aug. 31. Giles hit 12 homers and drove in 31 runs in August.

►**Sept. 15:** The Pirates knew they needed to make a special effort to extend Giles's contract. He was already signed through 2001 under terms inherited from Cleveland when he was acquired in a Nov. 18 trade. Last week Giles became the first Pirate since Barry Bonds in 1992 to both score and drive in at least 100 runs in a season..

►**Sept. 22:** Brant Brown became a part of Pirate history on Sept. 14 when he launched the team's 159th home run in a 2-1 loss at Arizona. The pinch-hit homer, which tied the score at 1-1, broke the club's season record of 158 set in 1966. Four Pirates—Brian Giles, left fielder Al Martin, third baseman Ed Sprague and first baseman Kevin Young—hit at least 20 homers, for the first time in team history.

►**Oct. 6:** Warren Morris was a candidate to win the NL Rookie of the Year award. He had a fine debut, finishing with a .288 average, 15 home runs and 73 RBI.

QUOTE OF THE YEAR

"It looks like Halloween came early."
—Right-hander Greg Hansell, on the Pirates' red, yellow and black futuristic uniforms

Team Leaders

Batting avg.	Hits	Wins	Strikeouts
.315 Brian Giles	174 Kevin Young	15 Todd Ritchie	148 Jason Schmidt
.298 Kevin Young	164 Brian Giles	13 Jason Schmidt	139 Kris Benson

HR	Runs	Losses	Innings
39 Brian Giles	109 Brian Giles	14 Kris Benson	212.2 Jason Schmidt
26 Kevin Young	103 Kevin Young	11 Jason Schmidt	196.2 Kris Benson

RBI	Stolen bases	ERA	Saves
115 Brian Giles	22 Jason Kendall	3.49 Todd Ritchie	23 Mike Williams
106 Kevin Young	22 Kevin Young	4.07 Kris Benson	4 Jose Silva

PITTSBURGH PIRATES 1999 final stats

BATTERS	BA	SLG	OBA	G	AB	R	H	TB	2B	3B	HR	RBI	BB	SO	SB	CS	E
Cruz	.400	.700	.400	5	10	3	4	7	0	0	1	2	0	2	0	0	0
Laker	.333	.333	.333	6	9	0	3	3	0	0	0	0	0	2	0	0	0
Kendall	.332	.511	.428	78	280	61	93	143	20	3	8	41	38	32	22	3	7
Giles	.315	.614	.418	141	521	109	164	320	33	3	39	115	95	80	6	2	3
Meares	.308	.352	.382	21	91	15	28	32	4	0	0	7	9	20	0	0	6
Young	.298	.522	.387	156	584	103	174	305	41	6	26	106	75	124	22	10	23
Morris	.288	.427	.360	147	511	65	147	218	20	3	15	73	59	88	3	7	14
Martin	.277	.506	.337	143	541	97	150	274	36	8	24	63	49	119	20	3	10
A. Brown	.270	.363	.364	116	226	34	61	82	5	2	4	17	33	39	5	3	4
Sprague	.267	.465	.352	137	490	71	131	228	27	2	22	81	50	93	3	6	29
Guillen	.267	.342	.321	40	120	18	32	41	6	0	1	18	10	21	1	0	3
Benjamin	.247	.364	.288	110	368	42	91	134	26	7	1	37	20	90	10	1	8
Hermansen	.233	.333	.324	19	60	5	14	20	3	0	1	1	7	19	2	2	0
B. Brown	.232	.449	.283	130	341	49	79	153	20	3	16	58	22	114	3	4	3
Nunez	.220	.251	.299	90	259	25	57	65	8	0	0	17	28	54	9	1	14
Sveum	.211	.437	.278	49	71	7	15	31	5	1	3	13	7	28	0	0	1
Oliver	.201	.284	.253	45	134	10	27	38	8	0	1	13	10	33	2	0	2
Osik	.186	.251	.239	66	167	12	31	42	3	1	2	13	11	30	0	0	1
Wehner	.185	.262	.264	39	65	6	12	17	2	0	1	4	7	12	1	0	1
Ramirez	.179	.250	.254	18	56	2	10	14	2	1	0	7	6	9	0	0	3
E. Brown	.143	.214	.143	6	14	0	2	3	1	0	0	0	0	3	0	0	0
Tremie	.071	.071	.188	9	14	1	1	1	0	0	0	1	2	4	0	0	0
Haad	.000	.000	.000	1	1	0	0	0	0	0	0	0	0	0	0	0	0

PITCHERS	W-L	ERA	BA	G	GS	CG	GF	SH	SV	IP	H	R	ER	HR	BB	SO
Garcia	1-0	1.29	.091	7	0	0	2	0	0	7.0	2	1	1	1	3	9
Sauerbeck	4-1	2.00	.220	65	0	0	16	0	2	67.2	53	19	15	6	38	55
Clontz	1-3	2.74	.254	56	0	0	16	0	2	49.1	49	21	15	6	24	40
Boyd	0-0	3.38	.250	4	0	0	0	0	0	5.1	5	2	2	0	2	4
Ritchie	15-9	3.49	.259	28	26	2	0	0	0	172.2	169	79	67	17	54	107
Wallace	1-0	3.69	.195	41	0	0	7	0	0	39.0	26	17	16	2	38	41
Hansell	1-3	3.89	.280	33	0	0	9	0	0	39.1	42	20	17	5	11	34
Anderson	2-1	3.99	.234	13	4	0	2	0	0	29.1	25	15	13	2	16	13
Christiansen	2-3	4.06	.198	39	0	0	17	0	3	37.2	26	17	17	2	22	35
Benson	11-14	4.07	.249	31	31	2	0	0	0	196.2	184	105	89	16	83	139
Schmidt	13-11	4.19	.262	33	33	2	0	0	0	212.2	219	110	99	24	85	148
Wilkins	2-3	4.24	.257	46	0	0	14	0	0	51.0	49	28	24	3	26	44
Cordova	8-10	4.43	.273	27	27	2	0	0	0	160.2	166	83	79	16	59	98
Williams	3-4	5.09	.276	58	0	0	50	0	23	58.1	63	36	33	9	37	76
Loiselle	3-2	5.28	.281	13	0	0	6	0	0	15.1	16	9	9	2	9	14
Schourek	4-7	5.34	.287	30	17	0	2	0	0	113.0	128	75	67	20	49	94
Silva	2-8	5.73	.281	34	12	0	9	0	4	97.1	108	70	62	10	39	77
Peters	5-4	6.59	.322	19	11	0	2	0	0	71.0	98	59	52	17	27	46
Dougherty	0-0	9.00	.333	2	0	0	0	0	0	2.0	3	3	2	0	3	1
Phillips	0-0	11.57	.393	6	0	0	0	0	0	7.0	11	9	9	2	6	7
Osik	0-0	36.00	.400	1	0	0	1	0	0	1.0	2	4	4	0	2	1

266

2000 preliminary roster

PITCHERS (20)
Jimmy Anderson
Bronson Arroyo
Kris Benson
Jason Boyd
Jason Christiansen
Francisco Cordova
Mike Garcia
Rich Loiselle
Brian O'Connor
Alex Pena
Chris Peters
Todd Ritchie
Scott Sauerbeck

Jason Schmidt
Pete Schourek
Jose Silva
Brian Smith
Jeff Wallace
Marc Wilkins
Mike Williams

CATCHERS (5)
Humberto Cota
Yamid Haad
Jason Kendall
Keith Osik
Rico Washington

INFIELDERS (7)
Mike Benjamin
Ivan Cruz
Pat Meares
Warren Morris
Abraham Nunez
Aramis Ramirez
Kevin Young

OUTFIELDERS (9)
Bruce Aven
Adrian Brown
Emil Brown
Wil Cordero
Brian Giles
Chad Hermansen
Alex Hernandez
Al Martin
Tike Redman

Games played by position

PLAYER	G	C	1B	2B	3B	SS	OF
Benjamin	110	0	0	12	6	93	0
A. Brown	116	0	0	0	0	0	96
B. Brown	130	0	7	0	0	0	82
E. Brown	6	0	0	0	0	0	6
Cruz	5	0	1	0	0	0	1
Garcia	55	0	0	0	9	0	24
Giles	141	0	0	0	0	0	138
Guillen	40	0	0	0	0	0	37
Haad	1	0	0	0	0	0	0
Hermansen	19	0	0	0	0	0	18
Kendall	78	75	0	0	0	0	0
Laker	6	2	0	0	0	0	0
Martin	143	0	0	0	0	0	134
Meares	21	0	0	0	0	21	0
Morris	147	0	0	144	0	0	0
Nunez	90	0	0	14	0	65	0
Oliver	45	44	0	0	0	0	0
Osik	66	50	0	0	0	0	0
Ramirez	18	0	0	0	17	0	0
Sprague	137	0	0	0	134	0	0
Sveum	49	0	4	2	12	4	1
Tremie	9	8	0	0	0	0	0
Ward	49	0	0	0	0	0	34
Wehner	39	0	0	1	2	2	17
Young	156	0	155	0	0	0	0

Sick call: 1999 DL report

PLAYER	Days on the DL
Mike Benjamin	19
Jason Christiansen	75**
Francisco Cordova	38
Ivan Cruz	92
Jason Kendall	91
Rich Loiselle	149
Javier Martinez	182
Pat Meares	150*
Keith Osik	22
Chris Peters	89
Todd Ritchie	15
Pete Schourek	15
Jose Silva	18
Ed Sprague	14
Doug Strange	182
Jeff Tabaka	182
Jeff Wallace	47
Turner Ward	63
Marc Wilkins	26
Mike Williams	15

Indicates two separate terms on Disabled List.

Minor Leagues

Tops in the organization

BATTER	CLUB	AVG.	G	AB	R	H	HR	RBI
Ramirez, Aramis	Nsh	.328	131	460	92	151	21	74
Washington, Rico	Lyn	.325	133	492	101	160	20	82
Brinkley, Darryl	Nsh	.323	111	372	68	120	14	75
Rivera, Carlos	Hic	.322	119	457	63	147	13	86
Hyzdu, Adam	Nsh	.308	105	389	70	120	29	91

HOME RUNS

Hermansen, Chad	Nsh	32
Hyzdu, Adam	Nsh	29
Cruz, Ivan	Nsh	25
Furniss, Eddy	Lyn	23
Sosa, Jovanny	Hic	22

WINS

Arroyo, Bronson	Nsh	15
Gonzalez, Mike	Alt	12
Ah Yat, Paul	Nsh	12
Anderson, Jimmy	Nsh	11
Van Poppel, Todd	Nsh	10

RBI

Hermansen, Chad	Nsh	97
Hyzdu, Adam	Nsh	91
Lankford, Derrick	Lyn	88
Furniss, Eddy	Lyn	87
Rivera, Carlos	Hic	86

SAVES

Pavlovich, Tony	Hic	20
Duff, Matt	Alt	12
Buirley, Matt	Hic	11
Several Players Tied at		10

STOLEN BASES

Dehaan, Kory	Alt	46
Alvarez, Antonio	WPT	38
Redman, Tike	Alt	29
Martin, Justin	Hic	28
Several Players Tied at		23

STRIKEOUTS

Grabow, John	Hic	164
Van Poppel, Todd	Nsh	157
Gonzalez, Mike	Alt	150
Ah Yat, Paul	Nsh	131
Arroyo, Bronson	Nsh	111

PITCHER	CLUB	W-L	ERA	IP	H	BB	SO
Williams, David	Hic	7-3	2.92	105	75	22	93
Bravo, Franklin	Hic	7-1	3.22	95	82	42	81
Wimberly, Larry	Lyn	8-4	3.41	103	109	24	98
France, Aaron	Alt	4-5	3.67	96	79	48	70
Duff, Matt	Alt	4-7	3.72	97	84	48	99

1999 salaries

	Bonuses	Total earned salary
Al Martin, of		2,700,000
Kevin Young, 1b		2,100,000
Pete Schourek, p		2,000,000
Pat Meares, ss		1,840,000
Jason Schmidt, p		1,450,000
Ed Sprague, 3b	250,000	1,300,000
Jason Kendall, c		1,250,000
Francisco Cordova, p		1,250,000
Brian Giles, of	250,000	1,116,666
Mike Benjamin, ss	175,000	875,000
Mike Williams, p	125,000	775,000
Jason Christiansen, p		725,000
Marc Wilkins, p	260,000	660,000
Doug Strange, 3b		550,000
Jeff Tabaka, p		500,000
Rich Loiselle, p		400,000
Keith Osik, c		350,000
Joe Oliver, c		350,000
Brad Clontz, p		350,000
Chris Peters, p		350,000
Brant Brown, of		290,000
Jose Silva, p		270,000
John Wehner, of		250,000
Greg Hansell, p		230,000
Todd Ritchie, p		225,000
Adrian Brown, of		220,000
Javier Martinez, p		220,000
Abraham Nunez, ss		210,000
Jeff Wallace, p		206,000
Ivan Cruz, 1b		205,000
Dale Sveum, 3b		200,000
Scott Sauerbeck, p		200,000
Jimmy Anderson, p		200,000
Kris Benson, p		200,000
Warren Morris, 2b		200,000

Average 1999 salary: $691,933
Total 1999 team payroll: $24,217,666
Termination pay: $485,246

Pittsburgh (1887-1999)

Runs: Most, career

1521	Honus Wagner, 1900-1917
1493	Paul Waner, 1926-1940
1416	Roberto Clemente, 1955-1972
1414	Max Carey, 1910-1926
1195	Willie Stargell, 1962-1982

Hits: Most, career

3000	Roberto Clemente, 1955-1972
2967	Honus Wagner, 1900-1917
2868	Paul Waner, 1926-1940
2416	Max Carey, 1910-1926
2416	Pie Traynor, 1920-1937

2B: Most, career

558	Paul Waner, 1926-1940
551	Honus Wagner, 1900-1917
440	Roberto Clemente, 1955-1972
423	Willie Stargell, 1962-1982
375	Max Carey, 1910-1926

3B: Most, career

232	Honus Wagner, 1900-1917
187	Paul Waner, 1926-1940
166	Roberto Clemente, 1955-1972
164	Pie Traynor, 1920-1937
156	Fred Clarke, 1900-1915

HR: Most, career

475	Willie Stargell, 1962-1982
301	Ralph Kiner, 1946-1953
240	Roberto Clemente, 1955-1972
176	BARRY BONDS, 1986-1992
166	Dave Parker, 1973-1983

RBI: Most, career

1540	Willie Stargell, 1962-1982
1475	Honus Wagner, 1900-1917
1305	Roberto Clemente, 1955-1972
1273	Pie Traynor, 1920-1937
1177	Paul Waner, 1926-1940

SB: Most, career

688	Max Carey, 1910-1926
639	Honus Wagner, 1900-1917
412	Omar Moreno, 1975-1982
312	Patsy Donovan, 1892-1899
271	Tommy Leach, 1900-1918

BB: Most, career

937	Willie Stargell, 1962-1982
918	Max Carey, 1910-1926
909	Paul Waner, 1926-1940
877	Honus Wagner, 1900-1917
795	Ralph Kiner, 1946-1953

BA: Highest, career

.340	Paul Waner, 1926-1940
.336	Kiki Cuyler, 1921-1927
.328	Honus Wagner, 1900-1917
.327	Matty Alou, 1966-1970
.324	Arky Vaughan, 1932-1941
.324	Elmer Smith, 1892-1901

On-base avg: Highest, career

.415	Arky Vaughan, 1932-1941
.415	Elmer Smith, 1892-1901
.410	George Grantham, 1925-1931
.407	Paul Waner, 1926-1940
.405	Ralph Kiner, 1946-1953

Slug pct: Highest, career

.567	Ralph Kiner, 1946-1953
.529	Willie Stargell, 1962-1982
.513	Kiki Cuyler, 1921-1927
.512	Dick Stuart, 1958-1962
.503	BARRY BONDS, 1986-1992

Games started: Most, career

477	Bob Friend, 1951-1965
369	Wilbur Cooper, 1912-1924
364	Vern Law, 1950-1967
353	Babe Adams, 1907-1926
299	Sam Leever, 1898-1910

Complete games: Most, career

263	Wilbur Cooper, 1912-1924
241	Sam Leever, 1898-1910
209	Deacon Phillippe, 1900-1911
206	Babe Adams, 1907-1926
167	Jim Galvin, 1887-1892

Saves: Most, career

188	Roy Face, 1953-1968
158	Kent Tekulve, 1974-1985
133	Dave Giusti, 1970-1976
61	STAN BELINDA, 1989-1993
59	Al McBean, 1961-1970

Shutouts: Most, career

44	Babe Adams, 1907-1926
39	Sam Leever, 1898-1910
35	Bob Friend, 1951-1965
33	Wilbur Cooper, 1912-1924
28	Vern Law, 1950-1967
28	Lefty Leifield, 1905-1912

Wins: Most, career

202	Wilbur Cooper, 1912-1924
194	Babe Adams, 1907-1926
194	Sam Leever, 1898-1910
191	Bob Friend, 1951-1965
168	Deacon Phillippe, 1900-1911

K: Most, career

1682	Bob Friend, 1951-1965
1652	Bob Veale, 1962-1972
1191	Wilbur Cooper, 1912-1924
1159	John Candelaria, 1975-1993
1092	Vern Law, 1950-1967

Win pct: Highest, career

.683	Nick Maddox, 1907-1910
.667	Jesse Tannehill, 1897-1902
.660	Sam Leever, 1898-1910
.659	Vic Willis, 1906-1909
.656	Emil Yde, 1924-1927

ERA: Lowest, career

2.08	Vic Willis, 1906-1909
2.38	Lefty Leifield, 1905-1912
2.47	Sam Leever, 1898-1910
2.50	Deacon Phillippe, 1900-1911
2.60	Bob Harmon, 1914-1918

Runs: Most, season

148	Jake Stenzel, 1894
145	Patsy Donovan, 1894
144	Kiki Cuyler, 1925
142	Paul Waner, 1928
140	Max Carey, 1922

Hits: Most, season

237	Paul Waner, 1927
234	Lloyd Waner, 1929
231	Matty Alou, 1969
223	Lloyd Waner, 1927
223	Paul Waner, 1928

2B: Most, season

62	Paul Waner, 1932
53	Paul Waner, 1936
50	Paul Waner, 1928
47	Adam Comorosky, 1930
45	Dave Parker, 1979
45	Andy Vanslyke, 1992
45	Honus Wagner, 1900

3B: Most, season

36	Chief Wilson, 1912
28	Harry Davis, 1897
27	Jimmy Williams, 1899
26	Kiki Cuyler, 1925
23	Adam Comorosky, 1930
23	Elmer Smith, 1893

HR: Most, season

54	Ralph Kiner, 1949
51	Ralph Kiner, 1947
48	Willie Stargell, 1971
47	Ralph Kiner, 1950
44	Willie Stargell, 1973

RBI: Most, season

131	Paul Waner, 1927	
127	Ralph Kiner, 1947	
127	Ralph Kiner, 1949	
126	Honus Wagner, 1901	
125	Willie Stargell, 1971	

SB: Most, season

96	Omar Moreno, 1980
77	Omar Moreno, 1979
71	Billy Sunday, 1888
71	Omar Moreno, 1978
70	Frank Taveras, 1977

BB: Most, season

137	Ralph Kiner, 1951
127	BARRY BONDS, 1992
122	Ralph Kiner, 1950
119	Elbie Fletcher, 1940
118	Elbie Fletcher, 1941
118	Arky Vaughan, 1936

BA: Highest, season

.385	Arky Vaughan, 1935
.381	Honus Wagner, 1900
.380	Paul Waner, 1927
.374	Jake Stenzel, 1895
.373	Paul Waner, 1936

On-base avg; Highest, season

.491	Arky Vaughan, 1935
.456	BARRY BONDS, 1992
.454	Elmer Smith, 1896
.453	Arky Vaughan, 1936
.452	Ralph Kiner, 1951

Slug pct: Highest, season

.658	Ralph Kiner, 1949
.646	Willie Stargell, 1973
.639	Ralph Kiner, 1947
.628	Willie Stargell, 1971
.627	Ralph Kiner, 1951

Games started: Most, season

55	Ed Morris, 1888
53	Mark Baldwin, 1892
51	Mark Baldwin, 1891
50	Jim Galvin, 1888
50	Pink Hawley, 1895
50	Frank Killen, 1896
42	Bob Friend, 1956 (12)

Complete games: Most, season

54	Ed Morris, 1888
49	Jim Galvin, 1888
48	Mark Baldwin, 1891
47	Jim Galvin, 1887
46	Harry Staley, 1889
32	Vic Willis, 1906 (19)

Saves: Most, season

34	Jim Gott, 1988
31	Kent Tekulve, 1978
31	Kent Tekulve, 1979
30	Dave Giusti, 1971
29	RICH LOISELLE, 1997

Shutouts: Most, season

8	Babe Adams, 1920
8	Jack Chesbro, 1902
8	Lefty Leifield, 1906
8	Al Mamaux, 1915
7	Steve Blass, 1968
7	Wilbur Cooper, 1917
7	Sam Leever, 1903
7	Bob Veale, 1965
7	Vic Willis, 1908

Wins: Most, season

36	Frank Killen, 1893
31	Pink Hawley, 1895
30	Frank Killen, 1896
29	Ed Morris, 1888
28	Jim Galvin, 1887
28	Jack Chesbro, 1902

K: Most, season

276	Bob Veale, 1965
250	Bob Veale, 1964
229	Bob Veale, 1966
213	Bob Veale, 1969
199	Larry McWilliams, 1983

Win pct: Highest, season

.947	Roy Face, 1959
.842	Emil Yde, 1924
.824	Jack Chesbro, 1902
.806	Howie Camnitz, 1909
.800	John Candelaria, 1977
.800	Ed Doheny, 1902
.800	Sam Leever, 1905

ERA: Lowest, season

1.56	Howie Camnitz, 1908
1.62	Howie Camnitz, 1909
1.66	Sam Leever, 1907
1.73	Vic Willis, 1906
1.87	Lefty Leifield, 1906

Most pinch-hit homers, season

4	Mark Johnson, 1996
3	Ham Hyatt, 1913
3	Al Rubeling, 1944
3	Ed Stevens, 1948
3	Bob Skinner, 1956
3	Dick Stuart, 1959
3	Gene Freese, 1964
3	Jose Pagan, 1969
3	Willie Stargell, 1982

Most pinch-hit homers, career

8	Willie Stargell 1962-1982
6	Dick Stuart, 1958-1962
6	John Milner, 1978-1982

Longest hitting streak

27	Jimmy Williams, 1899
26	Danny O'Connell, 1953
25	Charlie Grimm, 1923
25	Clyde Barnhart, 1925
25	Fred Lindstrom, 1933

Most consecutive scoreless innings

41	Jack Chesbro, 1902
36	Ed Morris, 1888

No-hit games

Nick Maddox, Pit vs Bro NL, 2-1; September 20, 1907.

Cliff Chambers, Pit at Bos NL, 3-0; May 6, 1951 (2nd game).

Harvey Haddix, Pit at Mil NL, 0-1; May 26, 1959 (lost on 1 hit in 13 innings after pitching 12 perfect innings).

Bob Moose, Pit at NY NL, 4-0; September 20, 1969.

Dock Ellis, Pit at SD NL, 2-0; June 12, 1970 (1st game).

John Candelaria, Pit vs LA NL, 2-0; August 9, 1976.

FRANCISCO CORDOVA (9 innings) and RICARDO RINCON (1 inning), Pit vs Hou NL, 3-0; July 12, 1997.

Lefty Leifield, six innings, darkness, Pit at Phi NL, 8-0; September 26, 1906 (2nd game).

Howie Camnitz, five innings, agreement, Pit at NY NL, 1-0; August 23, 1907 (2nd game).

ACTIVE PLAYERS in caps.

Players' years of service are listed by the first and last years with this team and are not necessarily consecutive; all statistics record performances for this team only.

By Anne Ryan, USA TODAY

Mark McGwire's assault on the home-run history books continued, but the Cardinals kept losing anyway.

1999 Cardinals: Enough about homers

All this home run stuff is getting old. Maybe not for a lot of fans but certainly to the guy most responsible. Sure, Mark McGwire is proud of his accomplishments—including hitting his 500th career home run in fewer at-bats than any player in history—but what he covets most is for the Cardinals to win again.

"I don't think anybody around here wants to deal with another season like this," McGwire said after St. Louis finished 11 games under .500 despite his 65 home runs. The previous year, McGwire hit a record 70, and it took a late-season surge for the Cardinals to finish four games above .500.

For his part, manager Tony La Russa has vowed spring training will be a boot camp: "If I see a team that's not running bases well, I'm going to say it's probably the manager. If I see a team that is not doing something that is pure baseball, like striking out too much, I blame the manager. So I'll take the heat."

A lot of the improvement could come from within. When the Cardinals lost young starting pitchers Matt Morris and Alan Benes to injuries, the hole was too big to plug. Imagine how bad things would have been had Kent Bottenfield not matched his career victory total and become a surprise 18-game winner.

General manager Walt Jocketty also wants to upgrade outfield production, though on-hand players might be sufficient. The right-field platoon of Eric Davis and Darren Bragg was gone for the season by mid-August with injuries, Ray Lankford struggled after undergoing surgery against the team's wishes, and J.D. Drew wasn't the phenom everyone expected.

"That's not our most critical need," Jocketty said. "But those guys are going to have to play better than they did this year."

Davis was already ahead of schedule in his latest comeback, at age 37. There could be another platoon situation at second base with Craig Paquette, a late-season surprise with 10 homers and 37 RBI in the last two months, and rookie Adam Kennedy. Catcher Eli Marrero is another reclama-

tion project after slumping to a .192 average and spending most of the last month and a half on the bench.

Then there's shortstop Edgar Renteria, who was better at the plate than on the field, where he committed 26 errors.

"Look at the plays he makes and his accurate, strong arm. If you find some lunatic out there, whatever his error total is, make him a big, big bet that he'll beat it by a lot next year. And give odds" La Russa said.

More than anything else, the Cardinals are hoping their run of bad luck is over. In addition to Morris and Benes, the team lost Donovan Osborne after the season began. Those injuries created a chain-reaction of juggling that sank a bullpen that was supposed to be a strength.

The Cardinals are trying not to count too heavily on Morris and Benes, who pitched a few times in September. Rick Ankiel, a 20-year-old left-hander who was winless yet impressive during the final month, should make the rotation but also will be handled carefully because of his youth.

One area that is not a problem is third base, where Fernando Tatis, 24, made a splash with two grand slams in one inning in April, and never slowed down. Tatis hit 34 homers, had 107 RBI and was strong defensively.

"I believe he's our MVP this year, and he hasn't gotten his due," McGwire said.

1999 Cardinals: Week-by-week notes

These notes were excerpted from the following issues of Baseball Weekly.

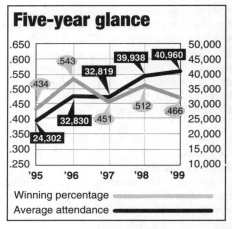

Five-year glance

Winning percentage
Average attendance

▶**April 14:** Third baseman Fernando Tatis hit three home runs in his first three games, marking the first time since the end of 1997 that someone other than first baseman Mark McGwire had led the Cardinals in homers.

▶**April 21:** Manager Tony La Russa said that batting shortstop Edgar Renteria second and dropping slumping rookie center fielder J.D. Drew to No. 6 "gives us a new look." Drew was then benched for a day after going 2-for-18. Right fielder Eric Davis, 4-for-28, was dropped out of the cleanup spot. When Drew returned, he went 1-for-8 with five strikeouts in two games and misplayed a ball in the field.

▶**April 28:** Before Fernando Tatis hit two grand slams in one inning on April 23, major leaguers had swatted 4,777 grand slams with no player ever accomplishing the double-slam. Tatis's eight RBI topped the modern-day RBI mark for an inning by two.

▶**May 5:** J.D. Drew scored a club-record-tying five runs when the Cards beat Montreal 16-5 on May 1. St. Louis lead-off hitters had batted only .209 before Drew singled, doubled, tripled, and walked twice.

▶**May 12:** Ray Lankford, slow to recover from offseason knee surgery, was starting only about two of every three games in left field. In just 31 at-bats through May 8, Lankford was hitting .355 with two home runs and four RBI. Joe McEwing cooled off, going hitless in four consecutive games to drop to .354. He saw one inning of duty at shortstop, giving him seven positions played—all but pitcher and catcher.

▶**May 19:** In 18 home games the Cardinals had given up 101 runs, including 60 (nearly seven per game) in the first nine games of a 10-game homestand. Their ERA of 5.07 ranked 15th in the NL.

▶**May 26:** Ray Lankford had a nine-game hitting streak in which he batted .400. He had two two-homer games, both against

Los Angeles. Mark McGwire was also heating up, with four homers in four games.

▶**June 16:** With a June 13 loss to Detroit, the Cardinals dropped to 1-19 in games in which they scored three runs or less. They were 29-12 when scoring four runs or more.

▶**June 23:** The Cardinals threw out 30 of the first 48 would-be base stealers through June 20. "These catchers [Eli Marrero and Alberto Castillo] are weapons," said Tony La Russa. "These guys get rid of the ball quick. There's a lot of arm strength and terrific accuracy."

▶**June 30:** Ricky Bottalico seemed to be recapturing his days as a closer in Philadelphia. He had 10 saves in 12 tries.

▶**July 7:** Joe McEwing extended his hitting streak to 25 games, eight short of the club record.

▶**July 21:** A three-homer burst in two games against the Chicago White Sox left Mark McGwire just 12 homers shy of 500. He has 57 multihomer games, placing him fourth on the career list, behind Babe Ruth (72), Willie Mays (63) and Henry Aaron (62).

▶**July 28:** The stress of the Cardinals' poor season might have gotten to Tony La Russa, who had to miss a week with stomach irritation. Third base coach Rene Lachemann took over the team and was 4-1 in five games as the Cardinals climbed back to the .500 level.

Aug. 4: Mark McGwire popped 12 homers in 16 games to roar past Lou Gehrig into 16th place on the career home run list with 496. McGwire also set a record for most homers hit over a five-year span, passing Babe Ruth, who had 256. McGwire had reached 258.

Aug. 11: The Cardinals lost much more often than they won when Mark McGwire homers. For his first 44 home runs, the Cardinals were 16-23 in games in which McGwire homered and 1-4 in games in which he homered twice.

Aug. 18: Through Aug. 15 McGwire had homered 78 times in his first 162 games at Busch Stadium. With 13 multihomer games there, McGwire had homered in an astonishing 40 percent of his games in St. Louis. Fernando Tatis was in the top 10 in the NL in walks, with 66 through Aug. 15. He drew just 36 walks last year in 532 at-bats.

Aug. 25: Right-hander Jose Jimenez went from no-hit hero to minor leaguer. Jimenez, who no-hit Arizona 1-0 on June 26 and then beat the Diamondbacks 1-0 again 10 days later, was given a ticket to AA Memphis after he lost 12 of 15 decisions. Craig Paquette had been a huge pickup. He homered five times and drove in 18 runs in his first 52 at-bats with the club and showed the ability to play left and right, first, second, and third.

Sept. 1: Left-hander Rick Ankiel, 20, allowed three runs in five innings in his debut against Montreal, on Aug. 23, and followed it up with a two-run effort in six innings on Aug. 29 against Atlanta.

Sept. 8: Right-hander Alan Benes was to be activated after making seven starts on rehab. Benes had two shoulder surgeries since he last pitched in the majors in July 1997. Right-hander Garrett Stephenson ran his winning streak to five with a 9-3 win against Florida on Sept. 1.

Sept. 15: The Cardinals lost six in a row to Atlanta in an 11-day span. The scores were 2-1, 3-0 in 13 innings, 4-3 in 12 innings, 4-1, 3-2 and 5-4. Mark McGwire was 2-for-25 in those games. One bright spot was Edgar Renteria, who has hit safely in 17 of 18 games, at a .366 clip. He had been in a 13-for-99 tailspin.

Sept. 22: Rick Ankiel had given the Cardinals chances to win in all five of his starts, but had not won any of those games, and neither has St. Louis. Ankiel (0-1, 3.72 ERA) was to spend the rest of the year in the bullpen to protect his arm.

Oct. 6: The Cardinals had their second-worst year in Tony La Russa's four seasons, finishing 11 games under .500. Mark McGwire finished with the third-highest home run total in major league history, 65. He outdistanced Chicago's Sammy Sosa in the last week, winning the home run title by two.

QUOTE OF THE YEAR

"He's taking baby steps. This is a tough league."
—Manager Tony La Russa, on rookie center fielder J.D. Drew's struggles

Team Leaders

Batting avg.	Hits	Wins	Strikeouts
.298 Fernando Tatis	161 Edgar Renteria	18 Kent Bottenfield	124 Kent Bottenfield
.278 Mark McGwire	160 Fernando Tatis	9 Darren Oliver	119 Darren Oliver

HR	Runs	Losses	Innings
65 Mark McGwire	118 Mark McGwire	14 Jose Jimenez	196.1 Darren Oliver
34 Fernando Tatis	104 Fernando Tatis	9 Darren Oliver	190.1 Kent Bottenfield

RBI	Stolen bases	ERA	Saves
147 Mark McGwire	37 Edgar Renteria	3.97 Kent Bottenfield	20 Ricky Bottalico
107 Fernando Tatis	21 Fernando Tatis	4.26 Darren Oliver	4 Juan Acevedo

ST. LOUIS CARDINALS 1999 final stats

BATTERS	BA	SLG	OBA	G	AB	R	H	TB	2B	3B	HR	RBI	BB	SO	SB	CS	E
Perez	.344	.500	.462	21	32	6	11	16	2	0	1	9	7	6	0	0	1
Lankford	.306	.493	.380	122	422	77	129	208	32	1	15	63	49	110	14	4	3
Tatis	.298	.553	.404	149	537	104	160	297	31	2	34	107	82	128	21	9	16
T. Howard	.292	.436	.353	98	195	16	57	85	10	0	6	28	17	26	1	1	1
Paquette	.287	.516	.309	48	157	21	45	81	6	0	10	37	6	38	1	0	3
McGwire	.278	.697	.424	153	521	118	145	363	21	1	65	147	133	141	0	0	13
Polanco	.277	.359	.321	88	220	24	61	79	9	3	1	19	15	24	1	3	8
Renteria	.275	.400	.334	154	585	92	161	234	36	2	11	63	53	82	37	8	26
McEwing	.275	.398	.333	152	513	65	141	204	28	4	9	44	41	87	7	4	11
Castillo	.263	.341	.326	93	255	21	67	87	8	0	4	31	24	48	0	0	5
Bragg	.260	.377	.369	93	273	38	71	103	12	1	6	26	44	67	3	0	3
Davis	.257	.403	.359	58	191	27	49	77	9	2	5	30	30	49	5	4	0
Kennedy	.255	.402	.284	33	102	12	26	41	10	1	1	16	3	8	0	1	4
McGee	.251	.277	.293	132	271	25	68	75	7	0	0	20	17	60	7	4	3
Drew	.242	.424	.340	104	368	72	89	156	16	6	13	39	50	77	19	3	7
Jensen	.235	.471	.350	16	34	5	8	16	5	0	1	1	6	12	0	0	1
D. Howard	.207	.293	.286	52	82	3	17	24	4	0	1	6	7	27	0	2	1
Marrero	.192	.297	.236	114	317	32	61	94	13	1	6	34	18	56	11	2	7
Ordaz	.111	.111	.200	10	9	3	1	1	0	0	0	2	1	2	1	0	3

PITCHERS	W-L	ERA	BA	G	GS	CG	GF	SH	SV	IP	H	R	ER	HR	BB	SO
Benes	0-0	0.00	.286	2	0	0	2	0	0	2.0	2	0	0	0	0	2
Slocumb	3-2	2.36	.243	40	0	0	12	0	2	53.1	49	16	14	3	30	48
Thompson	1-3	2.76	.241	5	5	0	0	0	0	29.1	26	12	9	1	17	22
Ankiel	0-1	3.27	.215	9	5	0	1	0	1	33.0	26	12	12	2	14	39
Bottenfield	18-7	3.97	.270	31	31	0	0	0	0	190.1	197	91	84	21	89	124
Croushore	3-7	4.14	.247	59	0	0	12	0	3	71.2	68	42	33	9	43	88
Stephenson	6-3	4.22	.275	18	12	0	1	0	0	85.1	90	43	40	11	29	59
Oliver	9-9	4.26	.265	30	30	2	0	1	0	196.1	197	96	93	16	74	119
Mohler	1-1	4.38	.255	48	0	0	16	0	1	49.1	47	26	24	3	23	31
Painter	4-5	4.83	.265	56	4	0	16	0	1	63.1	63	37	34	6	25	56
Radinsky	2-1	4.88	.270	43	0	0	13	0	3	27.2	27	16	15	2	18	17
Bottalico	3-7	4.91	.284	68	0	0	40	0	20	73.1	83	45	40	8	49	66
Mercker	6-5	5.12	.303	25	18	0	2	0	0	103.2	125	73	59	16	51	64
Luebbers	3-3	5.12	.261	8	8	1	0	0	0	45.2	46	27	26	8	16	16
Aybar	4-5	5.47	.272	65	1	0	22	0	3	97.0	104	67	59	13	36	74
Osborne	1-3	5.52	.298	6	6	0	0	0	0	29.1	34	18	18	4	10	21
Jimenez	5-14	5.85	.275	29	28	2	0	2	0	163.0	173	114	106	16	71	113
Acevedo	6-8	5.89	.291	50	12	0	21	0	4	102.1	115	71	67	17	48	52
Busby	0-1	7.13	.304	15	0	0	3	0	0	17.2	21	15	14	2	14	7
Heiserman	0-0	8.31	.400	3	0	0	0	0	0	4.1	8	4	4	2	4	4
Sodowsky	0-1	15.63	.455	3	1	0	0	0	0	6.1	15	11	11	1	6	2
King	0-0	18.00	.500	2	0	0	1	0	0	1.0	3	2	2	0	0	1

2000 preliminary roster

PITCHERS (21)
Juan Acevedo
John Ambrose
Rick Ankiel
Alan Benes
Ricky Bottalico
Kent Bottenfield
Justin Brunette
Luther Hackman
Rick Heiserman
Pat Hentgen
Chad Hutchinson

Darryl Kile
Mike Matthews
Mike Mohler
Matt Morris
Scott Radinsky
Heathcliff Slocumb
Paul Spoljaric
Gene Stechschulte
Garrett Stephenson
Mark Thompson

CATCHERS (1)
Eli Marrero

INFIELDERS (10)
Chris Haas
Adam Kennedy
Mark McGwire
Craig Paquette
Placido Polanco
Edgar Renteria
Chris Richard
Larry Sutton

Fernando Tatis
Jason Woolf

OUTFIELDERS (7)
Darren Bragg
Eric Davis
J.D. Drew
Ray Lankford
Joe McEwing
Dante Powell
Luis Saturria

Games played by position

PLAYER	G	C	1B	2B	3B	SS	OF
Bragg	93	0	0	0	0	0	88
Castillo	93	91	0	0	0	0	0
Davis	58	0	0	0	0	0	51
Drew	104	0	0	0	0	0	98
Dunston	62	0	8	0	5	7	23
D. Howard	52	0	9	9	4	13	5
T. Howard	98	0	0	0	0	0	48
Jensen	16	14	0	0	0	0	0
Kennedy	33	0	0	29	0	0	0
Lankford	122	0	0	0	0	0	106
Marrero	114	96	20	0	0	0	0
McEwing	152	0	2	96	6	1	66
McGee	132	0	3	0	0	0	89
McGwire	153	0	151	0	0	0	0
Ordaz	10	0	0	1	1	8	0
Paquette	48	0	6	7	10	0	27
Perez	21	0	5	0	0	0	6
Polanco	88	0	0	66	9	9	0
Renteria	154	0	0	0	0	151	0
Tatis	149	0	0	0	147	0	0

Sick call: 1999 DL report

PLAYER	Days on the DL
Alan Benes	153
Darren Bragg	62
Eric Davis	98
J.D. Drew	32
Shawon Dunston	16
David Howard	74*
Curtis King	72
Ray Lankford	19
Matt Morris	182
Donovan Osborne	150
Lance Painter	15
Scott Radinsky	69
Heathcliff Slocumb	23
Clint Sodowsky	33

Indicates two separate terms on Disabled List.

Minor Leagues

Tops in the organization

BATTER	CLUB	AVG.	G	AB	R	H	HR	RBI
Kennedy, Adam	Mem	.327	91	367	69	120	10	63
Perez, Eduardo	Mem	.320	119	416	67	133	18	82
Wilson, Jack	POT	.319	128	508	91	162	5	46
Ortega, Bill	Ark	.316	130	490	76	155	11	84
Ametller, Jesus	Mem	.307	118	401	53	123	10	53

HOME RUNS

			WINS		
Richard, Chris	Mem	30	Luebbers, Larry	Mem	13
Bevins, Andy	POT	25	Ankiel, Rick	Mem	13
Kim, Dave	POT	19	Prather, Scott	Peo	9
Farnsworth, Troy	Peo	19	Hutchinson, Chad	Mem	9
Several Players Tied at		18	Dewitt, Matt	Ark	9

RBI

			SAVES		
Richard, Chris	Mem	98	Marr, Jason	POT	21
Bevins, Andy	POT	97	Heiserman, Rick	Mem	20
Ortega, Bill	Ark	84	Stechschulte, G.	Ark	19
McNaughton, T.	Peo	84	Gooden, Derek	Peo	12
Perez, Eduardo	Mem	82	Griffin, Kirk	Peo	11

STOLEN BASES

			STRIKEOUTS		
Snead, Esix	Peo	64	Ankiel, Rick	Mem	194
Crisp, Covelli	JCY	27	Hutchinson, Chad	Mem	166
MaCrory, Bob	POT	27	Smith, Robert	POT	152
Hernandez, J.	NJY	24	Prather, Scott	Peo	132
Farley, Cordell	Ark	24	Stemle, Steve	Peo	113

PITCHER	CLUB	W-L	ERA	IP	H	BB	SO
Ankiel, Rick	Mem	13-3	2.35	138	98	62	194
Smith, Robert	POT	8-10	2.92	144	48	152	152
Prather, Scott	Peo	9-10	3.85	147	134	77	132
Sheredy, Kevin	POT	5-5	3.98	104	100	53	69
Luebbers, Larry	Mem	13-4	4.03	130	134	33	84

1999 salaries

	Bonuses	Total earned salary
Mark McGwire, 1b	475,334	9,358,667
Ray Lankford, of		6,600,000
Donovan Osborne, p		5,080,000
Darren Oliver, p		3,550,000
Eric Davis, of		3,420,840
Scott Radinsky, p		2,500,000
Ricky Bottalico, p	50,000	2,300,000
Edgar Renteria, ss	25,000	2,000,000
J.D. Drew, of	541,688	1,791,688
Willie McGee, of		1,000,000
David Howard, ss		950,000
Kent Bottenfield, p	25,000	850,000
Lance Painter, p		800,000
Darren Bragg, of		800,000
Alan Benes, p		550,000
Matt Morris, p		550,000
Mike Mohler, p	40,000	490,000
Juan Acevedo, p		475,000
Thomas Howard, of		325,000
Craig Paquette, of		300,000
Fernando Tatis, 3b		270,000
Alberto Castillo, c		225,000
Garrett Stephenson, p		215,000
Larry Luebbers, p		212,000
Manny Aybar, p		210,000
Eli Marrero, c		210,000
Curtis King, p		210,000
Rick Croushore, p		205,000
Heathcliff Slocumb, p		200,000
Joe McEwing, 2b		200,000
Adam Kennedy, 2b		200,000
Rick Ankiel, p		200,000

Average 1999 salary: $1,445,257
Total 1999 team payroll: $46,248,195
Termination pay: $163,934

St. Louis (1892-1999)

Runs: Most, career

1949	Stan Musial, 1941-1963	
1427	Lou Brock, 1964-1979	
1089	Rogers Hornsby, 1915-1933	
1071	Enos Slaughter, 1938-1953	
1025	Red Schoendienst, 1945-1963	

Hits: Most, career

3630	Stan Musial, 1941-1963
2713	Lou Brock, 1964-1979
2110	Rogers Hornsby, 1915-1933
2064	Enos Slaughter, 1938-1953
1980	Red Schoendienst, 1945-1963

2B: Most, career

725	Stan Musial, 1941-1963
434	Lou Brock, 1964-1979
377	Joe Medwick, 1932-1948
367	Rogers Hornsby, 1915-1933
366	Enos Slaughter, 1938-1953

3B: Most, career

177	Stan Musial, 1941-1963
143	Rogers Hornsby, 1915-1933
135	Enos Slaughter, 1938-1953
121	Lou Brock, 1964-1979
119	Jim Bottomley, 1922-1932

HR: Most, career

475	Stan Musial, 1941-1963
255	Ken Boyer, 1955-1965
193	Rogers Hornsby, 1915-1933
181	Jim Bottomley, 1922-1932
181	RAY LANKFORD, 1990-1999

RBI: Most, career

1951	Stan Musial, 1941-1963
1148	Enos Slaughter, 1938-1953
1105	Jim Bottomley, 1922-1932
1072	Rogers Hornsby, 1915-1933
1001	Ken Boyer, 1955-1965

SB: Most, career

888	Lou Brock, 1964-1979
549	Vince Coleman, 1985-1990
433	Ozzie Smith, 1982-1996
301	WILLIE McGEE, 1982-1999
239	RAY LANKFORD, 1990-1999

BB: Most, career

1599	Stan Musial, 1941-1963
876	Ozzie Smith, 1982-1996
838	Enos Slaughter, 1938-1953
681	Lou Brock, 1964-1979
660	Rogers Hornsby, 1915-1933

BA: Highest, career

.359	Rogers Hornsby, 1915-1933
.336	Johnny Mize, 1936-1941
.335	Joe Medwick, 1932-1948
.331	Stan Musial, 1941-1963
.326	Chick Hafey, 1924-1931

On-base avg: Highest, career

.427	Rogers Hornsby, 1915-1933
.419	Johnny Mize, 1936-1941
.417	Stan Musial, 1941-1963
.413	Joe Cunningham, 1954-1961
.402	Miller Huggins, 1910-1916

Slug pct: Highest, career

.600	Johnny Mize, 1936-1941
.568	Rogers Hornsby, 1915-1933
.568	Chick Hafey, 1924-1931
.559	Stan Musial, 1941-1963
.545	Joe Medwick, 1932-1948

Games started: Most, career

482	Bob Gibson, 1959-1975
401	Bob Forsch, 1974-1988
386	Jesse Haines, 1920-1937
320	Bill Doak, 1913-1929
243	Bill Sherdel, 1918-1932

Complete games: Most, career

255	Bob Gibson, 1959-1975
208	Jesse Haines, 1920-1937
196	Ted Breitenstein, 1892-1901
144	Bill Doak, 1913-1929
144	Bill Sherdel, 1918-1932

Saves: Most, career

160	Lee Smith, 1990-1993
129	Todd Worrell, 1985-1992
127	Bruce Sutter, 1981-1984
66	Dennis Eckersley, 1996-1997
64	Lindy McDaniel, 1955-1962

Shutouts: Most, career

56	Bob Gibson, 1959-1975
30	Bill Doak, 1913-1929
28	Mort Cooper, 1938-1945
25	Harry Brecheen, 1940-1952
24	Jesse Haines, 1920-1937

Wins: Most, career

251	Bob Gibson, 1959-1975
210	Jesse Haines, 1920-1937
163	Bob Forsch, 1974-1988
153	Bill Sherdel, 1918-1932
144	Bill Doak, 1913-1929

K: Most, career

3117	Bob Gibson, 1959-1975
1095	Dizzy Dean, 1930-1937
1079	Bob Forsch, 1974-1988
979	Jesse Haines, 1920-1937
951	Steve Carlton, 1965-1971

Win pct: Highest, career

.718	Ted Wilks, 1944-1951
.705	John Tudor, 1985-1990
.677	Mort Cooper, 1938-1945
.667	Al Hrabosky, 1970-1977
.641	Dizzy Dean, 1930-1937

ERA: Lowest, career

2.52	John Tudor, 1985-1990
2.67	Slim Sallee, 1908-1916
2.67	Jack Taylor, 1904-1906
2.74	Johnny Lush, 1907-1910
2.74	Red Ames, 1915-1919

Runs: Most, season

142	Jesse Burkett, 1901
141	Rogers Hornsby, 1922
135	Stan Musial, 1948
133	Rogers Hornsby, 1925
132	Joe Medwick, 1935

Hits: Most, season

250	Rogers Hornsby, 1922
237	Joe Medwick, 1937
235	Rogers Hornsby, 1921
230	Stan Musial, 1948
230	Joe Torre, 1971

2B: Most, season

64	Joe Medwick, 1936
56	Joe Medwick, 1937
53	Stan Musial, 1953
52	Enos Slaughter, 1939
51	Stan Musial, 1944

3B: Most, season

29	Perry Werden, 1893
25	Roger Connor, 1894
25	Tom Long, 1915
20	Duff Cooley, 1895
20	Rogers Hornsby, 1920
20	Jim Bottomley, 1928
20	Stan Musial, 1943
20	Stan Musial, 1946

HR: Most, season

70	MARK McGWIRE, 1998	
65	MARK McGWIRE, 1999	
43	Johnny Mize, 1940	
42	Rogers Hornsby, 1922	
39	Rogers Hornsby, 1925	
39	Stan Musial, 1948	

RBI: Most, season

154	Joe Medwick, 1937
152	Rogers Hornsby, 1922
147	MARK McGWIRE, 1998
147	MARK McGWIRE, 1999
143	Rogers Hornsby, 1925

SB: Most, season

118	Lou Brock, 1974
110	Vince Coleman, 1985
109	Vince Coleman, 1987
107	Vince Coleman, 1986
81	Vince Coleman, 1988

BB: Most, season

162	MARK McGWIRE, 1998
136	Jack Clark, 1987
136	Jack Crooks, 1892
133	MARK McGWIRE, 1999
121	Jack Crooks, 1893

BA: Highest, season

.424	Rogers Hornsby, 1924
.403	Rogers Hornsby, 1925
.401	Rogers Hornsby, 1922
.397	Rogers Hornsby, 1921
.396	Jesse Burkett, 1899

On-base avg; Highest, season

.507	Rogers Hornsby, 1924
.489	Rogers Hornsby, 1925
.470	MARK McGWIRE, 1998
.463	Jesse Burkett, 1899
.459	Jack Clark, 1987

Slug pct: Highest, season

.756	Rogers Hornsby, 1925
.752	MARK McGWIRE, 1998
.722	Rogers Hornsby, 1922
.702	Stan Musial, 1948
.697	MARK McGWIRE, 1999

Games started: Most, season

50	Ted Breitenstein, 1894
50	Ted Breitenstein, 1895
47	Jack Taylor, 1898
45	Kid Gleason, 1892
45	Kid Gleason, 1893
41	Bob Harmon, 1911 (11)

Complete games: Most, season

46	Ted Breitenstein, 1894
46	Ted Breitenstein, 1895
43	Kid Gleason, 1892
42	Jack Taylor, 1898
40	Jack Powell, 1899
40	Cy Young, 1899
39	Jack Taylor, 1904 (7)

Saves: Most, season

47	Lee Smith, 1991
45	Bruce Sutter, 1984
43	Lee Smith, 1992
43	Lee Smith, 1993
36	Dennis Eckersley, 1997
36	Bruce Sutter, 1982
36	Todd Worrell, 1986
36	Tom Henke, 1995

Shutouts: Most, season

13	Bob Gibson, 1968
10	Mort Cooper, 1942
10	John Tudor, 1985
7	Harry Brecheen, 1948
7	Mort Cooper, 1944
7	Dizzy Dean, 1934
7	Bill Doak, 1914

Wins: Most, season

30	Dizzy Dean, 1934
28	Dizzy Dean, 1935
27	Ted Breitenstein, 1894
26	Cy Young, 1899
24	Jesse Haines, 1927
24	Dizzy Dean, 1936

K: Most, season

274	Bob Gibson, 1970
270	Bob Gibson, 1965
269	Bob Gibson, 1969
268	Bob Gibson, 1968
245	Bob Gibson, 1964

Win pct: Highest, season

.811	Dizzy Dean, 1934
.810	Ted Wilks, 1944
.789	Harry Brecheen, 1945
.778	Johnny Beazley, 1942
.767	Bob Gibson, 1970

ERA: Lowest, season

1.12	Bob Gibson, 1968
1.72	Bill Doak, 1914
1.78	Mort Cooper, 1942
1.90	Max Lanier, 1943
1.93	John Tudor, 1985

Most pinch-hit homers, season

4	George Crowe, 1959
4	George Crowe, 1960
4	Carl Sawatski, 1961

Most pinch-hit homers, career

8	George Crowe, 1959-1961
6	Carl Sawatski, 1960-1963
6	Gerald Perry, 1991-1995

Longest hitting streak

33	Rogers Hornsby, 1922
30	Stan Musial, 1950
29	Harry Walker, 1943
29	Ken Boyer, 1959
28	Joe Medwick, 1935
28	Red Schoendienst, 1954

Most consecutive scoreless innings

47	Bob Gibson, 1968
37	George Bradley, 1876

No-hit games

George Bradley, StL vs Har NL, 2-0; July 15, 1876.

Jesse Haines, StL vs Bos NL, 5-0; July 17, 1924.

Paul Dean, StL at Bro NL, 3-0; September 21, 1934 (2nd game).

Lon Warneke, StL at Cin NL, 2-0; August 30, 1941.

Ray Washburn, StL at SF NL, 2-0; September 18, 1968.

Bob Gibson, StL at Pit NL, 11-0; August 14, 1971.

Bob Forsch, StL vs Phi NL, 5-0; April 16, 1978.

Bob Forsch, StL vs Mon NL, 3-0; September 26, 1983.

JOSE JIMENEZ, StL at Ari NL, 1-0; June 25, 1999

Stoney McGlynn, seven innings, agreement, StL at Bro NL, 1-1; September 24, 1906 (2nd game).

Ed Karger, seven perfect innings, agreement, StL vs Bos NL, 4-0; August 11, 1907 (2nd game).

Johnny Lush, six innings, rain, StL at Bro NL, 2-0; August 6, 1908.

ACTIVE PLAYERS in caps.

Players' years of service are listed by the first and last years with this team and are not necessarily consecutive; all statistics record performances for this team only.

Milwaukee Brewers

By Tom DiPace

Jeromy Burnitz brightened the Brewers' year with 30-plus homers and 100-plus RBI.

1999 Brewers: If it could go wrong, it did

Every disappointment that befell the Milwaukee Brewers in 1999 pales in comparison to the tragedy that took the lives of Jerome Starr, Jeffrey Wischer and William DeGrave.

The collapse of a 1,400-ton crane putting the retractable roof on the Brewer's new home, Miller Park, killed the three ironworkers in July and pushed the stadium opening back a full year. It was the lowest point of an exceptionally grim year in Milwaukee—on the field, in the clubhouse and in the front office.

"It's been an ordeal," infielder Mark Loretta said. "It was probably the toughest year of my professional life, and I'm sure it was that way for most of the other guys, too."

The Brewers started slowly and didn't speed up until they were mired near the bottom of the NL. Free-agent signings didn't pan out, veterans had lingering injuries, and the final upheaval was the firing of manager Phil Garner and resignation of general manager Sal Bando in August.

"The only thing this team can do is start over," said oufielder Marquis Grissom.

The management changes had little effect on the Brewers' seventh consecutive losing season and a 74-87 record that barely put them ahead of the even more disappointing Chicago Cubs.

Interim manager Jim Lefebvre went 22-27 after replacing Garner, but the former Cubs and Mariners skipper wasn't considered a candidate for the full-time job that was eventually turned over to Davey Lopes.

"We've had big problems, but at the end of the year we got it together and finished strong," said Lefebvre, who led the Brewers to 13 wins in their final 20 games.

Among the Brewers' first indications of how bad the season would be was the disappearance of second baseman Fernando Vina, who strained his quadriceps in May and missed the rest of the season.

All-Star catcher David Nilsson had one of his best seasons with a .310 average, 21 homers and 62 RBI, then became a free agent. Free-agent signee Sean Berry was a bust, and veterans Grissom,

Team MVP

Jeromy Burnitz: Sometimes lost in the sub-.500 season of the Brewers, Jeromy Burnitz has emerged as one of the more consistent power hitters in the game. He certainly is Milwaukee's most potent threat. Despite missing several weeks to injury, he topped the team with 33 home runs and 103 RBI. The missed time probably cost him the chance to improve on his career bests of 38 and 125 from 1998.

Loretta and Jose Valentin underperformed. Only Jeromy Burnitz, an All-Star starter who had 33 homers and 103 RBI, exceeded expectations.

The core of the offense came from solid young hitters Jeff Cirillo, Geoff Jenkins and rookie second baseman Ron Belliard. Cirillo easily led the club with his .326 average, his third .320-plus performance in the past four seasons.

But the search for a pitching nucleus continued. Milwaukee had just two bright spots on the mound: closer Bob Wickman, who set the team record with 37 saves, and Hideo Nomo, who went 12-8 and resurrected his career. But Nomo left as a free agent, leaving Steve Woodard as the top returning arm.

Bando's successor is Dean Taylor, former assistant general manager in Atlanta. When he arrived in Milwaukee, he readily acknowledged the Brewers didn't have the talent to win, something Milwaukee's management had steadfastly denied.

When the season began, the Brewers hoped to open the 2000 season in Miller Park, the state-of-the-art facility that has loomed as the light at the end of the Brewers' tunnel for nearly a decade. The accident pushed the stadium's opening back to 2001. That also at least partially delayed the club's plans to begin spending a bit more for on-field talent, a plan tied to the anticipated increase in revenue from the new ballpark.

1999 Brewers: Week-by-week notes

These notes were excerpted from the following issues of Baseball Weekly.

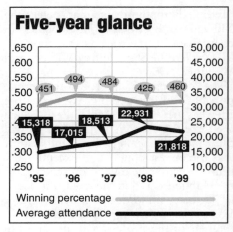

Five-year glance

.451 .494 .484 .425 .460

15,318 17,015 18,513 22,931 21,818

'95 '96 '97 '98 '99

Winning percentage
Average attendance

▶**April 14:** The concerns about pitching were already becoming reality as several starters and relievers pitched poorly in the first week. Left-handers Rafael Roque, Jim Abbott and Scott Karl all struggled, but perhaps of most concern was closer Bob Wickman, who blew a five-run lead in the opener against St. Louis and gave up the winning run in a 3-2 loss to the Astros on April 9. Only right-hander Steve Woodard really had a decent start during the first week, and he lost 4-1.

▶**April 21:** Manager Phil Garner has toyed with the idea of going with three pitchers for three innings each or two for four innings and one for one. Garner and his staff were looking for alternatives because of the failure of most of their starters to go deep into ball games.

▶**April 28:** Steve Woodard pitched the Brewers' first complete game in 113 contests in a 9-1 win against the Pirates on April 23. The complete-game drought was an NL record. Woodard allowed eight hits, struck out five and walked one. He had a shutout going until the bottom of the ninth.

▶**May 5:** After an encouraging first start, right-hander Cal Eldred was rocked for six runs on six hits in a 10-4 loss to the Dodgers on April 29. He walked three and threw 85 pitches in only three innings.

▶**May 12:** Right-hander Hideo Nomo made his Brewers debut in San Francisco on May 9, allowing one earned run over 6⅓ innings in a 3-2 win.

▶**May 19:** Catcher David Nilsson was swinging a hot bat, with three home runs and eight RBI last week. He hit two homers at Cincinnati on May 12 and drove in four runs with a homer and double at home against Florida on May 15.

▶**May 26:** The pitching was atrocious in giving up 21 runs in a doubleheader loss to the Mets on May 20. Jim Abbott struggled again, giving up seven runs on seven hits and watching his ERA balloon to 9.11. Scott Karl yielded six runs on nine

hits in 2⅓ innings in a 12-4 loss to the Expos two days later.

▶**June 2:** Infielder Ron Belliard had been slated to return to the minors when second baseman Fernando Vina came off the DL, but Belliard hit .293 and played well in the field, so the Brewers sent infielder Lou Collier to AAA Louisville instead.

▶**June 9:** The Brewers lost 9-8 and 12-11 to Colorado on June 4 and 5. Hideo Nomo, who had been the team's best starter, was roughed up in the 12-11 loss.

▶**June 16:** Left fielder Geoff Jenkins was moved up to sixth in the order after he continued to hit for both power (11 homers) and average (.323).

▶**June 23:** Jim Abbott got his first regular-season major league hit, against the Cubs on June 15. Abbott spent his career in the AL before joining the Brewers this season.

▶**June 30:** Hideo Nomo won his fourth consecutive start on June 26. Nomo, who was 6-1 with a 3.72 ERA, had seven strikeouts in a 7-4 win against Pittsburgh.

▶**July 7:** Right fielder Jeromy Burnitz was named the NL Player of the Month for June. He hit .317 (32-for-101) with 12 home runs and 32 RBI. Burnitz, who had 23 homers through July 4, hit his third career grand slam on June 27, against the Pirates.

▶**July 15:** Steve Woodard showed that he was becoming the ace of the staff by winning his 10th game in a 4-1 decision over

the Tigers on July 9. On July 14, a tragic construction accident killed three workers at the Brewers' new Miller Park.

▶**July 21:** For the first time in more than three months, the surging Brewers reached .500 on July 18 with a 5-4 victory against the White Sox. However, Jeromy Burnitz would miss at least three weeks after a pitch by Kansas City's Jose Rosado broke a bone in Burnitz's right hand on July 17. Burnitz was hitting .273 with 26 home runs and 73 RBI.

▶**July 28:** Jim Abbott was released on July 23 after he struggled (2-8, 6.91 ERA) in his comeback.

▶**Aug. 4:** The Brewers dedicated their game on July 30 to the three construction workers killed in the July 14 Miller Park accident and raised $100,000 for the families of the men. All Miller Park workers were admitted to the game free.

▶**Aug. 18:** The Brewers won their first game under interim manager Jim Lefebvre as Hideo Nomo beat the Diamondbacks 3-1 on Aug. 13. Lefebvre, the hitting coach under the ousted Phil Garner, had been told that his role was only interim. Club president Wendy Selig-Prieb said she did not want to talk about specifics regarding a new manager or general manager. Sal Bando left the latter job when Garner was let go; Bando was named special assistant to the team president.

▶**Sept. 1:** Shortstop Jose Valentin hit the only two home runs for the Brewers in a 15-game stretch, including a grand slam, but he continued to struggle in the field. Valentin, who was out from mid-April until mid-June with an injury, committed 21 errors in only 63 games.

▶**Sept. 15:** The Brewers allowed 56 runs in five games last week as their mound woes deepened. Changes in the rotation were made. Steve Woodard, who has been on the DL with a fractured left wrist, was activated and had his first start on Sept. 11. Right-hander Jason Bere, up from Louisville, started the next day in place of Cal Eldred, who suffered a right pectoral injury.

▶**Sept. 22:** The Brewers' sweep of the Cardinals on Sept. 14-16 was their first since July 4, when they completed one against the Pirates. Kevin Barker and third baseman Jeff Cirillo had some key hits in the series at St. Louis. Barker had made enough of an impression since being called up from Louisville that he very likely could be the starter next season at first base.

▶**Oct. 6:** New general manager Dean Taylor would wait to hire a new manager, because some of his top candidates were involved in postseason play. Taylor was also considering possible trades. Jeff Cirillo, Marquis Grissom, Scott Karl and Fernando Vina all have been subjects of trade rumors.

QUOTE OF THE YEAR

"I feel really needed by this team."
—Right-hander Hideo Nomo, on establishing himself in Milwaukee after being released earlier in the year by the Mets and the Cubs

Team Leaders

Batting avg.	Runs	Losses	Innings
.326 Jeff Cirillo	98 Jeff Cirillo	11 Scott Karl	197.2 Scott Karl
.295 Ron Belliard	93 Mark Loretta	8 Jim Abbott	185 Steve Woodard
		8 Cal Eldred	
HR	**Stolen bases**	8 Hideo Nomo	**Saves**
33 Jeromy Burnitz	24 Marquis Grissom	8 Bob Wickman	37 Bob Wickman
21 Geoff Jenkins	7 Jeromy Burnitz	8 Steve Woodard	2 David Weathers
21 Dave Nilsson	7 Jeff Cirillo		
		ERA	
RBI	**Wins**	4.52 Steve Woodard	
103 Jeromy Burnitz	12 Hideo Nomo	4.54 Hideo Nomo	
88 Jeff Cirillo	11 Scott Karl		
	11 Steve Woodard	**Strikeouts**	
Hits		161 Hideo Nomo	
198 Jeff Cirillo		119 Steve Woodard	
170 Mark Loretta			

MILWAUKEE BREWERS 1999 final stats

BATTERS	BA	SLG	OBA	G	AB	R	H	TB	2B	3B	HR	RBI	BB	SO	SB	CS	E
Cirillo	.326	.461	.401	157	607	98	198	280	35	1	15	88	75	83	7	4	15
Jenkins	.313	.564	.371	135	447	70	140	252	43	3	21	82	35	87	5	1	7
Nilsson	.309	.554	.400	115	343	56	106	190	19	1	21	62	53	64	1	2	5
Ochoa	.300	.466	.404	119	277	47	83	129	16	3	8	40	45	43	6	4	3
Belliard	.295	.429	.379	124	457	60	135	196	29	4	8	58	64	59	4	5	13
Loretta	.290	.390	.354	153	587	93	170	229	34	5	5	67	52	59	4	1	13
Barker	.282	.385	.331	38	117	13	33	45	3	0	3	23	9	19	1	0	1
Burnitz	.270	.561	.402	130	467	87	126	262	33	2	33	103	91	124	7	3	5
Grissom	.267	.415	.320	154	603	92	161	250	27	1	20	83	49	109	24	6	5
Vina	.266	.331	.339	37	154	17	41	51	7	0	1	16	14	6	5	2	1
Collier	.259	.370	.325	74	135	18	35	50	9	0	2	21	14	32	3	2	5
Hughes	.257	.366	.292	48	101	10	26	37	2	0	3	8	5	28	0	0	2
Becker	.252	.424	.395	89	139	15	35	59	5	2	5	16	33	38	5	0	2
Banks	.242	.352	.317	105	219	34	53	77	7	1	5	22	25	59	6	1	5
Berry	.228	.301	.281	106	259	26	59	78	11	1	2	23	17	50	0	0	5
Valentin	.227	.418	.347	89	256	45	58	107	9	5	10	38	48	52	3	2	22
Greene	.190	.214	.271	32	42	4	8	9	1	0	0	1	5	11	0	0	1
Cancel	.182	.227	.234	15	44	5	8	10	2	0	0	5	2	12	0	0	2
Mouton	.176	.412	.263	14	17	2	3	7	1	0	1	3	2	3	0	0	0
Zosky	.143	.143	.250	8	7	1	1	1	0	0	0	0	1	2	0	0	0

PITCHERS	W-L	ERA	BA	G	GS	CG	GF	SH	SV	IP	H	R	ER	HR	BB	SO
D'Amico	0-0	0.00	.250	1	0	0	1	0	0	1.0	1	0	0	0	0	1
Harris	0-0	3.00	.186	8	0	0	2	0	0	12.0	8	4	4	1	7	11
Wickman	3-8	3.39	.262	71	0	0	63	0	37	74.1	75	31	28	6	38	60
Ramirez	1-2	3.43	.247	15	0	0	5	0	0	21.0	19	8	8	1	11	9
Coppinger	5-3	3.68	.250	29	0	0	10	0	0	36.2	35	16	15	5	23	39
Reyes	2-0	4.25	.206	26	0	0	6	0	0	36.0	27	17	17	5	25	39
Woodard	11-8	4.52	.294	31	29	2	0	0	0	185.0	219	101	93	23	36	119
Nomo	12-8	4.54	.256	28	28	0	0	0	0	176.1	173	96	89	27	78	161
Peterson	4-7	4.56	.285	17	12	0	2	0	0	77.0	87	46	39	3	25	34
Weathers	7-4	4.65	.279	63	0	0	14	0	2	93.0	102	49	48	14	38	74
Karl	11-11	4.78	.312	33	33	0	0	0	0	197.2	246	121	105	21	69	74
Pittsley	0-1	4.82	.274	15	0	0	5	0	0	18.2	20	12	10	3	10	13
Plunk	4-4	5.02	.251	68	0	0	13	0	0	75.1	71	44	42	15	43	63
Myers	2-1	5.23	.291	71	0	0	14	0	0	41.1	46	24	24	7	13	35
Roque	1-6	5.34	.286	43	9	0	7	0	1	84.1	96	52	50	16	42	66
Pulsipher	5-6	5.98	.287	19	16	0	1	0	0	87.1	100	65	58	19	36	42
Bere	5-0	6.08	.302	17	14	0	0	0	0	66.2	79	52	45	9	50	47
De Los Santos	0-1	6.48	.343	7	0	0	3	0	0	8.1	12	6	6	1	7	5
Abbott	2-8	6.91	.317	20	15	0	3	0	0	82.0	110	71	63	14	42	37
Estrada	0-0	7.36	.313	4	0	0	2	0	0	7.1	10	6	6	4	4	5
Falteisek	0-0	7.50	.375	10	0	0	3	0	0	12.0	18	10	10	3	3	5
Eldred	2-8	7.79	.297	20	15	0	2	0	0	82.0	101	75	71	19	46	60
Fox	0-0	10.80	.355	6	0	0	2	0	0	6.2	11	8	8	1	4	12
Dale	0-1	20.25	.400	4	0	0	1	0	0	4.0	8	9	9	2	6	4

2000 preliminary roster

PITCHERS (21)
Jason Bere
Rocky Coppinger
Carl Dale
Jeff D'Amico
Valerio De Los Santos
Cal Eldred
Horacio Estrada
Chad Fox
Jose Garcia
Jimmy Haynes
Curtis Leskanic
Alen Levrault
Kyle Peterson
Bill Pulsipher
Hector Ramirez
Rafael Roque
Paul Stewart
Bob Wickman
Matt Williams
Steve Woodard
Jamey Wright

CATCHERS (3)
Henry Blanco
Robinson Cancel
Bobby Hughes

INFIELDERS (10)
Brian Banks
Kevin Barker
Ronnie Belliard
Sean Berry
Lou Collier
Jose Hernandez
Mark Loretta
Santiago Perez
Jose Valentin
Fernando Vina

OUTFIELDERS (6)
Jeromy Burnitz
Chad Green
Marquis Grissom
Geoff Jenkins
Lyle Mouton
Alex Ochoa

Games played by position

PLAYER	G	C	1B	2B	3B	SS	OF
Banks	105	40	44	0	0	0	5
Barker	38	0	31	0	0	0	0
Becker	89	0	0	0	0	0	50
Belliard	124	0	0	119	1	1	0
Berry	106	0	64	0	0	0	0
Burnitz	130	0	0	0	0	0	127
Cancel	15	15	0	0	0	0	0
Cirillo	157	0	0	0	155	0	0
Collier	74	0	0	4	7	31	10
Greene	32	31	0	0	0	0	0
Grissom	154	0	0	0	0	0	149
Hughes	48	44	0	0	0	0	0
Jenkins	135	0	0	0	0	0	128
Loretta	153	0	66	17	14	74	0
Mouton	14	0	0	0	0	0	3
Nilsson	115	101	0	0	0	0	0
Ochoa	119	0	0	0	0	0	85
Valentin	89	0	0	0	0	85	0
Vina	37	0	0	37	0	0	0
Zosky	8	0	0	2	4	0	0

Sick call: 1999 DL report

PLAYER	Days on the DL
Jeromy Burnitz	33
Jeff D'Amico	172
Valerio De Los Santos	156
Cal Eldred	60*
Chad Fox	166
Bobby Hughes	68*
Dave Nilsson	22
Bill Pulsipher	77
Jose Valentin	66
Fernando Vina	137*
Steve Woodard	29

* Indicates two separate terms on Disabled List.

Minor Leagues

Tops in the organization

BATTER	CLUB	AVG.	G	AB	R	H	HR	RBI
Sollmann, Scott	Hnt	.334	122	440	95	147	1	42
Pickler, Jeff	Hnt	.316	131	494	60	156	2	65
Mouton, Lyle	Lou	.310	127	467	89	145	23	94
Lopez, Mickey	Lou	.306	132	496	101	152	10	71
Darula, Bobby	Bel	.304	120	438	63	133	4	75

HOME RUNS
Kirby, Scott	Stk	27
Cromer, Brandon	Lou	24
Barker, Kevin	Lou	23
Mouton, Lyle	Lou	23
Hammond, Derry	Bel	17

WINS
Hawkins, Al	Hnt	11	
Mieses, Jose	Hel	10	
Stewart, Paul	Stk	10	
Levrault, Allen	Lou	10	
Beck, Greg	Hnt	10	

RBI
Mouton, Lyle	Lou	94
Krause, Scott	Lou	89
Cridland, Mark	Stk	87
Barker, Kevin	Lou	87
Kirby, Scott	Stk	83

SAVES
Harris, Reggie	Lou	16
Mosher, Andy	Hel	12
Ramirez, Hector	Lou	9
Poe, Ryan	Bel	9
Schubmehl, Brian	Stk	9

STOLEN BASES
Martinez, Greg	Lou	56
Sollmann, Scott	Hnt	49
Knox, Ryan	Hel	44
Lopez, Mickey	Lou	42
Azuaje, Jesus	Hnt	34

STRIKEOUTS
Johnson, James	Stk	135
Neugebauer, N.	Bel	125
Stewart, Paul	Stk	117
Levrault, Allen	Lou	115
Estrada, Horacio	Lou	112

PITCHER
PITCHER	CLUB	W-L	ERA	IP	H	BB	SO
Mieses, Jose	Hel	10-2	2.67	108	79	28	87
Peterson, Kyle	Lou	7-6	3.55	109	90	42	95
Poe, Ryan	Bel	6-10	3.56	96	94	16	108
Lee, Derek	Hnt	8-8	3.86	140	143	51	77
Stewart, Paul	Stk	10-11	3.96	170	171	61	117

1999 salaries

	Bonuses	Total earned salary
Dave Nilsson, c		5,694,133
Marquis Grissom, of		5,000,000
Cal Eldred, p		4,766,667
Jeromy Burnitz, of		3,612,500
Bob Wickman, p	1,100,000	3,300,000
Jose Valentin, ss		3,036,095
Jeff Cirillo, 3b		3,000,000
Scott Karl, p	100,000	2,900,000
Fernando Vina, 2b		2,000,000
Eric Plunk, p	50,000	1,850,000
Mark Loretta, ss		1,495,000
Sean Berry, 1b		1,050,000
Mike Myers, p		800,000
David Weathers, p	30,000	405,000
Steve Woodard, p		270,000
Bill Pulsipher, p		257,500
Chad Fox, p		255,000
Hideo Nomo, p		250,000
Alex Ochoa, of		245,000
Jeff D'Amico, p	7,500	242,500
Rocky Coppinger, p		220,000
Bobby Hughes, c		217,000
Geoff Jenkins, of		216,000
Lou Collier, ss		215,000
Rafael Roque, p		212,000
Valerio De Los Santos, p		210,000
Charlie Greene, c		205,000
Brian Banks, 1b		203,000
Hector Ramirez, p		200,000
Ron Belliard, 2b		200,000
Kevin Barker, 1b		200,000
Kyle Peterson, p		200,000

Average 1999 salary: $1,341,481
Total 1999 team payroll: $42,927,395
Termination pay: $49,180

283

Milwaukee NL (1998-1999), includes Milwaukee AL (1970-97) and Seattle AL (1969)

Runs: Most, career

1632	Robin Yount, 1974-1993
1275	Paul Molitor, 1978-1992
821	Cecil Cooper, 1977-1987
726	Jim Gantner, 1976-1992
596	Don Money, 1973-1983

Hits: Most, career

3142	Robin Yount, 1974-1993
2281	Paul Molitor, 1978-1992
1815	Cecil Cooper, 1977-1987
1696	Jim Gantner, 1976-1992
1168	Don Money, 1973-1983

2B: Most, career

583	Robin Yount, 1974-1993
405	Paul Molitor, 1978-1992
345	Cecil Cooper, 1977-1987
262	Jim Gantner, 1976-1992
215	Don Money, 1973-1983

3B: Most, career

126	Robin Yount, 1974-1993
86	Paul Molitor, 1978-1992
42	Charlie Moore, 1973-1986
38	Jim Gantner, 1976-1992
33	Cecil Cooper, 1977-1987

HR: Most, career

251	Robin Yount, 1974-1993
208	Gorman Thomas, 1973-1986
201	Cecil Cooper, 1977-1987
176	Ben Oglivie, 1978-1986
169	GREG VAUGHN, 1989-1996

RBI: Most, career

1406	Robin Yount, 1974-1993
944	Cecil Cooper, 1977-1987
790	Paul Molitor, 1978-1992
685	Ben Oglivie, 1978-1986
605	Gorman Thomas, 1973-1986

SB: Most, career

412	Paul Molitor, 1978-1992
271	Robin Yount, 1974-1993
137	Jim Gantner, 1976-1992
136	Tommy Harper, 1969-1971
112	Pat Listach, 1992-1996

BB: Most, career

966	Robin Yount, 1974-1993
755	Paul Molitor, 1978-1992
501	Gorman Thomas, 1973-1986
440	Don Money, 1973-1983
432	Ben Oglivie, 1978-1986

BA: Highest, career

.307	JEFF CIRILLO, 1994-1999
.303	Paul Molitor, 1978-1992
.302	Cecil Cooper, 1977-1987
.300	Kevin Seitzer, 1992-1996
.294	MARK LORETTA, 1995-1999

On-base avg: Highest, career

.385	JEFF CIRILLO, 1994-1999
.376	Kevin Seitzer, 1992-1996
.367	Paul Molitor, 1978-1992
.361	JOHN JAHA, 1992-1998
.359	MARK LORETTA, 1995-1999

Slug pct: Highest, career

.470	Cecil Cooper, 1977-1987
.463	JOHN JAHA, 1992-1998
.461	Gorman Thomas, 1973-1986
.461	Ben Oglivie, 1978-1986
.461	DAVE NILSSON, 1992-1999

Games started: Most, career

268	Jim Slaton, 1971-1983
231	Moose Haas, 1976-1985
217	Mike Caldwell, 1977-1984
216	Bill Wegman, 1985-1995
205	Teddy Higuera, 1985-1994

Complete games: Most, career

81	Mike Caldwell, 1977-1984
69	Jim Slaton, 1971-1983
55	Moose Haas, 1976-1985
51	Jim Colborn, 1972-1976
50	Teddy Higuera, 1985-1994
50	Lary Sorensen, 1977-1980

Saves: Most, career

133	DAN PLESAC, 1986-1992
97	Rollie Fingers, 1981-1985
79	MIKE FETTERS, 1992-1997
63	BOB WICKMAN, 1996-1999
61	DOUG HENRY, 1991-1994
61	Ken Sanders, 1970-1972

Shutouts: Most, career

19	Jim Slaton, 1971-1983
18	Mike Caldwell, 1977-1984
12	Teddy Higuera, 1985-1994
10	Bill Travers, 1974-1980
8	Chris Bosio, 1986-1992
8	Moose Haas, 1976-1985

Wins: Most, career

117	Jim Slaton, 1971-1983
102	Mike Caldwell, 1977-1984
94	Teddy Higuera, 1985-1994
91	Moose Haas, 1976-1985
81	Bill Wegman, 1985-1995

K: Most, career

1081	Teddy Higuera, 1985-1994
929	Jim Slaton, 1971-1983
800	Moose Haas, 1976-1985
749	Chris Bosio, 1986-1992
696	Bill Wegman, 1985-1995

Win pct: Highest, career

.606	Pete Vuckovich, 1981-1986
.595	Teddy Higuera, 1985-1994
.560	Mike Caldwell, 1977-1984
.535	Moose Haas, 1976-1985
.531	Lary Sorensen, 1977-1980

ERA: Lowest, career

3.61	Teddy Higuera, 1985-1994
3.65	Jim Colborn, 1972-1976
3.72	Lary Sorensen, 1977-1980
3.74	Mike Caldwell, 1977-1984
3.76	Chris Bosio, 1986-1992

Runs: Most, season

136	Paul Molitor, 1982
133	Paul Molitor, 1991
129	Robin Yount, 1982
121	Robin Yount, 1980
115	Paul Molitor, 1988

Hits: Most, season

219	Cecil Cooper, 1980
216	Paul Molitor, 1991
210	Robin Yount, 1982
205	Cecil Cooper, 1982
203	Cecil Cooper, 1983

2B: Most, season

49	Robin Yount, 1980
46	Robin Yount, 1982
46	JEFF CIRILLO, 1996
46	JEFF CIRILLO, 1997
44	Cecil Cooper, 1979

3B: Most, season

16	Paul Molitor, 1979
13	Paul Molitor, 1991
12	Robin Yount, 1982
11	Robin Yount, 1988
10	Robin Yount, 1980
10	Robin Yount, 1983
10	FERNANDO VINA, 1996

HR: Most, season

45	Gorman Thomas, 1979
41	Ben Oglivie, 1980
39	Gorman Thomas, 1982
38	JEROMY BURNITZ, 1998
38	Gorman Thomas, 1980

RBI: Most, season

126	Cecil Cooper, 1983
125	JEROMY BURNITZ, 1998
123	Gorman Thomas, 1979
122	Cecil Cooper, 1980
121	Cecil Cooper, 1982

SB: Most, season

73	Tommy Harper, 1969
54	Pat Listach, 1992
45	Paul Molitor, 1987
41	DARRYL HAMILTON, 1992
41	Paul Molitor, 1982
41	Paul Molitor, 1983
41	Paul Molitor, 1988

BB: Most, season

98	Gorman Thomas, 1979
95	Tommy Harper, 1969
91	JEROMY BURNITZ, 1999
89	Darrell Porter, 1975
89	GREG VAUGHN, 1993

BA: Highest, season

.353	Paul Molitor, 1987
.352	Cecil Cooper, 1980
.331	DAVE NILSSON, 1996
.331	Robin Yount, 1982
.327	Willie Randolph, 1991

On-base avg; Highest, season

.438	Paul Molitor, 1987
.424	Willie Randolph, 1991
.414	Sixto Lezcano, 1979
.407	DAVE NILSSON, 1996
.406	Kevin Seitzer, 1996

Slug pct: Highest, season

.578	Robin Yount, 1982
.573	Sixto Lezcano, 1979
.566	Paul Molitor, 1987
.563	Ben Oglivie, 1980
.561	JEROMY BURNITZ, 1999

Games started: Most, season

38	Jim Slaton, 1973
38	Jim Slaton, 1976
36	Marty Pattin, 1971
36	Jim Colborn, 1973
36	Lary Sorensen, 1978
36	CAL ELDRED, 1993

Complete games: Most, season

23	Mike Caldwell, 1978
22	Jim Colborn, 1973
17	Lary Sorensen, 1978
16	Mike Caldwell, 1979
16	Lary Sorensen, 1979

Saves: Most, season

37	BOB WICKMAN, 1999
36	DOUG JONES, 1997
33	DAN PLESAC, 1989
32	MIKE FETTERS, 1996
31	Ken Sanders, 1971

Shutouts: Most, season

6	Mike Caldwell, 1978
5	Marty Pattin, 1971
4	Bill Parsons, 1971
4	Jim Slaton, 1971
4	Jim Colborn, 1973
4	Mike Caldwell, 1979
4	Teddy Higuera, 1986

Wins: Most, season

22	Mike Caldwell, 1978
20	Jim Colborn, 1973
20	Teddy Higuera, 1986
18	Lary Sorensen, 1978
18	Pete Vuckovich, 1982
18	Teddy Higuera, 1987

K: Most, season

240	Teddy Higuera, 1987
207	Teddy Higuera, 1986
192	Teddy Higuera, 1988
180	CAL ELDRED, 1993
173	Chris Bosio, 1989

Win pct: Highest, season

.750	Pete Vuckovich, 1982
.727	Mike Caldwell, 1979
.727	Chris Bosio, 1992
.710	Mike Caldwell, 1978
.682	Bill Wegman, 1991

ERA: Lowest, season

2.36	Mike Caldwell, 1978
2.45	Teddy Higuera, 1988
2.79	Teddy Higuera, 1986
2.81	Bill Travers, 1976
2.83	Jim Lonborg, 1972

Most pinch-hit homers, season

4	Bob Hamelin, 1998

Most pinch-hit homers, career

4	Bob Hamelin, 1998
3	MATT MIESKE, 1993-1997

Longest hitting streak

39	Paul Molitor, 1987
24	Dave May, 1973
22	Cecil Cooper, 1980
19	Paul Molitor, 1989
19	Robin Yount, 1989
19	Paul Molitor, 1990
19	DARRYL HAMILTON, 1991

Most consecutive scoreless innings

32	Ted Higuera, 1987

No-hit games

Jim Wilson, Mil vs Phi NL, 2-0; June 12, 1954.

Lew Burdette, Mil vs Phi NL, 1-0; August 18, 1960.

Warren Spahn, Mil vs Phi NL, 4-0; September 16, 1960.

Warren Spahn, Mil vs SF NL, 1-0; April 28, 1961.

MAJOR LEAGUE REPORT

MILWAUKEE BREWERS / NL CENTRAL

By Anne Ryan, *USA TODAY*

Cubs fans packed Wrigley Field to see Sammy Sosa hit 60-plus homers for the second year in a row.

1999 Cubs: 'A season that hurt your soul'

Sammy Sosa's second consecutive season of slugging more than 60 homers wasn't enough to keep the Chicago Cubs from sinking out of sight in the National League. Coming just one year after they had won 90 games and gone to the playoffs, the Cubs' collapse was startling, even for a team that hasn't been to the World Series in 54 years. Over the final 2½ months, they won just 21 games, making a quick and emphatic plunge to the basement and finishing at 67-95.

"It was a season that hurt your soul," first baseman Mark Grace said. And one that cost Cubs' manager Jim Riggleman his job. "It was our fault," Grace said. "He just didn't have the horses."

The Cubs did some major housecleaning, opting for younger players such as Chad Meyers at second base and error-prone Jose Nieves at shortstop, and saying goodbye to veterans Gary Gaetti, Jeff Blauser, and Mickey Morandini, who faded after helping the team win the wild card in 1998.

The season was the Cubs' worst since 1980—not counting the strike years of 1981 and 1994. Their pitching staff allowed the most homers in club history (221), their team ERA was 5.27, they had their worst home record (35-46) in 25 years and they had a 26-51 mark after the All-Star break.

Thanks mostly to Sosa, though, the Cubs set a Wrigley Field attendance record, drawing 2.81 million fans.

The debacle began when Kerry Wood's elbow went pop in his first spring training appearance, causing the 1998 NL Rookie of the Year to undergo reconstructive surgery. The pitching staff never recovered.

Kevin Tapani, a 19-game winner in 1998, was hampered by injuries all season and finished on the DL with just six wins.

Jon Lieber, acquired from Pittsburgh before the season for outfielder Brant Brown, won only two games after the All-Star break, though he lost several chances when the bullpen faltered. He pitched well in his final three starts to finish 10-11 for the most wins on the staff.

Team MVP

Sammy Sosa: The Cubs' top slugger carried on another thrilling home run race with Mark McGwire, keeping the Wrigley Field fans enthralled long after they had given up on the team's fortunes. Sosa led the homer race much of the year and became the first player to hit 60 or more in two seasons, even though his total of 63 was two behind McGwire. Sosa led the majors with 397 total bases and drove in 141 runs.

The bullpen was a major problem. Beck struggled before elbow surgery, Rick Aguilera came over from Minnesota but spent time on the DL, and Terry Adams and Felix Heredia were inconsistent.

Nevertheless, the Cubs were second in early June before the cross-town White Sox came to Wrigley and pulled off a three-game sweep. The Cubs went from nine games above .500 on June 9 to 28 under at season's end.

Sosa kept swinging, challenging Mark McGwire for the home-run title for a second straight season and becoming the first player in major league history to reach 60 homers twice. He finished with 63, two behind McGwire.

Grace batted .300 for the ninth time in his career and finished the 1990s with 1,754 hits, the most in the majors. Henry Rodriguez had a strong season with 26 homers before being slowed for a second year in a row with injuries.

Once the Cubs were out of contention, reliever Rod Beck was shipped to the Red Sox, catcher Tyler Houston to the Indians, and shortstop Jose Hernandez and pitcher Terry Mulholland to the Braves. Riggleman kept his composure for the most part, but it was just a matter of time until Braves' coach Don Baylor was hired as the Cubs' new manager.

1999 Cubs: Week-by-week notes

These notes were excerpted from the following issues of Baseball Weekly.

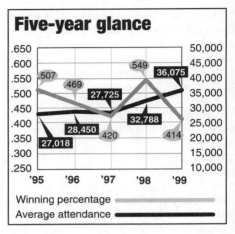

Five-year glance

Winning percentage
Average attendance

▶**April 14:** The Cubs insisted their offense was more than right fielder Sammy Sosa, but they scored only 17 runs in their first five games. (Sosa had only one hit.) Nine of the runs came in one game in Houston, so the Cubs averaged two runs in each of the other games.

▶**April 21:** Already weakened in starting pitching, the Cubs lost No. 1 starter Kevin Tapani for up to two weeks with shoulder soreness. They were scrambling for replacements. The original rotation involved right-handers Jon Lieber, Tapani, Steve Trachsel, Kerry Wood and left-hander Terry Mulholland. Wood was gone for the season with elbow surgery, and Mulholland was moved to help a weakened bullpen.

▶**May 12:** Management vowed a crackdown on rowdy Wrigley Field "bleacher bums" who litter the field. Play had to be halted on consecutive days while a cleanup crew removed debris that included liquor bottles and baseballs. Seventy-five fans were ejected on May 3.

▶**May 19:** When Jon Lieber threw his first shutout, on May 14, it was the first complete game by a Cub in 99 games, dating back to Mark Clark's on July 18, 1998. Manager Jim Riggleman reiterated that he was sticking with closer Rod Beck, even though he had blown four of 11 save chances.

▶**May 26:** With Rod Beck out for as much as 12 weeks, the Cubs would be using their fifth closer in five years after acquiring Rick Aguilera from the Twins. Terry Adams would be the main setup man for Aguilera, with Terry Mulholland rejoining the rotation.

▶**June 2:** Last June, Sammy Sosa hit 20 home runs, a record for a single month. This year he heated up in May by hitting 13 homers in 22 games, putting him ahead of his pace that produced 66 last season.

▶**June 16:** With center fielder Lance Johnson hurting again, the Cubs experimented with their "offensive outfield" of Henry Rodriguez in left, Sammy Sosa in center and Glenallen Hill in right. Jim Riggleman admitted that it is just average defensively.

▶**June 23:** All starting pitchers were struggling, the most noticeable being right-handed rookie Kyle Farnsworth, who lasted only 3⅓ innings on June 19 in San Francisco and who hadn't won in seven starts since May 11. Terry Mulholland had not won since May 23, and Steve Trachsel became the first NL pitcher to lose nine games.

▶**June 30:** Controversial No. 1 draft choice Ben Christensen was signed for what was believed to be $1 million and immediately said he was "sorry about everything's that happened. If I could take it back, I definitely would." As a pitcher for Wichita State, Christensen hit Evansville's Andy Molina in the on-deck circle during warmup pitches. Molina had to have eye surgery, and Christensen was suspended for the rest of his college career. Molina continued to have vision problems.

▶**July 7:** By the time Cubs pitchers had allowed the opposition double-digit runs in nine of 16 games and their ERA had risen to 5.65, the team found itself tied for last.

▶**July 21:** Kyle Farnsworth returned from Iowa as a reliever less than a month after being demoted from the Cubs' rotation

with a 2-3 record and 7.58 ERA. In his first appearance back, on July 17, he pitched six scoreless innings in relief.

▶**July 28:** First baseman Mark Grace, 35, would be a free agent after the season but said he wants to finish his career as a Cub. With 10/5 privileges that give him the right to veto any trade, Grace said it would take a two-year contract extension to sign him.

▶**Aug. 4:** The Cubs' youth movement began at the trading deadline with the acquisition of two pitchers from the Braves—left-hander Micah Bowie, 24, and right-hander Ruben Quevedo, 20—plus a player to be named. The Cubs dealt shortstop Jose Hernandez, 30, and Terry Mulholland, 36, to Atlanta.

▶**Aug. 11:** The promotion of Andrew Lorraine led to a pleasant pitching surprise. He pitched a three-hit shutout against the Astros on Aug. 6. Now with his fifth team, Lorraine, 26, threw the Cubs' first shutout by a lefty since Jamie Moyer did so in '88.

▶**Aug. 18:** Sammy Sosa reached the 100-RBI mark for the fifth consecutive year, tying Hack Wilson's club record set from 1926 to '30.

▶**Aug. 25:** Jim Riggleman would be with the Cubs through at least the end of the season, according to general manager Ed Lynch, who gave his endorsement on a day when the Cubs had lost 11 of 12 games and 22 of their last 27. The Cubs were one game behind Houston in the NL Central on June 8, with a 32-23 record. Their record of 20-47 from then through Aug. 22 is the worst in baseball.

▶**Sept. 1:** The team's previous worst record for August was 8-21 in 1921, but the Cubs were 5-22 this month with only three games remaining. Things became so bad that Sammy Sosa had the same number of home runs (53) as his team had victories. No player has ever had more homers than his team had victories.

▶**Sept. 22:** Sammy Sosa's 60th home run—and his 61st on Sept. 19—might have overshadowed it, but Sosa was responsible for the Cubs' first back-to-back victories in nearly two months. Sosa had a ninth-inning, game-winning double against Cincinnati on Sept. 16, then hit a 10th-inning sacrifice fly the next day against Milwaukee.

▶**Oct. 6:** For only the sixth time in their 124-year history—but the second in the past three years—the Cubs finished with 94 or more losses. Ed Lynch promised to upgrade the defense and get help for the pitching staff.

QUOTE OF THE YEAR

"In our minds he's an outstanding young man."
—GM Ed Lynch, on first-round draft choice Ben Christensen, who badly injured an opposing batter in college by beaning him while the batter stood in the on-deck circle

Team Leaders

Batting avg.	Hits	Wins	Strikeouts
.309 Mark Grace	183 Mark Grace	10 Jon Lieber	186 Jon Lieber
.304 Henry Rodriguez	180 Sammy Sosa	8 Steve Trachsel	149 Steve Trachsel

HR	Runs	Losses	Innings
63 Sammy Sosa	114 Sammy Sosa	18 Steve Trachsel	205.2 Steve Trachsel
26 Henry Rodriguez	107 Mark Grace	12 Kevin Tapani	203.1 Jon Lieber

RBI	Stolen bases	ERA	Saves
141 Sammy Sosa	13 Lance Johnson	4.07 Jon Lieber	13 Terry Adams
91 Mark Grace	7 Sammy Sosa	5.56 Steve Trachsel	8 Rick Aguilera

CHICAGO CUBS 1999 final stats

BATTERS	BA	SLG	OBA	G	AB	R	H	TB	2B	3B	HR	RBI	BB	SO	SB	CS	E
Grace	.309	.481	.390	161	593	107	183	285	44	5	16	91	83	44	3	4	8
Rodriguez	.304	.544	.381	130	447	72	136	243	29	0	26	87	56	113	2	4	6
Hill	.300	.581	.353	99	253	43	76	147	9	1	20	55	22	61	5	1	4
Sosa	.288	.635	.367	162	625	114	180	397	24	2	63	141	78	171	7	8	9
Alexander	.271	.356	.309	90	177	17	48	63	11	2	0	15	10	38	4	0	7
Molina	.263	.316	.333	10	19	3	5	6	1	0	0	1	2	4	0	0	0
Johnson	.260	.337	.332	95	335	46	87	113	11	6	1	21	37	20	13	3	3
Reed	.258	.371	.373	103	256	29	66	95	16	2	3	28	45	58	1	2	7
Nieves	.249	.343	.291	54	181	16	45	62	9	1	2	18	8	25	0	2	16
Santiago	.249	.377	.313	109	350	28	87	132	18	3	7	36	32	71	1	1	6
Goodwin	.242	.293	.298	89	157	15	38	46	6	1	0	9	13	38	2	4	2
Liniak	.241	.310	.267	12	29	3	7	9	2	0	0	2	1	4	0	1	0
Morandini	.241	.329	.319	144	456	60	110	150	18	5	4	37	48	61	6	6	5
Blauser	.240	.420	.347	104	200	41	48	84	5	2	9	26	26	52	2	2	7
Houston	.233	.386	.309	100	249	26	58	96	9	1	9	27	28	67	1	1	17
Meyers	.232	.296	.292	43	142	17	33	42	9	0	0	4	9	27	4	2	2
Brown	.219	.391	.239	33	64	6	14	25	6	1	1	10	2	14	1	0	1
Gaetti	.204	.339	.260	113	280	22	57	95	9	1	9	46	21	51	0	1	9
Jennings	.200	.200	.200	5	5	0	1	1	0	0	0	0	0	2	0	0	0
Andrews	.195	.368	.295	117	348	41	68	128	12	0	16	51	50	109	1	1	16
Porter	.192	.231	.250	24	26	2	5	6	1	0	0	0	2	13	0	0	1
Martinez	.167	.267	.167	17	30	1	5	8	0	0	1	1	0	11	0	0	2

PITCHERS	W-L	ERA	BA	G	GS	CG	GF	SH	SV	IP	H	R	ER	HR	BB	SO
Karchner	1-0	2.50	.235	16	0	0	2	0	0	18.0	16	5	5	3	9	9
Ayala	1-7	3.51	.228	66	0	0	21	0	0	82.0	71	43	32	10	39	79
Guthrie	0-2	3.65	.171	11	0	0	0	0	0	12.1	7	6	5	1	4	9
Aguilera	6-3	3.69	.254	44	0	0	25	0	8	46.1	44	22	19	6	10	32
Adams	6-3	4.02	.245	52	0	0	38	0	13	65.0	60	33	29	9	28	57
Lieber	10-11	4.07	.279	31	31	3	0	1	0	203.1	226	107	92	28	46	186
Myers	3-1	4.38	.289	46	0	0	5	0	0	63.2	71	34	31	10	25	41
Tapani	6-12	4.83	.280	23	23	1	0	0	0	136.0	151	81	73	12	33	73
Heredia	3-1	4.85	.272	69	0	0	15	0	1	52.0	56	35	28	7	25	50
Farnsworth	5-9	5.05	.271	27	21	1	1	1	0	130.0	140	80	73	28	52	70
Sanders	4-7	5.52	.277	67	6	0	16	0	2	104.1	112	69	64	19	53	89
Lorraine	2-5	5.55	.293	11	11	2	0	1	0	61.2	71	42	38	9	22	40
Trachsel	8-18	5.56	.280	34	34	4	0	0	0	205.2	226	133	127	32	64	149
Woodall	0-1	5.63	.270	6	3	0	3	0	0	16.0	17	12	10	5	6	7
King	0-0	5.91	.289	10	0	0	0	0	0	10.2	11	8	7	2	10	5
McNichol	0-2	6.75	.333	4	2	0	1	0	0	10.2	15	8	8	4	7	12
Serafini	3-2	6.93	.333	42	4	0	8	0	1	62.1	86	51	48	9	32	17
Barker	0-0	7.20	.300	5	0	0	1	0	0	5.0	6	4	4	0	4	3
Beck	2-4	7.80	.331	31	0	0	19	0	7	30.0	41	26	26	5	13	13
Rain	0-1	9.20	.418	16	0	0	5	0	0	14.2	28	17	15	1	7	12
Bowie	2-7	10.24	.363	14	11	0	2	0	0	51.0	81	60	58	9	34	41
Creek	0-0	10.50	.261	3	0	0	2	0	0	6.0	6	7	7	1	8	6
Gaetti	0-0	18.00	.400	1	0	0	1	0	0	1.0	2	2	2	1	1	1
Miller	0-0	18.00	.462	4	0	0	1	0	0	3.0	6	6	6	1	3	1

2000 preliminary roster

PITCHERS (24)
Rick Aguilera
Micah Bowie
Scott Downs
Kyle Farnsworth
Chris Gissell
Jeremi Gonzalez
Mark Guthrie
Felix Heredia
Matt Karchner
Ray King
Jon Lieber
Andrew Lorraine
Brian McNichol

Mike Meyers
Rodney Myers
Phillip Norton
Ruben Quevedo
Steve Rain
Scott Sanders
Dan Serafini
Kevin Tapani
Ismael Valdes
Kerry Wood
Danny Young

CATCHERS (4)
Pat Cline
Joe Girardi
Jose Molina
Jeff Reed

INFIELDERS (7)
Shane Andrews
Mark Grace
Cole Liniak
Chad Meyers
Jose Nieves
Eric Young
Julio Zuleta

OUTFIELDERS (5)
Roosevelt Brown
Damon Buford
Glenallen Hill
Henry Rodriguez
Sammy Sosa

Games played by position

PLAYER	G	C	1B	2B	3B	SS	OF
Alexander	90	0	0	17	22	30	2
Andrews	19	0	1	0	19	0	0
Blauser	104	0	0	25	18	22	1
Brown	33	0	0	0	0	0	18
Gaetti	113	0	8	0	81	1	0
Goodwin	89	0	0	0	0	0	76
Grace	161	0	160	0	0	0	0
Hernandez	99	0	1	0	0	92	20
Hill	99	0	0	0	0	0	62
Houston	100	18	2	0	63	0	1
Jennings	5	0	0	0	0	0	0
Johnson	95	0	0	0	0	0	91
Liniak	12	0	0	0	10	0	0
Martinez	17	12	0	0	0	0	0
Meyers	43	0	0	32	0	0	14
Molina	10	10	0	0	0	0	0
Morandini	144	0	0	132	0	0	0
Nieves	54	0	0	0	0	52	0
Porter	24	0	0	0	0	0	21
Reed	57	49	0	0	1	0	0
Rodriguez	130	0	0	0	0	0	122
Santiago	109	107	1	0	0	0	0
Sosa	162	0	0	0	0	0	162

Minor Leagues

Tops in the organization

BATTER	CLUB	AVG.	G	AB	R	H	HR	RBI
Brown, R.	low	.338	108	393	62	133	25	91
Choi, Hee	Lan	.321	79	290	71	93	18	70
Patterson, Corey	Lan	.320	112	475	94	152	20	79
Meyers, Chad	low	.317	108	413	84	131	3	45
Jennings, Robin	low	.311	80	312	58	97	14	60

HOME RUNS			WINS			
Porter, Bo	low	27	Meyers, Mike	WTn	14
Brown, R.	low	25	Zambrano, Carlos	Lan	13
Zuleta, Julio	WTn	21	Downs, Scott	WTn	13
Hinske, Eric	low	20	Norton, Phillip	low	12
Patterson, Corey	Lan	20	Wuertz, Mike	Lan	11

RBI			SAVES			
Zuleta, Julio	WTn	97	Rain, Steve	low	26
Brown, R.	low	91	Dant, Larry	Lan	12
Hinske, Eric	low	81	Gajkowski, Steve	low	9
Patterson, Corey	Lan	79	Fisher, Louis	Day	9
Nelson, Bry	WTn	78	Several Players Tied at		8

STOLEN BASES			STRIKEOUTS			
Meyers, Chad	low	39	Meyers, Mike	WTn	173
Patterson, Corey	Lan	33	Downs, Scott	WTn	151
Wilson, Brandon	low	31	Norton, Phillip	low	142
Abreu, Dennis	Day	29	Creek, Doug	low	140
Randolph, Jaisen	Day	25	Wuertz, Mike	Lan	127

PITCHER	CLUB	W-L	ERA	IP	H	BB	SO
Downs, Scott	WTn	13-2	1.44	138	104	45	151
Meyers, Mike	WTn	14-3	1.73	140	89	50	173
Yoder, Jeff	WTn	10-5	2.92	145	123	75	120
Palma, Ricardo	Lan	7-7	2.94	135	134	44	79
Ohman, Will	Day	4-7	3.46	107	102	41	97

Sick call: 1999 DL report

PLAYER	Days on the DL
Terry Adams	48*
Rick Aguilera	24
Rod Beck	65
Jeremi Gonzalez	87
Glenallen Hill	15
Robin Jennings	77
Lance Johnson	72
Matt Karchner	138*
Jon Lieber	17
Sandy Martinez	28
Kurt Miller	45*
Kevin Tapani	48*
Kerry Wood	182

Indicates two separate terms on Disabled List.

1999 salaries

	Bonuses	Total earned salary
Sammy Sosa, of		9,000,000
Steve Trachsel, p	100,000	5,250,000
Lance Johnson, of		5,100,000
Rick Aguilera, p	300,000	4,300,000
Jeff Blauser, 2b		4,200,000
Mark Grace, 1b		4,100,000
Henry Rodriguez, of		3,700,000
Kevin Tapani, p		3,500,000
Jon Lieber, p		2,100,000
Gary Gaetti, 3b		2,000,000
Mickey Morandini, 2b		2,000,000
Benito Santiago, c	200,000	1,700,000
Mark Guthrie, p		1,600,000
Glenallen Hill, of		1,150,000
Scott Sanders, p	225,000	825,000
Matt Karchner, p		776,000
Terry Adams, p		736,000
Kerry Wood, p		690,000
Manny Alexander, ss		475,000
Felix Heredia, p		275,000
Jeremi Gonzalez, p		265,000
Andrew Lorraine, p		220,000
Rodney Myers, p		205,000
Jose Nieves, ss		201,500
Jeff Reed, c		200,000
Jose Molina, c		200,000
Micah Bowie, p		200,000
Kyle Farnsworth, p		200,000
Chad Meyers, 2b		200,000

Average 1999 salary: $1,909,259
Total 1999 team payroll: $55,368,500
Termination pay: $51,148

Chicago (1876-1999)

Runs: Most, career

1719	Cap Anson, 1876-1897
1409	Jimmy Ryan, 1885-1900
1316	Ryne Sandberg, 1982-1997
1306	Billy Williams, 1959-1974
1305	Ernie Banks, 1953-1971

Hits: Most, career

2995	Cap Anson, 1876-1897
2583	Ernie Banks, 1953-1971
2510	Billy Williams, 1959-1974
2385	Ryne Sandberg, 1982-1997
2193	Stan Hack, 1932-1947

2B: Most, career

528	Cap Anson, 1876-1897
415	MARK GRACE, 1988-1999
407	Ernie Banks, 1953-1971
403	Ryne Sandberg, 1982-1997
402	Billy Williams, 1959-1974

3B: Most, career

142	Jimmy Ryan, 1885-1900
124	Cap Anson, 1876-1897
117	Frank Schulte, 1904-1916
106	Bill Dahlen, 1891-1898
99	Phil Cavarretta, 1934-1953

HR: Most, career

512	Ernie Banks, 1953-1971
392	Billy Williams, 1959-1974
337	Ron Santo, 1960-1973
307	SAMMY SOSA, 1992-1999
282	Ryne Sandberg, 1982-1997

RBI: Most, career

1879	Cap Anson, 1876-1897
1636	Ernie Banks, 1953-1971
1353	Billy Williams, 1959-1974
1290	Ron Santo, 1960-1973
1153	Gabby Hartnett, 1922-1940

SB: Most, career

400	Frank Chance, 1898-1912
399	Bill Lange, 1893-1899
369	Jimmy Ryan, 1885-1900
344	Ryne Sandberg, 1982-1997
304	Joe Tinker, 1902-1916

BB: Most, career

1092	Stan Hack, 1932-1947
1071	Ron Santo, 1960-1973
952	Cap Anson, 1876-1897
911	Billy Williams, 1959-1974
851	MARK GRACE, 1988-1999

BA: Highest, career

.336	Riggs Stephenson, 1926-1934
.330	Bill Lange, 1893-1899
.329	Cap Anson, 1876-1897
.325	Kiki Cuyler, 1928-1935
.323	Bill Everitt, 1895-1900

On-base avg: Highest, career

.412	Hack Wilson, 1926-1931
.408	Riggs Stephenson, 1926-1934
.401	Bill Lange, 1893-1899
.395	Cap Anson, 1876-1897
.394	Stan Hack, 1932-1947

Slug pct: Highest, career

.590	Hack Wilson, 1926-1931
.542	SAMMY SOSA, 1992-1999
.512	Hank Sauer, 1949-1955
.507	Andre Dawson, 1987-1992
.503	Billy Williams, 1959-1974

Games started: Most, career

347	Fergie Jenkins, 1966-1983
343	Rick Reuschel, 1972-1984
340	Charlie Root, 1926-1941
339	Bill Hutchison, 1889-1895
297	Bill Lee, 1934-1947

Complete games: Most, career

317	Bill Hutchison, 1889-1895
252	Larry Corcoran, 1880-1885
240	Clark Griffith, 1893-1900
206	Mordecai Brown, 1904-1916
188	Jack Taylor, 1898-1907

Saves: Most, career

180	Lee Smith, 1980-1987
133	Bruce Sutter, 1976-1980
112	Randy Myers, 1993-1995
63	Don Elston, 1953-1964
60	Phil Regan, 1968-1972

Shutouts: Most, career

48	Mordecai Brown, 1904-1916
35	Hippo Vaughn, 1913-1921
31	Ed Reulbach, 1905-1913
29	Fergie Jenkins, 1966-1983
28	Orval Overall, 1906-1913

Wins: Most, career

201	Charlie Root, 1926-1941
188	Mordecai Brown, 1904-1916
181	Bill Hutchison, 1889-1895
175	Larry Corcoran, 1880-1885
167	Fergie Jenkins, 1966-1983

K: Most, career

2038	Fergie Jenkins, 1966-1983
1432	Charlie Root, 1926-1941
1367	Rick Reuschel, 1972-1984
1224	Bill Hutchison, 1889-1895
1138	Hippo Vaughn, 1913-1921

Win pct: Highest, career

.800	Al Spalding, 1876-1878
.773	Jim McCormick, 1885-1886
.706	John Clarkson, 1884-1887
.686	Mordecai Brown, 1904-1916
.677	Ed Reulbach, 1905-1913

ERA: Lowest, career

1.80	Mordecai Brown, 1904-1916
1.85	Jack Pfiester, 1906-1911
1.91	Orval Overall, 1906-1913
2.14	Jake Weimer, 1903-1905
2.24	Ed Reulbach, 1905-1913

Runs: Most, season

156	Rogers Hornsby, 1929
155	Kiki Cuyler, 1930
155	King Kelly, 1886
152	Woody English, 1930
150	George Gore, 1886

Hits: Most, season

229	Rogers Hornsby, 1929
228	Kiki Cuyler, 1930
227	Billy Herman, 1935
214	Woody English, 1930
212	Frank Demaree, 1936

2B: Most, season

57	Billy Herman, 1935
57	Billy Herman, 1936
51	MARK GRACE, 1995
50	Kiki Cuyler, 1930
49	Riggs Stephenson, 1932
49	Ned Williamson, 1883

3B: Most, season

21	Vic Saier, 1913
21	Frank Schulte, 1911
19	Bill Dahlen, 1892
19	Bill Dahlen, 1896
19	Ryne Sandberg, 1984

HR: Most, season

66	SAMMY SOSA, 1998
63	SAMMY SOSA, 1999
56	Hack Wilson, 1930
49	Andre Dawson, 1987
48	Dave Kingman, 1979

RBI: Most, season

191	Hack Wilson, 1930
159	Hack Wilson, 1929
158	SAMMY SOSA, 1998
149	Rogers Hornsby, 1929
147	Cap Anson, 1886

SB: Most, season

84	Bill Lange, 1896
76	Walt Wilmot, 1890
74	Walt Wilmot, 1894
67	Bill Lange, 1895
73	Bill Lange, 1897
67	Frank Chance, 1903

BB: Most, season

147	Jimmy Sheckard, 1911
122	Jimmy Sheckard, 1912
116	Richie Ashburn, 1960
113	Cap Anson, 1890
108	Johnny Evers, 1910

BA: Highest, season

.389	Bill Lange, 1895
.388	King Kelly, 1886
.380	Rogers Hornsby, 1929
.372	Heinie Zimmerman, 1912
.371	Cap Anson, 1886

On-base avg; Highest, season

.483	King Kelly, 1886
.459	Rogers Hornsby, 1929
.456	Bill Lange, 1895
.454	Hack Wilson, 1930
.450	Frank Chance, 1905

Slug pct: Highest, season

.723	Hack Wilson, 1930
.679	Rogers Hornsby, 1929
.647	SAMMY SOSA, 1998
.635	SAMMY SOSA, 1999
.630	Gabby Hartnett, 1930

Games started: Most, season

70	John Clarkson, 1885
70	Bill Hutchison, 1892
66	Bill Hutchison, 1890
60	Al Spalding, 1876
60	Larry Corcoran, 1880
42	Fergie Jenkins, 1969 (18)

Complete games: Most, season

68	John Clarkson, 1885
67	Bill Hutchison, 1892
65	Bill Hutchison, 1890
57	Larry Corcoran, 1880
57	Larry Corcoran, 1884
57	Terry Larkin, 1879

Saves: Most, season

53	Randy Myers, 1993
51	ROD BECK, 1998
38	Randy Myers, 1995
37	Bruce Sutter, 1979
36	Lee Smith, 1987
36	Mitch Williams, 1989

Shutouts: Most, season

10	John Clarkson, 1885
9	Mordecai Brown, 1906
9	Mordecai Brown, 1908
9	Orval Overall, 1909
9	Pete Alexander, 1919
9	Bill Lee, 1938

Wins: Most, season

53	John Clarkson, 1885
47	Al Spalding, 1876
44	Bill Hutchison, 1891
43	Larry Corcoran, 1880
42	Bill Hutchison, 1890
29	Mordecai Brown, 1908 (14)

K: Most, season

314	Bill Hutchison, 1892
313	John Clarkson, 1886
308	John Clarkson, 1885
289	Bill Hutchison, 1890
274	Fergie Jenkins, 1970

Win pct: Highest, season

.941	Rick Sutcliffe, 1984
.875	Fred Goldsmith, 1880
.833	King Cole, 1910
.833	Jim McCormick, 1885
.826	Ed Reulbach, 1906

ERA: Lowest, season

1.04	Mordecai Brown, 1906
1.15	Jack Pfiester, 1907
1.17	Carl Lundgren, 1907
1.31	Mordecai Brown, 1909
1.33	Jack Taylor, 1902

Most pinch-hit homers, season

4	GLENALLEN HILL, 1999
3	Chuck Tanner, 1958
3	Willie Smith, 1969
3	Thad Bosley, 1985
3	Kevin Roberson, 1994
3	Dave Clark, 1997
3	Jeff Blauser, 1999

Most pinch-hit homers, career

6	Thad Bosley, 1983-1986
6	Kevin Roberson, 1993-1995
6	GLENALLEN HILL, 1998-99

Longest hitting streak

42	Bill Dahlen, 1894
30	Cal McVey, 1876
30	Jerome Walton, 1989
28	Bill Dahlen, 1894 (2nd streak)
28	Ron Santo, 1966

Most consecutive scoreless innings

50	Ed Reulbach, 1908-1909
39	Mordecai Brown, 1908
38	John Clarkson, 1885
38	Bill Lee, 1938

No-hit games

Larry Corcoran, Chi vs Bos NL, 6-0; August 19, 1880.

Larry Corcoran, Chi vs Wor NL, 5-0; September 20, 1882.

Larry Corcoran, Chi vs Pro NL, 6-0; June 27, 1884.

John Clarkson, Chi at Pro NL, 4-0; July 27, 1885.

Walter Thornton, Chi vs Bro NL, 2-0; August 21, 1898 (2nd game).

Bob Wicker, Chi at NY NL, 1-0; June 11, 1904 (won in 12 innings after allowing one hit in the tenth).

Jimmy Lavender, Chi at NY NL, 2-0; August 31, 1915 (1st game).

Hippo Vaughn, Chi vs Cin NL, 0-1; May 2, 1917 (lost on two hits in the 10th, Toney pitched a no-hitter in this game).

Sam Jones, Chi vs Pit NL, 4-0; May 12, 1955.

Don Cardwell, Chi vs StL NL, 4-0; May 15, 1960 (2nd game).

Ken Holtzman, Chi vs Atl NL, 3-0; August 19, 1969.

Ken Holtzman, Chi at Cin NL, 1-0; June 3, 1971.

Burt Hooton, Chi vs Phi NL, 4-0; April 16, 1972.

Milt Pappas, Chi vs SD NL, 8-0; September 2, 1972.

George Van Haltren, six innings, rain, Chi vs Pit NL, 1-0, June 21,1888.

King Cole, seven innings, called so Chicago could catch train, Chi at StL NL, 4-0; July 31, 1910 (2nd game).

ACTIVE PLAYERS in caps.

Players' years of service are listed by the first and last years with this team and are not necessarily consecutive; all statistics record performances for this team only.

MAJOR LEAGUE REPORT

293

CHICAGO CUBS / NL CENTRAL

Matt Williams' career year helped fuel the Diamondbacks' potent offense and division championship.

1999 Diamondbacks: The big turnaround

The Arizona Diamondbacks made all kinds of history. They just didn't make enough, as far as they were concerned.

"I think this team was as good as the San Diego team I played on that went to the World Series," Steve Finley said. "We had a team that could have won the World Series, but we didn't."

This team won 100 games, became the first to make the playoffs in its second season, turned in the biggest one-year turnaround in baseball history and won the National League West.

But the Diamondbacks won only one playoff game, losing a four-game Division Series to the New York Mets.

"We had a great regular season," said star pitcher Randy Johnson, the free-agent signing who was the cornerstone of the turnaround. "We won 100 games. We showed the people of Arizona what good major league baseball is all about. We have nothing to be ashamed of."

"With the talent we have on this team, no question we will be back," Johnson said. "It's not going out on a limb [to say that] with the players, the leadership, the coaches and the ownership we have, that we will be back in the playoffs."

Johnson, 36, had 364 strikeouts and a 2.48 ERA while throwing a career-high 271⅔ innings. Todd Stottlemyre, who started Arizona's Game Two playoff victory after Johnson lost his sixth consecutive postseason decision, will be 35 in May. Plus, he chose to come back without surgery from a 70 percent tear in his rotator cuff last season.

Yet there are many things that must fall neatly into place for Arizona to make a return trip to the postseason. Matt Williams, Jay Bell, Luis Gonzalez and Finley had among their best, if not the best, seasons of their careers. And the club generally avoided serious injuries.

Plenty fell into place in 1999. Williams and Bell were voted onto the All-Star team, and Gonzalez and Johnson were added. Gonzalez was perhaps the biggest surprise, putting together a 30-game hit-

Team MVP

Matt Williams: It's no coincidence the Diamondbacks' surge to the top of the National League West occurred in Matt Williams' most productive season. Staying healthy and playing in his most games (154) since 1991, Williams drove in 142 runs, 20 more than the career and league high he set in 1990. His .303 average, 190 hits and 37 doubles also were career highs, and he clubbed 35 home runs.

ting streak in April and May and finishing with a .336 batting average. Acquired from Detroit in the offseason, he also had four other double-digit hitting streaks, including a 12-gamer through the end of the season.

Williams, Bell, Gonzalez and Finley topped the 100-RBI mark, making the second-year Diamondbacks one of only seven NL teams ever to have four players top the century mark.

The biggest change during the season took place in mid-July. In advance of the trading deadline and after incumbent closer Gregg Olson had struggled for most of the first half, Arizona acquired Matt Mantei from the Florida Marlins. He had 22 saves the rest of the year for the Diamondbacks and a 2.79 earned run average.

The rest of the bullpen fell into place at about the same time, finishing the year with a 12-game winning streak and a 3.77 ERA, which that was second among the NL among relief corps. The bullpen ERA was 3.26 from July 9 through the end of the season.

A strong second half for the entire club—their .712 winning percentage after the All-Star break was the second-best of the decade to Atlanta's .740 in 1993—produced a 14-game margin over second-place San Francisco. Nobody has won the NL West by that much since Cincinnati's Big Red Machine dominated the 1975 season by 20 games.

1999 Diamondbacks: Week-by-week notes

These notes were excerpted from the following issues of Baseball Weekly.

Five-year glance

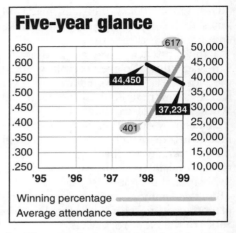

Winning percentage
Average attendance

▶**April 14:** Left-hander Randy Johnson suffered a frustrating no-decision in his Diamondbacks debut against the Dodgers on April 5, but he more than made up for it on April 10: He scattered six hits and struck out a club-record 15 as Arizona got its first victory, 8-3 over Atlanta.

▶**April 28:** Shortstop Tony Batista continued to have a roller-coaster season with the bat. He began with an 0-for-14 stumble, then had seven consecutive hits. Through April 24, though, he was hitless in 17 at-bats. First baseman Travis Lee also struggled, dropping to .197.

▶**May 5:** Arizona finished April with a 13-11 record, compared with 7-19 in its inaugural season. Leading the way were third baseman Matt Williams and second baseman Jay Bell. Williams batted .357 with eight homers and had 25 RBI. Bell was hitting .283 with seven homers and 16 RBI, and was among the league leaders in runs with 22.

▶**May 19:** Arizona grabbed a share of the NL West lead for the first time on May 15, but the talk of the town was the hitting streak of left fielder Luis Gonzalez, which by May 16 reached a club-record 28 games. Gonzalez has hit .396 (42-for-106) with 21 runs, six homers and 23 RBI during the stretch.

▶**May 26:** The Diamondbacks suffered a major setback when right-hander Todd Stottlemyre suffered partial tears of the rotator cuff and the labrum. He would be lost for a minimum of four weeks. Stottlemyre had been off to a solid start with a 4-1 record and 3.59 ERA.

▶**June 9:** Randy Johnson was heating up on the mound and with the bat. On June 4 he won his third consecutive start to raise his record to 7-2, yielding three hits in eight innings and striking out 11 in beating Texas 11-3. He also had a four-game hitting streak.

▶**June 16:** On June 12 the club acquired left-hander Dan Plesac, 37, from Toronto

for Tony Batista and right-hander John Frascatore. Plesac gave manager Buck Showalter more flexibility and another option for the closer's situation.

▶**June 30:** On June 25 Cardinals rookie Jose Jimenez threw a 1-0 no-hitter against Arizona—the first in the majors this season—after going 1-7 in his previous 11 starts. The loss was all the more frustrating considering that Randy Johnson scattered five hits and struck out 14, surrendering the only run with two outs in the ninth on a broken-bat single.

▶**July 15:** Arizona had blown 14 saves through July 10, including six by right-hander Gregg Olson, who saved 30 games in 1998. On July 9 the team acquired right-hander Matt Mantei from Florida for righty Vladimir Nunez, who had a 3-2 record in 27 games for Arizona; right-handed prospect Brad Penny; and a player to be named.

▶**July 21:** Jay Bell picked up where he left off before the break, slamming three home runs in the Texas series to give him 27 for the season, six more than his previous career high, with Kansas City in 1997.

▶**Aug. 4:** Travis Lee was in an 0-for-26 slump and was benched for three games through July 31 in favor of rookie Erubiel Durazo, who hit a combined .408 with 24 homers and 83 RBI in stops at AA El Paso and Tucson. He got three hits in his first start against San Diego and two more

against Kevin Brown of the Dodgers on July 30.

▶**Aug. 11:** Matt Williams hit his first home run in two weeks on Aug. 7. The three-run shot brought him within four RBI of becoming the first player to reach the 100 mark for Arizona.

▶**Aug. 18:** Gregg Olson, once the primary closer and now the main setup man, returned to his previous role to save two consecutive games against the Cubs. Through Aug. 15 he had allowed just one run in his previous 12 outings, spanning 12 innings.

▶**Aug. 25:** Matt Williams, one of the top MVP candidates, drove in 11 runs on the last road trip. Before being charged with an error on Aug. 22, he had played 41 consecutive games without a miscue and made just one in his previous 81.

▶**Sept. 1:** The number of victories Randy Johnson collected might not get him the Cy Young Award, but in every other way, he had proved to be deserving. On Aug. 26 in Florida he fanned nine to get his 14th win and pass 300 strikeouts for the season.

▶**Sept. 8:** The July 9 trade with Florida for Matt Mantei had solidified the bullpen. He struck out the side against the Braves in the ninth inning on Sept. 4 and did the same the next day to earn his 17th save since coming to Arizona. He had 27 overall, and was beginning to mix in his curveball more to set up his fastball, which commonly registers at 95-97 mph.

▶**Sept. 15:** Right-hander Andy Benes, tra-ditionally a second-half pitcher, struggled during the first half of the year. But just like the seasons, he came around. On Sept. 11 he evened his record at 11-11 by shutting out Philadelphia for eight innings on five hits. It was Benes's second consecutive victory and fourth in his last five starts.

▶**Sept. 22:** The Diamondbacks, fat cats in the NL West this season, had become a bit thin in the wallet. A drop in season-ticket sales was one of the primary culprits for the cash crunch, as was a player payroll that rose from $32 million in 1998 to almost $66 million in 1999.

▶**Sept. 29:** Arizona clinched the NL West title in only its second year of existence with an 11-3 victory against San Francisco at 3Com Park on Sept. 24. The next day Luis Gonzalez reached 200 hits in a season for the first time in his career.

▶**Oct. 6:** Arizona clinched the home-field advantage in the NL Division Series and would open with Randy Johnson on the mound. Johnson finished the 1999 season 17-9 with a 2.48 ERA, 12 complete games and 364 strikeouts.

QUOTE OF THE YEAR

"I think the four of us are going to get together and do an endorsement for Target."
—Left-hander Brian Anderson, after that many Arizona pitchers were hit by batted balls

Team Leaders

Batting avg.	Hits	Wins	Strikeouts
.336 Luis Gonzalez	206 Luis Gonzalez	17 Randy Johnson	364 Randy Johnson
.303 Matt Williams	190 Matt Williams	16 Omar Daal	148 Omar Daal

HR	Runs	Losses	Innings
38 Jay Bell	132 Jay Bell	12 Andy Benes	271.2 Randy Johnson
35 Matt Williams	112 Luis Gonzalez	9 Omar Daal	214.2 Omar Daal
		9 Randy Johnson	

RBI	Stolen bases	ERA	Saves
142 Matt Williams	72 Tony Womack	2.48 Randy Johnson	32 Matt Mantei
112 Jay Bell	17 Travis Lee	3.65 Omar Daal	14 Gregg Olson

ARIZONA DIAMONDBACKS 1999 final stats

BATTERS	BA	SLG	OBA	G	AB	R	H	TB	2B	3B	HR	RBI	BB	SO	SB	CS	E
Klassen	1.000	1.000	1.000	1	1	0	1	1	0	0	0	0	0	0	0	0	0
Diaz	.400	.800	.625	4	5	2	2	4	2	0	0	1	3	1	0	0	0
Dellucci	.394	.505	.463	63	109	27	43	55	7	1	1	15	11	24	2	0	0
Gonzalez	.336	.549	.403	153	614	112	206	337	45	4	26	111	66	63	9	5	5
Durazo	.329	.594	.422	52	155	31	51	92	4	2	11	30	26	43	1	1	0
Colbrunn	.326	.519	.392	67	135	20	44	70	5	3	5	24	12	23	1	1	1
Harris	.310	.396	.330	110	187	17	58	74	13	0	1	20	6	7	2	1	9
Williams	.303	.536	.344	154	627	98	190	336	37	2	35	142	41	93	2	0	10
Gilkey	.294	.500	.379	94	204	28	60	102	16	1	8	39	29	42	2	2	3
Bell	.289	.557	.374	151	589	132	170	328	32	6	38	112	82	132	7	4	22
Womack	.277	.370	.332	144	614	111	170	227	25	10	4	41	52	68	72	13	5
Frias	.273	.340	.391	69	150	27	41	51	3	2	1	16	29	18	4	3	5
Miller	.270	.446	.316	86	296	35	80	132	19	0	11	47	19	78	0	0	6
Finley	.264	.525	.336	156	590	100	156	310	32	10	34	103	63	94	8	4	2
Batista	.257	.396	.335	44	144	16	37	57	5	0	5	21	16	17	2	0	4
Fox	.255	.380	.351	99	274	34	70	104	12	2	6	33	33	61	4	1	14
Barajas	.250	.500	.294	5	16	3	4	8	1	0	1	3	1	1	0	0	0
Ryan	.241	.483	.267	20	29	4	7	14	1	0	2	5	1	8	0	0	0
Lee	.237	.363	.337	120	375	57	89	136	16	2	9	50	58	50	17	3	3
Ward	.237	.316	.326	59	114	8	27	36	3	0	2	15	15	15	2	2	2
Stinnett	.232	.426	.302	88	284	36	66	121	13	0	14	38	24	83	2	1	6
Young	.182	.182	.400	6	11	1	2	2	0	0	0	0	3	2	0	0	0
Powell	.160	.280	.222	22	25	4	4	7	3	0	0	1	2	6	2	1	1

PITCHERS	W-L	ERA	BA	G	GS	CG	GF	SH	SV	IP	H	R	ER	HR	BB	SO
Johnson	17-9	2.48	.208	35	35	12	0	2	0	271.2	207	86	75	30	70	364
Swindell	4-0	2.51	.230	63	0	0	15	0	1	64.2	54	19	18	8	21	51
Chouinard	5-2	2.68	.220	32	0	0	9	0	1	40.1	31	16	12	3	12	23
Mantei	1-3	2.76	.189	65	0	0	60	0	32	65.1	44	21	20	5	44	99
Plesac	2-1	3.32	.259	34	0	0	6	0	1	21.2	22	9	8	3	8	27
Daal	16-9	3.65	.236	32	32	2	0	1	0	214.2	188	92	87	21	79	148
Holmes	4-3	3.70	.262	44	0	0	9	0	0	48.2	50	21	20	3	25	35
Olson	9-4	3.71	.238	61	0	0	36	0	14	60.2	54	28	25	9	25	45
Stottlemyre	6-3	4.09	.268	17	17	0	0	0	0	101.1	106	51	46	12	40	74
Frascatore	1-4	4.09	.256	26	0	0	10	0	0	33.0	31	16	15	6	12	15
Reynoso	10-6	4.37	.276	31	27	0	1	0	0	167.0	178	90	81	20	67	79
Anderson	8-2	4.57	.279	31	19	2	4	1	1	130.0	144	69	66	18	28	75
Kim	1-2	4.61	.211	25	0	0	10	0	1	27.1	20	15	14	2	20	31
Benes	13-12	4.81	.273	33	32	0	0	0	0	198.1	216	117	106	34	82	141
Sabel	0-0	6.52	.300	7	0	0	1	0	0	9.2	12	7	7	1	6	6
Vosberg	0-1	8.18	.431	19	0	0	3	0	0	11.0	22	12	10	1	3	8
Carlson	0-0	9.00	.278	2	0	0	1	0	0	4.0	5	4	4	0	0	3
Padilla	0-1	16.88	.467	5	0	0	2	0	0	2.2	7	5	5	1	3	0

2000 preliminary roster

PITCHERS (20)
Brian Anderson
Nick Bierbrodt
Troy Brohawn
Bobby Chouinard
Brad Clontz
Omar Daal
Nelson Figueroa
Geraldo Guzman
Darren Holmes
Randy Johnson
Byung-Hyun Kim
Matt Mantei

Ben Norris
Vicente Padilla
Dan Plesac
Stephen Randolph
Armando Reynoso
Russ Springer
Todd Stottlemyre
Greg Swindell

CATCHERS (3)
Rod Barajas
Damian Miller
Kelly Stinnett

INFIELDERS (11)
Jay Bell
Greg Colbrunn
Erubiel Durazo
Andy Fox
Hanley Frias
Lenny Harris
Danny Klassen
Travis Lee
Luis Ordaz
Junior Spivey
Matt Williams

OUTFIELDERS (6)
Jason Conti
Dave Dellucci
Steve Finley
Bernard Gilkey
Luis Gonzalez
Tony Womack

Games played by position

PLAYER	G	C	1B	2B	3B	SS	OF
Barajas	5	5	0	0	0	0	0
Batista	44	0	0	0	0	43	0
Bell	151	0	0	148	0	1	0
Colbrunn	67	0	39	0	2	0	0
Dellucci	63	0	0	0	0	0	31
Diaz	4	0	0	2	0	2	0
Durazo	52	0	44	0	0	0	0
Finley	156	0	0	0	0	0	155
Fox	99	0	0	0	12	82	0
Frias	69	0	0	8	0	53	0
Gilkey	94	0	0	0	0	0	53
Gonzalez	153	0	0	0	0	0	148
Harris	19	0	0	0	5	0	2
Klassen	1	0	0	0	0	0	0
Lee	120	0	114	0	0	0	2
Miller	86	86	0	0	0	0	0
Powell	22	0	0	0	0	0	15
Ryan	20	0	0	0	0	0	5
Stinnett	88	86	0	0	0	0	0
Ward	10	0	0	0	0	0	5
Williams	154	0	0	0	153	0	0
Womack	144	0	0	19	0	19	123
Young	6	0	0	0	0	0	4

Minor Leagues
Tops in the organization

BATTER	CLUB	AVG.	G	AB	R	H	HR	RBI
Durazo, Erubiel	Tuc	.404	94	344	80	139	24	83
Urquiola, Carlos	SB	.362	93	384	66	139	0	35
Patterson, Jarrod	Tuc	.358	142	523	109	187	19	98
Overbay, Lyle	MSO	.343	75	306	66	105	12	101
Brooks, Jeff	MSO	.339	73	295	48	100	12	60

HOME RUNS			WINS		
Cust, Jack	HiD	32	Norris, Ben	EIP	12
Young, Ernie	Tuc	30	Good, Andrew	SB	11
Durazo, Erubiel	Tuc	24	Padilla, Vicente	Tuc	11
Meier, Dan	HiD	24	Figueroa, Nelson	Tuc	11
Nunez, Abraham	HiD	22	Several Players Tied at		9

RBI			SAVES		
Cust, Jack	HiD	112	Bloomer, Chris	SB	21
Overbay, Lyle	MSO	101	Batchelor, Rich	Tuc	12
Patterson, Jarrod	Tuc	98	Matzenbacher, B.	MSO	11
Barajas, Rod	EIP	95	Martines, Jason	HiD	9
Young, Ernie	Tuc	95	Several Players Tied at		8

STOLEN BASES			STRIKEOUTS		
Nunez, Abraham	HiD	40	Good, Andrew	SB	146
Santora, Jack	MSO	36	Patterson, John	Tuc	146
Martinez, Belvani	HiD	35	Norris, Ben	EIP	132
Hall, Victor	MSO	28	Wilson, Jeff	HiD	122
Terrero, Luis	MSO	27	Carlson, Dan	Tuc	118

PITCHER	CLUB	W-L	ERA	IP	H	BB	SO
Cervantes, Chris	HiD	8-5	3.59	115	114	35	90
Padilla, Vicente	Tuc	11-5	3.75	144	157	41	113
Figueroa, Nelson	Tuc	11-7	3.85	131	131	41	108
Sanchez, Martin	EIP	4-4	3.90	97	95	41	73
Good, Andrew	SB	11-10	4.10	154	160	42	146

Sick call: 1999 DL report

PLAYER	Days on the DL
Troy Brohawn	34
Dave Dellucci	71
Edwin Diaz	27
Andy Fox	15
Darren Holmes	45*
Byung-Hyun Kim	44
Russell Jacob	14
Travis Lee	26
Gregg Olson	15
Brian Shouse	16
Junior Spivey	45
Todd Stottlemyre	94
Greg Swindell	15
Amaury Telemaco	33
Turner Ward	15
Tony Womack	7

1999 salaries

	Bonuses	Total earned salary
Randy Johnson, p	300,000	9,700,000
Matt Williams, 3b	50,000	8,100,000
Todd Stottlemyre, p		8,000,000
Jay Bell, 2b	50,000	6,100,000
Andy Benes, p		6,000,000
Steve Finley, of		5,375,000
Bernard Gilkey, of		5,250,000
Omar Daal, p		2,625,000
Luis Gonzalez, of	25,000	2,050,000
Brian Anderson, p		1,800,000
Tony Womack, of		1,650,000
Armando Reynoso, p		1,625,000
Dan Plesac, p		1,500,000
Darren Holmes, p		1,466,666
Greg Swindell, p		1,333,333
Lenny Harris, 3b	25,000	1,125,000
Greg Colbrunn, 1b		900,000
Gregg Olson, p		850,000
Byung-Hyun Kim, p		762,500
Kelly Stinnett, c		750,000
Matt Mantei, p		735,000
Travis Lee, 1b	50,000	400,000
Andy Fox, ss		350,000
Dave Dellucci, of		260,000
Damian Miller, c		240,000
Bobby Chouinard, p		212,500
Hanley Frias, ss		211,000
Turner Ward, of		200,000
Troy Brohawn, p		200,000
Rob Ryan, of		200,000
Junior Spivey, 2b		200,000
Erubiel Durazo, 1b		200,000

Average 1999 salary: $2,199,094
Total 1999 team payroll: $70,370,999
Termination pay: $100,819

Arizona Diamondbacks (1998-1999)

Runs: Most, career

211	JAY BELL, 1998-1999
170	MATT WILLIAMS, 1998-1999
128	TRAVIS LEE, 1998-1999
112	LUIS GONZALEZ, 1999-1999
111	TONY WOMACK, 1999-1999

Hits: Most, career

326	MATT WILLIAMS, 1998-1999
308	JAY BELL, 1998-1999
240	TRAVIS LEE, 1998-1999
209	ANDY FOX, 1998-1999
206	LUIS GONZALEZ, 1999-1999

2B: Most, career

63	MATT WILLIAMS, 1998-1999
61	JAY BELL, 1998-1999
45	LUIS GONZALEZ, 1999-1999
36	TRAVIS LEE, 1998-1999
33	ANDY FOX, 1998-1999
33	DAMIAN MILLER, 1998-1999

3B: Most, career

13	DAVE DELLUCCI, 1998-1999
11	JAY BELL, 1998-1999
10	STEVE FINLEY, 1999-1999
10	TONY WOMACK, 1999-1999
8	ANDY FOX, 1998-1999
8	KARIM GARCIA, 1998-1998

HR: Most, career

58	JAY BELL, 1998-1999
55	MATT WILLIAMS, 1998-1999
34	STEVE FINLEY, 1999-1999
31	TRAVIS LEE, 1998-1999
26	LUIS GONZALEZ, 1999-1999

RBI: Most, career

213	MATT WILLIAMS, 1998-1999
179	JAY BELL, 1998-1999
122	TRAVIS LEE, 1998-1999
111	LUIS GONZALEZ, 1999-1999
103	STEVE FINLEY, 1999-1999

SB: Most, career

72	TONY WOMACK, 1999-1999
25	TRAVIS LEE, 1998-1999
22	DEVON WHITE, 1998-1998
18	ANDY FOX, 1998-1999
10	JAY BELL, 1998-1999

BB: Most, career

163	JAY BELL, 1998-1999
125	TRAVIS LEE, 1998-1999
84	MATT WILLIAMS, 1998-1999
76	ANDY FOX, 1998-1999
66	LUIS GONZALEZ, 1999-1999

BA: Highest, career

.336	LUIS GONZALEZ, 1999-1999
.288	DAVE DELLUCCI, 1998-1999
.287	MATT WILLIAMS, 1998-1999
.279	DEVON WHITE, 1998-1998
.277	TONY WOMACK, 1999-1999

On-base avg: Highest, career

.403	LUIS GONZALEZ, 1999-1999
.364	JAY BELL, 1998-1999
.353	ANDY FOX, 1998-1999
.349	DAVE DELLUCCI, 1998-1999
.342	TRAVIS LEE, 1998-1999

Slug pct: Highest, career

.549	LUIS GONZALEZ, 1999-1999
.525	STEVE FINLEY, 1999-1999
.496	JAY BELL, 1998-1999
.493	MATT WILLIAMS, 1998-1999
.478	TONY BATISTA, 1998-1999

Games started: Most, career

66	ANDY BENES, 1998-1999
55	OMAR DAAL, 1998-1999
51	BRIAN ANDERSON, 1998-1999
35	RANDY JOHNSON, 1999-1999
27	ARMANDO REYNOSO, 1999-1999

Complete games: Most, career

12	RANDY JOHNSON, 1999-1999
5	OMAR DAAL, 1998-1999
4	BRIAN ANDERSON, 1998-1999
1	ANDY BENES, 1998-1999
1	JEFF SUPPAN, 1998-1998

Saves: Most, career

44	GREGG OLSON, 1998-1999
22	MATT MANTEI, 1999-1999
5	FELIX RODRIGUEZ, 1998-1998
1	BRIAN ANDERSON, 1998-1999
1	Willie Banks, 1998-1998
1	ALAN EMBREE, 1998-1998
1	BOBBY CHOUINARD, 1998-1999
1	VLADIMIR NUNEZ, 1998-1999
1	BYUNG-HYUNKIM, 1999-1999
1	DAN PLESAC, 1999-1999
1	GREG SWINDELL, 1999-1999

Shutouts: Most, career

2	BRIAN ANDERSON, 1998-1999
2	MAR DAAL, 1998-1999
2	RANDY JOHNSON, 1999-1999

Wins: Most, career

27	ANDY BENES, 1998-1999
24	OMAR DAAL, 1998-1999
20	BRIAN ANDERSON, 1998-1999
17	RANDY JOHNSON, 1999-1999
12	GREGG OLSON, 1998-1999

K: Most, career

364	RANDY JOHNSON, 1999-1999
305	ANDY BENES, 1998-1999
280	OMAR DAAL, 1998-1999
170	BRIAN ANDERSON, 1998-1999
100	GREGG OLSON, 1998-1999

Win pct: Highest, career

.654	RANDY JOHNSON, 1999-1999
.625	ARMANDO REYNOSO, 1999-1999
.600	GREGG OLSON, 1998-1999
.571	BRIAN ANDERSON, 1998-1999
.533	OMAR DAAL, 1998-1999

ERA: Lowest, career

2.48	RANDY JOHNSON, 1999-1999
3.32	OMAR DAAL, 1998-1999
3.34	GREGG OLSON, 1998-1999
4.11	AMAURY TELEMACO, 1998-1999
4.36	ANDY BENES, 1998-1999

Runs: Most, season

132	JAY BELL, 1999
112	LUIS GONZALEZ, 1999
111	TONY WOMACK, 1999
100	STEVE FINLEY, 1999
98	MATT WILLIAMS, 1999

Hits: Most, season

206	LUIS GONZALEZ, 1999
190	MATT WILLIAMS, 1999
170	JAY BELL, 1999
170	TONY WOMACK, 1999
157	DEVON WHITE, 1998

2B: Most, season

45	LUIS GONZALEZ, 1999
37	MATT WILLIAMS, 1999
32	DEVON WHITE, 1998
32	JAY BELL, 1999
32	STEVE FINLEY, 1999

3B: Most, season

12	DAVE DELLUCCI, 1998
10	STEVE FINLEY, 1999
10	TONY WOMACK, 1999
8	KARIM GARCIA, 1998
6	ANDY FOX, 1998
6	JAY BELL, 1999

HR: Most, season

38	JAY BELL, 1999
35	MATT WILLIAMS, 1999
34	STEVE FINLEY, 1999
26	LUIS GONZALEZ, 1999
22	TRAVIS LEE, 1998
22	DEVON WHITE, 1998

RBI: Most, season

142	MATT WILLIAMS, 1999
112	JAY BELL, 1999
111	LUIS GONZALEZ, 1999
103	STEVE FINLEY, 1999
85	DEVON WHITE, 1998

SB: Most, season

72	TONY WOMACK, 1999
22	DEVON WHITE, 1998
17	TRAVIS LEE, 1999
14	ANDY FOX, 1998
9	LUIS GONZALEZ, 1999

BB: Most, season

82	JAY BELL, 1999
81	JAY BELL, 1998
67	TRAVIS LEE, 1998
66	LUIS GONZALEZ, 1999
63	STEVE FINLEY, 1999

BA: Highest, season

.336	LUIS GONZALEZ, 1999
.303	MATT WILLIAMS, 1999
.289	JAY BELL, 1999
.279	DEVON WHITE, 1998
.277	ANDY FOX, 1998

On-base avg; Highest, season

.403	LUIS GONZALEZ, 1999
.374	JAY BELL, 1999
.355	ANDY FOX, 1998
.353	JAY BELL, 1998
.346	TRAVIS LEE, 1998

Slug pct: Highest, season

.557	JAY BELL, 1999
.549	LUIS GONZALEZ, 1999
.536	MATT WILLIAMS, 1999
.525	STEVE FINLEY, 1999
.456	DEVON WHITE, 1998

Games started: Most, season

35	RANDY JOHNSON, 1999
34	ANDY BENES, 1998
32	BRIAN ANDERSON, 1998
32	ANDY BENES, 1999
32	OMAR DAAL, 1999

Complete games: Most, season

12	RANDY JOHNSON, 1999
3	OMAR DAAL, 1998
2	BRIAN ANDERSON, 1998
2	BRIAN ANDERSON, 1999
2	OMAR DAAL, 1999

Saves: Most, season

30	GREGG OLSON, 1998
22	MATT MANTEI, 1999
14	GREGG OLSON, 1999
5	FELIX RODRIGUEZ, 1998
1	BRIAN ANDERSON, 1999
1	Willie Banks, 1998
1	BOBBY CHOUINARD, 1999
1	ALAN EMBREE, 1998
1	BYUNG-HYUNKIM, 1999
1	VLADIMIR NUNEZ, 1999
1	DAN PLESAC, 1999
1	GREG SWINDELL, 1999

Shutouts: Most, season

2	RANDY JOHNSON, 1999
1	BRIAN ANDERSON, 1998
1	BRIAN ANDERSON, 1999
1	OMAR DAAL, 1998
1	OMAR DAAL, 1999

Wins: Most, season

17	RANDY JOHNSON, 1999
16	OMAR DAAL, 1999
14	ANDY BENES, 1998
13	ANDY BENES, 1999
12	BRIAN ANDERSON, 1998

K: Most, season

364	RANDY JOHNSON, 1999
164	ANDY BENES, 1998
148	OMAR DAAL, 1999
141	ANDY BENES, 1999
132	OMAR DAAL, 1998

Win pct: Highest, season

.654	RANDY JOHNSON, 1999
.640	OMAR DAAL, 1999
.625	ARMANDO REYNOSO, 1999
.520	ANDY BENES, 1999
.518	ANDY BENES, 1998

ERA: Lowest, season

2.48	RANDY JOHNSON, 1999
2.88	OMAR DAAL, 1998
3.65	OMAR DAAL, 1999
3.97	ANDY BENES, 1998
4.33	BRIAN ANDERSON, 1998

Most pinch-hit homers, season

1	TONY BATISTA, 1998
1	Yamil Benitez, 1998
1	HANLEY FRIAS, 1998
1	GREG COLBRUNN, 1999
1	ERUBIEL DURAZO, 1999
1	BERNARD GILKEY, 1999
1	KELLY STINNETT, 1999
1	TURNER WARD, 1999

Most pinch-hit homers, career

1	TONY BATISTA, 1998-1899
1	Yamil Benitez, 1998
1	HANLEY FRIAS, 1998-1999
1	GREG COLBRUNN, 1999
1	ERUBIEL DURAZO, 1999
1	BERNARD GILKEY, 1998-1999
1	KELLY STINNETT, 1998-1999
1	TURNER WARD, 1999

Longest hitting streak

30	LUIS GONZALEZ, 1999
19	MATT WILLIAMS, 1999

Most consecutive scoreless innings

27	ANDY BENES, 1998
23	RANDY JOHNSON, 1999
21	Willie Banks, 1998

No-hit games

Barry Bonds missed a third of the season and still led the Giants with 34 home runs.

By Tom DiPace

1999 Giants: Pitching worse than injuries

Barry Bonds missed seven weeks following elbow surgery. Bill Mueller fractured his big toe on opening day and did not return until mid-May. Ellis Burks and Jeff Kent each had stints on the disabled list.

The San Francisco Giants were hobbled by injuries in their final year at Candlestick Park.

The Giants opened the season with five straight wins and led the NL West by 2½ games at the All-Star break. But they lost 20 of their first 29 games after the break and never recovered, finishing 14 games behind the Arizona Diamondbacks.

The middle of the lineup—Bonds, Kent, Burks and J.T. Snow—was intact for just 48 games this season. The Giants went 27-21 in those contests.

Kent, who led the Giants in RBI for the third straight year with 101, said the team cannot point to the injuries as the only reason for the second-half slide.

"A lot needs to be done to be a championship ball club," he said. "We made a lot of mistakes that could be avoided—pitching, base running and scoring runs. There's no one in here exempt from making improvements. Injuries sure hurt us, but good teams overcome injuries."

Bonds, who hit .262 with 34 homers and 83 RBI, said the Giants stuck together despite the injuries.

"I don't have anything to be ashamed of this year. I feel like I did a pretty good job for having all the odds against me," Bonds said. "We as a team played very well."

Though no Giants player was in the top 10 in any major offensive category in the NL, the team set a franchise record with 307 doubles—breaking the mark of 292 it set last year—and five players hit more than 20 homers. Bonds (34), Burks (31), J.T. Snow (24), Kent (23) and Rich Aurilia (22) became the club's first such quintet since Willie McCovey, Willie Mays, Orlando Cepeda, Ed Bailey and Felipe Alou in 1963.

Bonds got his 2,000th hit in mid-September, set a major league record for career intentional walks and joined Ari-

Team MVP

Barry Bonds: Bonds led the Giants in home runs. That's hardly news, but consider that the All-Star left fielder was limited by injury to barely two-thirds of the team's games and still managed to slug 34 round-trippers and drive in 83 runs. Had he been able to amass the requisite number of at-bats, Bonds's .617 slugging percentage would've ranked among the top five in the league.

zona's Matt Williams as the only players with 20 homers in each year of the 1990s.

Aurilia led NL shortstops in homers, and set a San Francisco record for homers by a shortstop.

But the pitching was mediocre. The team had a 4.71 ERA and got disappointing performances from starters Mark Gardner (5-11) and Shawn Estes (11-11). The most reliable starter was second-year player Russ Ortiz (18-9, 164 strikeouts).

The bullpen was inconsistent. Though Robb Nen had 37 saves, he also had nine blown saves. What was once considered one of the league's deeper bullpens was erratic for most of the season.

The injuries and some of the performance problems did allow the Giants to get a good look at some promising young players. Pitcher Joe Nathan was 7-4 as he shuttled back and forth between San Francisco and AAA Fresno. And outfielder Armando Rios hit .327 with speed and power when filling in for Bonds and Burks.

The Giants drew more than 2 million fans, partly because of the novelty of bidding farewell to a park that most players and spectators hated because of its nasty weather. In 2000, the club moves to $319 million downtown Pacific Bell Park—a hitter's ballpark with very little foul territory and the shortest right field fence in the league.

1999 Giants: Week-by-week notes

These notes were excerpted from the following issues of Baseball Weekly.

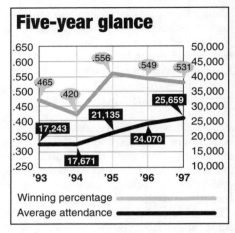

Five-year glance

Winning percentage

Average attendance

▶**April 14:** The Giants got off to their hottest start since 1997, winning five in a row before falling to the Padres. They had only two better starts in franchise history—9-0 in 1918 and 7-0 in 1930. In the first five games the Giants scored 45 runs and batted .343 against the Reds and the Padres.

▶**April 21:** Opening day pitcher Mark Gardner, who had an 11.77 ERA in his first three starts, was placed on the DL with shoulder inflammation. The right-hander was shelved one day after he allowed seven runs and nine hits in four innings in Arizona. On the season he had allowed 17 runs in 13 innings, including a league-high seven homers.

▶**May 5:** After owning a 13.50 ERA his first four starts, left-hander Kirk Rueter had just a 1.42 ERA in his past three outings. He earned a victory against Milwaukee despite allowing four runs (three unearned) in the first inning. The Giants rallied for a 6-4 victory.

▶**May 19:** The Astros continued to run wild on the Giants, stealing 15 bases in 17 attempts through May 16. On May 15 in Houston, the Astros attempted no steals against Kirk Rueter, who has a quick move to the plate. But after reliever Jeff Spradlin came in, they swiped four bags in four attempts.

▶**May 26:** Right fielder Ellis Burks, who had surgery on both knees last winter, was slowed by a tight quadriceps, but he's played through it. Burks, the No. 3 hitter in left fielder Barry Bonds's absence, is 18-for-77 (.234) in 22 games in that slot.

▶**June 2:** In his final start of the month, left-hander Shawn Estes lasted only three innings in a 7-4 loss to Montreal. It was his quickest hook of the season. Estes, 2-4, walked four batters in the game, pushing his league-leading total to 42.

▶**June 9:** Bonds looked like he might be returning ahead of schedule. He was taking batting practice and continued to throw regularly. Bonds, who had elbow surgery on April 20, was expected to come back sometime in June.

▶**June 23:** Bonds started hitting against the Cubs: He won the series opener on June 17 with a ninth-inning single, and the next day he blasted a home run.

▶**June 30:** The hidden-ball trick rarely works, but the Giants pulled it off against the Dodgers on June 26 when first baseman J.T. Snow stunned Carlos Perez. Snow hid the ball in his glove and waited for Perez, who had singled, to step off the bag. Once he did, Snow applied the tag.

▶**July 7:** Bonds hit three homers in two days against the Dodgers, helping the Giants return to first place. Before his power barrage, Bonds was in pain on the field, though an MRI on his elbow showed no further damage.

▶**July 15:** The Giants had won 22 times in Russ Ortiz's 30 career starts. The 25-year-old right-hander was 11-5 with a team-leading 3.32 ERA through July 11.

▶**July 21:** Second baseman Jeff Kent was 0-for-1 with a walk in his first All-Star Game. Without much attention, Bonds set the major league record for intentional walks. His historic free pass on July 15 in Oakland, delivered by Brad Rigby, was No. 294 in his career. Hank Aaron was intentionally walked 293 times, though the stat was not kept until after Aaron's rookie year of 1954.

▶**July 28:** J.T. Snow was the majors' most dangerous hitter in interleague contests. Since the beginning of interleague play in 1997, he had hit .350 with 17 homers and 54 RBI in 44 games against AL teams. This year he hit .310 with 20 RBI in 15 games.

▶**Aug. 4:** The Giants were concerned about Mark Gardner, who was 3-9 with a 6.88 ERA. Gardner signed a two-year, $5 million contract before the season but had become the team's least effective starter. Meanwhile, the Giants vowed to promote right-hander Joe Nathan from AAA Fresno and insert him in the rotation.

▶**Aug. 11:** Nathan was called up for one game and then returned to the minors. "Everything happened so quickly, I didn't have time to think about it," Nathan said. He allowed three homers in the first inning and was out by the second, replaced by Gardner, whose turn he had taken in the rotation.

▶**Aug. 18:** Jeff Kent left the Giants with an injury on Aug. 4 and returned to the Bay Area with seven games remaining on a 12-game, four-city road trip. The Giants won only once more and finished the journey at 3-9. In the standings they fell from 1 to 7 back of Arizona.

▶**Sept. 1:** The Giants were hot, but the first-place Diamondbacks weren't budging. Although the Giants won seven of eight—including a 6-1 road trip—their deficit in the NL West was 8 games, the same margin as before the streak. The Giants would have had a 7-0 trip if closer Robb Nen hadn't blown a save in the finale.

▶**Sept. 8:** Bonds hit 14 home runs in August, all after Aug. 14. His hot hitting helped the Giants reenter the race. They were as many as 8 games behind the Diamondbacks, but in one four-day stretch, they cut 3 games off the lead.

▶**Sept. 15:** Bonds collected his 2,000th career hit against Tom Glavine, a double that ignited the deciding rally in a 3-2 victory against the Braves on Sept. 11. He has 926 extra-base hits—441 homers, 65 triples and 420 doubles—plus 1,426 walks.

▶**Sept. 22:** When shortstop Rich Aurilia hit a home run on Sept. 17, it gave the Giants five players with 20 or more. Both Jeff Kent and J.T. Snow had hit their 20th two days earlier, joining Bonds (31) and Ellis Burks (29).

▶**Oct. 6:** The Giants lost their Candlestick Park finale 9-4 to the Dodgers and then staged an emotional ceremony in which 60 former players and managers were introduced and cheered by a sellout crowd. Juan Marichal threw out the first pitch, and Willie Mays threw the final one. Center fielder Marvin Benard made the last out and hit the last Giants home run in "the Stick."

305

QUOTE OF THE YEAR

"You learn in this business not to react, and I'm not reacting."

—Right-hander Mark Gardner, when asked to comment on his being replaced in the rotation

Team Leaders

Batting avg.	Hits	Wins	Strikeouts
.290 Marvin Benard	163 Marvin Benard	18 Russ Ortiz	164 Russ Ortiz
.290 Jeff Kent	157 Rich Aurilia	15 Kirk Rueter	159 Shawn Estes

HR	Runs	Losses	Innings
34 Barry Bonds	100 Marvin Benard	12 Livan Hernandez	207.2 Russ Ortiz
31 Ellis Burks	93 J.T. Snow	11 Shawn Estes	203 Shawn Estes
		11 Mark Gardner	

RBI	Stolen bases	ERA	Saves
101 Jeff Kent	27 Marvin Benard	3.81 Russ Ortiz	37 Robb Nen
98 J.T. Snow	15 Barry Bonds	4.64 Livan Hernandez	3 John Johnstone

SAN FRANCISCO GIANTS 1999 final stats

BATTERS	BA	SLG	OBA	G	AB	R	H	TB	2B	3B	HR	RBI	BB	SO	SB	CS	E
Canizaro	.444	.722	.474	12	18	5	8	13	2	0	1	9	1	2	1	0	0
Rios	.327	.527	.420	72	150	32	49	79	9	0	7	29	24	35	7	4	2
Mayne	.301	.419	.389	117	322	39	97	135	32	0	2	39	43	65	2	2	3
Benard	.290	.457	.359	149	562	100	163	257	36	5	16	64	55	97	27	14	4
Mueller	.290	.362	.388	116	414	61	120	150	24	0	2	36	65	52	4	2	12
Kent	.290	.511	.366	138	511	86	148	261	40	2	23	101	61	112	13	6	10
Burks	.282	.569	.394	120	390	73	110	222	19	0	31	96	69	86	7	5	2
Aurilia	.281	.444	.336	152	558	68	157	248	23	1	22	80	43	71	2	3	28
Snow	.274	.451	.370	161	570	93	156	257	25	2	24	98	86	121	0	4	6
Servais	.273	.399	.327	69	198	21	54	79	10	0	5	21	13	31	0	0	3
Martinez	.264	.410	.327	61	144	21	38	59	6	0	5	19	14	17	1	2	6
Murray	.263	.368	.333	15	19	1	5	7	2	0	0	5	2	4	1	0	0
Bonds	.262	.617	.389	102	355	91	93	219	20	2	34	83	73	62	15	2	3
Santangelo	.260	.386	.406	113	254	49	66	98	17	3	3	26	53	54	12	4	1
Delgado	.254	.310	.312	35	71	7	18	22	2	1	0	3	5	9	1	0	5
Mirabelli	.253	.356	.327	33	87	10	22	31	6	0	1	10	9	25	0	0	0
Hayes	.205	.314	.292	95	264	33	54	83	9	1	6	48	33	41	3	1	7
Guzman	.000	.000	.000	14	15	0	0	0	0	0	0	0	0	4	0	0	0

PITCHERS	W-L	ERA	BA	G	GS	CG	GF	SH	SV	IP	H	R	ER	HR	BB	SO
Johnstone	4-6	2.60	.203	62	0	0	11	0	3	65.2	48	24	19	8	20	56
Embree	3-2	3.38	.200	68	0	0	13	0	0	58.2	42	22	22	6	26	53
F. Rodriguez	2-3	3.80	.262	47	0	0	26	0	0	66.1	67	32	28	6	29	55
Ortiz	18-9	3.81	.244	33	33	3	0	0	0	207.2	189	109	88	24	125	164
Nen	3-8	3.98	.275	72	0	0	64	0	37	72.1	79	36	32	8	27	77
Del Toro	0-0	4.18	.264	14	0	0	2	0	0	23.2	24	11	11	5	11	20
Nathan	7-4	4.18	.243	19	14	0	2	0	1	90.1	84	45	42	17	46	54
Spradlin	3-1	4.19	.259	59	0	0	14	0	0	58.0	59	31	27	4	29	52
Hernandez	8-12	4.64	.286	30	30	2	0	0	0	199.2	227	110	103	23	76	144
Estes	11-11	4.92	.268	32	32	1	0	1	0	203.0	209	121	111	21	112	159
R. Rodriguez	3-0	5.24	.274	62	0	0	8	0	0	56.2	60	33	33	8	28	44
Rueter	15-10	5.41	.297	33	33	1	0	0	0	184.2	219	118	111	28	55	94
Brock	6-8	5.48	.291	19	19	0	0	0	0	106.2	124	69	65	18	41	76
Tavarez	2-0	5.93	.295	47	0	0	12	0	0	54.2	65	38	36	7	25	33
Gardner	5-11	6.47	.267	29	21	1	2	0	0	139.0	142	103	100	27	57	86
Patrick	1-0	10.13	.375	6	0	0	2	0	1	5.1	9	7	6	1	3	6

2000 preliminary roster

PITCHERS (18)
Miguel Del Toro
Alan Embree
Shawn Estes
Aaron Fultz
Mark Gardner
Livan Hernandez
Ryan Jensen
John Johnstone
Kevin Joseph
Scott Linebrink
David Maurer

Joe Nathan
Robb Nen
Russ Ortiz
Michael Riley
Felix Rodriguez
Kirk Rueter
Ben Weber

CATCHERS (5)
Giuseppe Chiaramonte
Bobby Estalella
Doug Mirabelli

Guillermo Rodriguez
Yorvit Torrealba

INFIELDERS (8)
Rich Aurilia
Jay Canizaro
Nelson Castro
Felipe Crespo
Wilson Delgado
Pedro Feliz
Jeff Kent
Ramon Martinez

Damon Minor
Bill Mueller
F.P. Santangelo
J.T. Snow

OUTFIELDERS (5)
Marvin Benard
Barry Bonds
Ellis Burks
Calvin Murray
Armando Rios

Games played by position

PLAYER	G	C	1B	2B	3B	SS	OF
Aurilia	152	0	0	0	0	150	0
Benard	149	0	0	0	0	0	142
Bonds	102	0	0	0	0	0	96
Burks	120	0	0	0	0	0	107
Canizaro	12	0	0	4	0	0	0
Delgado	35	0	0	15	0	20	0
Guzman	14	1	0	0	5	0	0
Hayes	95	0	20	0	55	0	1
Javier	112	0	0	0	0	0	94
Kent	138	0	1	133	0	0	0
Martinez	61	0	0	27	11	12	0
Mayne	117	105	0	0	0	0	0
Mirabelli	33	30	0	0	0	0	0
Mueller	116	0	0	3	108	0	0
Murray	15	0	0	0	0	0	9
Rios	72	0	0	0	0	0	53
Santangelo	113	0	0	11	3	1	81
Servais	69	62	1	0	0	0	0
Snow	161	0	160	0	0	0	0

Sick call: 1999 DL report

PLAYER	Days on the DL
Barry Bonds	52
Chris Brock	72
Ellis Burks	17
Mark Gardner	22
Charlie Hayes	19
Jeff Kent	18
Ramon Martinez	15
Bill Mueller	41
Armando Rios	72
Scott Servais	22
Julian Tavarez	31

Minor Leagues

Tops in the organization

BATTER	CLUB	AVG.	G	AB	R	H	HR	RBI
Murray, Calvin	Fre	.334	130	548	122	183	23	73
Otero, William	SJo	.333	96	402	81	134	10	56
Crespo, Felipe	Fre	.332	112	385	98	128	24	84
Woods, Ken	Fre	.324	124	469	77	152	6	73
Clark, Douglas	Shv	.315	133	470	73	148	12	64

HOME RUNS

Glendenning, M.	Shv	28
Canizaro, Jay	Fre	26
Flaherty, Tim	SJo	25
Crespo, Felipe	Fre	24
Murray, Calvin	Fre	23

WINS

Patrick, B.	Fre	14
Esteves, Jake	Shv	14
Jensen, Ryan	Fre	11
Several Players Tied at		10

RBI

Glendenning, M.	Shv	99
Flaherty, Tim	SJo	88
Crespo, Felipe	Fre	84
Minor, Damon	Shv	82
Serrano, Sammy	Bak	80

SAVES

Ozias, Todd	Bak	26
Davis, Jason	Shv	21
Miller, Benji	SJo	20
Bailey, Cory	Fre	18
Fields, Brian	S-K	9

STOLEN BASES

Murray, Calvin	Fre	42
Hill, Steve	Bak	39
Byas, Michael	Fre	33
Daeley, Scott	SJo	30
McDowell, Arturo	Bak	28

STRIKEOUTS

Fultz, Aaron	Fre	151
Jensen, Ryan	Fre	150
Urban, Jeff	SJo	143
Patrick, B.	Fre	142
Coscia, Tony	Bak	133

PITCHER	CLUB	W-L	ERA	IP	H	BB	SO
Riley, Michael	Shv	8-3	2.11	111	80	53	107
Esteves, Jake	Shv	14-3	2.93	163	135	40	109
Zerbe, Chad	Shv	8-10	3.23	167	156	43	97
Knoll, Brian	Shv	9-7	3.51	128	117	34	91
Prata, Danny	Bak	9-9	3.91	143	143	54	87

1999 salaries

	Bonuses	Total earned salary
Barry Bonds, of		9,381,057
Jeff Kent, 2b	25,000	5,750,000
Robb Nen, p	50,000	5,150,000
Ellis Burks, of		4,500,000
J.T. Snow, 1b		3,000,000
Kirk Rueter, p	60,000	2,810,000
Mark Gardner, p		2,000,000
Charlie Hayes, 3b	200,000	1,900,000
Livan Hernandez, p	300,000	1,875,000
Rich Aurilia, ss	150,000	950,000
Alan Embree, p		900,000
Shawn Estes, p		850,000
Marvin Benard, of	150,000	850,000
Brent Mayne, c		750,000
Rich Rodriguez, p	20,000	730,000
John Johnstone, p	10,000	702,500
Jerry Spradlin, p		687,500
F.P. Santangelo, of	50,000	550,000
Bill Mueller, 3b		525,000
Scott Servais, c		500,000
Felix Rodriguez, p		250,000
Russ Ortiz, p		220,000
Chris Brock, p		215,000
Doug Mirabelli, c		208,500
Ramon Martinez, 2b		205,000
Calvin Murray, of		200,000
Armando Rios, of		200,000
Joe Nathan, p		200,000

Average 1999 salary: $1,643,198
Total 1999 team payroll: $46,009,557
Termination pay: $57,377

307

San Francisco (1958-1999), includes New York (1883-1957)

Runs: Most, career

2011	Willie Mays, 1951-1972
1859	Mel Ott, 1926-1947
1313	Mike Tiernan, 1887-1899
1120	Bill Terry, 1923-1936
1113	Willie McCovey, 1959-1980

Hits: Most, career

3187	Willie Mays, 1951-1972
2876	Mel Ott, 1926-1947
2193	Bill Terry, 1923-1936
1974	Willie McCovey, 1959-1980
1835	Mike Tiernan, 1887-1899

2B: Most, career

504	Willie Mays, 1951-1972
488	Mel Ott, 1926-1947
373	Bill Terry, 1923-1936
308	Willie McCovey, 1959-1980
291	Travis Jackson, 1922-1936

3B: Most, career

162	Mike Tiernan, 1887-1899
139	Willie Mays, 1951-1972
131	Roger Connor, 1883-1894
117	Larry Doyle, 1907-1920
112	Bill Terry, 1923-1936

HR: Most, career

646	Willie Mays, 1951-1972
511	Mel Ott, 1926-1947
469	Willie McCovey, 1959-1980
269	BARRY BONDS, 1993-1999
247	MATT WILLIAMS, 1987-1996

RBI: Most, career

1860	Mel Ott, 1926-1947
1859	Willie Mays, 1951-1972
1388	Willie McCovey, 1959-1980
1078	Bill Terry, 1923-1936
929	Travis Jackson, 1922-1936

SB: Most, career

428	Mike Tiernan, 1887-1899
354	George Davis, 1893-1903
336	Willie Mays, 1951-1972
334	George Burns, 1911-1921
332	John Ward, 1883-1894

BB: Most, career

1708	Mel Ott, 1926-1947
1394	Willie Mays, 1951-1972
1168	Willie McCovey, 1959-1980
819	BARRY BONDS, 1993-1999
747	Mike Tiernan, 1887-1899

BA: Highest, career

.341	Bill Terry, 1923-1936
.332	George Davis, 1893-1903
.322	Ross Youngs, 1917-1926
.322	Frankie Frisch, 1919-1926
.308	Orlando Cepeda, 1958-1966 (12)

On-base avg: Highest, career

.439	BARRY BONDS, 1993-1999
.414	Mel Ott, 1926-1947
.403	Roger Bresnahan, 1902-1908
.402	Roger Connor, 1883-1894
.399	Ross Youngs, 1917-1926

Slug pct: Highest, career

.617	BARRY BONDS, 1993-1999
.564	Willie Mays, 1951-1972
.549	Johnny Mize, 1942-1949
.536	Kevin Mitchell, 1987-1991
.535	Orlando Cepeda, 1958-1966

Games started: Most, career

550	Christy Mathewson, 1900-1916
446	Juan Marichal, 1960-1973
432	Carl Hubbell, 1928-1943
412	Mickey Welch, 1883-1892
403	Amos Rusie, 1890-1898

Complete games: Most, career

433	Christy Mathewson, 1900-1916
391	Mickey Welch, 1883-1892
372	Amos Rusie, 1890-1898
260	Carl Hubbell, 1928-1943
244	Juan Marichal, 1960-1973 (6)

Saves: Most, career

199	ROD BECK, 1991-1997
127	Gary Lavelle, 1974-1984
125	Greg Minton, 1975-1987
83	Randy Moffitt, 1972-1981
78	Frank Linzy, 1963-1970

Shutouts: Most, career

79	Christy Mathewson, 1900-1916
52	Juan Marichal, 1960-1973
36	Carl Hubbell, 1928-1943
29	Amos Rusie, 1890-1898
28	Mickey Welch, 1883-1892

Wins: Most, career

372	Christy Mathewson, 1900-1916
253	Carl Hubbell, 1928-1943
238	Juan Marichal, 1960-1973
238	Mickey Welch, 1883-1892
234	Amos Rusie, 1890-1898

K: Most, career

2499	Christy Mathewson, 1900-1916
2281	Juan Marichal, 1960-1973
1835	Amos Rusie, 1890-1898
1677	Carl Hubbell, 1928-1943
1606	Gaylord Perry, 1962-1971

Win pct: Highest, career

.693	Sal Maglie, 1945-1955
.680	Tim Keefe, 1885-1891
.664	Christy Mathewson, 1900-1916
.656	Jesse Barnes, 1918-1923
.630	Juan Marichal, 1960-1973 (11)

ERA: Lowest, career

2.12	Christy Mathewson, 1900-1916
2.38	Joe McGinnity, 1902-1908
2.43	Jeff Tesreau, 1912-1918
2.45	Red Ames, 1903-1913
2.82	Gary Lavelle, 1974-1984 (12)

Runs: Most, season

147	Mike Tiernan, 1889
139	Bill Terry, 1930
138	Mel Ott, 1929
137	Johnny Mize, 1947
134	Bobby Bonds, 1970 (6)

Hits: Most, season

254	Bill Terry, 1930
231	Freddie Lindstrom, 1928
231	Freddie Lindstrom, 1930
226	Bill Terry, 1929
208	Willie Mays, 1958 (13)

2B: Most, season

46	Jack Clark, 1978
44	BARRY BONDS, 1998
43	Willie Mays, 1959
43	Bill Terry, 1931
42	George Kelly, 1921
42	Bill Terry, 1932

3B: Most, season

27	George Davis, 1893
25	Larry Doyle, 1911
22	Roger Connor, 1887
21	Mike Tiernan, 1890
21	Mike Tiernan, 1895
21	George Vanhaltren, 1896

HR: Most, season

52	Willie Mays, 1965
51	Willie Mays, 1955
51	Johnny Mize, 1947
49	Willie Mays, 1962

47	Willie Mays, 1964
47	Kevin Mitchell, 1989

RBI: Most, season

151	Mel Ott, 1929
142	Orlando Cepeda, 1961
141	Willie Mays, 1962
138	Johnny Mize, 1947
136	George Davis, 1897
136	George Kelly, 1924

SB: Most, season

111	John Ward, 1887
65	George Davis, 1897
62	George Burns, 1914
62	John Ward, 1889
58	Billy North, 1979 (7)

BB: Most, season

151	BARRY BONDS, 1996
145	BARRY BONDS, 1997
144	Eddie Stanky, 1950
137	Willie McCovey, 1970
130	BARRY BONDS, 1998

BA: Highest, season

.401	Bill Terry, 1930
.379	Freddie Lindstrom, 1930
.372	Bill Terry, 1929
.371	Roger Connor, 1885
.347	Willie Mays, 1958 (23)

On-base avg; Highest, season

.461	BARRY BONDS, 1996
.460	Eddie Stanky, 1950
.458	BARRY BONDS, 1993
.458	Mel Ott, 1930
.453	Willie McCovey, 1969

Slug pct: Highest, season

.677	BARRY BONDS, 1993
.667	Willie Mays, 1954
.659	Willie Mays, 1955
.656	Willie McCovey, 1969
.647	BARRY BONDS, 1994

Games started: Most, season

65	Mickey Welch, 1884
64	Tim Keefe, 1886
62	Amos Rusie, 1890
62	Amos Rusie, 1892
41	Gaylord Perry, 1970 (*)

Complete games: Most, season

62	Tim Keefe, 1886
62	Mickey Welch, 1884
59	Amos Rusie, 1892
56	Amos Rusie, 1890
56	Mickey Welch, 1886
30	Juan Marichal, 1968 (*)

Saves: Most, season

48	ROD BECK, 1993
40	ROBB NEN, 1998
37	ROD BECK, 1997
37	ROBB NEN, 1999
35	ROD BECK, 1996

Shutouts: Most, season

11	Christy Mathewson, 1908
10	Carl Hubbell, 1933
10	Juan Marichal, 1965
9	Joe McGinnity, 1904

Wins: Most, season

44	Mickey Welch, 1885
42	Tim Keefe, 1886
39	Mickey Welch, 1884
37	Christy Mathewson, 1908
36	Amos Rusie, 1894
26	Juan Marichal, 1968 (25)

K: Most, season

345	Mickey Welch, 1884
341	Amos Rusie, 1890
337	Amos Rusie, 1891
335	Tim Keefe, 1888
248	Juan Marichal, 1963 (11)

Win pct: Highest, season

.833	Hoyt Wilhelm, 1952
.818	Sal Maglie, 1950
.814	Joe McGinnity, 1904
.813	Carl Hubbell, 1936
.810	Doc Crandall, 1910
.806	Juan Marichal, 1966 (7)

ERA: Lowest, season

1.14	Christy Mathewson, 1909
1.28	Christy Mathewson, 1905
1.43	Christy Mathewson, 1908
1.44	Fred Anderson, 1917
1.57	Tim Keefe, 1885
1.99	Bobby Bolin, 1968 (16)

Most pinch-hit homers, season

4	Ernie Lombardi, 1946
4	Bill Taylor, 1955
4	Mike Ivie, 1978
4	Candy Maldonado, 1986
4	Ernie Riles, 1990

Most pinch-hit homers, career

13	Willie McCovey, 1959-1980
9	Bobby Hofman, 1949-1957

Longest hitting streak

33	George Davis, 1893
26	Jack Clark, 1978
24	Mike Donlin, 1908
24	Fred Lindstrom, 1930
24	Willie McCovey, 1963

Most consecutive scoreless innings

45	Carl Hubbell, 1933
45	Sal Maglie, -1950
40	Gaylord Perry, 1967
39	Christy Mathewson, 1901
39	Gaylord Perry, 1970

No-hit games

Amos Rusie, NY vs Bro NL, 6-0; July 31, 1891.

Christy Mathewson, NY at StL NL, 5-0; July 15, 1901.

Christy Mathewson, NY at Chi NL, 1-0; June 13, 1905.

Hooks Wiltse, NY vs Phi NL, 1-0; July 4, 1908 (1st game, ten innings).

Red Ames, NY vs Bro NL. 0-3; April 15, 1909 (lost on 7 hits in 13 innings after allowing the first hit in the tenth).

Jeff Tesreau, NY at Phi NL, 3-0; September 6, 1912 (1st game).

Rube Marquard, NY vs Bro NL, 2-0; April 15, 1915.

Jesse Barnes, NY vs Phi NL, 6-0; May 7, 1922.

Carl Hubbell, NY vs Pit NL, 11-0; May 8, 1929.

Juan Marichal, SF vs Hou NL, 1-0; June 15, 1963.

Gaylord Perry, SF vs StL NL, 1-0; September 17, 1968.

Ed Halicki, SF vs NY NL, 6-0; August 24, 1975 (2nd game).

John Montefusco, SF at Atl NL, 9-0; September 29, 1976.

Ed Crane, seven innings, darkness, NY vs Was NL, 3-0; September 27, 1888.

Red Ames, five innings, darkness, NY at StL NL, 5-0; September 14, 1903 (2nd game, first game in the major leagues).

Mike McCormick, five innings, rain, SF at Phi NL, 3-0; June 12, 1959. (allowed hit in 6th, but rain caused game to revert to 5 innings).

Sam Jones, seven innings, rain, SF at StL NL, 4-0; September 26, 1959.

ACTIVE PLAYERS in caps.

Players' years of service are listed by the first and last years with this team and are not necessarily consecutive; all statistics record performances for this team only.

Leader from the franchise's current location is included. If not in the top five, leader's rank is listed in parenthesis; asterisk (*) indicates player is not in top 25.

Los Angeles Dodgers

By Tom DiPace

With 34 homers and 112 RBI, Eric Karros was a model of consistency for the unsteady Dodgers.

1999 Dodgers: All talk, no walk

The Los Angeles Dodgers were the National League's biggest bust in 1999. Perhaps general manager Kevin Malone was asking for trouble last winter when he proclaimed, "There's a new sheriff in town," and talked about how exciting a Kevin Brown-Roger Clemens matchup would be in Game One of the World Series.

The Dodgers started the season with a payroll of $79.2 million, second in the majors behind the New York Yankees' $85.1 million. By that token, Malone's lofty expectations made more sense than the losing that followed.

Brown, one of the most dominant pitchers around, signed a record $105 million, seven-year contract to give the promising pitching staff an ace. Davey Johnson, a proven winner, was brought in as manager, and a handful of other offseason moves made the Dodgers heavy favorites to win their division, if not the National League pennant. At the very least, the Dodgers figured to win their first postseason game since 1988.

"With everything that was done this winter, the goal isn't just to win the NL West, the goal is to win the World Series," first baseman Eric Karros said in March.

A 5-1 start fueled hopes even more, and the Dodgers were in good shape after 35 games with a 20-15 record.

The collapse in June and July, when the Dodgers went 19-35, transformed them from a competitive 26-24 to a dismal 45-59. After that, the closest they came to .500 was six games under. They finished third with a miserable 77-85, their first losing record since 1992.

"It was definitely a frustrating season, with the expectations and experience we had," Karros said. "There are a lot of reasons why; it just depends on which route you want to take to analyze this team."

Pitching is a good place to start. Brown did fine, going 18-9 with a 3.00 ERA. But he couldn't make those around him better. In fact, the other starters, for the most part, weren't very good at all, especially Carlos Perez, who had a 2-10 record with a 7.43 ERA before being sent to the

Team MVP

Eric Karros: Some things are constant with the Dodgers: Eric Karros will be rumored to be on the trading block and Eric Karros will finish the season as one of the team's most consistent producers. In 1999, he hit .304, leading the club with 112 RBI and tying Gary Sheffield for the home run lead with 34. He also led the team in hits (176), total bases (318) and doubles (40).

minor leagues July 28. Chan Ho Park, Darren Dreifort and Ismael Valdes had their moments, but were inconsistent—the team ERA of 4.45 was by far the franchise's worst in 41 years.

Karros had his best year with 34 homers to equal a career-high and personal-bests of a .304 batting average, 40 doubles and 112 RBI. Others had impressive numbers, notably shortstop Mark Grudzielanek (.326), and outfielders Gary Sheffield (.301, 34 homers and 101 RBI) and Raul Mondesi, with career-high totals of 33 homers, 99 RBI and 36 stolen bases.

But several disappointments on offense added up to a .266 team batting average and 793 runs scored—both well below average in the NL. Catcher Todd Hundley was a major disappointment despite his 24 homers, hitting just .207, and center fielder Devon White batted .268. To make matters worse, the defense was suspect, especially up the middle. Hundley, for example, threw out less than 20 percent of opposing runners trying to steal.

The team's extreme frustration was exemplified in the plight of Mondesi. Despite becoming the first big-leaguer in 1999 to reach 30 homers and 30 stolen bases, he hit just .253 and was extremely unproductive in June and July, when the team hit the skids. On Aug. 11, he was so exasperated that he unleashed a profanity-laced tirade aimed at Malone and Johnson, and asked to be traded.

1999 Dodgers: Week-by-week notes

These notes were excerpted from the following issues of Baseball Weekly.

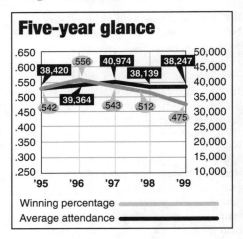

Five-year glance

Winning percentage

Average attendance

▶**April 14:** On opening day, right fielder Raul Mondesi hit a three-run homer to tie the score with the Dodgers down to their final out in the ninth inning. In the 11th, his two-run shot gave the Dodgers an 8-6 victory. Mondesi hit two other homers during the week, one that broke a 2-2 tie against Arizona and one that broke a scoreless tie against Colorado. Mondesi led the NL with 10 RBI.

▶**April 28:** The Dodgers averaged 4.7 runs through their first 18 games, but their .195 average (36-for-185) with runners in scoring position showed the opportunities they let get away. Catcher Todd Hundley (0-for-12), Raul Mondesi (4-for-22), first baseman Eric Karros (4-for-20) and left fielder Gary Sheffield (4-for-18) were among those struggling the most.

▶**May 5:** At 21, third baseman Adrian Beltre was providing the most consistent bat in the lineup. He had at least one hit in 20 of his first 23 games, reeled off a team-high 11-game hitting streak, then got six straight hits on April 29 and 30.

▶**May 12:** Todd Hundley extended his hitting streak to seven games on May 8. During the streak his average climbed from .148 to .256. Hundley ended his streak with a pinch-hitting appearance on May 9, fouling out.

▶**May 19:** In two starts last week right-hander Chan Ho Park, 3-3, took a comfortable lead into the sixth and let it slip away. The Marlins had hit only 12 home runs, but they whacked three off Park in two innings to erase a 4-0 deficit in their 6-4 Mother's Day victory at Dodger Stadium. On May 15 St. Louis feasted on a series of Park's off-speed pitches to rally from a 4-1 deficit for an 8-5 victory.

▶**May 26:** In his first 10 appearances closer Jeff Shaw went 1-0 with an 0.68 ERA. In his next nine games, through May 23, he went 0-2 with an 8.63 ERA.

▶**June 9:** Chan Ho Park kicked Angels pitcher Tim Belcher—spiking him with both feet—during an altercation that cleared both benches and bullpens on June 5. Belcher fielded Park's sacrifice bunt and tagged Park on the sternum too forcefully, Park said. Park punched him with a left forearm to the chin. Belcher pushed Park, and Park responded with the kick.

▶**June 16:** Right-hander Ismael Valdes lost his third consecutive decision on June 12, as the Dodgers scored just 10 runs in the losses. Valdes was 5-5 despite a 3.73 ERA.

▶**June 23:** Todd Hundley was relegated to backing up Angel Pena so he could focus on his catching mechanics. Hundley's struggles had hurt the Dodgers. He had thrown out just 12 percent (7-for-60) of would-be base stealers and had batted only .230 with seven home runs and 20 RBI.

▶**June 30:** Right-hander Kevin Brown continued his mastery against the Giants on June 25. He allowed two runs in 7⅓ innings, raising his record to 7-0 with an 0.78 ERA against San Francisco—5-0 and 0.63 at 3Com Park.

▶**July 7:** With their postseason hopes going up in flames anyway, the Dodgers took the extreme step of building a bonfire in the bullpen on July 3 and burning various articles from the clubhouse. Two hours later the Giants blasted the Dodgers 9-1, leaving Los Angeles 10 games out of first place.

▶**July 15:** The Dodgers slipped 12 games below .500 for the first time since 1992

before putting together a four-game winning streak. The Dodgers, with an $80 million payroll, had only one player on the All-Star team—Gary Sheffield.

▶**July 21:** Raul Mondesi finally ended his 39-day, 112-at-bat homerless string on July 17, taking Angels knuckleballer Steve Sparks deep, for his 20th home run of the season. While Mondesi has been cooling down, Eric Karros heated up. Karros had just seven home runs through the end of May but had 19 through July 18, including five in his past seven games.

▶**July 28:** Manager Davey Johnson benched second baseman Eric Young and bumped left-hander Carlos Perez from the rotation. A sore left ankle and sore right hamstring had bothered Young, making him a liability on defense. His .350 on-base percentage was sub-par for a leadoff hitter, so Johnson decided to let Young get healthy. Perez allowed 10 earned runs in a loss to Arizona on July 23, dropping him to 2-10 with a 7.43 ERA.

▶**Aug. 18:** Kevin Brown found himself back in the Cy Young contest by throwing seven shutout innings against both the Mets and the Braves. In his past five starts Brown was 4-0 with an 0.70 ERA, catapulting him to the top three in several pitching categories. He was 14-6 with a 3.14 ERA and 156 strikeouts.

▶**Aug. 25:** Todd Hundley thought hard about scrapping switch-hitting before actually doing so last week, deciding to swing exclusively from the left side. His average from the right side had slipped to .098 (4-for-41). All 19 of his home runs were hit left-handed.

▶**Sept. 8:** General manager Kevin Malone has big choices to make during this off-season. The key is whether to dismantle, with Raul Mondesi, Eric Karros and Eric Young seeming the most likely candidates to be moved. Malone said the team appears to be making progress. By going 17-11 in August, the Dodgers had their first winning month since April.

▶**Sept. 15:** Right-hander Darren Dreifort will be back in the rotation next season, Davey Johnson said. Dreifort (13-13) is on a roll that has seen him go 5-2 with a 2.96 ERA in his past seven starts. Right-hander Eric Gagne made a superb major league debut on Sept. 7, throwing six shutout innings at Florida in a no-decision.

▶**Sept. 22:** Ismael Valdes was 0-3 with an 18.00 ERA in his last three starts and said that persistent lower-back spasms had affected him. Meanwhile, Chan Ho Park improved to 5-0 in his past six starts with a victory on Sept. 18 at Colorado.

▶**Sept. 29:** The Dodgers broke their franchise record for home runs allowed in a season and had given up 185 through Sept. 26. The previous mark was 173 in 1958.

QUOTE OF THE YEAR

"I talked to him and said, 'Look, man, I know what you did. . . . I still love you.'"
—Manager Davey Johnson, on his response to right fielder Raul Mondesi's expletive-filled tirade against Johnson and GM Kevin Malone

Team Leaders

Batting avg.	Hits	Wins	Strikeouts
.326 Mark Grudzielanek	176 Eric Karros	18 Kevin Brown	221 Kevin Brown
.304 Eric Karros	165 Gary Sheffield	13 Darren Dreifort	174 Chan Ho Park
		13 Chan Ho Park	
HR	**Runs**		**Innings**
34 Eric Karros	103 Gary Sheffield	**Losses**	252.1 Kevin Brown
34 Gary Sheffield	98 Raul Mondesi	14 Ismael Valdes	203.1 Ismael Valdes
		13 Darren Dreifort	
RBI	**Stolen bases**		**Saves**
112 Eric Karros	51 Eric Young	**ERA**	34 Jeff Shaw
101 Gary Sheffield	36 Raul Mondesi	3.00 Kevin Brown	1 Jamie Arnold
		3.98 Ismael Valdes	1 Pedro Borbon
			1 Onan Masaoka

LOS ANGELES DODGERS 1999 final stats

BATTERS	BA	SLG	OBA	G	AB	R	H	TB	2B	3B	HR	RBI	BB	SO	SB	CS	E
Grudzielanek	.326	.436	.376	123	488	72	159	213	23	5	7	46	31	65	6	6	13
Hubbard	.314	.390	.387	82	105	23	33	41	5	0	1	13	13	24	4	3	1
Karros	.304	.550	.362	153	578	74	176	318	40	0	34	112	53	119	8	5	13
Sheffield	.301	.523	.407	152	549	103	165	287	20	0	34	101	101	64	11	5	7
Brumfield	.294	.412	.294	18	17	4	5	7	0	1	0	1	0	5	0	0	0
Hollandsworth	.284	.448	.345	92	261	39	74	117	12	2	9	32	24	61	5	2	3
Young	.281	.355	.371	119	456	73	128	162	24	2	2	41	63	26	51	22	9
Beltre	.275	.428	.352	152	538	84	148	230	27	5	15	67	61	105	18	7	29
White	.268	.407	.337	134	474	60	127	193	20	2	14	68	39	88	19	5	4
Mondesi	.253	.483	.332	159	601	98	152	290	29	5	33	99	71	134	36	9	6
Hansen	.252	.402	.404	100	107	14	27	43	8	1	2	17	26	20	0	0	3
Vizcaino	.252	.297	.304	94	266	27	67	79	9	0	1	29	20	23	2	1	7
Sanford	.250	.250	.250	5	8	1	2	2	0	0	0	2	0	1	0	0	0
LoDuca	.232	.337	.312	36	95	11	22	32	1	0	3	11	10	9	1	2	2
Counsell	.218	.259	.274	87	174	24	38	45	7	0	0	11	14	24	1	0	2
Pena	.208	.358	.276	43	120	14	25	43	6	0	4	21	12	24	0	1	3
Hundley	.207	.436	.295	114	376	49	78	164	14	0	24	55	44	113	3	0	16
Cookson	.200	.200	.200	3	5	0	1	1	0	0	0	0	0	1	0	0	0
Cromer	.192	.308	.263	33	52	5	10	16	0	0	2	8	5	10	0	0	0
Cora	.167	.200	.194	11	30	2	5	6	1	0	0	3	0	4	0	0	2
Castro	.000	.000	.000	2	1	0	0	0	0	0	0	0	0	1	0	0	0
Wilkins	.000	.000	.000	3	4	0	0	0	0	0	0	0	0	2	0	0	0

PITCHERS	W-L	ERA	BA	G	GS	CG	GF	SH	SV	IP	H	R	ER	HR	BB	SO
Gagne	1-1	2.10	.175	5	5	0	0	0	0	30.0	18	8	7	3	15	30
Shaw	2-4	2.78	.242	64	0	0	56	0	34	68.0	64	25	21	6	15	43
Brown	18-9	3.00	.222	35	35	5	0	1	0	252.1	210	99	84	19	59	221
Mills	3-4	3.73	.261	68	0	0	18	0	0	72.1	70	33	30	10	43	49
Maddux	1-1	3.77	.275	53	0	0	21	0	0	59.2	63	26	25	6	22	45
Valdes	9-14	3.98	.270	32	32	2	0	1	0	203.1	213	97	90	32	58	143
Herges	0-2	4.07	.255	17	0	0	9	0	0	24.1	24	13	11	5	8	18
Williams	2-0	4.08	.190	5	3	0	1	0	0	17.2	12	10	8	2	9	7
Borbon	4-3	4.09	.209	70	0	0	11	0	1	50.2	39	23	23	5	29	33
Masaoka	2-4	4.32	.222	54	0	0	12	0	1	66.2	55	33	32	8	47	61
Dreifort	13-13	4.79	.260	30	29	1	0	1	0	178.2	177	105	95	20	76	140
Mlicki	0-1	4.91	.323	2	0	0	0	0	0	7.1	10	4	4	1	2	1
Park	13-11	5.23	.276	33	33	0	0	0	0	194.1	208	120	113	31	100	174
Judd	3-1	5.46	.280	7	4	0	0	0	0	28.0	30	17	17	4	12	22
Arnold	2-4	5.48	.300	36	3	0	18	0	1	69.0	81	50	42	6	34	26
Bochtler	0-0	5.54	.224	12	0	0	4	0	0	13.0	11	8	8	3	6	7
Perez	2-10	7.43	.317	17	16	0	0	0	0	89.2	116	77	74	23	39	40
Osuna	0-0	7.71	.222	5	0	0	1	0	0	4.2	4	5	4	0	3	5
Checo	2-2	10.34	.333	9	2	0	1	0	0	15.2	24	20	18	5	13	11
Kubenka	0-1	11.74	.371	6	0	0	2	0	0	7.2	13	12	10	1	4	2

2000 preliminary roster

PITCHERS (19)
Terry Adams
Jamie Arnold
Kevin Brown
Darren Dreifort
Kris Foster
Eric Gagne
Randy Galvez
Apostol Garcia
Matt Herges
Mike Judd
Onan Masaoka
Alan Mills
Dan Naulty
Antonio Osuna
Chan Ho Park
Carlos Perez
Chad Ricketts
Jeff Shaw
Jeff Williams

CATCHERS (3)
Todd Hundley
Paul LoDuca
Angel Pena

INFIELDERS (10)
Adrian Beltre
Hiram Bocachica
Juan Castro
Alex Cora
Mark Grudzielanek
Dave Hansen
Eric Karros
Jorge Nunez
Kevin Orie
Jose Vizcaino

OUTFIELDERS (8)
Kevin Gibbs
Shawn Green
Todd Hollandsworth
Trenidad Hubbard
Terry Jones
Tony Mota
Gary Sheffield
Devon White

Games played by position

PLAYER	G	C	1B	2B	3B	SS	OF
Beltre	152	0	0	0	152	0	0
Brumfield	18	0	0	0	0	0	11
Castro	2	0	0	1	0	1	0
Cookson	3	0	0	0	0	0	3
Cora	11	0	0	3	0	8	0
Counsell	50	0	0	38	0	2	0
Cromer	33	0	1	9	2	9	2
Grudzielanek	123	0	0	0	0	119	0
Hansen	100	0	20	0	13	0	2
Hollandsworth	92	0	13	0	0	0	67
Hubbard	82	1	0	1	0	0	51
Hundley	115	108	0	0	0	0	0
Karros	153	0	151	0	0	0	0
LoDuca	36	34	0	0	0	0	0
Mondesi	159	0	0	0	0	0	158
Pena	43	43	0	0	0	0	0
Sanford	5	0	0	2	0	0	0
Sheffield	152	0	0	0	0	0	145
Vizcaino	94	0	0	30	9	44	1
White	134	0	0	0	0	0	128
Wilkins	3	1	0	0	0	0	0
Young	119	0	0	116	0	0	0

Sick call: 1999 DL report

PLAYER	Days on the DL
Robinson Checo	45
Alex Cora	83
Tripp Cromer	58
Kevin Gibbs	116
Mark Grudzielanek	33
Todd Hollandsworth	40*
Steve Montgomery	177
Antonio Osuna	165**
Carlos Perez	27
Jose Vizcaino	18
Eric Young	20

Indicates two separate terms on Disabled List.
**Indicates three separate terms on Disabled List.*

1999 salaries

	Bonuses	Total earned salary
Kevin Brown, p		10,714,286
Gary Sheffield, of	20,000	9,956,667
Raul Mondesi, of		9,000,000
Eric Karros, 1b		5,500,000
Todd Hundley, c		5,325,000
Eric Young, 2b		4,500,000
Ismael Valdes, p		4,275,000
Jeff Shaw, p	25,000	3,408,333
Jose Vizcaino, ss		3,000,000
Devon White, of		2,500,000
Chan Ho Park, p		2,300,000
Mark Grudzielanek, ss		1,900,000
Darren Dreifort, p		1,900,000
Alan Mills, p		1,250,000
Antonio Osuna, p		1,050,000
Todd Hollandsworth, of		850,000
Dave Hansen, 1b		450,000
Pedro Borbon, p		375,000
Tripp Cromer, ss	61,500	346,500
Trenidad Hubbard, of		300,000
Robinson Checo, p		300,000
Mike Maddux, p		265,000
Craig Counsell, 2b		245,000
Adrian Beltre, 3b		220,000
Mike Judd, p		205,000
Matt Herges, p		200,000
Paul LoDuca, c		200,000
Steve Montgomery, p		200,000
Onan Masaoka, p		200,000
Kevin Gibbs, of		200,000

Average 1999 salary: $2,371,193
Total 1999 team payroll: $71,135,786
Termination pay: $5,491,461

Minor Leagues

Tops in the organization

BATTER	CLUB	AVG.	G	AB	R	H	HR	RBI
Mota, Tony	SAn	.325	98	345	65	112	15	75
Gorr, Robb	SBr	.319	132	546	67	174	11	106
Grijak, Kevin	Alb	.317	119	401	58	127	18	80
Gonzalez, Jimmy	SBr	.316	111	471	78	149	5	53
Chen, Chin-Feng	SBr	.316	131	510	98	161	31	123

HOME RUNS
Chen, Chin-Feng	SBr	31
Cookson, Brent	Alb	28
Leach, Nick	VB	20
Several Players Tied at		18

WINS
Dorame, Randey	SBr	14
Castillo, Marcos	SBr	14
Gagne, Eric	SAn	12
Burnside, Adrian	SBr	10
Williams, Jeff	Alb	9

RBI
Chen, Chin-Feng	SBr	123
Gorr, Robb	SBr	106
Allen, Luke	SAn	82
Riggs, Adam	Alb	81
Grijak, Kevin	Alb	80

SAVES
Everly, Bill	SBr	34
Husted, Brent	VB	27
Montgomery, Matt	SAn	26
Kubenka, Jeff	Alb	11
Ruffin, Johnny	Alb	10

STOLEN BASES
Metcalfe, Mike	SAn	57
Chen, Chin-Feng	SBr	31
Bocachica, Hiram	SAn	30
Thurston, Joseph	SAn	27
Riggs, Eric	SBr	27

STRIKEOUTS
Gagne, Eric	SAn	185
Dorame, Randey	SBr	164
Beckett, Robbie	Alb	146
Stone, Ricky	Alb	132
Colyer, Stephen	SBr	131

PITCHER	CLUB	W-L	ERA	IP	H	BB	SO
Gagne, Eric	SAn	12-4	2.63	168	122	64	185
Alvarez, Victor	SAn	8-7	2.71	129	114	26	100
Dorame, Randey	SBr	14-5	2.72	165	145	38	164
Garcia, Apostol	SAn	7-5	3.36	102	110	45	50
Martin, Scott	GRF	4-4	3.86	103	115	23	69

Los Angeles (1958-1999), includes Brooklyn (1890-1957)

Runs: Most, career

1338	Pee Wee Reese, 1940-1958	
1255	Zack Wheat, 1909-1926	
1199	Duke Snider, 1947-1962	
1163	Jim Gilliam, 1953-1966	
1088	Gil Hodges, 1943-1961	

Hits: Most, career

2804	Zack Wheat, 1909-1926
2170	Pee Wee Reese, 1940-1958
2091	Willie Davis, 1960-1973
1995	Duke Snider, 1947-1962
1968	Steve Garvey, 1969-1982

2B: Most, career

464	Zack Wheat, 1909-1926
343	Duke Snider, 1947-1962
333	Steve Garvey, 1969-1982
330	Pee Wee Reese, 1940-1958
324	Carl Furillo, 1946-1960

3B: Most, career

171	Zack Wheat, 1909-1926
110	Willie Davis, 1960-1973
97	Hy Myers, 1909-1922
87	Jake Daubert, 1910-1918
82	John Hummel, 1905-1915
82	Duke Snider, 1947-1962

HR: Most, career

389	Duke Snider, 1947-1962
361	Gil Hodges, 1943-1961
242	Roy Campanella, 1948-1957
228	Ron Cey, 1971-1982
211	Steve Garvey, 1969-1982
211	ERIC KARROS, 1991-1999

RBI: Most, career

1271	Duke Snider, 1947-1962
1254	Gil Hodges, 1943-1961
1210	Zack Wheat, 1909-1926
1058	Carl Furillo, 1946-1960
992	Steve Garvey, 1969-1982

SB: Most, career

490	Maury Wills, 1959-1972
418	Davey Lopes, 1972-1981
335	Willie Davis, 1960-1973
298	Tom Daly, 1890-1901
290	Steve Sax, 1981-1988

BB: Most, career

1210	Pee Wee Reese, 1940-1958
1036	Jim Gilliam, 1953-1966
925	Gil Hodges, 1943-1961
893	Duke Snider, 1947-1962
765	Ron Cey, 1971-1982

BA: Highest, career

.352	Willie Keeler, 1893-1902
.339	Babe Herman, 1926-1945
.337	Jack Fournier, 1923-1926
.331	MIKE PIAZZA, 1992-1998
.317	Zack Wheat, 1909-1926

On-base avg: Highest, career

.421	Jack Fournier, 1923-1926
.416	Augie Galan, 1941-1946
.409	Jackie Robinson, 1947-1956
.405	Eddie Stanky, 1944-1947
.399	Mike Griffin, 1891-1898
.394	MIKE PIAZZA, 1992-1998 (7)

Slug pct: Highest, career

.572	MIKE PIAZZA, 1992-1998
.557	Babe Herman, 1926-1945
.553	Duke Snider, 1947-1962
.552	Jack Fournier, 1923-1926
.528	Reggie Smith, 1976-1981

Games started: Most, career

533	Don Sutton, 1966-1988
465	Don Drysdale, 1956-1969
335	Claude Osteen, 1965-1973
332	Brickyard Kennedy, 1892-1901
328	Dazzy Vance, 1922-1935

Complete games: Most, career

279	Brickyard Kennedy, 1892-1901
212	Dazzy Vance, 1922-1935
205	Burleigh Grimes, 1918-1926
186	Nap Rucker, 1907-1916
167	Don Drysdale, 1956-1969

Saves: Most, career

127	Todd Worrell, 1993-1997
125	Jim Brewer, 1964-1975
101	Ron Perranoski, 1961-1972
85	Jay Howell, 1988-1992
83	Clem Labine, 1950-1960

Shutouts: Most, career

52	Don Sutton, 1966-1988
49	Don Drysdale, 1956-1969
40	Sandy Koufax, 1955-1966
38	Nap Rucker, 1907-1916
34	Claude Osteen, 1965-1973

Wins: Most, career

233	Don Sutton, 1966-1988
209	Don Drysdale, 1956-1969
190	Dazzy Vance, 1922-1935
177	Brickyard Kennedy, 1892-1901
165	Sandy Koufax, 1955-1966

K: Most, career

2696	Don Sutton, 1966-1988
2486	Don Drysdale, 1956-1969
2396	Sandy Koufax, 1955-1966
1918	Dazzy Vance, 1922-1935
1759	Fernando Valenzuela, 1980-1990

Win pct: Highest, career

.715	Preacher Roe, 1948-1954
.682	Jay Hughes, 1899-1902
.674	Tommy John, 1972-1978
.658	Billy Loes, 1950-1956
.655	Sandy Koufax, 1955-1966

ERA: Lowest, career

2.31	Jeff Pfeffer, 1913-1921
2.42	Nap Rucker, 1907-1916
2.56	Ron Perranoski, 1961-1972
2.58	Rube Marquard, 1915-1920
2.62	Jim Brewer, 1964-1975

Runs: Most, season

148	Hub Collins, 1890
143	Babe Herman, 1930
140	Mike Griffin, 1895
140	Willie Keeler, 1899
136	Mike Griffin, 1897
130	Maury Wills, 1962 (10)

Hits: Most, season

241	Babe Herman, 1930
230	Tommy Davis, 1962
221	Zack Wheat, 1925
219	Lefty O'Doul, 1932
217	Babe Herman, 1929

2B: Most, season

52	Johnny Frederick, 1929
48	Babe Herman, 1930
47	Wes Parker, 1970
44	Johnny Frederick, 1930
43	Babe Herman, 1931
43	Augie Galan, 1944
43	Steve Sax, 1986

3B: Most, season

26	George Treadway, 1894
22	Hy Myers, 1920
20	Dan Brouthers, 1892
20	Tommy Corcoran, 1894
19	Jimmy Sheckard, 1901
16	Willie Davis, 1970 (12)

HR: Most, season

43	Duke Snider, 1956
42	Gil Hodges, 1954
42	Duke Snider, 1953
42	Duke Snider, 1955
41	Roy Campanella, 1953
40	MIKE PIAZZA, 1997 (6)

RBI: Most, season

153	Tommy Davis, 1962
142	Roy Campanella, 1953
136	Duke Snider, 1955
130	Jack Fournier, 1925
130	Babe Herman, 1930
130	Gil Hodges, 1954
130	Duke Snider, 1954

SB: Most, season

104	Maury Wills, 1962
94	Maury Wills, 1965
88	John Ward, 1892
85	Hub Collins, 1890
77	Davey Lopes, 1975

BB: Most, season

148	Eddie Stanky, 1945
137	Eddie Stanky, 1946
119	Dolph Camilli, 1938
116	Pee Wee Reese, 1949
114	Augie Galan, 1945
110	Jimmy Wynn, 1975 (6)

BA: Highest, season

.393	Babe Herman, 1930
.381	Babe Herman, 1929
.379	Willie Keeler, 1899
.375	Zack Wheat, 1924
.368	Lefty O'Doul, 1932
.361	MIKE PIAZZA, 1997 (7)

On-base avg; Highest, season

.467	Mike Griffin, 1894
.455	Babe Herman, 1930
.446	Jack Fournier, 1925
.444	Mike Griffin, 1895
.440	Jackie Robinson, 1952
.434	Wally Moon, 1961 (9)

Slug pct: Highest, season

.678	Babe Herman, 1930
.647	Duke Snider, 1954
.638	MIKE PIAZZA, 1997
.628	Duke Snider, 1955
.627	Duke Snider, 1953

Games started: Most, season

44	George Haddock, 1892
44	Brickyard Kennedy, 1893
44	Adonis Terry, 1890
43	Tom Lovett, 1891
42	Ed Stein, 1892
42	Don Drysdale, 1963
42	Don Drysdale, 1965

Complete games: Most, season

40	Brickyard Kennedy, 1893
39	George Haddock, 1892
39	Tom Lovett, 1890
39	Tom Lovett, 1891
38	Oscar Jones, 1904
38	Brickyard Kennedy, 1898
38	Ed Stein, 1892
38	Adonis Terry, 1890
27	Sandy Koufax, 1965 (*)
27	Sandy Koufax, 1966 (*)

Saves: Most, season

44	Todd Worrell, 1996
35	Todd Worrell, 1997
34	JEFF SHAW, 1999
32	Todd Worrell, 1995
28	Jay Howell, 1989

Shutouts: Most, season

11	Sandy Koufax, 1963
9	Don Sutton, 1972
8	TIM BELCHER, 1989
8	Don Drysdale, 1968
8	OREL HERSHISER, 1988
8	Sandy Koufax, 1965
8	Fernando Valenzuela, 1981

Wins: Most, season

30	Tom Lovett, 1890
29	George Haddock, 1892
28	Jay Hughes, 1899
28	Joe McGinnity, 1900
28	Dazzy Vance, 1924
27	Sandy Koufax, 1966 (6)

K: Most, season

382	Sandy Koufax, 1965
317	Sandy Koufax, 1966
306	Sandy Koufax, 1963
269	Sandy Koufax, 1961
262	Dazzy Vance, 1924

Win pct: Highest, season

.889	Freddie Fitzsimmons, 1940
.880	Preacher Roe, 1951
.864	OREL HERSHISER, 1985
.842	Ron Perranoski, 1963
.833	Sandy Koufax, 1963

ERA: Lowest, season

1.58	Rube Marquard, 1916
1.68	Ned Garvin, 1904
1.73	Sandy Koufax, 1966
1.74	Sandy Koufax, 1964
1.87	Kaiser Wilhelm, 1908

Most pinch-hit homers, season

6	Johnny Frederick, Bro-1932
5	Lee Lacy, 1978
5	Billy Ashley, 1996

Most pinch-hit homers, career

8	Johnny Frederick, 1929-1934
8	Lee Lacy, 1972-1978
7	Duke Snider, 1947-1962
7	Billy Ashley, 1992-1997

Longest hitting streak

31	Willie Davis, 1969
29	Zack Wheat, 1916
27	Joe Medwick, 1942
27	Duke Snider, 1953
26	Willie Keeler, 1902
26	Zack Wheat, 1918

Most consecutive scoreless innings

59	OREL HERSHISER, 1988
58	Don Drysdale, 1968
39	Don Newcombe, 1956

No hit games

Tom Lovett, Bro vs NY NL, 4-0; June 22, 1891.

Mal Eason, Bro at StL NL, 2-0; July 20, 1906.

Harry McIntyre, Bro vs Pit NL, 0-1; August 1, 1906 (lost on 4 hits in 13 innings after allowing the first hit in the 11th).

Nap Rucker, Bro vs Bos NL, 6-0; September 5, 1908 (2nd game).

Dazzy Vance, Bro vs Phi NL, 10-1; September 13, 1925 (1st game).

Tex Carleton, Bro at Cin NL, 3-0; April 30, 1940.

Ed Head, Bro vs Bos NL, 5-0; April 23, 1946.

Rex Barney, Bro at NY NL, 2-0; September 9, 1948.

Carl Erskine, Bro vs Chi NL, 5-0; June 19, 1952.

Carl Erskine, Bro vs NY NL, 3-0; May 12, 1956.

Sal Maglie, Bro vs Phi NL, 5-0; September 25, 1956.

Sandy Koufax, LA vs NY NL, 5-0; June 30, 1962.

Sandy Koufax, LA vs SF NL, 8-0; May 11, 1963.

Sandy Koufax, LA at Phi NL, 3-0; June 4, 1964.

Sandy Koufax, LA vs Chi NL, 1-0; September 9, 1965 (perfect game).

Bill Singer, LA vs Phi NL, 5-0; July 20, 1970.

Jerry Reuss, LA at SF NL, 8-0; June 27, 1980.

Fernando Valenzuela, LA vs StL NL, 6-0; June 29, 1990.

Kevin Gross, LA vs SF NL, 2-0; August 17, 1992.

RAMON MARTINEZ, LA vs Fla NL, 7-0; July 14, 1995.

HIDEO NOMO, LA at Col, 9-0; September 17, 1996.

Ed Stein, six innings, rain, Bro vs Chi NL, 6-0; June 2, 1894.

Fred Frankhouse, seven and two-thirds innings, rain, Bro vs Cin NL, 5-0; August 27, 1937.

ACTIVE PLAYERS in caps.

Players' years of service are listed by the first and last years with this team and are not necessarily consecutive; all statistics record performances for this team only.

317

Reggie Sanders led the Padres in both home runs and stolen bases.

By Tom DiPace

1999 Padres: From pennant to poorhouse

The San Diego Padres didn't finish last in the NL West like many thought they would following their post-World Series breakup—but they came pretty close.

San Diego's few highlights were top-notch: Tony Gwynn's 3,000th hit and a team-record 14-game winning streak in midsummer that showed a glimmer of hope. But the lowlights were too numerous to overcome. The Padres followed up their 1998 NL championship by finishing fourth in the division at 74-88, 26 games behind the second-year Arizona Diamondbacks.

When their brief shot at contention died out after the All-Star break, the Padres at least tried to finish ahead of the hated Los Angeles Dodgers. The Dodgers not only outspent the Padres by $30 million, but lured away their 1998 ace, Kevin Brown, for a record $105 million over seven seasons. But the Dodgers finished three games ahead of the Padres.

San Diego was limited by youth, injuries, an anemic offense, the worst road record in the majors, and having to pay $6 million to Randy Myers, who didn't throw a single pitch due to a shoulder injury.

"Coming off a season like we did last year, it makes it a little tougher to have a losing season," said manager Bruce Bochy, who was constantly juggling his lineup. "We knew it was going to be different with the changes we made. But I'm proud of them. They came out playing all season."

The Padres never quit. They just never had enough.

"We're not really disappointed," second baseman Quilvio Veras said. "We did the best we can with the team we have."

The Padres re-signed first baseman Wally Joyner and catcher Carlos Hernandez after the World Series loss to the New York Yankees. But Joyner slumped badly (.248, five homers), partly due to a shoulder injury, and Hernandez suffered a season-ending Achilles' heel injury in spring training.

The Padres felt they needed to let Steve Finley go in order to get a look at Ruben Rivera. What they saw was an extremely

erratic player who hit 23 homers and made some spectacular catches in center field, but hit just .195 and struck out 143 times.

George Arias was a bust as Ken Caminiti's replacement at third base. But Phil Nevin, acquired in spring training, shed his label as a utility player and not only took over at third, but got a two-year contract extension as well. Nevin, the first pick overall in the 1992 amateur draft, led the Padres with 85 RBI and was second with 24 homers.

The Padres saw Cincinnati and Oakland contend with much lower payrolls. Wanting to do a better job of producing home-grown talent, San Diego hired Ted Simmons to run both the farm system and the scouting department.

"We'll still be a younger club," said general manager Kevin Towers, "and we'll continue to get a bit younger. That's the way we need to go."

Except, of course, in the case of Gwynn. Sidelined twice by a nagging calf injury, Gwynn got his 3,000th hit on Aug. 6 at Montreal. He hit .338 for the season, one point below his lifetime average.

"Under the circumstances, I did O.K.," said Gwynn, an eight-time NL batting champion who now has 3,067 hits. "I wasn't as consistent as I wanted to be, but I started on a high note and I finished on a high note. In between was a roller coaster. I feel like I have a couple of years left where I can still be productive."

319

1999 Padres: Week by week notes

These notes were excerpted from the following issues of Baseball Weekly.

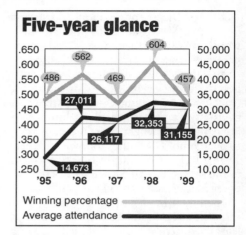

Five-year glance

Winning percentage
Average attendance

▶**April 7:** Because catcher-infielder Phil Nevin went on the DL with a pulled hamstring muscle only three days after the Padres acquired him from Anaheim (in a trade for infielder Andy Sheets), outfielder-infielder Eric Owens made the final cut. Owens, 28, had a great spring, hitting .466 (27-for-58) and playing every position but shortstop.

▶**April 14:** Right-hander Andy Ashby allowed one run over seven innings in his second effort, on April 10, after he was shelled for eight runs in less than two innings in his first outing. Before Ashby's strong outing, starters had worked 21⅓ innings in the first five games and the bullpen had worked 21⅔.

▶**April 21:** Center field had become a problem spot. Manager Bruce Bochy held a private meeting with Ruben Rivera on April 16 after the slumping player failed to run out a ground ball. Rivera was off to a 4-for-30 (.133) start with 13 strikeouts. The other option in center, Reggie Sanders, is 6-for-32 (.188), and he struck out three times on April 17 as Rivera sat out a second consecutive game.

▶**April 28:** Southpaw Sterling Hitchcock continued to struggle. He visited the video room after a third consecutive bad outing on April 22. Hitchcock had allowed 14 earned runs in 15 innings, giving up 19 hits (including five homers) and seven walks.

▶**May 5:** One of the Padres' all-time favorite streaks ended on April 28 with one Mike Piazza swing. Until the Mets catcher hit a two-run homer off closer Trevor Hoffman, the Padres had not lost a game in which they led after eight innings since July 24, 1996, a string of 181 consecutive wins.

▶**May 12:** Reggie Sanders is 17-for-45 (.378) with five homers, eight RBI and six stolen bases over his last 12 games. He had two or more hits in seven of the last eight games in which he hit safely.

▶**May 26:** Right fielder Tony Gwynn suffered a second-degree strain of his left calf while running out a ground ball in San Diego on May 21. Gwynn, who had 2,975 hits, was immediately placed on the disabled list and would probably be out until mid-June. First baseman Wally Joyner was lost for 15 days on May 20 due to a chip fracture of his left sterno-clavicular joint. Since April 21 Joyner had been 9-for-54.

▶**June 2:** Catcher Greg Myers was the unsung hero of the early season. Pressed into more action because of injuries to Carlos Hernandez and Jim Leyritz, Myers made 19 starts—compared with 37 all last season—and was 28-for-81 (.346).

▶**June 16:** Over eight games through June 14, the Padres were 4-4 although their pitching staff allowed only 20 runs for a 2.28 ERA. The offense scored just 17 runs in the same eight games, reaching five only once.

▶**June 30:** The Padres called up catcher Ben Davis from AAA Las Vegas after Jim Leyritz suffered a fracture of a bone in his left hand when struck by a Chan Ho Park pitch on June 22.

▶**July 7:** During the Padres' 14-game winning streak—a run unmatched by any NL team since San Diego joined the league in 1969—the Padres trailed at the end of a total of only nine innings. They scored in the first inning eight times and hit .302 during the streak.

▶**July 21:** The struggles continued for right-hander Woody Williams. He served

up the first two homers hit at Seattle's new Safeco Field on July 17, giving him nine homers allowed in his last three starts and 12 in his last five. He had allowed 21 home runs on the season.

▶**July 28:** Third base was becoming a black hole for the Padres. A night after the slumping George Arias (1-for-12, six strikeouts) botched a pair of potential double plays and made two errors, Carlos Baerga blew a double-play chance with a poor throw.

▶**Aug. 4:** Greg Myers went to Atlanta for Class A pitcher Doug Dent, and Jim Leyritz was sent to the Yankees for right-hander Geraldo Padua, 22, who was 25-4 with a 2.94 ERA in three seasons at Class A. Leyritz and Myers both became expendable because of the play of Ben Davis, who had an 11-game hitting streak snapped on July 31.

▶**Aug. 11:** On Aug. 6—the same night on which Tony Gwynn notched his 3,000th hit—second baseman Quilvio Veras tied a Padres record by scoring four runs in a game. The Padres had talked about extending Veras's contract. He was eligible for arbitration, and the Padres weren't eager to risk a $3.5 million loss.

▶**Aug. 18:** The Padres probably lost right-hander Brian Boehringer for the season. An MRI showed a strain in the rotator cuff. A career reliever, Boehringer was inserted into the rotation on June 12 and was 4-4 with a 3.23 ERA as a starter.

▶**Sept. 1:** The Padres suffered its worst back-to-back losses ever on Aug. 24 and 25, in Philadelphia. San Diego was outscored 18-2 and 15-1. Infielder Ed Giovanola pitched 1⅓ innings of scoreless relief to end the Philadelphia debacle. Giovanola hadn't pitched since Little League.

▶**Sept. 8:** Since becoming the everyday center fielder, Ruben Rivera was 3-for-46. Rivera's opportunity forced one of the Padres' top performers, Eric Owens, to the bench. Owens was tied for the team lead in steals and is hitting .274 to Rivera's .201.

▶**Sept. 15:** Phil Nevin was the brightest spot in a disappointing season, so the Padres extended his contract for the next three years. Since replacing George Arias as the regular third baseman at the end of July, Nevin went 50-for-157 (.318) with 12 homers and 41 RBI.

▶**Sept. 29:** Woody Williams and right-hander Matt Clement each were 4-0 over their last five starts. Clement was the fourth Padres rookie to win 10 or more games, and Williams had a 2.68 ERA in his last 37 innings.

▶**Oct. 6:** Tony Gwynn hit .338 for the year and equaled Honus Wagner's NL record of 17 consecutive seasons with a .300 average (minimum 50 games played).

QUOTE OF THE YEAR

"I'm a square. I'm a nerd. I'm not part of the entertainment world."
—Right fielder Tony Gwynn after his 3,000th hit, explaining why he turned down Leno and Letterman

Team Leaders

Batting avg.	Hits	Wins	Strikeouts
.285 Reggie Sanders	139 Tony Gwynn	14 Andy Ashby	194 Sterling Hitchcock
.280 Quilvio Veras	136 Reggie Sanders	12 Sterling Hitchcock	137 Woody Williams
		12 Woody Williams	

HR	Runs		Innings
26 Reggie Sanders	95 Quilvio Veras	**Losses**	208.1 Woody Williams
24 Phil Nevin	92 Reggie Sanders	14 Sterling Hitchcock	206 Andy Ashby
		12 Matt Clement	

RBI	Stolen bases	12 Woody Williams	Saves
85 Phil Nevin	36 Reggie Sanders		40 Trevor Hoffman
72 Reggie Sanders	34 Damian Jackson	**ERA**	2 Dan Miceli
		3.80 Andy Ashby	
		4.11 Sterling Hitchcock	

SAN DIEGO PADRES 1999 final stats

BATTERS	BA	SLG	OBA	G	AB	R	H	TB	2B	3B	HR	RBI	BB	SO	SB	CS	E
Gwynn	.338	.477	.381	111	411	59	139	196	27	0	10	62	29	14	7	2	1
Sanders	.285	.527	.376	133	478	92	136	252	24	7	26	72	65	108	36	13	6
Veras	.280	.379	.368	132	475	95	133	180	25	2	6	41	65	88	30	17	12
Magadan	.274	.355	.377	110	248	20	68	88	12	1	2	30	45	36	1	3	6
Vander Wal	.272	.419	.368	132	246	26	67	103	18	0	6	41	37	59	2	1	1
Darr	.271	.417	.340	25	48	6	13	20	1	0	2	3	5	18	2	1	0
Nevin	.269	.527	.352	128	383	52	103	202	27	0	24	85	51	82	1	0	5
Owens	.266	.391	.327	149	440	55	117	172	22	3	9	61	38	50	33	7	4
Gonzalez	.253	.410	.271	30	83	7	21	34	2	1	3	12	1	8	0	0	1
Gomez	.252	.308	.331	76	234	20	59	72	8	1	1	15	27	49	1	2	12
Baerga	.250	.338	.318	33	80	6	20	27	1	0	2	5	6	14	1	0	2
Joyner	.248	.350	.363	118	323	34	80	113	14	2	5	43	58	54	0	1	4
Davis	.244	.361	.307	76	266	29	65	96	14	1	5	30	25	70	2	1	7
Arias	.244	.421	.271	55	164	20	40	69	8	0	7	20	6	54	0	0	8
Leyritz	.239	.455	.331	50	134	17	32	61	5	0	8	21	15	37	0	0	3
Jackson	.224	.356	.320	133	388	56	87	138	20	2	9	39	53	105	34	10	26
Matthews	.222	.222	.378	23	36	4	8	8	0	0	0	7	9	9	2	0	0
Ru. Rivera	.195	.406	.295	147	411	65	80	167	16	1	23	48	55	143	18	7	8
Giovanola	.190	.224	.294	56	58	10	11	13	0	1	0	3	9	8	2	0	2
Garcia	.182	.182	.250	6	11	1	2	2	0	0	0	0	1	3	0	0	2
Newhan	.140	.302	.159	32	43	7	6	13	1	0	2	6	1	11	2	1	2

PITCHERS	W-L	ERA	BA	G	GS	CG	GF	SH	SV	IP	H	R	ER	HR	BB	SO
Giovanola	0-0	0.00	.200	1	0	0	1	0	0	1.1	1	0	0	0	2	0
Hoffman	2-3	2.14	.197	64	0	0	54	0	40	67.1	48	23	16	5	15	73
Wall	7-4	3.07	.219	55	0	0	12	0	0	70.1	58	31	24	11	23	53
Boehringer	6-5	3.24	.267	33	11	0	8	0	0	94.1	97	38	34	10	35	64
Whisenant	0-1	3.68	.200	19	0	0	4	0	0	14.2	10	6	6	0	10	10
Reyes	2-4	3.72	.254	65	0	0	23	0	1	77.1	76	38	32	11	24	57
Ashby	14-10	3.80	.258	31	31	4	0	3	0	206.0	204	95	87	26	54	132
Ro. Rivera	1-2	3.86	.240	12	0	0	3	0	0	7.0	6	4	3	1	3	3
Hitchcock	12-14	4.11	.254	33	33	1	0	0	0	205.2	202	99	94	29	76	194
Williams	12-12	4.41	.268	33	33	0	0	0	0	208.1	213	106	102	33	73	137
Miceli	4-5	4.46	.266	66	0	0	28	0	2	68.2	67	39	34	7	36	59
Clement	10-12	4.48	.273	31	31	0	0	0	0	180.2	190	106	90	18	86	135
Cunnane	2-1	5.23	.293	24	0	0	2	0	0	31.0	34	19	18	8	12	22
Murray	0-4	5.76	.297	22	8	0	1	0	0	50.0	60	33	32	7	26	25
Carlyle	1-3	5.97	.257	7	7	0	0	0	0	37.2	36	28	25	7	17	29
Almanzar	0-0	7.47	.316	28	0	0	11	0	0	37.1	48	32	31	6	15	30
Spencer	0-7	9.16	.335	9	8	0	1	0	0	38.1	56	44	39	11	11	36
Whiteside	1-0	13.91	.396	10	0	0	4	0	0	11.0	19	17	17	1	5	9
Guzman	0-1	21.60	.464	7	0	0	2	0	0	5.0	13	12	12	1	3	4

322

2000 preliminary roster

PITCHERS (20)
Carlos Almanzar
Brian Boehringer
Buddy Carlyle
Matt Clement
Will Cunnane
Domingo Guzman
Sterling Hitchcock
Trevor Hoffman
Brandon Kolb
Carlton Loewer
Rodrigo Lopez
Brian Meadows

Jason Middlebrook
Steve Montgomery
Randy Myers
Wascar Serrano
Kevin Walker
Donne Wall
Matt Whisenant
Woody Williams

CATCHERS (3)
Ben Davis
Wikleman Gonzalez
Carlos Hernandez

INFIELDERS (8)
Chris Gomez
Damian Jackson
Wally Joyner
Dave Magadan
Phil Nevin
David Newhan
Kevin Nicholson
Quilvio Veras

OUTFIELDERS (9)
Mike Darr
Kory DeHaan
Tony Gwynn
Gary Matthews
Eric Owens
Ruben Rivera
Reggie Sanders
Peter Tucci
John Vander Wal

Games played by position

PLAYER	G	C	1B	2B	3B	SS	OF
Arias	55	0	0	0	50	0	0
Baerga	33	0	2	13	13	0	0
Darr	25	0	0	0	0	0	22
Davis	76	74	0	0	0	0	0
Garcia	6	0	1	0	4	0	0
Giovanola	56	0	0	19	25	7	0
Gomez	76	0	0	0	0	75	0
Gonzalez	30	17	0	0	0	0	0
Gwynn	111	0	0	0	0	0	104
Jackson	133	0	0	21	0	100	3
Joyner	110	0	105	0	0	0	0
Leyritz	50	24	19	0	1	0	0
Magadan	116	0	42	0	52	0	0
Matthews	23	0	0	0	0	0	17
Myers	50	41	0	0	0	0	0
Nevin	128	31	11	0	67	0	13
Newhan	32	0	1	19	1	0	0
Owens	149	0	12	1	4	0	116
Rivera	147	0	0	0	0	0	143
Sanders	133	0	0	0	0	0	129
Vander Wal	132	0	28	0	0	0	48
Veras	132	0	0	118	0	0	0

Sick call: 1999 DL report

PLAYER	Days on the DL
Carlos Almanzar	33
George Arias	29
Andy Ashby	17
Brian Boehringer	50
Chris Gomez	59
Tony Gwynn	50*
Carlos Hernandez	181
Wally Joyner	39
Jim Leyritz	37
Greg Myers	27
Randy Myers	181
Phil Nevin	11
Reggie Sanders	15
Quilvio Veras	15
Ed Vosberg	19

Indicates two separate terms on Disabled List.

Minor Leagues

Tops in the organization

BATTER	CLUB	AVG.	G	AB	R	H	HR	RBI
Burroughs, Sean	RCu	.363	128	449	68	163	6	85
Nieves, Wilbert	RCu	.328	120	427	58	140	7	61
Gonzalez, W.	LV	.319	85	317	51	101	16	61
Ward, Brian	IDF	.317	68	287	50	91	7	60
Pelaez, Alex	RCu	.298	122	456	63	136	4	54

HOME RUNS

Curl, John	Mob	22
Pernell, Brandon	RCu	21
Schader, Troy	IDF	19
Eberwein, Kevin	RCu	19
Koonce, Graham	RCu	19

WINS

Guttormson, Rick	RCu	14
Lawrence, Brian	RCu	12
Several Players Tied at		11

RBI

Allen, Dusty	LV	89
Burroughs, Sean	RCu	85
Loggins, Joshua	FtW	85
Pernell, Brandon	RCu	84
Nicholson, Kevin	Mob	81

SAVES

Condrey, Clay	RCu	20
Aragon, Angel	RCu	19
Hite, Kevin	Mob	19
Verdugo, Oswaldo	IDF	13
Cunnane, Will	LV	11

STOLEN BASES

Owens, Jeremy	RCu	67
Faggett, Ethan	Mob	63
Donovan, Todd	IDF	40
Cook, Jon	FtW	39
Faison, Vince	FtW	37

STRIKEOUTS

Lawrence, Brian	RCu	166
Serrano, Wascar	Mob	158
Wolff, Bryan	LV	151
Lopez, Rodrigo	Mob	138
Carlyle, Buddy	LV	138

PITCHER	CLUB	W-L	ERA	IP	H	BB	SO
Lawrence, Brian	RCu	12-8	3.39	175	178	30	166
Kramer, Aaron	RCu	9-9	3.63	139	154	31	98
Guttormson, Rick	RCu	14-8	3.72	174	165	36	125
Serrano, Wascar	Mob	11-11	3.86	175	158	60	158
Lopez, Rodrigo	Mob	10-8	4.41	169	187	58	138

1999 salaries

	Bonuses	Total earned salary
Randy Myers, p		6,666,666
Andy Ashby, p	25,000	5,050,000
Trevor Hoffman, p	50,000	4,775,000
Tony Gwynn, of	50,000	4,400,000
Reggie Sanders, of		3,700,000
Sterling Hitchcock, p		3,500,000
Woody Williams, p		3,083,333
Wally Joyner, 1b		2,841,680
Chris Gomez, ss		2,200,000
Quilvio Veras, 2b	25,000	2,110,000
Carlos Hernandez, c		1,250,000
Dan Miceli, p		1,100,000
John Vander Wal, of	200,000	1,075,000
Dave Magadan, 3b		575,000
Carlos Reyes, p		400,000
Matt Whiteside, p		375,000
Donne Wall, p		275,000
Brian Boehringer, p		275,000
Eric Owens, of		275,000
Matt Whisenant, p	10,000	270,000
Ruben Rivera, of		265,000
Phil Nevin, 3b		265,000
Damian Jackson, ss		203,000
Heath Murray, p		201,500
Matt Clement, p		201,000
Earl Carlyle, p		200,000
Ben Davis, c		200,000
Wiklenman Gonzalez, c		200,000

Average 1999 salary: $1,640,435
Total 1999 team payroll: $45,932,179
Termination pay: $675,000

San Diego (1969-1999)

Runs: Most, career

1361 TONY GWYNN, 1982-1999
599 Dave Winfield, 1973-1980
484 Gene Richards, 1977-1983
442 Nate Colbert, 1969-1974
430 Garry Templeton, 1982-1991

Hits: Most, career

3067 TONY GWYNN, 1982-1999
1135 Garry Templeton, 1982-1991
1134 Dave Winfield, 1973-1980
994 Gene Richards, 1977-1983
817 Terry Kennedy, 1981-1986

2B: Most, career

522 TONY GWYNN, 1982-1999
195 Garry Templeton, 1982-1991
179 Dave Winfield, 1973-1980
158 Terry Kennedy, 1981-1986
134 STEVE FINLEY, 1995-1998

3B: Most, career

84 TONY GWYNN, 1982-1999
63 Gene Richards, 1977-1983
39 Dave Winfield, 1973-1980
36 Garry Templeton, 1982-1991
29 Cito Gaston, 1969-1974

HR: Most, career

163 Nate Colbert, 1969-1974
154 Dave Winfield, 1973-1980
133 TONY GWYNN, 1982-1999
121 KEN CAMINITI, 1995-1998
85 BENITO SANTIAGO, 1986-1992

RBI: Most, career

1104 TONY GWYNN, 1982-1999
626 Dave Winfield, 1973-1980
481 Nate Colbert, 1969-1974
427 Garry Templeton, 1982-1991
424 Terry Kennedy, 1981-1986

SB: Most, career

318 TONY GWYNN, 1982-1999
242 Gene Richards, 1977-1983
171 Alan Wiggins, 1981-1985
148 Bip Roberts, 1986-1995
147 Ozzie Smith, 1978-1981

BB: Most, career

771 TONY GWYNN, 1982-1999
463 Dave Winfield, 1973-1980
423 Gene Tenace, 1977-1980
350 Nate Colbert, 1969-1974
338 Gene Richards, 1977-1983

BA: Highest, career

.339 TONY GWYNN, 1982-1999
.298 Bip Roberts, 1986-1995
.295 KEN CAMINITI, 1995-1998
.291 Gene Richards, 1977-1983
.286 Johnny Grubb, 1972-1976

On-base avg: Highest, career

.403 Gene Tenace, 1977-1980
.389 TONY GWYNN, 1982-1999
.384 KEN CAMINITI, 1995-1998
.363 Johnny Grubb, 1972-1976
.361 Bip Roberts, 1986-1995

Slug pct: Highest, career

.540 KEN CAMINITI, 1995-1998
.468 Nate Colbert, 1969-1974
.464 Dave Winfield, 1973-1980
.459 TONY GWYNN, 1982-1999
.458 STEVE FINLEY, 1995-1998

Games started: Most, career

253 Randy Jones, 1973-1980
230 Eric Show, 1981-1990
208 Ed Whitson, 1983-1991
186 ANDY BENES, 1989-1995
185 ANDY ASHBY, 1993-1999

Complete games: Most, career

71 Randy Jones, 1973-1980
35 Eric Show, 1981-1990
34 Clay Kirby, 1969-1973
31 Steve Arlin, 1969-1974
29 Bruce Hurst, 1989-1993

Saves: Most, career

226 TREVOR HOFFMAN, 1993-1999
108 Rollie Fingers, 1977-1980
83 Rich Gossage, 1984-1987
78 Mark Davis, 1987-1994
64 Craig Lefferts, 1984-1992

Shutouts: Most, career

18 Randy Jones, 1973-1980
11 Steve Arlin, 1969-1974
11 Eric Show, 1981-1990
10 Bruce Hurst, 1989-1993
8 ANDY BENES, 1989-1995

Wins: Most, career

100 Eric Show, 1981-1990
92 Randy Jones, 1973-1980
77 Ed Whitson, 1983-1991
70 ANDY ASHBY, 1993-1999
69 ANDY BENES, 1989-1995

K: Most, career

1036 ANDY BENES, 1989-1995
951 Eric Show, 1981-1990
827 ANDY ASHBY, 1993-1999
802 Clay Kirby, 1969-1973
767 Ed Whitson, 1983-1991

Win pct: Highest, career

.591 Bruce Hurst, 1989-1993
.556 JOEY HAMILTON, 1994-1998
.535 Eric Show, 1981-1990
.530 ANDY ASHBY, 1993-1999
.517 Ed Whitson, 1983-1991

ERA: Lowest, career

3.12 Dave Dravecky, 1982-1987
3.27 Bruce Hurst, 1989-1993
3.30 Randy Jones, 1973-1980
3.57 ANDY BENES, 1989-1995
3.59 Eric Show, 1981-1990

Runs: Most, season

126 STEVE FINLEY, 1996
119 TONY GWYNN, 1987
112 GREG VAUGHN, 1998
110 RICKEY HENDERSON, 1996
109 KEN CAMINITI, 1996

Hits: Most, season

220 TONY GWYNN, 1997
218 TONY GWYNN, 1987
213 TONY GWYNN, 1984
211 TONY GWYNN, 1986
203 TONY GWYNN, 1989

2B: Most, season

49 TONY GWYNN, 1997
45 STEVE FINLEY, 1996
42 Terry Kennedy, 1982
41 TONY GWYNN, 1993
40 STEVE FINLEY, 1998

3B: Most, season

13 TONY GWYNN, 1987
12 Gene Richards, 1978
12 Gene Richards, 1981
11 Bill Almon, 1977
11 Gene Richards, 1977
11 TONY GWYNN, 1991

HR: Most, season

50 GREG VAUGHN, 1998
40 KEN CAMINITI, 1996
38 Nate Colbert, 1970
38 Nate Colbert, 1972
35 FRED McGRIFF, 1992

324

RBI: Most, season

130	KEN CAMINITI,	1996
119	TONY GWYNN,	1997
119	GREG VAUGHN,	1998
118	Dave Winfield,	1979
115	Joe Carter,	1990

SB: Most, season

70	Alan Wiggins,	1984
66	Alan Wiggins,	1983
61	Gene Richards,	1980
57	Ozzie Smith,	1980
56	Gene Richards,	1977
56	TONY GWYNN,	1987

BB: Most, season

132	Jack Clark,	1989
125	RICKEY HENDERSON,	1996
125	Gene Tenace,	1977
105	Gene Tenace,	1979
105	FRED McGRIFF,	1991

BA: Highest, season

.394	TONY GWYNN,	1994
.372	TONY GWYNN,	1997
.370	TONY GWYNN,	1987
.368	TONY GWYNN,	1995
.358	TONY GWYNN,	1993

On-base avg; Highest, season

.454	TONY GWYNN,	1994
.447	TONY GWYNN,	1987
.415	Gene Tenace,	1977
.410	RICKEY HENDERSON,	1996
.410	Jack Clark,	1989

Slug pct: Highest, season

.621	KEN CAMINITI,	1996
.597	GREG VAUGHN,	1998
.580	GARY SHEFFIELD,	1992
.568	TONY GWYNN,	1994
.558	Dave Winfield,	1979

Games started: Most, season

40	Randy Jones,	1976
39	Randy Jones,	1979
37	Steve Arlin,	1972
37	Gaylord Perry,	1978
36	Clay Kirby,	1971
36	Randy Jones,	1975
36	Randy Jones,	1978

Complete games: Most, season

25	Randy Jones,	1976
18	Randy Jones,	1975
14	Dave Roberts,	1971
13	Clay Kirby,	1971
13	Eric Show,	1988

Saves: Most, season

53	TREVOR HOFFMAN,	1998
44	Mark Davis,	1989
42	TREVOR HOFFMAN,	1996
40	TREVOR HOFFMAN,	1999
38	Randy Myers,	1992

Shutouts: Most, season

6	Fred Norman,	1972
6	Randy Jones,	1975
5	Randy Jones,	1976
4	Steve Arlin,	1971
4	Bruce Hurst,	1990
4	Bruce Hurst,	1992

Wins: Most, season

22	Randy Jones,	1976
21	Gaylord Perry,	1978
20	Randy Jones,	1975
18	KEVIN BROWN,	1998
18	Andy Hawkins,	1985

K: Most, season

257	KEVIN BROWN,	1998
231	Clay Kirby,	1971
194	STERLING HITCHCOCK, 1999	
189	ANDY BENES,	1994
185	Pat Dobson,	1970

Win pct: Highest, season

.778	Gaylord Perry,	1978
.720	KEVIN BROWN,	1998
.692	Andy Hawkins,	1985
.667	La Marr Hoyt,	1985
.654	ANDY ASHBY,	1998

ERA: Lowest, season

2.10	Dave Roberts,	1971
2.24	Randy Jones,	1975
2.38	KEVIN BROWN,	1998
2.60	Ed Whitson,	1990
2.66	Ed Whitson,	1989

Most pinch-hit homers, season

5	Jerry Turner,	1978
3	Luis Salazar,	1989
3	Archi Cianfrocco,	1995

Most pinch-hit homers, career

9	Jerry Turner,	1974-1983

Longest hitting streak

34	BENITO SANTIAGO,	1987
27	JOHN FLAHERTY,	1996
25	TONY GWYNN,	1983
23	Bip Roberts,	1994
21	Bobby Brown,	1983
21	STEVE FINLEY,	1996

Most consecutive scoreless innings

30	Randy Jones,	1980

No-hit games

ACTIVE PLAYERS in caps.

Players' years of service are listed by the first and last years with this team and are not necessarily consecutive; all statistics record performances for this team only.

Colorado Rockies

Larry Walker—the powerful Rockies' best hitter—won his second consecutive National League batting title.

By Tom DiPace

1999 Rockies: 'We were just no good'

In mid-June, Colorado manager Jim Leyland said, "We've got a shot." The Rockies were at .500 and within striking distance of first place in the National League West. It was exactly what the team envisioned when they signed Leyland to a $6 million, three-year contract.

Three weeks later, after a nine-game losing streak that included an 0-for-7 trip to San Diego and San Francisco, the Rockies were well on their way to the franchise's first last-place finish in its seven seasons.

"We had just begun to feel good about ourselves. The road trip took all that away," first baseman Todd Helton said. "Had we won some games on that road trip . . . our confidence would have just built instead of us having a collapse."

As losses mounted through the summer, word began to spread that general manager Bob Gebhard would be fired after the season. He resigned Aug. 20.

The Rockies got another jolt Sept. 6 when Leyland, 54, told his players he no longer had the passion needed to handle the daily grind of a 162-game season. He said on the season's final day he was embarrassed by the team's 72-90 finish and apologized to the fans.

"I just hope they don't get down because of this year," Leyland said. "I hope they get excited about the next manager and the next team. I just hope that they'll continue to give the Rockies a chance to get this thing righted, and I know they will."

Colorado's dismal record was the second-worst in franchise history, topped only by the 1993 expansion season (67-92). But the Rockies still managed to lead the National League in hitting at .279, and broke 69-year-old NL records for total bases (2,696) and extra-base hits (567). Helton, Dante Bichette, Larry Walker and Vinny Castilla were responsible for the bulk of the offense, each finishing with more than 30 home runs and 100 RBI.

The Rockies were done in by their horrible pitching and an inability to do the basics: bunt, take an extra base, or move a runner over.

"I guess you can finger-point at numerous things," Walker said. "Defense wasn't that good. We blew a lot of games. Base running, we were absolutely horrible. Getting signs, we were terrible at that all year. Really the fundamentals of baseball that Leyland usually brings to his teams, we didn't do it. That's not Jim's fault. That's our fault. We were just no good."

When healthy, Walker was phenomenal. His .379 average gave him his second consecutive NL batting title, and he also had 37 homers and 115 RBI before season-ending knee surgery.

Helton, runner-up for NL Rookie of the Year in 1998, dispelled any notion of a sophomore slump, hitting .320 with 35 homers and 113 RBI.

Bright spots on the pitching staff included Dave Veres' team-record 31 saves and a club-record-tying 17 victories by starter Pedro Astacio.

"You can talk all you want about personal stats, but we finished in last place," said Castilla, whose 33 homers gave him at least 30 for the fifth year in a row.

As always in Colorado, pitching will be a priority for new general manager manager Dan O'Dowd and first-year manager Buddy Bell. The Rockies gave up 1,700 hits and 1,028 runs—955 earned—and had the worst ERA in the majors (6.01). Those numbers were the worst by an NL team since Philadelphia in 1930, and the Rockies' 737 walks and 237 home runs allowed set league records.

327

1999 Rockies: Week-by-week notes

These notes were excerpted from the following issues of Baseball Weekly.

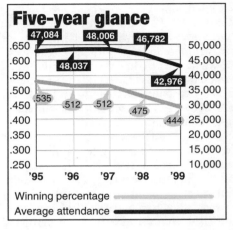

Five-year glance

47,084 48,006 46,782

48,037

42,976

.535 .512 .512 .475 .444

'95 '96 '97 '98 '99

Winning percentage
Average attendance

▶**April 14:** It took all of spring training and four games into the regular season for a decision to be made, but Dave Veres was finally the closer. However, manager Jim Leyland said that at times when the opponent has a tough lefty batting in the ninth, he might use one of his left-handed relievers, either Chuck McElroy or Bobby Jones.

▶**April 21:** The Rockies got off to a slow start, losing six of their first 10, but not because of poor pitching. They had quality starts in eight of the 10, and their 3.46 ERA away from Coors Field this year was better than the 3.82 mark the Yankees had last season while winning 114 games.

▶**April 28:** When an emotional Jerry McMorris, the team owner, told players they would not play the final two games of their season-opening homestand last week, everyone understood. Two Columbine High School gunmen had killed 12 fellow students and a teacher in a suburban Littleton shooting spree that shook the nation.

▶**May 5:** Never in their seven-year history had the Rockies boasted a hotter hitter than right fielder Larry Walker during a four-game stretch last week. Against St. Louis, Walker set a club record with 11 RBI over two consecutive games and 13 RBI in three. He then reset the three-game record to 15 and established a new four-game total of 17. He had five homers over the last three games.

▶**May 26:** Walker had 10 homers and 33 RBI and raised his batting average from .222 to .435 during a 21-game hitting streak that ended on May 22.

▶**June 9:** Second baseman Mike Lansing opted for physical therapy to try to repair the bulging disc in his lower vertebrae. Surgery almost certainly would have ended his season. Lansing was batting .310 with four home runs and 15 RBI in 35 games when he was sidelined on May 21. The second base duties would be shared by Terry Shumpert, Lenny Harris, Chris Sexton, and Kurt Abbott.

▶**June 16:** A .315 hitter during his rookie season in 1998, first baseman Todd Helton entered the June 12 game against Texas with a .262 average. But he came through when it mattered most, hitting several game-winning, late-inning home runs. Despite his overall average, he was batting .333 with runners in scoring position and two outs.

▶**June 23:** For the first time in their history, the Rockies were experiencing a real attendance drop. Through June 19, Coors Field crowds were down 9.7 percent from an average of 46,782 in 1998 to 42,223, and down 12.1 percent from the ballpark's high in 1996. After 203 consecutive sell-outs of 48,000-plus from June 12, 1995, until Sept. 6, 1997, the Rockies had just two in 29 dates this year.

▶**July 7:** Jim Leyland decided to go with a four-man rotation: right-handers Pedro Astacio and Darryl Kile and left-handers Brian Bohanon and Bobby Jones. The fifth starters this year—righties John Thomson and Mark Brownson—had a combined 0-7 record with a 9.43 ERA.

▶**July 21:** Four days after the All-Star break, the Rockies were eight games below .500, in their all-too-familiar fourth-place position in the NL West and 9 games behind the first-place San Francisco Giants. The Rockies had issued 401 walks

at the break (a whopping 4.7 per game) to lead the majors.

▶**July 28:** Dave Veres got three saves in a 24-hour period last week at Los Angeles. Through July 24 he had not allowed a run in his last 12 appearances, lowering his ERA from 4.34 to 3.31.

▶**Aug. 4:** For the first time in their seven-year history, the Rockies were rebuilding. Beating the July 31 deadline by five hours, they sent two veterans, center fielder Darryl Hamilton and Chuck McElroy, to the Mets for center fielder Brian McRae, left-handed reliever Rigo Beltran and Class A outfielder Tom Johnson.

▶**Aug. 18:** Pedro Astacio was charged on Aug. 13 with third-degree assault in a domestic dispute with his wife. He fled after she called 911 late in the night of Aug. 11, but he turned himself in to police the next day and was released after posting bond. Through an Aug. 15 victory against the Expos, Astacio was 13-9 with a rotation-best 4.81 ERA.

▶**Aug. 25:** General manager Bob Gebhard was forced to resign on Aug. 20. In a span of 10 months, the Rockies dumped their original manager, Don Baylor and the franchise's only GM, Gebhard. Gary Hughes, hired last fall as vice president of player personnel, was considered the leading candidate to replace Gebhard, though ownership was conducting a search.

▶**Sept. 1:** Talented catcher Ben Petrick was about to get the call to the big leagues. Petrick was hitting a combined .307 at AA Carolina and AAA Colorado Springs with 23 homers, 85 RBI and 12 stolen bases.

▶**Sept. 15:** Leyland made it official last week: He informed his players that he would resign as manager after the season. He surrendered $4.5 million of his $6 million contract. The person most frequently mentioned as Leyland's possible successor was Phil Garner, who was fired as Milwaukee's manager last month.

▶**Sept. 22:** Former Cleveland Indians executive Dan O'Dowd was named the club's new general manager on Sept. 20.

▶**Oct. 6:** In a chaotic season, Pedro Astacio was one of the Rockies' few steady performers. Astacio finished 17-11, tying Kevin Ritz for most wins in a season for Colorado. Larry Walker underwent arthroscopic surgery to repair frayed cartilage on his left knee on Sept. 30. With a .379 batting average, his second consecutive NL batting title was already clinched. He hit 37 homers and had 115 RBI while starting just 111 games.

QUOTE OF THE YEAR

"To say Dan O'Dowd is aggressive is an understatement."
—Indians manager Mike Hargrove, on the Rockies' new GM, formerly with Cleveland

329

Team Leaders

Batting avg.	Hits	Wins	Strikeouts
.379 Larry Walker	193 Neifi Perez	17 Pedro Astacio	210 Pedro Astacio
.320 Todd Helton	185 Todd Helton	12 Brian Bohanon	120 Brian Bohanon

HR	Runs	Losses	Innings
37 Larry Walker	114 Todd Helton	13 Darryl Kile	232 Pedro Astacio
35 Todd Helton	108 Neifi Perez	12 Brian Bohanon	197.1 Brian Bohanon
	108 Larry Walker		

RBI	Stolen bases	ERA	Saves
133 Dante Bichette	14 Terry Shumpert	5.04 Pedro Astacio	31 Dave Veres
115 Larry Walker	13 Neifi Perez	6.20 Brian Bohanon	1 Jerry DiPoto
			1 Roberto Ramirez

COLORADO ROCKIES 1999 final stats

BATTERS	BA	SLG	OBA	G	AB	R	H	TB	2B	3B	HR	RBI	BB	SO	SB	CS	E
Kelly	.500	1.000	.500	2	2	0	1	2	1	0	0	1	0	0	0	0	0
Walker	.379	.710	.458	127	438	108	166	311	26	4	37	115	57	52	11	4	4
Shumpert	.347	.584	.413	92	262	58	91	153	26	3	10	37	31	41	14	0	5
Petrick	.323	.565	.417	19	62	13	20	35	3	0	4	12	10	13	1	0	2
Helton	.320	.587	.395	159	578	114	185	339	39	5	35	113	68	77	7	6	9
Lansing	.310	.455	.344	35	145	24	45	66	9	0	4	15	7	22	2	0	2
Manwaring	.299	.409	.374	48	137	17	41	56	7	1	2	14	12	23	0	0	5
Bichette	.298	.541	.354	151	593	104	177	321	38	2	34	133	54	84	6	6	13
Echevarria	.293	.503	.360	102	191	28	56	96	7	0	11	35	17	34	1	3	1
Perez	.280	.403	.307	157	690	108	193	278	27	11	12	70	28	54	13	5	14
Castilla	.275	.478	.331	158	615	83	169	294	24	1	33	102	53	75	2	3	19
Abbott	.273	.430	.310	96	286	41	78	123	17	2	8	41	16	69	3	2	4
Barry	.268	.452	.344	74	168	19	45	76	16	0	5	26	19	29	0	4	0
Clemente	.253	.488	.282	57	162	24	41	79	10	2	8	25	7	46	0	0	3
Sexton	.237	.322	.357	35	59	9	14	19	0	1	1	7	11	10	4	2	2
Blanco	.232	.369	.320	88	263	30	61	97	12	3	6	28	34	38	1	1	5
Phillips	.231	.487	.250	25	39	5	9	19	4	0	2	4	0	13	0	0	1
McRae	.224	.358	.323	103	321	36	72	115	14	1	9	37	41	64	2	6	1
Sosa	.222	.222	.364	11	9	3	2	2	0	0	0	0	2	2	0	0	1
Gibson	.179	.429	.207	10	28	2	5	12	1	0	2	6	0	7	0	0	1
Cangelosi	.167	.333	.167	7	6	0	1	2	1	0	0	0	0	4	0	0	0
Petersen	.154	.154	.267	7	13	1	2	2	0	0	0	2	2	3	0	0	1
Watkins	.053	.053	.143	16	19	2	1	1	0	0	0	0	2	5	0	0	0

PITCHERS	W-L	ERA	BA	G	GS	CG	GF	SH	SV	IP	H	R	ER	HR	BB	SO
Lee	3-2	3.67	.247	36	0	0	11	0	0	49.0	43	21	20	4	29	38
DiPoto	4-5	4.26	.279	63	0	0	18	0	1	86.2	91	44	41	10	44	69
Beltran	1-1	4.50	.291	33	0	0	12	0	0	42.0	52	24	21	7	19	50
Wright	4-3	4.87	.308	16	16	0	0	0	0	94.1	110	52	51	10	54	49
Astacio	17-11	5.04	.285	34	34	7	0	0	0	232.0	258	140	130	38	75	210
Leskanic	6-2	5.08	.272	63	0	0	5	0	0	85.0	87	54	48	7	49	77
Veres	4-8	5.14	.290	73	0	0	63	0	31	77.0	88	46	44	14	37	71
Bohanon	12-12	6.20	.305	33	33	3	0	1	0	197.1	236	146	136	30	92	120
Jones	6-10	6.33	.292	30	20	0	1	0	0	112.1	132	91	79	24	77	74
Kile	8-13	6.61	.298	32	32	1	0	0	0	190.2	225	150	140	33	109	116
Wainhouse	0-0	6.91	.330	19	0	0	11	0	0	28.2	37	22	22	6	16	18
Brownson	0-2	7.89	.333	7	7	0	0	0	0	29.2	42	26	26	8	8	21
Thomson	1-10	8.04	.324	14	13	1	1	0	0	62.2	85	62	56	11	36	34
Ramirez	1-5	8.26	.368	32	4	0	6	0	1	40.1	68	42	37	8	22	32
DeJean	2-4	8.41	.335	56	0	0	17	0	0	61.0	83	61	57	13	32	31
Porzio	0-0	8.59	.328	16	0	0	3	0	0	14.2	21	14	14	5	10	10
Hackman	1-2	10.69	.371	5	3	0	0	0	0	16.0	26	19	19	5	12	10

COLORADO ROCKIES / NL WEST

330

2000 BASEBALL WEEKLY ALMANAC

2000 preliminary roster

PITCHERS (21)
Rolando Arrojo
Pedro Astacio
Manny Aybar
Stan Belinda
Rigo Beltran
Brian Bohanon
Shawn Chacon
Tim Christman
Rick Croushore
Mike DeJean
Lariel Gonzalez

Jose Jimenez
Bobby Jones
Josh Kalinowski
Scott Karl
David Lee
Mike Myers
Steve Shoemaker
Julian Tavarez
Travis Thompson
John Thomson

CATCHERS (2)
Brent Mayne
Ben Petrick

INFIELDERS (9)
Brent Butler
Jeff Cirillo
Todd Helton
Mike Lansing
Aaron Ledesma
Belvani Martinez
Neifi Perez

Terry Shumpert
Juan Sosa

OUTFIELDERS (8)
Jeff Barry
Edgard Clemente
Angel Echevarria
Derrick Gibson
Tom Goodwin
Jeffrey Hammonds
Chris Latham
Larry Walker

Games played by position

PLAYER	G	C	1B	2B	3B	SS	OF
Abbott	96	0	8	66	0	3	4
Barry	74	0	0	0	0	0	56
Bichette	151	0	0	0	0	0	144
Blanco	88	86	0	0	0	0	1
Cangelosi	7	0	0	0	0	0	1
Castilla	158	0	0	0	157	0	0
Clemente	57	0	0	0	0	0	49
Echevarria	102	0	10	0	0	0	49
Gibson	10	0	0	0	0	0	10
Hamilton	91	0	0	0	0	0	82
Harris	91	0	0	24	2	0	14
Helton	159	0	156	0	0	0	0
Kelly	2	0	0	0	0	0	1
Lansing	35	0	0	35	0	0	0
Manwaring	48	44	0	0	0	0	0
McRae	7	0	0	0	0	0	7
Perez	157	0	0	0	0	157	0
Petersen	7	0	0	6	0	1	0
Petrick	19	19	0	0	0	0	0
Phillips	25	0	4	0	0	0	7
Reed	46	36	0	0	0	0	0
Sexton	35	0	0	10	0	6	13
Shumpert	92	0	0	54	14	2	19
Sosa	11	0	0	0	0	2	6
Walker	127	0	0	0	0	0	114
Watkins	16	0	0	0	0	0	10

Sick call: 1999 DL report

PLAYER	Days on the DL
Kurt Abbott	30*
Mike DeJean	18
Mike Lansing	136
Kirt Manwaring	33
Kevin Ritz	182
Larry Walker	9

* Indicates two separate terms on Disabled List.

Minor Leagues

Tops in the organization

BATTER	CLUB	AVG.	G	AB	R	H	HR	RBI
Hatcher, Chris	CSp	.344	98	334	63	115	21	69
Pierre, Juan	Ash	.320	140	585	93	187	1	55
Tatum, Jim	CSp	.313	109	396	57	124	14	64
Petrick, Ben	CSp	.311	104	350	74	109	23	86
Phillips, J.R.	CSp	.311	124	479	87	149	41	100

HOME RUNS

Phillips, J.R.	CSp	41
Cotton, John	CSp	25
Petrick, Ben	CSp	23
Hatcher, Chris	CSp	21
Winchester, Jeff	Ash	18

WINS

Carter, Justin	Ash	13
Martin, Chandler	Car	13
Kalinowski, Josh	Sal	11
Lynch, Pat	Ash	11
Hackman, Luther	CSp	11

RBI

Phillips, J.R.	CSp	100
Petrick, Ben	CSp	86
Kirgan, Chris	Car	84
Colina, Javier	Ash	81
Bair, Rod	Car	81

SAVES

Thompson, T.	Sal	27
Wainhouse, D.	CSp	22
Gonzalez, Lariel	Car	14
Lee, David	CSp	13
House, Craig	Por	11

STOLEN BASES

Pierre, Juan	Ash	66
Sosa, Juan	CSp	39
Figgins, Chone	Sal	27
Several Players Tied at		25

STRIKEOUTS

Kalinowski, Josh	Sal	176
Carter, Justin	Ash	146
Price, Ryan	Sal	143
DiFelice, Mark	Sal	142
Walls, Doug	Car	140

PITCHER	CLUB	W-L	ERA	IP	H	BB	SO
Kalinowski, Josh	Sal	11-6	2.11	162	119	71	176
Lynch, Pat	Ash	11-6	3.48	140	141	24	120
Carter, Justin	Ash	13-6	3.56	144	138	72	146
Walls, Doug	Car	10-9	3.65	150	159	44	140
Martin, Chandler	Car	13-8	3.78	164	153	63	130

1999 salaries

	Bonuses	Total earned salary
Darryl Kile, p	25,000	8,442,981
Dante Bichette, of	250,000	7,250,000
Pedro Astacio, p	300,000	6,150,000
Vinny Castilla, 3b	250,000	6,000,000
Mike Lansing, 2b		5,750,000
Larry Walker, of	175,000	5,417,857
Kevin Ritz, p		3,000,000
Jerry DiPoto, p		2,250,000
Brian Bohanon, p	110,000	2,110,000
Dave Veres, p	100,000	1,166,666
Curtis Leskanic, p		1,050,000
Kurt Abbott, 2b	100,000	900,000
Todd Helton, 1b		750,000
Kirt Manwaring, c		700,000
Neifi Perez, ss		400,000
Jamey Wright, p		375,000
Mike DeJean, p		300,000
John Thomson, p		300,000
Terry Shumpert, 2b		220,000
Angel Echevarria, of		220,000
Henry Blanco, c		215,000
Rigo Beltran, p		215,000
Roberto Ramirez, p		206,000
Jeff Barry, of		202,000
Edgard Clemente, of		202,000
Chris Sexton, of		200,000
Mike Porzio, p		200,000
David Lee, p		200,000

Average 1999 salary: $1,942,589
Total 1999 team payroll: $54,392,504

Colorado (1993-1999)

Runs: Most, career

665	DANTE BICHETTE, 1993-1999	
518	LARRY WALKER, 1995-1999	
516	VINNY CASTILLA, 1993-1999	
476	Andres Galarraga, 1993-1997	
378	ERIC YOUNG, 1993-1997	

Hits: Most, career

1278	DANTE BICHETTE, 1993-1999
1044	VINNY CASTILLA, 1993-1999
843	Andres Galarraga, 1993-1997
765	LARRY WALKER, 1995-1999
626	ERIC YOUNG, 1993-1997

2B: Most, career

270	DANTE BICHETTE, 1993-1999
167	LARRY WALKER, 1995-1999
165	VINNY CASTILLA, 1993-1999
155	Andres Galarraga, 1993-1997
104	ELLIS BURKS, 1994-1998

3B: Most, career

30	NEIFI PEREZ, 1996-1999
28	ERIC YOUNG, 1993-1997
24	ELLIS BURKS, 1994-1998
20	LARRY WALKER, 1995-1999
18	DANTE BICHETTE, 1993-1999

HR: Most, career

203	VINNY CASTILLA, 1993-1999
201	DANTE BICHETTE, 1993-1999
172	Andres Galarraga, 1993-1997
163	LARRY WALKER, 1995-1999
115	ELLIS BURKS, 1994-1998

RBI: Most, career

826	DANTE BICHETTE, 1993-1999
610	VINNY CASTILLA, 1993-1999
579	Andres Galarraga, 1993-1997
471	LARRY WALKER, 1995-1999
337	ELLIS BURKS, 1994-1998

SB: Most, career

180	ERIC YOUNG, 1993-1997
105	DANTE BICHETTE, 1993-1999
92	LARRY WALKER, 1995-1999
55	Andres Galarraga, 1993-1997
52	ELLIS BURKS, 1994-1998

BB: Most, career

300	WALT WEISS, 1994-1997
268	LARRY WALKER, 1995-1999
254	ERIC YOUNG, 1993-1997
226	DANTE BICHETTE, 1993-1999
222	VINNY CASTILLA, 1993-1999

BA: Highest, career

.344	LARRY WALKER, 1995-1999
.316	Andres Galarraga, 1993-1997
.316	DANTE BICHETTE, 1993-1999
.315	TODD HELTON, 1997-1999
.306	ELLIS BURKS, 1994-1998

On-base avg: Highest, career

.423	LARRY WALKER, 1995-1999
.384	TODD HELTON, 1997-1999
.378	ELLIS BURKS, 1994-1998
.378	ERIC YOUNG, 1993-1997
.375	WALT WEISS, 1994-1997

Slug avg: Highest, career

.656	LARRY WALKER, 1995-1999
.579	ELLIS BURKS, 1994-1998
.577	Andres Galarraga, 1993-1997
.554	TODD HELTON, 1997-1999
.540	DANTE BICHETTE, 1993-1999

Games started: Most, career

98	Kevin Ritz, 1994-1998
91	JAMEY WRIGHT, 1996-1999
87	ARMANDO REYNOSO, 1993-1996
75	PEDRO ASTACIO, 1997-1999
67	DARRYL KILE, 1998-1999

Complete games: Most, career

7	PEDRO ASTACIO, 1997-1999
5	ARMANDO REYNOSO, 1993-1996
5	Roger Bailey, 1995-1997
5	JOHN THOMSON, 1997-1999
5	DARRYL KILE, 1998-1999

Saves: Most, career

60	Bruce Ruffin, 1993-1997
46	DARREN HOLMES, 1993-1997
39	DAVE VERES, 1998-1999
36	JERRY DIPOTO, 1997-1999
20	CURTIS LESKANIC, 1993-1999

Shutouts: Most, career

2	Roger Bailey, 1995-1997
1	David Nied, 1993-1996
1	MARK THOMPSON, 1994-1998
1	JOHN THOMSON, 1997-1999
1	DARRYL KILE, 1998-1999
1	BRIAN BOHANON, 1999-1999

Wins: Most, career

39	Kevin Ritz, 1994-1998
35	PEDRO ASTACIO, 1997-1999
31	CURTIS LESKANIC, 1993-1999
30	ARMANDO REYNOSO, 1993-1996
25	STEVE REED, 1993-1997
25	JAMEY WRIGHT, 1996-1999

K: Most, career

431	PEDRO ASTACIO, 1997-1999
415	CURTIS LESKANIC, 1993-1999
337	Kevin Ritz, 1994-1998
319	Bruce Ruffin, 1993-1997
297	DARREN HOLMES, 1993-1997

Win pct: Highest, career

.608	CURTIS LESKANIC, 1993-1999
.581	STEVE REED, 1993-1997
.574	PEDRO ASTACIO, 1997-1999
.507	Kevin Ritz, 1994-1998
.492	ARMANDO REYNOSO, 1993-1996

ERA: Lowest, career

3.68	STEVE REED, 1993-1997
3.84	Bruce Ruffin, 1993-1997
4.42	DARREN HOLMES, 1993-1997
4.65	ARMANDO REYNOSO, 1993-1996
4.90	Roger Bailey, 1995-1997

Runs: Most, season

143	LARRY WALKER, 1997
142	ELLIS BURKS, 1996
120	Andres Galarraga, 1997
119	Andres Galarraga, 1996
114	DANTE BICHETTE, 1996
114	TODD HELTON, 1999

Hits: Most, season

219	DANTE BICHETTE, 1998
211	ELLIS BURKS, 1996
208	LARRY WALKER, 1997
206	VINNY CASTILLA, 1998
198	DANTE BICHETTE, 1996

2B: Most, season

48	DANTE BICHETTE, 1998
46	LARRY WALKER, 1997
46	LARRY WALKER, 1998
45	CHARLIE HAYES, 1993
45	ELLIS BURKS, 1996

3B: Most, season

11	NEIFI PEREZ, 1999
10	NEIFI PEREZ, 1997
9	ERIC YOUNG, 1995
9	NEIFI PEREZ, 1998
8	ERIC YOUNG, 1993
8	Mike Kingery, 1994
8	ELLIS BURKS, 1996

HR: Most, season

49	LARRY WALKER, 1997
47	Andres Galarraga, 1996
46	VINNY CASTILLA, 1998
41	Andres Galarraga, 1997
40	DANTE BICHETTE, 1995
40	ELLIS BURKS, 1996
40	VINNY CASTILLA, 1996
40	VINNY CASTILLA, 1997

RBI: Most, season

150	Andres Galarraga, 1996
144	VINNY CASTILLA, 1998
141	DANTE BICHETTE, 1996
140	Andres Galarraga, 1997
133	DANTE BICHETTE, 1999

SB: Most, season

53	ERIC YOUNG, 1996
42	ERIC YOUNG, 1993
35	ERIC YOUNG, 1995
33	LARRY WALKER, 1997
32	ELLIS BURKS, 1996
32	ERIC YOUNG, 1997

BB: Most, season

98	WALT WEISS, 1995
80	WALT WEISS, 1996
78	LARRY WALKER, 1997
68	TODD HELTON, 1999
66	WALT WEISS, 1997

BA: Highest, season

.379	LARRY WALKER, 1999
.370	Andres Galarraga, 1993
.366	LARRY WALKER, 1997
.363	LARRY WALKER, 1998
.344	ELLIS BURKS, 1996

On-base avg; Highest, season

.458	LARRY WALKER, 1999
.452	LARRY WALKER, 1997
.445	LARRY WALKER, 1998
.408	ELLIS BURKS, 1996
.403	Andres Galarraga, 1993

Slug avg: Highest, season

.720	LARRY WALKER, 1997
.710	LARRY WALKER, 1999
.639	ELLIS BURKS, 1996
.630	LARRY WALKER, 1998
.620	DANTE BICHETTE, 1995

Games started: Most, season

35	DARRYL KILE, 1998
35	Kevin Ritz, 1996
34	PEDRO ASTACIO, 1998
34	JAMEY WRIGHT, 1998
34	PEDRO ASTACIO, 1999

Complete games: Most, season

7	PEDRO ASTACIO, 1999
5	Roger Bailey, 1997
4	ARMANDO REYNOSO, 1993
4	DARRYL KILE, 1998
3	MARK THOMPSON, 1996
3	BRIAN BOHANON, 1999

Saves: Most, season

31	DAVE VERES, 1999
25	DARREN HOLMES, 1993
24	Bruce Ruffin, 1996
19	JERRY DIPOTO, 1998
16	Bruce Ruffin, 1994
16	JERRY DIPOTO, 1997

Shutouts: Most, season

2	Roger Bailey, 1997
1	David Nied, 1994
1	MARK THOMPSON, 1996
1	JOHN THOMSON, 1997
1	BRIAN BOHANON, 1999
1	DARRYL KILE, 1998

Wins: Most, season

17	Kevin Ritz, 1996
17	PEDRO ASTACIO, 1999
13	PEDRO ASTACIO, 1998
13	DARRYL KILE, 1998
12	ARMANDO REYNOSO, 1993
12	BRIAN BOHANON, 1999

K: Most, season

210	PEDRO ASTACIO, 1999
170	PEDRO ASTACIO, 1998
158	DARRYL KILE, 1998
126	Bruce Ruffin, 1993
120	Kevin Ritz, 1995
120	BRIAN BOHANON, 1999

Win pct: Highest, season

.833	Marvin Freeman, 1994
.607	Kevin Ritz, 1996
.607	PEDRO ASTACIO, 1999
.522	ARMANDO REYNOSO, 1993

ERA: Lowest, season

4.00	ARMANDO REYNOSO, 1993
4.21	Kevin Ritz, 1995
4.29	Roger Bailey, 1997
4.71	JOHN THOMSON, 1997
4.96	ARMANDO REYNOSO, 1996

Most pinch-hit homers, season

4	Howard Johnson, 1994
4	JOHN VANDER WAL, 1995
3	JOHN VANDER WAL, 1998

Most pinch-hit homers, career

12	JOHN VANDER WAL, 1994-1998
4	Howard Johnson, 1994

Longest hitting streak

23	DANTE BICHETTE, 1995
22	VINNY CASTILLA, 1997
21	LARRY WALKER, 1999
20	LARRY WALKER, 1998
19	DANTE BICHETTE, 1995 (2nd streak)
19	ERIC YOUNG, 1995

Most consecutive scoreless innings

21	CURT LESKANIC, 1998
17	DARRYL KILE, 1998
16	Bruce Ruffin, 1993

No-hit games

ACTIVE PLAYERS in caps.

Players' years of service are listed by the first and last years with this team and are not necessarily consecutive; all statistics record performances for this team only.

Final American and National League team statistics

Batting	BA	SLG	OBA	AB	R	H	TB	2B	3B	HR	RBI	LOB	BB	SO	SB	CS	E
Anaheim	.272	.415	.335	5630	787	1530	2339	314	27	147	739	1180	510	1028	93	45	106
Baltimore	.273	.447	.347	5565	817	1520	2487	303	11	214	783	1187	593	903	86	48	81
Boston	.280	.463	.348	5601	876	1568	2591	338	35	205	827	1150	541	1049	72	39	105
Chicago	.271	.444	.339	5585	861	1516	2477	291	38	198	806	1104	551	916	127	46	140
Cleveland	.272	.448	.347	5616	850	1530	2518	334	30	198	811	1169	631	1061	143	60	110
Detroit	.264	.415	.323	5664	722	1494	2353	306	29	165	691	1131	455	1070	122	62	115
Kansas City	.263	.399	.324	5546	714	1459	2215	274	40	134	686	1140	475	984	135	50	125
Minnesota	.266	.389	.328	5641	734	1499	2193	285	32	115	691	1151	506	915	112	54	108
New York	.288	.460	.364	5643	965	1625	2598	290	31	207	907	1203	653	1025	153	63	98
Oakland	.257	.397	.338	5490	804	1413	2181	295	13	149	755	1159	633	1122	131	47	141
Seattle	.276	.468	.345	5628	859	1553	2632	321	28	234	822	1189	558	1081	115	39	125
Tampa Bay	.261	.385	.321	5555	620	1450	2136	267	43	111	579	1155	473	1107	120	73	94
Texas	.289	.462	.357	5672	940	1637	2618	314	32	201	894	1184	595	1045	82	47	121
Toronto	.266	.448	.340	5580	816	1482	2499	316	19	221	776	1133	564	1132	184	81	125
Totals	.271	.432	.340	78416	11365	21276	33837	4248	408	2499	10767	16235	7738	14438	1675	754	1594

Pitching	W-L	ERA	IP	CG	SHO	BB	SO	W-L	ERA	IP	SV	BB	SO	Total ERA
			Starters							Relievers				
Anaheim	60-53	4.78	960.1	3	1	424	675	25-24	3.91	483.2	52	206	416	4.49
Baltimore	56-64	4.89	956.0	16	4	298	659	23-19	4.45	471.1	37	237	406	4.74
Boston	64-50	4.36	937.2	5	2	300	675	28-20	3.86	498.1	53	204	350	4.18
Chicago	60-60	5.30	922.2	8	0	377	547	20-22	5.13	516.0	42	203	364	5.22
Cleveland	66-51	4.46	1005.1	9	3	378	662	23-22	4.43	454.2	47	185	375	4.44
Detroit	45-78	5.29	952.2	9	3	343	578	20-19	4.25	493.2	32	252	369	4.93
Kansas City	55-71	5.24	961.0	6	3	364	598	17-18	5.02	475.1	46	204	401	5.15
Minnesota	46-67	4.91	942.2	7	1	264	558	24-25	4.47	505.0	42	194	394	4.75
New York	86-39	3.85	1061.1	22	8	331	821	28-9	3.76	395.1	48	135	259	3.82
Oakland	52-60	4.92	986.1	12	3	359	608	22-28	4.62	447.2	39	170	314	4.81
Seattle	61-56	4.74	994.1	17	5	336	807	15-29	5.44	430.0	31	192	349	4.93
Tampa Bay	39-79	4.63	941.0	7	2	419	628	24-20	3.84	502.0	28	224	380	4.35
Texas	68-57	5.46	965.2	10	4	359	678	20-17	4.04	465.2	46	160	316	4.99
Toronto	67-51	4.14	1063.0	10	5	412	845	21-23	4.68	402.0	47	175	309	4.28
Totals	825-836	4.77	13650.0	141	44	4964	9339	310-295	4.42	6544.2	590	2741	5002	4.65

Batting	BA	SLG	OBA	AB	R	H	TB	2B	3B	HR	RBI	LOB	BB	SO	SB	CS	E
Arizona	.246	.393	.314	5491	665	1353	2157	235	46	159	621	1104	489	1239	73	38	100
Atlanta	.272	.453	.342	5484	826	1489	2483	297	26	215	794	1148	548	1062	98	43	91
Chicago	.264	.433	.337	5619	826	1484	2434	249	34	211	784	1158	599	1220	64	44	101
Cincinnati	.262	.402	.337	5496	750	1441	2209	298	28	138	723	1183	608	1107	95	42	122
Colorado	.291	.461	.347	5632	826	1640	2594	333	36	183	791	1138	469	949	67	47	102
Florida	.248	.373	.317	5558	667	1381	2072	277	36	114	621	1132	525	1119	115	57	129
Houston	.280	.436	.356	5641	874	1578	2458	326	28	166	818	1217	621	1122	155	51	108
Los Angeles	.252	.387	.310	5459	669	1374	2114	209	27	159	630	1069	447	1056	137	53	134
Milwaukee	.260	.396	.330	5541	707	1439	2195	266	17	152	673	1148	532	1039	81	59	110
Montreal	.249	.394	.310	5418	644	1348	2133	280	32	147	602	1068	439	1058	91	46	155
New York	.259	.394	.330	5510	706	1425	2170	289	24	136	671	1192	571	1049	62	46	101
Philadelphia	.264	.395	.326	5617	713	1482	2218	286	36	126	672	1179	508	1080	97	45	110
Pittsburgh	.254	.374	.311	5493	650	1395	2057	271	35	107	613	1089	393	1060	159	51	140
St. Louis	.258	.441	.341	5593	810	1444	2465	292	30	223	781	1200	676	1179	133	41	142
San Diego	.253	.409	.330	5490	749	1390	2243	292	30	167	715	1179	604	1072	79	37	104
San Francisco	.274	.422	.353	5596	842	1534	2359	292	25	161	797	1224	671	1034	102	51	101
Totals	.262	.410	.331	88638	11924	23197	36361	4492	490	2564	11306	18428	8700	17445	1608	751	1850

Pitching	W-L	ERA	IP	CG	SHO	BB	SO	W-L	ERA	IP	SV	BB	SO	Total ERA
			Starters							Relievers				
Arizona	46-76	4.57	999.0	7	2	285	601	19-21	4.80	433.1	37	204	307	4.63
Atlanta	90-40	3.06	1074.2	24	14	293	888	16-16	3.83	364.0	45	173	344	3.25
Chicago	66-49	4.57	1000.2	7	5	351	802	23-24	4.37	467.2	55	217	399	4.47
Cincinnati	53-60	4.53	932.0	6	3	353	717	24-25	4.28	509.1	42	220	381	4.44
Colorado	52-69	5.62	983.1	9	2	388	640	25-16	3.65	449.1	36	174	311	4.99
Florida	36-73	5.40	924.1	11	0	443	604	18-35	4.85	525.1	24	272	412	5.18
Houston	76-39	3.57	1059.1	12	7	288	825	26-21	3.32	412.0	44	177	362	3.50
Los Angeles	59-57	3.78	1043.2	16	6	411	843	24-22	3.88	403.2	47	176	335	3.81
Milwaukee	45-64	5.01	934.2	2	0	354	611	29-24	3.94	516.1	39	196	452	4.63
Montreal	42-69	4.61	906.2	4	0	309	599	23-28	4.01	520.1	39	224	418	4.38
New York	62-48	3.74	1022.2	9	3	334	759	26-26	3.85	435.1	46	198	370	3.76
Philadelphia	50-61	4.69	1004.0	21	3	356	795	25-26	4.53	459.0	32	188	380	4.64
Pittsburgh	53-68	4.16	990.2	7	2	307	692	16-25	3.36	458.1	41	223	420	3.91
St. Louis	58-57	4.38	936.0	6	2	344	613	25-22	4.23	533.2	44	214	359	4.31
San Diego	67-45	3.70	1033.2	14	5	327	828	31-19	3.46	421.0	59	174	389	3.63
San Francisco	59-50	4.72	959.1	6	3	365	656	30-23	3.16	509.2	44	195	430	4.17
Totals	914-925	4.36	15804.2	161	57	5508	11473	380-373	3.98	7418.1	674	3225	6069	4.23

League forecasts

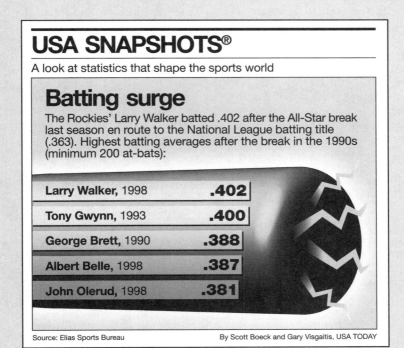

USA SNAPSHOTS®

A look at statistics that shape the sports world

Batting surge

The Rockies' Larry Walker batted .402 after the All-Star break last season en route to the National League batting title (.363). Highest batting averages after the break in the 1990s (minimum 200 at-bats):

Larry Walker, 1998	**.402**
Tony Gwynn, 1993	**.400**
George Brett, 1990	**.388**
Albert Belle, 1998	**.387**
John Olerud, 1998	**.381**

Source: Elias Sports Bureau   By Scott Boeck and Gary Visgaitis, USA TODAY

The future is in the stars, not the teams

It seems we're moving further into an era in baseball in which the same teams dominate the victory column. Given the economic structure of the game, it becomes increasingly likely our postseasons will be a battleground for the Yankees, Braves and Indians—and less likely we'll ever see the Twins, Brewers or Expos after September.

But with what lies ahead for baseball in the next year or so, the standings might actually be comforting. They might be the only constant. There's little doubt change will be rampant everywhere else.

It begins at the highest levels of the game. We enter the first year we've known without league presidents. The American and National League offices are now totally under the umbrella—or tentacles, depending on your view—of the commissioner's office. Certainly the new structure is more streamlined. What it will mean remains to be seen.

One of the issues to be handled by the new central structure is umpiring. No matter what labor lawyers and judges say and do, the role and position of the umpire will never be the same. On the surface, that's for the good. But even at the end of last season, we saw serious animosity among the "teams" assigned to police the game on the field. How long that potential ugliness lingers could have an effect on the project presented to us on the field.

The field. Lest we forget, that's what we all came to see. It's what we care about most. And we're already into a frenzy of change there. New ballparks open in Detroit, Houston and San Francisco in April. One in Milwaukee will close at the end of the season, and the holes are in the ground or the drawings on the board for a handful of others.

But it's the people in the uniforms on those fields who might confuse us most. It began through the winter, with significant names among the trades and signings. And we probably haven't seen anything yet.

When the 2000 season ends, the most talented—and potentially most costly—free-agent class in history will hit the open market. It's so full of star players that there may not be enough deep-pocketed bidders to go around. Combine the players' agents' awareness of that fact with some lesser-funded teams' desire to get something in return for players they can no longer afford, and you have a fluid marketplace.

Start with Ken Griffey, Alex Rodriguez, Craig Biggio, Manny Ramirez and many more, and the potential movement is at least explainable if not totally comprehensible.

The changes are and will continue to be staggering.

That's a major reason we're experiencing a change in the way so many fans approach baseball. When the faces and personalities of teams change so often, it's more difficult to grow attached to them. You might even find yourself with a cast of characters you don't exactly feel warmly about on what you like to think is your favorite team. And in a growing number of cities, the chance of getting any reward for rooting for your team is becoming more and more remote. It's difficult to get excited when you can be relatively certain on Opening Day that your team doesn't have a chance to win a championship—or even post a .500 record.

We're already starting to see the steady move to a more individual-based—even hero-based—form of rooting. Fans go to see specific players, even if they're with the visiting team. We attend games—or watch them on TV—hoping to see a special athlete produce a special event.

It's still easy for fans of the Yankees, Braves and Indians to root for the home team. But in so many other places, it has become much more satisfying to root for the exploits of a Sammy Sosa, a Mark McGwire or a Cal Ripken.

Maybe our game isn't changing as much as the way we approach it.

AL East: Yankees won't give up throne

It's the best division in the American League. And if there were any doubters, the 1999 season underlined the claim—from back-to-back World Series championships by the New York Yankees to the fact that Boston was the only team that won a postseason game against the Yanks and Toronto was the only over-.500 third-place team in the league.

Yes, that was last year. But there's little to indicate that the group is going to get any weaker. Even the trailing Tampa Bay Devil Rays are gradually adding young players from their farm system and should show steady improvement.

But the Devil Rays are a far cry from the talent atop the division. Whether the gap can be narrowed enough to prevent another Yankees championship will depend on pitching. Boston carries a distinct advantage at the top of their rotation with Cy Young Award winner and near-MVP Pedro Martinez. The key is being able to match the Yankees' depth. Let's face it, when you don't get around to five-time Cy Young winner Roger Clemens until Game Four of the World Series, you have plenty of weapons.

The most intriguing almost-new weapon for the Red Sox also is named Martinez. Pedro's older brother Ramon provided a brief glimpse in September and October of what quickly became a dynamite 1-2 punch. Recovering from shoulder surgery, Ramon flashed the form that made him one of the National League's premier pitchers in Los Angeles before he was hurt. That, plus the continued development of an excellent stable of mound prospects, should provide Boston with significant improvement from the patchwork rotation that Manager of the Year Jimy Williams was forced to use for most of 1999.

Speaking of managers, another one gets the opportunity to erase Baltimore's recent underachiever label. Mike Hargrove was snatched up by the Orioles shortly after Cleveland dismissed him. Beyond experience in dealing with Albert Belle, Hargrove brings along five consecutive post-season appearances. Playing into October is something the Orioles and their fans have expected, considering their huge payroll the past couple of years, but instead they have been plagued by lack of success in months like April, May and June.

Baltimore has an ace in Mike Mussina and could receive a big boost if Sidney Ponson is ready, as anticipated, to elevate his game into a No. 2 role. Offensively, the emergence of B.J. Surhoff into a team leader and the most consistent performer was the highlight of 1999. Assuming a more consistent season from Belle, the crucial questions will be how gracefully Cal Ripken and Brady Anderson age.

Toronto is going a different direction—right instead of left—with its premier slugger. Sending lefty Shawn Green to Los Angeles, the Blue Jays added right-handed right fielder Raul Mondesi to anchor the middle of the batting order.

The Blue Jays have had to toe the line on payroll for the past couple of years because of ownership uncertainty, but that hasn't prevented them from developing young players—especially pitchers—who are becoming the new nucleus of the club. Closer Billy Koch and starter Roy Halladay already are making an impact.

Tampa Bay figures to be much better, even if the same cast merely remains healthy. The Devil Rays were forced to give some young players big league experience much more quickly than expected. But they also got a glimpse of a brighter future that should include names like pitcher Ryan Rupe.

But for all those hopes up and down the Eastern Seaboard, what goes on along the Harlem River remains most important. The Yankees have rightfully established themselves as the benchmark for baseball excellence in this era. There's little reason to believe they'll allow themselves to slip from that perch.

AL Central: Indians *really* want that ring

It's no shock when a team that finishes 27½ games out of first place fires its manager. But when the team that ends up 21½ ahead makes a similar change, you understand where winning the American League Central division title stands in importance for the division's premier franchise.

Certainly, winning the division is the first priority for the Cleveland Indians—that's how they get to the playoffs every year. But after his fifth division championship in a row, manager Mike Hargrove was fired by the Indians. Why? Because general manager John Hart said the team needed to get to "the next level." Considering the highest the Indians have gotten in their playoff run is within one out of winning the World Series, there's little doubt what that next level can be. There isn't much left.

And when Cleveland lost the best-of-five Division Series to Boston after winning the first two games, management's opinion was that the Indians were way too far from that next level.

Few teams can reach the level of the Cleveland offense. With Manny Ramirez, Roberto Alomar and Jim Thome at the center of it, nobody has much chance of keeping up with the Indians, despite pitching problems that have plagued them for several seasons. While Hart annually searches for the right veteran pitcher, young fireballer Bartolo Colon probably will become the ace for whom the Indians have long searched.

No team figures to grab the division title from Cleveland anytime in the foreseeable future. A year ago, the Detroit Tigers were considered most likely, but they got mixed results from their talented young players, and manager Larry Parrish paid the price with his job in October. Former Milwaukee skipper Phil Garner was brought in, a solid choice even though the Tigers rankled the major league heirarchy, who thought minority candidates weren't considered.

More importantly, slugger Juan Gonza- lez was acquired in a controversial deal designed in part to help sell fans on the team as it moves into its new stadium in downtown Detroit. With promising outfielder Gabe Kapler and young pitchers Justin Thompson and Francisco Cordero leaving town, the concern was that the price was too high for a player who could become a free agent after the 2000 season.

While Detroit retooled, Chicago became the AL Central's up-and-coming team. The second-place White Sox had so much young talent that Frank Thomas had nearly become an afterthough by September. Right fielder Magglio Ordonez is the top offensive threat—for now. The progress shown by Paul Konerko, Chris Singleton and Carlos Lee indicates plenty of competition.

The stiffest young-talent competition comes from Kansas City. The Royals are a long way from a solid entity as a team but are putting together some exciting players, including Rookie of the Year Carlos Beltran and prospect Dee Brown in the outfield plus second baseman Carlos Febles.

The Minnesota Twins got plenty of production from young players in 1999, mostly because they were forced into the majors more quickly than the club would have preferred. But shortstop Cristian Guzman and outfielders Chad Allen, Torii Hunter and Jacque Jones showed they belong—and Eric Milton's late-season no-hitter indicated he's becoming an ace-quality pitcher.

The questions for the Twins—as well as the Royals—are how much the young players will continue to improve and whether limited budgets can provide enough other talent to make these smaller-market teams contenders.

It's highly unlikely that anyone will significantly gain on Cleveland, but the AL Central has more quality young talent than any division in the majors.

AL West: Rangers hope pitching holds up

The Texas Rangers have moved up to the next level—the one with Cleveland, where winning the division no longer is enough. The Rangers proved they can win the American League West with three titles in the past four seasons, but they don't yet have a postseason series victory to back it up.

After an offensive meltdown against the New York Yankees in the Division Series for the second consecutive year, aggressive new owner Tom Hicks said, in essence, that just won't do anymore. This is a guy who bought a hockey team (the Dallas Stars), saw a similar scenario unfold, and kept at it until he won the sport's ultimate championship.

So that was Hicks's message to general manager Doug Melvin, who built one of baseball's most potent offensive teams and assembled a bullpen that repeatedly bailed out Texas's inconsistent starters until the big bats could take over.

Just before Rangers catcher Ivan "Pudge" Rodriguez was named American League MVP, Melvin shipped out two-time MVP Juan Gonzalez, underscoring the message that things were going to change. The Rangers still have Rodriguez along with MVP candidate Rafael Palmeiro and supporting cast members Rusty Greer and Lee Stevens, but the Gonzalez trade heralded the injection of new blood.

Powerful young outfielder Gabe Kapler is the key offensive piece of the nine-player deal. He'll fill Gonzalez's spot in right field at the ballpark. Next to him likely will be the most exciting part of the change: center fielder Ruben Mateo, who got his first taste of the big leagues late last season before he was felled by an injury.

But even if their offense doesn't suffer, the Rangers still must make certain pitching doesn't drag them down. Rick Helling has developed into a consistent winner, and Texas hopes the arm troubles of Justin Thompson—part of the Gonzalez deal—are over.

The other interesting arm Texas got from Detroit was that of reliever Francisco Cordero. The fireballer could eventually be the successor to closer deluxe John Wetteland and, for now, will be part of an outstanding setup crew featuring right-hander Jeff Zimmerman and lefty Mike Venafro.

The Rangers can't be sure where to look for their challengers. A scrappy young Oakland team, led by veteran bangers John Jaha, Jason Giambi and Matt Stairs, couldn't quite keep up with Texas last year but hung in the wild-card race into September.

The Athletics were able to keep pitcher Kevin Appier, whom they acquired in a stretch-drive deal with Kansas City, and they should get more production from the youthful part of the lineup, including outfielder Ben Grieve, third baseman Eric Chavez and catcher Ramon Hernandez.

Anaheim actually could be a bigger threat. The Angels never were a factor in 1999 but much of that has to be attributed to a long string of injuries. If Mo Vaughn and Tim Salmon return to form, this suddenly is a potent lineup that can make up for some of the club's pitching deficiencies. The Angels clubhouse deteriorated in last year's frustration, so repairing that is a major task for new manager Mike Scioscia and first-year general manager Bill Stoneman.

Uncertainty continues as the Seattle Mariners redefine themselves, a several-year process that began with the departure of Randy Johnson and will continue through the impending losses of Ken Griffey and Alex Rodriguez. In addition to the influx of young talent led by pitchers Freddy Garcia and John Halama, the Mariners are in the midst of changing the style of their team after moving last July from the homer-happy Kingdome to Safeco Field, a stadium that favors pitching and defense.

NL East: Mets will badger, Braves will win

The New York Mets made gains on the Atlanta Braves in 1999, and they aren't likely to leave the perennial National League East champions alone anytime soon. But don't expect the Braves to relinquish their stranglehold.

Atlanta proved last September and again in October that they're still the best team in the division and in the National League. But the Mets' performance in the League Championship Series finally got them believing they can be Atlanta's equal.

The Braves are well positioned to stay on top, having nearly completed a transformation of the roster—especially on the offensive side—while remaining one of the game's elite teams. That difficult task has been made easier by the emergence of Chipper Jones as the most potent element of the Atlanta offense. The third baseman won the 1999 NL Most Valuable Player award not only for his stellar season but because he carried the team through September, especially in showdown games with the Mets.

A team that was winning division championships with Terry Pendleton, Fred McGriff and David Justice now is doing the same thing with Chipper Jones, Andruw Jones and Brian Jordan.

Plus, the Braves get the equivalent of three free-agent signings at no cost over the team that went to the World Series. Andres Galarraga is scheduled to be back at first base after his year off for cancer treatment, catcher Javy Lopez returns another good young bat to the lineup after missing most of the second half of 1999 because of knee surgery, and erstwhile closer Kerry Ligtenberg should be back in the bullpen.

Whether Ligtenberg can reclaim his role remains to be seen, but the point could be moot because of the development of John Rocker as Atlanta's ninth-inning man in Ligtenberg's absence.

Pitching remains the Braves' bread and butter. The frightening thing for opponents is that Kevin Millwood, the youngest of Atlanta's top four starters

and the only one without a Cy Young Award, probably was the team's best pitcher for the last few months of 1999.

The Mets still can't match Atlanta's pitching, but their star-power offense, led by Mike Piazza and Robin Ventura, can hold its own with any team in the league, and New York has one of the best defensive teams in recent memory.

The NL East isn't about to become a wide-open division, thanks to the presence of the Montreal Expos and Florida Marlins, but the Philadelphia Phillies are quietly lurking on the horizon. The Phillies faded badly late in the past two seasons, but they're building a hustling young team with a load of talent.

Third baseman Scott Rolen and outfielders Bobby Abreu and Doug Glanville already have emerged as stars, and catcher Mike Lieberthal broke through with a Gold Glove and over-.300 season in 1999. Hot prospect Pat Burrell could add his lively bat to the lineup this year.

The Phillies got Andy Ashby from San Diego to begin the task of shoring up a pitching staff that hasn't developed as quickly as the offense.

Montreal and Florida both are assembling some promising talent, but both franchises have been moving slowly as they work out issues revolving around hopes for new stadiums. The Expos are building around mega-talented outfielder Vladimir Guerrero and likely will bring more youngsters on board—possibly outfielders Peter Bergeron and Milton Bradley, plus pitchers Tony Armas and Ted Lilly.

Florida, forced by previous ownership to sell off the higher-salaried players who brought the Marlins their 1997 World Series championship, have continued to stockpile top prospects. Outfielder Preston Wilson and shortstop Alex Gonzalez were top rookies last season, and pitchers Vladimir Nunez and Brad Penny, both acquired in last year's trade of closer Matt Mantei, should quickly make their marks.

NL Central: Challengers game for Astros

The Houston Astros have three consecutive National League Central Division championships, but this is hardly a division that is dominated by one team. Houston went to the final day of last season to hold off the Cincinnati Reds and claim the division title. The previous year, the Chicago Cubs were the second-place team and the wild card. The year before that, Pittsburgh chased the Astros into the final week.

The Astros have to be considered the favorite again, based on their experience, depth and star quality, led by MVP runnerup Jeff Bagwell and Cy Young Award runnerup Mike Hampton. And the law of averages would seem to guarantee not nearly as much could go wrong for Houston as it did in 1999, when manager Larry Dierker missed time with a seizure, outfielder Moises Alou missed the entire season, and several other key players spent significant time on the disabled list.

So whose turn is it to give Houston a battle?

Cincinnati's Cinderella season was no fluke—the Reds have too much talent to turn into pumpkins. Sean Casey will be an offensive force for a long time and he'll have help from slugger Dante Bichette, acquired from Colorado. The deep bullpen, led by Rookie of the Year Scott Williamson, should ensure the Reds will stay close in most games.

St. Louis is the team with the potential to make the most significant jump. Despite Mark McGwire's heroics and the rapid development of third baseman Fernando Tatis, the Cardinals have been doomed in recent seasons by numerous pitching injuries.

In order to buy time and take pressure off the returns of promising Matt Morris and Alan Benes, St. Louis got veterans Darryl Kile and Pat Hentgen in trades. Factor in last year's big season from unheralded Kent Bottenfield, and the Cardinals suddenly have the potential for a strong rotation. And that's before mentioning Rick Ankiel, possibly the brightest pitching prospect coming into the majors this season.

Pittsburgh rebounded from a disappointing finish in 1998 to get its youth movement back on track in '99. Second baseman Warren Morris was a serious Rookie of the Year candidate, and outfielder Brian Giles became a major power-and-average threat after several seasons of platooning in Cleveland.

The biggest boost for the Pirates and their solid young pitching staff will be the return of catcher Jason Kendall, the heart and soul of the team. His solid hitting and baserunning ability were sorely missed when he lost the second half of 1999 because of a broken leg.

The rest of the teams in the division included managerial changes as part of their overhauls. Milwaukee's new management includes general manager Dean Taylor and manager Davey Lopes. The Brewers, who had hoped to be in their new Miller Park this season, will play one more year at County Stadium because of delays caused by a construction accident at the new facility last summer.

The Chicago Cubs sunk to last place in 1999, despite record attendance. Sammy Sosa—the main reason for the throngs at Wrigley Field—will have to continue to provide most of the offense, but the more crucial concern for new manager Don Baylor is his pitching.

There's no firm timetable for the return of 1998 Rookie of the Year Kerry Wood, but indications are that he'll be able to recover from elbow ligament surgery. The loss of Wood for the entire season, coupled with a later injury to Kevin Tapani, decimated the Chicago rotation and ruined the Cubs' chances.

If recent history is any indication, the NL Central will provide another good race and it likely will be Houston and somebody. And there are enough indications that if the Astros slip even in the least, there could be several somebodies ready to challenge.

NL West: Money talks, mostly to Arizona

The Los Angeles Dodgers are determined to get it right. The Arizona Diamondbacks already have. The rest of the National League West has to wonder what it will take to compete on a long-term basis with these free-spenders.

Last season opened with a head-to-head matchup between the free-agent jewels of the previous offseason: Kevin Brown and Randy Johnson. The Dodgers won the game in extra innings, but Johnson won the Cy Young Award and the Diamondbacks won the division in just their second season. The Dodgers never meshed as a team and tumbled to a distant third place.

Well, they're at it again in L.A., trying to fix a couple of things in one fell swoop by sending Raul Mondesi to Toronto for Shawn Green. The change of faces in right field at Dodger Stadium does more than remove Mondesi, who was frustrated and angry by the end of last season and begged out. It addresses the biggest problem of the Los Angeles offense: an extreme right-handedness. Green adds a potent lefty bat to the middle of the order.

But making up for a 23-game deficit in the standings is a formidable task, especially because the Diamondbacks appeared to improve as last season wore on. They added closer Matt Mantei at midseason and slugging first baseman Erubiel Durzao a bit later, and continued building a farm system of prospects like young pitcher John Patterson.

Arizona's biggest fear has to be that some of its offensive players won't be able to repeat their 1999 seasons. Outfielder Luis Gonzalez batted 59 points above his career average. Steve Finley, at age 34, boosted his average 15 points over 1998 and more than doubled his home run output. Second baseman Jay Bell's homers jumped from 20 to 38 and his average climbed 38 points.

But the Diamondbacks figure to remain strong thanks to the deepest starting pitching in the division, led by Johnson and still-developing Omar Daal.

San Francisco hung with Arizona longer than any other team in the 1999 race, and this year the Giants get the boost of moving into their new downtown stadium. Or will they miss the home advantage from the effect of the biting winds at Candlestick Point on their sometimes reluctant opponents?

With an offensive nucleus of Barry Bonds, Jeff Kent and improving center fielder Marvin Benard already in place, the Giants are trying to develop a competitive pitching staff from within the organization. Russ Ortiz matured into an 18-game winner in his first full season and Joe Nathan showed second-half flashes of being the next major contributor.

Colorado and San Diego have even more ground to make up than the Dodgers—and it's the Rockies who appear of a mind to do it more quickly. Former Cleveland assistant Dan O'Dowd took over the general manager's chair in Denver, immediately hiring Buddy Bell as manager and moving out high-priced veterans Dante Bichette and Darryl Kile in an attempt to inject more young talent into the roster.

San Diego is moving more slowly, still in a payroll-reduction mode that began after its trip to the 1998 World Series. That season helped the Padres build impetus for a new downtown stadium, and their rebuilding process is geared toward the move to the new playground.

Of course, new facilities are not automatic guarantees of increased spending. Even the Giants have indicated they will proceed cautiously until they see how their move affects their revenue stream.

Meanwhile, the revenue stream in Los Angeles and Arizona will be more like a torrent, at least in comparison with the other clubs in the NL West. That kind of spending doesn't mean that a team becomes a certain contender, as the Dodgers proved last season. But it allows the richer teams to make a few more mistakes and stretches the odds against the other clubs.

Final player statistics

2000 Baseball Weekly Almanac

American League

National League

Stats key for pitchers:

T–Throws right or left; **W**–Wins;
L–Losses; **ERA**–Earned run average;
G–Games; **GS**–Games started;
CG–Complete games; **SHO**–Shutouts;
GF–Games finished in relief; **SV**–Saves;
IP–Innings pitched; **H**–Hits; **R**–Runs;
ER–Earned runs; **HR**–Home runs;
BB–Bases on balls; **SO**–Strikeouts;
WP–Wild pitches; **BA**–Batting average
against; **RV**–Rotisserie value.

*Rotisserie values are provided by John
Hunt. Dollar values are based on each
player occupying a roster spot on a
standard Rotisserie league team for an
entire season. Players with no value (NV)
had no effect or a negative effect on a
Rotisserie team in 1999. In a standard
12-team league only 276 players can be
active at one time.*

Stats key for batters:

B–Bats right, left, or both; **BA**–Batting
average; **G**–Games; **AB**–At-bats;
R–Runs; **H**–Hits; **TB**–Total Bases;
2B–Doubles; **3B**–Triples; **HR**–Home
runs; **RBI**–Runs batted in; **SH**–Sacrifice
hits; **SF**–Sacrifice flies; **BB**–Bases on
balls; **SO**–Strikeouts; **SB**–Stolen bases;
CS–Caught stealing; **SLG**–Slugging percentage; **OBA**–On-base average;
RV–Rotisserie value.

Players are listed alphabetically by
position within each league. Each player
is listed at the position where he played
the most games in 1999; statistics are
for all games played in 1999.

*Statistics are provided by the Elias
Sports Bureau.*

American League designated hitters

Name/Team	B	BA	G	AB	R	H	TB	2B	3B	HR	RBI	SH	SF	BB	SO	SB	CS	SLG	OBA	RV
Alvarez, Gabe, Det.	R	.208	22	53	5	11	20	3	0	2	4	0	0	3	9	0	0	.377	.250	NV
Baines, Harold, Bal.-Cle.	L	.312	135	430	62	134	229	18	1	25	103	0	2	54	48	1	2	.533	.387	22
Berroa, Geronimo, Tor.	R	.194	22	62	11	12	18	3	0	1	6	0	0	9	15	0	0	.290	.315	NV
Canseco, Jose, T.B.	R	.279	113	430	75	120	242	18	1	34	95	0	7	58	135	3	0	.563	.369	21
Cordova, Marty, Min.	R	.285	124	425	62	121	197	28	3	14	70	0	6	48	96	13	4	.464	.365	16
Davis, Chili, N.Y.	B	.269	146	476	59	128	212	25	1	19	78	0	3	73	100	4	1	.445	.366	13
Giambi, Jeremy, K.C.	L	.285	90	288	34	82	106	13	1	3	34	1	4	40	67	0	0	.368	.373	3
Greene, Todd, Ana.	R	.243	97	321	36	78	140	20	0	14	42	0	2	12	63	1	4	.436	.275	4
Greene, Willie, Tor.	L	.204	81	226	22	46	89	7	0	12	41	0	2	20	56	0	1	.394	.266	1
Hollins, Dave, Tor.	B	.222	27	99	12	22	33	5	0	2	6	0	0	5	22	0	0	.333	.260	NV
Jaha, John, Oak.	R	.276	142	457	93	126	254	23	0	35	111	0	3	101	129	2	0	.556	.414	22
Jefferies, Gregg, Det.	B	.200	70	205	22	41	67	8	0	6	18	0	3	13	11	3	4	.327	.258	NV
Jefferson, Reggie, Bos.	L	.277	83	206	21	57	87	13	1	5	17	0	0	17	55	0	0	.422	.338	1
Leyritz, Jim, N.Y.	R	.227	31	66	8	15	21	4	1	0	5	0	0	13	17	0	0	.318	.354	NV
Martinez, Edgar, Sea.	R	.337	142	502	86	169	278	35	1	24	86	0	3	97	99	7	2	.554	.447	26
McRae, Brian, Tor.	B	.195	31	82	11	16	30	3	1	3	11	1	0	16	22	0	1	.366	.340	NV
Palmeiro, Rafael, Tex.	L	.324	158	565	96	183	356	30	1	47	148	0	9	97	69	2	4	.630	.420	37
Polonia, Luis, Det.	L	.324	87	333	46	108	175	21	8	10	32	2	2	16	32	17	9	.526	.357	15
Strawberry, Darryl, N.Y.	L	.327	24	49	10	16	30	5	0	3	6	0	0	17	16	2	0	.612	.500	1
Sweeney, Mike, K.C.	R	.322	150	575	101	185	299	44	2	22	102	0	4	54	48	6	1	.520	.387	25
Thomas, Frank, Chi.	R	.305	135	486	74	148	229	36	0	15	77	0	8	87	66	3	3	.471	.414	16
Witt, Kevin, Tor.	L	.206	15	34	3	7	11	1	0	1	5	1	0	2	9	0	0	.324	.250	NV

American League catchers

Name/Team	B	BA	G	AB	R	H	TB	2B	3B	HR	RBI	SH	SF	BB	SO	SB	CS	SLG	OBA	RV
Alomar, Sandy, Cle.	R	.307	37	137	19	42	73	13	0	6	25	1	2	4	23	0	1	.533	.322	4
Ausmus, Brad, Det.	R	.275	127	458	62	126	190	25	6	9	54	3	1	51	71	12	9	.415	.365	11
Borders, Pat, Cle.-Tor.	R	.265	12	34	3	9	14	0	1	1	6	0	0	1	5	0	1	.412	.286	NV
Brown, Kevin, Tor.	R	.444	2	9	1	4	6	2	0	0	1	0	0	0	3	0	0	.667	.444	NV
Dalesandro, Mark, Tor.	R	.185	16	27	3	5	5	0	0	0	1	0	1	0	2	1	0	.185	.207	NV
Davis, Tommy, Bal.	R	.167	5	6	0	1	1	0	0	0	0	0	0	0	2	0	0	.167	.167	NV
Decker, Steve, Ana.	R	.238	28	63	5	15	21	6	0	0	5	1	1	13	9	0	0	.333	.372	NV
Diaz, Einar, Cle.	R	.281	119	392	43	110	142	21	1	3	32	6	1	23	41	11	4	.362	.328	7
DiFelice, Mike, T.B.	R	.307	51	179	21	55	84	11	0	6	27	0	1	8	23	0	0	.469	.346	4
Fasano, Sal, K.C.	R	.233	23	60	11	14	31	2	0	5	16	0	1	7	17	0	1	.517	.373	NV
Fick, Rob, Det.	L	.220	15	41	6	9	18	0	0	3	10	0	1	7	6	1	0	.439	.327	NV
Figga, Mike, N.Y.-Bal.	R	.221	43	86	12	19	26	4	0	1	5	2	1	2	27	0	2	.302	.236	NV
Flaherty, John, T.B.	R	.278	144	463	53	124	185	19	0	14	71	1	10	19	64	0	0	.415	.310	10
Fletcher, Darrin, Tor.	L	.291	115	412	48	120	200	26	0	18	80	0	4	26	47	0	0	.485	.339	14
Fordyce, Brook, Chi.	R	.297	105	333	36	99	153	25	1	9	49	3	2	21	48	2	0	.459	.343	9
Girardi, Joe, N.Y.	R	.239	65	209	23	50	74	16	1	2	27	8	2	10	26	3	1	.354	.271	NV
Gubanich, Creighton, Bos.	R	.277	18	47	4	13	20	2	1	1	11	0	0	3	13	0	0	.426	.346	NV
Haselman, Bill, Det.	R	.273	48	143	13	39	59	8	0	4	14	0	0	10	26	2	0	.413	.320	1
Hatteberg, Scott, Bos.	L	.275	30	80	12	22	30	5	0	1	11	0	1	18	14	0	0	.375	.410	NV
Hemphill, Bret, Ana.	B	.143	12	21	3	3	3	0	0	0	2	1	1	4	4	0	0	.143	.269	NV
Hernandez, Ramon, Oak.	R	.279	40	136	13	38	54	7	0	3	21	1	2	18	11	1	0	.397	.363	2
Hinch, A.J., Oak.	R	.215	76	205	26	44	71	4	1	7	24	9	1	11	41	6	2	.346	.260	1
Johnson, Charles, Bal.	R	.251	135	426	58	107	176	19	1	16	54	4	3	55	107	0	0	.413	.340	6
Johnson, Mark, Chi.	L	.227	73	207	27	47	70	11	0	4	16	1	2	36	58	3	1	.338	.344	NV
Kreuter, Chad, K.C.	B	.225	107	324	31	73	103	15	0	5	35	2	2	34	65	0	0	.318	.309	NV
Lampkin, Tom, Sea.	L	.291	76	206	29	60	102	11	2	9	34	1	2	13	32	1	3	.495	.345	6
Levis, Jesse, Cle.	L	.154	10	26	0	4	4	0	0	0	3	1	0	1	6	0	0	.154	.214	NV
Lomasney, Steve, Bos.	R	.000	1	2	0	0	0	0	0	0	0	0	0	0	2	0	0	.000	.000	NV
Macfarlane, Mike, Oak.	R	.243	81	226	24	55	84	17	0	4	31	1	5	13	52	0	0	.372	.282	NV
Matheny, Mike, Tor.	R	.215	57	163	16	35	50	6	0	3	17	2	1	12	37	0	0	.307	.271	NV
Molina, Ben, Ana.	R	.257	31	101	8	26	34	5	0	1	10	0	0	6	6	0	1	.337	.312	NV
O'Brien, Charlie, Ana.	R	.097	27	62	3	6	9	0	0	1	4	1	1	1	12	0	0	.145	.136	NV
Paul, Josh, Chi.	R	.222	6	18	2	4	5	1	0	0	1	0	0	0	4	0	0	.278	.222	NV
Pierzynski, A.J., Min.	L	.273	9	22	3	6	8	2	0	0	3	0	0	1	4	0	0	.364	.333	NV
Posada, Jorge, N.Y.	B	.245	112	379	50	93	152	19	2	12	57	0	2	53	91	1	0	.401	.341	5
Rodriguez, Ivan, Tex.	R	.332	144	600	116	199	335	29	1	35	113	0	5	24	64	25	12	.558	.356	40
Spehr, Tim, K.C.	R	.206	60	155	26	32	66	7	0	9	26	2	2	22	47	1	0	.426	.324	1
Steinbach, Terry, Min.	R	.284	101	338	35	96	132	16	4	4	42	0	2	38	54	2	2	.391	.358	5
Turner, Chris, Cle.	R	.190	12	21	3	4	4	0	0	0	0	0	0	1	8	1	0	.190	.227	NV
Valentin, Javier, Min.	B	.248	78	218	22	54	83	12	1	5	28	1	5	22	39	0	0	.381	.313	1
Varitek, Jason, Bos.	B	.269	144	483	70	130	233	39	2	20	76	5	8	46	85	1	2	.482	.330	12
Walbeck, Matt, Ana.	B	.240	107	288	26	69	88	8	1	3	22	3	1	26	46	2	3	.306	.308	NV
Webster, Lenny, Bal.-Bos.	R	.120	22	50	1	6	7	1	0	0	4	0	0	10	7	0	0	.140	.290	NV

American League catchers

Name/Team	B	BA	G	AB	R	H	TB	2B	3B	HR	RBI	SH	SF	BB	SO	SB	CS	SLG	OBA	RV
Wilson, Dan, Sea.	R	.266	123	414	46	110	158	23	2	7	38	10	2	29	83	5	0	.382	.315	5
Zaun, Greg, Tex.	B	.247	43	93	12	23	30	2	1	1	12	1	2	10	7	1	0	.323	.314	NV

American League first basemen

Name/Team	B	BA	G	AB	R	H	TB	2B	3B	HR	RBI	SH	SF	BB	SO	SB	CS	SLG	OBA	RV
Blowers, Mike, Sea.	R	.239	19	46	2	11	18	1	0	2	7	0	0	4	12	0	0	.391	.300	NV
Catalanotto, Frank, Det.	L	.276	100	286	41	79	131	19	0	11	35	0	5	15	49	3	4	.458	.327	6
Clark, Tony, Det.	B	.280	143	536	74	150	272	29	0	31	99	0	3	64	133	2	1	.507	.361	20
Clark, Will, Bal.	L	.303	77	251	40	76	121	15	0	10	29	0	3	38	42	2	2	.482	.395	7
Conine, Jeff, Bal.	R	.291	139	444	54	129	201	31	1	13	75	1	7	30	40	0	3	.453	.335	12
Coomer, Ron, Min.	R	.263	127	467	53	123	198	25	1	16	65	0	3	30	69	2	1	.424	.307	9
Cox, Steve, T.B.	L	.211	6	19	0	4	5	1	0	0	0	0	0	0	2	0	0	.263	.211	NV
Daubach, Brian, Bos.	L	.294	110	381	61	112	214	33	3	21	73	0	0	36	92	0	1	.562	.360	14
Delgado, Carlos, Tor.	L	.272	152	573	113	156	327	39	0	44	134	0	7	86	141	1	1	.571	.377	26
Erstad, Darin, Ana.	L	.253	142	585	84	148	219	22	5	13	53	2	3	47	101	13	7	.374	.308	9
Franco, Julio, T.B.	R	.000	1	1	0	0	0	0	0	0	0	0	0	0	1	0	0	.000	.000	NV
Giambi, Jason, Oak.	L	.315	158	575	115	181	318	36	1	33	123	0	8	105	106	1	1	.553	.422	28
Jackson, Ryan, Sea.	L	.235	32	68	4	16	19	3	0	0	10	0	2	6	19	3	3	.279	.299	NV
King, Jeff, K.C.	R	.236	21	72	14	17	28	2	0	3	11	0	1	15	10	2	0	.389	.385	NV
Konerko, Paul, Chi.	R	.294	142	513	71	151	262	31	4	24	81	1	3	45	68	1	0	.511	.352	17
Leius, Scott, K.C.	R	.203	37	74	8	15	19	1	0	1	10	0	3	4	8	1	0	.257	.244	NV
Martinez, Tino, N.Y.	L	.263	159	589	95	155	270	27	2	28	105	0	4	69	86	3	4	.458	.341	17
McGriff, Fred, T.B.	L	.310	144	529	75	164	292	30	1	32	104	0	4	86	107	1	0	.552	.405	25
Mientkiewicz, Doug, Min.	L	.229	118	327	34	75	108	21	3	2	32	3	2	43	51	1	1	.330	.324	NV
Ortiz, David, Min.	L	.000	10	20	1	0	0	0	0	0	0	0	0	5	12	0	0	.000	.200	NV
Pickering, Calvin, Bal.	L	.125	23	40	4	5	9	1	0	1	5	0	0	11	16	0	0	.225	.314	NV
Pritchett, Chris, Ana.	L	.156	20	45	3	7	11	1	0	1	2	1	1	2	9	1	1	.244	.188	NV
Segui, David, Sea.-Tor.	B	.298	121	440	57	131	206	27	3	14	52	1	4	40	60	1	1	.468	.355	11
Sexson, Richie, Cle.	R	.255	134	479	72	122	246	17	7	31	116	0	8	34	117	3	3	.514	.305	19
Simms, Mike, Tex.	R	.500	4	2	0	1	1	0	0	0	0	0	0	0	0	0	0	.500	.500	NV
Stanley, Mike, Bos.	R	.281	136	427	59	120	199	22	0	19	72	0	4	70	94	0	0	.466	.393	12
Stevens, Lee, Tex.	L	.282	146	517	76	146	251	31	1	24	81	0	7	52	132	2	3	.485	.344	16
Sutton, Larry, K.C.	L	.225	43	102	14	23	35	6	0	2	15	1	2	13	17	1	0	.343	.308	NV
Thorne, Jim, Cle.	L	.277	146	494	101	137	267	27	2	33	108	0	4	127	171	0	0	.540	.426	20
Vaughn, Mo, Ana.	L	.281	139	524	63	147	266	20	0	33	108	0	3	54	127	0	0	.508	.358	21
Vitiello, Joe, K.C.	R	.146	13	41	4	6	10	1	0	1	4	0	0	2	9	0	0	.244	.222	NV

American League second basemen

Name/Team	B	BA	G	AB	R	H	TB	2B	3B	HR	RBI	SH	SF	BB	SO	SB	CS	SLG	OBA	RV
Alicea, Luis, Tex.	B	.201	68	164	33	33	52	10	0	3	17	3	1	28	32	2	1	.317	.316	NV
Alomar, Roberto, Cle.	B	.323	159	563	138	182	300	40	3	24	120	12	13	99	96	37	6	.533	.422	39
Bell, David, Sea.	R	.268	157	597	92	160	258	31	2	21	78	3	7	58	90	7	4	.432	.331	14
Bush, Homer, Tor.	R	.320	128	485	69	155	204	26	4	5	55	8	3	21	82	32	8	.421	.353	23
Cairo, Miguel, T.B.	R	.295	120	465	61	137	171	15	5	3	36	7	5	24	46	22	7	.368	.335	13
Davidson, Cleatus, Min.	B	.136	12	22	3	3	3	0	0	0	3	2	0	0	4	2	0	.136	.136	NV
DeShields, Delino, Bal.	L	.264	96	330	46	87	120	11	2	6	34	5	1	37	52	11	8	.364	.339	6
Durham, Ray, Chi.	B	.296	153	612	109	181	266	30	8	13	60	3	2	73	105	34	11	.435	.373	24
Durrington, Trent, Ana.	B	.180	43	122	14	22	24	2	0	0	2	5	0	9	28	4	3	.197	.237	NV
Easley, Damion, Det.	R	.266	151	549	83	146	238	30	1	20	65	2	6	51	124	11	3	.434	.346	14
Febles, Carlos, K.C.	R	.256	123	453	71	116	186	22	9	10	53	12	3	47	91	20	4	.411	.336	12
Fonville, Chad, Bos.	B	.000	3	2	1	0	0	0	0	0	0	0	0	2	0	1	0	.000	.500	NV
Frye, Jeff, Bos.	R	.281	41	114	14	32	38	3	0	1	12	1	1	14	11	2	2	.333	.362	NV
Graffanino, Tony, T.B.	R	.315	39	130	20	41	64	9	4	2	19	2	0	9	22	3	2	.492	.364	3
Grebeck, Craig, Tor.	R	.363	34	113	18	41	48	7	0	0	10	3	1	15	13	0	1	.425	.443	2
Hairston, Jerry, Bal.	R	.269	50	175	26	47	73	12	1	4	17	4	0	11	24	9	4	.417	.323	4
Hansen, Jed, K.C.	R	.203	49	79	16	16	26	1	0	3	5	4	1	10	32	0	1	.329	.289	NV
Huson, Jeff, Ana.	L	.262	97	225	21	59	68	7	1	0	18	1	3	16	27	10	1	.302	.307	3
Kelly, Pat, Tor.	R	.267	37	116	17	31	56	7	0	6	20	1	3	10	23	0	1	.483	.318	2
Knoblauch, Chuck, N.Y.	R	.292	150	603	120	176	274	36	4	18	68	3	5	83	57	28	9	.454	.393	24
Lopez, Mendy, K.C.	R	.400	7	20	2	8	10	0	1	0	3	0	0	5	0	0	0	.500	.429	NV
Macias, Jose, Det.	B	.250	5	4	2	1	4	0	0	1	2	0	0	0	1	0	1	1.000	.250	NV
Martin, Norberto, Tor.	R	.222	9	27	3	6	8	2	0	0	0	0	0	4	4	0	0	.296	.364	NV
McDonald, Jed, Cle.	R	.333	18	21	2	7	7	0	0	0	0	0	0	0	3	0	1	.333	.333	NV
McLemore, Mark, Tex.	B	.274	144	566	105	155	207	20	7	6	45	9	6	83	79	16	8	.366	.363	10
Offerman, Jose, Bos.	B	.294	149	586	107	172	255	37	11	8	69	2	7	96	79	18	12	.435	.391	17
Phillips, Tony, Oak.	B	.244	106	406	76	99	176	24	4	15	49	0	2	71	94	11	3	.433	.362	8

FINAL PLAYER STATISTICS

American League second basemen

Name/Team	B	BA	G	AB	R	H	TB	2B	3B	HR	RBI	SH	SF	BB	SO	SB	CS	SLG	OBA	RV
Rodriguez, Liu, Chi.	B	.237	39	93	8	22	31	2	2	1	12	3	0	12	11	0	0	.333	.343	NV
Silvestri, Dave, Ana.	R	.091	3	11	0	1	2	1	0	0	1	0	0	0	1	0	0	.182	.091	NV
Spiezio, Scott, Oak.	B	.243	89	247	31	60	108	24	0	8	33	1	3	29	36	0	0	.437	.324	2
Velandia, Jorge, Oak.	R	.188	63	48	4	9	10	1	0	0	2	0	0	2	13	2	0	.208	.235	NV
Velarde, Randy, Ana.-Oak.	R	.317	156	631	105	200	287	25	7	16	76	4	0	70	98	24	8	.455	.390	27
Walker, Todd, Min.	L	.279	143	531	62	148	211	37	4	6	46	0	2	52	83	18	10	.397	.343	12

American League third basemen

Name/Team	B	BA	G	AB	R	H	TB	2B	3B	HR	RBI	SH	SF	BB	SO	SB	CS	SLG	OBA	RV
Baerga, Carlos, Cle.	B	.228	22	57	4	13	16	0	0	1	5	1	1	4	10	1	1	.281	.274	NV
Bellinger, Clay, N.Y.	R	.200	32	45	12	9	14	2	0	1	2	0	0	1	10	1	0	.311	.217	NV
Blake, Casey, Tor.	R	.256	14	39	6	10	15	2	0	1	1	0	0	2	7	0	0	.385	.293	NV
Boggs, Wade, T.B.	L	.301	90	292	40	88	110	14	1	2	29	0	4	38	23	1	0	.377	.377	4
Branyan, Russell, Cle.	L	.211	11	38	4	8	13	2	0	1	6	0	0	3	19	0	0	.342	.286	NV
Brosius, Scott, N.Y.	R	.247	133	473	64	117	196	26	1	17	71	2	9	39	74	9	3	.414	.307	10
Chavez, Eric, Oak.	L	.247	115	356	47	88	152	21	2	13	50	0	0	46	56	1	1	.427	.333	5
Davis, Russ, Sea.	R	.245	124	432	55	106	188	17	1	21	59	7	2	32	111	3	3	.435	.304	8
Fernandez, Tony, Tor.	B	.328	142	485	73	159	218	41	0	6	75	0	4	77	62	6	7	.449	.427	17
Fryman, Travis, Cle.	R	.255	85	322	45	82	132	16	2	10	48	0	2	25	57	2	1	.410	.309	5
Gates, Brent, Min.	R	.255	110	306	40	78	104	13	2	3	38	2	3	34	56	1	3	.340	.328	1
Glaus, Troy, Ana.	R	.240	154	551	85	132	248	29	0	29	79	0	3	71	143	5	1	.450	.331	12
Houston, Tyler, Cle.	L	.148	13	27	2	4	8	1	0	1	3	0	0	3	11	0	0	.296	.233	NV
Jimenez, D'Angelo, N.Y.	B	.400	7	20	3	8	10	2	0	0	4	0	0	3	4	0	0	.500	.478	NV
Koskie, Corey, Min.	L	.310	117	342	42	106	160	21	0	11	58	2	3	40	72	4	4	.468	.387	12
Manto, Jeff, Cle.-N.Y.	R	.182	18	33	5	6	9	0	0	1	2	1	0	13	15	0	0	.273	.413	NV
Minor, Ryan, Bal.	R	.194	46	124	13	24	40	7	0	3	10	0	1	8	43	1	0	.323	.241	NV
Norton, Greg, Chi.	B	.255	132	436	62	111	185	26	0	16	50	1	2	69	93	4	4	.424	.358	7
Otanez, Willis, Bal.-Tor.	R	.237	71	207	28	49	81	11	0	7	24	1	1	15	46	0	0	.391	.293	NV
Palmer, Dean, Det.	R	.262	150	560	92	147	290	25	2	38	100	0	4	57	153	3	3	.518	.339	20
Perry, Herb, T.B.	R	.254	66	209	29	53	83	10	1	6	32	0	4	16	42	0	0	.397	.331	2
Randa, Joe, K.C.	R	.314	156	628	92	197	297	36	8	16	84	1	7	50	80	5	4	.473	.363	20
Reboulet, Jeff, Bal.	R	.162	99	154	25	25	29	4	0	0	4	3	0	33	29	1	0	.188	.317	NV
Ripken, Cal, Bal.	R	.340	86	332	51	113	194	27	0	18	57	3	3	13	31	0	1	.584	.368	16
Saenz, Olmedo, Oak.	R	.275	97	255	41	70	121	18	0	11	41	0	3	22	47	1	1	.475	.363	6
Sheldon, Scott, Tex.	R	.000	2	2	0	0	0	0	0	0	0	0	0	0	0	0	0	.000	.000	NV
Smith, Robert, T.B.	R	.181	68	199	18	36	51	4	1	3	19	2	1	16	64	4	4	.256	.244	NV
Sojo, Luis, N.Y.	R	.252	49	127	20	32	44	6	0	2	16	2	0	4	17	1	0	.346	.275	NV
Valentin, John, Bos.	R	.254	113	449	58	114	179	27	1	12	70	1	8	40	68	0	1	.399	.315	6
Veras, Wilton, Bos.	R	.286	36	119	14	34	47	5	1	2	13	0	2	5	14	0	2	.395	.320	NV
Wilson, Craig, Chi.	R	.238	98	252	28	60	82	8	1	4	26	6	1	23	22	1	1	.325	.301	NV
Wilson, Enrique, Cle.	B	.262	113	332	41	87	117	22	1	2	24	4	6	25	41	5	4	.352	.310	2
Wood, Jason, Det.	R	.159	27	44	5	7	11	1	0	1	8	1	0	2	13	0	0	.250	.196	NV
Zeile, Todd, Tex.	R	.293	156	587	80	172	287	41	1	24	98	1	7	56	94	1	2	.489	.355	19

American League shortstops

Name/Team	B	BA	G	AB	R	H	TB	2B	3B	HR	RBI	SH	SF	BB	SO	SB	CS	SLG	OBA	RV
Batista, Tony, Tor.	R	.285	98	375	61	107	212	25	1	26	79	3	5	22	79	2	0	.565	.328	17
Bordick, Mike, Bal.	R	.277	160	631	93	175	254	35	7	10	77	8	10	54	102	14	4	.403	.334	15
Bournigal, Rafael, Sea.	R	.274	55	95	16	26	37	5	0	2	14	4	2	7	6	0	0	.389	.317	NV
Caruso, Mike, Chi.	B	.250	136	529	60	132	157	11	4	2	35	11	1	20	36	12	14	.297	.280	3
Cedeno, Domingo, Sea.	B	.214	21	42	4	9	17	2	0	2	8	0	0	5	9	1	1	.405	.313	NV
Clayton, Royce, Tex.	R	.288	133	465	69	134	207	21	5	14	52	9	3	39	100	8	6	.445	.346	12
Cruz, Deivi, Det.	R	.284	155	518	64	147	221	35	0	13	58	14	5	12	57	1	4	.427	.302	10
Dellaero, Jason, Chi.	B	.091	11	33	1	3	3	0	0	0	2	0	1	1	13	0	0	.091	.114	NV
DiSarcina, Gary, Ana.	R	.229	81	271	32	62	74	7	1	1	29	9	1	15	32	2	2	.273	.273	NV
Dransfeldt, Kelly, Tex.	R	.189	16	53	3	10	14	1	0	1	5	1	0	3	12	0	0	.264	.232	NV
Garcia, Jesse, Bal.	R	.207	17	29	6	6	12	0	0	2	2	3	0	2	3	0	0	.414	.258	NV
Garcia, Luis, Det.	R	.111	8	9	0	1	2	1	0	0	0	0	0	0	2	0	0	.222	.111	NV
Garciaparra, Nomar, Bos.	R	.357	135	532	103	190	321	42	4	27	104	0	4	51	39	14	3	.603	.418	35
Gonzalez, Alex, Tor.	R	.292	38	154	22	45	64	13	0	2	12	0	0	16	23	4	2	.416	.370	2
Guevara, Giomar, Sea.	B	.250	10	12	2	3	5	2	0	0	2	0	0	2	0	0	0	.417	.250	NV
Guillen, Carlos, Sea.	B	.158	5	19	2	3	6	0	0	1	3	1	0	1	6	0	0	.316	.200	NV
Guzman, Cristian, Min.	B	.226	131	420	47	95	116	12	3	1	26	7	4	22	90	9	7	.276	.267	NV
Hocking, Dennis, Min.	B	.267	136	386	47	103	146	18	2	7	41	4	6	22	54	11	7	.378	.307	8
Holbert, Ray, K.C.	R	.280	34	100	14	28	31	3	0	0	5	6	1	8	20	7	4	.310	.330	1
Jeter, Derek, N.Y.	R	.349	158	627	134	219	346	37	9	24	102	3	6	91	116	19	8	.552	.438	36

American League shortstops

Name/Team	B	BA	G	AB	R	H	TB	2B	3B	HR	RBI	SH	SF	BB	SO	SB	CS	SLG	OBA	RV
Lamb, David, T.B.	B	.226	55	124	18	28	38	5	1	1	13	0	0	10	18	0	1	.306	.284	NV
Ledesma, Aaron, T.B.	R	.265	93	294	32	78	93	15	0	0	30	1	0	14	35	1	1	.316	.305	NV
Martinez, Felix, K.C.	B	.143	6	7	1	1	1	0	0	0	0	0	0	0	0	0	0	.143	.143	NV
Menechino, Frank, Oak.	R	.222	9	9	0	2	2	0	0	0	0	0	0	0	4	0	0	.222	.222	NV
Merloni, Lou, Bos.	R	.254	43	126	18	32	42	7	0	1	13	3	1	8	16	0	0	.333	.307	NV
Rodriguez, Alex, Sea.	R	.285	129	502	110	143	294	25	0	42	111	1	8	56	109	21	7	.586	.357	32
Sadler, Donnie, Bos.	R	.280	49	107	18	30	37	5	1	0	4	3	0	5	20	2	1	.346	.313	NV
Sanchez, Rey, K.C.	R	.294	134	479	66	141	177	18	6	2	56	10	3	22	48	11	5	.370	.329	11
Scarsone, Steve, K.C.	R	.206	46	68	2	14	19	5	0	0	6	1	1	9	24	1	0	.279	.295	NV
Shave, Jon, Tex.	R	.288	43	73	10	21	25	4	0	0	9	3	0	5	17	1	0	.342	.350	NV
Sheets, Andy, Ana.	R	.197	87	244	22	48	67	10	0	3	29	6	5	14	59	1	2	.275	.236	NV
Soriano, Alfonso, N.Y.	R	.125	9	8	2	1	4	0	0	1	1	0	0	0	3	0	1	.500	.125	NV
Stocker, Kevin, T.B.	B	.299	79	254	39	76	94	11	2	1	27	4	0	24	41	9	7	.370	.369	6
Tejada, Miguel, Oak.	R	.251	159	593	93	149	253	33	4	21	84	9	5	57	94	8	7	.427	.325	13
Vizquel, Omar, Cle.	B	.333	144	574	112	191	250	36	4	5	66	17	7	65	50	42	9	.436	.397	31
Woodward, Chris, Tor.	R	.231	14	26	1	6	7	1	0	0	2	0	1	2	6	0	0	.269	.276	NV

American League outfielders

Name/Team	B	BA	G	AB	R	H	TB	2B	3B	HR	RBI	SH	SF	BB	SO	SB	CS	SLG	OBA	RV
Abbott, Jeff, Chi.	R	.158	17	57	5	9	15	0	0	2	6	1	1	5	12	1	1	.263	.222	NV
Allen, Chad, Min.	R	.277	137	481	69	133	190	21	3	10	46	1	2	37	89	14	7	.395	.330	11
Amaral, Rich, Bal.	R	.277	91	137	21	38	48	8	1	0	11	1	2	15	20	9	6	.350	.348	2
Anderson, Brady, Bal.	L	.282	150	564	109	159	269	28	5	24	81	1	7	96	105	36	7	.477	.404	28
Anderson, Garret, Ana.	L	.303	157	620	88	188	291	36	2	21	80	0	6	34	81	3	4	.469	.336	19
Bartee, Kimera, Det.	R	.195	41	77	11	15	22	1	3	0	3	3	0	9	20	3	3	.286	.279	NV
Becker, Rich, Oak.	L	.264	40	125	21	33	39	3	0	1	10	1	0	25	43	3	2	.312	.395	NV
Belle, Albert, Bal.	R	.297	161	610	108	181	330	36	1	37	117	0	4	101	82	17	3	.541	.400	32
Beltran, Carlos, K.C.	B	.293	156	663	112	194	301	27	7	22	108	0	10	46	123	27	8	.454	.337	29
Brown, Dee, K.C.	L	.080	12	25	1	2	2	0	0	0	0	0	0	2	7	0	0	.080	.148	NV
Brumfield, Jacob, Tor.	R	.235	62	170	25	40	60	8	3	2	19	3	3	19	39	1	2	.353	.307	NV
Buford, Damon, Bos.	R	.242	91	297	39	72	109	15	2	6	38	1	3	21	74	9	2	.367	.294	4
Buhner, Jay, Sea.	R	.222	87	266	37	59	112	11	0	14	38	0	3	69	100	0	0	.421	.388	2
Butler, Rich, T.B.	L	.150	7	20	2	3	4	1	0	0	0	0	0	2	4	0	0	.200	.227	NV
Butler, Rob, Tor.	L	.143	8	7	1	1	1	0	0	0	1	0	0	0	0	0	0	.143	.250	NV
Cabrera, Jolbert, Cle.	R	.189	30	37	6	7	8	1	0	0	0	0	0	1	8	3	0	.216	.231	NV
Christensen, McKay, Chi.	L	.226	28	53	10	12	16	1	0	1	6	1	2	4	7	2	1	.302	.271	NV
Christenson, Ryan, Oak.	R	.209	106	268	41	56	82	12	1	4	24	8	4	38	58	7	5	.306	.305	NV
Clyburn, Danny, T.B.	R	.198	28	81	8	16	29	4	0	3	5	0	0	7	21	0	0	.358	.270	NV
Colangelo, Mike, Ana.	R	.500	1	2	0	1	1	0	0	0	0	0	0	1	0	0	0	.500	.667	NV
Coleman, Michael, Bos.	R	.200	2	5	1	1	1	0	0	0	0	0	0	1	0	0	0	.200	.333	NV
Cordero, Wil, Cle.	R	.299	54	194	35	58	97	15	0	8	32	0	2	15	37	2	0	.500	.364	6
Cruz, Jacob, Cle.	L	.330	32	88	14	29	45	5	1	3	17	1	1	5	13	0	2	.511	.368	2
Cruz, Jose, Tor.	B	.241	106	349	63	84	151	19	3	14	45	1	0	64	91	14	4	.433	.358	9
Cummings, Midre, Min.	B	.263	16	38	1	10	13	0	0	1	9	0	1	3	7	2	0	.342	.310	NV
Curtis, Chad, N.Y.	R	.262	96	195	37	51	72	6	0	5	24	1	3	43	35	8	4	.369	.398	4
Damon, Johnny, K.C.	L	.307	145	583	101	179	278	39	9	14	77	3	4	67	50	36	6	.477	.379	29
DaVanon, Jeff, Ana.	B	.200	7	20	4	4	9	0	1	1	4	0	0	2	7	0	1	.450	.273	NV
Dye, Jermaine, K.C.	R	.294	158	608	96	179	320	44	8	27	119	0	6	58	119	2	3	.526	.354	23
Edmonds, Jim, Ana.	L	.250	55	204	34	51	87	17	2	5	23	0	1	28	45	5	4	.426	.339	2
Encarnacion, Juan, Det.	R	.255	132	509	62	130	229	30	6	19	74	4	2	14	113	33	12	.450	.287	21
Garcia, Karim, Det.	L	.240	96	288	38	69	127	10	3	14	32	0	1	20	67	2	4	.441	.288	4
Gipson, Charles, Sea.	R	.225	55	80	16	18	27	5	2	0	9	2	0	6	13	3	4	.338	.287	NV
Gonzalez, Juan, Tex.	R	.326	144	562	114	183	338	36	1	39	128	0	12	51	105	3	3	.601	.378	33
Goodwin, Curtis, Tor.	L	.000	2	8	0	0	0	0	0	0	0	0	0	3	3	0	0	.000	.000	NV
Goodwin, Tom, Tex.	L	.259	109	405	63	105	138	12	6	3	33	7	3	40	61	39	11	.341	.324	15
Green, Scarboroug, Tex.	R	.308	18	13	4	4	4	0	0	0	0	0	0	1	2	0	1	.308	.357	NV
Green, Shawn, Tor.	L	.309	153	614	134	190	361	45	0	42	123	0	5	66	117	20	7	.588	.384	38
Greer, Rusty, Tex.	L	.300	147	556	107	167	274	41	3	20	101	0	5	96	67	2	2	.493	.405	20
Grieve, Ben, Oak.	L	.265	148	486	80	129	234	21	0	28	86	0	1	63	108	4	0	.481	.358	16
Griffey, Ken, Sea.	L	.285	160	606	123	173	349	26	3	48	134	0	2	91	108	24	7	.576	.384	38
Guillen, Jose, T.B.	R	.244	47	168	24	41	57	10	0	2	13	0	1	10	36	0	0	.339	.312	NV
Higginson, Bobby, Det.	L	.239	107	377	51	90	144	18	0	12	46	0	2	64	66	4	6	.382	.351	4
Hunter, Brian, Det.-Sea.	R	.232	139	539	79	125	162	13	6	4	34	4	7	37	91	44	8	.301	.280	12
Hunter, Torii, Min.	R	.255	135	384	52	98	146	17	2	9	35	1	5	26	72	10	6	.380	.309	6
Huskey, Butch, Sea.-Bos.	R	.282	119	386	62	109	190	15	0	22	77	0	3	34	65	3	1	.492	.338	15
Ibanez, Raul, Sea.	L	.258	87	209	23	54	88	7	0	9	27	0	1	17	32	5	1	.421	.313	4
Jackson, Darrin, Chi.	R	.275	73	149	22	41	64	9	1	4	16	2	1	3	20	4	1	.430	.288	2
Jones, Jacque, Min.	L	.289	95	322	54	93	148	24	2	9	44	1	3	17	63	3	4	.460	.329	8

American League outfielders

Name/Team	B	BA	G	AB	R	H	TB	2B	3B	HR	RBI	SH	SF	BB	SO	SB	CS	SLG	OBA	RV
Justice, David, Cle.	L	.287	133	429	75	123	204	18	0	21	88	0	5	94	90	1	3	.476	.413	16
Kapler, Gabe, Det.	R	.245	130	416	60	102	186	22	4	18	49	4	4	42	74	11	5	.447	.315	9
Kelly, Roberto, Tex.	R	.300	87	290	41	87	130	17	1	8	37	0	2	21	57	6	1	.448	.355	9
Kingsale, Gene, Bal.	B	.247	28	85	9	21	23	2	0	0	7	2	1	5	13	1	3	.271	.301	NV
Latham, Chris, Min.	B	.091	14	22	1	2	2	0	0	0	3	0	2	0	13	0	0	.091	.083	NV
Lawton, Matt, Min.	L	.259	118	406	58	105	144	18	0	7	54	0	7	57	42	26	4	.355	.353	13
Ledee, Ricky, N.Y.	L	.276	88	250	45	69	119	13	5	9	40	0	2	28	73	4	3	.476	.346	7
Lee, Carlos, Chi.	R	.293	127	492	66	144	228	32	2	16	84	1	7	13	72	4	2	.463	.312	16
Lennon, Patrick, Tor.	R	.207	9	29	3	6	11	2	0	1	6	0	0	2	12	0	0	.379	.281	NV
Lewis, Darren, Bos.	R	.240	135	470	63	113	145	14	6	2	40	14	4	45	52	16	10	.309	.311	4
Liefer, Jeff, Chi.	L	.248	45	113	8	28	37	7	1	0	14	0	1	8	28	2	0	.327	.295	NV
Lofton, Kenny, Cle.	L	.301	120	465	110	140	201	28	6	7	39	5	5	79	84	25	6	.432	.405	17
Lowery, Terrell, T.B.	R	.259	66	185	25	48	71	15	1	2	17	0	1	19	53	0	2	.384	.330	NV
Luke, Matt, Ana.	L	.300	18	30	4	9	18	0	0	3	6	0	0	2	10	0	0	.600	.344	NV
Mabry, John, Sea.	L	.244	87	262	34	64	105	14	0	9	33	2	1	20	60	2	1	.401	.297	3
Martinez, Dave, T.B.	L	.284	143	514	79	146	199	25	5	6	66	10	5	60	76	13	6	.387	.361	13
Mateo, Ruben, Tex.	R	.238	32	122	16	29	55	9	1	5	18	0	0	4	28	3	0	.451	.268	1
May, Derrick, Bal.	L	.265	26	49	5	13	25	0	0	4	12	0	1	4	6	0	0	.510	.315	NV
McCracken, Quinton, T.B.	B	.250	40	148	20	37	48	6	1	1	18	1	1	14	23	6	5	.324	.317	1
McDonald, Jason, Oak.	B	.209	100	187	26	39	52	2	1	3	8	4	1	25	48	6	3	.278	.310	NV
Mieske, Matt, Sea.	R	.366	24	41	11	15	27	0	0	4	7	0	0	2	9	0	0	.659	.395	1
Monahan, Shane, Sea.	L	.133	16	15	3	2	2	0	0	0	0	0	0	0	6	0	0	.133	.133	NV
Nixon, Trot, Bos.	L	.270	124	381	67	103	180	22	5	15	52	2	8	53	75	3	1	.472	.357	9
Nunnally, Jon, Bos.	L	.286	10	14	4	4	5	1	0	0	1	0	0	0	6	0	0	.357	.286	NV
O'Leary, Troy, Bos.	L	.280	157	596	84	167	295	36	4	28	103	0	5	56	91	1	2	.495	.343	19
O'Neill, Paul, N.Y.	L	.285	153	597	70	170	274	39	4	19	110	0	10	66	89	11	9	.459	.353	21
Ordonez, Magglio, Chi.	R	.301	157	624	100	188	318	34	3	30	117	0	5	47	64	13	6	.510	.349	29
Palmeiro, Orlando, Ana.	L	.278	109	317	46	88	105	12	1	1	23	6	3	39	30	5	5	.331	.364	3
Pose, Scott, K.C.	L	.285	86	137	27	39	42	3	0	0	12	1	1	21	22	6	2	.307	.377	2
Quinn, Mark, K.C.	R	.333	17	60	11	20	44	4	1	6	18	0	0	4	11	1	0	.733	.385	3
Raines, Tim, Oak.	B	.215	58	135	20	29	46	5	0	4	17	1	2	26	17	4	1	.341	.337	NV
Ramirez, Alex, Cle.	R	.299	48	97	11	29	46	6	1	3	18	1	0	3	26	1	1	.474	.327	2
Ramirez, Manny, Cle.	R	.333	147	522	131	174	346	34	3	44	165	0	9	96	131	2	4	.663	.442	39
Roberts, Dave, Cle.	L	.238	41	143	26	34	44	4	0	2	12	3	1	9	16	11	3	.308	.281	2
Salmon, Tim, Ana.	R	.266	98	353	60	94	173	24	2	17	69	0	6	63	82	4	1	.490	.372	11
Sanders, Anthony, Tor.	R	.286	3	7	1	2	3	1	0	0	2	0	0	0	2	0	0	.429	.286	NV
Simmons, Brian, Chi.	B	.230	54	126	14	29	50	3	3	4	17	0	0	9	30	4	0	.397	.281	1
Singleton, Chris, Chi.	L	.300	133	496	72	149	243	31	6	17	72	4	6	22	45	20	5	.490	.328	22
Sorrento, Paul, T.B.	L	.235	99	294	40	69	118	14	1	11	42	0	1	49	101	1	1	.401	.351	3
Spencer, Shane, N.Y.	R	.234	71	205	25	48	80	8	0	8	20	0	1	18	51	0	4	.390	.301	NV
Stairs, Matt, Oak.	L	.258	146	531	94	137	283	26	3	38	102	0	1	89	124	2	7	.533	.366	19
Stewart, Shannon, Tor.	R	.304	145	608	102	185	250	28	2	11	67	3	4	59	83	37	14	.411	.371	27
Surhoff, B.J., Bal.	L	.308	162	673	104	207	331	38	1	28	107	1	8	43	78	5	1	.492	.347	26
Tarasco, Tony, N.Y.	L	.161	14	31	5	5	7	2	0	0	3	0	1	3	5	1	0	.226	.229	NV
Timmons, Ozzie, Sea.	R	.114	26	44	4	5	10	2	0	1	3	0	0	4	12	0	1	.227	.188	NV
Trammell, Bubba, T.B.	R	.290	82	283	49	82	143	19	0	14	39	0	1	43	37	0	2	.505	.384	8
Unroe, Tim, Ana.	R	.241	27	54	5	13	18	2	0	1	6	0	0	4	16	0	0	.333	.305	NV
Wells, Vernon, Tor.	R	.261	25	88	8	23	31	5	0	1	8	0	0	4	18	1	1	.352	.293	NV
Whiten, Mark, Cle.	B	.160	8	25	2	4	8	1	0	1	4	0	0	3	4	0	0	.320	.250	NV
Williams, Bernie, N.Y.	B	.342	158	591	116	202	317	28	6	25	115	0	5	100	95	9	10	.536	.435	32
Williams, Reggie, Ana.	B	.222	30	63	8	14	22	1	2	1	6	1	1	5	21	2	1	.349	.286	NV
Winn, Randy, T.B.	B	.267	79	303	44	81	111	16	4	2	24	1	2	17	63	9	9	.366	.307	4

American League relief pitchers (batting)

Name/Team	B	BA	G	AB	R	H	TB	2B	3B	HR	RBI	SH	SF	BB	SO	SB	CS	SLG	OBA
Barber, Brian, K.C.	R	.000	8	0	0	0	0	0	0	0	0	1	0	0	0	0	0	.000	.000
Bones, Ricky, Bal.	R	.000	31	0	1	0	0	0	0	0	0	0	0	0	0	0	0	.000	.000
Byrdak, Tim, K.C.	L	.500	33	2	1	1	2	1	0	0	0	0	0	0	0	0	0	1.000	.500
Cloude, Ken, Sea.	R	.000	31	2	0	0	0	0	0	0	0	0	0	0	0	0	0	.000	.000
Coppinger, Rocky, Bal.	R	1.000	11	1	0	1	1	0	0	0	0	0	0	0	0	0	0	1.000	1.000
Duvall, Mike, T.B.	R	.000	40	0	0	0	0	0	0	0	0	0	0	1	0	0	0	.000	1.000
Florie, Bryce, Det.-Bos.	R	.000	41	1	0	0	0	0	0	0	0	0	0	0	1	0	0	.000	.000
Foulke, Keith, Chi.	R	.000	67	2	0	0	0	0	0	0	0	0	0	0	1	0	0	.000	.000
Johns, Doug, Bal.	R	.000	32	1	0	0	0	0	0	0	0	0	0	0	1	0	0	.000	.000
Koch, Billy, Tor.	R	.000	56	1	0	0	0	0	0	0	0	0	0	0	1	0	0	.000	.000
Langston, Mark, Cle.	L	.500	25	2	0	1	1	0	0	0	0	0	0	0	0	0	0	.500	.500
Mathews, Terry, K.C.	L	.000	24	1	0	0	0	0	0	0	0	0	0	0	1	0	0	.000	.000
Mays, Joe, Min.	B	.000	49	3	0	0	0	0	0	0	0	0	0	2	1	0	0	.000	.400

American League relief pitchers (batting)

Name/Team	B	BA	G	AB	R	H	TB	2B	3B	HR	RBI	SH	SF	BB	SO	SB	CS	SLG	OBA
Nitkowski, C. j., Det.	L	.000	69	1	0	0	0	0	0	0	0	0	0	0	1	0	0	.000	.000
Patterson, Danny, Tex.	R	.000	53	1	0	0	0	0	0	0	0	0	0	0	0	0	0	.000	.000
Perkins, Dan, Min.	R	.500	29	2	0	1	1	0	0	0	0	0	0	0	1	0	0	.500	.500
Rekar, Bryan, T.B.	R	.200	27	5	0	1	1	0	0	0	0	0	0	0	2	0	0	.200	.200
Rodriguez, Frank, Sea.	R	.333	30	3	1	1	1	0	0	0	1	0	0	0	0	0	0	.333	.333
Sampson, Benj, Min.	R	.000	30	3	0	0	0	0	0	0	0	0	0	0	2	0	0	.000	.000
Santana, Julio, T.B.	R	1.000	22	1	0	1	1	0	0	0	1	0	0	0	0	0	0	1.000	1.000
Stanton, Mike, N.Y.	L	.000	73	1	0	0	0	0	0	0	0	0	0	0	1	0	0	.000	.000
Wakefield, Tim, Bos.	R	.000	49	3	0	0	0	0	0	0	0	0	0	0	3	0	0	.000	.000
Ward, Bryan, Chi.	L	.000	40	0	0	0	0	0	0	0	0	0	0	1	0	0	0	.000	1.000

American League starting pitchers (batting)

Name/Team	B	BA	G	AB	R	H	TB	2B	3B	HR	RBI	SH	SF	BB	SO	SB	CS	SLG	OBA
Alvarez, Wilson, T.B.	L	.000	28	3	0	0	0	0	0	0	0	0	0	0	1	0	0	.000	.000
Appier, Kevin, K.C.-Oak.	R	.000	34	2	0	0	0	0	0	0	0	0	0	0	1	0	0	.000	.000
Arrojo, Rolando, T.B.	R	.000	24	0	0	0	0	0	0	0	0	0	0	0	0	0	0	.000	.000
Baldwin, James, Chi.	R	.500	35	2	1	1	3	0	1	0	1	0	0	0	1	0	0	1.500	.500
Belcher, Tim, Ana.	R	.200	24	5	0	1	2	1	0	0	0	0	0	0	2	0	0	.400	.200
Borkowski, Dave, Det.	R	.000	17	3	0	0	0	0	0	0	1	0	0	0	2	0	0	.000	.000
Burba, Dave, Cle.	R	.333	34	3	0	1	1	0	0	0	0	0	0	1	0	0	0	.333	.500
Burkett, John, Tex.	R	.000	30	2	0	0	0	0	0	0	0	0	0	0	2	0	0	.000	.000
Callaway, Mickey, T.B.	R	.667	6	3	0	2	2	0	0	0	1	0	0	0	0	0	0	.667	.667
Candiotti, Tom, Oak.-Cle.	R	.000	18	0	0	0	0	0	0	0	0	0	0	0	0	0	0	.000	.000
Carpenter, Chris, Tor.	R	.000	24	1	0	0	0	0	0	0	0	0	0	1	1	0	0	.000	.500
Cho, Jin Ho, Bos.	R	.000	9	1	0	0	0	0	0	0	0	0	0	0	0	0	0	.000	.000
Clark, Mark, Tex.	R	.000	15	2	0	0	0	0	0	0	0	0	0	0	2	0	0	.000	.000
Clemens, Roger, N.Y.	R	.000	30	4	0	0	0	0	0	0	0	1	0	0	3	0	0	.000	.000
Colon, Bartolo, Cle.	R	.143	32	7	0	1	1	0	0	0	0	1	0	0	5	0	0	.143	.143
Cone, David, N.Y.	L	.333	31	3	1	1	2	1	0	0	1	0	0	0	0	0	0	.667	.333
Cooper, Brian, Ana.	R	.000	5	0	0	0	0	0	0	0	0	0	0	0	0	0	0	.000	.000
Daneker, Pat, Chi.	R	.000	3	2	0	0	0	0	0	0	0	0	0	1	0	0	0	.000	.000
Eiland, Dave, T.B.	R	.000	21	1	0	0	0	0	0	0	0	1	0	0	0	0	0	.000	.000
Erickson, Scott, Bal.	R	.000	34	6	0	0	0	0	0	0	0	1	0	0	2	0	0	.000	.000
Escobar, Kelvim, Tor.	R	.000	33	1	0	0	0	0	0	0	0	0	0	0	1	0	0	.000	.000
Fassero, Jeff, Sea.-Tex.	L	.000	37	7	0	0	0	0	0	0	0	0	0	0	5	0	0	.000	.000
Finley, Chuck, Ana.	L	.000	33	4	0	0	0	0	0	0	0	1	0	0	3	0	0	.000	.000
Garcia, Freddy, Sea.	R	.250	34	4	0	1	1	0	0	0	1	2	0	1	0	0	0	.250	.250
Glynn, Ryan, Tex.	R	.000	13	1	0	0	0	0	0	0	0	0	0	0	0	0	0	.000	.000
Gooden, Dwight, Cle.	R	.500	26	2	1	1	4	0	0	1	2	0	0	1	1	0	0	2.000	.667
Graterol, Beiker, Det.	R	.000	1	0	0	0	0	0	0	0	0	0	0	0	0	0	0	.000	.000
Guzman, Juan, Bal.	R	.167	21	6	0	1	1	0	0	0	1	0	0	0	4	0	0	.167	.167
Halama, John, Sea.	L	.200	38	5	1	1	2	1	0	0	0	0	0	1	2	0	0	.400	.333
Halladay, Roy, Tor.	R	.000	36	2	0	0	0	0	0	0	0	1	0	0	2	0	0	.000	.000
Hamilton, Joey, Tor.	R	.000	22	2	0	0	0	0	0	0	0	0	0	0	1	0	0	.000	.000
Hawkins, LaTroy, Min.	R	.000	33	2	0	0	0	0	0	0	0	0	0	0	1	0	0	.000	.000
Haynes, Jimmy, Oak.	R	.000	30	4	0	0	0	0	0	0	0	1	0	0	1	0	0	.000	.000
Helling, Rick, Tex.	R	.000	35	2	0	0	0	0	0	0	0	0	0	0	2	0	0	.000	.000
Henry, Butch, Sea.	L	.000	7	0	0	0	0	0	0	0	0	0	0	0	0	0	0	.000	.000
Hentgen, Pat, Tor.	R	.167	34	6	0	1	1	0	0	0	0	0	0	0	4	0	0	.167	.167
Heredia, Gil, Oak.	R	.000	33	6	0	0	0	0	0	0	0	1	0	1	1	0	0	.000	.143
Hernandez, O., N.Y.	R	.333	33	3	1	1	1	0	0	0	0	0	0	0	0	0	0	.333	.333
Hill, Ken, Ana.	R	.000	26	3	0	0	0	0	0	0	0	0	0	0	0	0	0	.000	.000
Hudson, Tim, Oak.	R	.250	24	4	0	1	1	0	0	0	0	0	0	1	2	0	0	.250	.400
Irabu, Hideki, N.Y.	R	.000	32	4	0	0	0	0	0	0	0	2	0	1	3	0	0	.000	.200
Johnson, Jason, Bal.	R	.000	22	2	0	0	0	0	0	0	0	0	0	1	0	0	0	.000	.000
Juden, Jeff, N.Y.	R	.000	2	0	0	0	0	0	0	0	0	0	0	0	0	0	0	.000	.000
Laxton, Brett, Oak.	L	.000	3	0	0	0	0	0	0	0	0	0	0	0	0	0	0	.000	.000
Lincoln, Mike, Min.	R	.000	18	1	0	0	0	0	0	0	0	0	0	0	0	0	0	.000	.000
Linton, Doug, Bal.	R	.000	14	0	0	0	0	0	0	0	0	0	0	0	0	0	0	.000	.000
Loaiza, Esteban, Tex.	R	.000	30	0	0	0	0	0	0	0	0	0	0	0	0	0	0	.000	.000
Martinez, Pedro, Bos.	R	.000	31	2	0	0	0	0	0	0	0	0	0	0	1	0	0	.000	.000
Martinez, Ramon, Bos.	R	.000	4	0	0	0	0	0	0	0	0	0	0	0	0	0	0	.000	.000
McDowell, Jack, Ana.	R	.000	4	0	0	0	0	0	0	0	0	0	0	0	0	0	0	.000	.000
Meche, Gil, Sea.	R	.000	16	0	0	0	0	0	0	0	0	0	0	0	0	0	0	.000	.000
Mercker, Kent, Bos.	L	.000	5	0	0	0	0	0	0	0	0	0	0	0	0	0	0	.000	.000
Milton, Eric, Min.	L	.000	34	2	0	0	0	0	0	0	0	0	0	1	1	0	0	.000	.333
Mlicki, Dave, Det.	R	.000	31	4	0	0	0	0	0	0	0	0	0	2	3	0	0	.000	.333
Moehler, Brian, Det.	R	.000	32	1	0	0	0	0	0	0	0	0	0	1	1	0	0	.000	.500

American League starting pitchers (batting)

Name/Team	B	BA	G	AB	R	H	TB	2B	3B	HR	RBI	SH	SF	BB	SO	SB	CS	SLG	OBA
Morgan, Mike, Tex.	R	.250	34	4	0	1	1	0	0	0	0	0	0	0	2	0	0	.250	.250
Moyer, Jamie, Sea.	L	.500	32	2	0	1	1	0	0	0	0	1	0	1	1	0	0	.500	.667
Mussina, Mike, Bal.	R	.273	31	11	1	3	4	1	0	0	4	0	0	0	1	0	0	.364	.273
Myette, Aaron, Chi.	R	.000	4	0	0	0	0	0	0	0	0	0	0	0	0	0	0	.000	.000
Nagy, Charles, Cle.	L	.000	34	6	0	0	0	0	0	0	0	0	0	0	5	0	0	.000	.000
Navarro, Jaime, Chi.	R	.000	32	3	0	0	0	0	0	0	0	1	0	0	1	0	0	.000	.000
Olivares, Omar, Ana.-Oak.	R	.333	32	6	0	2	3	1	0	0	0	1	0	0	1	0	0	.500	.333
Oquist, Mike, Oak.	R	.000	28	2	0	0	0	0	0	0	0	0	0	0	1	0	0	.000	.000
Ortiz, Ramon, Ana.	R	.000	9	0	0	0	0	0	0	0	0	0	0	0	0	0	0	.000	.000
Parque, Jim, Chi.	L	.400	31	5	0	2	2	0	0	0	0	1	0	0	1	0	0	.400	.400
Pena, Juan, Bos.	R	.000	2	0	0	0	0	0	0	0	0	0	0	0	0	0	0	.000	.000
Pettitte, Andy, N.Y.	L	.200	31	5	0	1	1	0	0	0	0	0	0	1	2	0	0	.200	.333
Pittsley, Jim, K.C.	R	.000	5	0	0	0	0	0	0	0	0	0	0	0	0	0	0	.000	.000
Ponson, Sidney, Bal.	R	.000	32	3	0	0	0	0	0	0	0	1	0	0	0	0	0	.000	.000
Portugal, Mark, Bos.	R	.000	31	3	0	0	0	0	0	0	0	1	0	0	0	0	0	.000	.000
Radke, Brad, Min.	R	.000	33	5	0	0	0	0	0	0	0	0	0	0	2	0	0	.000	.000
Ramsay, Robert, Sea.	L	.000	6	0	0	0	0	0	0	0	0	0	0	0	0	0	0	.000	.000
Rapp, Pat, Bos.	R	.000	37	2	0	0	0	0	0	0	0	0	0	0	1	0	0	.000	.000
Reichert, Dan, K.C.	R	.333	8	3	0	1	1	0	0	0	0	1	0	0	2	0	0	.333	.333
Riley, Matt, Bal.	L	.000	3	0	0	0	0	0	0	0	0	0	0	0	0	0	0	.000	.000
Rogers, Kenny, Oak.	L	.000	19	3	0	0	0	0	0	0	0	1	0	0	1	0	0	.000	.000
Rosado, Jose, K.C.	L	.000	33	5	0	0	0	0	0	0	0	0	0	0	4	0	0	.000	.000
Rose, Brian, Bos.	R	.000	22	2	0	0	0	0	0	0	0	1	0	0	0	0	0	.000	.000
Rupe, Ryan, T.B.	R	.000	24	4	0	0	0	0	0	0	0	0	0	0	1	0	0	.000	.000
Ryan, Jason, Min.	B	.000	8	0	0	0	0	0	0	0	0	0	0	0	0	0	0	.000	.000
Saberhagen, Bret, Bos.	R	.000	22	4	0	0	0	0	0	0	0	0	0	1	2	0	0	.000	.200
Saunders, Tony, T.B.	L	.000	9	0	0	0	0	0	0	0	0	0	0	0	0	0	0	.000	.000
Sele, Aaron, Tex.	R	.000	33	4	0	0	0	0	0	0	0	1	0	1	2	0	0	.000	.200
Sirotka, Mike, Chi.	L	.250	32	8	1	2	2	0	0	0	0	0	0	0	3	0	0	.250	.250
Snyder, John, Chi.	R	.000	25	0	0	0	0	0	0	0	0	0	0	0	0	0	0	.000	.000
Sparks, Steve, Ana.	R	.333	29	3	0	1	2	1	0	0	2	0	0	0	1	0	0	.667	.333
Stein, Blake, Oak.-K.C.	R	.000	13	0	0	0	0	0	0	0	0	0	0	0	0	0	0	.000	.000
Sturtze, Tanyon, Chi.	R	.000	1	0	0	0	0	0	0	0	0	0	0	0	0	0	0	.000	.000
Suppan, Jeff, K.C.	R	.200	32	5	0	1	1	0	0	0	0	1	0	0	0	0	0	.200	.200
Thompson, Justin, Det.	L	.000	24	5	0	0	0	0	0	0	0	0	0	0	2	0	0	.000	.000
Washburn, Jarrod, Ana.	L	.000	16	0	0	0	0	0	0	0	0	0	0	0	0	0	0	.000	.000
Weaver, Jeff, Det.	R	.500	31	4	2	2	3	1	0	0	0	1	0	0	1	0	0	.750	.500
Wells, David, Tor.	L	.000	34	6	0	0	0	0	0	0	0	1	0	0	0	0	0	.000	.000
Wells, Kip, Chi.	R	.000	7	0	0	0	0	0	0	0	0	0	0	0	0	0	0	.000	.000
Wheeler, Dan, T.B.	R	.000	6	0	0	0	0	0	0	0	0	0	0	0	0	0	0	.000	.000
Witasick, Jay, K.C.	R	.000	32	5	0	0	0	0	0	0	0	0	0	0	4	0	0	.000	.000
Witt, Bobby, T.B.	R	.000	32	2	0	0	0	0	0	0	0	0	0	0	1	0	0	.000	.000
Wright, Jaret, Cle.	R	.000	26	1	0	0	0	0	0	0	0	0	0	0	1	0	0	.000	.000

National League catchers

Name/Team	B	BA	G	AB	R	H	TB	2B	3B	HR	RBI	SH	SF	BB	SO	SB	CS	SLG	OBA	RV
Bako, Paul, Hou.	L	.256	73	215	16	55	77	14	1	2	17	3	3	26	57	1	1	.358	.332	NV
Barajas, Rod, Ari.	R	.250	5	16	3	4	8	1	0	1	3	1	0	1	1	0	0	.500	.294	NV
Bennett, Gary, Phi.	R	.273	36	88	7	24	31	4	0	1	21	0	2	4	11	0	0	.352	.298	NV
Blanco, Henry, Col.	R	.232	88	263	30	61	97	12	3	6	28	3	2	34	38	1	1	.369	.320	NV
Cancel, Robinson, Mil.	R	.182	15	44	5	8	10	2	0	0	5	1	0	2	12	0	0	.227	.234	NV
Castillo, Alberto, St.L.	R	.263	93	255	21	67	87	8	0	4	31	5	4	24	48	0	0	.341	.326	NV
Castro, Ramon, Fla.	R	.179	24	67	4	12	22	4	0	2	4	0	1	10	14	0	0	.328	.282	NV
Cox, Darron, Mon.	R	.240	15	25	2	6	10	1	0	1	2	0	0	5	0	0	0	.400	.296	NV
Davis, Ben, S.D.	B	.244	76	266	29	65	96	14	1	5	30	0	2	25	70	2	1	.361	.307	NV
Estalella, Bobby, Phi.	R	.167	9	18	2	3	3	0	0	0	1	0	0	4	7	0	1	.167	.318	NV
Eusebio, Tony, Hou.	R	.272	103	323	31	88	115	15	0	4	33	0	0	40	67	0	0	.356	.353	1
Fabregas, Jorge, Fla.-Atl.	L	.199	88	231	20	46	69	10	2	3	21	4	5	26	27	0	0	.299	.280	NV
Garcia, Guillermo, Fla.	R	.250	4	4	0	1	1	0	0	0	0	0	0	0	2	0	0	.250	.250	NV
Gonzalez, W., S.D.	R	.253	30	83	7	21	34	2	1	3	12	0	0	1	8	0	0	.410	.271	NV
Greene, Charlie, Mil.	R	.190	32	42	4	8	9	1	0	0	1	1	1	5	11	0	0	.214	.271	NV
Haad, Yamid, Pit.	R	.000	1	1	0	0	0	0	0	0	0	0	0	0	0	0	0	.000	.000	NV
Hughes, Bobby, Mil.	R	.257	48	101	10	26	37	2	0	3	8	0	0	5	28	0	0	.366	.292	NV
Hundley, Todd, L.A.	B	.207	115	376	49	78	164	14	0	24	55	1	3	44	113	3	0	.436	.295	4
Jensen, Marcus, St.L.	L	.235	16	34	5	8	16	5	0	1	1	2	0	6	12	0	0	.471	.350	NV
Johnson, Brian, Cin.	R	.231	45	117	12	27	49	7	0	5	18	1	0	9	31	0	0	.419	.286	NV
Kendall, Jason, Pit.	R	.332	78	280	61	93	143	20	3	8	41	0	4	38	32	22	3	.511	.428	16
Knorr, Randy, Hou.	R	.167	13	30	2	5	6	1	0	0	0	0	0	1	8	0	0	.200	.194	NV

National League catchers

Name/Team	B	BA	G	AB	R	H	TB	2B	3B	HR	RBI	SH	SF	BB	SO	SB	CS	SLG	OBA	RV
Laker, Tim, Pit.	R	.333	6	9	0	3	3	0	0	0	0	0	0	0	2	0	0	.333	.333	NV
LaRue, Jason, Cin.	R	.211	36	90	12	19	35	7	0	3	10	0	0	11	32	4	1	.389	.311	NV
Leyritz, Jim, S.D.	R	.239	50	134	17	32	61	5	0	8	21	0	1	15	37	0	0	.455	.331	NV
Lieberthal, Mike, Phi.	R	.300	145	510	84	153	281	33	1	31	96	1	8	44	86	0	0	.551	.363	20
LoDuca, Paul, L.A.	R	.232	36	95	11	22	32	1	0	3	11	1	2	10	9	1	2	.337	.312	NV
Lopez, Javy, Atl.	R	.317	65	246	34	78	131	18	1	11	45	0	0	20	41	0	3	.533	.375	8
Machado, Robert, Mon.	R	.182	17	22	3	4	5	1	0	0	0	0	0	2	6	0	0	.227	.250	NV
Manwaring, Kirt, Col.	R	.299	48	137	17	41	56	7	1	2	14	0	1	12	23	0	0	.409	.374	NV
Marrero, Eli, St.L.	R	.192	114	317	32	61	94	13	1	6	34	4	3	18	56	11	2	.297	.236	NV
Martinez, Sandy, Chi.	L	.167	17	30	1	5	8	0	0	1	1	0	0	0	11	0	0	.267	.167	NV
Matos, Pascual, Atl.	R	.125	6	8	0	1	1	0	0	0	2	0	0	0	1	0	0	.125	.125	NV
Mayne, Brent, S.F.	L	.301	117	322	39	97	135	32	0	2	39	1	3	43	65	2	2	.419	.389	5
Meluskey, Mitch, Hou.	B	.212	10	33	4	7	11	1	0	1	3	0	0	5	6	1	0	.333	.316	NV
Miller, Damian, Ari.	R	.270	86	296	35	80	132	19	0	11	47	0	3	19	78	0	0	.446	.316	5
Mirabelli, Doug, S.F.	R	.253	33	87	10	22	31	6	0	1	10	0	1	9	25	0	0	.356	.327	NV
Molina, Jose, Chi.	R	.263	10	19	3	5	6	1	0	0	1	0	0	2	4	0	0	.316	.333	NV
Myers, Greg, S.D.-Atl.	L	.265	84	200	19	53	74	6	0	5	24	0	1	26	30	0	0	.370	.348	NV
Nilsson, Dave, Mil.	L	.309	115	343	56	106	190	19	1	21	62	2	4	53	64	1	2	.554	.400	14
Oliver, Joe, Pit.	R	.201	45	134	10	27	38	8	0	1	13	0	2	10	33	2	0	.284	.253	NV
Osik, Keith, Pit.	R	.186	66	167	12	31	42	3	1	2	13	1	1	11	30	0	0	.251	.239	NV
Pena, Angel, L.A.	R	.208	43	120	14	25	43	6	0	4	21	1	2	12	24	0	1	.358	.276	NV
Perez, Eddie, Atl.	R	.249	104	309	30	77	115	17	0	7	30	4	3	17	40	0	1	.372	.299	NV
Petrick, Ben, Col.	R	.323	19	62	13	20	35	3	0	4	12	0	0	10	13	1	0	.565	.417	1
Piazza, Mike, N.Y.	R	.303	141	534	100	162	307	25	0	40	124	0	7	51	70	2	2	.575	.361	28
Pratt, Todd, N.Y.	R	.293	71	140	18	41	54	4	0	3	21	0	2	15	32	2	0	.386	.369	1
Prince, Tom, Phi.	R	.167	4	6	1	1	1	0	0	0	0	0	0	1	1	0	0	.167	.286	NV
Redmond, Mike, Fla.	R	.302	84	242	22	73	85	9	0	1	27	5	0	26	34	0	0	.351	.381	2
Reed, Jeff, Col.-Chi.	L	.258	103	256	29	66	95	16	2	3	28	0	2	45	58	1	2	.371	.373	NV
Roskos, Johnny, Fla.	R	.167	13	12	0	2	4	2	0	0	1	0	0	1	7	0	0	.333	.231	NV
Santiago, Benito, Chi.	R	.249	109	350	28	87	132	18	3	7	36	0	2	32	71	1	1	.377	.313	NV
Servais, Scott, S.F.	R	.273	69	198	21	54	79	10	0	5	21	3	0	13	31	0	0	.399	.327	NV
Stinnett, Kelly, Ari.	R	.232	88	284	36	66	121	13	0	14	38	2	2	24	83	2	1	.426	.302	3
Taubensee, Eddie, Cin.	L	.311	126	424	58	132	221	22	2	21	87	1	5	30	67	0	2	.521	.354	17
Tremie, Chris, Pit.	R	.071	9	14	1	1	1	0	0	0	1	0	0	2	4	0	0	.071	.188	NV
Widger, Chris, Mon.	R	.264	124	383	42	101	169	24	1	14	56	0	1	28	86	1	4	.441	.325	6
Wilkins, Rick, L.A.	L	.000	3	4	0	0	0	0	0	0	0	0	0	0	2	0	0	.000	.000	NV
Wilson, Vance, N.Y.	R	.000	1	0	0	0	0	0	0	0	0	0	0	0	0	0	0	.000	.000	NV

National League first basemen

Name/Team	B	BA	G	AB	R	H	TB	2B	3B	HR	RBI	SH	SF	BB	SO	SB	CS	SLG	OBA	RV
Bagwell, Jeff, Hou.	R	.304	162	562	143	171	332	35	0	42	126	0	7	149	127	30	11	.591	.454	39
Banks, Brian, Mil.	B	.242	105	219	34	53	77	7	1	5	22	3	2	25	59	6	1	.352	.317	1
Barker, Kevin, Mil.	L	.282	38	117	13	33	45	3	0	3	23	0	1	9	19	1	0	.385	.331	1
Berry, Sean, Mil.	R	.228	106	259	26	59	78	11	1	2	23	0	2	17	50	0	0	.301	.281	NV
Brogna, Rico, Phi.	L	.278	157	619	90	172	281	29	4	24	102	0	4	54	132	8	5	.454	.336	19
Casey, Sean, Cin.	L	.332	151	594	103	197	320	42	3	25	99	0	5	61	88	0	2	.539	.399	24
Colbrunn, Greg, Ari.	R	.326	67	135	20	44	70	5	3	5	24	0	2	12	23	1	1	.519	.392	3
Cruz, Ivan, Pit.	L	.400	5	10	3	4	7	0	0	1	2	0	0	0	2	0	0	.700	.400	NV
Durazo, Erubiel, Ari.	L	.329	52	155	31	51	92	4	2	11	30	0	3	26	43	1	1	.594	.422	6
Franco, Matt, N.Y.	L	.235	122	132	18	31	48	5	0	4	21	0	1	28	21	0	0	.364	.366	NV
Fullmer, Brad, Mon.	L	.277	100	347	38	96	161	34	2	9	47	0	3	22	35	2	3	.464	.321	5
Grace, Mark, Chi.	L	.309	161	593	107	183	285	44	5	16	91	0	10	83	44	3	4	.481	.390	18
Hansen, Dave, L.A.	L	.252	100	107	14	27	43	8	1	2	17	0	1	26	20	0	0	.402	.404	NV
Helton, Todd, Col.	L	.320	159	578	114	185	339	39	5	35	113	0	4	68	77	7	6	.587	.395	30
Howell, Jack, Hou.	L	.212	37	33	2	7	12	2	0	1	1	0	0	8	9	0	0	.364	.366	NV
Hunter, Brian, Atl.	R	.249	114	181	28	45	77	12	1	6	30	5	2	31	40	0	1	.425	.367	NV
Joyner, Wally, S.D.	L	.248	110	323	34	80	113	14	2	5	43	0	3	58	54	0	1	.350	.363	NV
Karros, Eric, L.A.	R	.304	153	578	74	176	318	26	0	34	112	0	6	53	119	8	5	.550	.362	27
Klesko, Ryan, Atl.	L	.297	133	404	55	120	215	28	2	21	80	0	7	53	69	5	2	.532	.376	16
Lee, Derrek, Fla.	R	.206	70	218	21	45	71	9	1	5	20	0	1	17	70	2	1	.326	.263	NV
Lee, Travis, Ari.	L	.237	120	375	57	89	136	16	2	9	50	0	3	58	50	17	3	.363	.337	7
Lovullo, Torey, Phi.	B	.211	17	38	3	8	14	0	0	2	5	0	0	3	11	0	0	.368	.368	NV
McGuire, John, Mon.	L	.221	88	140	17	31	48	7	2	2	18	3	0	27	33	1	1	.343	.347	NV
McGwire, Mark, St.L.	R	.278	153	521	118	145	363	21	1	65	147	0	5	133	141	0	0	.697	.424	34
Millar, Kevin, Fla.	R	.285	105	351	48	100	152	17	4	9	67	1	8	40	64	1	0	.433	.362	8
Morris, Hal, Cin.	L	.284	80	102	10	29	38	9	0	0	16	0	0	10	21	0	0	.373	.348	NV
Olerud, John, N.Y.	L	.298	162	581	107	173	269	39	0	19	96	0	6	125	66	3	0	.463	.427	18
Seguignol, F., Mon.	B	.257	35	105	14	27	51	9	0	5	10	0	2	5	33	0	0	.486	.328	NV

National League first basemen

Name/Team	B	BA	G	AB	R	H	TB	2B	3B	HR	RBI	SH	SF	BB	SO	SB	CS	SLG	OBA	RV
Simon, Randall, Atl.	L	.317	90	218	26	69	100	16	0	5	25	0	1	17	25	2	2	.459	.367	4
Snow, J. t., S.F.	B	.274	161	570	93	156	257	25	2	24	98	1	6	86	121	0	4	.451	.370	15
Sweeney, Mark, Cin.	L	.355	37	31	6	11	20	3	0	2	7	0	0	4	9	0	0	.645	.429	NV
Toca, Jorge, N.Y.	R	.333	4	3	0	1	1	0	0	0	0	0	0	0	2	0	0	.333	.333	NV
Young, Kevin, Pit.	R	.298	156	584	103	174	305	41	6	26	106	0	4	75	124	22	10	.522	.387	28

National League second basemen

Name/Team	B	BA	G	AB	R	H	TB	2B	3B	HR	RBI	SH	SF	BB	SO	SB	CS	SLG	OBA	RV
Abbott, Kurt, Col.	R	.273	96	286	41	78	123	17	2	8	41	2	1	16	69	3	2	.430	.310	5
Alfonzo, Edgardo, N.Y.	R	.304	158	628	123	191	315	41	1	27	108	1	9	85	85	9	2	.502	.385	25
Anderson, Marlon, Phi.	L	.252	129	452	48	114	163	26	4	5	54	4	2	24	61	13	2	.361	.292	6
Baerga, Carlos, S.D.	B	.250	33	80	6	20	27	1	0	2	5	1	0	6	14	1	0	.338	.318	NV
Bell, Jay, Ari.	R	.289	151	589	132	170	328	32	6	38	112	4	9	82	132	7	4	.557	.374	26
Belliard, Ronnie, Mil.	R	.295	124	457	60	135	196	29	4	8	58	6	4	64	59	4	5	.429	.379	9
Biggio, Craig, Hou.	R	.294	160	639	123	188	292	56	0	16	73	5	6	88	107	28	14	.457	.386	23
Blauser, Jeff, Chi.	R	.240	104	200	41	48	84	5	2	9	26	2	2	26	52	2	2	.420	.347	1
Boone, Bret, Atl.	R	.252	152	608	102	153	253	38	1	20	63	9	2	47	112	14	9	.416	.310	11
Canizaro, Jay, S.F.	R	.444	12	18	5	8	13	2	0	1	9	0	0	1	2	1	0	.722	.474	NV
Castillo, Luis, Fla.	B	.302	128	487	76	147	178	23	4	0	28	6	3	67	85	50	17	.366	.384	22
Castro, Juan, L.A.	R	.000	2	1	0	0	0	0	0	0	0	0	0	0	1	0	0	.000	.000	NV
Counsell, Craig, Fla.-L.A.	L	.218	87	174	24	38	45	7	0	0	11	5	2	14	24	1	0	.259	.274	NV
Cromer, Tripp, L.A.	R	.192	33	52	5	10	16	0	0	2	8	0	0	5	10	0	0	.308	.263	NV
Diaz, Edwin, Ari.	R	.400	4	5	2	2	4	2	0	0	1	0	0	3	1	0	0	.800	.625	NV
Doster, David, Phi.	R	.196	99	97	9	19	30	2	0	3	10	2	1	12	23	1	0	.309	.282	NV
Garcia, Amaury, Fla.	R	.250	10	24	6	6	14	0	1	2	2	0	0	3	11	0	0	.583	.333	NV
Guerrero, Wilton, Mon.	B	.292	132	315	42	92	127	15	7	2	31	10	0	13	38	7	6	.403	.324	5
Harris, Lenny, Col.-Ari.	L	.310	110	187	17	58	74	13	0	1	20	0	1	6	7	2	1	.396	.330	2
Hernandez, Carlos, Hou.	R	.143	16	14	4	2	2	0	0	0	1	1	0	0	0	3	1	.143	.143	NV
Kennedy, Adam, St.L.	L	.255	33	102	12	26	41	10	1	1	16	1	2	3	8	0	1	.402	.284	NV
Kent, Jeff, S.F.	R	.290	138	511	86	148	261	40	2	23	101	0	8	61	112	13	6	.511	.366	22
Lansing, Mike, Col.	R	.310	35	145	24	45	66	9	0	4	15	1	1	7	22	2	0	.455	.344	2
Lockhart, Keith, Atl.	L	.261	108	161	20	42	50	3	1	1	21	0	3	19	21	3	1	.311	.337	NV
Martinez, Ramon, S.F.	R	.264	61	144	21	38	59	6	0	5	19	6	1	14	17	1	2	.410	.327	NV
McEwing, Joe, St.L.	R	.275	152	513	65	141	204	28	4	9	44	9	5	41	87	7	4	.398	.333	7
Meyers, Chad, Chi.	R	.232	43	142	17	33	42	9	0	0	4	2	0	9	27	4	2	.296	.292	NV
Morandini, Mickey, Chi.	L	.241	144	456	60	110	150	18	5	4	37	7	4	48	61	6	6	.329	.319	NV
Mordecai, Mike, Mon.	B	.235	109	226	29	53	82	10	2	5	25	1	2	20	31	2	5	.363	.297	NV
Morris, Warren, Pit.	L	.288	147	511	65	147	218	20	3	15	73	4	5	59	88	3	7	.427	.360	12
Newhan, David, S.D.	L	.140	32	43	7	6	13	1	0	2	6	0	0	1	11	2	1	.302	.159	NV
Petersen, Chris, Col.	R	.154	7	13	1	2	2	0	0	0	2	0	0	2	3	0	0	.154	.267	NV
Polanco, Placido, St.L.	R	.277	88	220	24	61	79	9	3	1	19	3	2	15	24	1	3	.359	.321	NV
Reese, Pokey, Cin.	R	.285	149	585	85	167	244	37	5	10	52	5	5	35	81	38	7	.417	.330	21
Sanford, Chance, L.A.	L	.250	5	8	1	2	2	0	0	0	2	0	0	1	0	0	0	.250	.250	NV
Shumpert, Terry, Col.	R	.347	92	262	58	91	153	26	3	10	37	4	5	31	41	14	0	.584	.413	14
Stynes, Chris, Cin.	R	.239	73	113	18	27	34	1	0	2	14	3	1	12	13	5	2	.301	.310	NV
Veras, Quilvio, S.D.	B	.280	132	475	95	133	180	25	2	6	41	1	2	65	88	30	17	.379	.368	15
Vidro, Jose, Mon.	B	.304	140	494	67	150	235	45	2	12	59	2	2	29	51	0	4	.476	.346	11
Vina, Fernando, Mil.	L	.266	37	154	17	41	51	7	0	1	16	3	2	14	6	5	2	.331	.339	NV
Young, Eric, L.A.	R	.281	119	456	73	128	162	24	2	2	41	6	4	63	26	51	22	.355	.371	21

National League third basemen

Name/Team	B	BA	G	AB	R	H	TB	2B	3B	HR	RBI	SH	SF	BB	SO	SB	CS	SLG	OBA	RV
Andrews, S., Mon.-Chi.	R	.195	117	348	41	68	128	12	0	16	51	0	5	50	109	1	1	.368	.295	NV
Arias, George, S.D.	R	.244	55	164	20	40	69	8	0	7	20	0	0	6	54	0	0	.421	.271	NV
Barrett, Michael, Mon.	R	.293	126	433	53	127	189	32	3	8	52	0	1	32	39	0	2	.436	.345	7
Battle, Howard, Atl.	R	.353	15	17	2	6	9	0	0	1	5	0	0	2	3	0	0	.529	.421	NV
Beltre, Adrian, L.A.	R	.275	152	538	84	148	230	27	5	15	67	4	5	61	105	18	7	.428	.352	15
Boone, Aaron, Cin.	R	.280	139	472	56	132	210	26	5	14	72	5	5	30	79	17	6	.445	.330	16
Caminiti, Ken, Hou.	B	.286	78	273	45	78	130	11	1	13	56	0	7	46	58	6	2	.476	.386	10
Castilla, Vinny, Col.	R	.275	158	615	83	169	294	24	1	33	102	0	5	53	75	2	3	.478	.331	19
Cirillo, Jeff, Mil.	R	.326	157	607	98	198	280	35	1	15	88	3	7	75	83	7	4	.461	.401	22
Clapinski, Chris, Fla.	B	.232	36	56	6	13	18	1	2	0	2	0	0	9	12	1	0	.321	.348	NV
Coquillette, Trace, Mon.	R	.265	17	49	2	13	16	3	0	0	4	1	0	4	7	1	0	.327	.333	NV
Fernandez, Jose, Mon.	R	.208	8	24	0	5	7	2	0	0	1	0	0	1	7	0	0	.292	.240	NV
Gaetti, Gary, Chi.	R	.204	113	280	22	57	95	9	1	9	46	0	5	21	51	0	1	.339	.260	NV
Garcia, Carlos, S.D.	R	.182	6	11	1	2	2	0	0	0	0	0	0	1	3	0	0	.182	.250	NV

National League third basemen

Name/Team	B	BA	G	AB	R	H	TB	2B	3B	HR	RBI	SH	SF	BB	SO	SB	CS	SLG	OBA	RV
Giovanola, Ed, S.D.	L	.190	56	58	10	11	13	0	1	0	3	1	1	9	8	2	0	.224	.294	NV
Guzman, Edwards, S.F.	L	.000	14	15	0	0	0	0	0	0	0	1	0	0	4	0	0	.000	.000	NV
Hayes, Charlie, S.F.	R	.205	95	264	33	54	83	9	1	6	48	0	3	33	41	3	1	.314	.292	NV
Houston, Tyler, Chi.	L	.233	100	249	26	58	96	9	1	9	27	1	1	28	67	1	1	.386	.309	NV
Johnson, Russ, Hou.	R	.282	83	156	24	44	69	10	0	5	23	4	3	20	31	2	3	.442	.358	2
Jones, Chipper, Atl.	B	.319	157	567	116	181	359	41	1	45	110	0	6	126	94	25	3	.633	.441	39
Jordan, Kevin, Phi.	R	.285	120	347	36	99	134	17	3	4	51	0	3	24	34	0	0	.386	.339	4
Lewis, Mark, Cin.	R	.254	88	173	18	44	78	16	0	6	28	2	2	7	24	0	0	.451	.280	1
Liniak, Cole, Chi.	R	.241	12	29	3	7	9	2	0	0	2	0	0	1	4	0	1	.310	.267	NV
Lowell, Mike, Fla.	R	.253	97	308	32	78	129	15	0	12	47	0	5	26	69	0	0	.419	.317	4
Magadan, Dave, S.D.	L	.274	116	248	20	68	88	12	1	2	30	0	7	45	36	1	3	.355	.377	1
Mueller, Bill, S.F.	B	.290	116	414	61	120	150	24	0	2	36	8	2	65	52	4	2	.362	.388	4
Nevin, Phil, S.D.	R	.269	128	383	52	103	202	27	0	24	85	1	5	51	82	1	0	.527	.352	13
Orie, Kevin, Fla.	R	.254	77	240	26	61	95	16	0	6	29	0	2	22	43	1	0	.396	.322	1
Ramirez, Aramis, Pit.	R	.179	18	56	2	10	14	2	1	0	7	1	1	6	9	0	0	.250	.254	NV
Rolen, Scott, Phi.	R	.268	112	421	74	113	221	28	1	26	77	0	6	67	114	12	2	.525	.368	17
Spiers, Bill, Hou.	L	.288	127	393	56	113	153	18	5	4	39	3	1	47	45	10	5	.389	.363	7
Sprague, Ed, Pit.	R	.267	137	490	71	131	228	27	2	22	81	1	6	50	93	3	6	.465	.352	12
Sveum, Dale, Pit.	B	.211	49	71	7	15	31	5	1	3	13	1	1	7	28	0	0	.437	.278	NV
Tatis, Fernando, St.L.	R	.298	149	537	104	160	297	31	2	34	107	0	4	82	128	21	9	.553	.404	30
Ventura, Robin, N.Y.	L	.301	161	588	88	177	311	38	0	32	120	1	5	74	109	1	1	.529	.379	24
Williams, Matt, Ari.	R	.303	154	627	98	190	336	37	2	35	142	0	8	41	93	2	0	.536	.344	29
Zosky, Eddie, Mil.	R	.143	8	7	1	1	1	0	0	0	0	0	0	1	2	0	0	.143	.250	NV

National League shortstops

Name/Team	B	BA	G	AB	R	H	TB	2B	3B	HR	RBI	SH	SF	BB	SO	SB	CS	SLG	OBA	RV
Alexander, Manny, Chi.	R	.271	90	177	17	48	63	11	2	0	15	1	1	10	38	4	0	.356	.309	NV
Arias, Alex, Phi.	R	.303	118	347	43	105	139	20	1	4	48	1	2	36	31	2	2	.401	.373	6
Aurilia, Rich, S.F.	R	.281	152	558	68	157	248	23	1	22	80	3	5	43	71	2	3	.444	.336	14
Batista, Tony, Ari.	R	.257	44	144	16	37	57	5	0	5	21	0	2	16	17	2	0	.396	.335	NV
Benjamin, Mike, Pit.	R	.247	110	368	42	91	134	26	7	1	37	11	3	20	90	10	1	.364	.288	2
Berg, Dave, Fla.	R	.286	109	304	42	87	116	18	1	3	25	3	0	27	59	2	2	.382	.348	2
Blum, Geoff, Mon.	B	.241	45	133	21	32	67	7	2	8	18	3	0	17	25	1	0	.504	.327	NV
Bogar, Tim, Hou.	R	.239	107	309	44	74	106	16	2	4	31	0	3	38	52	3	5	.343	.328	NV
Cabrera, Orlando, Mon.	R	.254	104	382	48	97	154	23	5	8	39	4	0	18	38	2	2	.403	.293	2
Cedeno, Domingo, Phi.	B	.152	32	66	5	10	17	4	0	1	5	1	0	5	22	0	1	.258	.211	NV
Collier, Lou, Mil.	R	.259	74	135	18	35	50	9	0	2	21	1	2	14	32	3	2	.370	.325	NV
Cora, Alex, L.A.	L	.167	11	30	2	5	6	1	0	0	3	0	0	0	4	0	0	.200	.194	NV
Dawkins, Travis, Cin.	R	.143	7	7	1	1	1	0	0	0	0	0	0	0	4	0	0	.143	.250	NV
Delgado, Wilson, S.F.	B	.254	35	71	7	18	22	2	1	0	3	1	0	5	9	1	0	.310	.312	NV
DeRosa, Mark, Atl.	R	.000	7	8	0	0	0	0	0	0	0	0	0	0	2	0	0	.000	.000	NV
Fox, Andy, Ari.	L	.255	99	274	34	70	104	12	2	6	33	1	3	33	61	4	1	.380	.351	2
Frias, Hanley, Ari.	B	.273	69	150	27	41	51	3	2	1	16	1	0	29	18	4	3	.340	.391	NV
Gomez, Chris, S.D.	R	.252	76	234	20	59	72	8	1	1	15	2	1	27	49	1	2	.308	.331	NV
Gonzalez, Alex, Fla.	R	.277	136	560	81	155	241	28	8	14	59	1	3	15	113	3	5	.430	.308	9
Grudzielanek, Mark, L.A.	R	.326	123	488	72	159	213	23	5	7	46	2	3	31	65	6	6	.436	.376	13
Guillen, Ozzie, Atl.	L	.241	92	232	21	56	75	16	0	1	20	5	3	15	17	4	2	.323	.284	NV
Gutierrez, Ricky, Hou.	R	.261	85	268	33	70	90	7	5	1	25	3	1	37	45	2	5	.336	.354	NV
Hernandez, Jose, Chi.-Atl.	R	.266	147	508	79	135	216	20	2	19	62	2	1	52	145	11	3	.425	.339	12
Howard, David, St.L.	R	.207	52	82	3	17	24	4	0	1	6	1	0	7	27	0	2	.293	.286	NV
Jackson, Damian, S.D.	R	.224	133	388	56	87	138	20	2	9	39	0	3	53	105	34	10	.356	.320	11
Klassen, Danny, Ari.	R	1.000	1	1	0	1	1	0	0	0	0	0	0	0	0	0	0	1.000	1.000	NV
Larkin, Barry, Cin.	R	.293	161	583	108	171	245	30	4	12	75	5	4	93	57	30	8	.420	.390	22
Lopez, Luis, N.Y.	B	.212	68	104	11	22	32	4	0	2	13	1	1	12	33	1	1	.308	.300	NV
Loretta, Mark, Mil.	R	.290	153	587	93	170	229	34	5	5	67	9	6	52	59	4	1	.390	.354	9
Meares, Pat, Pit.	R	.308	21	91	15	28	32	4	0	0	7	2	0	9	20	0	0	.352	.382	NV
Nieves, Jose, Chi.	R	.249	54	181	16	45	62	9	1	2	18	3	3	8	25	0	2	.343	.291	NV
Nunez, Abraham, Pit.	B	.220	90	259	25	57	65	8	0	0	17	13	0	28	54	9	1	.251	.299	NV
Ordaz, Luis, St.L.	R	.111	10	9	3	1	1	0	0	0	2	1	0	1	2	1	0	.111	.200	NV
Ordonez, Rey, N.Y.	R	.258	154	520	49	134	165	24	2	1	60	11	7	49	59	8	4	.317	.319	4
Perez, Neifi, Col.	B	.280	157	690	108	193	278	27	11	12	70	9	4	28	54	13	5	.403	.307	14
Relaford, Desi, Phi.	B	.242	65	211	31	51	69	11	2	1	26	6	0	19	34	4	3	.327	.322	NV
Renteria, Edgar, St.L.	R	.275	154	585	92	161	234	36	2	11	63	6	7	53	82	37	8	.400	.334	20
Valentin, Jose, Mil.	B	.227	89	256	45	58	107	9	5	10	38	2	5	48	52	3	2	.418	.347	1
Vizcaino, Jose, L.A.	B	.252	94	266	27	67	79	9	0	1	29	9	2	20	23	2	1	.297	.304	NV
Weiss, Walt, Atl.	B	.226	110	279	38	63	90	13	4	2	29	6	4	35	48	7	3	.323	.315	NV

National League outfielders

Name/Team	B	BA	G	AB	R	H	TB	2B	3B	HR	RBI	SH	SF	BB	SO	SB	CS	SLG	OBA	RV
Abreu, Bobby, Phi.	L	.335	152	546	118	183	300	35	11	20	93	0	4	109	113	27	9	.549	.446	32
Agbayani, Benny, N.Y.	R	.286	101	276	42	79	145	18	3	14	42	0	3	32	60	6	4	.525	.363	9
Allensworth, J., N.Y.	R	.219	40	73	14	16	27	2	0	3	9	2	1	9	23	2	1	.370	.310	NV
Aven, Bruce, Fla.	R	.289	137	381	57	110	169	19	2	12	70	0	6	44	82	3	0	.444	.370	11
Barker, Glen, Hou.	B	.288	81	73	23	21	26	2	0	1	11	4	1	11	19	17	6	.356	.384	5
Barry, Jeff, Col.	B	.268	74	168	19	45	76	16	0	5	26	0	3	19	29	0	4	.452	.344	1
Bautista, Danny, Fla.	R	.288	70	205	32	59	86	10	1	5	24	0	1	4	30	3	0	.420	.303	3
Becker, Rich, Mil.	L	.252	89	139	15	35	59	5	2	5	16	2	0	33	38	5	0	.424	.395	1
Bell, Derek, Hou.	R	.236	128	509	61	120	178	22	0	12	66	0	5	50	129	18	6	.350	.306	9
Benard, Marvin, S.F.	L	.290	149	562	100	163	257	36	5	16	64	1	1	55	97	27	14	.457	.359	21
Bergeron, Peter, Mon.	L	.244	16	45	12	11	13	2	0	0	1	1	0	9	5	0	0	.289	.370	NV
Berkman, Lance, Hou.	B	.237	34	93	10	22	36	2	0	4	15	0	1	12	21	5	1	.387	.321	NV
Bichette, Dante, Col.	R	.298	151	593	104	177	321	38	2	34	133	0	10	54	84	6	6	.541	.354	28
Bonds, Barry, S.F.	L	.262	102	355	91	93	219	20	2	34	83	0	3	73	62	15	2	.617	.389	21
Bonilla, Bobby, N.Y.	B	.160	60	119	12	19	36	5	0	4	18	0	2	19	16	0	1	.303	.277	NV
Bragg, Darren, St.L.	L	.260	93	273	38	71	103	12	1	6	26	5	0	44	67	3	0	.377	.369	1
Brown, Adrian, Pit.	B	.270	116	226	34	61	82	5	2	4	17	6	1	33	39	5	3	.363	.364	1
Brown, Brant, Pit.	L	.232	130	341	49	79	153	20	3	16	58	0	4	22	114	3	4	.449	.283	5
Brown, Emil, Pit.	R	.143	6	14	0	2	3	1	0	0	0	0	0	0	3	0	0	.214	.143	NV
Brown, Roosevelt, Chi.	L	.219	33	64	6	14	25	6	1	1	10	3	1	2	14	1	0	.391	.239	NV
Brumfield, Jacob, L.A.	R	.294	18	17	4	5	7	0	1	0	1	0	0	0	5	0	0	.412	.294	NV
Burks, Ellis, S.F.	R	.282	120	390	73	110	222	19	0	31	96	0	4	69	86	7	5	.569	.394	20
Burnitz, Jeromy, Mil.	L	.270	130	467	87	126	262	33	2	33	103	0	6	91	124	7	3	.561	.402	20
Cameron, Mike, Cin.	R	.256	146	542	93	139	254	34	9	21	66	5	3	80	145	38	12	.469	.357	22
Cangelosi, John, Col.	B	.167	7	6	0	1	2	1	0	0	0	0	0	0	4	0	0	.333	.167	NV
Cedeno, Roger, N.Y.	L	.313	155	453	90	142	185	23	4	4	36	7	2	60	100	66	17	.408	.396	31
Clemente, Edgard, Col.	R	.253	57	162	24	41	79	10	2	8	25	1	1	7	46	0	0	.488	.282	1
Cookson, Brent, L.A.	R	.200	3	5	0	1	1	0	0	0	0	0	0	0	1	0	0	.200	.200	NV
Darr, Mike, S.D.	L	.271	25	48	6	13	20	1	0	2	3	0	0	5	18	2	1	.417	.340	NV
Davis, Eric, St.L.	R	.257	58	191	27	49	77	9	2	5	30	0	1	30	49	5	4	.403	.359	2
Dellucci, David, Ari.	L	.394	63	109	27	43	55	7	1	1	15	0	0	11	24	2	0	.505	.463	3
Diaz, Alex, Hou.	B	.220	30	50	3	11	16	2	0	1	7	0	0	3	13	2	2	.320	.264	NV
Drew, J.D., St.L.	L	.242	104	368	72	89	156	16	6	13	39	3	3	50	77	19	3	.424	.340	9
Ducey, Rob, Phi.	L	.261	104	188	29	49	87	10	2	8	33	0	1	38	57	2	1	.463	.383	3
Dunston, S., St.L.-N.Y.	R	.321	104	243	35	78	110	11	3	5	41	3	2	2	39	10	4	.453	.337	10
Dunwoody, Todd, Fla.	L	.220	64	186	20	41	59	6	3	2	20	0	1	12	41	3	4	.317	.270	NV
Echevarria, Angel, Col.	R	.293	102	191	28	56	96	7	0	11	35	0	0	17	34	1	3	.503	.360	5
Everett, Carl, Hou.	B	.325	123	464	86	151	265	33	3	25	108	2	8	50	94	27	7	.571	.398	33
Finley, Steve, Ari.	L	.264	156	590	100	156	310	32	10	34	103	2	5	63	94	8	4	.525	.336	20
Floyd, Cliff, Fla.	L	.303	69	251	37	76	130	19	1	11	49	0	2	30	47	5	6	.518	.379	9
Gant, Ron, Phi.	R	.260	138	516	107	134	222	27	5	17	77	0	3	85	112	13	3	.430	.364	13
Garcia, Freddy, Pit.-Atl.	R	.235	57	132	17	31	57	5	0	7	24	0	1	5	42	0	0	.432	.261	NV
Gibson, Derrick, Col.	R	.179	10	28	2	5	12	1	0	2	6	0	0	0	7	0	0	.429	.207	NV
Giles, Brian, Pit.	L	.315	141	521	109	164	320	33	3	39	115	0	8	95	80	6	2	.614	.418	30
Gilkey, Bernard, Ari.	R	.294	94	204	28	60	102	16	1	8	39	1	5	29	42	2	2	.500	.379	5
Glanville, Doug, Phi.	R	.325	150	628	101	204	287	38	6	11	73	5	5	48	82	34	2	.457	.376	29
Gonzalez, Luis, Ari.	L	.336	153	614	112	206	337	45	4	26	111	1	5	66	63	9	5	.549	.403	30
Goodwin, Curtis, Chi.	L	.242	89	157	15	38	46	6	1	0	9	4	1	13	38	2	4	.293	.298	NV
Grissom, Marquis, Mil.	R	.267	154	603	92	161	250	27	1	20	83	4	5	49	109	24	6	.415	.320	19
Guerrero, Vladimir, Mon.	R	.316	160	610	102	193	366	37	5	42	131	0	2	55	62	14	7	.600	.378	36
Guillen, Jose, Pit.	R	.267	40	120	18	32	41	6	0	1	18	1	1	10	21	1	0	.342	.321	NV
Gwynn, Tony, S.D.	L	.338	111	411	59	139	196	27	0	10	62	0	4	29	14	7	2	.477	.381	16
Halter, Shane, N.Y.	R	.000	7	0	0	0	0	0	0	0	0	0	0	0	0	0	0	.000	.000	NV
Hamilton, Darryl, Col.-N.Y.L	R	.315	146	505	82	159	213	19	4	9	45	3	1	57	39	6	8	.422	.386	12
Hammonds, Jeffrey, Cin.	R	.279	123	262	43	73	137	13	0	17	41	2	1	27	64	3	6	.523	.347	8
Henderson, Rickey, N.Y.	R	.315	121	438	89	138	204	30	0	12	42	1	3	82	82	37	14	.466	.423	24
Hermansen, Chad, Pit.	R	.233	19	60	5	14	20	3	0	1	1	1	0	7	19	2	2	.333	.324	NV
Hidalgo, Richard, Hou.	R	.227	108	383	49	87	161	25	2	15	56	0	5	56	73	8	5	.420	.328	5
Hill, Glenallen, Chi.	R	.300	99	253	43	76	147	9	1	20	55	0	3	22	61	5	1	.581	.353	13
Hollandsworth, Todd, L.A.L	L	.284	92	261	39	74	117	12	2	9	32	0	1	24	61	5	2	.448	.345	5
Howard, Thomas, St.L.	B	.292	98	195	16	57	85	10	0	6	28	0	1	17	26	1	1	.436	.353	3
Hubbard, Trenidad, L.A.	R	.314	82	105	23	33	41	5	0	1	13	1	1	13	24	4	3	.390	.387	1
Hyers, Tim, Fla.	L	.222	58	81	8	18	30	4	1	2	12	0	1	14	11	0	0	.370	.333	NV
Javier, Stan, S.F.-Hou.	B	.285	132	397	61	113	145	19	2	3	34	8	2	38	63	16	7	.365	.347	8
Jenkins, Geoff, Mil.	L	.313	135	447	70	140	252	43	3	21	82	3	1	35	87	5	1	.564	.371	19
Jennings, Robin, Chi.	L	.200	5	5	0	1	1	0	0	0	0	0	0	0	2	0	0	.200	.200	NV
Johnson, Lance, Chi.	L	.260	95	335	46	87	113	11	6	1	21	4	1	37	20	13	3	.337	.332	2
Jones, Andruw, Atl.	R	.275	162	592	97	163	286	35	5	26	84	0	2	76	103	24	12	.483	.365	23
Jones, Terry, Mon.	B	.270	17	63	4	17	20	1	1	0	3	0	0	3	14	1	2	.317	.303	NV
Jordan, Brian, Atl.	R	.283	153	576	100	163	268	28	4	23	115	0	9	51	81	13	8	.465	.346	22

National League outfielders

Name/Team	B	BA	G	AB	R	H	TB	2B	3B	HR	RBI	SH	SF	BB	SO	SB	CS	SLG	OBA	RV
Kelly, Mike, Col.	R	.500	2	2	0	1	2	1	0	0	1	0	0	0	0	0	0	1.000	.500	NV
Kinkade, Mike, N.Y.	R	.196	28	46	3	9	19	2	1	2	6	0	0	3	9	1	0	.413	.275	NV
Kotsay, Mark, Fla.	L	.271	148	495	57	134	199	23	9	8	50	2	9	29	50	7	6	.402	.306	6
Lankford, Ray, St.L.	L	.306	122	422	77	129	208	32	1	15	63	0	2	49	110	14	4	.493	.380	17
Lombard, George, Atl.	L	.333	6	6	1	2	2	0	0	0	0	0	0	1	2	2	0	.333	.429	NV
Long, Terrence, N.Y.	L	.000	3	3	0	0	0	0	0	0	0	0	0	0	2	0	0	.000	.000	NV
Magee, Wendell, Phi.	R	.357	12	14	4	5	12	1	0	2	5	0	0	1	4	0	0	.857	.400	NV
Martin, Al, Pit.	L	.277	143	541	97	150	274	36	8	24	63	0	2	49	119	20	3	.506	.337	19
Martinez, Manny, Mon.	R	.245	137	331	48	81	113	12	7	2	26	6	3	17	51	19	6	.341	.279	4
Matthews, Gary, S.D.	B	.222	23	36	4	8	8	0	0	0	7	0	0	9	9	2	0	.222	.378	NV
McGee, Willie, St.L.	B	.251	132	271	25	68	75	7	0	0	20	0	2	17	60	7	4	.277	.293	NV
McRae, Brian, N.Y.-Col.	B	.224	103	321	36	72	115	14	1	9	37	0	2	41	64	2	6	.358	.323	NV
Merced, Orlando, Mon.	B	.268	93	194	25	52	90	12	1	8	26	0	1	26	27	2	1	.464	.353	2
Mieske, Matt, Hou.	R	.284	54	109	13	31	51	5	0	5	22	1	2	6	22	0	0	.468	.316	1
Mondesi, Raul, L.A.	R	.253	159	601	98	152	290	29	5	33	99	0	5	71	134	36	9	.483	.332	28
Mora, Melvin, N.Y.	R	.161	66	31	6	5	5	0	0	0	1	3	0	4	7	2	1	.161	.278	NV
Mouton, James, Mon.	R	.262	95	122	18	32	45	5	1	2	13	3	1	18	31	6	2	.369	.364	NV
Mouton, Lyle, Mil.	R	.176	14	17	2	3	7	1	0	1	3	0	0	2	3	0	0	.412	.263	NV
Murray, Calvin, S.F.	R	.263	15	19	1	5	7	2	0	0	5	0	0	2	4	1	0	.368	.333	NV
Nixon, Otis, Atl.	B	.205	84	151	31	31	35	2	1	0	8	1	1	23	15	26	7	.232	.309	4
Ochoa, Alex, Mil.	R	.300	119	277	47	83	129	16	3	8	40	0	2	45	43	6	4	.466	.404	8
Owens, Eric, S.D.	R	.266	149	440	55	117	172	22	3	9	61	2	2	38	50	33	7	.391	.327	17
Paquette, Craig, St.L.	R	.287	48	157	21	45	81	6	0	10	37	1	2	6	38	1	0	.516	.309	5
Payton, Jay, N.Y.	R	.250	13	8	1	2	3	1	0	0	1	0	0	0	2	1	2	.375	.333	NV
Perez, Eduardo, St.L.	R	.344	21	32	6	11	16	2	0	1	9	0	0	7	6	0	0	.500	.462	NV
Phillips, J. R., Col.	L	.231	25	39	5	9	19	4	0	2	4	0	0	0	13	0	0	.487	.250	NV
Porter, Bo, Chi.	R	.192	24	26	2	5	6	1	0	0	0	1	0	2	13	0	0	.231	.250	NV
Powell, Dante, Ari.	R	.160	22	25	4	4	7	3	0	0	1	1	0	2	6	2	1	.280	.222	NV
Ramirez, Julio, Fla.	R	.143	15	21	3	3	4	1	0	0	2	0	0	1	6	0	1	.190	.182	NV
Rios, Armando, S.F.	L	.327	72	150	32	49	79	9	0	7	29	1	1	24	35	7	4	.527	.420	7
Rivera, Ruben, S.D.	R	.195	147	411	65	80	167	16	1	23	48	0	4	55	143	18	7	.406	.295	7
Robinson, Kerry, Cin.	L	.000	9	1	4	0	0	0	0	0	0	0	0	0	1	0	1	.000	.000	NV
Rodriguez, Henry, Chi.	L	.304	130	447	72	136	243	29	0	26	87	0	1	56	113	2	4	.544	.381	19
Ryan, Rob, Ari.	L	.241	20	29	4	7	14	1	0	2	5	0	0	1	8	0	0	.483	.267	NV
Sanders, Reggie, S.D.	R	.285	133	478	92	136	252	24	7	26	72	0	1	65	108	36	13	.527	.376	27
Santangelo, F. P., S.F.	B	.260	113	254	49	66	98	17	3	3	26	5	2	53	54	12	4	.386	.406	4
Sefcik, Kevin, Phi.	R	.278	111	209	28	58	82	15	3	1	11	3	0	29	24	9	4	.392	.368	2
Sexton, Chris, Cin.	R	.237	35	59	9	14	19	0	1	1	7	0	0	11	10	4	2	.322	.357	NV
Sheffield, Gary, L.A.	R	.301	152	549	103	165	287	20	0	34	101	0	9	101	64	11	5	.523	.407	26
Sosa, Juan, Col.	R	.222	11	9	3	2	2	0	0	0	0	0	0	2	2	0	0	.222	.364	NV
Sosa, Sammy, Chi.	R	.288	162	625	114	180	397	24	2	63	141	0	6	78	171	7	8	.635	.367	37
Stowers, Chris, Mon.	L	.000	4	2	0	0	0	0	0	0	0	0	0	0	0	0	0	.000	.000	NV
Thompson, Ryan, Hou.	R	.200	12	20	2	4	8	1	0	1	5	0	0	2	7	0	0	.400	.273	NV
Tucker, Michael, Cin.	L	.253	133	296	55	75	126	8	5	11	44	0	4	37	81	11	4	.426	.338	7
Vander Wal, John, S.D.	L	.272	132	246	26	67	103	18	0	6	41	0	3	37	59	2	1	.419	.368	3
Vaughn, Greg, Cin.	R	.245	153	550	104	135	294	20	2	45	118	0	5	85	137	15	2	.535	.347	25
Walker, Larry, Col.	L	.379	127	438	108	166	311	26	4	37	115	0	6	57	52	11	4	.710	.458	38
Ward, Daryle, Hou.	L	.273	64	150	11	41	71	6	0	8	30	0	2	9	31	0	0	.473	.311	2
Ward, Turner, Pit.-Ari.	B	.237	59	114	8	27	36	3	0	2	15	3	2	15	15	2	2	.316	.326	NV
Watkins, Pat, Col.	R	.053	16	19	2	1	1	0	0	0	0	1	0	2	5	0	0	.053	.143	NV
Wehner, John, Pit.	R	.185	39	65	6	12	17	2	0	1	4	3	0	7	12	1	0	.262	.264	NV
White, Devon, L.A.	B	.268	134	474	60	127	193	20	2	14	68	0	2	39	88	19	5	.407	.337	14
White, Rondell, Mon.	R	.312	138	539	83	168	272	26	6	22	64	0	6	32	85	10	6	.505	.359	20
Williams, Gerald, Atl.	R	.275	143	422	76	116	193	24	1	17	68	4	2	33	67	19	11	.457	.335	16
Wilson, Preston, Fla.	R	.280	149	482	67	135	242	21	4	26	71	0	6	46	156	11	4	.502	.350	17
Womack, Tony, Ari.	L	.277	144	614	111	170	227	25	10	4	41	9	7	52	68	72	13	.370	.332	29
Young, Dmitri, Cin.	B	.300	127	373	63	112	188	30	2	14	56	0	4	30	71	3	1	.504	.352	11
Young, Ernie, Ari.	R	.182	6	11	1	2	2	0	0	0	0	0	0	3	2	0	0	.182	.400	NV

National League relief pitchers (batting)

Name/Team	B	BA	G	AB	R	H	TB	2B	3B	HR	RBI	SH	SF	BB	SO	SB	CS	SLG	OBA
Acevedo, Juan, St.L.	R	.050	50	20	0	1	1	0	0	0	0	2	0	0	16	0	0	.050	.050
Adams, Terry, Chi.	R	.000	52	2	0	0	0	0	0	0	0	0	0	0	2	0	0	.000	.000
Aguilera, Rick, Chi.	R	.000	44	1	0	0	0	0	0	0	0	0	0	0	0	0	0	.000	.000
Aldred, Scott, Phi.	L	.000	29	1	0	0	0	0	0	0	0	0	0	0	1	0	0	.000	.000
Alfonseca, Antonio, Fla.	R	.000	73	2	0	0	0	0	0	0	0	0	0	0	2	0	0	.000	.000
Almanza, Armando, Fla.	L	.000	14	3	0	0	0	0	0	0	0	0	0	0	2	0	0	.000	.000
Almanzar, Carlos, S.D.	R	.000	28	1	0	0	0	0	0	0	0	0	0	0	1	0	0	.000	.000

National League relief pitchers (batting)

Name/Team	B	BA	G	AB	R	H	TB	2B	3B	HR	RBI	SH	SF	BB	SO	SB	CS	SLG	OBA
Anderson, Jimmy, Pit.	L	.333	13	9	2	3	4	1	0	0	1	0	0	0	2	0	0	.444	.333
Arnold, Jamie, L.A.	R	.200	36	10	1	2	2	0	0	0	1	1	0	0	3	0	0	.200	.200
Ayala, Bobby, Mon.-Chi.	R	.000	66	1	0	0	0	0	0	0	0	0	0	0	0	0	0	.000	.000
Aybar, Manuel, St.L.	R	.083	67	12	0	1	1	0	0	0	1	1	0	0	7	0	0	.083	.083
Batista, Miguel, Mon.	R	.200	39	35	6	7	11	1	0	1	3	4	0	2	19	0	0	.314	.243
Belinda, Stan, Cin.	R	.250	29	4	0	1	1	0	0	0	0	0	0	0	1	0	0	.250	.250
Beltran, Rigo, N.Y.-Col.	L	.333	33	3	0	1	1	0	0	0	0	0	0	0	0	0	0	.333	.333
Benitez, Armando, N.Y.	R	.000	77	5	0	0	0	0	0	0	1	0	0	0	2	0	0	.000	.000
Bennett, Shayne, Mon.	R	.000	5	2	0	0	0	0	0	0	0	0	0	0	1	0	0	.000	.000
Boehringer, Brian, S.D.	B	.063	33	16	0	1	1	0	0	0	0	2	0	2	9	0	0	.063	.167
Borbon, Pedro, L.A.	R	.000	70	2	0	0	0	0	0	0	0	1	0	0	1	0	0	.000	.000
Bottalico, Ricky, St.L.	L	.000	68	3	0	0	0	0	0	0	0	0	0	0	0	0	0	.000	.000
Boyd, Jason, Pit.	R	.000	4	1	0	0	0	0	0	0	0	0	0	0	1	0	0	.000	.000
Checo, Robinson, L.A.	R	.333	9	3	0	1	1	0	0	0	2	1	0	0	2	0	0	.333	.333
Chen, Bruce, Atl.	B	.000	16	11	0	0	0	0	0	0	0	1	0	0	6	0	0	.000	.000
Chouinard, Bobby, Ari.	R	.000	32	3	0	0	0	0	0	0	0	1	0	0	3	0	0	.000	.000
Christiansen, Jason, Pit.	R	.000	40	1	0	0	0	0	0	0	0	0	0	0	1	0	0	.000	.000
Clontz, Brad, Pit.	R	.000	56	3	0	0	0	0	0	0	0	0	0	0	2	0	0	.000	.000
Cook, Dennis, N.Y.	L	.000	71	1	0	0	0	0	0	0	0	0	0	0	1	0	0	.000	.000
Coppinger, Rocky, Mil.	R	.000	29	2	0	0	0	0	0	0	0	0	0	0	0	0	0	.000	.000
Corbin, Archie, Fla.	R	.000	17	1	0	0	0	0	0	0	0	0	0	0	1	0	0	.000	.000
Cornelius, Reid, Fla.	R	.200	5	5	0	1	1	0	0	0	0	1	0	0	2	0	0	.200	.200
Croushore, Rich, St.L.	R	.333	59	3	1	1	1	0	0	0	0	0	0	1	1	0	0	.333	.500
Cunnane, Will, S.D.	R	.000	24	3	0	0	0	0	0	0	0	0	0	0	1	0	0	.000	.000
Darensbourg, Vic, Fla.	L	.000	56	0	0	0	0	0	0	0	0	0	0	1	0	0	0	.000	1.000
DeJean, Mike, Col.	R	.000	57	2	0	0	0	0	0	0	0	0	0	0	1	0	0	.000	.000
DelToro, Miguel, S.F.	R	.000	14	4	0	0	0	0	0	0	0	1	0	0	3	0	0	.000	.000
Dipoto, Jerry, Col.	R	.000	63	5	0	0	0	0	0	0	0	0	0	1	2	0	0	.000	.167
Dougherty, Jim, Pit.	R	.000	2	0	0	0	0	0	0	0	0	0	0	1	0	0	0	.000	1.000
Ebert, Derrin, Atl.	R	.000	5	1	0	0	0	0	0	0	0	0	0	0	1	0	0	.000	.000
Edmondson, Brian, Fla.	R	.364	68	11	0	4	6	2	0	0	2	0	0	0	4	0	0	.545	.364
Elarton, Scott, Hou.	R	.192	43	26	1	5	5	0	0	0	1	7	0	0	10	0	0	.192	.192
Estrada, Horacio, Mil.	L	.000	4	2	0	0	0	0	0	0	0	0	0	0	0	0	0	.000	.000
Falteisek, Steve, Mil.	R	.000	11	1	1	0	0	0	0	0	0	0	0	0	1	0	0	.000	.000
Fox, Chad, Mil.	R	.000	6	1	0	0	0	0	0	0	0	0	0	0	0	0	0	.000	.000
Gomes, Wayne, Phi.	R	.000	73	1	0	0	0	0	0	0	0	0	0	0	1	0	0	.000	.000
Grace, Mike, Phi.	R	.000	27	7	1	0	0	0	0	0	0	3	0	1	4	0	0	.000	.125
Grahe, Joe, Phi.	R	.143	13	7	1	1	1	0	0	0	0	0	0	1	3	0	0	.143	.250
Graves, Danny, Cin.	R	.000	75	5	0	0	0	0	0	0	0	0	0	0	2	0	0	.000	.000
Greene, Rick, Cin.	R	.000	1	2	0	0	0	0	0	0	0	0	0	0	2	0	0	.000	.000
Hansell, Greg, Pit.	R	.000	33	2	0	0	0	0	0	0	0	0	0	0	2	0	0	.000	.000
Harris, Reggie, Mil.	R	.000	8	1	0	0	0	0	0	0	0	0	0	0	1	0	0	.000	.000
Heiserman, Rick, St.L.	R	.000	3	1	0	0	0	0	0	0	0	0	0	0	0	0	0	.000	.000
Henry, Doug, Hou.	R	.000	35	1	0	0	0	0	0	0	0	0	0	0	1	0	0	.000	.000
Heredia, Felix, Chi.	L	.500	69	4	0	2	2	0	0	0	1	0	0	0	0	0	0	.500	.500
Herges, Matt, L.A.	L	.000	17	1	0	0	0	0	0	0	0	0	0	0	1	0	0	.000	.000
Hoffman, Trevor, S.D.	R	.333	64	3	0	1	2	1	0	0	2	0	0	0	0	0	0	.667	.333
Holmes, Darren, Ari.	R	.000	44	2	0	0	0	0	0	0	0	0	0	0	2	0	0	.000	.000
Hudek, John, Cin.-Atl.	R	.000	17	1	0	0	0	0	0	0	0	0	0	0	1	0	0	.000	.000
Isringhausen, Jason, N.Y.	R	.083	13	12	2	1	2	1	0	0	1	1	0	0	4	0	0	.167	.083
Johnson, Mike, Mon.	L	.250	3	4	1	1	1	0	0	0	0	0	0	0	1	0	0	.250	.250
Kim, Byung-Hyun, Ari.	R	.000	25	1	0	0	0	0	0	0	0	0	0	0	0	0	0	.000	.000
King, Ray, Chi.	L	.000	10	1	0	0	0	0	0	0	0	0	0	0	1	0	0	.000	.000
Kline, Steve, Mon.	B	.000	82	1	0	0	0	0	0	0	0	1	0	0	1	0	0	.000	.000
Kubenka, Jeff, L.A.	R	1.000	6	1	1	1	1	0	0	0	0	0	0	0	0	0	0	1.000	1.000
Lee, David, Col.	R	.200	36	5	1	1	1	0	0	0	0	0	0	0	2	0	0	.200	.200
Leskanic, Curtis, Col.	R	.500	63	4	1	2	5	0	0	1	3	0	0	0	2	0	0	1.250	.500
Lilly, Ted, Mon.	L	.200	9	5	0	1	1	0	0	0	0	1	0	0	1	0	0	.200	.200
Loiselle, Rich, Pit.	R	.000	13	0	0	0	0	0	0	0	0	1	0	0	0	0	0	.000	.000
Mahomes, Pat, N.Y.	R	.313	41	16	2	5	8	3	0	0	3	0	0	0	6	0	0	.500	.313
Manzanillo, Josias, N.Y.	R	1.000	13	1	0	1	1	0	0	0	0	0	0	0	0	0	0	1.000	1.000
Masaoka, Onan, L.A.	R	.000	54	4	0	0	0	0	0	0	0	1	0	0	2	0	0	.000	.000
McElroy, Chuck, Col.-N.Y.	L	.000	56	1	0	0	0	0	0	0	0	1	0	0	0	0	0	.000	.000
McGlinchy, Kevin, Atl.	R	.000	64	2	0	0	0	0	0	0	0	0	0	0	1	0	0	.000	.000
Miceli, Dan, S.D.	R	.000	66	1	0	0	0	0	0	0	0	0	0	0	1	0	0	.000	.000
Miller, Trever, Hou.	R	.000	47	3	0	0	0	0	0	0	0	2	0	0	1	0	0	.000	.000
Miller, Wade, Hou.	R	.000	5	1	0	0	0	0	0	0	0	0	0	0	1	0	0	.000	.000
Mills, Alan, L.A.	R	.000	68	2	0	0	0	0	0	0	0	0	0	0	1	0	0	.000	.000
Mlicki, Dave, L.A.	R	1.000	2	1	0	1	1	0	0	0	0	2	0	0	0	0	0	1.000	1.000
Mohler, Mike, St.L.	R	.000	48	3	0	0	0	0	0	0	0	0	0	0	1	0	0	.000	.000

National League relief pitchers (batting)

Name/Team	B	BA	G	AB	R	H	TB	2B	3B	HR	RBI	SH	SF	BB	SO	SB	CS	SLG	OBA
Montgomery, Steve, Phi.	R	1.000	53	1	1	1	1	0	0	0	0	0	0	0	0	0	0	1.000	1.000
Mota, Guillermo, Mon.	R	1.000	51	1	1	1	4	0	0	1	3	0	0	0	0	0	0	4.000	1.000
Murray, Heath, S.D.	L	.154	22	13	1	2	2	0	0	0	0	1	0	1	9	0	0	.154	.214
Myers, Mike, Mil.	L	.000	71	1	0	0	0	0	0	0	0	0	0	0	1	0	0	.000	.000
Myers, Rodney, Chi.	R	.429	46	7	2	3	4	1	0	0	1	0	0	0	2	0	0	.571	.429
Nunez, Vladimir, Ari.-Fla.	R	.143	44	28	0	4	4	0	0	0	2	2	0	0	6	0	0	.143	.143
Olson, Gregg, Ari.	R	.000	61	0	0	0	0	0	0	0	0	0	0	1	0	0	0	.000	1.000
Painter, Lance, St.L.	L	.000	56	7	0	0	0	0	0	0	0	0	0	0	5	0	0	.000	.000
Patrick, Bronswell, S.F.	R	.000	6	1	0	0	0	0	0	0	0	0	0	0	1	0	0	.000	.000
Perez, Yorkis, Phi.	L	.000	35	2	0	0	0	0	0	0	0	0	0	0	2	0	0	.000	.000
Pittsley, Jim, Mil.	R	.000	15	1	0	0	0	0	0	0	0	0	0	1	1	0	0	.000	.500
Plesac, Dan, Ari.	L	.000	34	1	0	0	0	0	0	0	0	0	0	0	1	0	0	.000	.000
Poole, Jim, Phi.	L	.000	51	2	0	0	0	0	0	0	0	0	0	0	1	0	0	.000	.000
Ramirez, Hector, Mil.	R	.000	15	3	0	0	0	0	0	0	0	0	0	0	2	0	0	.000	.000
Ramirez, Roberto, Col.	L	.143	32	7	1	1	1	0	0	0	0	1	0	0	0	0	0	.143	.250
Remlinger, Mike, Atl.	R	.000	73	2	1	0	0	0	0	0	0	2	0	0	2	0	0	.000	.000
Reyes, Carlos, S.D.	B	.000	65	1	0	0	0	0	0	0	0	0	0	0	1	0	0	.000	.000
Reyes, Dennys, Cin.	L	.000	65	4	0	0	0	0	0	0	0	0	0	0	3	0	0	.000	.000
Reyes, Alberto, Mil.	R	.000	26	2	0	0	0	0	0	0	0	0	0	0	0	0	0	.000	.000
Rodriguez, Felix, S.F.	R	.333	47	6	3	2	6	1	0	1	3	1	0	0	1	0	0	1.000	.429
Rodriguez, Rich, S.F.	L	1.000	62	1	1	1	1	0	0	0	1	1	0	0	0	0	0	1.000	1.000
Roque, Rafael, Mil.	L	.059	43	17	0	1	1	0	0	0	0	1	0	2	10	0	0	.059	.158
Sabel, Erik, Ari.	R	.000	7	2	0	0	0	0	0	0	0	0	0	0	2	0	0	.000	.000
Sanchez, Jesus, Fla.	L	.083	60	12	0	1	1	0	0	0	0	2	0	1	5	0	0	.083	.154
Sanders, Scott, Chi.	R	.278	67	18	0	5	7	2	0	0	1	2	0	0	6	0	0	.389	.278
Sauerbeck, Scott, Pit.	R	.000	65	1	0	0	0	0	0	0	0	1	0	0	1	0	0	.000	.000
Schrenk, Steve, Phi.	R	.000	32	3	0	0	0	0	0	0	0	1	0	0	2	0	0	.000	.000
Seanez, Rudy, Atl.	R	.000	56	1	1	0	0	0	0	0	0	0	0	1	1	0	0	.000	.500
Serafini, Dan, Chi.	B	.083	42	12	1	1	1	0	0	0	0	1	0	3	7	0	0	.083	.267
Silva, Jose, Pit.	R	.100	34	20	0	2	2	0	0	0	3	2	0	0	10	0	0	.100	.100
Sodowsky, Clint, St.L.	L	.000	3	1	0	0	0	0	0	0	0	0	0	0	1	0	0	.000	.000
Speier, Justin, Atl.	R	.333	19	3	0	1	1	0	0	0	0	0	0	0	2	0	0	.333	.333
Springer, Russ, Atl.	R	.000	49	0	0	0	0	0	0	0	0	0	0	0	0	0	0	.000	.000
Sullivan, Scott, Cin.	R	.000	79	15	1	0	0	0	0	0	0	0	0	0	11	0	0	.000	.000
Swindell, Greg, Ari.	R	.000	63	4	0	0	0	0	0	0	0	2	0	0	1	0	0	.000	.000
Tavarez, Julian, S.F.	R	.200	47	5	0	1	1	0	0	0	0	0	0	0	2	0	0	.200	.200
Telemaco, A., Ari.-Phi.	R	.000	49	0	0	0	0	0	0	0	0	0	0	0	0	0	0	.000	.000
Telford, Anthony, Mon.	R	.000	79	2	0	0	0	0	0	0	0	1	2	0	1	1	0	0	.000	.333
Urbina, Ugueth, Mon.	R	.000	71	5	0	0	0	0	0	0	0	0	0	0	2	0	0	.000	.000
Veres, Dave, Col.	R	.000	73	1	0	0	0	0	0	0	0	0	0	0	0	0	0	.000	.000
Wainhouse, Dave, Col.	L	.000	19	1	0	0	0	0	0	0	0	0	0	0	1	0	0	.000	.000
Wall, Donne, S.D.	R	.000	55	1	0	0	0	0	0	0	0	0	0	0	1	0	0	.000	.000
Wallace, Jeff, Pit.	L	.000	41	0	0	0	0	0	0	0	0	0	0	1	0	0	0	.000	1.000
Watson, Allen, N.Y.	L	.300	14	10	0	3	4	1	0	0	0	0	0	0	1	0	0	.400	.300
Weathers, Dave, Mil.	R	.143	63	7	1	1	1	0	0	0	0	0	0	1	4	0	0	.143	.250
Wendell, Turk, N.Y.	B	.000	80	6	0	0	0	0	0	0	0	0	0	1	3	0	0	.000	.143
Wilkins, Marc, Pit.	R	.000	46	1	0	0	0	0	0	0	0	0	0	0	1	0	0	.000	.000
Williams, Brian, Hou.	R	.333	50	3	0	1	1	0	0	0	1	0	0	0	1	0	0	.333	.333
Williams, Mike, Pit.	R	.000	58	2	0	0	0	0	0	0	0	0	0	0	0	0	0	.000	.000
Williamson, Scott, Cin.	R	.000	62	7	0	0	0	0	0	0	0	3	0	1	6	0	0	.000	.125
Wohlers, Mark, Atl.	R	.000	2	0	0	0	0	0	0	0	0	0	0	0	0	0	0	.000	.000

National League starting pitchers (batting)

Name/Team	B	BA	G	AB	R	H	TB	2B	3B	HR	RBI	SH	SF	BB	SO	SB	CS	SLG	OBA
Abbott, Jim, Mil.	L	.095	20	21	0	2	2	0	0	0	3	3	0	0	10	0	0	.095	.095
Anderson, Brian, Ari.	L	.132	32	38	4	5	10	0	1	1	2	1	1	2	10	1	0	.263	.171
Ankiel, Rick, St.L.	L	.100	9	10	0	1	1	0	0	0	0	1	0	0	3	0	0	.100	.100
Armas, Tony, Mon.	R	.000	1	2	0	0	0	0	0	0	0	0	0	0	1	0	0	.000	.000
Ashby, Andy, S.D.	R	.129	31	62	3	8	10	2	0	0	2	7	0	3	25	0	0	.161	.169
Astacio, Pedro, Col.	R	.233	37	86	5	20	24	2	1	0	7	7	0	1	24	0	0	.279	.241
Avery, Steve, Cin.	L	.077	19	26	1	2	2	0	0	0	1	2	0	0	11	0	0	.077	.077
Benes, Andy, Ari.	R	.155	33	58	6	9	12	0	0	1	5	10	0	4	17	0	0	.207	.222
Bennett, Joel, Phi.	R	.000	5	4	1	0	0	0	0	0	0	1	0	1	1	0	0	.000	.200
Benson, Kris, Pit.	R	.154	31	65	7	10	13	3	0	0	7	6	0	3	24	0	0	.200	.191
Bere, Jason, Cin.-Mil.	R	.318	17	22	3	7	7	0	0	0	1	2	0	2	9	0	0	.318	.400
Bergman, Sean, Hou.-Atl.	R	.107	25	28	4	3	9	0	0	2	2	1	0	0	12	0	0	.321	.107
Bohanon, Brian, Col.	L	.197	34	71	6	14	19	2	0	1	7	5	0	5	20	0	0	.268	.250
Bottenfield, Kent, St.L.	B	.148	31	61	4	9	12	3	0	0	5	8	0	1	26	0	0	.197	.161

National League starting pitchers (batting)

Name/Team	B	BA	G	AB	R	H	TB	2B	3B	HR	RBI	SH	SF	BB	SO	SB	CS	SLG	OBA
Bowie, Micah, Atl.-Chi.	L	.214	14	14	0	3	3	0	0	0	3	0	0	1	3	0	0	.214	.267
Brock, Chris, S.F.	R	.200	19	35	4	7	7	0	0	0	4	4	0	3	8	0	0	.200	.263
Brown, Kevin, L.A.	R	.064	35	78	1	5	5	0	0	0	3	13	1	2	24	0	0	.064	.086
Brownson, Mark, Col.	L	.111	7	9	1	1	1	0	0	0	0	2	0	0	2	0	0	.111	.111
Burnett, A.J., Fla.	R	.118	7	17	1	2	2	0	0	0	0	0	0	0	10	0	0	.118	.118
Byrd, Paul, Phi.	R	.127	32	55	6	7	7	0	0	0	4	11	0	5	11	0	0	.127	.200
Carlyle, Buddy, S.D.	L	.222	7	9	1	2	2	0	0	0	1	0	0	2	3	0	0	.222	.364
Clement, Matt, S.D.	R	.077	31	52	7	4	4	0	0	0	1	6	0	4	28	0	0	.077	.143
Cordova, Francisco, Pit.	R	.163	27	49	2	8	8	0	0	0	2	5	0	2	15	0	0	.163	.196
Daal, Omar, Ari.	L	.232	32	69	8	16	18	2	0	0	4	6	0	2	10	0	0	.261	.254
Dempster, Ryan, Fla.	R	.102	26	49	5	5	6	1	0	0	2	1	0	1	22	0	0	.122	.120
Dotel, Octavio, N.Y.	R	.125	19	24	2	3	3	0	0	0	1	1	0	4	17	0	0	.125	.276
Dreifort, Darren, L.A.	R	.210	30	62	7	13	20	4	0	1	9	4	0	3	23	1	0	.323	.246
Eldred, Cal, Mil.	R	.083	23	24	3	2	3	1	0	0	2	4	0	2	13	0	0	.125	.154
Estes, Shawn, S.F.	B	.164	42	61	8	10	14	4	0	0	5	10	0	3	21	0	1	.230	.215
Farnsworth, Kyle, Chi.	R	.086	27	35	3	3	3	0	0	0	2	6	0	2	10	0	0	.086	.158
Fernandez, Alex, Fla.	R	.233	25	43	3	10	20	1	0	3	7	3	0	0	5	0	0	.465	.233
Gagne, Eric, L.A.	R	.200	5	10	1	2	2	0	0	0	1	0	0	0	3	0	0	.200	.200
Gardner, Mark, S.F.	R	.103	39	39	2	4	7	0	0	1	3	6	0	3	15	0	0	.179	.167
Glavine, Tom, Atl.	L	.138	36	65	3	9	10	1	0	0	4	7	0	5	17	0	0	.154	.200
Guzman, Juan, Cin.	R	.115	12	26	1	3	3	0	0	0	2	3	0	1	10	0	0	.115	.148
Hackman, Luther, Col.	R	.200	5	5	1	1	1	0	0	0	0	0	0	0	3	0	0	.200	.200
Hampton, Mike, Hou.	R	.311	34	74	10	23	32	3	3	0	10	5	1	7	18	0	0	.432	.373
Harnisch, Pete, Cin.	B	.152	33	66	6	10	17	4	0	1	5	8	0	1	20	0	0	.258	.164
Hermanson, Dustin, Mon.	R	.047	34	64	1	3	3	0	0	0	2	8	0	3	39	0	0	.047	.090
Hernandez, L., Fla.-S.F.	R	.270	31	63	6	17	25	2	0	2	8	7	1	1	10	0	0	.397	.288
Hershiser, Orel, N.Y.	R	.145	32	62	3	9	10	1	0	0	3	3	2	1	18	1	0	.161	.154
Hitchcock, Sterling, S.D.	L	.082	33	61	4	5	5	0	0	0	0	7	0	3	34	0	0	.082	.125
Holt, Chris, Hou.	R	.067	32	45	3	3	3	0	0	0	2	7	0	3	14	0	0	.067	.125
Jimenez, Jose, St.L.	R	.094	31	53	5	5	7	0	1	0	2	2	0	0	22	0	0	.132	.094
Johnson, Randy, Ari.	R	.124	35	97	1	12	16	4	0	0	6	7	0	0	46	0	0	.165	.124
Jones, Bobby, N.Y.	R	.313	12	16	1	5	8	0	0	1	1	1	0	0	4	0	0	.500	.313
Jones, Bobby, Col.	R	.148	30	27	3	4	5	1	0	0	4	4	1	2	7	0	0	.185	.200
Judd, Mike, L.A.	R	.000	7	5	0	0	0	0	0	0	0	3	0	1	1	0	0	.000	.167
Karl, Scott, Mil.	L	.183	33	60	5	11	19	2	0	2	7	12	1	3	17	0	0	.317	.219
Kile, Darryl, Col.	R	.135	32	52	3	7	7	0	0	0	4	8	0	4	20	0	0	.135	.196
Leiter, Al, N.Y.	L	.105	32	57	1	6	8	2	0	0	5	11	0	2	29	0	0	.140	.136
Lieber, Jon, Chi.	L	.121	31	58	8	7	8	1	0	0	2	7	1	5	23	0	0	.138	.188
Lima, Jose, Hou.	R	.080	36	75	4	6	6	0	0	0	2	13	0	3	24	0	0	.080	.115
Loewer, Carlton, Phi.	R	.227	20	22	0	5	5	0	0	0	1	2	0	1	9	0	0	.227	.261
Lorraine, Andrew, Chi.	L	.133	12	15	1	2	3	1	0	0	0	4	0	1	9	0	0	.200	.188
Luebbers, Larry, St.L.	R	.125	8	16	1	2	2	0	0	0	0	1	0	1	2	0	0	.125	.176
Maddux, Greg, Atl.	R	.172	33	64	7	11	20	1	1	2	7	13	0	1	18	0	0	.313	.197
McNichol, Brian, Chi.	L	.000	4	2	0	0	0	0	0	0	0	1	0	0	1	0	0	.000	.000
Meadows, Brian, Fla.	R	.140	31	50	6	7	10	3	0	0	1	7	0	2	21	0	0	.200	.173
Mercker, Kent, St.L.	L	.179	26	28	5	5	6	1	0	0	2	4	0	2	10	0	0	.214	.233
Millwood, Kevin, Atl.	R	.154	33	78	4	12	17	2	0	1	6	6	0	2	29	0	0	.218	.175
Mulholland, Terry, Chi.-Atl.	R	.104	42	48	2	5	5	0	0	0	3	5	0	2	21	0	0	.104	.140
Nathan, Joe, S.F.	R	.179	19	28	1	5	6	1	0	0	1	5	0	2	6	0	0	.214	.233
Neagle, Denny, Cin.	L	.162	20	37	1	6	7	1	0	0	2	5	0	1	9	0	0	.189	.184
Nomo, Hideo, Mil.	R	.214	29	56	3	12	16	2	1	0	5	7	0	1	22	0	0	.286	.228
Ogea, Chad, Phi.	R	.091	36	44	1	4	4	0	0	0	0	7	0	4	25	0	0	.091	.167
Oliver, Darren, St.L.	R	.274	35	73	7	20	24	4	0	0	6	8	0	3	23	0	0	.329	.303
Ortiz, Russ, S.F.	R	.197	33	71	7	14	19	2	0	1	8	7	0	3	17	0	0	.268	.230
Osborne, Donovan, St.L.	B	.100	6	10	1	1	2	1	0	0	0	1	0	0	2	0	0	.200	.100
Park, Chan Ho, L.A.	R	.153	33	59	4	9	11	2	0	0	6	6	2	2	26	0	0	.186	.175
Parris, Steve, Cin.	R	.158	22	38	1	6	6	0	0	0	4	5	0	0	11	0	0	.158	.158
Pavano, Carl, Mon.	R	.061	19	33	1	2	2	0	0	0	2	5	0	1	14	0	0	.061	.088
Perez, Carlos, L.A.	L	.296	17	27	2	8	13	2	0	1	2	3	0	2	8	0	0	.481	.345
Perez, Odalis, Atl.	L	.133	18	30	1	4	4	0	0	0	3	4	0	0	10	0	0	.133	.133
Person, Robert, Phi.	R	.073	31	41	3	3	3	0	0	0	1	4	0	1	23	0	0	.073	.116
Peters, Chris, Pit.	L	.273	19	22	5	6	6	0	0	0	1	1	0	2	10	1	0	.273	.333
Peterson, Kyle, Mil.	L	.136	17	22	2	3	3	0	0	0	1	2	0	1	9	0	0	.136	.174
Powell, Jeremy, Mon.	R	.133	17	30	2	4	5	1	0	0	0	1	0	3	8	0	0	.167	.212
Pulsipher, Bill, Mil.	L	.143	19	21	1	3	3	0	0	0	0	8	0	0	14	0	0	.143	.143
Reed, Rick, N.Y.	R	.244	27	45	2	11	13	2	0	0	5	8	0	1	14	0	0	.289	.261
Reynolds, Shane, Hou.	R	.167	35	66	4	11	16	2	0	1	14	17	1	2	27	0	0	.242	.188
Reynoso, Armando, Ari.	R	.163	31	49	3	8	10	2	0	0	2	8	0	1	26	0	0	.204	.180
Ritchie, Todd, Pit.	R	.151	29	53	3	8	9	1	0	0	1	8	0	1	16	0	0	.170	.167
Rogers, Kenny, N.Y.	L	.120	12	25	2	3	3	0	0	0	1	3	0	2	10	0	0	.120	.185

National League starting pitchers (batting)

Name/Team	B	BA	G	AB	R	H	TB	2B	3B	HR	RBI	SH	SF	BB	SO	SB	CS	SLG	OBA
Rueter, Kirk, S.F.	L	.155	33	58	6	9	11	2	0	0	5	8	1	3	6	0	0	.190	.194
Schilling, Curt, Phi.	R	.100	24	50	5	5	8	1	1	0	3	9	0	7	28	0	0	.160	.211
Schmidt, Jason, Pit.	R	.083	33	60	2	5	5	0	0	0	1	12	0	5	33	0	0	.083	.154
Schourek, Pete, Pit.	L	.000	30	25	1	0	0	0	0	0	1	3	0	3	13	0	0	.000	.107
Shumaker, Anthony, Phi.	L	.200	8	5	0	1	1	0	0	0	0	0	0	1	3	0	0	.200	.333
Smith, Dan, Mon.	R	.083	20	24	3	2	2	0	0	0	1	3	0	3	15	0	0	.083	.185
Smoltz, John, Atl.	R	.274	29	62	11	17	24	4	0	1	7	4	0	5	28	0	0	.387	.338
Spencer, Stan, S.D.	R	.000	9	10	0	0	0	0	0	0	0	1	0	0	3	0	0	.000	.091
Spoljaric, Paul, Phi.	R	.000	5	2	0	0	0	0	0	0	0	2	0	0	0	0	0	.000	.000
Springer, Dennis, Fla.	R	.120	38	50	2	6	7	1	0	0	2	3	1	0	17	0	0	.140	.118
Stephenson, Garrett, St.L.	R	.074	18	27	1	2	3	1	0	0	0	3	0	0	5	0	0	.111	.074
Stottlemyre, Todd, Ari.	L	.125	17	32	0	4	5	1	0	0	3	0	0	5	12	0	0	.156	.243
Tapani, Kevin, Chi.	R	.051	23	39	1	2	3	1	0	0	3	5	0	3	21	0	0	.077	.119
Thompson, Mark, St.L.	R	.000	5	8	0	0	0	0	0	0	0	1	0	0	6	0	0	.000	.000
Thomson, John, Col.	R	.167	14	18	1	3	4	1	0	0	1	0	0	2	7	0	0	.222	.250
Thurman, Mike, Mon.	R	.025	29	40	1	1	1	0	0	0	0	4	0	1	31	0	0	.025	.071
Tomko, Brett, Cin.	R	.213	33	47	3	10	12	2	0	0	2	8	0	3	17	0	0	.255	.260
Trachsel, Steve, Chi.	R	.111	34	63	4	7	8	1	0	0	0	7	0	1	25	1	0	.127	.125
Valdes, Ismael, L.A.	R	.086	32	58	1	5	5	0	0	0	2	10	0	1	18	1	0	.086	.102
Vazquez, Javier, Mon.	R	.286	26	42	4	12	14	2	0	0	5	8	0	3	8	0	0	.333	.333
Villone, Ron, Cin.	L	.070	29	43	0	3	3	0	0	0	0	5	0	1	10	0	0	.070	.091
Williams, Woody, S.D.	R	.178	34	73	4	13	17	4	0	0	6	4	1	2	19	0	1	.233	.197
Williams, Jeff, L.A.	R	.200	5	5	2	1	1	0	0	0	0	1	0	1	4	0	0	.200	.333
Wolf, Randy, Phi.	L	.233	22	30	2	7	8	1	0	0	0	7	0	2	8	0	0	.267	.281
Woodall, Brad, Chi.	B	.500	6	2	0	1	1	0	0	0	0	0	0	2	0	0	0	.500	.750
Woodard, Steve, Mil.	L	.132	31	53	5	7	8	1	0	0	0	10	0	6	16	0	0	.151	.220
Wright, Jamey, Col.	R	.125	16	32	0	4	5	1	0	0	2	3	0	0	13	0	0	.156	.125
Yoshii, Masato, N.Y.	R	.164	31	55	1	9	9	0	0	0	2	6	0	0	16	0	1	.164	.164

American League relief pitchers

Name/Team	T	ERA	W	L	G	GS	CG	SHO	GF	SV	IP	H	R	ER	HR	BB	SO	WP	BA	RV
Abbott, Paul, Sea.	R	3.10	6	2	25	7	0	0	8	0	72.2	50	31	25	9	32	68	2	.193	11
Aguilera, Rick, Min.	R	1.27	3	1	17	0	0	0	16	6	21.1	10	3	3	2	2	13	1	.135	12
Aldred, Scott, T.B.	L	5.18	3	2	37	0	0	0	9	0	24.1	26	15	14	1	14	22	1	.274	NV
Alvarez, Juan, Ana.	L	3.00	0	1	8	0	0	0	1	0	3.0	1	1	1	0	4	4	1	.111	NV
Anderson, Matt, Det.	R	5.68	2	1	37	0	0	0	9	0	38.0	33	27	24	8	35	32	3	.232	NV
Assenmacher, Paul, Cle.	L	8.18	2	1	55	0	0	0	8	0	33.0	50	32	30	6	17	29	1	.347	NV
Bale, John, Tor.	L	13.50	0	0	1	0	0	0	0	0	2.0	2	3	3	1	2	4	0	.250	NV
Barber, Brian, K.C.	R	9.64	1	3	8	3	0	0	1	1	18.2	31	20	20	6	10	7	0	.383	NV
Beck, Rod, Bos.	R	1.93	0	1	12	0	0	0	8	3	14.0	9	3	3	0	5	12	0	.184	4
Blair, Willie, Det.	R	6.85	3	11	39	16	0	0	8	0	134.0	169	107	102	29	44	82	5	.308	NV
Boggs, Wade, T.B.	R	6.75	0	0	1	0	0	0	1	0	1.1	3	1	1	0	0	1	0	.429	NV
Bones, Ricky, Bal.	R	5.98	0	3	30	2	0	0	7	0	43.2	59	29	29	7	19	26	3	.322	NV
Bradford, Chad, Chi.	R	19.64	0	0	3	0	0	0	0	0	3.2	9	8	8	1	5	0	1	.474	NV
Brocail, Doug, Det.	R	2.52	4	4	70	0	0	0	22	2	82.0	60	23	23	7	25	78	4	.206	15
Brower, Jim, Cle.	R	4.56	3	1	9	2	0	0	1	0	25.2	27	13	13	8	10	18	0	.270	2
Brunson, Will, Det.	L	6.00	1	0	17	0	0	0	1	0	12.0	18	9	8	3	6	9	0	.367	NV
Buddie, Mike, N.Y.	R	4.50	0	0	2	0	0	0	0	0	2.0	3	1	1	1	0	1	0	.333	NV
Bullinger, Kirk, Bos.	R	4.50	0	0	4	0	0	0	0	0	2.0	2	1	1	0	2	0	0	.286	NV
Bunch, Melvin, Sea.	R	11.70	0	0	5	1	0	0	4	0	10.0	20	13	13	3	7	4	0	.426	NV
Byrdak, Tim, K.C.	L	7.66	0	3	33	0	0	0	5	1	24.2	32	24	21	5	20	17	3	.308	NV
Carmona, Rafael, Sea.	R	7.94	1	0	9	0	0	0	3	0	11.1	13	11	10	3	9	0	0	.409	NV
Carrasco, Hector, Min.	R	4.96	2	3	39	0	0	0	10	1	49.0	48	29	27	3	18	35	4	.261	1
Carter, Lance, K.C.	R	5.06	0	1	6	0	0	0	3	0	5.1	3	3	3	2	3	3	0	.167	NV
Castillo, Carlos, Chi.	R	5.71	2	2	18	2	0	0	6	0	41.0	45	26	26	10	14	23	0	.274	NV
Charlton, Norm, T.B.	L	4.44	2	3	42	0	0	0	9	0	50.2	49	29	25	4	36	45	4	.257	NV
Cloude, Ken, Sea.	R	7.96	4	4	31	6	0	0	8	1	72.1	106	67	64	10	46	35	8	.346	NV
Coppinger, Rocky, Bal.	R	8.31	0	1	11	2	0	0	7	0	21.2	25	21	20	8	19	17	0	.294	NV
Cordero, Francisco, Det.	R	3.32	2	2	20	0	0	0	4	0	19.0	19	7	7	2	18	19	1	.284	NV
Cormier, Rheal, Bos.	L	3.69	2	0	60	0	0	0	7	0	63.1	61	34	26	4	18	39	1	.246	4
Corsi, Jim, Bos.-Bal.	R	4.34	1	3	36	0	0	0	8	0	37.1	40	19	18	6	20	22	0	.288	NV
Crabtree, Tim, Tex.	R	3.46	5	1	68	0	0	0	21	0	65.0	71	26	25	4	18	54	5	.280	6
Cruz, Nelson, Det.	R	5.67	2	5	29	6	0	0	10	0	66.2	74	44	42	11	23	46	2	.281	NV
Davenport, Joe, Chi.	R	0.00	0	0	3	0	0	0	2	0	1.2	1	0	0	0	2	0	0	.200	NV
Davey, Tom, Tor.-Sea.	R	4.71	2	1	45	0	0	0	15	1	65.0	62	41	34	5	40	59	6	.250	NV
Davis, Doug, Tex.	L	33.75	0	0	2	0	0	0	0	0	2.2	12	10	10	3	0	3	0	.600	NV
DeLucia, Rich, Cle.	R	6.75	0	1	6	0	0	0	2	0	9.1	13	7	7	4	9	7	1	.317	NV
DePaula, Sean, Cle.	R	4.63	0	0	11	0	0	0	4	0	11.2	8	6	6	0	3	18	0	.200	1

American League relief pitchers

Name/Team	T	ERA	W	L	G	GS	CG	SHO	GF	SV	IP	H	R	ER	HR	BB	SO	WP	BA	RV
Durbin, Chad, K.C.	R	0.00	0	0	1	0	0	0	0	0	2.1	1	0	0	0	1	3	1	.125	NV
Duvall, Mike, T.B.	L	4.05	1	1	40	0	0	0	7	0	40.0	46	21	18	5	27	18	4	.293	NV
Erdos, Todd, N.Y.	R	3.86	0	0	4	0	0	0	1	0	7.0	5	4	3	2	4	4	1	.192	NV
Eyre, Scott, Chi.	L	7.56	1	1	21	0	0	0	8	0	25.0	38	22	21	6	15	17	1	.339	NV
Falkenborg, Brian, Bal.	R	0.00	0	0	2	0	0	0	0	0	3.0	2	0	0	0	2	1	0	.200	NV
Fetters, Mike, Bal.	R	5.81	1	0	27	0	0	0	10	0	31.0	35	23	20	5	22	22	1	.278	NV
Florie, Bryce, Det.-Bos.	R	4.65	4	1	41	5	0	0	10	0	81.1	94	50	42	8	35	65	8	.288	NV
Fossas, Tony, N.Y.	L	36.00	0	0	5	0	0	0	0	0	1.0	6	4	4	1	1	0	0	.667	NV
Foulke, Keith, Chi.	R	2.22	3	3	67	0	0	0	31	9	105.1	72	28	26	11	21	123	1	.188	25
Franklin, Ryan, Sea.	R	4.76	0	0	6	0	0	0	2	0	11.1	10	6	6	2	8	6	0	.238	NV
Frascatore, John, Tor.	R	3.41	7	1	33	0	0	0	14	1	37.0	42	16	14	5	9	22	5	.292	8
Fussell, Chris, K.C.	R	7.39	0	5	17	8	0	0	3	2	56.0	72	51	46	9	36	37	6	.329	NV
Fyhrie, Mike, Ana.	R	5.05	0	4	16	7	0	0	5	0	51.2	61	32	29	8	21	26	0	.286	NV
Gaillard, Eddie, T.B.	R	2.08	1	0	8	0	0	0	1	0	8.2	12	9	2	1	4	7	0	.324	NV
Garces, Rich, Bos.	R	1.55	5	1	30	0	0	0	4	2	40.2	25	9	7	1	18	33	0	.171	12
Glover, Gary, Tor.	R	0.00	0	0	1	0	0	0	1	0	1.0	0	0	0	0	1	0	0	.000	NV
Gordon, Tom, Bos.	R	5.60	0	2	21	0	0	0	15	11	17.2	17	11	11	2	12	24	0	.246	4
Grimsley, Jason, N.Y.	R	3.60	7	2	55	0	0	0	25	1	75.0	66	39	30	7	40	49	8	.231	7
Groom, Buddy, Oak.	L	5.09	3	2	76	0	0	0	6	0	46.0	48	29	26	1	18	32	2	.274	NV
Gross, Kip, Bos.	R	7.82	0	2	11	1	0	0	7	0	12.2	15	11	11	3	8	9	1	.294	NV
Guardado, Eddie, Min.	L	4.50	2	5	63	0	0	0	13	2	48.0	37	24	24	6	25	50	0	.222	3
Gunderson, Eric, Tex.	L	7.20	0	0	11	0	0	0	3	0	10.0	20	8	8	1	2	6	3	.417	NV
Guthrie, Mark, Bos.	L	5.83	1	1	46	0	0	0	15	2	46.1	50	32	30	9	20	36	2	.275	NV
Haney, Chris, Cle.	L	4.69	0	2	13	4	0	0	1	0	40.1	43	22	21	3	16	22	0	.270	NV
Harikkala, Tim, Bos.	R	6.23	1	1	7	0	0	0	2	0	13.0	15	9	9	0	6	7	1	.306	NV
Harville, Chad, Oak.	R	6.91	0	2	15	0	0	0	8	0	14.1	18	11	11	2	10	15	3	.310	NV
Hasegawa, S., Ana.	R	4.91	4	6	64	1	0	0	26	2	77.0	80	45	42	14	34	44	4	.276	NV
Hernandez, Roberto, T.B.	R	3.07	2	3	72	0	0	0	66	43	73.1	68	27	25	1	33	69	3	.244	28
Hiljus, Erik, Det.	R	5.19	0	0	6	0	0	0	0	0	8.2	7	5	5	2	5	1	0	.241	NV
Hinchliffe, Brett, Sea.	R	8.80	0	4	11	4	0	0	2	0	30.2	41	31	30	10	21	14	2	.323	NV
Holtz, Mike, Ana.	L	8.06	2	3	28	0	0	0	9	0	22.1	26	20	20	3	15	17	3	.295	NV
Howry, Bobby, Chi.	R	3.59	5	3	69	0	0	0	54	28	67.2	58	34	27	8	38	80	3	.229	21
Hudek, John, Tor.	R	12.27	0	0	3	0	0	0	1	0	3.2	8	5	5	1	1	2	0	.471	NV
Isringhausen, Jason, Oak.	R	2.13	0	1	20	0	0	0	18	8	25.1	21	6	6	2	12	20	2	.223	6
Jackson, Mike, Cle.	R	4.06	3	4	72	0	0	0	65	39	68.2	60	32	31	11	26	55	0	.232	26
Jarvis, Kevin, Oak.	R	11.57	0	1	4	1	0	0	0	0	14.0	28	19	18	6	6	11	0	.418	NV
Johns, Doug, Bal.	L	4.47	6	4	32	5	0	0	2	0	86.2	81	45	43	9	25	50	1	.248	6
Johnson, Jonathan, Tex.	R	15.00	0	0	1	0	0	0	0	0	3.0	9	5	5	0	2	3	0	.529	NV
Jones, Doug, Oak.	R	3.55	5	5	70	0	0	0	35	10	104.0	106	43	41	10	24	63	2	.267	14
Jones, Todd, Det.	R	3.80	4	4	65	0	0	0	62	30	66.1	64	30	28	7	35	64	2	.259	19
Kamieniecki, Scott, Bal.	R	4.95	2	4	43	3	0	0	18	2	56.1	52	32	31	4	29	39	4	.250	NV
Karsay, Steve, Cle.	R	2.97	10	2	50	3	0	0	13	1	78.2	71	29	26	6	30	68	5	.247	14
Kida, Masao, Det.	R	6.26	1	0	49	0	0	0	21	1	64.2	73	48	45	6	30	50	7	.289	NV
Koch, Billy, Tor.	R	3.39	0	5	56	0	0	0	48	31	63.2	55	26	24	5	30	57	0	.235	19
Kolb, Danny, Tex.	R	4.65	2	1	16	0	0	0	6	0	31.0	33	18	16	2	15	15	2	.268	NV
Kubinski, Tim, Oak.	L	5.84	0	0	14	0	0	0	4	0	12.1	14	8	8	3	5	7	0	.280	NV
Langston, Mark, Cle.	L	5.25	1	2	25	5	0	0	2	0	61.2	69	40	36	9	29	43	2	.287	NV
Lee, Corey, Tex.	L	27.00	0	1	1	0	0	0	1	0	1.0	2	3	3	1	1	0	0	.400	NV
Leiter, Mark, Sea.	R	6.75	0	0	2	0	0	0	0	0	1.1	2	1	1	0	0	1	0	.333	NV
Levine, Alan, Ana.	R	3.39	1	1	50	1	0	0	12	0	85.0	76	40	32	13	29	37	3	.247	5
Lidle, Cory, T.B.	R	7.20	1	0	5	1	0	0	1	0	5.0	8	4	4	0	2	4	0	.364	NV
Lira, Felipe, Det.	R	10.80	0	0	2	0	0	0	0	0	3.1	7	5	4	2	2	3	0	.389	NV
Lloyd, Graeme, Tor.	L	3.62	5	3	74	0	0	0	25	3	72.0	68	36	29	11	23	47	1	.250	9
Lopez, Albie, T.B.	R	4.64	3	2	51	0	0	0	14	1	64.0	64	40	33	8	24	37	3	.263	1
Lowe, Derek, Bos.	R	2.63	6	3	74	0	0	0	32	15	109.1	84	35	32	7	25	80	1	.208	28
Lowe, Sean, Chi.	R	3.67	4	1	64	0	0	0	13	0	95.2	90	39	39	10	46	62	4	.262	3
Ludwick, Eric, Tor.	R	27.00	0	0	1	0	0	0	0	0	1.0	3	3	3	0	2	0	0	.500	NV
Lundquist, David, Chi.	R	8.59	1	1	17	0	0	0	7	0	22.0	28	21	21	3	12	18	0	.315	NV
Magnante, Mike, Ana.	L	3.38	5	2	53	0	0	0	13	0	69.1	68	30	26	2	29	44	3	.262	5
Mahay, Ron, Oak.	L	1.86	2	0	6	1	0	0	2	1	19.1	8	4	4	2	3	15	0	.123	7
Marte, Damaso, Sea.	L	9.35	0	1	5	0	0	0	2	0	8.2	16	9	9	3	6	3	0	.390	NV
Martin, Tom, Cle.	L	8.68	0	1	6	0	0	0	0	0	9.1	13	9	9	2	3	8	0	.325	NV
Mathews, Terry, K.C.	R	4.38	2	1	24	1	0	0	7	1	39.0	44	21	19	4	17	19	0	.289	NV
Mathews, T. j., Oak.	R	3.81	9	5	50	0	0	0	15	3	59.0	46	28	25	9	20	42	2	.215	14
Mays, Joe, Min.	R	4.37	6	11	49	20	2	1	8	0	171.0	179	92	83	24	67	115	6	.270	1
McMichael, Greg, Oak.	R	5.40	0	0	17	0	0	0	4	0	15.0	15	9	9	3	12	3	0	.283	NV
Mecir, Jim, T.B.	R	2.61	0	1	17	0	0	0	3	0	20.2	15	7	6	0	14	15	0	.203	1
Mendoza, Ramiro, N.Y.	R	4.29	9	9	53	6	0	0	15	3	123.2	141	68	59	13	27	80	2	.284	9
Mesa, Jose, Sea.	R	4.98	3	6	68	0	0	0	60	33	68.2	84	42	38	11	40	42	7	.305	12
Miller, Travis, Min.	L	2.72	2	2	52	0	0	0	12	0	49.2	55	19	15	3	16	40	6	.284	3

American League relief pitchers

Name/Team	T	ERA	W	L	G	GS	CG	SHO	GF	SV	IP	H	R	ER	HR	BB	SO	WP	BA	RV
Mintz, Steve, Ana.	R	3.60	0	0	3	0	0	0	2	0	5.0	8	2	2	1	2	2	0	.381	NV
Molina, Gabe, Bal.	R	6.65	1	2	20	0	0	0	7	0	23.0	22	19	17	4	16	14	4	.256	NV
Montgomery, Jeff, K.C.	R	6.84	1	4	49	0	0	0	36	12	51.1	72	40	39	7	21	27	1	.343	NV
Moreno, Orber, K.C.	R	5.63	0	0	7	0	0	0	3	0	8.0	4	5	5	1	6	7	0	.143	NV
Morman, Alvin, K.C.	L	4.05	2	4	49	0	0	0	2	1	53.1	66	27	24	6	23	31	1	.307	NV
Morris, Jim, T.B.	L	5.79	0	0	5	0	0	0	3	0	4.2	3	3	3	1	2	3	0	.167	NV
Munoz, Mike, Tex.	L	3.93	2	1	56	0	0	0	11	1	52.2	52	24	23	5	18	27	2	.263	3
Munro, Peter, Tor.	R	6.02	0	2	31	2	0	0	9	0	55.1	70	38	37	6	23	38	3	.318	NV
Murray, Dan, K.C.	R	6.48	0	0	4	0	0	0	0	0	8.1	9	8	6	4	4	8	0	.265	NV
Naulty, Dan, N.Y.	R	4.38	1	0	33	0	0	0	20	0	49.1	40	24	24	8	22	25	2	.225	1
Nelson, Jeff, N.Y.	R	4.15	2	1	39	0	0	0	8	1	30.1	27	14	14	2	22	35	2	.245	NV
Newman, Alan, T.B.	R	6.89	2	2	18	0	0	0	5	0	15.2	22	12	12	2	9	20	2	.333	NV
Nitkowski, C. J., Det.	L	4.30	4	5	68	7	0	0	7	0	81.2	63	44	39	11	45	66	4	.213	3
Ohka, Tomokazu, Bos.	R	6.23	1	2	8	2	0	0	3	0	13.0	21	12	9	2	6	8	0	.362	NV
Orosco, Jesse, Bal.	L	5.34	0	2	65	0	0	0	12	1	32.0	28	21	19	5	20	35	2	.239	NV
Paniagua, Jose, Sea.	R	4.06	6	11	59	0	0	0	16	3	77.2	75	37	35	5	52	74	6	.264	2
Patterson, Danny, Tex.	R	5.67	2	0	53	0	0	0	18	0	60.1	77	38	38	5	19	43	2	.304	NV
Pena, Jesus, Chi.	L	5.31	0	0	26	0	0	0	1	0	20.1	21	15	12	3	23	20	3	.259	NV
Percival, Troy, Ana.	R	3.79	4	6	60	0	0	0	50	31	57.0	38	24	24	9	22	58	3	.186	26
Perisho, Matt, Tex.	L	2.61	0	0	4	1	0	0	3	0	10.1	8	3	3	0	2	17	1	.211	1
Perkins, Dan, Min.	R	6.54	1	7	29	12	0	0	7	0	86.2	117	69	63	14	43	44	6	.326	NV
Person, Robert, Tor.	R	9.82	0	2	11	0	0	0	7	2	11.0	9	12	12	1	15	12	2	.231	NV
Petkovsek, Mark, Ana.	R	3.47	10	4	64	0	0	0	18	1	83.0	85	37	32	6	21	43	3	.269	13
Pisciotta, Marc, K.C.	R	8.64	0	2	8	0	0	0	3	0	8.1	9	8	8	1	10	3	1	.281	NV
Plesac, Dan, Tor.	L	8.34	0	3	30	0	0	0	5	0	22.2	28	21	21	4	9	26	2	.308	NV
Poole, Jim, Cle.	L	18.00	1	0	3	0	0	0	0	0	1.0	2	2	2	0	3	0	0	.667	NV
Pote, Lou, Ana.	R	2.15	1	1	20	0	0	0	10	3	29.1	23	9	7	1	12	20	1	.219	6
Quantrill, Paul, Tor.	R	3.33	3	2	41	0	0	0	13	0	48.2	53	19	18	5	17	28	0	.282	3
Radlosky, Rob, Min.	R	12.46	0	1	7	0	0	0	2	0	8.2	15	12	12	7	4	3	1	.375	NV
Rakers, Jason, Cle.	R	4.50	0	0	1	0	0	0	0	0	2.0	2	1	1	1	1	0	0	.250	NV
Rath, Gary, Min.	L	11.57	0	1	5	1	0	0	1	0	4.2	6	6	6	1	5	1	2	.300	NV
Ray, Ken, K.C.	R	8.74	1	0	13	0	0	0	4	0	11.1	23	12	11	2	6	0	0	.460	NV
Redman, Mark, Min.	L	8.53	1	0	5	1	0	0	0	0	12.2	17	13	12	3	7	11	0	.298	NV
Reed, Steve, Cle.	R	4.23	3	2	63	0	0	0	15	0	61.2	69	33	29	10	20	44	2	.285	1
Rekar, Bryan, T.B.	R	5.80	6	6	27	12	0	0	2	0	94.2	121	68	61	14	41	55	4	.313	NV
Reyes, Alberto, Bal.	R	4.85	2	3	27	0	0	0	6	0	29.2	23	16	16	4	16	28	1	.225	1
Rhodes, Arthur, Bal.	L	5.43	3	4	43	0	0	0	11	3	53.0	43	37	32	9	45	59	4	.221	NV
Rigby, Brad, Oak.-K.C.	R	5.06	4	6	49	0	0	0	11	0	83.2	102	51	47	11	31	36	6	.303	NV
Rincon, Ricardo, Cle.	L	4.43	2	3	59	0	0	0	14	0	44.2	41	22	22	6	24	30	2	.248	NV
Riske, David, Cle.	R	8.36	1	1	12	0	0	0	3	0	14.0	20	15	13	2	6	16	0	.333	NV
Rivera, Mariano, N.Y.	R	1.83	4	3	66	0	0	0	63	45	69.0	43	15	14	2	18	52	2	.176	42
Rizzo, Todd, Cle.	R	6.75	0	2	3	0	0	0	2	0	1.1	4	2	1	0	3	2	0	.500	NV
Roberts, Willis, Det.	R	13.50	0	0	1	0	0	0	0	0	1.1	3	4	2	0	0	0	0	.500	NV
Rodriguez, Frank, Sea.	R	5.65	2	4	28	5	0	0	10	3	73.1	94	47	46	11	30	47	1	.314	NV
Rodriguez, Nerio, Tor.	R	13.50	0	1	2	0	0	0	1	0	2.0	2	3	3	2	2	2	0	.250	NV
Rojas, Mel, Det.	R	22.74	0	0	5	0	0	0	2	0	6.1	12	16	16	3	4	6	0	.387	NV
Romano, Mike, Tor.	R	11.81	0	0	3	0	0	0	1	0	5.1	8	8	7	1	5	3	1	.364	NV
Romero, J.C., Min.	L	3.72	0	0	5	0	0	0	3	0	9.2	13	4	4	0	0	4	0	.333	NV
Runyan, Sean, Det.	L	3.38	0	1	12	0	0	0	2	0	10.2	9	4	4	2	3	6	2	.237	1
Rusch, Glendon, K.C.	L	15.75	0	1	3	0	0	0	1	0	4.0	7	7	7	1	3	4	0	.368	NV
Ryan, B.J., Bal.	L	2.95	1	0	13	0	0	0	3	0	18.1	9	6	6	0	12	28	1	.150	2
Sampson, Benj, Min.	L	8.11	3	2	30	4	0	0	2	0	71.0	107	65	64	17	34	56	2	.351	NV
Santana, Julio, T.B.	R	7.32	1	4	22	5	0	0	7	0	55.1	66	49	45	10	32	34	0	.300	NV
Santana, Marino, Bos.	R	15.75	0	0	3	0	0	0	1	0	4.0	8	7	7	3	3	4	1	.444	NV
Santiago, Jose, K.C.	R	3.42	3	4	34	0	0	0	15	2	47.1	46	23	18	7	14	15	2	.251	6
Scheffer, Aaron, Sea.	R	1.93	0	0	4	0	0	0	3	0	4.2	6	5	1	0	3	4	0	.353	NV
Schoeneweis, Scott, Ana.	L	5.49	1	1	30	0	0	0	6	0	39.1	47	27	24	4	14	22	1	.294	NV
Service, Scott, K.C.	R	6.09	5	5	68	0	0	0	29	6	75.1	87	51	51	13	42	68	3	.294	NV
Shuey, Paul, Cle.	R	3.53	8	5	72	0	0	0	28	6	81.2	68	37	32	8	40	103	8	.223	13
Simas, Bill, Chi.	R	3.75	6	3	70	0	0	0	21	2	72.0	73	36	30	6	32	41	4	.263	6
Sinclair, Steve, Tor.-Sea.	L	6.52	0	1	21	0	0	0	6	0	19.1	22	16	14	5	14	18	0	.278	NV
Slocumb, Heathcliff, Bal.	R	12.46	0	0	10	0	0	0	7	0	8.2	15	12	12	2	9	12	1	.395	NV
Sparks, Jeff, T.B.	R	5.40	0	0	8	0	0	0	2	1	10.0	6	6	6	1	12	17	1	.171	NV
Spencer, Sean, Sea.	L	21.60	0	0	2	0	0	0	0	0	1.2	5	4	4	0	3	2	0	.556	NV
Spoljaric, Paul, Tor.	L	4.65	2	2	37	2	0	0	7	0	62.0	62	41	32	9	32	63	1	.258	NV
Spradlin, Jerry, Cle.	R	18.00	0	0	4	0	0	0	1	0	3.0	6	6	6	1	3	2	0	.400	NV
Stanton, Mike, N.Y.	L	4.33	2	2	73	1	0	0	10	0	62.1	71	30	30	5	18	59	2	.289	NV
Stark, Dennis, Sea.	R	9.95	0	0	5	0	0	0	2	0	6.1	10	8	7	0	4	4	0	.370	NV
Stevens, Dave, Cle.	R	10.00	0	0	5	0	0	0	0	0	9.0	10	10	10	1	8	6	1	.286	NV
Suzuki, Mac, Sea.-K.C.	R	6.79	2	5	38	13	0	0	6	0	110.0	124	92	83	16	64	68	11	.286	NV

American League relief pitchers

Name/Team	T	ERA	W	L	G	GS	CG	SHO	GF	SV	IP	H	R	ER	HR	BB	SO	WP	BA	RV
Tam, Jeff, Cle.	R	81.00	0	0	1	0	0	0	0	0	0.1	2	3	3	0	1	0	0	1.000	NV
Taylor, Billy, Oak.	R	3.98	1	5	43	0	0	0	38	26	43.0	48	23	19	3	14	38	1	.287	15
Tessmer, Jay, N.Y.	R	14.85	0	0	6	0	0	0	4	0	6.2	16	11	11	1	4	3	0	.444	NV
Timlin, Mike, Bal.	R	3.57	3	9	62	0	0	0	52	27	63.0	51	30	25	9	23	50	1	.221	22
Trombley, Mike, Min.	R	4.33	2	8	75	0	0	0	56	24	87.1	93	42	42	15	28	82	6	.272	14
Venafro, Mike, Tex.	L	3.29	3	2	65	0	0	0	11	0	68.1	63	29	25	4	22	37	0	.251	6
Vizcaino, Luis, Oak.	R	5.40	0	0	1	0	0	0	1	0	3.1	3	2	2	1	3	2	1	.231	NV
Wagner, Paul, Cle.	R	4.15	1	0	3	0	0	0	1	0	4.1	5	4	2	0	3	0	0	.263	NV
Wakefield, Tim, Bos.	R	5.08	6	11	49	17	0	0	28	15	140.0	146	93	79	19	72	104	1	.266	3
Wallace, Derek, K.C.	R	3.24	0	1	8	0	0	0	4	0	8.1	7	4	3	2	5	5	0	.259	NV
Ward, Bryan, Chi.	L	7.55	0	1	40	0	0	0	8	0	39.1	63	36	33	10	11	35	2	.368	NV
Wasdin, John, Bos.	R	4.12	8	3	45	0	0	0	17	2	74.1	66	38	34	14	18	57	2	.236	12
Watson, Allen, Sea.-N.Y.	L	2.89	4	1	24	0	0	0	8	0	37.1	36	17	12	8	13	32	2	.254	6
Weaver, Eric, Sea.	R	10.61	0	1	8	0	0	0	2	0	9.1	14	12	11	2	8	14	5	.318	NV
Wells, Bob, Min.	R	3.81	8	3	76	0	0	0	18	1	87.1	79	41	37	8	28	44	4	.245	11
Wengert, Don, K.C.	R	9.25	0	1	11	1	0	0	2	0	24.1	41	26	25	6	5	10	0	.376	NV
Wetteland, John, Tex.	R	3.68	4	4	62	0	0	0	59	43	66.0	67	30	27	9	19	60	0	.262	30
Whisenant, Matt, K.C.	L	6.35	4	4	48	0	0	0	21	1	39.2	40	28	28	4	26	27	1	.267	NV
White, Rick, T.B.	R	4.08	5	3	63	1	0	0	11	0	108.0	132	56	49	8	38	81	3	.304	NV
Williams, Todd, Sea.	R	4.66	0	0	13	0	0	0	7	0	9.2	11	5	5	1	7	7	0	.289	NV
Wolcott, Bob, Bos.	R	8.10	0	0	4	0	0	0	1	0	6.2	8	6	6	1	3	2	0	.333	NV
Worrell, Tim, Oak.	R	4.15	2	2	53	0	0	0	17	0	69.1	69	38	32	6	34	62	1	.256	NV
Yan, Esteban, T.B.	R	5.90	3	4	50	1	0	0	15	0	61.0	77	41	40	8	32	46	2	.326	NV
Yarnall, Ed, N.Y.	L	3.71	1	0	5	2	0	0	2	0	17.0	17	8	7	1	10	13	0	.254	NV
Zimmerman, Jeff, Tex.	R	2.36	9	3	65	0	0	0	14	3	87.2	50	24	23	9	23	67	2	.166	25
Zimmerman, Jordan, Sea.	L	7.87	0	0	12	0	0	0	2	0	8.0	14	8	7	0	4	3	1	.389	NV

American League starting pitchers

Name/Team	T	ERA	W	L	G	GS	CG	SHO	GF	SV	IP	H	R	ER	HR	BB	SO	WP	BA	RV
Alvarez, Wilson, T.B.	L	4.22	9	9	28	28	1	0	0	0	160.0	159	92	75	22	79	128	3	.260	3
Appier, Kevin, K.C.-Oak.	R	5.17	16	14	34	34	1	0	0	0	209.0	230	131	120	27	84	131	10	.279	1
Arrojo, Rolando, T.B.	R	5.18	7	12	24	24	2	0	0	0	140.2	162	84	81	23	60	107	2	.296	NV
Baldwin, James, Chi.	R	5.10	12	13	35	33	1	0	1	0	199.1	219	119	113	34	81	123	11	.278	NV
Belcher, Tim, Ana.	R	6.73	6	8	24	24	0	0	0	0	132.1	168	104	99	27	46	52	7	.315	NV
Borkowski, Dave, Det.	R	6.10	2	6	17	12	0	0	2	0	76.2	86	58	52	10	40	50	3	.283	NV
Burba, Dave, Cle.	R	4.25	15	9	34	34	1	0	0	0	220.0	211	113	104	30	96	174	13	.254	11
Burkett, John, Tex.	R	5.62	9	8	30	25	0	0	1	0	147.1	184	95	92	18	46	96	4	.307	NV
Callaway, Mickey, T.B.	R	7.45	1	2	5	4	0	0	0	0	19.1	30	20	16	2	14	11	1	.357	NV
Candiotti, Tom, Oak.-Cle.	R	7.32	4	6	18	13	0	0	1	0	71.1	86	64	58	14	30	41	13	.300	NV
Carpenter, Chris, Tor.	R	4.38	9	8	24	24	4	1	0	0	150.0	177	81	73	16	48	106	9	.294	2
Cho, Jin Ho, Bos.	R	5.72	2	3	9	7	0	0	1	0	39.1	45	26	25	7	8	16	0	.287	NV
Clark, Mark, Tex.	R	8.60	3	7	15	15	0	0	0	0	74.1	103	73	71	17	34	44	7	.329	NV
Clemens, Roger, N.Y.	R	4.60	14	10	30	30	1	1	0	0	187.2	185	101	96	20	90	163	8	.261	5
Colon, Bartolo, Cle.	R	3.95	18	5	32	32	1	1	0	0	205.0	185	97	90	24	76	161	4	.242	21
Cone, David, N.Y.	R	3.44	12	9	31	31	1	1	0	0	193.1	164	84	74	21	90	177	7	.229	16
Cooper, Brian, Ana.	R	4.88	1	1	5	5	0	0	0	0	27.2	23	15	15	3	18	15	0	.228	NV
Daneker, Pat, Chi.	R	4.20	0	0	3	2	0	0	1	0	15.0	14	8	7	1	6	5	0	.255	NV
Eiland, Dave, T.B.	R	5.60	4	8	21	15	0	0	0	0	80.1	98	59	50	8	27	53	2	.294	NV
Erickson, Scott, Bal.	R	4.81	15	12	34	34	6	3	0	0	230.1	244	127	123	27	99	106	10	.280	2
Escobar, Kelvim, Tor.	R	5.69	14	11	33	30	1	0	2	0	174.0	203	118	110	19	81	129	6	.293	NV
Fassero, Jeff, Sea.-Tex.	L	7.20	5	14	37	27	0	0	0	0	156.1	208	135	125	35	83	114	9	.318	NV
Finley, Chuck, Ana.	L	4.43	12	11	33	33	1	0	0	0	213.1	197	117	105	23	94	200	15	.246	8
Garcia, Freddy, Sea.	R	4.07	17	8	33	33	2	1	0	0	201.1	205	96	91	18	90	170	12	.263	11
Glynn, Ryan, Tex.	R	7.24	2	4	13	10	0	0	2	0	54.2	71	46	44	10	35	39	3	.316	NV
Gooden, Dwight, Cle.	R	6.26	3	4	26	22	0	0	0	0	115.0	127	90	80	18	67	88	4	.282	NV
Graterol, Beiker, Det.	R	15.75	0	1	1	1	0	0	0	0	4.0	4	7	7	3	4	2	0	.250	NV
Guzman, Juan, Bal.	R	4.18	5	9	21	21	1	1	0	0	122.2	124	63	57	18	65	95	7	.264	NV
Halama, John, Sea.	L	4.22	11	10	38	24	1	1	7	0	179.0	193	88	84	20	56	105	4	.281	8
Halladay, Roy, Tor.	R	3.92	8	7	36	18	1	1	2	1	149.1	156	76	65	19	79	82	6	.270	2
Hamilton, Joey, Tor.	R	6.52	7	8	22	18	0	0	1	0	98.0	118	73	71	13	39	56	4	.298	NV
Hawkins, LaTroy, Min.	R	6.66	10	14	33	33	1	0	0	0	174.1	238	136	129	29	60	103	9	.323	NV
Haynes, Jimmy, Oak.	R	6.34	7	12	30	25	0	0	2	0	142.0	158	112	100	21	80	93	7	.282	NV
Helling, Rick, Tex.	R	4.84	13	11	35	35	3	0	0	0	219.1	228	127	118	41	85	131	8	.272	3
Henry, Butch, Sea.	L	5.04	2	0	7	4	0	0	0	0	25.0	30	15	14	1	10	15	0	.303	NV
Hentgen, Pat, Tor.	R	4.79	11	12	34	34	1	0	0	0	199.0	225	115	106	32	65	118	8	.286	1
Heredia, Gil, Oak.	R	4.81	13	8	33	33	1	0	0	0	200.1	228	119	107	22	34	117	2	.283	9
Hernandez, Orlando, N.Y.	R	4.12	17	9	33	33	2	1	0	0	214.1	187	108	98	24	87	157	4	.233	18
Hill, Ken, Ana.	R	4.77	4	11	26	22	0	0	0	0	128.1	129	72	68	14	76	76	5	.270	NV

American League starting pitchers

Name/Team	T	ERA	W	L	G	GS	CG	SHO	GF	SV	IP	H	R	ER	HR	BB	SO	WP	BA	RV
Hudson, Tim, Oak.	R	3.23	11	2	21	21	1	0	0	0	136.1	121	56	49	8	62	132	6	.237	14
Irabu, Hideki, N.Y.	R	4.84	11	7	32	27	2	1	2	0	169.1	180	98	91	26	46	133	7	.267	6
Johnson, Jason, Bal.	R	5.46	8	7	22	21	0	0	0	0	115.1	120	74	70	16	55	71	5	.266	NV
Juden, Jeff, N.Y.	R	1.59	0	1	2	1	0	0	0	0	5.2	5	9	1	1	3	9	0	.200	NV
Laxton, Brett, Oak.	R	7.45	0	1	3	2	0	0	0	0	9.2	12	12	8	1	7	9	3	.316	NV
Lincoln, Mike, Min.	R	6.84	3	10	18	15	0	0	0	0	76.1	102	59	58	11	26	27	4	.321	NV
Linton, Doug, Bal.	R	5.95	1	4	14	8	0	0	0	0	59.0	69	41	39	14	25	32	4	.296	NV
Loaiza, Esteban, Tex.	R	4.56	9	5	30	15	0	0	4	0	120.1	128	65	61	10	40	77	2	.275	5
Martinez, Pedro, Bos.	R	2.07	23	4	31	29	5	1	1	0	213.1	160	56	49	9	37	313	6	.205	53
Martinez, Ramon, Bos.	R	3.05	2	1	4	4	0	0	0	0	20.2	14	8	7	2	8	15	0	.192	4
McDowell, Jack, Ana.	R	8.05	0	4	4	4	0	0	0	0	19.0	31	17	17	4	5	12	0	.369	NV
Meche, Gil, Sea.	R	4.73	8	4	16	15	0	0	0	0	85.2	73	48	45	9	57	47	1	.237	2
Mercker, Kent, Bos.	L	3.51	2	0	5	5	0	0	0	0	25.2	23	12	10	0	13	17	0	.235	2
Milton, Eric, Min.	L	4.49	7	11	34	34	5	2	0	0	206.1	190	111	103	28	63	163	2	.243	8
Mlicki, Dave, Det.	R	4.60	14	12	31	31	2	0	0	0	191.2	209	108	98	24	70	119	0	.276	6
Moehler, Brian, Det.	R	5.04	10	16	32	32	2	2	0	0	196.1	229	116	110	22	59	106	4	.294	NV
Morgan, Mike, Tex.	R	6.24	13	10	34	25	1	0	1	0	140.0	184	108	97	25	48	61	3	.323	NV
Moyer, Jamie, Sea.	L	3.87	14	8	32	32	4	0	0	0	228.0	235	108	98	23	48	137	3	.267	19
Mussina, Mike, Bal.	R	3.50	18	7	31	31	4	0	0	0	203.1	207	88	79	16	52	172	2	.268	24
Myette, Aaron, Chi.	R	6.32	0	2	4	3	0	0	0	0	15.2	17	11	11	2	14	11	2	.266	NV
Nagy, Charles, Cle.	R	4.95	17	11	33	32	1	0	0	0	202.0	238	120	111	26	59	126	3	.293	5
Navarro, Jaime, Chi.	R	6.09	8	13	32	27	0	0	1	0	159.2	206	126	108	29	71	74	9	.313	NV
Olivares, Omar, Ana.-Oak.	R	4.16	15	11	32	32	4	0	0	0	205.2	217	105	95	19	81	85	6	.276	9
Oquist, Mike, Oak.	R	5.37	9	10	28	24	0	0	1	0	140.2	158	86	84	18	64	89	2	.283	NV
Ortiz, Ramon, Ana.	R	6.52	2	3	9	9	0	0	0	0	48.1	50	35	35	7	25	44	2	.265	NV
Parque, Jim, Chi.	L	5.13	9	15	31	30	1	0	0	0	173.2	210	111	99	23	79	111	3	.299	NV
Pena, Juan, Bos.	R	0.69	2	0	2	2	0	0	0	0	13.0	9	1	1	0	3	15	0	.196	5
Pettitte, Andy, N.Y.	L	4.70	14	11	31	31	0	0	0	0	191.2	216	105	100	20	89	121	3	.289	NV
Pittsley, Jim, K.C.	R	6.94	1	2	5	5	0	0	0	0	23.1	33	22	18	2	15	7	2	.337	NV
Ponson, Sidney, Bal.	R	4.71	12	12	32	32	6	0	0	0	210.0	227	118	110	35	80	112	4	.282	2
Portugal, Mark, Bos.	R	5.51	7	12	31	27	1	0	1	0	150.1	179	100	92	28	41	79	2	.292	NV
Radke, Brad, Min.	R	3.75	12	14	33	33	4	0	0	0	218.2	239	97	91	28	44	121	4	.280	15
Ramsay, Robert, Sea.	L	6.38	0	2	6	3	0	0	1	0	18.1	23	13	13	3	9	11	1	.324	NV
Rapp, Pat, Bos.	R	4.12	6	7	37	26	0	0	3	0	146.1	147	78	67	13	69	90	5	.263	1
Reichert, Dan, K.C.	R	9.08	2	2	8	8	0	0	0	0	36.2	48	38	37	2	32	20	1	.327	NV
Riley, Matt, Bal.	L	7.36	0	3	3	3	0	0	0	0	11.0	17	9	9	4	13	6	0	.378	NV
Rogers, Kenny, Oak.	L	4.30	5	3	19	19	3	0	0	0	119.1	135	66	57	8	41	68	3	.288	NV
Rosado, Jose, K.C.	L	3.85	10	14	33	33	5	0	0	0	208.0	197	103	89	24	72	141	9	.248	13
Rose, Brian, Bos.	R	4.87	7	6	22	18	0	0	1	0	98.0	112	59	53	19	29	51	0	.280	2
Rupe, Ryan, T.B.	R	4.55	8	9	24	24	0	0	0	0	142.1	136	81	72	17	57	97	4	.253	5
Ryan, Jason, Min.	R	4.87	1	4	8	8	1	0	0	0	40.2	46	23	22	9	17	15	0	.286	NV
Saberhagen, Bret, Bos.	R	2.95	10	6	22	22	0	0	0	0	119.0	122	43	39	11	11	81	1	.265	20
Saunders, Tony, T.B.	L	6.43	3	3	9	9	0	0	0	0	42.0	53	39	30	6	29	30	3	.315	NV
Sele, Aaron, Tex.	R	4.79	18	9	33	33	2	2	0	0	205.0	244	115	109	21	70	186	4	.293	5
Sirotka, Mike, Chi.	L	4.00	11	13	32	32	3	1	0	0	209.0	236	108	93	24	57	125	4	.283	8
Snyder, John, Chi.	R	6.68	9	12	25	25	1	0	0	0	129.1	167	103	96	27	49	67	11	.311	NV
Sparks, Steve, Ana.	R	5.42	5	11	28	26	0	0	1	0	147.2	165	101	89	21	82	73	8	.281	NV
Stein, Blake, Oak.-K.C.	R	4.56	1	2	13	12	0	0	0	0	73.0	65	38	37	11	47	47	3	.241	NV
Sturtze, Tanyon, Chi.	R	0.00	0	0	1	1	0	0	0	0	6.0	4	0	0	0	2	2	0	.200	1
Suppan, Jeff, K.C.	R	4.53	10	12	32	32	4	1	0	0	208.2	222	113	105	28	62	103	5	.274	5
Thompson, Justin, Det.	L	5.11	9	11	24	24	0	0	0	0	142.2	152	85	81	24	59	83	2	.274	NV
Washburn, Jarrod, Ana.	L	5.25	4	5	16	10	0	0	3	0	61.2	61	36	36	6	26	39	2	.261	NV
Weaver, Jeff, Det.	R	5.55	9	12	30	29	0	0	1	0	163.2	176	104	101	27	56	114	0	.278	NV
Wells, David, Tor.	L	4.82	17	10	34	34	7	1	0	0	231.2	246	132	124	32	62	169	1	.271	11
Wells, Kip, Chi.	R	4.04	4	1	7	7	0	0	0	0	35.2	33	17	16	2	15	29	1	.248	4
Wheeler, Dan, T.B.	R	5.87	0	4	6	6	0	0	0	0	30.2	35	20	20	7	13	32	1	.287	NV
Witasick, Jay, K.C.	R	5.57	9	12	32	28	1	1	2	0	158.1	191	108	98	23	83	102	5	.304	NV
Witt, Bobby, T.B.	R	5.84	7	15	32	32	3	2	0	0	180.1	213	130	117	23	96	123	9	.304	NV
Wright, Jaret, Cle.	R	6.06	8	10	26	26	0	0	0	0	133.2	144	99	90	18	77	91	4	.277	NV

National League relief pitchers

Name/Team	T	ERA	W	L	G	GS	CG	SHO	GF	SV	IP	H	R	ER	HR	BB	SO	WP	BA	RV
Acevedo, Juan, St.L.	R	5.89	6	8	50	12	0	0	21	4	102.1	115	71	67	17	48	52	5	.291	NV
Adams, Terry, Chi.	R	4.02	6	3	52	0	0	0	38	13	65.0	60	33	29	9	28	57	6	.245	10
Aguilera, Rick, Chi.	R	3.69	6	3	44	0	0	0	25	8	46.1	44	22	19	6	10	32	3	.254	10
Aldred, Scott, Phi.	L	3.90	1	1	29	0	0	0	5	1	32.1	33	15	14	1	15	19	3	.277	NV
Alfonseca, Antonio, Fla.	R	3.24	4	5	73	0	0	0	49	21	77.2	79	28	28	4	29	46	1	.274	13
Almanza, Armando, Fla.	L	1.72	0	1	14	0	0	0	2	0	15.2	8	4	3	1	9	20	0	.154	NV

National League relief pitchers

Name/Team	T	ERA	W	L	G	GS	CG	SHO	GF	SV	IP	H	R	ER	HR	BB	SO	WP	BA	RV
Almanzar, Carlos, S.D.	R	7.47	0	0	28	0	0	0	11	0	37.1	48	32	31	6	15	30	2	.316	NV
Almonte, Hector, Fla.	R	4.20	0	2	15	0	0	0	6	0	15.0	20	7	7	1	6	8	2	.339	NV
Anderson, Jimmy, Pit.	L	3.99	2	1	13	4	0	0	2	0	29.1	25	15	13	2	16	13	4	.234	NV
Arnold, Jamie, L.A.	R	5.48	2	4	36	3	0	0	18	1	69.0	81	50	42	6	34	26	3	.300	NV
Ayala, Bobby, Mon.-Chi.	R	3.51	1	7	66	0	0	0	21	0	82.0	71	43	32	10	39	79	5	.228	1
Aybar, Manny, St.L.	R	5.47	4	5	65	1	0	0	22	3	97.0	104	67	59	13	36	74	1	.272	NV
Barker, Richie, Chi.	R	7.20	0	0	5	0	0	0	1	0	5.0	6	4	4	0	4	3	1	.300	NV
Batista, Miguel, Mon.	R	4.88	8	7	39	17	2	1	3	1	134.2	146	88	73	10	58	95	6	.280	NV
Beck, Rod, Chi.	R	7.80	2	4	31	0	0	0	19	7	30.0	41	26	26	5	13	13	1	.331	NV
Belinda, Stan, Cin.	R	5.27	3	1	29	0	0	0	12	2	42.2	42	26	25	11	18	40	3	.258	NV
Beltran, Rigo, N.Y.-Col.	L	4.50	1	1	33	0	0	0	12	0	42.0	50	24	21	7	19	50	7	.291	NV
Benes, Alan, St.L.	R	0.00	0	0	2	0	0	0	2	0	2.0	2	0	0	0	2	0	0	.286	NV
Benitez, Armando, N.Y.	R	1.85	4	3	77	0	0	0	42	22	78.0	40	17	16	4	41	128	2	.148	24
Bennett, Shayne, Mon.	R	14.29	0	1	5	1	0	0	1	0	11.1	24	18	18	4	3	4	0	.444	NV
Billingsley, Brent, Fla.	L	16.43	0	0	8	0	0	0	3	0	7.2	11	14	14	3	10	3	1	.379	NV
Bochtler, Doug, L.A.	R	5.54	0	0	12	0	0	0	4	0	13.0	11	8	8	3	6	7	1	.224	NV
Boehringer, Brian, S.D.	R	3.24	6	5	33	11	0	0	8	0	94.1	97	38	34	10	35	64	2	.267	5
Borbon, Pedro, L.A.	L	4.09	4	3	70	0	0	0	11	1	50.2	39	23	23	5	29	33	1	.209	2
Bottalico, Ricky, St.L.	R	4.91	3	7	68	0	0	0	40	20	73.1	83	45	40	8	49	66	6	.284	1
Boyd, Jason, Pit.	R	3.38	0	0	4	0	0	0	0	0	5.1	5	2	2	0	2	4	1	.250	NV
Brantley, Jeff, Phi.	R	5.19	1	2	10	0	0	0	9	5	8.2	5	6	5	0	8	11	0	.161	1
Brewer, Billy, Phi.	L	7.01	1	1	25	0	0	0	8	2	25.2	30	20	20	4	14	28	1	.294	NV
Busby, Mike, St.L.	R	7.13	0	1	15	0	0	0	3	0	17.2	21	15	14	2	14	7	1	.300	NV
Cabrera, Jose, Hou.	R	2.15	4	0	26	0	0	0	11	0	29.1	21	7	7	3	9	28	4	.196	6
Carlson, Dan, Ari.	R	9.00	0	0	2	0	0	0	1	0	4.0	5	4	4	0	0	3	0	.278	NV
Cather, Mike, Atl.	R	10.13	1	0	4	0	0	0	0	0	2.2	5	3	3	2	1	0	0	.417	NV
Checo, Robinson, L.A.	R	10.34	2	2	9	2	0	0	1	0	15.2	24	20	18	5	13	11	2	.333	NV
Chen, Bruce, Atl.	L	5.47	2	2	16	7	0	0	3	0	51.0	38	32	31	11	27	45	0	.208	NV
Chouinard, Bobby, Ari.	R	2.68	5	2	32	0	0	0	9	1	40.1	31	16	12	3	12	23	1	.220	8
Christiansen, Jason, Pit.	L	4.06	2	3	39	0	0	0	17	3	37.2	26	17	17	2	22	35	0	.198	2
Clontz, Brad, Pit.	R	2.74	1	3	56	0	0	0	16	2	49.1	49	21	15	6	24	40	2	.254	1
Cook, Dennis, N.Y.	L	3.86	10	5	71	0	0	0	12	3	63.0	50	27	27	11	27	68	0	.216	11
Coppinger, Rocky, Mil.	R	3.68	5	3	29	0	0	0	10	0	36.2	35	16	15	5	23	39	1	.250	1
Corbin, Archie, Fla.	R	7.29	0	1	17	0	0	0	4	0	21.0	25	20	17	2	15	30	3	.291	NV
Cornelius, Reid, Fla.	R	3.26	1	0	5	2	0	0	0	0	19.1	16	7	7	0	5	12	1	.229	1
Cortes, David, Atl.	R	4.91	0	0	4	0	0	0	4	0	3.2	3	3	2	0	4	2	2	.214	NV
Creek, Doug, Chi.	L	10.50	0	0	3	0	0	0	2	0	6.0	6	7	7	1	8	6	1	.261	NV
Croushore, Rich, St.L.	R	4.14	3	7	59	0	0	0	12	3	71.2	68	42	33	9	43	88	9	.247	NV
Cunnane, Will, S.D.	R	5.23	2	1	24	0	0	0	2	0	31.0	34	19	18	8	12	22	3	.293	NV
Dale, Carl, Mil.	R	20.25	0	1	4	0	0	0	1	0	4.0	8	9	9	2	6	4	0	.400	NV
D'Amico, Jeff, Mil.	R	0.00	0	0	1	0	0	0	1	0	1.0	1	0	0	0	0	1	0	.250	NV
Darensbourg, Vic, Fla.	L	8.83	0	1	56	0	0	0	5	0	34.2	50	36	34	3	21	16	1	.340	NV
DeHart, Rick, Mon.	L	21.60	0	0	3	0	0	0	0	0	1.2	6	4	4	2	3	1	0	.545	NV
DeJean, Mike, Col.	R	8.41	2	4	56	0	0	0	17	0	61.0	83	61	57	13	32	31	3	.335	NV
De Los Santos, Valerio, Mil.	L	6.48	0	1	7	0	0	0	3	0	8.1	12	6	6	1	7	5	1	.343	NV
DelToro, Miguel, S.F.	R	4.18	0	0	14	0	0	0	2	0	23.2	24	11	11	5	11	20	0	.264	NV
Dipoto, Jerry, Col.	R	4.26	4	5	63	0	0	0	18	1	86.2	91	44	41	10	44	69	6	.279	NV
Dougherty, Jim, Pit.	R	9.00	0	0	2	0	0	0	0	0	2.0	3	3	2	0	3	1	0	.333	NV
Ebert, Derrin, Atl.	L	5.63	0	1	5	0	0	0	3	1	8.0	9	5	5	2	5	4	0	.300	NV
Edmondson, Brian, Fla.	R	5.84	5	8	68	0	0	0	14	1	94.0	106	65	61	11	44	58	5	.290	NV
Elarton, Scott, Hou.	R	3.48	9	5	42	15	0	0	8	1	124.0	111	55	48	8	43	121	3	.238	12
Embree, Alan, S.F.	L	3.38	3	2	68	0	0	0	13	0	58.2	42	22	22	6	26	53	3	.200	5
Estrada, Horacio, Mil.	L	7.36	0	0	4	0	0	0	0	0	7.1	10	6	6	4	4	5	0	.313	NV
Falteisek, Steve, Mil.	R	7.50	0	0	10	0	0	0	3	0	12.0	18	10	10	3	3	5	0	.375	NV
Fox, Chad, Mil.	R	10.80	0	0	6	0	0	0	0	0	6.2	11	8	8	1	4	12	1	.355	NV
Franco, John, N.Y.	L	2.88	0	2	46	0	0	0	34	19	40.2	40	14	13	1	19	41	0	.255	8
Franco, Matt, N.Y.	R	13.50	0	0	2	0	0	0	2	0	1.1	3	2	2	1	3	2	0	.429	NV
Frascatore, John, Ari.	R	4.09	1	4	26	0	0	0	10	0	33.0	31	16	15	6	12	15	0	.256	NV
Gaetti, Gary, Chi.	R	18.00	0	0	1	0	0	0	1	0	1.0	2	2	2	1	1	1	0	.400	NV
Garcia, Michael, Pit.	R	1.29	1	0	7	0	0	0	2	0	7.0	2	1	1	1	3	9	0	.091	NV
Giovanola, Ed, S.D.	R	0.00	0	0	1	0	0	0	1	0	1.1	1	0	0	0	2	0	0	.200	NV
Gomes, Wayne, Phi.	R	4.26	5	5	73	0	0	0	58	19	74.0	70	38	35	5	56	58	3	.255	6
Grace, Mike, Phi.	R	7.69	1	4	27	5	0	0	1	0	55.0	80	48	47	5	30	28	4	.346	NV
Grahe, Joe, Phi.	R	3.86	1	4	13	5	0	0	4	0	32.2	40	16	14	1	17	16	2	.308	NV
Graves, Danny, Cin.	R	3.08	8	7	75	0	0	0	56	27	111.0	90	42	38	10	49	69	3	.227	25
Greene, Rick, Cin.	R	4.76	0	1	7	0	0	0	0	0	5.2	7	4	3	2	1	3	0	.292	NV
Guthrie, Mark, Chi.	L	3.65	0	2	11	0	0	0	0	0	12.1	7	6	5	1	4	9	1	.171	NV
Guzman, Domingo, S.D.	R	21.60	0	1	7	0	0	0	2	0	5.0	13	12	12	1	3	4	0	.464	NV
Hansell, Greg, Pit.	R	3.89	1	3	33	0	0	0	9	0	39.1	42	20	17	5	11	34	2	.280	NV
Harris, Reggie, Mil.	R	3.00	0	0	8	0	0	0	2	0	12.0	8	4	4	1	7	11	2	.186	NV

National League relief pitchers

Name/Team	T	ERA	W	L	G	GS	CG	SHO	GF	SV	IP	H	R	ER	HR	BB	SO	WP	BA	RV
Heiserman, Rick, St.L.	R	8.31	0	0	3	0	0	0	0	0	4.1	8	4	4	2	4	4	2	.400	NV
Henry, Doug, Hou.	R	4.65	2	3	35	0	0	0	17	2	40.2	45	24	21	8	24	36	0	.281	NV
Heredia, Felix, Chi.	L	4.85	3	1	69	0	0	0	15	1	52.0	56	35	28	7	25	50	2	.272	NV
Herges, Matt, L.A.	R	4.07	0	2	17	0	0	0	9	0	24.1	24	13	11	5	8	18	0	.255	NV
Hoffman, Trevor, S.D.	R	2.14	2	3	64	0	0	0	54	40	67.1	48	23	16	5	15	73	4	.197	30
Holmes, Darren, Ari.	R	3.70	4	3	44	0	0	0	9	0	48.2	50	21	20	3	25	35	0	.262	NV
Hudek, John, Cin.-Atl.	R	7.64	0	2	17	0	0	0	12	0	17.2	25	17	15	2	14	18	0	.325	NV
Isringhausen, Jason, N.Y.	R	6.41	1	3	13	5	0	0	2	1	39.1	43	29	28	7	22	31	2	.279	NV
Johnson, Mike, Mon.	R	8.64	0	0	3	1	0	0	0	0	8.1	12	8	8	2	7	6	2	.324	NV
Johnstone, John, S.F.	R	2.60	4	6	62	0	0	0	11	3	65.2	48	24	19	8	20	56	2	.203	11
Karchner, Matt, Chi.	R	2.50	1	0	16	0	0	0	2	0	18.0	16	5	5	3	9	9	1	.235	NV
Kim, Byung-Hyun, Ari.	R	4.61	1	2	25	0	0	0	10	1	27.1	20	15	14	2	20	31	4	.211	NV
King, Curtis, St.L.	R	18.00	0	0	2	0	0	0	1	0	1.0	3	2	2	0	0	1	0	.500	NV
King, Ray, Chi.	L	5.91	0	0	10	0	0	0	0	0	10.2	11	8	7	2	10	5	1	.289	NV
Kline, Steve, Mon.	L	3.75	7	4	82	0	0	0	18	0	69.2	56	32	29	8	33	69	2	.218	6
Kubenka, Jeff, L.A.	L	11.74	0	1	6	0	0	0	2	0	7.2	13	12	10	1	4	2	0	.371	NV
Lee, David, Col.	R	3.67	3	2	36	0	0	0	11	0	49.0	43	21	20	4	29	38	3	.247	NV
Leskanic, Curtis, Col.	R	5.08	6	2	63	0	0	0	5	0	85.0	87	54	48	7	49	77	5	.272	NV
Lilly, Ted, Mon.	L	7.61	0	1	9	3	0	0	1	0	23.2	30	20	20	7	9	28	1	.309	NV
Loiselle, Rich, Pit.	R	5.28	3	2	13	0	0	0	6	0	15.1	16	9	9	2	9	14	1	.281	NV
Looper, Braden, Fla.	R	3.80	3	3	72	0	0	0	22	0	83.0	96	43	35	7	31	50	2	.293	NV
Maddux, Mike, Mon.-L.A.	R	3.77	1	1	53	0	0	0	21	0	59.2	63	26	25	6	22	45	1	.275	NV
Mahomes, Pat, N.Y.	R	3.68	8	0	39	0	0	0	12	0	63.2	44	26	26	7	37	51	2	.197	7
Mantei, Matt, Fla.-Ari.	R	2.76	1	3	65	0	0	0	60	32	65.1	44	21	20	5	44	99	2	.189	18
Manzanillo, Josias, N.Y.	R	5.79	0	0	12	0	0	0	1	0	18.2	19	12	12	5	4	25	0	.264	NV
Masaoka, Onan, L.A.	L	4.32	2	4	54	0	0	0	12	1	66.2	55	33	32	8	47	61	3	.222	NV
McCurry, Jeff, Hou.	R	15.75	0	1	5	0	0	0	1	0	4.0	11	8	7	1	2	3	0	.478	NV
McElroy, Chuck, Col.-N.Y.	L	5.50	3	1	56	0	0	0	19	0	54.0	60	34	33	9	36	44	5	.286	NV
McGlinchy, Kevin, Atl.	R	2.82	7	3	64	0	0	0	21	0	70.1	66	25	22	6	30	67	1	.255	7
McMichael, Greg, N.Y.	R	4.82	1	1	19	0	0	0	4	0	18.2	20	10	10	3	8	18	4	.270	NV
Medina, Rafael, Fla.	R	5.79	1	1	20	0	0	0	4	0	23.1	20	15	15	3	20	16	2	.227	NV
Miceli, Dan, S.D.	R	4.46	4	5	66	0	0	0	28	2	68.2	67	39	34	7	36	59	2	.266	NV
Miller, Kurt, Chi.	R	18.00	0	0	4	0	0	0	1	0	3.0	6	6	6	1	3	1	0	.462	NV
Miller, Trever, Hou.	L	5.07	3	2	47	0	0	0	11	1	49.2	58	29	28	6	29	37	4	.299	NV
Miller, Wade, Hou.	R	9.58	0	1	5	1	0	0	2	0	10.1	17	11	11	4	5	8	0	.362	NV
Mills, Alan, L.A.	R	3.73	3	4	68	0	0	0	18	0	72.1	70	33	30	10	43	49	3	.261	NV
Mlicki, Dave, L.A.	R	4.91	0	1	2	0	0	0	0	0	7.1	10	4	4	1	2	1	1	.323	NV
Mohler, Mike, St.L.	L	4.38	1	1	48	0	0	0	16	1	49.1	47	26	24	3	23	31	1	.254	NV
Montgomery, Steve, Phi.	R	3.34	1	5	53	0	0	0	21	3	64.2	54	25	24	10	31	55	4	.229	3
Mota, Guillermo, Mon.	R	2.93	2	4	51	0	0	0	18	0	55.1	54	24	18	5	25	27	1	.257	1
Murray, Dan, N.Y.	R	13.50	0	0	1	0	0	0	1	0	2.0	4	3	3	0	2	1	1	.444	NV
Murray, Heath, S.D.	L	5.76	0	4	22	8	0	0	1	0	50.0	60	33	32	7	26	25	1	.297	NV
Myers, Mike, Mil.	L	5.23	2	1	71	0	0	0	14	0	41.1	46	24	24	7	13	35	1	.291	NV
Myers, Rodney, Chi.	R	4.38	3	1	46	0	0	0	5	0	63.2	71	34	31	10	25	41	2	.289	NV
Nen, Robb, S.F.	R	3.98	3	8	72	0	0	0	64	37	72.1	79	36	32	8	27	77	5	.275	17
Nunez, Vladimir, Ari.-Fla.	R	4.06	7	10	44	12	0	0	12	1	108.2	95	63	49	11	54	86	8	.242	4
Ojala, Kirt, Fla.	L	14.34	0	1	8	1	0	0	2	0	10.2	21	17	17	1	6	5	0	.438	NV
Olson, Gregg, Ari.	R	3.71	9	4	61	0	0	0	36	14	60.2	54	28	25	9	25	45	1	.238	14
Osik, Keith, Pit.	R	36.00	0	0	1	0	0	0	1	0	1.0	2	4	4	0	2	1	0	.400	NV
Osuna, Antonio, L.A.	R	7.71	0	0	5	0	0	0	1	0	4.2	4	5	4	0	3	5	1	.222	NV
Padilla, Vicente, Ari.	R	16.88	0	1	5	0	0	0	2	0	2.2	7	5	5	1	3	0	0	.467	NV
Painter, Lance, St.L.	L	4.83	4	5	56	4	0	0	10	1	63.1	63	37	34	6	25	56	4	.265	NV
Patrick, Bronswell, S.F.	R	10.13	1	0	6	0	0	0	2	1	5.1	9	7	6	1	3	6	0	.375	NV
Perez, Yorkis, Phi.	L	3.94	3	1	35	0	0	0	4	0	32.0	29	15	14	4	15	26	5	.244	1
Phillips, Jason, Pit.	R	11.57	0	0	6	0	0	0	0	0	7.0	11	9	9	2	6	7	2	.393	NV
Pittsley, Jim, Mil.	R	4.82	0	1	15	0	0	0	5	0	18.2	20	12	10	3	10	13	2	.274	NV
Plesac, Dan, Ari.	L	3.32	2	1	34	0	0	0	6	1	21.2	22	9	8	3	8	27	1	.259	1
Plunk, Eric, Mil.	R	5.02	4	4	68	0	0	0	13	0	75.1	71	44	42	15	43	63	5	.251	NV
Politte, Cliff, Phi.	R	7.13	1	0	13	0	0	0	0	0	17.2	19	14	14	2	15	15	2	.275	NV
Poole, Jim, Phi.	L	4.33	1	1	51	0	0	0	12	0	35.1	48	20	17	3	15	22	4	.327	NV
Porzio, Mike, Col.	L	8.59	0	0	16	0	0	0	3	0	14.2	21	14	14	5	10	10	0	.328	NV
Powell, Jay, Hou.	R	4.32	5	4	67	0	0	0	26	4	75.0	82	38	36	3	40	77	5	.282	NV
Radinsky, Scott, St.L.	L	4.88	2	1	43	0	0	0	13	3	27.2	27	16	15	2	18	17	3	.270	NV
Rain, Steve, Chi.	R	9.20	0	1	16	0	0	0	5	0	14.2	28	17	15	1	7	12	1	.418	NV
Ramirez, Hector, Mil.	R	3.43	1	2	16	0	0	0	6	0	21.0	19	8	8	1	11	9	0	.247	NV
Ramirez, Roberto, Col.	L	8.26	1	5	32	4	0	0	6	1	40.1	68	42	37	8	22	32	4	.368	NV
Remlinger, Mike, Atl.	L	2.37	10	1	73	0	0	0	14	1	83.2	66	24	22	9	35	81	5	.215	15
Reyes, Carlos, S.D.	R	3.72	2	4	65	0	0	0	23	1	77.1	76	38	32	11	24	57	7	.254	2
Reyes, Dennis, Cin.	L	3.79	2	2	65	1	0	0	12	2	61.2	53	30	26	5	39	72	5	.232	NV
Reyes, Alberto, Mil.	R	4.25	2	0	26	0	0	0	6	0	36.0	27	17	17	5	25	39	2	.206	NV

National League relief pitchers

Name/Team	T	ERA	W	L	G	GS	CG	SHO	GF	SV	IP	H	R	ER	HR	BB	SO	WP	BA	RV
Rivera, Roberto, S.D.	L	3.86	1	2	12	0	0	0	3	0	7.0	6	4	3	1	3	3	1	.240	NV
Rocker, John, Atl.	L	2.49	4	5	74	0	0	0	61	38	72.1	47	24	20	5	37	104	7	.180	27
Rodriguez, Felix, S.F.	R	3.80	2	3	47	0	0	0	26	0	66.1	67	32	28	6	29	55	2	.262	NV
Rodriguez, Rich, S.F.	L	5.24	3	0	62	0	0	0	8	0	56.2	60	33	33	8	28	44	1	.274	NV
Rojas, Mel, L.A.-Mon.	R	14.09	0	0	8	0	0	0	3	0	7.2	10	12	12	3	5	4	1	.313	NV
Roque, Rafael, Mil.	L	5.34	1	6	43	9	0	0	7	1	84.1	96	52	50	16	42	66	4	.286	NV
Rusch, Glendon, N.Y.	L	0.00	0	0	1	0	0	0	1	0	1.0	1	0	0	0	0	0	0	.333	NV
Ryan, Ken, Phi.	R	6.32	1	2	15	0	0	0	5	0	15.2	16	11	11	2	11	9	1	.267	NV
Ryan, B.J., Cin.	L	4.50	0	0	1	0	0	0	0	0	2.0	4	1	1	0	1	1	0	.500	NV
Sabel, Erik, Ari.	R	6.52	0	0	7	0	0	0	1	0	9.2	12	7	7	1	6	6	1	.300	NV
Sanchez, Jesus, Fla.	L	6.01	5	7	59	10	0	0	8	0	76.1	84	53	51	16	60	62	5	.291	NV
Sanders, Scott, Chi.	R	5.52	4	7	67	6	0	0	16	2	104.1	112	69	64	19	53	89	5	.277	NV
Sauerbeck, Scott, Pit.	L	2.00	4	1	65	0	0	0	16	2	67.2	53	19	15	6	38	55	3	.220	8
Schrenk, Steve, Phi.	R	4.29	1	3	32	2	0	0	8	1	50.1	41	24	24	6	14	36	2	.223	2
Seanez, Rudy, Atl.	R	3.35	6	1	56	0	0	0	13	3	53.2	47	21	20	3	21	41	3	.234	7
Serafini, Dan, Chi.	L	6.93	3	2	42	4	0	0	8	1	62.1	86	51	48	9	32	17	3	.333	NV
Shaw, Jeff, L.A.	R	2.78	2	4	64	0	0	0	56	34	68.0	64	25	21	6	15	43	1	.242	23
Silva, Jose, Pit.	R	5.73	2	8	34	12	0	0	9	4	97.1	108	70	62	10	39	77	4	.281	NV
Slocumb, Heathcliff, St.L.	R	2.36	3	2	40	0	0	0	12	2	53.1	49	16	14	3	30	48	3	.243	4
Slusarski, Joe, Hou.	R	0.00	0	0	3	0	0	0	1	0	3.2	1	0	0	0	3	3	0	.083	NV
Smart, J.D., Mon.	R	5.02	0	1	29	0	0	0	6	0	52.0	56	30	29	4	17	21	0	.276	NV
Sodowsky, Clint, St.L.	R	15.63	0	1	3	1	0	0	0	0	6.1	15	11	11	1	6	2	0	.455	NV
Speier, Justin, Ari.	R	5.65	0	0	19	0	0	0	8	0	28.2	28	18	18	8	13	22	0	.248	NV
Spradlin, Jerry, S.F.	R	4.19	3	1	59	0	0	0	14	0	58.0	59	31	27	4	29	52	2	.259	NV
Springer, Russ, Atl.	R	3.42	2	1	49	0	0	0	8	1	47.1	31	20	18	5	22	49	0	.185	4
Strickland, Scott, Mon.	R	4.50	0	1	17	0	0	0	5	0	18.0	15	10	9	3	11	23	0	.231	NV
Stull, Everett, Atl.	R	13.50	0	0	1	0	0	0	0	0	0.2	2	3	1	0	2	0	0	.500	NV
Sullivan, Scott, Cin.	R	3.01	5	4	79	0	0	0	16	3	113.2	88	41	38	10	47	78	6	.216	12
Swindell, Greg, Ari.	L	2.51	4	0	63	0	0	0	15	1	64.2	54	19	18	8	21	51	0	.230	8
Tam, Jeff, N.Y.	R	3.18	0	0	9	0	0	0	3	0	11.1	6	4	4	3	8	8	0	.150	NV
Tavarez, Julian, S.F.	R	5.93	2	0	47	0	0	0	12	0	54.2	65	38	36	7	25	33	4	.295	NV
Taylor, Billy, N.Y.	R	8.10	0	1	18	0	0	0	5	0	13.1	20	12	12	2	9	14	0	.345	NV
Tejera, Michael, Fla.	L	11.37	0	0	3	1	0	0	1	0	6.1	10	8	8	1	5	7	0	.385	NV
Telemaco, A., Ari.-Phi.	R	5.77	4	0	49	0	0	0	10	0	53.0	52	34	34	10	26	43	5	.259	NV
Telford, Anthony, Mon.	R	3.94	5	4	79	0	0	0	21	2	96.0	112	52	42	3	38	69	3	.295	NV
Urbina, Ugueth, Mon.	R	3.69	6	6	71	0	0	0	62	41	75.2	59	35	31	6	36	100	6	.208	26
Veres, Dave, Col.	R	5.14	4	8	73	0	0	0	63	31	77.0	88	46	44	14	37	71	8	.290	9
Vosberg, Ed, Ari.-S.D.	L	8.18	0	1	19	0	0	0	3	0	11.0	22	12	10	1	3	8	1	.431	NV
Wagner, Billy, Hou.	L	1.57	4	1	66	0	0	0	55	39	74.2	35	14	13	5	23	124	2	.135	37
Wainhouse, Dave, Col.	R	6.91	0	0	19	0	0	0	11	0	28.2	37	22	22	6	16	18	1	.330	NV
Wall, Donne, S.D.	R	3.07	7	4	55	0	0	0	12	0	70.1	58	31	24	11	23	53	6	.219	10
Wallace, Jeff, Pit.	L	3.69	1	0	41	0	0	0	7	0	39.0	26	17	16	2	38	41	5	.195	NV
Watson, Allen, N.Y.	L	4.08	2	2	14	4	0	0	6	1	39.2	36	18	18	5	22	32	2	.252	NV
Weathers, Dave, Mil.	R	4.65	7	4	63	0	0	0	14	2	93.0	102	49	48	14	38	74	1	.279	NV
Wendell, Turk, N.Y.	R	3.05	5	4	80	0	0	0	14	3	85.2	80	31	29	9	37	77	2	.245	7
Whisenant, Matt, S.D.	L	3.68	0	1	19	0	0	0	6	0	14.2	10	6	6	0	10	10	0	.200	NV
White, Gabe, Cin.	L	4.43	1	2	50	0	0	0	18	0	61.0	68	31	30	13	14	61	0	.281	NV
Whiteside, Matt, S.D.	R	13.91	1	0	10	0	0	0	4	0	11.0	19	17	17	1	5	9	1	.396	NV
Wickman, Bob, Mil.	R	3.39	3	8	71	0	0	0	63	37	74.1	75	31	28	6	38	60	2	.262	18
Wilkins, Marc, Pit.	R	4.24	2	3	46	0	0	0	14	0	51.0	49	28	24	3	26	44	4	.257	NV
Williams, Brian, Hou.	R	4.41	2	1	50	0	0	0	15	0	67.1	69	35	33	4	35	53	7	.272	NV
Williams, Mike, Pit.	R	5.09	3	4	58	0	0	0	50	23	58.1	63	36	33	9	37	76	4	.276	5
Williamson, Scott, Cin.	R	2.41	12	7	62	0	0	0	40	19	93.1	54	29	25	8	43	107	13	.171	30
Winkelsas, Joe, Atl.	R	54.00	0	0	1	0	0	0	0	0	0.1	4	2	2	0	1	0	0	1.000	NV
Wohlers, Mark, Atl.	R	27.00	0	0	2	0	0	0	0	0	0.2	1	2	2	0	6	0	0	.333	NV

National League starting pitchers

Name/Team	T	ERA	W	L	G	GS	CG	SHO	GF	SV	IP	H	R	ER	HR	BB	SO	WP	BA	RV
Abbott, Jim, Mil.	L	6.91	2	8	20	15	0	0	3	0	82.0	110	71	63	14	42	37	7	.317	NV
Anderson, Brian, Ari.	L	4.57	8	2	31	19	2	1	4	1	130.0	144	69	66	18	28	75	0	.279	4
Ankiel, Rick, St.L.	L	3.27	0	1	9	5	0	0	1	0	33.0	26	12	12	2	14	39	2	.215	1
Armas, Tony, Mon.	R	1.50	0	1	1	1	0	0	0	0	6.0	8	4	1	0	2	2	2	.320	NV
Ashby, Andy, S.D.	R	3.80	14	10	31	31	4	3	0	0	206.0	204	95	87	26	54	132	6	.258	16
Astacio, Pedro, Col.	R	5.04	17	11	34	34	7	0	0	0	232.0	258	140	130	38	75	210	5	.285	2
Avery, Steve, Cin.	L	5.16	6	7	19	19	0	0	0	0	96.0	75	62	55	11	78	51	4	.222	NV
Benes, Andy, Ari.	R	4.81	13	12	33	32	0	0	0	0	198.1	216	117	106	34	82	141	10	.273	NV
Bennett, Joel, Phi.	R	9.00	2	1	5	3	0	0	0	0	17.0	26	17	17	10	7	13	0	.351	NV
Benson, Kris, Pit.	R	4.07	11	14	31	31	2	0	0	0	196.2	184	105	89	16	83	139	2	.249	7

National League starting pitchers

Name/Team	T	ERA	W	L	G	GS	CG	SHO	GF	SV	IP	H	R	ER	HR	BB	SO	WP	BA	RV
Bere, Jason, Cin.-Mil.	R	6.07	5	0	17	14	0	0	0	0	66.2	79	52	45	9	50	47	6	.302	NV
Bergman, Sean, Hou.-Atl.	R	5.21	5	6	25	16	2	1	2	0	105.1	135	62	61	9	29	44	3	.325	NV
Bohanon, Brian, Col.	L	6.20	12	12	33	33	3	1	0	0	197.1	236	146	136	30	92	120	6	.304	NV
Bottenfield, Kent, St.L.	R	3.97	18	7	31	31	0	0	0	0	190.1	197	91	84	21	89	124	1	.270	9
Bowie, Micah, Atl.-Chi.	L	10.24	2	7	14	11	0	0	2	0	51.0	81	60	58	9	34	41	4	.363	NV
Brock, Chris, S.F.	R	5.48	6	8	19	19	0	0	0	0	106.2	124	69	65	18	41	76	8	.291	NV
Brown, Kevin, L.A.	R	3.00	18	9	35	35	5	1	0	0	252.1	210	99	84	19	59	221	4	.222	36
Brownson, Mark, Col.	R	7.89	0	2	7	7	0	0	0	0	29.2	42	26	26	8	8	21	2	.333	NV
Burnett, A.J., Fla.	R	3.48	4	2	7	7	0	0	0	0	41.1	37	23	16	3	25	33	0	.242	1
Byrd, Paul, Phi.	R	4.60	15	11	32	32	1	0	0	0	199.2	205	119	102	34	70	106	11	.265	6
Carlyle, Buddy, S.D.	R	5.97	1	3	7	7	0	0	0	0	37.2	36	28	25	7	17	29	1	.257	NV
Clement, Matt, S.D.	R	4.48	10	12	31	31	0	0	0	0	180.2	190	106	90	18	86	135	11	.273	NV
Cordova, Francisco, Pit.	R	4.43	8	10	27	27	2	0	0	0	160.2	166	83	79	16	59	98	5	.273	1
Daal, Omar, Ari.	L	3.65	16	9	32	32	2	1	0	0	214.2	188	92	87	21	79	148	3	.236	19
Dempster, Ryan, Fla.	R	4.71	7	8	25	25	0	0	0	0	147.0	146	77	77	21	93	126	8	.262	NV
Dotel, Octavio, N.Y.	R	5.38	8	3	19	14	0	0	1	0	85.1	69	52	51	12	49	85	3	.226	NV
Dreifort, Darren, L.A.	R	4.79	13	13	30	29	1	1	0	0	178.2	177	105	95	20	76	140	9	.260	3
Eldred, Cal, Mil.	R	7.79	2	8	20	15	0	0	2	0	82.0	101	75	71	19	46	60	8	.297	NV
Estes, Shawn, S.F.	L	4.92	11	11	32	32	1	1	0	0	203.0	209	121	111	21	112	159	15	.268	NV
Farnsworth, Kyle, Chi.	R	5.05	5	9	27	21	1	1	0	0	130.0	140	80	73	28	52	70	7	.271	NV
Fernandez, Alex, Fla.	R	3.38	7	8	24	24	1	0	0	0	141.0	135	60	53	10	41	91	2	.252	10
Gagne, Eric, L.A.	R	2.10	1	1	5	5	0	0	0	0	30.0	18	8	7	3	15	30	1	.175	3
Gardner, Mark, S.F.	R	6.47	5	11	29	21	1	0	2	0	139.0	142	103	100	27	57	86	3	.267	NV
Glavine, Tom, Atl.	L	4.12	14	11	35	35	2	0	0	0	234.0	259	115	107	18	83	138	2	.287	5
Guzman, Juan, Cin.	R	3.03	6	3	12	12	1	0	0	0	77.1	70	33	26	10	21	60	5	.238	9
Hackman, Luther, Col.	R	10.69	1	2	5	3	0	0	0	0	16.0	26	19	19	5	12	10	0	.371	NV
Hampton, Mike, Hou.	L	2.90	22	4	34	34	3	2	0	0	239.0	206	86	77	12	101	177	9	.241	29
Harnisch, Pete, Cin.	R	3.68	16	10	33	33	2	2	0	0	198.1	190	86	81	25	57	120	3	.252	18
Hermanson, Dustin, Mon.	R	4.20	9	14	34	34	0	0	0	0	216.1	225	110	101	20	69	145	4	.271	4
Hernandez, Livan, Fla.-S.F.	R	4.64	8	12	30	30	2	0	0	0	199.2	227	110	103	23	76	144	2	.286	NV
Hershiser, Orel, N.Y.	R	4.58	13	12	32	32	0	0	0	0	179.0	175	92	91	14	77	89	6	.260	4
Hitchcock, Sterling, S.D.	L	4.11	12	14	33	33	1	0	0	0	205.2	202	99	94	29	76	194	15	.254	8
Holt, Chris, Hou.	R	4.66	5	13	32	26	0	0	0	1	164.0	193	92	85	12	57	115	5	.303	NV
Jimenez, Jose, St.L.	R	5.85	5	14	29	28	2	2	0	0	163.0	173	114	106	16	71	113	10	.275	NV
Johnson, Randy, Ari.	L	2.48	17	9	35	35	12	2	0	0	271.2	207	86	75	30	70	364	4	.208	43
Jones, Bobby, N.Y.	R	5.61	3	3	12	9	0	0	0	0	59.1	69	37	37	3	11	31	0	.295	NV
Jones, Bobby, Col.	L	6.33	6	10	30	20	0	0	1	0	112.1	132	91	79	24	77	74	4	.292	NV
Judd, Mike, L.A.	R	5.46	3	1	7	4	0	0	0	0	28.0	30	17	17	4	12	22	3	.280	NV
Karl, Scott, Mil.	L	4.78	11	11	33	33	0	0	0	0	197.2	246	121	105	21	69	74	4	.312	NV
Kile, Darryl, Col.	R	6.61	8	13	32	32	1	0	0	0	190.2	225	150	140	33	109	116	13	.298	NV
Leiter, Al, N.Y.	L	4.23	13	12	32	32	1	1	0	0	213.0	209	107	100	19	93	162	4	.262	5
Lieber, Jon, Chi.	R	4.07	10	11	31	31	3	1	0	0	203.1	226	107	92	28	46	186	2	.279	7
Lima, Jose, Hou.	R	3.58	21	10	35	35	3	0	0	0	246.1	256	108	98	30	44	187	8	.265	26
Loewer, Carlton, Phi.	R	5.12	2	6	20	13	2	1	2	0	89.2	100	54	51	9	26	48	3	.287	NV
Lorraine, Andrew, Chi.	L	5.55	2	5	11	11	2	1	0	0	61.2	71	42	38	9	22	40	3	.293	NV
Luebbers, Larry, St.L.	R	5.12	3	3	8	8	1	0	0	0	45.2	46	27	26	8	16	16	1	.261	NV
Maddux, Greg, Atl.	R	3.57	19	9	33	33	4	0	0	0	219.1	258	103	87	16	37	136	1	.294	18
McNichol, Brian, Chi.	L	6.75	0	2	4	2	0	0	1	0	10.2	15	8	8	4	7	12	0	.333	NV
Meadows, Brian, Fla.	R	5.60	11	15	31	31	0	0	0	0	178.1	214	117	111	31	57	72	4	.302	NV
Mercker, Kent, St.L.	L	5.12	6	5	25	18	0	0	2	0	103.2	125	73	59	16	51	64	3	.303	NV
Millwood, Kevin, Atl.	R	2.68	18	7	33	33	2	0	0	0	228.0	168	80	68	24	59	205	5	.202	39
Mulholland, Terry, Chi.-Atl.	L	4.39	10	8	42	24	0	0	7	1	170.1	201	95	83	21	45	83	3	.297	2
Nathan, Joe, S.F.	R	4.18	7	4	19	14	0	0	2	1	90.1	84	45	42	17	46	54	2	.243	3
Neagle, Denny, Cin.	L	4.27	9	5	20	19	0	0	0	0	111.2	95	54	53	23	40	76	4	.229	8
Nomo, Hideo, Mil.	R	4.54	12	8	28	28	0	0	0	0	176.1	173	96	89	27	78	161	10	.256	NV
Ogea, Chad, Phi.	R	5.63	6	12	36	28	0	0	3	0	168.0	192	110	105	36	61	77	5	.288	NV
Oliver, Darren, St.L.	L	4.26	9	9	30	30	2	1	0	0	196.1	197	96	93	16	74	119	6	.265	3
Ortiz, Russ, S.F.	R	3.81	18	9	33	33	3	0	0	0	207.2	189	109	88	24	125	164	13	.244	9
Osborne, Donovan, St.L.	L	5.52	1	3	6	6	0	0	0	0	29.1	34	18	18	4	10	21	1	.298	NV
Park, Chan Ho, L.A.	R	5.23	13	11	33	33	0	0	0	0	194.1	208	120	113	31	100	174	11	.276	NV
Parris, Steve, Cin.	R	3.50	11	4	22	21	2	1	0	0	128.2	124	59	50	16	52	86	3	.260	10
Pavano, Carl, Mon.	R	5.63	6	8	19	18	1	1	0	0	104.0	117	66	65	8	35	70	1	.285	NV
Perez, Carlos, L.A.	L	7.43	2	10	17	16	0	0	0	0	89.2	116	77	74	23	39	40	2	.317	NV
Perez, Odalis, Atl.	L	6.00	4	6	18	17	0	0	0	0	93.0	100	65	62	12	53	82	5	.275	NV
Person, Robert, Phi.	R	4.27	10	5	31	22	0	0	1	0	137.0	130	72	65	23	70	127	3	.252	3
Peters, Chris, Pit.	L	6.59	5	4	19	11	0	0	2	0	71.0	98	59	52	17	27	46	2	.322	NV
Peterson, Kyle, Mil.	R	4.56	4	7	17	12	0	0	0	0	77.0	87	46	39	3	25	34	1	.285	NV
Powell, Jeremy, Mon.	R	4.73	4	8	17	17	0	0	0	0	97.0	113	60	51	14	44	44	4	.302	NV
Pulsipher, Bill, Mil.	L	5.98	5	6	19	16	0	0	1	0	87.1	100	65	58	19	36	42	4	.286	NV
Reed, Rick, N.Y.	R	4.58	11	5	26	26	1	1	0	0	149.1	163	77	76	23	47	104	1	.281	3

National League starting pitchers

Name/Team	T	ERA	W	L	G	GS	CG	SHO	GF	SV	IP	H	R	ER	HR	BB	SO	WP	BA	RV
Reynolds, Shane, Hou.	R	3.85	16	14	35	35	4	2	0	0	231.2	250	108	99	23	37	197	4	.275	18
Reynoso, Armando, Ari.	R	4.37	10	6	31	27	0	0	1	0	167.0	178	90	81	20	67	79	7	.276	1
Ritchie, Todd, Pit.	R	3.49	15	9	28	26	2	0	0	0	172.2	169	79	67	17	54	107	7	.259	16
Rogers, Kenny, N.Y.	L	4.03	5	1	12	12	2	1	0	0	76.0	71	35	34	8	28	58	1	.253	3
Rueter, Kirk, S.F.	L	5.41	15	10	33	33	1	0	0	0	184.2	219	118	111	28	55	94	2	.297	NV
Schilling, Curt, Phi.	R	3.54	15	6	24	24	8	1	0	0	180.1	159	74	71	25	44	152	4	.237	22
Schmidt, Jason, Pit.	R	4.19	13	11	33	33	2	0	0	0	212.2	219	110	99	24	85	148	6	.262	5
Schourek, Pete, Pit.	L	5.34	4	7	30	17	0	0	2	0	113.0	128	75	67	20	49	94	0	.287	NV
Shumaker, Anthony, Phi.	L	5.96	0	3	8	4	0	0	2	0	22.2	23	17	15	3	14	17	1	.261	NV
Smith, Dan, Mon.	R	6.02	4	9	20	17	0	0	0	0	89.2	104	64	60	12	39	72	3	.293	NV
Smoltz, John, Atl.	R	3.19	11	8	29	29	1	1	0	0	186.1	168	70	66	14	40	156	2	.245	22
Spencer, Stan, S.D.	R	9.16	0	7	9	8	0	0	1	0	38.1	56	44	39	11	11	36	1	.335	NV
Spoljaric, Paul, Phi.	L	15.09	0	3	5	3	0	0	1	0	11.1	23	24	19	1	7	10	0	.426	NV
Springer, Dennis, Fla.	R	4.86	6	16	38	29	3	2	3	1	196.1	231	121	106	23	64	83	2	.303	NV
Stephenson, Garrett, St.L.	R	4.22	6	3	18	12	0	0	1	0	85.1	90	43	40	11	29	59	0	.275	2
Stottlemyre, Todd, Ari.	R	4.09	6	3	17	17	0	0	0	0	101.1	106	51	46	12	40	74	2	.268	1
Tapani, Kevin, Chi.	R	4.83	6	12	23	23	1	0	0	0	136.0	151	81	73	12	33	73	3	.280	NV
Thompson, Mark, St.L.	R	2.76	1	3	5	5	0	0	0	0	29.1	26	12	9	1	17	22	1	.241	NV
Thomson, John, Col.	R	8.04	1	10	14	13	1	0	1	0	62.2	85	62	56	11	36	34	2	.324	NV
Thurman, Mike, Mon.	R	4.05	7	11	29	27	0	0	1	0	146.2	140	84	66	17	52	85	4	.251	5
Tomko, Brett, Cin.	R	4.92	5	7	33	26	1	0	1	0	172.0	175	103	94	31	60	132	8	.263	NV
Trachsel, Steve, Chi.	R	5.56	8	18	34	34	4	0	0	0	205.2	226	133	127	32	64	149	8	.280	NV
Valdes, Ismael, L.A.	R	3.98	9	14	32	32	2	1	0	0	203.1	213	97	90	32	58	143	6	.270	7
Vazquez, Javier, Mon.	R	5.00	9	8	26	26	3	1	0	0	154.2	154	98	86	20	52	113	2	.255	1
Villone, Ron, Cin.	L	4.23	9	7	29	22	0	0	2	2	142.2	114	70	67	8	73	97	6	.219	7
Williams, Woody, S.D.	R	4.41	12	12	33	33	0	0	0	0	208.1	213	106	102	33	73	137	9	.268	5
Williams, Jeff, L.A.	L	4.08	2	0	5	3	0	0	1	0	17.2	12	10	8	2	9	7	0	.190	1
Wolf, Randy, Phi.	L	5.55	6	9	22	21	0	0	0	0	121.2	126	78	75	20	67	116	4	.266	NV
Woodall, Brad, Chi.	L	5.63	0	1	6	3	0	0	3	0	16.0	17	12	10	5	6	7	1	.270	NV
Woodard, Steve, Mil.	R	4.52	11	8	31	29	2	0	0	0	185.0	219	101	93	23	36	119	4	.294	4
Wright, Jamey, Col.	R	4.87	4	3	16	16	0	0	0	0	94.1	110	52	51	10	54	49	3	.307	NV
Yoshii, Masato, N.Y.	R	4.40	12	8	31	29	1	0	1	0	174.0	168	86	85	25	58	105	1	.260	8

Minor league report

2000 Baseball Weekly Almanac

▶ **1999 AAA World Series**
▶ **Player of the year**
▶ **All-Star team**
▶ **Overall leaders**

▶ **1999 league wrap-ups**
▶ **Final AAA and AA player stats**

USA SNAPSHOTS®

A look at statistics that shape the sports world

Pitching prosperity

The Atlanta Braves seemingly own the Cy Young Award in the 1990s. Three of their pitchers have won the award at least once this decade. Teams with the most Cy Young Award winners all time:

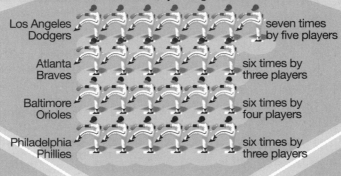

Los Angeles Dodgers	seven times by five players
Atlanta Braves	six times by three players
Baltimore Orioles	six times by four players
Philadelphia Phillies	six times by three players

Source: USA TODAY research

By Ellen J. Horrow and Sam Ward, USA TODAY

The Vancouver Canadians posted a league-best 84-58 record and beat the Oklahoma Redhawks for the Pacific Coast League title en route to the 1999 AAA World Series championship.

Vancouver wins 1999 AAA World Series

The Vancouver Canadians (Oakland A's) played "Long" ball to edge the Charlotte Knights (Chicago White Sox), three games to two, and win the 1999 AAA World Series.

Center fielder **Terrence Long** was named the series Most Valuable Player, hitting .429 with a double, two triples and 10 RBI while making several sparkling catches. The Athletics acquired Long from the New York Mets in July in a trade for left-handed pitcher Kenny Rogers. Long, a left-handed hitter, was the 20th overall pick by the Mets from high school in Alabama in 1994 and is regarded as a player with five-tool potential. The Canadians, who will be moving to Sacramento, Calif., in 2000, were down two games to one in the best-of-five series before winning the last two games. It was the second time in a row that the Pacific Coast League beat the International League to take the title.

Game One:
Charlotte 6, Vancouver 5

Vancouver starter **Mark Mulder** brought a 17-inning postseason scoreless streak with him into the game and kept it alive for 2⅓ innings before giving up one run.

The Canadians scored three runs in the seventh on RBI singles from **Jeff Ball** and Terrence Long. A run-scoring fielder's choice by Mike Neill made it 5-1, Vancouver.

But Mulder tired in the bottom of the seventh, allowing a sacrifice fly by **Dave Hollins** and a two-run double by **Jeff Liefer**, to bring Charlotte within a run (5-4). The Knights tied the score in the eighth on an RBI single by Hollins and won it in the ninth, as **Eric Christopherson** hit a chopper over reliever **Anthony Chavez**'s head with two outs, driving in Chad Mottola for the winning run.

Game Two:
Vancouver 5, Charlotte 4

Vancouver's Long tripled in the fifth to snap a 4-4 tie, pacing the Canadians to the win. It was his third RBI of the night. Long had also delivered sacrifice flies in the first and third.

Charlotte had rallied for a 3-1 lead on groundouts by Liefer, **Tilson Brito,** and Hollins after Mottola had homered to tie the score.

Game Three:
Charlotte 4, Vancouver 2

The Knights rallied from an early 2-0 deficit to take a 2-1 lead in the series with the victory. **Jeff Abbott,** Liefer and **Luis Raven** each homered for Charlotte. Vancouver scored its runs in the second on a two-run double by **Danny Ardoin.**

Game Four:
Vancouver 9, Charlotte 7

Vancouver chased Charlotte starter **Jason Secoda** from the game with a five-run first inning. But Brito hit a pair of homers for the Knights and **Esteban Beltre** tied the game on a wild pitch by reliever **Bert Snow.** In the eighth, Vancouver's **Josue Espada** drove in **Eric Martins** for the tiebreaker, and Long singled Ardoin home for the insurance run.

Game Five:
Vancouver 16, Charlotte 2

Long and **Roberto Vaz** had four RBI apiece to back the stellar pitching of Mulder and lead the Canadians to the championship. Vancouver jumped out to an early 8-0 lead and chased Knights starter **Tanyon Sturtze** in the fourth inning.

Shortstop **Jose Ortiz** hit a three-run homer in the second and Vaz added a two-run shot, his second of the series, in the fourth.

Vancouver put the game away with a seven-run sixth inning, fueled by a two-run homer by **Adam Piatt.**

Mulder allowed just one earned run, walking one and striking out four for the victory.

—*by Lisa Winston*

By Barbara Jean Germano, Baseball Weekly

Piatt won the Texas League Triple Crown in 1999.

Player of the Year:
Adam Piatt

Adam Piatt has become the Oakland Athletics' poster boy for batting practice—as much for what he doesn't do as for what he does.

He doesn't put on a BP show, crushing tape-measure homers over the outfield walls—he saves that for game time. Instead, the third baseman works on the little things, like hitting to the opposite field. It may not dazzle the fans, but it pays off during the game.

It paid off so well that the Midland RockHounds' slugger won the Texas League's first Triple Crown in 72 years and led the minors in several offensive categories.

Piatt's .345 edged out former teammate Jeff DaVanon by .002 and current teammate Josue Espada by .007. Piatt's 39 homers ranked second in the minors and led Wichita's Sean McNally by three for the league title.

His 135 RBI topped the league by 24, over another teammate, T.R. Marcinczyk, and he added three more at Triple A Vancouver for a minor-league-best 138. Piatt also led the minors in runs scored (129), extra-base hits (91) and slugging percentage with an astounding .704 mark.

To put these numbers in perspective, even in a league known as a hitters' haven, the last man to lead in all three categories was Del Pratt of the Waco Cubs in 1927.

Piatt did it all with aplomb, despite being in the spotlight for the first time in his three-year pro career.

"The whole situation has been a great experience," said Piatt, who was promoted to Triple A Vancouver and helped it win both the Pacific Coast League and Triple A World Series titles. "I'd never been in the limelight before like I was with this. Every day there were reporters asking about [the quest for the Triple Crown]."

But Piatt's remarkable season wasn't a total shock to Keith Lieppman, Oakland's director of player development. Lieppman had worked with Piatt for five grueling weeks in 1998 at the Athletics' instructional league in Phoenix.

Every afternoon, in 100-degree heat, Lieppman hit ball after ball to Piatt and a few other third base prospects, getting them to dive, leap, and sprawl in the dirt.

"He dedicated himself to defense and mental toughness, and when he got a glimpse of how much better he was getting defensively, it taught him that he could handle adversity," Lieppman said. "It got to the point that if we were late for the drill, he'd come to get us. He really turned his whole career around with that commitment."

Piatt, the A's eighth-round draft pick in 1997 from Mississippi State, started his 1999 preseason training early, at the advice of fellow A's farmhand Todd Mensik. Sure enough, Piatt got the season off to a blazing start, leading the minors in homers in April. He never looked back.
—by Lisa Winston

Pitcher of the Year: Rick Ankiel

Few pitchers have received the amount of attention, praise or hype, as has Rick Ankiel, the left-hander from Florida who is barely 20 years old.

But Ankiel proved worthy of all the hype and was promoted to the big leagues—and to the starting rotation of the St. Louis Cardinals—in late August.

Between AA Arkansas and AAA Memphis, the teenage sensation had a combined 13-3 record with a 2.35 ERA, striking out 194 batters in 138 innings.

Had he stuck around for three more starts, he probably would've finished the season leading the minors in strikeouts for the second consecutive year. Ankiel, 6-1 and 210 pounds, was the Cards' second-round draft pick in 1997.

Manager of the Year: DeMarlo Hale

DeMarlo Hale guided the Trenton Thunder (Boston Red Sox) to a 92-50 record in 1999, steering the team from a season-opening nine-game win streak to a 14-game lead over second-place Norwich (Yankees) in the final AA Eastern League standings. The 92 wins broke the franchise record of 86, as the squad became just the fourth Eastern League team to win 90 games since 1954.

The club posted four winning streaks of eight games or more, including a 12-game stretch in May. The Thunder never lost more than three games in a row.

For pitching coach Mike Griffin, who had just joined the organization in 1999, the season with Hale was a revelation.

"I had heard many, many great things about DeMarlo when I was assigned to Trenton, and they were all true," said Griffin. "The way the players respond to him is just unbelievable. His patience, his work ethic, the way he treats every single player on the ballclub is just astounding."

Baseball Weekly Minor League All-Star Team

▶1B—Aaron McNeal, Michigan Battle Cats/A (Houston Astros): The Midwest League MVP boosted his average to .310 in the final days of the season. His 38 homers easily led the league, and his 131 RBI set a single-season record for an Astros minor league player. At 6-3 and 230 pounds, the 21-year-old right-handed hitter is a formidable presence at the plate.

▶2B—Marcus Giles, Myrtle Beach Pelicans/A (Atlanta Braves): The younger brother of Pittsburgh Pirates outfielder Brian Giles, the 5-8, 180-pounder won his second consecutive league MVP award in 1999. He took the batting title at .326, adding 13 homers, a league-best 40 doubles and 73 RBI. He was second in the league with a .513 slugging percentage and third with a .393 on-base average.

▶SS—Rafael Furcal, Macon Braves and Myrtle Beach Pelicans/A (Atlanta Braves): Furcal, who didn't turn 19 until the last week of the season, ran onto the All-Star team with 96 stolen bases, tops in the minors this decade. But his game is not one-dimensional. The leadoff hitter batted .322 between his two stops and played outstanding defense in his first full season.

▶3B—Adam Piatt, Midland Rock-Hounds/AA and Vancouver Canadians/AAA (Oakland A's): Baseball Weekly Player of the Year.

▶OF—Chin-Feng Chen, San Bernardino Stampede/A (Los Angeles Dodgers): In his U.S. debut, the first Taiwanese player in more than 20 years became the first 30-30 man in the California League. The 21-year-old Chen was league MVP as he tied for the lead in RBI with 123 while hitting .316 with 31 homers and 31 steals.

▶OF—Jack Cust, High Desert Mavericks/A (Arizona Diamondbacks): Though he lost out to Chen in Cal League MVP voting, Cust finished second in the batting race at .334, and first in homers (32), slugging percentage (.651), and on-base average (.450). He was named the league's top rookie. Cust also finished in the top five in RBI (112), doubles (42), extra-base hits (77) and runs (107).

▶OF—Dee Brown, Wilmington Blue Rocks/A and Wichita Wranglers/AA (Kansas City Royals): The Royals' top pick in 1996 may be the best pure athlete in their system. The former high school football star—5-11, 210 pounds—was on a Triple-Crown pace in Class A (.308, 13 HR, 46 RBI) before he was promoted to AA in early June. Then he picked it up a notch and finished the season with combined stats of .331-25-102 and 30 steals.

▶C—Javier Cardona, Jacksonville Suns/AA (Detroit Tigers): Despite playing in just 107 of 140 games, Cardona managed to finish among the Southern League leaders in nearly every key offensive category. His 26 homers led the league, while his .312 average and 92 RBI both ranked third. His .575 slugging percentage also led the league, and he finished fifth in extra-base hits with 57.

▶SP—Rick Ankiel, Arkansas Travelers/AA and Memphis Redbirds/AAA (St. Louis Cardinals): Baseball Weekly Pitcher of the Year.

▶SP—Scott Comer, Brevard County Manatees/A (Florida Marlins): The 6-foot-5 southpaw was limited to 19 starts due to an early injury, but he posted a 2.35 ERA and walked only five batters in 130 innings. Originally a 10th-round pick by the Mets, Comer was dealt to the Marlins during the 1997 winter meetings for left-handed reliever Dennis Cook.

▶SP—Eric Gagne, San Antonio Missions/AA (Los Angeles Dodgers): While recovering from Tommy John surgery, which had cost him the 1997 season, the hockey fanatic from Montreal seriously considered retiring to accept a hockey scholarship from the University of Vermont. But he stuck with baseball and was Texas League Pitcher of the Year in 1999 (12-4, 2.63 ERA, 185 strikeouts in 168 innings). Gagne finished the year with five double-digit strikeout performances in a row, the first minor leaguer to accomplish that in three years.

▶SP—Mike Meyers, Daytona Cubs/A and West Tenn Diamond Jaxx/AA (Chicago Cubs): The 6-2, 210-pound righty from Canada went 14-3 with a 1.73 ERA in 1999. He walked just 50 and allowed just

89 hits over 140 innings while striking out 150. Meyers added a curveball to his arsenal in 1999 and won Florida State League All-Star honors despite being promoted to West Tenn in early August.

▶SP—Tomokazu Ohka, Trenton Thunder/AA and Pawtucket Red Sox/AAA (Boston Red Sox): In his U.S. debut, the Japanese-born 23-year-old went 15-0 with a 2.31 ERA, striking out 116 while walking just 36 in 140 innings. The Yokohama BayStars system (Japanese Central League) allowed Ohka to sign with the Red Sox as a gesture of thanks for help that the Boston organization gave the BayStars' scouting department.

▶Closer—Francisco Cordero, Jacksonville Suns/AA (Detroit Tigers): Though he missed the last month of the season after being called up to Detroit, Cordero still was named the Southern League's Most Outstanding Pitcher, an unusual honor for a reliever. Cordero collected 27 saves with Jacksonville while posting a 1.38 ERA, best among minor league closers.

and barely missed a beat. Overall, Broussard finished the regular season with a .332 average, 24 homers, and 75 RBI in just 78 games.

▶OF—Chad Durham, Bristol Sox, Appalachian League (Chicago White Sox): If the name, the position and the organization sound familiar, it's because they are. This is the younger brother of White Sox second baseman Ray Durham. Drafted as a second baseman like big brother, this Durham has moved to the outfield where he can utilize his blazing speed. That speed netted him 59 stolen bases, tops in the organization, in just 75 games while batting .314.

▶2B—Ruben Salazar, Elizabethton Twins, Appalachian League (Minnesota Twins): The 21-year-old Venezuelan, in his second year in the U. S., batted .401 to win not only the Appy League batting crown, but the MVP award as well. Salazar added 14 homers and 65 RBI to his other season totals.

Short-season standouts

Though the *Baseball Weekly* All-Star Team honors players who have turned in top performances over the course of a full season, a handful of short-season players deserve notice for their spectacular showings.

▶1B—Lyle Overbay, Missoula Osprey, Pioneer League (Arizona Diamondbacks): The Diamondbacks' 19th-round pick (spring 1999) from the University of Nevada-Reno set a new standard in RBI for all short-season leagues as he drove in 101 runs. It was the first time in minor league history that a short-season player topped the century mark. Overbay also hit .343 with 12 homers.

▶1B/OF—Ben Broussard, Billings Mustangs, Pioneer League; Clinton Lumber-Kings, Midwest League; and Chattanooga Lookouts, Southern League (Cincinnati Reds): Broussard, the Reds' second-round pick (1999) from McNeese State, tore up Pioneer League pitching so completely that he was catapulted from Billings to Clinton to playoff-bound Chattanooga

Final AAA and AA Player Stats

International League

Buffalo Bisons (Indians) AAA

BATTING	AVG	AB	R	H	2B	3B	HR	RBI	BB	SO	SB
Alomar, Sandy, C	.273	33	9	9	2	1	2	10	6	3	0
Borders, Pat, C	.237	198	17	47	7	0	5	23	12	31	0
*Branyan, Russell, 3B	.208	395	51	82	11	1	30	67	52	187	8
*Budzinski, Mark, OF	.286	133	24	38	7	3	2	17	22	36	4
Cabrera, Jolbert, OF	.265	279	44	74	13	4	0	27	26	43	20
*Cruz, Jacob, OF	.272	202	29	55	7	2	7	31	21	39	4
Fryman, Travis, 3B	.182	11	1	2	0	0	1	2	0	3	0
Harriss, Robin, C	.000	3	0	0	0	0	0	0	0	1	0
Manto, Jeff, 1B	.296	203	47	60	9	0	23	44	66	47	3
McDonald, John, SS	.316	237	30	75	12	1	0	25	11	23	6
*Miller, David, OF	.240	325	37	78	21	3	2	37	33	57	12
Miller, Orlando, SS	.258	233	27	60	17	0	7	33	12	52	5
Morgan, Scott, OF	.257	171	32	44	9	0	8	31	18	38	2
Ortiz, Nick, SS	.255	51	7	13	4	0	0	1	3	10	0
Perry, Chan, 1B	.282	273	44	77	17	0	10	59	19	34	5
Ramirez, Alex, OF	.305	305	50	93	20	2	12	50	17	52	5
*Roberts, David, OF	.271	350	65	95	17	10	0	38	43	52	39
Scutaro, Marcos, 2B	.273	462	76	126	24	2	8	51	61	69	21
*Selby, Bill, DH	.295	447	75	132	32	5	20	85	57	63	4
Soliz, Steve, C	.259	112	15	29	6	0	2	14	6	24	0
Turner, Chris, C	.273	231	36	63	9	0	9	33	34	45	2
#Whiten, Mark, OF	.280	175	32	49	10	0	6	19	22	38	3

PITCHING	W	L	ERA	G	SV	IP	H	R	ER	BB	SO
Brower, Jim	11	11	4.73	27	0	160.0	164	101	84	59	76
Brown, Jamie	1	0	5.40	1	0	5.0	8	4	3	1	2
*Cadaret, Greg	0	0	2.70	10	0	6.2	6	3	2	7	8
*Cairncross, Cam	0	3	5.21	19	0	19.0	22	13	11	6	13
Camp, Jared	0	0	.84	10	1	10.2	4	2	1	13	14
De Paula, Sean	0	0	.00	5	2	5.0	0	0	0	3	7
Dedrick, Jim	2	2	4.08	30	0	46.1	49	23	21	27	26
DeLucia, Rich	2	3	4.18	44	19	47.1	39	24	22	29	46
Dougherty, Tony	0	2	5.63	16	0	24.0	28	17	15	15	8
Driskill, Travis	9	8	4.83	31	0	132.1	146	78	71	32	90
Gooden, Doc	0	1	2.45	1	0	3.2	6	1	1	3	3
*Haney, Chris	2	5	3.22	13	0	58.2	50	25	21	22	37
*Langston, Mark	0	1	3.86	4	0	18.2	16	9	8	8	11
*Martin, Tom	1	0	3.00	5	0	6.0	5	2	2	1	6
Martinez, Willie	2	2	6.85	4	0	22.1	28	17	17	7	12
*Matthews, Mike	1	2	7.59	25	0	21.1	23	18	18	18	16
Menhart, Paul	2	1	4.85	7	0	13.0	18	7	7	4	10
Rakers, Jason	7	8	4.92	23	0	131.2	151	83	72	31	85
Rigdon, Paul	7	4	4.53	19	0	103.1	114	60	52	28	60
Riske, David	3	0	.65	23	6	27.2	14	3	2	7	22
Sanders, Frankie	0	1	9.00	1	0	5.0	6	5	5	4	3
Sexton, Jeff	0	1	6.52	23	0	29.0	47	24	21	14	22
Stevens, Dave	1	0	1.52	20	12	23.2	12	4	4	14	28
Tam, Jeff	2	3	2.53	32	3	46.1	47	16	13	11	23
Telgheder, Dave	8	8	3.95	29	0	107.0	109	56	47	21	60
Wagner, Paul	8	4	3.82	23	0	129.2	123	67	55	55	95
Walker, Mike	2	1	5.60	29	2	35.1	43	29	22	26	15
Wright, Jaret	0	0	.00	1	0	3.0	0	0	0	0	4

Charlotte Knights (White Sox) AAA

BATTING	AVG	AB	R	H	2B	3B	HR	RBI	BB	SO	SB
Abbott, Jeff, OF	.318	277	42	88	24	1	9	37	16	27	2
*Beamon, Trey, OF	.259	54	11	14	5	0	1	6	3	10	4
Beltre, Esteban, SS	.262	435	72	114	27	3	3	40	30	80	9
Brito, Tilson, 2B	.318	406	60	129	30	5	11	58	34	66	6
*Christensen, M., OF	.250	4	0	1	0	0	0	0	0	0	1
Christopherson, E., C	.314	188	36	59	17	0	3	27	30	39	4
Eddie, Steve, 3B	.273	143	17	39	6	0	2	15	8	20	0
Gonzalez, Jose, 2B	.286	14	3	4	1	0	0	1	0	3	1
#Gonzalez, M., OF	.310	129	14	40	6	1	1	25	5	20	1
#Hollins, Dave, 3B	.317	199	49	63	18	0	8	33	33	37	5

Class AAA WRAP-UPS

International League

The International League wild card Charlotte Knights upset the Durham Bulls to win the Governors Cup. Bulls first baseman **Steve Cox**, league MVP, won the batting title (.341) and had a league-best 127 RBI. Knights DH **Luis Raven** took the homer crown (33); Louisville RiverBats outfielder **Greg Martinez** led the league with 48 steals. Indianapolis Indians ace **Giovanni Carrara** edged out **Ed Yarnall** of the Columbus Clippers by less than .01 of a percentage point for the ERA crown (3.47). Yarnall, Pitcher of the Year, was second in wins (13) and third in strikeouts (146). **Jay Tessmer** of Columbus led the league with 28 saves. Teammate **Kurt Bierek** was Rookie of the Year (.279, 22 HR, 89 RBI).

INTERNATIONAL (AAA)

North Division

	W	L	Pct.	GB
Scranton-W.B.	78	66	.542	—
Pawtucket	76	68	.528	2
Syracuse	73	71	.507	5
Buffalo	72	72	.500	6
Rochester	61	83	.424	17
Ottawa	59	85	.410	19

South Division

	W	L	Pct.	GB
Durham	83	60	.580	—
Charlotte	82	62	.569	1.5
Norfolk	77	63	.550	4.5
Richmond	64	78	.451	18.5

West Division

	W	L	Pct.	GB
Columbus	83	58	.589	—
Indianapolis	75	69	.521	9.5
Louisville	63	81	.438	21.5
Toledo	57	87	.396	27.5

Switch-hitter
* Left-handed

Class AAA WRAP-UPS

Pacific Coast League

The Vancouver Canadians, who will become the Sacramento River Cats in 2000, took the title. Fresno Grizzlies outfielder **Calvin Murray** was MVP; Omaha Goldenspikes outfielder **Mark Quinn** won the batting crown (.360); and Colorado Springs SkySox veteran **J.R. Phillips** hit 41 homers—the only player in the minors to top 40. Salt Lake Buzz slugger **David Ortiz** won the RBI title (110). Tacoma Rainiers **Mel Bunch** won the ERA crown (3.10); Oklahoma Redhawks ace **Matt Perisho** led in wins (15); and Nashville Sounds hurler **Todd Van Poppel** led in strikeouts (157). The Sky Sox **David Wainhouse** led the loop in saves (22).

PACIFIC COAST (AAA)
East Division

	W	L	Pct.	GB
Oklahoma	83	59	.585	—
Nashville	80	60	.571	2
Memphis	74	64	.536	7
New Orleans	55	85	.393	27

North Division

	W	L	Pct.	GB
Vancouver	84	58	.592	—
Tacoma	69	70	.496	13.5
Edmonton	65	74	.468	17.5
Calgary	57	82	0.41	25.5

Central Division

	W	L	Pct.	GB
Omaha	81	60	.574	—
Col. Springs	66	73	.475	14
Albuquerque	65	74	.468	15
Iowa	65	76	.461	16

South Division

	W	L	Pct.	GB
Salt Lake	73	68	.518	—
Fresno	73	69	.514	0.5
Las Vegas	67	75	.472	6.5
Tucson	66	76	.465	7.5

Switch-hitter
* Left-handed

BATTING	AVG	AB	R	H	2B	3B	HR	RBI	BB	SO	SB
#Hollins, Dave, 3B	.308	214	51	66	19	0	8	34	34	42	5
Inglin, Jeff, OF	.205	39	8	8	0	0	3	8	4	9	0
Lee, Carlos, 3B	.351	94	16	33	5	0	4	20	8	14	2
*Liefer, Jeff, 1B	.339	171	36	58	17	1	9	34	21	26	2
Lydy, Scott, OF	.212	66	11	14	2	0	2	13	8	15	1
Magdaleno, Ricky, SS	.235	81	7	19	5	1	0	7	7	20	0
Martinez, Gabby, SS	.286	49	8	14	1	0	4	5	5	6	3
Moore, Brandon, SS	.284	299	44	85	21	2	1	41	21	41	3
Mottola, Chad, OF	.321	511	95	164	32	4	20	94	60	83	18
Ramirez, Dan, OF	.143	14	2	2	1	0	0	2	1	3	1
Raven, Luis, DH	.282	532	97	150	32	4	33	125	50	127	5
#Simmons, Brian, OF	.270	285	53	77	14	0	10	44	37	60	8
Simons, Mitch, 2B	.289	474	85	137	32	1	7	52	45	67	22
Toth, Dave, C	.245	261	36	64	14	0	6	33	24	38	1
*Valdez, Mario, 1B	.274	402	78	110	17	2	26	76	76	91	1

PITCHING	W	L	ERA	G	SV	IP	H	R	ER	BB	SO
Andujar, Luis	4	5	3.00	52	16	60.0	62	21	20	13	59
Beirne, Kevin	5	5	5.42	20	0	113.0	134	75	68	36	63
Bradford, Chad	9	3	1.94	47	5	74.1	63	19	16	15	56
Castillo, Carlos	9	6	5.15	20	0	136.1	150	88	78	30	105
Daneker, Pat	4	4	6.57	9	0	49.1	64	36	36	16	36
Davenport, Joe	0	0	8.00	6	0	9.0	13	8	8	1	6
*Eyre, Scott	6	4	3.82	12	0	68.1	75	32	29	23	63
*Fordham, Tom	4	7	7.31	29	0	112.0	144	101	91	66	101
Hasselhoff, Derek	6	0	4.82	49	4	71.0	83	46	38	25	65
Heathcott, Mike	10	8	5.17	32	0	139.1	177	89	80	64	77
Lundquist, David	0	0	0.00	3	0	3.2	3	0	0	1	4
Olsen, Jason	2	4	7.11	22	0	62.0	84	59	49	29	49
*Rizzo, Todd	4	5	4.06	53	8	71.0	68	37	32	31	46
Secoda, Jason	2	5	5.28	7	0	44.1	54	35	26	10	33
Snyder, John	3	0	4.24	3	0	17.0	17	9	8	5	9
Sturtze, Tanyon	9	4	4.05	33	3	104.1	83	53	47	41	107
*VanRyn, Ben	3	2	5.93	47	5	68.1	83	47	45	30	54
Virchis, Adam	0	0	1.42	3	0	6.1	6	1	1	1	4
*Ward, Bryan	2	0	3.52	14	1	15.1	15	7	6	3	15

Columbus Clippers (Yankees) AAA

BATTING	AVG	AB	R	H	2B	3B	HR	RBI	BB	SO	SB
Ashby, Chris, OF	.267	206	46	55	13	1	9	32	21	39	6
Bellinger, Clay, 3B	.234	141	19	33	10	1	2	14	13	32	6
*Bierek, Kurt, 1B	.280	532	84	149	42	4	23	95	48	99	5
*Carpenter, Bubba, OF	.283	325	78	92	20	2	22	81	75	68	7
Cedeno, Andujar, 3B	.293	215	27	63	14	3	6	38	11	31	1
Coolbaugh, Mike, 3B	.276	391	65	108	31	2	15	66	38	112	5
*Glass, Chip, OF	.277	159	32	44	7	3	2	30	22	32	5
#Jimenez, D'Angelo, SS	.327	526	97	172	32	5	15	88	59	75	26
*Ledee, Ricky, OF	.252	115	18	29	7	1	4	15	17	29	4
Molina, Izzy, C	.246	338	44	83	16	1	4	51	18	47	4
Powell, Alonzo, DH	.315	470	97	148	23	1	24	90	82	110	1
Raabe, Brian, 2B	.327	493	93	161	35	5	11	77	48	19	5
Soriano, Alfonso, SS	.183	82	8	15	5	1	2	11	5	18	1
Spencer, Shane, OF	.360	50	17	18	2	0	2	10	9	8	0
Stankiewicz, Andy, 2B	.276	163	34	45	8	3	1	20	23	27	6
*Strawberry, Darryl, DH	.288	73	12	21	5	1	4	15	11	13	1
*Tarasco, Tony, OF	.295	346	72	102	23	0	19	61	49	39	9
Waszgis, B.J., C	.277	191	36	53	12	0	6	31	27	55	4

PITCHING	W	L	ERA	G	SV	IP	H	R	ER	BB	SO
Bradley, Ryan	5	12	6.21	29	0	145.0	163	112	100	73	118
Buddie, Mike	9	2	2.86	49	0	78.2	80	30	25	22	68
De Los Santos, Luis	3	4	4.77	12	0	66.0	81	42	35	24	45
Erdos, Todd	3	2	6.56	27	0	59.0	70	47	43	25	53
Ford, Ben	6	3	4.73	53	3	70.1	69	42	37	39	40
*Fossas, Tony	1	0	4.05	26	0	20.0	17	10	9	6	15
Juden, Jeff	11	12	5.56	27	0	176.1	164	124	109	76	151
*McCarthy, Greg	2	1	3.86	29	1	35.0	24	19	15	19	21
Naulty, Dan	2	1	4.35	7	0	10.1	14	6	5	4	5
Nichting, Chris	8	5	5.29	25	0	127.2	135	80	75	47	110
Pavlas, Dave	4	2	4.04	38	1	62.1	69	32	28	9	49
Spence, Cam	0	1	5.14	1	0	7.0	8	4	4	1	4
Tessmer, Jay	3	3	3.34	51	28	56.2	52	22	21	12	42
*Watson, Allen	0	0	6.14	2	0	7.1	7	5	5	2	5
*Williams, Matt	0	2	3.86	13	0	21.0	15	9	9	11	22
*Wilson, Trevor	3	2	3.56	19	1	48.0	47	25	19	12	41
*Yarnall, Ed	13	4	3.47	23	0	145.0	136	61	56	57	146
*Zancanaro, Dave	7	2	4.17	13	0	77.2	85	40	36	28	45

Durham Bulls (Devil Rays) AAA

BATTING	AVG	AB	R	H	2B	3B	HR	RBI	BB	SO	SB
*Butler, Rich, OF	.289	332	52	96	28	2	10	63	41	70	6
Clyburn, Danny, OF	.234	303	38	71	11	1	9	33	19	74	2
*Cox, Steve, 1B	.341	534	107	182	49	4	25	127	67	74	3
Fraraccio, Dan, 2B	.267	30	5	8	3	0	1	4	4	4	2
#Garcia, Neil, C	.091	33	1	3	1	0	1	2	2	8	1
Graffanino, Tony, 2B	.313	345	66	108	25	6	9	58	37	46	16
Guillen, Jose, OF	.382	34	8	13	1	0	3	12	7	7	0
Holbert, Aaron, 2B	.311	347	77	108	18	4	12	56	25	56	14
*Kieschnick, B., DH	.200	75	6	15	5	0	1	5	5	14	0
#Lamb, David, SS	.233	30	7	7	3	0	0	7	2	4	0
Ledesma, Aaron, 2B	.100	10	0	1	0	0	0	0	0	1	0
*Levis, Jesse, C	.330	94	20	31	5	0	1	8	15	9	0
Lowery, Terrell, OF	.335	275	69	92	20	5	15	57	43	62	10
Martin, Chris, SS	.273	399	64	109	20	1	9	53	48	61	14
McClain, Scott, 3B	.251	533	106	134	33	1	28	104	73	156	4
*Mendoza, Carlos, OF	.293	266	57	78	8	3	1	25	32	38	9
Oliver, Joe, C	.301	219	27	66	18	1	7	43	7	50	1
Perry, Herbert, DH	.311	103	21	32	8	0	5	20	6	21	0
*Sanchez, Alex, OF	.200	10	2	2	1	0	0	0	1	0	0
Silvestri, Dave, 2B	.000	3	0	0	0	0	0	0	0	0	0
Smith, Bobby, 3B	.333	225	52	75	15	3	14	47	27	61	13
Trammell, Bubba, OF	.269	186	25	50	12	0	7	31	15	36	0
*Wilcox, Luke, OF	.328	134	32	44	12	5	9	34	22	18	1
Wilson, Tom, C	.279	215	41	60	19	0	16	44	49	59	0
#Winn, Randy, OF	.353	207	38	73	20	3	3	30	16	27	9

PITCHING	W	L	ERA	G	SV	IP	H	R	ER	BB	SO
Bailey, Roger	1	0	5.67	7	0	27.0	28	21	17	13	17
Barnett, Marty	1	0	5.46	16	0	28.0	30	17	17	14	19
Callaway, Mickey	7	1	4.20	15	0	81.1	86	45	38	28	56
*Charlton, Norm	3	2	3.69	18	1	31.2	27	13	13	10	29
Daniels, John	2	0	4.89	21	0	35.0	37	19	19	9	25
*Davis, Tim	0	0	9.00	3	0	2.0	2	2	2	1	1
*Duvall, Mike	2	2	5.40	19	2	30.0	32	20	18	12	27
Eiland, Dave	5	3	3.36	10	0	59.0	60	26	22	9	46
Gaillard, Eddie	3	6	2.89	59	26	62.1	67	30	20	23	67
Hernandez, Santos	0	2	10.80	6	0	18.1	34	25	22	11	12
Kieschnick, Brooks	0	0	0.00	1	0	2.0	1	1	0	1	1
Lidle, Cory	0	0	4.76	3	0	5.2	9	3	3	1	6
*Morris, James	3	1	5.48	18	0	23.0	21	14	14	19	16
Munoz, Bobby	3	3	4.39	39	5	55.1	55	35	27	31	50
*Newman, Alan	10	0	2.24	50	0	80.1	59	24	20	20	76
Nunez, Maximo	1	0	5.40	21	2	31.2	25	20	19	28	31
Ortega, Pablo	0	1	34.71	1	0	2.1	10	9	9	0	2
Rekar, Bryan	4	1	3.86	6	0	35.0	29	15	15	8	26
*Saunders, Tony	0	0	2.57	1	0	7.0	8	3	2	2	7
Small, Aaron	5	7	6.88	32	0	120.1	156	104	92	47	63
Sparks, Jeff	3	0	3.38	18	0	24.0	16	11	9	14	31
Strong, Joe	0	1	7.98	6	1	14.2	20	13	13	8	12
*Tatis, Ramon	12	8	5.50	28	0	155.1	178	100	95	74	97
Valdes, Marc	1	2	5.18	9	0	40.0	39	25	23	12	23
*Wade, Terrell	1	7	9.49	34	0	98.2	140	112	104	80	61
Wheeler, Dan	7	5	4.92	14	0	82.1	103	59	45	25	58

Indianapolis Indians (Reds) AAA

BATTING	AVG	AB	R	H	2B	3B	HR	RBI	BB	SO	SB
#Baerga, Carlos, 3B	.290	221	32	64	10	0	3	27	10	18	2
Boone, Aaron, 3B	.341	41	6	14	2	1	0	7	3	4	2
*Branson, Jeff, SS	.253	430	57	109	18	2	7	56	46	86	2
*Cromer, D.T., OF	.310	535	83	166	37	4	30	107	44	98	4
Davis, James, C	.288	52	7	15	4	1	0	10	3	6	0
*Frank, Mike, OF	.296	433	73	128	36	7	9	62	36	55	10
Garcia, Guillermo, C	.288	233	30	67	9	0	10	28	22	44	1
#Hardtke, Jason, 2B	.329	416	74	137	37	2	12	61	35	43	7
Hiatt, Phil, 1B	.238	311	46	74	11	0	18	54	30	103	0
Hollins, Damon, OF	.262	328	58	86	19	0	9	43	31	44	11
Johnson, Brian, C	.211	19	2	4	3	0	0	4	1	3	0
LaRue, Jason, C	.251	263	42	66	12	2	12	37	15	52	0
*McCall, Rod, 1B	.259	139	21	36	7	0	6	28	32	49	1
#Melo, Juan, SS	.240	150	23	36	9	1	4	16	10	33	9
Owens, Jayhawk, C	.208	53	7	11	1	0	4	10	4	18	0
*Robinson, Kerry, OF	.264	129	24	34	3	2	1	14	4	12	14
Salzano, Jerry, PH	.091	11	0	1	0	0	0	2	0	6	0
Snopek, Chris, 3B	.281	381	66	107	24	3	9	64	42	51	17

Class AA WRAP-UPS

Eastern League

The Harrisburg Senators defended their Eastern League title. Norwich Navigators first baseman **Nick Johnson** won the batting crown (.345) and led the minors in on-base average (.525). Chris Norton of Portland led the loop in homers (38), while Harrisburg's **Andy Tracy** led in RBI (128). Portland Sea Dogs **Julio Ramirez** led in steals (64). **Pat Ahearne** of the New Haven Ravens won the ERA crown (2.61); Norwich's **Jason Beverlin** and Altoona Curve's **Bronson Arroyo** each had 15 wins. New Haven ace **Ryan Anderson**, the 6-11 "Little Unit," fanned 162; Norwich's **Joe Lisio** had 33 saves.

EASTERN (AA)
Northern Division

	W	L	Pct.	GB
Trenton	92	50	.648	—
Norwich	78	64	.549	14
Portland	65	77	.458	27
New Haven	65	77	.458	27
New Britain	59	82	.418	32.5
Binghamton	54	88	.380	38

Southern Division

	W	L	Pct.	GB
Erie	81	61	.570	—
Harrisburg	76	66	.535	5
Reading	73	69	.514	8
Bowie	70	71	.496	10.5
Akron	69	71	.493	11
Altoona	67	73	.479	13

Switch-hitter
* Left-handed

Class AA WRAP-UPS

Southern League

The Orlando Rays, who are moving to the Disney World Sports Complex in 2000, won the league title. Chattanooga Lookouts outfielder **Brady Clark** earned MVP honors and the batting crown (.326), while Jacksonville Suns catcher **Javier Cardona** led the league in homers (26) and Knoxville Smokies **Tim Giles** took the RBI title (114). **Ethan Faggett** of the Mobile Baybears had a league-best 63 steals. Chattanooga's **Jeff Yoder** had the best ERA (3.08); Jacksonville's **David Darwin** had 14 wins and teammate **Victor Santos** won the strikeout crown (146). Jacksonville closer **Francisco Cordero** was Most Outstanding Pitcher (27 saves, 1.38 ERA) before being called up to Detroit Aug. 2.

SOUTHERN (AA)

East Division

	W	L	Pct.	GB
Orlando	40	31	.563	—
Jacksonville	39	32	.549	1
Knoxville	33	37	.471	6.5
Carolina	29	41	.414	10.5
Greenville	27	43	.386	12.5

West Division

	W	L	Pct.	GB
West Tenn	45	25	.643	—
Chattanooga	41	29	.586	4
Birmingham	39	31	.557	6
Mobile Bay	32	38	.457	13
Huntsville	26	44	.371	19

BATTING	AVG	AB	R	H	2B	3B	HR	RBI	BB	SO	SB
Snopek, Chris, SS	.275	462	76	127	31	3	12	74	47	66	19
*Sweeney, Mark, OF	.322	311	66	100	17	1	12	51	59	40	3
#Tinsley, Lee, OF	.211	76	5	16	2	2	1	6	5	14	1
*Whitmore, Darrell, OF	.282	238	39	67	17	1	10	42	24	64	2
Williams, Jason, 2B	.381	160	30	61	18	2	2	19	14	25	4

PITCHING	W	L	ERA	G	SV	IP	H	R	ER	BB	SO
*Atchley, Justin	2	1	5.40	5	1	23.1	39	14	14	2	6
Barrios, Manny	2	7	5.28	49	0	90.1	94	60	53	35	73
Belinda, Stan	2	0	2.38	10	0	11.1	7	3	3	6	10
Carrara, Giovanni	12	7	3.47	39	0	158.0	144	68	61	58	114
Etler, Todd	2	1	6.39	26	0	38.0	42	29	27	29	35
Flury, Pat	1	1	7.04	23	6	23.0	27	18	18	20	20
Glauber, Keith	3	3	5.82	12	0	68.0	84	49	44	20	51
Greene, Rick	5	7	3.69	61	9	78.0	78	37	32	35	40
Harriger, Denny	14	6	4.08	27	0	172.0	183	82	78	36	110
Janzen, Marty	1	1	4.86	9	0	16.2	16	9	9	8	8
Klingenbeck, Scott	4	4	4.82	14	1	74.2	89	44	40	26	53
LeBlanc, Eric	1	2	7.11	14	1	44.1	57	43	35	19	26
Meacham, Rusty	1	3	6.98	16	1	29.2	38	27	23	15	19
Merrell, Phil	0	3	14.73	3	0	11.0	21	21	18	4	6
*Neagle, Denny	2	0	4.67	3	0	17.1	11	9	9	2	9
Pall, Donn	1	0	8.44	4	0	5.1	9	7	5	1	1
Parris, Steve	0	2	4.04	6	0	35.2	39	16	16	9	31
*Priest, Eddie	6	5	5.35	18	2	69.0	86	41	41	20	35
Riedling, John	1	0	1.54	24	1	35.0	19	9	6	18	26
*Robertson, Rich	0	0	9.82	9	0	7.1	17	9	8	4	7
Sager, A.J.	6	3	4.67	24	0	52.0	79	45	27	25	18
Therneau, Dave	0	2	8.17	7	0	36.1	52	36	33	14	22
Thompson, Mark	2	6	5.13	11	0	54.1	50	31	31	29	28
*Tolar, Kevin	1	0	2.08	8	0	13.0	8	4	3	7	18
Tomko, Brett	2	0	4.97	2	0	12.2	15	7	7	1	9
*Villone, Ron	2	0	1.42	18	1	19.0	9	3	3	13	23
Williams, Todd	1	3	5.10	38	24	42.1	38	24	24	13	35

Louisville Riverbats (Brewers) AAA

BATTING	AVG	AB	R	H	2B	3B	HR	RBI	BB	SO	SB
*Andreopoulos, A., C	.264	201	19	53	8	0	5	31	25	21	1
#Banks, Brian, 1B	.208	24	3	5	2	1	1	6	2	5	0
*Barker, Kevin, 1B	.278	442	89	123	27	5	23	87	59	94	2
Belliard, Ron, 2B	.241	108	14	26	4	0	1	8	14	13	12
Benitez, Yamil, OF	.214	341	47	73	24	2	12	49	29	103	13
Brito, Jorge, C	.056	18	0	1	0	0	0	0	0	9	0
Cancel, Robinson, C	.368	117	22	43	8	0	5	28	14	28	6
Collier, Lou, 3B	.385	91	25	35	10	0	4	11	15	14	6
*Cromer, Brandon, 2B	.215	330	46	71	12	1	24	61	40	103	6
Greene, Charlie, C	.211	161	16	34	8	0	4	15	7	26	0
Hughes, Bobby, C	.188	32	5	6	2	0	1	2	2	7	0
#Iapoce, Anthony, OF	.169	83	6	14	2	0	0	0	7	30	6
Krause, Scott, OF	.277	499	57	138	26	7	15	89	33	104	10
#Lopez, Mickey, 2B	.320	181	43	58	17	2	5	31	37	25	11
#Martinez, Greg, OF	.265	419	79	111	13	4	4	29	53	50	48
Mouton, Lyle, OF	.310	467	89	145	43	3	23	94	40	98	22
Ortiz, Luis, DH	.263	304	36	80	11	0	11	33	23	41	0
#Perez, Santiago, SS	.263	407	57	107	23	8	7	38	31	94	21
*Valentin, Jose, SS	.250	20	6	5	0	0	3	3	4	3	0
*Williamson, A., DH	.239	184	21	44	7	0	5	20	30	29	0
Zosky, Eddie, 3B	.294	415	60	122	22	3	12	47	23	68	5

PITCHING	W	L	ERA	G	SV	IP	H	R	ER	BB	SO
Bere, Jason	2	3	5.36	10	0	43.2	46	28	26	27	35
Borowski, Joe	6	2	5.46	58	4	89.0	94	59	54	44	70
Converse, Jim	4	3	5.81	30	0	62.0	76	43	40	34	40
D'Amico, Jeff	0	0	13.50	1	0	3.1	6	5	5	2	1
Dale, Carl	0	1	4.63	7	1	11.2	8	6	6	5	8
Eldred, Cal	0	1	5.30	4	0	18.2	19	12	11	10	21
*Estrada, Horacio	6	6	5.67	25	0	131.2	128	87	83	65	112
Falteisek, Steve	5	11	6.84	42	0	76.1	98	65	58	41	34
*Granger, Jeff	1	6	4.73	56	3	59.0	72	40	31	25	50
Harris, Reggie	3	4	4.73	41	16	40.0	43	21	21	20	45
Henderson, Rod	7	11	6.34	28	0	120.2	119	109	85	64	76
Levrault, Allen	1	3	8.65	9	0	34.1	48	37	33	16	33
Minor, Blas	4	4	4.58	21	0	108.0	118	59	55	32	77
Ontiveros, Steve	5	1	4.44	8	0	48.2	47	26	24	12	33
*Passini, Brian	2	3	7.48	6	0	27.2	34	23	23	17	14
Peterson, Kyle	7	6	3.55	18	0	109.0	90	52	43	42	95
Pittsley, Jim	2	4	8.77	8	0	39.0	55	42	38	16	26

Switch-hitter
* Left-handed

PITCHING	W	L	ERA	G	SV	IP	H	R	ER	BB	SO
*Pulsipher, Bill	0	2	4.28	6	0	27.1	22	14	13	19	21
Ramirez, Hector	3	3	3.80	58	9	94.2	91	45	40	33	55
Reyes, Al	0	2	8.38	6	0	9.2	12	9	9	7	8
*Roque, Rafael	1	0	.00	2	0	10.0	4	0	0	3	3
VanEgmond, Tim	0	5	5.06	8	0	26.2	28	25	15	17	15
*Wunsch, Kelly	2	1	4.75	16	0	41.2	52	23	22	14	20

Norfolk Tides (Mets) AAA

BATTING	AVG	AB	R	H	2B	3B	HR	RBI	BB	SO	SB
Agbayani, Benny, OF	.356	101	21	36	8	1	8	32	16	19	5
Allensworth, J., OF	.264	273	44	72	20	5	5	20	36	39	10
Baez, Kevin, 2B	.270	215	19	58	8	0	1	33	28	25	3
Bell, Mike, 2B	.274	135	11	37	11	1	1	25	9	23	4
#Bonilla, Bobby, DH	.231	13	1	3	0	0	0	1	0	1	0
Brooks, Jerry, 1B	.237	241	32	57	13	1	9	27	34	50	0
Buccheri, Jim, OF	.220	100	11	22	4	0	0	7	6	15	6
Darden, Tony, 3B	.121	33	4	4	1	0	0	3	7	4	2
Grifol, Pedro, C	.260	177	11	46	5	0	4	27	12	33	1
Halter, Shane, SS	.274	474	77	130	22	3	6	35	60	90	19
Haltiwanger, G., OF	.000	13	2	0	0	0	0	0	0	8	0
Haney, Todd, 2B	.311	447	82	139	25	6	5	48	73	43	7
Kinkade, Mike, 3B	.308	312	53	96	20	2	7	49	21	31	7
*Livingstone, Scott, 1B	.318	157	15	50	11	0	1	27	14	13	3
*Long, Terrence, OF	.326	304	41	99	20	4	7	47	23	41	14
Mora, Melvin, SS	.303	304	55	92	17	2	8	36	41	54	18
Neubart, Garrett, OF	.158	38	6	6	0	0	0	2	6	7	5
Paquette, Craig, 3B	.272	283	40	77	20	3	15	54	10	47	3
Payton, Jay, OF	.389	144	27	56	13	2	8	35	12	13	2
Rodriguez, Sammy, C	.222	9	2	2	0	0	2	4	3	2	0
#Romero, Mandy, C	.233	240	15	56	13	0	4	31	22	44	0
Toca, Jorge, 1B	.335	176	25	59	12	1	5	29	6	23	0
*Tomberlin, Andy, OF	.310	303	60	94	21	1	16	61	40	74	2
*Tyner, Jason, OF	.000	8	0	0	0	0	0	0	0	5	0
Valera, Yohanny, C	.154	65	3	10	2	0	1	6	4	16	0
Wilson, Vance, C	.264	53	10	14	3	0	3	5	4	8	1

PITCHING	W	L	ERA	G	SV	IP	H	R	ER	BB	SO
Baez, Kevin	0	0	3.38	2	0	2.2	5	1	1	1	0
Bautista, Jose	7	4	5.33	20	0	82.2	111	53	49	21	41
Bautista, Jose	7	5	5.43	36	4	111.0	144	72	67	26	65
*Beltran, Rigo	2	1	1.61	21	0	22.1	16	5	4	12	27
Cammack, Eric	0	0	3.12	9	4	8.2	7	3	3	1	17
Darden, Tony	0	0	.00	2	0	2.1	2	2	0	0	1
Dotel, Octavio	5	2	3.84	13	0	70.1	52	33	30	34	90
Fleetham, Ben	1	2	14.85	6	0	6.2	11	15	11	10	9
Gonzalez, Dicky	0	1	2.70	1	0	6.2	5	2	2	1	3
Guerra, Mark	8	3	2.93	63	0	89.0	90	45	29	39	70
Henderson, Ryan	1	2	6.84	28	0	48.2	49	45	37	34	46
Henriquez, Oscar	3	4	4.00	53	23	54.0	54	31	24	38	65
Isringhausen, Jason	3	1	2.29	12	0	51.0	33	18	13	20	51
Jones, Bobby	2	0	2.45	2	0	11.0	11	3	3	3	8
Lewis, Richie	7	8	5.06	20	0	122.2	128	82	69	49	101
Lopez, Johan	3	5	4.15	33	1	102.0	98	49	47	44	84
Lyons, Mike	0	0	21.00	2	0	3.0	7	7	7	3	5
Mahomes, Pat	4	1	3.49	6	0	38.2	38	17	15	12	24
McMichael, Greg	0	0	2.70	3	0	3.1	4	1	1	3	4
*Mercado, Hector	0	0	1.50	2	0	6.0	3	1	1	1	2
Mercedes, Jose	2	1	2.53	6	0	32.0	36	15	9	11	19
Murray, Dan	12	10	4.97	29	0	145.0	149	91	80	70	96
Neubart, Garrett	0	0	3.38	2	0	2.2	3	1	1	0	1
Palacios, Vicente	2	1	1.86	7	1	9.2	9	2	2	4	9
Pontes, Dan	0	0	9.39	14	0	23.0	36	25	24	11	14
Reed, Rick	0	1	27.00	1	0	3.0	10	9	9	2	2
Roberts, Grant	2	1	4.50	5	0	28.0	32	15	14	11	30
*Ruebel, Matt	3	0	4.50	7	0	40.0	40	20	20	17	23
*Stewart, Scott	6	4	4.42	35	0	99.2	109	55	49	36	85
Treadwell, Jody	1	2	9.93	11	0	22.2	27	25	25	18	19
Turrentine, Rich	0	1	6.75	2	0	2.2	6	2	2	1	3
Villano, Mike	0	0	4.50	2	0	2.0	3	1	1	2	1
Wallace, Derek	2	5	3.60	36	7	55.0	53	24	22	25	38
Welch, Mike	3	4	5.81	37	0	66.2	78	47	43	26	28

Ottawa Lynx (Expos) AAA

BATTING	AVG	AB	R	H	2B	3B	HR	RBI	BB	SO	SB
Adolfo, Carlos, OF	.189	53	5	10	2	1	2	9	3	11	0
Andrews, Shane, 3B	.250	8	1	2	0	0	1	4	0	2	0

Class AA WRAP-UPS

Texas League

The Wichita Wranglers won the league title with a sweep of the defending champion Tulsa Drillers. **Adam Piatt** of the Midland RockHounds, *Baseball Weekly*'s 1999 Minor League Player of the Year, was a shoo-in MVP with the first Triple Crown in the circuit since 1927 (.345, 39 HR, 135 RBI). He also led the minors with a .704 slugging percentage, 128 runs scored and 90 extra-base hits. Mike Metcalfe of the San Antonio Missions led in steals (57); **Eric Gagne** of San Antonio was Pitcher of the Year at 12-4 with a league-best 2.63 ERA and 185 strikeouts. The Jackson Generals' **Jeriome Robertson** led the league with 15 wins; San Antonio's **Matt Montgomery** led with 26 saves.

TEXAS (AA)
East Division

	W	L	Pct.	GB
Tulsa	40	32	.556	—
Jackson	38	34	.528	2
Shreveport	32	40	.444	8
Arkansas	28	44	.389	12

West Division

	W	L	Pct.	GB
Wichita	45	27	.625	—
Midland	38	34	.528	7
San Antonio	37	35	.514	8
El Paso	30	42	.417	15

Switch-hitter
* Left-handed

Class A WRAP-UPS

California League

The San Bernardino Stampede won the league championship and made history with Taiwanese outfielder **Chin-Feng Chen,** who in his first U.S. season became the league's first 30-30 man. Feng was MVP (.316, 31 HR, 31 steals, 123 RBI). His RBI mark tied Modesto A's **Jason Hart** and the Visalia Oaks' **Todd Mensik** for the league lead. High Desert Mavericks outfielder **Jack Cust** was second in the batting race at .334, first in homers (32) and fourth in RBI (112). **Eric Byrnes** of Modesto took the batting crown (.337); Lake Elsinore Storm's **Nelson Castro** led in steals (53). San Bernardino's **Randey Dorame** was Most Valuable Pitcher (14-3, 2.51). Lake Elsinore's **Steve Fish** had 180 strikeouts; **Bill Everly** of San Bernardino tied a league record with 34 saves and was the Rolaids Reliever of the Year in the National Association.

CALIFORNIA (A)
North Division

	W	L	Pct.	GB
Modesto	44	26	.629	—
Visalia	43	27	.614	1
San Jose	37	33	.529	7
Bakersfield	28	42	.400	16
Stockton	23	47	.329	21

South Division

	W	L	Pct.	GB
San Bernardino	38	32	.543	—
High Desert	38	32	.543	—
Rancho Cuca.	34	36	.486	4
Lake Elsinore	33	37	.471	5
Lancaster	32	38	.457	6

Switch-hitter
* Left-handed

BATTING	AVG	AB	R	H	2B	3B	HR	RBI	BB	SO	SB
Barrett, Michael, 3B	.429	7	1	3	0	0	0	2	1	0	0
*Bergeron, Peter, OF	.314	194	36	61	12	3	3	20	23	40	14
#Blum, Geoff, SS	.265	268	43	71	14	1	10	37	37	39	6
*Bradshaw, Terry, OF	.197	127	13	25	5	3	0	10	16	31	4
Burkhart, Lance, OF	.125	8	1	1	0	0	0	0	0	5	0
Camilli, Jason, 2B	.265	102	12	27	6	0	0	8	11	19	4
Carvajal, Jhonny, SS	.231	355	28	82	20	4	0	34	21	67	7
Coquillette, Trace, 2B	.326	334	56	109	32	3	14	55	44	68	10
Cox, Darron, C	.000	9	0	0	0	0	0	0	1	2	0
Fernandez, Jose, 3B	.271	465	73	126	30	2	14	68	31	136	14
*Fullmer, Brad, 1B	.317	142	31	45	9	0	11	32	12	16	2
#Hosey, Dwayne, OF	.181	94	16	17	3	1	1	11	15	26	6
Hunter, Scott, OF	.226	460	42	104	17	0	16	64	29	106	8
Jones, Terry, OF	.262	332	49	87	17	2	0	23	24	66	30
Machado, Robert, C	.217	129	10	28	8	0	2	10	4	26	0
Malave, Jaime, DH	.250	8	2	2	0	0	0	0	1	4	0
*McGuire, Ryan, 1B	.251	183	23	46	6	1	4	27	35	37	1
Morales, Francisco, C	.229	345	43	79	11	1	10	44	31	93	1
Pachot, John, C	.214	56	7	12	4	0	0	6	6	9	0
Post, Dave, 2B	.259	375	49	97	17	2	10	36	34	56	12
#Seguignol, F., 1B	.285	312	54	89	17	3	23	74	40	96	3
Snusz, Chris, C	.286	63	6	18	3	0	3	9	1	18	0
*Staton, T.J., OF	.190	42	5	8	3	1	0	5	10	11	2
*Stowers, Chris, OF	.237	431	60	102	17	4	5	37	39	92	28

PITCHING	W	L	ERA	G	SV	IP	H	R	ER	BB	SO
Baker, Jason	1	0	8.53	11	0	12.2	18	12	12	14	9
Batista, Miguel	0	1	2.25	3	0	8.0	3	2	2	4	7
Bennett, Shayne	3	9	5.04	38	8	89.1	96	53	50	37	70
*Benz, Jake	2	3	5.93	18	1	30.1	42	27	20	20	34
*DeHart, Rick	2	4	4.78	15	0	26.1	33	19	14	11	22
DeSilva, John	4	1	2.89	22	0	90.1	73	35	29	41	75
*Duran, Roberto	1	1	5.25	5	0	12.0	10	8	7	13	10
Durocher, Jayson	1	3	1.51	17	4	35.2	17	12	6	20	22
Evans, Keith	2	13	4.80	24	0	122.0	143	79	65	22	74
Field, Nathan	0	0	3.00	2	0	3.0	4	1	1	4	4
*Forster, Scott	0	4	5.16	53	2	52.1	49	32	30	47	32
Johnson, Mike	6	12	5.38	28	0	147.1	174	105	88	63	120
*Lilly, Ted	8	5	3.84	16	0	89.0	81	40	38	23	78
Marquez, Robert	1	1	4.88	18	1	27.2	33	19	15	14	16
Mitchell, Scott	4	4	5.63	18	0	62.1	78	43	39	25	28
*Moraga, David	1	2	6.19	4	0	16.0	24	14	11	5	10
Mota, Guillermo	2	0	1.89	14	5	19.0	16	6	4	5	17
Parker, Christian	0	1	7.59	7	0	10.2	10	9	9	7	5
Pavano, Carl	0	1	9.00	2	0	5.0	7	5	5	0	3
Powell, Jeremy	3	5	2.97	16	0	91.0	85	37	30	37	72
Rojas, Mel	0	1	5.14	12	2	21.0	25	13	12	12	16
Salyers, Jeremy	0	0	1.50	1	0	6.0	6	2	1	2	2
Small, Mark	4	5	5.54	42	2	66.2	85	50	41	32	43
Smart, J.D.	0	1	2.61	6	0	20.2	22	7	6	6	9
Smith, Dan	5	4	3.68	11	0	71.0	61	31	29	27	59
Stevenson, Rod	2	1	3.93	17	2	18.1	15	9	8	7	12
Strickland, Scott	3	0	1.63	19	5	27.2	23	5	5	11	34
Vazquez, Javier	4	2	4.85	7	0	42.2	45	24	23	16	46

Pawtucket Red Sox (Red Sox) AAA

BATTING	AVG	AB	R	H	2B	3B	HR	RBI	BB	SO	SB
*Abad, Andy, OF	.297	377	61	112	21	4	15	65	51	50	1
Alcantara, Israel, OF	.272	81	13	22	3	0	9	23	9	29	0
Chamblee, James, 2B	.274	464	84	127	21	3	24	88	43	126	5
Coleman, Michael, OF	.268	467	95	125	29	2	30	74	51	128	14
*Daubach, Brian, DH	.290	31	4	9	2	0	1	6	6	8	0
Depastino, Joe, C	.253	257	35	65	13	0	13	52	27	40	1
#Fonville, Chad, 2B	.253	257	31	65	3	2	1	14	20	31	6
Frye, Jeff, 2B	.333	9	0	3	0	0	0	2	2	1	0
Gubanich, Creighton, C	.283	92	12	26	3	0	5	10	6	23	0
*Hatteberg, Scott, C	.176	34	3	6	2	0	0	4	4	6	0
Hyzdu, Adam, OF	.229	35	4	8	0	0	1	6	4	13	0
Ingram, Garey, OF	.247	296	49	73	15	3	9	39	17	52	11
Jackson, Gavin, SS	.164	140	17	23	3	0	0	5	27	32	2
*Jefferson, Reggie, 1B	.000	10	1	0	0	0	0	0	2	3	0
Liniak, Cole, 3B	.264	348	55	92	25	0	12	42	40	57	0
Merloni, Lou, SS	.279	229	45	64	14	1	7	36	30	38	1
Mitchell, Keith, OF	.258	431	71	111	32	4	12	52	78	69	9
*Nunnally, Jon, OF	.267	494	90	132	24	3	23	76	85	103	26
Rodriguez, Luis, C	.000	3	0	0	0	0	0	0	0	1	0
Sadler, Donnie, SS	.291	172	25	50	12	4	1	17	16	36	4

BATTING	AVG	AB	R	H	2B	3B	HR	RBI	BB	SO	SB
*Stenson, Dernell, 1B	.270	440	64	119	28	2	18	82	55	119	2
#Tebbs, Nate, SS	.600	5	1	3	1	0	0	1	2	1	0

PITCHING	W	L	ERA	G	SV	IP	H	R	ER	BB	SO
Adams, Willie	4	5	5.15	11	0	64.2	82	46	37	10	37
*Adamson, Joel	2	4	6.02	25	2	43.1	60	35	29	8	14
*Baptist, Travis	4	2	5.31	17	0	42.1	49	27	25	19	30
*Barkley, Brian	0	1	5.14	3	0	14.0	11	9	8	7	5
Bullinger, Kirk	0	2	2.39	35	15	37.2	37	14	10	13	27
Cho, Jin Ho	9	3	3.45	17	0	109.2	99	46	42	29	80
*Cumberland, Chris	4	3	4.45	36	0	62.2	56	33	31	30	35
*Dixon, Tim	0	1	8.53	4	0	6.1	9	6	6	3	5
Farrell, Jim	2	3	4.19	14	0	43.0	45	25	20	16	35
Fernandez, Jared	12	9	4.24	27	0	163.1	172	88	77	39	76
Garces, Rich	1	0	3.25	21	7	27.2	24	11	10	10	24
Gross, Kip	1	0	5.40	10	0	21.2	24	14	13	12	16
Harikkala, Tim	1	2	5.40	14	0	30.0	44	19	18	7	19
Martinez, Ramon	0	1	9.00	2	0	9.0	10	9	9	6	7
Mix, Greg	4	4	3.69	46	1	85.1	89	45	35	40	79
Ohka, Tomokazu	7	0	1.58	12	0	68.1	60	17	12	11	63
Pena, Juan	4	2	4.13	10	0	48.0	44	28	22	13	61
*Ramsay, Robert	6	6	5.35	20	0	114.1	114	81	68	36	79
Rose, Brian	2	1	2.89	7	0	28.0	28	10	9	8	30
Santana, Marino	2	3	2.95	25	1	39.2	28	15	13	17	45
Sekany, Jason	0	1	4.76	1	0	5.2	7	4	3	4	1
Stanifer, Rob	3	1	2.04	31	3	39.2	34	21	9	15	29
*Urso, Sal	1	0	3.52	4	0	7.2	10	4	3	5	6
Wasdin, John	1	1	2.12	5	0	29.2	19	9	7	7	28
Wolcott, Bob	6	13	3.59	26	2	125.1	131	67	50	28	69

Richmond Braves (Braves) AAA

BATTING	AVG	AB	R	H	2B	3B	HR	RBI	BB	SO	SB
#Bass, Jayson, OF	.209	153	20	32	4	1	1	10	19	46	9
Battle, Howard, 3B	.284	454	80	129	29	1	24	74	33	66	2
De Rosa, Mark, SS	.272	364	41	99	16	2	1	40	21	49	7
*Johnson, Adam, OF	.333	42	7	14	2	0	1	6	2	5	1
*Lombard, George, OF	.206	233	25	48	11	3	7	29	35	98	21
Mahoney, Mike, C	.228	145	10	33	7	0	2	20	6	25	0
*Malloy, Marty, 2B	.292	407	58	119	23	1	7	36	53	52	19
#Martinez, Pablo, SS	.194	186	18	36	7	3	1	18	25	42	13
Matos, Pascual, C	.210	224	17	47	7	0	3	21	6	47	3
*McNabb, Buck, OF	.229	48	8	11	0	0	1	8	6	9	0
#Roberts, Lonell, OF	.262	442	66	116	19	5	3	41	33	95	17
Rumfield, Toby, C	.274	383	57	105	23	1	15	62	31	57	1
Schall, Gene, 1B	.293	355	49	104	25	1	12	53	35	84	0
*Simon, Randall, 1B	.271	59	7	16	4	0	1	8	3	10	0
Sisco, Steve, 2B	.311	495	80	154	36	2	18	76	38	74	13
*Tyler, Brad, OF	.286	413	73	118	20	2	21	79	69	99	18
*Whatley, Gabe, OF	.271	251	35	68	14	2	8	34	38	65	8

PITCHING	W	L	ERA	G	SV	IP	H	R	ER	BB	SO
*Bowie, Micah	4	4	2.96	13	0	73.0	65	24	24	14	82
*Brooks, Antone	3	5	3.86	43	1	56.0	57	28	24	21	39
*Butler, Adam	0	1	2.25	9	3	8.0	10	4	2	3	6
Cather, Mike	2	7	6.78	45	1	67.2	71	57	51	44	60
*Chen, Bruce	6	3	3.81	14	0	78.0	73	36	33	26	90
Cortes, David	2	3	3.35	47	22	45.2	50	19	17	14	42
Dawley, Joey	0	3	5.18	7	0	40.0	43	26	23	12	31
*Ebert, Derrin	8	7	4.30	25	0	150.2	173	79	72	44	82
Harrison, Tommy	0	1	8.10	4	0	10.0	17	9	9	6	6
Iglesias, Mike	0	2	15.75	3	0	4.0	6	7	7	4	7
Nelson, Joe	2	3	4.54	12	1	33.2	33	18	17	15	31
Pisciotta, Marc	3	2	6.06	23	0	35.2	34	25	24	17	27
Quevedo, Ruben	6	5	5.37	21	0	105.2	112	65	63	34	98
Ratliff, Jon	5	12	4.45	27	0	157.2	154	88	78	44	129
Seelbach, Chris	6	1	5.15	13	0	57.2	51	34	33	34	48
Speier, Justin	2	4	5.62	27	3	41.2	51	28	26	22	39
Springer, Russ	1	0	1.17	11	2	15.1	9	2	2	1	13
Stull, Everett	8	8	4.47	30	0	139.0	124	75	69	73	126
Villegas, Ismael	6	7	4.40	44	1	92.0	93	51	45	39	61
Wengert, Don	0	1	6.75	7	0	21.1	32	16	16	3	8

Class A WRAP-UPS

Carolina League

Hurricane Floyd forced the league to cancel the final game, naming the Wilmington Blue Rocks and the Myrtle Beach co-champions. Myrtle Beach second baseman **Marcus Giles** earned his second MVP award in a row and won the batting title (.326). Pitcher of the Year was the Salem Avalanche's **Josh Kalinowski** (11-6, 2.11, 176 strikeouts). Potomac Cannons **Andy Bevins** led the league in both homers (25) and RBI (97) while Kinston infielder **Scott Pratt** led with 47 steals. The Kinston Indians also had the top winner in **Tim Drew**, with 13 victories. Salem had the top closer in the loop with **Travis Thompson**, who notched 27 saves.

CAROLINA (A)
Northern Division

	W	L	Pct.	GB
Wilmington	38	31	.551	—
Frederick	30	38	.441	7.5
Potomac	30	40	.429	8.5
Lynchburg	29	39	.426	8.5

Southern Division

	W	L	Pct.	GB
Myrtle Beach	44	26	.629	—
Kinston	42	26	.618	1
Salem	35	33	.515	8
Winston-Salem	27	42	.391	16.5

Switch-hitter
* Left-handed

Class A WRAP-UPS

Florida State League

The Kissimmee Cobras won the league title in four games. Dunedin Blue Jays outfielder **Vernon Wells** was MVP at the All-Star Game and at season's end. St. Lucie Mets outfielder **Allen Dina** won the batting crown (.344); Sarasota Red Sox first baseman **Morgan Burkhart**, in his first year out of the indies at age 27, led the league with 23 homers; and Clearwater Phillies outfielder Eric Valent led the way with 106 RBI. Lakeland Tigers outfielder **Rod Lindsay** led the league with 61 steals. Kissimmee ace **Eric Ireland**, who tossed a perfect game during the season, won the ERA title (2.06) as teammate **Wilfredo Rodriguez** led the league in wins (15) and strikeouts (148). Tampa Yankees closer **Jason Ellison's** 35 saves were tops in the minors.

FLORIDA STATE (A)

East Division

	W	L	Pct.	GB
Kissimmee	41	29	.586	—
St. Lucie	37	33	.529	4
Brevard County	34	34	.500	6
Jupiter	34	36	.486	7
Daytona	33	37	.471	8
Vero Beach	22	43	.338	16.5

West Division

	W	L	Pct.	GB
Dunedin	41	27	.603	—
Tampa	39	29	.574	2
Charlotte	40	30	.571	2
St. Petersburg	35	34	.507	6.5
Fort Myers	35	35	.500	7
Lakeland	32	37	.464	9.5
Clearwater	31	36	.463	9.5
Sarasota	28	42	.400	14

Switch-hitter
* Left-handed

Rochester Red Wings (Orioles) AAA

BATTING	AVG	AB	R	H	2B	3B	HR	RBI	BB	SO	SB
*Clark, Howie, OF	.294	279	33	82	19	4	6	28	34	24	1
Davis, Tommy, C	.257	413	49	106	18	0	11	56	24	65	1
*Dent, Darrell, OF	.133	30	4	4	0	0	2	5	3	8	4
*DeCinces, Tim, C	.264	53	7	14	5	0	2	8	0	12	0
Dunn, Todd, OF	.196	204	22	40	6	1	7	31	22	67	3
Forbes, P.J., 3B	.264	349	49	92	16	1	0	19	26	40	5
Foster, Jim, C	.229	118	6	27	3	1	0	11	12	19	4
Garcia, Jesse, SS	.255	220	25	56	10	2	2	23	11	21	9
Hairston, Jerry, 2B	.291	413	65	120	24	5	7	48	30	50	19
*Herrera, Jose, OF	.205	127	11	26	7	1	2	16	2	20	3
Isom, Johnny, OF	.345	119	19	41	12	0	2	10	10	28	1
#Kingsale, Eugene, OF	.309	191	31	59	9	0	2	20	13	23	10
*May, Derrick, OF	.278	295	39	82	19	3	5	43	22	28	4
Minor, Ryan, 3B	.256	383	56	98	24	1	21	67	37	119	3
Murphy, Mike, OF	.226	217	35	49	6	3	1	21	34	63	7
#Ojeda, Augie, SS	.000	1	1	0	0	0	0	0	0	0	0
#Otero, Ricky, OF	.231	199	16	46	11	4	4	21	16	23	5
*Pickering, Calvin, 1B	.285	372	63	106	20	0	16	63	60	99	1
Rust, Brian, 3B	.000	3	0	0	0	0	0	1	0	0	0
Vinas, Julio, DH	.312	484	67	151	32	2	20	83	25	73	4
Webster, Lenny, C	.302	43	8	13	5	0	3	9	4	8	0

PITCHING	W	L	ERA	G	SV	IP	H	R	ER	BB	SO
Blood, Darin	0	4	8.66	12	0	43.2	53	43	42	38	21
*Burrows, Terry	1	6	3.97	17	0	93.0	74	49	41	39	75
Clark, Howie	0	0	9.00	2	0	2.0	4	2	2	2	0
Coppinger, Rocky	2	2	3.66	5	0	32.0	28	13	13	12	37
Corsi, Jim	0	0	3.48	10	2	10.1	12	4	4	3	7
Delahoya, Javier	4	3	5.09	14	0	81.1	88	49	46	26	58
*Dykhoff, Radhames	2	0	3.94	47	1	82.1	69	42	36	31	57
Evans, David	2	11	5.35	60	2	70.2	70	48	42	27	65
Fetters, Mike	0	0	0.00	4	0	3.2	0	0	0	2	6
*Hamilton, Jimmy	1	2	5.81	29	0	26.1	25	25	17	31	27
*Hartmann, Pete	1	5	8.93	34	0	44.1	56	45	44	27	43
*Johns, Doug	1	1	4.85	6	0	29.2	34	20	16	6	18
Johnson, Jason	4	2	3.65	8	0	44.1	35	19	18	27	47
Kamieniecki, Scott	1	2	5.09	4	0	23.0	23	13	13	6	14
Linton, Doug	7	5	3.65	18	0	118.1	120	58	48	27	97
Maduro, Calvin	11	11	3.99	29	0	169.0	179	88	75	60	149
McCommon, Jason	7	10	4.98	29	0	124.2	143	73	69	50	68
Molina, Gabe	2	2	3.14	45	18	57.1	45	22	20	23	58
Pina, Rafael	8	10	4.37	48	5	111.1	113	60	54	48	88
*Plantenberg, Erik	7	5	5.91	40	0	80.2	100	59	53	41	72
*Rogers, Jason	0	2	8.10	9	0	10.0	15	9	9	6	7
*Ryan, B.J.	1	0	3.09	22	1	23.1	17	8	8	7	32
Snyder, Matt	6	6	5.21	48	1	84.2	95	60	49	30	59

Scranton-W.B. Red Barons (Phillies) AAA

BATTING	AVG	AB	R	H	2B	3B	HR	RBI	BB	SO	SB
Alvarez, Clemente, C	.250	28	4	7	4	0	0	6	3	9	0
Burrell, Pat, 1B	.152	33	4	5	0	0	1	4	4	8	0
#Burton, Darren, OF	.262	409	61	107	30	3	13	63	44	96	7
Carter, Mike, OF	.161	31	2	5	1	1	1	4	0	8	0
*Carver, Steve, 1B	.236	288	33	68	18	1	11	38	34	101	4
Estalella, Bobby, C	.231	386	58	89	23	2	15	62	55	100	4
Finn, John, SS	.218	124	18	27	1	0	4	10	15	12	2
Flores, Jose, SS	.246	228	35	56	6	2	0	18	37	43	13
#Frazier, Lou, OF	.247	308	54	76	16	7	6	32	44	79	21
Guiliano, Matt, SS	.190	216	20	41	15	0	2	24	17	61	3
Huff, Larry, 2B	.235	17	4	4	2	0	0	1	5	2	0
#Lovullo, Torey, 2B	.279	519	90	145	36	3	21	106	78	89	5
Lucca, Lou, 3B	.268	533	61	143	33	2	12	70	22	94	4
Magee, Wendell, OF	.283	566	95	160	34	2	20	79	55	124	10
*McMillon, Billy, OF	.304	464	97	141	38	4	16	85	65	79	11
Millan, Adan, C	.000	2	0	0	0	0	0	0	1	2	0
Prince, Tom, C	.091	22	2	2	0	0	1	1	3	5	1
#Rollins, Jimmy, SS	.077	13	0	1	1	0	0	0	1	1	1
*Ronan, Marc, C	.165	115	14	19	5	0	2	10	8	28	1
*Zuber, Jon, 1B	.295	387	69	114	24	2	6	54	86	48	7

PITCHING	W	L	ERA	G	SV	IP	H	R	ER	BB	SO
Bennett, Joel	10	4	4.61	20	0	127.0	134	71	65	47	125
Bolton, Rod	11	10	3.82	24	0	153.0	161	76	65	52	85
*Brewer, Billy	6	1	3.78	33	2	69.0	59	32	29	28	57
*Dodd, Robert	4	0	0.91	6	1	29.2	19	5	3	6	23

PITCHING	W	L	ERA	G	SV	IP	H	R	ER	BB	SO
Eaton, Adam	1	1	3.00	3	0	21.0	17	10	7	6	10
*Fesh, Sean	4	3	4.39	45	1	53.1	50	29	26	31	38
Fiore, Tony	0	0	6.64	13	0	20.1	28	19	15	15	13
Grace, Mike	2	2	4.44	10	0	46.2	52	25	23	17	27
Grahe, Joe	3	1	3.00	23	10	36.0	38	15	12	15	25
Green, Tyler	4	6	7.69	19	0	50.1	78	47	43	24	31
*Jacquez, Thomas	0	1	2.45	3	0	3.2	4	1	1	0	4
Johnson, Barry	6	10	5.02	31	0	136.1	157	83	76	49	88
*Looney, Brian	4	0	5.70	50	2	71.0	70	47	45	50	64
Montgomery, Steve	0	0	6.23	14	7	13.0	17	9	9	11	13
Myers, Jimmy	1	0	6.50	14	1	18.0	26	14	13	5	8
Nye, Ryan	5	4	5.10	14	0	65.1	69	41	37	20	63
Ryan, Ken	2	2	5.66	31	6	41.1	54	30	26	19	33
Schrenk, Steve	3	1	2.93	32	2	43.0	38	17	14	21	34
Scott, Darryl	7	6	4.09	57	10	105.2	100	53	48	47	91
*Shumaker, Anthony	3	5	5.72	14	0	89.2	119	60	57	32	49
Williams, Shad	0	2	19.80	2	0	5.0	17	11	11	3	2
*Wolf, Randy	4	5	3.61	12	0	77.1	73	36	31	29	72
*Zuber, Jon	0	0	0.00	1	0	2.0	0	0	0	0	0

Syracuse Sky Chiefs (Blue Jays) AAA

BATTING	AVG	AB	R	H	2B	3B	HR	RBI	BB	SO	SB
Berroa, Geronimo, OF	.273	33	7	9	0	0	3	8	8	5	0
Blake, Casey, 3B	.245	387	69	95	16	2	22	75	61	82	9
Brown, Kevin, C	.258	295	39	76	18	2	13	51	21	79	0
*Carter, Shannon, OF	.111	9	0	1	0	0	0	0	0	2	0
#Cruz, Jose, OF	.184	103	17	19	3	1	3	14	28	20	5
Dalesandro, Mark, OF	.225	71	3	16	2	0	0	5	1	7	1
Delgado, Alex, C	.206	107	11	22	7	0	2	12	14	14	0
*Fletcher, Darrin, C	.267	15	0	4	0	0	0	0	1	1	0
Freel, Ryan, OF	.299	77	15	23	3	2	1	11	8	13	10
Grebeck, Craig, 2B	.250	16	3	4	1	0	1	2	1	1	0
*Greene, Willie, OF	.327	52	12	17	1	0	5	11	6	14	0
Hurst, Jimmy, OF	.282	103	18	29	3	0	3	10	15	32	4
Jones, Chris, DH	.237	279	45	66	12	3	8	40	19	74	11
Lopez, Luis, 1B	.322	531	76	171	35	2	4	69	40	58	1
Martin, Norberto, SS	.295	319	45	94	11	2	5	34	12	33	14
#Melhuse, Adam, C	.282	71	15	20	5	0	2	16	10	20	1
Mummau, Rob, 2B	.242	433	52	105	29	3	5	58	28	61	2
Pohle, Matthew, C	.200	5	0	1	0	0	0	0	0	2	0
Probst, Alan, C	.220	59	6	13	2	0	1	5	4	18	0
Sanders, Anthony, OF	.244	496	71	121	22	5	18	59	46	111	18
Solano, Fausto, SS	.214	28	4	6	0	0	1	3	1	2	0
Soriano, Fred, SS	.389	18	3	7	0	0	0	2	0	4	0
Strange, Mike, DH	.156	32	4	5	3	0	0	2	8	13	1
Thompson, Andy, OF	.293	229	42	67	17	2	16	42	21	45	5
Wells, Vernon, OF	.310	129	20	40	8	1	4	21	10	22	5
*Witt, Kevin, 1B	.278	421	72	117	24	3	24	71	64	109	0
Woodward, Chris, SS	.292	281	46	82	20	3	1	20	38	49	4

PITCHING	W	L	ERA	G	SV	IP	H	R	ER	BB	SO
*Andrews, Clayton	0	1	7.80	3	0	15.0	10	14	13	13	9
*Arroyo, Luis	0	1	8.53	9	0	12.2	18	13	12	9	10
*Bale, John	0	3	3.97	6	0	22.2	16	14	10	10	10
Bochtler, Doug	4	0	2.63	14	0	27.1	18	9	8	10	28
*Bogott, Kurt	8	6	4.62	46	1	85.2	80	52	44	44	76
Bovee, Mike	0	2	7.32	19	1	35.2	49	29	29	20	32
Bradford, Josh	0	1	18.00	1	0	4.0	9	8	8	3	2
Croghan, Andy	0	0	0.00	2	2	3.1	0	0	0	2	4
Davey, Tom	1	2	3.48	6	0	33.2	30	15	13	19	20
Delgado, Ernie	0	4	9.43	14	0	27.2	38	29	29	19	15
Donnelly, Brendan	5	6	3.03	42	2	71.1	61	27	24	22	70
Glover, Gary	4	6	5.19	14	0	76.1	93	50	44	35	57
Hamilton, Joey	0	1	5.11	3	0	12.1	15	8	7	5	9
Harris, D.J.	0	0	7.71	7	0	14.0	20	15	12	10	6
Hudek, John	0	2	5.83	24	1	29.1	31	20	19	13	32
Koch, Billy	3	0	3.86	5	0	25.2	27	11	11	10	22
*Lukasiewicz, Mark	4	4	5.34	37	3	97.2	109	59	58	40	77
Mann, Jim	6	5	4.64	47	5	66.0	53	35	34	39	72
McClellan, Sean	0	0	3.86	8	2	7.0	6	4	3	4	5
Moore, Marcus	0	1	11.25	7	0	12.0	14	15	15	13	12
Munro, Peter	6	1	3.10	18	0	69.2	70	29	24	33	68
*Pennington, Brad	3	0	4.24	27	1	34.0	30	20	16	30	34
Probst, Alan	0	0	4.50	2	0	2.0	1	1	1	0	1
Quantrill, Paul	0	0	0.00	2	0	2.0	1	0	0	0	1
*Reece, Dana	0	0	0.00	1	0	2.0	1	0	0	2	1
Rodriguez, Nerio	10	8	4.54	27	0	162.2	161	84	82	53	137

Class A WRAP-UPS

Midwest League

The Burlington Bees won the league title, but Michigan Battle Cats first baseman **Aaron McNeal** cruised to the MVP award at .310, with 131 RBI—second best in the minors. He also led the loop in homers (38)—tied for third in the minors. South Bend Silver Hawks **Carlos Urquiola** won the batting crown (.362). Prospect of the Year was Lansing Lugnuts outfielder **Corey Patterson**. In his pro debut, he hit .320 with 20 HR, 79 RBI and 33 steals. **Robert Averette** of the Rockford Cubbies won the ERA crown (2.58); **Doug Bridges** of the Cedar Rapids Kernels led the league with 15 wins and added three more with the Lake Elsinore Storm (California League) to finish tops in the minors with 18 wins. Quad City River Bandits **Juan Rincon** had a league-best 153 strikeouts and the Clinton Lumber Kings' **Brandon Puffer** led in saves (34), tied for second in the minors.

MIDWEST (A)

Eastern Division

	W	L	Pct.	GB
Michigan	41	28	.594	—
West Michigan	39	31	.557	2.5
South Bend	36	34	.514	5.5
Lansing	35	35	.500	6.5
Fort Wayne	32	38	.457	9.5

Central Division

	W	L	Pct.	GB
Wisconsin	40	30	.571	—
Kane County	38	32	.543	2
Beloit	34	36	.486	6
Rockford	31	39	.443	9
Peoria	26	44	.371	14

Western Division

	W	L	Pct.	GB
Burlington	40	30	.571	—
Quad City	39	31	.557	1
Cedar Rapids	31	39	.443	9
Clinton	27	42	.391	12.5

Switch-hitter
* Left-handed

Class A WRAP-UPS

South Atlantic League

The Augusta Greenjackets took the league title. The Greensboro Bats' **Scott Seabol**, whose 35-game hitting streak mid-season was the best in the minors, was MVP (.315, 15 HR, 89 RBI). Pitcher of the Year was Jason Standridge of the Charleston (S.C.) River Dogs, who went 9-1 and took the ERA crown (2.02). Most Outstanding Major League Prospect was the Macon Braves' **Rafael Furcal**, who won the batting crown (.337) and stole 73 bases before his promotion to the Myrtle Beach Pelicans, where he brought his season steal total to 96, easily the best in the minors. **Travis Hafner** of the Savannah Sand Gnats and **Earl Snyder** of the Capital City Bombers tied for the league homer lead with 28, while Hafner led with 111 RBI. Delmarva ace **John Stephens** led the minors with 217 strikeouts. Macon's **Jimmy Osting** led the league with 14 wins; Augusta's **Mark Cisar** and Hagerstown Suns **Jarrod Kingrey** shared the lead with 27 saves.

SOUTH ATLANTIC (A)
Northern Division
	W	L	Pct.	GB
Cape Fear	37	32	.536	—
Hagerstown	36	33	.522	1
Delmarva	32	36	.471	4.5
Charleston-WV	31	38	.449	6

Central Division
	W	L	Pct.	GB
Greensboro	40	29	.58	—
Columbia	39	31	.557	1.5
Hickory	35	35	.500	5.5
Asheville	35	35	.500	5.5
Piedmont	33	36	.478	7
Charleston-SC	33	37	.471	7.5

Southern Division
	W	L	Pct.	GB
Augusta	40	30	.571	—
Macon	34	34	.500	5
Savannah	34	35	.493	5.5
Columbus	26	44	.371	14

Switch-hitter
* Left-handed

384

2000 BASEBALL WEEKLY ALMANAC

PITCHING	W	L	ERA	G	SV	IP	H	R	ER	BB	SO
Romano, Mike	12	8	4.13	29	0	174.1	160	90	80	84	104
*Sinclair, Steve	2	2	2.06	34	18	39.1	24	11	9	12	31
Smith, Brian	7	4	3.50	29	7	46.1	45	22	18	24	46
Stevenson, Jason	1	2	6.05	7	0	38.2	52	30	26	21	15
Yennaco, Jay	2	6	6.86	15	0	80.0	107	68	61	42	45

Toledo Mud Hens (Tigers) AAA

BATTING	AVG	AB	R	H	2B	3B	HR	RBI	BB	SO	SB
Alvarez, Gabe, 3B	.285	410	70	117	24	0	21	67	57	80	1
Ashley, Billy, DH	.286	112	19	32	9	0	9	25	9	32	0
#Bartee, Kimera, OF	.286	416	64	119	13	8	12	43	38	76	21
Bonnici, Jim, DH	.224	58	10	13	3	0	2	4	6	25	0
#Casanova, Raul, C	.206	160	21	33	9	0	6	23	7	28	0
#Clark, Tony, 1B	.000	3	0	0	0	0	0	0	1	1	0
Cradle, Rickey, OF	.239	348	57	83	27	2	10	52	42	82	11
*Fick, Robert, 1B	.313	48	11	15	0	1	2	8	8	5	1
Garcia, Luis, SS	.266	308	30	82	19	1	3	34	5	41	3
*Hamelin, Bob, DH	.221	149	20	33	9	0	5	20	24	29	4
#Jefferies, Gregg, DH	.250	8	0	2	0	0	0	0	0	2	0
Kapler, Gabe, OF	.315	54	11	17	6	2	3	14	9	10	0
Lennon, Pat, OF	.287	414	75	119	21	1	30	83	55	106	4
#Macias, Jose, 2B	.244	438	44	107	18	8	2	36	36	60	10
Maxwell, Jason, SS	.236	419	60	99	17	2	15	62	53	87	6
McCarty, Dave, 1B	.268	466	85	125	24	3	31	77	70	110	6
McKeel, Walt, C	.242	215	21	52	9	1	7	37	26	32	2
*Polonia, Luis, OF	.323	161	20	52	7	1	3	22	10	28	13
*Siddall, Joe, C	.193	244	29	47	15	0	8	33	34	74	4
*Swann, Pedro, OF	.259	332	51	86	14	2	10	37	36	67	3
Wood, Jason, 3B	.286	185	34	53	11	0	6	24	22	43	0

PITCHING	W	L	ERA	G	SV	IP	H	R	ER	BB	SO
Alberro, Jose	2	2	5.25	14	0	24.0	28	16	14	11	21
Anderson, Matt	0	4	6.39	24	5	38.0	32	27	27	31	35
Borkowski, David	6	8	3.50	19	0	126.0	119	59	49	43	94
*Brunson, Will	3	1	4.53	38	3	47.2	45	28	24	17	41
Checo, Robinson	0	0	0.00	2	0	5.0	2	0	0	1	6
Corey, Bryan	5	2	2.86	48	2	69.1	63	27	22	34	36
Cruz, Nelson	7	1	2.73	10	0	62.2	47	20	19	21	41
Drews, Matt	2	14	8.27	28	0	136.0	171	136	125	91	70
Drumright, Mike	6	10	5.97	21	0	120.2	116	88	80	59	76
Goldsmith, Gary	0	3	6.95	6	0	22.0	29	21	17	9	14
Graterol, Beiker	3	9	5.83	17	0	78.2	89	55	51	38	47
Greisinger, Seth	0	1	5.87	2	0	7.2	9	5	5	3	4
Grzanich, Mike	1	0	9.28	14	1	21.1	21	24	22	25	17
Hiljus, Erik	2	3	4.40	33	5	59.1	49	31	29	16	73
Keagle, Greg	1	4	7.16	7	0	32.2	50	29	26	13	19
Kida, Masao	0	0	3.18	3	0	5.2	6	2	2	1	4
Lira, Felipe	2	11	6.71	30	1	114.0	163	97	85	35	70
Martinez, Romulo	0	0	5.40	6	0	6.2	7	5	4	6	2
*McCarty, Dave	0	0	4.50	2	0	2.0	1	1	1	6	0
*Ramirez, Jose	0	0	1.80	1	0	5.0	3	1	1	4	3
Reed, Brandon	8	5	4.14	44	3	91.1	101	53	42	26	59
*Roach, Peter	1	1	4.50	4	0	8.0	6	4	4	2	5
Roberts, Willis	5	8	6.26	31	0	92.0	112	68	64	59	52
*Runyan, Sean	0	0	3.48	10	0	10.1	7	4	4	6	7

Pacific Coast League

Albuquerque Dukes (Dodgers) AAA

BATTING	AVG	AB	R	H	2B	3B	HR	RBI	BB	SO	SB
*Anthony, Eric, OF	.300	20	4	6	2	0	1	3	3	5	0
Castro, Juan, SS	.274	423	52	116	25	4	7	51	34	70	2
Chamberlain, Wes, 1B	.307	375	53	115	19	3	18	78	24	66	3
*Clark, Dave, OF	.324	108	19	35	7	1	3	17	26	26	2
Cookson, Brent, OF	.321	277	57	89	18	1	28	70	38	56	7
*Cora, Alex, SS	.308	302	51	93	11	7	4	37	12	37	9
Cromer, Tripp, 2B	.267	15	1	4	2	0	0	1	1	3	0
#Gibbs, Kevin, OF	.286	21	4	6	3	0	0	1	4	6	2
Gilbert, Shawn, OF	.304	421	88	128	35	3	10	52	62	84	25
*Grijak, Kevin, OF	.317	401	58	127	28	1	18	80	19	50	2
Hubbard, Trenidad, OF	.333	123	24	41	8	2	5	24	16	27	16
*Livingstone, Scott, 1B	.205	78	11	16	1	0	1	4	9	12	2
LoDuca, Paul, C	.368	76	17	28	9	0	1	8	10	1	1
Mejia, Roberto, 3B	.146	41	6	6	0	0	1	5	1	8	0

BATTING	AVG	AB	R	H	2B	3B	HR	RBI	BB	SO	SB
*Newson, Warren, OF	.260	285	42	74	22	0	8	38	44	70	2
Ortiz, Hector, C	.305	164	21	50	9	0	6	20	7	27	2
Pena, Angel, C	.291	127	15	37	10	1	1	24	10	24	3
Riggs, Adam, 2B	.292	513	87	150	29	7	13	81	54	114	25
*Sanford, Chance, 3B	.247	227	37	56	14	1	8	29	31	55	6
Steed, Dave, 1B	.210	62	8	13	4	0	0	5	7	17	0
#Stovall, DaRond, OF	.207	266	40	55	15	3	10	34	33	109	8
*Wilkins, Rick, C	.253	300	39	76	8	1	8	33	29	87	1

PITCHING	W	L	ERA	G	SV	IP	H	R	ER	BB	SO
Alston, Garvin	1	2	5.06	5	0	10.2	12	6	6	4	5
Arnold, Jamie	0	2	5.59	7	0	19.1	28	14	12	7	13
*Beckett, Robbie	1	3	7.57	15	0	44.0	48	39	37	37	54
Bochtler, Doug	3	4	3.18	18	3	22.2	16	9	8	11	25
Boskie, Shawn	4	8	5.84	15	0	86.1	111	66	56	37	62
Checo, Robinson	3	6	4.33	16	0	79.0	68	40	38	39	98
Croghan, Andy	2	1	2.81	35	2	41.2	43	16	13	14	31
Garrett, Hal	0	1	15.43	1	0	2.1	3	4	4	2	1
Herges, Matt	8	3	4.73	21	0	131.1	135	82	69	47	88
*Jordan, Ricardo	4	1	7.20	37	2	30.0	33	26	24	21	35
Judd, Mike	8	7	6.67	21	0	110.2	132	90	82	47	122
*Kubenka, Jeff	4	4	3.22	51	11	67.0	62	33	24	23	63
Mitchell, Dean	2	1	7.36	31	0	47.2	61	41	39	28	42
*Osteen, Gavin	6	8	5.12	34	2	103.2	127	64	59	33	65
*Perez, Carlos	3	3	5.92	6	0	38.0	46	28	25	10	14
Ruffin, Johnny	1	1	3.17	46	10	54.0	41	21	19	26	66
Stone, Ricky	6	10	5.50	27	0	167.0	205	123	102	71	132
*Weber, Neil	1	2	10.43	18	0	29.1	53	35	34	13	30
*West, David	0	1	6.43	2	0	7.0	9	5	5	0	7
*Williams, Jeff	9	7	5.01	42	4	125.2	151	77	70	47	86

Calgary Cannons (Marlins) AAA

BATTING	AVG	AB	R	H	2B	3B	HR	RBI	BB	SO	SB
Bautista, Danny, OF	.319	135	25	43	8	1	8	28	11	18	3
Castro, Ramon, C	.258	349	43	90	22	0	15	61	24	64	0
#Clapinski, Chris, 3B	.322	267	51	86	21	6	8	35	30	53	5
Duncan, Mariano, SS	.200	5	0	1	1	0	0	0	0	2	0
*Dunwoody, Todd, OF	.272	246	35	67	16	7	9	36	10	56	7
*Floyd, Cliff, OF	.387	31	6	12	1	0	3	8	2	8	0
Franco, Raul, SS	.273	55	7	15	0	0	0	4	2	4	0
Garcia, Amaury, 2B	.317	479	94	152	37	9	17	53	44	79	17
Gil, Benji, SS	.279	412	74	115	29	1	17	64	27	101	17
Gulan, Mike, 3B	.276	286	41	79	23	2	13	51	10	82	2
Hastings, Lionel, C	.267	75	8	20	4	1	1	4	5	13	2
*Hyers, Tim, OF	.268	179	25	48	12	0	4	20	14	22	1
*Jones, Jaime, OF	.246	138	12	34	6	0	0	7	10	30	1
Lee, Derrek, 1B	.283	339	60	96	20	1	19	73	30	90	3
Lobaton, Jose, SS	.189	90	9	17	6	0	0	4	6	26	2
Lowell, Mike, 3B	.313	83	11	26	3	0	2	9	8	19	0
Millar, Kevin, OF	.301	143	24	43	11	1	7	26	11	19	2
Morman, Russ, 1B	.327	52	10	17	1	0	3	12	7	6	1
Orie, Kevin, 3B	.319	72	10	23	9	0	3	8	13	7	0
Reese, Nate, C	.250	20	4	5	1	0	0	2	1	5	0
Reeves, Glenn, OF	.216	236	33	51	8	1	2	21	37	42	3
*Robertson, Ryan, C	.302	169	16	51	10	0	1	19	26	29	0
Roskos, John, OF	.320	506	85	162	44	0	24	90	52	112	2
Walton, Jerome, OF	.321	84	12	27	8	1	0	12	5	12	5

PITCHING	W	L	ERA	G	SV	IP	H	R	ER	BB	SO
Alberro, Jose	3	2	6.64	24	0	59.2	79	46	44	16	43
*Almanza, Armando	2	2	10.90	15	0	17.1	29	27	21	18	20
*Arroyo, Luis	2	1	6.48	22	0	33.1	42	33	24	17	26
*Benz, Jake	1	0	0.00	2	0	4.0	3	1	0	3	4
*Billingsley, Brent	2	9	5.55	21	0	116.2	133	81	72	48	79
*Burgus, Travis	1	0	5.40	20	1	23.1	33	17	14	8	15
Corbin, Archie	0	1	6.75	12	0	13.1	13	11	10	10	16
Cornelius, Reid	10	6	4.49	27	0	172.1	184	96	86	68	135
*Darensbourg, Vic	0	0	4.63	9	1	11.2	13	6	6	0	12
Dempster, Ryan	1	1	4.99	5	0	30.2	30	17	17	10	29
Drumright, Mike	0	2	13.71	12	0	21.0	39	33	32	13	15
Duncan, Geoff	1	0	4.00	5	1	9.0	4	4	4	10	5
Fontenot, Joe	3	2	5.11	8	0	44.0	52	26	25	19	18
*Gonzalez, Gabe	1	1	4.18	24	0	28.0	27	15	13	9	23
Grilli, Jason	8	10	6.16	27	0	141.2	180	117	97	62	103
Lobaton, Jose	0	1	18.00	2	0	2.0	4	4	4	3	1
Ludwick, Eric	11	6	3.86	48	14	58.1	65	33	25	36	61
Medina, Rafael	1	2	3.34	25	1	35.0	29	15	13	21	34

Class A WRAP-UPS

New York-Penn League (SS)

Hudson Valley won the league title. The newly aligned league named MVPs for each division: Williamsport's **Tony Alvarez** for the Pinckney Division, and Hudson Valley's **Andrew Beinbrink** for the McNamara Division. Hudson Valley's **Dan Grummitt** aced the home-run crown (22), but Auburn's **Jason Lane** took the RBI title—59 to Grummitt's 58. Vermont's **Matt Watson** took the batting title (.380) and tied teammate **Valentino Pascucci** with seven homers. Pascucci edged out Watson in RBI, 58-57. Mahoning Valley's **Alexander Requena** led with 44 steals. Auburn's **Jairo Pineda** led with nine wins, but Utica's **Todd Moser** went 8-2 and won the ERA title (1.53). Hudson Valley's **Joe Kennedy** fanned 101 in 95 innings. Oneonta's **Gregory Watson** easily won the saves title (19).

NEW YORK-PENN (SS-A)

Pinckney Division

	W	L	Pct.	GB
Mahoning Valley	43	33	.566	—
Batavia	42	34	.553	1
Auburn	39	37	.513	4
Jamestown	38	38	.500	5
St. Catharines	34	42	.447	9
Williamsport	32	44	.421	11

McNamara Division

	W	L	Pct.	GB
Utica	42	33	.560	—
Hudson Valley	42	34	.553	.5
Oneonta	41	34	.547	1
Pittsfield	41	35	.539	1.5
Staten Island	39	35	.527	2.5
Lowell	34	42	.447	8.5
Vermont	33	43	.434	9.5
New Jersey	30	46	.395	12.5

Switch-hitter
* Left-handed

Class A WRAP-UPS

Northwest League (SS)

Spokane won the league title with the help of batting champ **Kenneth Harvey** (.397). But Boise's **Robb Quinlan** was MVP (.322, 9 HR, league-high 77 RBI). Southern Oregon's **Kirk Asche** and Yakima's **Lamont Matthews** shared the home run crown (17). Southern Oregon's **Carlos Rosario** was the stolen base king (31). Boise's **Wesley Crawford** led the league with a 2.21 ERA while Everett's **Craig Anderson** led in wins (10) and teammate **Aquilino Lopez** led in strikeouts (93). Spokane's **Jay Gehrke** notched a league-best 13 saves.

NORTHWEST (SS-A)

North Division

	W	L	Pct.	GB
Spokane	44	32	.579	—
Boise	43	33	.566	1
Everett	41	35	.539	3
Yakima	33	43	.434	11

South Division

	W	L	Pct.	GB
Portland	39	37	0.513	—
So. Oregon	38	38	.500	1
Salem-Keizer	37	39	.487	2
Eugene	29	47	.382	10

Switch-hitter
* Left-handed

PITCHING	W	L	ERA	G	SV	IP	H	R	ER	BB	SO
Menhart, Paul	5	5	5.89	17	0	81.0	106	60	53	37	51
Mercedes, Jose	3	8	4.03	19	0	114.0	140	70	51	23	70
*Ojala, Kirt	3	8	7.21	16	0	78.2	110	70	63	44	54
Perez, Dario	7	13	5.73	28	0	132.0	150	94	84	31	66
Salkeld, Roger	1	1	4.63	27	1	35.0	37	21	18	20	32
*Sanchez, Jesus	0	0	5.79	4	1	9.1	8	6	6	5	14
Stanifer, Rob	1	2	12.38	16	0	16.0	32	23	22	6	15
*Tejera, Michael	0	2	12.00	2	0	9.0	19	14	12	4	5
Villano, Mike	1	5	6.21	36	2	58.0	87	43	40	17	48

Colorado Springs Sky Sox (Rockies) AAA

BATTING	AVG	AB	R	H	2B	3B	HR	RBI	BB	SO	SB
#Barry, Jeff, OF	.341	185	36	63	15	0	10	27	19	31	6
Blanco, Henry, C	.333	57	8	19	4	0	3	12	1	12	0
#Cangelosi, John, OF	.330	109	22	36	7	0	1	13	24	16	4
Clemente, Edgard, OF	.304	273	45	83	24	1	16	59	20	55	5
*Cotton, John, 3B	.315	235	50	74	18	1	15	48	14	64	4
Gibson, Derrick, OF	.275	385	68	106	19	6	17	67	30	82	12
Hajek, Dave, 2B	.295	533	84	157	43	3	8	58	25	42	13
Hatcher, Chris, OF	.344	334	63	115	24	2	21	69	23	89	12
Kelly, Mike, OF	.277	394	69	109	27	3	9	50	57	93	10
Manwaring, Kirt, C	.227	22	3	5	0	0	1	2	1	2	0
#Pena, Elvis, SS	.163	43	5	7	1	0	0	1	3	7	4
Petersen, Chris, SS	.259	370	56	96	21	1	6	33	29	85	4
Petrick, Ben, C	.312	282	56	88	16	5	19	64	44	58	9
*Phillips, J.R., 1B	.311	479	87	149	22	0	41	100	54	143	4
Sexton, Chris, SS	.339	171	23	58	9	0	0	17	28	22	5
Shumpert, Terry, 3B	.380	79	15	30	8	1	6	17	4	9	3
Sosa, Juan, OF	.393	28	3	11	1	1	1	5	0	1	1
Strittmatter, Mark, C	.215	195	16	42	10	1	4	31	20	45	0
Tatum, Jim, 3B	.313	396	57	124	23	1	14	64	33	85	1
Watkins, Pat, OF	.333	30	4	10	1	0	0	2	2	6	0

PITCHING	W	L	ERA	G	SV	IP	H	R	ER	BB	SO
Bailey, Roger	0	0	7.06	4	0	21.2	31	19	17	14	15
*Beltran, Rigo	1	0	2.25	6	0	8.0	12	3	2	5	12
Bost, Heath	5	4	5.53	38	0	86.1	120	59	53	12	67
Briggs, Anthony	1	1	7.64	10	0	17.2	30	25	15	10	5
Brownson, Mark	6	6	6.20	17	0	103.0	120	75	71	24	81
De La Rosa, Maximo	0	1	2.45	8	0	11.0	12	3	3	4	5
De La Rosa, Maximo	0	3	4.91	23	1	33.0	46	21	18	14	29
*Farmer, Michael	8	10	7.86	25	0	113.1	170	111	99	44	75
Gonzalez, Lariel	0	1	10.13	11	0	13.1	18	16	15	12	9
Hackman, Luther	7	6	3.74	15	0	101.0	106	49	42	44	88
*Holzemer, Mark	3	2	5.69	41	1	55.1	77	39	35	24	49
*Jones, Bobby	2	1	5.40	3	0	16.2	17	13	10	15	14
Lee, David	0	0	0.00	6	3	5.2	0	0	0	1	7
*Phillips, J.R.	0	0	0.00	2	0	3.1	2	0	0	0	1
*Porzio, Mike	5	1	3.38	35	0	42.2	44	16	16	30	33
*Ramirez, Roberto	3	2	3.50	10	0	61.2	64	26	24	17	55
Randall, Scott	1	4	7.93	9	0	42.0	62	41	37	22	25
Rossiter, Mike	2	0	3.89	24	0	37.0	37	16	16	20	31
Saipe, Mike	1	5	4.83	11	0	54.0	62	36	29	20	39
Seifert, Ryan	0	0	4.50	1	0	4.0	4	2	2	2	2
Shoemaker, Stephen	4	6	6.00	16	0	81.0	100	59	54	47	46
Stoops, Jim	3	7	5.18	55	3	88.2	93	54	51	56	57
Thomson, John	0	2	9.45	5	0	20.0	36	25	21	8	19
Wainhouse, David	1	3	3.19	38	22	42.1	42	19	15	7	42
Walker, Pete	8	4	4.48	48	5	62.1	64	37	31	28	57
Wright, Jamey	5	7	6.46	17	0	100.1	133	87	72	38	75

Edmonton Trappers (Angels) AAA

BATTING	AVG	AB	R	H	2B	3B	HR	RBI	BB	SO	SB
t'Hoen, E.J., 2B	.138	29	2	4	0	0	0	0	2	7	0
Betten, Randy, 3B	.379	29	5	11	1	0	0	3	0	5	0
Burke, Jamie, 3B	.336	149	29	50	9	0	3	16	23	18	0
#Carvajal, Jovino, OF	.245	367	38	90	15	3	5	40	20	63	17
#Christian, Eddie, OF	.236	148	24	35	5	1	5	15	12	31	4
Colangelo, Mike, OF	.362	105	13	38	7	1	0	9	13	18	2
#DaVanon, Jeff, OF	.326	132	35	43	8	3	6	19	20	27	11
Decker, Steve, 3B	.284	225	51	64	19	2	15	51	44	38	0
Foster, Jim, C	.289	114	17	33	11	0	2	18	8	15	1
Graves, Bryan, C	.400	5	2	2	1	0	0	1	1	2	0
Greene, Todd, OF	.243	74	10	18	6	0	5	14	0	12	0
#Hemphill, Bret, C	.313	246	29	77	16	1	7	31	31	58	1
*Herrick, Jason, OF	.208	72	6	15	3	0	1	7	1	27	0

BATTING	AVG	AB	R	H	2B	3B	HR	RBI	BB	SO	SB
#Hutchins, Norm, OF	.250	521	80	130	27	6	7	51	40	127	25
Johns, Keith, SS	.208	236	32	49	9	2	3	26	26	38	2
*Kieschnick, B., DH	.314	296	54	93	20	3	23	73	19	60	0
*Luke, Matt, OF	.429	21	7	9	2	1	5	15	6	4	0
Luuloa, Keith, 2B	.285	396	54	113	23	1	4	46	44	53	7
Molina, Ben, C	.286	241	28	69	16	0	7	41	15	17	1
Pennyfeather, Will, OF	.212	99	16	21	5	1	2	10	5	21	3
#Perez, Tomas, SS	.260	296	31	77	17	1	4	40	19	43	2
*Pritchett, Chris, 1B	.279	348	60	97	15	1	12	45	47	70	1
Sheets, Andy, SS	.289	45	6	13	1	1	0	4	2	11	0
Silvestri, Dave, 2B	.318	318	55	101	18	0	6	42	22	43	4
Stoner, Mike, OF	.363	102	14	37	6	1	3	18	6	14	0
Tejero, Fausto, C	.294	17	3	5	0	0	1	2	3	3	0
#Williams, Reggie, OF	.314	137	25	43	9	1	6	31	16	29	3

PITCHING	W	L	ERA	G	SV	IP	H	R	ER	BB	SO
*Alvarez, Juan	0	3	3.49	27	0	28.1	30	13	11	8	25
Borland, Toby	2	1	7.00	21	0	27.0	31	24	21	23	34
Brow, Scott	1	6	5.70	64	15	79.0	94	53	50	31	48
Burke, Jamie	1	0	0.00	1	0	3.0	1	0	0	1	3
Cooper, Brian	2	1	3.77	5	0	31.0	30	17	13	10	32
Edsell, Geoff	1	4	5.01	30	0	46.2	46	27	26	25	37
Etherton, Seth	0	2	5.48	4	0	21.1	25	13	13	6	19
Fyhrie, Mike	9	5	3.47	19	0	114.0	90	47	44	40	113
Hawblitzel, Ryan	4	4	5.34	24	0	64.0	81	47	38	24	37
*Holtz, Mike	2	1	2.30	20	1	27.1	20	7	7	11	39
Jacobsen, Joe	0	1	7.20	12	0	15.0	24	13	12	5	6
James, Mike	1	2	8.64	8	0	8.1	16	14	8	2	3
Lomon, Kevin	7	8	5.75	23	0	123.2	170	86	79	35	91
*Lubozynski, Matt	0	0	0.00	1	0	2.0	1	0	0	1	1
McDowell, Jack	1	0	5.73	2	0	11.0	12	7	7	3	2
Mintz, Steve	4	3	2.35	31	9	30.2	31	11	8	6	17
*Montoya, Norm	4	1	5.61	38	0	67.1	92	49	42	17	30
Morse, Paul	1	5	7.11	10	0	49.1	64	44	39	34	30
Ortiz, Ramon	5	3	4.05	9	0	53.1	46	26	24	19	64
Pote, Lou	7	9	4.50	24	0	150.0	171	80	75	41	118
*Schoeneweis, Scott	2	4	7.64	9	0	35.1	58	35	30	12	29
Troutman, Keith	1	0	3.54	6	0	20.1	23	12	8	2	22
*Washburn, Jarrod	1	5	4.73	11	0	59.0	50	31	31	17	55
Williams, Shad	5	3	3.72	16	0	75.0	73	36	31	19	35

Fresno Grizzlies (Giants) AAA

BATTING	AVG	AB	R	H	2B	3B	HR	RBI	BB	SO	SB
#Byas, Michael, OF	.364	22	4	8	2	0	0	2	5	4	2
Campusano, C., 3B	.283	46	2	13	2	0	0	3	2	9	0
Canizaro, Jay, 2B	.280	364	77	102	20	2	26	78	49	79	16
#Crespo, Felipe, 1B	.332	385	98	128	27	5	24	84	78	73	17
#Delgado, Wilson, SS	.300	213	28	64	10	3	1	33	18	35	4
*Faircloth, Chad, PH	.000	1	0	0	0	0	0	0	0	0	0
*Guzman, Edwards, 3B	.274	358	48	98	13	0	7	48	17	50	6
*Leach, Jalal, OF	.294	371	58	109	19	5	15	75	27	67	8
Martinez, Ramon, SS	.325	114	13	37	7	1	2	17	10	17	2
Marval, Raul, SS	.300	280	41	84	15	1	7	46	16	48	2
Mashore, Damon, OF	.262	347	62	91	20	1	20	69	38	98	7
*Mayes, Craig, C	.260	169	19	44	12	0	3	16	8	26	1
Mirabelli, Doug, C	.313	320	63	100	24	1	14	51	48	56	8
#Mueller, Bill, 3B	.417	12	3	5	0	1	0	6	6	0	0
Murray, Calvin, OF	.334	548	122	183	31	7	23	73	49	88	42
*Rios, Armando, OF	.275	109	24	30	3	0	4	21	11	22	3
Servais, Scott, C	.273	11	3	3	1	1	0	2	0	1	0
#Tavarez, Jesus, 1B	.167	6	0	1	0	0	0	0	0	0	0
Torrealba, Yorvit, C	.254	63	9	16	2	0	2	10	4	11	0
Voigt, Jack, 1B	.194	67	12	13	4	1	1	5	17	21	1
Williams, Keith, OF	.282	294	46	83	23	3	11	50	34	50	4
Woods, Ken, 3B	.324	469	77	152	23	4	6	73	33	45	19
Young, Travis, 2B	.250	92	15	23	1	1	2	11	9	23	3

PITCHING	W	L	ERA	G	SV	IP	H	R	ER	BB	SO
Bailey, Cory	2	1	3.30	43	18	46.1	47	24	17	17	52
Connelly, Steve	6	4	5.25	54	2	72.0	93	58	42	32	47
Corps, Edwin	0	0	3.86	4	0	7.0	9	7	3	3	11
Crabtree, Robbie	1	4	5.24	22	1	34.1	37	23	20	10	40
Del Toro, Miguel	4	2	4.42	40	0	71.1	76	41	35	29	71
Estrella, Luis	0	1	12.34	8	0	11.2	23	16	16	7	5
*Fultz, Aaron	9	8	4.98	37	0	137.1	141	87	76	51	151
Jensen, Ryan	11	10	5.12	27	0	156.1	160	96	89	68	150
McMullen, Mike	2	2	4.36	41	0	66.0	52	36	32	41	56

Rookie League WRAP-UPS

Appalachian League

Martinsville won the league title and Elizabethton's **Ruben Salazar** won the MVP award. Salazar batted .401 in 64 games with 14 homers and 65 RBI, missing the Triple Crown by two homers. Pulaski's **Kevin Mench** won the homer race (16). Bristol's **Chad Durham** led the league—and the entire White Sox organization—with 57 steals. Pitcher of the Year was Pulaski's **Aaron Harang** (9-2, 2.30, 87 strikeouts in 78 innings). He beat out Martinsville's **Carlos Hernandez**, who led the loop with a 1.46 ERA and struck out a minor-league-high 18 batters in his last game of the year.

APPALACHIAN (ADV. ROOKIE)
East Division

	W	L	Pct.	GB
Martinsville	41	29	.586	—
Danville	38	31	.551	2.5
Bluefield	25	45	.368	15
Princeton	25	45	.357	16
Burlington	21	49	.300	20

West Division

	W	L	Pct.	GB
Pulaski	48	21	.696	—
Bristol	45	24	.652	3
Elizabethton	40	30	.571	8.5
Kingsport	34	36	.486	14.5
Johnson City	30	39	.435	18

Switch-hitter
* Left-handed

Rookie League WRAP-UPS

Pioneer League

The Missoula Osprey moved from Canada and won the league championship. They had help from MVP **Lyle Overbay** (.343, 12 HR, and a short-season record 101 RBI). Billings's **Casey Bookout** won the batting crown (.363) while Idaho Falls' **Troy Schader** was the home run king (19). Helena's **Ryan Knox** swiped a league-best 44 bases. Teammate **Jose Mieses** was the top pitcher (10-2, 2.67); he finished his season by winning a minor-league-best nine consecutive starts. Great Falls's **Adam Williams** struck out a league-best 95 batters while Idaho Falls's **Oswaldo Verdugo** led the league with 13 saves.

PIONEER (ADV. ROOKIE)
North Division

	W	L	Pct.	GB
Helena	26	11	.703	—
Missoula	17	21	.447	9.5
Medicine Hat	17	21	.447	9.5
Great Falls	15	23	.395	11.5

South Division

	W	L	Pct.	GB
Idaho Falls	24	13	.649	—
Billings	20	17	.541	4
Ogden	16	22	.421	8.5
Butte Copper	15	22	.405	9

Pioneer League

PITCHING	W	L	ERA	G	SV	IP	H	R	ER	BB	SO
Nathan, Joe	6	4	4.46	13	0	74.2	68	44	37	36	82
*Oropesa, Eddie	6	5	4.85	21	0	102.0	113	69	55	49	61
Patrick, Bronswell	14	11	4.88	28	0	164.0	194	116	89	42	142
Soderstrom, Steve	2	8	6.78	22	0	71.2	90	64	54	35	58
Tavarez, Julian	0	0	2.25	4	0	8.0	3	2	2	3	9
Verdugo, Jason	1	0	4.87	9	0	20.1	19	14	11	9	29
Weber, Ben	2	4	3.34	51	8	86.1	78	34	32	28	67

Iowa Cubs (Cubs) AAA

BATTING	AVG	AB	R	H	2B	3B	HR	RBI	BB	SO	SB
Almanzar, Richard, 2B	.215	93	13	20	2	3	1	4	6	7	6
Battle, Allen, DH	.245	110	16	27	7	0	3	14	14	30	2
*Brown, Roosevelt, OF	.358	268	50	96	25	2	22	79	19	54	3
Cline, Pat, C	.228	290	27	66	20	1	6	42	26	73	1
Gazarek, Marty, OF	.320	128	13	41	12	0	5	16	5	13	0
*Hinske, Eric, 1B	.267	15	3	4	0	1	1	2	1	4	0
*Jennings, Robin, OF	.309	259	47	80	20	5	9	43	25	34	6
King, Brett, SS	.196	112	16	22	6	0	4	10	17	27	6
Lisanti, Bob, PH	.173	52	5	9	3	0	0	1	1	14	0
*Martinez, Sandy, C	.232	125	8	29	6	0	2	18	5	29	1
Meyers, Chad, 2B	.354	175	39	62	13	2	0	16	29	20	17
Molina, Jose, C	.263	240	24	63	11	1	4	26	20	54	0
Nieves, Jose, SS	.268	392	55	105	25	3	11	59	24	65	11
Porter, Bo, OF	.292	414	86	121	24	2	27	64	65	121	15
Quinlan, Tom, 3B	.250	472	62	118	26	1	17	58	41	159	1
#Rennhack, Mike, OF	.226	146	8	33	7	1	2	11	20	40	2
*Stahoviak, Scott, 1B	.237	274	51	65	16	1	14	44	44	88	4
White, Derrick, OF	.262	503	75	132	31	0	13	77	47	94	10
Wilson, Brandon, 2B	.278	472	82	131	28	6	12	49	34	76	31
#Zinter, Alan, 1B	.255	51	7	13	2	0	3	8	5	13	0

PITCHING	W	L	ERA	G	SV	IP	H	R	ER	BB	SO
Barker, Richie	4	4	4.26	55	7	74.0	72	37	35	30	52
Beck, Rod	0	0	0.00	2	0	2.0	1	0	0	0	2
Cole, Victor	2	1	4.69	19	0	40.1	41	24	21	23	33
*Creek, Doug	7	3	3.79	25	1	130.2	116	66	55	62	140
Farnsworth, Kyle	2	2	3.20	6	0	39.1	38	16	14	9	29
Gajkowski, Steve	5	8	3.73	58	9	79.2	79	36	33	25	64
Gonzalez, Jeremi	0	1	4.50	3	0	10.0	10	8	5	6	10
Juelsgaard, Jarod	4	7	5.59	23	0	83.2	92	57	52	26	54
Karchner, Matt	0	0	6.35	5	0	5.2	6	4	4	1	6
*King, Ray	4	4	1.88	37	2	43.0	31	11	9	22	41
Lacy, Kerry	3	8	5.44	49	0	92.2	105	65	56	44	69
*Lorraine, Andrew	9	8	3.71	22	0	143.0	149	67	59	34	96
Manning, David	0	0	4.66	7	0	9.2	9	6	5	8	7
*McNichol, Brian	10	11	5.58	28	0	161.1	194	108	100	55	120
Miller, Kurt	1	2	5.09	8	1	17.2	17	10	10	8	23
Myers, Rodney	2	4	4.06	20	2	31.0	29	18	14	11	24
Nomo, Hideo	1	1	3.71	3	0	17.0	12	7	7	12	18
*Norton, Phillip	5	6	6.67	14	0	79.2	98	63	59	33	61
Quevedo, Ruben	3	1	3.45	7	0	44.1	34	18	17	21	50
Rain, Steve	0	1	2.00	8	2	9.0	7	2	2	4	9
*Serafini, Dan	0	0	2.77	2	0	13.0	12	6	4	5	11
*Watkins, Scott	1	2	6.14	47	0	63.0	71	47	43	33	54
*Woodall, Brad	2	2	6.84	15	1	52.2	67	40	40	23	41

Las Vegas Stars (Padres) AAA

BATTING	AVG	AB	R	H	2B	3B	HR	RBI	BB	SO	SB
Allen, Dusty, 1B	.273	454	68	124	30	3	18	89	79	143	3
Arias, George, 3B	.284	95	30	27	7	2	10	30	17	28	1
#Baerga, Carlos, 3B	.286	91	15	26	7	0	2	9	9	5	0
Charles, Frank, C	.246	272	25	67	19	2	2	28	10	61	2
*Darr, Mike, OF	.298	383	57	114	34	0	10	62	50	103	10
#Davis, Ben, C	.308	201	27	62	18	1	7	44	24	41	4
Garcia, Carlos, 1B	.281	274	36	77	19	0	3	28	17	61	5
*Giovanola, Ed, 3B	.283	106	23	30	6	1	2	10	16	23	2
Gomez, Chris, SS	.333	27	3	9	1	0	0	4	2	6	0
Gonzalez, Jimmy, C	.295	112	10	33	9	1	3	19	14	29	0
Gonzalez, W., C	.272	92	13	25	6	0	6	12	5	10	0
*Guiel, Aaron, OF	.245	257	46	63	25	2	12	39	44	86	5
Hamel, Jon, C	.000	2	0	0	0	0	0	0	1	1	0
*Joyner, Wally, 1B	.235	17	4	4	0	0	0	2	3	2	0
*Kirby, Wayne, OF	.300	160	29	48	7	3	10	31	28	36	2
LaRocca, Greg, 3B	.275	51	3	14	2	0	0	2	2	10	2
Leyritz, Jim, 1B	.000	8	0	0	0	0	0	0	0	5	0
Lidle, Kevin, C	.276	29	5	8	3	0	2	5	3	8	0

Switch-hitter
* Left-handed

BATTING	AVG	AB	R	H	2B	3B	HR	RBI	BB	SO	SB
#Matthews, Gary, OF	.256	422	57	108	22	3	9	52	58	104	17
#Melo, Juan, SS	.201	169	17	34	3	2	2	13	7	34	1
*Mitchell, Mike, 1B	.241	87	7	21	5	0	1	11	12	20	0
Nevin, Phil, C	.200	10	2	2	0	0	2	2	0	2	0
*Newhan, David, 2B	.286	374	49	107	25	1	14	49	30	84	22
Pelaez, Alex, 3B	.308	13	1	4	0	0	0	0	0	2	0
*Prieto, Chris, OF	.241	348	66	84	14	6	6	29	46	51	21
Rossy, Rico, SS	.255	259	42	66	12	0	10	29	41	27	4
Snellgrove, Clay, 2B	.667	3	1	2	2	0	0	0	0	0	0
#Thrower, Jake, 2B	.288	267	40	77	17	4	4	30	27	56	4

PITCHING	W	L	ERA	G	SV	IP	H	R	ER	BB	SO
Almanzar, Carlos	1	3	9.53	11	0	22.2	32	25	24	8	18
*Carlyle, Buddy	11	8	4.89	25	0	160.0	180	99	87	42	138
*Cooke, Steve	0	0	30.00	1	0	3.0	6	10	10	12	0
Cunnane, Will	2	1	0.98	28	11	36.2	30	5	4	16	54
Darwin, Jeff	1	1	13.50	8	0	10.0	19	17	15	5	9
*Dennis, Shane	3	10	5.59	34	0	116.0	140	83	72	60	104
*Drumheller, Al	6	4	4.90	20	0	60.2	72	36	33	22	46
Kolb, Brandon	2	1	3.94	42	4	61.2	72	36	27	29	63
*Murray, Heath	5	4	4.26	15	0	82.1	99	45	39	32	65
*Rivera, Roberto	1	2	10.16	20	0	33.2	61	39	38	14	25
Rossy, Rico	0	0	18.00	1	0	2.0	5	4	4	1	0
Sak, Jim	2	2	3.58	23	6	27.2	22	11	11	17	32
Skrmetta, Matt	2	1	3.45	20	1	28.2	20	13	11	11	25
Smith, Pete	6	8	4.76	21	0	109.2	130	75	58	29	82
Spencer, Stan	5	4	5.47	12	0	54.1	69	35	33	15	50
Sullivan, Brendan	2	4	7.60	45	0	66.1	88	60	56	38	50
Tollberg, Brian	1	2	4.85	5	0	29.2	34	17	16	6	23
Whiteside, Matt	9	5	5.12	47	7	89.2	99	59	51	29	88
Wolff, Bryan	8	12	4.66	28	0	177.2	199	99	92	57	151

Memphis Redbirds (Cardinals) AAA

BATTING	AVG	AB	R	H	2B	3B	HR	RBI	BB	SO	SB
*Ametller, Jesus, 2B	.250	4	0	1	0	0	0	0	0	0	0
Belk, Tim, 1B	.200	55	10	11	4	0	3	8	9	9	1
*Bieser, Steve, OF	.306	193	28	59	14	2	4	19	18	34	8
*Clapp, Stubby, 2B	.260	393	72	102	26	2	14	62	53	96	7
*Dishington, Nate, OF	.209	196	34	41	11	1	8	32	25	96	1
*Drew, J.D., OF	.299	87	11	26	5	1	2	15	8	20	6
*Haas, Chris, 3B	.229	397	63	91	19	2	18	73	66	155	4
#Howard, Dave, 2B	.263	19	3	5	0	0	0	2	1	6	2
#Howard, Thomas, OF	.361	119	24	43	10	2	2	21	13	21	1
*Hulse, David, OF	.335	200	37	67	13	2	4	31	9	39	4
#Jensen, Marcus, C	.291	237	38	69	19	4	8	44	30	59	0
*Kennedy, Adam, 2B	.327	367	69	120	22	4	10	63	29	36	20
Lariviere, Jason, OF	.286	497	90	142	35	3	9	47	47	64	18
Little, Mark, OF	.296	196	40	58	11	5	3	22	10	48	12
McDonald, Keith, C	.301	113	20	34	7	0	5	27	20	25	1
Ordaz, Luis, SS	.285	362	31	103	25	4	1	45	24	40	3
Pemberton, Rudy, OF	.260	73	13	19	7	0	2	11	6	13	1
Perez, Eduardo, 1B	.320	416	67	133	31	0	18	82	45	92	7
Polanco, Placido, 2B	.275	120	18	33	4	1	0	10	3	11	2
*Richard, Chris, 1B	.412	17	3	7	2	0	1	4	1	2	0
Stefanski, Mike, C	.299	201	27	60	12	0	4	22	17	28	3
Warner, Ron, OF	.290	245	35	71	14	1	11	33	32	70	8

PITCHING	W	L	ERA	G	SV	IP	H	R	ER	BB	SO
*Ankiel, Rick	7	3	3.16	16	0	88.1	73	37	31	46	119
*Barnes, Brian	4	3	5.50	36	0	90.0	104	55	55	33	88
Benes, Alan	0	1	3.18	3	0	5.2	8	3	2	2	3
Busby, Mike	3	4	7.43	29	0	72.2	112	69	60	36	50
Crafton, Kevin	0	1	22.85	4	0	4.1	12	12	11	0	2
Croushore, Rich	1	0	6.75	7	4	6.2	8	5	5	6	11
*Detmers, Kris	6	8	5.10	23	0	125.1	135	74	71	44	90
*Eversgerd, Bryan	6	6	2.86	59	2	66.0	56	26	21	15	46
Heiserman, Rick	2	3	5.11	52	20	61.2	67	37	35	21	57
Hutchinson, Chad	2	0	2.19	2	0	12.1	4	3	3	8	16
Jimenez, Jose	2	2	3.04	4	0	26.2	30	10	9	9	18
King, Curtis	2	2	2.61	27	7	31.0	21	13	9	10	25
*Lovingier, Kevin	3	4	4.85	51	0	78.0	66	44	42	40	66
Luebbers, Larry	13	4	4.03	21	0	129.2	134	61	58	33	84
Mlicki, Doug	3	1	5.78	38	0	67.0	78	48	43	26	26
*Mohler, Mike	2	1	3.07	10	1	14.2	16	5	5	5	17
Nussbeck, Mark	6	10	8.23	36	0	101.2	145	100	93	37	82
Opipari, Mario	0	0	10.13	3	0	2.2	2	3	3	3	0
Slocumb, Heathcliff	0	0	4.50	2	0	2.0	3	1	1	0	2

Rookie League WRAP-UPS

Arizona League

The Athletics ran away with the regular-season title in the eight-team complex league, finishing at 39-17, seven games ahead of the second-place Mariners. **German Chirinos** of the Oakland club led the league with 56 RBI, a full 15 ahead of his runner-up. **Michael Wenner** was second in the batting race with a .386 mark and also was named the league's MVP. Three Athletics pitchers—**Kurt Nantkes** (2.19), **Claudio Galva** (2.38) and southpaw **Javier Calzada** (2.54)—ranked among the top 10 in ERA for the loop while closer **Corey Miller**'s 11 saves led the league. **Juan Ventura** of the Rockies won the batting title with a .399 mark, while Padres right-hander **Jacob Peavy** led the league with a 1.34 ERA. Peavy also tied for the league lead with his 7-1 record and struck out 90 batters in just 74 innings.

ARIZONA (ROOKIE)

	W	L	Pct.	GB
Athletics	39	17	.696	—
Mariners	32	24	.571	7
Padres	31	24	.564	7.5
Mexico	28	27	.509	10.5
Rockies	27	28	.491	11.5
Diamondbacks	24	32	.429	15
White Sox	23	33	.411	16
Cubs	18	37	.327	20.5

MINOR LEAGUE REPORT

389

Switch-hitter
* Left-handed

Rookie League WRAP-UPS

Gulf Coast League

The Mets swept the Twins for the championship. The Rangers' **Hank Blalock** won the Gulf Coast League batting title (.361), edging out Marlin **Chip Ambres** by eight points. Blalock's 38 RBI, 69 hits, 17 doubles, six triples and .560 slugging percentage all led the league as well. Oriole **Charlie Dees** led in homers (nine). The Phillies had the top two base stealers: **Ian Rauls** (27) and **Julio Collazo** (25). The Braves' **Kyle Colton** won the ERA crown (1.79); **David Tavarez** of the Orioles went 9-0 (2.14); and Yankee **David Martinez**, who threw a no-hitter in his final start, led the league with 67 strikeouts.

GULF COAST (ROOKIE)

Eastern Division

	W	L	Pct.	GB
Mets	39	21	.650	—
Expos	29	31	.483	10
Braves	27	33	.450	12
Marlins	25	35	.417	14

Northern Division

	W	L	Pct.	GB
Royals	33	27	.550	—
Yankees	32	28	.533	1
Tigers	29	31	.483	4
Phillies	26	34	.433	7

Western Division

	W	L	Pct.	GB
Rangers	37	23	.617	—
Twins	33	26	.559	3.5
Orioles	31	28	.525	5.5
Red Sox	30	29	.508	6.5
Pirates	24	35	.407	12.5
Reds	23	37	.383	14

PITCHING (continued)

PITCHING	W	L	ERA	G	SV	IP	H	R	ER	BB	SO
Sodowsky, Clint	4	5	4.82	19	3	80.1	85	55	43	32	52
Stechschulte, Gene	0	0	7.71	2	0	2.1	2	2	2	5	2
Stephenson, Garrett	1	1	3.16	4	0	25.2	22	9	9	7	19
Thompson, Mark	4	2	2.94	9	0	52.0	50	22	17	20	27
Weibl, Clint	1	0	5.40	5	0	8.1	10	9	5	2	8

Nashville Sounds (Pirates) AAA

BATTING	AVG	AB	R	H	2B	3B	HR	RBI	BB	SO	SB
Brinkley, Darryl, OF	.323	372	68	120	35	2	14	75	31	58	5
#Brown, Adrian, OF	.321	56	10	18	3	1	0	4	11	8	6
Brown, Emil, OF	.307	430	97	132	20	5	18	60	35	80	16
*Cruz, Ivan, 1B	.326	273	57	89	20	1	25	81	21	56	0
Garcia, Freddy, 3B	.000	9	0	0	0	0	0	0	0	3	0
Guillen, Jose, OF	.333	132	28	44	10	0	5	22	8	21	0
Hermansen, Chad, OF	.270	496	89	134	27	3	32	97	35	119	19
Howard, Matt, 2B	.293	399	41	117	17	2	2	44	25	24	13
Hyzdu, Adam, OF	.250	44	6	11	1	0	5	13	4	11	0
Laker, Tim, C	.269	405	48	109	29	3	12	65	29	68	3
Meares, Pat, SS	.167	18	3	3	0	0	0	0	1	3	1
Montgomery, Ray, OF	.331	272	57	90	23	2	16	52	24	49	5
#Nunez, Abraham, SS	.310	58	12	18	0	0	0	3	5	8	1
Osik, Keith, C	.091	11	0	1	0	0	0	0	0	1	0
#Patzke, Jeff, 2B	.220	173	20	38	5	1	2	14	32	29	2
Polcovich, Kevin, SS	.240	233	37	56	10	1	3	25	20	52	6
Ramirez, Aramis, 3B	.328	460	92	151	35	1	21	74	73	56	5
*Robertson, Mike, 1B	.309	220	34	68	16	1	9	31	10	32	2
*Secrist, Reed, C	.265	102	12	27	8	1	2	15	8	22	1
#Strange, Doug, 2B	.077	13	2	1	1	0	0	0	0	2	0
#Sveum, Dale, SS	.297	192	28	57	15	1	4	29	21	53	1
Tremie, Chris, C	.248	121	20	30	7	0	3	16	14	29	4
Wehner, John, SS	.431	58	14	25	3	0	8	15	3	6	0

PITCHING	W	L	ERA	G	SV	IP	H	R	ER	BB	SO
*Ah Yat, Paul	4	3	5.71	13	0	64.2	75	45	41	24	41
*Anderson, Jimmy	11	2	3.84	21	0	133.2	153	67	57	41	93
Arroyo, Bronson	0	2	10.38	3	0	13.0	22	15	15	10	11
Boyd, Jason	6	5	4.26	49	5	80.1	78	42	38	27	62
Castillo, Frank	7	5	4.68	19	0	119.1	139	72	62	32	90
*Christiansen, Jason	0	0	0.00	2	0	2.0	0	0	0	0	1
Clontz, Brad	0	2	3.50	12	7	18.0	12	8	7	6	23
Cordova, Francisco	2	0	0.75	2	0	12.0	10	2	1	1	7
Davis, Kane	3	2	6.75	12	0	49.1	65	38	37	17	31
Dougherty, Jim	3	3	5.43	53	10	59.2	69	38	36	27	55
*Dunbar, Matt	1	0	4.35	11	0	10.1	13	6	5	4	9
Garcia, Mike	0	2	3.95	23	2	27.1	24	12	12	10	35
Giard, Ken	0	0	4.32	14	0	16.2	16	10	8	11	21
Hansell, Greg	3	3	2.00	22	2	27.0	18	8	6	9	36
*Long, Joey	2	1	4.50	35	0	36.0	39	25	18	22	37
Milacki, Bob	6	8	4.86	22	0	111.0	130	82	60	43	79
*Peters, Chris	3	1	2.19	11	1	49.1	54	18	12	15	34
Phillips, Jason	0	0	15.00	1	0	3.0	6	6	5	5	5
Ritchie, Todd	0	0	1.80	1	0	5.0	6	1	1	1	2
*Robertson, Rich	2	4	7.94	10	0	34.0	46	32	30	23	33
Ryan, Ken	1	1	3.86	6	0	7.0	7	3	3	8	9
Ryan, Matt	6	5	4.42	48	8	79.1	87	48	39	35	52
*Sauveur, Rich	5	2	1.95	53	7	64.2	62	21	14	16	61
Scott, Tim	1	3	5.09	19	0	23.0	29	14	13	7	21
Silva, Jose	2	0	1.50	2	0	12.0	14	4	2	4	10
Sparks, Jeff	5	3	3.83	34	0	49.1	37	25	21	23	69
Van Poppel, Todd	10	6	4.95	27	0	163.2	173	95	90	62	157
*Wallace, Jeff	2	2	8.79	15	3	14.1	18	15	14	8	14
Wilkins, Marc	1	1	0.79	8	3	11.1	9	3	1	3	8

New Orleans Zephyrs (Astros) AAA

BATTING	AVG	AB	R	H	2B	3B	HR	RBI	BB	SO	SB
Alexander, Chad, OF	.240	96	7	23	5	0	2	8	6	22	0
*Bako, Paul, C	.191	47	2	9	3	1	1	4	1	11	0
#Berkman, Lance, OF	.323	226	42	73	20	0	8	49	39	47	7
Betzsold, James, OF	.217	198	29	43	15	0	7	27	14	64	3
#Caminiti, Ken, 3B	.350	20	6	7	4	0	0	3	2	1	0
#Candaele, Casey, 2B	.266	467	56	124	34	3	7	42	47	54	3
Gonzales, Rene, 1B	.253	79	9	20	4	0	0	11	11	11	1
Gutierrez, Ricky, SS	.214	14	0	3	0	0	0	1	2	3	0
Hernandez, Carlos, SS	.293	355	56	104	14	0	0	43	27	65	22
Incaviglia, Pete, OF	.181	94	9	17	7	1	1	13	9	26	2
Johnson, Russ, 2B	.351	77	17	27	6	0	1	12	16	13	1

Batting leaders across all leagues

BATTING	AVG	AB	R	H	2B	3B	HR	RBI	BB	SO	SB
Knorr, Randy, C	.352	270	33	95	22	1	11	41	20	41	0
Lopez, Pedro, C	.267	60	11	16	4	0	2	11	7	8	0
Miller, Ryan, PH	.276	174	19	48	8	0	1	25	5	29	0
Neal, Mike, OF	.202	243	33	49	10	1	6	28	27	61	3
Ramirez, Omar, OF	.253	379	56	96	15	2	6	51	30	49	8
Russo, Paul, 1B	.263	133	19	35	6	0	4	18	21	28	1
*Saylor, Jamie, OF	.224	330	38	74	14	5	4	36	34	83	8
Thompson, Ryan, OF	.309	404	60	125	23	2	16	58	37	78	4
Thurston, Jerrey, C	.220	59	7	13	0	0	0	4	4	15	0
Villalobos, Carlos, 3B	.283	499	82	141	33	1	9	50	54	100	11
*Ward, Daryle, 1B	.353	241	56	85	15	1	28	65	23	43	1
#Williams, George, C	.284	328	56	93	21	1	9	45	55	70	1

PITCHING	W	L	ERA	G	SV	IP	H	R	ER	BB	SO
Bergman, Sean	0	1	9.95	3	0	6.1	9	8	7	2	2
Cabrera, Jose	3	1	2.82	31	7	51.0	34	18	16	12	41
Creek, Ryan	1	2	3.98	6	0	31.2	30	17	14	16	20
Crow, Dean	2	6	7.04	34	3	46.0	71	36	36	12	22
Diorio, Mike	2	3	6.40	50	1	70.1	85	59	50	31	32
Ellis, Robert	7	12	5.43	27	0	155.2	176	106	94	51	105
Henry, Doug	0	0	4.50	3	0	4.0	4	2	2	3	3
Huisman, Rick	3	1	3.61	35	3	52.1	42	23	21	16	67
Maxcy, John	0	0	12.38	4	0	8.0	12	11	11	2	6
McCurry, Jeff	0	7	4.15	40	14	43.1	48	23	20	14	26
Meacham, Rusty	3	4	4.94	17	1	47.1	56	26	26	9	47
Miller, Wade	11	9	4.38	26	0	162.1	156	85	79	64	135
*Mounce, Tony	0	1	2.45	14	0	11.0	10	3	3	13	10
Powell, Brian	4	4	6.19	9	0	48.0	54	39	33	21	36
Scanlan, Bob	8	15	5.61	28	0	163.2	208	116	102	55	78
Sikorski, Brian	7	10	4.95	28	0	158.1	169	92	87	58	122
Slusarski, Joe	1	4	3.64	40	1	64.1	71	31	26	13	40
Wallace, Kent	2	2	4.14	36	1	58.2	61	30	27	13	43

Oklahoma Redhawks (Rangers) AAA

BATTING	AVG	AB	R	H	2B	3B	HR	RBI	BB	SO	SB
*Barkett, Andy, 1B	.307	486	70	149	32	5	10	76	44	71	7
Bournigal, Rafael, 2B	.375	56	16	21	6	0	3	14	12	5	1
*Bridges, Kary, 2B	.343	239	38	82	14	0	7	39	21	14	6
*Bridges, Kary, 2B	.322	264	39	85	14	0	7	39	22	19	6
Brumbaugh, Cliff, OF	.250	12	1	3	0	0	0	1	0	2	0
Clayton, Royce, SS	.143	7	1	1	0	0	0	1	3	3	0
#Cuyler, Milt, OF	.173	52	3	9	4	0	0	6	2	12	1
*Demetral, Chris, 2B	.262	183	29	48	7	1	4	18	28	35	1
Dransfeldt, Kelly, SS	.237	359	55	85	21	2	10	44	24	108	6
Evans, Tom, 3B	.280	439	84	123	35	3	12	68	66	100	5
Forbes, P.J., 2B	.104	67	4	7	1	0	0	2	5	12	0
#Green, S., OF	.248	359	68	89	16	6	3	29	34	86	26
Hubbard, Mike, C	.283	392	48	111	19	0	9	49	25	70	4
*Lamb, Mike, 3B	.500	2	0	1	0	0	0	0	1	0	0
Marzano, John, C	.244	160	15	39	10	0	2	16	8	19	0
Mateo, Ruben, OF	.336	253	53	85	12	0	18	62	14	36	6
Monroe, Craig, OF	.250	16	2	4	1	0	0	1	1	4	0
Reeder, Cory, C	.190	21	3	4	2	0	0	1	0	6	0
#Rosario, Mel, C	.192	26	2	5	1	0	0	3	0	8	1
*Sagmoen, Marc, OF	.272	268	42	73	11	3	13	43	24	58	3
Sheldon, Scott, 2B	.311	453	94	141	35	3	28	97	56	112	0
Simms, Mike, DH	.274	73	7	20	1	0	2	16	16	25	0
Solano, Danny, SS	.000	6	0	0	0	0	0	1	0	4	0
*Valdes, Pedro, DH	.327	394	72	129	27	1	21	72	52	60	1
Zywica, Mike, OF	.265	495	80	131	31	3	9	79	33	119	4

PITCHING	W	L	ERA	G	SV	IP	H	R	ER	BB	SO
*Davis, Doug	7	0	3.00	13	0	78.0	77	27	26	31	74
Dickey, R.A.	2	2	4.37	6	0	22.2	23	12	11	7	17
*Frey, Steve	1	2	4.47	30	9	44.1	51	25	22	15	38
Glynn, Ryan	6	2	3.39	16	0	90.1	81	46	34	36	55
*Gunderson, Eric	0	1	8.10	5	1	6.2	11	6	6	1	3
Hudson, Joe	1	1	5.00	5	0	9.0	15	6	5	4	4
Johnson, Jonathan	8	4	6.25	21	2	67.2	91	53	47	23	38
*Karp, Ryan	2	2	7.49	8	0	39.2	62	34	33	14	28
Knight, Brandon	9	8	4.91	27	0	163.0	173	96	89	47	97
Kolb, Dan	5	5	5.10	11	0	60.0	74	35	34	27	21
*Lee, Corey	3	0	2.03	4	0	26.2	21	6	6	8	25
Loaiza, Esteban	0	0	.00	2	0	4.1	3	0	0	3	6
*McDill, Allen	1	3	3.72	42	18	48.1	45	22	20	17	46
Moody, Eric	7	4	3.42	39	4	73.2	78	33	28	13	31
Patterson, Danny	1	0	.00	2	0	3.0	1	0	0	1	4

BATTING AVERAGE
(minimum 383 TPA)

Player	Club	Lg.	BA
T*Durazo, E.	Tuc	PCL	.404
T*Burroughs, S.	RCu	Cal	.363
*Urquiola, Carlos	SB	Mid	.362
Quinn, Mark	Oma	PCL	.360
T*Patterson, J.	Tuc	PCL	.358
*Johnson, Nick	Nrw	East	.345
T*Nunnari, T.	Har	East	.344
*Cox, Steve	Dur	Int	.341
T Piatt, Adam	Van	PCL	.340
T Williams, Jason	Ind	Int	.339
T#Davanon, Jeff	Edm	PCL	.338
T*Brown, R.	Iow	PCL	.338
T*Cummings, M.	Slk	PCL	.336
T Espada, J.	Van	PCL	.336
Gonzalez, Raul	Tre	East	.335

SLUGGING PERCENTAGE

Player	Club	Lg.	SLUG
T*Durazo, Erubiel	Tuc	PCL	.703
T Piatt, Adam	Van	PCL	.688
*Cust, Jack	HiD	Cal	.651
T*Brown, R.	Iow	PCL	.634
Norton, Chris	Por	East	.633
#Crespo, Felipe	Fre	PCL	.616
*Phillips, J.R.	Csp	PCL	.614
T Petrick, Ben	Csp	PCL	.603
T Burrell, Pat	SWB	Int	.602
T Alcantara, Israel	Paw	Int	.599
Quinn, Mark	Oma	PCL	.598
*Patterson, Corey	Lan	Mid	.592
McNally, Sean	Wch	Tex	.591
*Ortiz, David	SLk	PCL	.590
T*Patterson, J.	Tuc	PCL	.589

ON BASE AVERAGE

Player	Club	Lg.	OBA
*Johnson, Nick	Nrw	East	.525
T*Durazo, Erubiel	Tuc	PCL	.489
T*Burroughs, S.	RCu	Cal	.467
TPiatt, Adam	Van	PCL	.450
*Cust, Jack	HiD	Cal	.450
T*Patterson, J.	Tuc	PCL	.448
#Crespo, Felipe	Fre	PCL	.447
T*Sollmann, S.	Hnt	Sou	.446
Robinson, Bo	Wis	Mid	.446
Schaeffer, Jon	QC	Mid	.444
T#Melhuse, A.	Knx	Sou	.442
Eckstein, David	Tre	East	.440
T*Brown, Dee	Wch	Tex	.436
Kiil, Skip	Clr	FSL	.436

Switch-hitter
* Left-handed
T Player has been with more than one team; listed with last team.
(Players in major leagues are listed with last minor league club.)

Batting leaders across all leagues

(Cont'd from previous page)

HOME RUNS

Players	Club	Lg.	HR
*Phillips, J.R.	Csp	PCL	41
T Piatt, Adam	Van	PCL	39
Norton, Chris	Por	East	38
McNeal, Aaron	Mch	Mid	38
*Tracy, Andy	Har	East	37
McNally, Sean	Wch	Tex	36
Pellow, Kit	Oma	PCL	35
T#Burkhart, M.	Tre	East	35
T Morgan, Scott	Buf	Int	34
Raven, Luis	Chr	Int	33
Hermansen, C.	Nsh	PCL	32
*Cust, Jack	HiD	Cal	32
McCarty, Dave	Tol	Int	31
T Thompson, A.	Syr	Int	31
Chen, Chin-Feng	SBr	Cal	31

RUNS BATTED IN

Player	Club	Lg.	RBI
T Piatt, Adam	Van	PCL	138
McNeal, Aaron	Mch	Mid	131
*Tracy, Andy	Har	East	128
*Cox, Steve	Dur	Int	127
Raven, Luis	Chr	Int	125
*Mensik, Todd	Vis	Cal	123
Hart, Jason	Mod	Cal	123
Chen, Chin-Feng	SBr	Cal	123
*Giles, Tim	Knx	Sou	114
*Cust, Jack	HiD	Cal	112
Landry, Jacques	Mod	Cal	111
Marcinczyk, T.R.	Mid	Tex	111
*Hafner, Travis	Sav	SAL	111
*Ortiz, David	SLk	PCL	110
McNally, Sean	Wch	Tex	109

PITCHING	W	L	ERA	G	SV	IP	H	R	ER	BB	SO
*Perisho, Matt	15	7	4.61	27	0	156.1	160	86	80	78	150
*Pickett, Ricky	3	4	8.13	29	2	55.1	77	53	50	43	55
Raggio, Brady	6	11	5.14	30	1	168.0	193	100	96	49	114
Sievert, Mark	0	0	10.32	7	0	11.1	17	13	13	8	5
Smith, Chuck	5	4	2.96	32	4	85.0	73	31	28	28	76
*Venafro, Mike	0	0	5.40	6	1	11.2	16	7	7	0	7
Zimmerman, Jeff	1	0	.00	2	1	3.2	0	0	0	0	2

Omaha Goldenspikes (Royals) AAA

BATTING	AVG	AB	R	H	2B	3B	HR	RBI	BB	SO	SB
Brito, Juan, C	.286	7	1	2	2	0	0	0	0	2	0
Byington, Jimmie, OF	.206	228	28	47	10	1	2	23	20	46	3
Carr, Jeremy, OF	.262	275	47	72	12	1	4	25	42	58	15
Fasano, Sal, C	.275	280	63	77	15	0	21	49	42	69	4
*Giambi, Jeremy, OF	.346	127	31	44	5	1	12	28	31	30	1
Gibralter, Steve, OF	.266	417	77	111	21	1	28	78	27	97	6
Hansen, Jed, 2B	.274	175	35	48	8	5	7	22	32	72	8
Holbert, Ray, SS	.297	128	26	38	4	0	4	12	12	35	13
Lopez, Mendy, SS	.311	222	41	69	8	0	12	40	18	41	2
#Martinez, Felix, SS	.304	23	2	7	5	0	0	2	2	6	0
Medrano, Tony, 2B	.313	112	14	35	6	1	2	23	10	15	0
Mendez, Carlos, 1B	.280	293	38	82	25	0	10	37	6	32	4
Mercedes, Henry, C	.244	193	27	47	8	0	6	32	27	63	4
Norman, Les, OF	.273	333	53	91	20	2	13	40	14	45	7
Pellow, Kit, 3B	.286	475	88	136	28	4	35	99	20	117	6
Quinn, Mark, OF	.360	428	67	154	27	0	25	84	28	69	7
Roberge, J.P., 2B	.314	437	77	137	31	3	13	66	26	59	16
Scarsone, Steve, SS	.172	58	9	10	1	0	5	7	7	21	1
*Sutton, Larry, 1B	.277	148	28	41	8	1	3	12	27	24	4
Unroe, Tim, OF	.333	66	14	22	5	1	6	20	5	14	0
Vitiello, Joe, DH	.318	447	70	142	33	0	28	98	66	84	3

PITCHING	W	L	ERA	G	SV	IP	H	R	ER	BB	SO
Barber, Brian	9	5	4.56	19	0	120.1	128	68	61	29	75
Bluma, Jaime	0	0	3.22	17	2	22.1	21	10	8	4	19
*Byrdak, Tim	3	1	1.81	33	4	49.2	39	19	10	28	51
D'Amico, Jeff	3	5	3.53	26	5	35.2	45	19	14	13	22
Evans, Bart	4	5	8.10	30	2	33.1	33	34	30	36	34
Fussell, Chris	10	3	3.54	14	0	81.1	66	35	32	27	80
*Gooding, Jason	0	1	6.00	1	0	6.0	8	4	4	1	2
Hanson, Erik	5	9	5.90	24	0	108.1	126	75	71	48	85
*Krivda, Rick	6	8	5.70	21	0	115.1	154	94	73	41	70
Lineweaver, Aaron	0	1	6.00	1	0	6.0	6	4	4	3	2
Mathews, Terry	1	0	1.65	7	0	16.1	11	4	3	5	11
Montgomery, Jeff	0	0	0.00	4	1	5.0	1	0	0	1	3
Moreno, Orber	3	1	2.10	16	4	25.2	17	6	6	4	30
*Morman, Alvin	0	0	3.14	8	1	14.1	8	5	5	1	15
*Mullen, Scott	6	7	6.26	20	0	119.1	150	91	83	53	87
Pisciotta, Marc	0	1	11.20	10	0	13.2	18	18	17	11	8
Ray, Ken	1	0	5.19	27	8	43.1	41	27	25	12	36
Reichert, Dan	9	2	3.71	17	0	111.2	92	51	46	50	123
Rios, Dan	10	4	6.07	47	8	89.0	111	64	60	39	44
Ruffcorn, Scott	1	0	5.02	8	0	14.1	14	10	8	10	8
*Rusch, Glendon	4	7	4.42	20	0	114.0	143	68	56	33	102
Saier, Matt	4	4	5.09	9	0	58.1	69	37	33	8	44
Veras, Dario	1	2	4.35	12	0	20.2	19	10	10	3	17
*Walker, Jamie	0	1	4.67	4	0	17.1	22	12	9	4	11
Wengert, Don	4	0	4.17	16	1	41.0	41	20	19	9	24
Wilson, Kris	0	1	8.44	1	0	5.1	8	5	5	0	3

Salt Lake Buzz (Twins) AAA

BATTING	AVG	AB	R	H	2B	3B	HR	RBI	BB	SO	SB
#Alvarez, Rafael, OF	.375	16	3	6	1	0	0	2	0	1	0
Buchanan, Brian, OF	.297	391	67	116	24	1	10	60	28	85	11
Cey, Dan, 2B	.295	403	63	119	18	3	11	56	32	66	10
*Cummings, Midre, OF	.322	261	50	84	19	4	13	68	23	43	4
Ferguson, Jeff, 3B	.265	298	44	79	16	2	4	48	28	39	7
Hacker, Steve, DH	.150	20	2	3	0	0	2	3	5	7	0
Huls, Steve, OF	.233	30	6	7	0	0	0	2	5	7	0
*Jones, Jacque, OF	.298	198	32	59	13	2	4	26	9	36	9
#Latham, Chris, OF	.322	382	93	123	24	8	15	51	54	95	18
Lecroy, Matthew, C	.303	119	23	36	4	1	10	30	5	22	0
Marsters, Brandon, C	.200	25	4	5	1	0	1	8	2	6	0
Moriarty, Mike, SS	.258	380	63	98	21	7	4	51	56	62	6
Nicholas, Darrell, OF	.293	348	55	102	19	2	5	44	33	76	14
*Ortiz, David, 1B	.315	476	85	150	35	3	30	110	79	105	2

\# Switch-hitter
* Left-handed
T Player has been with more than one team; listed with last team.
(Players in major leagues are listed with last minor league club.)

BATTING	AVG	AB	R	H	2B	3B	HR	RBI	BB	SO	SB
*Pierzynski, A.J., C	.259	228	29	59	10	0	1	25	16	29	0
Richardson, Brian, 3B	.277	451	77	125	23	4	18	73	54	104	0
Rupp, Chad, 1B	.193	119	18	23	3	0	7	18	17	48	3
*Smith, Jeff, C	.389	18	5	7	3	0	1	3	0	1	0
Williams, Eddie, DH	.316	345	56	109	24	0	17	57	35	68	0

PITCHING	W	L	ERA	G	SV	IP	H	R	ER	BB	SO
*Baptist, Travis	1	3	5.35	17	1	38.2	46	24	23	17	23
Bell, Jason	5	5	6.37	18	0	76.1	96	58	54	35	72
Bowers, Shane	7	4	5.68	31	0	122.0	149	86	77	54	103
Carrasco, Hector	1	0	0.00	3	1	4.1	3	0	0	1	3
*Carroll, Dave	0	1	6.55	36	2	34.1	34	25	25	19	26
Fiore, Tony	2	1	3.47	40	19	46.2	45	21	18	26	38
Gandarillas, Gus	2	2	4.55	42	2	61.1	73	37	31	20	47
Harris, Jeff	4	3	6.90	36	0	45.2	61	38	35	26	20
Lincoln, Mike	5	2	7.78	9	0	59.0	82	52	51	21	39
*Mahaffey, Alan	1	2	5.48	7	0	21.1	28	17	13	15	11
*Miller, Travis	1	2	2.50	16	1	18.0	16	7	5	6	19
*Ohme, Kevin	5	3	3.83	51	2	82.1	94	44	35	31	48
Perkins, Dan	0	0	4.26	3	0	12.2	11	6	6	4	7
Radlosky, Rob	8	4	3.91	22	0	101.1	98	49	44	38	68
Rath, Fred	7	5	3.92	56	3	82.2	88	41	36	24	36
*Rath, Gary	3	8	5.62	20	0	99.1	129	76	62	27	67
*Redman, Mark	9	9	5.05	24	0	133.2	141	87	75	51	114
Rodriguez, Frank	3	4	6.70	9	0	43.0	40	34	32	14	33
*Romero, J.C.	4	1	3.20	15	1	19.2	18	11	7	14	20
Ryan, Jason	4	4	5.13	9	0	54.1	57	36	31	24	34
*Sampson, Benj	1	1	8.04	3	0	15.2	25	16	14	1	7
Stentz, Brent	0	3	11.22	23	3	25.2	43	34	32	21	23
Williams, Eddie	0	1	10.13	2	0	2.2	5	3	3	2	0

Tacoma Rainiers (Mariners) AAA

BATTING	AVG	AB	R	H	2B	3B	HR	RBI	BB	SO	SB
Akers, Chad, SS	.313	192	31	60	9	3	1	14	18	25	7
Alcala, Juan, PH	.000	1	0	0	0	0	0	0	0	0	0
Blowers, Mike, 1B	.231	13	1	3	1	0	0	2	0	4	0
Brown, Randy, 2B	.256	156	15	40	7	1	6	27	9	48	4
Buhner, Shawn, 1B	.240	146	17	35	8	0	1	12	10	43	0
Carroll, Mark, PH	.000	1	0	0	0	0	0	0	0	1	0
#Cedeno, D., SS	.268	112	17	30	8	1	1	13	7	36	1
Chavez, Raul, C	.268	354	39	95	20	1	3	40	28	63	1
#Durango, Ariel, 2B	.000	4	0	0	0	0	0	0	0	0	0
Flores, Jose, SS	.308	143	33	44	6	1	3	15	37	23	4
Gipson, Charles, SS	.299	174	26	52	6	3	0	21	14	24	18
#Guevara, Giomar, SS	.293	116	15	34	13	0	3	15	12	22	0
Hills, Rich, 3B	.000	4	0	0	0	0	0	0	0	0	0
*Ibanez, Raul, OF	.355	31	6	11	1	0	3	5	1	7	1
*Jackson, Ryan, 1B	.308	409	57	126	25	2	8	62	36	64	12
#Johnson, Earl, OF	.236	55	6	13	2	0	0	4	8	6	5
*Mathis, Joe, OF	.250	92	8	23	5	1	0	7	6	25	3
Matos, Francisco, 2B	.310	393	43	122	24	3	3	33	18	41	4
*Monahan, Shane, OF	.256	399	51	102	21	2	7	32	19	81	9
Murphy, Mike, OF	.295	129	22	38	7	3	2	22	13	36	10
*Pledger, Kinnis, DH	.275	153	20	42	8	1	8	30	19	37	0
*Radmanovich, R., OF	.286	420	69	120	24	3	17	80	53	83	10
*Robinson, Kerry, OF	.322	335	53	108	16	9	0	34	14	44	30
*Sachse, Matt, OF	.200	35	2	7	1	0	0	0	4	13	1
Sealy, Scot, C	.184	201	22	37	4	0	6	24	20	56	0
Seitzer, Brad, 3B	.287	474	80	136	34	1	9	66	89	86	1
Timmons, Ozzie, OF	.273	297	56	81	22	0	21	66	53	81	0

PITCHING	W	L	ERA	G	SV	IP	H	R	ER	BB	SO
Abbott, Paul	1	1	6.43	2	0	14.0	21	11	10	4	10
*Adamson, Joel	2	2	5.15	14	0	36.2	48	25	21	15	15
*Bertotti, Mike	0	2	10.29	3	0	7.0	6	8	8	17	6
Bunch, Mel	10	2	3.10	21	0	125.0	112	53	43	40	117
Carmona, Rafael	1	3	3.53	27	2	43.1	39	18	17	20	38
Cloude, Ken	5	1	2.33	6	0	38.2	19	11	10	15	33
Delgado, Danny	0	1	6.00	2	0	3.0	4	2	2	2	2
Fleetham, Ben	1	2	3.38	14	1	18.2	19	9	7	10	26
*Flener, Huck	4	4	5.45	22	1	66.0	72	41	40	26	48
Franklin, Ryan	6	9	4.71	29	2	135.2	142	81	71	33	94
*Henry, Butch	2	0	.00	4	0	5.0	4	0	0	1	3
Hinchliffe, Brett	9	7	5.15	21	0	131.0	141	78	75	44	107
Hodges, Kevin	4	6	4.24	19	1	110.1	122	54	52	38	58
Holdridge, David	5	6	4.34	41	10	66.1	67	38	32	23	68
Kroon, Marc	3	2	6.11	13	0	35.1	31	24	24	21	38

Batting leaders across all leagues

(Cont'd from previous page)

STOLEN BASES

Player	Club	Lg.	SB
T#Furcal, Rafael	MYR	Caro	96
T*Curry, Mike	Wil	Caro	85
T Owens, Jeremy	RCu	Cal	67
Gomez, Richard	WM	Mid	66
*Pierre, Juan	Ash	SAL	66
T#Snead, Esix	Peo	Mid	64
Ramirez, Julio	Por	East	64
*Faggett, Ethan	Mob	Sou	63
T Lindsey, R.	Lkl	FSL	61
#Metcalfe, Mike	SAn	Tex	57
T#Martinez, Greg	Lou	Int	56
*Foster, Quincy	BC	FSL	56
#McDonald, D.	Nrw	East	54

RUNS

Player	Club	Lg.	R
T Piatt, Adam	Van	PCL	129
T#DaVanon, Jeff	Edm	PCL	122
Murray, Calvin	Fre	PCL	122
Nunez, Jorge	Hag	SAL	116
*Johnson, Nick	Nrw	East	114
T Owens, Jeremy	RCu	Cal	113
*Clark, Jermaine	Lan	Cal	112
T Byrnes, Eric	Mod	Cal	111
Eckstein, David	Tre	East	109
T*Patterson, J.	Tuc	PCL	109
Abernathy, Brent	Knx	Sou	108
T*Brown, Dee	Wch	Tex	107
*Cox, Steve	Dur	Int	107
German, Esteban	Mod	Cal	107
*Cust, Jack	HiD	Cal	107

WALKS

Player	Club	Lg.	BB
*Johnson, Nick	Nrw	East	123
T#Melhuse, A.	Knx	Sou	118
Robinson, Bo	Wis	Mid	108
Schrager, Tony	Lan	Mid	103
German, Esteban	Mod	Cal	102
#Machado, A.	CF	SAL	102
T Piatt, Adam	Van	PCL	99
T Paz, Richard	Bow	East	98
*Cust, Jack	HiD	Cal	96
*Furniss, Eddy	Lyn	Caro	94
Edwards, Mike	Kin	Caro	93
McNally, Sean	Wch	Tex	93
#Torres, Andres	WM	Mid	92
Schaeffer, Jon	QC	Mid	92
Hankins, Ryan	Bur	Mid	91

Switch-hitter
*   Left-handed
T   Player has been with more than one team; listed with last team.
(Players in major leagues are listed with last minor league club.)

Batting leaders across all leagues

(Cont'd from previous page)

TOTAL BASES

Player	Club	Lg.	TB
T Piatt, Adam	Van	PCL	340
McNeal, Aaron	Mch	Mid	315
*Cox, Steve	Dur	Int	314
T*Patterson, J.	Tuc	PCL	308
*Cromer, D.T.	Ind	Int	301
T*Lamb, Mike	Ok	PCL	301
Landry, Jacques	Mod	Cal	297
Murray, Calvin	Fre	PCL	297
Chen, Chin-Feng	SBr	Cal	296
*Cust, Jack	HiD	Cal	296
*Phillips, J.R.	Csp	PCL	294
Raven, Luis	Chr	Int	289
T#DaVanon, Jeff	Edm	PCL	287
Seabol, Scott	Grn	SAL	283
T#Burkhart, M.	Tre	East	283

STRIKEOUTS

Player	Club	Lg.	K
*Branyan, Russell	Buf	Int	187
*Gainey, Bryon	Bng	East	184
Flaherty, Tim	SJo	Cal	168
T Owens, Jeremy	RCu	Cal	166
*Zapp, A.J.	Mac	SAL	163
#Cameron, Troy	Mac	SAL	161
*Bass, Jayson	NHv	East	160
#Blakely, Darren	LkE	Cal	159
Quinlan, Tom	Iow	PCL	159
#Lopez, Felipe	Hag	SAL	157
McClain, Scott	Dur	Int	156
Pernell, Brandon	RCu	Cal	156
*Haas, Chris	Mem	PCL	155
T Eberwein, K.	RCu	Cal	155
T Brignac, Junior	MYR	Caro	152

HITS

Player	Club	Lg.	H
T*Patterson, J.	Tuc	PCL	187
*Pierre, Juan	Ash	SAL	187
Murray, Calvin	Fre	PCL	183
*Cox, Steve	Dur	Int	182
T*Lamb, Mike	Ok	PCL	177
Gorr, Robb	SBr	Cal	174
#Jimenez, D.	Col	Int	172
T*Nunnari, T.	Har	East	172
Seabol, Scott	Grn	SAL	171
T#DaVanon, Jeff	Edm	PCL	171
Lopez, Luis	Syr	Int	171
Gonzalez, Raul	Tre	East	169
T Piatt, Adam	Van	PCL	168
Hart, Jason	Mod	Cal	168
Abernathy, Brent	Knx	Sou	168

Switch-hitter
* Left-handed
T Player has been with more than one team; listed with last team.
(Players in major leagues are listed with last minor league club.)

PITCHING	W	L	ERA	G	SV	IP	H	R	ER	BB	SO
Leiter, Mark	0	0	4.50	1	0	2.0	2	1	1	0	3
Luce, Robert	0	3	8.44	3	0	16.0	22	15	15	7	6
*Marte, Damaso	3	3	5.13	31	0	73.2	79	43	42	40	59
*McCarthy, Greg	0	1	2.05	18	0	22.0	18	6	5	13	14
Meche, Gil	2	2	3.19	6	0	31.0	31	12	11	13	24
*Ramsay, Robert	4	1	1.08	5	0	33.1	20	6	4	14	37
Scheffer, Aaron	2	3	2.87	35	9	59.2	47	25	19	23	62
*Sinclair, Steve	1	0	4.50	2	0	2.0	2	1	1	1	1
*Spencer, Sean	2	1	3.47	44	7	49.1	41	21	19	23	53
Steenstra, Kennie	1	4	5.57	13	0	51.2	60	40	32	15	24
Stevens, Dave	1	1	12.60	7	0	10.0	14	14	14	6	8
Sweeney, Brian	0	2	6.75	5	0	16.0	26	17	12	2	10
Weaver, Eric	1	2	3.86	16	1	25.2	22	11	11	7	22
*Zimmerman, Jordan	0	0	5.14	9	0	7.0	13	4	4	4	4

Tucson Sidewinders (Diamondbacks) AAA

BATTING	AVG	AB	R	H	2B	3B	HR	RBI	BB	SO	SB
#Belliard, F., 2B	.143	7	0	1	0	0	0	2	1	3	0
*Conti, Jason, OF	.290	520	100	151	23	8	9	57	55	89	22
Coolbaugh, Scott, 3B	.255	212	28	54	14	1	7	31	32	49	1
Diaz, Edwin, 2B	.311	415	72	129	24	1	11	50	17	77	6
*Durazo, Erubiel, 1B	.407	118	27	48	7	0	10	28	14	18	1
#Frias, Hanley, 3B	.300	80	15	24	3	0	0	6	7	15	3
Hanel, Marcus, C	.067	15	1	1	0	0	0	0	4	2	0
Huckaby, Ken, C	.301	355	44	107	20	1	2	42	13	33	0
Johnson, Keith, 2B	.287	356	61	102	19	0	12	46	30	71	2
Klassen, Danny, SS	.269	245	38	66	16	3	6	33	20	51	5
Koeyers, Ramsey, SS	.128	39	6	5	1	0	0	1	4	7	0
Pachot, John, C	.265	102	10	27	4	0	1	11	3	10	1
*Patterson, Jarrod, 3B	.336	274	46	92	25	3	11	47	36	37	4
Powell, Dante, OF	.332	187	29	62	14	2	7	30	14	38	22
Rios, Eduardo, 2B	.375	8	1	3	1	0	1	2	0	3	0
*Ryan, Rob, OF	.290	414	72	120	30	5	19	88	56	70	4
*Sell, Chip, OF	.357	84	12	30	5	2	1	18	3	14	4
#Ward, Turner, OF	.318	129	24	41	5	1	4	25	23	18	7
White, Walt, 2B	.203	153	18	31	8	1	3	13	14	39	0
*Wilson, Desi, 1B	.323	452	65	146	27	7	6	62	34	76	2
*Womack, Tony, OF	.250	16	1	4	1	0	1	3	2	3	0
Young, Ernie, OF	.294	453	78	133	25	1	30	95	57	129	4

PITCHING	W	L	ERA	G	SV	IP	H	R	ER	BB	SO
*Anderson, Brian	0	1	5.40	2	0	6.2	9	5	4	1	8
Batchelor, Rich	0	4	4.50	30	12	28.0	29	19	14	12	23
*Bierbrodt, Nick	1	4	7.27	11	0	43.1	57	42	35	30	43
*Brohawn, Troy	1	0	3.29	3	0	13.2	22	8	5	3	12
Bross, Terry	0	0	11.57	2	0	2.1	6	3	3	1	0
Carlson, Dan	4	9	5.43	32	0	117.2	130	82	71	52	118
Chouinard, Bobby	4	1	4.06	12	0	62.0	70	33	28	13	63
Clemons, Chris	6	4	5.93	45	1	68.1	77	53	45	44	75
Coolbaugh, Scott	0	0	3.00	1	0	3.0	3	1	1	1	3
*Cummings, John	1	1	8.31	11	0	21.2	33	24	20	9	18
*Eischen, Joey	1	3	9.07	27	1	41.2	63	47	42	26	36
Figueroa, Nelson	11	6	3.94	24	0	128.0	128	59	56	41	106
Hernandez, Fernando	0	2	8.44	5	0	16.0	22	16	15	4	14
*Jensen, Jason	0	1	3.86	1	0	4.2	6	6	2	4	3
Kim, Byung-Hyun	4	0	2.40	11	1	30.0	21	9	8	15	40
*Michalak, Chris	6	0	4.29	45	3	92.1	92	50	44	40	66
Nunez, Vladimir	1	0	6.75	3	0	2.2	5	2	2	0	3
Padilla, Vicente	7	4	3.75	18	0	93.2	107	47	39	24	58
Patterson, John	1	5	7.04	7	0	30.2	43	26	24	18	29
Peters, Don	0	1	3.86	3	0	4.2	1	2	2	2	2
*Randolph, Steve	0	7	6.91	11	0	41.2	47	37	32	32	26
*Ruebel, Matt	1	3	7.00	6	0	27.0	32	26	21	10	19
Sabel, Erik	5	2	3.34	22	2	72.2	79	36	27	24	38
*Shouse, Brian	3	4	6.25	30	0	44.2	63	35	31	18	32
Swartzbaugh, Dave	0	0	6.23	13	0	21.2	27	16	15	14	20
Telemaco, Amaury	0	3	5.09	13	0	17.2	21	11	10	6	17
Tuttle, Dave	2	5	6.51	35	0	84.1	100	62	61	48	55
Verplancke, Joe	0	0	0.00	2	0	2.1	1	0	0	1	4
*Vosberg, Ed	1	0	0.84	34	8	43.0	29	6	4	12	42

Vancouver Canadians (Athletics) AAA

BATTING	AVG	AB	R	H	2B	3B	HR	RBI	BB	SO	SB
Ardoin, Danny, C	.253	336	53	85	13	2	6	46	50	78	3
Ball, Jeff, 3B	.309	346	50	107	22	2	8	51	37	57	7
Christenson, Ryan, OF	.344	128	30	44	8	1	1	16	22	21	7

BATTING

BATTING	AVG	AB	R	H	2B	3B	HR	RBI	BB	SO	SB
Encarnacion, Mario, OF	.241	145	18	35	5	0	3	17	6	44	5
Espada, Josue, 2B	.308	26	2	8	1	0	0	0	3	4	1
Freeman, Ricky, 1B	.223	202	27	45	14	0	4	24	20	39	0
Hernandez, Ramon, C.	.261	291	38	76	11	3	13	55	23	37	1
Hinch, A.J., C	.377	61	9	23	3	0	2	7	3	12	1
Lesher, Brian, 1B	.292	387	66	113	29	2	14	64	41	71	8
*Long, Terrence, OF	.247	154	16	38	6	2	2	21	10	29	7
Luderer, Brian, C	.321	28	6	9	1	0	0	4	4	2	0
Martins, Eric, 2B	.239	301	39	72	15	5	3	33	31	47	2
#McDonald, Jason, OF	.326	129	27	42	9	1	4	18	19	33	8
Menechino, Frank, 3B	.309	501	103	155	31	9	15	88	73	97	4
Morales, Willie, 1B	.143	14	2	2	1	0	0	2	1	4	0
*Neill, Mike, OF	.296	365	61	108	23	2	10	61	57	97	10
Newfield, Marc, OF	.143	28	1	4	0	0	0	1	1	2	0
Ortiz, Jose, SS	.284	377	66	107	29	2	9	45	29	50	13
Piatt, Adam, 3B	.222	18	1	4	1	0	0	3	6	2	0
Saenz, Olmedo, 3B	.600	5	1	3	1	0	0	2	0	0	0
Sheff, Chris, OF	.287	421	62	121	24	1	15	70	45	87	9
#Spiezio, Scott, 2B	.390	105	27	41	7	1	6	27	15	16	0
*Vaz, Roberto, OF	.264	367	54	97	18	4	7	38	51	72	7

PITCHING

PITCHING	W	L	ERA	G	SV	IP	H	R	ER	BB	SO
*Baez, Benito	0	2	3.50	11	1	18.0	18	7	7	7	19
Chavez, Anthony	4	6	3.91	54	14	69.0	67	42	30	37	72
Clark, Terry	3	4	4.79	14	0	41.1	47	25	22	14	17
Dale, Carl	4	3	3.48	29	4	44.0	41	19	17	18	27
De La Maza, Roland	0	0	12.00	4	0	3.0	5	4	4	4	4
Gregg, Kevin	1	0	3.60	1	0	5.0	6	2	2	2	4
Harville, Chad	1	0	1.75	22	11	25.2	24	5	5	11	36
Hudson, Tim	4	0	2.20	8	0	49.0	38	16	12	21	61
Jarvis, Kevin	10	2	3.41	17	0	103.0	110	47	39	26	64
Jones, Marcus	2	1	2.40	3	0	15.0	23	11	4	5	5
King, Bill	9	6	3.49	45	4	98.0	105	52	38	22	60
*Kubinski, Tim	5	3	3.44	46	6	73.1	70	30	28	27	56
*Lawrence, Sean	2	2	4.81	25	0	39.1	51	25	21	21	37
Laxton, Brett	13	8	3.46	25	0	161.1	158	68	62	49	112
*Mahay, Ron	7	2	4.29	32	0	107.0	116	57	51	45	73
Manwiller, Tim	4	2	6.46	11	0	54.1	72	42	39	14	30
*Mulder, Mark	6	7	4.06	22	0	128.2	152	69	58	31	81
Oquist, Mike	1	0	0.00	1	0	6.0	2	0	0	1	2
*Perez, Juan	0	4	6.96	20	0	32.1	42	25	25	15	22
Rigby, Brad	0	1	1.93	1	0	4.2	6	3	1	2	6
Snow, Bert	1	0	3.86	2	0	2.1	3	1	1	1	3
Stein, Blake	4	2	4.10	19	0	109.2	94	54	50	43	111
Vizcaino, Luis	0	1	1.38	7	0	13.0	13	4	2	6	7
*Zito, Barry	1	0	1.50	1	0	6.0	5	1	1	2	6

Eastern League

Akron Aeros (Indians) AA

BATTING	AVG	AB	R	H	2B	3B	HR	RBI	BB	SO	SB
Alomar, Sandy, C	.310	29	8	9	0	0	1	6	3	2	1
#Bady, Ed, OF	.243	230	42	56	13	3	2	33	32	68	19
Benefield, Brian, 2B	.193	145	14	28	3	2	3	14	16	32	3
Betances, Junior, 2B	.294	306	41	90	14	5	2	28	31	53	9
*Betts, Todd, 3B	.280	375	60	105	24	1	19	67	61	65	2
*Budzinski, Mark, OF	.283	297	58	84	17	6	6	46	48	63	9
Cordero, Wil, OF	.364	11	2	4	2	0	0	0	0	3	0
*Dishington, Nate, DH	.237	59	12	14	2	0	5	14	6	30	0
Dorman, John, 2B	.143	7	0	1	0	0	0	0	0	1	0
Fryman, Travis, DH	.250	12	4	3	0	0	1	4	2	4	0
Harriss, Robin, C	.167	48	9	8	1	0	2	6	1	12	1
Hayes, Heath, C	.266	418	51	111	15	2	16	68	41	111	2
Hernaiz, Juan, DH	.190	21	3	4	0	0	1	1	0	7	0
#Huelsmann, Mike, OF	.277	177	20	49	5	1	1	10	15	30	12
*Kilburg, Joe, 2B	.271	144	20	39	8	0	1	14	23	28	1
McDonald, John, SS	.296	226	31	67	12	0	1	26	19	26	7
*McKinley, Dan, OF	.257	463	70	119	20	6	3	37	24	87	3
Mohr, Dustan, OF	.167	42	3	7	2	1	0	2	5	7	0
Morgan, Scott, OF	.282	344	72	97	26	2	26	70	38	96	6
Ortiz, Nick, SS	.267	195	24	52	15	2	2	13	17	40	1
Peoples, Danny, 1B	.251	494	75	124	23	3	21	78	55	142	2
Perry, Chan, DH	.279	154	24	43	14	0	7	30	11	27	1
Robinson, Adam, 2B	.277	238	37	66	12	4	5	30	20	49	4

Batting leaders across all leagues

(Cont'd from previous page)

DOUBLES

Player	Club	Lg.	2B
Seabol, Scott	Grn	SAL	55
T*Patterson, J.	Tuc	PCL	52
T*Lamb, Mike	Ok	PCL	51
Robinson, Bo	Wis	Mid	50
*Cox, Steve	Dur	Int	49
T Piatt, Adam	Van	PCL	49
Hart, Jason	Mod	Cal	48
Landry, Jacques	Mod	Cal	46
T Williams, Jason	Ind	Int	45
Vieira, Scott	WTn	Sou	44
Roskos, John	Cal	PCL	44
T Mouton, Lyle	Lou	Int	43
Hajek, Dave	Csp	PCL	43

TRIPLES

Player	Club	Lg.	3B
Salazar, Oscar	Mod	Cal	18
*Patterson, Corey	Lan	Mid	17
T#DaVanon, Jeff	Edm	PCL	14
Romano, Jason	Chr	FSL	14
*Guzman, Elpidio	CR	Mid	13
Melian, Jackson	Tam	FSL	13
Ross, Jason	MYR	Caro	13
*Wise, Dewayne	Rfd	Mid	13
Castro, Nelson	LkE	Cal	12
Gomez, Richard	WM	Mid	12
German, Esteban	Mod	Cal	12
#Izturis, Cesar	Dun	FSL	12
*Allen, Luke	SAn	Tex	12
*Redman, Tike	Alt	East	12
T Owens, Jeremy	RCu	Cal	12

EXTRA-BASE HITS

Player	Club	Lg.	EBH
T Piatt, Adam	Van	PCL	91
Landry, Jacques	Mod	Cal	79
*Cox, Steve	Dur	Int	78
T*Lamb, Mike	Ok	PCL	77
T*Patterson, J.	Tuc	PCL	77
*Cust, Jack	HiD	Cal	77
Seabol, Scott	Grn	SAL	76
*Patterson, C.	Lan	Mid	72
T Morgan, Scott	Buf	Int	71
T*Wilcox, Luke	Dur	Int	71
*Cromer, D.T.	Ind	Int	71
McNeal, Aaron	Mch	Mid	70

Switch-hitter

* Left-handed*

T *Player has been with more than one team; listed with last team.*

(Players in major leagues are listed with last minor league club.)

Batting leaders across all leagues

(Cont'd from previous page)

SACRIFICE HITS

Player	Club	Lg.	SH
T#Ojeda, Augie	Bow	East	25
Halter, Shane	Nor	Int	17
#Izturis, Cesar	Dun	FSL	17
#Mateo, Henry	Jup	FSL	17
#Cintron, Alex	HiD	Cal	17
#Figueroa, Luis	Alt	East	16
T Moore, B.	Chr	Int	15
T Keck, Brian	Car	Sou	14
#Figgins, Chone	Sal	Caro	14
Perez, Nestor	StP	FSL	14

SACRIFICE FLIES

Player	Club	Lg.	SF
*Barnes, Larry	ERI	East	16
*Cridland, Mark	Stk	Cal	16
*Wise, Dewayne	Rfd	Mid	14
Landry, Jacques	Mod	Cal	12
Truby, Chris	JCK	Tex	12
T Matos, Luis	Bow	East	11
Seabol, Scott	Grn	Sal	11
*Pond, Simon	Jup	FSL	11

HIT-BY-PITCH

Player	Club	Lg.	HBP
*Johnson, Nick	Nrw	East	37
T Miller, Corky	Cht	Sou	31
Fasano, Sal	Oma	PCL	26
Eckstein, David	Tre	East	25
Coquillette, Trace	Ott	Int	24
#Blakely, Darren	LkE	Cal	20
Schaeffer, Jon	QC	Mid	20
Zuleta, Julio	WTn	Sou	20
Hairston, Jerry	ROC	Int	19
Wilson, Craig	Alt	East	19
Schreimann, Eric	Pie	Sal	19
Haverbusch, K.	Alt	East	19
*Graham, Jess	Sar	FSL	19

Switch-hitter
* Left-handed
T Player has been with more than one team; listed with last team.
(Players in major leagues are listed with last minor league club.)

BATTING	AVG	AB	R	H	2B	3B	HR	RBI	BB	SO	SB
Schwab, Chris, OF	.000	6	0	0	0	0	0	0	1	3	0
Soliz, Steve, C	.130	23	1	3	0	0	0	3	1	4	0
*Taveras, Frank, 3B	.190	42	6	8	1	0	1	4	4	17	0
*Whitaker, Chad, OF	.322	149	18	48	12	2	5	38	15	40	0

PITCHING	W	L	ERA	G	SV	IP	H	R	ER	BB	SO
Atkins, Ross	6	8	5.77	33	3	87.1	90	60	56	47	43
*Bacsik, Mike	11	11	4.64	26	0	149.1	164	84	77	47	84
Brammer, J.D.	3	2	4.76	47	8	75.2	53	44	40	60	69
Brown, Jamie	5	9	4.57	23	0	138.0	140	72	70	39	98
Camp, Jared	1	2	6.50	17	7	18.0	22	17	13	16	18
De Paula, Sean	1	0	3.54	14	1	28.0	20	11	11	17	31
Dedrick, Jim	1	0	9.00	2	0	3.0	4	3	3	0	0
Deschenes, Marc	3	2	3.31	43	3	65.1	57	28	24	31	64
Garza, Albert	3	5	9.35	10	0	42.1	54	46	44	41	38
Gooden, Doc	0	0	3.00	1	0	3.0	3	2	1	1	2
*Hamilton, Jimmy	0	2	3.73	25	2	31.1	19	14	13	24	27
*Martin, Tom	0	0	1.00	3	0	9.0	4	1	1	3	9
Martinez, Willie	9	8	4.09	24	0	147.1	163	83	67	45	91
Negrette, Richard	1	3	6.13	33	1	47.0	49	35	32	47	34
*Poole, Jim	0	0	0.00	2	0	2.2	0	0	0	0	4
Rigdon, Paul	7	0	0.90	8	0	50.0	20	5	5	10	25
Riske, David	0	0	1.90	22	13	23.2	5	6	5	13	33
Sanders, Frankie	6	6	4.85	33	2	120.2	139	72	65	51	72
Sexton, Jeff	1	0	3.60	15	2	20.0	24	10	8	9	16
St. Pierre, Bob	0	0	18.00	1	0	4.0	9	8	8	4	2
Turnbow, Mark	1	0	3.00	1	0	6.0	4	3	2	3	4
*Watson, Mark	9	8	4.34	19	0	110.0	143	64	53	38	57
Wright, Jaret	1	0	0.00	1	0	5.0	3	0	0	1	6

Altoona Curve (Pirates) AA

BATTING	AVG	AB	R	H	2B	3B	HR	RBI	BB	SO	SB
Asche, Mike, OF	.412	17	3	7	2	0	0	3	1	3	1
*Bieser, Steve, 3B	.209	148	24	31	5	2	4	23	21	32	3
Bryant, Matt, SS	.250	24	1	6	0	0	0	1	2	7	0
*Cruz, Ivan, DH	.154	13	1	2	1	0	0	3	1	8	0
*Dehaan, Kory, OF	.268	190	26	51	13	2	3	24	11	46	14
Dunn, Todd, OF	.167	30	0	5	2	0	0	2	2	10	0
#Figueroa, Luis, SS	.263	418	61	110	15	5	3	50	52	44	9
Haad, Yamid, C	.182	137	20	25	3	0	6	10	19	32	7
Haverbusch, Kevin, 3B	.286	332	57	95	22	2	14	61	12	60	6
*Hernandez, A., OF	.257	475	76	122	26	3	15	63	54	110	11
Hyzdu, Adam, OF	.316	345	64	109	26	2	24	78	40	62	8
Iglesias, Luis, 3B	.241	89	13	25	6	0	6	16	14	26	0
*Jorgensen, Tim, 3B	.130	23	1	3	1	0	0	2	0	6	0
Long, Garrett, OF	.245	355	61	87	12	4	18	56	63	100	6
Lorenzana, Luis, 3B	.216	74	9	16	2	1	2	8	14	17	0
*Mackowiak, Rob, 2B	.262	195	21	51	15	3	3	27	8	34	0
#Patzke, Jeff, 2B	.298	198	31	59	12	1	2	25	33	45	4
*Redman, Tike, OF	.269	532	84	143	20	12	3	60	52	52	29
*Robertson, Mike, 1B	.280	175	31	49	12	0	9	28	24	26	0
#Rosario, Mel, C	.241	87	11	21	9	0	1	11	6	15	0
*Secrist, Reed, C	.168	95	9	16	5	0	0	10	13	23	0
*Sweet, Jonathan, C	.257	105	15	27	5	1	2	13	11	15	0
#Ward, Turner, DH	.000	3	1	0	0	0	0	0	2	2	0
Wehner, John, 3B	.167	12	2	2	0	0	0	2	0	0	1
Wilson, Craig, DH	.268	362	57	97	21	3	20	69	40	104	1
Wimmer, Chris, 2B	.252	107	9	27	5	2	1	6	8	12	5
Wright, Ron, 1B	.213	80	2	17	6	0	0	4	9	27	0

PITCHING	W	L	ERA	G	SV	IP	H	R	ER	BB	SO
*Ah Yat, Paul	8	4	3.02	16	0	95.1	86	41	32	30	90
Arroyo, Bronson	15	4	3.65	25	0	153.0	167	73	62	58	100
*Ayers, Mike	0	0	1.59	11	0	17.0	10	4	3	11	16
*Baron, Jim	9	9	3.97	29	0	145.0	141	73	64	44	75
Beltran, Alonso	0	2	9.00	13	1	18.0	27	18	18	9	18
*Burgos, Enrique	0	1	2.25	5	0	4.0	1	1	1	3	2
*Christiansen, Jason	0	0	.00	2	0	3.0	1	0	0	1	2
Cordova, Francisco	1	1	4.66	2	0	9.2	13	8	5	4	12
Daniels, David	2	2	2.67	55	8	67.1	55	21	20	19	63
Davis, Kane	4	6	3.78	16	0	95.1	97	51	40	41	53
Donnelly, Brendan	0	0	7.71	2	1	2.1	4	2	2	2	0
Duff, Matt	2	4	2.81	44	12	57.2	43	19	18	35	59
*Dunbar, Matt	3	5	3.42	49	2	47.1	35	19	18	23	35
France, Aaron	4	5	3.67	33	0	95.2	79	50	39	48	70
Garcia, Al	0	0	4.50	2	0	4.0	6	4	2	3	1

PITCHING	W	L	ERA	G	SV	IP	H	R	ER	BB	SO
Giard, Ken	2	2	1.71	38	6	42.0	34	12	8	25	48
*Gonzalez, Mike	2	3	8.10	7	0	26.2	34	25	24	19	31
*Long, Joey	0	0	5.91	8	0	10.2	16	8	7	4	5
Martinez, Javier	0	0	6.10	10	0	10.1	11	8	7	14	16
*Mathews, Del	1	1	6.00	9	0	12.0	21	15	8	6	8
*McConnell, Sam	1	7	6.64	13	0	62.1	82	52	46	33	40
*O'Connor, Brian	7	11	4.70	28	0	153.1	152	98	80	92	106
Pena, Alex	1	0	3.86	9	0	21.0	22	12	9	9	20
Runion, Tony	1	0	3.59	31	2	42.2	52	23	17	9	39
Wilkins, Marc	0	1	1.50	4	0	6.0	4	2	1	4	5

Binghamton Mets (Mets) AA

BATTING	AVG	AB	R	H	2B	3B	HR	RBI	BB	SO	SB
*Beamon, Trey, OF	.240	246	32	59	13	0	2	20	29	41	13
Bennett, Ryan, C	.000	4	1	0	0	0	0	0	0	2	0
Bruce, Mo, 2B	.270	500	80	135	25	4	9	76	61	134	33
Buccheri, Jim, OF	.294	17	1	5	1	1	0	1	0	4	0
Darden, Tony, DH	.354	164	25	58	8	1	5	23	19	30	5
Dina, Allen, OF	.229	192	25	44	10	3	0	15	9	46	9
*Dubose, Brian, DH	.174	69	8	12	3	0	0	4	14	19	5
*Gainey, Bryon, 1B	.237	502	68	119	28	6	25	78	40	184	1
Haltiwanger, G., OF	.273	11	1	3	0	0	1	2	1	1	0
Huff, B.J., OF	.249	205	26	51	9	1	7	32	19	46	9
Lopez, Jose, OF	.145	55	2	8	2	0	0	6	2	24	2
Mashore, Justin, OF	.259	58	7	15	4	2	1	8	1	17	2
Meggers, Mike, OF	.161	56	6	9	4	0	1	6	7	29	0
Neubart, Garrett, OF	.288	260	36	75	14	4	3	21	22	40	17
Phillips, Jason, C	.227	141	13	32	5	0	7	23	13	20	0
Rodriguez, Sammy, C	.227	203	15	46	10	0	3	24	21	49	2
#Sanchez, Yuri, SS	.231	381	43	88	10	1	5	30	37	135	6
Stoffels, Alex, DH	.000	8	0	0	0	0	0	0	2	4	0
#Tamargo, John, 3B	.215	363	27	78	13	3	4	37	40	55	7
Toca, Jorge, OF	.308	279	60	86	15	1	20	67	32	43	5
*Tyner, Jason, OF	.313	518	91	162	19	5	0	33	62	46	49
Valera, Yohanny, C	.289	204	33	59	14	3	9	39	17	57	2
Zamora, Junior, 3B	.239	255	28	61	17	0	10	33	12	62	2

PITCHING	W	L	ERA	G	SV	IP	H	R	ER	BB	SO
*Arteaga, J.D.	3	1	5.72	11	0	28.1	32	21	18	14	24
Bohannon, Gary	0	0	49.50	2	0	2.0	12	13	11	3	0
Brittan, Corey	2	4	2.78	54	7	90.2	84	36	28	23	60
Cammack, Eric	4	2	2.38	45	15	56.2	28	17	15	38	83
Corey, Mark	7	13	5.40	29	0	155.0	175	108	93	64	111
Della Ratta, Pete	1	4	2.18	41	0	82.2	75	22	20	13	68
Hafer, Jeff	0	2	3.14	7	0	14.1	12	5	5	0	9
Henderson, Ryan	0	2	7.04	5	0	7.2	9	6	6	6	8
Herbison, Brett	5	13	5.85	27	0	149.1	161	115	97	81	60
Jones, Bobby	1	2	3.86	3	0	11.2	11	5	5	5	12
Lopez, Johan	0	0	13.50	2	0	2.0	3	3	3	3	1
Lyons, Mike	4	7	3.40	53	5	79.1	76	41	30	37	70
McCrary, Scott	1	5	4.86	17	0	53.2	72	34	29	21	29
*McEntire, Ethan	0	2	13.17	4	0	13.2	26	23	20	8	7
McMichael, Greg	0	0	0.00	2	0	3.0	2	1	0	1	5
Neubart, Garrett	0	0	0.00	1	0	2.0	1	0	0	0	1
Pontes, Dan	3	1	5.01	19	1	32.1	29	18	18	15	37
Pumphrey, Ken	6	9	4.80	25	0	131.1	146	95	70	71	84
Reed, Rick	0	0	1.80	1	0	5.0	1	1	1	1	5
Roberts, Grant	7	6	4.87	23	0	131.1	135	81	71	49	94
*Ruebel, Matt	2	0	2.73	6	0	26.1	24	13	8	8	25
Short, Barry	0	7	3.48	24	0	41.1	43	29	16	16	22
*Stewart, Scott	1	0	0.00	1	0	5.0	3	0	0	0	5
Turrentine, Rich	0	2	4.66	17	0	19.1	20	13	10	20	16
*Vasquez, Leo	1	2	3.83	27	1	42.1	39	18	18	28	43
Walker, Tyler	6	4	6.22	13	0	68.0	78	49	47	32	59

Bowie Baysox (Orioles) AA

BATTING	AVG	AB	R	H	2B	3B	HR	RBI	BB	SO	SB
#Alley, Charles, C	.111	9	4	1	1	0	0	0	1	3	0
Almonte, Wady, OF	.293	482	68	141	27	4	17	83	31	72	10
Casimiro, Carlos, 2B	.221	526	73	116	23	1	18	64	39	101	7
*Clark, Howie, DH	.294	126	17	37	6	0	2	12	10	12	2
*Coffie, Ivanon, 3B	.185	195	21	36	9	3	3	23	20	46	2
*Dent, Darrell, OF	.212	250	41	53	9	2	0	17	37	58	24
Devarez, Cesar, C	.265	200	25	53	11	0	4	29	16	24	2
*DeCinces, Tim, C	.260	258	38	67	15	0	12	36	54	52	0

Batting leaders across all leagues

(Cont'd from previous page)

CAUGHT STEALING

Player	Club	Lg.	CS
T#Furcal, Rafael	MYR	Caro	30
Martinez, Belvani	HiD	Cal	30
#Machado, A.	CF	SAL	28
T*Sanchez, Alex	Dur	Int	27
Randolph, Jaisen	DAY	FSL	26
Perez, Antonio	Rfd	Mid	24
*Hill, Willy	KnC	Mid	24
T#Valera, Ramon	Wis	Mid	23
*McDowell, A.	BAK	Cal	23
*Foster, Quincy	BC	FSL	23
Brown, Tonayne	AUG	SAL	22
T*Sollmann, S.	Hnt	Sou	22
T*Curry, Mike	Wil	Caro	22
#Caceres, Wilmy	CLN	Mid	22
*Taylor, Reggie	REA	East	22

TOUGHEST TO STRIKE OUT

Player	Club	Lg.	TPA/SO
Raabe, Brian	Col	Int	29.63
T Hall, Toby	ORL	Sou	22.00
T*Ametller, Jesus	Mem	PCL	19.81
Azuaje, Jesus	Hnt	Sou	18.46
Howard, Matt	Nsh	PCL	18.21
*Pierre, Juan	Ash	SAL	17.51
#Miles, Aaron	Mch	Mid	15.55
Amado, Jose	Wch	Tex	14.11
Abernathy, Brent	Knx	Sou	13.83
T Cepeda, Jose	GRV	Sou	13.80
Hajek, Dave	Csp	PCL	13.52
*Gallo, Ismael	SBr	Cal	13.37
*Urquiola, Carlos	SB	Mid	12.97
T Walther, Chris	ERI	East	12.83
Eckstein, David	Tre	East	12.81

SWITCH-HITTERS

Player	Club	Lg.	BA
T#DaVanon, Jeff	Edm	PCL	.338
#Crespo, Felipe	Fre	PCL	.332
#Hardtke, Jason	Ind	Int	.329
#Bradley, Milton	Har	East	.329
#Jimenez, D.	Col	Int	.327
#Mota, Tony	SAn	Tex	.325
T#Furcal, Rafael	MYR	Caro	.322
#Latham, Chris	SLk	PCL	.322
#Miles, Aaron	Mch	Mid	.317
#Theodorou, N.	SBr	Cal	.310
#Izturis, Cesar	Dun	FSL	.308
#Cintron, Alex	HiD	Cal	.307
T#Lopez, Mickey	Lou	Int	.306
#Smith, Demond	GRV	Sou	.305
#Punto, Nick	Clr	FSL	.305

Switch-hitter
* Left-handed
T Player has been with more than one team; listed with last team.
(Players in major leagues are listed with the last minor league club.)

Pitching leaders across all leagues

ERA (MINIMUM 112 IP)

Player	Club	Lg.	ERA
T Meyers, Mike	WTn	Sou	1.73
*Kalinowski, Josh	Sal	Caro	2.11
T Hebson, Bryan	Jup	FSL	2.17
T Ireland, Eric	Kis	FSL	2.24
Baisley, Brad	Pie	SAL	2.26
T Ohka, T.	Paw	Int	2.31
T Guerrero, J.	Wil	Caro	2.31
Norton, Jason	AUG	SAL	2.32
T*Downs, Scott	WTn	Sou	2.35
*Comer, Scott	BC	FSL	2.35
T*Ankiel, Rick	Mem	PCL	2.35
Lewis, Derrick	MYR	Caro	2.40
T Abreu, Winston	MYR	Caro	2.48
T Standridge, J.	StP	FSL	2.57
T Gonzalez, E.	CWV	SAL	2.60

WINS

Player	Club	Lg.	W
T*Bridges, D.	LkE	Cal	18
T Fernandez, J.	Paw	Int	15
T Ohka, T.	Paw	Int	15
*Perisho, Matt	Ok	PCL	15
T*Watson, Mark	Akr	East	15
Beverlin, Jason	Nrw	East	15
T Coco, Pasqual	Dun	FSL	15
*Robertson, J.	JCK	Tex	15
*Rodriguez, W.	Kis	FSL	15
T*Blank, Matt	Har	East	15
T Arroyo, B.	Nsh	PCL	15
T Knotts, Gary	Por	East	15

COMPLETE GAMES

Player	Club	Lg.	CG
T Cooper, Brian	Edm	PCL	6
*Hundley, Jeff	CR	Mid	6
T Manning, D.	WTn	Sou	6
Towers, Josh	Bow	East	5
Fish, Steve	LkE	Cal	5
T Green, Steve	ERI	East	
T*Bridges, D.	LkE	Cal	5
T Emanuel, B.	LkE	Cal	5
Castillo, Carlos	Chr	Int	5
Stewart, Paul	Stk	Cal	5
Knight, Brandon	Ok	PCL	5
T Ireland, Eric	Kis	FSL	5
*Comer, Scott	BC	FSL	5
T*McConnell, S.	Alt	East	5

Switch-hitter
* Left-handed
T Player has been with more than one team; listed with last team.
(Players in major leagues are listed with last minor league club.)

BATTING	AVG	AB	R	H	2B	3B	HR	RBI	BB	SO	SB
*DeShields, Delino, 2B	.267	15	2	4	1	0	0	0	3	2	0
*Hage, Tom, 1B	.277	426	53	118	21	4	8	65	50	60	1
Isom, Johnny, OF	.228	127	19	29	6	0	2	16	12	25	0
#Kingsale, Eugene, OF	.235	268	43	63	11	4	3	23	33	46	14
*Lopez-Cao, Mike, C	.255	47	5	12	1	0	2	7	2	8	0
Matos, Luis, OF	.237	283	41	67	11	1	9	36	15	39	14
#Ojeda, Augie, SS	.267	460	73	123	18	4	10	60	57	47	6
Paz, Richard, 3B	.286	273	39	78	12	2	2	20	51	35	11
#Rivera, Roberto, OF	.222	36	0	8	0	0	0	1	1	9	2
Ronca, Joe, OF	.242	153	12	37	12	1	5	25	13	43	1
Rust, Brian, 1B	.309	149	24	46	11	0	4	21	17	29	2
Short, Rick, OF	.314	392	60	123	19	0	16	62	43	48	6
Werth, Jayson, C	.273	121	18	33	5	1	1	11	17	26	7

PITCHING	W	L	ERA	G	SV	IP	H	R	ER	BB	SO
*Bell, Mike	7	7	4.59	41	1	131.1	134	80	67	49	79
Blazier, Ron	1	1	7.39	19	0	31.2	40	27	26	12	28
Delahoya, Javier	9	1	3.36	12	0	77.2	64	29	29	18	68
*Eibey, Scott	2	0	2.63	27	0	51.1	49	17	15	25	29
Falkenborg, Brian	3	6	3.78	16	0	83.1	77	40	35	36	77
Gentile, Scott	1	2	8.36	10	0	14.0	15	13	13	9	12
*Hartmann, Pete	1	1	1.72	11	0	15.2	11	4	3	8	12
Heredia, Maximo	6	4	4.24	50	0	76.1	80	42	36	33	56
Iglesias, Mario	1	4	7.52	14	0	26.1	28	23	22	16	27
Kamieniecki, Scott	0	1	3.60	1	0	5.0	6	2	2	0	1
Kohlmeier, Ryan	3	7	3.16	55	23	62.2	44	23	22	29	78
*Lynch, Ryan	1	0	6.89	9	1	15.2	23	15	12	16	11
Maloney, Sean	0	0	3.38	4	0	10.2	10	4	4	3	17
McDougal, Mike	5	7	4.26	48	0	61.1	70	34	29	31	47
*McNatt, Josh	0	1	5.14	2	0	7.0	8	5	4	6	1
*Medina, Carlos	3	6	5.54	15	0	78.0	86	52	48	37	70
Moreno, Julio	2	2	5.28	10	0	44.1	46	29	26	27	25
Paronto, Chad	0	4	8.12	15	0	41.0	59	39	37	32	27
*Parrish, John	0	2	4.04	12	0	55.2	49	28	25	43	42
*Riley, Matt	10	6	3.22	20	0	125.2	113	53	45	42	131
*Rogers, Jason	0	1	1.54	7	0	11.2	11	5	2	9	9
*Rosenkranz, Terry	3	1	3.98	26	0	43.0	36	20	19	26	36
Rust, Brian	0	0	.00	2	0	2.1	1	0	0	1	0
Towers, Josh	12	7	3.76	29	0	189.0	204	86	79	26	106

Erie Seawolves (Angels) AA

BATTING	AVG	AB	R	H	2B	3B	HR	RBI	BB	SO	SB
t'Hoen, E.J., 3B	.203	187	18	38	12	1	2	21	13	52	6
Abbott, Chuck, SS	.239	444	70	106	13	1	6	46	47	138	9
*Barnes, Larry, 1B	.286	497	73	142	25	9	20	100	49	99	14
Betten, Randy, SS	.150	20	3	3	0	1	0	1	0	7	3
#Christian, Eddie, OF	.283	205	29	58	11	1	3	27	20	34	14
Colangelo, Mike, OF	.339	109	24	37	10	3	1	13	14	22	3
Dewey, Jason, C	.223	139	17	31	7	0	4	14	17	50	0
DiSarcina, Gary, SS	.300	20	1	6	0	0	0	2	0	4	0
Durrington, Trent, 2B	.288	396	84	114	26	1	3	34	52	66	59
Foster, Jim, C	.250	16	2	4	1	0	1	3	2	0	0
Graves, Bryan, C	.194	103	22	20	2	1	1	8	32	32	1
*Guiel, Jeff, OF	.263	175	34	46	10	3	6	24	33	33	3
*Haynes, Nathan, OF	.158	19	3	3	1	0	0	0	5	5	0
*Herrick, Jason, OF	.167	78	9	13	5	1	2	6	8	28	1
#Leggett, Adam, 2B	.167	72	8	12	0	0	1	6	21	14	2
*Murphy, Nate, OF	.267	359	48	96	17	8	14	56	54	85	6
Pennyfeather, W., OF	.205	39	4	8	1	0	0	4	5	13	1
Rapp, Travis, C	.250	8	1	2	1	0	0	2	0	4	0
Simonton, Benji, OF	.242	182	13	44	10	1	1	19	28	55	4
Stoner, Mike, DH	.339	62	10	21	4	0	3	15	2	8	0
Tejero, Fausto, SS	.213	211	19	45	9	0	3	18	13	38	0
Tolentino, Juan, OF	.252	489	61	123	19	5	9	61	47	116	47
Walther, Chris, DH	.355	31	5	11	2	1	1	6	4	4	0
Wolff, Mike, DH	.248	307	43	76	21	3	10	40	63	85	4
Wooten, Shawn, 3B	.292	518	70	151	27	1	19	88	50	102	3

PITCHING	W	L	ERA	G	SV	IP	H	R	ER	BB	SO
*Alvarez, Juan	1	2	2.05	23	4	30.2	20	14	7	6	22
Anderson, Bill	1	1	5.40	5	0	18.1	20	12	11	8	12
*Beaumont, Matt	5	6	4.73	32	1	106.2	97	64	56	59	76
Bovee, Mike	1	1	1.32	26	12	34.0	26	6	5	5	33
Brown, Alvin	4	2	6.55	13	2	33.0	38	28	24	24	21
Cooper, Brian	10	5	3.30	22	0	158.0	146	61	58	29	143
Cummings, Ryan	1	1	5.09	3	0	17.2	18	12	10	10	7
Edsell, Geoff	2	3	3.46	26	2	39.0	45	20	15	13	28

PITCHING	W	L	ERA	G	SV	IP	H	R	ER	BB	SO
Etherton, Seth	10	10	3.27	24	0	167.2	153	72	61	43	153
Green, Steve	3	1	3.32	6	0	40.2	34	25	15	19	32
Hancock, Ryan	0	1	5.27	8	1	13.2	23	8	8	2	6
Harriger, Mark	2	1	4.70	6	0	30.2	31	16	16	15	13
*Hill, Jason	1	2	9.96	23	0	28.0	37	37	31	24	14
*Johnson, Greg	0	0	12.00	2	0	3.0	8	4	4	1	4
Mintz, Steve	1	1	2.23	26	9	32.1	26	12	8	12	33
Morse, Paul	8	6	3.33	15	0	97.1	83	44	36	54	52
Nina, Elvin	3	0	4.07	4	0	24.1	20	12	11	15	19
Ortiz, Ramon	9	4	2.82	15	0	102.0	88	38	32	40	86
Petroff, Dan	0	0	9.45	8	0	13.1	21	17	14	4	8
Salter, Cody	6	2	4.10	27	0	52.2	65	29	24	14	16
Shields, Scot	4	4	2.89	10	0	74.2	57	26	24	26	81
Troutman, Keith	5	4	4.12	38	6	59.0	66	32	27	19	49
Wise, Matt	8	5	3.77	16	0	98.0	102	48	41	24	72

Harrisburg Senators (Expos) AA

BATTING	AVG	AB	R	H	2B	3B	HR	RBI	BB	SO	SB
Adolfo, Carlos, OF	.271	221	37	60	16	0	10	41	25	51	3
*Bergeron, Peter, OF	.327	162	29	53	14	2	4	18	24	29	9
#Bradley, Milton, OF	.329	346	62	114	22	5	12	50	33	61	14
#Bravo, Danny, 3B	.143	28	0	4	1	0	0	2	1	6	0
Camilli, Jason, 3B	.214	154	26	33	7	0	4	16	23	31	0
Carroll, Jamey, 2B	.292	561	78	164	34	5	5	63	48	58	21
Cossins, Tim, C	.172	93	8	16	2	0	4	14	4	21	0
De La Rosa, Tomas, SS	.261	467	70	122	22	3	6	43	42	64	28
#James, Kenny, OF	.255	102	8	26	4	2	0	6	1	19	7
Johannes, Todd, C	.250	4	0	1	0	0	0	0	0	2	0
Malave, Jaime, C	.222	18	4	4	0	0	3	4	2	4	0
*Nunnari, Talmadge, 1B	.331	239	45	79	17	1	6	29	39	46	7
Post, Dave, OF	.381	21	5	8	1	0	1	3	1	2	0
Preston, Brian, C	.067	15	1	1	0	0	0	2	1	4	0
*Schneider, Brian, C	.264	421	48	111	19	1	17	66	32	56	2
Snusz, Chris, C	.308	13	2	4	1	0	0	3	1	3	0
*Tracy, Andy, 3B	.274	493	96	135	26	2	37	128	70	139	6
*Tucker, Jon, 1B	.257	362	53	93	21	2	13	55	50	85	4
Ware, Jeremy, OF	.262	381	57	100	23	2	9	56	41	79	12
*Wilkerson, Brad, OF	.235	422	66	99	21	3	8	49	88	100	3
Zech, Scott, 3B	.278	72	8	20	4	1	1	10	4	13	3

PITCHING	W	L	ERA	G	SV	IP	H	R	ER	BB	SO
Agamennone, Brandon	5	2	3.10	22	5	52.1	44	19	18	14	41
Armas, Tony	9	7	2.89	24	0	149.2	123	62	48	55	106
Baker, Jason	1	3	6.03	23	2	31.1	29	22	21	28	24
*Blank, Matt	6	3	3.92	15	0	85.0	94	41	37	26	42
*Duran, Roberto	2	2	8.31	19	1	21.2	15	20	20	31	20
Durocher, Jayson	1	3	3.48	29	4	51.2	44	29	20	25	36
Evans, Keith	0	2	3.67	5	0	27.0	29	14	11	5	21
*Forster, Scott	0	0	0.00	2	0	5.0	3	0	0	0	1
Lara, Yovanny	0	0	7.90	9	0	13.2	19	12	12	8	10
Marquez, Robert	2	2	4.56	18	1	25.2	31	15	13	8	22
Mattes, Troy	5	8	5.36	20	0	97.1	114	67	58	38	58
Mitchell, Scott	2	0	4.26	3	0	19.0	16	9	9	3	10
*Moraga, David	1	0	.00	1	0	3.0	1	0	0	0	0
*Niebla, Ruben	2	0	5.58	29	1	30.2	31	22	19	22	23
Parker, Christian	8	5	3.65	36	3	88.2	86	39	36	37	45
*Phelps, Tommy	3	6	5.71	13	0	64.2	76	53	41	26	36
Quezada, Edward	0	0	1.80	3	0	5.0	2	1	1	1	4
Salyers, Jeremy	1	0	2.81	12	0	25.2	20	9	8	11	9
Saylor, Ryan	6	1	3.62	28	7	59.2	50	28	24	24	55
Stevenson, Rod	2	9	4.38	37	4	51.1	54	32	25	21	34
Strickland, Scott	1	1	2.48	14	3	29.0	25	8	8	10	36
Tucker, T.J.	8	5	4.10	19	0	116.1	110	55	53	38	85
Westbrook, Jake	11	5	3.92	27	0	174.2	180	88	76	63	90

New Britain Rock Cats (Twins) AA

BATTING	AVG	AB	R	H	2B	3B	HR	RBI	BB	SO	SB
Barnes, John, OF	.263	452	62	119	21	1	13	58	49	40	10
Cranford, Joey, 3B	.208	159	19	33	4	1	5	14	10	38	0
*Cummings, Midre, OF	.376	93	28	35	7	0	2	15	17	14	3
#Davidson, Cleatus, 2B	.244	491	88	120	16	10	2	40	53	110	40
*Felston, Anthony, OF	.207	135	17	28	3	2	0	12	13	15	12
Gunderson, Shane, OF	.253	154	15	39	11	1	3	16	7	37	1
Hacker, Steve, DH	.302	461	71	139	36	0	27	97	39	103	0
Huls, Steve, 3B	.217	152	13	33	1	0	0	10	23	32	4
Lane, Ryan, 3B	.286	49	6	14	0	1	3	6	7	10	2

Pitching leaders across all leagues

(Cont'd from previous page)

SHUTOUTS

Player	Club	Lg.	SO
T Green, Steve	ERI	East	4
T Merrell, Phil	Cht	Sou	3
T*Haring, Brett	Cht	Sou	3
Lawrence, Brian	RCu	Cal	3
T Knotts, Gary	Por	East	3
T Standridge, J.	StP	FSL	3

LOSSES

Player	Club	Lg.	L
*Root, Derek	JCK	Tex	16
T Bump, Nate	Por	East	16
T Robbins, Jake	Tam	FSL	15
Pineiro, Joel	NHv	East	15
Scanlan, Bob	NO	PCL	15
T Evans, Keith	Ott	Int	15
*Bausher, Andy	Lyn	Caro	15

WALKS

Player	Club	Lg.	BB
*Caraccioli, L.	SBr	Cal	126
Howard, Ben	FTW	Mid	110
T*Beckett, R.	Alb	PCL	105
Bennett, Tom	Vis	Cal	94
T Shumate, J.	GRV	Sou	94
T Hutchinson, C.	Mem	PCL	93
*O'Connor, B.	Alt	East	92
Drews, Matt	Tol	Int	91
T Morse, Paul	ERI	East	88
*Mills, Ryan	FtM	FSL	87
Bruback, Matt	Lan	Mid	87
*Jones, Chris	SJo	Cal	87
*Anderson, Ryan	NHv	East	86
*Colyer, Stephen	SBr	Cal	86
*Crowell, Jim	Cht	Sou	85

Notes

\# Switch-hitter

* Left-handed

T Player has been with more than one team; listed with last team.

(Players in major leagues are listed with last minor league club.)

Pitching leaders across all leagues

(Cont'd from previous page)

WILD PITCHES

Player	Club	Lg	WP
Bennett, Tom	Vis	Cal	39
Jacobs, Dwayne	W-S	Caro	28
Casey, Joe	Hag	SAL	25
*Johnson, James	Stk	Cal	23
Bradley, Ryan	Col	Int	23
Price, Ryan	Sal	Caro	22
*O'Connor, Brian	Alt	East	21
Smith, Cam	NHv	East	20
*Mills, Ryan	FtM	FSL	20
*Ridenour, Ryan	Grn	SAL	20
Maness, Nick	CLB	SAL	20
T Hutchinson, C.	Mem	PCL	20
Mendoza, H.	SB	Mid	20

BALKS

Player	Club	Lg.	B
T Sequea, J.	Del	SAL	9
*Tatis, Ramon	Dur	Int	9
*Robertson, J.	JCK	Tex	7
*Buehrle, Mark	Bur	Mid	6
Matos, Josue	Wis	Mid	6
Torres, Melqui	Wis	Mid	6
Ulloa, Enmanuel	Wis	Mid	6
Book, Jeremy	Peo	Mid	6
T Keagle, Greg	Tol	Int	6
T Serrano, W.	Mob	Sou	6
Martin, Chandler	Car	Sou	6

SAVES

Player	Club	Lg.	SV
Ellison, Jason	Tam	FSL	35
Puffer, Brandon	CLN	Mid	34
Everly, Bill	SBr	Cal	34
Lisio, Joe	Nrw	East	33
T Brink, Jim	Mod	Cal	29
Nickle, Douglas	Clr	FSL	28
Tessmer, Jay	Col	Int	28
Cisar, Mark	AUG	SAL	27
Cordero, F.	JAX	Sou	27
Kingrey, Jarrod	Hag	SAL	27
Husted, Brent	VB	FSL	27
Thompson, T.	Sal	Caro	27
T Reyes, Eddy	ORL	Sou	27

 # Switch-hitter
** Left-handed*
T Player has been with more than one team; listed with last team. (Players in major leagues are listed with last minor league club.)

BATTING	AVG	AB	R	H	2B	3B	HR	RBI	BB	SO	SB
Lewis, Marc, OF	.260	384	38	100	27	0	9	52	38	79	6
Moeller, Chad, C	.248	250	29	62	11	3	4	24	21	44	0
*Moss, Rick, 3B	.270	252	28	68	13	0	4	29	24	37	0
*Mucker, Kelcey, OF	.272	368	26	100	16	0	1	25	32	57	0
*Peterman, Tommy, 1B	.262	538	68	141	28	0	20	84	61	84	1
Rivas, Luis, SS	.254	527	78	134	30	7	7	49	41	92	31
*Smith, Jeff, C	.253	265	25	67	13	0	6	31	23	40	1

PITCHING	W	L	ERA	G	SV	IP	H	R	ER	BB	SO
Babineaux, Darrin	0	0	6.52	5	0	9.2	14	10	7	4	7
Bell, Jason	3	3	3.42	7	0	47.1	46	21	18	11	34
Cressend, Jack	8	10	4.61	28	0	160.0	171	91	82	57	136
*Downs, Scott	0	0	8.69	6	0	19.2	33	21	19	10	22
Espinal, Jose	3	12	5.54	29	0	131.2	160	100	81	41	90
Gandarillas, Gus	1	3	8.63	18	1	32.1	38	32	31	21	26
*Garza, Chris	1	0	2.08	31	0	30.1	14	10	7	19	40
*Guardado, Eddie	0	0	1.93	3	0	4.2	3	1	1	0	5
Haigler, Phil	1	4	6.32	19	0	52.2	74	53	37	20	18
Harris, Jeff	3	1	1.48	20	0	24.1	21	5	4	14	12
Hooten, David	6	6	3.56	52	1	103.2	94	55	41	49	89
Kinney, Matt	4	7	7.12	14	0	60.2	69	54	48	36	50
Lohse, Kyle	3	4	5.89	11	0	70.1	87	49	46	23	41
*Mahaffey, Alan	8	6	4.12	33	1	98.1	109	47	45	34	89
Mota, Danny	0	1	3.55	6	0	12.2	11	5	5	5	12
Niedermaier, Brad	2	2	4.35	41	9	49.2	50	29	24	27	47
Padilla, Juan	1	1	6.63	11	2	19.0	31	15	14	7	12
*Romero, J.C.	4	4	3.40	36	7	53.0	51	25	20	34	53
Ryan, Jason	2	4	4.80	8	0	50.2	48	29	27	24	42
*Spiers, Corey	5	2	3.47	8	0	46.2	50	21	18	12	21
Stentz, Brent	0	1	3.73	32	9	31.1	23	13	13	12	44
Yeskie, Nate	5	11	5.28	25	0	129.2	157	83	76	47	102

New Haven Ravens (Mariners) AA

BATTING	AVG	AB	R	H	2B	3B	HR	RBI	BB	SO	SB
*Bass, Jayson, OF	.265	431	79	114	23	5	21	67	72	160	34
Brown, Randy, 3B	.257	167	30	43	7	5	6	22	19	37	0
Cruz, Cirilo, DH	.158	57	5	9	3	0	0	9	10	13	0
#Estrada, Marco, DH	.150	20	3	3	1	0	0	1	3	8	0
Gipson, Charles, 2B	.000	18	2	0	0	0	0	0	3	2	1
*Harrison, Adonis, 2B	.272	449	54	122	16	0	2	45	38	75	22
Hills, Rich, 3B	.262	282	30	74	15	0	4	29	40	47	1
Horner, Jim, C	.270	278	29	75	17	0	6	50	17	51	1
#Johnson, Earl, OF	.245	139	18	34	3	0	0	10	8	31	11
Kingman, Brendan, 1B	.279	509	58	142	20	0	10	56	26	71	0
Lopez, Rafael, OF	.188	32	1	6	1	0	0	1	0	5	0
Magdaleno, Ricky, SS	.271	258	30	70	13	1	1	24	21	45	1
Maness, Dwight, OF	.241	87	11	21	2	1	5	12	11	18	9
Marn, Kevin, OF	.286	7	0	2	0	0	0	1	1	3	1
Martinez, Victor, DH	.000	4	0	0	0	0	0	0	1	3	0
*Mathis, Joe, OF	.271	240	29	65	13	5	2	30	15	45	9
Regan, Jason, 3B	.213	150	12	32	9	1	3	13	17	46	2
*Sachse, Matt, OF	.113	97	12	11	1	0	1	4	10	36	1
Thomas, Juan, DH	.243	267	47	65	13	0	16	51	14	92	0
*Vazquez, Ramon, SS	.258	438	58	113	27	3	5	45	62	77	8
Wathan, Dusty, C	.279	333	37	93	16	2	4	37	24	60	4
*Weber, Jake, OF	.256	489	64	125	22	2	11	59	66	73	5

PITCHING	W	L	ERA	G	SV	IP	H	R	ER	BB	SO
Ahearne, Pat	8	3	2.61	17	0	124.0	114	41	36	27	80
*Anderson, Ryan	9	13	4.50	24	0	134.0	131	77	67	86	162
*Brosnan, Jason	3	0	2.34	28	6	50.0	32	14	13	15	44
De La Rosa, Maximo	0	1	2.53	10	4	10.2	9	4	3	3	7
Dunham, Pat	0	1	2.57	3	0	7.0	1	2	2	16	5
*Fitzgerald, Brian	2	2	3.83	29	3	54.0	58	24	23	18	37
*Fuentes, Brian	3	3	4.95	15	0	60.0	53	36	33	46	66
Gryboski, Kevin	2	5	2.89	47	10	62.1	67	27	20	20	41
Kirkreit, Daron	2	2	2.63	5	0	24.0	33	8	7	7	15
Luce, Robert	0	0	8.59	2	0	7.1	11	10	7	3	3
McClaskey, Tim	0	0	2.25	4	0	8.0	4	2	2	1	7
Meche, Gil	3	4	3.05	10	0	59.0	51	24	20	26	56
Montane, Ivan	4	2	2.47	41	10	54.2	38	16	15	22	70
*Newton, Geronimo	2	1	3.97	31	0	59.0	60	32	26	26	48
Pineiro, Joel	10	15	4.72	28	0	166.0	190	105	87	52	116
Scheffer, Aaron	2	0	3.71	10	0	17.0	19	9	7	8	24
Smith, Cam	1	4	5.07	41	0	55.0	42	39	31	61	59
Stark, Dennis	9	11	4.40	26	0	147.1	151	82	72	62	103
Sweeney, Brian	4	6	4.69	23	1	111.1	125	65	58	31	83
*Zimmerman, Jordan	1	4	1.08	22	2	33.1	26	8	4	19	33

Norwich Navigators (Yankees) AA

BATTING	AVG	AB	R	H	2B	3B	HR	RBI	BB	SO	SB
Ashby, Chris, OF	.250	108	11	27	5	1	3	16	11	20	3
*Brown, Richard, OF	.261	383	46	100	18	8	6	54	34	81	5
Brown, Vick, 2B	.251	482	86	121	19	1	5	48	83	101	50
Dennis, Les, SS	.250	176	27	44	10	0	0	12	27	50	0
Emmons, Scott, C	.235	102	13	24	1	0	3	16	6	25	0
*Glass, Chip, OF	.251	239	36	60	9	3	6	34	31	49	5
*Johnson, Nick, 1B	.345	420	114	145	33	5	14	87	123	88	8
#Leon, Donny, 3B	.302	457	69	138	34	2	21	100	34	102	0
#McDonald, D., OF	.272	533	95	145	19	10	4	33	90	110	54
#McLamb, Brian, 3B	.159	126	11	20	5	0	2	14	4	46	1
#Mirizzi, Marc, 3B	.106	47	6	5	0	0	1	6	5	13	0
Morris, Jeremy, DH	.247	392	50	97	16	1	9	52	31	91	8
*Ottavinia, Paul, OF	.288	191	26	55	11	3	7	31	14	40	5
Shumpert, Derek, OF	.217	166	25	36	8	0	7	15	13	63	3
#Smith, Rod, DH	.600	5	1	3	0	0	0	1	0	1	2
Soriano, Alfonso, SS	.305	361	57	110	20	3	15	68	32	67	24
Thames, Marcus, OF	.225	182	25	41	6	2	4	26	22	40	0
Valencia, Victor, C	.222	396	57	88	18	0	22	72	45	142	0

PITCHING	W	L	ERA	G	SV	IP	H	R	ER	BB	SO
Beverlin, Jason	15	9	3.69	28	0	173.1	153	91	71	81	147
*Carroll, Dave	0	0	0.00	3	1	6.0	5	3	0	2	4
De La Cruz, Francisco	6	5	4.59	29	0	133.1	141	89	68	73	91
Dingman, Craig	8	6	1.57	55	9	74.1	56	16	13	12	90
Einertson, Darrell	2	2	4.97	21	0	29.0	39	23	16	10	16
*Flores, Randy	0	1	6.48	4	0	25.0	32	20	18	11	19
Johnson, Mark	9	3	3.68	16	0	88.0	88	51	36	39	52
Kaufman, Brad	3	2	4.12	40	1	83.0	76	45	38	38	81
*Keisler, Randy	3	4	4.57	8	0	43.1	45	24	22	17	33
Lail, Denny	5	0	1.74	6	0	41.1	24	12	8	11	29
Lisio, Joe	2	6	4.13	59	33	56.2	58	27	26	27	49
Maeda, Kats	3	2	4.34	25	1	76.2	82	41	37	40	48
*Mairena, Oswaldo	4	3	2.67	49	2	57.1	48	24	17	27	47
Resz, Greg	3	2	4.36	20	0	43.1	40	25	21	20	45
Robbins, Jake	3	12	5.43	20	0	111.0	118	80	67	60	63
Spence, Cam	5	5	5.79	19	0	91.2	118	75	59	32	62
*Williams, Matt	1	1	2.40	22	0	30.0	22	9	8	18	44
*Zancanaro, Dave	6	1	2.28	15	0	79.0	64	25	20	32	61

Portland Sea Dogs (Marlins) AA

BATTING	AVG	AB	R	H	2B	3B	HR	RBI	BB	SO	SB
#Bates, Fletcher, OF	.253	537	72	136	28	9	9	55	39	109	18
*Erickson, Matt, 2B	.269	361	38	97	20	2	0	35	51	65	2
Funaro, Joe, 3B	.366	268	42	98	19	1	3	40	31	22	6
Hastings, Lionel, C	.228	197	26	45	5	1	3	14	32	45	2
Heinrichs, Jon, OF	.227	176	25	40	11	1	3	17	16	23	4
*Jones, Jaime, OF	.254	244	39	62	16	0	7	31	47	81	2
Kleinz, Larry, 3B	.261	276	30	72	21	1	5	43	39	50	2
Kuilan, Hector, C	.261	245	22	64	11	0	2	32	11	42	0
Lobaton, Jose, 3B	.250	32	2	8	2	0	0	0	2	13	1
#Niles, Drew, 2B	.230	135	12	31	3	0	0	9	21	34	0
Norton, Chris, DH	.291	406	74	118	25	0	38	97	71	124	1
Ozuna, Pablo, SS	.281	502	62	141	25	7	7	46	13	50	31
Ramirez, Julio, OF	.261	568	87	148	30	10	13	64	39	150	64
Reese, Nate, PH	.000	3	0	0	0	0	0	0	0	0	0
Reeves, Glenn, OF	.000	9	0	0	0	0	0	0	0	6	0
*Robertson, Ryan, C	.246	130	15	32	6	0	2	10	22	17	0
Rodriguez, Victor, 3B	.206	97	13	20	3	1	1	12	10	9	0
*Rolison, Nate, 1B	.299	438	71	131	20	1	17	69	68	112	0
Schifano, Tony, 3B	.239	67	9	16	1	1	0	6	5	9	0

PITCHING	W	L	ERA	G	SV	IP	H	R	ER	BB	SO
*Almanza, Armando	0	0	3.97	10	3	11.1	5	5	5	4	20
Almonte, Hector	1	4	2.84	47	23	44.1	42	14	14	26	42
*Arroyo, Luis	0	1	3.29	9	1	13.2	14	11	5	8	10
*Benz, Jake	1	0	4.32	23	0	33.1	30	19	16	23	24
Bump, Nate	2	6	6.07	8	0	43.0	57	38	29	12	33
Burnett, A.J.	6	12	5.52	26	0	120.2	132	91	74	71	121
Cames, Aaron	3	6	5.55	23	0	95.2	110	64	59	46	66
Clark, Chris	1	0	7.50	4	0	6.0	5	5	5	7	4
Duncan, Geoff	2	3	2.85	43	4	66.1	59	24	21	26	59
*Gonzalez, Gabe	2	4	3.55	26	0	38.0	38	19	15	8	34
Henderson, Scott	6	3	2.96	46	7	85.0	67	32	28	26	83
Knotts, Gary	6	3	3.75	12	0	81.2	79	39	34	33	63
Larkin, Andy	1	1	7.11	7	0	12.2	16	10	10	4	7

Pitching leaders across all leagues

(Cont'd from previous page)

GAMES

Player	Club	Lg.	G
T Flury, Pat	Ind	Int	66
Brow, Scott	Edm	PCL	64
T Riedling, John	Ind	Int	64
Guerra, Mark	Nor	Int	63
Greene, Rick	Ind	Int	61
T Snyder, Bill	JAX	Sou	61
Nickle, Douglas	Clr	FSL	60
T Gandarillas, G.	SLk	PCL	60
Rivera, Saul	QC	Mid	60
T*Dunbar, Matt	Nsh	PCL	60
*Noriega, Ray	Vis	Cal	60
Evans, David	ROC	Int	60
Everly, Bill	SBr	Cal	60
*Enders, Trevor	ORL	Sou	60

INNINGS PITCHED

Player	Club	Lg.	IP
Fish, Steve	LkE	Cal	196.2
*Robertson, J.	JCK	Tex	191.0
Towers, Josh	Bow	East	189.0
T Cooper, Brian	Edm	PCL	189.0
T Etherton, Seth	Edm	PCL	189.0
*Darwin, David	JAX	Sou	187.1
T*Pettyjohn, A.	JAX	Sou	186.1
T*Bridges, D.	LkE	Cal	185.2
T Cummings, R.	ERI	East	185.1
T Ireland, Eric	Kis	FSL	185.0
T Fernandez, J.	Paw	Int	182.0
T Shields, Scot	ERI	East	182.0
T Padua, G.	RCu	Cal	180.1
Wolff, Bryan	LV	PCL	177.2

STRIKEOUTS

Player	Club	Lg.	SO
Stephens, John	Del	SAL	217
T Padua, G.	RCu	Cal	196
T Shields, Scot	ERI	East	194
T*Ankiel, Rick	Mem	PCL	194
*Riley, Matt	Bow	East	189
T Figueroa, Juan	W-S	Caro	189
Gagne, Eric	SAn	Tex	185
T Guerrero, J.	Wil	Caro	181
Fish, Steve	LkE	Cal	180
Cassidy, Scott	Hag	SAL	178
*Kalinowski, Josh	Sal	Caro	176
T Cooper, Brian	Edm	PCL	175
T Meyers, Mike	WTn	Sou	173
T*Downs, Scott	WTn	Sou	173
T Etherton, Seth	Edm	PCL	172

Switch-hitter
* Left-handed
T Player has been with more than one team; listed with last team.
(Players in major leagues are listed with last minor league club.)

Pitching leaders across all leagues

(Cont'd from previous page)

HIT-BY-PITCH

Player	Club	Lg.	HBP
Cassidy, Scott	Hag	SAL	21
T Harper, Travis	ORL	Sou	20
Matcuk, Steve	Sal	Caro	20
Van Buren, J.	Ash	SAL	19
Lampley, Daniel	Sar	FSL	18
T Loux, Shane	Lkl	FSL	18
*Saenz, Jason	CLB	SAL	18
Bermudez, M.	BAK	Cal	18
Garrett, Josh	Sar	FSL	17
Juden, Jeff	Col	Int	17
T Parker, C.	Har	East	17
Estrella, Leo	Dun	FSL	17

HITS ALLOWED

Player	Club	Lg.	HA
Fish, Steve	LkE	Cal	220
Scanlan, Bob	NO	PCL	208
T Saier, Matt	Oma	PCL	206
Stone, Ricky	Alb	PCL	205
Towers, Josh	Bow	East	204
Wolff, Bryan	LV	PCL	199
Price, Ryan	Sal	Caro	198
*Knott, Eric	ELP	Tex	198
T*Mullen, Scott	Oma	PCL	197
T*Pettyjohn, A.	JAX	Sou	196
*Darwin, David	JAX	Sou	194
Patrick, B.	Fre	PCL	194
*McNichol, B.	Iow	PCL	194
Raggio, Brady	Ok	PCL	193

ERA (WORST)

Player	Club	Lg.	ERA
Drews, Matt	Tol	Int	8.27
T Nussbeck, M.	Mem	PCL	8.02
*Farmer, Michael	Csp	PCL	7.86
*Fordham, Tom	Chr	Int	7.31
T Drumright, M.	Cal	PCL	7.12
Tynan, Chris	Sav	SAL	6.99
T Small, Aaron	Dur	Int	6.88
Lira, Felipe	Tol	Int	6.71
Cook, Aaron	Ash	SAL	6.44
*Teut, Nate	DAY	FSL	6.38
Henderson, Rod	Lou	Int	6.34
T Yennaco, Jay	Knx	Sou	6.28
Bradley, Ryan	Col	Int	6.21
T Stevenson, J.	Syr	Int	6.18
T Grilli, Jason	Cal	PCL	6.16

\# Switch-hitter
* Left-handed
T Player has been with more than one team; listed with last team.
(Players in major leagues are listed with last minor league club.)

2000 BASEBALL WEEKLY ALMANAC

PITCHING	W	L	ERA	G	SV	IP	H	R	ER	BB	SO
Leese, Brandon	4	4	5.73	20	0	81.2	110	66	52	20	52
Pageler, Mick	4	2	4.76	31	1	51.0	70	33	27	13	44
Penny, Brad	1	0	3.90	6	0	32.1	28	15	14	14	35
Rector, Bobby	0	4	3.59	13	0	42.2	43	23	17	14	19
Rodgers, Bobby	5	10	5.43	26	0	122.2	147	85	74	70	109
*Tejera, Michael	13	4	2.62	25	0	154.2	137	55	45	45	152
Vardijan, Dan	0	1	29.08	5	0	4.1	12	15	14	8	5
Villafuerte, Brandon	6	8	3.50	22	0	100.1	97	45	39	40	85

Reading Phillies (Phillies) AA

BATTING	AVG	AB	R	H	2B	3B	HR	RBI	BB	SO	SB
Alvarez, Clemente, C	.176	142	12	25	5	1	2	12	11	38	1
Antczak, Chuck, C	.000	19	0	0	0	0	0	0	0	6	0
*Burnham, Gary, 1B	.249	354	47	88	20	0	12	49	41	49	11
Burrell, Pat, 1B	.333	417	84	139	28	6	28	90	79	103	3
Finn, John, 3B	.209	115	15	24	8	1	0	9	20	16	7
*Francia, David, OF	.271	339	41	92	22	5	4	43	21	57	13
#Harris, Brian, 2B	.221	380	42	84	13	3	5	41	46	58	9
*Horne, Tyrone, OF	.267	262	37	70	13	2	5	37	43	64	13
Huff, Larry, 3B	.260	427	72	111	28	3	3	54	60	69	28
McNamara, Rusty, 3B	.249	177	26	44	9	1	5	20	17	22	0
Pierce, Kirk, C	.259	255	37	66	10	0	9	40	42	56	4
Raynor, Mark, 2B	.209	43	4	9	0	1	0	3	6	4	0
#Rollins, Jimmy, SS	.273	532	81	145	21	8	11	56	51	47	24
Royster, Aaron, OF	.291	309	53	90	17	2	8	48	48	90	11
Stewart, Andy, C	.300	190	23	57	19	0	7	40	16	18	0
*Taylor, Reggie, OF	.266	526	75	140	17	10	15	61	18	79	38
Tinoco, Luis, OF	.271	96	18	26	4	0	1	10	22	23	2

PITCHING	W	L	ERA	G	SV	IP	H	R	ER	BB	SO
Bailie, Matt	1	0	0.00	1	0	6.2	3	0	0	1	6
Barnett, Marty	2	3	2.53	35	7	53.1	43	19	15	24	33
Brannan, Ryan	0	0	16.62	5	0	4.1	9	8	8	4	1
*Brester, Jason	7	5	3.76	16	0	105.1	105	48	44	26	87
Burger, Rob	0	6	13.50	9	0	27.1	29	43	41	45	23
Cedeno, Blas	2	2	4.26	19	0	31.2	30	16	15	12	18
*Censale, Silvio	1	6	11.77	16	0	52.0	74	76	68	48	36
Coggin, Dave	2	5	7.50	9	0	42.0	55	37	35	20	21
*Dodd, Robert	10	2	3.83	42	5	80.0	78	38	34	23	79
Eason, Clay	0	2	10.38	10	1	13.0	14	15	15	14	13
Eaton, Adam	5	4	2.92	12	0	77.0	60	30	25	28	67
Grahe, Joe	0	0	.90	7	4	10.0	7	3	1	2	12
Herbert, Russ	3	5	4.75	26	3	83.1	90	53	44	32	55
Hubbs, Dan	0	0	5.63	3	0	8.0	10	5	5	5	8
*Jacquez, Thomas	6	5	5.28	38	1	122.2	149	84	72	32	68
Kawabata, Kyle	0	0	6.00	8	0	12.0	20	9	8	2	7
*Kershner, Jason	4	4	5.73	57	8	92.2	99	67	59	40	86
Politte, Cliff	9	8	3.63	37	5	109.0	112	45	44	33	97
*Pyc, David	5	2	4.33	17	0	81.0	95	44	39	15	51
Rutherford, Mark	1	0	.98	4	0	18.1	11	3	2	9	10
*Shumaker, Anthony	4	3	1.78	10	0	60.2	48	17	12	17	60
Thomas, Evan	9	5	3.25	36	3	127.1	123	53	46	50	127
Williams, Shad	2	2	3.13	16	2	31.2	30	17	11	10	19

Trenton Thunder (Red Sox) AA

BATTING	AVG	AB	R	H	2B	3B	HR	RBI	BB	SO	SB
Alcantara, Israel, OF	.294	293	48	86	26	0	20	60	27	78	4
#Burkhart, M., DH	.230	239	40	55	14	1	12	41	31	43	3
Chevalier, Virgil, OF	.293	509	81	149	29	4	13	76	50	73	9
Depastino, Joe, DH	.217	23	5	5	1	0	2	5	3	3	1
Eckstein, David, 2B	.313	483	109	151	22	5	6	52	89	48	32
#Epperson, Chad, DH	.197	188	24	37	10	1	2	15	31	46	1
Espinal, Juan, 3B	.185	65	11	12	1	0	2	7	5	19	0
Everett, Adam, SS	.263	338	56	89	11	0	10	44	41	64	21
Faurot, Adam, 2B	.250	108	11	27	4	1	0	8	6	20	1
Gibralter, David, 1B	.299	448	76	134	22	1	24	97	32	68	5
Gonzalez, Raul, OF	.335	505	80	169	33	4	18	103	51	71	12
Hillenbrand, Shea, C	.259	282	41	73	15	0	7	36	14	27	6
Jackson, Gavin, SS	.211	71	11	15	1	0	0	5	15	12	2
Lomasney, Steve, C	.245	151	24	37	6	0	12	31	31	44	7
Newfield, Marc, OF	.154	13	3	2	1	0	1	2	1	3	1
Rodriguez, Luis, C	.272	114	10	31	7	0	4	14	3	25	2
Soriano, Jose, OF	.253	166	38	42	9	1	2	20	12	31	15
#Tebbs, Nate, OF	.271	365	49	99	14	1	4	35	29	67	21
Veras, Wilton, 3B	.281	474	65	133	23	2	11	75	43	55	7

PITCHING	W	L	ERA	G	SV	IP	H	R	ER	BB	SO
Adams, Willie	1	1	4.63	2	0	11.2	17	6	6	2	6
*Barkley, Brian	5	0	2.55	7	0	35.1	32	10	10	6	18
Beale, Chuck	2	5	5.95	29	1	59.0	71	45	39	36	41
Betancourt, Rafael	6	2	3.62	39	13	54.2	50	24	22	10	57
Bullinger, Kirk	1	1	0.53	17	10	17.0	6	2	1	5	16
Crawford, Paxton	7	8	4.08	28	0	163.1	151	81	74	59	111
*Cumberland, Chris	2	0	0.43	14	1	21.0	12	1	1	13	18
*Dixon, Tim	2	1	3.52	10	0	23.0	19	10	9	8	14
Dougherty, Tony	0	0	7.71	15	1	23.1	41	27	20	13	16
Farrell, Jim	2	2	3.33	7	0	27.0	26	13	10	9	26
Fernandez, Jared	3	0	3.38	7	1	18.2	18	9	7	8	10
*Hazlett, Andy	9	9	4.16	27	1	164.1	155	84	76	41	123
Kim, Sun	9	8	4.89	26	0	149.0	160	86	81	44	130
*Matthews, Mike	0	5	7.47	9	0	37.1	47	37	31	24	18
*McMullen, Jerry	1	0	6.00	3	0	3.0	4	2	2	2	2
Ohka, Tomokazu	8	0	3.00	12	0	72.0	63	26	24	25	53
Saberhagen, Bret	1	0	0.00	1	0	6.0	2	0	0	0	5
Sekany, Jason	14	4	3.35	27	0	161.1	143	65	60	64	116
*Smetana, Steve	5	4	3.99	39	1	85.2	90	39	38	26	61
Stanifer, Rob	0	0	0.00	5	1	9.0	6	0	0	4	11
Taglienti, Jeff	0	0	2.79	10	2	19.1	9	6	6	5	17
Tweedlie, Brad	6	0	3.65	44	3	56.2	59	28	23	21	31
*Urso, Sal	2	2	1.86	22	5	29.0	25	11	6	14	39
*Young, Tim	4	4	4.37	31	2	45.1	38	26	22	26	52

Southern League

Birmingham Barons (White Sox) AA

BATTING	AVG	AB	R	H	2B	3B	HR	RBI	BB	SO	SB
Aude, Rich, 1B	.290	486	63	141	33	2	12	85	34	90	15
#Bravo, Danny, 3B	.281	270	49	76	12	1	2	38	41	39	6
*Christensen, M., OF	.290	293	53	85	8	6	3	28	31	46	18
Connacher, Kevin, 2B	.222	18	1	4	0	0	0	0	2	5	1
Crede, Joe, 3B	.251	291	37	73	14	1	4	42	22	47	2
#Dellaero, Jason, SS	.268	272	40	73	13	3	10	44	14	76	6
Eaglin, Mike, 2B	.227	75	7	17	2	0	0	8	4	17	1
Eddie, Steve, 3B	.197	157	15	31	8	0	1	12	12	30	0
Gomez, Ramon, OF	.285	274	47	78	10	5	0	26	31	81	26
Hyde, Brandon, C	.278	18	4	5	3	0	0	2	3	4	0
Inglin, Jeff, OF	.292	432	63	126	26	4	15	63	58	62	20
Lydy, Scott, OF	.265	400	74	106	25	1	20	65	67	61	18
Moore, Brandon, SS	.193	119	11	23	3	2	0	13	17	20	4
*Newstrom, Doug, C	.285	253	30	72	11	1	3	23	29	42	3
*Olson, Dan, OF	.165	97	14	16	4	0	6	13	15	44	1
Paul, Josh, C	.279	319	47	89	19	3	4	42	29	68	6
Pemberton, Rudy, DH	.277	307	49	85	14	3	18	60	27	55	8
Ramirez, Dan, OF	.197	127	16	25	5	0	0	10	3	31	6
*Rexrode, Jackie, 2B	.268	213	34	57	7	5	0	25	28	30	14
#Rodriguez, Liu, 2B	.291	244	42	71	11	1	3	37	22	35	5
Ryder, Derek, C	.148	27	4	4	1	0	0	2	2	3	0

PITCHING	W	L	ERA	G	SV	IP	H	R	ER	BB	SO
Barcelo, Lorenzo	0	1	3.60	4	0	20.0	14	8	8	6	14
Chantres, Carlos	6	8	3.50	28	2	141.1	122	64	55	61	105
Daneker, Pat	6	8	3.22	16	0	109.0	106	46	39	30	71
Davenport, Joe	3	5	3.10	40	10	49.1	43	26	17	19	24
Fogg, Josh	3	2	5.89	10	0	55.0	66	37	36	18	40
Garland, Jon	3	1	4.38	7	0	39.0	39	22	19	18	27
Iglesias, Mario	5	3	4.68	23	0	50.0	51	29	26	21	29
Lakman, Jason	0	0	15.00	3	0	3.0	3	5	5	9	3
Myette, Aaron	12	7	3.66	28	0	164.2	138	76	67	77	135
Olsen, Jason	1	3	3.82	9	0	33.0	33	15	14	10	25
*Pena, Jesus	3	2	2.36	40	5	45.2	31	12	12	18	49
Roberts, Mark	5	8	3.40	33	2	124.1	108	64	47	41	84
Schmack, Brian	4	4	3.43	46	6	63.0	60	31	24	18	56
Secoda, Jason	8	7	3.44	22	0	115.0	100	49	44	39	94
Tokarse, Brian	0	1	5.06	6	0	10.2	12	7	6	3	11
Tucker, Julien	2	1	5.33	37	5	49.0	52	30	29	22	32
*Vining, Ken	0	2	9.26	3	0	11.2	20	16	12	9	8
Virchis, Adam	0	0	0.00	1	0	3.0	3	0	0	0	1
Wells, Kip	8	2	2.94	11	0	70.1	49	24	23	31	44
*Whitley, Curtis	4	2	5.01	36	1	50.1	58	31	28	25	24

Pitching leaders across all leagues

(Cont'd from previous page)

LOW-HITTERS (0,-1,-2,-3-HIT)

Player	Club	Lg.	LH
Stephens, John	Del	SAL	3
T Manning, D.	WTn	Sou	3
T Standridge, J.	StP	FSL	3

SO/9 IP RATIO (STARTERS)

Player	Club	Lg.	SO/9 IP
Neugebauer, N.	BLT	Mid	13.95
T*Ankiel, Rick	Mem	PCL	12.68
Stephens, John	Del	SAL	11.47
T Abreu, Winston	MYR	Caro	11.15
T Checo, R.	Alb	PCL	11.12
T Meyers, Mike	WTn	Sou	11.10
*Anderson, Ryan	NHv	East	10.88
T Guerrero, J.	Wil	Caro	10.46
Sobkowiak, S.	MYR	Caro	10.40
Brea, Lesli	SLU	FSL	10.14
T Patterson, J.	Tuc	PCL	10.06
T Sneed, John	Knx	Sou	10.02
T Vogelsong, R.	Shv	Tex	10.01
*Bowers, C.	ORL	Sou	9.94

AVERAGE AGAINST (STARTERS)

Player	Club	Lg.	BA
Neugebauer, N.	BLT	Mid	.178
T Meyers, Mike	WTn	Sou	.179
*Miller, Aaron	QC	Mid	.188
*Vega, Rene	CLB	SAL	.192
T Abreu, Winston	MYR	Caro	.195
T*Ankiel, Rick	Mem	PCL	.196
Sobkowiak, S.	MYR	Caro	.199
*Rodriguez, W.	Kis	FSL	.199
Gagne, Eric	SAn	Tex	.201
T*Spiegel, Mike	Kin	Caro	.206
*Kalinowski, J.	Sal	Caro	.207
McClellan, Matt	Dun	FSL	.213
T Guerrero, J.	Wil	Caro	.214
T Vogelsong, R.	Shv	Tex	.214

Switch-hitter
* Left-handed
T Player has been with more than one team; listed with last team.
(Players in major leagues are listed with last minor league club.)

403

Pitching leaders across all leagues

(Cont'd from previous page)

SO/9 IP RATIO (RELIEVERS)

Player	Club	Lg.	SO/9IP
T Cammack, Eric	Nor	Int	13.78
Rivera, Saul	QC	Mid	13.18
Heams, Shane	WM	Mid	13.17
T Donaldson, Bo	Cht	Sou	12.95
T Miller, Matt	TUL	Tex	12.82
T Snow, Bert	Van	PCL	12.78
T Ruhl, Nathan	StP	FSL	12.56
Hiles, Cary	Pie	SAL	12.39
*Lontayo, A.	AUG	SAL	12.27
T Sparks, Jeff	Dur	Int	12.27
T Hiljus, Erik	Tol	Int	12.27
T De Paula, Sean	Buf	Int	12.06
*Moreno, Juan	TUL	Tex	11.92
T Montane, Ivan	NHv	East	11.76
Jacobs, Dwayne	W-S	Caro	11.59

AVERAGE AGAINST (RELIEVERS)

Player	Club	Lg.	BA
T Riske, David	Buf	Int	.113
*Moreno, Juan	TUL	Tex	.153
T Voyles, Brad	MYR	Caro	.155
T Cammack, Eric	Nor	Int	.160
File, Bob	Dun	FSL	.164
Heams, Shane	WM	Mid	.165
Jacobs, Dwayne	W-S	Caro	.166
T Donaldson, Bo	Cht	Sou	.167
Rivera, Saul	QC	Mid	.171
T*Franklin, W.	JCK	Tex	.178
T Ruhl, Nathan	StP	FSL	.180
T Montane, Ivan	NHv	East	.182
Serrano, Jim	Jup	FSL	.182
Cordero, F.	JAX	Sou	.183

Carolina Mudcats (Rockies) AA

BATTING	AVG	AB	R	H	2B	3B	HR	RBI	BB	SO	SB
*Anthony, Brian, 3B	.222	171	20	38	9	1	7	20	11	39	1
Bair, Rod, OF	.303	472	70	143	34	6	13	81	28	78	14
Barthol, Blake, C	.280	322	41	90	18	3	8	27	32	62	0
Berry, Mike, 3B	.242	306	36	74	15	2	9	38	26	61	0
*Cotton, John, 3B	.282	163	27	46	9	0	10	21	10	48	0
Feuerstein, Dave, OF	.220	287	27	63	9	3	1	18	18	43	6
Keck, Brian, 3B	.200	15	0	3	0	1	0	2	4	3	2
Kirgan, Chris, 1B	.222	474	55	105	27	2	13	84	60	115	1
Light, Tal, OF	.185	259	26	48	18	0	9	30	16	121	0
Livingston, Doug, 2B	.202	119	11	24	2	1	1	9	13	24	4
Malave, Jose, OF	.274	146	21	40	10	1	10	26	16	28	0
#Pena, Elvis, 2B	.301	356	57	107	24	6	2	31	48	64	21
Petrick, Ben, C	.309	68	18	21	5	1	4	22	9	15	3
Raleigh, Matt, 3B	.209	115	13	24	8	0	4	12	23	60	0
Sosa, Juan, SS	.276	490	70	135	22	5	7	42	31	65	38
Vidal, Gilbert, C	.240	129	10	31	8	0	2	12	8	30	0
Watkins, Pat, OF	.298	312	38	93	27	1	3	40	24	49	6

PITCHING	W	L	ERA	G	SV	IP	H	R	ER	BB	SO
Bailey, Roger	0	3	7.00	4	0	18.0	21	16	14	10	14
*Bevel, Bobby	3	7	4.43	48	7	67.0	70	37	33	27	58
*Brester, Jason	2	6	5.76	11	0	59.1	71	45	38	26	44
Briggs, Anthony	0	1	11.25	4	0	4.0	7	5	5	4	4
Colmenares, Luis	0	0	8.10	8	0	10.0	16	9	9	8	10
*DeWitt, Scott	1	2	3.92	45	2	66.2	84	34	29	21	65
Gonzalez, Lariel	2	1	5.29	30	14	34.0	39	27	20	22	41
Hackman, Luther	4	3	4.04	11	0	62.1	53	33	28	28	50
*Hartvigson, Chad	0	5	6.28	30	1	43.0	48	35	30	11	32
*Jacobs, Ryan	6	12	5.29	28	0	114.0	120	76	67	68	89
Lee, David	0	0	1.04	16	10	17.1	8	3	2	3	16
Martin, Chandler	13	8	3.78	27	0	164.1	153	82	69	63	130
Randall, Scott	5	8	3.43	16	0	99.2	101	52	38	34	102
*Rawitzer, Kevin	3	2	3.60	33	1	70.0	73	33	28	26	54
*Roberts, Chris	5	4	3.78	43	1	81.0	76	46	34	36	52
*Robertson, Rich	3	2	3.21	11	0	47.2	48	20	17	16	42
Rossiter, Mike	0	1	2.08	16	2	21.2	11	5	5	9	24
*Vavrek, Mike	1	5	7.38	10	0	46.1	71	42	38	19	41
Walls, Doug	10	9	3.65	26	0	150.1	159	74	61	44	140
Zamarripa, Mark	2	1	4.43	5	0	20.1	20	11	10	14	12

Chattanooga Lookouts (Reds) AA

BATTING	AVG	AB	R	H	2B	3B	HR	RBI	BB	SO	SB
*Broussard, Ben, OF	.213	127	26	27	5	0	8	21	11	41	1
Burress, Andy, OF	.272	257	42	70	12	1	7	28	18	41	11
Clark, Brady, OF	.326	506	103	165	37	4	17	75	89	58	25
Conner, Decomba, OF	.179	123	17	22	3	2	5	19	17	31	1
Davis, James, C	.241	54	7	13	5	0	4	16	1	5	0
Dawkins, Travis, SS	.364	129	24	47	7	0	2	13	14	17	15
Diaz, Alejandro, OF	.264	220	27	58	9	8	7	35	8	31	6
Florez, Tim, 2B	.252	139	24	35	8	1	5	22	15	23	7
Garcia, Guillermo, C	.310	42	11	13	3	3	1	7	2	6	0
Ingram, Darron, OF	.221	267	42	59	11	3	11	40	28	95	5
*Larkin, Stephen, 1B	.299	264	34	79	16	2	4	42	31	44	7
Larson, Brandon, 3B	.285	172	28	49	10	0	12	42	10	51	4
Lawrence, Tony, C	.125	8	0	1	0	0	0	1	1	4	0
Miller, Corky, C	.221	104	20	23	10	0	4	16	11	30	0
Milliard, Ralph, SS	.294	102	19	30	3	1	4	23	20	13	2
Monds, Wonderful, OF	.260	311	48	81	14	2	11	32	17	49	14
Nevers, Tom, SS	.295	380	61	112	23	2	17	65	15	74	3
Owens, Jayhawk, C	.222	153	24	34	6	1	6	21	31	45	3
Presto, Nick, SS	.268	224	34	60	8	0	2	28	38	34	5
Salzano, Jerry, 3B	.327	263	44	86	19	1	4	38	39	38	14
Saunders, Chris, 1B	.315	216	31	68	13	1	7	35	34	42	0
Snusz, Chris, C	.500	6	0	3	1	0	0	2	1	0	0
Stegall, Randy, 2B	.207	29	0	6	0	0	0	1	2	5	0
Williams, Jason, 2B	.319	332	65	106	27	2	7	45	46	40	3

PITCHING	W	L	ERA	G	SV	IP	H	R	ER	BB	SO
*Atchley, Justin	4	9	3.42	17	0	97.1	114	48	37	22	70
Averette, Robert	2	1	5.20	6	0	36.1	42	22	21	19	15
Bell, Rob	3	6	3.13	12	0	72.0	75	30	25	17	68
*Crowell, Jim	10	5	5.10	27	0	148.1	173	98	84	85	80
Donaldson, Bo	5	3	2.98	38	6	51.1	30	18	17	16	67
Etler, Todd	0	0	2.35	14	0	23.0	17	6	6	8	26
Flury, Pat	1	1	2.87	43	15	53.1	36	20	17	31	69

Switch-hitter
* Left-handed
T Player has been with more than one team; listed with last team.
(Players in major leagues are listed with last minor league club.)

PITCHING	W	L	ERA	G	SV	IP	H	R	ER	BB	SO
Glauber, Keith	5	0	1.98	7	0	50.0	42	12	11	8	26
*Haring, Brett	2	1	3.72	7	0	36.1	46	18	15	12	15
Janzen, Marty	1	3	4.94	30	0	54.2	54	32	30	29	41
LeBlanc, Eric	3	3	3.84	15	0	65.2	63	33	28	20	37
MacRae, Scott	8	7	4.42	39	0	128.1	139	76	63	49	81
Mallard, Randi	4	5	6.78	14	0	71.2	92	61	54	45	45
Merrell, Phil	2	2	6.62	7	0	35.1	47	32	26	14	15
Meyer, Jake	2	2	5.96	20	0	22.2	24	17	15	14	16
*Pearsall, J.J.	3	1	5.90	32	0	39.2	40	31	26	28	36
*Priest, Eddie	4	3	3.97	12	0	77.0	99	42	34	14	60
Riedling, John	9	5	3.43	40	5	42.0	41	23	16	20	38
Rose, Ted	2	0	4.24	13	2	17.0	17	8	8	9	23
*Ryan, B.J.	2	1	2.59	35	6	41.2	33	13	12	17	46
Thereneau, Dave	2	0	2.57	3	0	21.0	22	7	6	8	11
*Tolar, Kevin	4	4	4.97	47	1	54.1	61	32	30	45	60

Greenville Braves (Braves) AA

BATTING	AVG	AB	R	H	2B	3B	HR	RBI	BB	SO	SB
Cepeda, Jose, 2B	.276	196	19	54	8	2	1	17	13	15	2
*Glavine, Mike, 1B	.269	305	47	82	24	0	17	52	49	65	0
Goodell, Steve, 3B	.299	338	69	101	25	2	15	58	55	61	8
Helms, Wes, 1B	.301	113	15	34	6	0	8	26	7	34	1
Horn, Jeff, C	.229	166	19	38	6	0	2	27	16	28	0
*Johnson, Adam, OF	.289	394	50	114	27	2	14	72	31	74	1
Lackey, Steve, SS	.292	315	50	92	18	3	4	38	21	55	9
Lunar, Fernando, C	.224	343	33	77	15	1	3	35	12	64	0
#Martinez, Pablo, SS	.237	228	28	54	9	3	1	19	20	41	6
*McNabb, Buck, OF	.323	93	9	30	4	0	0	5	5	18	2
Mortimer, Mark, OF	.233	30	4	7	1	0	0	5	3	7	0
Norris, Dax, 1B	.278	403	59	112	27	0	15	66	41	59	2
#Pendergrass, T., OF	.262	344	60	90	12	3	6	31	37	61	19
Pimentel, Jose, OF	.214	364	55	78	18	1	8	45	24	80	20
*Smith, Demond, OF	.305	416	70	127	20	7	9	59	55	72	31
*Trippy, Joe, OF	.221	131	26	29	5	0	2	15	30	25	6
Williams, Glenn, 2B	.225	204	19	46	11	0	4	15	7	58	1

PITCHING	W	L	ERA	G	SV	IP	H	R	ER	BB	SO
*Beasley, Ray	7	4	4.63	50	3	81.2	84	45	42	26	71
Bullard, Jason	0	1	18.78	5	0	7.2	16	18	16	12	5
*Butler, Adam	1	3	7.65	27	1	42.1	71	44	36	12	29
Carlyle, Ken	1	6	5.93	17	0	71.1	89	60	47	42	33
*Cruz, Charlie	1	0	3.45	11	1	15.2	23	6	6	9	11
Dawley, Joey	5	3	4.03	26	0	91.2	76	54	41	37	89
Dishman, Richard	6	13	4.19	30	1	139.2	146	76	65	58	131
Flach, Jason	1	2	6.63	12	1	36.2	44	29	27	10	15
Forney, Rick	3	3	2.99	12	0	72.1	67	27	24	19	70
Harrison, Tommy	3	7	7.39	16	0	63.1	75	59	52	43	42
Iglesias, Mike	0	3	7.07	4	0	14.0	19	11	11	6	5
Manzano, Adrian	5	2	3.21	42	2	61.2	61	24	22	22	51
Marquis, Jason	3	4	4.58	12	0	55.0	52	33	28	29	35
*Milburn, Adam	1	0	4.74	14	0	19.0	23	10	10	7	10
*Moss, Damian	1	3	8.54	7	0	32.2	50	33	31	21	22
Nelson, Joe	1	1	2.37	25	8	30.1	19	15	8	14	37
Norris, Dax	0	0	0.00	2	0	2.1	1	0	0	3	0
Salamon, John	2	4	8.29	28	1	42.1	42	41	39	42	41
Seelbach, Chris	3	2	3.89	8	0	39.1	31	18	17	19	47
Shumate, Jacob	3	4	4.74	14	0	57.0	43	30	30	61	48
Smoltz, John	0	0	4.50	2	0	4.0	5	2	2	1	7
Steenstra, Kennie	2	1	3.79	8	0	19.0	25	8	8	1	12
Steinmetz, Earl	0	2	6.75	6	0	10.2	13	9	8	16	6
*Trippy, Joe	0	0	14.54	5	0	4.1	10	7	7	3	1
Winkelsas, Joe	4	4	3.75	55	12	62.1	71	32	26	30	38
Yankosky, L.J.	5	8	4.24	20	0	108.1	122	70	51	43	62

Huntsville Stars (Brewers) AA

BATTING	AVG	AB	R	H	2B	3B	HR	RBI	BB	SO	SB
Alfano, Jeff, C	.247	247	20	61	15	0	5	31	35	65	4
Azuaje, Jesus, SS	.281	391	63	110	21	0	10	60	70	26	34
Brito, Jorge, C	.299	67	11	20	2	1	3	7	4	15	0
Cancel, Robinson, C	.251	223	35	56	10	1	5	32	23	38	8
*Dipace, Dan, OF	.115	26	2	3	1	0	0	2	3	9	0
Elliott, Dave, OF	.233	404	69	94	23	0	12	55	59	111	11
Faurot, Adam, PH	.260	50	5	13	2	0	0	7	1	7	1
#Green, Chad, OF	.246	422	56	104	22	3	10	46	46	109	28
#Iapoce, Anthony, OF	.263	133	17	35	7	0	0	5	12	25	2
Jacobsen, Buck, OF	.193	150	20	29	6	1	3	19	20	32	4

Batting leaders by position

CATCHER

Player	Club	Lg.	BA
Hammock, R.	HiD	Cal	.332
Nieves, Wilbert	RCu	Cal	.328
Barajas, Rod	ELP	Tex	.318
T Petrick, Ben	Csp	PCL	.311
Cardona, Javier	JAX	Sou	.309
Flores, Javier	Vis	Cal	.296
T Werth, Jayson	Bow	East	.294
*McKay, Cody	Mid	Tex	.294
Heintz, Chris	W-S	Caro	.293
T Cancel, R.	Lou	Int	.291
Schaeffer, Jon	QC	Mid	.290
Hill, Jason	CR	Mid	.287
T Dewey, Jason	LkE	Cal	.286
T Lecroy, M.	SLk	PCL	.285
T Williams, G.	NO	PCL	.284

FIRST BASE

Player	Club	Lg.	BA
T*Durazo, E.	Tuc	PCL	.404
*Johnson, Nick	Nrw	East	.345
T*Nunnari, T.	Har	East	.344
*Cox, Steve	Dur	Int	.341
#Crespo, Felipe	Fre	PCL	.332
*Wilson, Desi	Tuc	PCL	.323
Lopez, Luis	Syr	Int	.322
*Rivera, Carlos	HIC	SAL	.322
Perez, Eduardo	Mem	PCL	.320
T Burrell, Pat	SWB	Int	.320
Gorr, Robb	SBr	Cal	.319
T Toca, Jorge	Nor	Int	.319
*Ortiz, David	SLk	PCL	.315
*Phillips, J.R.	Csp	PCL	.311
*Giles, Tim	Knx	Sou	.311

Cepeda

Batting leaders by position

(Cont'd from previous page)

SECOND BASE

Player	Club	Lg.	BA
*Urquiola, Carlos	SB	Mid	.362
T Williams, J.	Ind	Int	.339
T Espada, J.	Van	PCL	.336
Otero, William	SJo	Cal	.333
Martinez, Belvani	HiD	Cal	.333
T Medrano, Tony	Oma	PCL	.331
#Hardtke, Jason	Ind	Int	.329
Raabe, Brian	Col	Int	.327
*Kennedy, Adam	Mem	PCL	.327
Giles, Marcus	MYR	Caro	.326
Coquillette, Trace	Ott	Int	.326
Brito, Tilson	Chr	Int	.318
T Meyers, Chad	Iow	PCL	.317
#Miles, Aaron	Mch	Mid	.317
Garcia, Amaury	Cal	PCL	.317

THIRD BASE

Player	Club	Lg.	BA
T*Patterson, J.	Tuc	PCL	.358
T Piatt, Adam	Van	PCL	.340
Robinson, Bo	Wis	Mid	.329
Ramirez, Aramis	Nsh	PCL	.328
T*Washington, R.	Lyn	Caro	.325
T*Lamb, Mike	Ok	PCL	.324
Woods, Ken	Fre	PCL	.324
Gonzalez, Jimmy	SBr	Cal	.316
Seabol, Scott	Grn	SAL	.315
Tatum, Jim	Csp	PCL	.313
Landry, Jacques	Mod	Cal	.311
Menechino, F.	Van	PCL	.309
Ball, Jeff	Van	PCL	.309
Turnquist, Tyler	Mch	Mid	.309

BATTING	AVG	AB	R	H	2B	3B	HR	RBI	BB	SO	SB
*Klimek, Josh, 3B	.239	431	46	103	28	0	14	71	33	78	3
Kominek, Toby, OF	.232	456	56	106	20	3	12	59	52	118	7
Lobaton, Jose, SS	.281	128	23	36	6	0	2	18	13	34	2
#Lopez, Mickey, 2B	.298	315	58	94	16	5	5	40	46	46	31
Macalutas, Jon, 1B	.265	306	50	81	20	1	5	45	38	32	4
*Marrero, Oreste, 1B	.216	37	2	8	3	0	1	7	1	8	0
#Martinez, Greg, OF	.276	98	18	27	3	2	0	6	12	13	8
Mathis, Jared, SS	.225	218	23	49	5	1	2	24	8	32	2
*Pickler, Jeff, 2B	.279	183	20	51	8	1	1	23	15	25	9
*Sollmann, Scott, OF	.314	191	34	60	4	5	1	9	34	31	17
*Williamson, A., 1B	.342	38	5	13	3	0	0	6	7	6	3

PITCHING	W	L	ERA	G	SV	IP	H	R	ER	BB	SO
*Akin, Jay	2	5	4.18	46	0	84.0	93	51	39	31	62
Beck, Greg	10	9	4.45	26	0	151.2	157	79	75	48	93
Chavez, Carlos	0	3	10.64	13	0	22.0	37	27	26	13	12
Converse, Jim	1	1	2.86	16	5	22.0	14	8	7	7	25
D'Amico, Jeff	0	1	36.00	1	0	2.0	6	8	8	2	2
*Dawsey, Jason	1	0	9.00	4	0	18.0	22	18	18	10	8
*Dixon, Tim	0	0	2.75	24	6	39.1	33	16	12	19	43
Eldred, Cal	0	1	7.50	2	0	12.0	13	10	10	3	10
Gordon, Mike	0	1	0.00	7	0	6.1	8	8	0	7	5
Hawkins, Al	8	9	5.33	19	0	99.2	126	71	59	29	56
Helmer, Chad	1	0	8.38	7	0	9.2	15	12	9	9	7
Henderson, Ryan	2	0	0.63	12	6	14.1	12	2	1	6	13
Huntsman, Scott	1	4	3.63	47	5	69.1	72	33	28	25	31
Johnston, Doug	7	11	5.01	21	0	118.2	128	72	66	43	80
*Kelley, Rich	1	3	5.72	25	3	28.1	30	19	18	8	26
*Lee, Derek	8	8	3.86	26	0	140.0	143	70	60	51	77
Levrault, Allen	9	2	3.43	16	0	99.2	77	44	38	33	82
Minor, Blas	0	1	9.39	2	0	7.2	11	12	8	5	6
Nomo, Hideo	1	0	0.00	1	0	7.0	5	0	0	1	7
Paredes, Roberto	2	3	3.96	28	1	52.1	48	26	23	29	35
*Passini, Brian	0	4	3.62	8	0	37.1	33	19	15	19	22
*Priebe, Kevin	0	0	2.57	3	0	7.0	7	2	2	2	4
Smith, Travis	3	2	5.87	7	0	38.1	40	27	25	18	23
Theodile, Robert	3	7	5.75	47	0	92.1	118	71	59	56	60
VanEgmond, Tim	0	1	3.27	3	0	11.0	11	6	4	6	9
*Wunsch, Kelly	4	1	1.95	22	1	50.2	40	13	11	23	35

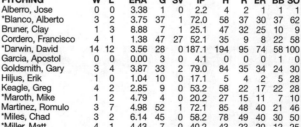

Jacksonville Suns (Tigers) AA

BATTING	AVG	AB	R	H	2B	3B	HR	RBI	BB	SO	SB
Airoso, Kurt, OF	.272	536	95	146	28	6	10	72	89	113	10
*Candelaria, Ben, OF	.269	464	65	125	31	3	18	77	35	93	6
Cardona, Javier, C	.309	418	84	129	31	0	26	92	46	69	4
Freire, Alejandro, 1B	.296	243	45	72	20	0	10	43	23	44	2
*Gillespie, Eric, OF	.306	474	80	145	28	6	19	88	53	89	12
#Ibarra, Jesse, DH	.157	70	9	11	1	0	1	6	10	20	0
Jones, Ryan, 1B	.253	487	66	123	21	3	19	73	50	115	1
*Lemonis, Chris, 2B	.283	265	35	75	16	1	5	38	19	45	1
Lindsey, Rod, OF	.185	27	3	5	1	0	0	2	1	6	0
Lindstrom, David, C	.271	214	30	58	17	1	7	35	24	35	1
Mitchell, Derek, SS	.242	422	56	102	17	1	7	49	53	117	4
#Riley, Marquis, OF	.255	161	30	41	4	0	0	16	30	29	16
Rivera, Mike, C	.174	23	3	4	1	0	2	6	2	5	0
Santana, Pedro, 2B	.279	512	89	143	35	6	5	49	34	98	34
Sasser, Rob, 3B	.283	424	60	120	38	1	7	61	57	101	9
*Wakeland, Chris, OF	.321	212	42	68	16	3	13	36	35	53	6

PITCHING	W	L	ERA	G	SV	IP	H	R	ER	BB	SO
Alberro, Jose	0	0	3.38	1	0	2.2	4	2	1	1	1
*Blanco, Alberto	3	2	3.75	37	1	72.0	58	37	30	37	62
Bruner, Clay	1	3	8.88	7	1	25.1	47	32	25	10	9
Cordero, Francisco	4	1	1.38	47	27	52.1	35	9	8	22	58
*Darwin, David	14	12	3.56	28	0	187.1	194	95	74	58	100
Garcia, Apostol	0	0	0.00	3	0	4.1	0	0	0	1	0
Goldsmith, Gary	3	4	3.87	33	2	79.0	84	35	34	24	30
Hiljus, Erik	1	0	1.04	10	0	17.1	5	4	2	5	28
Keagle, Greg	4	2	2.85	9	0	53.2	58	22	17	22	28
*Maroth, Mike	1	2	4.79	4	0	20.2	27	15	11	7	10
Martinez, Romulo	3	7	4.98	52	1	72.1	85	48	40	21	46
*Miles, Chad	3	2	6.14	45	0	58.2	78	49	40	30	50
*Miller, Matt	4	1	4.43	7	0	40.2	43	23	20	12	25
*Pettyjohn, Adam	9	5	4.69	20	0	126.2	134	75	66	35	92
Romo, Greg	2	2	8.27	8	0	20.2	29	20	19	7	15
Santos, Victor	12	6	3.49	28	0	173.0	150	86	67	58	146
Smith, Keilan	1	2	6.61	19	0	31.1	35	25	23	23	24

PITCHING	W	L	ERA	G	SV	IP	H	R	ER	BB	SO
Snyder, Bill	1	0	2.50	14	2	18.0	6	6	5	5	17
Swartzbaugh, Dave	0	4	10.25	6	0	26.1	36	31	30	12	22
Villafuerte, Brandon	0	2	1.88	15	5	24.0	17	6	5	12	20
Weaver, Jeff	0	0	3.00	1	0	6.0	5	2	2	0	6
*Webb, Alan	9	9	4.95	26	0	140.0	140	88	77	64	88

Knoxville Smokies (Blue Jays) AA

BATTING	AVG	AB	R	H	2B	3B	HR	RBI	BB	SO	SB
Abernathy, Brent, 2B	.291	577	108	168	42	1	13	62	55	47	34
*Butler, Rob, OF	.337	258	48	87	13	6	2	36	19	21	4
Chiaffredo, Paul, C	.077	39	3	3	1	0	1	3	0	10	0
*Cripps, Bobby, DH	.172	87	13	15	6	0	2	9	6	37	0
Freel, Ryan, OF	.283	46	9	13	5	1	1	9	8	4	4
*Giles, Tim, 1B	.311	505	76	157	24	2	18	114	56	93	0
Gomez, Rudy, SS	.281	427	74	120	26	3	17	92	75	63	10
Hayes, Chris, 3B	.287	129	25	37	11	1	2	16	18	29	4
*Langaigne, S., OF	.244	123	18	30	4	1	0	10	10	25	3
Lawrence, Joe, 3B	.264	250	52	66	16	2	7	24	56	48	7
Loyd, Brian, C	.280	364	53	102	18	1	11	65	46	57	9
*Melhuse, Adam, OF	.294	374	79	110	25	0	19	69	108	76	5
Probst, Alan, C	.212	66	5	14	3	0	1	7	5	23	0
Rupp, Chad, OF	.257	241	49	62	19	2	16	44	44	73	7
Schifano, Tony, OF	.272	92	12	25	4	1	0	15	3	15	5
Solano, Fausto, SS	.305	348	62	106	18	0	14	61	57	54	11
Strange, Mike, DH	.093	54	10	5	0	0	0	4	26	24	1
Stromsborg, Ryan, OF	.249	377	54	94	17	3	9	45	28	91	5
Thompson, Andy, OF	.244	254	56	62	16	3	15	53	34	55	7
Wells, Vernon, OF	.340	106	18	36	6	2	3	17	12	15	6

PITCHING	W	L	ERA	G	SV	IP	H	R	ER	BB	SO
*Andrews, Clayton	10	8	3.93	25	0	132.2	143	85	58	69	93
*Arroyo, Luis	0	0	1.35	5	1	6.2	2	1	1	0	7
*Bale, John	2	2	3.75	33	1	62.1	64	32	26	16	91
Bleazard, David	5	3	3.22	15	0	86.2	81	36	31	34	49
Bradford, Josh	5	4	5.31	34	2	105.0	109	65	62	53	83
Delgado, Ernie	4	1	3.51	31	0	51.1	49	27	20	23	33
Glover, Gary	8	2	3.56	13	0	86.0	70	39	34	27	77
Harris, D.J.	2	4	7.05	25	0	60.0	73	50	47	31	36
Hartshorn, Ty	4	1	4.79	10	0	47.0	60	32	25	15	24
*Hendrickson, Mark	2	7	6.63	12	0	55.2	73	46	41	21	39
Hibbard, Billy	0	0	8.10	3	0	3.1	7	3	3	1	0
*Lowe, Benny	4	6	5.14	58	3	68.1	68	44	39	40	70
Mann, Jim	1	2	0.93	6	0	9.2	6	2	1	1	12
McClellan, Sean	1	0	3.48	14	1	20.2	18	8	8	11	24
Rivette, Scott	4	7	3.81	56	10	78.0	85	40	33	29	74
Schaffer, Trevor	1	3	5.67	38	1	54.0	69	43	34	38	23
Smith, Brian	1	2	5.14	29	13	35.0	42	25	20	6	27
Sneed, John	3	1	5.08	6	0	28.1	33	17	16	21	28
Stevenson, Jason	4	7	6.24	21	0	92.1	99	69	64	57	73
Yennaco, Jay	3	4	6.60	8	0	43.2	52	34	32	17	30

Mobile Baybears (Padres) AA

BATTING	AVG	AB	R	H	2B	3B	HR	RBI	BB	SO	SB
*Ahrendt, Jay, C	.200	15	2	3	1	0	0	2	4	8	0
#Balfe, Ryan, 3B	.280	400	69	112	31	3	11	70	50	95	0
*Curl, John, OF	.285	474	79	135	30	3	22	76	77	137	9
Eberwein, Kevin, 3B	.171	35	5	6	1	0	1	2	3	16	0
*Faggett, Ethan, OF	.243	527	82	128	18	11	6	43	53	126	63
Gonzalez, Jimmy, C	.265	68	15	18	3	0	2	8	7	16	0
Gonzalez, W., C	.338	225	38	76	16	2	10	49	29	28	0
Johnson, A.J., OF	.243	136	12	33	7	0	4	18	6	35	1
*Jorgensen, Randy, 1B	.321	252	41	81	15	0	7	54	36	46	2
Kent, Robbie, 2B	.271	336	48	91	17	3	8	56	44	71	2
Lidle, Kevin, C	.222	180	23	40	8	0	6	26	30	40	1
Luzinski, Ryan, C	.279	233	28	65	20	0	2	30	37	58	1
*McClure, Brian, 2B	.207	169	17	35	10	3	1	27	17	34	0
*Morenz, Shea, DH	.263	57	6	15	5	0	0	7	4	27	1
#Nicholson, Kevin, SS	.288	489	84	141	38	3	13	81	46	92	16
*Paciorek, Pete, 1B	.221	226	38	50	9	2	4	17	38	60	2
#Prieto, Rick, OF	.287	359	61	103	14	4	6	43	57	55	28
Schmidt, Bryan, 2B	.188	32	7	6	1	0	0	3	5	8	0
#Thrower, Jake, 2B	.242	149	15	36	9	2	3	26	21	26	3
Tucci, Pete, OF	.250	312	45	78	15	0	11	35	26	83	11

PITCHING	W	L	ERA	G	SV	IP	H	R	ER	BB	SO
*Agosto, Stevenson	3	3	5.89	40	0	81.0	81	61	53	59	59
Anderson, Bill	0	0	7.00	4	0	18.0	20	14	14	13	19

Batting leaders by position

(Cont'd from previous page)

SHORTSTOP

Player	Club	Lg.	BA
#Jimenez, D.	Col	Int	.327
T#Furcal, Rafael	MYR	Caro	.322
Lugo, Julio	JCK	Tex	.319
T Wilson, Jack	POT	Caro	.319
*Gallo, Ismael	SBr	Cal	.314
#Izturis, Cesar	Dun	FSL	.308
T McDonald, J.	Buf	Int	.307
#Cintron, Alex	HiD	Cal	.307
#Punto, Nick	Clr	FSL	.305
T Dawkins, T.	Cht	Sou	.300
#Lara, Eddie	Vis	Cal	.299
T Solano, Fausto	Knx	Sou	.298
Nevers, Tom	Cht	Sou	.295
Prieto, Alejandro	Wch	Tex	.294

OUTFIELD

Player	Club	Lg.	BA
Quinn, Mark	Oma	PCL	.360
T#DaVanon, Jeff	Edm	PCL	.338
T*Brown, R.	Iow	PCL	.338
T*Cummings, M.	SLk	PCL	.336
Gonzalez, Raul	Tre	East	.335
T*Sollmann, S.	Hnt	Sou	.334
T Wells, Vernon	Syr	Int	.334
Murray, Calvin	Fre	PCL	.334
*Cust, Jack	HiD	Cal	.334
T*Brown, Dee	Wch	Tex	.331
#Bradley, Milton	Har	East	.329
Clark, Brady	Cht	Sou	.326
#Mota, Tony	SAn	Tex	.325

407

| Switch-hitter
* | Left-handed
T | Player has been with more than one team; listed with last team.
(Players in major leagues are listed with last minor league club.)

Error leaders by position

CATCHER

Player	Club	Lg.	E
Taveras, Luis	Chr	FSL	22
T Lomasney, S.	Tre	East	21
Smith, Casey	Kin	Caro	20
Valera, Yohanny	Bng	East	18
Hammock, R.	HiD	Cal	18
Miller, Corky	Cht	Sou	17
Loyd, Brian	Knx	Sou	17
Heintz, Chris	WS	Caro	16
Valencia, Victor	Nrw	East	16
Ortiz, Hector	Alb	PCL	16
Ross, David	VB	FSL	16
Sandusky, Scott	Jup	FSL	16
Priess, Matthew	Shv	TEX	16

FIRST BASE

Player	Club	Lg.	E
*Stenson, Dernell	Paw	Int	34
T Kirby, Scott	Stk	Cal	34
*Sears, Todd	Sal	Caro	26
T*Hinske, Eric	Iow	PCL	23
#Burns, Pat	SLu	FSL	22
Vaughn, Clint	CLN	Mid	21
*Johnson, Nick	Nrw	East	20
*Ortiz, David	SLk	PCL	20
*Wilson, Desi	Tuc	PCL	20
*Delgado, Ariel	CR	Mid	18
*Zapp, A.J.	Mac	SAL	18
*Choi, Hee	Lan	Mid	18
*Leach, Nick	VB	FSL	18
Flaherty, Tim	SJo	Cal	18

PITCHING	W	L	ERA	G	SV	IP	H	R	ER	BB	SO
Doughty, Brian	8	10	4.77	36	1	137.2	161	85	73	29	69
*Drumheller, Al	5	2	4.33	12	0	68.2	78	40	33	29	55
Estes, Eric	0	1	10.90	8	0	17.1	33	22	21	9	4
Giron, Isabel	11	12	5.46	28	0	158.1	168	108	96	54	126
Guzman, Domingo	1	2	5.47	41	6	51.0	60	33	31	25	38
*Hart, Len	0	0	3.38	2	0	2.2	4	1	1	2	4
Herndon, Junior	10	9	4.69	26	0	163.0	172	96	85	52	87
Hite, Kevin	2	4	4.32	51	15	58.1	71	30	28	17	52
Kolb, Brandon	0	2	0.79	7	2	11.1	8	4	1	4	14
Lopez, Rodrigo	10	8	4.41	28	0	169.1	187	91	83	58	138
*Maurer, Dave	4	4	3.63	54	3	72.0	59	30	29	26	59
Middlebrook, Jason	4	6	8.06	13	0	63.2	78	59	57	30	38
Ricken, Ray	7	7	5.37	20	0	110.2	122	73	66	55	67
Sak, Jim	4	1	1.69	18	2	26.2	15	11	5	15	37
Serrano, Wascar	2	3	5.53	7	0	42.1	48	27	26	17	29
Skrmetta, Matt	1	3	6.27	25	1	37.1	42	28	26	24	45
Szymborski, Tom	1	0	5.40	6	0	6.2	10	9	4	5	3
Walters, Brett	0	1	5.40	9	0	13.1	13	8	8	9	12

Orlando Rays (Devil Rays) AA

BATTING	AVG	AB	R	H	2B	3B	HR	RBI	BB	SO	SB
#Badeaux, Brooks, 2B	.500	2	1	1	0	0	1	1	0	0	0
Becker, Brian, 1B	.252	480	67	121	24	1	18	74	42	89	0
Bucceri, Jim, OF	.311	161	18	50	8	1	1	16	15	24	5
Cairo, Miguel, 2B	.385	13	1	5	2	0	0	1	0	1	0
Carr, Dustin, 2B	.302	461	76	139	22	3	6	63	70	62	7
*Colina, Roberto, DH	.273	315	45	86	20	1	6	53	37	47	0
Cruz, Luis, 2B	.281	32	2	9	2	0	0	1	1	6	0
De Los Santos, E., SS	.275	448	53	123	24	4	3	49	29	69	3
Fraraccio, Dan, OF	.287	254	48	73	19	3	7	28	25	43	1
#Garcia, Neil, O	.284	95	13	27	6	0	1	11	10	16	0
Hall, Toby, C	.254	173	20	44	7	0	9	34	4	10	1
Hawkins, Kraig, OF	.301	296	41	89	10	1	0	27	38	45	19
*Huff, Aubrey, 3B	.301	491	85	148	40	3	22	78	64	77	2
*Levis, Jesse, C	.396	48	6	19	7	0	1	11	6	4	0
Long, Ryan, OF	.233	30	2	7	1	0	0	4	1	3	0
Mosquera, Julio, C	.305	259	36	79	13	1	4	37	15	40	1
Pigott, Anthony, OF	.250	8	0	2	1	0	0	0	0	2	0
*Pomierski, Joe, OF	.261	188	31	49	10	3	9	33	22	44	1
Quatraro, Matt, C	.250	4	1	1	0	0	1	2	0	2	0
*Sanchez, Alex, OF	.254	500	68	127	12	4	2	29	26	88	48
*Wilcox, Luke, OF	.270	333	60	90	24	1	20	64	35	54	3
Wilson, Tom, C	.288	104	12	30	2	0	7	23	18	34	0

PITCHING	W	L	ERA	G	SV	IP	H	R	ER	BB	SO
Aquino, Julio	0	0	18.47	5	0	6.1	18	15	13	0	4
*Belitz, Todd	9	9	5.77	28	0	160.2	169	114	103	65	118
*Bowers, Cedrick	6	9	5.98	27	0	125.0	125	94	83	76	138
Brown, Elliot	0	2	7.71	10	0	18.2	25	18	16	12	12
Callaway, Mickey	1	1	4.50	2	0	10.0	15	6	5	2	7
Daniels, John	3	2	1.90	38	14	52.0	33	14	11	15	40
*Enders, Trevor	8	2	3.30	60	1	95.1	86	37	35	33	63
Fraraccio, Dan	0	0	9.00	2	0	2.0	4	2	2	0	1
Gardner, Lee	0	0	9.00	1	0	2.0	3	2	2	1	1
Harper, Travis	6	3	5.38	14	0	72.0	73	45	43	26	68
Hernandez, Santos	5	4	3.70	35	5	56.0	43	31	23	15	47
*Kaufman, John	1	3	8.83	21	0	35.2	54	39	35	14	22
LeRoy, John	0	0	4.50	4	0	6.0	7	3	3	5	5
Manon, Julio	3	3	5.10	30	0	67.0	80	43	38	23	53
*Morris, James	0	1	1.80	3	1	5.0	6	1	1	1	6
Nunez, Maximo	0	2	3.46	26	9	26.0	23	11	10	17	19
Ortega, Pablo	8	10	3.87	22	0	130.1	147	77	56	47	74
Pujals, Denis	5	3	3.86	42	0	72.1	82	35	31	19	39
Reyes, Eddy	1	3	4.08	18	2	28.2	31	16	13	11	25
Rupe, Ryan	2	2	2.73	5	0	26.1	18	13	8	6	22
*Seay, Bobby	1	2	7.94	6	0	17.0	22	15	15	15	16
Strong, Joe	1	4	5.68	11	0	38.0	40	24	24	18	34
Valdes, Marc	0	1	5.87	2	0	7.2	7	5	5	2	5
Wheeler, Dan	3	0	3.26	9	0	58.0	56	27	21	8	53
Zambrano, Victor	7	2	4.59	40	1	82.1	92	55	42	38	81

West Tenn Diamond Jaxx (Cubs) AA

BATTING	AVG	AB	R	H	2B	3B	HR	RBI	BB	SO	SB
Almanzar, Richard, 2B	.305	151	27	46	7	0	2	16	18	19	13
*Bowers, Brent, OF	.160	100	10	16	4	0	2	9	11	16	4
*Brock, Tarrik, OF	.233	407	69	95	20	5	8	32	72	127	16

Switch-hitter
* Left-handed
T Player has been with more than one team; listed with last team.
(Players in major leagues are listed with last minor league club.)

BATTING	AVG	AB	R	H	2B	3B	HR	RBI	BB	SO	SB
*Brown, Roosevelt, OF	.296	125	12	37	12	0	3	12	14	29	6
Encarnacion, Angelo, C	.257	101	11	26	6	1	1	10	4	12	2
Font, Franklin, 2B	.344	96	14	33	2	1	1	17	8	14	4
Gazarek, Marty, OF	.297	128	16	38	9	1	6	27	4	7	2
*Jennings, Robin, OF	.321	53	11	17	3	0	5	17	5	7	1
King, Brad, C	.228	232	29	53	10	0	0	25	38	34	2
King, Brett, SS	.218	142	27	31	6	0	3	13	39	49	7
Manning, Nate, 3B	.222	27	0	6	2	0	0	5	2	8	1
Meyers, Chad, 2B	.290	238	45	69	19	2	3	29	26	40	22
*Micucci, Mike, C	.169	124	7	21	1	0	0	7	7	32	1
Molina, Jose, C	.171	35	2	6	3	0	0	5	2	14	0
#Nelson, Bry, 3B	.268	471	66	126	24	5	16	78	42	52	10
Polanco, Enohel, SS	.240	354	44	85	21	5	3	30	20	89	12
#Rennhack, Mike, OF	.254	189	29	48	11	0	5	21	34	46	4
Rivers, Jonathan, OF	.182	88	10	16	3	0	1	6	8	20	5
Speed, Dorian, OF	.267	415	70	111	21	8	14	57	27	106	22
Vieira, Scott, OF	.292	455	63	133	44	4	10	58	53	126	10
Walker, Ron, 3B	.219	302	42	66	20	1	9	42	39	86	2
Zuleta, Julio, 1B	.295	482	75	142	37	4	21	97	35	122	4

PITCHING	W	L	ERA	G	SV	IP	H	R	ER	BB	SO
Adams, Terry	0	0	16.88	2	0	2.2	5	6	5	2	2
Cole, Victor	3	1	3.91	17	0	23.0	21	11	10	18	17
*Downs, Scott	8	1	1.35	13	0	80.0	56	13	12	28	101
Duncan, Courtney	1	7	7.13	11	0	41.2	44	42	33	42	42
Gissell, Chris	3	8	5.99	20	0	97.2	121	76	65	62	57
Gonzalez, Jeremi	0	0	1.74	3	0	10.1	7	2	2	9	12
Hernandez, Elvin	9	9	4.94	29	1	151.1	174	100	83	50	98
Manning, David	8	5	3.94	23	0	123.1	113	59	54	51	78
Meyers, Mike	4	0	1.09	5	0	33.0	21	5	4	10	51
Negrette, Richard	1	0	5.40	3	0	3.1	3	2	2	2	2
Newman, Eric	5	3	3.20	58	8	84.1	61	37	30	49	90
*Norton, Phillip	7	4	2.39	14	0	86.2	72	32	23	42	81
Piersoll, Chris	0	0	0.63	8	1	14.1	12	1	1	3	14
Rain, Steve	3	1	1.59	40	24	45.1	32	9	8	16	55
Ricketts, Chad	6	4	3.09	57	8	67.0	55	25	23	21	80
Ryan, Jason	5	0	1.41	8	0	44.2	29	12	7	15	53
*Schutz, Carl	3	1	4.38	40	1	51.1	54	30	25	30	46
*Smith, Dan	5	3	4.22	56	2	74.2	70	38	35	31	78
Yoder, Jeff	10	5	3.08	29	0	134.1	115	54	46	70	109
*Young, Danny	3	5	3.28	27	0	60.1	48	25	22	38	67

Texas League

Arkansas Travelers (Cardinals) AA

BATTING	AVG	AB	R	H	2B	3B	HR	RBI	BB	SO	SB
*Ametller, Jesus, 2B	.307	397	53	122	26	2	10	53	5	21	2
Butler, Brent, SS	.269	528	68	142	21	1	13	54	26	47	0
*Deck, Billy, 1B	.061	33	1	2	1	0	0	0	1	16	0
Eckelman, Alex, 3B	.241	116	5	28	4	3	1	13	5	20	0
Farley, Cordell, OF	.259	421	43	109	16	8	8	41	19	97	24
Feramisco, Derek, OF	.182	121	10	22	5	0	2	9	19	27	1
Garcia, Ossie, PH	.125	8	0	1	0	0	0	1	1	2	0
Hardge, Mike, OF	.227	141	15	32	3	1	5	11	25	43	3
Hogan, Todd, OF	.200	280	36	56	7	6	4	21	21	68	8
Kleiner, Stacy, C	.221	235	23	52	8	2	2	16	24	60	2
Leon, Jose, 3B	.233	335	37	78	17	0	18	54	25	114	3
Martine, Chris, C	.150	40	3	6	1	0	0	1	2	12	0
McDonald, Keith, C	.307	163	21	50	10	0	2	14	15	35	1
*Munoz, Juan, OF	.667	3	1	2	0	0	0	0	0	0	0
Ortega, Bill, OF	.377	69	10	26	9	0	2	10	10	9	0
*Richard, Chris, 1B	.294	442	78	130	26	3	29	94	43	75	7
Saturria, Luis, OF	.244	484	66	118	30	4	16	61	35	134	16
*Schmidt, Dave, C	.221	113	6	25	4	0	3	15	11	34	1
#Woolf, Jason, SS	.272	320	46	87	18	4	8	15	28	86	11

PITCHING	W	L	ERA	G	SV	IP	H	R	ER	BB	SO
Ambrose, John	4	12	4.73	34	9	106.2	108	65	56	68	78
*Ankiel, Rick	6	0	0.91	8	0	49.1	25	6	5	16	75
Avrard, Corey	1	1	3.12	25	6	26.0	15	12	9	14	31
Benes, Adam	1	1	5.36	28	0	40.1	51	30	24	15	19
Benes, Alan	0	0	6.23	2	0	4.1	6	3	3	1	0
*Brunette, Justin	1	2	1.96	18	0	18.1	21	12	4	7	23
Crafton, Kevin	7	2	7.58	42	2	46.1	57	41	39	16	41
Dewitt, Matt	9	8	4.43	26	0	148.1	153	87	73	59	107
*Geis, John	2	5	6.83	45	0	55.1	65	44	42	29	29

Error leaders by position

(Cont'd from previous page)

SECOND BASE

Player	CLUB	Lg.	E
Fajardo, A.	Pie	SAL	47
German, Esteban	Mod	Cal	38
Myers, Tootie	CF	SAL	38
#Hill, Steve	Bak	Cal	37
T Espada, Josue	Van	PCL	36
*Ryan, Mike	FtM	FSL	35
#Santos, Angel	Aug	SAL	34
Bush, Ron	WM	Mid	33
Martinez, Belvani	HiD	Cal	33
T Benefield, Brian	AKR	East	32
Nunez, Jorge	HAG	SAL	32
#Castro, Jose	Mid	Tex	31
Bocachica, H.	SAn	Tex	31
T#Cesar, Dionys	Vis	Cal	28
*Terrell, Jeff	Clr	FSL	28

THIRD BASE

Player	Club	Lg.	E
*Allen, Luke	SAn	Tex	53
Ramirez, Aramis	Nsh	PCL	42
Santos, Jose	KnC	Mid	40
Collier, Lamonte	Clr	FSL	39
*LaForest, Pete	CSC	SAL	37
Holliday, Matt	Ash	SAL	37
Sandberg, Jared	StP	FSL	37
Deardorff, Jeff	Stk	Cal	36
#Leon, Donny	Nrw	East	35
T Sasser, Rob	Jax	Sou	35
#Cameron, Troy	Mac	SAL	35
Ensberg, Morgan	Kis	FSL	35
Christensen, M.	CR	Mid	34
Villalobos, Carlos	NO	PCL	34

Switch-hitter
* Left-handed
T Player has been with more than one team; listed with last team.
(Players in major leagues are listed with last minor league club.)

Error leaders by position

(Cont'd from previous page)

SHORTSTOP

Player	Club	Lg.	E
T Suarez, Luis	WS	Caro	52
Rowan, Chris	Stk	Cal	45
#Figgins, Chone	Sal	Caro	45
#Caceres, Wilmy	CLN	Mid	42
Bautista, Juan	Tul	Tex	41
T Lackey, Steve	GRV	Sou	41
Cosme, C.	Mod	Cal	40
#Soler, Ramon	CSC	SAL	40
T#Dellaero, J.	Brm	Sou	39
Jimenez, Carlos	WM	Mid	39
Calderon, Henry	CWV	SAL	39
Rivas, Luis	NB	East	39
De Los Santos, E.	Orl	Sou	39
Uribe, Juan	Ash	SAL	38

OUTFIELD

Player	Club	Lg.	E
T Sosa, Juan	Csp	PCL	25
Peeples, Mike	Dun	FSL	22
Tyler, Josh	Shv	Tex	21
German, Franklin	Lan	Mid	21
T#Metzler, Rod	Wch	Tex	20
T Owens, Jeremy	RCu	Cal	18
Pimentel, Jose	Gvl	Sou	16
Byington, Jimmie	Oma	PCL	15
T Ramirez, Dan	Chr	Int	15
*Foster, Quincy	BC	FSL	15
Daedelow, Craig	Fre	Caro	14
#Nunez, A.	HiD	Cal	14
T*Sanchez, Alex	Dur	Int	14

Jackson (continued tables on right)

PITCHING	W	L	ERA	G	SV	IP	H	R	ER	BB	SO
Hardge, Mike	0	0	22.50	3	0	2.0	7	5	5	2	3
Hutchinson, Chad	7	11	4.72	25	0	141.0	127	79	74	85	150
Karnuth, Jason	7	11	5.22	26	0	160.1	175	105	93	55	71
*Matthews, Mike	2	0	0.00	2	0	12.0	3	0	0	1	10
Nussbeck, Mark	0	1	6.17	2	0	11.2	12	8	8	9	11
Opipari, Mario	1	0	3.51	20	0	25.2	30	11	10	11	16
*Painter, Lance	0	0	0.00	1	0	2.0	1	0	0	0	4
Reed, Steve	4	8	5.42	36	0	81.1	87	59	49	28	45
*Rodriguez, Jose	1	2	3.25	30	0	36.0	38	16	13	25	30
Stechschulte, Gene	2	6	3.40	39	19	42.1	41	26	16	20	41
Stephenson, Garrett	0	0	3.38	1	0	5.1	8	3	2	1	2
Weibl, Clint	4	9	4.66	28	0	110.0	121	59	57	49	75
Woodward, Finley	0	2	4.94	5	0	27.1	36	19	15	10	15

El Paso Diablos (Diamondbacks) AA

BATTING	AVG	AB	R	H	2B	3B	HR	RBI	BB	SO	SB
Barajas, Rod, C	.318	510	77	162	41	2	14	95	24	73	2
Bautista, Juan, 2B	.000	3	0	0	0	0	0	0	0	2	0
Brock, J.J., 2B	.191	136	13	26	4	2	0	8	4	26	0
*Calloway, Ronald, OF	.219	32	4	7	0	0	0	1	7	7	1
Clark, Kevin, DH	.298	373	44	111	24	3	8	64	21	75	0
Coolbaugh, Scott, 3B	.279	61	12	17	3	0	3	17	13	9	1
*Durazo, Erubiel, 1B	.403	226	53	91	18	3	14	55	44	37	2
Gann, Jamie, OF	.262	443	69	116	24	6	9	56	32	141	7
Hartman, Ron, 3B	.195	82	6	16	3	1	0	7	5	8	0
*Herrick, Jason, OF	.301	173	23	52	18	1	6	20	14	45	2
Johnson, Keith, 2B	.300	70	17	21	10	1	3	15	4	17	0
Koeyers, Ramsey, C	.208	77	6	16	9	0	1	10	4	20	0
*Maddox, Garry, OF	.295	492	80	145	35	9	15	75	31	106	22
#Martin, Jared, 2B	.258	62	9	16	4	0	1	5	4	13	0
Matos, Julius, SS	.280	425	54	119	17	5	5	41	13	37	5
McKinnon, Sandy, OF	.250	12	1	3	0	0	0	2	0	2	0
Neubart, Adam, OF	.209	43	7	9	3	0	1	4	5	14	0
Owens, Ryan, 3B	.319	113	11	36	5	1	1	18	8	36	1
*Patterson, Jarrod, 3B	.382	249	63	95	27	3	8	51	51	45	3
*Rexrode, Jackie, 2B	.319	144	30	46	7	2	2	11	29	16	7
Rios, Eduardo, 2B	.283	60	8	17	3	0	0	10	4	6	0
Sandoval, Jhensy, OF	.222	126	10	28	6	1	1	23	7	42	1
*Sell, Chip, OF	.307	329	50	101	16	1	8	35	20	66	19
Spivey, Junior, 2B	.293	164	40	48	10	4	3	19	36	27	14
*Van Rossum, C., OF	.280	75	11	21	5	0	3	9	8	21	1
White, Walt, SS	.120	50	4	6	3	0	0	1	2	13	0
*Wolff, Mike, 1B	.226	155	14	35	8	1	1	17	11	23	0

PITCHING	W	L	ERA	G	SV	IP	H	R	ER	BB	SO
Andrews, Jeff	3	8	5.30	35	7	73.0	87	47	43	24	40
*Bierbrodt, Nick	5	6	4.62	14	0	76.0	78	45	39	37	55
*Burgus, Travis	1	1	4.33	17	2	27.0	26	14	13	13	32
Crews, Jason	3	4	5.66	35	0	55.2	73	47	35	23	30
*Dace, Derek	2	2	5.19	40	0	52.0	58	33	30	23	34
Jacob, Russell	0	0	6.75	3	0	2.2	5	4	2	2	3
*Jensen, Jason	0	1	8.49	4	0	11.2	20	11	11	9	8
Kermode, Al	4	4	3.01	12	0	71.2	68	31	24	12	56
Kim, Byung-Hyun	2	0	2.11	10	0	21.1	6	5	5	9	32
*Knott, Eric	7	11	4.57	27	0	161.1	198	95	82	42	83
Mayo, Blake	3	3	5.68	56	4	76.0	104	56	48	33	49
*McCutcheon, Mike	1	1	6.23	3	0	8.2	7	8	6	9	8
Miadich, Bart	0	2	8.10	12	1	20.0	37	22	18	7	16
*Norris, Ben	10	6	4.16	20	0	119.0	132	61	55	53	87
Patterson, John	8	6	4.77	18	0	100.0	98	61	53	42	117
Penny, Brad	2	7	4.80	17	0	90.0	109	56	48	25	100
Peters, Don	3	3	5.71	32	4	41.0	57	36	26	16	29
*Randolph, Steve	2	2	2.64	8	0	44.1	39	14	13	23	38
Sabel, Erik	0	1	6.30	8	1	10.0	16	9	7	4	7
Sanchez, Martin	4	4	3.90	42	6	97.0	95	57	42	41	73
Schroeffel, Scott	5	4	6.72	41	2	64.1	75	55	48	34	52
Ward, Jeremy	1	1	2.45	19	7	25.2	18	7	7	9	26

Jackson Generals (Astros) AA

BATTING	AVG	AB	R	H	2B	3B	HR	RBI	BB	SO	SB
Alexander, Chad, OF	.309	317	42	98	27	3	9	44	34	58	9
Barr, Tucker, C	.252	107	8	27	0	0	5	15	12	20	0
Bearden, Doug, SS	.181	83	7	15	3	0	0	3	2	24	0
Betzsold, James, OF	.238	126	30	30	6	1	6	17	22	35	4
*Burns, Kevin, 1B	.281	352	55	99	21	2	12	58	42	74	6
Cole, Eric, OF	.167	54	4	9	1	0	2	8	1	11	0

Bottom legend

Switch-hitter
* Left-handed
T Player has been with more than one team; listed with last team.
(Players in major leagues are listed with last minor league club.)

BATTING	AVG	AB	R	H	2B	3B	HR	RBI	BB	SO	SB
Dallimore, Brian, 2B	.267	251	38	67	13	1	5	19	16	44	13
Duffy, Jim, OF	.133	60	5	8	0	0	0	2	4	15	0
Ginter, Keith, 2B	.382	34	9	13	1	0	1	6	4	6	0
Gutierrez, Ricky, SS	.333	12	4	4	1	0	0	1	4	3	0
*Howell, Jack, 1B	.375	8	2	3	1	0	2	3	0	2	0
Johnson, A.J., OF	.241	187	21	45	7	0	4	16	9	38	4
Johnson, J.J., OF	.252	437	57	110	28	2	18	69	47	119	11
Johnson, Ric, OF	.245	323	28	79	19	1	1	27	13	44	5
Lopez, Pedro, C	.184	255	20	47	11	0	6	28	12	52	1
Lugo, Julio, SS	.319	445	77	142	24	5	10	42	44	53	25
Miller, Ryan, PH	.147	75	5	11	0	1	0	4	2	11	5
Perez, Jhonny, 2B	.250	276	37	69	16	4	4	25	19	44	7
#Rose, Mike, C	.244	45	8	11	0	0	3	8	13	10	0
Samboy, Nelson, OF	.300	170	20	51	9	0	0	14	11	14	6
Sanchez, Victor, 1B	.251	407	61	102	18	0	17	68	40	93	11
Truby, Chris, 3B	.282	465	78	131	21	3	28	87	36	88	20

PITCHING	W	L	ERA	G	SV	IP	H	R	ER	BB	SO
Bennett, Erik	0	3	4.13	20	1	28.1	23	14	13	12	32
*Braswell, Bryan	9	10	4.52	28	0	171.1	180	104	86	54	131
Creek, Ryan	4	3	4.57	8	0	43.1	47	25	22	25	32
*Franklin, Wayne	3	1	1.61	46	0	50.1	31	11	9	16	40
Green, Jason	3	3	3.40	33	10	42.1	41	20	16	20	50
Henry, Doug	0	1	4.50	2	0	2.0	2	1	1	1	3
Hodges, Kevin	1	4	2.94	8	0	49.0	48	22	16	16	21
Ireland, Eric	0	1	4.30	3	0	14.2	19	9	7	2	15
Kester, Tim	8	5	3.72	43	1	75.0	91	43	31	19	51
McKnight, Tony	9	9	2.75	24	0	160.1	134	60	49	44	118
*Mounce, Tony	5	2	3.69	31	0	68.1	64	33	28	30	80
Narcisse, Tyrone	0	2	7.30	10	0	12.1	14	12	10	7	8
O'Malley, Paul	1	3	5.60	36	0	70.2	75	53	44	48	65
Persails, Mark	1	0	1.37	12	0	19.2	15	5	3	10	20
*Robertson, Jeriome	15	7	3.06	28	0	191.0	184	81	65	45	133
*Root, Derek	7	16	4.65	28	0	156.2	167	103	81	79	129
Wallace, Kent	0	1	2.30	13	0	15.2	13	4	4	6	16
Walter, Mike	2	1	4.81	34	4	48.2	35	32	26	31	44

Midland RockHounds (Athletics) AA

BATTING	AVG	AB	R	H	2B	3B	HR	RBI	BB	SO	SB
#Bellhorn, Mark, 2B	.298	57	12	17	3	0	2	8	11	13	1
Berroa, Angel, SS	.059	17	3	1	1	0	0	0	0	2	0
*Bowles, Justin, OF	.286	489	73	140	27	8	20	73	44	122	10
Byrnes, Eric, OF	.238	164	25	39	14	0	1	22	17	32	6
#Castro, Jose, 2B	.261	368	69	96	17	3	7	42	38	90	21
#Cesar, Dionys, 2B	.190	105	15	20	4	3	3	15	18	28	1
Chirinos, German, IF	.214	14	1	3	1	0	0	0	3	3	1
#DaVanon, Jeff, OF	.342	374	87	128	29	11	11	60	53	68	18
Encarnacion, Mario, OF	.309	353	69	109	21	4	18	71	47	86	9
Espada, Josue, SS	.338	435	85	147	15	2	6	51	62	51	22
Garland, Tim, OF	.289	463	84	134	23	10	6	55	29	58	22
Garrison, Webster, 1B	.274	124	17	34	9	0	4	21	16	15	1
Marcinczyk, T.R., 1B	.279	477	87	133	39	1	23	111	62	109	2
*McKay, Cody, C	.294	333	59	98	21	1	6	43	38	40	1
Morales, Willie, C	.280	343	43	96	27	0	16	71	24	54	2
Piatt, Adam, 3B	.345	476	128	164	48	3	39	135	93	101	7
Skeels, David, C	.273	66	6	18	5	0	1	12	6	15	2
Stucknschneider, E., OF	.163	92	17	15	4	2	0	16	17	22	6
*Vaz, Roberto, OF	.406	32	4	13	3	0	1	12	8	5	0

PITCHING	W	L	ERA	G	SV	IP	H	R	ER	BB	SO
*Anderson, Jason	4	9	6.89	23	0	111.0	148	103	85	47	74
*Baez, Benito	5	1	5.47	37	3	54.1	68	35	33	15	51
*Bertotti, Mike	2	3	8.42	20	1	25.2	30	26	24	37	25
Brink, Jim	1	1	7.88	5	0	8.0	10	7	7	1	4
D'Amico, Jeff	1	2	4.96	32	3	45.1	53	31	25	16	38
*Dubose, Eric	4	2	5.49	21	1	77.0	89	57	47	44	68
Enochs, Chris	3	5	10.00	13	0	45.0	69	57	50	34	33
Gorrell, Chris	2	0	7.83	30	1	56.1	92	63	49	23	41
Gregg, Kevin	4	7	3.74	16	0	91.1	75	45	38	31	66
Harville, Chad	2	0	2.01	17	7	22.1	13	6	5	9	35
Hudson, Tim	3	0	0.50	3	0	18.0	9	1	1	3	18
Kimball, Andy	9	5	5.44	47	2	89.1	112	64	54	40	87
Leyva, Julian	3	4	6.03	12	0	62.2	86	46	42	12	39
Manwiller, Tim	6	2	3.51	17	0	84.2	95	43	33	24	58
Nelson, Chris	1	1	7.92	19	0	30.2	45	30	27	22	24
Niles, Randy	4	6	5.73	23	0	88.0	126	78	56	47	46
Nina, Elvin	3	2	4.80	7	0	30.0	36	21	16	18	18
O'Dell, Jake	0	2	11.31	9	0	24.2	36	31	31	15	16

Independent League standings

Atlantic League

	W	L	Pct.	GB
Bridgeport	78	42	.650	—
Atlantic	61	58	.513	16.5
Somerset	60	60	.500	18
Newark	55	64	.462	22.5
Nashua	52	67	.437	25.5
Lehigh Valley	52	67	.437	25.5

Northern League
East Division

	W	L	Pct.	GB
Schaumburg	44	42	.512	—
St. Paul	40	47	.460	4.5
Madison	37	47	.440	6
Duluth-Superior	35	49	.417	8

West Division

	W	L	Pct.	GB
Fargo-Moorhd.	50	35	.588	—
Winnipeg	48	38	.558	4
Sioux City	51	44	.537	8
Sioux Falls	37	48	.435	13

Northeast League
North Division

	W	L	Pct.	GB
Albany	45	41	.523	—
Quebec	43	43	.500	2
Adirondack	43	43	.500	2
Mass.	41	45	.477	4

South Division

	W	L	Pct.	GB
Allentown	47	39	.547	—
New Jersey	45	40	.529	1.5
Elmira	43	42	.506	3.5
Waterbury	36	50	.419	11

Switch-hitter
* Left-handed
T Player has been with more than one team; listed with last team.
(Players in major leagues are listed with last minor league club.)

Independent League standings

(Cont'd from previous page)

Western League
	W	L	Pct.	GB
Chico	63	27	.700	—
Tri-City	48	42	.533	15
Zion	41	49	.456	22
Sonoma	41	49	.456	22
Reno	41	49	.456	22
Sacramento	36	54	.400	27

Texas-Louisiana League
	W	L	Pct.	GB
Amarillo	63	21	.750	—
Alexandria	48	36	.571	15
Abilene	46	38	.548	17
Rio Grande Val.	45	38	.542	17.5
Ozark Mtn.	32	50	.390	30
Lafayette	32	51	.386	30.5
Greenville	26	58	.310	37

Frontier League
West Division
	W	L	Pct.	GB
Evansville	43	41	.512	—
Dubois	42	42	.500	1
Cook County	41	43	.488	2
Springfield	39	45	.464	4
River City	39	45	.464	4

East Division
	W	L	Pct.	GB
London	54	30	.643	—
Chillicothe	45	38	.542	8.5
Johnstown	43	41	.512	11
Richmond	40	43	.482	13.5
Canton	33	51	.393	21

\# Switch-hitter
* Left-handed
T Player has been with more than one team; listed with last team.
(Players in major leagues are listed with last minor league club.)

PITCHING	W	L	ERA	G	SV	IP	H	R	ER	BB	SO
*Perez, Juan	2	2	6.94	23	3	35.0	47	29	27	18	30
Skeels, David	0	0	18.00	2	0	2.0	5	4	4	1	2
Snow, Bert	1	1	1.71	21	13	21.0	14	4	4	9	32
*Vasquez, Leo	3	1	3.09	13	1	23.1	18	11	8	13	24
Vizcaino, Luis	8	7	5.85	25	0	104.2	120	74	68	48	88
Wagner, Denny	1	2	4.23	5	0	27.2	28	22	13	14	12
*Zito, Barry	2	1	4.91	4	0	22.0	22	15	12	11	29

San Antonio Missions (Dodgers) AA

BATTING	AVG	AB	R	H	2B	3B	HR	RBI	BB	SO	SB
*Allen, Luke, 3B	.281	533	90	150	16	12	14	82	44	102	14
Bocachica, Hiram, 2B	.291	477	84	139	22	10	11	60	60	71	30
Collins, Michael, 2B	.333	12	1	4	0	0	0	0	5	2	0
Cuevas, Trent, 3B	.500	2	0	1	0	0	0	0	0	0	0
#Davis, Glenn, OF	.260	492	72	128	33	4	10	63	69	130	6
Diaz, Juan, 1B	.303	254	42	77	21	1	9	52	26	77	0
*Dubose, Brian, 1B	.264	121	15	32	9	3	3	22	11	25	0
Gil, Geronimo, C	.283	343	47	97	26	1	15	59	49	58	2
#Metcalfe, Mike, SS	.293	461	78	135	25	3	3	57	65	47	57
Moreta, Ramon, OF	.305	397	56	121	13	3	2	42	18	66	26
#Mota, Tony, OF	.325	345	65	112	31	2	15	75	41	56	13
*Myers, Roderick, OF	.252	147	21	37	11	0	2	16	18	35	2
Ortiz, Hector, C	.240	121	10	29	4	0	0	13	10	17	0
Ortiz, Nicky, SS	.175	40	4	7	1	0	0	2	3	7	0
*Phoenix, Wynter, OF	.249	169	22	42	6	1	5	22	21	41	1
Saitta, Rich, SS	.291	254	25	74	11	4	2	34	8	43	7
*Skeels, Andy, PH	.000	1	0	1	0	0	0	0	0	0	0
#Snow, Casey, C	.253	170	21	43	8	2	4	16	13	45	0
#Stovall, Darond, OF	.367	49	9	18	3	0	4	11	7	10	1
*Warner, Mike, OF	.330	191	35	63	16	5	3	25	34	29	12

PITCHING	W	L	ERA	G	SV	IP	H	R	ER	BB	SO
*Alvarez, Victor	4	3	3.67	9	0	56.1	58	27	23	10	43
*Beckett, Robbie	7	7	5.18	18	1	97.1	82	63	56	68	92
*Davis, Allen	7	10	4.22	29	0	130.0	140	83	61	46	87
Foster, Kris	0	2	3.59	33	4	52.2	43	24	21	26	53
Gagne, Eric	12	4	2.63	26	0	167.2	122	55	49	64	185
Garcia, Apostol	7	5	3.36	32	1	101.2	110	57	38	45	50
Garrett, Hal	5	9	3.61	42	2	94.2	70	47	38	55	76
*Jarvis, Matt	0	1	27.00	3	0	3.0	10	10	9	3	1
Mitchell, Dean	1	2	3.13	10	0	31.2	36	20	11	14	28
Montgomery, Matt	5	6	2.60	58	26	55.1	65	35	16	17	39
*Newton, Geronimo	0	1	3.21	11	0	14.0	17	6	5	10	14
*Niebla, Ruben	2	1	3.77	12	0	14.1	19	7	6	5	12
*Pearsall, J.J.	0	0	4.50	10	0	16.0	14	11	8	8	13
Prokopec, Luke	8	12	5.42	27	0	157.2	172	113	95	46	128
*Weber, Neil	4	2	5.24	12	0	55.0	62	39	32	24	31
Workman, Widd	1	5	6.97	9	0	50.1	73	48	39	27	27
*Zamora, Pete	2	1	6.08	35	3	63.2	79	48	43	30	41

Shreveport Captains (Giants) AA

BATTING	AVG	AB	R	H	2B	3B	HR	RBI	BB	SO	SB
#Byas, Michael, OF	.271	487	76	132	9	1	0	41	68	79	31
Campusano, C., SS	.154	39	5	6	0	2	1	6	3	10	1
Chiaramonte, C., C	.245	400	54	98	20	2	19	74	40	88	4
*Clark, Douglas, OF	.220	50	6	11	3	0	1	6	4	9	0
#Dilone, Juan, OF	.253	340	52	86	19	6	5	44	46	87	11
*Faircloth, Chad, PH	.216	37	4	8	2	0	0	3	2	14	0
Feliz, Pedro, 3B	.253	491	52	124	24	6	13	77	19	90	4
Glendenning, Mike, OF	.264	106	14	28	6	0	5	19	12	30	1
*Gulseth, Mark, PH	.228	145	13	33	6	0	1	17	18	26	1
#Magruder, Chris, OF	.256	476	78	122	21	4	6	60	69	85	17
Marval, Raul, SS	.250	4	0	1	0	0	0	0	0	1	0
#Mendoza, Carlos, SS	.202	332	35	67	16	4	3	34	36	65	1
*Minor, Damon, 1B	.273	473	76	129	33	4	20	82	80	115	1
Priess, Matthew, C	.167	12	1	2	0	0	1	1	1	3	0
Ransom, Cody, SS	.122	41	6	5	0	0	2	4	4	22	0
Torrealba, Yorvit, C	.244	217	25	53	10	1	4	19	9	34	0
Tyler, Josh, OF	.263	331	41	87	17	0	3	39	30	53	14
Young, Travis, 2B	.264	416	68	110	28	2	5	38	33	75	6

PITCHING	W	L	ERA	G	SV	IP	H	R	ER	BB	SO
Bump, Nate	4	10	3.31	17	0	92.1	85	40	34	32	59
Chavarria, David	0	1	7.47	10	0	15.2	24	22	13	9	16
Corps, Edwin	4	4	4.59	24	0	84.1	98	54	43	29	34
Crabtree, Robbie	4	2	2.56	36	2	63.1	50	21	18	18	65
*Davis, Jason	5	1	1.27	52	21	64.0	42	9	9	22	54

PITCHING	W	L	ERA	G	SV	IP	H	R	ER	BB	SO
Esteves, Jake	8	2	3.63	15	0	91.2	76	40	37	23	53
Estrella, Luis	6	4	3.02	40	4	92.1	77	33	31	33	75
*Heckman, Andy	10	6	4.08	23	0	132.1	142	67	60	43	70
Joseph, Kevin	0	2	1.42	7	0	12.2	8	4	2	5	16
Knoll, Brian	9	7	3.51	33	1	128.1	117	54	50	34	91
Linebrink, Scott	1	8	6.44	10	0	43.1	48	31	31	14	33
Malloy, Bill	2	0	6.26	17	1	27.1	31	20	19	15	16
Nathan, Joe	0	1	3.12	2	0	8.2	5	4	3	7	7
Ricabal, Dan	2	0	4.91	8	0	11.0	15	6	6	5	4
*Riley, Michael	8	3	2.11	30	1	111.0	80	35	26	53	107
Tucker, Ben	3	3	4.18	18	1	28.0	37	19	13	12	12
*Urban, Jeff	2	7	5.81	14	0	69.2	100	54	45	19	54
Verdugo, Jason	2	3	3.02	40	8	62.2	58	34	21	12	46
Vogelsong, Ryan	0	2	7.31	6	0	28.1	40	25	23	15	23
*Zerbe, Chad	1	3	1.96	7	0	41.1	32	13	9	10	16

Tulsa Drillers (Rangers) AA

BATTING	AVG	AB	R	H	2B	3B	HR	RBI	BB	SO	SB
Bautista, Juan, SS	.246	471	60	116	14	3	8	45	25	114	18
Brumbaugh, Cliff, OF	.281	513	94	144	35	3	25	89	71	88	18
#Cuyler, Milt, OF	.326	138	30	45	4	4	0	13	18	29	7
#Diaz, Freddie, DH	.096	52	5	5	3	0	0	9	6	15	1
Gallagher, Shawn, 1B	.283	452	61	128	30	3	18	78	26	84	1
Goodwin, Joe, C	.235	98	15	23	7	0	0	8	7	16	0
*Grabowski, Jason, DH	.167	6	1	1	0	0	0	0	2	2	0
#Ibarra, Jesse, DH	.222	325	32	72	10	1	11	49	41	88	0
King, Cesar, C	.227	321	41	73	19	2	11	45	32	70	2
*Lamb, Mike, 3B	.324	544	98	176	51	5	21	100	53	65	4
Lane, Ryan, DH	.273	264	38	72	23	5	9	48	26	47	5
*Morris, Bobby, DH	.333	21	0	7	2	0	0	2	4	1	0
Myers, Adrian, OF	.235	357	60	84	12	4	1	28	44	63	33
Piniella, Juan, OF	.264	458	69	121	23	2	9	46	61	120	15
*Podsednik, Scott, OF	.155	116	10	18	4	0	0	1	5	13	6
#Rosario, Mel, C	.208	96	12	20	3	0	8	19	3	28	1
Sasser, Rob, OF	.263	19	3	5	2	0	0	0	1	2	0
*Sergio, Tom, 2B	.291	512	88	149	38	6	10	72	58	59	19
*Valdes, Pedro, DH	.353	34	3	12	4	0	1	4	8	6	0

PITCHING	W	L	ERA	G	SV	IP	H	R	ER	BB	SO
Buckles, Bucky	10	4	3.73	36	1	72.1	71	40	30	34	39
Burkett, John	0	1	2.70	2	0	6.2	7	5	2	3	3
*Cobb, Trevor	4	5	5.26	35	1	75.1	79	52	44	33	44
Cook, Derrick	7	6	5.67	21	0	114.1	137	81	72	45	71
*Davis, Doug	4	4	2.42	12	0	74.1	65	26	20	25	79
Dickey, R.A.	6	7	4.55	35	10	95.0	105	60	48	40	59
Elder, David	1	0	8.10	3	0	6.2	8	7	6	6	7
Johnson, Jonathan	0	0	9.53	1	0	5.2	12	6	6	0	4
*Karp, Ryan	2	2	2.78	11	0	64.2	50	21	20	21	49
Kolb, Dan	1	2	2.79	7	0	38.2	38	16	12	18	32
*Lee, Corey	8	5	4.44	22	0	127.2	132	76	63	44	121
Martinez, Jose	4	4	5.42	33	3	98.0	112	69	59	36	70
Miller, Matt	6	4	3.38	34	7	56.0	42	24	21	28	83
*Moreno, Juan	4	3	2.30	42	3	62.2	33	20	16	32	83
*Poland, Trey	5	8	4.93	21	0	118.2	139	74	65	56	80
*Quarnstrom, Robert	1	0	1.98	10	0	13.2	12	3	3	4	7
Silva, Ted	6	3	4.00	13	0	72.0	64	34	32	14	48
Sollecito, Gabe	5	4	2.43	53	11	96.1	85	28	26	29	80
Woodman, Hank	0	4	5.46	6	0	29.2	27	24	18	19	25

Wichita Wranglers (Royals) AA

BATTING	AVG	AB	R	H	2B	3B	HR	RBI	BB	SO	SB
Amado, Jose, 1B	.290	459	71	133	29	2	13	93	54	37	5
Brito, Juan, C	.091	11	0	1	0	0	0	0	2	3	0
*Brown, Dee, OF	.353	235	58	83	14	3	12	56	35	41	10
*Brown, Ray, 1B	.318	44	8	14	4	0	1	11	8	5	0
*Dodson, Jeremy, OF	.257	452	63	116	20	1	21	58	51	95	9
Escamilla, Roman, C	.244	201	21	49	13	0	1	28	13	46	3
*Escandon, E., DH	.259	340	59	88	18	5	7	57	73	46	5
Goodwin, David, 1B	.300	10	3	3	0	0	0	0	1	3	0
Hallmark, Pat, OF	.285	242	35	69	7	2	5	24	21	62	14
*Layne, Jason, 1B	.217	92	13	20	4	0	2	12	15	24	1
#Martinez, Felix, SS	.269	327	57	88	22	2	4	37	37	43	19
McNally, Sean, 3B	.282	440	97	124	24	2	36	109	93	132	7
Medrano, Tony, 2B	.339	257	45	87	15	1	5	32	21	23	4
#Metzler, Rod, OF	.500	10	5	5	2	0	2	4	0	3	0
Moore, Kenderick, OF	.251	243	36	61	11	0	0	27	20	55	19

1999 Top Attendance Rankings

Team	Attendance	No. of Games
Buffalo	684,051	68
Indianapolis	658,250	71
Pawtucket	596,624	71
Akron	522,459	69
Salt lake	505,547	65
Richmond	499,459	67
New Orleans	472,665	70
Oklahoma	471,722	67
Rochester	467,730	68
Durham	464,001	70
Lansing	462,515	67
West Michigan	457,350	69
Columbus	453,423	65
Kane County	451,165	64
Reading	448,367	70
Syracuse	446,026	69
Trenton	440,033	71
Scranton-WB	439,171	68
Norfolk	431,245	62
Bowie	421,398	69
Iowa	416,804	65
Omaha	410,706	64
Portland	402,582	71
Memphis	397,177	70
Edmonton	385,913	65
Nashville	366,684	67
Louisville	361,419	72
Tulsa	351,929	66
Las Vegas	345,969	70
Bridgeport	342,857	75
Charlotte	337,720	69
Somerset	335,056	64
Altoona	323,932	69
Rancho Ccmng	321,682	69
Wilmington	321,143	70
Albuquerque	319,339	68
San Antonio	318,590	68
Birmingham	314,010	70
El Paso	313,622	65
Frederick	313,603	66
Fresno	311,804	70
West Tenn	302,203	68
Delmarva	296,004	69
Toledo	295,183	68
Mobile	293,147	69
Lake Elsinore	281,521	70
Huntsville	275,000	68
Tacoma	271,026	69
Calgary	269,002	61
St. Paul	265,818	42
Greenville	257,171	67
Tucson	254,817	69
Harrisburg	253,399	66
Winnipeg	248,488	41
Norwich	244,442	69
Vancouver	241,569	63
Charleston-SC	238,184	69

MINOR LEAGUE REPORT

413

Team	Attendance	No. of Games
Carolina	238,002	66
Schaumburg	236,476	43
Erie	234,257	67
Jacksonville	233,630	70
Myrtle Beach	232,619	66
Wisconsin	222,814	66
Chattanooga	218,946	69
Lancaster	218,479	69
Potomac	209,168	68
Atlantic City	206,538	76
Portland	206,136	38
Salem	206,012	67
Colorado Spr.	205,992	62
Binghamton	203,674	70
Mahoning V.	203,073	36
South Bend	200,518	65
Fort Wayne	199,027	68
New Haven	197,163	68
Ottawa	195,232	70
Arkansas	191,346	57
Spokane	187,315	38
Wichita	181,403	66
Lowell	180,077	37
Fargo-Mrhd	179,919	41
Hickory	179,340	68
New Britain	177,026	66
Midland	176,369	67
San Bernardino	167,437	69
Hudson Valley	161,698	38
San Jose	157,598	70
Augusta	156,685	65
Shreveport	155,416	67
Ozark	154,752	42
River City	151,661	40
Greensboro	151,573	69
Amarillo	151,222	41
Peoria	150,182	65
Quad City	146,043	66
High desert	145,888	69
Asheville	137,836	64
New Jersey	135,775	38
Winston-Salem	134,764	64
Modesto	133,847	68
Columbia	133,273	64
Boise	132,773	38
Savannah	132,017	66
New Jersey	129,179	39
Cedar Rapids	127,862	69
Chico	126,525	45
Newark	126,407	35
Salem-Keizer	124,627	37
Kinston	124,010	66
Eugene	122,500	36
Knoxville	119,571	67
Piedmont	119,563	64
Sioux Falls	118,765	41
Sioux City	118,333	43
Staten Island	117,765	37
Allentown	116,402	42
Macon	115,900	62
Brevard Cty	115,145	66

BATTING	AVG	AB	R	H	2B	3B	HR	RBI	BB	SO	SB
Phillips, Paul, C	.267	393	58	105	20	2	3	56	26	38	8
Prieto, Alejandro, SS	.294	360	56	106	23	4	6	41	35	47	12
*Tomlinson, Goef, OF	.280	479	100	134	31	4	4	46	72	82	24

PITCHING	W	L	ERA	G	SV	IP	H	R	ER	BB	SO
Austin, Jeff	3	1	4.46	6	0	34.1	40	19	17	11	21
Bluma, Jaime	2	6	5.40	30	6	38.1	40	25	23	16	21
Brewer, Ryan	5	2	5.54	42	3	66.2	85	45	41	17	34
Calero, Kiko	9	3	4.11	26	1	129.1	143	67	59	57	92
Carter, Lance	5	2	0.78	44	13	69.2	49	10	6	27	77
*Chapman, Jake	3	0	4.39	52	3	69.2	87	38	34	29	53
Durbin, Chad	8	10	4.64	28	0	157.0	154	88	81	49	122
*Gooding, Jason	13	7	4.73	23	0	139.0	176	80	73	39	63
Lineweaver, Aaron	4	3	5.28	9	1	44.1	49	32	26	15	20
Mathews, Terry	0	0	4.50	1	0	2.0	2	1	1	0	2
Morrison, Robbie	2	0	2.01	15	5	22.1	26	7	5	7	21
*Mullen, Scott	4	3	4.01	9	0	49.1	47	28	22	18	30
*Prihoda, Steve	6	3	4.00	49	2	78.2	91	43	35	15	51
Ray, Ken	0	0	5.06	14	7	21.1	23	12	12	10	18
Saier, Matt	9	7	5.01	19	0	109.2	137	64	61	34	61
Santiago, Jose	0	1	2.00	4	0	9.0	8	2	2	0	0
Smith, Toby	5	2	2.94	22	1	79.2	86	30	26	18	40
Wilson, Kris	5	7	5.45	23	0	74.1	91	51	45	14	45

Clubhouse

- ▶Youth league results
- ▶Little League
  World Series
- ▶Yankees honor Little
  League finalists
- ▶List of all Little League
  Champions
- ▶American Legion
  leads Hall inductees
- ▶Youth league directory

USA SNAPSHOTS®

A look at statistics that shape the sports world

Blasting to the top

In the fall of 1997, baseball fans ranked Ken Griffey Jr. as baseball's greatest active player. Two years later, Mark McGwire has shot to the top. Top player in the game today:

Player	Sept. '97 Pct. (rank)	Sept. '99 Pct. (rank)
Mark McGwire	4% (4)	23% (1)
Sammy Sosa	—	16% (2)
Ken Griffey Jr.	24% (1)	8% (3)
Cal Ripken	12% (2)	5% (4)

Source: USA TODAY/CNN/Gallup Poll   By Scott Boeck and Alejandro Gonzalez, USA TODAY

Little League World Series scores

▶**Little League (9-12):**
Osaka (Japan) 5,
Phenix City (Ala.) 0

▶**Junior League (13-14):**
Arroyo, Puerto Rico 1,
Hermosillo, Sonora (Mexico) 0

▶**Senior League (13-16):**
Kissimmee (Fla.) 10,
Venezuela 2

▶**Big League (16-18):**
Fla. Dist. 14 (Fla.) 14,
Canada 2

PONY championship scores

▶**Mustang (ages 9-10):**
Garden Grove (Calif.) 12,
Irving (Texas) 4

▶**Bronco (11-12):**
Tai-Tong (Taiwan) 5,
Corona (Calif.) 0

▶**Pony (13-14):**
West Covina (Calif.) 9,
Tai Tung (Taiwan) 1

▶**Colt (15-16):**
Hoosier North (Ind.) 10,
Danville (Calif.) 4

▶**Palomino (17-18):**
Santa Clara (Calif.) 15,
Houston (Texas) 2

RBI World Series champions

▶**Senior Boys (16-18):**
San Juan, Puerto Rico

▶**Junior Boys (13-15):**
San Juan, Puerto Rico

Courtesy of Little League Baseball Inc.

Hirakata little league brought Japan its fourth world title.

Osaka, Japan, wins 53rd Little League World Series

Kazuki Sumiyama—the 12-year-old pitcher who struck out nine Phenix City, Alabama, players in the final game of the Little League World Series to win the championship for Osaka, Japan—wields a double-edged sword.

He can hit, too.

In two games against Phenix City, he batted .615. At 5-7 and 122 pounds, Sumiyama is a formidable opponent on the mound and at the plate. He struck out 19 batters and did not allow a single run in 11 innings at the series.

"The kids were coming back to the dugout and saying, 'The ball's just jumping out at us,'" Phenix City manager Tony Rasmus said.

Sumiyama's arsenal includes a fastball and a couple of nasty variations: the "Kazuball" and the "Thunderball." He is so effective that he is already being heavily recruited by Japanese high schools.

Meanwhile, in the USA, his career was helped by Phenix City catcher Cory Rasmus's second-inning throwing error on a steal attempt. Osaka's Toshi Adachi, on third base, seized the opportunity to score the first run of the game.

Rasmus helped Osaka again in the fourth inning. Kazunori Morishita and Kazuya Yamasaki hit consecutive doubles, and Yamasaki scored when a low pitch bounced off Rasmus's glove: Osaka 3, Phenix City 0.

Osaka added a two-run fifth inning, and Phenix City was history. The Hirakata Little League of Osaka, managed by former Hanshin Tigers outfielder Tsutomu Kameyama, was the fourth Japanese team to win the Little League world championship.

Yankees honor both Little League finalists

Major league baseball's 1998 world champions tipped their caps to both finalists in the 1999 Little League World Series in a pregame ceremony the day after Osaka beat Phenix City 5-0.

Before the game, the Little Leaguers met some big leaguers, including David Cone and Hideki Irabu. Then they ran out on the field with the Yankees and took their positions for the national anthem.

After that, the youngsters were taken to a luxury suite, where they watched the Yankees play the Seattle Mariners. The Yankees gave them T-shirts, caps and other gifts.

Little League world champions

- ▶1998—Toms River, NJ 12, Kashima, Japan 9
- ▶1997—Guadalupe, Mexico 5, Mission Viejo, CA 4
- ▶1996—Taiwan 13, Cranston, RI 3 (5 innings)
- ▶1995—Taiwan 17, Spring, TX 3
- ▶1994—Venezuela 4, Northridge, CA 3
- ▶1993—Long Beach, CA 3, Panama 2
- ▶1992—Long Beach, CA 6, Philippines 0-x (forfeit)
- ▶1991—Taiwan 11, Danville, CA 0
- ▶1990—Taiwan 9, Shippensburg, PA 0
- ▶1989—Trumbull, CT 5, Taiwan 2
- ▶1988—Taiwan 10, Pearl City, HI 0
- ▶1987—Taiwan 21, Irvine, CA 1
- ▶1986—Taiwan 12, Tucson, AZ 0
- ▶1985—Seoul, South Korea 7, Mexicali, Mexico 1
- ▶1984—Seoul, South Korea 6, Altamonte Springs, FL 2
- ▶1983—Marietta, GA 3, Barahona, Dominican Republic 1
- ▶1982—Kirkland, WA 6, Chai-Yi-Hsien, Taiwan 0
- ▶1981—Taiwan 4, Tampa Bay, FL 2
- ▶1980—Taiwan 4, Tampa Bay, FL 3
- ▶1979—Taiwan 2, Campbell, CA 1
- ▶1978—Taiwan 11, Danville, CA 1
- ▶1977—Taiwan 7, El Cajon, CA 2
- ▶1976—Tokyo, Japan 10, Campbell, CA 3
- ▶1975—Lakewood, NJ 4, Tampa Bay, FL 3
- ▶1974—Taiwan 12, Red Bluff, CA 1
- ▶1973—Taiwan 12, Tucson, AZ 0
- ▶1972—Taiwan 6, Hammond, IN 0
- ▶1971—Taiwan 12, Gary, IN 3
- ▶1970—Wayne, NJ 2, Campbell, CA 0
- ▶1969—Taiwan 5, Santa Clara, CA 0

NABF championship scores

▶**Rookie (10 and under):**
Nashville 9,
Joliet (Ill.) 3

▶**Freshman (12 and under):**
Lavonia (Mich.) 10,
Cincinnati 4

▶**Sophomore (14 and under):**
Westchester (Ohio) 9,
Cincinnati 2

▶**Junior (16 and under):**
Indianapolis 9,
Long Island (N.Y.) 8

▶**High School (17 and under):**
Germantown (Tenn.) 11,
Long Island (N.Y.) 8

▶**Senior (18 and under):**
Hammond (La.) 11,
Chicago 3

▶**College (22 and under):**
Salisbury (Md.) 3,
Mt. Airy, (Md.) 2

▶**Major (unlimited age):**
Long Island (N.Y.) 13,
Buffalo (N.Y.) 10

American Legion World Series score

New Brighton (Minn.) 11,
Kennewick (Wash.) 5

Dixie champions

▶**Dixie Majors (11-12):**
Hilton Head (S.C.)

▶**Dixie AAA (9-10):**
North Gwinnett (Ga.)

Babe Ruth World Series scores

▶**Bambino (11-12):**
Danbury (Conn.) 3,
Honolulu (Hawaii) 1

▶**13-year-olds:**
Tallahassee (Fla.) 7,
JPRD East Bank (La.) 5

▶**13- to 15-year-olds:**
Sarasota (Fla.) 4,
JPRD East Bank, (La.) 2

▶**14-year-olds:**
Peabody (Mass.) 9,
Brooklyn (N.Y.) 3

▶**16-year-olds:**
San Gabriel Valley (Calif.) 12,
Redmond (Wash.) 4

▶**16- to 18-year-olds:**
San Gabriel Valley (Calif.) 5,
Kent (Wash.) 3

▶1968—Wakayama, Japan 1, Richmond, VA 0
▶1967—West Tokyo, Japan 4, Chicago, IL 1
▶1966—Houston 8, West New York, NJ 2
▶1965—Windsor Locks, CT 3, Stoney Creek, Canada (Ontario) 1
▶1964—Staten Island, NY 4, Monterrey, Mexico 0
▶1963—Granada Hills, CA 2, Stratford, CT 1
▶1962—San Jose, CA 3, Kankakee, IL 0
▶1961—El Cajon, CA 4, El Campo, TX 2
▶1960—Levittown, PA 5, Fort Worth, TX 0
▶1959—Hamtramack, MI 12, Auburn, CA 0
▶1958—Monterrey, Mexico 10, Kankakee, IL 1
▶1957—Monterrey, Mexico 4, La Mesa, CA 0
▶1956—Roswell, NM 3, Delaware Township, NJ 1
▶1955—Morrisville, PA 4, Delaware Township, NJ
▶1954—Schenectady, NY 7, Colton, CA 5
▶1953—Birmingham, AL 1, Schenectady, NY 0
▶1952—Norwalk, CT 4, Monongahela, PA 3
▶1951—Stamford, CT 3, Austin, TX 0
▶1950—Houston, TX 2, Bridgeport, CT 1
▶1949—Hammonton, NJ 5, Pensacola, FL 0
▶1948—Lock Haven, PA 6, St. Petersburg, FL 5
▶1947—Williamsport, PA 16, Lock Haven, PA 7

x—Philippines won final, 15-4, but was stripped of title for using ineligible players.

AABC championship scores

▶**Roberto Clemente (8 and under):**
Puerto Rico 13,
Jefferson County (Colo.) 7

▶**Willie Mays (9-10):**
Vega Baja (P.R.) 9,
Memphis (Tenn.) 8

▶**Pee Wee Reese (10-12):**
Dallas (Texas) 8,
Puerto Rico 7
(8 innings)

▶**Sandy Koufax (13-14):**
Las Lomas (P.R.) 7,
Memphis (Tenn.) 2

▶**Mickey Mantle (15-16):**
Orange County (Calif.) 9,
Dallas (Texas) 3

▶**Connie Mack (17-18):**
Marietta (Ga.) 9,
Puerto Rico 4

American Legion leads youth leagues in Hall inductees

Forty former American Legion players have been inducted into the National Baseball Hall of Fame in Cooperstown. That's more than any other amateur baseball league. American Legion Hall of Famers are:
▶George Brett—1999
▶Robin Yount—1999
▶Nellie Fox—1997
▶Phil Niekro—1997
▶Jim Bunning—1996
▶Richie Ashburn—1995
▶Steve Carlton—1994
▶Reggie Jackson—1993
▶Tom Seaver—1991
▶Rollie Fingers—1991
▶Hal Newhouser—1991
▶Gaylord Perry—1991
▶Jim Palmer—1990
▶Joe Morgan—1990
▶Carl Yastrzemski—1989

Royals great George Brett was inducted into the Baseball Hall of fame in 1999.

▶Johnny Bench—1989
▶Willie Stargell—1988
▶Jim "Catfish" Hunter—1987
▶Bobby Doerr—1986
▶Hoyt Wilhelm—1985
▶Pee Wee Reese—1984
▶Don Drysdale—1984
▶Harmon Killebrew—1984
▶Brooks Robinson—1983
▶George Kell—1983
▶Frank Robinson—1982
▶Bob Gibson—1981
▶Al Kaline—1980
▶Eddie Mathews—1978
▶Bob Lemon—1976
▶Ralph Kiner—1975
▶Warren Spahn—1973
▶Yogi Berra—1972
▶Early Wynn—1972
▶Lou Boudreau—1970
▶Roy Campanella—1969
▶Stan Musial—1969
▶Joe Medwick—1968
▶Ted Williams—1966
▶Bob Feller—1962

CABA World Series scores

▶**9-year-olds:**
Cincinnati, OH 12,
Honolulu, HI 3

▶**10-year-olds:**
Woolsey, GA 11,
Austin, TX

▶**11-year-olds:**
Marietta, GA 10,
Baltimore, MD 7

▶**12-year-olds:**
Miami, FL 7,
Dallas, TX 5

▶**13-year-olds:**
Houston, TX 5,
Encinitas, CA 1

▶**14-year-olds:**
Denver, CO 13,
West Covina, CA 6

▶**15-year-olds:**
Issaquah, WA 6,
West Covina, CA 4

▶**16-year-olds:**
Duluth, GA 18,
Dallas, TX 0

▶**High School:**
Brooklyn, NY 10,
Nashville, TN 9

▶**18-year-olds:**
Bayside, NY 9,
Duluth, GA 7

USABF World Series scores

▶**12 and under:**
California 8,
South San Diego (Calif.) 5

▶**14 and under:**
Encinitas (Calif.) 12,
USABF South 6

▶**16 and under:**
Oceanside (Calif.) 8,
Arizona 2

▶**18 and under:**
Colton (Calif.) 8,
Sylmar (Calif.) 5

Youth baseball for every age

▶**American Amateur Baseball Congress**
Founded: 1935. Ages: 8 and up
National office: 118-19 Redfield Plaza, P.O. Box 467, Marshall, MI 49068; (616) 630-1213
Official web site: www.voyager.net/aabc
Interesting fact: The AABC says it is the nation's largest amateur baseball league for players above junior age.

▶**American Legion Baseball**
Founded: 1925. Ages: 16-18
National office: P.O. Box 1055, Indianapolis, IN 46206; (317) 630-1213
Official web site: www.legion.org/baseball/home.htm
Interesting fact: Forty former American Legion players are in the Hall of Fame at Cooperstown.

▶**Babe Ruth Baseball**
Founded: 1951. Ages: 5-18
National office: 1771 Brunswick Ave., P.O. Box 5000, Trenton, NJ 08638; (609) 695-1434
Official web site: www.baberuthleague.org
Interesting fact: John Smoltz, John Olerud and David Wells are among the famous alumni of Babe Ruth Baseball.

▶**Continental Amateur Baseball Association**
Founded: 1984. Ages: 9-18
National office: 82 University St., Westerville, OH 43081; (614) 899-2103
Official web site: http://cababaseball.com
Interesting fact: The CABA has single-age divisions to encourage a more equitable level of competition.

▶**Dixie Youth Baseball**
Founded: 1956. **Ages:** 4-12
National office: P.O. Box 877, Marshall, TX 75671; (903) 927-2255
Official web site: www.dixie.org
Interesting fact: Most Dixie games are played on a scaled-down diamond to suit the age group.

▶**Little League Baseball, Inc.**
Founded: 1939. Ages: 5-18
National office: P.O. Box 3485, Williamsport, PA 17701; (717) 326-1921
Official web site: www.littleleague.org

Interesting fact: More than 2.5 million kids play Little League worldwide.

▶**National Amateur Baseball Federation**
Founded: 1914. Ages: 12 and up (including 30-and-over leagues)
National office: P.O. Box 705, Bowie, MD 20718; (301) 262-5005
Official web site: www.nabf.net
Interesting fact: The NABF claims to be the oldest continuously operating amateur baseball league in the country.

▶**National Police Athletic League Baseball**
Founded: 1960. Ages: 14-16
National office: 614 U.S. Hwy. 1, Ste. 20, North Palm Beach, FL 33408; (407) 844-1823
Interesting fact: The PAL prevents crime through athletics, by building a bond between kids and police.

▶**Pony League**
Founded: 1951. Ages: 5-18
National office: P.O. Box 225, Washington, PA 15301-0225; (412) 225-1060
Official web site: www.pony.org
Interesting fact: Originally formed for the graduates of Little League.

▶**United States Amateur Baseball Federation**
Founded: 1997. Ages: 10-18
National office: 7355 Peter Pan Ave., San Diego, CA 92114; (619) 527-9205
Official web site: www.usabf.com
Interesting fact: 23 major league scouts came to a 1999 tournament.

—*Contributing: Dana Heiss, Liz Barrett*

High school/ college baseball

▶1999 Super 25 high schools

▶All-USA high school team

▶1999 College World Series

▶Baseball Weekly/ ESPN Top 25 college coaches poll

▶2000 college preview

USA SNAPSHOTS®

A look at statistics that shape the sports world

Sharpshooters

Pitchers with the best winning percentages after the All-Star break (minimum 10 decisions):

Rick Sutcliffe, 1984 **12-0**

Burt Hooton, 1975 **12-0**

Roger Clemens, 1998 **11-0**

Mark Portugal, 1993 **11-0**

Orel Hershiser, 1985 **11-0**

Source: Elias Sports Bureau   By Scott Boeck and Quin Tian, USA TODAY

Final 1999 high school rankings

▶1. **Bellaire, Houston, Texas (38-2)**
Won seventh Class 5A state title and first USA TODAY national championship. Set school records for wins (38), batting average (.384), home runs (66), stolen bases (194), ERA (1.10), no-hitters (six), one-hitters (nine) and shutouts (18). Kyle Smith set school records with 19 home runs and 67 RBI while batting .449. Junior Enrique Cruz set records with a .512 batting average, 62 hits, 18 doubles. Matt Laird was 14-0 with a 0.97 ERA.

▶2. **Lassiter, Marietta, Ga. (35-2)** Won last 33 games and first Class 4A state title. Jarrod Schmidt was 12-1 with a 2.05 ERA and batted .471 with 18 home runs, 55 runs and 54 RBI. Michael DeRosa batted .476 with 19 HRs, 50 runs and 51 RBI.

▶3. **Westminster Academy, Fort Lauderdale, Fla. (33-2)**
Won last 15 games and first Class 2A state title. Danny Core was 12-0 with a 1.42 ERA, striking out 119 in 84 innings. Von David Stertzbach was 12-0 with a 1.14 ERA. Bobby Van Kirk batted .450 with eight home runs and 50 RBI.

▶4. **Arlington, Riverside, Calif. (29-2)**
Won last 11 games and first Southern Section Division I title, setting school records with 38 home runs and a .380 team batting average. The nation's No. 1 catcher, Ryan Christianson, batted .512 with 40 runs, 10 doubles, 32 walks and 43 RBI while throwing out 14 of 15 runners attempting to steal. Bill Murphy was 13-1 with a 2.40 ERA and a school-record 123 strikeouts.

▶5. **Rose, Greenville, N.C. (28-0)**
Won third Class 4A state title while setting school records with 46 home runs, 12 shutouts and fewest runs allowed (50). Ryan Gordon was 12-0 with a 0.27 ERA, striking out 144 in 92 innings. He had three no-hitters and seven shutouts, both school records. Will Brinson was 8-0 and batted .433.

▶6. **Wellington, West Palm Beach, Fla. (33-4)** Won first Class 6A state title while setting school records for wins (33) and ERA (1.09). Bobby Bradley was 12-1 with three saves and eight one-hitters. He struck out 156, walked 13 and allowed 38 hits in 92 innings compiling a 0.38 ERA. Larry Broadway batted .429 with 39 runs.

▶7. **Englewood, Jacksonville, Fla. (30-5)** Won first Class 4A state title. Brett Myers posted an 8-2 record with a 0.80 ERA, striking out 131 in 78 innings, and batted .408 with 12 home runs and 41 RBI. Charlie Farah was 11-0 with a 2.02 ERA.

▶8. **Chatsworth, Calif. (27-3)** Won third Class 4A Los Angeles city title, setting a school record with a .391 batting average. Steve Kracow batted .493 with 28 runs, 11 doubles and 22 RBI. Mike Kunes was 13-1 with a 2.60 ERA and batted .396 with 24 RBI.

▶9. **El Dorado, Placentia, Calif. (26-5)** Won last 12 games and first Southern Section Division III title. Set school records with 26 wins and 37 home runs. J.P. Frid was 10-0 with a 1.45 ERA and batted .346 with 26 RBI. Dan Franklin set a school record with 46 RBI and tied another record with 10 home runs.

▶10. **Merritt Island, Fla. (31-4)** Won last 12 games and first Class 5A state title, hitting a state-record 59 home runs. Tommy Parrott hit a state-record 19 home runs and set school records with 58 hits, 16 doubles and 67 RBI. Junior Kevin Deaton (6-4, 290) was 15-1 with a 1.20 ERA, striking out 133 in 99 innings.

▶11. **Oakland, Murfreesboro, Tenn. (37-2)** Won last 22 games and first Class AAA state title. Set school records with a .390 batting average, 60 home runs, 375 runs, 37 wins, 95 doubles and 14 triples. Brennan King batted .506 with 10 doubles and 31 RBI. Casey Rauschenberger batted .421 with 12 home runs, 16 doubles, 49 RBI and had a record 32-game hitting streak.

▶12. **Catholic Central, Redford, Mich. (38-1)** Won last 18 games and third Division I state title. Michigan's Mr. Baseball, Casey Rogowski, batted .491 with

11 home runs, 58 runs, 41 walks and 55 RBI. Anthony Tomey was 11-1 with a 1.68 ERA and batted .404 with 43 RBI.

▶**13. Steinert, Hamilton Township, N.J. (29-3)** Won last 13 games and fifth Group IV state title (third in a row). Mike Stanton batted .394 with 13 doubles and 37 RBI. Sophomore Michael Rogers had a school-record 11 wins (two losses) with a 1.21 ERA. Junior Scott Rich batted .382 with a school-record 42 RBI.

▶**14. Vestavia Hills, Birmingham, Ala. (30-4)** Won state-record sixth consecutive Class 6A title and eighth in last nine years. Brent Speigner was 12-1 with a 1.15 ERA and batted .375. Kent Krupicka batted .465 with 33 RBI. Robert Evans batted .358.

▶**15. Desert Vista, Tempe, Ariz. (34-5)** Set state records with 34 wins and 435 runs (11.2 average per game) while winning first Class 5A state title. Corey Myers set state records with 70 hits, 22 home runs, 70 runs and 81 RBI while batting .560. Travis Hinton batted .433 with 12 home runs and 55 RBI.

▶**16. Owasso, Okla. (39-5)** Won second consecutive Class 6A state title as Tommy Pratt batted .500 with 66 runs, 44 walks and 32 RBI. Junior Scott Campbell batted .443 with 47 runs and 36 RBI. Junior Mark Roberts was 14-1 with a 2.05 ERA.

▶**17. Richland, Wash. (23-3)** Set school records with 39 home runs and 105 extra-base hits. Won first Class 4A state title. Steve Mortimer batted .349 with a school-record 46 RBI. Sophomore Grant Richardson batted .441 with 35 RBI and a school-record 11 home runs.

▶**18. Riverdale Baptist, Upper Marlboro, Md. (35-4)** Won third consecutive Maryland State Private Schools title. Junior Kenny Nelson was 9-2 with four saves, a 1.79 ERA and 103 strikeouts in 62 innings. He also hit a state-record 14 home runs and batted .369 with 13 doubles and 45 RBI. Ryan Dulaney was 9-1 with a 2.26 ERA and led the team with a .446 batting average.

▶**19. Lexington, S.C. (32-3)** Won fifth Class 4A state title, setting a school record for wins. James Cown batted .434 with six home runs and 33 RBI. Junior Britt Bearden batted .407 with nine home runs and 42 RBI.

▶**20. Wilson, Long Beach, Calif. (26-5)** Southern Section Division I runner-up. Set school records with 26 wins, a .367 batting average, 246 runs and a 1.67 ERA. Jeremy Hess was 11-2 with a 1.13 ERA. Chris Miller batted .484 with a school-record 44 hits. He had 31 runs and 21 RBI while amassing a 20-game hitting streak.

▶**21. Chambersburg, Pa. (27-2)** Defeated Shaler (Pittsburgh) 4-3, extending winning streak to 20, to win its second Class AAA state title. Shaler had won 13 games in a row. Aaron Edwards (10-1) pitched a five-hitter. Dustin Negley was 2-for-3 and Scott Folmar 2-for-4.

▶**22. Durango, Las Vegas, Nev. (35-4)** Had school-record 35 wins and 50 home runs en route to first Class 4A state title. Eric Kitchen scored a school record with 10 HR, tied the record with 56 RBI and batted .509. Junior Chris Kelly also had 56 RBI.

▶**23. Blue Springs, Mo. (28-2)** Won last 11 games and first Class 5A state title. Gatorade state player of the year Rusty Meyer batted .451 with 11 home runs and 40 RBI. Rick Wilson was 11-0 with a 1.91 ERA and batted .438 with 28 RBI.

▶**24. Mills Godwin, Richmond, Va. (24-4)** Won last 15 games and second Group AAA state title. Set school records with 296 hits, 238 runs, 24 home runs, 72 doubles. Tommy Edelbut was 12-0 with a 0.50 ERA and set a school record with 28 career wins. Doug McCray was 9-1 with a 2.29 ERA.

▶**25. Southington, Conn. (19-1)** Won third Class LL state title. Had 210-28 scoring margin, nine shutouts, 0.85 ERA, .410 batting average, and 12 errorless games. Brian Mascaro was 12-1 with a 0.72 ERA and batted .458 with 29 RBI. Jay Maule batted .477 with 28 runs and 27 RBI.

First Team

▶Josh Beckett, RHP

School: Spring, Texas

Ht.: 6-5 / **Wt.:** 203 / **Class:** Senior / **B-T:**R-R.
1999: 10-1, two no-hitters, 0.46 ERA, 17 strikeouts in one game. 155 strikeouts, 28 walks, 10 runs (five earned), 30 hits in 75⅓ innings. Career five no-hitters and 484 strikeouts.
Signed with: Texas A&M or Blinn Junior College (Texas).
Drafted by: Florida, first round.

▶Bobby Bradley, RHP

School: Wellington (W. Palm Beach, Fla.)

Ht.: 6-1 / **Wt.:** 171 / **Class:** Senior / **B-T:** R-R
1999: 12-1, 0.38 ERA, 156 strikeouts, 13 walks, and 38 hits in 92 innings.
Signed with: Florida State.
Drafted by: Pittsburgh, first round.

▶Cody Ross, OF/LHP

School: Carlsbad, N.M.

Ht.: 5-11 / **Wt.:** 195 / **Class:** Senior / **B-T:** R-L.
1999: Batted .515, 11 HR (school record), 41 runs, 14 doubles, four triples, 16 walks and 43 RBI. 11-0, 0.68 ERA.
Signed with: Arizona State.
Drafted by: Detroit, fourth round.

▶Corey Myers, IF

School: Desert Vista (Phoenix)

Ht.: 6-2 / **Wt.:** 215 / **Class:** Senior / **B-T:** R-R.
1999: Batted .560, 14 doubles, 27 walks, 11 strikeouts. 70 hits, 22 HR, 70 runs, and 81 RBI (state records).
Signed with: Arizona.
(first-round draft pick)

▶Ryan Christianson, C

School: Arlington (Riverside, Calif.)

Ht.: 6-2 / **Wt.:** 210 / **Class:** Senior / **B-T:** R-R.
1999: Batted .512, 10 doubles, eight HR, 40 runs, 43 RBI, 32 walks, 12 stolen bases.
Signed with: UCLA.
Drafted by: Seattle, first round.

▶Pat Manning, IF

School: Mater Dei (Santa Ana, Calif.)

Ht.: 6-0 / **Wt.:** 185 / **Class:** Senior / **B-T:** R-R
1999: Batted .494, 33 runs, 37 RBI. 1.052 slugging percentage (school record); 12 HR, 27 walks (tied school record).
Signed with: Southern California.
Drafted by: Atlanta, third round.

▶B.J. Garbe, OF/LHP

School: Moses Lake, Wash.

Ht.: 6-2 / **Wt.:** 195 / **Class:** Senior / **B-T:** R-R.
1999: Batted .486, six HR, 22 RBI, 23 walks, five doubles, four triples, five strikeouts. 9-0, 0.48 ERA, 115 strikeouts in 58 innings.
Signed with: Minnesota.
(first-round draft pick).

▶Pat Osborn, IF

School: Bakersfield, Calif.

Ht.: 6-3 / **Wt.:** 200 / **Class:** Senior / **B-T:** R-R.
1999: Batted .555, five HR, 36 runs, six doubles, 22 walks, 25 RBI. Struck out twice in 63 at-bats.
Signed with: Florida.
Drafted by: Anaheim, 22nd round.

▶Josh Hamilton, OF/LHP

School: Athens Drive (Raleigh, N.C.)

Ht.: 6-4 / **Wt.:** 210 / **Class:** Senior / **B-T:** L-L.
1999: Batted .514 with 13 HR (school record), 27 runs, nine doubles, four triples, 21 walks and 35 RBI. 18-for-19 in stolen bases. 7-1, 2.72 ERA, 94 strikeouts in 55 innings.
Signed with: Tampa Bay
(first-round draft pick).

▶Brennan King, IF

School: Oakland (Murfreesboro, Tenn.)

Ht.: 6-3 / **Wt.:** 175 / **Class:** Senior / **B-T:** R-R.
1999: Batted .506, six HR, 10 doubles, 19 walks, 7 strikeouts, 31 RBI.
Signed with: Mississippi State.
Drafted by: Los Angeles, second round.

Miami title lets Morris leave pain of '96 behind

When Miami coach Jim Morris flipped on the television on June 12 in search of the College World Series game between Florida State and Texas A&M, he found instead a replay of the ninth inning of the 1996 Louisiana State–Miami championship game.

Bottom of the ninth. Two outs, one man on, Miami ahead 8-7. Miami closer Robbie Morrison unleashes a curveball away to Warren Morris. Ping! The LSU second baseman cranks the ball into the right-field bleachers. Game over.

In 1999, Jim Morris was back on network TV, coaching Miami in the CWS championship game against rival Florida State. With first baseman Kevin Brown's three-run double in the fifth inning, Miami took a 6-2 lead. Morris was relaxed; his bullpen hadn't blown a big lead all year. But when FSU scored two runs in the seventh, and then another in the eighth on John Ford Griffin's sacrifice fly, Morris's stomach turned. Pitcher Alex Santos got up from the bench and headed for the clubhouse. He couldn't watch.

Miami closer Michael Neu struck out the first batter of the ninth, then got FSU catcher Jeremiah Klosterman to pop up to third baseman Lale Esquivel. With a 2-2 count on third baseman Kevin Cash, pitching coach Lazer Collazo instructed Neu to throw a curve away—the same pitch that he had asked Morrison to throw to Warren Morris in 1996. "That pitch has haunted me for three years," Collazo said. This time, Cash swung through it. Strikeout. Game over. After six consecutive trips to Omaha, Jim Morris and the Hurricanes finally left the College World Series as national champions. After marching undefeated through nine postseason games, winning with the same pitching, defense and timely hitting that had carried them all season, the Hurricanes celebrated their first championship since 1985.

Exuberant Miami players celebrate the Hurricanes' first title in six straight trips to the CWS.

"It's a huge thing to lift the monkey off my back," Morris said.

The final victory over FSU featured some of Miami's heroes. Kris Clute, a sophomore who started the year as a third-string infielder but finished as the team's starting second baseman, went 1-for-3 with an RBI. Sophomore Kevin Brown, the big bat on a team that stresses defense, drove in four runs with his 22nd homer and a three-run double. Team captain and shortstop Bobby Hill went 2-for-2 and stole his 52nd base. Santos earned his 13th win by giving up two runs on four hits in five innings, and Neu earned his 16th save.

1999 series notes

▶**Fantasy baseball:** Actor Kevin Costner, a Cal State–Fullerton alumnus, sat behind the third base dugout during the game to cheer on the Titans — and invited all the teams in the series to a private screening of his new baseball movie, *For Love of the Game.* Costner plays an aging pitcher who throws a perfect game in his final outing.

▶**Attendance:** Sunday's record crowd of 24,859 fans pushed the 1999 total attendance to 91,173 for the tournament. The first six games of the tournament averaged a record 22,793.

HIGH SCHOOL/COLLEGE BASEBALL

By Ted Kirk, AP/Wide World Photos

425

Baseball Weekly/ESPN
Top 25 college coaches poll

▶1. **Miami (50-13)**
Poll points: 1,000 (40 No. 1 votes). Tournament results: 1st, College World Series.

▶2. **Florida State (57-14)**
Poll points: 960. Tournament results: 2nd, CWS.

▶3. **Stanford (50-15)**
Poll points: 919. Tournament results: Tied for 3rd, CWS.

▶4. **Alabama (53-16)**
Poll points: 868. Tournament results: Tied for 3rd, CWS.

▶5. **Rice (59-15)**
Poll points: 832. Tournament results: Tied for 5th, CWS.

▶6. **Cal State-Fullerton (50-14)**
Poll points: 814. Tournament results: Tied for 5th, CWS.

▶7. **Texas A&M (52-18)**
Poll points: 761. Tournament results: Tied for 7th, CWS.

▶8. **Oklahoma State (46-21)**
Poll points: 703. Tournament results: Tied for 7th, CWS.

▶9. **Baylor (50-15)**
Poll points: 648. Tournament results: 2nd at Waco super regional.

▶10. **Wake Forest (47-16)**
Poll points: 596. Tournament results: 2nd at Coral Gables super regional.

▶11. **Auburn (46-19)**
Poll points: 566. Tournament results: 2nd at Tallahassee super regional.

▶12. **Ohio State (50-14)**
Poll points: 533. Tournament results: 2nd at Columbus super regional.

▶13. **Southern California (36-26)**
Poll points: 506. Tournament results: 2nd at Palo Alto super regional.

▶14. **Clemson (42-27)**
Poll points: 466. Tournament results: 2nd at College Station super regional.

▶15. **Wichita State (59-14)**
Poll points: 431. Tournament results: 2nd at Wichita regional.

▶16. **Louisiana State (41-24-1)**
Poll points: 405. Tournament results: 2nd at Alabama super regional.

▶17. **Pepperdine (46-16)**
Poll points: 343. Tournament results: 2nd at Los Angeles regional.

▶18. **Southwestern Louisiana (42-24)**
Poll points: 308. Tournament results: 2nd at Houston super regional.

▶19. **Tulane (48-17)**
Poll points: 269. Tournament results: 2nd at Auburn regional.

▶20. **Arkansas (42-23)**
Poll points: 250. Tournament results: 3rd at Fayetteville super regional.

▶21. **Texas Tech (42-17)**
Poll points: 190. Tournament results: 2nd at Lubbock regional.

▶22. **Florida Atlantic (54-9)**
Poll points: 169. Tournament results: 2nd at Coral Gables super regional.

▶23. **East Carolina (46-16)**
Poll points: 147. Tournament results: 2nd at Baton Rouge regional.

▶24. **Mississippi State (42-21)**
Poll points: 97. Tournament results: 2nd at Columbus super regional.

▶25. **Nebraska (42-18)**
Poll points: 56. Tournament results: 3rd at Columbus super regional.

—The Baseball Weekly/ESPN *Top 25 College Coaches Poll as selected by 40 Division I head coaches representing the American Baseball Coaches Association (ABCA)*

2000 College preview: Top contenders

▶Alabama: The Crimson Tide wrapped up a 56-13 season with a third-place finish at the 1999 College World Series. Nearly everyone returns in 2000, except for two key elements: power-hitting shortstop Andy Phillips (the most celebrated player in Alabama history) and outfielder G.W. Keller. Sophomore first-baseman Jeremy Brown (.354, 14 HR, 20 doubles, 65 RBI) is the best among several returning big bats, including catcher Kelley Gulledge (.356, 11 HR). The Tide also has an experienced group of pitchers back, led by starter Jonathan Blankenship (10-2) and reliever Rheal Cormier (11 saves).

▶Auburn : This season, coach Hal Baird's 15th at Auburn, will be his last. The Tigers would like to give him his first College World Series appearance as a retirement present. A trio of talented juniors could make it happen. Hayden Gliemmo, a southpaw, tied for the Southeastern Conference lead with 13 wins. Outfielder Mailon Kent led the Tigers with a .379 batting average and set the school single-season stolen base record with 40 steals. Second baseman Dominic Rich had an All-Star summer on Cape Cod, where he finished third with a .348 average in the prestigious wood-bat summer league.

▶UCLA: The Bruins have a roster full of pro prospects, yet the team consistently plays below potential. Now that many of UCLA's top players are entering their crucial junior seasons, the Bruins are again expected to be one of the nation's top teams. Juniors Bill Scott, Garrett Atkins and Chase Utley are the ones to watch in 2000. Scott, an outfielder, hit 28 homers in 1999 and excelled for Team USA during the summer. Atkins and Utley, both infielders, also starred in summer ball, playing alongside each other for Cape Cod Baseball League–champion Cotuit. All three are potential high picks in the June draft. Highly touted pitching prospects Jon Brandt, Josh Karp and closer Chad Cislak will be joined by starter Rob Henkel, finally healthy after two injury-plagued seasons. Henkel was drafted in the 20th round by the Mets but chose school over signing.

▶Louisiana State: Leading the Tigers back to the top in 2000 will be two familiar faces: senior catcher Brad Cresse and senior third baseman Blair Barbier. Other top players returning include Brad Hawpe, who battled injuries last season but still managed 12 homers in 117 at-bats, and top reliever Hunter Gomez, who is expected to move into LSU's weekend rotation this season. Starting pitching is a question mark for the second straight year, as LSU is counting on two junior college transfers—right-hander Heath McMurray and right-hander Jason Scobie—to contribute right away.

▶Florida State: The Seminoles are celebrating the return of second baseman Marshall McDougall, who hit a record six homers in a game last season and led the NCAA with 106 RBI. McDougall declined signing with Boston to play his senior season for FSU. He was the offensive heart of the Seminoles in 1999, leading them to the title game of the College World Series with a .419 batting average and 28 home runs. Also returning to action are starting pitchers Jon McDonald and Blair Varnes. The latter's solid pitching effort against Miami despite torn knee ligaments was the most endearing image of Omaha.

▶Miami: The Hurricanes already are talking about a repeat College World Series title, even though many heroes from last season have hung up their Miami spikes. Ace Alex Santos graduated and closer Michael Neu signed professionally, leaving senior David Gil (12-0, 3.19 ERA) and sophomore Vince Vasquez as Miami's top returning pitchers. The biggest all-around loss is talented shortstop Bobby Hill. Picked in the second round of the June draft by the Chicago White Sox, Hill was still unsigned when the fall semester started at Miami but declined enrolling to continue negotiations with the Sox. Miami still has a formidable lineup without him, complete with power (first baseman Kevin

Brown and outfielder Mike Rodriguez) and speed.

▶**Stanford:** Here's a phrase you've heard before: The Cardinals have the top rotation in the nation. Following in the footsteps of Mike Mussina, Jack McDowell and countless other pitching prospects who developed at Stanford are a trio of talented right-handers: Jason Young, Justin Wayne and Brian Sager. The three pitchers combined to go 28-4 with a 4.11 ERA last season. Young (12-3) took the summer off after pitching a school-record 154 innings and collecting 178 strikeouts last season. He's a potential first-round draft choice in 2000, as is Wayne (10-1, 4.94). Sager had an outstanding freshman year, going 6-0 with a 3.98 ERA. Stanford's outfield also ranks among the nation's best, with highly touted Joe Borchard (.372, 11 HR), John Gall (.337, 70 RBI) and Edmund Muth (.305, six HR). Gall and Muth were both drafted in June but decided to return to school for their senior seasons. Scheduling note: Stanford will spend its first month of the season with a tough non-conference slate including Cal State–Fullerton, Florida State and Texas.

▶**Cal State–Fullerton:** With a pitching staff loaded with experienced juniors and with a speedy lineup, the Titans are ready for another trip to Omaha in 2000. All four regular starters—Matt Sorensen (12-0), Adam Johnson (10-4), Jon Smith (7-1) and Jordan DeJong (4-1)—return for their draft-eligible junior seasons. Closer Kirk Saarloos (seven saves) also returns. Offensively, the Titans took a hit in the June draft, losing top players Spencer Osborn, Ryan Owens and Reed Johnson to professional baseball. However, first baseman Chris Beck (.408, 75 RBI, 27 steals) declined signing and returned. Also back is Aaron Rifkin, who also stole 27 bases last season.

▶**Texas A&M:** Outfielder Daylan Holt is a national player-of-the-year candidate in 2000. Holt clubbed an NCAA-high 34 homers last season after hitting just seven as a freshman. The supporting cast around the surefire Holt isn't as clear, however, because many players from last season's College World Series team either signed professionally or graduated. Some of the names that you'll hear next season are: returning outfielder Chad Hudson, infielder Shawn Heaney and two-sport star Greg Porter. Pitching is also a question mark since all three weekend starters left after last season, among them first-round draft pick Chance Caple and second-rounder Casey Fossum. Two hurlers with little starting pitching experience are leading candidates for starting roles: Chris Russ, who won 12 games and posted a 2.64 ERA in a team-high 28 appearances, and Khalid "KB" Ballouli (7-2). Russ is Mr. Versatile, with experience at third base, shortstop, second base and left field.

▶**Rice:** The most successful season in Rice baseball history concluded with the Owls' second College World Series appearance in three seasons and a school-record 59 wins. Seven seniors played for Rice in 1999, an unusually high number for a competitive college club. This year, expect yet another large senior contingent, led by pitchers Jeff Nichols and Marc Gwyn. Nichols won 15 games last season and is already Rice's most successful pitcher ever with 37 career victories. Offensively, the Owls lost their three top hitters in Will Ford, Damon Thames and Charles Williams, but power-hitting senior outfielder Jason Gray (20 homers, eight triples, 72 RBI) returns, as does infielder Brett Smith (.299, eight homers). The 2000 season will be Rice's first in its new $6.4-million campus stadium, Reckling Park.

—by Dana Heiss, Baseball Weekly

Where are they now?

▶1969 'Miracle Mets' honored 30 years later

▶The inside story on Hank Aaron's home-run chase

USA SNAPSHOTS®

A look at statistics that shape the sports world

Jersey hangers

Nolan Ryan is the only player in major league baseball history to have his number retired by three teams, though he wore two different numbers. The players who have had their numbers retired by more than one team:

Henry Aaron	No. 44	Atlanta & Milwaukee
Rod Carew	No. 29	Anaheim & Minnesota
Rollie Fingers	No. 34	Milwaukee & Oakland
Frank Robinson	No. 20	Cincinnati & Baltimore
Nolan Ryan	No. 30 & No. 34	Anaheim, Houston & Texas
Casey Stengel	No. 37	N.Y. Mets & N.Y. Yankees

Source: USA TODAY research

By Ellen J. Horrow and Sam Ward, USA TODAY

30 years later, the 1969 Miracle Mets prove they still have heart

Ed Charles (left), Jerry Koosman and Jerry Grote celebrate the Miracle Mets' 1969 World Series victory.

Jim Palmer approached Tom Seaver, the look on his face as incredulous as it had been three decades earlier.

"How the heck did you beat us thirty years ago?" asked Palmer, the Baltimore Orioles Hall of Famer, who is still confounded by one of the biggest upsets in World Series history.

"Thirty years, Jim. Get over it," replied Seaver, the New York Mets Hall of Famer, who enjoys chiding his pal. "It's like golf. You double-bogey a hole, you forget it and go on to the next tee."

The year 1969 is difficult to forget in Baltimore—its teams were beaten by New York opponents in the Super Bowl, World Series and NBA playoffs. For the Mets, it's a different story.

"The bragging rights get better, the lies get bigger," Seaver said. "But still we love it."

The '69 Miracle Mets, those 100-to-1 long shots, were honored at the annual Baseball Assistance Team (BAT) dinner in New York. The event raised about $500,000 to help former players who are suffering financial hardships.

The formal program began with a clip from the old *Ed Sullivan Show,* where the world champions sang "You Gotta Have Heart." The camera panned the chorus, identifying each player, including "L. Nolan Ryan" and "G. Thomas Seaver." A bit too formal, perhaps, for a team that came out of nowhere to cap the summer of Woodstock and man's first steps on the moon.

"The handwriting was on the wall," said outfielder Cleon Jones, suggesting a theory of predestination. "We're just actors, you know. We were just playing it out.

"We didn't go to spring training that year thinking we'd win the World Series. We went in with a program to improve. But Gil [Hodges, the manager] had other ideas. He was the right guy for a young team still learning to play. We needed a good teacher."

The Mets had finished ninth with a 73-89

record the year before. But in the first year of divisional alignment, they overcame a 9½-game deficit to the Cubs, won 100 games and swept the Atlanta Braves in the first National League Championship Series.

The Mets were huge underdogs to the Orioles, who had won 109 games, but they split two games in Baltimore. Then the fun began.

Agee was unforgettable

Game Three belonged to center fielder Tommie Agee. He led off with a home run against Palmer and made two sensational catches in a 5-0 win. He robbed catcher Elrod Hendricks by going to his right, then center fielder Paul Blair by diving to his left.

"I don't know if they were the two best catches I ever made, but coming in the World Series like that, everybody remembers them," Agee said. "I was probably in the wrong position on the second one. With Nolan Ryan pitching [in relief], I should have realized [Blair] wouldn't have been able to pull the ball. I should have shaded him more to right-center. But the wind held it up for me."

The next day it was right fielder Ron Swoboda's turn. Seaver carried a 1-0 lead into the ninth inning. The O's had runners on the corners with one out. Brooks Robinson hit a looping fly ball, which Swoboda snared with a tumbling, shoe-string catch. The tying run scored, although Swoboda's catch kept the go-ahead run on first.

"My full backhand layout position," Swoboda joked. "I caught it just before I hit the ground. The worst thing was trying to get all the grass off my tongue."

"I just reacted to the ball. [Coach] Joe Pignatano used to tell me, 'Don't think. When you think, you hurt the ballclub.' My mind was as clear as an unopened box of Pampers.

"Everybody says it would have been a triple and two runs would have scored if I don't catch it. But I don't buy that. Boog Powell was on first. Do you know how far you have to hit it for Boog to score from first base with his big butt? The best he can do is get to third. That's my guess."

The Mets won in the 10th inning on a disputed play. The Orioles thought that pinch-hitter J.C. Martin was running out of the baseline after laying down a sacrifice bunt. Pitcher Pete Richert's throw deflected off Martin's wrist, allowing the winning run to score. Despite Orioles manager Earl Weaver's best tantrum, plate umpire Shag Crawford sided with the Mets.

The Orioles died in Game Five. The Mets trailed 3-0 at one point, but their comeback was ignited in the sixth inning on another disputed play, when a Dave McNally pitch hit Cleon Jones on the foot. The ball ricocheted into the Mets' dugout. When Hodges brought the ball to umpire Lou DiMuro and pointed to a smudge of shoe polish, Jones was awarded first base.

Clendendon was Series MVP

After the Jones hit-by-pitch, Series MVP Donn Clendenon hit a two-run homer, his third of the series. Clendenon, now a lawyer in Sioux Falls, S.D., talked about the trade that had brought him to the Mets after eight seasons in Pittsburgh and half a year with Montreal. He drove in the tying or winning run in his first 16 games as a Met.

"With the Pirates, I was overshadowed by two Hall of Famers, [Roberto] Clemente and [Willie] Stargell. And playing for the Mets made me realize how great it was to play behind great pitching."

Clendenon won a purple 1970 Dodge Challenger as Series MVP. "I left it on the Grand Central [Parkway]," he joked. "It had too much stuff on it for me."

In the end, the Mets had too much stuff for the Orioles. And 30 years later, at a dinner that Palmer compared to a trip to the dentist, the great Baltimore hurler made his belated concession speech.

"The bottom line," he said, "is they were better, they deserved to win, and as painful as it is, I'm glad I'm here tonight."

—by Bill Koenig

Hate mail and death threats marred Aaron's historic home-run chase

When Hank Aaron chased Babe Ruth's record, he got death threats and jeers as well as cheers.

"There's a new home run champion of all time, and it's Henry Aaron."

With those words, Atlanta broadcaster Milo Hamilton called home run No. 715 for Hank Aaron. That was 25 years ago.

But the "soon-to-be" home run king had not been treated like royalty. When the 1974 major league season began, Hank Aaron—the black ballplayer who was about to break Babe Ruth's immortal record—was a virtual prisoner.

For his own safety, he was escorted through secret exits from stadiums. He couldn't enter the front door of hotels. Atlanta Braves teammate Paul Casanova often brought meals to Aaron's room. Aaron was escorted by an armed bodyguard at all times.

On April 8, 1974, Aaron hit his 715th home run, surpassing Ruth and hoping to liberate himself from the bigotry that had engulfed his road to the top.

"I wish I could have enjoyed it as much

as Sammy Sosa or Mark McGwire enjoyed it [in 1998]," Aaron said 25 years later.

The whole world reveled in Sosa and McGwire's chase of Roger Maris's single-season mark—a far cry from the racist hate mail and death threats sent to Aaron from people who did not want a black man to eclipse the beloved Bambino in the record book.

"My daughter [who also received threats] was in college at Fisk University," Aaron, 65, says. "She couldn't enjoy it. I had to put my two boys in private school. They weren't able to be there with me as batboys that night. I couldn't enjoy what should have been a joyous occasion for me and my family."

Entering the season, Aaron needed one home run to tie the record. The Braves were scheduled to open with three games in Cincinnati—an area about to be hit with its worst tornadoes in nearly 50 years. But another storm was brewing as well.

The Braves wanted to keep Aaron out of the Reds series to make sure that he would break the record at home. Commissioner Bowie Kuhn said no.

"He [Kuhn] took the lineup card out of the hands of Eddie Mathews, our manager," says Bill Bartholomay, the chairman of the Braves' board of directors. "It was the only time I know of in baseball history when somebody other than the manager set the team's lineup. I objected, and it got resolved."

A compromise was reached: Aaron would play two of the three games against the Reds. Indeed, he hit the record-tying 714th homer on his first swing of the season on Opening Day against pitcher Jack Billingham. But that was it, and he came home tied with Ruth.

On April 8, with a packed stadium and national TV audience looking on, Aaron took five pitches and drew a walk from Dodgers left-hander Al Downing in his first at-bat.

"I've always been a very patient type of

hitter," Aaron says. "I always knew what I wanted to hit. I wasn't a wild swinger."

In the fourth inning, with a runner aboard and none out, Aaron took another pitch. Downing then tried to go down and away with a sinking fastball. Plate umpire Satch Davidson says he was ready to call Ball Two.

"I think it would have been a ball," Davidson says, "but he saw a pitch he could handle. He had the strongest wrists I've ever seen, and he turned on it."

Aaron unloaded.

"I knew it had a very good chance to go out," Aaron says. "But you never know. I followed it and saw it go out."

Tommy House was a nondescript Braves relief pitcher who won 29 games and saved 33 during his eight-year career. That night, he was Tommy-on-the-spot.

"Each guy in the bullpen had his own 10-yard area to stand," House, 51, says. "We all respected each other's territory. I was farthest from the foul line. I didn't think I'd have a chance. But as soon as it left the bat, I knew it was coming right to me. I didn't have to move. Everybody said, 'Nice catch,' but if I didn't lift my glove up, it would have hit me in the forehead.

"That catch was the highlight of my pitching career. It's how I'm introduced at every dinner or clinic. It got me in the Hall of Fame. It got me a card in Trivial Pursuit. Is that immortality or what?"

Ironically, House caught the ball right in front of a BankAmericard sign that read: "Think of it as Money." But House never thought of it that way.

"Some people today say the ball might be worth between $4.5 and $6 million," House says. "I do remember that right before the game, Sammy Davis Jr. walked through our clubhouse and offered $30,000 if one of us caught it. He wanted the ball for his act in Las Vegas. But I never thought about keeping it, and nobody else in the bullpen would have, either."

House raced in to the ceremony at home plate and held the ball up in front of Aaron's face.

"There was a tear on his cheek," House says. "I never saw him show emotion like that. All he said was, 'Thanks, kid.' Then I got pushed out of the way. But Hank made it clear over the years that if I ever needed help, he would help me."

Safe in the ballpark

As Aaron rounded the bases, two fans jumped from the stands and ran toward the infield. They caught up with him near shortstop and shook his hand. Despite the threats, Aaron wasn't alarmed.

"It didn't bother me one bit," he says. "I thought I was in the safest place I could be. When I was in a ballpark, I always felt surrounded by angels, like God's hand was on my shoulder."

He recalls that Dodgers second baseman Davey Lopes and shortstop Bill Russell also congratulated him during his homerun trot.

Davidson had one more task as Aaron headed home.

"I had to make sure he touched home plate," Davidson says. "I knew people would be rushing out to meet him, and I didn't want to go down in history as the guy who called him out [for failure to touch the plate]."

In the middle of the receiving line, among players and coaches, was Aaron's mother, Estella.

"My mother was there waiting before I got to home plate," he says with a laugh. "I don't know how she got there so fast. My dad [Herbert] was on the field, too, having his own celebration somewhere." Aaron doesn't even rate this as the most important home run of his career. That would be the 11th-inning shot off the Cardinals' Billy Muffett that clinched the 1957 National League pennant for the Milwaukee Braves.

—by Bill Koenig

Aaron rates the all-time great sluggers

Hank Aaron gave *Baseball Weekly* his personal "scouting report" on several of the top home-run hitters of all time.

▶**Willie Mays:** "Easily one of the best athletes who played the game. He was what I call a flair kind of player. He did things with a flair. The one thing that people don't know about Willie is that he could always time himself to get to home plate just as the ball came in, so that the ball was going one way and he another. He could do it all."

▶**Frank Robinson:** "I have to put Frank in the same category as Willie. He didn't have the flair, but he brought the one thing to a ballclub that very few players can bring: He made other players good around him. He went from Cincinnati to Baltimore, and Baltimore won championship after championship. The only reason they won it was because of Frank Robinson. Frank made Brooks good, Brooks made Boog Powell good. Everybody was good because of Frank."

▶**Willie McCovey:** "One of the strongest guys ever to play the game. They talk about [Mark] McGwire, but nobody could hit balls any harder or farther than this guy. His career was cut short by his legs, but he was a tremendous ballplayer."

▶**Ted Williams:** "If there was anything against him, it would be that he would sometimes take balls too close to the plate. But Ted was Ted. When he speaks, it's like E.F. Hutton; everybody listens."

▶**Eddie Mathews:** "When I came on the ballclub, Eddie was an average third baseman. But he made himself an All-Star third baseman. Eddie was very strong. He was the only guy who could hit a home run by just dropping his bat. His bat was very quick, and he was surprisingly fast for a big man. He was not a Brooks Robinson, but he was a very gifted athlete."

▶**Ernie Banks:** "The thing about Ernie is that if he had gotten to the big leagues a lot quicker, I think he could have hit 60 to 70 more home runs. [He finished with 512 .] He was the only guy I've ever seen, no matter who was pitching, if he threw something down around his kneecaps, he would hit it out of the ballpark. He was a dead low-ball hitter."

▶**Mickey Mantle:** "If he had taken care of himself, he would have hit at least another 100 home runs. Despite all the things he was guilty of, he still had an outstanding career....He was probably the best switch-hitter in baseball and when he was young, nobody could get down to first faster than him. He played through a lot of pain."

▶**Harmon Killebrew:** "He, too, played through a lot of injuries. He didn't hit for average, but he hit a lot of home runs. He reminds me a little bit of McGwire. He could hit the ball a long ways. He didn't hit for much of an average. He didn't steal any bases. But he did some great things."

▶**Reggie Jackson:** "He was another flair ballplayer. Reggie could have probably been a better ballplayer if he wanted to. Reggie was a very good outfielder. He had the reputation of not being one. He probably dropped a ball somewhere. But it's funny how things stick with you if you do something funny in the minor leagues. Reggie had a good arm. Also I think he could have stolen a lot more bases than he did."

AMERICAN LEAGUE

ANAHEIM ANGELS

▸**Owner:** Walt Disney Co.
▸**General manager:** Bill Stoneman
▸**Ballpark:**
Edison International Field of Anaheim
2000 Gene Autry Way
Anaheim, Calif.
714-940-2000
Capacity 45,050
Parking for 15,000 vehicles; public transportation available; family and wheelchair sections, elevators, ramps
▸**Team publications:** *Halo Insider Magazine*, media guide, yearbook
714-937-6700, ext. 7281
▸**TV, radio stations:**
KLAC 570 AM, KCAL Channel 9, Fox Sports West
▸**Camps and/or clinics:** Angels Clinic, on Saturdays during the season, 714-940-7204
▸**Spring training:**
Tempe Diablo Stadium
Tempe, Ariz.
Capacity 7,285
(9,785 including lawn)
602-438-4300

BALTIMORE ORIOLES

▸**Owner:** Peter Angelos
▸**General manager:** Syd Thrift
▸**Ballpark:**
Oriole Park at Camden Yards,
Baltimore, Md.
410-685-9800
Capacity 48,188
Public transportation available; disability seating, ramps, elevators, sound-amplification devices for the hearing-impaired
▸**Team publications:** *Orioles Magazine*, media guide
410-685-9800
▸**TV, radio stations:**
WBAL 1090 AM, WJZ Channel 13, Home Team Sports Cable
▸**Camps and/or clinics:** Fantasy Camp (ages 30-plus), February,
410-799-0005
Elrod Hendricks Camp,
Reistertown, Md., July,
410-685-9800
Summer clinics, the Orioles region, during the season
410-685-9800
▸**Spring training:**
Ft. Lauderdale Stadium
Ft. Lauderdale, Fla.
Capacity 8,346
954-776-1921

BOSTON RED SOX

▸**Owners:** JRY Corporation and John Harrington
▸**General manager:** Dan Duquette
▸**Ballpark:**
Fenway Park
4 Yawkey Way
Boston, Mass.
617-267-9440
Capacity 33,871
Public transportation available; family, wheelchair, and vision-impaired sections, ramps, sound- amplification, and TDD ticket information for hearing-impaired
▸**Team publications:** Media guide, official scorebook, yearbook
617-267-9440
▸**TV, radio stations:**
WEEI 850 AM, WB56, New England Sports Network Cable TV
▸**Spring training:**
City of Palms Park
Fort Myers, Fla.
Capacity 6,850
941-534-4799

CHICAGO WHITE SOX

▸**Owner:** Jerry Reinsdorf (chairman), Eddie Einhorn (vice-chairman) and a board of directors
▸**General manager:** Ron Schueler
▸**Ballpark:**
Comiskey Park
333 W. 35th St.
Chicago, Ill.
312-674-1000
Capacity 44,321
Parking for 7,000 vehicles; public transportation available; Kids Corner (with photo booth and uniforms for imitation baseball cards), elevators and seating for the handicapped, escalators, ramps, cash station, Hall of Fame
▸**Team publications:** Program, yearbook, media guide, calendar, team photos and player photos
312-451-5300
▸**TV, radio stations:**
ESPN Radio 1000 AM, WGN TV-9, Fox Sports Chicago
▸**Camps and/or clinics:** Chicago White Sox Training Centers
708-752-9225
▸**Spring training:**
Kino Veterans Memorial Sports Park
Tucson, Ariz.
Capacity 11,000
520-740-2680

CLEVELAND INDIANS

▸**Owner:** Larry Dolan
▸**General manager:** John Hart
▸**Ballpark:**
Jacobs Field
2401 Ontario St.
Cleveland, Ohio
216-420-4200
Capacity 43,368
Downtown parking available; public transportation; handicapped seating, extremely accessible with escalators, elevators and ramps; all 38 bathrooms have diaper-changing areas; two unisex bathrooms for the physically challenged and kids.
▸**Team publications:** *Game Face Magazine, Tribe Talk;*
216-420-4200
▸**TV, radio stations:**
WTAM 1100 AM, WUAB Channel 43, Fox Sports Ohio
▸**Camps and/or clinics:** Cleveland Indians Fantasy Camp, January,
888-588-1975

435

▶Spring training:
Chain O'Lakes Park
Winter Haven, Fla.
Capacity 7,900
813-291-5803

DETROIT TIGERS

▶Owner: Michael Ilitch
▶General manager: Randy Smith
▶Ballpark:
Comerica Park
2121 Trumbull Ave.
Detroit, Mich.
313-962-4000
Capacity 40,000
Pay parking lot; public trans-
portation available; wheelchair
section ramps
▶Team publications: Scorebook/
program
▶TV, radio stations:
WJR 760 AM, WKBD
Channel 50, Fox Sports Detroit
▶Camps and/or clinics:
Tigers' Fantasy Camp
941-686-8075
▶Spring training:
Marchant Stadium
Lakeland, Fla.
Capacity 7,100
941-688-9589

KANSAS CITY ROYALS

▶Owner: Greater Kansas
Community Foundation, Board
of Directors; David Glass,
Chairman of the Board; Michael
Herman, President
▶General manager:
Herk Robinson
▶Ballpark:
Ewing Kauffman Stadium
1 Royal Way
Kansas City, Mo.
816-921-2200
Capacity 40,625
Pay parking lot; public trans-
portation available; wheelchair
section and ramps, handicapped
accessible
▶Team publications: Yearbook,
scorecard, media guide
▶TV, radio stations:
KMBZ 980 AM, KMBC Chan-
nel 9, KCWE Channel 29,
Fox Sports Midwest
▶Spring training:
Baseball City Stadium
Baseball City, Fla.
Capacity 7,000 (1,000 on grass)
941-424-2500

MINNESOTA TWINS

▶Owner: Carl R. Pohlad
▶General manager: Terry Ryan
▶Ballpark:
Hubert H. Humphrey
Metrodome
34 Kirby Puckett Place
Minneapolis, Minn.
612-375-1366
Capacity 48,678
Public transportation available;
family and wheelchair sections,
elevators
▶Team publications: Twins Mag-
azine, 612-375-7458
▶TV, radio stations:
WCCO 830 AM, KMSP-TV
Channel 9, Midwest Sports-
Channel
▶Camps and/or clinics: Twins
Clinics, weekends throughout
the summer,
612-375-7498
▶Spring training:
Lee County Sports Complex
Fort Myers, Fla.
Capacity 7,500
813-768-4200

NEW YORK YANKEES

▶Owner: George Steinbrenner
▶General manager:
Brian Cashman
▶Ballpark:
Yankee Stadium
161st Street and River Avenue
Bronx, N.Y.
718-293-4300
Capacity 57,545
Parking (independently owned);
public transportation available;
family and wheelchair sections,
ramps, senior citizen discount ($2
tickets day of game), group dis-
counts, monument park behind
left-center field with plaques hon-
oring famous Yankees
▶Team publications: Yankees
Magazine, media guide, score-
card, yearbook,
718-293-4300
▶TV, radio stations:
WABC 770 AM, WNYW Chan-
nel 5, MSG Network
▶Spring training:
Legends Field
3802 Martin Luther King Blvd.
Tampa, Fla.
813-879-2244
Capacity: 10,382

OAKLAND ATHLETICS

▶Owners: Steve Schott and Ken
Hofmann
▶General manager: Billy Beane
▶Ballpark:
Oakland Coliseum
Nimitz Frwy & Hegenberger Rd.
Oakland, Calif.
510-568-5600
Capacity 43,662
Public transportation available;
wheelchair sections and ramps,
picnic areas
▶Team publications:
A's Magazine, media guide,
510-638-4900, ext. 2328
▶TV, radio stations:
KABL 960 AM, KICU Channel
36, Fox Sports Bay Area
▶Spring training:
Phoenix Municipal Stadium
Phoenix, Ariz.
Capacity 8,776
602-392-0074

SEATTLE MARINERS

▶Owner: Baseball Club of Seattle
▶General manager: Pat Gillick
▶Ballpark:
Safeco Field
First and Atlantic
Seattle, Wash.
206-346-4000
Capacity 47,145
Public transportation available;
parking for 2,400 cars, 30,000
within a mile; family and wheel-
chair sections, birthday package,
anniversary package
▶Team publications: Mariners
Magazine, Mariners Newsletter,
scorecard, media guide
206-346-4000
▶TV, radio stations:
KIRO 710 AM, KIRO Channel 7,
Fox Sports Northwest Cable
▶Spring training:
Peoria Sports Complex
Peoria, Ariz.
Capacity 10,000 (3,000 on grass)
602-412-9000

TAMPA BAY DEVIL RAYS

▶Owners: Vincent J. Naimoli and
a partnership
▶General manager: Chuck LaMar
▶Ballpark:
Tropicana Field
One Tropicana Drive
St. Petersburg, Fla.
813-825-3137
Capacity 45,200

Parking for 7,000 vehicles; public transportation available; family and wheelchair areas, elevators, ramps
▶**TV, radio stations:** WFLA 970 AM, WWWB Channel 32, WTSP Channel 10, SportsChannel Florida
▶**Spring training:** Al Lang Stadium St. Petersburg, Fla. Capacity 7,227

TEXAS RANGERS

▶**Owner:** Thomas O. Hicks
▶**General manager:** Doug Melvin
▶**Ballpark:** The Ballpark in Arlington 1000 Ballpark Way Arlington, Texas 817-273-5222 Capacity 49,166 Parking for 12,500 cars; no public transportation; approximately 480 wheelchair seats with additional handicap seating; restrooms with diaper-changing areas; ramps, escalators and elevators to serve all areas
▶**Team publications:** *On Deck Newsletter*, yearbook, *Program Magazine* 817-273-5222
▶**TV, radio stations:** KRLD-AM 1080, KXAS Channel 5, KXTX Channel 39, Fox Sports Southwest
▶**Camps and/or clinics:** Texas Ranger Youth Summer Clinic (boys and girls), June; Coaches Clinic, April; Parent/Child Clinic, June 817-273-5222
▶**Spring training:** Charlotte County Stadium Port Charlotte, Fla. Capacity 6,026 813-625-9500

TORONTO BLUE JAYS

▶**Owners:** Inter-Brew S.A. (Canadian Imperial Bank of Commerce owns 10%)
▶**General manager:** Gord Ash
▶**Ballpark:** SkyDome Toronto, Ontario, Canada 416-341-1000 Capacity 51,516 Public transportation available; family and wheelchair sections, no-alcohol sections, ramps, Playland

▶**Team publications:** *Scorebook Magazine* (Buzz Communications) 416-961-3319
▶**TV, radio stations:** CHUM AM 1050 TSN, CBC,
▶**Spring training:** Dunedin Stadium at Grant Field 311 Douglas Ave. Dunedin, Fla. Capacity 6,218 813-733-9302

NATIONAL LEAGUE

ARIZONA DIAMONDBACKS

▶**Owners:** Jerry Colangelo and a limited partnership
▶**General manager:** J. Garagiola Jr.
▶**Ballpark:** BankOne Ballpark 201 E. Jefferson St. Phoenix, Ariz. 602-514-8500 Parking 1,500-car garage; 18,600 spaces within 15-minute walk; wheelchair sections, ramps
▶**Team publications:** *Diamondbacks Quarterly* 602-462-6500
▶**TV, radio:** KTAR 620 AM, KTVK Channel 3, Fox Sports Arizona
▶**Spring training:** Tucson Electric Park Tucson, Ariz. 520-434-1400

ATLANTA BRAVES

▶**Owner:** Ted Turner
▶**General manager:** John Schuerholz
▶**Ballpark:** Turner Field P.O. Box 4064 Atlanta, Ga. 30302 404-522-7630 Capacity 49,831 Parking for 3,500 cars; public transportation available by bus; family and wheelchair sections
▶**Team publications:** *Fan Magazine*, 404-522-7630; *Chop Talk*, 1-800-700-CHOP
▶**TV, radio stations:** WSB 750 AM, WTBS Channel 17, Fox Sports South
▶**Spring training:** Disney's Wide World of Sports Orlando, Fla.

CHICAGO CUBS

▶**Owner:** Tribune Company
▶**General manager:** Ed Lynch
▶**Ballpark:** Wrigley Field Clark and Addison Streets, Chicago, Ill. 773-404-2827 Capacity 38,884 Parking for 900 (private lots available); public transportation available; family and wheelchair sections, ramps and elevators
▶**Team publications:** *Vineline*, *Scorecard Magazine*, *Cubs Quarterly*, 312-404-2827
▶**TV, radio stations:** WGN 720 AM, WGN Channel 9, Fox Sports Chicago
▶**Spring training:** HoHoKam Park Mesa, Ariz. Capacity 12,500 800-283-6372

CINCINNATI REDS

▶**Owners:** Carl Lindner
▶**General manager:** James G. Bowden
▶**Ballpark:** Cinergy Stadium Pete Rose Way Cincinnati, Ohio 513-421-4510 Capacity 52,952 Parking for 5,022 cars; wheelchair locations, ramps
▶**Team publications:** Media guide, yearbook/program, *Reds Report*, 800-760-2862
▶**TV, radio stations:** WLW 700 AM, Fox Sports Ohio
▶**Spring training:** Ed Smith Stadium Sarasota, Fla. Capacity 7,500 941-954-4101

COLORADO ROCKIES

▶**Owner:** Jerry McMorris (Colorado Baseball Partnership)
▶**General manager:** Dan O'Dowd
▶**Ballpark:** Coors Field 2001 Blake St., Denver, Colo. 303-762-5437 Capacity 50,249 Parking for 5,200 cars, 171 permanent handicap spaces, 18,000 more spaces within a 15-minute walk; public transporta-

tion available; wheelchair section, family sections in all price ranges
▶**Team publications:** Media guide, game program, yearbook
▶**TV, radio stations:** KOA 850 AM, KWGN Channel 2, Fox Sports Rocky Mountain
▶**Spring training:** Hi Corbett Field Tucson, Ariz. Capacity 9,500 602-327-9467

FLORIDA MARLINS

▶**Owner:** John Henry
▶**General manager:** David Dombrowski
▶**Ballpark:** Pro Player Stadium 2267 N.W. 199th St. Miami, Fla. 305-626-7400 Capacity 41,855 Parking 24,137 cars; public transportation available; wheelchair section, ramps and elevators
▶**TV, radio stations:** WQAM 560 AM, WAMI Channel 69, Sports Channel Florida
▶**Spring training:** Space Coast Stadium Melbourne, Fla. Capacity 7,200 407-633-9200

HOUSTON ASTROS

▶**Owner:** Drayton McLane Jr.
▶**General manager:** Gerry Hunsicker
▶**Ballpark:** Enron Field PO Box 288 Houston, Texas 713-799-9500 Capacity 42,000 Parking for 2,030 cars on-site; 25,179 spaces within ½ mile; public transportation by bus; wheelchair section and ramps
▶**Team publications:** *Astros Magazine, Astros Media Guide,* 713-799-9600
▶**TV, radio stations:** KTRH 950 AM, KNWS-TV, Channel 51, Fox Sports Southwest
▶**Camps and/or clinics:** Astros Youth Clinics, during the season, 713-799-9877
▶**Spring training:** Osceola County Stadium Kissimmee, Fla. Capacity 5,130 407-933-6500

LOS ANGELES DODGERS

▶**Owner:** FOX Network
▶**General manager:** Kevin Malone
▶**Ballpark:** Dodger Stadium 1000 Elysian Park Ave. Los Angeles, Calif. 213-224-1400 Capacity 56,000 Parking for 16,000 cars; wheelchair section and ramps
▶**Team publications:** Dodger Yearbook, *Dodger On-Line* (bi-monthly), *Dodger Magazine,* media guide, *Line Drive*
▶**TV, radio stations:** KXTA 1150 AM, KTLA Channel 5, Fox Sports West
▶**Camps and/or clinics:** Twenty clinics per year, 213-224-1435
▶**Spring training:** Holman Stadium Dodgertown Vero Beach, Fla. Capacity 7,000 407-569-4900

MILWAUKEE BREWERS

▶**Owner:** Wendy Selig-Prieb
▶**General manager:** Dean Taylor
▶**Ballpark:** Milwaukee County Stadium 201 South 46th St. Milwaukee, Wis. 414-933-4114 Capacity 53,192 Parking for approximately 11,000 cars; public transportation available; family and wheelchair sections, ramps, Designated Driver Program including free taxi transportation for single-ticket holders participating in the DDP
▶**Team publications:** Media guide, *Lead Off Magazine*
▶**TV, radio stations:** WTMJ 620 AM, WCGV-TV 24
▶**Camps and/or clinics:** Gatorade Youth Camp, during the season, 414-933-4114 Fantasy Camp, winter, 414-933-4114, 800-336-CAMP
▶**Spring training:** Maryville Baseball Park Maryville, Ariz. Capacity 7,000 602-247-7177

MONTREAL EXPOS

▶**Owner:** Montreal Baseball Club Inc., Claude R. Brochu (president and general partner)

▶**General manager:** Jim Beattie
▶**Ballpark:** Olympic Stadium 4549 Ave. Pierre-de-Coubertin, Montreal, Quebec, Canada 514-253-3434 Capacity 46,500 Parking for 4,000 cars; public transportation available; wheelchair sections, ramps, extensive food concessions, outfield bleachers
▶**Team publications:** Media guide, *Expos Magazine,* P.O. Box 500, Station M, Montreal, Quebec H1V 3P2
▶**TV, radio stations:** CIQC 600 AM, TSN (English); CKAC 730 AM, CBC, CTV (English); RDS TQS (French)
▶**Spring training:** Roger Dean Stadium 4751 Main Street Jupiter, Fla. Capacity 7,000 561-775-1818

NEW YORK METS

▶**Owners:** Fred Wilpon (president and CEO) and Nelson Doubleday (chairman of the board)
▶**President of baseball operations:** Steve Phillips
▶**Ballpark:** William A. Shea Municipal Stadium 126th St. and Roosevelt Ave. Flushing, N.Y. 718-507-METS Capacity 55,777 Parking for 6,000 cars; public transportation available; family and wheelchair sections, ramps, elevators
▶**Team publications:** Yearbook, scorecard, press guide 919-688-0218
▶**TV, radio stations:** WFAN 660 AM, WPIX Channel 11, Fox Sports New York
▶**Camps and/or clinics:** Baseball Heaven, 800-898-METS
▶**Spring training:** Thomas J. White Stadium Port St. Lucie, Fla. Capacity 7,347 407-871-2100

PHILADELPHIA PHILLIES

▶**Owner:** David Montgomery, Bill Giles and a limited partnership
▶**General manager:** Ed Wade
▶**Ballpark:** Veterans Stadium

Broad St. and Pattison Ave.,
Philadelphia, Pa.
215-463-1000
Capacity 62,363
Parking for 10,000 cars; public
transportation available; wheel-
chair section and ramps, TDD
ticket information for hearing
impaired (215-463-2998)
▶Team publications: Media guide,
scorebook, *Phillies Magazine*
▶TV, radio stations:
WPHT 1210 AM, UPN Chan-
nel 57, Comcast Sportsnet
▶Spring training:
Jack Russell Memorial Stadium
Clearwater, Fla.
Capacity 6,926
813-441-8638

PITTSBURGH PIRATES

▶Owner: Kevin McClatchy
▶General manager: Cam Bonifay
▶Ballpark:
Three Rivers Stadium
600 Stadium Circle
Pittsburgh, Pa.
412-323-5000
Capacity 47,972
Pay parking lot; public trans-
portation available; family and
wheelchair sections, ramps,
guest relations
▶Team publications: Yearbook,
scorecard, *Info Guide*, *On Deck*
▶TV, radio stations:
KDKA 1020 AM, Fox Sports
Pittsburgh
▶Camps and/or clinics: Youth
Camps, 412-323-5098
▶Spring training:
McKechnie Field
Bradenton, Fla.
Capacity 6,562
941-747-3031

ST. LOUIS CARDINALS

▶Owner: St. Louis Cardinals LP
▶General manager: Walt Jocketty
▶Ballpark:
Busch Stadium
250 Stadium Plaza
St. Louis, Mo.
314-421-3060
Capacity 49,676 (includes
1,500 standing)
Parking for more than 7,000
cars; public transportation avail-
able; wheelchair section, ramps
▶Team publications: Media
guide, *The Cardinals* magazine,
314-982-7336
▶TV, radio stations:
KMOX 1120 AM, KPLR Chan-

nel 11, Fox Sports Midwest
▶Spring training:
Roger Dean Stadium
4751 Main Street
Jupiter, Fla.
Capacity 7,000
561-775-1818

SAN DIEGO PADRES

▶Owner: John Moores
▶General manager: Kevin Towers
▶Ballpark:
QualComm Park
9449 Friars Road
San Diego, Calif.
619-283-4494
Capacity 56,975
Parking for 18,751 cars; public
transportation available; wheel-
chair sections, ramps, pre-
registration for telephone pag-
ing, ATM machines
▶Team publications: *Padre Maga-
zine*, 619-881-6500
▶TV, radio stations:
KFMB 760 AM, Channel 4
▶Spring training:
Peoria Sports Complex
Peoria, Ariz.
Capacity 10,000 (with grass
seating)
602-878-4337

SAN FRANCISCO GIANTS

▶Owner: Peter Magowan
(president and managing general
partner)
▶General manager: Brian Sabean
▶Ballpark:
Pacific Bell Park
King and Third Sts.
San Francisco, Calif.
415-468-3700
Capacity 40,800
Parking for 17,000 cars; public
transportation available; family
and wheelchair sections, ramps,
battery charger plug-ins for
wheelchairs, designated handi-
capped pick-up and drop-off
sites
▶Team publications: *Giants
Magazine*, *Giants Info Guide*,
415-468-3700, ext. 478
▶TV, radio stations:
KNBR 680 AM, KTVU Chan-
nel 2, Fox Sports Bay Area
▶Camps and/or clinics: Rob
Andrews Baseball, June and July
510-935-3505
▶Spring training:
Scottsdale Stadium
Scottsdale, Ariz.
Capacity 7,500 (plus 2,500 on

outfield grass)
602-990-7972

Buffalo Bisons (Indians)
Dunn Tire Park
P.O. Box 450
Buffalo, NY 14205
(716) 846-2000
Capacity: 20,050
Charlotte Knights (White Sox)
Knights Castle
P.O. Box 1207
Fort Mill, SC 29716
(704) 357-8071
Capacity: 10,917
Columbus Clippers (Yankees)
Harold Cooper Stadium
1155 W. Mound St.
Columbus, OH 43223
(614) 462-5250
Capacity: 15,000
Durham Bulls (Devil Rays)
Durham Bulls Athletic Park
P.O. Box 507
Durham, NC 27702
(919) 687-6500
Capacity: 6,500
Indianapolis Indians (Brewers)
Victory Field
1501 W 16th St.
Indianapolis, IN 46202
(317) 269-3545
Capacity: 15,400
Louisville River Bats (Reds)
Slugger Field
P.O. Box 36407
Louisville, KY 40233
(502) 367-9121
Capacity: 13,000
Norfolk Tides (Mets)
Harbor Park
150 Park Ave.
Norfolk, VA 23510
(804) 622-2222
Capacity: 12,000
Ottawa Lynx (Expos)
JetForm Park
300 Conventry Rd.
Ottawa, ON K1K 4P5
Canada
(613) 747-5969
Capacity: 10,000
Pawtucket Red Sox (Red Sox)
McCoy Stadium
P.O. Box 2365
Pawtucket, RI 02861
(401) 724-7300
Capacity: 7,002
Richmond Braves (Braves)
The Diamond
P.O. Box 6667

Richmond, VA 23230
(804) 359-4444
Capacity: 12,500
Rochester Red Wings (Orioles)
Frontier Field
1 Morrie Silver Way
Rochester, NY 14608
(716) 454-1001
Capacity: 10,000
Scranton/Wilkes-Barre Red Barons (Phillies)
Lackawanna County Stadium
P.O. Box 3449
Scranton, PA 18505
(717) 969-2255
Capacity: 10,800
Syracuse Sky Chiefs (Blue Jays)
P & C Stadium
Syracuse, NY 13208
(315) 474-7833
Capacity: 11,400
Toledo Mud Hens (Tigers)
Ned Skeldon Stadium
P.O. Box 6212
Toledo, OH 43614
(419) 893-9483
Capacity: 10,917

Albuquerque Dukes (Dodgers)
Albuquerque Sports Stadium
1601 Stadium Blvd. SE
Albuquerque, NM 87106
(505) 243-1791
Capacity: 10,510
Calgary Cannons (Marlins)
Burns Stadium
2255 Corwchild Trail NW
Calgary, AB T2M 4S7
CANADA
(403) 284-1111
Capacity: 7,500
Colorado Springs Sky Sox (Rockies)
Sky Sox Stadium
4385 Tutt Blvd
Colorado Springs, CO 80922
(719) 597-1449
Capacity: 6,130
Edmonton Trappers (Athletics)
Telus Field
10233 96th Ave.
Edmonton, AB T5K 0A5
Canada
(403) 429-2934
Capacity: 10,000
Fresno Grizzlies (Giants)
Beiden Field
1231 N St.
Fresno, CA 93740
(209) 442-1994
Capacity: 6,500

Iowa Cubs (Cubs)
Sec Taylor Stadium
350 SW 1st St.
Des Moines, IA 50309
(515) 243-6111
Capacity: 11,000
Las Vegas Stars (Padres)
Cashman Field
850 Las Vegas Blvd. N.
Las Vegas, NV 89101
(702) 386-7200
Capacity: 9,334
Memphis Redbirds (Cardinals)
Tim McCarver Stadium
800 Home Run Lane
Memphis, TN 38104
(901) 272-1687
Capacity: 10,000
Nashville Sounds (Pirates)
Herschel Greer Stadium
P.O. Box 23290
Nashville, TN 37202
(615) 242-4371
Capacity: 17,000
New Orleans Zephyrs (Astros)
Zephyr Field
6000 Airline Highway
New Orleans, LA 70003
(504) 734-5155
Oklahoma Redhawks (Rangers)
All-Sports Stadium
P.O. Box 75089
Oklahoma City, OK 73147
(405) 946-8989
Capacity: 15,000
Omaha Golden Spikes (Royals)
Rosenblatt Stadium
P.O. Box 3665
Omaha, NE 68103
(402) 734-2550
Capacity: 22,000
Salt Lake Buzz (Twins)
Franklin Quest Field
P.O. Box 4108
Salt Lake City, UT 84110
(801) 485-3800
Capacity: 15,000
Tacoma Rainiers (Mariners)
Cheney Stadium
P.O. Box 11087
Tacoma, WA 98411
(206) 752-7707
Capacity: 9,800
Tucson Sidewinders (Diamondbacks)
Tucson Electric Park
P.O. Box 27045
Tucson, AZ 85726
(520) 325-2621
Capacity: 12,000
Sacramento (River Cats) (Athletics)
Raley Field
1001 2nd St.
Sacramento, Calif.

916-319-4700
Capacity: 10,400

Akron Aeros (Indians)
Canal Park
300 S. Main St.
Akron, OH 44308
(330) 253-5151
Capacity: 10,000
Altoona Curve (Pirates)
Lakemont Stadium
P.O. Box 1029
Altoona, PA 16603
(814) 943-5400
Capacity 6,022
Binghamton Mets (Mets)
Municipal Stadium
P.O. Box 598
Binghamton, NY 13902
(607) 723-6387
Capacity: 6,012
Bowie Baysox (Orioles)
Prince Georges Stadium
P.O. Box 1661
Bowie, MD 20717
(301) 805-6000
Capacity: 10,000
Erie Seawolves (Angels)
Jerry Uht Stadium
P.O. Box 1776
Erie, PA 16507
Capacity 6,000
Harrisburg Senators (Expos)
Riverside Stadium
P.O. Box 15757
Harrisburg, PA 17105
(717) 231-4444
Capacity: 6,300
New Britain Rock Cats (Twins)
New Britain Stadium
P.O. Box 1718
New Britain, CT 06051
(860) 224-8383
Capacity: 6,146
New Haven Ravens (Mariners)
Yale Field
252 Derby Ave.
New Haven, CT 06516
(203) 782-1666
Capacity: 6,200
Norwich Navigators (Yankees)
Dodd Stadium
P.O. Box 6003
Yantic, CT 06389
(203) 887-7962
Capacity: 6,000
Portland Sea Dogs (Marlins)
Hadlock Field
P.O. Box 636
Portland, ME 04104
(207) 874-9300
Capacity: 6,000

Reading Phillies (Phillies)
Municipal Stadium
P.O. Box 15050
Reading, PA 19612
(610) 375-8469
Capacity: 7,500
Trenton Thunder (Red Sox)
Waterfront Park
One Thunder Rd.
Trenton, NJ 08611
(609) 394-3000
Capacity: 6,341

SOUTHERN LEAGUE-CLASS AA

Birmingham Barons (White Sox)
Hoover Met
P.O. Box 360007
Birmingham, AL 35236
(205) 988-3200
Capacity: 10,000
Carolina Mudcats (Rockies)
Five County Stadium
P.O. Drawer 1218
Zebulon, NC 27597
(919) 269-2287
Capacity: 6,000
Chattanooga Lookouts (Reds)
Engel Stadium
P.O. Box 11002
Chattanooga, TN 37403
(423) 267-2208
Capacity: 7,500
Greenville Braves (Braves)
Municipal Stadium
P.O. Box 16683
Greenville, SC 29606
(864) 299-3456
Capacity: 7,027
Huntsville Stars (Brewers)
Joe W. Davis Stadium
P.O. Box 2769
Huntsville, AL 35804
(205) 882-2562
Capacity: 10,200
Jacksonville Suns (Tigers)
Wolfson Park
P.O. Box 4756
Jacksonville, FL 32201
(904) 358-2846
Capacity: 8,200
Mobile Bay Bears (Padres)
Hank Aaron Stadium
P.O. Box 161663
Mobile, AL 36616
(334) 479-2327
Capacity: 6,000
Orlando Rays (Devil Rays)
Disney Wide World of Sports
287 Tampa Ave. S
Orlando, FL 32805
(407) 649-7297
Capacity: 9,500

Tennessee Smokies (Blue Jays)
Bill Meyer Stadium
633 Jessamine St.
Knoxville, TN 37917
(615) 637-9494
Capacity: 6,412
West Tenn Diamond Jaxx (Cubs)
Pringles Park
1861 N. Highland, Suite 1998
Jackson, TN 38305
(901) 664-2020
Capacity: 6,000

TEXAS LEAGUE- CLASS AA

Arkansas Travelers (Cardinals)
Ray Winder Field
P.O. Box 55066
Little Rock, AK 72215
(501) 664-1555
Capacity: 6,083
El Paso Diablos (Diamondbacks)
Cohen Stadium
P.O. Drawer 4797
El Paso, TX 79914
(915) 755-2000
Capacity: 10,000
Midland Rockhounds (Athletics)
Christensen Stadium
P.O. Box 51187
Midland, TX 79710
(915) 683-4251
Capacity: 5,000
Round Rock Express (Astros)
Express Stadium
P.O. Box 5309
Round Rock, TX 78683
(512) 255-2255
Capacity: 7,816
San Antonio Missions (Dodgers)
Nelson Wolff Municipal
   Stadium
5757 Highway 90 W
San Antonio, TX 78227
(210) 675-7275
Capacity: 6,500
Shreveport Captains (Giants)
Fairgrounds Field
P.O. Box 3448
Shreveport, LA 71133
(318) 636-5555
Capacity: 6,200
Tulsa Drillers (Rangers)
Drillers Stadium
P.O. Box 4448
Tulsa, OK 74159
(918) 744-5998
Capacity: 10,995
Wichita Wranglers (Royals)
Lawrence-Dumont Stadium
P.O. Box 1420
Wichita, KS 67201
(316) 267-3372
Capacity: 6,058

CALIFORNIA LEAGUE-CLASS A

Bakersfield Blaze (Giants)
Sam Lynn Ballpark
P.O. Box 10031
Bakersfield, CA 93389
(805) 322-1363
Capacity: 4,300
High Desert Mavericks
(Diamondbacks)
Maverick Stadium
12000 Stadium West
Adelanto, CA 92301
(619) 246-6287
Capacity: 3,808
Lake Elsinore Storm (Angels)
Lake Elsinore Diamond
P.O. Box 535
Lake Elsinore, CA 92531
(909) 245-4487
Capacity: 6,000
Lancaster Jethawks (Mariners)
The Hangar
45116 Valley Central Way
Lancaster, CA 93536
(805) 726-5400
Capacity: 7,000
Modesto A's (Athletics)
Thurman Field
P.O. Box 883
Modesto, CA 95353
(209) 572-4487
Capacity: 4,500
Mudville Nine (Brewers)
Billy Hebert Field
P.O. Box 8550
Stockton, CA 95208
(209) 944-5943
Capacity: 3,500
Rancho Cucamonga Quakes
(Padres)
The Epicenter
P.O. Box 4139
Rancho Cucamonga, CA 91729
(909) 481-5000
Capacity: 6,500
San Bernardino Stampede
(Dodgers)
San Bernardino Stadium
P.O. Box 1806
San Bernardino, CA 92402
(909) 888-9922
Capacity: 5,000
San Jose Giants (Giants)
Municipal Stadium
P.O. Box 21727
San Jose, CA 95151
(408) 297-1435
Capacity: 4,500
Visalia Oaks (Athletics)
Recreation Park
P.O. Box 48
Visalia, CA 93279
(209) 625-0480
Capacity: 2,000

Frederick Keys (Orioles)
Harry Grove Stadium
P.O. Box 3169
Frederick, MD 21705
(301) 662-0013
Capacity: 5,700

Kinston Indians (Indians)
Grainger Stadium
P.O. Box 3542
Kinston, NC 28502
(919) 527-9111
Capacity: 4,100

Lynchburg Hillcats (Pirates)
City Stadium
P.O. Box 10213
Lynchburg, VA 24506
(804) 528-1144
Capacity: 4,200

Myrtle Beach Pelicans (Braves)
Coastal Federal Field
2411 Oak St., Suite 308
Myrtle Beach, SC 29577
(803) 946-7557

Potomac Cannons (Cardinals)
Pfitzner Memorial Stadium
P.O. Box 2148
Woodbridge, VA 22193
(703) 590-2311
Capacity: 6,000

Salem Avalanche (Rockies)
Salem Mem. Baseball Stadium
P.O. Box 842
Salem, VA 24153
(540) 389-3333
Capacity: 6,300

Wilmington Blue Rocks (Royals)
Frawley Stadium
801 South Madison St.
Wilmington, DE 19801
(302) 888-2015
Capacity: 5,500

Winston-Salem Warthogs
(White Sox)
Ernie Shore Field
P.O. Box 4488
Winston-Salem, NC 27115
(910) 759-2233
Capacity: 6,280

FLORIDA STATE LEAGUE-CLASS A

Brevard County Manatees
(Marlins)
Space Coast Stadium
5600 Stadium Parkway
Melbourne, FL 32940
(407) 633-9200
Capacity: 7,200

Charlotte Rangers (Rangers)
Charlotte County Stadium
2300 El Jobean Rd.
Port Charlotte, FL 33948

(813) 625-9500
Capacity: 6,026

Clearwater Phillies (Phillies)
Jack Russell Stadium
P.O. Box 10336
Clearwater, FL 10336
(813) 441-8638
Capacity: 6,917

Daytona Cubs (Cubs)
Jackie Robinson Ballpark
P.O. Box 15080
Daytona Beach, FL 32114
(904) 257-3172
Capacity: 4,900

Dunedin Blue Jays (Blue Jays)
Dunedin Stadium
P.O. Box 957
Dunedin, FL 34697
(813) 733-9302
Capacity: 6,218

Fort Myers Miracle (Twins)
Lee County Complex
14400 Six Miles Cypress Pkwy.
Fort Myers, FL 33912
(941) 768-4210
Capacity: 7,500

Lakeland Tigers (Tigers)
Joker Marchant Stadium
P.O. Box 90187
Lakeland, FL 33804
(941) 688-7911
Capacity: 7,000

St. Lucie Mets (Mets)
Thomas J.White Stadium
525 N.W. Blvd.
Port St. Lucie, FL 34986
(561) 871-2100
Capacity: 7,350

St. Petersburg Devil Rays
(Devil Rays)
Al Lang Stadium
P.O. Box 12557
St. Petersburg, FL 33733
(813) 822-3384
Capacity: 7,004

Sarasota Red Sox (Red Sox)
Ed Smith Stadium
P.O. Box 2816
Sarasota, FL 34230
(941) 365-4460
Capacity: 7,500

Tampa Yankees (Yankees)
Legends Field
3802 W. Dr. MLK Blvd.
Tampa, FL 33614
(813) 875-7753
Capacity: 10,000

Vero Beach Dodgers (Dodgers)
Holman Stadium
P.O. Box 2887
Vero Beach, FL 32961
(407) 569-4900
Capacity: 6,500

MIDWEST LEAGUE-CLASS A

Beloit Snappers (Brewers)
Pohlman Field
P.O. Box 855
Beloit, WI 53512
(608) 362-2272
Capacity: 3,500

Burlington Bees (White Sox)
Community Field
P.O. Box 824
Burlington, IA 52601
(319) 754-5705
Capacity: 3,500

Cedar Rapids Kernels (Angels)
Veterans Memorial Ballpark
P.O. Box 2001
Cedar Rapids, IA 52406
(319) 363-3887
Capacity: 6,000

Clinton Lumber Kings (Reds)
Riverview Stadium
P.O. Box 1295
Clinton, IA 52733
(319) 242-0727
Capacity: 3,400

Dayton Dragons (Reds)
Fifth Third Field
Dayton, OH
(937) 228-2287
Capacity: 7,500

Fort Wayne Wizards (Padres)
Memorial Stadium
4000 Parnell Ave.
Fort Wayne, IN 46805
(219) 482-6400
Capacity: 6,000

Kane County Cougars (Marlins)
Elfstrom Stadium
34W002 Cherry Ln.
Geneva, IL 60134
(630) 232-8811
Capacity: 5,900

Lansing Lugnuts (Cubs)
Oldsmobile Park
505 E. Michigan Ave.
Lansing, MI 48912
(517) 485-4500
Capacity: 12,000

Michigan Battle Cats (Astros)
C.O. Brown Stadium
1392 Capital Ave. NE
Battle Creek, MI 49017
(616) 660-2287
Capacity: 6,200

Peoria Chiefs (Cardinals)
Pete Vonachen Stadium
1524 W. Nebraska Ave.
Peoria, IL 61604
(309) 688-1622
Capacity: 5,200

Quad City River Bandits (Twins)
John O'Donnell Stadium
P.O. Box 3496

Davenport, IA 52808
(319) 324-2032
Capacity: 5,500
South Bend Silver Hawks
(Diamondbacks)
Coveleski Stadium
P.O. Box 4218
South Bend, IN 46634
(219) 235-9988
Capacity: 5,000
West Michigan Whitecaps
(Tigers)
Old Kent Park
P.O. Box 428
Comstock Park, MI 49321
(616) 784-4131
Capacity: 5,500
Wisconsin Timber Rattlers
(Mariners)
Fox Cities Stadium
P.O. Box 464
Appleton, WI 54912
(414) 733-4152
Capacity: 5,200

SOUTH ATLANTIC
LEAGUE-CLASS A

Asheville Tourists (Rockies)
McCormick Field
P.O. Box 1556
Asheville, NC 28802
(704) 258-0428
Capacity: 3,400
Augusta Greenjackets (Red Sox)
Lake Olmstead Stadium
P.O. Box 3746 Hill Station
Augusta, GA 30904
(706) 736-7889
Capacity: 4,500
Cape Fear Crocs (Expos)
J.P. Riddle Stadium
P.O. Box 64939
Fayetteville, NC 28306
(910) 424-6500
Capacity: 3,200
Capital City Bombers (Mets)
Capital City Stadium
P.O. Box 7845
Columbia, SC 29202
(803) 256-4110
Capacity: 6,000
Charleston (SC) River Dogs
(Devil Rays)
Joseph P. Riley Jr. Park
P.O. Box 20849
Charleston, SC 29413
(803) 965-4096
Capacity: 5,900
Charleston (WVa) Alley Cats
(Royals)
Watt Powell Park
P.O. Box 4669
Charleston, WV 25304
(304) 344-2287
Capacity: 6,000

Columbus Redstixx (Indians)
Golden Park
P.O. Box 1886
Columbus, GA 31902
(706) 571-8866
Capacity: 4,000
Delmarva Shorebirds (Orioles)
Perdue Stadium
P.O. Box 1552
Salisbury, MD 21802
(410) 219-3112
Capacity: 5,200
Greensboro Bats (Yankees)
War Memorial Stadium
510 Yanceyville St.
Greensboro, NC 27405
(910) 333-2287
Capacity: 7,500
Hagerstown Suns (Blue Jays)
Municipal Stadium
P.O. Box 230
Hagerstown, MD 21740
(301) 791-6266
Capacity: 4,500
Hickory Crawdads (Pirates)
L.P. Frans Stadium
P.O. Box 1268
Hickory, NC 28603
(704) 322-3000
Capacity: 5,200
Macon Braves (Braves)
Luther Williams Field
P.O. Box 4525
Macon, GA 31208
(912) 745-8923
Capacity: 4,000
Piedmont Boll Weevils (Phillies)
Fieldcrest Cannon Stadium
P.O. Box 64
Kannapolis, NC 28082
(704) 932-3267
Capacity: 4,800
Savannah Sand Gnats (Rangers)
Grayson Stadium
P.O. Box 3783
Savannah, GA 31414
(912) 351-9150
Capacity: 8,000

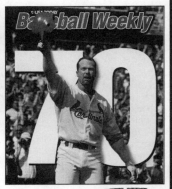